Principles and Practice of Marketing

David Jobber and Fiona Ellis-Chadwick

Seventh edition

London Boston Burr Ridge, IL Dubuque, IA Madison, WI New York San Francisco St. Louis Bangkok Bogotá Caracas Kuala Lumpur Lisbon Madrid Mexico City Milan Montreal New Delhi Santiago Seoul Singapore Sydney Taipei Toronto

Principles and Practice of Marketing seventh edition
David Jobber and Fiona Ellis-Chadwick
ISBN-13 9780077140007
ISBN-10 0077140001

Published by McGraw-Hill Education
Shoppenhangers Road
Maidenhead
Berkshire
SL6 2QL
Telephone: 44 (0) 1628 502 500
Fax: 44 (0) 1628 770 224
Website: www.mcgraw-hill.co.uk

British Library Cataloguing in Publication Data
A catalogue record for this book is available from the British Library

Library of Congress Cataloguing in Publication Data
The Library of Congress data for this book has been applied for from the Library of Congress

Executive Editor: Caroline Prodger
Commissioning Editor: Peter Hooper
Development Editor: Jennifer Yendell
Head of Production: Beverley Shields
Head of Marketing: Vanessa Boddington

Text Design by Kamae Design, Oxford
Cover design by Adam Renvoize
Printed and bound in Markono Print Media Pte Ltd, Singapore

ISBN-13 9780077140007
ISBN-10 0077140001

To Janet, Paul and Matthew

Brief Table of Contents

Detailed Table of Contents

Vignettes

Mini Cases

Marketing Ethics and Corporate Social Responsibility in Action

Read the Research

Case guide

This guide shows the key concepts covered in each of the cases in both the book and the Online Learning Centre so you can easily pick out which cases are relevant to a particular part of your course. Go to **www.mcgraw-hill.com/ textbooks/jobber** to find a pdf of this guide, and search by company, industry or topic to find the ideal case to use.

Chapter	Case number	Case title and author	Key concepts covered
1	Case 1	Coca-Cola vs Pepsi: Cola Wars in a Changing Marketing Environment *David Jobber, Professor of Marketing, University of Bradford*	marketing orientation, competition, leading brands, positioning
	Case 2	Nokia: Disconnecting People *Tony Rowe, Principal of Marketing Mentors, and Tony Lindley, Managing Director of Tony Lindley Consultants Ltd.*	global marketing, technology, internal orientation, mobile telecoms industry
	OLC case 1	H&M Gets Hotter: Fashion at its Fastest *David Jobber, Professor of Marketing, University of Bradford*	marketing orientation, effectiveness and efficiency, customer value, fashion industry
2	Case 3	Dixons Retail PLC: Planning for a Multichannel Future *Fiona Ellis-Chadwick, Senior Lecturer in Marketing, The Open University*	marketing strategy and planning, values, mission
	Case 4	Volvo: Putting the *Vroom* Back into Sales *Conor Carroll, Lecturer in Marketing, University of Limerick*	brands, market share, competition, marketing environment, SWOT, strategic options, car industry
	OLC case 2	Daloon Spring Rolls *Poul Faarup, Associate Professor, University of Southern Denmark*	marketing planning, SWOT, 4Ps, food industry
3	Case 5	Saving Sony: The Demise of an Industrial Giant *Conor Carroll, Lecturer in Marketing, University of Limerick*	product innovation, SWOT, marketing environment, strategic options
	Case 6	Made in Amazonia *Fiona Ellis-Chadwick, Senior Lecturer in Marketing, The Open University*	social, cultural and environmental forces and physical forces on production
	OLC case 3	Marketing Environment: PEEST Analysis Exercise *David Jobber, Professor of Marketing, University of Bradford*	elements of marketing environment analysis, legal, political, technology, economics, social and physical environment

Chapter	Case number	Case title and author	Key concepts covered
4	Case 7	Cappuccino Wars: The Battle for the High Street *David Jobber, Professor of Marketing, University of Bradford*	market development, competitive positioning, consumer choice
	Case 8	Red Bull: 'Gives You Wings' *David Cosgrave, Teaching Assistant, Department of Marketing and Management, University of Limerick*	buying decision process, marketing communications, choice criteria, social influences on consumer behaviour
	OLC case 4	Consumer Behaviour: How Do You Decide? *David Jobber, Professor of Marketing, University of Bradford*	consumer behaviour, decision-making, choice criteria
5	Case 9	Trading Television Formats is Big Business: Do You Want to Be a Millionaire? *Fiona Ellis-Chadwick, Senior Lecturer in Marketing, The Open University*	organizational behaviour, buying process in the entertainment industry. worldwide buying and trade exhibitions
	Case 10	Sleeping with the Enemy? The Delicate Art of Managing Different Roles at Ericsson's Purchasing Unit *Marlene Johansson, Lecturer in Marketing, and Helena Renström, Assistant Professor, Umeå School of Business and Economics, Sweden*	business to business, characteristics of organizational buying, internal buying, relationship management, choice criteria, services
	OLC case 5	Winters Company: Understanding Organizational Decision-Making *David Jobber, Professor of Marketing, University of Bradford*	organizational buyer behaviour, roles in decision making units, organizational decision-making
6	Case 11	The Co-operative: Leading the Way in CSR *Brian Searle, Lecturer in Marketing, Loughborough University*	ethical production, influences on industry standards
	Case 12	Nestlé vs Greenpeace: Giving the Rainforest a Break *Loïc Plé, Associate Professor, IÉSEG School of Management, France*	ethical marketing, ethical production, CSR, public health, public relations
	OLC case 6	Fairtrade Coffee: Grounds for a Fresh Look at Ethical Consumption? *Ken Peattie, Professor of Marketing and Strategy, Cardiff University*	fair trade movement, marketing ethics, pricing issues
7	Case 13	iPod: Researching Consumers' Perceptions *Nina Reynolds, Professor of Marketing, University of Southampton, and Sheena MacArthur, Senior Lecturer in Marketing, Glasgow Caledonian University*	questionnaires, survey methods, sampling methods, marketing research
	Case 14	Market Force *Dr Raffaele Filieri, Lecturer in Marketing, Newcastle Business School, Northumbria University*	market research methods, innovation, mystery shopping
	OLC case 7	Nectar: Loyalty Brings Sweet Rewards *Conor Carroll, Lecturer in Marketing, and Sara Kate Hurley, Research Assistant, University of Limerick*	customer loyalty, loyalty programmes

Chapter	Case number	Case title and author	Key concepts covered
8	Case 15	Utilization of Loyalty Card Data for Segmentation: Morelli's Story *Dr Christina Donnelly, Lecturer in Marketing, NUI Maynooth, and Dr Gillian Armstrong, Head of Department of Accounting, Business and Management Research Institute, University of Ulster*	marketing strategy, consumer segmentation, branding
	Case 16	Mercedes-Benz: 'The Best or Nothing' *David Cosgrave, Teaching Assistant, Department of Marketing and Management, University of Limerick*	segmenting in organizational markets, positioning strategy
	OLC case 8	Dell Hell: Strategic Change for a Fallen Market Leader *David Jobber, Professor of Marketing, University of Bradford*	positioning, marketing environment, 4Cs framework
9	Case 17	iPhone: Design is Everything *Fiona Ellis-Chadwick, Senior Lecturer in Marketing, The Open University*	competition, new product development, product design, mobile technology industry
	Case 18	Burberry: Reinventing the Brand *David Jobber, Professor of Marketing, University of Bradford*	product management, brand stretching, brand extension, global branding
	OLC case 9	Levi Jeans: Branding for the Youth Market *David Jobber, Professor of Marketing, University of Bradford*	brand positioning, market segmentation, managing products, clothing industry
10	Case 19	Sandals Resorts International (SRI): Positioning Services *Deneise Dadd, The Open University*	nature of services, managing services, customer relationship management
	Case 20	Marketing Care: A Healthy Challenge? *Clare Brindley, Professor of Marketing and Entrepreneurship, Dr Carley Foster, Reader, Dr Sheilagh Resnick, Senior Lecturer in Services Marketing, Nottingham Trent University, and Dr Ranis Cheng, University of Sheffield Management School*	managing service quality
	OLC case 10	Services Marketing in a Recession: The Tale of Five Supermarkets *David Jobber, Professor of Marketing, University of Bradford*	marketing strategies, service marketing, economic downturn, supermarkets
11	Case 21	Unilever's Quest for Growth *David Jobber, Professor of Marketing, University of Bradford*	brand extension, brand portfolio, global marketing, emerging markets
	Case 22	Intel Inside Out: The Search for Growth *David Jobber, Professor of Marketing, University of Bradford*	product life-cycle, product management, IT industry
	OLC case 11	Champagne De Castelnau: Branding and Growth Strategies *Dr. Nicolas Kfuri. Professor of Strategy, Marketing, International Business and Entrepreneurship, GISMA Business School*	global and domestic marketing, consumer profiling, competitor strategy

Chapter	Case number	Case title and author	Key concepts covered
12	Case 23	UGG Australia: Fad of the Season to Fashion Staple of the Decade, Establishing an International Fashion Brand *Fiona Armstrong-Gibbs, Senior Lecturer in Fashion Marketing, London Metropolitan University, and Tamsin Mclaren, Consultant and Senior Lecturer, Southampton Solent University*	innovation, new product development, product life-cycle, brand management
	Case 24	In the Dragons' Den *Fiona Ellis-Chadwick, Senior Lecturer in Marketing, The Open University*	commercialization, innovation culture, managing for success
	OLC case 12	Absolut Vodka *Super Premium Vodka in an Age of Austerity* *Conor Carroll, Lecturer in Marketing*	new products, brand extension, new product development, drinks industry
13	Case 25	EasyJet and Ryanair: Flying High with Low Prices *David Jobber, Professor of Marketing, University of Bradford*	pricing strategies, marketing strategy, low price strategy, airline industry
	Case 26	Limited Range Discounters: In a Recession Discounters are Booming *Conor Carroll, Lecturer in Marketing, University of Limerick*	everyday low pricing, limited range discounters, retail discounters, price wars, competitive strategy
	OLC case 13	Pricing at Hansen Bathrooms *David Jobber, Professor of Marketing, University of Bradford*	pricing strategies, internal marketing
14	Case 27	The Budweiser Ice Cold Index App: 'The Hotter the Day, the Less You Pay' *Marie O'Dwyer, Lecturer in Marketing, Waterford Institute of Technology, Ireland*	IMC, digital and social media, advertising
	Case 28	Comparethemarket.com: 'Simples' *David Cosgrave, Teaching Assistant, Department of Marketing and Management, University of Limerick*	IMC – off and online communications, brand identity, promotional mix
	OLC case 14	Cadbury and 'A Glass Half Full Productions' *Marie O'Dwyer, Lecturer in Marketing, Waterford Institute of Technology, Ireland*	advertising objectives, virtual advertising, television advertising
15	Case 29	Toyota and Buddy *Adele Berndt, Associate Professor, Jönköping International Business School, Sweden*	marketing strategy, IMC, rebuilding a brand
	Case 30	White Horse Whisky: Developing a New Advertising Strategy *Ann Murray Chatterton, Director of Training and Development, Institute of Practitioners in Advertising*	advertising, branding, repositioning, drinks industry
	OLC case 15	Ambush Marketing and the London 2012 Olympic Games *Ran Liu and Dr Des Thwaites, Leeds University Business School.*	sports marketing, ambush marketing

Chapter	Case number	Case title and author	Key concepts covered
16	Case 31	Charles Tyrwhitt: Bricks, Clicks and Flips *Brian Searle, Lecturer in Marketing, Loughborough University*	direct marketing, online and offline catalogue retailing: clothing
	Case 32	Selling in China: Harnessing the Power of the *Guanxi* *David Jobber, Professor of Marketing, University of Bradford*	international marketing, cultural issues, self reference criteria
	OLC case 16	Tesco's Club Card CRM Programme: The Challenges of Coming to Terms with a Changing Market *Colin Gilligan, Emeritus Professor of Marketing, Sheffield Hallam University and Visiting Professor of Marketing, Newcastle Business School*	relationship marketing strategies, CRM programmes, loyalty schemes, grocery retailers
17	Case 33	ASOS: Setting the Pace in Online Fashion *David Jobber, Professor of Marketing, University of Bradford*	online fashion retailing, customer service, promotion strategy, SWOT analysis
	Case 34	Thorntons *Adrian Pritchard, Senior Lecturer in Marketing, Coventry University*	multichannel strategy, types of retail distribution, franchising
	OLC case 17	iTunes: Apple's Profitable Trojan Horse *Conor Carroll, Lecturer in Marketing, University of Limerick*	digital technologies, halo effect, distribution of digital products, digital download industry
18	Case 35	Buy4Now: Powering eCommerce Solutions *Aileen Kennedy, Lecturer Dublin Institute of Technology*	search engine marketing, online retailing
	Case 36	Google Has All the Answers? *Fiona Ellis-Chadwick, Senior Lecturer in Marketing, The Open University*	competitive advantage, differentiation, online resources and competencies
	OLC case 18	Yankee.ie *Roisin Vize, Researcher, Aileen Kennedy, Lecturer, and Dr Joseph Coughlan, Lecturer, Dublin Institute of Technology*	search engine marketing (SEM), online retailing, social media
19	Case 37	General Meltdown: Too Big to Fail *Conor Carroll, Lecturer in Marketing, University of Limerick*	competitive advantage, competitive forces, recovery strategy, global automobile markets
	Case 38	Wal-Mart and Asda: Battling for Retail Success *David Jobber, Professor of Marketing, University of Bradford*	competitive advantage, international acquisitions, retail information systems, global supermarket operations
	OLC case 19	The Wii Fits Us All! Nintendo Regains Video Game Supremacy *Loïc Plé, Assistant Professor, IÉSEG School of Management, France*	competitor analysis, competitive advantage, marketing mix, computer games industry

Preface to the 7th edition

Marketing is constantly adapting to meet the demands of dynamic business environments. Exploring both theoretical principles and business practices is the key to understanding this highly dynamic and complex subject. The seventh edition aims to bring these aspects together and engage readers in an illuminating journey through the discipline of marketing. The book provides many illustrative examples from many different perspectives.

The principle and practice of marketing supports marketing education for students and practitioners of the subject. Students can enjoy learning from applying the principles to real-world marketing problems and, in doing so, gain a richer knowledge of marketing.

Becoming a successful marketing practitioner also requires understanding of the principles of marketing together with the practical experience of implementing marketing ideas, processes and techniques. This book provides a framework for understanding important marketing topics such organizational and consumer behaviour, segmentation, targeting and positioning, brand building, innovation, pricing, communications and digital technology, and implementation – core subject areas within the discipline, which form the backbone of marketing.

Technology is changing the way we do business and communicate, which has profound implications for the way organizations operate. By understanding how to interpret the marketing environment, apply principal concepts and plan for the future, students and practitioners can benefit from developing their knowledge of marketing.

I am joined in the writing of the 7th edition by Fiona Ellis-Chadwick, who as co-author brings to the book her expert knowledge of digital and retail marketing and detailed insight into the practical application of marketing.

Marketing is a very strong discipline, and around Europe there are specialist conferences which present the latest research: for example, the European Marketing Academy, and the Academy of Marketing in the UK. Such conferences highlight the variety and extent of marketing and ensure that there is a growing community of academics, researchers and students who are prepared to take on the challenges of modern marketing and build rewarding careers in this field.

Most students and practitioners enjoy marketing, find it rewarding and relevant not only from an academic but also a practical perspective. We hope this book adds to your knowledge of the subject of marketing and enhances your skills and understanding.

How to study

This book has been designed to help you to learn and to understand the important principles behind successful marketing and how these are applied in practice. We hope that you find the book easy to use and that you are able to follow the ideas and concepts explained in each chapter. As soon as you don't grasp something, go back and read it again. Try to think of *other* examples to which the theory could be applied. To check you really understand the new concepts you are reading about, try completing the exercises and questions at the end of each chapter. You can also test your understanding and expand your knowledge by exploring the Online Learning Centre.

To assist you in working through this text, we have developed a number of distinctive study and design features. To familiarize yourself with these features, please turn to the Guided Tour on pages xxii–xxiv.

New to the 7th edition

As always, recent events are reflected throughout this book. Here is a brief summary of the **key content changes** for this edition:

- **New authorship:** Fiona Ellis-Chadwick as co-author brings considerable teaching experience from Loughborough University and The Open University along with her expert knowledge of digital and retail marketing and detailed insight into the practical application of marketing.

- **Revised structure:** in response to review feedback, this edition has moved away from Advertising and towards the more modern Integrated Marketing Communications, bringing services to the fore as befits such a large sector of the economy.

- **New content:** in response to reviewers who want to teach social media topics, there is a new chapter on *Digital Marketing and Social Media*. Digital coverage has been increased throughout the text with new content including e-procurement, SOE, mobile technologies, new hardware such as smartphones and tablets, and more.

    Other topics covered include social marketing issues such as anti-consumerism, ethical brand value over shareholder value, the social impact of social media marketing and anti-branding. Also coverage of global sourcing, more qualitative market research techniques such as ethnographic research, service dominant logic and guerrilla and ambient marketing.

- **Brand new vignettes, case studies and advertisements throughout the book:** the principles of marketing cannot be fully grasped without solid examples of how these apply in practice. That is why in every chapter you will find a wealth of examples to support the concepts presented. These include current advertisements, and vignettes spanning Marketing in Action, Digital Marketing, and Marketing Ethics and Corporate Social Responsibility in Action, as well as a brand-new *Read the Research* feature and *Mini Cases* that ask you to apply the principles learnt for yourself. Two case studies at the end of each chapter provide more in-depth examples. These features will not only help you to absorb the key principles of marketing, but will also allow you to make links between the various topics and demonstrate the marketing mix at work in real-life situations.

- **An exciting new package of supporting online resources,** including new video resources and cases, as well as a rich choice of activities designed to help students develop and apply their understanding of marketing concepts. See pages xxv–xxvi for further details.

Guided tour

Real marketing

Throughout the text, marketing principles are illustrated with examples of real marketing practice. The following features encourage you to pause to consider the decisions taken by a rich variety of companies.

Marketing in Action vignettes provide additional practical examples to highlight the application of concepts, and encourage you to critically analyse and discuss real-world issues.

Digital Marketing vignettes demonstrate how organizations have used new technologies in their marketing strategies.

Mini Cases are new to this edition. Providing additional practice examples to highlight the application of key concepts, they also have questions to help you critically analyse the principles discussed in each chapter.

Read the Research 10.1   Service Dominant Logic

Service dominant logic challenges the status quo of marketing thinking by putting service rather than the production of goods at the heart of business activity.

Vargo, Stephen L. and Robert F. Lusch (2004) Evolving to a New Dominant Logic for Marketing, Journal of Marketing 68(1), 1–17.

In 2004 Stephen Vargo and Robert Lusch proposed that marketing had changed significantly during past decades and consequently should be viewed from a different perspective. These authors suggested that rather than looking at marketing using a logic based on tangible resources and the economic exchange process, more attention should be given to intangible resources, relationships and co-creation of value. This paper sets out the key ideas of service dominant logic and in doing so has sparked off a controversial academic debate.

Read the Research boxes provide additional information to help guide you to key readings to allow you to explore the concepts discussed in more detail.

Marketing Ethics and CSR in Action vignettes examine ethical dilemmas and examples of how companies can engage in corporate social responsibility.

Real advertisements demonstrate how marketers have presented their products in real promotions and campaigns.

machines. An important choice criterion for business customers is economic value to the customer, which takes into account not only price, but also other costs. The advertisement for Michelin HydroEdge Green X tyres targets business people, explaining that when longevity and fuel efficiency are taken into account, Michelin tyres are better value than the competition.

Decision-making unit structure

Another way of segmenting organizational markets is based on decision-making unit (DMU) composition: members of the DMU and its size may vary between buying organizations. As discussed in Chapter 5, the DMU consists of all those people in a buying organization who have an effect on supplier choice. One segment might be characterized by the influence of top management on the decision; another by the role played by engineers; and a third segment might comprise

In every chapter video clips from television and online campaigns are available on the Online Learning Centre. Look out for the **Ad Insight** boxes.

Go to the website to compare how car manufacturers highlight different benefits depending on the target segment of each car.
www.mcgraw-hill.co.uk/
textbooks/jobber

Each chapter concludes with two **case studies**. These up-to-date examples encourage you to apply what you have learned in each chapter to a real-life marketing problem.

CASE 9

Trading Television Formats is Big Business
Do You Want to Be a Millionaire?

What do the programmes *Pointless*, *Million Pound Drop* and *Who Wants to be a Millionaire* have in common? They are all television quiz shows, with a presenter and teams of contestants. What separates them from each other is that each show has its own unique format, which includes

You can test yourself by trying out the **questions** at the end of each case study section.

Questions

1. Discuss the extent to which the organizational buying decision process is applicable to the buying of television formats.

2. Imagine you are going to the MIPTV exhibition in Cannes to buy new television formats for your television station. Make a list of the criteria you would use to guide your purchasing.

3. Many production companies and broadcasters have their headquarters in London. Suggest why it might be beneficial to be located in a particular area.

Studying effectively

At the beginning of each chapter, the main learning objectives are listed to show you what topics are covered in the chapter. Keep these aims in mind to help focus your reading and then check your understanding in the review at the end of the chapter.

LEARNING OBJECTIVES

After reading this chapter, you should be able to:

1 explain how to develop an IMC strategy and set relevant communication objectives
2 describe the elements of integrated marketing communications
3 explain the distinction between mass and direct communications
4 discuss the promotional communication mix
5 explain the key characteristics of each of the main media channels
6 consider the implications for planning communications for different audiences and contexts

At the beginning of each chapter, the main **learning objectives** are listed to show you what topics are covered in the chapter. Keep these aims in mind to help focus your reading and then check your understanding in the review at the end of the chapter.

Key Terms

advertising any paid form of non-personal communication of ideas or products in the prime media: i.e. television, the press, posters, cinema and radio, the Internet and direct marketing

agency an organization that specializes in providing services such as media selection, creative work, production and campaign planning to clients

digital promotion the promotion of products to consumers and businesses through electronic media

direct marketing (1) acquiring and retaining customers without the use of an intermediary; (2) the distribution of products, information and promotional benefits to target consumers through interactive communication in a way that allows

media planning an advertising strategy most commonly employed to target consumers using a variety of informational outlets. Media planning is generally conducted by a professional media planning or advertising agency and typically finds the most appropriate media outlets to reach the target market

media relations the communication of a product or business by placing information about it in the media without paying for time or space directly

media type (also referred to as a *content type*) is a general category of data content, such as: application (executable program), audio content, an image, a text message, a video stream, and so forth

media vehicle decision the choice of the particular

Use the **key terms** list at the end of each chapter to look up any unfamiliar words, and as a handy aid for quick revision and review.

Study Questions

1 Compare the possible use of advertising and personal selling in an IMC campaign.

2 Discuss how communication messages can be used to build a brand.

3 Explain the difference between mass and direct communications.

4 Explain the consideration a company might use to help with the selection of the promotional mix.

5 Media class decisions should always be based on creative considerations, while media vehicle decisions should be determined solely by cost per thousand calculations. Do you agree?

6 Outline the stages in the IMC planning framework.

Use the **study questions** to review and apply the knowledge you have acquired from each chapter. These questions can be undertaken either individually or as a focus for group discussion in seminars or tutorials.

References

1. Hegarty J. (2011) *Hegarty on advertising: turning intelligence into magic*, London: Thames & Hudson, 95.
2. Hegarty (2011) op. cit., 42.
3. Fill, C. (2011) *Essentials of Marketing Communications*, London: Prentice Hall, 7–8.
4. Hegarty (2011) op. cit., 113.
5. Duncan, T. and S. Everett, (1993) Client perceptions of integrated communications, *Journal of Advertising Research*, 3(3), 30–39.
6. Schultz, D. (1993) Integrated marketing communications: maybe definition is in the point of view, *Marketing News*, 18 January, 17.
7. Hegarty (2011) op. cit., 39.
8. Based on Fill (2011) op. cit., 117.
9. Fill (2011) op. cit., 118.
10. Hall, B. (2012) Campaign Viral Chart: 'the bark side' rises for VW, *Campaign.co.uk*, 27 January, http://www.campaignlive.co.uk/news/1114282/Campaign-Viral-Chart-the-bark-side-rises-VW/?DCMP=ILC-SEARCH.
11. Fill (2011) op. cit., 118.
32. Fill (2011) op. cit., 41.
33. Doherty, N. F., F. E. Ellis-Chadwick and C. A. Hart (1999) Cyber retailing: the potential in the UK of the Internet as a retail channel, *International Journal of Retail & Distribution Management* 27(1).
34. Gladwell, M. (2000) *The Tipping Point*, London: Abacus, 3–5.
35. Mehta, A. (2000) Advertising Attitudes and Advertising Effectiveness, *Journal of Advertising Research*, May/June, 67–72.
36. Cordiner R. (2009) Set free your core native: the brand as a storyteller, *Admap*, October.
37. Chaffey, D. and F. E. Ellis-Chadwick (2012) *Digital Marketing: Strategy, Implementation and Practice*, 5th edn, Harlow: Pearson.
38. Caemmerer, B. (2009) The planning and implementation of integrated marketing communications, *Marketing Intelligence and Planning* 27(4), 524–38.
39. Syedain, H. (1992) Taking the Expert Approach to Media, *Marketing*, 4 June, 20–1.
40. Ellis-Chadwick, F., N. F. Doherty and L. Anastasakis (2007) E-strategy in the UK retail grocery sector: a resource-based analysis,

Use the **references** at the end of the chapter to research an idea in greater depth.

Tour our video and digital resources

In addition to the great study tools available for students and lecturers through **Connect** there are a host of support resources available to you via our website.
Visit www.mcgraw-hill.co.uk/textbooks/jobber today

Online Learning Centre

Visit **www.mcgraw-hill.co.uk/textbooks/jobber today**

Resources for Students:
- Marketing weblinks
- Learning objectives
- Case study guidelines
- Glossary
- Ad Insight videos

Also available for lecturers:
- Case study teaching notes
- PowerPoint slides
- New case studies
- An image bank of artwork from the textbook
- Marketing Showcase videos

Ad Insight

On the student centre of the OLC you will find a wealth of TV advertising campaigns, many of which are linked to topics in the book. Look out for the Ad Insight icon in the text to refer you to watch the relevant clip and put your marketing skills into practice by answering the accompanying questions.

Marketing Showcase

We are excited to offer an exclusive set of new video cases to lecturers adopting this text. Each video illustrates a number of core marketing concepts linked to the book to help students to see how marketing works in the real world. This fantastic video resource will add real value to lectures, providing attention-grabbing content that helps students to make the connection between theory and practice.

What do the videos cover?

The videos offer students insights into how different organizations have successfully harnessed the elements of the marketing mix, including discussions about new product development, pricing, promotion, packaging, market research, and relationship and digital marketing. The videos feature interviews with business leaders and marketing professionals, and ensure seamless integration with the content of the new edition of this text.

How can I use them?

To ensure maximum flexibility for teaching purposes, the videos have been edited to focus on key topics so that short extracts can be easily integrated into a lecture presentation or be delivered in a tutorial setting to spark class discussion. To ensure painless preparation for teaching, each video is accompanied by teaching notes and discussion questions.

Some highlights of the video package include:

- **innocent's** Head of Creative responding to criticism of their pricing policy

- A first-hand account of how a young student entrepreneur set up the thriving **SuperJam** brand, taking his homemade preserves from the kitchen table to the supermarket

- How **Hungry House** took on the Dragons' Den and the take-away market

- An interview with **BMW** revealing how they grow their market without damaging their reputation as a luxury brand

How do I get the videos?

The full suite of videos is available exclusively to lecturers adopting this textbook. For ultimate flexibility, they are available to lecturers:

- through **Connect**
- online at **www.mcgraw-hill.co.uk/textbooks/jobber**

If you are interested in this resource, please contact your McGraw-Hill representative or visit **www.mcgraw-hill.co.uk/textbooks/jobber** to request a demonstration.

Lecturer Test bank in EZ Test

A test bank of hundreds of questions is available to lecturers adopting this book for their module, either through Connect, or if preferred, direct through EZ Test online. A range of questions is provided for each chapter including multiple choice, true or false, and short answer or essay questions. The questions are identified by type, difficulty and topic to help you to select questions that best suit your needs. **McGraw-Hill EZ Test Online** is accessible to busy academics virtually anywhere. They also have access to hundreds of banks and thousands of questions created for other McGraw-Hill titles. Multiple versions of tests can be saved for delivery on paper or online through WebCT, Blackboard and other course management systems.

To register for this FREE resource, visit www.eztestonline.com or contact your McGraw-Hill representative.

STUDENTS...

Want to get **better grades**? *(Who doesn't?)*

Prefer to do your **homework online**? *(After all, you are online anyway...)*

Need **a better way** to **study** before the big test?

(A little peace of mind is a good thing...)

With **McGraw-Hill's** *Connect*™ *Plus Marketing,*

STUDENTS GET:

- **Easy online access** to homework, tests and quizzes assigned by your instructor.

- **Immediate feedback** on how you're doing. (No more wishing you could call your instructor at 1 a.m.)

- **Quick access** to lectures, practice materials, eBook, and more. (All the material you need to be successful is right at your fingertips.)

- A Self-Quiz and Study tool that **assesses your knowledge** and **recommends** specific readings, supplemental study materials, and additional practice work.

- Access to the e-book of this text.

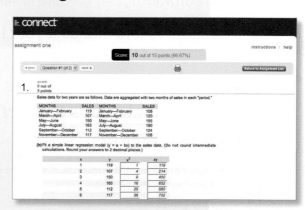

Less managing. More teaching. Greater learning.

 INSTRUCTORS...

Would you like your **students** to show up for class **more prepared**?
(Let's face it, class is much more fun if everyone is engaged and prepared...)

Want an **easy way to assign** homework online and track student **progress**?
(Less time grading means more time teaching...)

Want an **instant view** of student or class performance? *(No more wondering if students understand...)*

Need to **collect data and generate reports** required for administration or accreditation? *(Say goodbye to manually tracking student learning outcomes...)*

Want to **record and post your lectures** for students to view online?

 With **McGraw-Hill's *Connect*™ *Plus Marketing*,**

INSTRUCTORS GET:

- Simple **assignment management**, allowing you to spend more time teaching.
- **Auto-graded** assignments, quizzes and tests.
- **Detailed visual reporting** where student and section results can be viewed and analysed.
- Sophisticated **online testing** capability.
- A **filtering and reporting** function that allows you to easily assign and report on materials that are correlated to sections in the book and level of difficulty.
- An easy-to-use **lecture capture** tool.
- The option to **upload course documents** for student access.

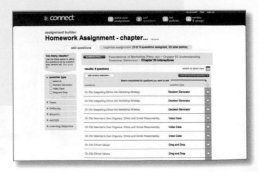

Want an online, **searchable version** of your textbook?

Wish your textbook could be **available online** while you're doing your assignments?

 Connect™ Plus Marketing eBook

If you choose to use *Connect™ Plus Marketing*, you have an affordable and searchable online version of your book integrated with your other online tools.

Connect™ Plus Marketing eBook offers a media-rich version of the book, including:

- Topic search
- Direct links from assignments
- Adjustable text size
- Jump to page number
- Print by section

 Want to get more **value** from your textbook purchase?

Think learning marketing should be a bit more **interesting**?

 Check out the STUDENT RESOURCES section under the *Connect™* Library tab.

Here you'll find a wealth of resources designed to help you achieve your goals in the course. Every student has different needs, so explore the STUDENT RESOURCES to find the materials best suited to you.

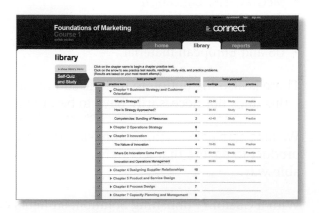

Let us help make our content your solution

At McGraw-Hill Education our aim is to help lecturers to find the most suitable content for their needs delivered to their students in the most appropriate way. Our **custom publishing solutions** offer the ideal combination of content delivered in the way which best suits lecturer and students.

Our custom publishing programme offers lecturers the opportunity to select just the chapters or sections of material they wish to deliver to their students from a database called CREATE™ at

www.mcgrawhillcreate.co.uk

CREATE™ contains over two million pages of content from:
- textbooks
- professional books
- case books – Harvard Articles, Insead, Ivey, Darden, Thunderbird and BusinessWeek
- Taking Sides – debate materials

Across the following imprints:
- McGraw-Hill Education
- Open University Press
- Harvard Business Publishing
- US and European material

There is also the option to include additional material authored by lecturers in the custom product – this does not necessarily have to be in English.

We take care of everything from start to finish in the process of developing and delivering a custom product to ensure that lecturers and students receive exactly the material needed in the most suitable way.

With a Custom Publishing Solution, students enjoy the best selection of material deemed to be the most suitable for learning everything they need for their courses – something of real value to support their learning. Teachers are able to use exactly the material they want, in the way they want, to support their teaching on the course.

Please contact **your local McGraw-Hill representative** with any questions or alternatively contact Warren Eels e: **warren_eels@mcgraw-hill.com**.

About the Authors

David Jobber is an internationally recognized marketing academic. He is Professor of Marketing at the University of Bradford School of Management. He holds an honours degree in Economics from the University of Manchester, a master's degree from the University of Warwick and a doctorate from the University of Bradford.

Before joining the faculty at the Bradford Management Centre, David worked for the TI Group in marketing and sales, and was Senior Lecturer in Marketing at the University of Huddersfield. He has wide experience of teaching core marketing courses at undergraduate, postgraduate and post-experience levels. His specialisms are industrial marketing, sales management and marketing research. He has a proven, ratings-based record of teaching achievements at all levels. His competence in teaching is reflected in visiting appointments at the universities of Aston, Lancaster, Loughborough and Warwick in the UK, and the University of Wellington, New Zealand. He has taught marketing to executives of such international companies as BP, Allied Domecq, the BBC, Bass, Croda International, Rolls-Royce and Rio Tinto.

Supporting his teaching is a record of achievement in academic research. David has over 150 publications in the marketing area in such journals as the *International Journal of Research in Marketing, MIS Quarterly, Strategic Management Journal, Journal of International Business Studies, Journal of Management, Journal of Business Research, Journal of Product Innovation Management* and the *Journal of Personal Selling and Sales Management*. David has served on the editorial boards of the *International Journal of Research in Marketing, Journal of Personal Selling and Sales Management, European Journal of Marketing* and the *Journal of Marketing Management*. He has also acted as Special Adviser to the Research Assessment Exercise panel that rated research output from business and management schools throughout the UK. In 2008 he received the Academy of Marketing's Life Achievement award for distinguished and extraordinary services to marketing.

Fiona-Ellis Chadwick has a successful professional business and academic career. She is a Senior Lecturer at The Open University Business School, where she leads the Retail Management and Marketing programme. As part of this role, Fiona is a very active researcher and innovative educator, and frequently leads the development of innovative multi-media teaching materials, bringing together research and business. Fiona has made a series of educational films for the Open University, which looks at retail marketing, digital technology and economic growth from the perspective of international business leaders. As an academic consultant for the OU/BBC productions, she has worked on highly successful and award-winning series: *The Virtual Revolution, Foods That Make Billions, Evans Business Challenges* and Radio 4's *The Bottom Line* programme. Fiona had a successful commercial career in retailing before becoming an academic and completing her PhD. Having made a significant contribution in the area of online retailing, she continues to focus her research and academic publications on the strategic impact of the Internet and digital technologies on marketing and retailing. Her work on these topics has been widely published in the *Journal of Business Research, European Journal of Marketing, Internet Research, International Journal of Retail Distribution and Management* plus additional textbooks and practitioner journals. Fiona is passionate about how technology and education can help business development in the future.

Acknowledgements for the 7th edition

Authors' Acknowledgements

We would like to thank colleagues, contributors and the reviewers who have offered advice and helped develop this text. We would also like to thank our editors Peter Hooper, Caroline Prodger and Jennifer Yendell for their invaluable support and assistance.

Publisher's Acknowledgements

Our thanks go to the following reviewers for their comments at various stages in the text's development:

Sree Begg, *University of Surrey*
Joan Buckley, *University College Cork*
Sally Chan, *University of Leeds*
Scott Dacko, *Warwick University*
Nathalie Dens, *Universiteit Antwerpen*
Declan Fleming, *NUI Galway*
Jocelyn Hayes, *University of York*
Krzszof Kubacki, *Keele University*
Ed Little, *University of the West of England*
Boris Maciejovsky, *Imperial College London*
Danielle McCartan Quinn, *University of Ulster*
Nikki Newman, *Sheffield University*
Norman Peng, *University of Westminster*
Carsten Rennhak, *Reutlingen University*
Finn Rolighed Andersen, *Aarhus Kobmandsskole*
Eleri Rosier, *Cardiff University*
Agnes Salajczyk, *London South Bank University*
Elo Simoni, *VIA University College*
Graeme Stephen, *Robert Gordon University*
Liane Voerman, *University of Groningen*

We would also like to thank the following contributors for the material which they have provided for this textbook and its accompanying online resources:

Dr Gillian Armstrong, *University of Ulster*
Fiona Armstrong-Gibbs, *London Metropolitan University*
Glyn Atwal, *ESC Dijon-Bourgogne*
Adele Berndt, *Jönköping International Business School*
Claire Brindley, *Nottingham Trent University*
Douglas Bryson, *ESC Rennes School of Business*
Jane Burns-Nurse, *Imperial College London*

Marylyn Carrigan, *The Open University*
Conor Carroll, *University of Limerick*
David Cosgrave, *University of Limerick*
Deneise Dadd, *The Open University*
Dr Christina Donnelly, *NUI Maynooth*
David Edmundson-Bird, *Manchester Metropolitan University*
Dr Raffaele Filieri, *Newcastle Business School*
Marlene Johansson, *Umeå School of Business and Economics*
Aileen Kennedy, *Dublin Institute of Technology*
Nicholas Kfuri, *GISMA Business School*
Tony Lindley, *Tony Lindley Consultants Ltd and University of Bradford*
Sheena MacArthur, *Glasgow Caledonian University*
Tamsin Mclaren, *Southampton Solent University*
Marie O'Dwyer, *Waterford Institute of Technology*
Dr Michele O'Dwyer, *University of Limerick.*
Loïc Plé, *IÉSEG School of Management*
Adrian Pritchard, *Coventry University*
Helena Renström, *Umeå School of Business and Economics*
Nina Reynolds, *Bradford University*
Tony Rowe, *Marketing Mentors*
Brian Searle, *Loughborough University*
Fred Silcock, *Loughborough University*
Ran Lui, *Leeds University Business School*

Paulo Alves, *BMW*
Dan Germain, *Innocent*
Russell Jones, *Diageo*
Shane Lake, *HungryHouse.co.uk*

Picture Acknowledgements

The authors and publishers would like to extend thanks to the following for the reproduction of company advertising and/or logos:

Part Opening Images
Part 1: Thanks to Kraft Foods Inc.; Part 2: Thanks to Diageo; Part 3: Thanks to Innocent/The Coca-Cola Company; Part 4: Thanks to BMW; Part 5: Thanks to Intel

Chapter Opening Images
1: Thanks to Kraft Foods Inc.; 2: Thanks to Kraft Foods Inc.; 3: Thanks to Diageo; 4: Thanks to Diageo; 5: Thanks to Diageo; 6: Thanks to Diageo; 7: Thanks to Diageo; 8: Thanks to Diageo; 9: Thanks to Innocent/The Coca-Cola Company; 10: Thanks to Innocent/The Coca-Cola Company; 11: Thanks to Innocent/The Coca-Cola Company; 12: Thanks to Innocent/The Coca-Cola Company; 13: Thanks to Innocent/The Coca-Cola Company; 14: Thanks to Innocent/The Coca-Cola Company; 15: Thanks to Innocent/The Coca-Cola Company; 16: Thanks to Innocent/The Coca-Cola Company; 17: Thanks to Innocent/The Coca-Cola Company; 18: Thanks to Innocent/The Coca-Cola Company; 19: Thanks to BMW; 20: Thanks to BMW; 21: Thanks to BMW; 22: Thanks to Intel

Chapter Images:
1.1: Thanks to Toyota Motor Europe; 1.2: Thanks to Innocent/The Coca-Cola Company; 1.3: Thanks to Leon Restaurants; 1.4: Thanks to MolsonCoors Brewing Company UK Ltd; 2.1: Virgin Atlantic; 2.2: Thanks the Stobart and Transportation Distribution Group; 2.3: Thanks to Apple Inc.; 2.4: Thanks to Iglo Foods Group Limited; Mini Case 3.1: Thanks to iStockphoto

© Merijn van der Vliet; 3.1: Thanks to Honda Motor Europe Ltd.; 3.2: Thanks to Royal Philips Electronics; 3.3: Thanks to Kraft Foods Inc.; 4.1: Thanks to Mars; 4.2: Thanks to Bulgari; 4.3: Thanks to Audi UK/Volkswagen Group United Kingdom Ltd.; 4.4: Thanks to Pernod Ricard UK; Marketing in Action 4.2: Thanks to iStockphoto © Eleonora Nazarova, © Serhiy Kobyakov, © ideeone, © Carmen Martínez Banús; 5.1: Thanks to Xerox Europe; 5.2: Thanks to Renault UK Ltd; 5.3: Thanks to SAP © Stephen Wilkes; 6.1: Thanks to Nissan Motor (GB) Ltd.; 6.2: Thanks to Sean Click © www.seanclick.com; 6.3: Thanks to Electrolux; 6.4: Thanks to Clipper Teas Ltd; 7.1: Thanks to Dubit Ltd.; 7.2: Thanks to Alamy Ltd © Jeffrey Blackler; Mini Case 7.1: Thanks to Google.com; 7.3: Thanks to Oxfam GB; Digital Marketing 7.2: Thanks to Conquest Research & Consultancy Ltd.; 8.1: Thanks to Fanny Karst; 8.2: Thanks to Michelin; 8.3: Thanks to iStockphoto © peng wu; 8.4: Thanks to The Advertising Archives; 9.1: Thanks to eBay Inc.; 9.2: Thanks to the LEGO Group; 9.3: Thanks to News International; 9.4: Thanks to Unilever; 9.5: Thanks to Samsung; 10.1: Thanks to iStockphoto © Horst Gerlach; 10.2: Thanks to Sainsbury's Supermarkets Ltd; 10.3: Thanks to easyJet Airline Company Limited; 10.4: Thanks to Singapore Airlines; 11.1: Thanks to Samsung; 11.2: Thanks to Heinz; 11.3: Thanks to Cadbury; 11.4: Thanks to ŠKODA AUTO; Digital Marketing 12.1: Thanks to the British Sky Broadcasting Group Plc.; 12.2: License All rights reserved by Digital Forming; 13.1: Thanks to Aldi; Marketing in Action 13.1: Thanks to the Tata Group; 14.1: Thanks to Marks & Spencer; 14.2: Thanks to Volkswagen of America Inc.; 14.3: Thanks to British Airways and the London Olympic Games; 14.4: Thanks to Levis; 14.5: Thanks to Thames Reach; 14.6: Thanks to the Benetton Group; 14.7: Thanks to iStockphoto © GYI NSEA; 15.1: Thanks to GoCompare.com; 15.2: Thanks to the GlaxoSmithKline Group; 15.3: Thanks to Procter & Gamble © Wieden + Kennedy; 15.4: Thanks to the Advertising Archives; Marketing in Action 15.1: Barter Books; 15.5: Thanks to Diageo; 15.6: Thanks to FedEx; Digital Marketing 15.1: Thanks to Häagen-Dazs; 16.1: Thanks to Who's Next; Mini Case 16.1: Thanks to Stella McCartney Limited; 17.1: Thanks to Welcome Break; 17.2: Thanks to Yum!; 17.3: Thanks to iStockphoto © LifesizeImages; 17.4: Thanks to DHL; 18.1: Thanks to Facebook; 18.2: Thanks to Dailymail.co.uk; 18.3 www.lastexittonowhere.com; Mini Case 18.1: Thanks to Zynga Inc.; 19.1: Thanks to Nespresso; 19.2: Thanks to Apple Inc.; 19.3: Thanks to Bang & Olufsen; 19.4: Thank to the Advertising Archives; Marketing in Action 20.1: Thanks to iStockphoto © Danil Melekhin; 20.1: Thanks to Kraft Foods Inc.; 21.1: Thanks to iStockphoto © Nikada; 21.2: Thanks to HSBC; 21.3: Thanks to A.G. BARR p.l.c.; Marketing in Action 22.1: Thanks to Xerox Corporation; 22.1: Thanks to iStockphoto © GYI NSEA; 22.2: Thanks to Lloyds Banking Group; 22.3: Thanks to B&Q.

Case Images
1: Thanks to iStockphoto© NoDerog; 2: Thanks to Nokia; 3: Reprinted with permission from Dixons Retail plc.; 4: Thanks to Volvo Car Corporation; 5: Thanks to Sony Europe Ltd; 6: Thanks to iStockphoto © ranplett; 7: Thanks to iStockphoto © Andrea Zanchi; 8: Thanks to RedBull/Instagram; 9: Thanks to BBC; 10: Thanks to iStockphoto © Anthony Seebaran; 11: Thanks to iStockphoto © Carlos Daniel Gawronski; 12: Thanks to Nestlé; 13: Thanks to Apple Inc.; 14: Thanks to iStockphoto © Brian Jackson; 15: Thanks to Morelli's Gelato Limited; 16: Thanks to iStockphoto © Trevor Smith; 17: Thanks to Apple Inc.; 18: Thanks to iStockphoto © Andrea Zanchi; 19: Thanks to iStockphoto © Martin Valigursky; 20: Thanks to iStockphoto © Dean Mitchell; 21: Thanks to Getty Images © AFP/Getty Images; 22: Thanks to iStockphoto © 4kodiak; 23: Thanks to iStockphoto © Gordon Heeley; 24: Thanks to Levi Roots; 25: Thanks to Getty Images © Bloomberg; 26: Thanks to Alamy Ltd. © vario images GmbH & Co.KG; 27: Thanks to Anheuser-Busch InBev; 28: Thanks to comparethemarket.com; 29: Thanks to Toyota; 30: Thanks to iStockphoto © Aydin Mutlu; 31: Thanks to iStockphoto © Monique Heydenrych; 32: Thanks to iStockphoto © Robert Churchill; 33: Thanks to Alamy Ltd. © Newscast; 34: Thanks to iStockphoto © Courtney Keating; 35: Thanks to Alamy Ltd. © cyberstock; 36: Thanks to iStockphoto © Cliff Wassmann; 37: Thanks to iStockphoto © Shaun Lowe; 38: Thanks to Alamy Ltd.© Maurice Savage; 39: Thanks to Alamy Ltd.© European

Pressphoto Agency; 40: Thanks to Nikon; 41: Thanks to iStockphoto © omer sukru goksu; 42: Thanks to Diageo; 43: Thanks to Getty Images © Ian Walton; 44: Thanks to Glyn Atwal © Glyn Atwal. The publishers would also like to extend special thanks to Leonie Sloman for her assistance with image research.

Fundamentals of Modern Marketing Thought

1 Marketing in the modern organization   2

CHAPTER 1

Marketing in the modern organization

> *Management must think of itself not as producing products, but as providing customer-creating value satisfactions. It must push this idea (and everything it means and requires) into every nook and cranny of the organization. It has to do this continuously and with the kind of flair that excites and stimulates the people in it.*
>
> **THEODORE LEVITT**

LEARNING OBJECTIVES

After reading this chapter, you should be able to:

1. identify the fundamental principles of marketing
2. define the marketing concept and identify its key components and limitations
3. compare a production orientation and a marketing orientation
4. differentiate between the characteristics of market-driven and internally driven businesses
5. compare the roles of efficiency and effectiveness in achieving corporate success
6. describe how to create customer value and satisfaction
7. describe how an effective marketing mix is designed
8. discuss the criticisms of the 4-Ps approach to marketing management
9. explain the relationship between marketing characteristics, market orientation and business performance
10. identify relevant business and research examples, which illustrate the principles of marketing in a modern organization

What is Marketing?

Marketing drives successful organizations but it is often misinterpreted and sometimes gets bad press. Critics use phrases like marketing '*gimmicks*', '*ploys*' and '*tricks*' to undermine the valuable effect that marketing *can* deliver. This is unfortunate because the essence of marketing is value creation not trickery. Successful companies rely on customers returning to repurchase, and the goal of marketing is long-term satisfaction, not short-term deception. This theme is reinforced by the writings of top management consultant, the late Peter Drucker, who stated:[1]

> Because the purpose of business is to create and keep customers, it has only two central functions—marketing and innovation. The basic function of marketing is to attract and retain customers at a profit.

What can we learn from this statement? First, it places marketing in a central role for business success and focuses managers' attention on attracting and keeping customers. Second, it implies that the purpose of marketing is not to chase any customer at any price. Drucker used profit as a criterion. Please note that profit may be used by many commercial organizations, whereas in the non-profit sector other measures of success might be used, such as reduction of social deprivation or hunger. Consequently, the concepts, principles and techniques described in this book are as applicable to Oxfam as to Apple.

Third, it is much more expensive to attract new customers than to retain existing ones. Indeed, the costs of attracting a new customer have been found to be up to six times higher than the costs of retaining old ones.[2] Companies which apply the principles of marketing recognize the importance of building relationships with customers by providing satisfaction and attracting new customers by creating added value. Grönroos stressed the importance of relationship building in his definition of marketing in which he describes the objective of marketing as to establish, develop and commercialize long-term customer relationships so that the objectives of the parties involved are met.[3] Finally, most markets—e.g., consumer, industrial and not-for-profit—are characterized by strong competition. This means organizations need not only to understand what their customers want but also to understand what their competitors provide. If customers' needs are not met, they may switch to a rival supplier.

Marketing exists through exchanges. **Exchange** is the act or process of receiving something from someone by giving something in return. The 'something' could be a physical good, service, idea or money. Money facilitates exchanges so that people can concentrate on working at things they are good at, earn money (itself an exchange) and spend it on products or services that someone else has supplied. The objective is for all parties in the exchange to feel satisfied and gain something of value. The idea of satisfaction is particularly important to suppliers of products, because satisfied customers are more likely than dissatisfied ones to return to buy more. Hence, the notion of customer satisfaction as the central pillar of marketing is fundamental to the creation of a stream of exchanges upon which commercial success depends.

The rest of this chapter discusses the fundamental principles of marketing and provides an introduction to how marketing can create customer value and satisfaction.

The Marketing Concept

The above discussion introduces the notion of the marketing concept—that is, that companies achieve their profit and other objectives by satisfying (even delighting) customers.[4] This is the traditional idea underlying marketing. However, it neglects a fundamental aspect of commercial life: competition. The traditional marketing concept is a necessary but not a sufficient condition for corporate success. To achieve success, companies must go further than mere customer satisfaction; they must do better than the competition. Mercedes-Benz constantly focuses on the competition, and year-on-year builds on its success through successful marketing and innovation. In 2011 Mercedes-Benz was ranked top super brand in the luxury car market continuing to increase market share by 3.4 per cent.[5]

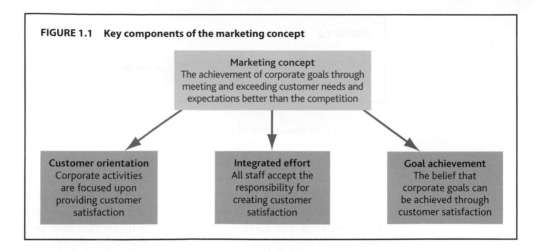

FIGURE 1.1 Key components of the marketing concept

The modern **marketing concept** can be expressed as:

The achievement of corporate goals through meeting and exceeding customer needs and expectations better than the competition.

To apply this concept, three conditions should be met: 1) company activities should focus on providing customer satisfaction rather than making things easier and better for the producer or manufacturer. This is not an easy condition to meet but it is a necessity to place the customer at the centre of all activity; 2) the achievement of customer satisfaction relies on integrated effort. The responsibility for the implementation of the concept lies not just within the marketing department. The belief that customer needs are central to the operation of a company should run right through production, finance, research and development, engineering and other departments. The role of the marketing department is to play *champion* for the concept and to coordinate activities. But the concept is a business philosophy, not a departmental duty; 3) for integrated effort to work successfully, management must believe that corporate goals can be achieved through satisfied customers (see Fig. 1.1).

Marketing versus Production Orientation

There is no guarantee that all companies will adopt the marketing concept. Researchers suggest the **marketing orientation** is an evolutionary process and companies can move from unawareness to complete acceptance of the importance of the marketing concept[6,7] as a means of defining the orientation of a business. A competing philosophy is production orientation.* This is an inward-looking stance, where managers can become focused on the internal aspects of their business. This is particularly evident, in manufacturing companies, where employees spend their working day at the point of production, so it is easy to understand how this can happen.

Production orientation manifests itself in two ways. First, management becomes cost-focused and believes that the central focus of its job is to attain economies of scale by

---

*This, of course, is not the only alternative business philosophy. For example, companies can be financially or sales orientated. If financially orientated, companies focus on short-term returns, basing decisions more on financial ratios than customer value; and sales-orientated companies emphasize sales push rather than adaptation to customer needs. Some textbooks even allude to the existence of eras of business orientation—production, product, selling and marketing—each with its own time zone, and this has entered marketing folklore. However, research has shown that such a sequence is based on the flimsiest of evidence and is oversimplified and misleading.[8] We shall concentrate on the fundamental difference in corporate outlook: marketing versus production orientation.

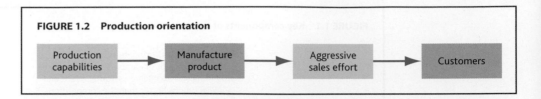

FIGURE 1.2 Production orientation

Production capabilities → Manufacture product → Aggressive sales effort → Customers

producing a limited range of products (at the extreme, just one) in a form that minimizes production costs. Henry Ford is quoted as an example of a production-orientated manager because he built just one car in one colour—the black Model T—in order to minimize costs. However, this is unfair to Mr. Ford since his objective was customer satisfaction: bringing the car to new market segments through low prices. The real production-orientated manager has no such virtues. The objective is cost reduction for its own sake, an objective at least partially fuelled by the greater comfort and convenience that comes from producing a narrow product range.

The second way in which production orientation is manifest is in the belief that the business should be defined in terms of its production facilities. Figure 1.2 illustrates production orientation in its crudest form. The focus is on current production capabilities that define the business mission. The purpose of the organization is to manufacture products and aggressively sell them to unsuspecting customers. A classic example of the catastrophe that can happen when this philosophy drives a company is that of Pollitt and Wigsell, a steam engine producer that sold its products to the textile industry. It made the finest steam engine available and the company grew to employ over 1000 people on a 30-acre (12-hectare) site. Its focus was on steam engine production, so when the electric motor superseded the earlier technology, it failed to respond. The 30-acre site is now a housing estate. Contrast the fortunes of Pollitt and Wigsell with another company operating in the textile industry at about the same time. This company made looms and achieved great success when it launched the type G power loom, which allowed one person to oversee 50 machines. Rather than defining its business as a power loom producer, the company adopted a marketing orientation and sought new opportunities in emerging markets. In 1929 the type G power loom patent was sold to fund the creation of a car division. The company was Toyota.[9] Tension between the product and market orientation continues to define business success today. Kodak is a company that failed to adapt to the market and recognize changes in the film and photography industry. Consequently, it struggled to cope with the emergence of competitors,[10] who offered the market products more suited to their needs. Despite being the first company to introduce a digital camera in 1991, Kodak lost market share to the smart phone—e.g., iPhone 4s, and other catch-all electronic devices that meet consumers' photographic and movie needs, on-demand and on the move. There has been a significant shift in the needs of the consumer in the electronics industry and a merging of the boundaries between communications, photography and film.

Marketing-orientated companies focus on customer needs. Change is recognized as endemic and adaptation considered a Darwinian condition for survival. Changing needs present potential market opportunities, which drive the company. For example, the change towards ethical consumption has created opportunities for existing companies, such as Danone—in 2011 the company launched the Fundooz brand aimed at improving nutritional intake of children in India—as well as opportunities for the creation and growth of new companies such as One Water, that donates 100 per cent of profits to life-saving projects in Africa, and Toms Shoes where one pair of shoes is donated every time a pair is sold. Within the boundaries of their distinctive competences, market-driven companies seek to adapt their product and service offerings to the demands of current and latent markets. This orientation is shown in Figure 1.3.

Marketing-orientated companies get close to their customers so that they can get to understand their needs and problems. For example, Dürr AG, the German paint and assembly systems

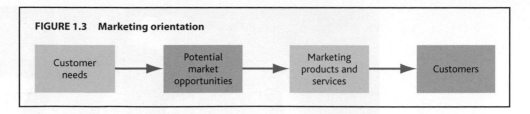

FIGURE 1.3   Marketing orientation

Customer needs → Potential market opportunities → Marketing products and services → Customers

manufacturer, gets close to its customers by assigning over half its workforce to the sites of its customers, such as Ford and Audi. When personal contact is insufficient or not feasible, formal marketing research is commissioned to understand customer motivations and behaviour.

Part of the success of German machine tool manufacturers can be attributed to their willingness to develop new products with lead customers: those companies who themselves are innovative.[11] This contrasts sharply with the attitude of UK machine tool manufacturers, who saw marketing research as merely a tactic to delay new product proposals and who feared that involving customers in new product design would have adverse effects on the sales of current products. Marketing orientation is related to the strategic aims of companies. Marketing-orientated firms adopt a proactive search for market opportunities, use market information as a base for analysis and organizational learning, and adopt a long-term strategic perspective on markets and brands.[12]

Understanding Market-Driven Businesses

A deeper understanding of the marketing concept and orientation can be gained by contrasting a market-driven business with an internally focused business that focuses mainly on production-orientation. Table 1.1 summarizes the key differences.

Market-driven companies display customer concern throughout the business. All departments recognize the importance of the customer to the success of the business. Nestlé, for example, has placed the customer at the centre of its business philosophy by giving the company's head of marketing responsibility for the company's seven strategic business units. Marketers also control strategy, research and development, and production.[13] For internally

TABLE 1.1   Contrasting businesses: market versus internal focus

Market focus	Internal focus
Customer concern throughout business	Convenience comes first
Knowledge of customer choice criteria enables matching with marketing mix	Assumes price and product performance is key to generating sales
Segment by customer differences	Segment by product
Invest in market research (MR) and track market changes	Rely on anecdotes and received wisdom
Welcome change	Cherish status quo
Try to understand competition	Ignore competition
Marketing spend regarded as an investment	Marketing spend regarded as a luxury
Innovation rewarded	Innovation punished
Search for latent markets	Stick with the same
Being fast	Why rush?
Strive for competitive advantage	Happy to be me-too
Efficient and effective	Efficient

Go to the website to watch Toyota's 'Gadget Guy' advert to see how they communicate the car's benefits to customers. www.mcgraw-hill.co.uk/ textbooks/jobber

⬆EXHIBIT 1.1   The Toyota Yaris 'Gadget Guy' advert displays how product benefits are used to communicate with customers.

focused businesses convenience comes first. If customer wants are inconvenient or expensive to produce, excuses are often used as avoidance tactics.

Market-driven businesses know how their products and services are being evaluated against those of the competition. They understand the choice criteria that customers are using and ensure that their marketing mix matches those criteria better than that of the competition.

Businesses that are driven by the market base their segmentation analyses on customer differences that have implications for marketing strategy. Businesses that are focused internally segment by product and, consequently, are vulnerable when customers' requirements change. Bombardier manufactures products for two industrial sectors: aerospace and rail transportation. However, this world-leading business also recognizes the importance of its customers, who have very specific needs.

A key feature of market-driven businesses is their recognition that marketing research expenditure is an investment that can yield rich rewards through better customer understanding. Toyota is a market-led company which uses market research extensively. The Yaris was specially designed to meet the needs of the European consumer and Toyota's Optimal Drive technology was designed to provide their customers with the benefit of enhanced performance, lower emissions and better fuel economy.

Internally driven businesses see marketing research as a non-productive intangible and prefer to rely on anecdotes and received wisdom. Market-orientated businesses welcome the organizational changes that are bound to occur as an organization moves to maintain strategic fit between its environment and its strategies. In contrast, internally orientated businesses cherish the status quo and resist change. Read Digital Marketing 1.1 to find out how technology companies are changing the way everyone does business.

Attitudes towards competition also differ. Market-driven businesses try to understand competitive objectives and strategies, and anticipate competitive actions. Internally driven companies are content to ignore the competition. Marketing spend is regarded as an investment that has long-term consequences in market-driven businesses. The alternative view is that marketing expenditure is viewed as a luxury that never appears to produce benefits.

In marketing-orientated companies those employees who take risks and are innovative are rewarded. Recognition of the fact that most new products fail is reflected in a reluctance to punish those people who risk their career championing a new product idea. Internally

Digital Marketing 1.1 Googleyzed, Facebooked and eBayed: The Internet is Changing How Everyone Does Business

In 1986 the first .co.uk address was registered. Less than 25 years later almost three-quarters of households and businesses in the UK have access to the Internet via broadband connections. According to the Boston Consulting Group 'The Internet is transforming the UK economy'. Nearly everyone in the UK has taken to e-commerce in a big way. It has been estimated that the Internet contributed almost £100 billion to the UK economy. It is not easy to visualize, but it amounts to more trade than each of the construction, transportation and utilities industries and means that more than 7 per cent of Gross Domestic Product (GDP) comes via the Internet. This is important as GDP is an indicator of the health of a country's economy; if it is showing positive growth then the economy is expanding. GDP is measured in three ways: 1) *output*, which is the value of goods produced by all sectors of the economy; 2) *expenditure*, the value of all goods purchased by households and government departments; 3) *income*, which is all the wages of individuals and company profits. So, there is a further £400 billion of commercial activities generated by business-to-business e-commerce, online advertising and productivity improvements, conducted via the Internet, which are not included in GDP calculations. The reach of the Internet is having an impact not only on the economy but also on the way companies do business and how consumers shop. Even those who do not trade or buy online may refer to websites to check out products and services before they buy, and the financial benefits of this activity are calculated to a further £40 billion per year (in offline purchases).

Based on: BCG (2011);[14] *BBC News Business (2011)*[15]

↑EXHIBIT 1.2
Natural smoothies enable Innocent to access emerging niche markets.

Go to the website to see how Innocent markets its smoothies and how the advertising has changed since the launch of the product.
www.mcgraw-hill.co.uk/ textbooks/jobber

orientated businesses reward time-serving and the ability not to make mistakes. This results in risk avoidance and the continuance of the status quo. Market-driven businesses search for latent markets: markets that no other company has yet exploited. 3M's Post-it product filled a latent need for a quick, temporary attachment to documents, while eBay, the online auction site, exploited the latent market for individuals who wished to sell products directly to others. Nintendo identified a latent market for a new style of home entertainment with the launch of its Wii console and software. The new product targets families, and the electronic games promise health and fitness for everyone who plays. Internally driven businesses are happy to stick with their existing products and markets.

Intensive competition means market-driven companies should respond quickly to latent markets. They need to innovate, manufacture and distribute their products and services rapidly if they are to succeed before the *strategic window* of opportunity closes.[16] In contrast;

Test your knowledge about who owns whom by matching the parent company with the brands they own (answers below the table)	
A Kraft owns ?	1 Rachel's Organic
B PepsiCo owns ?	2 Innocent
C Groupe Lactalis owns ?	3 Abel & Cole
D Wellness Foods owns ?	4 Green & Black's
E Lloyds Banking Group majority shareholder in ?	5 Buxton
F Unilever owns ?	6 Tyrrell's
G Coca Cola majority shareholder in ?	7 Seeds of Change
H Nestlé owns ?	8 Dorset Cereals
I Mars owns ?	9 Copella
J Langholm Capital majority shareholder in ?	10 Ben & Jerry's
A 4 B 9 C 1 D 8 E 3 F 10 G 2 H 5 I 7 J 6	

internally driven companies tend to take their time. An example of a company which was slow to respond to the opportunities in the mobile computer is Microsoft. It introduced the tablet PC and carved a niche market in the health sector, but in 2010 Apple launched the iPad, widened market demand and now dominates this sector.

A key feature of marketing-orientated companies is that they strive for competitive advantage. They seek to serve customers better than the competition. Internally orientated companies are happy to produce me-too copies of offerings already on the market.

Finally, marketing-orientated companies are both efficient and effective; internally orientated companies achieve only efficiency. The concepts of efficiency and effectiveness are discussed in the next section.

Marketing in Action 1.1 Corporate Strategies to Access Niche Markets

New markets are emerging for natural products. A report by the Co-operative identified that markets for ethically sourced and produced food have grown almost three-fold in less than ten years and demand is driving these markets towards becoming more mainstream. While the rate of growth slowed a little in 2008/9, overall demand has continued to be positive, and a Euromonitor International report forecasts year-on-year growth of 4 per cent during 2011–2015. So it might come as no surprise that major corporate food manufacturers are seeking ways to access these emerging and potentially lucrative markets. According to a report by *Which? Magazine* (2011), 'Wholesome-sounding brands have become household names, from Rachel's Organics to Green & Blacks and many of us buy them partly because we like their principles and want to support small independents'. However, *Which? Magazine* also discovered that multinational corporations have become parent companies of many niche organic and ethical brands and, while they may share their principles, the 'corporate parents often keep quiet about their ethical offspring'. Many ethical brands do not display the parent company name on the product or on associated websites, and those that do tend to be in very small print on an obscure part of the product packaging. According to academic experts there are advantages to adopting this approach: access to target markets that are difficult to reach, and *off-the-shelf* products with ready-made branding and strong market positioning, giving easy access to the market.

Based on: *Euromonitor International (2011)*;[17] *Which? Magazine (2011)*[18]

Efficiency versus Effectiveness

Another perspective on business philosophy can be gained by understanding the distinction between efficiency and effectiveness.[19] **Efficiency** is concerned with inputs and outputs. An efficient firm produces goods economically: it does things right. The benefit is that the cost per unit of output is low and, therefore, the potential for offering low prices to gain market share, or charging medium to high prices and achieving high profit margins, is present. For example, car companies attempt to achieve efficiency by gaining economies of scale and building several models on the same sub-frame and with the same components. However, to be successful, a company needs to be more than just efficient—it needs to be effective as well. **Effectiveness** means doing the right things. This implies operating in attractive markets and making products that customers want to buy. Conversely, companies that operate in unattractive markets or are not producing what customers want to buy will go out of business; the only question is one of timing.

The link between performance and combinations of efficiency and effectiveness can be conceived as shown in Figure 1.4. A company that is both inefficient and ineffective will go out of business quickly, because it is a high-cost producer of products that customers do not want to buy. One company that has suffered through a combination of

FIGURE 1.4 Efficiency and effectiveness

	Ineffective	Effective
Inefficient	Goes out of business quickly	Survives
Efficient	Dies slowly	Does well Thrives

inefficiency and ineffectiveness is General Motors. The inefficiency is the result of the legacy of paying healthcare costs to its current and retired workers—this adds $1500 to the cost of each of its cars; the ineffectiveness stems from a history of making unreliable and undesirable cars.[20]

A company that is efficient and ineffective may last a little longer because its low cost base may generate more profits from the dwindling sales volume it is achieving. Kodak is an example of an efficient and ineffective company that has slowly died. It was an efficient producer of photographic film but has become ineffective as consumers have moved to digital photography.[21] Firms that are effective but inefficient are likely to survive because they are operating in attractive markets and are marketing products that customers want to buy. Mercedes used to fall into this category, with its emphasis on over-engineering pushing up costs and lowering efficiency, while still making cars that people wanted to buy (driving an S500 has been likened to 'being wrapped in a freshly laundered silk sheet and blown up the road by a warm wind')[22] and so achieving effectiveness. The problem is that their inefficiency is preventing them from reaping the maximum profits from their endeavours. Many small companies that operate in niche markets fall into the effective/inefficient category. One example is Morgan Motor Company, which manufactures bespoke, high-specification sports cars. Prices for the basic model start at less than £30,000 and, as a result, the company has a long waiting list of customer orders but the factory continues to manufacture fewer than 20 cars a week.

A combination of efficiency and effectiveness leads to optimum business success. Such firms do well and thrive because they are operating in attractive markets, are supplying products that consumers want to buy and are benefiting from a low cost base.

Toyota is an example of an efficient and effective manufacturing company. Its investment in modern production practices ensures efficiency, while effectiveness is displayed by research and development investment into new products that consumers want to buy. Similarly, Dixons Retail Plc is an example of a company that has streamlined the supply side of its operation, so it can handle the growing demands of a multichannel retail operation efficiently. The company has also reinvented its store operations with a two-in-one format bringing together the leading brands of Currys and PC World to maximize consumer convenience and satisfaction. These investments have put the company in a strong position in consumer electronic markets.

Another company that has thrived through a combination of efficiency and effectiveness is Zara, the Spanish fashion chain. By using its own highly automated manufacturing and distribution facilities, seamstresses in 350 independently owned workshops in Spain and Portugal, and low advertising expenditures (its shops have always been its primary marketing tool), Zara has achieved high levels of efficiency. It is also highly effective through its ability to match quickly changing fashion trends by means of an extremely fast and responsive supply chain. The result is that Zara has become the world's largest clothing retailer.[23]

The essential difference between efficiency and effectiveness, then, is that the former is cost focused while the latter is customer focused. An effective company has the ability to attract and retain customers, while remaining cost-efficient.

Limitations of the Marketing Concept

Academics have raised important questions regarding the value of the marketing concept. The four key issues are:
1 The marketing concept as an ideology
2 Marketing and society
3 Marketing as a constraint on innovation
4 Marketing as a source of dullness.

The marketing concept as an ideology

Brownlie and Saren argue the marketing concept has assumed many of the characteristics of an ideology or an article of faith that should dominate the thinking of organizations.[24] They

⬆**EXHIBIT 1.3**   Leon Restaurants offer a different 'fast food' experience.

recognize the importance of a consumer orientation for companies but ask why, after 40 years of trying, the concept has not been fully implemented. They argue that there are other valid considerations that companies must take into account when making decisions (e.g. economies of scale) apart from giving customers exactly what they want. Marketers' attention should focus not only on propagation of the ideology but also on its integration with the demands of other core business functions in order to achieve a compromise between the satisfaction of consumers and the achievement of other company requirements.

Marketing and society

A second limitation of the marketing concept concerns its focus on individual market transactions. Since many individuals focus on personal benefits rather than the societal impact of their purchases, the adoption of the marketing concept will result in the production of goods and services that do not adequately correspond to societal welfare. Providing customer satisfaction is simply a means to achieve a company's profit objective and does not guarantee protection of the consumer's welfare. This view is supported by Wensley, who regards consumerism as a challenge to the adequacy of the atomistic and individual view of market transactions.[25] Bloom and Greyser present an alternative view. They regard consumerism as the ultimate expression of the marketing concept, compelling marketers to consider consumer needs and wants that hitherto may have been overlooked:[26] 'The resourceful manager will look for the positive opportunities created by consumerism rather than brood over its restraints.'

Companies are responding to the challenge of societal concerns in various ways. Marketing Ethics and Corporate Social Responsibility in Action 1.1 describes how company and government collaboration resulted in a social marketing campaign to control obesity. Other companies are responding to society's concern for the environment. Leon restaurants are aiming to change the fast food experience by only using natural, sustainably farmed produce in their menus.

Go to the website to watch the Change4Life TV commercial.
www.mcgraw-hill.co.uk/ textbooks/jobber

Marketing as a constraint on innovation

Tauber presented a third criticism of marketing—that is, how marketing research discourages major innovation.[27] The thrust of his argument was that relying on customers to guide the development of new products has severe limitations. This is because customers have difficulty articulating needs beyond the realm of their own experience. This suggests that the ideas gained from marketing research will be modest compared to those coming from the 'science push' of the research and development laboratory. Brownlie and Saren agree that, particularly for discontinuous innovations (e.g. Xerox, penicillin), the role of product development ought to be far more proactive than this.[28] Indeed technological innovation is the process that 'realizes' market demands that were previously unknown—e.g., search engines, social networks, cloud computing—are changing the very structure of society and were unimaginable by most consumers less than a decade ago.

It is important to note that these criticisms are not actually directed at the marketing concept itself but towards its faulty implementation: an overdependence on customers as a source of new product ideas.[29] The marketing concept does not suggest that companies must depend solely on the customer for new product ideas; rather the concept implies that new product development should be based on sound interfacing between perceived customer needs and technological research. For example, at Google innovation is encouraged and innovations are tested and launched—e.g., froogle (product search engine, launched

Marketing Ethics and Corporate Social Responsibility in Action 1.1 Using Social Marketing to Combat the Obesity Crisis

Overeating has become a pressing health issue in many developed countries. In the UK there are 9000 premature deaths per year linked to obesity. Government data suggest that obesity-related illnesses will cost the taxpayer £50 billion by 2050, and up to 90 per cent of today's children will be obese or overweight by the same year if current trends continue. In an attempt to raise public awareness of the link between obesity and life-threatening diseases such as coronary heart disease and diabetes, the UK Government financed a £75 million social marketing campaign, which drew an additional £200 million-worth of services and marketing support from a variety of companies and organizations, including supermarkets, large food producers, health clubs, the London Marathon, voluntary groups and a wide-ranging media coalition. Rather than shocking people into healthier lifestyles, the Change4Life TV campaign used light-hearted animation to inform consumers of the threats posed by sedentary lifestyles, and drew particular attention to the need for children to eat more healthily and become more active.

The campaign is a social marketing effort aimed at employing the power of marketing tools and concepts to achieve specific behavioural goals for increased societal welfare. Although the initiative has been welcomed by most stakeholders, some have criticized the government's choice to engage in corporate partnerships, as food corporations and supermarkets are seen as part of the issue by selling junk food and pushing foods high in salt, fat and sugar as cheap and credit crunch-friendly options for hard-pressed consumers. Critics have suggested that the use of legislation to protect children from junk food marketing and effective nutritional labelling enforcement would be far better investments than the Change4Life campaign. Others suggest private partnerships will have a positive effect by putting junk food companies under the spotlight, and making them subject to public scrutiny through their commitments to a health-related cause.

In 2010 HM Government reported on the Change4Life campaign, and found that, in its first year, the Change4Life movement has become more widespread than expected and there are many more supporters in the form of government and commercial sector partners. The focus of the campaign has widened and now includes Let's Dance with Change4Life, Bike4Life, and Walk4Life and Start4Life, targeting pregnant mums and families with very young children. The Change4Life campaign has exceeded all of the initial targets, and the number of families signing up to the schemes is double the year one target. The report also states that 'over 1 million mums are already claiming to have made changes to their children's diets or activity levels as a result of Change4Life'.

Based on: HM Government (2010);[30] Boseley (2009);[31] Sweeney (2009);[32] Watts (2009);[33] National Social Marketing Centre[34]

November 2004, sidelined and renamed 2007), Google Sidewiki (web annotation tool launched 2009, discontinued December 2011), Google Buzz (social networking launched in September 2010). However, innovations only succeed if they satisfy the user and there is widespread uptake. Google is very well informed about which of its innovations are effective and which need to be discontinued.

Marketing as a source of dullness

A fourth criticism of marketing is that its focus on analysing customers and developing offerings that reflect their needs leads to dull marketing campaigns, me-too products, copycat promotion and marketplace stagnation. Instead, marketing should create demand rather than simply reflect it. Britain's retail industry provides some evidence to support this premise: in 2005 a NEF report[35] concluded that there was increasing uniformity across high streets up and down the country and suggested the level of *blandness* was a new threat to retail development. The report blamed concentration of ownership among retailers, who have rolled out their formulaic retail solutions in high streets and shopping malls and the result is 'corporate sameness'—a style, which continues to shape today's high streets. Retail guru Mary Portas raised her concerns with the UK Government about the 'sameness' of malls and shopping centres and the impact on town centres, and got their commitment to invest in developing more diverse retailing to attract shoppers to city centres.

Brown also feels marketing should tease, tantalize and torment target markets to create insatiable desire'.[36] He introduced 'retro marketing' as an approach built on five principles: exclusivity, secrecy, amplification, entertainment and 'tricksterism'.

1 *Exclusivity* is created by deliberately holding back supplies and delaying gratification. Consumers are encouraged to 'buy now while stocks last'. The lucky ones are happy in the knowledge that they are the select few, the discerning elite. Short supply of brands like Harley-Davidson (motorcycles), certain models of Mercedes cars and even the BMW Mini, has created an aura of exclusivity.

2 *Secrecy* has the intention of teasing would-be purchasers and was a tactic used by the Harry Potter marketing team. The pre-launch of the blockbuster *Harry Potter and the Goblet of Fire* involved a complete blackout of advance information with the book's title, price and review copies being withheld prior to its launch.

3 *Amplification* is designed to get consumers talking about the new product or service. This can be achieved by controversial adverts—e.g. Benetton, viral social media videos, Cadbury's Gorilla playing the drums, Cravendale cats with thumbs. The growth in online advertising has facilitated wider use of such campaigns by many companies—e.g., Apple, Samsung and many other leading brands.

4 *Entertainment* ensures that marketing efforts are engaging target audiences. Brown claims 'modern marketing's greatest failure' is that it has lost its sense of fun in its quest to be rigorous and analytical.

5 *Tricksterism* means marketing with 'panache and audacity'. For example, Britvic made what appeared to be a public service announcement for television. Viewers were told that some rogue grocery stores were selling an imitation of its brand, Tango. The difference could be detected because it was not fizzy, and they were asked to call a freefone number to name the outlets. Around 30,000 people rang, only to be informed that they had been tricked ('Tango'd') as part of the company's promotion for a new, non-carbonated version of the drink. Despite attracting censure for abusing the public information service format, the promotion had succeeded in amplifying the brand extension launch and reinforcing Tango's irreverent image.

These four emerging issues help prompt discussion about the value of the marketing concept, and together are useful for highlighting how aspects of the concept are evolving.

Creating Customer Value, Satisfaction and Loyalty

Go to the website to see how Procter & Gamble establishes its value to customers through iconic brands like Fairy washing up liquid.
www.mcgraw-hill.co.uk/textbooks/jobber

Customer value

Marketing-orientated companies attempt to create **customer value** in order to attract and retain customers. Their aim is to deliver superior value to their target customers. In doing so, they implement the marketing concept by meeting and exceeding customer needs better than the competition. For example, the global success of McDonald's has been based on creating added value for its customers, which is based not only on the food products it sells but on the complete delivery system that goes to make up a fast-food restaurant. It sets high standards in quality, service, cleanliness and value (termed QSCV). Customers can be sure that the same high standards will be found in all of the McDonald's outlets around the world. This example shows that customer value can be derived from many aspects of what the company delivers to its customers—not just the basic product.

Customer value is dependent on how the customer perceives the benefits of an offering and the sacrifice that is associated with its purchase. Therefore:

customer value = perceived benefits – perceived sacrifice

Perceived benefits can be derived from the product (for example, the taste of the hamburger), the associated service (for example, how quickly customers are served and the cleanliness of the outlet) and the image of the company (for example, whether the image of the company/product is favourable). If one of those factors—for example, product benefits—

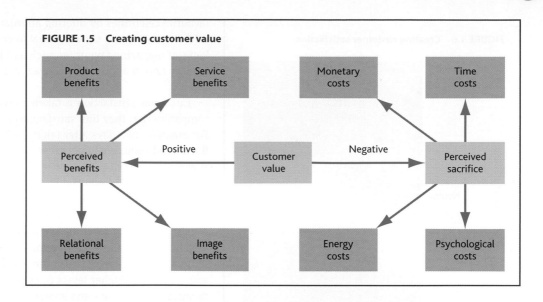

FIGURE 1.5 Creating customer value

changes then the perceived benefits and customer value also change. For instance, the downturn in the fortunes of McDonald's a few years ago was largely attributed to the trend towards healthier eating. This caused some consumers to regard the product benefits of its food to be less, resulting in lower perceived benefits and reduced customer value. In an attempt to redress the situation, McDonald's has introduced healthy-eating options including salad and fruit[37] and is developing allegiances with Weight Watchers and its popular weight-loss programme.[38]

A further source of perceived benefits is the relationship between customer and supplier. Customers may enjoy working with suppliers with whom they have developed close personal and professional friendships, and value the convenience of working with trusted partners.

Perceived sacrifice is the total cost associated with buying a product. This consists of not just monetary cost but the time and energy involved in purchase. For example, with fast-food restaurants, good location can reduce the time and energy required to find a suitable eating place. But marketers need to be aware of another critical sacrifice in some buying situations. This is the potential psychological cost of not making the right decision. Uncertainty means that people perceive risk when purchasing: for example, McDonald's attempts to reduce perceived risk by standardizing its complete offer so that customers can be confident of what they will receive before entering its outlets. In organizational markets companies offer guarantees to reduce the risk of purchase. Figure 1.5 illustrates how perceived benefits and sacrifice affect customer value. It provides a framework for considering ways of maximizing value. The objective is to find ways of raising perceived benefits and reducing perceived sacrifice.

Customer satisfaction

Exceeding the value offered by competitors is key to marketing success. Consumers decide upon purchases on the basis of judgements about the values offered by suppliers. Once a product has been bought, **customer satisfaction** depends upon its perceived performance compared to the buyer's expectations. Customer satisfaction occurs when perceived performance matches or exceeds expectations. Successful companies, such as Canon, Nokia, Toyota, Samsung, H&M, Waitrose, Apple and Virgin, all place customer satisfaction at the heart of their business philosophy. Companies facing difficulties, such as General Motors, Chrysler, Gap and Kodak, have failed to do so as customers' needs and expectations have changed.

ASOS, a successful online fashion retailer, is succeeding by creating customer satisfaction. The company succeeds in satisfying young women's desire to replicate the look of their

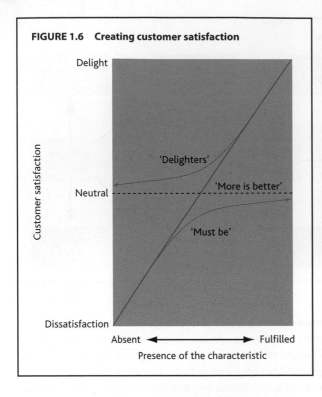

FIGURE 1.6 **Creating customer satisfaction**

favourite celebrities by offering affordable versions of celebrity styles, and showing how to copy the designer looks of magazine favourites such as Victoria Beckham, Lindsay Lohan and Jennifer Lopez at a fraction of the cost.[39]

Customer satisfaction is taken so seriously by some companies that they link satisfaction to financial bonuses. For example, two days after taking delivery of a new car, BMW (and Mini) customers receive a telephone call to check on how well they were treated in the dealership. The customer is asked various questions, and their responses are measured. Dealerships have to be capable of achieving good performance scores, and existing dealerships that consistently fail to meet these standards are under threat of franchise termination. This approach makes a great deal of sense as higher levels of customer satisfaction are associated with higher levels of customer retention, financial performance and shareholder value.[40]

In today's competitive climate it is often not enough to match performance and expectations. Expectations need to be exceeded for commercial success so that customers are delighted with the outcome. In order to understand the concept of customer satisfaction the so-called 'Kano model' (see Fig. 1.6) helps to separate characteristics that cause dissatisfaction, satisfaction and delight. Three characteristics underlie the model: 'Must be', 'More is better' and 'Delighters'.

'Must be' characteristics are expected to be present and are taken for granted. For example, in a hotel, customers expect service at reception and a clean room. The lack of these characteristics causes annoyance, but their presence only brings dissatisfaction up to a neutral level. 'More is better' characteristics can take satisfaction past neutral into the positive satisfaction range. For example, no response to a telephone call can cause dissatisfaction, but a fast response may cause positive satisfaction or even delight. 'Delighters' are the unexpected characteristics that surprise the customer. Their absence does not cause dissatisfaction but their presence delights the customer. For example, a UK hotel chain provides a free basket of fruit on arrival in visitors' rooms. This delights many of its customers, who were not expecting this treat. Another way to delight the customer is to under-promise and over-deliver (for example, by saying that a repair will take about five hours but getting it done in two).[41]

A problem for marketers is that, over time, delighters become expected. For example, some car manufacturers provided small unexpected delighters such as pen holders and delay mechanisms on interior lights so that there is time to find the ignition socket at night. These are standard on most cars now and have become 'Must be' characteristics as customers expect them. This means that marketers must constantly strive to find new ways of delighting. Innovative thinking and listening to customers are key ingredients in this. Mini Case 1.1 explains how to listen to customers.

The importance of customer satisfaction is supported by studies which show that higher levels of customer satisfaction lead to higher financial (profits and sales) performance,[42] greater customer loyalty[43] and the willingness of customers to pay higher prices.[44]

Customer Loyalty

Customer satisfaction is linked to customer loyalty and profitability.[45] It can cost up to five times more to attract a new customer than to serve an existing one.[46]

Mini Case 1.1 Listening to Customers

Leading companies recognize the importance of listening to their customers as part of their strategy to manage satisfaction. Customer satisfaction indices are based on surveys of customers, and the results plotted over time to reveal changes in satisfaction levels. The first stage is to identify those characteristics (choice criteria) that are important to customers when evaluating competing products. The second stage involves the development of measurement scales (often statements followed by strongly agree/strongly disagree response boxes) to assess satisfaction quantitatively. Customer satisfaction data should be collected over a period of time to measure change. Only long-term measurement of satisfaction ratings will provide a clear picture of what is going on in the marketplace. However, the marketplace is changing and use of new data-capture methods and technologies means that some customers are more aware of how their data are being used. Consequently, customers must see some benefit from the use of their data if an effective relationship is to develop. Furthermore, customers (both satisfied and dissatisfied) are making themselves heard across the web, via Facebook, Twitter, so that understanding the digital arena is critical for marketers. Marks & Spencer discovered via Facebook that their tiered pricing of bras caused much dissatisfaction among their customers.[47]

The critical role of listening to customers in marketing success was emphasized by Sir Terry Leahy, former chief executive of Tesco, the successful UK supermarket chain, when talking to a group of business people. 'Let me tell you a secret,' he said, 'the secret of successful retailing. Are you ready? It's this: never stop listening to customers, and giving them what they want. I'm sorry if that is a bit of an anticlimax … but it is that simple.'

Marketing research can also be used to question new customers about why they first bought, and lost customers (defectors) on why they have ceased buying. In the latter case a second objective would be to stage a last-ditch attempt to keep the customer. One bank found that a quarter of its defecting customers would have stayed had the bank attempted to rescue the situation.

Kwik-Fit, the car repair group, places listening to customers high on its list of priorities. Customer satisfaction is monitored by its customer survey unit, which telephones 5000 customers a day within 72 hours of their visit to a Kwik-Fit centre.

A strategy also needs to be put in place to manage customer complaints, comments and questions. A system needs to be set up that solicits feedback on product and service quality, and feeds the information to the appropriate employees. To facilitate this process, front-line employees need training to ask questions, to listen effectively, to capture the information and to communicate it so that corrective action can be taken.

In addition, companies must make provision to find out what their customers are saying online. Companies can listen to what is being said about them and their brands by using a blog search engine such as Technorati, which also identifies the writer of the blog. This means that companies not only have a major research tool but also a means of responding to comments—both positive and negative. TripAdvisor is the world's largest online travel site, and it helps people plan their holiday and business trips by providing advice from over 60 million reviews and opinions from other travellers who have experience of services provided by hotels, restaurants and travel companies. Each service provider is ranked by a number of performance indicators, and this can make a big difference to future trade as the opinions of other travellers can have a powerful influence.

Consumers can write blogs, which can contain positive and/or negative comments about companies and brands. A blog is a personal commentary, a collection of thoughts and comments, which creates a kind of personal diary on the Internet.

Companies can also launch websites to solicit customers' ideas. Dell did this after it received a flood of criticism over poor customer service, while also reaching out to online bloggers. The feedback led to a customer services overhaul and a fall in negative buzz. Finally, Google listens to customers by releasing most products in 'beta' (which means they are not quite finished), allowing users to suggest improvements. This approach has led to the refinement of such products as Google News, Gmail and the Chrome browser.

Questions:

1. Explain why feedback from social media sites can be more accurate than surveys.
2. What strategy would you suggest for a business in handling customer complaints, comments and questions?
3. How would you explain the blog search engine site Technorati to a friend and the benefits it offers?

Based on: Jones and Sasser Jr (1995);[48] Morgan (1996);[49] White (1999);[50] Roythorne (2003);[51] Ryle (2003);[52] Mitchell (2005);[53] Wright (2006);[54] Jarvis (2009);[55] Hilpern (2011), TripAdvisor (2012)[56]

Read the Research 1.1 Branding and the Marketing Mix

1. Love is all around—that is if you're a brand. Brand love is the one of the new paradigms in marketing. The aim of 'brand love' is to engender greater affection amongst customers and prospects for the brand or business. Ultimately, building brand loyalty and word-of-mouth recommendations. This study adds to the understanding of the managerial potential of brand love by proposing and testing two actionable antecedents of brand love: brand identification and sense of community.

Lars Bergkvist and Tino Bech-Larsen (2010) Two studies of consequences and actionable antecedents of brand love,
Journal of Brand Management 17, 504–18.

2. One of the great marketing frameworks from the 1960s is still with us today: the marketing mix. Over the years there has been great debate about its influence and relevance as the gaps between current marketing theory and marketing practice are exposed. However, this article suggests that combining the marketing mix with another worthy concept, relationship marketing, has the potential to produce a new marketing paradigm.

Uolevi Lehtinen (2011) Combining mix and relationship marketing, The Marketing Review 11(2), 117–36.

In most situations a returning customer is beneficial to an organization as they can increase sales volumes through repeat purchases. Loyalty is a response which a customer shows over time. Typically, they will repeatedly return to the same supplier if they are satisfied with the products and services they receive.[57] Customer loyalty can be built on convenience, quality of service and social interaction, for example. However, loyalty can take different forms and be triggered by different marketing initiatives. For example, Tesco uses sales promotions through its loyalty card programme to trigger repeat customer behaviour. Arguably, this type of loyalty is driven by price, and the promotion acts as an incentive to trigger repeat purchases. At the other end of the scale is a form of loyalty which transcends emotional boundaries: brand love. Brand love is an extension of the concept of loyalty.[58] Researchers have found that the connections between individuals and the brands they choose are closely associated with the concept of interpersonal physical love. However, while brand love was found to involve passion, positive emotional connections, long-term relationships, positive attitudes, and distress at the thought of separation, it does not leave the *brand lover* as profoundly committed to a product as they might be to a personal partner. Nevertheless, there are consequences for marketing managers and they should look for ways to turn *liked* brands into *loved* brands. Looking for ways to maintain this high level of commitment to the relationship can be achieved by maximizing three key opportunities: 1) *facilitate 'passion-driven behaviour'*, which is a strong commitment to use the brand as in the case of luxury designer brands—e.g., Gucci, Rolex, Porsche; 2) *build brands that engender self-brand integration*. This is the way the brand connects to an individual's values and deeper thought processes. Rewards can be used effectively to emphasise the benefits of this higher-level commitment. Samsung is an example of a brand attempting to connect with customers by engendering self-identity through brand values associated with the environment; 3) *Create positive emotional connections*. Brands which succeed in being regarded as 'an old friend' and creating a strong bond with the customer benefit by finding a place in the customer's heart. Anita Roddick succeeded in making this type of connection with Body Shop customers.[59] The concept of relationship marketing is covered in greater detail in Chapter 16.

Whether the aim is to build closely connected, deep and meaningful relationships with their customers or to offer short-term incentives to foster customer loyalty, marketing strategies need to pay close attention to how to apply the marketing mix. Read the research to develop a more in-depth knowledge of customer satisfaction and loyalty.

Developing an Effective Marketing Mix

Using its understanding of its customers as a basis, a company develops its **marketing mix**. The original concept of the marketing mix consists of four major elements: product, price, promotion and place. These '4-Ps' are the four key decision areas that marketers must manage so that they satisfy or exceed customer needs better than the competition. However, the growth of the service industries has given rise to an extended marketing mix of '7-Ps' which adds people, process and physical evidence into the mix. The emphasis of each of the elements of the mix will vary depending on the products and services offered by an organization. For example, BMW cars and Rolex watches are market-orientated companies that focus primarily on the 4-Ps as they are product manufacturers, but Pizza Hut and Kentucky Fried Chicken focus primarily on the elements of the extended mix, as service, process and the physical evidence are at the heart of their fast-food restaurants.

In other words, decisions regarding the marketing mix form a major aspect of marketing concept implementation. At this point we briefly examine the 4-Ps to provide an essence of marketing mix decision-making. Later we look at each of the 4-Ps in considerable detail (Chapters 9, 11–18) and the service mix (people, process and physical in Chapter 10).

Product

The **product** decision involves deciding what goods or services should be offered to a group of customers. An important element is new product development. As technology and tastes change, products become out of date and inferior to those of the competition, so companies must replace them with features that customers value. As new products are developed that give greater benefits than old ones, market leadership can change. For example, the Samsung MP3 player was the market leader in digital music players, but following its launch, the Apple iPod soon outsold the MP3 player. Samsung has been market leader in various consumer electronic markets from batteries for digital gadgets to flat-screen televisions. Currently, the company is making a move into more sustainable products. Samsung envisages in the future that it will be a market leader in technology markets which are vital to society.

Product decisions also involve choices regarding brand names, guarantees, packaging and the services that should accompany the product offering. Guarantees can be an important component of the product offering. For example, the operators of the AVE, Spain's high-speed train, capable of travelling at 300 kmph, are so confident of its performance that they guarantee to give customers a full refund of their fare if they are more than five minutes late.

Price

Price is a key element of the marketing mix because it represents on a unit basis what the company receives for the product or service that is being marketed. All of the other elements represent costs—for example, expenditure on product design (product), advertising and salespeople (promotion), and transportation and distribution (place). Marketers, therefore, need to be very clear about pricing objectives, methods and the factors that influence price setting. They must also take into account the necessity to discount and give allowances in some transactions. These requirements can influence the level of list price chosen, perhaps with an element of negotiation margin built in. Payment periods and credit terms also affect the real price received in any transaction. These kinds of decisions can affect the perceived value of a product.

Because price affects the value that customers perceive they get from buying a product, it can be an important element in the purchase decision. Some companies attempt to position themselves as offering lower prices than their rivals. For example, supermarkets such as Asda (Wal-Mart) in the UK, Aldi in Germany, Netto in Denmark and Super de Boer in the Netherlands employ a low-price positioning strategy. Another strategy is to launch a low-price version of an existing product targeted at price-sensitive consumers.

Digital Marketing 1.2 What Opportunities Do Social Media Environments Offer?

Social networking environments, such as Facebook and Twitter, provide opportunities for organizations to engage in a direct dialogue with individuals. The promise of an economically viable, direct, one-to-one dialogue between customers and companies seems to be a nirvana that marketers have been seeking for years. Examples of this include Glasses Direct, which uses the Twitter application to publicly respond to direct queries from customers browsing its website. This creates a kind of on-the-fly FAQ (frequently asked questions) as well as demonstrating a swift level of customer response. Microsoft employees actively use their staff blogs to engage with software developer customers, by opening up the process of software design for others to see and comment on. However, environments such as Facebook and Twitter have emerging problems that companies are finding difficult to grasp. Social networker 'conversations' may not be in the best interests of a company or brand. Many Facebook groups have been set up by users to complain vociferously about organizations: HSBC famously reversed a policy decision on student debt after thousands of graduates and undergraduates of British universities joined a group to voice their opposition to the action.

Used well, social media environments can be a new channel into difficult-to-reach markets. But many organizations are still learning the hard way that such environments can actually be very negative places to engage with customers.

Useful further reading: Charles (2007)[60]

Promotion

Decisions have to be made with respect to the **promotional mix**: advertising, personal selling, sales promotions, public relations, direct marketing and online promotion. Target audiences are made aware of the existence of a product or service, and the benefits (both economic and psychological) it gives to customers. Each element of the promotional mix has strengths and weaknesses. Advertising, for example, is able to reach wide audiences very quickly. Procter & Gamble used advertising to reach the emerging market of 290 million Russian consumers. It ran a 12-minute commercial on Russian television as its first promotional venture in order to introduce the company and its range of products.[61] Sales promotions can be used to stimulate an immediate uplift in sales but this effect can be short-term. The Internet now attracts more advertising revenue than any other media and has become an important promotional tool. A great advantage of the Internet is its global reach. This means that companies that did not have the resources to promote overseas can reach consumers worldwide by creating a website. However, social networks pose challenges for marketing managers. Find out more by reading Digital Marketing 1.2. In business-to-business markets, the promotional mix is used to communicate with suppliers and customers. Personal selling can be used to good effect as this promotional tool offers face-to-face interactions which are an important part of sales negotiations.

Place

Place concerns decisions about distribution channels. Key management decisions focus on locations of outlets, methods of transportation and inventory levels held. The objective is to ensure products and services are available in required quantities, at the right time and place. Distribution channels consist of organizations such as retailers or wholesalers through which goods pass on their way to customers. Producers need to manage their relationships with these organizations well because they may provide the only cost-effective access to the marketplace. They also need to be aware of new methods of distribution that can create a competitive advantage. For example, Dell revolutionized the distribution of computers selling direct to customers rather than using traditional computer outlets. Music and film is increasingly being distributed by downloading from the Internet rather than being bought at music shops.

Following this trend, Radiohead offered fans the opportunity to pay whatever they liked to download their new album, and the rock band Nine Inch Nails released theirs as a free download from the band's website.[62]

Key Characteristics of an Effective Marketing Mix

There are four hallmarks of an effective marketing mix (see Fig. 1.7).

The marketing mix matches customer needs

Sensible marketing mix decisions can be made only when the target customer is identified and understood (choosing customer groups, targeting, segmentation and positioning are explored in Chapter 8). Once the target market(s) is identified, marketing management needs to understand how customers choose between rival offerings. Managers should consider the product or service through customers' eyes and understand, among other factors, the choice criteria they use.

Figure 1.8 illustrates the link between customer choice criteria and the marketing mix. The starting point is the realization that customers evaluate products on economic and psychological criteria. Economic criteria include factors such as performance, availability, reliability, durability and productivity gains to be made by using the product. Examples of psychological criteria are self-image, a desire for a quiet life, pleasure, convenience and risk reduction (see Chapter 4). The important point at this stage is to note that an analysis of customer choice criteria reveals a set of key customer requirements that must be met in order to succeed in the marketplace. Meeting or exceeding these requirements better than the competition leads to the creation of a competitive advantage.

The marketing mix creates a competitive advantage

A **competitive advantage** is the achievement of superior performance through differentiation to provide superior customer value or by managing to achieve lowest delivered cost. It can be derived from decisions about the 4-Ps. Apple's iPad is an

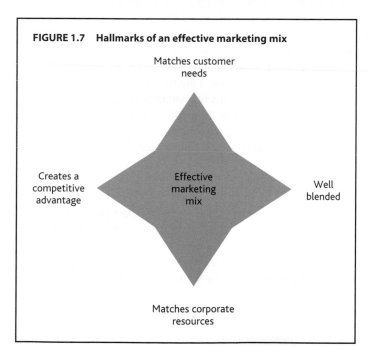

FIGURE 1.7 Hallmarks of an effective marketing mix

Matches customer needs

Creates a competitive advantage

Effective marketing mix

Well blended

Matches corporate resources

FIGURE 1.8 Matching the marketing mix to customer needs

Customer needs

Economic	Psychological
Performance	Self-image
Availability	Quiet life
Reliability	Pleasure
Durability	Convenience
Productivity	Risk reduction

Key customer requirements

Competitive advantage

Marketing mix
Product
Price
Promotion
Place

↑**EXHIBIT 1.4** Cobra Premium Beer: traditional Indian Beer adapted for contemporary tastes.

example of a company using product features to convey customer benefits which exceed the competition's offerings. The iPad's portability, range of applications and its ability to download, display and store, pdf document audio, music, films can, therefore, be regarded as the creation of competitive advantages over the previous market leader in the tablet computer market, Microsoft. Aldi, the German supermarket chain, achieves a competitive advantage by severely controlling costs, allowing it to make profits even though its prices are low, a strategy that is attractive to price-sensitive shoppers. Marketing in Action 1.2 explains how Cobra beer has gained a competitive advantage.

The strategy of using advertising as a tool for competitive advantage is often employed when product benefits are particularly subjective and amorphous in nature. Thus the advertising for perfumes such as those produced by Chanel, Givenchy and Yves St Laurent is critical in preserving the exclusive image established by such brands. The size and quality of the sales force can act as a competitive advantage. A problem that a company such as Rolls-Royce, the aero engine manufacturer, faces is the relatively small size of its sales force compared to those of its giant competitors Boeing and General Electric. Finally, distribution decisions need to be made with the customer in mind, not only in terms of availability but also with respect to service levels, image and customer convenience. The Radisson SAS hotel at Manchester Airport is an example of creating a competitive advantage through customer convenience. It is situated five minutes' walk from the airport terminals, which are reached by covered walkways. Guests at rival hotels have to rely on taxis or transit buses to reach the airport.

The marketing mix should be well blended

The third characteristic of an effective marketing mix is that the four elements—product, price, promotion and place—should be well blended to form a consistent theme. If a product gives superior benefits to customers, price, which may send cues to customers regarding quality, should reflect those extra benefits. All of the promotional mix should be designed with the objective of communicating a consistent message to the target audience about these

---

Marketing in Action 1.2 Spare the Gas with Cobra Beer

Before Cobra beer, British Asian curry eaters faced a problem: what drink to order with a curry. Often Asian cuisine overpowered the taste of wine, and standard beers or lagers were too gassy. Cobra beer's competitive advantages were its 'less gassy' nature and its Indian heritage. Positioned as an Indian lager, since 2009 Cobra has been jointly owned by Molson Coors UK and Lord Bilimoria, an India-born British peer who established the brand. Cobra is now regarded as a natural accompaniment to Asian meals. It is available in a selection of ranges, including the double-fermented King Cobra and Cobra 0%. The company has also signed new deals to offer the drink in bottles and on draught.

It is now available in bars, pubs and restaurants in almost 50 countries around the world. Its success is based on marketing fundamentals: meeting a customer need (a less gassy, suitable accompaniment for Asian food) better than the competition (wine and standard beers and lagers). Cobra has won many industry awards for its consistently high quality products.

Based on: Fernandez (2008)[63,64]

benefits, and distribution decisions should be consistent with the overall strategic position of the product in the marketplace. The use of exclusive outlets for upmarket fashion and cosmetics brands—Armani, Christian Dior and Calvin Klein, for example—is consistent with their strategic position.

The marketing mix should match corporate resources

The choice of marketing mix strategy may ultimately be down to the available financial resources of the company. For example, Amazon was only able to establish its global presence by massive financial investment in online advertising. Certain media—for example, television advertising—require a minimum threshold investment before they are regarded as feasible. In the UK a rule of thumb is that at least £5 million per year is required to achieve impact in a national advertising campaign. Clearly those brands that cannot afford such a promotional budget must use other less expensive media—for example, digital marketing, posters or sales promotion—to attract and hold customers.

A second internal resource constraint may be the internal competences of the company. A marketing mix strategy may be too ambitious for the limited marketing skills of personnel to implement effectively. While an objective may be to reduce or eliminate this problem in the medium to long term, in the short term marketing management may have to heed the fact that strategy must take account of competences. An area where this may manifest itself is within the place dimension of the 4-Ps. A company lacking the personal selling skills to market a product directly to end users may have to use intermediaries (distributors or sales agents) to perform that function.

Criticisms of the 4-Ps Approach to Marketing Management

Some critics of the 4-Ps approach to the marketing mix argue that it oversimplifies the reality of marketing management. Booms and Bitner, for example, argue for a 7-Ps approach to services marketing.[65] Their argument, discussed in some detail in Chapter 10 on services marketing, is that the 4-Ps do not take sufficient account of people, process and physical evidence. In services, people often *are* the service itself; the process or how the service is delivered to the customer is usually a key part of the service; and the physical evidence—the décor of the restaurant or shop, for example—is so critical to success that it should be considered as a separate element in the services marketing mix.

Rafiq and Ahmed argue that this criticism of the 4-Ps can be extended to include industrial marketing.[66] The interaction approach to understanding industrial marketing stresses that success does not come solely from manipulation of the marketing mix components but long-term relationship building, whereby the bond between buyer and seller becomes so strong that it effectively acts as a barrier to entry for out-suppliers.[67] This phenomenon undoubtedly exists to such an extent that industrial buyers are now increasingly seeking long-term supply relationships with suppliers. For example, car manufacturers have drawn up long-term contracts with preferred suppliers that provide stability in supply and improvements in new component development. Bosch, the German producer of industrial and consumer goods, conducts quality audits of its suppliers. These kinds of activities are not captured in the 4-Ps approach, it is claimed.

However, the strength of the 4-Ps approach is that it represents a memorable and practical framework for marketing decision-making and has proved useful for many years.

Marketing and Business Performance

The basic premise of the marketing concept is that its adoption will improve business performance. Marketing is not an abstract concept: its acid test is the effect that its use has on key corporate indices such as profitability and market share. Research in Europe and North America has examined the relationship between marketing and performance and the results suggest that the relationship is positive.

24

Marketing characteristics and business performance

In a study of 1700 senior marketing executives, Hooley and Lynch reported the marketing characteristics of high- versus low-performing companies.[68] The approach that they adopted was to isolate the top 10 per cent of companies (based on such measures as profit margin, return on investment and market share) and to compare their marketing practices with the remainder of the sample. The 'high fliers' differed from the 'also-rans' as follows:

- more committed to marketing research
- more likely to be found in new, emerging or growth markets
- adopted a more proactive approach to marketing planning
- more likely to use strategic planning tools
- placed more emphasis on product performance and design, rather than price, for achieving a competitive advantage
- worked more closely with the finance department
- placed greater emphasis on market share as a method of evaluating marketing performance.

Marketing orientation and business performance

Narver and Slater studied the relationship between marketing orientation and business performance.[69] Marketing orientation was based on three measures: customer orientation, competitor orientation, and degree of inter-functional coordination. They collected data from 113 strategic business units (SBUs) of a major US corporation.

The businesses comprised 36 commodity businesses (forestry products) and 77 non-commodity businesses (speciality products and distribution businesses). They related each SBU's profitability, as measured by return on assets in relation to competitors over the last year in the SBU's principal served market, to their three-component measure of market orientation.

Figure 1.9 shows the results of their study. For commodity businesses the relationship was U-shaped, with low and high market-orientation businesses showing higher profitability than the businesses in the mid-range of market orientation. Businesses with the highest market orientation had the highest profitability and those with the lowest market orientation had the second highest profitability. Narver and Slater explained this result by suggesting that the businesses lowest in market orientation may achieve some profit success through a low cost strategy, though not the profit levels of the high market-orientation businesses, an explanation supported by the fact that they were the largest companies of the three groups.

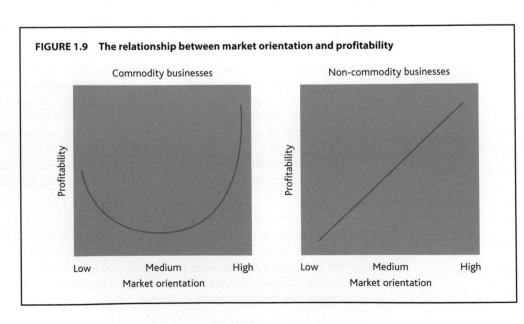

FIGURE 1.9   The relationship between market orientation and profitability

For the non-commodity businesses the relationship was linear, with the businesses displaying the highest level of market orientation achieving the highest levels of profitability and those with the lowest scores on market orientation having the lowest profitability figures. As the authors state, 'The findings give marketing scholars and practitioners a basis beyond mere intuition for recommending the superiority of a market orientation.'

Recent studies have found a positive relationship between market orientation and business performance. Market orientation has been found to have a positive effect on sales growth, market share and profitability,[70] sales growth,[71] sales growth and new product success,[72] perception of product quality[73] and overall business performance.[74]

Finally, a study by Kirca, Jayachandran and Bearden analysed the empirical findings from a wide range of studies that sought to identify the antecedents and consequences of marketing orientation.[75] Their findings showed that a marketing orientation led to higher overall business performance (higher profits, sales and market share), better customer consequences (higher perceived quality, customer loyalty and customer satisfaction), better innovative consequences (higher innovativeness and better new product performance) and beneficial employee consequences (higher organizational commitment, team spirit, customer orientation and job satisfaction, and lower role conflict). Their analysis of the antecedents of marketing orientation showed the importance of top management emphasis on marketing, good communications between departments and systems that reward employees for market success for the implementation of marketing orientation.

So, what overall conclusions can be drawn from these studies? In order to make a balanced judgement limitations must be recognized. Most were cross-sectional studies based on self-reported data. With any such survey there is the question of the direction of causality. However, this clearly did not occur with the commodity sample in the Narver and Slater study.[76] What these studies have consistently and unambiguously shown is a strong association between marketing and business performance. As one condition for establishing causality, this is an encouraging result for those people concerned with promoting the marketing concept as a guiding philosophy for business.

Online
LearningCentre

When you have read this chapter

log on to the Online Learning Centre at **www.mcgraw-hill.co.uk/textbooks/jobber** to explore chapter-by-chapter test questions, links and further online study tools for marketing.

Review

1 **Identify the fundamental principles of marketing**
- The marketing concept sets out the core ideas which underpin the nature of marketing and provides central planks on which to build a market-orientated organization.
- The marketing-orientation provides a guiding philosophy that enables an organization to concentrate its activities on its customers.
- Focusing on efficiency and effectiveness enables an organization to ensure that it is doing things *right* and doing the *right* things. Getting the balance correct between the two can mean the difference between success and failure.
- Customers are at the heart of marketing; consequently understanding how to create customer value and satisfaction is very important.
- Designing an effective marketing mix is an essential element of marketing and is the means by which customers are satisfied and marketing objectives are achieved.

2 **The marketing concept: an understanding of the nature of marketing, its key components and limitations**
- The marketing concept is the achievement of corporate goals through meeting and exceeding customer needs better than the competition.
- It exists through exchanges where the objective is for all parties in the exchange to feel satisfied.
- Its key components are customer orientation, integrated effort and goal achievement (e.g. profits).
- The limitations of the concept are that the pursuit of customer satisfaction is only one objective companies should consider (others, such as achieving economies of scale, are equally valid), the adoption of the marketing concept may result in a focus on short-term personal satisfaction rather than longer-term societal welfare, the focus on customers to guide the development of new products will lead to only modest improvements compared to the innovations resulting from technological push, and the emphasis on reflecting rather than creating demand can lead to dull marketing campaigns and me-too products.

3 **The difference between a production orientation and marketing orientation**
- Marketing orientation focuses on customer needs to identify potential market opportunities, leading to the creation of products that create customer satisfaction.
- Production orientation focuses on production capabilities, which defines the business mission and the products that are manufactured. These are then sold aggressively to customers.

4 **The differences between market-driven and internally orientated businesses**
- Customer concern vs convenience.
- Know customer choice criteria and match with marketing mix vs the assumption that price and performance are key.
- Segment by customer differences vs segment by product.
- Marketing research vs anecdotes and received wisdom.
- Welcome change vs cherish status quo.
- Understand competition vs ignore competition.
- Marketing spend is an investment vs marketing spend is a luxury.
- Innovation rewarded and reluctance to punish failure vs avoidance of mistakes rewarded and a failure to innovate is conspicuously punished.
- Search for latent markets vs stick with the same.
- Recognize the importance of being fast vs content to move slowly.
- Strive for competitive advantage vs happy to be me-too.
- Efficiency and effectiveness vs efficiency.

5 **The differing roles of efficiency and effectiveness in achieving corporate success**
- Efficiency is concerned with inputs and outputs. Business processes are managed to a high standard so that cost per unit of output is low. Its role is to 'do things right'—that is, use processes that result in low-cost production.
- Effectiveness is concerned with making the correct strategic choice regarding which products to make for which markets. Its role is to 'do the right things'—that is, make the right products for attractive markets.

6 **How to create customer value and satisfaction**
- Customer value is created by maximizing perceived benefits (e.g. product or image benefits) and minimizing perceived sacrifice (e.g. monetary or time costs).
- Customer satisfaction once a product is bought is created by maximizing perceived performance compared to the customer's expectations. Customer satisfaction occurs when perceived performance matches or exceeds expectations.

7 **How an effective marketing mix is designed**
- The classical marketing mix consists of product, price, promotion and place (the '4-Ps').
- An effective marketing mix is designed by ensuring that it matches customer needs, creates a competitive advantage, is well blended and matches corporate resources.

8 **Criticisms of the 4-Ps approach to marketing management**
- Criticisms of the 4-Ps approach to marketing management are that it oversimplifies reality. For example, for services marketing three further Ps—people, process and physical evidence—should be added and, for industrial (business-to-business) marketing, the marketing mix approach neglects the importance of long-term relationship building.

and Powerade, an energy drink, following the success of Red Bull and Gatorade in this sector.

PepsiCo's diversification programme and its brand-building expertise has made it the world's fourth largest food and beverage company, ranking behind Nestlé, Kraft and Unilever. Its sales were more than $66 billion compared with Coke's $47 billion in 2011; it owns 6 of the 15 top-selling food and drink brands in US supermarkets—more than any other company, including Coke, which has two. Coke, on the other hand, is market leader in carbonated drinks (43 per cent versus 32 per cent).

TABLE C1.1	Cola wars: who owns what
Coca-Cola brands	**PepsiCo brands**
Coca-Cola	Pepsi
Diet Coke	Diet Pepsi
Coke Zero	Gatorade
Powerade	Tropicana
Minute Maid	Aquafina
Dasani	Lipton Iced Tea
Fanta	Frappuccino
Lilt	Mountain Dew
Sprite	Walkers crisps
Calypso	Lay's potato crisps
Oasis	Quaker Oats
Just Juice	Quavers
Kia Ora	Doritos
Five Alive	Wotsits
Malvern water	Sugar Puffs
	7-Up

Life since Mr Goizueta also saw Coke criticized for its fall in marketing investments, including advertising and marketing research, in an effort to maintain short-term profits, and the lack of iconic brand-building advertising. Its culture was also questioned and its high-rise headquarters in central Atlanta was known in the industry as 'the Kremlin' because of the political intrigue and bureaucratic culture that pervaded its corridors.

A new era?

In response to its problems, Coca-Cola brought an ex-employee, Neville Isdell, out of retirement to become chairman and chief executive in 2004. One of his first acts was to allocate an additional $400 million a year to

marketing and innovation. This was in recognition of the under-investment in brands and product development. Emerging markets such as China and India were also targeted more aggressively. He also briefed advertising agencies around the world in an attempt to create new iconic campaigns to revive the core brand and reconnect with consumers. In the face of research that showed the proportion of Americans agreeing that cola is 'liked by everyone' falling from 56 per cent in 2003 to 44 per cent in 2005, and those agreeing that the drink was 'too fattening' increasing from 48 per cent to 59 per cent, Coke increased investment in sugar-free brands such as Diet Coke and Sprite Zero. Sugar-free colas have also been launched, such as Coke Zero, which comes in black cans and bottles, and is targeted at calorie-conscious young males who have failed to connect with Diet Coke, believing that it lacks a masculine image. The brand is designed to compete with PepsiMax, which is also a diet cola targeted at men. Overall, marketing spend for the category doubled. Isdell also oversaw the acquisition of a number of small water and fruit juice companies in Europe. Isdell resisted the temptation to follow Pepsi with the acquisition of a snacks company. Instead his strategy was to focus on building a portfolio of branded drinks. Following this strategy, Coca-Cola purchased the US firm Energy Brands, which owns Glaceau, a vitamin-enhanced water brand, and bought a stake of between 10 and 20 per cent of Innocent (increased to 58 per cent in 2010), the market leader (68 per cent) of fruit smoothie drinks in the UK. Innocent has built a reputation for making only natural healthy products, and using only socially and environmentally aware products. At the time of the deal (2009), Innocent operated in the UK, Ireland, France, Scandinavia, Germany and Austria. Coca-Cola also launched an energy drink Relentless aimed at 18–40-year-old men.

Meanwhile, PepsiCo has introduced its own labelling system in the USA to identify healthier products, using criteria set by an independent board of health experts. Now 40 per cent of sales derive from products with the green 'Smart Spot' given to healthier brands such as sugar-free colas and baked rather than fried crisps. Most of its research and development is focused on healthier products such as Tropicana-branded fruit bars, which provide the nutritional equivalent to fresh fruit. Sales of Smart Spot products are growing at twice the rate of those without the designation, and account for over half of Pepsi's product portfolio.

Continuing its focus on healthy drinks, PepsiCo launched PurVia which uses Stevia, a South American herb used to create natural sugar substitutes, as a zero-calorie sweetener. It was first used in flavours in PepsiCo's water brand SoBe Life. Coca-Cola followed this launch with its own equivalent, Truvia. PepsiCo has continued its move into healthier fare with yoghurt drinks, hummus and oatmeal bars.

Both companies have also attempted to arrest the decline in the carbonated soft drinks sector by launching a flurry of new products such as lime- and cherry-flavoured colas. Nevertheless, colas have come under attack for their contribution to obesity with some schools banning the sale of all carbonated drinks on their premises.

Other ethical controversies have been encroaching upon Coca-Cola's global hold on the drinks market. Concern at American foreign policy and anti-American sentiment around the world has led to the launch of brands such as Mecca Cola to provide an alternative to US colas.

Under Mr Isdell Coca Cola achieved steady international sales and profit growth. In 2008 he returned to retirement and was succeeded by Muhtar Kent who has successfully built sales of Coke's brands globally. For example, in 2011 China accounted for 7 per cent of Coca-Cola's total sales volume. In the same year, his investment in core brands saw Diet Coke overtake Pepsi as North America's second-selling soft drink.

References

Based on: Devaney, P. (2006) As US Tastes Change, Coca-Cola's Supremacy Drip, Drip, Drips Away, *Marketing Week*, 6 April, 30–1; Teather, D. (2005) Bubble Bursts for the Real Thing as PepsiCo Ousts Coke from Top Spot, *Guardian*, 27 December, 26; Ward, A. (2005) A Better Model? Diversified Pepsi Steals Some of Coke's Sparkle, *Financial Times*, 28 February, 21; Ward, A. (2005) Coke Gets Real: The World's Most Valuable Brand Wakes Up to a Waning Thirst for Cola, *Financial Times*, 22 September, 17; Sweeney, M. and C. Tryhorn (2009) The Day Innocent Lost Its Innocence, *Guardian*, 7 April, 3; Bokai, J. (2008) Soft Drinks Eye Herbal 'Sugar', *Marketing*, 6 August, 2; Bokai, J. (2008) Soft Drinks Eye Premium Boost, *Marketing*, 19 March, 2; Rappeport, A. (2011) China the Real Thing for Business rather than US, *Financial Times*, 27 September, 17; Anonymous (2012) At Pepsi a Renewed Focus on Pepsi, *Bloomberg BusinessWeek*, 6 January–12 February, 25; Eleftheriou-Smith, L.-M. (2011) Pepsi and Coke Fill War Chests, *Marketing*, 15 February, 7.

Questions

1. Compare Coca-Cola's response to the changing marketing environment before the arrival of Neville Isdell to that of PepsiCo.

2. Assess both companies in terms of their level of marketing orientation.

3. How would you position Coca-Cola and PepsiCo on the efficiency–effectiveness matrix? Justify your answer.

4. What advantages, if any, does PepsiCo's greater diversification give the company over Coca-Cola?

5. Assess Coca Cola's part-ownership of Innocent drinks from the point of view of both companies.

6. What future challenges is Coca-Cola likely to face?

The case was written by David Jobber, Professor of Marketing, University of Bradford.

In 1998 Nokia became the world's biggest mobile phone manufacturer, with its share price peaking at over $60 in June 2000. It remained in a strong position until the first quarter of 2012 when its share price fell to just over $3.00 and Samsung overtook them. Nokia's market capitalization stands at less than $12 billion, compared to Samsung's $137 billion.

This case seeks to provide some insight into how Nokia found itself in decline, and asks what Nokia can do, if anything, to engineer a turnaround when faced with rivals who seem to be becoming stronger.

Company background

Since its establishment in the mid-nineteenth century Nokia has made one of the most remarkable business transformations ever. In 1966 Nokia restructured itself into three business units: forestry, rubber, and electronics. Back then, it was not certain that electronics would win out as the most important division because the traditional businesses within the group could point to stability, longevity, market share and cash generation—so why change?

Several factors were soon to make mobile communications not only a natural but also strategic choice—an opportunity where there is a strong fit between the resources and capabilities of the organization and an identified opportunity from the external environment.

The key opportunity arrived in the 1970s when the Nordic countries, who had already established a great degree of cooperation in various areas of trade, planned to have a common telephone network. At the time, it was thought that there was no way Finland could take the lead in this enterprise. It had a small population and too many lakes, which ruled out interconnecting cables between the islands because it was far too expensive.

However, Nokia decided to turn that problem into an opportunity. They believed that the aerial route for electronic signals was the best, maybe the only, solution and the Nordic Mobile Telephone (NMT) network was born, with Nokia appointed supplier of hardware to NMT. This enabled Nokia to set the industry standards right from the start—potentially a huge market advantage.

Nokia built on its successful pioneering and market development efforts as well as a track record of innovation

in the 1990s with milestones such as the development and launch of the first global mobile communications network—GSM (Global System for Mobile Communications) with the very first GSM call in 1991.

As the market expanded, portability, design, style and services increased in importance and segments of consumers with different needs clearly emerged. Identifying these segments and developing value propositions which met each segment's clearly defined needs were the key reasons why Nokia handsets became the popular handset of choice for users.

From 2000 to 2005

In 2000 things looked very promising for Nokia—sales and profits were at record levels, as was its share price. It was also Europe's biggest brand and the fifth biggest brand on the planet (according to Interbrand).

However, within a couple of years the wheels on the Nokia bandwagon started to wobble, perhaps best demonstrated by the dramatic 80 per cent fall in its share price to just under $11.00 in August 2002.

Having had such a dominant market position, how could Nokia's fall from grace be so dramatic? Surely, the company was still customer and market–oriented and performing well against the 'market-driven business' criteria shown in

▶ Table 1.1? **(Go to www.mcgraw-hill.co.uk/textbooks/ jobber to read the table.)**

Early warning signs

As early as 2001/2, Nokia was starting to get complacent as a remark by the then CEO, Olli-Pekka Kallasvuo, shows: 'The complexity of the new devices benefits us. We know this industry better than anyone. Complexity improves our competitive position.'

In addition, Microsoft, which has the reputation of being an aggressive competitor, had announced its decision to enter the mobile phones market but this only belatedly set alarm bells ringing in Nokia.

In mid-2004 an article in the *Economist* highlighted the potential contributory factors:

1 *Competitive blindness: not constantly monitoring the competitive environment*

'When a firm dominates a market, especially one that is driven by constant technological advances, it becomes so fixated with trying to ward off what it reckons to be its most powerful challenger, that it leaves itself vulnerable to attack from other directions'.

By just focusing on Microsoft, Nokia seemed to ignore the challenges from other competitors, thereby failing not only to follow what established players like Motorola and Sony Ericsson were doing, but also emerging competitors such as Samsung.

2 *Failing to track market demands*

Obsessed with warding off competition from Microsoft, Nokia failed to read market signals like growing demand for clamshell phones, colour monitors and camera options, while Asian players like Samsung, LG and Sharp quickly introduced new models at better prices. Companies like Motorola and Sony Ericsson also proved more agile than Nokia in adapting to new market demands. 'We read the signs in the marketplace a bit wrong. While Nokia was focused on functional advantages like phone size and ease of use, the competition was emphasizing "experiential" factors such as colour richness and screen size. That proved to be attractive at the point of sale,' said Anssi Vanjoki, head of Nokia's multimedia operations.

3 *Line reduction for internal convenience, not in response to customer segment needs*

Nokia restricted the range of their models, mainly to reap the rewards of manufacturing cost reduction and thereby increase the bottom line. However, important segments of the market wanted more variation than Nokia was giving them. The competitors were much more in tune with the needs of younger buyers.

The re-emergence of smartphones (2006–2009)

From 2005 things seemed to improve. In the second quarter of 2006 alone, Nokia shipped 78.4 million mobile phone units, 34 per cent of the total market. At the time, Nokia seemed to be putting renewed emphasis on new product development and branding.

In April 2005 Nokia launched two new smartphone sub-brands, the N Series and the E Series (although the company referred to the E Series as 'business devices' rather than smartphones), in a departure from its normal 'umbrella branding' approach. Analysts felt that these helped Nokia to capture the new/emerging market for high-end multimedia mobile phones and business-oriented mobile phones respectively.

In addition, Nokia entered the Internet space with the 'OVI' brand in August 2007. 'OVI' was an umbrella brand for a range of Internet services offered by Nokia—an online music store, games store and navigation service. The above initiatives led to improvements in Nokia's overall performance, which was reflected in its share price. In January 2005 it stood at around $15.00; by the end of 2007 it was hovering around the $40.00 mark, an increase of more than 250 per cent.

However, once again, this proved to be an illusion. Some analysts felt that the emerging markets of India and China were largely responsible for Nokia's revival in the mid-2000s, rather than their NPD initiatives. As the old saying goes, 'a rising tide lifts all boats', and this might have led to more complacency and not delving deep enough into the drivers of their performance improvements.

Although Nokia had launched the first smartphone back in 2005 and had 53 per cent of this market in the fourth quarter of 2007, according to Canalys, it was about to lose this leadership to iPhone and BlackBerry. While Nokia's mobile phones were generally praised for their robust construction and ease of use, its competitors' smartphones were perceived as more powerful and even easier to use—especially the Apple iPhone—and BlackBerry phones had fantastic email integration. Nokia smartphones simply didn't possess the cachet of their rivals.

Bloomberg BusinessWeek put it thus: 'As iPhone sales took off in 2007, Nokia remained strangely detached, say a dozen current and former executives. The company didn't sit still, exactly. Yes, it opened its own app store, OVI—but never put marketing muscle behind it. With no runaway hit like the iPhone, app developers largely ignored it. However, "It was an ignorant complacency, not an arrogant complacency," said Nokia human resources head Juha Akras.'

2010 onwards

In September 2010 Nokia appointed its first non-Finnish CEO as a replacement for Olli-Pekka Kallasvuo. Stephen Elop was recruited from Microsoft, where he had been Head of Business for Microsoft Office.

Within six months, Elop conducted his own strategic review of Nokia and he didn't hold back on his assessment of the dire situation facing the company. As the *Economist* reported in February 2011:

> Apocalyptic language fuels the technology industry as much as venture capital does. But Stephen Elop, Nokia's new boss, may have set a new standard. 'We are standing on a burning [oil] platform,' he wrote in a memo to all 132,000 employees of the world's biggest handset-maker. If Nokia did not want to be consumed by the flames, it had no choice but to plunge into the 'icy waters' below. In plainer words, the company must change its ways radically.

In 1996 Andy Grove, founder of Intel said: 'Business success contains the seeds of its own destruction…Success breeds complacency, and complacency breeds failure.' This is a key lesson, which successive CEOs before Elop didn't really apply.

Elop's predecessor, Olli-Pekka Kallasvuo, was openly and infamously dismissive about the threat from Apple in 2007. He confidently informed his executives that Apple's new iPhone would 'not in any way necessitate us changing our thinking'. He obviously had forgotten the lessons of the early 2000s, and yet again complacency seemed to be rearing its ugly head.

And as Mark Ritson wrote in June 2011:

> The eternal problem for brands such as Nokia is that markets are fluid and companies are not. If executives could have their way, they would draw up a list of brands allowed to compete in a market and competition would then commence, uninterrupted by game-changing entrants. In Nokia's case it was a short list of handset manufacturers that included Sony, Ericsson, Motorola and Samsung.
>
> But sadly for Nokia, consumers don't think within categories, they think across them. To them, Apple was just as much an option as Nokia because of its brand and its proven relationship with consumers in other areas.

Elop was not going to make the same mistake. In March 2011, he announced that Nokia were to dump their homemade Symbian software (shipped already on around 400 million phones), and replace it with Microsoft's

Windows Phone 7 software, then running on around 4 million. To the 2000 employees in the announcement meeting in Finland, this was a humiliating climb-down, but Elop was unapologetic. Apple and Google had changed the industry, he said, from handset-focused to software-focused, while Nokia just stood and watched.

As *Bloomberg BusinessWeek* put it in June 2011, 'Pride can kill a company. So can bad management. Nokia suffered from both—and terrible timing, too.' Elop couldn't put the clock back, but at least he was trying to lead the jump from the burning platform.

> 'When you go through a transition like this,' Elop said, 'there are going to be bumps in the road. Investors hate uncertainty, and we've entered a period of uncertainty.' 'Bumps' and 'uncertainty' maybe understate it, but Elop insists he knew things would get worse before they got better. He remains committed, he says, to his process, and especially to the 'management journey' he undertook to get Nokia back on track.

The future

What, then, does the future look like for Nokia? As the Nokia website puts it, the future will look like this:

> To help us achieve our mission, Nokia has formed a strategic partnership with Microsoft that will, we hope, see us regain lost ground in the smartphone market. Together, we intend to build a global ecosystem that surpasses anything currently in existence. The Nokia-Microsoft ecosystem will deliver differentiated and innovative products with unrivalled scale in terms of product breadth, geographical reach and brand identity.

Elop's master plan, according to *Bloomberg BusinessWeek*, has two main components:

> **Windows-based smartphones are the first stage.** With an estimated $1.4 billion annual savings from discontinuing Symbian, he says he will invest more to protect and build Nokia's massive low-end phone business in emerging and yet-to-emerge nations in Asia and Africa, which brought in 33 per cent of Nokia's sales in 2010.
>
> **Elop's second priority has been dubbed 'New Disruptions'.** It's a fully sanctioned skunkworks (skunkworks means a group within an organization given a high degree of autonomy and unhampered by bureaucracy, tasked with working on advanced or secret projects, according to Wikipedia).

The goal of the skunkworks, as Elop told a group of engineers in Berlin on Feb. 29, is once again to 'find that next big thing that blows away Apple, Android, and everything we're doing with Microsoft right now and makes it irrelevant—all of it. So go for it, without having to worry about saving Nokia's rear end in the next 12 months. I've taken off the handcuffs.'

Lumia 900: the next big thing?

It didn't take long for this big shift in strategy to show signs of promise. Prior to going on sale in North America in April 2012, there was an unmistakable buzz around Nokia's new Lumia 900 touchscreen, which runs the new Windows Phone OS (Operating System) and can operate on fourth-generation, or LTE (Long Term Evolution), wireless networks. The phone won 'best of' accolades at the 2012 Consumer Electronics Show (CES 2012).

There was also a lot of goodwill amongst the UK pundits. The *Sunday Times* gave the Lumia a very good report when it launched. And *Marketing Week*, in November 2011, gave Nokia a great piece of PR. They reported that Charmaine Eggberry, Nokia's senior vice-president of Marketing and Marketplace Activation, is one of the marketers enacting the new strategy. Well known in the technology world, Eggberry joined from BlackBerry maker RIM in July 2010 and reports to CMO Jerri DeVard.

Part of the refocus is to focus on the youth market, a market segment that has become very important for BlackBerry, because of its free instant messaging application, BBM. Eggberry says the Lumia range's social hub and inbuilt music streaming service will be the functions that will revive the brand among this particular segment.

But can Nokia, a brand that has been typically favoured by older, more conservative consumers, speak the language of today's youth? Eggberry is quoted by *Marketing Week* saying the company's research and insight department has been exploring the global youth market to help inform Nokia's strategy.

> 'If you want to be consumer-centric, the first thing you have to do is talk to consumers. I have been blown away by the consumer research and insights group here. We have been doing intensive research on every continent and really looking hard at what Nokia means to them, who they are, what do they aspire to, what are their passions and what resonates with them,' Eggberry explains. But was that confidence misplaced?

It's going to be difficult—maybe Gloomia for Lumia?

In 2012 Nokia warned investors that it would post losses for the third and fourth quarters of the year. This sent its shares plunging to just over $3.00, a level not seen since 1996.

Then came reports that the Lumia 900 was marred by an embarrassing software glitch, and that several big European carriers didn't think it was good enough to compete with Apple's iPhone or Samsung's Galaxy phones. Some have even questioned whether Elop bet on the wrong horse by hitching Nokia's fortunes to Microsoft's, rather than going with the 'open' OS Android.

In the first quarter of 2012, Nokia said it had sold 2 million Lumia handsets. By comparison, Apple claimed to have sold 1 million iPhone 4s handsets in the 24 hours after it went on sale, according to *PC Pro*.

It all just highlights how difficult it can be to engineer a quick turnaround when up against giants like Apple, Google and Samsung. Having a phone which generates buzz is one thing, but convincing people to buy it is quite another.

The figures published by IDC for smartphone sales in February 2012 show the huge job still to be done:

TABLE C2.1   Smartphone sales February 2012

Manufacturer	Market Share
Apple	23.5%
Samsung	22.8%
Nokia	12.4%
RIM (Blackberry)	6.5%
HTC	10.8%
Others	24.0%

Rupert Englander, Nokia's head of Innovation and Services, gave an interview to *The Marketer* in the May–June 2012 edition in which he was very sanguine about the future, especially as Nokia builds stronger relationships with developers. 'We're being recognised as an ecosystem for developers,' he says. 'We're actively courting new ideas.'

The objective to regain lost ground in the smartphone market, and 'build a global ecosystem that surpasses anything currently in existence', seems an almost unattainable target at the moment. But who would bet against a company that has made a series of staggering business transformations in the past. Can it do it again?

References

The Economist 12 February 2005: 'The giant in the palm of your hand'.

Ewing, J. (2009) Nokia: Bring on the employee rants, *Business Week*, 22 June, 50.

Interbrand/Business Week: Best Global Brands 2006: published 1 August 2006.

Interbrand/Business Week (2009) 100 Best Global Brands, 28 September, 50–60.

Nokia website: Nokia in Brief 2005 (published June 2006).

Nokia website: Nokia Firsts.

Nokia.com 1975–1999 turnover.

Sunday Times, 25 June 2006.

The Mobile Revolution—Dan Steinbock (Kogan Page 2005).

Wikipedia.

Wray, R. (2009) Nokia turns to Android in battle of the smartphones, *Guardian*, 6 July, 22.

Questions

1 If you were to pick just one reason why Nokia finds itself in its current predicament, what would it be, and how would you justify your choice?

2 Which of the Internal focus criteria in Table 1.1 do you feel contributed to Nokia's decline? Again, justify your choice!

3 Evaluate Nokia's recent attempts to regain a leading position in the market. How likely is it that it will succeed? What other options does Nokia have?

This case was prepared by Tony Rowe, Principal of Marketing Mentors, and Tony Lindley, Managing Director of Tony Lindley Consultants Ltd.

CHAPTER 2

Marketing planning: an overview of marketing

> **The firm's DNA is communicated to both internal and external stakeholders, and stakeholders' concerns should be an influence on strategic marketing planning.**
> (CRITTENDEN 2011)[1]

> **Life is what happens to you while you're busy making other plans.**
> JOHN LENNON ('Beautiful Boy')

LEARNING OBJECTIVES

After reading this chapter, you should be able to:

1. describe the role of marketing planning within businesses
2. identify the key planning questions
3. discuss the process of marketing planning
4. describe the concept of the business mission
5. explain the marketing audit and SWOT analysis
6. discuss the nature of marketing objectives
7. identify the components of core strategy and how to test its effectiveness
8. explain marketing mix decisions in relation to the planning process
9. discuss implementation and control in the marketing planning process
10. describe the rewards and problems associated with marketing planning
11. discuss recommendations to overcoming marketing planning problems

Chapter 1 introduced the marketing concept and made a case for adopting it as a guiding business philosophy for improving performance. However, to gain the potential advantages that marketing might bring, managers must make many decisions. For example, which customer groups to serve; how to create value-added products and services; which technology to use and which marketing strategies are most likely to deliver competitive advantages. To add to these complex choices, managers must also consider the impact of the environment, and determine how to get the best strategic fit between their organization's capabilities and resources and the market opportunities.

This chapter presents the **marketing planning** framework, which addresses many of the key questions and decisions a manager might encounter. Additionally, it acts as a framework for all the elements of marketing we consider in the rest of the book. We begin the chapter by considering the marketing planning context. Then we delve into the key functions of marketing planning, before exploring the stages in the marketing planning process. The chapter concludes by looking at the rewards and problems of marketing planning.

Marketing Planning Context

Marketing planning is part of a broader concept of *corporate strategic planning* which involves all business functions: marketing, operations, finance, human resources, information management, distribution and the trading environment. The aim of corporate strategic planning is to provide direction for a company so its activities constantly meet high-level corporate objectives: e.g., being market leader, improving profitability. Marketing links to this high level of strategic planning by managing the interface between a company and its environment, e.g., a corporate objective to be market leader will take account of the economic forces and their impact on a particular market. So the marketing planning team carrying out a marketing audit, for example, should produce sufficient knowledge to enable the corporate management team to make their long-term strategic decisions, thereby creating a link between strategy and marketing planning.

In reality, the role of marketing planning in strategy development is complex and can vary considerably in terms of what is involved. At the simplest level a company may market only one product in one market. In this case, the role of marketing planning is to ensure the marketing plan for the product matches its customers' needs. Also the company can use all available resources to achieve its marketing objectives—for example, to sell more products. This should also enable the marketing plan to feed into the corporate objective of becoming market leader. However, this is rarely the case, as companies tend to offer many products and/or services to many different target markets. In this situation decisions have to be made about the allocation of resources to each product and/or service. This is far from a straightforward process as resource allocation is dependent on the attractiveness of the market for each product, and the capabilities and resources of the company.

To add to the complexity, a company may comprise a number of discrete but connected divisions (or totally separate companies) each of which serves distinct groups of customers and has a distinct set of competitors.[2] For example: the Virgin Group operates many companies in different activity sectors, e.g. media (Virgin Media); music (Virgin Megastore); travel (Virgin Atlantic Airways).

Each business may be strategically autonomous and thus form a **strategic business unit** (SBU). For example, the Virgin Group is made up of a *community* of independently operating companies. A major component of a strategic plan—at the corporate level—is allocation of resources to each SBU. Strategic decisions at the corporate level are normally concerned with acquisition, divestment and diversification.[3] In the Virgin Group example, each company contributes to the over-arching aims of the Group—i.e. Virgin Media was created through mergers with NTL, Telewest and Virgin Mobile. The decisions to add or release a business are taken at the corporate and strategic planning level. Richard Branson, the founder of the Virgin empire, expanded the business's reach by entering markets as diverse as cosmetics, weddings and hotels. Marketing feeds into such corporate decision-making by identifying

Go to the website and suggest why Sky allows its competitor Virgin Media to provide viewers with Sky channels.
www.mcgraw-hill.co.uk/textbooks/jobber

⬆EXHIBIT 2.1   Virgin Atlantic Airways makes a contribution to the Virgin Group's corporate identity.

opportunities and threats in the environment. So, the opportunity to develop the travel arm of the Virgin group by adding Virgin hotels is likely to have emerged from marketing planning actions.

In summary, marketing planning is part of the overarching corporate strategic planning process and provides a range of insights from the trading environment to target markets and customer needs. Thinking about where marketing planning fits in the wider business planning process is only part of the challenge managers encounter. There are two other aspects of marketing planning to consider: the core functions and key planning processes of marketing planning, which are discussed in more detail in the following sections.

The Functions of Marketing Planning

Arguably, the core function of a marketing plan is to answer the following questions:

1   Where are we now?
2   Where would we like to be?
3   How do we get there?
4   Are we on course?

For the marketing planning team at Virgin Atlantic answering these questions means considering:

- Where are we now? Looking at the current position of the business in terms of its past performance, considering the effectiveness of previous marketing plans and questioning what might happen if there were no changes in current practice. In 2011 Virgin Atlantic performed well against its objectives, managing its resources effectively through tough economic conditions.
- Where would we like to be? The future direction of the business is defined by its marketing objectives. Virgin's corporate objective is to 'offer *the best business* product in the air'[4] so the implications for the marketing planning team are setting suitable objectives which ensure improved customer service of its *business* products.

TABLE 2.1   Key questions and the process of marketing planning

Key questions	Stages in marketing planning
Where are we now?	Business mission, marketing audit, SWOT analysis
Where would we like to be?	Marketing objectives
How do we get there?	Core strategy, marketing mix decisions, organization, implementation
Are we on course?	Control

- How do we get there? This can be answered in the Virgin case by looking at the needs of *business* travellers, considering their expectations and experiences. Virgin has won industry awards for its Upper Class Suite, which is designed to be a first-class product for a business class fare. The marketing planning team looked at this key target audience (business travellers), and devised a marketing mix strategy which they could implement to achieve their marketing objectives.
- Are we on course? This question is answered by looking at performance measures. Like many companies, Virgin measures sales and profitability but it uses other measures such as increase in fuel efficiency and reduction in carbon emissions, targeting the use of sustainable products and renewable resources.

The core functions of marketing planning addressed by these questions link into specific stages in the marketing planning process (see Table 2.1). 'Where are we now?' is forecast by reference to the marketing audit and SWOT analysis. 'Where would we like to be?' is determined by the setting of marketing objectives. 'How do we get there?' refers to core strategy, marketing mix decisions, organization and implementation. Finally 'Are we on course?' is answered by the establishment of a control system.

The next section discusses the process of marketing planning in detail.

The Process of Marketing Planning

In reality, planning is rarely straightforward. Different people are involved at various stages of the planning process. The key marketing planning process can broadly be divided into distinct areas:

- the business unit level—e.g. Virgin Atlantic
- the product level—e.g. Virgin flights to America.

The process of marketing planning is outlined in Figure 2.1. This overview of framework provides a systematic way for understanding the analysis and the decision-making processes involved in marketing planning. Additionally, the framework shows how key elements of marketing—discussed in subsequent chapters—relate to each other and fit into the planning process.

Business mission

Russell Ackoff, an American organizational theorist defined **business mission** as:

> A broadly defined, enduring statement of purpose that distinguishes a business from others of its type.[5]

This definition captures two essential ingredients in mission statements: they are enduring and specific to the individual organization.[6] Two fundamental questions that need to be addressed are 'What business are we in?' and 'What business do we want to be in?' The answers define the scope and activities of the company. The business mission explains the reason for its existence and focuses on the present. The mission statement should not be confused with a vision statement, which looks to the future: for example, Samsung's 2020

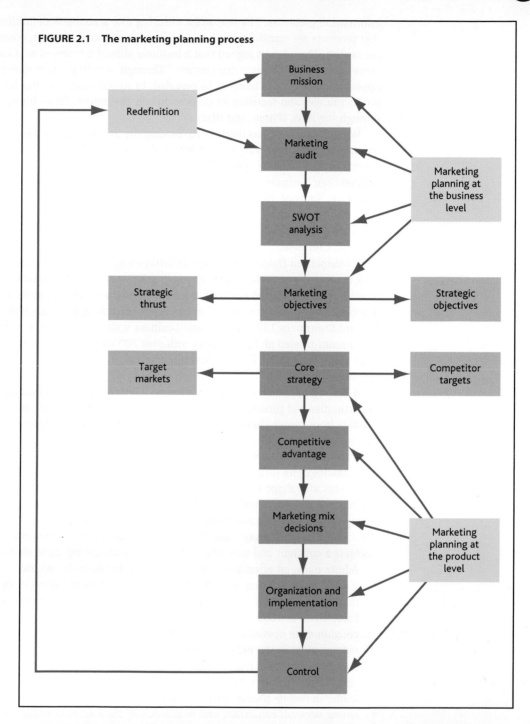

FIGURE 2.1 The marketing planning process

vision statement for the coming decade is 'Inspire the World, Create the Future' (Samsung 2012), whereas Google's mission statement is 'to organize the world's information and make it universally accessible and useful' (Google 2012). Consider how each statement has different implications for marketing planning.[7,8]

A mission statement can take many forms, but it should reflect the customer groups being served (the market), refer to the customer needs being satisfied, and describe the process by which a customer need can be satisfied. The inclusion of market and needs ensures that the business definition is market focused rather than product based. Thus, the purpose of a company such as Apple Inc. is not to manufacture computers but to solve customers' information problems. The reason for ensuring that a business definition is market focused is that products are transient, but basic needs such as transportation, entertainment and eating are lasting. Thus, Levitt argued that a business should be viewed as a customer-satisfying process, not a goods-producing process.[9] Through adopting a customer perspective, new opportunities are more likely to be revealed. In Apple's case this has led to streamlining its product ranges and focusing its innovations on customers' needs for mobile computing, through the iPod, iPhone and iPad.

While this advice has merit in advocating the avoidance of a narrow business definition, management must be wary of a definition that is too wide. Theodore Levitt, a leading American economist, suggested that railroad companies would have survived had they defined their business as transportation and moved into the airline business. But this is to ignore the limits of the business competence of the railroads. Did they possess the necessary skills and resources to run an airline? Clearly a key constraint on a business definition can be the competences (both actual and potential) of management, and the resources at their disposal. Conversely, competences can act as the motivator for widening a business mission. Asda (Associated Dairies) redefined its business mission as a producer and distributor of milk to a retailer of fast-moving consumer goods partly on the basis of its distribution skills, which it rightly believed could be extended to products beyond milk. The Virgin Group is another example of a company that has adapted to changing market demands. Founded by Richard Branson in 1970 in the music business with Virgin records, the group has developed into a multi-faceted global business with over 300 successful companies in sectors ranging from mobile telephony through to transportation, travel, financial services, media, music and fitness.[10]

A second influence on business mission is macro-environmental change. Change provides opportunities and threats that influence mission definition. Asda saw that changes in retail practice from corner shops to high-volume supermarkets presented an opportunity that could be exploited by its skills. Its move redefined its business.

A third influence on business mission is the background of the company and the personalities of its senior management. The personalities and beliefs of the people who run businesses also shape the business mission and influence its success. This last factor emphasizes the judgemental nature of business definition and indicates there is no right or wrong way to write a business mission statement. However, the mission should be based on the vision that top management and its subordinates have of the future of the business. This vision is a coherent and powerful statement of what the business should aim to become.[11]

Additionally, an effective mission statement should be based on:

- *a solid understanding of the business*, and the forces acting on its operations, which might change in the future. The vision of its business was crucial to the success of Nokia. Established in 1865 by Fredrik Idestam as a paper manufacturer, it expanded into a conglomerate operating in industries such as paper, chemicals and rubber. The vision of management in the early 1990s transformed the company by redefining its mission. Nokia abandoned life as a conglomerate to focus on mobile phone technology, a strategic decision that led to it becoming one of Europe's most successful companies and the world leader in mobile phones early in the 21st century.[12]

- *strong personal conviction and motivation of the leader*, who has the ability to make his or her vision contagious. For example, it was Walt Disney who founded his company's mission statement 'To make people happy', which is both contagious and motivating for staff.[13] Jeff Bezos's vision and mission for Amazon is 'to be the earth's most customer-centric company, to build a place where people can come to find and discover anything they might want to buy online.'[14,15] His passion and commitment has led the company through challenging times to become the world's leading consumer e-commerce company.

- *creating strategic intent of winning throughout the organization*. This helps to build a sense of common purpose, and stresses the need to create competitive advantages rather than settle for imitative moves.

- *enabling success*. Managers must believe they have the latitude to make decisions about strategy without being second-guessed by top management.

In summary, the mission statement provides the framework within which managers decide which opportunities and threats to address, and which to disregard. A well-defined mission statement is a key element in the marketing planning process, as it defines boundaries within which new opportunities are sought and motivates staff to succeed in the implementation of marketing strategy.

Read the Research 2.1 Elements of Marketing Planning

Quite often mission and vision statements have become part of business speak. Many organizations offer a wide variety of terms to express themselves in these statements with little empirical evidence to guide their choice.

This article has conducted extensive research on mission and vision statements, and looks at over 300 organizations with nearly 500 statements to ascertain how many distinct concepts could be identified and the most commonly used ones.

Their conclusion comes up with some interesting results.

Steven H. Cady, Jane V. Wheeler, Jeff DeWolf and Michelle Brodke (2011) Mission, Vision, and Values: What Do They Say?
Organization Development Journal, 1 April, 63–78.

This website offers sample business plans from a variety of sectors and practical advice on the content and process of business planning. This link starts with the SWOT analysis of a brewery business and continues through the entire process. Just click on the link to get started. http://www.bplans.com/brewery_business_plan/swot_analysis_fc.php#.UGHEb0LiM-b.

Marketing Audit

The **marketing audit** is a systematic examination of a business's marketing environment, objectives, strategies and activities, with a view to identifying key strategic issues, problem areas and opportunities. The marketing audit provides the basis for developing a plan of action to improve marketing performance and in doing so should provide answers to the question: where are we now? And the supplemental issues of: how did we get here? where are we heading?

Answers to these questions depend upon an analysis of the internal and external environment of a business. This analysis benefits from a clear mission statement, since the latter defines the boundaries of the environmental scan and helps decisions regarding which strategic issues and opportunities are important.

The internal audit focuses on those areas that are under the control of marketing management, whereas the external audit is concerned with those forces over which management has no control. The results of the marketing audit are a key determinant of the future direction of the business and may give rise to a redefined business mission statement. Alongside the marketing audit, a business may conduct audits of other functional areas such as production, finance and personnel. The coordination and integration of these audits produces a composite business plan in which marketing issues play a central role, since they concern decisions about which products to manufacture for which markets. These decisions clearly have production, financial and personnel implications, and successful implementation depends upon each functional area acting in concert.

A checklist of issues that may be examined in a marketing audit is given in Tables 2.2 (external) and 2.3 (internal). External analysis covers the macroenvironment and the microenvironment. The **macroenvironment** consists of broad environmental issues that may

TABLE 2.2   External marketing audit checklist

Forces	Key topics / Trends
MACROENVIRONMENT	
Political/legal	EU and national laws; codes of practice; political instability
Economic	Economic growth; unemployment; interest and exchange rates; global economic trends (e.g. the growth of the BRICS economies)
Ecological/physical environmental	Global warming; pollution; energy and other scarce resources; environmentally friendly ingredients and components; recycling and non-wasteful packaging
Social/cultural	Changes in world population, age distribution and household structure; attitude and lifestyle changes; subcultures within and across national boundaries; consumerism
Technological	Innovations; communications; technology infrastructures; bio-technology
MICROENVIRONMENT	
Market	Size; growth rates
Customers	Who they are, their choice criteria, how, when and where they buy; how they rate the competition on product, promotion, price and distribution; how customers group (market segmentation), and what benefits each group seeks
Competitors	Who are the major competitors (actual and potential); their objectives and strategies; strengths and weaknesses; size, market share and profitability; entry barriers to new competitors
Distributors	Channel attractiveness; distributor decision-making unit, decision-making process and choice criteria; strengths and weaknesses; power changes; physical distribution methods
Suppliers	Who they are and location; strengths and weaknesses; power changes

affect business performance. These are political/legal, economic, ecological/physical, social/cultural and technological forces. Auditing these issues is known by the acronym PEEST analysis, which adds the influence of changes in the physical environment. Originally, Francis J. Aguilar alerted the attention of managers to the importance of scanning the business environment and he is credited with inventing the PEST acronym, a structured method of analysis that assisted an organization's future planning.[16] Since then various acronyms have been used in management literature, e.g. STEP, STEEP, PESTLE.[17] The key point to remember is that scanning the business environment in a systematic manner is crucially important for all organizations as changes in the environment can have dramatic effects on long-term success.

Table 2.2 lists the forces and key topics that fall within each area. Chapter 3 explores marketing environment in-depth. Mini Case 2.1 looks at how macro forces influence how the Highways Agency plans.

Mini Case 2.1 Highways Agency and the Influence of the Macroenvironment

The Highways Agency is part of the Department for Transport (DfT) and is responsible for looking after the road network in England. Maintaining and improving 4300 miles of motorways and trunk roads, which carry around a third of all traffic, means the Highways Agency has to plan carefully, to ensure traffic keeps moving and that the services provided by the agency satisfy its customers: over 4 million drivers per day. Many changes in the macroenvironment have affected the use of the major roads in England: for example, the increase in transporting of goods by road; technology infrastructure and changing digital equipment like speed detection and variable traffic messages; the pressure to reduce carbon emissions. This means the Highways Agency has to keep in touch with the business environment in which it operates and develop its marketing plan in a way that enables the agency to continue to meet the needs of all of its stakeholders.

The Highways Agency has several core roles to consider when planning its future actions; operating, maintaining and improving the major road network in England. To do this successfully, it has to consider the influences of various macroenvironmental forces, both political and legal. As a result of the UK Government's 2010 spending review (looking at expenditure across all agencies) the Highways Agency's budget was reduced and the senior team had to devise a strategy that would enable them to manage the roads network until 2015. The Agency is an important part of the DfT vision for the future and much responsibility falls on the Highways Agency to ensure that England has 'a transportation system that is the engine of economic growth'. Furthermore, many of the Highways Agency's actions are informed and controlled by legislation from the DfT. Economic forces—for example, the influence of the 2008/9 recession—means the agency has had to *deliver more for less*, while the changing economic environment means it has to prioritize actions and road improvement plans. The physical environment is at the heart of the agency's environmental policies and is central to strategy development. Environmental issues include: climate change, air quality and pollution, noise and vibrations, drainage and water quality, nature conservation and the landscape. Social and cultural issues involve planning traffic management for major events—e.g. the Olympic Games, city marathons. The agency has to ensure that the road network is fit for purpose and can cope with increased congestion resulting from such events, as well as ensuring road user safety. Traffic services and road improvements are developed with the aim of reducing deaths and serious injuries. Technological innovations have also enabled the agency to lower the cost of its operation at the roadside through the deployment of new fibre optic cables, which has streamlined communications, and made improvements to the technology infrastructure, while the addition of CCTV and the MIDAS signalling system keep road networks flowing.

Analysing the macroenvironment is very important to the Highways Agency due to the nature of the activities it is involved with: developing the road network and ensuring future sustainability.

Questions:

1   Explain why there is no mention of any of the microenvironmental factors in the article. Discuss each factor in turn.
2   The uncontrollable macroenvironment has a dramatic influence on the planning processes of the Highways Agency. Suggest ways the agency might reduce the risks associated with this uncertainty.

Source: Highways Agency (2012)[18]

The **microenvironment** consists of the actors in the firm's immediate environment that affect its capabilities to operate effectively in its chosen markets. The key actors are customers, distributors, suppliers and competitors and microenvironmental analysis will consist of an analysis of issues relating to these actors and an overall analysis of market size, growth rates and trends (see Table 2.2).

More specifically, microenvironmental analysis consists of:

•   **market analysis**, which involves the statistical analysis of market size, growth rates and trends
•   **customer analysis** of buyer behaviour—how they rate competitive offerings, and how they segment
•   **competitor analysis**, which examines the nature of actual and potential competitors, and their objectives and strategies. It also seeks to identify their strengths and weaknesses,

TABLE 2.3 Internal marketing audit checklist	
Operating results (by product, customer, geographic region)	**Marketing mix effectiveness**
Sales	Product
Market share	Price
Profit margins	Promotion
Costs	Distribution
Strategic issues analysis	**Marketing structures**
Marketing objectives	Marketing organization
Market segmentation	Marketing training
Competitive advantage	Intra- and interdepartmental communication
Core competences	**Marketing systems**
Positioning	Marketing information systems
Portfolio analysis	Marketing planning system
	Marketing control system

⬆ EXHIBIT 2.2 Eddie Stobart transformed the image of his dad's haulage company by focusing on presenting the company as smart and clean.

⬆ EXHIBIT 2.3 Apple's iPad—Advanced design. Thin. Light. Fully loaded.

size, market share and profitability. Finally, entry barrier analysis identifies the key financial and non-financial barriers that protect the industry from competitor attack

- **distribution analysis**, which covers an examination of the attractiveness of different distribution channels, distributor buyer behaviour, their strengths and weaknesses, movements in power bases, and alternative methods of physical distribution

- **supplier analysis** examines who and where they are located, their strengths and weaknesses, power changes and trends in the supply chain.

The internal audit allows the performance and activities of the business to be assessed in the light of environmental developments. Operating results form a basis of assessment through analysis of sales, market share, profit margins and costs. **Strategic issues analysis** examines the suitability of marketing objectives and segmentation bases in the light of changes in the marketplace. Competitive advantages and the core competences on which they are based would be reassessed and the positioning of products in the market critically reviewed. Core competences are the principal distinctive capabilities possessed by a company, which define what it really is good at.

An example of a company that has invested in its core competences is Eddie Stobart Ltd. When Eddie set about transforming his dad's haulage business he knew that customers 'hated slovenly drivers and old dirty lorries' and so focusing on dress code and cleanliness helped him to transform not only his own company but the whole of the haulage industry in the UK. Other core competencies included just-in-time stock management and highly effective logistics solutions.[19] Apple Inc. is another company that has built a leading global business by investing in developing innovative digital technology products.

One danger that companies face is moving away from their core competences into areas where their skills and capabilities do not provide a competitive advantage. Management can become distracted, leading to poor performance, as Marketing in Action 2.1 describes veteran brands that are struggling to survive.

Marketing in Action 2.1 Focusing on Core Competences: Veteran Brands Struggle to Stay Alive

Thomas Cook has been established for over 100 years but attempts to diversify and move into new markets have not proved so successful. By contrast, Lego, a slightly younger company founded in 1916, is turning a corner, with healthy profits, despite having a difficult trading period in recent years through diversifying into unprofitable new product ranges.

Thomas Cook is the world's oldest travel agency, but its future is uncertain; it has reported substantial losses, and the closure of 200 of its UK high street travel shops puts many jobs at risk. In order to protect its future, the company has also sold its Spanish hotel chain. CEO Sam Weihagen said '. . . this transaction will significantly reduce Thomas Cook's net debt and demonstrate our ongoing commitment to strengthen the balance sheet'. Part of the problem is that Thomas Cook invested in market growth in Russia but then blamed political unrest in Egypt and Tunisia and floods in Thailand for falling sales as holiday makers in the new target markets failed to book in the expected volumes. The company has also failed to make the best of the opportunities afforded by the Internet, where many consumers now prefer to go to make their own travel arrangements. So investment in new markets has proved to be highly risky, and existing markets are also underperforming.

Lego's mistake was to diversify into the manufacture of new product ranges—clothing, bags and accessories—areas that required very different skills from the manufacture and marketing of toy bricks. The result was an overcomplicated product portfolio and an overstretching of the Lego brand. Lego's remedy was to refocus on its core, brick-based product range and place more emphasis on its key target group: boys aged five to nine. The company has also formed partnerships with famous film studios and created popular ranges of themed toys—for example, *Pirates of the Caribbean*, *Harry Potter* and *Star Wars*. It has also diversified by creating an online community and the Lego Universe gaming portal. This has enabled the Lego group to increase significantly revenues on a year-on-year basis and the group has seen market growth in the USA, Britain, Russia and Eastern Europe.

The moral of these tales is that it is important to be aware of changes taking place in the wider trading environment and to ensure that any diversification is undertaken only when the core competences to succeed are in place or can be acquired.

Sources: BBC (2011), Thomas Cook to close 200 UK branches, http://www.bbc.co.uk/news/business-16173578, 14 December.

Based on: Amos (2011);[20] BBC Business News (2011);[21] Bowers (2011);[22] Chapman (2011);[23] Jackson (2011);[24] The Lego Group (2010);[25] Sibun (2008)[26]

Finally, **product portfolios** should be analysed to determine future strategic objectives. Each element of the marketing mix is reviewed in the light of changing customer requirements and competitor activity. The **marketing structures** on which marketing activities are based should be analysed. Marketing structure consists of the marketing organization, training, and intra- and interdepartmental communication that takes place within an organization. Marketing organization is reviewed to determine fit with strategy and the market, and marketing training requirements are examined. Finally, communications and the relationship within the marketing department and between marketing and other functions (e.g. R&D, engineering, production) need to be appraised.

Marketing systems are audited for effectiveness. These consist of the marketing information, planning and control systems that support marketing activities. Shortfalls in information provision are analysed; the marketing planning system is critically appraised for cost-effectiveness; and the marketing control system is assessed in the light of accuracy, timeliness (does it provide evaluations when managers require them?) and coverage (does the system evaluate the key variables affecting company performance?).

Marketing systems can be vital assets. For example, marketing information systems at British Airways, Qantas and Singapore Airlines provide knowledge regarding repeat passengers' preferred seats, newspapers, food and drinks, allowing customization of their offerings.

This checklist provides the basis for deciding on the topics to be included in the marketing audit. However, to give the same amount of attention and detailed analysis to every item would grind the audit to a halt under a mass of data and issues. In practice, the judgement of those conducting the audit is critical in deciding the key items to focus upon. Those factors that are considered of crucial importance to the company's performance will merit most attention. One by-product of the marketing audit may be a realization that information about key environmental issues is lacking.

All assumptions should be made explicit as an ongoing part of the marketing audit: for example, key assumptions might be:

- inflation will average 3 per cent during the planning period
- VAT levels will not be changed
- worldwide overcapacity will remain at 150 per cent
- no new entrants into the market will emerge.

The marketing audit should be an ongoing activity, not a desperate attempt to turn round an ailing business. Some companies conduct an annual audit as part of their annual planning system; others operating in less turbulent environments may consider two or three years an adequate period between audits. Others might consider the use of an outside consultant to coordinate activities and provide an objective, outside view to be beneficial, while some may believe that their own managers are best equipped to conduct the analyses. Clearly there is no set formula for deciding when and by whom the audit is conducted. The decision ultimately rests on the preferences and situation facing the management team.

SWOT analysis

A **SWOT analysis** is a structured approach to evaluating the strategic position of a business by identifying its strengths, weaknesses, opportunities and threats. It provides a simple method of synthesizing the results of the marketing audit. Internal strengths and weaknesses are summarized as they relate to external opportunities and threats (see Fig. 2.2).

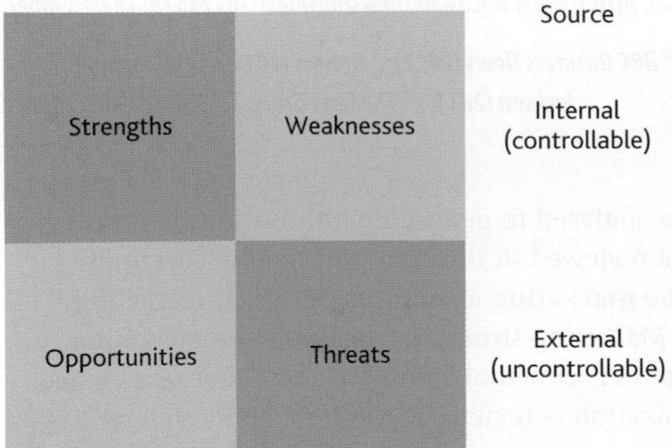

When evaluating strengths and weaknesses, only those resources or capabilities that would be valued by the customer should be included.[27] Thus strengths such as 'We are an old established firm', 'We are a large supplier' and 'We are technologically advanced' should be questioned for their impact on customer satisfaction. It is conceivable that such bland generalizations confer as many weaknesses as strengths. Also, opportunities and threats should be listed as anticipated events or trends *outside* the business that have implications for performance. Figure 2.3 shows an example of a SWOT chart for a specialist, low-volume US sports car manufacturer.

FIGURE 2.2 Strengths, weaknesses, opportunities and threats (SWOT) analysis

		Source
Strengths	Weaknesses	Internal (controllable)
Opportunities	Threats	External (uncontrollable)

FIGURE 2.3   SWOT chart

Strengths	Weaknesses
1 Reliable products 2 Well-respected brand name worldwide 3 Competitive prices 4 Tightly focused on a specialist niche market	1 Production limited to 20 cars per week, resulting in six-month waiting lists 2 Outdated production methods 3 Lack of marketing expertise 4 Limited marketing research information 5 Only distributed in UK (mainly) and USA 6 Low profit margin
Opportunities	**Threats**
1 Growing market in USA 2 High market potential in Germany, France, Benelux and Scandinavia 3 Untapped market potential in UK	1 Volume manufacturers could target specialist niche market 2 Increasing number of specialist car manufacturers setting up in Europe 3 Tough European legislation on exhaust emission standards likely

FIGURE 2.4   SWOT analysis and strategy development

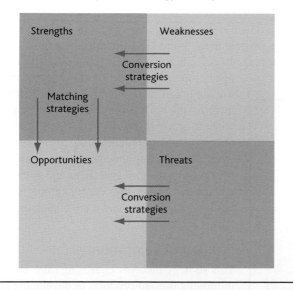

Once a SWOT analysis has been completed, thought can be given to how to turn weaknesses into strengths and threats into opportunities. For example, a perceived weakness in customer care might suggest the need for staff training to create a new strength. A threat posed by a new entrant might call for a strategic alliance to combine the strengths of both parties to exploit a new opportunity. Because these activities are designed to convert weaknesses into strengths and threats into opportunities, they are called *conversion strategies* (see Fig. 2.4). Another way to use a SWOT analysis is to match strengths with opportunities. An example of a company that successfully matched strengths with opportunities is Charles Tyrwhitt, the gents' clothing retailer, whose founder Nick Wheeler saw an opportunity in the growing demand for online sales. One of the company's strengths was the fact that it had run its own catalogue business for more than a decade to service its existing home shopping operation. The result is that Charles Tyrwhitt has created a highly profitable online business, outselling its rivals Thomas Pink and TM Lewin in terms of online sales.

Using the SWOT chart for the specialist sports car manufacturer (Fig. 2.3), conversion strategies might include building a new manufacturing facility to raise production levels to 50 cars per week and to incorporate more modern production methods, establishing a marketing function and (if marketing research supports it) raising price levels. The company could also seek to eliminate the threat of tougher European standards on exhaust emissions by redesigning its engines to meet them. Marketing strategies might include building on the company's strengths in producing reliable products and possessing a well-respected global brand name to establish distribution in Germany, France, Benelux and Scandinavia, while building sales in the USA and UK (opportunities). Given the company's lack of marketing expertise, the geographic expansion would need to be carefully planned (with full input from the newly created marketing department) at a rate of growth compatible with its managerial capabilities and production capacity. International marketing research would be conducted to establish the relative attractiveness of the new European markets to decide the order of entry. Such a phased entry strategy would enable the company to learn progressively about what is needed to market successfully in Europe.

Marketing Objectives

The results of the marketing audit and SWOT analysis lead to the definition of **marketing objectives**. These objectives also link through the business mission to corporate objectives. Imagine you are responsible for managing Danone's yogurt portfolio, which includes Activia, Shape and Actimel product ranges. The corporate objective is to become number one in the yogurt markets, overtaking Muller, the existing market leader. You will need to develop a marketing plan, which contributes to this corporate objective. How you do this involves deciding on which markets to target with which products and then setting specific objectives for individual products. There are two levels of objectives, used in marketing planning:

1 *Strategic thrust objectives* which shape the direction of the plan and involve deciding on which markets to target and which products/service to sell. So, in the Danone case you might decide to target new customers (Muller yogurt eaters) with existing products (Activia fruit yogurts).

2 *Strategic objectives* set specific objectives for individual products. So, to implement your plan you will need to build market share of (Activia fruit yogurts).

Each type of objectives is now discussed in more detail.

Strategic thrust

Objectives should be set in terms of which products to sell in which markets.[28] This describes the **strategic thrust** of the business. The strategic thrust defines the future direction and areas of potential growth for a business. The alternatives comprise:

- existing products in existing markets (market penetration or expansion)
- new/related products for existing markets (product development)
- existing products in new/related markets (market development)
- new/related products for new/related markets (entry into new markets).

Market penetration

This strategy is to take the existing product in the existing market and to attempt increased penetration. Existing customers may become more brand loyal (brand-switch less often) and/or new customers in the same market may begin to buy the brand. Other tactics to increase penetration include getting existing customers to use the brand more often (e.g. wash their hair more frequently) and to use a greater quantity when they use it (e.g. two spoonfuls of tea instead of one). The latter tactic would also have the effect of expanding the market: e.g. Glasses Direct, the online reseller of spectacles and sunglasses, launched a 2-for-1 offer encouraging existing customers to buy several pairs of glasses at a time.[29]

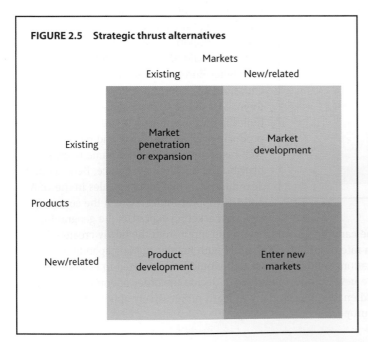

FIGURE 2.5 **Strategic thrust alternatives**

Markets

	Existing	New/related
Existing (Products)	Market penetration or expansion	Market development
New/related	Product development	Enter new markets

Product development

This strategy involves increasing sales by improving present products or developing new products for current markets. New product replacements that fail to provide additional benefits may disappoint, as with the Vista version of Microsoft Windows, which was intended to replace XP. Many users did not change systems, preferring the XP product.[30] Product development may take the form of brand extensions (Cadbury's Dairy Milk Caramel bars and Caramel Nibbles,

Cadbury's Crunchie Bars and Crunchie Rocks) that provide slightly modified features for target customers.

Market development

This strategy is used when current products are sold in new markets. This may involve moving into new geographical markets. Many consumer durable brands, such as cars, consumer electronics and household appliance brands, are sold in overseas markets with no or only very minor modifications to those sold at home. An alternative market development strategy is to move into new market segments. For example, BSkyB has expanded its market share through the acquisition of Virgin Media's TV channel. This has enabled BSkyB to gain access to Virgin's customers by providing Sky's existing content. Santander, one of the world's largest banking groups, has also developed markets for its existing financial products in both Latin America and the UK.[31]

Marketing in Action 2.2 discusses how Tesco has used both strategies with great success.

Marketing in Action 2.2 Market Development at Tesco

Tesco is the UK's most successful supermarket chain and accounts for a staggering £1 of every £8 of consumer spending in British shops. The traditional Tesco supermarket was the large superstore offering large food and non-food (e.g. clothing, consumer electronics goods, petrol, CDs) product ranges. These superstores tend to be on the edge of town, with free parking and facilities that include cafés and petrol stations. They target customers who want big, trolley-based family shopping. This one-stop-shopping experience, backed by a good-quality, value-for-money positioning strategy based on the 'Every Little Helps' strap-line, ensured healthy sales and profit growth for many years.

In an effort to continue this growth, Tesco embarked on a market development strategy based on entering a new market segment. This was the convenience shopper who wishes to 'top up' their shopping or replace home essentials such as milk or bread. Two new store formats were created, both small but differing in terms of location. Tesco Metro stores allow convenience shopping in town centres, while Tesco Express stores are usually found at petrol stations, providing drivers and local customers with a convenient place to shop for groceries. Both stores carry the same grocery products, albeit a smaller range than their superstore counterparts.

Tesco has also pursued market development through moving into new geographical markets with similar products. It has expanded into the USA, China, India, South Korea, Thailand, Hungary, Poland and Turkey as it seeks to compete globally with Wal-Mart. However, overseas expansion has sometimes been met with difficulties—most notably in the USA, where the Fresh & Easy chain of stores continues to make losses.

Nevertheless, Tesco continues with its two-pronged market development strategy of seeking to serve new market segments at home and moving into new geographical markets abroad, which has been highly successful in maintaining sales and profit growth.

Based on: http://www.imaginerecruitment.com;[32] Singh (2008);[33] Wood (2011);[34] Jackson (2011);[35] Chapman (2011)[36]

Entry into new markets

This strategy occurs when new products are developed for new markets. This is the most risky strategy but may be necessary when a company's current products and markets offer few prospects for future growth. When there is synergy between the existing and new products, this strategy is more likely to work. For example, Apple's experience and competences in computer electronics provided the platform for designing a new product, the iPod, targeting a different market: young people who want downloadable music on a portable music player.[37] This, in turn, has been followed by the launch of the iPhone, which has placed Apple in a strong position in the market for smartphones[38] and the development of the tablet computer

Digital Marketing 2.1 Google+ Challenges Facebook

Google+ is a social network that enables friends to share ideas, contacts, images and other content through friendship 'circles'; it also provides 'hangouts' where members of the network can have face-to-face conversations using their computers and mobile phones. As one of the giants of the Internet era, Google has the technological resources and competencies to ensure that Google+ delivers on its technological promises. The biggest challenge is how to enter the market successfully and take on Facebook, the market leader and most well-established social network. Entering the market is proving difficult. Only a few months after its launch reports from the business press suggested that 'Google+ is dead', the issue behind the headline being that in the early months after the launch businesses were discouraged from creating brand profiles on the network. Nevertheless, in the first 100 days it was reported that over 40 million individual users had uploaded images, but taken in context this is a small number compared to the 800 million active Facebook users and 900 million objects, which users interact with on a daily basis. However, perhaps the biggest challenge for Google+ is not driving users to its network—as it is integrated into the Google search interface—but what they do when they get there. Currently, levels of interactivity appear to be static and even though new features have been added, they have limited impact on levels of traffic and user engagement. Critics of Google+ blame its step-by-step approach of starting small with an innovation and developing its features as it goes along, as they feel that in order to compete with Facebook everything should have been *right* at the launch date. However, gmail—one of the world's most popular email programs—was developed in this way and enabled Google to become a major competitor for Microsoft. So only time will tell whether Google+ will sustain its entry into the social network market and compete with Facebook as market leader.

Based on: Monjoo (2011);[39] *Facebook (2012);*[40] *Morphy (2012)*[41]

market with the iPad. Intel also believes it has the core competence required to move into smartphones, net books and tablet computing. Players in technology markets are constantly investing in new developments and looking for markets for their offers. Google has entered the social networking with the introduction of Google+ as Digital Marketing 2.1 describes.

Strategic objectives

Alongside objectives for product/market direction, **strategic objectives** for each product need to be agreed. This begins the process of planning at the product level. There are four options:

1 build
2 hold
3 harvest
4 divest

For new products, the strategic objective will inevitably be to build sales and market share. For existing products, the appropriate strategic objective will depend on the particular situation associated with the product. This will be determined in the marketing audit, SWOT analysis and evaluation of the strategic options outlined earlier. In particular, product portfolio planning tools such as the Boston Consulting Group Growth–Share Matrix, the General Electric Market Attractiveness–Competitive Position Model and the Shell Directional Policy Matrix may be used to aid this analysis. These will be discussed in detail in Chapter 11, which deals with managing products.

The important point to remember at this stage is that *building* sales and market share is not the only sensible strategic objective for a product. As we shall see, *holding* sales and market share may make commercial sense under certain conditions; *harvesting*, where sales and market share are allowed to fall but profit margins are maximized, may also be preferable to building; finally, *divestment*, where the product is dropped or sold, can be the logical outcome of the situation analysis.

Together, strategic thrust and strategic objectives define where the business and its products intend to go in the future.

Core Marketing Strategy

Once objectives have been set, the next stage in the plan involves deciding how to meet the objectives and answer the question: how do we get there? The **core marketing strategy** focuses on how objectives can be accomplished. There are three key elements to consider: target markets, competitor targets and establishing a competitive advantage. Each element is interlinked and together they form the key aspects of **competitive positioning**.[42] We will consider each of the three elements in turn.

Target markets

A central plank of core strategy is the choice of **target market(s)**. Marketing is not about chasing any customer at any price. Decisions should be taken about which groups of customers (segments) are most attractive to the business and best fit with its capabilities. The *Economist* targets business professionals who wish to be regarded as well-informed about business matters. This periodical is able to 'offer authoritative insight and opinion on international news, politics, business, finance, science and technology'. It is able to achieve high standards of journalism across a wide range of subject as it attracts many writers who wish to work together to produce thought-provoking articles. This is an example of a company which has a clear target market and it is able to use its capabilities and resources to produce a product which satisfies the needs of its customers.

The choice of target market can result from the SWOT analysis and the setting of marketing objectives (strategic thrust). For example, Samsung has identified an opportunity to use its technological know-how, research and development expertise and extensive resources to respond to changes in the marketing environment. As a result, the company is entering the solar energy business. There are several possible segments (customer groups) of varying attractiveness—industrial, resellers, consumers. Samsung needs to assess the attractiveness of each potential market, by considering measures such as size of the market, growth potential, level of competitor activity and customer requirements. Much of this information should have been compiled during the marketing audit, and this analysis together with the SWOT should also provide the basis for judging Samsung's capabilities to be able to respond to the opportunities presented.

For existing products marketing management should also consider its current target markets and their changing needs. Consequently, Samsung should focus on customers' needs across its established product ranges. For example, tablet computers are constantly evolving in response to changing customer needs, and to retain its market share Samsung will make changes to the marketing mix to adapt to new requirements. In other cases current target markets may have decreased in attractiveness, so products will need to be repositioned to target different market segments. The process of market segmentation and targeting is examined in depth in Chapter 8.

Competitor targets

Competitor targets are the organizations against which the company chooses to compete directly. Samsung competes directly with Apple in the tablet computer market. Weak competitors may be viewed as easy prey and resources channelled to attack them. The importance of understanding competitors and strategies for attacking and defending against competitors are discussed in Chapters 19 and 20, which examine in detail the areas of competitor analysis and competitive strategy.

Competitive advantage

The link between target markets and competitor targets is the establishment of a competitive advantage. A competitive advantage is the achievement of superior performance through differentiation to provide superior customer value, or by managing to achieve lowest delivered cost. For major success, businesses need to achieve a clear performance differential over competition on factors that are important to target customers. The most successful methods are built upon some combination of three advantages:[43]

Go to the website and work out Fiat's marketing objectives.
www.mcgraw-hill.co.uk/
textbooks/jobber

Go to the website and find out how Birds Eye is positioning its peas against the competition.
www.mcgraw-hill.co.uk/textbooks/jobber

⬆ EXHIBIT 2.4 Birds Eye aims to be better than the competition by providing *field fresh peas,* which are processed and packaged within two and a half hours of being picked so they retain more vitamins than rival products.

1 *being better*—superior quality or service (e.g. Mercedes-Benz, Dulux paints, Singapore Airlines)
2 *being faster*—anticipate or respond to customer needs faster than the competition (e.g. Zara)
3 *being closer*—establishing close long-term relationships with customers (e.g. Ford Retail, Pitney Bowes, Marks & Spencer).

Another route to competitive advantage is achieving the lowest relative rate cost position of all competitors.[44] Lowest cost can be translated into a competitive advantage through low prices, or by producing standard items at price parity when comparative success may be achieved through higher profit margins than those of competitors. Achieving a highly differentiated product is not incompatible with a low cost position, however.[45] Inasmuch as high-quality products suffer lower rejection rates through quality control and lower repair costs through their warranty period, they may incur lower total costs than their inferior rivals. Methods of achieving competitive advantages and their sources are analysed in Chapter 19.

Tests of an effective core strategy

Figure 2.6 shows six key considerations, which can be used to test a core strategy. The six considerations are that the strategy should:

1 be based upon a *clear definition of target customers and their needs*.
2 show understanding of competitors and be able to create *competitive advantage*.
3 *incur acceptable risk*. Challenging a strong competitor with a weak competitive advantage and a low resource base would not incur acceptable risk.
4 be *resourced and managerially supportable*. The strategy should match the resources, capabilities and managerial competences of the business.
5 be derived from the *product and marketing objectives* established as part of the planning process. Extensive use of promotions that makes commercial logic when following a build objective may make no sense when following a harvesting objective.
6 be *internally consistent*. Each of the elements of the core strategy should be consistent with the rest of the marketing plan.

Marketing mix decisions

At this stage in the planning process, managers consider the marketing mix. The tools they use and the choices they make will be informed by the core strategy. Decisions about use of

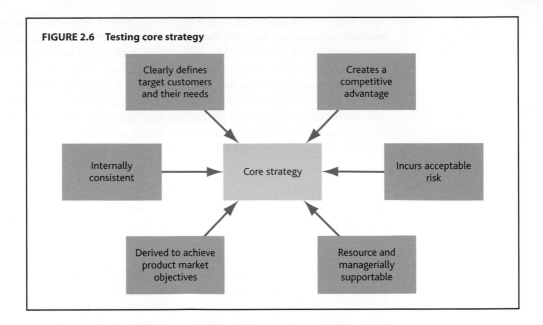

FIGURE 2.6 Testing core strategy

each of the elements of the mix will vary depending on whether the focus is on a product or service. Nevertheless, decisions will consist of judgements about how to select and blend each of the relevant elements of the mix. Such decisions will not be taken in isolation, as they will also consider how their close competitors use the mix. For example, major supermarkets Tesco, Sainsbury's, Morrisons and Asda constantly vie for market share. As there is limited growth in the overall size of the grocery market, so each of these major players grows its share of the market by attracting its competitors' customers. This is achieved through the marketing mix and each of these supermarket brands uses the mix differently. At a basic level, Asda creates its competitive advantage by focusing on keeping prices very low. Sainsbury's creates competitive advantage through the quality of its products. Morrisons differentiates itself through the freshness of its products and its store destinations, and Tesco positions its brand on offering the greatest value across the widest product range. Currently, *place* is an element of the mix which is challenging supermarket marketing managers. The Internet and online shopping is proving very popular. Many retailers are devising multichannel strategies to enable customers to shop from home, while on the move and in-store. This in turn is having an impact on the number and size of stores needed to meet corporate objectives.

As with all of the other stages of the marketing plan there are many complex choices involved in selecting an effective marketing mix, which is why the third part of the book devotes several chapters to exploring each of elements of the mix in detail: Product (Chapters 9, 11 and 12), Services (Chapter 10), Price (Chapter 13), Promotion (Chapters 14, 15, 16 and 18) and Place (Chapter 17).

Organization and implementation

No marketing plan will succeed unless it 'degenerates into work'.[46] Consequently, the business must design an organization that has the capability of implementing the plan. Indeed, organizational weaknesses discovered as part of the SWOT analysis may restrict the feasible range of strategic options. Reorganization could mean the establishment of a new marketing organization or department in the business. In the past many manufacturing organizations did not have a marketing department.[47] In some cases marketing was done by the chief executive, or the sales department dealt with customer enquiries so there was no further need for other marketing input. In other situations environmental change caused strategy change and subsequent reorganization of marketing and sales business functions.

More recently, the growth of large corporate customers with enormous buying power has resulted in businesses focusing their resources more firmly on meeting their needs (strategy change), which in turn has led to dedicated marketing and sales teams being organized to service these accounts (reorganization). Organizational issues are explored in Chapter 22.

Because strategy change and reorganization affect the balance of power in businesses, and the daily life and workloads of people, resistance may occur. Consequently marketing personnel need to understand the barriers to change, the process of change management and the techniques of persuasion that can be used to effect the implementation of the marketing plan. These issues are dealt with in Chapter 22.

Control

The final stage in the marketing planning process is **control**. The aim of control systems is to evaluate the results of the marketing plan so that corrective action can be taken if performance does not match objectives. Short-term control systems can plot results against objectives on a weekly, monthly, quarterly and/or annual basis. Measures include sales, profits, costs and cash flow. There is a growing need for marketing managers to assess the payoff from their investments and justify them. This has resulted in the use of marketing metrics, which are quantitative measures of the outcomes of marketing activities and expenditures. There is extensive coverage of them in Chapter 22, Managing Marketing Implementation, Organization and Control, and on the Online Learning Centre that accompanies this book. Strategic control systems are more long term. Managers need to stand back from week-by-week and month-by-month results to reassess critically whether their plans are in line with their capabilities and the environment.

Lack of this long-term control perspective may result in the pursuit of plans that have lost strategic credibility. New competition, changes in technology and moving customer requirements may have rendered old plans obsolete. This, of course, returns the planning process to the beginning, since this kind of fundamental review is conducted in the marketing audit. It is the activity of assessing internal capabilities and external opportunities and threats that result in a SWOT analysis. This outcome may be a redefinition of the business mission, and, as we have seen, changes in marketing objectives and strategies to realign the business with its environment.

So how do the stages of marketing planning relate to the fundamental planning questions stated earlier in this chapter? Table 2.1 illustrates this relationship. The question 'Where are we now?' is answered by the business mission definition, the marketing audit and SWOT analysis.

The Rewards of Marketing Planning

Various authors have attributed the following benefits to marketing planning.[48,49,50]

1 *Consistency*: the plan provides a focal point for decisions and actions. By reference to a common plan, management decisions should be more consistent and actions better coordinated.

2 *Encourages the monitoring of change*: the planning process forces managers to step away from day-to-day problems and review the impact of change on the business from a strategic perspective.

3 *Encourages organizational adaptation*: the underlying premise of planning is that the organization should adapt to match its environment. Marketing planning, therefore, promotes the necessity to accept the inevitability of change. This is important as the capability to adapt has been linked to superior performance.[51]

4 *Stimulates achievement*: the planning process focuses on objectives, strategies and results. It encourages people to ask, 'What can we achieve given our capabilities?' As such it motivates people to set new horizons for objectives when they otherwise might be content to accept much lower standards of performance.

5   *Resource allocation*: the planning process asks fundamental questions about resource allocation. For example, which products should receive high investment (build), which should be maintained (hold), which should have resources withdrawn slowly (harvest) and which should have resources withdrawn immediately (divest)?

6   *Competitive advantage*: planning promotes the search for sources of competitive advantage.

However, it is important to realize that this logical planning process (sometimes called *synoptic planning*) may conflict with the culture of the business, which may plan effectively using an *incremental approach*.[52] The style of planning should match business culture.[53] Saker and Speed argue that the considerable demands on managers in terms of time and effort implied by the synoptic marketing planning process may mean that alternative planning schemes are more appropriate, particularly for small companies.[54]

Incremental planning is more problem-focused in that the process begins with the realization of a problem (for example, a fall-off in orders) and continues with an attempt to identify a solution. As solutions to problems form, so strategy emerges. However, little attempt is made to integrate consciously the individual decisions that could possibly affect one another. Strategy is viewed as a loosely linked group of decisions that are handled individually. Nevertheless, its effect may be to attune the business to its environment through its problem-solving nature. Its drawback is the lack of a broad situation analysis and strategy option generation, which renders the incremental approach less comprehensive. For some companies, however, its inherent practicality may support its use rather than its rationality.[55]

Problems in Making Planning Work

Empirical work into the marketing planning practices has found that most commercial companies did not practise the kinds of systematic planning procedures described in this chapter and, of those that did, many did not enjoy the rewards described in the previous section.[56] However, others have shown that there is a relationship between planning and commercial success (see, for example, Armstrong and McDonald).[57,58] The problem is that the *contextual difficulties* associated with the process of marketing planning are substantial and need to be understood. Inasmuch as forewarned is forearmed, the following is a checklist of potential problems that have to be faced by those charged with making marketing planning work.

Political

Marketing planning is a resource allocation process. The outcome of the process is an allocation of more funds to some products and departments, the same or less to others. Since power bases, career opportunities and salaries are often tied to whether an area is fast or slow growing, it is not surprising that managers view planning as a highly political activity. An example is a European bank, whose planning process resulted in the decision to insist that its retail branch managers divert certain types of loan application to the industrial/merchant banking arm of the group where the return was greater. This was required because the plan was designed to optimize the return to the group as a whole. However, the consequence was considerable friction between the divisions concerned because the decision lowered the performance of the retail branch.

In another European bank the introduction of a series of market-based products was blocked by managers of existing product-orientated offerings who feared their launch would mean, for them, losing their jobs. Both these examples demonstrate how political factors can be a barrier to marketing planning initiatives.

Opportunity cost

Some busy managers view marketing planning as a time-wasting ritual that conflicts with the need to deal with day-to-day problems. They view the opportunity cost of spending two or three days away at a hotel thrashing out long-term plans as too high. This difficulty may be compounded by the fact that people who are attracted to the hectic pace of managerial life may be the type who prefer to live that way.[59] Hence, they may be ill at ease with the thought of a long period of sedate contemplation.

Reward systems

The reward systems of many businesses are geared to the short term. Incentives and bonuses may be linked to quarterly or annual results. Managers may thus overweight short-term issues and underweight medium- and long-term concerns if there is a conflict of time. Thus marketing planning may be viewed as of secondary importance.

Information

To function effectively, a systematic marketing planning system needs informational inputs. Market share, size and growth rates are basic inputs into the marketing audit but may be unavailable. More perversely, information may be wilfully withheld by vested interests who, recognizing that knowledge is power, distort the true situation to protect their position in the planning process.

Culture

The establishment of a systematic marketing planning process may be at variance with the culture of the organization. As has already been stated, businesses may 'plan' by making incremental decisions. Hence, the strategic planning system may challenge the status quo and be seen as a threat. In other cases, the values and beliefs of some managers may be hostile to a planning system altogether.

Personalities

Marketing planning usually involves a discussion between managers about the strategic choices facing the business and the likely outcomes. This can be a highly charged affair where personality clashes and pent-up antagonisms can surface. The result can be that the process degenerates into abusive argument and sets up deep chasms within the management team.

Lack of knowledge and skills

Another problem that can arise when setting up a marketing planning system is that the management team does not have the knowledge and skills to perform the tasks adequately.[60] Basic marketing knowledge about market segmentation, competitive advantage and the nature of strategic objectives may be lacking. Similarly, skills in analysing competitive situations and defining core strategies may be inadequate.

How to Handle Marketing Planning Problems

Some of the problems revealed during the market planning process may be deep-seated managerial inadequacies rather than being intrinsic to the planning process itself. As such, the attempt to establish the planning system may be seen as a benefit to the business by revealing the nature of these problems. However, various authors have proposed recommendations for minimizing the impact of such problems.[61,62]

1 *Senior management support*: top management must be committed to planning and be seen by middle management to give it total support. This should be ongoing support, not a short-term fad.

2 *Match the planning system to the culture of the business*: how the marketing planning process is managed should be consistent with the culture of the organization. For example, in some organizations the top-down/bottom-up balance will move towards top-down; in other less directive cultures the balance will move towards a more bottom-up planning style.

3 *The reward system*: this should reward the achievement of longer-term objectives rather than focus exclusively on short-term results.

4 *Depoliticize outcomes*: less emphasis should be placed on rewarding managers associated with build (growth) strategies. Recognition of the skills involved in defending share and harvesting products should be made. At General Electric managers are classified as 'growers', 'caretakers' and 'undertakers', and matched to products that are being built, defended or harvested in recognition of the fact that the skills involved differ according to the strategic objective. No stigma is attached to caretaking or undertaking; each is acknowledged as contributing to the success of the organization.

5 *Clear communication*: plans should be communicated to those charged with implementation.

6 *Training*: marketing personnel should be trained in the necessary marketing knowledge and skills to perform the planning job. Ideally the management team should attend the same training course so that they each share a common understanding of the concepts and tools involved and can communicate using the same terminology.

Online
LearningCentre

When you have read this chapter

log on to the Online Learning Centre at **www.mcgraw-hill.co.uk/textbooks/jobber** to explore chapter-by-chapter test questions, links and further online study tools for marketing.

Review

❶ The role of marketing planning within business
- Marketing planning is part of a broader concept known as strategic planning.
- For one-product companies, its role is to ensure that the product continues to meet customers' needs as well as seeking new opportunities.
- For companies marketing a range of products in a number of markets, marketing planning's role is as above plus the allocation of resources to each product.
- For companies comprising a number of businesses (SBUs), marketing planning's role is as above plus a contribution to the allocation of resources to each business.

❷ The key planning questions
- These are: 'Where are we now?', 'How did we get there?', 'Where are we heading?', 'Where would we like to be?', 'How do we get there?' and 'Are we on course?'

❸ The process of marketing planning
- The steps in the process are: deciding the business mission, conducting a marketing audit, producing a SWOT analysis, setting marketing objectives (strategic thrust and strategic objectives), deciding core strategy (target markets, competitive advantage and competitor targets), making marketing mix decisions, organizing and implementing, and control.

❹ The concept of the business mission
- A business mission is a broadly defined, enduring statement of purpose that distinguishes a business from others of its type.
- A business mission should answer two questions: 'What business are we in?' and 'What business do we want to be in?'

5 **The nature of the marketing audit and SWOT analysis**

- The marketing audit is a systematic examination of a business's marketing environment, objectives, strategies and activities, with a view to identifying key strategic issues, problem areas and opportunities.
- It consists of an examination of a company's external and internal environments. The external environment is made up of the macroenvironment, the market and competition. The internal environmental audit consists of operating results, strategic issues analysis, marketing mix effectiveness, marketing structures and systems.
- A SWOT analysis provides a simple method of summarizing the results of the marketing audit. Internal issues are summarized under strengths and weaknesses, and external issues are summarized under opportunities and threats.

6 **The nature of marketing objectives**

- There are two types of marketing objective: (i) strategic thrust, which defines the future direction of the business in terms of which products to sell in which markets; and (ii) strategic objectives, which are product-level objectives relating to the decision to build, hold, harvest or divest products.

7 **The components of core strategy and the criteria for testing its effectiveness**

- The components are target markets, competitor targets and competitive advantage.
- The criteria for testing its effectiveness are that core strategy clearly defines target customers and their needs, creates a competitive advantage, incurs acceptable risk, is resource and managerially supportable, is derived to achieve product–market objectives and is internally consistent.

Each element is inter-linked and together they form the core aspects of competitive positioning.[63]

8 **Where marketing mix decisions are placed within the marketing planning process**

- Marketing mix decisions follow those of core strategy as they are based on an understanding of target customers' needs and the competition so that a competitive advantage can be created.

9 **The importance of organization, implementation and control within the marketing planning process**

- Organization is needed to support the strategies decided upon. Strategies are unlikely to be effective without attention to implementation issues. For example, techniques to overcome resistance to change and the training of staff who are required to implement strategic decisions are likely to be required.
- Control systems are important so that the results of the marketing plan can be evaluated and corrective action taken if performance does not match objectives.

10 **The rewards and problems associated with marketing planning**

- The rewards are consistency of decision-making, encouragement of the monitoring of change, encouragement of organizational adaptation, stimulation of achievement, aiding resource allocation and promotion of the creation of a competitive advantage.
- The potential problems with marketing planning revolve around the context in which it takes place and are political, high opportunity cost, lack of reward systems tied to longer-term results, lack of relevant information, cultural and personality clashes, and lack of managerial knowledge and skills.

11 **Recommendations for overcoming marketing planning problems**

- Recommendations for minimizing the impact of marketing planning problems are: attaining senior management support, matching the planning system to the culture of the business, creating a reward system that is focused on longer-term performance, depoliticizing outcomes, communicating clearly to those responsible for implementation, and training in the necessary marketing knowledge and skills to conduct marketing planning.

Key Terms

business mission the organization's purpose, usually setting out its competitive domain, which distinguishes the business from others of its type

competitive positioning consists of three key elements: target markets, competitor targets and establishing a competitive advantage

competitor analysis an examination of the nature of actual and potential competitors, and their objectives and strategies

competitor targets the organizations against which a company chooses to compete directly

control the stage in the marketing planning process or cycle when the performance against plan is monitored so that corrective action, if necessary, can be taken

core marketing strategy the means of achieving marketing objectives, including target markets, competitor targets and competitive advantage

customer analysis a survey of who the customers are, what choice criteria they use, how they rate competitive offerings and on what variables they can be segmented

distribution analysis an examination of movements in power bases, channel attractiveness, physical distribution and distribution behaviour

macroenvironment a number of broader forces that affect not only the company but the other actors in the environment, e.g. social, political, technological and economic

market analysis the statistical analysis of market size, growth rates and trends

marketing audit a systematic examination of a business's marketing environment, objectives, strategies and activities with a view to identifying key strategic issues, problem areas and opportunities

marketing objectives there are two types of marketing objective: strategic thrust, which dictates which products should be sold in which markets, and strategic

objectives, i.e. product-level objectives, such as build, hold, harvest and divest

marketing planning the process by which businesses analyse the environment and their capabilities, decide upon courses of marketing action and implement those decisions

marketing structures the marketing frameworks (organization, training and internal communications) upon which marketing activities are based

marketing systems sets of connected parts (information, planning and control) that support the marketing function

microenvironment the actors in the firm's immediate environment that affect its capability to operate effectively in its chosen markets—namely, suppliers, distributors, customers and competitors

product portfolio the total range of products offered by the company

strategic business unit a business or company division serving a distinct group of customers and with a distinct set of competitors, usually strategically autonomous

strategic issues analysis an examination of the suitability of marketing objectives and segmentation bases in the light of changes in the marketplace

strategic objectives product-level objectives relating to the decision to build, hold, harvest or divest products

strategic thrust the decision concerning which products to sell in which markets

supplier analysis an examination of who and where suppliers are located, their competences and shortcomings, the trends affecting them and the future outlook for them

SWOT analysis a structured approach to evaluating the strategic position of a business by identifying its strengths, weaknesses, opportunities and threats

target market a market segment that has been selected as a focus for the company's offering or communications

Study Questions

1 Discuss the importance of situation analysis and explain the significance of macro and micro level influences.

2 Explain how each stage of the marketing planning process links with the fundamental planning questions identified in Table 2.1.

3 Evaluate the extent to which the marketing planning process is a true reflection of how businesses plan their marketing strategies.

4 Why is a clear business mission statement a help to marketing planners?

5 What is meant by core marketing strategy? What role does it play in the process of marketing planning?

6 Distinguish between strategic thrust and strategic objectives.

7 Suggest how the Internet is changing marketing planning.

References

1. Crittenden, V. L., W. F. Crittenden, L. K. Ferrell, O. C. Ferrell and C. C. Pinney (2011) Market-oriented sustainability: a conceptual framework and propositions, *Journal of the Academy of Marketing Science* 39(1), 71–85, DOI: 10.1007/s11747-010-0217-2.

2. Day, G. S. (1984) *Strategic Marketing Planning: The Pursuit of Competitive Advantage*, St Paul, MN: West, 41.

3. Weitz, B. A. and R. Wensley (1988) *Readings in Strategic Marketing*, New York: Dryden, 4.

4. Virgin Atlantic: http://www.virginatlantic.com/en/cn/allaboutus/pressoffice/faq/strategy.jsp (accessed May 2012).

5. Ackoff, R. I. (1987) Mission Statements, *Planning Review* 15(4), 30–2.

6. Hooley, G. J., A. J. Cox and A. Adams (1992) Our Five Year Mission: To Boldly Go Where No Man Has Been Before . . . , *Journal of Marketing Management* 8(1), 35–48.

7. Samsung: http://www.samsung.com/uk/aboutsamsung/corporateprofile/vision.html (accessed 15 January 2012).

8. Google: http://www.google.com/about/corporate/company/ (accessed 15 January 2012).

9. Levitt, T. (1960) Marketing Myopia, *Harvard Business Review*, July–August, 45–6.

10. Virgin Group: http://www.virgin.com/about-us (accessed January 2012).

11. Wilson, I. (1992) Realizing the Power of Strategic Vision, *Long Range Planning* 25(5), 18–28.

12. Davidson, H. (2002) *The Committed Enterprise*, Oxford: Heinemann.

13. Sanghera, S. (2005) Why So Many Mission Statements are Mission Impossible, *Financial Times*, 22 July, 13.

14. http://www.company-statements-slogans.info/list-of-companies-a/amazon-com.htm.

15. Gapper, J. and B. Jopson (2011) An inventor with fire in his belly and Jobs in his sights, *Financial Times*, 30 September.

16. Aguilar, Francis J. (1967) *Scanning the Business Environment*, New York, NY: Macmillan.

17. Gillespie, A. (2007) Foundation of Economics, *Oxford University Press*, 12: http://www.oup.com/uk/orc/bin/9780199296378/01student/additional/page_12.htm.

18. Highways Agency: http://www.highways.gov.uk/aboutus/documents/S100277_Business_Plan_2011-12_Web_4.pdf (accessed January 2012).

19. Madden, R. (2011) The best form of innovation is simply doing things better, *Marketing Week*, 5 May, 12.

20. Amos, S. (2011) Lego: The Danish toymaker's idea became a classic design and has expanded into a multimedia business, *Marketing*, 13 July, 16.

21. BBC Business News (2011) Thomas Cook sells Spanish hotel chain for £61m: http://www.bbc.co.uk/news/business-16155134.

22. Bowers, S. (2011) Thomas Cook makes 398 loss, putting up to 1000 jobs at risk, *Guardian*, 14 December: http://www.guardian.co.uk/business/2011/dec/14/thomas-cook-posts-398m-loss.

23. Chapman, H. (2011) Kodak: The veteran imaging brand is struggling to keep up with digital developments, *Marketing*, 26 October, 20.

24. Jackson, T. (2011) Eastman Kodak fell victim to disruptive technology, *Financial Times*, 3 October, 20.

25. The Lego Group (2010) Annual Report: http://cache.lego.com/upload/contentTemplating/AboutUsAboutUsContent/otherfiles/downloadE994290D230BFB0E2A914F4DC3B6531C.pdf.

26. Sibun, J. (2008) Lego Renaissance Builds on Key Strengths, *The Telegraph*, 27 January.

27. Piercy, N. (2008) *Market-led Strategic Change: Transforming the Process of Going to Market*, Oxford: Butterworth-Heinemann, 259.

28. McDonald, M. H. B. (2007) *Marketing Plans*, London: Butterworth-Heinemann, 2nd edn.

29. Glasses Direct: http://www.glassesdirect.co.uk/about/story/#os2006 (accessed 15 January 2012).

30. *The Economist* (2008) After Bill, 28 June, 92–4.

31. *The Economist* (2010) Breaking and entering: Why it is hard to copy Santander, 13 May: http://www.economist.com/node/16078452 (accessed January 2012).

32. http://www.imaginerecruitment.com/jobs/featured/tesco.

33. Singh, S. (2008) Is India the Gateway to Global Domination for Tesco? *Marketing Week*, 21 August.

34. Wood, Z. (2011) Tesco back loss-making Fresh & Easy with 12 new US stores, *Guardian*, 4 March, 30.

35. Jackson, T. (2011) Eastman Kodak fell victim to disruptive technology, *Financial Times*, 3 October, 20.

36. Chapman, H. (2011) Kodak: The veteran imaging brand is struggling to keep up with digital developments, *Marketing*, 26 October, 20.

37. Helmore, E. (2005) Big Apple, *Observer*, 16 January, 3.

38. Allison, K. (2008) Apple Unveils iPhone Grand Plan, *Financial Times*, 10 March, 23.

39. Monjoo, F. (2011) Google+ is dead, *Slate*, 8 November: http://www.slate.com/articles/technology/technology/2011/11/google_had_a_chance_to_compete_with_facebook_not_anymore_.html.

40. Facebook (2012) Facebook Statistics: http://www.facebook.com/press/info.php?statistics.

41. Morphy, E. (2012) Will the new feature at Google+ lead to more user engagement and why do we even care? *Forbes*, 30 October: http://www.forbes.com/sites/erikamorphy/2011/10/30/will-the-new-features-at-google-lead-to-more-engagement-and-why-do-we-even-care/.

42. Hooley, G., N. F. Piercy and B. Nicoulaud (2012) *Marketing Strategy & Competitive Positioning*, Harlow: FT Prentice Hall, 32.

43. Day (1999) op. cit., 9.

44. Porter, M. E. (1980) *Competitive Strategy: Techniques for Analysing Industries and Competitors*, New York: Free Press, Ch. 2.

45. Phillips, L. W., D. R. Chang and R. D. Buzzell (1983) Product Quality, Cost Position and Business Performance: A Test of Some Key Hypotheses, *Journal of Marketing* 47(Spring), 26–43.

46. Drucker, P. F. (1993) *Management Tasks, Responsibilities, Practices*, New York: Harper and Row, 128.

47. Piercy, N. (1986) The Role and Function of the Chief Marketing Executive and the Marketing Department, *Journal of Marketing Management* 1(3), 265–90.

48. Leppard, J. W. and M. H. B. McDonald (1991) Marketing Planning and Corporate Culture: A Conceptual Framework which Examines Management Attitudes in the Context of Marketing Planning, *Journal of Marketing Management* 7(3), 213–36.

49. Greenley, G. E. (1986) *The Strategic and Operational Planning of Marketing*, Maidenhead: McGraw-Hill, 185–7.

50. Terpstra, V. and R. Sarathy (1991) *International Marketing*, Orlando, FL: Dryden, Ch. 17.

51. Oktemgil, M. and G. Greenley (1997) Consequences of High and Low Adaptive Capability in UK Companies, *European Journal of Marketing* 31(7), 445–66.

52. Raimond, P. and C. Eden (1990) Making Strategy Work, *Long Range Planning* 23(5), 97–105.

53. Driver, J. C. (1990) Marketing Planning in Style, *Quarterly Review of Marketing* 15(4), 16–21.

54. Saker, J. and R. Speed (1992) Corporate Culture: Is it Really a Barrier to Marketing Planning?, *Journal of Marketing Management* 8(2), 177–82. For information on marketing and planning in small and medium-sized firms see Carson, D. (1990) Some Exploratory Models for Assessing Small Firms' Marketing Performance: A Qualitative Approach, *European Journal of Marketing* 24(11), 8–51, and Fuller, P. B. (1994) Assessing Marketing in Small and Medium-Sized Enterprises, *European Journal of Marketing* 28(12), 34–9.

55. O'Shaughnessy, J. (1995) *Competitive Marketing*, Boston, Mass: Allen & Unwin.

56. Greenley, G. (1987) An Exposition into Empirical Research into Marketing Planning, *Journal of Marketing Management* 3(1), 83–102.

57. Armstrong, J. S. (1982) The Value of Formal Planning for Strategic Decisions: Review of Empirical Research, *Strategic Management Journal* 3(3), 197–213.

58. McDonald, M. H. B. (1984) The Theory and Practice of Marketing Planning for Industrial Goods in International Markets, Cranfield Institute of Technology, PhD thesis. A more recent study has also confirmed that marketing planning is linked to commercial success: Pulendran, S., R. Speed and R. E. Wildin II (2003) Marketing Planning, Marketing Orientation and Business Performance, *European Journal of Marketing* 37(3/4), 476–97.

59. Mintzberg, H. (1975) The Manager's Job: Folklore and Fact, *Harvard Business Review*, July–August, 49–61.

60. McDonald, M. H. B. (1989) The Barriers to Marketing Planning, *Journal of Marketing Management* 5(1), 1–18.

61. McDonald (1984) op. cit.

62. Abell, D. F. and J. S. Hammond (1979) *Strategic Market Planning*, Englewood Cliffs, NJ: Prentice-Hall.

Dixons Retail PLC
Planning for a Multichannel Future

Dixons has grown from a one-man band into a fully orchestrated international retail and service operation, which attracts over 100 million shoppers to its stores and online businesses. How did the company get started and then develop into Europe's leading specialist electrical retailer? This case explores the significance of adopting a market-orientated approach to planning in developing a *family* of successful international retail brands.

Background: Start-up to market leader

Dixons started out in the photography business during challenging trading times in the early 1940s (first store opened in 1937). By the 1960s the original photographic studio had developed into a relatively large public limited company, with an expanding mail order business and high street retail operation. The business continued to grow in the UK, by opening high street stores selling photographic equipment, computers and other high-tech gadgetry. In the 1990s, the acquisition of PC World, opening tax-free travel stores in airports (Dixons Travel) and expansion into European markets with the acquisition of Elkjøp, a leading Nordic retailer, enabled the business to grow further and more rapidly. More acquisitions in Italy (UniEuro), Russia and the Ukraine (in Russia it explored a joint venture with an existing ElDorado but decided not to pursue it) and expansion into Ireland, Greece and the Czech Republic enabled Dixons Retail plc to become Europe's largest specialist electrical retailer and services company, which employs over 38,000 people spread over 26 countries (see Table C3.1 for details of Dixons Retail's brands).

Products to markets: 'stack-em high—sell-em cheap' to 'bringing life to technology'

Clearly, over its history, Dixons has developed a robust business model but the customer has not always been at the heart of business planning. In the past the Group's competitive position largely revolved around a product-focused approach and the strategy was 'stack-em high—sell-em cheap' in brightly coloured stores, which attracted customers by being packed with new and exciting electrical goods. However, customer satisfaction was often overlooked as it was not central to this strategic approach—something which had not been missed by some of the brand's competitors.

Table C3.1	Dixon Retail plc Pan-European brands			
Location	**UK & Ireland**	**Nordics**	**Other International**	**e-commerce**
Brands	Currys, PC World, Dixons Travel, DSGi Business	Elkjøp, Gigantti, El Giganten, Lefdal	Unieuro (Italy), Kotsovolos (Greece), Electro World (Czech Republic and Slovakia)	PIXmania (pan-European), Dixons.co.uk (UK)
Sales	£3.8 billion	£2.3 billion	£1.2 billion	£0.8 billion
Market position	No 1	No 1	No 1 in Greece, No 2 in Italy and Czech Republic	Leading pureplay retailer in Europe

Change was needed and the condition of the marketing environment and the behaviour of competitors prompted Dixons to consider where the company was heading. In 2006 economic forces were threatening to affect market performance. Signs of trouble in global financial markets and recession were looming large. As a result the competition for market share intensified. Dixons and other UK retailers like Kesa (owner of Comet Plc until 2012) set about developing strategies to secure their future. Global players also showed interest in UK markets. Best Buy, the leading US retailer, believed it had spotted an opportunity in the UK consumer electronics market. The company thought consumers in the UK were getting a bad deal in terms of the service they received from electronic goods retailers like Currys and Comet. So Best Buy committed to an expansion strategy based on building market share, providing better customer service and supply-chain improvements. However, Best Buy was slow to roll out its strategy and waited until summer 2009 to enter the UK. By this time Dixons Retail had revolutionized its approach, moving into a transformation strategy, which put the customers at the heart of the business, and its approach to planning was guided by a new positioning statement 'bringing life to technology'.

A transformation strategy

Faced with intensified competition, global recession and poorly performing retail markets, the senior management team at Dixons, headed by then CEO John Browett, devised a service-led business model which transformed every aspect of the business (see Figure C3.1). This strategy gave the company the competitive edge not only to survive and grow during the severest economic collapse since the Great Depression of the 1930s, but also to fend off the competition and become an international market leader in specialist consumer electronics.

Every area of the business had to contribute to the implementation of the new strategy. At an operational level, stores were remodelled so they became 'easy to shop'; channels were extended to a fully integrated multichannel approach; products were selected based on giving the widest, best and most exclusive product choice based on customer needs. After-sales service and support were completely restructured and rebranded in accordance with the strategic plan.

The strategic plan had five clear objectives:

1 focus on the customer
2 focus the portfolio on winning positions
3 transform the business
4 win in the Internet market
5 reduce costs.

At the corporate level, decisions were taken to 'clean up' the business. This meant exiting poorly performing areas, identifying process improvements and reducing costs. From a marketing perspective the core strategy focused on

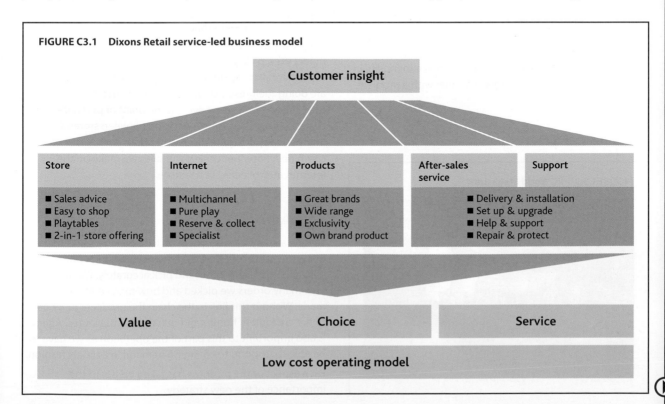

FIGURE C3.1   Dixons Retail service-led business model

customer needs and how to get the voice of the customer heard throughout the business, and at the same time making cost efficiencies. Every part of the business made a contribution to the success of the strategy. Since its launch the marketing strategy has been evolving but the concepts of value range and service remain central. In order to make the strategy happen, the marketing team had to get the range right by reviewing all the product ranges and target markets. The review identified that ranges were too narrow, and there was a need for more price point in order to satisfy all customers' needs. The segmentation strategy changed as a result and Dixons now has seven or eight target segments in the UK based on lifestyle, lifecycle, income.

Integrated effort

Getting the plan to work involved all areas of the business. Members of the senior management team explained how their area of the business contributed to the implementation of the plan.

Niall O'Keefe, KNOWHOW Development Director

'The KNOWHOW brand was created to consolidate sales and after service elements of the business. We believed that where we could make a difference was around service so we chose to put all of our existing brands (e.g. Tech Guys, Partmaster) together under one service umbrella brand and so we created KNOWHOW . . . After sales service is hugely important for the customer. What it does is it differentiates Dixons as a brand. We believe we are going to drive shareholder values through having this service mentality in our business and never leaving a customer with a problem unsolved.'

FIGURE C3.2   PC World Megastore

Boyd Glover, Head of Skills Training, Dixons Retail

'When the strategy began in 2008, we put the customers at the heart of everything we do at Dixons Retail. The key challenge (for skills training) became how do we get our colleagues (Dixons employees) to deliver the service promise. So we made investment in training to ensure everyone across the business understood that customer service was now at the heart of everything we do. Every penny we invest in training is about the customers. We have found ingenious ways to deliver appropriate cost-effective training. All of the investment (in training) is evaluated so we can measure the benefits. To allow KNOWHOW to deliver on its promise we support the customer and colleagues.'

Jeremy Fennel, E-Commerce Director

'Our focus on a multichannel approach is really contributing to the growth of the business and its structure. The majority of retail growth in the next 3–4 years will come from multichannel and this will continue to be the growth engine of our sales.

'There are multiple touch points for the customer. So it could mean that advertising is a point at which they touch. We know they go on to the website and 70 per cent of the people who shop in our stores have been on the website prior to coming to our stores. This is a very important number because it says that people are researching away from the stores before they come in. We also know that people are increasingly reading reviews and using social media sites, picking up opinions from other people. Multichannel is the understanding of where the customers are doing their research and where the customers are doing their shopping because even at the point of purchase customers aren't making a decision between stores and the Internet; they are quite often using both channels combined. Forty per cent of the sales we make on the Internet are collected at the store.'

Tim Allinson, UK Logistics Director

'People are key—from operators to leaderships—as they make the processes work and meet our customer KPIs, e.g. deliver on time and in full and pick accurately. We measure how many orders we picked and how many errors we've made. Without this link in the chain the products don't get to the customers' homes and don't get to the stores. Agility is also important to this part of the operation as we have to be able to respond to changing demand in a timely fashion.'

Each aspect of the business has taken on board the importance of the new strategy.

The marketing mix and implementation

The mix was adapted to reflect the strategic initiatives and this had implications for implementation:

- *Place*: store formats were redesigned and the 2-in-1 Currys and PC World store format was rolled out. Other changes in-store included the introduction of play tables to allow customers to explore products, and storyboards to help with selecting complex TV and satellite products (interesting to note that this initiative was suggested by a member of staff, and then applied across the business). Distribution and supply were streamlined and made more efficient and cost-effective through the development of a high-tech distribution centre in Nottinghamshire.

- *Service*: KNOWHOW was launched replacing a myriad of different customer case and support services. The new after-sales service and support brand offers a multiple touch-point approach to customer care from the 'cradle to the grave' customer experience. KNOWHOW services provide delivery and installation; help with setting up and upgrading complex technology products; help and support online, on the phone and in-store; and repair and protection to give peace of mind when things go wrong. Additionally, the Fives training scheme was introduced to ensure that staff in-store and throughout the business have the *right* knowledge and behaviour to respond to all customer needs regardless of where they 'touched' the business.

- *Product*: The product portfolio was revised to offer wider product choice from brand leaders like Apple, but also to include own-brands; Currys and PC World Essentials range included TVs, DVD, white goods, computers, keyboards, printers and other peripheral devices.

- *Promotion*: significant investment was made in repositioning of the brand aims to engage the interest of consumers in different target markets. And customer service rather than products feature strongly in advertising campaigns.[1]

- *Price*: rapid innovation of high-tech products drives up volumes of purchasing and this means pricing was tailored to follow market demand.

Success was measured by monitoring customer satisfaction, customer advocacy (recommendations and referrals), profitability, sales, tracking store transformations.

Debrief

Dixons Retail has confounded its critics by succeeding in transforming its business model by shifting from a product-led to a service-led model that puts the customer at the heart of the business. Being informed by the marketing environment, the needs of the customers, the behaviour of the competitors and the contribution of the staff, the company has built a strong new competitive positioning.

The transformation strategy applied by Dixons is a solid example of how the marketing concept can help a business succeed. This case has highlighted the benefits of setting corporate goals that acknowledge the importance of meeting and exceeding customer needs better than the competition. Furthermore, it has emphasized the importance of an integrated effort across the business; the strategy reinforces the need for everyone in the business to be involved with creating customer satisfaction. Nevertheless, the business environment is constantly changing; major competitors, such as Best Buy, have made a strategic withdrawal because, although their 'big box stores . . . delivered exceptional customer satisfaction scores', they did not have the national reach to offer this experience to customers on a national scale in the UK. Additionally, Comet was sold off for £2 with a massive debt burden, which leaves the market open for Dixons. However, even in this climate the biggest challenge for Dixons in the future is to ensure that its transformation strategy continues to gather momentum and drive the business forward.

References

Baker, R. (2011) Best Buy to withdraw from UK, *Marketing Week*, 7 November, http://www.marketingweek.co.uk/best-buy-to-withdraw-from-uk/3031624.article.

Dixons Retail PLC group Presentation, September 2011.

Dixons Retail PLC (2007) Press Releases Extra Colleagues for the Newark Distributions centre, http://www.dixonsretail.com/dixons/en/mediacentre/mediapressreleases?id=413.

Kesa Electricals (2012) Sale of Comet, http://kesaelectricals.com/index.php?cID=304&cType=news

Black Book (2010) *Dixons Retail: Ambitious self-help in the midst of structural pressure*, Bernstein Research, 77–93.

1 See making of the Star wars campaign at: http://www.youtube.com/watch?feature=endscreen&v=8OA0-ylOMnQ&NR=1.

Questions

1   Consider the extent to which Dixons has applied a formal marketing planning process, when devising its marketing strategy. Illustrate your answer with specific examples.

2   Discuss how each of the business functions explored in this case have contributed to the success of Dixon's marketing strategy plan.

3   Explain how the KNOWHOW customer service brand has contributed to the performance of the marketing strategy.

4   Debate the extent to which the marketing environment has influenced senior management decision-making and marketing planning at Dixons.

5   Find current evidence from the external marketing environment which is likely to have implications for the future direction of Dixons' marketing strategy.

This case was prepared by Fiona Ellis-Chadwick, Senior Lecturer in Marketing, The Open University.

CASE 4

Volvo
Putting the *Vroom* Back into Sales

Over the years Volvo (www.volvocars.com) had developed an image of being stodgy, and designing cars resembling large boxes on wheels for county gentry. A typical Volvo owner was seen to be middle-aged, has 2.5 kids and a golden retriever dog barking in the boot. This image of functionality over styling prevailed. A newer suite of car models attempted to move Volvo away from these traditional boxy lines. Volvo developed a suite of cars that seemed to turn around the fortunes of the company, and deliver stable revenues and profits for the firm. Volvo became one of the most successful automotive brands for its then parent Ford Motor Corporation. However, sales for Volvo were down by 18.3 per cent in 2008, and sales continued to underperform in 2009, given the global economic turmoil. This unprecedented downturn has led to leading companies filing for bankruptcy and to the demise of several automotive brands (its fellow Swedish arch-rival Saab being one of them). A white knight in the form of Chinese manufacturer Geely paid Ford $1.8 billion for the car brand, hoping to reverse Volvo's downward trajectory.

Volvo is a relatively small car manufacturer with less than 1 per cent of global market share. It lost more than $1.5 billion in 2008, a colossal figure in any industry. The Volvo name is over 90 years old and has become a Swedish international icon. In 1999 AB Volvo sold Volvo cars to Ford Motor Company for $6.45 billion, much to the chagrin of many Swedes. Many feared that Volvo would lose its unique appeal, and that the brand would be destroyed by the takeover. AB Volvo still continues to make commercial trucks and buses. The Volvo brand is managed under a unique dual-partnership brand committee to ensure that the brand's equity is protected. Ford wanted a slice of the luxury car market to compete successfully against the likes of the increasingly successful Toyota and Lexus brands. Volvo was part of Ford's four-pronged strategy to enter the luxury car marque sector, which failed to realise its potential. It formed the Premier Automotive Group, PAG, by buying Volvo, Land Rover, Aston Martin and Jaguar. Volvo consistently made large profits for the group, ranging from $750 million to $1 billion per year, whereas other investments such as Jaguar continued to haemorrhage money for Ford. In 2008 Ford bailed out of this aspirational project by selling the Jaguar, Aston Martin and Land Rover brands in a firesale. They sold Jaguar and Land Rover to Indian car manufacturer Tata for $2.3 billion. When Ford bought Volvo, they bought not only

a successful brand but a unique culture, which had never been forced into being just a Ford subsidiary. Volvo maintained independence but benefited from platform sharing, shared research and development, and combined buying power.

TABLE C4.1   Volvo—at a glance

Headquarters based in Göteborg, Sweden.

Volvo has a presence in over 120 countries.

Sold through a network of 2400 dealers, 1500 in Europe, and 400 in the USA.

Employs 20,000, many based in Sweden.

Mission statement—'Designed Around You'.

Sold 373,525 in 2010, 449,255 in 2011, an increase of 20%

Manufacturing plants in Göteborg, Sweden and Ghent, Belgium.

Is establishing several manufacturing sites in China, where it hopes to sell 200,000 by 2015.

The brand values include Safety, Modern Scandinavian Design, Environmental Care, Premium Quality, Customer Experience, and Driving Dynamics.

The Volvo brand was primarily about two key aspects—big estate cars, and safety. Over the years Volvo developed a reputation for big estate cars that would last for long periods of time. Entry-level models were somewhat affordable, with high-end models priced at a premium, with big engine options. The company sells basic models and has a whole host of optional extras and accessories, ranging from metallic paint, leather seats and roof racks to grocery holders. All of these optional extras help boost the final selling price, and provide a certain level of customisation sought after by Volvo customers. Now Volvo has four main types of models, the S-Type (saloons), the V-Type (estates), the XC (SUVs), and the C-Type (coupes). Its XC range became the company's biggest seller, being particularly successful in America, where big cars typically equated to big success. Now with rising petrol prices Volvo's SUV market is under threat. The big XC range accounts for 36 per cent of total sales. Furthermore, consumers are moving away from Volvo's large engines, seeking more fuel-efficient options. The company is pioneering eco-friendly initiatives like eco-drive, fuel-efficient, low-emission engines, and electric plug-in hybrid cars.

Competition in the global automotive market is fierce. The company's key competitors would be Volkswagen's Audi, Toyota's Lexus, Mercedes-Benz and BMW. The industry is faced with continued economic turmoil, with their nearest Scandinavian rival Saab being abandoned by the bankrupt General Motors. The industry is faced with some notable challenges: the impact of globalization, increasing regulation, growing environmental/energy concerns, rising fuel prices, rising commodity prices, calls for more safety initiatives, large taxation on the automotive trade, manufacturing overcapacity, pressure on margins, and the changing socio-cultural influences. Many are relying on demand surges in developing countries like China and Brazil, to buffet them against the economic turmoil in Western countries. Companies have had to adapt or face death.

Toyota has achieved huge success through their winning combination of value for money and fuel-efficient and reliable cars. This is what the industry is labelling 'guzzler fatigue', where consumers are migrating to smaller fuel-efficient cars. Also, governments are putting in place taxation structures that penalize large cars with high CO_2 emissions. Governments are providing tax incentives for consumers who buy fuel-efficient hybrid and flexi-fuel cars, and possibly other incentives such as free road tolls, parking, etc. With the rising price of oil, all of the major automotive players have seen sales shrink, as consumers move towards more fuel-efficient cars. Volvo is now offering flexi-fuel (combination of petrol and ethanol) in certain geographic markets. This provides consumers with a more eco-friendly alternative, and cheaper fuel prices. These cars produce 80 per cent less carbon gas emissions. Electric cars are seen by the industry as the way forward. Volvo too have launched the electric alternative with C30 Electric competing against the Nissan Leaf and Chevrolet Volt. Will the electric car finally spark in a time of 'peak oil' prices?

Volvo states that its vision is 'To be the world's most progressive and desired luxury car brand', whereas in its mission statement it aims to 'create the safest most exciting car experience for modern families'. This continued

TABLE C4.2   Volvo Market 2011 in figures

Sales by model			Ten biggest markets		
	2011	2010		2011	2010
S40	23,621	31,688	USA	67,273	53,952
S60	68,330	14,786	Sweden	58,463	52,894
S80	14,681	19,162	China	47,140	30,522
S80L	10,018	11,778	Germany	33,167	25,207
V50	45,970	56,098	UK	32,770	37,940
V60	49,820	4,609	Belgium	20,320	17,644
V70	36,842	48,877	Russia	19,209	10,650
XC60	97,183	80,723	Italy	18,705	17,509
XC70	26,156	22,068	Netherlands	15,981	14,308
XC90	39,631	37,597	France	15,678	12,211
C30	27,090	35,981			
C70	9,913	10,158			
Total	**449,255**	**373,525**			

TABLE C4.3   Volvo's product range

	Description
C30	Small hatchback
S40	Mid-sized saloon (entry level), prices from £15,700 (€23,100)
S60	Mid-sized saloon
S80	Large luxury saloon
V50	Mid-sized estate, V stands for versatile
V60	Mid-sized estate, now second most popular seller
V70	Large estate
XC60	New crossover small premium utility launched in 2008
XC70	Cross-country sport utility vehicle (SUV)
XC90	Large SUV, most popular seller, prices from £33,000 (€48,000) to £54,000 (€79,000)
C70	Turbo-charged convertible

emphasis on creating a luxury automotive brand means that research and development is crucial, and that Volvo needs to create models that exude quality, performance and safety. Probably an interesting aspect of their mission statement is their concentration on the family sector, especially in light of declining birth rates in Europe, smaller families and more couples choosing to remain childless. Many cars on the road today are used by single occupants, commuting to work. The firm sees its future as delivering 'safe', 'premium', and 'exciting driving' suitable for families. In a radical departure from this philosophy the firm has launched a new sporty hatchback called the S30, destined to compete against high-end versions of VW's Golf. A key challenge for Volvo is to attract younger drivers to their car marque, as its target audience of 15 years ago is downsizing and migrating to smaller fuel-efficient cars, as they approach retirement. Luring the next generation of Volvo drivers is essential in ensuring long-term success. Volvo's design philosophy is that 'good design is not only a matter of styling the surface. It is just as important to make the product easy to understand and use. If the product is not functional, it can't be beautiful'. The Volvo car brand has three distinct values that it wants to project: 'Designed around people; Contemporary luxury experience; Strength in every sense'. However, sales for this model are in decline. Evidence that Volvo has yet to shake off the shackles of being seen as a big estate car manufacturer.

The company's overall long-term aim is to sell 800,000 cars a year by 2020. The company ceased assembly operations in South Africa, and has now started ramping up production in China. The company has established state-of-the-art

dealerships in the country. Volvo has even decided to sell in India also, initially with its premium ranges in three dealerships. It priced its cars in the same price range as luxury German car brands, which failed to yield dividends. Now the company has reduced prices to build up a base in this developing market. The company sponsors the internationally renowned Volvo Global Ocean race, and golf events that complement its core target market. This has proved an excellent brand platform with exciting media coverage lasting several months, and the company being able to leverage experiential marketing opportunities through events and competitions. Volvo has created a museum to showcase Volvo's brand philosophy called the 'Volvo Experience', full of interactive exhibits to showcase the company, its brand and its achievements. In order to be successful in the premium sector, it believes that customers' satisfaction in the Volvo brand experience is vital. This can be achieved through excellent superior product performance, and excellent dealership service.

The company has built a factory in China with a capacity to produce 100,000 cars a year, with a second plant in the pipeline to build an additional 100,000. Geely has big plans for Volvo in China. It believes that success can be achieved through strategic positioning and operational effectiveness (e.g. shared technologies, cost advantages). Their emphasis is on design, safety and sustainability. The company has launched the DRIVe initiative aimed at reducing the carbon emissions of its popular models. Furthermore, it also aims at launching further plug-in hybrid models.

Volvo has launched Volvo Vision 2020, where the firm aims to differentiate itself from its competitors. The two central planks of this strategy are an ongoing commitment to the environment and to safety, a transfer from the concept of the 'common good' to the 'private good', where a fun, exciting driving experience is created for the customer. By doing so, the firm aims to create a brand that is well respected and trustworthy. It aims to create cars that are exciting to drive, and drivers feel good about driving them. In relation to the environment the firm plans to improve energy efficiency, and health-related technology through the incorporation of recycled materials, alternative fuel types and reduced emissions. The continued emphasis on safety aims to focus on preventive and protective safety through reducing accidents, fatalities and injuries. Volvo has placed great emphasis on creating a safer world, in relation to the environment, and driving. This will represent Volvo's core positioning strategy, but will it yield increased dividends, in a market where competitors are mimicking this strategic focus?

The company is extremely proud of its innovation in car safety enhancements, being pioneers of the safety cage, crumple zones, side impact protection, anti-lock brakes, whiplash protection, and airbags. Volvo invests heavily in safety research and development; its Göteberg Safety centre is world-renowned. The company continues to innovate with 'Blind Spot' and collision warning systems. Yet branding a car as just safe is never going to win over large numbers of would-be consumers. Performance, styling, reliability, handling and value for money are all vitally important. Volvo's core positioning statement of producing the safest cars in the market remains, yet more and more of its competitors have also successfully integrated safety into their customer propositions (e.g. Renault). It needs to offer something else to consumers.

The company uses the tag line 'Volvo. For Life'. A key question remains for Volvo, will Volvo maintain its tried and tested marketing formula, or will the firm have to pursue a radical rethinking of its business philosophy in the wake of a changing marketing environment? The company is under threat from the changing automotive landscape, but how will it adapt?

Questions

1 Outline and discuss the macro- and microenvironmental factors that are influencing Volvo's strategy.

2 Conduct a SWOT analysis on the Volvo cars.

3 Outline the strategic options available to Volvo cars, recommending what you believe to be the best option available, giving reasons for your answer.

This case was written by Conor Carroll, Lecturer in Marketing, University of Limerick. Copyright © Conor Carroll (2012). The material in the case has been drawn from a variety of published sources.

PART 2
Marketing Analysis

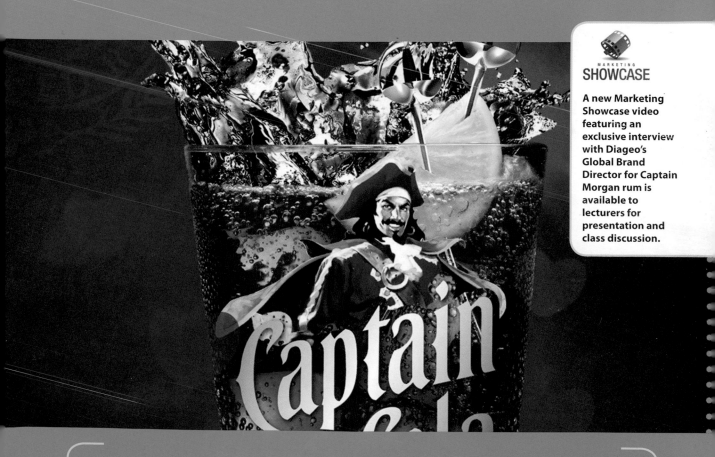

MARKETING SHOWCASE

A new Marketing Showcase video featuring an exclusive interview with Diageo's Global Brand Director for Captain Morgan rum is available to lecturers for presentation and class discussion.

CHAPTER 3

The marketing environment

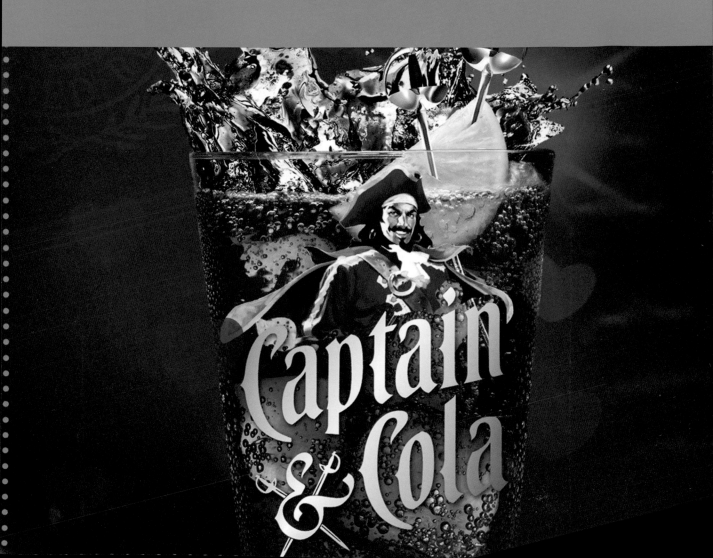

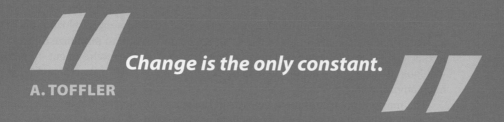

Change is the only constant.

A. TOFFLER

LEARNING OBJECTIVES

After reading this chapter, you should be able to:

1 describe the nature of the marketing environment
2 explain the distinction between the microenvironment and the macroenvironment
3 discuss the impact of political and legal, economic, ecological/physical environmental, social/cultural and technological forces on marketing decisions
4 explain how to conduct environmental scanning
5 discuss how companies respond to environmental change

Amarketing-orientated firm looks outwards to the environment in which it operates, adapting to take advantage of emerging opportunities and to minimize potential threats. In this chapter we will examine how to monitor the marketing environment. In particular, we will look at some of the major forces acting on companies in their macro- and microenvironments.

The **marketing environment** consists of the actors and forces that affect a company's capability to operate effectively in providing products and services to its customers. As we saw in Chapter 2 it is useful to classify these forces into the macroenvironment and the microenvironment (see Fig. 3.1). The **macroenvironment** consists of a number of broad forces that affect not only the company but also the other actors in the microenvironment. Traditionally four forces—political/legal, economic, social/cultural and technological—have been the focus of attention, with the result that the term 'PEST analysis' has been used to describe macroenvironmental analysis. However, the growing importance of ecological/physical environmental forces on companies has led to the acronym being expanded to **PEEST analysis**. The microenvironment consists of the actors in the firm's immediate environment that affect its capabilities to operate effectively in its chosen markets. The key actors are customers, competitors, distributors and suppliers. The macro- and microenvironments shape the character of the opportunities and threats facing a company and are largely uncontrollable.

This chapter focuses on the macroenvironmental forces—political/legal, economic, ecological/physical, social/cultural and technological—which affect marketing decisions. Later in the chapter the four dimensions of the microenvironment—customers, competitors, distributors and suppliers—are introduced and then examined in greater detail throughout the book. The influence of customers on marketing decisions are discussed in Chapters 4 and 5 and the changing nature of the supply chain examined in Chapter 5. Distribution and competitive forces will be analysed in Chapters 17, and 19 and 20 respectively.

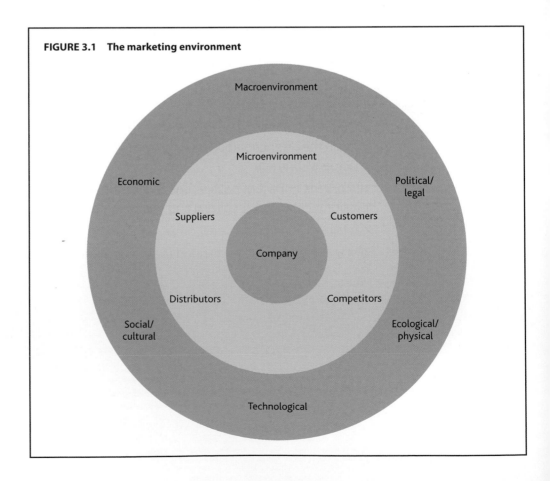

FIGURE 3.1   The marketing environment

Political and Legal Forces

Political and legal forces can influence marketing decisions by setting the rules by which business is conducted. For example, smoking bans in public places can have dramatic short- and long-term effects on the demand for cigarettes. Because of politicians' power to affect business activities, companies try to cultivate close relationships with them, both to monitor political moods and also to influence them. Sometimes, sizeable contributions to the funds of political parties are made in an attempt to maintain favourable relationships. Never has the relationship between political forces and business been more apparent than in the recent period of recession, which has forced governments to support banks financially and, in the case of the British Government (taxpayers), acquire Northern Rock and become the major shareholder in the Royal Bank of Scotland.[1] Political forces are complex to analyse and the impact difficult to determine. However, unrest in the North African countries of Libya, Egypt, Tunisia, has affected various industries: for example, the oil industry raising prices of a barrel of oil on the wholesale markets due to fear of loss of supply; the travel and tourism industry reducing demand for holidays and travel in these regions. Thomas Cook is a company that has attributed some of its losses to these events. Mini Case 3.1 focuses on how service cuts and changes in taxation can affect behaviour in unusual ways.

Mini Case 3.1 Wall Street Staked Out by Angry Protestors

For several decades, continuing economic growth has engendered a relatively peaceful life for financial districts around the world (e.g. New York, London, Athens and Rome). However, global recession, changes in taxation and austerity measures introduced by national governments, designed to reduce national debts, sparked an unexpected response. In September 2011 protestors gathered and set up camp in New York's financial district to protest about social inequalities. This inspired others around the globe to follow suit. In Rome the protests turned violent as demonstrators set cars alight and hurled rocks at police. Greek workers demonstrated against yet another set of austerity measures. Public anger was fuelled by economic troubles but the link between economic conditions and unrest is complex. UK politician Ken Livingstone suggested that an economic downturn and government cuts create unrest as it is a combination of events which intensifies social divisions. Service cuts tend to have more impact on those with lower incomes, and these people can easily become disenfranchised. This contrasts with tax increases which tend to have a greater impact on those with higher incomes, and these people are less likely to protest. This means the greater the level of actual and perceived inequality between incomes, the greater the likelihood of unrest and civil disturbances.

The Occupy Wall Street demonstrators had placards and banners stating 'We are the 99%'. This slogan refers to figures which estimate that '58% of the real economic growth in America of the past 30 years was captured by the top 1% of earners' and this highlights the trend towards a polarization in the American labour force into high- and low-skilled segments, especially in technology industries. While changes in the macroenvironment can be incremental and occur over a lengthy period, a steady build-up can lead to far-reaching implications, which can reshape society.

Question:

1 The article concludes that the steady build up of political, economic and legal factors from the macroenvironment is reshaping society as we know it.

   Is their argument that technological factors or environmental factors are endeavouring to do the same? Illustrate your answer with examples.

Based on: **The Economist (2011);**[2] *Alesina, and Perotti (1966)*[3]

In Europe companies are affected by legislation at EU and national levels. We will first examine EU-wide laws before discussing the impact of national laws on business life.

European Union-wide laws

EU laws exist at two levels: (i) regulations that are binding on member states, and (ii) directives that are binding only through enactment of a law within the member state in line with the directive. A major influence at European level is EU competition, which is based on the belief that business competitiveness benefits from intense competition. The role of competition policy, then, is to encourage competition in the EU by removing restrictive practices and other anti-competitive activities. This is accomplished by tackling barriers to competition through rules that form a legal framework within which EU firms must operate. The objects of these legal rules are to prevent firms from:

- *colluding* by price fixing, cartels and other collaborative activities. Competition is encouraged by preventing firms joining forces to act in a monopolistic way. The European Commission enforces EU rules, and has had considerable success in disbanding and fining cartels. For example, the Commission broke up a cartel between producers of cathode ray tubes (CRT) glass used in televisions and computer screens (Asahi Glass (AGC), Nippon Electric Glass (NEG) and Germany's Schott AG). They were fined a total of €128 million for operating a cartel that ultimately affected consumers in Europe.[4] British Airways was also fined £270 million for conspiring with Virgin Airways (who escaped prosecution because it alerted the regulators about the price fixing) to fix the price of passenger fuel surcharges on transatlantic flights;[5] and glass manufacturers Saint-Gobain, Pilkington, Asahi Glass and Soliver were fined a total of over €1 billion for illegally fixing the price of glass used in the car industry.[6] Such actions are having a real impact on firms' behaviour. The success the European Commission has had in locating and punishing those firms that collude acts as a major deterrent through both the severity of the fines imposed and the bad publicity that results. Marketing in Action 3.1 explains further.

- *abusing a position of market dominance*. They are discouraged from taking such actions as monopoly and discriminatory pricing, which could harm small buyers with little bargaining power. Market dominance was successfully challenged when Italian cigarette producer and distributor AAMS was found to be abusing its dominant position for the wholesale distribution of cigarettes. AAMS was protecting its own sales by imposing restrictive distribution contracts on foreign manufacturers, which limited the access of foreign cigarettes to the Italian market.[7] Possibly the most high-profile case occurred when Microsoft was fined £340 million for its alleged misuse of its near monopoly in operating systems, when trying to squeeze out rivals by bundling Media Player into the Windows operating system.[8] Microsoft was fined £650 million for failing to disclose technical information on 'reasonable terms' to allow rivals to develop products that would work with Windows.[9]

- *acquiring excessive market power* through acquisition. The objective is to control the size that firms grow to through acquisition or merging with other firms within defined markets, in order to stop the creation of monopolistic profits. Actions to prevent the build-up of excess power include blocking mergers, as in the case of the Swedish truck and coach builders Volvo which wanted to acquire Scania. The reason was that such a merger would create a near monopoly. Less severe action is to apply strict conditions to any merger such as the requirement that Nestlé sell a number of Perrier brands to encourage a third force to emerge in the French mineral water market to compete with Nestlé and BSN, the second major supplier of bottled water in France.

- *relying on state aid*. It can be in a nation's interest for its government to give state aid to ailing firms within its boundaries; on a broader scale this can give artificial competitive advantages to recipient firms, enabling them to charge lower prices than their unsupported rivals; recipients may also be unfairly shielded from the full force of the competitive pressures affecting their markets. EC approval of state aid is usually given as part of a restructuring or rescue package for ailing firms. The general principle is that such payments should be 'one-offs' to prevent uncompetitive firms being repeatedly bailed out by their governments. When the Icelandic volcano erupted, the ash cloud caused many European airlines to be grounded for several days, resulting in the loss of billions of pounds of revenue, lost travel and compensation to passengers and, consequently, several airlines applied for state assistance. The European Commission's response was that Brussels would have to sanction national government bail-outs if they amounted to state aid. The EC cautioned that non-state aid would be allowed, but warned against providing 'unfair assistance' that could undermine competition.[10] Generally, the level of state aid given to firms in most of the EU member states is declining.

Marketing in Action 3.1 The European Commission's Crusade Against Cartels

In the USA and the EU the battle against price-fixing cartels has never been so strongly fought.

In the USA auction houses Sotheby's and Christie's were convicted of fixing the prices they charge clients. For many years America has been obsessed by bringing down price-fixing cartels, but the message is now spreading, with new measures against anti-competitive cartel behaviour.

Since 2000 the European Commission has crusaded with renewed vigour against cartels across a diverse range of industries from pharmaceuticals, airlines, tobacco, glass, carbonless paper and banking services to e-publishing. The Commission's investigation into the sale of ebooks is concerned with publishers' pricing policies (e.g. HarperCollins, Penguin and Simon & Schuster), and is questioning whether those content providers are engaged in anti-competitive practices by setting prices at a certain level instead of competing. Such actions have stretched its resources to the limit, which is one reason it has published a Green Paper designed to encourage customers and competitors to make private claims for damages resulting from anti-competitive practices, an action that moves it towards the US anti-trust regime, which relies heavily on private litigation.

One of the driving forces behind the EC's efforts to drive out anti-competitive behaviour is the desire to create a genuine single market in Europe, where geographic 'market sharing' is seen as highly damaging. Companies are responding by educating themselves: for example, Roche, the global pharmaceutical giant, has put thousands of its managers through training to teach them to follow the law.

Based on: Savov (2011);[11] Ritson (2002);[12] Buck (2005);[13] Murphy and Yuk (2008)[14]

National laws

In addition to EU laws, member states also have the right to make their own legislation governing business practice. This can mean inconsistencies across Europe. For example, national laws governing advertising across Europe mean that what is acceptable in one country is banned in another. For example, toys cannot be advertised in Greece; tobacco advertising is illegal in Scandinavia, the UK and Italy; alcohol advertising is banned on television in France and at sports grounds; and in Germany any advertisement believed to be in bad taste can be prohibited. This patchwork of national advertising regulations means that companies attempting to create a brand image across Europe often need to make substantial changes to advertising strategy on a national basis.

Supplementing the work of the European Commission are national bodies set up to investigate anti-competitive practices—e.g. the Competition Commission in the UK, the Bundeskartellamt in Germany and the Competition Council in France provide national protection against anti-competitive behaviour. Self-regulation also occurs at national level, with industries drawing up codes of practice to protect consumer interests; for example in the advertising industry: Deutscher Werbat (Germany), Stichting Reclame Code (Netherlands), Marknads Etiska Radet (Sweden) and the Advertising Standards Authority (UK). The

Go to the website and check out how McDonald's is using the alphabet to reinforce its healthy credentials. www.mcgraw-hill.co.uk/textbooks/jobber

marketing research industry also has drawn up codes of practice to protect people from unethical activities such as using marketing research as a pretext for selling.

The political and legal environment exerts constraints on marketing management activities, and consequently staff involved in the marketing function must assess these forces and consider how they might influence political decisions that may affect their operations. They should also determine the degree to which industry practice needs to be self-regulated in order to maintain high standards of customer satisfaction and service. Above all, companies need to ensure that their activities are in accord with EU and national laws and codes of practice.

Economic Forces

The *economic environment* can have a critical impact on the success of companies through its effect on supply and demand. Companies must choose those economic influences that are relevant to their business and monitor them. We will examine four major economic influences on the marketing environment of companies: economic growth and unemployment, interest and exchange rates, the eurozone, and the growth of the 'Bric' economies (Brazil, Russia, India and China).

Economic growth and unemployment

The general state of national and international economies can have a profound effect on a company's prosperity. Economies tend to fluctuate according to the business cycle, although more enlightened economic management has reduced the depth of the contraction in some countries. Most of the world's economies have gone through a period of significant growth since the mid-1990s, driven partly by productivity gains brought about by developments in computing and telecommunications technologies. This growth was followed by a period of economic slump which began in 2008 with a period referred to as the 'credit crunch'; this was followed by deepening recession and the eurozone debt crisis,[15] which threatened to impact on the worldwide economy. During periods of boom, well-managed companies experience an expansion in the demand for their products, while periods of slump may bring a decline in sales as consumers became wary of discretionary expenditures. A major marketing problem is predicting the next boom or slump. Investments made during periods of high growth can become massive cash drains when consumer spending falls suddenly. Retailers are often the first to be affected; Carrefour, Tesco, Walmart, Dixons Retail are only too aware that they must plan to manage their national and international operations in anticipation of rising and falling consumer demand. Derived demand also affects manufacturers because, as consumer demand falls, manufacturers are affected too.

Within an economy, different sectors experience varying growth rates, leading to changing degrees of market attractiveness. Undoubtedly, the services sector has experienced the fastest growth and become the dominant force in most western economies. For example, among the 27 EU countries, services account for over 70 per cent of gross domestic product, which is a measure of the total value of goods and services produced within an economy.

Low growth rates are reflected in high unemployment levels, which in turn affect consumer spending power. The recent period of recession has caused unemployment rates to rise and consumer spending to fall in many European economies: e.g. in Greece, Portugal and Ireland. This has led to calls for state aid for ailing companies—for example, in the motor industry—to help them through the slump. However, this is not the case in emerging economies in BRIC countries, where economic growth is positive and employment and spending on the increase. China is predicted to become the largest global economy by 2020.[16]

Interest and exchange rates

A key monetary tool that governments use to manage the economy is interest rates. Interest rates represent the price that borrowers have to pay lenders for the use of their money over a specified period of time. Most western economies lowered interest rates during the credit crunch to encourage borrowing and lending, in an effort to avert a major slump in consumer and business demand.

An exchange rate is the price of one currency in terms of another (e.g. an exchange rate of £1 = €1.20 means that £1 buys €1.20). Fluctuations in exchange rates mean that the price a consumer in one country pays for a product and/or the money that a supplier in an overseas country receives for selling that product can change. For example, if the exchange rate between the pound sterling and the euro changes, such that a pound buys fewer euros, a German car manufacturer who receives payment in euros will receive fewer euros if the price of the car remains unchanged in the UK. In an attempt to maintain a constant euro price, the German car manufacturer may raise the UK pound sterling price to UK distributors and consumers. The following example illustrates these points.

At £1 = €1, a German car manufacturer would receive €10,000 for a £10,000 car. If the exchange rate changed to £1 = €0.5, the German car manufacturer's receipts would fall to €5000. To maintain euro receipts at €10,000 the UK price would have to rise to £20,000.

The exchange rates between most European countries are now fixed, thus avoiding such problems. However, the rates at which major currencies such as the US dollar, the euro, the pound sterling and the yen are traded are still variable. As seen in the example above this can have significant implications for sales revenues and hence the profitability of a firm's international operations. For example, during the credit crunch, the pound fell against the dollar. This meant that UK goods and services exported to eurozone countries could be sold cheaper, or, if sold at the same price, would realize higher sterling profit margins.

The European Union and the Eurozone

The EU is a massive, largely deregulated market and it has far-reaching implications for marketing as the barriers to the free flow of goods, services, capital and people among the member states are removed. A key objective of the EU is to lower the costs of operating throughout Europe and to create an enormous free market in which companies can flourish. As we have already seen, competition is encouraged through the enactment and enforcement of laws designed to remove restrictive practices and other anti-competitive activities. The EU currently consists of 27 member states and it is continually expanding. Croatia is expected to become the 28th member state in 2013. Table 3.1 shows the spread of the member states, when they joined and candidate countries that are likely to become members in the future.

As the EU has expanded, new member states have contributed to the development of the community and helped with the economic growth of union. Expansion to include eastern European countries has brought a low-cost, technically skilled workforce which has proved to be competitive with those in China and India. The strengths of the economies of member states have been boosted by EU membership and have led to considerable inward investment—for example, the Korean firm LG Electronic, which is the world's second largest producer of televisions, committed to invest US$110 million to build a plant to produce plasma and LCD televisions.[17]

The eurozone is an economic and monetary union (EMU) between 17 of the member states of the EU. Each state has adopted the euro (€) as a common currency, which is managed and controlled by the European Central Bank (ECB). A primary responsibility of the ECB is to control inflation and manage debt and economic reforms, and a common currency brings advantages through facilitating the flow of free trade within the community. However, turbulence in economic markets has exposed weaknesses in areas of the eurozone, which potentially have far-reaching implications for economies around the world.

China and India

Why are western nations watching the economies of China and India like hawks? First, both economies are growing at high and consistent rates, although both, like other major

TABLE 3.1 European Union member states

Membership Year	Member States	Total population (in millions)
Founding members	France, Netherlands, Belgium, Luxembourg, Germany, Italy	235
1970–1980	United Kingdom, Ireland, Denmark	72
1981–1990	Spain, Portugal, Greece	69
1991–2000	Austria, Sweden, Finland	23
2001–present	Poland, Estonia, Latvia, Lithuania, Czech Republic, Slovakia, Hungary, Slovenia, Romania, Bulgaria, Cyprus, Malta	103
Candidate countries	Iceland, Croatia, the former Yugoslav Republic of Macedonia, Turkey	80
		582

Statistics Source: European Commission Eurostat (2012), http://epp.eurostat.ec.europa.eu

Marketing in Action 3.2 Trouble in the Eurozone

The expansion of the EU into Eastern Europe brought significant economic advantages through expansion of the labour force, and in the period from 2004 onwards many of the countries joining the union enjoyed rapidly growing economies, which attracted investment from China and India. However, the global economic crisis has impacted on member states, revealing divergence in competitiveness between the stronger core economies and the weaker peripheral economies. In terms of gross domestic product (GDP)—a measure of economic activity that enables the comparison of the dynamics of development of economies of varying sizes—eurozone economies in Greece and Portugal are contracting, in Spain and Italy they are stagnant but in Germany and Estonia they are growing. Credit ratings are another indicator of financial health. Germany, the Netherlands, Finland and Luxembourg have retained their 'triple A credit ratings' but Italy, Spain, Portugal and others have had their ratings downgraded. The credit ratings of countries operate on similar principles to those given to individuals but at a much higher level of sophistication. Standard and Poor's (S&P) is the world's leader in providing credit rating indices. These indicate how investable a country might be and the basic premise is that the credit rating gives an indication of future economic performance. S&P feel EU leaders have focused too much on tackling budget deficits rather than the divergence in competitiveness between the strong and weak economies in the eurozone. In addition, actions by the European Central Bank (ECB) to support its commitment to low inflation, on the one hand, have contributed to a collapse in demand and raised fears that the single currency may not survive.[18] On the other hand, its actions in increasing lending appear to have secured bank financing and helped to rally some struggling economies.

Turbulence in the eurozone can affect the US economy and contribute to an overall slowdown in expected growth, and so it remains central to the health of the global economy. Ultimately, this means that a downturn in the EU economy is likely to mean weaker consumer and business confidence, which affects spending, investment and development.

To find out more about the development of Standard and Poor's and its 500 index visit the following web link and view the video and interactive timeline. Visit http://www.standardandpoors.com/about-sp/timeline/en/us/

Based on: S&P (2012); European Commission Eurostat (2012);[19] The Economist (2012);[20] Economist Intelligence Unit (2011)[21]

economies, have suffered during the recent recession. For the past 20 years China's economy has been growing at an average of 9.5 per cent and is predicted to become the largest economy in the world by 2020.[22] India's growth is less at 6 per cent.[23] Second, both nations possess considerable strengths in low-cost labour, but increasingly also in technical and managerial skills. China possesses strengths in mass manufacturing, and is currently building massive electronics and heavy industrial factories. India, on the other hand, is an emerging power in software, design, services and precision industry. These complementary skills are persuading some electronics multinationals to have their products built in China with software and circuitry designed in India.

Third, China and India not only pose threats to western companies, they also provide opportunities. Chinese consumers are spending their growing incomes on all manner of consumer durables from cars to shampoo. The Chinese buy more cars than the Americans (13.5 million compared to 11.6 million) and western brands are becoming increasingly popular—from Burberry to Tesco, Bosch, Nestlé, Procter & Gamble.[24] However, companies wishing to expand in these booming markets must do adequate research as it is very important to get things right. M&S made a mistake on opening its stores in China as they filled their rails with clothes of the wrong sizes. Chinese women are smaller and slimmer than European women and have smaller feet. In fact many Chinese students studying in the UK often buy their shoes in children's shoe shops.[25]

In India the consumer market is also growing rapidly but Indian consumers are not as wealthy as the Chinese. However, in less than 15 years India's economy could be as large as China's is today so the prospects are good. Nestlé has operated in India for nearly a century and today runs seven factories making many varieties of yogurt, milk products and chocolates. Nestlé has invested in the infrastructure, training and education programmes which have taught local farmers how to do things better and more efficiently. Hindustan Unilever is another European firm taking opportunities in India to create competitive advantage. Nationally, Indians' preference for soap and shampoo vary much less than their taste in food, so Unilever is doing even better than Nestlé with an 18 per cent increase in profits.

Fourth, China's and India's economies are not just booming in the physical world, but are also rapidly expanding online and in mobile markets. Read Digital Marketing 3.1 and find out more about online shopping and social networks in China.

Digital Marketing 3.1 China: The Greatest Connected Market in the World?

Less than ten years ago fewer than 3 per cent of the Chinese population were online (about 33.7 million people). However, in the past four years China has seen an internet boom. Around 145 million people shop online and it is predicted that by 2015 each consumer will spend the equivalent of $1000 a year (which is about what the Americans were spending in 2012). The boom is being driven by the Chinese government, which is heavily subsidizing the roll-out of high-speed internet access, and, surprisingly, by the inefficiency of existing bricks-and-mortar retailers. Many shoppers go online because they cannot find the goods in the stores. Taobao is a giant online retailer, and with Alibaba is said to account for 50 per cent of all of the parcels delivered in China. As well as shopping, the Chinese have taken to socializing and sharing information online. The online shoppers are fearful of being tricked by fraudsters so they like to share their experiences. According to research, over 40 per cent of online shoppers read and post product reviews, making them more active in this area than Americans and Indians. Social networking, like e-commerce, started slowly but there are now three large social networks in China: QQ, Weibo and RenRen. Weibo is the Chinese equivalent of Twitter and its top stars have more fans than their celebrity counterparts on Twitter. Also, there are over 200 million people with a social network account. Facebook, Twitter and YouTube are banned in China, which has created an opportunity for these homegrown networks to emerge. Furthermore, Chinese society is being changed extensively by the internet. Traditionally, families were reluctant to socialize with those outside their known circle of close friends and family, tending to be shy and reserved. However, now families use social networks to organize vacations and find families with similar interests from distant towns, arranging to meet, share car journeys and lots more.

Based on: Chaffey et al. (2002);[26] The Economist (2011);[27] Muller (2011)[28]

In the Indian mobile phone industry there are over 600 million active mobile phone subscribers, which is about one phone per two head of population; the country also has the lowest prices anywhere in the world. Bharti Airtel is the main mobile network operator in India and it is bringing phone access to everyone regardless of where they live. However, for international competitors trying to operate in or enter the mobile market, there are limited profits to be made and massive investment required to improve network operations and services.[29]

There are also major cultural and logistic barriers to overcome, although these apply to both on- and offline markets. The retail industry in both China and India is underdeveloped. There are potentially big opportunities for western retailers (especially supermarkets) to enter Asian markets. However, in the Indian subcontinent 'there are 20 officially recognized languages, 14 main types of cuisines and countless religious and ethnic festivals as well as a passion for cricket',[30] which presents exhaustive challenges for developing a national retail operation.

While both countries possess considerable strengths, they also have weaknesses. Neither country has a strong track record in global brand building. A survey of *Financial Times* readers conducted by McKinsey, the management consultancy, to find out what business people around the world consider are the top Chinese brands, rated Haier, a white goods and home appliances company, first and Lenovo, a computer company and famous for buying IBM's personal computer division, second. Neither company is a major global player in its respective market.[31] India, similarly, does not possess major global brands. However, the conglomerate Tata is building a global presence with its purchase of Jaguar and Land Rover from Ford, the acquisition of Corus (steel) and the growth of Tata Consultancy Services, Asia's largest software company.[32] Both countries suffer from the risk of social strife—resulting from the widening gap between rich and poor—as well as from corruption.[33] Additionally, they have paid a steep ecological price for rapid industrial and population growth, with millions of deaths attributed to air and water pollution each year.[34] China is the world's largest producer of carbon emissions. Another issue is wage levels which are rising fast, particularly in skilled areas, reducing their advantage in low labour costs.[35] Also bureaucracy can make doing business in both countries difficult. China, in particular, has been a destination for western goods and foreign investment, but great care needs to be taken when entering the Chinese market, as Marketing in Action 3.3 explains.

Russia and Brazil

Russia and Brazil are emerging economies with market development potential and, while both have suffered during the 2008–9 recessions, they are recovering.

Russia's economy has changed dramatically since the collapse of the communist state, and its centrally planned economy has moved into a globally integrated economy.[36] However, despite becoming the world's largest exporter of natural gas, the second largest in oil and third largest in steel, in 2009 the Russian economy was hit hard by the recession caused by its reliance on such commodities. In an attempt to reduce this reliance, Russia has been investing in building up its high-tech industries but with limited success. High oil prices in 2011 helped economic recovery and put Russia back on a growth trajectory. However, it still faces long-term challenges in the form of a shrinking workforce, a high level of corruption, difficulty in accessing capital for smaller, non–energy companies, and poor infrastructure. Retail markets are also recovering, showing growth rates of around 13 per cent, but this is considerably slower than in the pre-recessionary period.

Russia is interesting for having one of the lowest income tax rates in the world: a flat rate of 13 per cent. Also all Russians own their own homes, having been given their own flat or house free as the Soviet era ended (most of these, however, are in a poor state of repair). Wealth tends to be centred around Moscow and there are cash-rich consumers present, as the fact that Russia is the fourth biggest consumer of luxury goods after the USA, Japan and China testifies.[37]

Marketing in Action 3.3   Doing Business in China

Marketing in any overseas country is difficult because of differences in culture, and local laws and regulations. China is particularly troublesome, with many companies—such as Whirlpool, a US white-goods manufacturer that lost more than £26 million in a series of joint ventures, and food multinational Kraft, which was forced to close its loss-making dairy business after eight years—finding life uncomfortable in the Chinese market.

In order to succeed, overseas companies need to observe a number of guidelines. First, they must appreciate the diversity of the market. A country with 1.3 billion people speaking 100 dialects is vastly diverse, and the need to segment the market is essential. For example, Samsung discovered that consumers living in humid Guangdong Province needed larger refrigerators than those in the more temperate north, so it started marketing bigger fridges in the south. P&G has targeted consumers in less affluent rural districts with a budget detergent called Tide Clean White, while targeting richer city consumers with the more expensive Tide Triple Action. To understand customers, domestic and multinational companies are conducting focus groups and surveys. For example, the Grey Global Group, a Chinese advertising agency, has segmented Chinese consumers into 11 categories based on their lifestyle and aspirations. These groups range from independents who do not follow consumer trends to shoppers on the cutting edge.

Western firms often enter China by means of a joint venture, but they need to be aware of the different business scenarios there. In China there is no effective rule of law governing business. One potential drawback is that western companies can fall prey to the theft of intellectual property. Other problems about which western companies complain include the siting of projects in inappropriate locations so local authorities can charge inflated land use costs, and inflation of costs by joint venture partners. Bureaucracy and governmental interference can also bring difficulties. Thames Water reportedly had to pull out of a 20-year water treatment project in Shanghai after the government ruled that the guaranteed rate of return to investors was illegal. Technical problems can also hamper joint ventures. For example, Chrysler ended its small-car venture with Cherry Automobile because of that company's failure to bring the cars' safety and environmental performance up to western standards. However, the Swedish firm Ericsson, the world's largest telecommunications equipment producer, successfully entered into contracts with China's two biggest mobile phone companies, China Mobile and China Unicom. Ericsson has begun providing the service for managed services for China Mobile, which could turn into the largest managed services contract the company has received in China.

Western companies also need to understand the importance of *guanxi* networks. *Guanxi* is a set of personal relationships/connections on which a person can draw to obtain resources or an advantage when doing business. *Guanxi* is one reason why working with a Chinese partner is usually better than going it alone. When entering into business relationships, the Chinese seek stability and trust more than intimacy. They want to feel comfortable that western companies will not spring surprises that may hurt them, but they do not need to feel that they are the company's best friend. It is claimed that the failure of Rupert Murdoch's News Corp. to penetrate China is largely because the company did not spend enough time and effort on building *guanxi*.

The media also have to be handled with care. Severely restrained in reporting domestic politics and social issues, Chinese media feel much freer to attack foreign companies. Chinese reporters need to be educated about the western company's business, treated with respect, and regular contact to develop personal relationships is recommended.

Based on: Ericsson (2010);[38] McGregor (2005);[39] Roberts and Rocks (2005);[40] Singh (2005);[41] Anderlini and Reed (2008);[42] Bulkley (2008);[43] Ibison (2008)[44]

Russia's large population of 140 million, which has rapidly become richer, has attracted international food and drink companies such as Unilever, PepsiCo, Kellogg, Kraft, Nestlé, Coca-Cola and Carlsberg, which have entered by acquisition. For example, PepsiCo purchased the Russian food and drinks group Lebedyansky for over £1 billion.[45] Working in Russia can be highly profitable for western companies, but can be fraught with problems, as the battle for control of the TNK-BP joint venture showed. Although BP managed to keep 50 per cent of the ownership, it was forced to sacrifice its chief executive and agree to international expansion, even when that meant competing with existing BP interests.[46]

Brazil's was one of the first emerging markets to show signs of recovery from the global recession, with a 7.5 per cent growth in GDP in 2010, but it has since experienced a slow-down. However, high interest rates still make Brazil a destination for foreign investors, and in

2012 the country was ranked eighth in the world in terms of its GDP purchasing power parity (a measure used by economists to compare the living conditions and resources of different countries). Brazil's industry is linked to agribusiness and other primary products. Its main output comes from sugar, steel, oil and iron. It also has an important technological sector that ranges from submarines to aircraft, and it is involved in space research. Its economy has benefited from high levels of foreign investment by such companies as Procter & Gamble, IBM, Ford, DuPont, Peugeot Citroën, Anheuser-Busch InBev and PepsiCo. Among its largest companies are Petrobas (energy) and Vale (material), ITau Unibanco Holding (finance) and BRF—Brazil Foods (consumables). The country is also a major producer of ethanol, a sugar-based biofuel. Growth in the economy has led to rising demand for cars, mobile phones, computers and televisions among the large population of 190 million. However, like the other Bric nations, Brazil has not developed significant brand-building capabilities.[47]

Companies need to be aware of the economic forces that may affect their operations and be wary of assuming that the benign economic environment will last for ever. Sudden changes in growth, interest and/or exchange rates can alter the economic climate quickly so that contingency plans are needed to cope with economy-induced downturns in demand. Firms also need to monitor the international economic environment, including the change to market-driven economies and the move into the EU by central and eastern European countries, and the opportunities and threats posed by the rise of China and India as major economic forces.

Ecological/ Physical Environmental Forces

Ecology is the study of living things within their environmental context. In a marketing context it concerns the relationship between people and the physical environment. Environmentalists attempt to protect the physical environment from the costs associated with producing and marketing products. They are concerned with the environmental costs of consumption, not just the personal costs to the consumer. Five environmental issues are of particular concern. These are climate change, pollution control, energy conservation (and that of other scarce resources), use of environmentally friendly ingredients and components, and the use of recyclable and non-wasteful packaging.

Climate change

Concerns about climate change and the problems associated with global warming originate from a quadrupling of carbon dioxide emissions over the past 50 years, evidenced by more extreme weather conditions, such as hurricanes, storms and flooding. There is much discussion about whether or not climate change is caused by human activity and associated with carbon dioxide-induced emission. However, industries such as insurance, agriculture and oil have felt the impact from natural disasters like Hurricane Katrina in the USA.[48] At the heart of the debate is the rate at which the planet is warming and the impact on global average temperature changes, which is different from the temperature changes we experience in our daily lives. In the history of the world, ice ages, super-volcano eruptions and 'nuclear' winters have been responsible for wiping out species and reshaping the geography of the planet.[49]

In 1992 countries joined in an international treaty to 'cooperatively consider what they could do to limit average global temperature increases and the resulting climate change and to cope with whatever impacts were, by then, inevitable'.[50] The United Nations Framework Convention on Climate Change (UNFCCC) realized that the measures in place to control climate change were insufficient. Accordingly, they developed the Kyoto Protocol (KP), which is an international agreement that focuses member countries on how to keep global temperature increases below 2 degrees Celsius. 37 industrialized nations and the European community which have signed up to the KP have committed themselves to the reduction by 2012 of four greenhouse gases: carbon dioxide, methane, nitrous oxide and sulphur hexafluoride, by 5 per cent.[51] This means consumers and organizations have to alter their behaviour. In 2011 Tesco (UK), Concentrica (UK), Schneider (France), Suntech (USA),

⬆EXHIBIT 3.1   Honda was keen to boost its environmentally friendly image with the launch of the Jazz hybrid.

Go to the website to see how EDF communicates how the company is helping to preserve the planet.
www.mcgraw-hill.co.uk/ textbooks/jobber

Swisscom (Switzerland) and Philips (Netherlands) won Gigaton awards for being businesses which have showing outstanding performance in measurable carbon reduction.[52] Car manufacturers also have a responsibility to reduce their carbon footprint. Toyota's environmentally friendly image has also helped to sell over 3 million of its car worldwide[53] and has made a major contribution in establishing the hybrid car market. Honda lagged behind in the race, but its strategic investments in hybrid technology has led to the launch of the Jazz hybrid, which has won awards for its fuel efficiency and lower carbon emission. Luxury performance car manufacturer Jaguar has given its C-X16 the eco treatment and made it cleaner and more efficient. Porsche has launched its Panamera as part of its strategy to comply with new fuel standards in the USA.[54]

Phillips Electronics is also taking steps to reduce $CO2$ emissions with consumer and professional electronics (see Exhibit 3.2).

Pollution

The manufacture, use and disposal of products can have a harmful effect on the quality of the physical environment. The production of chemicals that pollute the atmosphere, the use of nitrates as a fertilizer that pollutes rivers, and the disposal of by-products into the sea have caused considerable public concern. For example, there is a garbage patch in the northern Pacific Ocean, which is an accumulation of plastics, chemical sludge and debris deposited by ocean currents. The 'Trash Vortex', as it is called by Greenpeace, is equivalent in size to the state of Texas USA, and is a major pollution problem for the marine environment. As the waste degrades, it is being ingested by marine animals, poisoning them and thereby entering the food chain.[55] The list of manufactured products that have found their way to the vortex is extensive and includes plastic bottles, polystyrene packaging, traffic cones, disposable lighters, vehicle tyres and even toothbrushes.

In response to pollution issues, Denmark has introduced a series of anti-pollution measures, including a charge on pesticides and a CFC tax. The Netherlands has imposed higher taxes on pesticides, fertilizers and carbon monoxide emissions. The EU has made an agreement with car manufacturers to produce colour-coded labels to make it easier for car users to understand the environmental impact of the vehicle they choose to drive.[56] Not all initiatives mean adding costs, however. In Germany, for example, one of the marketing benefits of its involvement in green technology has been a thriving export business in pollution-control equipment.

Energy and scarce resource conservation

The finite nature of the world's resources is driving conservation. Energy conservation is reflected in the demand for energy-efficient housing and fuel-efficient cars. In Europe Sweden has taken the lead in developing an energy policy based on renewable resources. The tax system penalizes the use of polluting energy sources such as coal and oil, while less polluting resources such as peat and woodchip receive favourable tax treatment. In addition, it is planning to become the world's first oil-free economy by 2020, not by building nuclear power stations but by utilizing renewable resources such as wind and wave power, geothermal

energy and waste heat. The plan is a response to warnings that the world may be running out of oil, together with global climate change and rising petrol prices. The UK government is responding by committing to green energy production on a large scale and investing in offshore wind farms, anticipating being able to produce 70 per cent of the energy needed to meet its 2020 targets by 2017.[57] Companies are also making more energy-efficient products. For example, Philips manufactures energy-efficient consumer products (see Exhibit 3.2).

Another concern of environmentalists is the consumption of wood. Forest depletion by the deforestation activities of companies and the effects of acid rain damage the ecosystem. Consumers' desire for soft and hardwood furniture and window frames is at odds with the need to preserve forests. Trees' leaves absorb carbon dioxide and their roots help to stabilize slopes: a landslide in the Philippines that cost many lives was allegedly caused by illegal logging. A solution is the replanting of forests to maintain the long-term stock of trees. In Brazil major initiatives have largely stopped deforestation of the rain forest. Read Case 6, Made in Amazonia to find out more.

⬆ **EXHIBIT 3.2** **Philips encourages consumers to save by using its energy-efficient products.**

Environmentally friendly ingredients and components

Environmentalists favour the use of biodegradable and natural ingredients and components when practicable, and PETA (People for the Ethical Treatment of Animals) campaigns against cruelty to animals. Companies have responded to the challenge by launching products such as the Estée Lauder Origins skincare and cosmetics range of vegetable-based products containing no animal ingredients. Plastic products and components have been the target of criticism because of their non-biodegradability, but biodegradable polymers are now available. For example, Biopol, developed by ICI, is the first fully biodegradable commercial plastic; its applications include disposable nappies, rubbish bags and other plastic-coated disposable household items.

Concern has also been expressed over the use of genetically modified (GM) ingredients in food products, since the health implications are uncertain. Pressure from consumer groups and the media has forced Monsanto, a pioneer in genetic modification, to stop further development, and persuaded supermarkets to banish such products from their shelves, and countries such as Austria, France, Germany, Greece, Italy and Luxembourg to impose import bans.

Recycling and non-wasteful packaging

Germany took the lead in the recycling of packaging when it introduced the Verpackvo, a law that allows shoppers to return packaging to retailers and retailers to pass it back to suppliers. In response, suppliers promised to assume responsibility for the management of packaging waste. Over 400 companies have created a mechanism called the Dual System Deutschland (DSD). Consumers are asked to return glass bottles and waste paper to recycling bins and are also encouraged to separate other recyclable materials such as plastics, composite packaging and metals, and place them in yellow bags and bins supplied by the DSD. Collection takes place every month and (together with separation of the refuse) is paid for by the DSD and the cost is eventually absorbed by the packaging manufacturers. Recycling is also important in Sweden, where industry has established a special company to organize the collection and sorting of waste for recycling, and in Finland where over 35 per cent of packaging is recycled.

Fast food companies can promote recycling by using recycled paper for burger containers rather than polystyrene, which is non-biodegradable. Not only is cutting out waste in packaging environmentally friendly, it also makes commercial sense. Thus, companies have introduced concentrated detergents and refill packs, and removed the cardboard around some brands of toothpaste, for example. The savings can be substantial: in Germany, Lever GmbH saved 15 per cent of paper, carton and corrugated board; 30 per cent by introducing concentrated detergents; 20 per cent by using lightweight plastic bottles; and the introduction of refills for concentrated liquids reduced the weight of packaging materials by half. Henkel has introduced special 22-gram 'light packs', which are polyethylene bottles that save 270 tons of plastic a year.

Marketing managers need to be aware of the environmental consequences of their decisions and activities, and recognize the danger of environmentally irresponsible actions to the reputation of their companies and brands. Managers should also be alert to the opportunities created by a greater focus on the environment. For example, in the services industry hoteliers are making operational savings by encouraging guests to reuse towels,

Digital Marketing 3.2 Fish Fighters' Campaign Uses Digital to Recruit Supporters

The problem:

Fish could soon be off the menu as stocks of cod, tuna and salmon are being severely depleted and the mackerel, currently the most abundant fish in the sea, could suffer the same fate. Currently, half the fish caught in the North Sea are thrown back—dead—because of quota restrictions. The EU is trying to stop the throwing back of 'out of quota' fish, but this puts emphasis on landing less popular types of fish.

The protagonist:

Hugh Fearnley-Whittingstall is a celebrity chef, writer, television presenter and campaigner. His interest in organic food production has sparked his interest in various projects: most notably the 'Chicken Out!' campaign, which exposed farm animal welfare issues, and also the 'Fish Fighters' campaign.

The campaign:

Hugh's overarching aim was to 'try to change those laws' and was supported by 'a wide coalition of environmental Non-Governmental Organisations (NGOs) and, we hope, by a growing number of fishermen and policy makers too'.

From a communication perspective Hugh wanted to get as many people as possible to sign up to the fish-fighters campaign.

The media:

A three-part television series was used to highlight fish-eating habits in the UK, showing the majority of fish consumed was either cod, tuna or salmon and making viewers aware of how EU fishing quotas lead to many fish being discarded.

A website was built to enable supporters to sign up. Over 700,000 people signed the petition and 43,000 emailed their MEPs in protest about the EU policies over fish discards.

Social media Twitter and Facebook also played a pivotal role in getting signatures. The Twitter pages had over 26,000 followers.

Postscript:

Hugh's campaign is not over despite the EU having agreed in July 2011 to include recommendations for banning fish discards in its new Common Fisheries Policy. But the innovative use of broadcast and digital media used in this campaign means not only has awareness of the cause reached millions of potential supporters, but that it continues to be debated through the website, social media and email.

Based on: Nightingale (2011);[58] *Wikipedia (2012);*[59] *Fish Fight (2012)*[60]

which reduces the laundry bill; key cards, which switch off all the lights when a guest leaves the room; dual flush toilets which use less water.[61] Ultimately, managers should also consider communicating their environmentally conscious credentials. For environmental groups, marketing provides the tools to spread awareness of their campaigns, which can have widespread impact on consumer behaviour as Digital Marketing 3.2 explains.

We shall explore in more detail how marketing should respond to environmental issues in Chapter 6, which deals with understanding marketing ethics and corporate social responsibility.

Social/Cultural Forces

Three key *social/cultural forces* that have implications for marketing are the changes in the demographic profile of the population, cultural differences within and between nations, and the influence of consumerism. Each will now be examined.

Demographic forces

Demographic forces concern changes in populations in terms of their size and characteristics. **Demography** is important to marketers because it helps to predict the size and growth rates of markets, and the need for products such as schools, one-person housing and homes for the elderly. Three major demographic forces are world population growth, the changing age distribution and the changing structure of households in western countries.

World population growth

Overall, the global population is expanding at an increasing rate. However, the rate of growth is uneven across the world. In particular, the population in developed economies is expected to be stable or shrinking, whereas countries of Africa, India, 'other Asia' and Latin America are expected to account for over 90 per cent of the projected population increase during the twenty-first century (see Fig. 3.2).[62] As these countries grow more youthful, the developed countries will play host to an ageing population. In 2025 half the population of Europe will be over 45 years old. For the next decade, the world population is expected to grow by an average of 97 million per year.

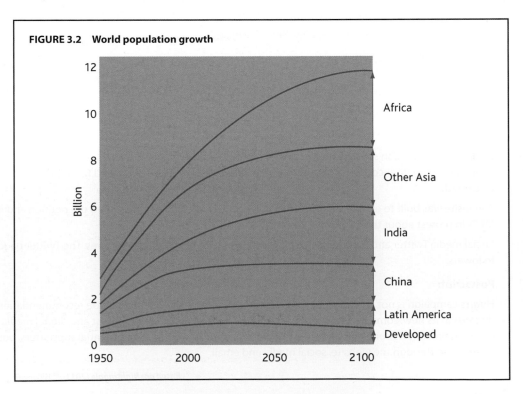

FIGURE 3.2   World population growth

The changing world population distribution suggests that new markets outside the developed economies may provide attractive opportunities, although the extent to which this force progresses will depend on a concomitant rise in income levels in the less developed world. The problem is that the major growth is predicted to be in countries that are already poor. Concern for their well-being is growing among people in the developed world. One response is the social marketing of family planning and birth control. Companies such as Hewlett-Packard and Citibank are increasingly focusing their attention on these so-called 'pre-markets' (i.e. those not yet sufficiently developed to be considered consumer markets). For example, Hewlett-Packard aims to sell, lease or donate a billion dollars worth of computer equipment and services to these under-served markets.[63]

Age distribution

A major demographic change that will continue to affect the demand for products is the rising proportion of people over the age of 45 in the EU, and the decline in the younger age group. The rise in over-45s creates substantial marketing opportunities because of their high level of per capita income. They have higher disposable income and higher levels of savings than younger people, tend to benefit from inheritance wealth, and are healthier than ever before. In France, for example, the average per capita disposable income for households headed by a retired person is now higher than the average for all households, and people over 60 (who constitute 18 per cent of the population) consume more than 22 per cent of the French gross domestic product (GDP).

Another demographic change is the growth in the numbers of retired people in Europe. This is partly because people are living longer but also because of early retirement. For example, although the official UK retirement age is 65 and likely to rise, early retirement schemes and redundancies have meant that a high proportion of people below this age group are, in effect, retired (over 30 per cent of men aged 55–64 have left the labour market early). High disposable income, coupled with increasing leisure time, means that the demand for holidays and recreational activities such as golf, fishing and walking should continue to increase. Also there should be increasing demand for medical products and services, housing designed for elderly couples and singles, and single-portion foods. Understanding the needs of the over-45s presents a huge marketing opportunity, so that products can be created that possess the differential advantages valued by these people. In reality it is likely that there are a number of subgroups according to age band, which will allow market segmentation to be used. The overall implication of these trends is that many consumer companies may need to reposition their product offerings to take account of the rise in 'grey' purchasing power.

Household structure

Changes in household structure and behaviour that have marketing implications are the rise in one-person households, households with no children and the growth in dual-income families.

More people are living alone by choice, through divorce or bereavement. This suggests that a key market segment is people who demand products that meet their particular needs, such as one-bedroom houses or apartments, and single-portion foods. The proportion of couples who have no children has also increased. This may reflect a desire to maintain high standards of living for longer. The implication is an increase in the attractiveness of markets where couples are likely to spend their disposable income, such as restaurant meals, luxury holidays and designer clothing.

Households are also changing behaviour regarding employment. In many European countries there has been a growth in dual-earner families. In the UK, for example, over half of couples with dependent children are double-income families. The rise of two-income households means this market segment possibly has higher disposable income, which can lead to reduced price sensitivity and the capacity to buy luxury furniture and clothing products (e.g. upmarket furniture and clothing) and expensive services (e.g. foreign holidays, restaurant meals).

Cultural forces

Culture is the combination of traditions, taboos, values and attitudes of the society in which an individual lives. A number of distinctive subcultures in the UK provide a rich tapestry of lifestyles and the creation of new markets. The Asian population, for example, has provided restaurants and stores supplying food from that part of the world. This influence is now seen in supermarkets, where Asian foods are readily available. The free movement of workers around the EU has also encouraged the growth of subcultures—for example, the flow of workers from central and eastern Europe to older, established EU countries. To meet the needs of the Polish community in the UK, for example, Tesco now runs a groceries website in the Polish language.[64]

Subcultures can also span national boundaries. For example, the existence of a youth subculture across Europe has allowed brands such as Levi's jeans, Coca-Cola, Pepsi and MTV to be marketed with only modest adaptation to local tastes. Young consumers spend considerable time communicating with others via the Internet. The popularity of social networking sites, e.g. Facebook, Twitter, Google+, means that they can share information, post photographs and download music. These sites provide huge opportunities and challenges for marketers to reach young audiences.

Attitudes towards food among some sections of society in Europe are also changing. Pressures towards healthy eating have prompted moves towards food with less fat, sugar and salt, and towards health labelling. For example, the Nestlé-branded cereal range targeted at children has been reformulated with 10 per cent less sugar. New brands focusing on their healthy credentials have emerged, like Innocent smoothies, and even MacDonald's has a nutrition calculator which enables savvy consumers to check what they are eating.[65] Market segments have appeared, based on the concept of ethical consumption, and leading to demand for fair trade and organic products, together with avoidance of companies and brands that are associated with dubious labour practices. The growth in healthy eating and ethical consumption has prompted the acquisition of small ethical brands by larger corporates: for example, Rachel's organic yogurts by Group Lactilis, a subsidiary of BSA international, and Ben & Jerry's by Unilever.[66]

Successful marketing depends on knowing the cultural differences that exist between European consumers. The German preference for locally brewed beer has proved a major barrier to entry for foreign brewers, such as Guinness, which have attempted to penetrate that market. The slower than expected take-off of the Euro Disney complex near Paris was partly attributed to French consumers' reluctance to accede to the US concept of spending a lot of money on a one-day trip to a single site. Once there, the French person, being an individualist, 'hates being taken by the hand and led around'.[67]

Cultural differences also have implications for business-to-business marketing. Within Europe cultural variations affect the way business should be conducted. Humour in business life is acceptable in the UK, Italy, Greece, the Netherlands and Spain but less commonplace in France and Germany. These facts of business life need to be recognized when interacting with European business customers.

A study by Mole examined business culture in the EU and the USA.[68] Management styles were analysed using two dimensions:

GREEN
&BLACK'S.
The Original Organic
Chocolate

Aspire to be the first

41

⬆ **EXHIBIT 3.3**　**Green & Black's ethical brand is owned by Kraft Food Inc.**

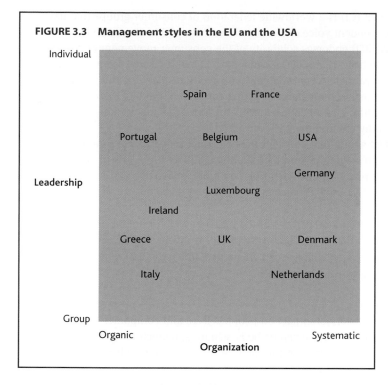

FIGURE 3.3   Management styles in the EU and the USA

type of leadership and organization. Figure 3.3 shows the position of each of the 13 nations according to these two characteristics. Individual leadership (autocratic, directive) is to be found in Spain and France, whereas organic leadership style (democratic, equalitarian) tends to be found in Italy and the Netherlands. Systematic organization (formal, mechanistic) is found in Germany, Denmark and the Netherlands, while organic companies (informal, social) are more likely to exist in Spain, Italy, Portugal and Greece.

On the basis of the Mole survey, Wolfe describes business life in Italy, Spain and the Netherlands.[69] As Figure 3.3 shows, Italian organizations tend to be informal, with democratic leadership. Decisions are taken informally, usually after considerable personal contact and discussion. Italian managers are flexible improvisers who have a temperamental aversion to forecasting and planning. Interpersonal contact with deciders and influencers in the decision-making unit (DMU) is crucial for suppliers. Finding the correct person to talk to is not easy since DMUs tend to be complex, with authority vested in trusted individuals outside the apparent organizational structure. Suppliers must demonstrate commitment to a common purpose with their Italian customers.

In Spain, on the other hand, business is typified by the family firm where the leadership style is autocratic and the organizational system informal. Communications tend to be vertical, with little real teamwork. Important purchasing decisions are likely to be passed to top management for final approval, but good personal relationships with middle management are vital to prevent them blocking approaches.

Leadership in the Netherlands is more democratic, although organizational style tends to be systematic, with rigorous management systems designed to involve multilevel consensus decision-making. Buying is, therefore, characterized by large DMUs and long decision-making processes as members attempt to reach agreement without conflict or one-sided outcomes.

Consumerism

Consumerism takes the form of organized action against business practices that are not in the interests of consumers. Organized action is taken through the consumer movement, which is an organized collection of groups and organizations whose objective is to protect the rights of consumers. Pressure from the consumer movement, environmentalists, individuals who engage in ethical consumption and the media has resulted in many organizations adopting corporate social responsibility as a guide to their business practices. **Corporate social responsibility** (CSR) refers to the ethical principle that an organization should be accountable for how its behaviour might affect society and the environment. The importance of CSR is reflected in the large proportion of Chapter 6 (Understanding Marketing Ethics and Corporate Social Responsibility) that is devoted to coverage of this topic.

The consumer movement has had notable successes, including improvements in car safety, the encouragement of fast-food restaurants to provide healthy-eating options, health labelling of food products, and the banning of smoking in public places in some European countries including Ireland and the UK.

Consumers International (CI) is a worldwide federation of consumer groups that have joined together as an independent voice of the consumer.[70] On 15 March every year, World Consumer Rights Day (WCRD) endorses solidarity of the consumer movement and is an opportunity to promote the basic rights of the consumer. CI tackles issues from around the world. For example, in Kenya there were problems with product safety and inappropriate use of labelling, which could cause serious harm to young consumers; in Asia there is a great deal of marketing of unhealthy food to children; in Latin America CI is working to protect consumers' right to a healthy environment.

Marketing management should not consider the consumer movement a threat to business but rather an opportunity to create new product offerings to meet the needs of emerging market segments. For example, in the detergent market brands have been launched that are more environmentally friendly, while food companies have reduced the fat and salt content of some of their products.

Changes in the social and cultural aspects of the marketing environment need to be monitored and understood so that marketing management is aware of the changing tastes and behaviour of consumers. Such changes can create demand shifts that may act as either opportunities or threats for European companies.

Technological Forces

Technology can have a substantial impact on people's lives and companies' fortunes. Technological breakthroughs have given us body scanners, biotechnology, the Internet, mobile phones, computers and many other products. Many technological breakthroughs change the rules of the competitive game: the launch of the computer and wordprocessing software destroyed the market for typewriters; email largely replaced the fax machine; compact discs decimated the market for records and cassette tapes. Technological change can provide opportunities for new product development, create new markets, change marketing practices and communications, and revolutionize society.

Research and development

Technology investments require sound understanding of the market. Marketing and R&D staff should work closely together to ensure that investments are purposeful and not just for the sake of technology. The classic example of a high-technology initiative driven by technologists rather than by the market is Concorde. Although technologically sophisticated, management knew before launch that it never stood a chance of being commercially viable. By contrast, the development of the Airbus A380, the world's biggest passenger plane, has been market-based, taking into account the need for greater passenger comfort on long-haul flights, pressure to reduce carbon emissions and increasing demand for these flights. By using aircraft like the A380, the predicted increase in passenger demand can be accommodated using the same number of planes.[71]

R&D in new technology can pay handsome dividends and secure market share. ICI, for example, invested heavily in the biotechnology area and became market leader in equipment used for genetic fingerprinting.

Technological investment can deliver high market potential in both existing and new markets. For example, Teflon, a major marketing success in the coating of non-stick frying pans, was first developed as a coating on the nose cone of space rockets. Visco foam, developed by NASA for the space programme to absorb the tremendous forces that astronauts are subjected to during lift-off, has been successfully used to create Visco memory foam beds that adjust to body position, minimizing pressure points and maximizing body support.

A lack of investment in high-potential technological areas can severely affect the fortunes of companies. For example, Sony—once regarded as a leader in high-tech product innovation—lost ground due to its lack of early investment in developing flat-screen television, liquid crystal display allowing Samsung to gain a competitive advantage in flat-screen televisions. Similarly, Apple superseded the Sony Walkman with its iPod, which not only allows high-quality mobile listening but also the downloading of music.

Information and data management

Technology also affects the way in which marketing is conducted. Developments in information technology have revolutionized marketing practices. Information technology describes the broad range of processes and products within the fields of computing and telecommunications. Accessibility of information has been found to be a source of competitive advantage and data warehouses are an important new technology that offers organizations the potential to leverage such advantage from their information resources effectively. Data warehouses facilitate sharing of information and enable information to be accessible at the point of need. Indeed research has found that accessibility of strategic information can facilitate commercial benefits.[72] Using better quality information, managers can make more informed decisions, save time and make a greater contribution to corporate and marketing success.

Information systems and data warehouses are used in many areas of business. Salesforce automation is improving the efficiency of salesforces, and these are described and the implications examined in Chapter 16, on direct communications, personal selling and sales management. Customer relationship management (CRM), founded on data technologies, has enabled companies to improve communications and relationships with customers. Multichannel retailing is underpinned by information and data technology and is discussed in Chapter 17.

Communications

The Internet and mobile phone technology have allowed companies to use new channels of communication and distribution (e.g. music downloads) to reach consumers. New technology speeds up communications and enables multiple interactions using various media. In the multichannel world we communicate and gather information from multiple points—websites, apps, a multitude of television channels, printed publications and perhaps more importantly each other. Digital technologies have completely altered modes of communication but in so doing are eroding the boundaries between the message, the media, the channel and the product. The applications, issues and implications of digital communication technology are covered in detail in Chapters 14, 15, 16 and 18.

Society

Digital technologies are becoming increasingly important in most sectors of economic activity. The Internet has provided the impetus for many companies to rethink the role of technology and it has also had a significant effect on society. For its users, the Internet has not only provided the means to find, buy and sell products, but has also created an environment for building communities, where like-minded people can network, socialize and be entertained. The emergence of social networking sites such as Facebook, LinkedIn, Google+ and microblogging sites like Twitter have had a significant impact on global society. Social media have given a voice to masses of individuals, businesses and communities around the world, and its influence can be powerful. Social media have been used to communicate, organize protests and influence politics and governments. It has also been argued that 'Social media is reshaping human language through the unprecedented mixing of idioms, dialects, and alphabets' and this is bringing into question whether the technology will have long-term effects on the way we speak, write and listen.[73] The importance of such developments for marketing is considered in detail in Chapter 18.

In summary, marketing-led companies seek not only to monitor technological trends but also to pioneer technological breakthroughs that can transform markets and shift competitive advantage in their favour. They also seek to use technology to improve the efficiency and effectiveness of their marketing operations.

The Microenvironment

The **microenvironment** consists of the actors in the firm's immediate environment that affect its capabilities to operate effectively in its chosen markets. Those actors—customers, competitors, distributors and suppliers—will now be introduced and analysed in more depth throughout the book.

Customers

As we saw in Chapter 1, customers are at the centre of the marketing philosophy and effort, and it is the task of marketing management to satisfy their needs and expectations better than the competition. The starting point is an understanding of them and this is considered in Chapter 4 (Understanding Consumer Behaviour) and Chapter 5 (Understanding Organizational Buying Behaviour). The techniques for gathering and analysing customer and other marketing information are discussed in Chapter 7, on marketing research. The grouping of consumers to form market segments that can be targeted with specific marketing mix offerings is the subject of Chapter 8 (Market Segmentation and Positioning).

Changing customer tastes, lifestyles, motivations and expectations need to be monitored so that companies supply the appropriate targeted marketing mix strategies that meet their needs. Changes in consumer behaviour also need to be monitored. For example, consumers are using social network sites like Twitter to communicate—a fact not lost on marketers, as Digital Marketing 3.2 explains. Marketers should also seek out the latest customer needs.

Competition

Competitors have a major bearing on the performance of companies. For example, when competitors price-cut, the attractiveness of the market can fall and their ability to innovate can ruin once highly profitable brands. Marketing history is littered with brands that were once successful (e.g. Olivetti typewriters, Amstrad computers and Lotus software) but are now defunct because rivals developed and marketed better alternatives. No longer is it sufficient to meet customer needs and expectations—success is dependent on doing it better than the competition.

Marketing-orientated companies not only monitor and seek to understand customers but also research competitors and their brands to understand their strengths, weaknesses, strategies and response patterns. In this book, the importance of these issues is reflected in a section being devoted to such analysis and the strategies that can be employed to anticipate and combat competitive moves. These matters are discussed in Chapter 19 (Analysing Competitors and Creating a Competitive Advantage) and Chapter 20 (Competitive Marketing Strategy).

Distributors

Some companies, such as those providing services, dispense with the use of distributors, preferring to deal directly with end-user customers. The others use the services of distributors such as wholesalers and retailers to supply end users. As we shall see in Chapter 17, on distribution, these channel intermediaries perform many valuable services, including breaking bulk, making products available to customers where and when they want them, and providing specialist services such as maintenance and installation.

Distributors can reduce the profitability of suppliers by putting pressure on profit margins. For example, large retailers such as Wal-Mart and Tesco have enormous buying power and can demand low prices from their suppliers, a fact that has been criticized in the media when applied to small farmers.

Distribution trends need to be monitored. For example, the trend towards downloading music has hit traditional music outlets that sell CDs, and the growth of the Internet-based sellers such as Amazon has impacted on traditional bricks-and-mortar booksellers. As the attractiveness of distribution channels changes so suppliers must alter their strategies to keep in touch with customers.

Suppliers

The fortunes of companies are not only dependent on customers, competitors and distributors, they are also influenced by their suppliers. Increases in supply costs can push up prices, making other alternatives more attractive. For example, increases in the price of aluminium make plastic more attractive. Also, as with distributors, powerful suppliers can force up prices. The rise in the price of gas has been blamed on powerful European suppliers who, it is alleged, restricted supply in order to force prices higher.

Companies need to monitor supply availability, such as shortages due to labour strikes or political factors, as these can cause customer dissatisfaction and lost sales. They also need to be sensitive to alternative input materials that can be substituted for those of existing suppliers if the latter's prices rise or availability diminishes significantly.

The importance of suppliers is reflected in discussion of their relationship with customers in Chapter 5, which focuses on organizational buying behaviour. Many customers are increasingly forming partnerships with selected suppliers in order to enhance value delivery.

All the elements of the microenvironment need to be monitored and assessed so that opportunities can be exploited and threats combated. This forms an essential ingredient in maintaining strategic fit between a company and its marketing environment.

Environmental Scanning

The process of monitoring and analysing the marketing environment of a company is called **environmental scanning**. Research[74] has found that formal environmental scanning can deliver potential benefits:

- better general awareness of, and responsiveness to, environmental changes
- better strategic planning and decision-making
- greater effectiveness in dealing with government
- improved industry and market analysis
- better foreign investment and international marketing
- improved resource allocation and diversification decisions
- superior energy planning.

Additionally, environmental scanning provides the essential informational input to create strategic fit between a company's strategies, its organizational operations and the marketing environment (see Fig. 3.4). Marketing strategy should reflect the environment even if this means a fundamental reorganization of operations.

The most appropriate organizational arrangement for scanning will depend on the unique circumstances facing a firm. A judgement needs to be made regarding the costs and benefits of each alternative approach. The size and profitability of the company and the perceived degree of environmental turbulence will be factors that impinge on this decision. Clearly, in theory, every event in the world has the potential to affect a company's operations, but to establish a scanning system that covers every conceivable force would be unmanageable. Consequently, there are two key questions for managers when establishing environmental scanning; 1) what to scan, and 2) how to organize the process. In order to answer these questions and develop an effective scanning system, action should be taken to:

1 *define a feasible range of forces that require monitoring*. These are the *potentially relevant environmental forces* that have the most likelihood of affecting future business

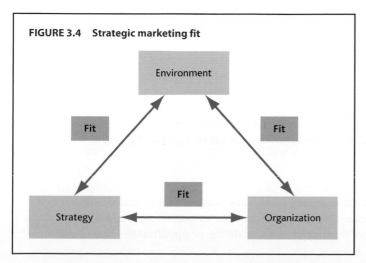

FIGURE 3.4   Strategic marketing fit

prospects. Research[75] suggests that companies should monitor and analyse trends, issues and events which have implications for their company. Ansoff identified that environmental scanning monitors a company's environment for signals of the development of *strategic issues* which have an influence on company performance.[76] For example, Google was slow to respond to the social media phenomenon, which could have been the result of not scanning the right forces. Not only has this allowed Facebook to develop a very powerful member base for its social network, but it is now also a potential threat to one of Google's core revenue streams: online advertising.

2 *design a system that provides a fast response* to events. Some events are only partially predictable, emerge as surprises and grow very rapidly. It is essential for companies to be informed if they are to manage in increasing turbulent marketing environments. Research[77] suggests environmental scanning should enable a company to:

- develop forecasts, scenarios and issues analysis as input to strategic decision-making
- provide a focal point for the interpretation and analysis of environmental information identified by other people in the company
- establish a library or database for environmental information
- provide expertise on environmental affairs
- disseminate information on the business environment through newsletters, reports and lectures
- evaluate and revise the scanning system itself by applying new tools and procedures.

In order to develop such a system for environmental scanning, four approaches are open to the organization:[78]

1 *Line management*: functional managers (e.g. sales, marketing, procurement) can conduct environmental scanning in addition to their existing duties. The problem with this approach is that the scanning can suffer if employees are resistant to taking on additional duties. They may also lack the specialist research and analytical skills required for scanning.

2 *Strategic planner*: in this case environmental scanning is part of the strategic planner's job. The drawback is that a head office planner may not have the depth of understanding of a business unit's operations to be able to do the job effectively.

3 *Separate organizational unit*: sometimes regular and ad hoc scanning is conducted by a separate organizational unit which is then responsible for disseminating relevant information to managers. The advantage with this approach is a dedicated team concentrating its efforts on the scanning task. The disadvantage is that it is very costly and unlikely to be feasible except for large, profitable companies.

4 *Joint line/general management teams*: a temporary planning team consisting of line and general (corporate) management may be set up to identify trends and issues that may have an impact on the business. Alternatively, an environmental trend or issue may have emerged that requires closer scrutiny. A joint team may be set up to study its implications.

The benefits of environmental scanning appear straightforward; better understanding of the trading environment gives a company the knowledge to respond effectively to environmental changes. However, despite potential positive outcomes companies respond differently to environmental change.

Responses to Environmental Change

Companies respond in various ways to environmental change (see Fig. 3.5).

Ignorance

Because of poor environmental scanning, companies may not realize that salient forces are affecting their future prospects. They therefore continue as normal, ignorant of the environmental issues that are threatening their existence, or opportunities that could be seized. No change is made.

Read the Research 3.1 Understanding the Environment

High street booksellers are going through turbulent times. Hit by recession and the ever-growing threat from ebooks, their profitability and status are eroding.

This study investigates the market environment of the UK high street bookselling business with emphasis on Waterstones. The authors carry out a SWOT analysis, and Porter's Five Forces to help Waterstones to reinvent themselves, and offer strategies for consideration on customer service and profitability.

Uzoechi Nwagbara (2011) Waterstones and the Changing Bookselling Environment in the UK: the Journey so far and Prospects,
Economic Science Series, 63(3), 14–26.

Environmental scanning has become a prerequisite for effective strategy formulation. However, is there a link between the length of tenure of a CEO in the industry and the emphasis placed on environmental scanning? The authors look at 90 computer and food-processing companies and the background characteristics of their CEOs to find evidence of any causal links with their adoption of environmental scanning and ultimately the nature of strategic decision-making.

Arifin Angriawan and Michael Abebe (2011) Chief Executive background characteristics and environmental scanning emphasis:
an empirical investigation, Journal of Business Strategies, 28(1).

Go to the website to see how Cobra used its Indian heritage as part of its latest communications campaign.
www.mcgraw-hill.co.uk/textbooks/jobber

Delay

The second response is to delay action once the force is understood. This can be caused by *bureaucratic decision processes* that stifle swift action. The slow response by Swiss watch manufacturers to the introduction of digital watches was thought, in part, to be caused by the bureaucratic nature of their decision-making. *Marketing myopia* can slow response through management being product rather than customer focused. CompuServe, followed by America On-line, created an online market by providing customized content and services as well as Internet Service Providers (ISP) for their subscribers. In the 1990s when Internet access was relatively new, subscribers were prepared to pay to access the Internet through such custom portals. However, both companies failed to respond effectively to technological and market changes and the move to a more commoditized market place. In 2003 CompuServe became a division of AOL, and by 2009 announced it would no longer operate as an ISP. AOL was rated as 'the worst tech product of all time' by *PC World Magazine*.[79]

A third source of delay is *technological myopia*, where a company fails to respond to technological change. An example is Kodak's slow response to the emergence of digital technology in cameras. The fourth reason for delay is *psychological recoil* by managers who see change as a threat and defend the status quo. These are four powerful contributors to inertia.

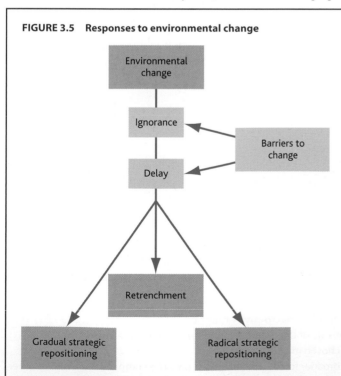

FIGURE 3.5   Responses to environmental change

Retrenchment

This response tackles efficiency problems but ignores effectiveness issues. As sales and profits decline, management cuts costs; this leads to a period of higher profits but does nothing to stem declining sales. Costs (and capacity) are reduced once more but the fundamental strategic problems remain. Retrenchment policies only delay the inevitable.

Gradual strategic repositioning

This involves a gradual, planned and continuous adaptation to the changing marketing environment. Tesco is a company that has continually repositioned itself in response to changing social and economic trends. Originally a supermarket based on a 'pile it high, sell it cheap' philosophy, it maintained its low price positioning while moving to higher-quality products. It has also expanded the range of products it sells (including CDs, electrical goods, financial services and clothing) to provide one-stop shopping, and has expanded into new market segments (Tesco Express convenience stores) and international markets including the Far East, the USA and central and eastern Europe.

Radical strategic repositioning

Radical strategic repositioning involves changing the direction of the entire business. An example is Nokia, which radically repositioned itself from being a conglomerate operating in such industries as paper, chemicals and rubber into a world leader in mobile phones and provider of Internet services through Ovi. Samsung also successfully repositioned itself, transferring from a copy-cat producer of consumer electronics into a technology company marketing mobile phones, flat-screen televisions, and flash memory technology. This is followed by a move away from electronics into energy technology and solar panels.[80] Such radical strategic repositioning is much riskier than gradual strategic repositioning and could have dramatic consequences should such a venture fail.

This chapter has explored a number of major forces occurring in the marketing environment, and has discussed methods of scanning for these and other changes that may fundamentally reshape the fortunes of companies. Failure to respond to a changing environment can lead to business collapse.

Online **LearningCentre**

When you have read this chapter

log on to the Online Learning Centre at **www.mcgraw-hill.co.uk/textbooks/jobber** to explore chapter-by-chapter test questions, links and further online study tools for marketing.

Review

1 **The nature of the marketing environment**
- The marketing environment consists of the microenvironment (customers, competitors, distributors and suppliers) and the macroenvironment (economic, social, political, legal, physical and technological forces). These shape the character of the opportunities and threats facing a company and yet are largely uncontrollable.

2 **The distinction between the microenvironment and the macroenvironment**
- As can be seen above, the microenvironment consists of those actors in the firm's immediate environment that affect its capabilities to operate effectively in its chosen markets.
- The macroenvironment consists of a number of broader forces that affect not only the company but also the other actors in the microenvironment.

3 **The impact of political and legal, economic, ecological/physical environmental, social/cultural and technological forces on marketing decisions**

- Political and legal forces influence marketing decisions by determining the rules for conducting business. In Europe marketing decisions are affected by legislation at EU and national levels. EU laws seek to prevent collusion, prevent abuse of market dominance, control mergers and acquisitions, and restrict state aid to firms. National laws also affect marketing decisions by regulating anti-competitive practices.
- Economic forces can impact marketing decisions through their effect on supply and demand. Key factors are economic growth, unemployment, interest and exchange rates and changes in the global economic environment such as growth of the EU and the eurozone and the rise of the BRIC economies. Marketers need to have contingency plans in place to cope with economic turbulence and downturns, and to be aware of the opportunities and threats arising from changes in the global marketing environment.
- Ecological/physical environmental forces are concerned with the environmental costs of consumption. Five issues that impact marketing decisions are combating global warming, pollution control, conservation of energy and other scarce resources, use of environmentally friendly ingredients and components, and the use of recyclable and non-wasteful packaging. Marketers need to be aware of the environmental consequences of their actions, and the opportunities and threats associated with ecological issues.
- Social/cultural forces can have an impact on marketing decisions by changing demand patterns (e.g. the growth of the over-50s market) and creating new opportunities and threats. Three major influences are changes in the demographic profile of the population, cultural differences within and between nations, and the impact of consumerism.
- Technological forces can impact marketing decisions by changing the rules of the competitive game. Technological change can provide major opportunities and also pose enormous threats to companies. Marketers need to monitor technological trends and pioneer technological breakthroughs.

4 **How to conduct environmental scanning**

- Two key decisions are what to scan and how to organize the activity.
- Four approaches to the organization of environmental scanning are to use line management, the strategic planner, a separate organizational unit and joint line/general management teams.
- The system should monitor trends, develop forecasts, interpret and analyse internally produced information, establish a database, provide environmental experts, disseminate information, and evaluate and revise the system.

5 **How companies respond to environmental change**

- Response comes in five forms: ignorance, delay, retrenchment, gradual strategic repositioning and radical strategic repositioning.

Key Terms

consumerism organized action against business practices that are not in the interests of consumers

corporate social responsibility the ethical principle that an organization should be accountable for how its behaviour might affect society and the environment

culture the combination of traditions, taboos, values and attitudes of the society in which an individual lives

demography changes in the population in terms of its size and characteristics

ecology the study of living things within their environment

environmental scanning the process of monitoring and analysing the marketing environment of a company

macroenvironment a number of broader forces that affect not only the company but also the other actors in the microenvironment

marketing environment the actors and forces that affect a company's capability to operate effectively in providing products and services to its customers

microenvironment the actors in the firm's marketing environment: customers, suppliers, distributors and competitors

PEEST analysis the analysis of the political/legal, economic, ecological/physical, social/cultural and technological environments

Study Questions

1 Choose an organization (if you are in paid employment use your own organization) and identify the major forces in the environment that are likely to affect its prospects in the next five to 10 years.

2 What are the major ecological/physical environmental forces acting on marketing? What are their implications for marketing management?

3 What are the major opportunities and threats to EU businesses arising from the move to market-driven economies of former eastern bloc countries?

4 Generate two lists of products and services. The first list will identify those products and services that are likely to be associated with falling demand as a result of changes in the age structure in Europe. The second list will consist of those that are likely to see an increase in demand. What are the marketing implications for their providers?

5 How does technological change affect marketing? What should marketing management do to take account of technological forces?

6 Evaluate the marketing opportunities and threats posed by the growing importance of the socially conscious consumer.

References

1. Royal Bank of Scotland Plc (2012) http://uk.finance.yahoo.com/q/bc?s=RBS.L&t=my.
2. *The Economist* (2011) Unrest in peace: protestors in the West have roots beyond austerity, http://www.economist.com/node/21533365, October, 94 (accessed January 2012).
3. Alesina, A. and R. Perotti (1966) Income distribution, political instability, and investment, *European Economic Review* 109, 465–89.
4. European Commission (2011) Antitrust: Commission fines producers of CRT glass €128 million in fourth cartel settlement, http://europa.eu/rapid/pressReleasesAction.do?reference=IP/11/1214&format=HTML&aged=0&language=EN&guiLanguage=en (accessed January 2012).
5. Milmo, D. (2008) British Airways executives charged over price-fixing scandal, *Guardian*, 7 August, 26.
6. Tait, N. and P. Hollinger (2008) Record EU Fine for Glass Cartel, *Financial Times*, 13 November, 27.
7. Mercado, S., R. Welford and K. Prescott (2001) *European Business: An Issue-Based Approach*, Harlow: FT Pearson.
8. Helmore, E. (2004) Do Not Pass Go Says EC, *Observer*, 28 March, 3.
9. Tait, N. and K. Allison (2008) Brussels Hits Microsoft with €899m Antitrust Fine, *Financial Times*, 28 February, 27.
10. http://www.thisislondon.co.uk/standard-business/article-23828536-airlines-given-hope-for-state-aid-over-volcanic-ash-crisis.do, *Evening Standard*, 27 April 2012.
11. European Commission investigating collusion among ebook sellers, Apple's involvement, Vlad Savov, 6 December 2011, http://www.theverge.com/2011/12/6/2614954/european-commission-antitrust-investigation-ebooks (accessed January 2012).
12. Ritson, M. (2002) Companies Walk a Tightrope as EU Free Trade Law Begins to Bite, *Marketing*, 7 November, 16.
13. Buck, T. (2005) EU Targets Cartels in Antitrust Overhaul, *Financial Times*, 21 December, 1.
14. Murphy, M. and P. K. Yuk (2008) Record Fine Over Price Fixes, *Financial Times*, 13 July, 1.
15. IMF: Without Action, Debt Crisis May Force 4% Euro-Area Contraction, *Wall Street Journal*, 12 January 2012, http://online.wsj.com/article/BT-CO-20120124-709079.html.
16. Costa, M. (2011) Heading East? *Marketing Week*, 7 April, 16–20.
17. LG Electronics Inc: http://www.lg.com/us/download/pressrelease/700339858050412PolandDTV.pdf (accessed January 2012).
18. *The Economist* (2011) Who killed the euro zone? 28 November, http://www.economist.com/blogs/freeexchange/2011/11/euro-crisis-21 (accessed January 2012).
19. European Commission Eurostat (2012) http://epp.eurostat.ec.europa.eu
20. *The Economist* (2012) France goes soft-core, 14 January, http://www.economist.com/blogs/freeexchange/2012/01/euro-zone-crisis (accessed January 2012).
21. Economist Intelligence Unit (2011) World economy: EIU forecast—Downgrading the euro zone and the US, 20 October, http://performance.ey.com/wp-content/uploads/downloads/2011/11/World-economy-EIU-forecast-downgrading-the-euro-zone-and-the-US.pdf (accessed January 2012).
22. Costa (2011) op. cit.
23. India Sustainability report (2011) http://www.imf.org/external/np/country/2011/mapindia.pdf.
24. Wood, Z. (2011) P&G boss who made a difference for China's dandruff-afflicted, *Guardian*, 4 March, 31.
25. *The Marketer* (2011) Target China, July/August, 32–4.
26. Chaffey, D. and F.E. Ellis-Chadwick (2012) *Digital Marketing: Strategy, Implementation and Practice*, 5th edn, Harlow: Pearson.
27. *The Economist* (2011) E-commerce from China: The great leap online, 26 November, 81.
28. Muller, R. (2011) Target: China, *The Marketer*, 32–34.
29. *The Economist* (2011) Happy Customers, no profits, 18 June, 71.

30. *The Economist* (2011) Send for the supermarkets, 16 April, 69–70.
31. McGregor, R. (2005) China's Companies Count Down to Lift-off, *Financial Times*, 30 August, 9.
32. *The Economist* (2011) The magical mystery tour, 26 November, 82.
33. *The Economist* (2011) The price of graft, 26 March, 78–9.
34. Engardio, P. (2005) Crouching Tigers, Hidden Dragons, *Business Week*, 22/29 August, 40–1.
35. *The Economist* (2011) Taxing times ahead, 29 October, 73.
36. The World Facts Book (2012) Russia, https://www.cia.gov/library/publications/the-world-factbook/geos/rs.html (accessed Jan 2012).
37. Connon, H. (2008) Brazil and Russia: Giants of a New Economic World Order, *Observer*, 25 August, 6–7.
38. Ericsson (2010) China Mobile selects Ericsson managed services, http://www.ericsson.com.news/1432272 (accessed February 2012).
39. McGregor, J. (2005) How China Learned to Love Capitalism, *Observer*, 6 November, 4.
40. Roberts, D. and D. Rocks (2005) Let a Thousand Brands Bloom, *Business Week*, 17 October, 58–60.
41. Singh, S. (2005) Western Brands Vie to Fulfil Eastern Promise, *Marketing Week*, 21 April, 24–6.
42. Anderlini, J. and J. Reed (2008) Chrysler Ends Small Car Deal with Cherry, *Financial Times*, 10 December, 23.
43. Bulkley, K. (2008) Partnerships are key, *Media Guardian*, 29 September, 1.
44. Ibison, D. (2008) Ericsson Clinches Deals With China Duo, *Financial Times*, 15 April, 24.
45. Wiggins, J. (2008) Multinationals Eat into the Russian Market, *Financial Times*, 18 June, 22.
46. Hoyos, C., E. Crooks and C. Belton (2008) Strained Relations Thaw over TNK-BP, *Financial Times*, 5 September, 19.
47. Connon (2008) op. cit.
48. Macalister, T. (2006) BP to Make Biggest Profit in UK History, *Guardian*, 12 January, 26.
49. Lynas, M. (2008) *Six Degrees: Our Future on a Hotter Planet*, London: Harper Collins.
50. UNFCCC (2012) Background on the UNFCCC http://unfccc.int/essential_background/items/6031.php.
51. UNFCCC (2012) op. cit.
52. Gigaton Awards, http://www.gigaton-awards.com/about/ (accessed February 2012).
53. http://www.fastcompany.com/1736964/why-it-matters-that-three-million-toyota-priuss-have-been-sold (accessed January 2012).
54. Barnett, M. (2011) Driving home the benefits of greener wheels, *Marketing Week*, 7 April, 23–26. The 10 key cars from Frankfurt, http://www.parkers.co.uk/cars/advice/news/2011/september/the-10-most-important-cars-from-frankfurt/.
55. Greenpeace, http://www.greenpeace.org/international/en/campaigns/oceans/pollution/trash-vortex/ (accessed January 2012).
56. http://www.environmental-protection.org.uk/transport/car-pollution/.
57. Department of Energy and Climate Change (2011) Clegg and Huhne set out government commitment to renewables, http://www.decc.gov.uk/en/content/cms/news/pn11_85/pn11_85.aspx, 20 October.
58. Nightingale, J. (2011) Biteback, *Dive*, August, 15.
59. Wikipedia (2012), http://en.wikipedia.org/wiki/Hugh_Fearnley-Whittingstall.
60. Fish fighters (2011) About Hugh's Fish Fight, http://www.fishfight.net/the-campaign/.
61. hotel-industry.co.uk (2011) Green Technology for hoteliers, http://www.hotel-industry.co.uk/2011/09/green-technology-for-hoteliers/.
62. Brown, P. (1992) Rise of Women Key to Population Curb, *Guardian*, 30 April, 8.
63. James, D. (2001) B2-4B Spells Profits, *Marketing News*, 5 November, 13.
64. *The Economist* (2008) Poles Apart, 30 August, 33–4.
65. http://www.mcdonalds.ca/ca/en/food/nutrition_calculator.html#.
66. *Which ? Magazine* (2011) Food & drink brands unwrapped, February, 28–31.
67. *Financial Times* (1992) Queuing for Flawed Fantasy, 13/14 June, 5.
68. Mole, J. (1990) *Mind Your Manners*, London: Industrial Society.
69. Wolfe, A. (1991) The 'Eurobuyer', How European Businesses Buy, *Market Intelligence and Planning* 9(5), 9–15.
70. Consumers International (2012) Who we are, http://www.consumersinternational.org/who-we-are.
71. Edemariam, A. (2006) Wings of Desire, *Guardian*, 23 February, 6–17.
72. Doherty, N. F. and G. Doig (2011) The role of enhanced information accessibility in realizing the benefits from data warehousing investments, *Journal of Organisational Transformation and Social Change* 8(2), 163–82.
73. Schillinger, R (2011) *Huff Post: The Blog* Social Media and the Arab Spring: What Have We Learned? http://www.huffingtonpost.com/raymond-schillinger/arab-spring-social-media_b_970165.html 2 September.
74. Dieffenbach, J. (1983) Corporate Environmental Analysis in Large US Corporations, *Long-Range Planning* 16(3), 107–16.
75. Brownlie, D. (2002) Environmental Analysis, in Baker, M. J. (ed.) *The Marketing Book*, Oxford: Butterworth-Heinemann.
76. Ansoff, H. I. (1991) *Implementing Strategic Management*, Englewood Cliffs, NJ: Prentice-Hall.
77. Brownlie (2002) op. cit.
78. Brownlie (2002) op. cit.
79. Tynan, D. (2006) The worst tech products of all time, *PCWorld* magazine, 26 May.
80. *The Economist* (2011) The next big bet, 1 October, 73–5.

Saving Sony

The Demise of an Industrial Giant

All is not well in the Sony dynasty. The company's performance in recent years has been less than stellar for this once global brand icon. The Sony brand (www.sony.com) was once a byword for innovation, being a company known for firsts. In 2011 Sony had a traumatic year: the devastating Japanese tsunami, a strong Japanese Yen currency, computer hackers stealing customers' personal information on its online gaming network, and spiralling losses. The company has failed to tap into new opportunities, and been criticized for being complacent and over-reliant on past successes. Its pioneering electronics division is struggling, with sales plummeting. Aggressive competitors are stealing market share in key markets where once it dominated. Now the company is being criticized for its lack of focus, and for failing to avail itself of strategic windows of opportunity that its competitors have rapidly exploited. The biggest surprise is that Sony, although earning huge revenues from the variety of industries in which it operates, still lost $6.7 billion in 2011. So, what is happening at Sony? Faced with intensification of price competition, a strong currency and the global economic slowdown, it is fighting for its very survival.

Following the ravages of the Second World War, Akito Morita and Masaru Ibuka joined together to form a small electronics firm that would become a global colossus. In the ramshackle remains of a bombed-out department store in Tokyo the pair started to make radio components and repair radios. Morita was the consummate salesman, while Ibuka was a technical expert, forming a perfect partnership. Both guided the firm for over 50 years. One of the company's first engineering forays was an electric rice cooker and electrically heated seat cushions. In the early years the company set upon an innovation focus, always looking for potentially lucrative markets, and exploiting new technology. The founders would frequently visit other countries with a view to exploiting new opportunities. Ibuka visited the USA in 1952, and brought back the idea of exploiting new transistor technology and developing radios. This became the launch pad for Sony's early success, when people bought hundreds of thousands of transistor radios to listen to the new rock 'n' roll. The company went from strength to strength through a combination of leading-edge technology products and miniaturization. Sony became the embodiment of postwar Japanese industry: entrepreneurial, creative, pioneering and highly successful.

The company was always at the forefront of technology, entering untested new markets, and creating one hit product after another.

TABLE C5.1   Sony at a glance

Headquarters based in Tokyo, Japan
Employs over 168,200 people worldwide
Annual sales exceed over $78 billion dollars. Revenue was down 12.9%
Loses 540 billion Yen or $6.7 billion in 2011 financial year
Makes $2.5 billion in profit from music, film and financial services
Pioneers of groundbreaking technology such as the 'Walkman', 'Playstation', transistor radios, tape recorders, video recorders, CD players and video cameras
Owns second largest music company in the world
Large investment in the motion picture and television industry, with Sony Pictures

From these humble origins Sony has now become a highly respected global brand name, manufacturing audio, video, communications and information technology products for both consumer and industrial markets worldwide. The Sony brand has developed into a well-respected and sought-after

TABLE C5.2   The major divisions of Sony

Name	Details
Sony Electronics	Manufactures a wide variety of electronic products for both consumer and industrial markets. Products include DVD players, LCD/LED screens, digital audio players, semiconductors, camcorders, notebook computers and a variety of other electronic products. TV business has lost money for eight straight years.
Sony Computer Entertainment	Markets the Sony Playstation family of products and produces gaming content for these devices. Over 60 million Playstation 3 have been sold.
Sony DADC	Manufactures media storage discs such as CD, DVD, Blu-Ray and Universal Media Discs.
Sony Mobile (Formerly Sony- Ericcson)	Formerly a 50:50 joint venture with Swedish firm Ericsson, focused on the mobile telephony industry. Joint venture established in October 2001, ended in 2012. The division develops innovative mobile phones integrating camera, digital audio and gaming technology. Sony paid €1 billion cash to buy out Ericsson from the venture.
Sony Pictures	Produces and distributes motion pictures and television programmes worldwide. Films include the Spiderman series, Skyfall (James Bond Series), and Men in Black series. Television shows include a variety of game shows, soap operas, comedies and drama. Owns several studios including Columbia, Tristar and Screen Gems. Also owns a variety of television stations. The company recently bought MGM studios through a consortium bid, strengthening its position in the movie business. The MGM film library has over 4000 films.
Sony Music Entertainment	Second largest music publisher in the world. A music colossus owning several music labels in a variety of genres. Artists on roster include Adele, Beyonce, Jennifer Lopez, One Direction, Bruce Springsteen, Olly Murs and Rod Stewart. Owns huge back catalogue of master works including Elvis Presley, Johnny Cash and Louis Armstrong.
Sony/ATV Music Publishing	Joint venture with estate of the late Michael Jackson, which owns a treasure trove of a music back catalogue including music from the Beatles, Bob Dylan and Jimi Hendrix. The firm owns and administers the copyright of these songs.

brand, instantly recognizable the world over. Its products have the reputation of being highly innovative, extremely reliable, and possessing high-quality standards. The company has evolved to become more than just an electronics business. There are several key divisions within the group (see Table C5.2).

One of the biggest hopes was Sony mobile devices. However, these have failed as yet to capture the product allure of its rival Apple with its iPhone success. Their hopes lie in their range of phones equipped with high-end camera capabilities and Walkman-branded capabilities, turning the mobile phones into portable digital music devices. It is hoped that these devices will be the future 'iPod Killer', and help Sony regain the portable music market which it once dominated. Similarly, it missed the boat when Apple successfully launched the iPad tablet device, which created a burgeoning category of its own. It now is seen as a follower within the technology sector. It needs to be seen as creating category-defining products.

The company has initiated a raft of changes to turn around its performance, including radical cost-saving initiatives to stop the haemorrhaging losses, but with little success. One of the biggest areas of concern for Sony is its electronics business, which is the cornerstone of the business. At present the firm is over-reliant on the success of the Playstation games console business, involved in intense price competition and experiencing ever-tightening price margins. Prices have deflated by 30 per cent in some cases, and it is losing ground to competitors. Mobile games sales are burgeoning through sales on mobile phone devices. The company's sales of Cybershot digital cameras, Vaio laptops, Handycam camcorders are seeing decreased demand. The company is still yearning for a blockbuster product that will revitalize the company. Its Bravia television screens are finding it difficult to compete against low-priced competitors. Its iconic status as the world's leading electronics brand is losing its lustre; other firms have taken the lead, such as its Korean archrival Samsung and the rejuvenated Apple. It has tried to take the lead in new platforms like e-readers only to be surprisingly trounced by Amazon.com with its Kindle device, thanks to wireless connectivity and abundance of content, while Apple's iPhone and iPad devices are dominating the smartphone and tablet computing categories.

Some blame Sony's current problems on its past successes, making it complacent in the face of the

TABLE C5.3   Sony milestones

1946	Founded by Masaru Ibuka and Akito Morita in post-war Tokyo, using a bombed-out department store and employing 20 people. Called the company Tokyo Tsuchin Kogyo KK (Tokyo Telecommunications Engineering Corporation).
1954	Produces Japan's first transistor radio
1958	Name changed to Sony (derived from *sonus*, Latin for 'sound')
1962	Releases the world's smallest transistor television
1968	Manufactures Trinitron colour television
1971	Sells the first videocassette recorder
1975	Launches the ill-fated Betamax home video recorder, loses format war to VHS standard
1979	Launches the Sony Walkman, the personal portable stereo that becomes a worldwide phenomenon
1983	Releases the first consumer camcorder
1988	Launches American acquisitions phase and diversifies by buying CBS Records
1989	Acquires Columbia Pictures, which now forms Sony Pictures
1995	Enters the games console market with the first Sony Playstation
1999	Founder Akito Morita dies, aged 78
2000	Playstation 2 launched
2001	Sony Ericsson venture launched
2004	Sony BMG Music Entertainment launched after successful merger
2005	Launches the Playstation Portable, the PSP
2005	Welshman Sir Howard Stringer appointed as chairman and CEO of Sony
2006	Launches the Playstation 3. Forecasts a 10-year lifecycle for its latest console
2007	Cancels Sony Connect, music distribution platform
2008	Announces a ¥95 billion (£590 million) loss
2009	Demoes the motion-sensitive Sony Playstation Move for the Playstation 3
2011	Japanese tsunami and flooding in Thailand disrupt supply chain
2012	New Japanese CEO Kazuo Hirai takes the reins
2012	Launches Playstation Vita (portable handheld gaming device)

changing needs of the market. The company is facing intense competition from several key competitors in the several diverse markets in which it operates. In televisions, where it was once so dominant, it has lost the impetus by failing to provide a viable LCD screen and plasma screen offering. Competitors like Samsung devoured the market, while Sony continued to focus on the traditional bulky televisions. Sony completely missed the market. In the mid-1990s it decided to stay out of the LCD market because it felt that the technology was simply not good enough. It failed to invest in LCD manufacturing capabilities. In trying to catch up with the market, Sony had to buy in LCD screen technology from competitors, as it didn't have the expertise or production capacity when the market's demand for flat screen televisions took off. Losing market leadership in the television sector could have very serious consequences for the Sony brand and sales of other products. Typically a television in the home was the centrepiece, to which other electronics peripherals would be attached, such as camcorders and DVD players. Consumers bought devices that worked well with their television. Having a Sony-branded television had a knock-on effect for the sales of other peripherals. Now Sony is losing market share against aggressive Korean competition from LG and Samsung, coupled with the emergence of manufacturers from China and Taiwan. Its television business has lost money for eight straight years. Should it pull out?

In other markets they are feeling the pressure of intense competition on multiple fronts. Competitors are offering very good-quality technology products, at competitive price points. Apple iPods have become this generation's new Walkman. While Apple pioneered the market, Sony was more concerned with piracy and copyright issues associated with the digital music revolution. It was reluctant to manufacture devices that could impinge on its music business. The company has ultimately failed to rekindle the Walkman brand as a digital music device. It is fighting Dell, Acer, Asus, Toshiba and HP in its mobile computing business. Nikon and Canon have retaken their lead in the digital photography market. It faces strenuous competition in the games console market against Microsoft X-Box 360 and their online gaming platform Microsoft Live. Samsung and now Apple dominate the mobile telephone market. Traditionally Sony was regarded as a premium brand because of its reputation for quality, higher specifications, reliability and innovation. This strong reputation enabled it to charge consumers premium prices. Consumers are now being enticed by the competition's high quality and competitive pricing, leaving Sony unable to justify its higher prices. Sony needs to develop 'must have' consumer electronics gadgets that consumers want. The company is now focusing intensively on several 'champion products' including Playstation 3, PSP (Playstation Portable), Walkman, OLED and Bravia LCD televisions. However, these champion products aren't beating their competitors.

The company has diversified widely from being solely an electronics firm. The purchase of Columbia Pictures cost Sony $3.4 billion in 1989, and it purchased CBS Records for $2 billion, which were both bold moves for an electronics company. This was during the heady times of the Japanese bubble economy. Sony felt it wanted to create a global entertainment empire combining technology with the best entertainment content. The acquisition of CBS Records and Columbia Pictures garnered a mixed reception from industry commentators, with many casting doubt on the rationale of a technology firm, which specialized in gadgets, knowing anything about the entertainment industry. The company decided to diversify into entertainment in the hope that synergies could emerge between both the hardware and software aspects of the business. Sony now has the opportunity to set the standard, and provide content which works on its devices. Convergence is seen as the 'Holy Grail'; however, the vision and successful integration of both Sony's hardware and entertainment division remain elusive. The entertainment divisions are providing a substantial contribution to the business. However, critics of the strategy see it as sidetracking the business, and losing focus on its central business—electronics. Also, success can be fickle in these sectors, dependent on notoriously unreliable blockbuster movies,

and a new record superstar to emerge. Furthermore, digital piracy is a huge concern.

In the music arena the industry is consolidating even further. The Sony Music Entertainment division has an impressive roster of talent and is now the second largest music label behind Universal Music Group. The strategy of owning the content and the technology has yet to reap its full potential. Some question the logic behind the strategy, citing that Apple's success in becoming the dominant player in the digital music landscape was not due to it owning a record label. Some commentators view the entertainment division as an unnecessary distraction for Sony, and consider that it curtailed the development of digital technology because it was too concerned with the effects of piracy and the copyright of its entertainment division. Other rival electronics firms have no such qualms, trying to placate their entertainment divisions, and developing hit products quickly. The music business itself is facing enormous challenges as sales are falling, and most revenue is generated through touring rather than sales of albums.

One of the main challenges facing Sony is leveraging the content that they own through their entertainment ventures with their hardware technology. Sony had to abandon its Sony Connect initiative as an alternative music distribution channel similar to iTunes. This was due to a lack of popularity in comparison to rivals. The market wanted content that was 'DRM free', where consumers could transfer content with ease to multiple devices. Innovation within Sony remains the core challenge. For the company to maintain its product leadership status, and command price premium—developing products that are cutting edge, and that the market wants—is pivotal to its future. The company is investing heavily in Organic Light Emitting Diode (OLED) technology which it hopes will set standards in high-definition, flat-screen technology. One big hope for Sony is the medical industry, where the company hopes to leverage its technology in the areas of diagnostic and surgical equipment. Furthermore, it is abandoning pet R&D projects, like robotic dogs.

Back in the early 1980s, Sony lost a bitter technology standard war, which damaged the brand and left thousands of disgruntled Sony customers. Sony backed the losing video-recording technology called Betamax. Betamax was indeed a superior product; however, the mass market chose a rival format called VHS, which became the industry standard for all videotapes. Now Sony has won the latest format war, with its Blu-ray format winning the war to be the next generation of DVD. Blu-ray boasts greater storage capacities, can record, possesses anti-piracy technology and has the ability to deal with high-definition broadcasts. Sony beat its Japanese rival Toshiba who with their partners were backing HD-DVD, an alternative format. Sony won thanks to the support of all of the major movie studios. However, this may be a pyrrhic victory as digital downloads surge in popularity with consumers downloading content through their broadband connection, rather than using disc storage.

A major element of its business is the Playstation suite of products. The games industry is very cyclical with new consoles fighting for market dominance. Sales of the games console have been less than stellar due to strong competition from Microsoft and Nintendo. Although Playstation 3 was the most technologically sophisticated, their rivals exploited different gaps in the market to enormous success. The Nintendo Wii with its fun, innovative gameplay—with less graphical finesse, but addictive gameplay—became a runaway surprise success. Furthermore, the Xbox 360 continues to thrive thanks to a strong games portfolio and online gaming capability (with over 50 million units sold and 30 million active online subscribers to Microsoft Live). In addition, the company faces strong competition from Nintendo and Apple in the handheld gaming market. The future of gaming relies on immersive games like the Grand Theft Auto series, addictive gameplay, games that cater for divergent markets (e.g. Nintendo sells 54 per cent of its DS consoles to females), and motion sensitive technology (where physical movement is captured on screen in gaming environments). The biggest threat to the category is the emergence of smartphones and tablet devices as a gaming platform. The portable gaming market is worth $25 billion.

After several years in charge, the Sony president Sir Howard Stringer has stepped down. The Welsh-born US citizen and former television producer who spoke little or no Japanese had the onerous task of turning around the fortunes at Sony. He tried to transform the core business. Sony was seen by many as top-heavy in terms of top management, too bureaucratic, and with not enough cohesion between divisions. The firm has undertaken several initiatives to turn around the business. These initiatives have focused on cutting costs, removing layers of management, greater coordination of expenditure on research and development, streamlining the business, and consolidating important business activities such as warehousing and information technology. The Sony chief bemoaned the fact that Apple has a higher market value based on a small handful of products, whereas Sony has thousands. His turnaround

efforts failed to quell the problems at Sony. In 2012 a Japanese Sony insider, Kazuo Hirai, took over the reins. He is deploying a five-pronged strategy of: focus on core business; leveraging the games business; concentration on burgeoning developing countries; more of an innovation focus; and optimizing resources across divisions.

It is not all doom and gloom in the Sony camp, its entertainment division is doing well, and the brand still enjoys massive retailer support. Sony has adopted a new tagline for its business using the 'make.believe' slogan. Sony's brand status is being eroded by strong competition, with competitors such as Samsung, LG and HTC investing in high-profile global sponsorships and brand advertising. However, the Sony brand is not as strong as it once was within the electronics sector. Sony may be tempted to sell off non-core activities, but ironically these businesses are contributing a healthy profit to the business.

The company under a new management initiative wants greater cross-company collaboration, removing the silos that developed within the company and hindered the cross-fertilization of ideas, inhibiting growth and innovation. The new CEO has a number of challenges facing him at the helm of Sony. He has to stem the losses in Sony's electronics business, make a greater profit, improve the coordination between Sony's disparate divisions, renew the focus on research and development, and figure out where Sony is headed in the next five years.

Questions

1. Discuss the importance of product innovation to the future success of Sony, in regard to the changing marketing environment.

2. Conduct a SWOT analysis on Sony.

3. What are the strategic options available to Sony? Furthermore, recommend a course of action for Sony, giving reasons for your answer.

This case was written by Conor Carroll, Lecturer in Marketing, University of Limerick. Copyright © Conor Carroll (2012). The material in the case has been drawn from a variety of published sources.

CASE 6
Made in Amazonia

The Amazon rainforest is known as *Amazonia*. The forest produces around a fifth of the world's oxygen as the lush vegetation constantly recycles carbon dioxide. However, many years of deforestation has led to over 20 per cent of this valuable world resource being destroyed to make way for intensive farming. The case explores how Brazil is responding to macroenvironmental forces and changing its approach to using its natural resources.

Brazil is known for producing beef products, from canned corned beef to leather for shoes. However, according to Greenpeace campaigners, beef farming is a main cause of the destruction of the Amazon rainforest and there have been various incidents relating to the care and treatment of the beef cattle and related products which have led to large recalls of such products. Brazilian cattle ranchers cut down swathes of forest to create large grazing lands for their cattle. The herds are frequently moved to new grazing lands as the soil becomes exhausted and unable to sustain future grazing lands. For decades much of the produce from these farms has ended up in Europe.

Now, however, manufacturers, retailers and consumers are more aware of the issues associated with the environmental impact of deforestation and destruction of the equatorial rainforest and have begun to make demands which have far-reaching implications for Brazilian producers. For example, Clarks, Timberland, Adidas and Nike have demanded that leather suppliers from Brazil cease destruction of the rainforest. Leather for shoe production has to be supplied from farms that are not involved in illegal deforestation. In 2012 Tesco customers in the UK were made aware that potentially they were contributing to this problem as meat from JBS, a large Brazilian meat supplier, did not conform to ethical standards and policies. Tesco responded by terminating contracts with JBS. Tesco has been changing its sourcing policies to ensure that they comply with sustainability and also address ethical and environmental concerns. Many other European retailers and manufacturers are also taking this approach.

Green politics

Carlos Minc, Brazil's environment minister, is only too aware of the issues caused by deforestation and illegal farming practices. However, he saw pressure from consumers, retailers and manufacturers as very positive as this is giving

the government the legitimacy it needs to crack down on environmental criminals, illegal farming practices and deforestation.

Moves to protect the environment stem for the Rio Earth Summit in 1992, which introduced the idea of sustainable development and sparked action from the government and non-governmental organizations (NGOs). This was a ground-breaking event, and nearly all the world's leaders signed up to two treaties on climate change and protecting biodiversity. However, two decades later positive moves to protect the environment have been overshadowed by raging consumption. Carbon dioxide emissions are up by 40 per cent and human consumption of natural resources has doubled in the past 20 years. Moreover, the Rio+20 Earth Summit in 2012 is said to have produced 'a largely meaningless document that failed to address the daunting environment challenges the world faces'.[1] Interest from politicians appears diluted compared to the commitment seen at the 1992 summit, and many of the proposed agreements and changes to international laws were not agreed. Director of the UN Environmental Programme Achim Steiner is quoted as saying 'a world at a loss what to do'. On a more positive note—even though in his view it is not possible to legislate for sustainable development—he suggested that 'underneath that failure there is an extraordinary array of activity and innovation' which might put the world on a greener path.

▶ A green economy?

Ilha das Cinzas is an isolated part of the rainforest which is half a day's boat ride from Macapa. The indigenous peoples of this region have been driven to move to an area where a hydroelectric dam is being built. Despite the disruption, the people who live here are 'in tune' with the environment. Their houses are sustainably built from local materials, their water is filtered and recycled and their economic activity contributes to the green agenda. Rio 1992 helped these people, as NGOs and the government helped improve their farming and fishing practices to make them more efficient and economically sustainable. Slight changes to the way prawns were caught improved yields and freed up villagers' time so they could gather acai berries and harvest timber. An upturn in demand for the berries from surfers at Malibu and Ipanema helped double the villagers' monthly income.

Another example of sustainable green economic activities is the Natex condom factory. Sebastiao Mendes comes from a long line of rubber tappers. For generations his family has relied on the Amazon forest for their livelihood. In the 1980s his cousin Chico took on the farmers and lumberjacks who were intent on cutting down trees to create pasture for cattle. His fight for the land drew the world's attention to the destruction of the rainforest. In 1988 Chico was murdered, but he left a legacy: Chico Mendes Extraction Reserve, which is a remote settlement in the Amazon rainforest. Sebastiao and his sons work in a harsh environment which they share with snakes, spiders, monkeys and the occasional big cat, and daily are likely to encounter tropical downpours. To harvest the rubber, the men work on around 200 rubber trees, and to safeguard the business for the future more rubber trees are regularly planted. The end product is latex, which used to be sold to the rubber tappers cooperative in Xapuri to make tyres and shoes. The government set up the Natex condom factory to produce condoms for the Brazilian Department of Health. The factory pays a good price for the latex and this has led to significant improvement in local incomes for Sebastiao, his family and other rubber tappers.

While these are examples of how Brazilians are addressing the environmental challenges and devising sustainable business models, there are strong economic forces that are driving less environmentally friendly consumption. Brazil is experiencing economic change, and in 2012 was said to be the world's sixth largest economy. Its main exports are manufactured goods, iron ore, coffee, oranges and other agricultural products. Brazil has a population of around 200 million, many of whom are contributing to over-consumption, but the 'green economy' is working in parts of Brazil.

The new forest code

According to Kumi Naidoo, the International Director of Greenpeace, Brazil's President Dilma Rousseff has an important decision to make in the fight to save the environment and prevent destruction of the Amazon rainforest. The Brazilian Congress has voted to relax the rules which have been introduced to control deforestation in the Amazon region. The new forest code means that the rules on the amount of land farmers have to replant will be increased, but the federal states will be able to decide how much forest to replace and make it possible for the larger farming states to act with leniency towards farmers. There is also a change in the way landowners measure their acreage, as under the proposal they can include river margins and hilltops in the total proportion of their land that must be legally preserved. The net outcome is seen to be a reduction in the total area of protected land. The shift towards state control away from central government is also likely to mean long delays to replanting and this will impact on the recovery of the area. Environmentalists say that to have any impact farmers would need to replant an area which is equivalent to the combined acreage of Germany, Austria and Italy.

Over 80 per cent of Brazilians are against the new forest code and a further million and a half people from Europe and the USA have petitioned President Rousseff to stop the new bill. The fears are that the new land use bill will be ruled by rural interests rather than wider environmental concerns and could reverse the past 20 years' efforts to protect the Amazon rainforest.

References

1 Pearce, F. (2012) Beyond Rio, green economics can give us hope, *The Guardian*, 28 June.

2 Peck, J. (2012) The Future/who/wants (or needs)? http://www.energybulletin.net/stories/2012-07-12

Questions

1   Explain how Brazil is responding to forces in the macroenvironment.

2   Politicians have the power to influence business practices through changes in the law. Discuss the extent to which you feel the Brazilian Government is being effective in implementing changes.

3   The Natex condom factory is an example of an environmentally sustainable business. Suggest the wider social and cultural benefits of this government initiative.

4   Discuss how the European Union might influence economic growth and development in Brazil.

This case was written by Fiona Ellis-Chadwick, Senior Lecturer in Marketing, The Open University.

CHAPTER 4

Understanding consumer behaviour

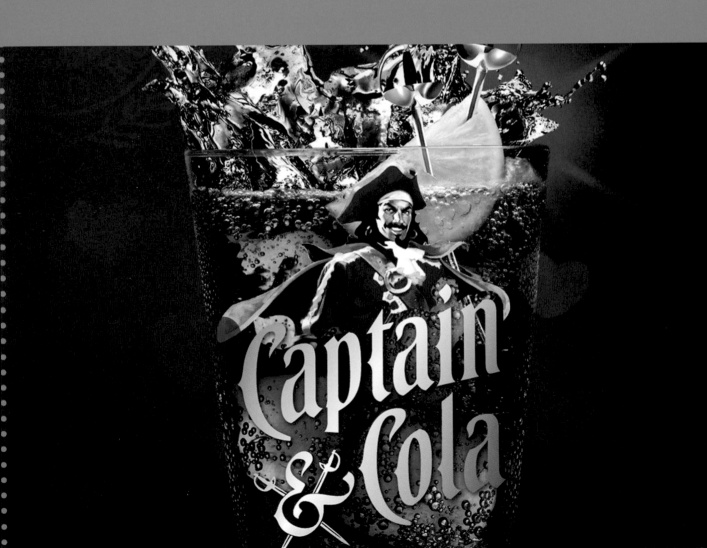

" **The customer is always right.** "
HARRY GORDON SELFRIDGE[1]

" **A brand isn't only made by the people who buy it, but also by the people who know about it.** "
JOHN HEGARTY[2]

LEARNING OBJECTIVES

After reading this chapter, you should be able to:

1 define the dimensions of consumer buyer behaviour

2 describe the role of the buying centre (who buys) and its implications

3 describe the consumer decision-making process (how people buy)

4 discuss the marketing implications of need recognition, information search, evaluation of alternatives, purchase and post-purchase stages

5 compare the differences in evaluation of high- versus low-involvement situations

6 describe the nature of choice criteria (what are used) and their implications

7 explain the influences on consumer behaviour—the buying situation, personal and social influences—and their marketing implications

In Chapter 2 we saw that a fundamental marketing decision was the choice of target customer. Marketing-orientated companies make clear decisions about the type of customer to engage with particular product and service offerings. The implications are that an in-depth knowledge of customers is a prerequisite of successful marketing. Consumer and buyer behaviour influences the choice of target market and the composition of the marketing mix, so understanding customers is a cornerstone of marketing.

In this chapter we will explore consumer behaviour and, in Chapter 5, we examine organizational buyer behaviour. You will find there are similarities and key differences between each type of purchaser (individual consumers and professional **buyers**), which have important implications for marketing. More specifically, this chapter examines three key areas which are important for understanding consumer behaviour and its implications for marketing: 1) *the dimensions*; 2) *the processes*; 3) *the influences*.

Understanding consumer behaviour is important because consumers are changing. While average incomes rise, income distribution is more uneven in most nations and household size is gradually decreasing. In all EU nations more women have jobs outside the home, the consumption of services is rising at the expense of consumer durables and demand for (and supply of) health, green (ecological), fun/luxury and convenience products is increasing. Concern for the environment and European legislation have led to an increase in recyclable and reusable packaging, while concern for value for money and increasing retailer concentration have led to an increase in market share for private-label (own-label) brands.[3]

The marketing environment impacts on consumer behaviour and often leads to significant changes in what we buy. For example, children are losing interest in traditional toys like building bricks, dolls and toy cars at a younger age as they are being replaced by tablet computers, mobile phones and computer games. This trend has resulted in changes in demand and losses for companies like Mattell and Lego. To ensure survival, these companies have to adapt: for example, Mattel's best-selling doll Barbie comes with a range of modern attributes—inbuilt video camera, tattoos—and Lego has ranges which include *Star Wars*, *Harry Potter* and *Pirates of the Caribbean*. The lesson is that companies need to have a deep understanding of their customers and be alert to their changing behaviours. This chapter provides the foundations for developing such understanding and sensitivity.

The Dimensions of Buyer Behaviour

Consumers are individuals who buy products or services for personal consumption. Organizational buying, on the other hand, focuses on the purchase of products and services for use in an organization's activities. Sometimes it is difficult to classify a product as being either a consumer or an organizational good. Cars, for example, sell to consumers for personal consumption and to organizations for use in carrying out their activities (e.g. to provide transport for a sales executive). For both types of buyer, an understanding of customers can be gained only by answering the following questions (see also Fig. 4.1).

1 *Who* is important in the buying decision?
2 *How* do they buy?
3 *What* are their choice criteria?
4 *Where* do they buy?
5 *When* do they buy?

These questions define the key dimensions of behaviour (and are relevant to both consumer and organizational purchasers). In this chapter we focus on the consumer perspective and in Chapter 5 the organizational perspective. Understanding the dimensions identified by these questions is important and has implications for different levels of marketing planning.

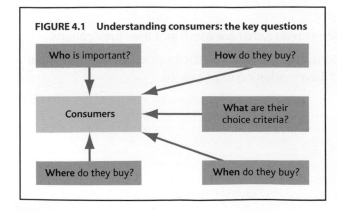

FIGURE 4.1   Understanding consumers: the key questions

Who is important? → Consumers
How do they buy? → Consumers
What are their choice criteria? → Consumers
Where do they buy? → Consumers
When do they buy? → Consumers

These issues are discussed throughout in the following sections. The next section examines the processes of consumer behaviour.

Consumer Behaviour

Who buys?

Many consumer purchases are individual. When purchasing a Snickers (probably the best-selling chocolate bar in the world with sales of over $2 billion) a person may make an impulse purchase upon seeing an array of confectionery at a newsagent's counter. However, decision-making can also be made by a group such as a household. In such a situation a number of individuals may interact to influence the purchase decision. Each person may assume a role in the decision-making process. Blackwell et al. describe five roles, as outlined below.[4] Each may be taken by parents, children or other members of the **buying centre**.

1 *Initiator*: the person who begins the process of considering a purchase. Information may be gathered by this person to help the decision.
2 *Influencer*: the person who attempts to persuade others in the group concerning the outcome of the decision. Influencers typically gather information and attempt to impose their choice criteria on the decision.
3 *Decider*: the individual with the power and/or financial authority to make the ultimate choice regarding which product to buy.
4 *Buyer*: the person who conducts the transaction. The buyer calls the supplier, visits the store, makes the payment and effects delivery.
5 *User*: the actual consumer/user of the product.

One person may assume multiple roles in the buying group. In a toy purchase, for example, a girl may be the *initiator*, and attempt to *influence* her parents, who are the *deciders*. The girl may be *influenced* by her sister to buy a different brand. The *buyer* may be one of the parents, who visits the store to purchase the toy and brings it back to the home. Finally, both children may be *users* of the toy. Although the purchase was for one person, in this example marketers have four opportunities—two children and two parents—to affect the outcome of the purchase decision. Much of the research into the roles of household members has been carried out in the USA. Woodside and Mote, for example, found that roles differed according to product type, with the woman's influence stronger for carpets and washing machines while the man's influence was stronger for television sets.[5] Also the respective roles may change as the purchasing process progresses. In general, one or other partner will tend to dominate the early stages, then joint decision-making tends to occur as the process moves towards final purchase. Joint decision-making is more common when the household consists of two income-earners.

As roles and the marketing environment change so does our purchasing behaviour; consumers are eating more convenience food than ever before and more working family members and single person households mean that convenience is a high priority for many people.[6] Consumers are also getting heavier—Europe has the highest number of overweight people in the world[7]—and this influences what they buy: that is, the likelihood of buying healthy convenience food is affected by overall liking of the meal,[8] so chicken meals are favoured over salmon. Technology is enabling sophisticated analysis of consumer decision-making, which has implications for

Go to the website to see who this Snickers' advert is targeting.
www.mcgraw-hill.co.uk/textbooks/jobber

IF YOU'RE READING THIS OUT LOUD, YOU'RE PROBABLY HUNGRY.

YOU'RE NOT YOU WHEN YOU'RE HUNGRY.

SNICKERS

REALLY SATISFIES.

⬆ **EXHIBIT 4.1** Snickers uses advertising messages to stimulate impulse purchasing.

marketing initiatives. Research for Carlsberg Sweden, using special glasses that track exactly what consumers are looking at, found that point-of-sale materials are more important in influencing the purchase decision than previously thought.[9]

The marketing implications of understanding who buys lie within the areas of marketing communications and segmentation. An identification of the roles played within the buying centre is a prerequisite for targeting persuasive communications. As the previous discussion has demonstrated, the person who actually uses or consumes the product may not be the most influential member of the buying centre, nor the decision-maker. Even when the user does play the predominant role, communication with other members of the buying centre can make sense when their knowledge and opinions may act as persuasive forces during the decision-making process. The second implication is that the changing roles and influences within the family buying centre are providing new opportunities to creatively segment hitherto stable markets (e.g. cars). Read Mini Case 4.1 Pre-family Man, to understand more about influences on consumer decision-making and fine-tuning marketing directed at the previously stable age 21–35 male segment.

How they buy

How consumers buy may be regarded as a decision-making process beginning with the recognition that a problem exists. For example, a personal computer may be bought to solve a perceived problem: for example, lack of access to the Internet. Problem-solving may thus be considered a thoughtful reasoned action undertaken to bring about need satisfaction. In this example, the need was fast and accurate calculations. Blackwell et al. define a series of steps a consumer may pass through before choosing a brand.[10] Figure 4.2 shows these stages, which form the **consumer decision-making process**.

Need recognition/problem awareness

FIGURE 4.2   The consumer decision-making process

Need recognition/ problem awareness

↓

Information search

↓

Evaluation of alternatives

↓

Purchase

↓

Post-purchase evaluation of decision

In the computer example, *need recognition* is essentially *functional*, and recognition may take place over a period of time. Other problems may occur as a result of routine depletion (e.g. petrol, food) or unpredictability (e.g. the breakdown of a television set or washing machine). In other situations consumer purchasing may be initiated by more *emotional* or *psychological* needs. For example, the purchase of Aqua Pour Homme Cologne for Men by Bulgari is likely to be motivated by status needs rather than any marginal functional superiority over other perfumes.

The degree to which the consumer intends to resolve the problem depends on two issues: the magnitude of the discrepancy between the desired and present situation, and the relative importance of the problem.[11] A problem may be perceived, but if the difference between the *current and desired situation* is small, then the consumer may not be sufficiently motivated to move to the next step in the decision-making process. For example, a person considering upgrading their mobile phone from a basic handset to a smartphone model will only make the purchase if they consider the difference in benefits to be sufficient to incur the costs involved (even though they might desire the more sophisticated product).

Conversely, a large discrepancy may be perceived but the person may not proceed to information search because the *relative importance* of the problem is small. A person may feel that a smartphone has significant advantages over a mobile phone, but that the relative importance of the advantages compared with other purchase needs (for example, the mortgage or a holiday) might be small.

The existence of a need, however, may not activate the decision-making process in all cases. This is due to the existence of *need inhibitors*.[12] For example, someone may want to buy an item on eBay but may be inhibited by fear of paying online and not receiving the goods. In such circumstances, the need remains passive.

There are a number of marketing implications in the need-recognition stage, and marketing managers should be aware of:

Mini Case 4.1 Pre-family Man

Things you ought to know about Pre-Family Man (PFM):

- 92 per cent are online across multiple devices
- 67 per cent don't see their friends as much as they did
- 75 per cent see love as a top priority[13]
- 92 per cent use email at least once a day
- 55 per cent use social networks at least once a day
- 91 per cent watch short videos online
- 72 per cent of PFM buy online at least once a month

Microsoft has its eye on PFM, young men aged between 21–35, as they make up a large market. In the seven largest countries in Europe there are over 21 million PFM and this group is predicted to grow. Research has revealed that PFM, who is between secondary education and having a family, should not be targeted as one group. According to Microsoft, PFM is evolving, he moves from living with parents, through living on his own or with a friend, to living with a partner. During this evolution PFM has to achieve a balance between his desire for fun and the need to be responsible, has to work out how to manage the things he wants to do and to set priorities as there are always too many things he wants to do. PFM is *always switched on* to digital technology devices, and access to the Internet is critical for managing his busy life.

However, depending on where PFM is on the evolutionary track, his priorities will vary according to which country he lives in. For example, between the age of 21 and 23 in Sweden 20 per cent of PFM are living with parents, whereas in Spain the figure is 80 per cent. Priorities are different too; in Germany 35 per cent are looking for more money, while in Sweden the figure is only 15 per cent. Career aspirations appear to be higher in Sweden with 31 per cent looking for a better job, whereas in the Netherlands the figure is 7 per cent.

As technology has enabled marketers to become more informed about consumer behaviour, a complex set of rules emerge, which could give more insight into how better to serve the needs of various customers. The study by Microsoft provides guidance on targeting PFM, and suggests there are four golden rules that marketers should adhere to when targeting him:

1 Life stages—if targeting by age it is key to also factor in life stages; when PFM is living with parents, his focus is on fun and he is interested in flats to rent and sports events. For the marketer in-game advertising is very important. When PFM is living alone or with friends, marketers should target money, fashion, health and fitness websites. His priorities change when living with a partner. The focus is no longer on fun, he becomes more responsive to messages about DIY, holidays, property, cooking and money. Social media and review sites are good places to advertise to capture his attention.

2 Cultural differences—the PFM evolution goes at a different speed depending on which country he lives in; he makes use of the Internet, social media and email to stay in touch through the evolution.

3 Priorities—PFM has many hurdles to overcome during his evolution. Advertisers should be aware of these and seek to give him the information he needs to achieve different priorities.

4 Information—marketers should always aim to give PFM the right type of information he needs at the point he wants it, whether that is online, or on the move.

Questions:

1 Suggest how you would advise a company manufacturing tablet computers to communicate with PFM.
2 Explain how the priorities of PFM change during his evolution and suggest what the implications are for marketing managers.
3 Using the available information suggest which country (Sweden, Germany, Netherlands, Spain) and which accompanying PFM life-stage you might target if you were responsible for developing a communication campaign for:
    a) an international property company
    b) state-of-the-art gaming console
    c) a shopping app.

Based on: Microsoft (2012)

↑ **EXHIBIT 4.2** Bulgari Aqua uses personal emotional triggers to communicate with target audiences.

1 *the needs* of consumers and the problems that they face. By being more attuned to customers' needs, companies have the opportunity to create a competitive advantage. This may be accomplished by intuition. For example, intuitively a marketing manager of a washing machine company may believe that consumers would value a silent machine. Alternatively, marketing research could be used to assess customer problems or needs. For example, group discussions could be carried out among people who use washing machines, to assess their dissatisfaction with current models, what problems they encountered and what their ideal machine would be. This could be followed by a large-scale survey to determine how representative the views of the group members were. The results of such research can have significant effects on product redesign.

2 *need inhibitors* which potentially stop a purchase. For example, eBay has recognized that overcoming the need inhibitor lack of trust in being sent the product is important. To overcome this need inhibitor, eBay introduced its PayPal system, which acts as financial insurance against non-receipt of goods, and has developed a feedback system that allows buyers to post information on their transactions and their experiences with particular vendors.

3 *need stimulation* which might encourage a purchase. Marketers' activities, such as developing advertising campaigns and training salespeople to sell product benefits, may act as cues to needs arousal. For example, an advertisement displaying the features and benefits of a smartphone may stimulate customers to regard their lack of a computer, or the limitations of their current model, to be a problem that warrants action.

As we have seen, activating problem recognition depends on the size of the discrepancy between the current and desired situation, and the relative importance of the problem. The advertisement could therefore focus on the advantages of a smartphone over a mobile phone, to create awareness of a large discrepancy, and also stress the importance of owning a top-of-the-range model as a symbol of innovativeness and professionalism (thereby increasing the relative importance of purchasing a computer relative to other products).

Not all consumer needs are obvious. Consumers often engage in exploratory behaviour such as being early adopters of new products and retail outlets, taking risks in making product choices, recreational shopping and seeking variety in purchasing products. Such activities can satisfy the need for novel purchase experiences, offer a change of pace and relief from boredom, and satisfy a thirst for knowledge and the urge of curiosity.[14]

Information search

If problem recognition is sufficiently strong, the consumer decision-making process is likely to move to the second stage: **information search**. This involves the identification of alternative ways of problem solution. The search may be internal or external. *Internal search* involves a review of relevant information from memory. This review would include potential solutions, methods of comparing solutions, reference to personal experiences and marketing communications. If a satisfactory solution is not found, then *external search* begins. This involves *personal sources* such as friends, the family, work colleagues and neighbours, and *commercial sources* such as advertisements and salespeople. *Third-party reports*, such as blogs and product-testing reports in newspapers and magazines and on the Internet, may provide unbiased information, and *personal experiences* may be sought such as asking for demonstrations and viewing, touching or tasting the product.

The objective of information search is to build up the **awareness set**—that is, the array of brands that may provide a solution to the problem. Using the smartphone example again, an advertisement may not only stimulate a search for more unbiased information regarding the advertised smartphone, but also stimulate an external search for information about rival brands.

Information search by consumers is facilitated by the growth of Internet usage and companies that provide search facilities, such as Yahoo! and Google. Consumers are increasingly using the Internet to gather information before buying a product. For example, many purchases only take place after consumers have researched brands online. Of growing importance are recommendation and review sites, as Digital Marketing 4.1 explains.

Digital Marketing 4.1 Recommendation and Review Sites

One of the significant outcomes of the 'powerful consumer' phenomenon is the role of personal recommendation as part of the marketing process. Word of mouth is an important form of communication, and the influence of individuals' comments has also become increasingly important online. Web businesses have emerged that specialize in providing a platform for customer reviews—for example, TripAdvisor (travel and tourism industry), Epinions (retail industry) and other websites like Amazon have facilities for feedback and comments on products and customer service.

According to some research, 70 per cent of Internet shoppers find the personal ratings and reviews section of a retail website the most useful to them, particularly when both positive and negative reviews of a product are shown. In the USA more than 60 per cent of respondents trust reviews from 'a person like themselves' more than an expert in the field or an academic. This is most significant for purchases such as travel, recreation and leisure, where 82 per cent of US consumers checked a personal review before making a purchase decision.

Amazon has an interesting take on personal reviews, in that it encourages other customers to say if they found particular reviews useful. The reviews that are found to be most useful are found nearer the top of the list of reviews (whether positive or negative).

TripAdvisor, however, leads the way in the use of personal customer reviews, with over 41.6 million users a month and 40 million reviews on hotels, cities, airlines and even excursions. Reviews by previous travellers have been found to influence future consumer purchasing behaviour. TripAdvisor's commentaries have become so important in the travel industry that many firms, such as Kuoni, now include TripAdvisor reviews on their own websites as part of the process of increasing sales likelihood, because both good and bad reviews are shown.

Nevertheless, TripAdvisor has a problem, emanating from dishonest reviews and, despite having a policy in place to deter competing hoteliers and travel providers from posting such reviews, legal cases are coming to court. Commentators suggest the 'nit-picking' nature of some reviews and the false nature of others are making it more difficult to assess the usefulness of reviews. KwikChex, a company that specializes in protecting online reputations, estimates there are more than 27,000 defamatory comments posted on TripAdvisor.

Despite this controversy TripAdvisor is growing at a rate of 21 new reviews per minute, which can lead to information excess for wary travellers. The implication for marketing managers is not only that they have to produce excellent products that people want but they must also manage online reviews, as poor reviews that people trust can have a significant impact on consumer decision-making.

Based on: www.kwikchex.com (2012);[15] Cochrane (2011);[16] www.eMarketer.com (March, April, July 2008)

Evaluation of alternatives and the purchase

The first step in *evaluation* is to reduce the awareness set to a smaller set of brands for serious consideration. The awareness set of brands passes through a screening filter to produce an **evoked set**: those brands that the consumer seriously considers before making a purchase. In a sense, the evoked set is a shortlist of brands for careful evaluation. The screening process may use different choice criteria from those used when making the final choice, and the number of choice criteria used is often fewer.[17] One choice criterion used for screening may be price. Those smartphones priced below a certain level may form the evoked set. Final choice may then depend on such choice criteria as ease of use, speed of connection to the Internet and reliability. The range of choice criteria used by consumers will be examined in more detail later in this chapter.

Although brands may be perceived as similar, this does not necessarily mean they will be equally preferred. This is because different product attributes (e.g. benefits, imagery) may be used by people when making similarity and preference judgements. For example, two brands may be perceived as similar because they provide similar functional benefits, yet one may be preferred over the other because of distinctive imagery.[18]

A key determinant of the extent to which consumers evaluate a brand is their level of *involvement*. Involvement is the degree of perceived relevance and personal importance accompanying the brand choice.[19] When a purchase is highly involving, the consumer is more likely to carry out extensive evaluation. High-involvement purchases are likely to include those incurring high expenditure or personal risk, such as buying a car or a home. In contrast, low-involvement situations are characterized by simple evaluations about purchases. Consumers use simple choice tactics to reduce time and effort rather than maximize the consequences of the purchase.[20] For example, when purchasing baked beans or breakfast cereal, consumers are likely to make quick choices rather than agonize over the decision.

This distinction between high- and low-involvement situations implies different evaluative processes. For high-involvement purchases the Fishbein and Ajzen theory of reasoned action[21] has proven robust in predicting purchase behaviour,[22] while in low-involvement situations, work by Ehrenberg and Goodhart has shown how simple evaluation and decision-making can be.[23] Each of these models will now be examined.

Fishbein and Ajzen model: this model suggests that an attitude towards a brand is based upon a set of **beliefs** about the brand's attributes (e.g. value for money, durability). These are the perceived consequences resulting from buying the brand. Each attribute is weighted by how good or bad the consumer believes the attribute to be. Those attributes that are weighted highly will be that person's choice criteria and have a large influence in the formation of attitude. **Attitude** is the degree to which someone likes or dislikes the brand overall. The link between personal beliefs and attitudes is shown in Figure 4.3a. However, evaluation of a brand is not limited to personal beliefs about the consequences of buying a brand. Outside influences also play a part. Individuals will thus evaluate the extent to which *important others* believe that they should or should not buy the brand. These beliefs may conflict with their personal beliefs. People may personally believe that buying a sports car may have positive consequences (providing fun driving, being more attractive to other people) but refrain from doing so if they believe that important others (e.g. parents, boss) would disapprove of the purchase. This collection of *normative beliefs* forms an overall evaluation of the degree to which these outside influences approve or disapprove of the purchase (*subjective norms*). The link between normative beliefs and subjective norms is shown in Figure 4.3a. This clearly is a *theory of reasoned action*. Consumers are highly involved in the purchase to the extent that they evaluate the consequences of the purchase *and* what others will think about it. Only after these considerations have taken place are purchase intention formed and the ultimate purchase result.

The Fishbein and Ajzen model can be illustrated by using the smartphone again. Having conducted the search for information, the evoked set comprises an iPhone and BlackBerry.

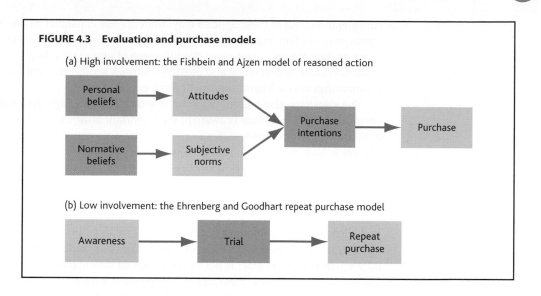

FIGURE 4.3 Evaluation and purchase models

(a) High involvement: the Fishbein and Ajzen model of reasoned action

Personal beliefs → Attitudes → Purchase intentions → Purchase

Normative beliefs → Subjective norms → Purchase intentions

(b) Low involvement: the Ehrenberg and Goodhart repeat purchase model

Awareness → Trial → Repeat purchase

The buyer believes that buying an iPhone would result in a significant cost saving and that both models are virtually identical on other attributes (e.g. reliability, design and speed). Cost savings are very important to this person and so are rated as a very good attribute to possess. The buyer, therefore, has a more favourable attitude towards the iPhone. Furthermore, a close friend, whose opinion the buyer regards as important, owns an iPhone, rates it highly and would strongly approve of such a purchase. Therefore, subjective norms also favour the iPhone. This leads to a purchase intention to buy the iPhone and subsequently its purchase. If the friend was perceived to disapprove of the iPhone purchase, the decision would depend on the relative strengths of the attitude and subjective norm components. When attitudes outweigh subjective norms, the iPhone would be purchased and, for the opposite case, the BlackBerry would be chosen.

Ehrenberg and Goodhart model: in low-involvement situations the amount of information processing implicit in the earlier model may not be worthwhile or sensible. A typical low-involvement situation is the *repeat purchase* of fast-moving consumer goods. The work of Ehrenberg and Goodhart suggests that a very simple process may explain purchase behaviour (see Fig. 4.3b). According to this model, awareness precedes trial, which, if satisfactory, leads to repeat purchase. This is an example of a behavioural model of consumer behaviour: the behaviour becomes *habitual* with little conscious thought or formation of attitudes preceding behaviour. The limited importance of the purchase simply does not warrant the reasoned evaluation of alternatives implied in the Fishbein and Ajzen model. The notion of low involvement suggests that awareness precedes behaviour and behaviour precedes attitude. In this situation the consumer does not actively seek information but is a passive recipient. Furthermore, since the decision is not inherently involving, the consumer is likely to satisfice (i.e. search for a satisfactory solution rather than the best one).[24] Consequently any of several brands that lie in the evoked set may be considered adequate.

Distinguishing between high- and low-involvement situations: the distinction between these two purchasing situations is important because the variations in how consumers evaluate products and brands leads to contrasting marketing implications. The complex evaluation outlined in the high-involvement situation suggests that marketing managers need to provide a good deal of information about the positive consequences of buying. Messages with *high information content* would enhance knowledge about the brand; because the consumer is actively seeking information, high levels of repetition are not needed.[25] Print media and websites may be appropriate in the high-involvement case since they allow detailed and repeated scrutiny of information. Car advertisements often provide information about the comfort, reliability and performance of the model, and also appeal to status considerations. All of these appeals may influence the consumer's beliefs about the consequences of buying the model. However, persuasive communications should also focus on how the consumer views the influence of important others. This is an area that is underdeveloped in marketing and provides avenues for further development of communications for high-involvement products.

The salesforce also has an important role to play in the high-involvement situation by ensuring that the customer is aware of the important attributes of the product and correctly evaluates their consequences. For example, if the differential advantage of a particular model of a car is fuel economy the salesperson would raise fuel economy as a salient product attribute and explain the cost benefits of buying that model vis-à-vis the competition.

For low-involvement situations, as we have seen, the evaluation of alternatives is much more rudimentary, and attitude change is likely to follow purchase. In this case, attempting to gain *top-of-mind awareness* through advertising and providing positive *reinforcement* (e.g. through sales promotion) to gain trial may be more important than providing masses of information about the consequences of buying the brand. Furthermore, as this is of little interest, the consumer is not actively seeking information but is a passive receiver. Consequently advertising messages should be *short* with a small number of key points but with *high repetition* to enhance learning.[26] Television may be the best medium since it allows passive reception to messages while the medium actively transmits them. Also, it is ideal for the transmission of short, highly repetitive messages. Much soap powder advertising follows this format.[27]

Marketers must be aware of the role of emotion in consumer evaluation of alternatives. A major source of high emotion is when a product is high in symbolic meaning. Consumers believe that the product helps them to construct and maintain their self-concept and sense of identity. Furthermore, ownership of the product will help them communicate the desired image to other people. In such cases, non-rational preferences may form and information search is confined to providing objective justification for an emotionally based decision. Studies have shown the effects of emotion on judgement to be less thought, less information-seeking, less analytical reasoning and less attention to negative factors that might contradict the decision.[28] Instead, consumers consult their feelings for information about a decision: 'How do I feel about it?' Consequently, many marketers attempt to create a feeling of warmth about their brands. The mere exposure to a brand name over time, and the use of humour in advertisements, can create such feelings.

Impulse buying is another area that can be associated with emotions. Consumers have described a compelling feeling that was 'thrilling', 'wild', 'a tingling sensation', 'a surge of energy', and 'like turning up the volume'.[29]

Post-purchase evaluation of the decision

Effective marketing aims to create **customer** satisfaction in both high- and low-involvement situations. Marketing managers want to create positive experiences from the purchase of their products or services. Nevertheless, it is common for customers to experience some post-purchase concerns; this is called **cognitive dissonance**. These concerns arise because of uncertainty about making the right decision. This is because the choice of one product often means the rejection of the attractive features of the alternatives.

Dissonance is likely to increase in four ways: with the *expense* of purchase; when the decision is *difficult* (e.g. many alternatives, many choice criteria and each alternative offering benefits not available with the others); when the decision is *irrevocable*; and when the purchaser has a tendency *to experience anxiety*.[30] Thus, it is often associated with high-involvement purchases. Shortly after purchase, car buyers may attempt to reduce dissonance by looking at advertisements, websites and brochures for their model, and seeking reassurance from owners of the same model. Volkswagen buyers are more likely to look at Volkswagen advertisements and avoid Renault or Ford ads. Clearly, advertisements can act as positive reinforcers in such situations, and follow-up sales efforts can act similarly.

Car dealers can reduce *buyer remorse* by contacting recent purchasers by letter to reinforce the wisdom of their decision and to confirm the quality of their after-sales service.

However, the outcome of post-purchase evaluation is dependent on many factors besides this kind of reassurance. The quality of the product or service is obviously a key determinant, and the role of the salesperson acting as a problem-solver for the customer rather than simply pushing the highest-profit-margin product can also help create customer satisfaction, and thereby reduce cognitive dissonance.

What are the choice criteria?

Choice criteria are the various attributes (and benefits) a consumer uses when evaluating products and services. They provide the grounds for deciding to purchase one brand or another. Different members of the buying centre may use different choice criteria. For example, a child may use the criterion of self-image when choosing shoes, whereas a parent may use price. The same criterion may be used differently. For example, a child may want the most expensive smartphone while the parent may want a less expensive alternative. Choice criteria can change over time due to changes in income through the family life cycle. As disposable income rises, so price may no longer be the key criterion but is replaced by considerations of status or social belonging.

Table 4.1 lists four types of choice criteria and gives examples of each. Technical criteria are related to the performance of the product or service, and include reliability, durability, comfort and convenience. Convenience is often synonymous with ease of use and Apple products have often been leaders in this area. For example, it was Apple's Macintosh that led the way in icon-based graphical interfaces that are now standard in PCs; it was the iPod that made digital mobile music players user friendly; it was the iPhone that first introduced an elegant, easy-to-use touchscreen[31] and the iPad, which incorporates all these easy to use features and provides mobile Internet access.

Economic criteria concern the cost aspects of purchase and include price, running costs and residual values (e.g. the trade-in value of a car). Exhibit 4.3 shows an advertisement for the Audi TT TDI that announces the higher fuel economy (and hence lower running costs) of the new model, as well as its more responsible credentials (an ethical consideration). Social criteria concern the impact that the purchase makes on the person's perceived relationships

TABLE 4.1   Choice criteria used when evaluating alternatives

Type of criteria	Examples	Type of criteria	Examples
Technical	Reliability	Social	Status
	Durability		Social belonging
	Performance		Convention
	Style/looks		Fashion
	Comfort	Personal	Self-image
	Delivery		Risk reduction
	Convenience		Ethics
	Taste		Emotions
Economic	Price		
	Value for money		
	Running costs		
	Residual value		
	Life-cycle costs		

Vorsprung durch Technik   Audi

The new Audi TT TDI. The World's first 50mpg sportscar.

↑**EXHIBIT 4.3   Audi uses a clean, clear image to convey a message of fuel efficiency for its Audi TT TDI.**

with other people, and the influence of social norms on the person. The purchase of a BMW car may be based on status considerations as much as to any technical advantages over its rivals. Choosing a brand of trainer may be determined by the need for social belonging. Nike and Reebok recognize the need for their trainers to have 'street cred'. The need to project success gives rise to celebrity endorsements where a product is associated with a high profile sports or television personality, film star, team. In 2000 Nike paid £300 million to ensure that Manchester United wore its shirts and shorts for 13 years[32] and then subsequently embarked on negotiations to renew the deal for a figure of £450[33] million. Social norms such as convention and fashion can also be important choice criteria, with some brands being rejected as too unconventional (e.g. fluorescent spectacles) or out of fashion (e.g. 'shell' tracksuits).

Personal criteria are to do with how the product or service relates to the individual psychologically. Self-image is our personal view of ourselves. Some people might view themselves as 'cool' and successful, and only buy fashion items such as Paul Smith, Super Dry, Hugo Boss or Burberry clothes which reflect that perception of themselves. Risk reduction can affect choice decisions since some people are risk averse and prefer to choose 'safe' brands; an example is the purchase of designer labels, which reduces the risk of being seen wearing unfashionable clothing. Ethical criteria can also be employed. For example, brands may be rejected because they are manufactured by companies that have offended a person's ethical code of behaviour. Research has shown that consumers weigh up the ethical arguments for buying products against other more personal criteria.[34] For example, for many young consumers the importance of image, fashion and price outweighs ethical issues as an influence on purchase behaviour.[35] The market for ethical products has grown in recent years. Some of the products currently deemed ethical include fairly traded foods and drinks that guarantee a fair deal to producers in developing countries, but a company's *green credential* can be confusing, and it is difficult for consumers to choose the 'best' products because, although organic may be seen as the greener and healthier food option, many scientific studies have cast doubts on such conclusions. Although ethical consumption is important in shaping and maintaining empowered ethical consumer identities and markets, there is much uncertainty about the choices to be made, and at times ethical trade-offs occur (i.e. products are not always organic as well as fair trade). This, in turn, generates much

INTRODUCING
ABSOLUT GRÄPEVINE
Cocktails Perfected

⬆ EXHIBIT 4.4   Absolut maintains the brand's success using wit and humour rather than more tangible product features.

inconsistency with regard to what it is possible to achieve. Although people feel empowered and responsible for environmental issues at an individual level, this is coupled with the insecurity of not knowing what the 'right choices' are, and such contradictions pose huge challenges to policy-makers and marketers alike. Marketing ethics and corporate social responsibility are discussed in more detail in Chapter 6.

Emotional criteria can be important in decision-making. The rejection of new-formula Coca-Cola in 1985, despite product tests that showed it to be preferred on taste criteria to traditional Coca-Cola, has been explained in part by emotional reactions to the withdrawal of an old, well-loved brand.[36] Many purchase decisions are experiential in that they evoke feelings such as fun, pride, pleasure, boredom or sadness. Research by Elliot and Hamilton showed that a decision about out-of-home leisure activities such as going for a drink, a meal, to the cinema, a disco or to play sport is affected by the desire to 'do something different for a change' and 'do what I'm in the mood to do', both of which reflect emotional criteria.[37] In another survey of consumers, 31 per cent claimed that many of their purchases were motivated by a desire to 'cheer themselves up'.[38] The importance of experiences to consumers has led to the growth in experiential consumption, as Marketing in Action 4.1 explains.

Marketing in Action 4.1 Experiences and Consumer Behaviour

What drives fans to pay excessive prices to see their favourite artists? Tickets for the Rolling Stones at Carnegie Hall New York were sold at $1882 per seat, Pet Shop Boys tickets sold for £2200 for two tickets to see them perform live in London. Why did thousands of tickets for an Arctic Monkeys tour priced at £14 sell for over £60 each on eBay? What explains the demand for 112,000 Glastonbury Festival tickets, which took less than four hours to sell? And how come tickets for Led Zeppelin's gig at London's O2 arena sold for over £7000? The answer lies in the concept of experiential consumption.

A Rolling Stones or Pet Shop Boys CD can be bought for around £10, so what extra were those fans seeking that persuaded them to pay so much more for a ticket? We can imagine that the experience of seeing your favourite group play live engendered feelings of nostalgia, fun and pleasure at attending a rare event (especially as both bands only had two gigs in their 'tour'). Fans may also have valued the experience of being with a crowd of like-minded fans, all of which would contribute to the feeling of excitement at being there.

In a world that can often seem bland, consumers are willing to pay premium prices for experiences that can arouse both positive feelings and emotions. The implications for marketers are that products that tap into this trend—such as music concerts, football matches, white-water rafting and piloting an aircraft—are likely to grow in demand in the future. This is borne out by the price of the tickets for the London 2012 Olympics, where the most expensive ticket in Olympic history was £2012 ($3250) for the Opening Ceremony of the Summer Olympics.

Based on: Guinness World Records (2012);[39] Seatgeek.com (2012);[40] Smith (2005);[41] Gibson (2008)[42]

Go to the website to see how Absolut Vodka is leading the way in creative advertising in Europe. **www.mcgraw-hill.co.uk/ textbooks/jobber**

Concern about store design and ambience at shops such as H&M and Zara reflects the importance of creating the right feeling or atmosphere when shopping for clothes. Saab ran a two-page advertising campaign that combined technical and economic appeals with an emotional one. The first page was headlined '21 Logical Reasons to Buy a Saab'. The second page ran the headline 'One Emotional Reason'. The first page supported the headline with detailed body copy explaining the technical and economic rationale for purchase. The second page showed a Saab powering along a rain-drenched road. Another brand that has successfully appealed to emotions is Absolut Vodka, one of the world's biggest spirits brands. Its clever, simple ads—featuring the now famous clear bottle and tag-lines such as 'Absolut Grapevine'—have appealed to consumers' sense of fun. Gordon Lundquist, the former president of the Swedish company, claimed that it is Absolut's wit rather than its taste that is the reason for the brand's success. 'Absolut is a personality,' he says 'We like certain people but some people are just more fun and interesting.'

When a product scores well on a combination of choice criteria the outcome can be global success. For example, the success of the BlackBerry derives from the convenience of being able to access emails and websites on the move (technical), and the status (social) and high self-image (personal) that is associated with owning one. The popularity of the iPod can also be understood by its high performance, access to a large library of music via iTunes, stylish looks (technical), affordability (economic), and the status (social) and high self-image (personal) associated with owning one.

Marketing managers need to understand the choice criteria that are being used by customers to evaluate their products and services. Such knowledge has implications for priorities in product design (e.g. are style/looks more important than performance?) and the type of appeals to use in marketing communications, which should be linked to the key choice criteria used by buying centre members.

Influences on Consumer Behaviour

Our discussion of *evaluation of alternatives*, highlights that not all decisions follow the same decision-making process, involve the same purchasers (buying centre) or use identical choice criteria. Neither do they occur at the same place or time. The consumer behaviour process, the buying centre, choice criteria, purchase situation and timing can be influenced by a number of factors: 1) the buying situation, 2) personal influences, 3) social influences (see Table 4.2).

TABLE 4.2   Influences on consumer purchasing behaviour

Areas of influence	Factors affecting decision-making	Examples of marketing implications/considerations
The buying situation	Extended problem-solving Limited problem-solving Habitual problem-solving	Level of information to provide to for consumers to make informed decisions.
Personal influences	Information processing Motivations Beliefs and attitudes Personality Lifestyle Life-cycle and age	Extent to which personal influences inform decision-making, e.g. an individual's perceptions can distort marketing messages; lifestyle can determine interest and opinions.
Social influences	Culture Social class Geodemographics Reference groups	Extent to which social influences inform decision-making, e.g. culture can determine societal values, which might affect individual behaviour.

The buying situation

Three types of buying situation can be identified: extended problem-solving, limited problem-solving, and habitual problem-solving.

Extended problem-solving

Extended problem-solving involves a high degree of information search, and close examination of alternative solutions using many choice criteria.[43] It is commonly seen in the purchase of cars, video and audio equipment, houses and expensive clothing, where it is important to make the right choice. Information search and evaluation may focus not only on which brand/model to buy but also on where to make the purchase. The potential for cognitive dissonance is greatest in this buying situation.

Extended problem-solving is usually associated with three conditions: the alternatives are differentiated and numerous; there is an adequate amount of time available for deliberation; and the purchase has a high degree of involvement.[44]

Figure 4.4 summarizes these relationships. High involvement means that the purchase is personally relevant and is seen as important with respect to basic motivations and needs.[45] Differentiation affects the extent of problem-solving because more comparisons need to be made and uncertainty is higher. Problem-solving is likely to be particularly extensive when all alternatives possess desirable features that others do not have. If alternatives are perceived as being similar, then less time is required in assessment.

Extended problem-solving is inhibited by time pressure. If the decision has to be made quickly, by definition the extent of problem-solving activity is curtailed. However, not all decisions follow extended problem-solving even though the alternatives may be differentiated and there is no time pressure. The decision-maker must also feel a high degree of involvement in the choice. Involvement—how personally relevant and important the choice is to the decision-maker—varies from person to person.

Research by Laurent and Kapferer identified four factors that affect involvement:[46]

1 *Self-image*: involvement is likely to be high when the decision potentially affects one's self-image. Thus, purchase of jewellery, cars and clothing invokes more involvement than choosing a brand of soap or margarine.

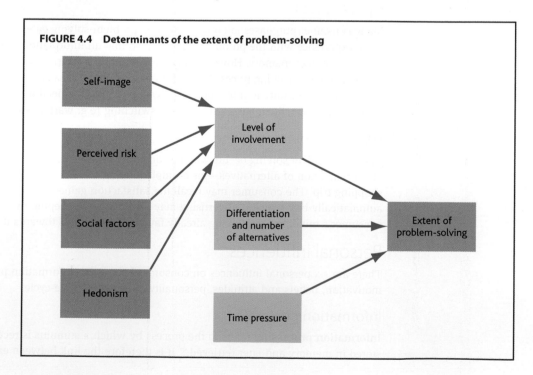

FIGURE 4.4　Determinants of the extent of problem-solving

2 *Perceived risk*: involvement is likely to be high when the perceived risk of making a mistake is high. The risk of buying the wrong house is much higher than buying the wrong chewing gum, because the potential negative consequences of the wrong decision are higher. Risk usually increases with the price of the purchase.

3 *Social factors*: when social acceptance is dependent upon making a correct choice, involvement is likely to be high. Buying of the *right* golf clubs may be highly involved, as making a *wrong* decision may affect social standing among fellow golfers; the principle may apply to clothes, trainers and other products that can affect the purchase's acceptance within a social group.

4 *Hedonistic influences*: when the purchase is capable of providing a high degree of pleasure, involvement is usually high. The choice of restaurant when on holiday can be highly involving since the difference between making the right or wrong choice can severely affect the amount of pleasure associated with the experience.

Marketers can help in this buying situation by providing information-rich communications—for example, press advertisements and websites are particularly suited to information-rich content, supported by a well-trained salesforce where appropriate.

Table 4.3 shows how the consumer decision-making process changes between high- and low-involvement purchases.

TABLE 4.3 **The consumer decision-making process and level of purchase involvement**

Stage	Low involvement	High involvement
Need recognition/problem awareness	Minor	Major, *personally* important
Information search	*Limited* search	*Extensive* search
Evaluation of alternatives and the purchase	Few *alternatives* evaluated on few choice criteria	Many *alternatives* evaluated on many choice criteria
Post-purchase evaluation of the decision	*Limited* evaluation	*Extensive* evaluation including media search

Limited problem-solving

Many consumer purchases fall into the limited problem-solving category. The consumer has some experience with the product in question so that an information search may be mainly internal, through memory. However, a certain amount of external search and evaluation may take place (e.g. checking prices) before purchase is made. This situation provides marketers with some opportunity to affect purchase by stimulating the need to conduct search (e.g. advertising) and reducing the risk of brand switching (e.g. warranties).

Habitual problem-solving

Habitual problem-solving occurs when a consumer repeat-buys the same product with little or no evaluation of alternatives—for example, buying the same breakfast cereal on a weekly shopping trip. The consumer may recall the satisfaction gained by purchasing a brand and automatically buy it again. Advertising may be effective in keeping the brand name in the consumer's mind and reinforcing already favourable attitudes towards it.

Personal influences

There are six personal influences on consumer behaviour: information processing, motivation, beliefs and attitudes, personality, lifestyle, and life-cycle.

Information processing

Information processing refers to the process by which a stimulus is received, interpreted, stored in memory and later retrieved.[47] It is therefore the link between external influences, including marketing activities and the consumer's decision-making process. Two key aspects of information processing are perception and learning.

Perception is the complex process by which people select, organize and interpret sensory stimulation into a meaningful picture of the world.[48] Three processes may be used to sort out the masses of stimuli that could be perceived into a manageable amount. These are selective attention, selective distortion and selective retention.

Selective attention is the process by which we screen out stimuli that are neither meaningful nor consistent with our experiences and beliefs. On entering a supermarket there are thousands of potential stimuli (brands, point-of-sale displays, prices, etc.) to which we could pay attention. To do so would be unrealistic in terms of time and effort. Consequently we are selective in attending to these messages. Selective attention has obvious implications for advertising considering that studies have shown that consumers consciously attend to only 5–25 per cent of the advertisements to which they are exposed.[49]

A number of factors influence attention. We pay more attention to stimuli that contrast with their background than to stimuli that blend with it. Computer and smartphone manufacturers use names of fruit to act as attention-getting brand names (e.g., Apple, BlackBerry, Raspberry Pi) because they contrast with the technologically orientated names usually associated with computers. Read more about Raspberry Pi in Digital Marketing 4.2. The size, colour and movement of a stimulus also affect attention. Position is critical too. Objects placed near the centre of the visual range are more likely to be noticed than those on the periphery. This is why there is intense competition to obtain eye-level positions on supermarket shelves. We are also more likely to notice those messages that relate to our needs (benefits sought)[50] and those that provide surprises (for example, large price reductions).

Selective distortion occurs when consumers distort the information they receive according to their existing beliefs and attitudes. We may distort information that is not in accord with our existing views. Methods of doing this include thinking that we misheard the message, and discounting the message source. Consequently, it is very important to present messages clearly without the possibility of ambiguity and to use a highly credible source, which reduces the scope for selective distortion of the message on the part of the recipient.

Distortion can occur because people interpret the same information differently. Interpretation is a process whereby messages are placed into existing categories of meaning. A cheaper price, for example, may be categorized not only as providing better value for money but also as implying lower quality. **Information framing** can affect interpretation. Framing refers to ways in which information is presented to people. Levin and Gaeth asked people to taste minced beef after telling half the sample that it was 70 per cent lean and

---

Digital Marketing 4.2 Raspberry Pi

Raspberry Pi, tiny cheap computers for kids, are the hope for future computer scientists. Several generations of children have been learning ICT in schools, which has given them a set of skills that enable them to word process, manipulate spreadsheets, build databases and web pages, and publish documents. What they haven't been learning *en masse* is how to program a computer. Eben Upton noticed a significant drop in the skill level of A-level computer science students in 2006 while working at Cambridge University. Eben and a few colleagues felt they had to try to do something about this trend and they identified the cost and complexity of computers to be at the heart of the problem. By 2012 the trustees of the Raspberry Pi foundation had produced their first batch of affordable credit-card-sized computers at a cost of £16. The machine has 128MB RAM and can perform to the same level as a Pentium II machine.

Based on: Raspberry Pi (2012);[51] Graham-Rowe (2012)[52]

the other half that it was 30 per cent fat.[53] Despite the fact that the two statements are equivalent, the sample that had the information framed positively (70 per cent lean) recorded higher levels of taste satisfaction. The implications for marketing are that there is benefit in framing communication messages in a positive manner. Words, images, colours and even smell can influence interpretations. For example, blue and green are viewed as cool, and evoke feelings of security. Red and yellow are regarded as warm and cheerful. Black is seen as an indication of strength. By using the appropriate colour in pack design it is possible to affect the consumer's feelings about the product. Marketers often base complete branding concepts on colour. For example, mobile phone company Orange uses 'colour as brand' approach. The colour orange is distinctive in its sector and conveys feelings of energy and warmth.[54] The Virgin group uses 'red' throughout its branding. Smell can influence interpretation. For example, British Airways announced its intention to introduce a new fragrance and by doing so recreate a uniform experience for travellers similar to walking into an expensive department store.[55] Singapore Airlines has been using the aroma created by the infusion of Stefan Floridian Waters cologne into its hot towels and cabins for many years. It receives consistently positive feedback from passengers and is described as exotic and feminine. Singapore Airlines was the first airline to market itself as a sensory experience appealing to the emotions as opposed to the approach of its competitors, which emphasized price, food and comfort.[56]

Selective retention refers to the fact that only a selection of messages may be retained in memory. We tend to remember messages that are in line with existing beliefs and attitudes. In an experiment 12 statements were given to a group of Labour and Conservative supporters. Six of the statements were favourable to Labour and six to the Conservatives. The group members were asked to remember the statements and to return after seven days. The result was that Labour supporters remembered the statements that were favourable to Labour and Conservative supporters remembered the pro-Conservative statements. Selective retention has a role to play in reducing cognitive dissonance: when reading reviews of a recently purchased car, positive messages are more likely to be remembered than negative ones.

Learning is any change in the content or organization of long-term memory, and is the result of information processing.[57] There are numerous ways in which learning can take place. These include *conditioning* and *cognitive learning*. **Classical conditioning** is the process of using an established relationship between a stimulus and response to cause the learning of the same response to a different stimulus. Thus, in advertising, humour, which is known to elicit a pleasurable response, may be used in the belief that these favourable feelings will carry over to the product. Red Bull is a brand that benefits from such associations. The humour in its advertising conveys a fun image, and the promotion of Red Bull on the body of racing cars projects the feeling of excitement for the brand by association.

Operant conditioning differs from classical conditioning by way of the role and timing of the reinforcement. In this case reinforcement results from rewards: the more rewarding the response, the stronger the likelihood of the purchase being repeated. Operant conditioning occurs as a result of product trial. The use of free samples is based on the principles of operant conditioning. For example, free samples of a new shampoo are distributed to a large number of households. This means the shampoo can be used (desired response) without making an initial purchase. Olay introduced its body wash using this tactic. The rewards for the consumer are that they benefit by experiencing the desirable properties of the product at no cost. These experiences can then reinforce the likelihood of the consumer making a purchase. Thus, the sequence of events is different between classical and operant conditioning. In classic conditioning liking precedes trial, whereas in operant conditioning trial precedes liking.

For marketers, introducing a series of rewards (reinforcements) may encourage repeat buying of a product. A free sample may be accompanied by a coupon to buy the product at a discounted rate (reinforcement). On the pack may be another discount coupon to encourage repeat buying. After this purchase the product relies on its own intrinsic reward—product performance—to encourage purchase. This process is known as *shaping*. Repeat purchase behaviour will have been shaped by the application of repeated reinforcers so that the consumer will have learned that buying the product is associated with pleasurable experiences.

Cognitive learning involves the learning of knowledge and development of beliefs and attitudes without direct reinforcement. **Rote learning** involves the learning of two or more concepts without conditioning. Having seen the headline 'Lemsip is for flu attacks' the consumer may remember that Lemsip is a remedy for flu attacks without the kinds of conditioning and reinforcement previously discussed.

Vicarious learning involves learning from others without direct experience or reward. It is the promise of the reward that motivates. Thus, we may learn the type of clothes that attract potential admirers by observing other people. In advertising, the 'admiring glance' can be used to signal approval of the type of clothing being worn. We imagine that the same may happen to us if we dress in a similar way.

Reasoning is a more complex form of cognitive learning and is usually associated with high-involvement situations. For example, some advertising messages rely on the recipient to draw their own conclusions, through reasoning.

Whichever type of learning has taken place, the result of the learning process is the creation of *product positioning*. The market objective is to create a clear and favourable position in the mind of the consumer.[58]

One technique that holds great potential for understanding how consumers process information is neuroscience, as Marketing in Action 4.2 discusses.

Motivation

An understanding of **motivation** lies in the relationship between needs, drives and goals.[59] The basic process involves needs (deprivations) that set drives in motion (deprivations with direction) to accomplish goals (anything that alleviates a need and reduces a drive). Motives can be grouped into five categories as proposed by Maslow[60] (see Fig. 4.5).

1 *Physiological*: the fundamentals of survival, e.g. hunger or thirst.
2 *Safety*: protection from the unpredictable happening in life, e.g. accidents, ill-health.
3 *Belongingness and love*: striving to be accepted by those to whom we feel close, and to be an important person to them. The popularity of social network site Facebook has been driven by this premise.

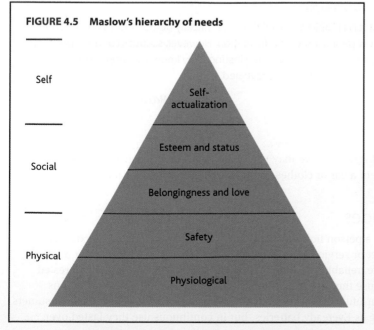

FIGURE 4.5   Maslow's hierarchy of needs

Self

Social

Physical

Self-actualization

Esteem and status

Belongingness and love

Safety

Physiological

4 *Esteem and status*: striving to achieve a high standing relative to other people; a desire for prestige and a high reputation.
5 *Self-actualization*: the desire for self-fulfilment in achieving what one is capable of for one's own sake.

Maslow's model is widely used in management teaching, but you should be aware that it was devised in the mid-twentieth century and centred on American society where individualism was very important, especially to the *middle classes*.[61] Arguably, this is rather one-dimensional, as the model does not accommodate the influences of others on an individual's motivations—e.g. family, children, work colleagues, society (see Read the Research 4.1 for more in-depth analysis).

It is important to understand the motives that drive consumers, because they determine choice criteria. For example, a consumer who is

Marketing in Action 4.2   Neuromarketing: New Horizon or False Dawn?

Which image would you choose to sell milk?

According to one of the world's leading neuromarketing experts, Dr A K Pradeep, 'the one that always wins out is the cows'. He suggests the underlying reasoning is that the source of a product hits a spot deep in the subconscious which is more evocative than any of the other associated images. Pradeep says that neuroscience allows marketers to find out what a brand means in the subconscious mind. One brand that he feels understands how to 'market to the buying brain' is Jo Malone. This perfume brand uses images of ingredients to trigger positive emotions, which he advocates are far more powerful than images of a man and woman in passionate embraces.

For marketers, the key question is how consumers process information because it sheds light on how they make purchasing choices—for example, what clothes we buy or what music we like to listen to. Potentially, neuroscience and its study of the brain and nervous system by means of functional magnetic resonance imaging (fMRI) scanning has all the answers. The brain is made up of networks of neurons. When these cell clusters are stimulated, they use more energy. These active areas light up on fMRI scans, allowing researchers to map emotion and cognition. The scanner produces a colour-coded image of the brain that is helpful in revealing a person's unconscious feelings about a brand, an advertisement or, even, a media channel. For example, the effects of different media channels (e.g. print versus the Internet) on brain stimulation have been found to be useful when making media decisions. This application of the techniques of neuroscience to marketing is called neuromarketing.

Neuromarketing advocates like Pradeep argue that it is an objective tool that scientifically demonstrates and quantifies human reactions and provides new insights into how people process information. However, sceptics counter that it has not revealed huge insights into human behaviour that are not already instinctively known. As applications of neuromarketing develop, the truth about its worth to marketers will be revealed.

Based on: McCormick (2011);[62] Lovell (2008)[63]

driven by the esteem and status motive may use self-image as a key choice criterion when considering the purchase of a car or clothes. Understanding this enables marketers to tap into motives directly.

Beliefs and attitudes

A *belief* is a thought that a person holds about something. In a marketing context, it is a thought about a product or service on one or more choice criteria. Beliefs about a Volvo car might be that it is safe, reliable and high status. Marketing people are very interested in consumer beliefs because they are related to attitudes. In particular, misconceptions about products can be harmful to brand sales. Duracell batteries were believed by consumers to last three times as long as Eveready batteries, but in continuous use they lasted over

Go to the website to see how Marmite 'lovers' are reminded about the brand. www.mcgraw-hill.co.uk/ textbooks/jobber

Read the Research 4.1 Consumer Motivations

Consumer motivation has been widely explored through academic study. Read the research which examines the latest thinking in this area.

Motivation is the force that drives us to do something. Understanding this force has been a prime objective of marketers and managers over a number of years to help explain what motivates people to buy or perform better in the workplace.

Two enduring, but contrasting theories—Maslow's hierarchy of needs and Herzberg's motivation-hygiene theory—are discussed and critiqued in this article on staff turnover in a correctional facility. The step-by-step approach offers an insightful understanding of the theories to help marketing managers adopt the appropriate strategy to accomplish their objectives.

Ikwukananne Udechukwu (2009) Correctional Officer Turnover: Of Maslow's Needs Hierarchy and Herzberg's Motivation Theory, Public Personnel Management 38(2), 69–82.

Today, impulse buying grossly violates the assumptions of *homo economicus* (economic human). For instance, impulse buying is often associated with joy and pleasure but has also been linked to negative emotions and low self-esteem. This article explores a variety of perspectives on impulse buying, and the results lead to ask if consumers should be protected from their impulsivity via legislation or is self-regulation a more obvious solution.

Bas Verplanken and Ayana Sato: The Psychology of Impulse Buying: An Integrative Self-Regulation Approach, Journal of Consumer Policy, published online: 26 March 2011, 197–210.

six times as long. This prompted Duracell to launch an advertising campaign to correct this misconception. The promotion for Marmite crisps recognizes that the beliefs of some consumers will be favourable towards the brand and others negative. By presenting the brand in this way, the advertisement is inviting consumers to try the crisps to discover which group they are in.

An *attitude* is an overall favourable or unfavourable evaluation of a product or service. The consequence of a set of beliefs may be a positive or negative attitude towards the product or service. Beliefs and attitudes play an important part in the evaluation of alternatives in the consumer decision-making process. They may be developed as part of the information search activity and/or as a result of product use, and play an important role in product design (matching product attributes to beliefs and attitudes); in persuasive communications (reinforcing existing positive beliefs and attitudes, correcting misconceptions and establishing new beliefs, e.g. Skoda is a quality car brand); and in pricing (matching price with customers' beliefs about what a 'good' product would cost).

Personality

Our everyday dealings with people tell us that they differ enormously in their personalities. **Personality** is the inner psychological characteristics of individuals that lead to consistent responses to their environment.[64] A person may tend to be warm–cold, dominant–subservient, introvert–extrovert, sociable–loner, adaptable–inflexible, competitive–cooperative, etc. If we find from marketing research that our product is being purchased by people with a certain personality profile, then advertising could show people of the same type using the product.

The concept of personality is also relevant to brands. *Brand personality* is their characterization as perceived by consumers. Brands may be characterized as 'for young people' (Tommy Hilfiger), 'for winners' (Nike), or 'intelligent' (Toyota iQ). This is a dimension over and above the physical (e.g. colour) or functional (e.g. taste) attributes of a brand. By creating a brand personality, a marketer may create appeal to people who value that characterization. Research into brand personalities of beers showed that most consumers preferred the brand of beer that matched their own personality.[65]

Economic circumstances

During periods of economic growth, consumer spending is fuelled by rising income levels and confidence in job security. Products that are the subject of discretionary spending, such as luxury brands, expensive holidays, restaurant meals and top-of-the-range consumer durables, thrive. However, during economic recession fears about employment prospects drive many consumers to postpone purchases, become more price sensitive and change their shopping habits. Economic circumstances, therefore, can have a major effect on consumer behaviour, as Marketing in Action 4.3 explains.

Marketing in Action 4.3 How Consumer Behaviour Changes During a Recession

During an economic recession many people experience financial hardship and respond to changing circumstances by changing their purchasing behaviour. Lengthy periods of economic downturn can affect all socioeconomic groups, even the wealthiest; the Office for National Statistics (ONS) predicted that households with annual incomes of £62,000 or above would reduce their annual spend by around £3000 in an economic recession. Economies in household spending might be achieved by:

- *Downsizing*: buying small, fuel-efficient cars rather than large gas-guzzlers. This has meant consumers have moved from SUVs and sports cars to compacts and hybrid (petrol-electric) cars.
- *Discounting*: shopping more at discount supermarkets such as Aldi, Lidl and Netto rather than Marks & Spencer and Waitrose.
- *Eating out less*: visiting restaurants less often, while buying more premium-priced supermarket ready meals and door-delivered foods like Domino's pizzas.
- *Buying low-priced basics*: moving from branded products to lower-priced own-label brands (e.g. Sainsbury's 'Basics' range) for basic items such as frozen peas, bread and rice.
- *De-greening*: being more reluctant to buy environmentally friendly products where cheaper alternatives are available.
- *Inexpensive treating*: looking for inexpensive treats such as eating chocolate.
- *Delaying*: putting off purchases of consumer durables such as cars and household furnishings.

The tendency for many shoppers to place greater emphasis on searching for value has caused markets to respond by launching fighter brands. Rather than drop price across the entire product range, supermarkets like Tesco and Sainsbury's extended their value ranges, and in the case of Tesco introduced a second-tier 'discounter' range targeted at shoppers who are reluctant to trade down to 'value' items but, nevertheless, wanted to save money from their normal branded products. Another response was to emphasize lifetime costs rather than price. For example, Lexus, the premium-priced car brand, ran advertisements with the tag-line 'Lowest Cost of Ownership', based on its decent fuel economy and high resale value. Marks & Spencer's toyed with smart consumers looking for a different means to get the same end by offering them a meal deal for £20 to stay in on St Valentine's Day.

Based on: Cooper (2011);[66] *Alarcon (2008);*[67] *Finch (2008);*[68] *Helm (2008)*[69]

Lifestyle

Lifestyle patterns have attracted much attention from marketing research practitioners. **Lifestyle** refers to the pattern of living as expressed in a person's activities, interests and opinions. Lifestyle analysis (psychographics) groups consumers according to their beliefs, activities, values, and demographic characteristics such as education and income. For example, the advertising agency Young & Rubicam has identified the following major lifestyle groups that can be found throughout Europe and the USA.

1 *The mainstreamers*: the largest group. Attitudes include conventional, trusting, cautious and family centred. Leisure activities include spectator sports and gardening; purchase behaviour is habitual, brand loyal and in approved stores.

2 *The aspirers*: members of this group tend to be ambitious, suspicious and unhappy. Leisure activities include trendy sports and fashion magazines; they buy fads, are impulse shoppers and engage in conspicuous consumption.

3 *The succeeders*: these people are leaders, industrious, confident and happy. Leisure activities include travel, sports, sailing and dining out. Purchase decisions are based on choice criteria such as quality, status and luxury.

4 *The transitionals*: members of this group are liberal, rebellious, self-expressive and intuitive. They have unconventional tastes in music, travel and movies; and enjoy cooking, and arts and crafts. Shopping behaviour tends to be impulsive and to involve unique products.

5 *The reformers*: these people are self-confident and involved, have broad interests and are issues orientated. They like reading, cultural events, intelligent games and educational TV. They have eclectic tastes, enjoy natural foods, and are concerned about authenticity and ecology.

6 *The struggling poor*: members of this group are unhappy, suspicious and feel left out. Their interests are in sports, music and television; their purchase behaviour tends to be price-based, and they are looking for instant gratification.

7 *The resigned poor*: people in this group are unhappy, isolated and insecure. Television is their main leisure activity and their shopping behaviour is price-based, although they also look for the reassurance of branded goods.

Lifestyle analysis has implications for marketing since lifestyles have been found to correlate with purchasing behaviour.[70] A company may choose to target a particular lifestyle group (e.g. the succeeders) with a product offering, and use communications which reflect the values and beliefs of this group. An example of how changing lifestyles affect consumer behaviour is the popularity of on-the-go products with people who live very busy lives. On-the-go drinks, such as bottled water and takeaway coffee, and on-the-go food, such as cereal-based breakfast snack bars, have found favour among time-pressured consumers.

Life-cycle and age

Consumer behaviour might depend on the stages reached during their lives. A person's *life-cycle stage* (shown in Fig. 4.6) is relevant since disposable income and purchase requirements may vary according to stage. For example, young couples with no children may have high disposable income if both work, and may be heavy purchasers of home furnishings and appliances since they may be setting up home. When they have children, disposable income may fall, particularly if they become a single-income family and the purchase of baby- and child-related products increases. At the empty-nester stage, disposable income may rise due to the absence of dependent children, low mortgage repayments and high personal income. This type of person may be a high-potential target for financial services and holidays. BMW uses life-cycle stage to segment consumers with its 4 × 4 X5 model targeted at young couples with children, and the 4 × 4 X6 model targeted at empty nesters. The X6 is designed for someone who previously owned an X5, or something similar, but now is looking for an SUV that 'doesn't scream "family"'.[71]

However, not all people follow the classic family life-cycle stages. Figure 4.6 also shows alternative paths that may have consumer behaviour and market segmentation implications.

Age is an effective discriminator of consumer behaviour. For example, young people have very different tastes in product categories such as clothing, drinks, holidays and television viewing compared to older people. The young have always been a prime target for marketers because of their capacity to spend.

Social influences

There are four social influences on consumer behaviour: culture, social class, geodemographics and reference groups.

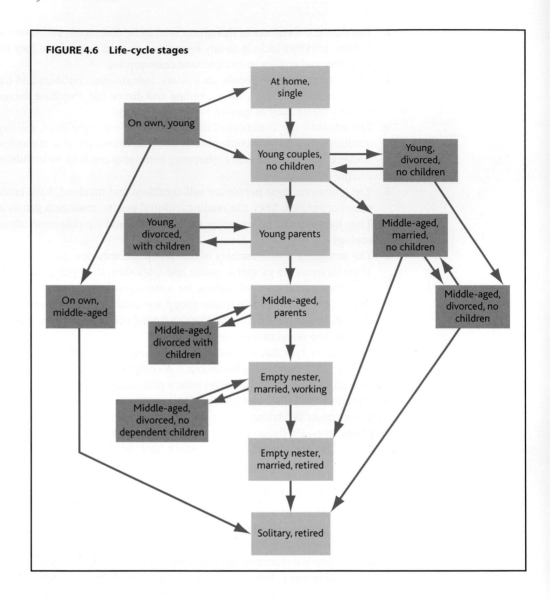

FIGURE 4.6 Life-cycle stages

Culture

Culture refers to the traditions, taboos, values and basic attitudes of the whole society within which an individual lives. It provides the framework within which individuals and their lifestyles develop. Cultural norms are the rules that govern behaviour, and are based upon values: beliefs about what attitudes and behaviour are desirable. Conformity to norms is created by reward-giving (e.g. smiling) and sanctioning (e.g. criticism). Cultural values affect how business is conducted. Culture also affects consumption behaviour.

The spread of global communications technology and greater global mobility has led to a degree of social and cultural convergence. This does not mean that a global culture is replacing the diversity of local and national cultures in the world. Deep-rooted beliefs and values, and religious differences prevent that. However, the emergence of a global consumer, or at least consumers with common preferences across a large part of the world, has created opportunities for global brands (e.g. Chanel, BMW, Apple and IBM), supported by global marketing campaigns with only slight modifications to accommodate national differences.[72]

Social class

Social class has long been regarded as an important determinant of consumer behaviour. In the UK it is largely based on occupation, and respondents to marketing research surveys are often classified in this way. Advertising media (e.g. newspapers) usually give readership/ viewership figures broken down by social class groupings. Every country has its own method of grouping and, in the UK, the National Statistics Socio-economic Classification system identifies eight categories based on occupation (see Table 4.4).

The implication is that social class is a predictive measure of consumption although consumption patterns are likely to vary within each of the groups (e.g. some people may be more inclined to spend their money on consumer durables, while others may have more hedonistic preferences). It is important to note that the influence of social class should be tempered by life-cycle, lifestyle and age.

Geodemographics

Another method of classifying households is based on geographic location. This analysis—called **geodemographics**—is based on population census data. Households are grouped into geographic clusters based on information such as type of accommodation, car ownership, age, occupation, number and age of children, and ethnicity. These clusters can be identified by postcodes, which makes targeting by mail easier. A number of systems are use in the UK, including PINPOINT and MOSAIC, but the best known is ACORN (A Classification Of Residential Neighbourhoods). The ACORN system identified 11 neighbourhood types (discussed in more detail in Chapter 8) which can be used for market segmentation and positioning. Geodemographics is an effective method of segmenting many markets, including financial services and retailing and is a powerful discriminator between different lifestyles, purchasing patterns and media exposure.[73]

Reference groups

The term **reference group** indicates a group of people that influences an individual's attitude or behaviour. Where a product is conspicuous—for example, clothing or cars—the brand or model chosen may have been strongly influenced by what buyers perceive as acceptable to their reference group. This group may consist of family members, a group of friends or work colleagues. Some reference groups may be formal (e.g. members of a club or society), while others may be informal (friends with similar interests). Reference groups influence their members by the roles and norms expected of them. For example, students may have to play

TABLE 4.4 Social class categories

Classification	Descriptors	Occupations
1	Higher managerial and professional occupations	Senior managers, directors and professionals
2	Lower managerial and professional occupations	Higher technical and supervisory occupations, e.g., department managers
3	Intermediate occupations	Clerical/administrative, sales/service, technical/auxiliary and engineering occupations
4	Small employers and sole traders	Non-professional and agricultural occupations, and self-employed sole traders
5	Lower supervisory and technical occupations	Technical craft and process operative occupations, e.g., shift manager in a factory
6	Semi-routine occupations	Service and technical operatives, agricultural, clerical and childcare occupations
7	Routine occupations	Production, technical, operative and agricultural occupations
8	Never worked and long-term unemployed	Never worked, long-term unemployed and students

several roles: to lecturers, the student's role may be that of learner; to other students, their role may vary from peer to social companion. Depending on the role, various behaviours may be expected based upon group norms. To the extent that group norms influence values and attitudes, these reference groups may be seen as an important determinant of behaviour. Sometimes reference group norms can conflict, as when reference to the learning role suggests different patterns of behaviour from that of social companion. In terms of consumption, reference group influence can affect student purchasing of clothing, beverages, social events and textbooks, for example. The more conspicuous the choice is to the reference group, the stronger its influence.

There are two main types of reference group: membership and aspirant groups. *Membership groups* are the groups to which a person already belongs. What is believed to be suitable, acceptable and/or impressive to this group may play a major role in consumption behaviour. What other people think at a party, at work or generally socializing is of great importance. *Aspirant groups* are the groups to which the individual would like to belong. Stereotypically, men supposedly want to look/feel like their favourite sport stars and women want to look/feel like famous film stars or models. This motivates the purchase of football shirts with 'Ronaldo' on the back, and the buying of clothing seen to be worn by Adele or Kate Moss. ASOS, the online fashion retailer, bases its marketing strategy on aspirant group theory. It copies the style of clothing worn by film stars and models, and sells its clothes to aspirant women who wish to dress like them. Celebrities such as David Beckham, Ronaldo, Kate Moss and Angelina Jolie also act as opinion leaders to aspirant group members, influencing their consumption behaviour.

When you have read this chapter

log on to the Online Learning Centre at **www.mcgraw-hill.co.uk/textbooks/jobber** to explore chapter-by-chapter test questions, links and further online study tools for marketing.

Review

① **The dimensions of buyer behaviour**
- Looking at the dimensions of the buying decision: how they buy, what their choice criteria are, where they buy and when they buy, helps identify what is important and has implication for the marketing mix.

② **The role of the buying centre (who buys) and its implications**
- Some buying decisions are made individually, others by a group. A group decision may be in the hands of a buying centre with up to five roles: initiator, influencer, decider, buyer and user. The interaction between these roles determines whether a purchase is made.
- Marketers need to understand the formulation of buying groups as this can be helpful in targeting and segmenting of markets, and planning the core strategy.

③ **The consumer decision-making process (how people buy)**
- The decision to purchase a consumer product may pass through a number of stages: need recognition/problem awareness, information search, evaluation of alternatives, purchase, and post-purchase evaluation of the decision.

4 **The marketing implications of the consumer decision-making process**
Each stage in the process potentially has implications for marketing managers:
- *Need recognition*: awareness of consumer problems can create opportunities for building a competitive advantage and planning strategies to overcome any *need* inhibitors; stimulating need recognition through marketing communications might help initiate the decision-making process.
- *Information search*: where consumers look for information to help solve their decision-making can aid marketing planning. Communication can direct consumers to suitable sources of information. One objective is to ensure that the company's brand appears in the consumer's awareness set.
- *Evaluation of alternatives*: when a consumer is highly involved, they might require much information about the positives of making a particular buying decision. In this situation it is important to provide sufficiently detailed information to aid decision-making. For low-involvement decisions, creating top-of-mind awareness through repetitive advertising and trial (e.g. through sales promotion) can aid the decision-making. For all consumer decisions, marketing managers must understand the choice criteria used to evaluate brands, including the importance of emotion.
- *Post-purchase evaluation*: consumers can experience cognitive dissonance after making a purchase and might need reassurance. Advertisements, direct mail or reviews and other communications can act as positive reinforcers.

5 **The differences in evaluation of high- versus low-involvement situations**
- *High-involvement situations*: the consumer is more likely to carry out extensive evaluation and take into account beliefs about the perceived consequences of buying the brand, the extent to which important others believe they should or should not buy the brand, attitudes (which are the degree to which the consumer likes or dislikes the brand overall), and subjective norms (which form an overall evaluation of the degree to which important others approve or disapprove of the purchase).
- *Low-involvement situations*: the consumer carries out a simple evaluation and uses simple choice tactics to reduce time and effort. Awareness precedes trial, which, if satisfactory, leads to repeat purchase. The behaviour may become habitual, with little conscious thought or formation of attitudes before purchase.

6 **The nature of choice criteria (what are used) and their implications**
- Choice criteria are the various attributes (and benefits) a consumer uses when evaluating products and services. These may be technical (e.g. reliability), economic (e.g. price), social (e.g. status) or personal (e.g. self-image).
- The implications are that knowledge of the choice criteria used by members of the buying centre aids product design (e.g. are style/looks more important than performance?) and the choice of the appeals to use in advertising and personal selling, which should be linked to the key choice criteria used by those members.

7 **The influences on consumer behaviour—the buying situation, personal and social influences—and implications for marketing**
- *Buying situation*: the three types are extended problem-solving, limited problem-solving and habitual problem-solving. The marketing implications for each type are: extended problem-solving—provide information-rich communications; limited problem-solving—stimulate the need to conduct a search (when their brand is not currently bought) or reduce the risk of brand switching; habitual problem-solving—repetitive advertising should be used to create awareness and reinforce already favourable attitudes.
- *Personal influences*: the six types are information processing, motivation, beliefs and attitudes, personality, lifestyle, and life-cycle and age, and have implications for marketing:
  1) *Information processing* involves perceptions and learning. *Perceptions* help consumers sort out the masses of stimuli into manageable amounts of information through a process called (i) *selective attention* (which implies that advertisements, logos and packaging need to be attention-getting); (ii) *selective distortion* (which implies that messages should be presented clearly, using a credible source and with supporting evidence); (iii) *selective retention* (which implies that messages that are in line with existing beliefs and attitudes are more likely to be remembered).
     Learning involves conditioning and cognitive learning. *Conditioning* suggests that associating a brand with humour (e.g. in advertisements) or excitement (e.g. motor racing sponsorship) will carry over to the brand, and also that the use of free samples and coupons (reinforcers) can encourage sales by inducing trial and repeat

buying. Through the reinforcers the consumer will have learnt to associate the brand with pleasurable experiences.

Cognitive learning suggests that statements in an advertisement may be remembered, the promise of a reward may influence behaviour, as may communications that allow the recipient to draw his/her own conclusions. The result of the learning process is the creation of product positioning.

2) *Motives* influence choice criteria and include physiological, safety, belongingness and love, esteem and status, and self-actualization.

3) *Beliefs* and attitudes are linked in that the consequence of a set of beliefs may be a positive or negative attitude. Marketers attempt to match product attributes to desired beliefs and attitudes, and use communications to influence these and establish new beliefs.

4) *Personality* of the type of person who buys a brand may be reflected in the type of person used in its advertisements. Brand personality is used to appeal to people who identify with that characterization.

5) *Lifestyles* have been shown to be linked to purchase behaviour. Lifestyle groups can be used for market segmentation and targeting purposes.

6) *Life-cycle and age* stage may affect consumer behaviour as the level of disposable income and purchase requirements (needs) may depend on the stage that people have reached during their life. For similar reasons, age may affect consumer behaviour.

- There are four types of social influence: culture, social class, geodemographics and reference groups.

1) *Culture* affects how business is conducted and consumption behaviour. Marketers have to adjust their behaviour and the marketing mix to accommodate different cultures.

2) *Social class* can predict some consumption patterns, and so can be used for market segmentation and targeting purposes.

3) *Geodemographics* classifies consumers according to their location, and is used for market segmentation and targeting purposes.

4) *Reference groups* influence their members by the roles and norms expected of them. Marketers attempt to make their brands acceptable to reference groups, and target opinion leaders to gain brand acceptability.

Key Terms

attitude the degree to which a customer or prospect likes or dislikes a brand

awareness set the set of brands that the consumer is aware may provide a solution to the problem

beliefs descriptive thoughts that a person holds about something

buyers generally refers to professionals in procurement. A buyer makes business decisions on purchasing

buying centre a group that is involved in the buying decision (also known as a *decision-making unit*)

choice criteria the various attributes (and benefits) people use when evaluating products and services

classical conditioning the process of using an established relationship between a stimulus and a response to cause the learning of the same response to a different stimulus

cognitive dissonance post-purchase concerns of a consumer arising from uncertainty as to whether a decision to purchase was the correct one

cognitive learning the learning of knowledge and development of beliefs and attitudes without direct reinforcement

consumer a person who buys goods and services for personal use

consumer decision-making process the stages a consumer goes through when buying something—namely, problem awareness, information search, evaluation of alternatives, purchase and post-purchase evaluation

customers a term used in both consumer and organizational purchasing situations. These are individuals and companies that have an established relationship with a seller (e.g. retailers, producers, manufacturers)

evoked set the set of brands that the consumer seriously evaluates before making a purchase

geodemographics the process of grouping households into geographic clusters based on information such as type of accommodation, occupation, number and age of children, and ethnic background

information framing the way in which information is presented to people

information processing the process by which a stimulus is received, interpreted, stored in memory and later retrieved

information search the identification of alternative ways of problem-solving

learning any change in the content or organization of long-term memory as the result of information processing

lifestyle the pattern of living as expressed in a person's activities, interests and opinions

motivation the process involving needs that set drives in motion to accomplish goals

operant conditioning the use of rewards to generate reinforcement of response

perception the process by which people select, organize and interpret sensory stimulation into a meaningful picture of the world

personality the inner psychological characteristics of individuals that lead to consistent responses to their environment

reasoning a more complex form of cognitive learning where conclusions are reached by connected thought

reference group a group of people that influences an individual's attitude or behaviour

rote learning the learning of two or more concepts without conditioning

selective attention the process by which people screen out those stimuli that are neither meaningful to them nor consistent with their experiences and beliefs

selective distortion the distortion of information received by people according to their existing beliefs and attitudes

selective retention the process by which people only retain a selection of messages in memory

vicarious learning learning from others without direct experience or reward

Study Questions

1. **Choose a recent purchase which involved you and other people in the decision-making. Explain what role(s) you played in the buying centre. What roles did these other people play and how did they influence your choice?**

2. **What decision-making process did you go through? At each stage (need recognition, information search, etc.), try to remember what you were thinking about and what activities took place.**

3. **What choice criteria did you use? Did they change between drawing up a shortlist and making the final choice?**

4. **Think of the last time you made an impulse purchase. What stimulated you to buy? Have you bought the brand again? Why or why not? Did your thoughts and actions resemble those suggested by the Ehrenberg and Goodhart model?**

5. **Can you think of a brand that has used the principles of classical conditioning in its advertising?**

6. **Are there any brands that you buy (e.g. beer, perfume) that have personalities that match your own?**

7. **To what kind of lifestyle do you aspire? How does this affect the types of product (particularly visible ones) you buy now and in the future?**

8. **Are you influenced by any reference groups? How do these groups influence what you buy?**

References

1. Barnett, M. (2011) Why the customer is the kingmaker, *Marketing Week* 3 November, 16.
2. Hegarty, J. (2011) *Hegarty on Advertising: turning intelligence into magic*, London: Thames & Hudson, 43.
3. Leeflang, P. S. H. and W. F. van Raaij (1995) The Changing Consumer in the European Union: A Meta-Analysis, *International Journal of Research in Marketing* 12, 373–87.
4. Blackwell, R. D., P. W. Miniard and J. F. Engel (2005) *Consumer Behavior*, Orlando, FL: Dryden.
5. Woodside, A. G. and W. H. Mote (1979) Perceptions of Marital Roles in Consumer Processes for Six Products, in Beckwith *et al.* (eds) *American Marketing Association Educator Proceedings*, Chicago: American Marketing Association, 214–19.
6. Costa, A. I. A., D. Schoolmeester, M. Dekker and W. M. F. Jongen (2007) To cook or not to cook: A means-end study of motives for choice of meal solutions, *Food Quality and Preference* 18, 77–88.
7. http://www.euro.who.int/en/who-we-are/regional-director/news/news/2010/12/2570-of-adults-in-europe-are-overweight.
8. Olsen, N. V., E. Menichelli, O. Sørheim and T. Næs (2012) Likelihood of buying healthy convenience food: An at-home testing procedure for ready-to-heat meals, *Food Quality and Preference* 24(1), 171–8.
9. Barda, T. (2011) Beer Googles, *The Marketer*, April, 20–22.
10. Blackwell, Miniard and Engel (2005) op. cit.
11. Neal, C., P. Quester and D. I. Hawkins (2007) *Consumer Behavior: Implications for Marketing Strategy*, Boston, Mass: Irwin.
12. O'Shaughnessey, J. (1987) *Why People Buy*, New York: Oxford University Press, 161.
13. Microsoft (2012) The Evolution of Pre-family Man, http://advertising.microsoft.com/europe/WWDocs/User/Europe/ResearchLibrary/ResearchReport/8.%20The%20Evolution%20of%20Pre-family%20man.pdf.
14. Baumgartner, H. and J. Bem Steenkamp (1996) Exploratory Consumer Buying Behaviour: Conceptualisation and Measurement, *International Journal of Research in Marketing* 13, 121–37.
15. http://www.kwikchex.com/ (accessed January 2012).
16. Cochrane, K. (2011) Why TripAdvisor is getting a bad review, *Guardian*, 25 January, 6.
17. Kuusela, H., M. T. Spence and A. J. Kanto (1998) Expertise Effects on Prechoice Decision Processes and Final Outcomes: A Protocol Analysis, *European Journal of Marketing* 32(5/6), 559–76.
18. Creusen, M. E. H. and J. P. L. Schoormans (1997) The Nature of Differences between Similarity and Preference Judgements: A Replication and Extension, *International Journal of Research in Marketing* 14, 81–7.
19. Blackwell, Miniard and Engel (2005) op. cit.
20. Elliott, R. and E. Hamilton (1991) Consumer Choice Tactics and Leisure Activities, *International Journal of Advertising* 10, 325–32.
21. Ajzen, I. and M. Fishbein (1980) *Understanding Attitudes and Predicting Social Behavior*, Englewood Cliffs, NJ: Prentice-Hall.
22. See e.g. Budd, R. J. and C. P. Spencer (1984) Predicting Undergraduates' Intentions to Drink, *Journal of Studies on Alcohol* 45(2), 179–83; Farley, J., D. Lehman and M. Ryan (1981) Generalizing from 'Imperfect' Replication, *Journal of Business* 54(4), 597–610; Shimp, T. and A. Kavas (1984) The Theory of Reasoned Action Applied to Coupon Usage, *Journal of Consumer Research* 11, 795–809.
23. Ehrenberg, A. S. C. and G. J. Goodhart (1980) *How Advertising Works*, J. Walter Thompson/MRCA.
24. Wright, P. L. (1974) The Choice of a Choice Strategy: Simplifying vs Optimizing, Faculty Working Paper no. 163, Champaign, Ill: Department of Business Administration, University of Illinois.
25. Rothschild, M. L. (1978) Advertising Strategies for High and Low Involvement Situations, *American Marketing Association Educator's Proceedings*, Chicago, 150–62.
26. Rothschild (1978) op. cit.
27. For a discussion of the role of involvement in package labelling see Davies, M. A. P. and L. T. Wright (1994) The Importance of Labelling Examined in Food Marketing, *European Journal of Marketing* 28(2), 57–67.
28. Elliott, R. (1997) Understanding Buyers: Implications for Selling, in D. Jobber (ed.) *The CIM Handbook of Selling and Sales Strategy*, Oxford: Butterworth-Heinemann.
29. See Elliott, R. (1998) A Model of Emotion-Driven Choice, *Journal of Marketing Management* 14, 95–108; Rook, D. (1987) The Buying Impulse, *Journal of Consumer Research* 14(1), 89–99.
30. Neal, Quester and Hawkins (2007) op. cit.
31. *The Economist* (2008) Follow the Leader, 14 June, 82–3.
32. Bedell, G. (2003) The *Observer Review*, 19 January, 1–2.
33. Manchester United (2011) http://www.united-latest.com/1/post/2011/04/united-demand-450-million-nike-kit-deal.html.
34. See Carrigan, M. and A. Attala (2001) The Myth of the Ethical Consumer—Do Ethics Matter in Purchase Behaviour? *Journal of Consumer Marketing* 18(7), 560–77; and Follows, S. B. and D. Jobber (1999) Environmentally Responsible Behaviour: A Test of a Consumer Model, *European Journal of Marketing* 34(5/6), 723–46.
35. Carrigan and Attala (2001) op. cit.; www.ethicalconsumer.org/Portals/0/Downloads/ETHICAL%20CONSUMER%20REPORT.pdf.
36. Mowen, J. C. (1988) Beyond Consumer Decision Making, *Journal of Consumer Research* 5(1), 15–25.
37. Elliot and Hamilton (1991) op. cit.
38. Carter, M. (2002) Ruthlessly Shopping for Comfort, *Financial Times*, 20 May, 12.
39. http://www.guinnessworldrecords.com/records-9000/most-expensive-olympic-ticket-/.
40. http://seatgeek.com/rolling-stones-tickets/.
41. Smith, L. (2005) Ten Sales a Second: Glastonbury Tickets Go in Record Rush, *Guardian*, 4 April, 7.
42. Gibson, O. (2008) Led Zep Tickets Fetch £7425 as Online 'Touts' Strike Gold in £200m Bonanza, *Guardian*, 8 January, 13.
43. Neal, Quester and Hawkins (2007) op. cit.
44. Blackwell, Miniard and Engel (2005) op. cit.
45. Bettman, J. R. (1982) A Functional Analysis of the Role of Overall Evaluation of Alternatives and Choice Processes, in Mitchell, A. (ed.) *Advances in Consumer Research 8*, Ann Arbor, Michigan: Association for Consumer Research, 87–93.
46. Laurent, G. and J. N. Kapferer (1985) Measuring Consumer Involvement Profiles, *Journal of Marketing Research* 12 (February), 41–53.
47. Blackwell, Miniard and Engel (2005) op. cit.
48. Williams, K. C. (1981) *Behavioural Aspects of Marketing*, London: Heinemann.
49. Neal, Quester and Hawkins (2007) op. cit.
50. Ratneshwar, S., L. Warlop, D. G. Mick and G. Seegar (1997) Benefit Salience and Consumers' Selective Attention to Product Features, *International Journal of Research in Marketing* 14, 245–9.
51. http://www.raspberrypi.org/sample-page.
52. Graham-Rowe, D. (2012) Raspberry Pi: Britain's £16 computer (and what powers it), *Wired Magazine*, www.wired.co.uk/magazine/archive/2012/03/start/finally-16-pound-computer (accessed February 2012).
53. Levin, L. P. and G. J. Gaeth (1988) Framing of Attribute Information Before and After Consuming the Product, *Journal of Consumer Research* 15 (December), 374–78.
54. Key, A. (2000) The Colour-Coded Secrets of Brands, *Marketing*, 6 January, 21.
55. http://sg.news.yahoo.com/fragrance-flight-planned-improve-cabin-experience-110046669.html.

56. Lindstrom, M. (2005) Sensing the Opportunity, *The Marketeer*, February, 4–17.

57. Neal, Quester and Hawkins (2007) op. cit.

58. Ries, A. and J. Trout (2001) *Positioning: The Battle for Your Mind*, New York: Warner.

59. Luthans, F. (2001) *Organisational Behavior*, San Francisco: McGraw-Hill.

60. Maslow, A. H. (1954) *Motivation and Personality*, New York: Harper & Row, 80–106.

61. Bennet, B. (2011) Another criticism of Maslow's hierarchy of needs, http://billbennett.co.nz/2011/07/02/criticism-maslows-hierarchy/.

62. McCormick, A. (2011) Marketing on the brain, *Marketing*, 2 November, 24–5.

63. Lovell, C. (2008) Is Neuroscience Making a Difference?, *Campaign*, 3 October, 11.

64. Kassarjan, H. H. (1971) Personality and Consumer Behaviour Economics: A Review, *Journal of Marketing Research*, November, 409–18.

65. Ackoff, R. L. and J. R. Emsott (1975) Advertising at Anheuser-Busch, Inc., *Sloan Management Review*, Spring, 1–15.

66. Cooper, L. (2011) Brands feeling the pinch need to tailor the offer, *Marketing Week*, 5 May, 25–8.

67. Alarcon, C. (2008) M&S to be Hardest Hit As Consumers Change Food Buying Patterns, *Marketing Week*, 16 October, 6.

68. Finch, J. (2008) Sainsbury's Feels the Difference in Eating Habits, *Guardian*, 19 June, 27.

69. Helm, B. (2008) How to Sell Luxury to Penny-Pinchers, *Business Week*, 10 November, 60.

70. O'Brien, S. and R. Ford (1988) Can We at Last Say Goodbye to Social Class?, *Journal of the Market Research Society* 30(3), 289–332.

71. Smith, G. (2008) On the Road, *Guardian Weekend*, 21 June, 99.

72. Johnson, D. and C. Turner (2006) *European Business*, London: Routledge.

73. Baker, K., J. Germingham and C. Macdonald (1979) The Utility to Market Research of the Classification of Residential Neighbourhoods, *Market Research Society Conference*, Brighton, March, 206–17.

Cappuccino Wars
The Battle for the High Street

The UK has come a long way from the days when a request for coffee would bring a cup of uniformly grey, unappealing liquid, sometimes served in polystyrene cups, which bore no relation to the rich, flavoursome coffee experienced on trips to continental Europe. The origin of this change was not Europe, however, but the USA, where the coffee bar culture was grounded.

Recent years have seen an explosion of coffee bars on UK high streets, with over 5 million lattés, cappuccinos and espressos served per week. The market is dominated by the US-owned Starbucks, with over 700 coffee bars, Costa Coffee (backed by Whitbread), with over 1300, and an independent, Caffè Nero, with around 400 bars. In total, the UK has over 3000 coffee shops, all charging over £2 (€2.90) for a small coffee. Often three or more bars will be located within 100 yards of each other.

The first US West Coast-style coffee shop was opened in the UK in 1995 and was called the Seattle Coffee Company. The owners were Americans who saw an opportunity to serve the British with good-quality coffee in relaxed surroundings just like they experienced in the USA. The concept was a huge success, and by 1997 the company had 49 coffee outlets. It was joined by Coffee Republic and Caffè Nero, which also grew rapidly. In 1997, however, the coffee market in the UK was to change dramatically with the arrival of the US-based Starbucks coffee bar giant, which bought the Seattle Coffee Company.

Its strategy was to gain market share through fast rollout. For the first five years Starbucks opened an average of five shops a month in the UK: in 1999 it had 95 shops, by 2012 this had increased to over 700. Today, Starbucks is in the Fortune Top 500 US companies and has nearly 15,000 coffee shops in more than 40 countries. Its approach is simple: blanket an area completely, even if the shops cannibalize one another's business. A new coffee bar will often capture about 30 per cent of the sales of a nearby Starbucks, but the company considered this was more than offset by lower delivery and management costs (per shop), shorter queues at individual shops and increased foot traffic for all the shops in an area as new shops take custom from competitors too. Twenty million people buy coffee at Starbucks every week, with the average Starbucks customer visiting 18 times a month.

One of its traditional strengths was the quality of its coffee. Starbucks has its own roasting plant, from which the media are banned lest its secrets are revealed. In its coffee shops, coffee is mixed with a lot of milk and offered in hundreds of flavours. Its Frappuccino is positioned as a midday break in advertisements where a narrator explains 'Starbucks Frappuccino coffee drink is a delicious blend of coffee and milk to smooth out your day'. The tag-line is 'Smooth out your day, everyday'.

A key problem is that Starbucks' major competitors—Costa Coffee and Caffè Nero—have also followed a fast roll-out strategy causing rental prices to spiral upwards. For example, Starbucks' Leicester Square coffee shop in London was part of a £1.5 million (€2.2 million) two-shop rental deal. Many coffee shops are not profitable and, with Starbucks continuing to operate them, it has been accused of unfairly trying to squeeze out the competition. Nevertheless, after sustaining losses in the early years all three major players are now profitable.

The typical consumer at these coffee bars is young, single and a high earner. They are likely to be professionals, and senior or middle managers with company cars. Students also are an important part of the market. Coffee bars are seen as a 'little bit of heaven', a refuge where consumers can lounge on sofas, read broadsheet newspapers and view New-Age poetry on the walls. They provide an oasis of calm for people between their homes and offices. They are regarded as a sign of social mobility for people who may be moving out of an ordinary café or low-end department store into something more classy. Even the language is important for these consumers, where terms such as latté, cappuccino and espresso allow them to demonstrate connoisseurship.

Coffee bars also cater for the different moods of consumers. For example, Sahar Hashemi, a founding partner of Coffee Republic, explains 'If I'm in my routine, I'll have a tall, skinny latté. But if I'm feeling in a celebratory mood or like spoiling myself, it's a grand vanilla mocha with whip and marshmallows.'

Starbucks has expanded the services it provides by offering a Wi-Fi service that allows laptop and personal digital assistant users to gain high-speed Internet access. This service has been copied by Costa Coffee and Caffè Nero.

Starbucks, Costa Coffee and Caffè Nero offer food alongside drinks. Starbucks targets breakfast, lunch and snack times with a limited range of both indulgent and healthy eating options. Costa Coffee has been offering hot foods and salads since 2002. Caffè Nero's food offer is integral to its Italian-style positioning, with most of the ingredients for its meals coming from Italy.

The chains have also embraced the fair trade coffee idea, with Costa Coffee offering Cafédirect products since 2000 and Starbucks introducing fair trade coffee in 2002. Starbucks has also met with considerable success for its low-calorie version of its Frappuccino iced drinks.

Declining performance at Starbucks led to the reappointment in 2008 of Howard Schultz as chief executive, the man who grew the firm from just four outlets to nearly 15,000 today. He identified Starbucks' problems as stemming from their outlets losing their 'romance and theatre'. He pointed out that the distinctive aroma of fresh coffee was less evident because of the advent of vacuum-sealed, flavour-locked packaging. Also, the use of new automated machines meant that customers could not see their drinks being prepared—eliminating an 'intimate experience' with the barista and impairing the spectacle of coffee-making. The result he concluded was that some customers found Starbucks coffee shops sterile places that no longer reflected a passion for coffee. The situation was made worse by the smell of sandwiches which often overpowered the aroma of coffee. Some Starbucks staff were also criticized as being unfriendly.

The problems facing Starbucks were worsened by a strong challenge from McDonald's who opened McCafés in some of their outlets where customers can buy similar drinks at a cheaper price. Their woes continued with a report from the consumer magazine *Which?* that showed that Starbucks coffee was inferior to Costa Coffee and Caffè Nero, which won. It was also the most expensive.

Mr Schultz has begun to address some of these problems by introducing new smaller expresso machines so customers can once again see the baristas making their drink. Coffee is once again being ground by hand, restoring the aroma, and a less potent-smelling cheese is being used in their sandwiches. The baristas have all been retrained not only in the art of making excellent coffee but also in connecting better with customers. The interiors of many of their coffee shops are being renovated. Stores in the USA have been closed and expansion of the chain abroad has been slowed as management realize that the market is saturated.

To make the outlets more attractive during the recession, a new instant coffee brand, Via, was launched which Starbucks claims tastes as good as ground coffee but at a much cheaper price. The company also introduced a loyalty card which allowed free extras such as a shot of whipped cream, syrup or soy in the coffee. Like Wi-Fi this innovation was copied by its rivals. A further change was the dropping of the 'Starbucks Coffee' logo from its mugs and changing the colour of its 'siren' figure from black to green.

Meanwhile, Costa Coffee has moved into the self-service market by buying Coffee Nation and its 900 vending machines. The new offering carries the Costa Express branding.

References

Based on: Cree, R. (2003) Sahar Hashemi, *The Director*, January, 44–7; Daniels, C. (2003) Mr Coffee, *Fortune*, 14 April, 139–40; Hedburg, A. and M. Rowe (2001) UK Goes Coffee House Crazy, *Marketing Week*, 4 January, 28–9; Sutter, S. (2003) Staff the Key to Marketing Success, *Marketing Magazine*, 19 May, 4; Bainbridge, J. (2005) Off the Boil, *Marketing*, 13 April, 28–9; Anonymous (2004) Starbucks to Offer 'Music to Go', *BBC News*, 12 March, http://news.bbc.co.uk.; Clark, A. (2008) Wall St Gets Palpitations Over Caffeine Fuelled Growth, *Guardian*, 7 January, 25; Anonymous (2008) Coffee Wars, *The Economist*, 12 January, 57–8; Fernandez, J. (2009) Back To Basics, *Marketing Week*, 26 February, 18–19; Charles, E. (2011) Change Brewing at Starbucks, *Marketing*, 12 January, 14–15; Reynolds, J. (2011) Costa Targets Tesco with Express Self-Service Offer, *Marketing*, 9 March, 9; Roberts, J. (2012) Quality Quest Keeps Sector Full of Beans, *Marketing Week*, 9 February, 22–3.

Questions

1. Why have coffee bars been so popular with consumers in the UK?

2. You are considering visiting a coffee bar for the first time. What would influence your choice of coffee bar to visit? Is this likely to be a high- or low-involvement decision?

3. Assess the coffee chains' moves to expand the offerings they provide for their customers.

4. Coffee bars are mainly located in the centres of towns and cities. Are there other locations where they could satisfy customer needs?

This case was written by David Jobber, Professor of Marketing, University of Bradford.

Dietrich Mateschitz is probably not a name that most people are familiar with. However, he is one of the most successful entrepreneurs of our age, a man who single-handedly changed the landscape of the beverage industry by creating not just a new brand but a whole new category: the energy drink. Mateschitz is the founder and co-owner of Red Bull GmbH, a privately held energy beverages production and marketing firm based in Fuschl am See, Austria. Founded in 1984, Red Bull GmbH produces the energy drink named Red Bull and markets it all around the world. Red Bull GmbH has had high growth since its launch as a premium energy drink thanks to its innovative marketing strategies and innate ability to understand its customers and the market.

How it all started

A chance trip to Thailand in 1982 would prove to be the turning point in Mateschitz's life. Here Mateschitz became aware of a local uncarbonated 'tonic drink' called Krating Daeng (Thai for water buffalo), which enjoyed widespread popularity throughout the Far East. Mateschitz was further intrigued when he read in a magazine that the top corporate taxpayer in Japan that year was a maker of such tonics. In 1984 Mateschitz approached Chaleo Yoovidhya, a Thai businessman who was selling the tonic in Southeast Asia, and suggested that the two introduce the drink to the rest of the world, with one crucial change: it would be carbonated. Yoovidhya liked the idea, and they agreed to invest $500,000 each to establish a 49/49 partnership, with the remaining 2 per cent going to Yoovidhya's son. (Yoovidhya remains a silent partner in the company). Mateschitz then returned to Austria where he founded Red Bull establishing the company's headquarters in Fuschl am See, not far from Salzburg, and began to plan the all-important packaging and slogan. For help, he turned to his university friend Johannes Kastner, who owned his own ad agency in Frankfurt, finally deciding on the distinctive blue-and-silver can emblazoned with the logo of two muscular bulls about to smash heads in front of a yellow sun. A slogan was harder to come by, with Kastner stating that the eventual slogan 'Gives You Wings' came to him at 3 a.m. and was his last attempt after telling Mateschitz to find another agency. Mateschitz developed a unique marketing strategy to sell Red Bull as an ultra-premium drink in a category all its own by making it far-and-away the most expensive

carbonated drink on the market. In 1987 Mateschitz started selling Red Bull Energy Drink on the Austrian market. This was not only the launch of a completely new product; it was in fact the birth of a totally new product category.

While the consumption was doubling year on year in Austria, Red Bull arrived in its first foreign markets, Singapore and Hungary in 1989 and 1992 respectively. The authorization for Germany was granted in 1994, the UK followed in 1995 and in 1997 Red Bull entered the US market over a five-year period starting in California. Since 1987 around 30 billion cans of Red Bull have been consumed, A total of 4.631 billion cans of Red Bull were sold worldwide in 2011 (more than a billion in the USA alone), representing an increase of 11.4 per cent against 2010. Company turnover increased by 12.4 per cent from €3.785 billion to €4.253 billion. In all key areas such as sales, revenues, productivity and operating profit, the figures recorded were the best in the company's history so far. The main reasons for such positive figures include outstanding sales, especially in key markets such as the USA (+11 per cent) and Germany (+10 per cent), and also in other markets such as Turkey (+86 per cent), Japan (+62 per cent), France (+35 per cent) and Scandinavia (+34 per cent), combined with efficient cost management and ongoing brand investment. Energy drinks were the second fastest growing segment in the global beverage industry, with a 25 per cent growth rate in 2011. Red Bull is now a mature product in the energy drinks sector, with an estimated 33.8 per cent market share around the world, yet this is without a strong presence in some of the world's largest markets, including China and India. The responsibility for the success of the world's No. 1 energy drink is shared by the company's 8,294 employees around the world (compared to 7,758 in 2010) in 164 countries.

Understanding the customer

Red Bull has been particularly successful in communicating its core brand values of individuality, humour, innovation and nonconformism. Red Bull actively describes its target market as a 'post-modern hedonistic group'. Mateschitz positioned Red Bull as the original energy drink with a believable and proven effect. Red Bull's positioning is a conscious decision by the company to differentiate the brand from other carbonates through premium pricing. However, Red Bull originally needed to secure food-and-drug authority approval of its contents and was delayed from entering a number of key markets (notably Germany, Norway, Denmark and France). While this was an initial source of frustration for Mateschitz, it turned out to provide exactly the marketing strategy he needed. Red Bull contains the active ingredients caffeine and taurine – the main reasons why drug approval was needed. However, because Red Bull was essentially illegal until approval was granted, rumours began circulating that the drink 'contained ecstasy', was 'made with bulls' testicles' and was 'liquid amphetamine'. These rumours spread among the clubbing community, a key target audience for the energy drink sector, and an audience for whom the idea of an illegal drink was distinctly inviting. Instead of attempting to quash the rumours, Red Bull added a 'rumours' section to its website to enhance the myth. This worked so well that when the drink was finally licensed, a group of worried mothers campaigned to have it banned, asserting that it led to drug use. Again, this just served to increase the attractiveness of the drink among its core market and Red Bull capitalized on this by launching guerrilla campaigns in bars and clubs. Red Bull affectionately became known as 'speed in a can' or even 'liquid cocaine'. Such health concerns simply reaffirmed Red Bull's reputation as an icon of the counter-culture, and the flag-bearer of anti-brands. This initial mystique and intrigue drove Red Bull's brand in its early years. To enhance its attachment within the Generation Y community, Red Bull utilized regional marketing targeting trendy nightlife spots and student life, and specifically employed students as brand representatives.

Extreme marketing

Marketing remains central to the brand's success, with 30–40 per cent of sales invested in marketing and promotion activity. Red Bull's marketing has historically been a 3-pronged approach incorporating buzz marketing, sponsorship and TV advertising.

The brand has engaged its core male l8-to-34 demographic and a broader mainstream audience through diverse platforms, third-party media, and, perhaps most important, its own channels. The central pillar of Red Bull's marketing campaign has always been its claim that it can improve athletic performance. In order to effectively communicate this message, Mateschitz zeroed in on the extreme-sports market. The first such involvement came in 1991, with the creation of the Red Bull Flugtag event, first hosted in Vienna, Austria. The Flugtag, which calls on participants to design and build flying contraptions to be launched off a 9.1-metre-high ramp, aligning perfectly with Red Bull's 'Gives You Wings' slogan. Since the advent of the Flugtag event, Red Bull has been ever-present in adventure and 'new-age' sports, spending an estimated US$300 million per year on sports marketing, including sponsoring and heavily branding over 500 action sports events and athletes. Red Bull has even created its own sport known as Red Bull Crashed Ice. Red Bull's initial involvement in newly created sports and non-traditional adventure sports that were on the margins of mainstream popularity in the 1990s opened the door for Mateschitz to enter more traditional, high-profile sports with a degree of authority and authenticity. This is a key element of Red Bull's brand identity—to be considered both as an established drinks company and as a brand with a successful sporting history. Today Red Bull underwrites more than 500 athletes in 97 sports. Red Bull's place in sport, as well as positioning its energy drink as being beneficial for athletes and a driver of performance, has led to the creation both of new and innovative sports properties, and the sponsorship and eventual ownership of mainstream sports properties. Red Bull boasts an arguably unrivalled international sporting empire, including, among others: EC Red Bull Salzburg (Hockey League, Austria), FC Red Bull Salzburg (Austrian Bundesliga), Fl teams Red Bull Racing and Scuderia Toro Rosso, Major League Soccer's New York Red Bulls, NASCAR's Team Red Bull, Red Bull Brasil FC (Segunda Divisão Paulista, Brazilian second division) and, most recently, a fifth-division German football club. Each of Red Bull's properties, purchased or created, bears the Red Bull name in some way, and has been branded or rebranded to fit the company's colour scheme and identity. Mateschitz has used sport to further promote and grow the Red Bull brand and reach a broader audience of consumers internationally. By stressing authenticity and establishing the brand as an icon of the extreme sports subculture, the company has pioneered not only the energy drinks market, but also the use of sport as a brand extension.

Content is key

The proliferation of new media channels and user-generated content has resulted in a frightening loss of control for many marketers. In keeping with its brand values 2011 saw an extremely dynamic expansion of Red Bull's media activities. Red Bull became an early adopter of Instagram, the photo-sharing app recently bought by Facebook for $1bn. It now has 230,000 followers on this site. The visual images associated with the themes provided a more compelling call to action and structure for consumers to create on behalf of the brand versus a standard promotional call to action. Red Bull's business plan defies conventional advertising in favour of marketing through its own events, shows, and publications. Red Bull established its content arm, Red Bull Media House, in Europe in 2007 and expanded stateside last year. In 2011 alone it filmed movies, signed a partnership deal with NBC for a show called *Red Bull Signature Series*, developed reality-TV ideas with big-time producer Bunim/Murray and MTV, honed its own Web and mobile outlets, and became a partner in YouTube's new plan to publish original content among others. It also expanded its magazine *Red Bulletin* into the USA, giving it a global distribution of 4.8 million. The development of Media House demonstrates Red Bull's ambition to use all possible channels to capture the maximum young audience within the energy drinks market using original content to reinforce the core values of the brand.

Conclusion

Red Bull continues to comfortably lead the global energy drinks market in both volume and value terms. However, the threat from The Coca-Cola Company (TCCC) and PepsiCo has been mounting through agreements with energy drinks such as Monster and Rockstar. Long-term focus for Red Bull is to remain relevant with the core audience and retain its edgy image with its consumer group, which may become increasingly difficult with the brand's status as a major global brand which has achieved mass-market success. New market entrants may become more attractive to the new generation of young consumers who want to be different and for whom the mass-market Red Bull may no longer be 'cool' or 'trendy' enough.

In spite of this competition and difficult financial and global economic climate, Red Bull's plans for growth and investment remain just as ambitious. While it remains to be seen what future endeavours and extensions Mateschitz and Red Bull have planned, the foundations laid within youth culture leading to the company's market dominance have been thanks to an innate ability of Red Bull to understand its customers.

Questions

1. Using your understanding of who is important in the buying decision process, evaluate the significance of these roles in terms of creating marketing communications for Red Bull.

2. Discuss the potential choice criteria used by consumers when evaluating alternative energy drinks.

3. 'Red Bull actively describes its target market as a post-modern hedonistic group.' Critically evaluate the social influences on consumer behaviour with respect to the target market of Red Bull.

4. Discuss the potential benefits of sports marketing as a tool in the consumer decision-making process.

This case was written by David Cosgrave, Teaching Assistant, Department of Marketing and Management, University of Limerick.

CHAPTER 5

Understanding organizational buying behaviour

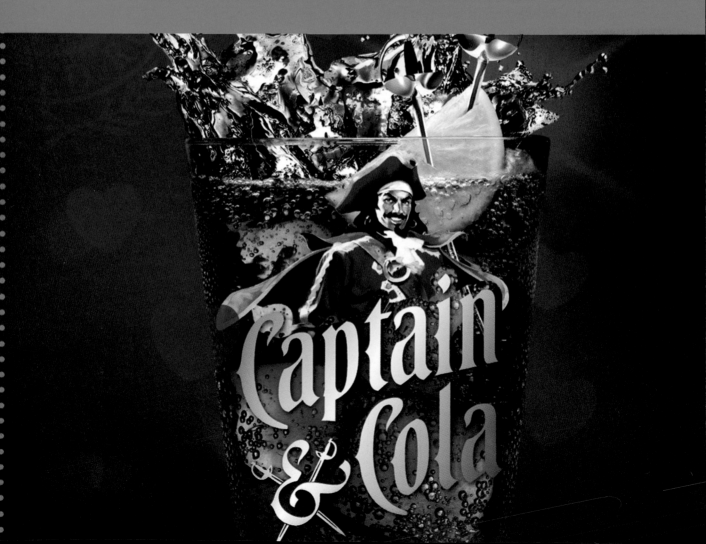

People are people at work or at play.

ANONYMOUS

LEARNING OBJECTIVES

After reading this chapter, you should be able to:

1   discuss the characteristics of organizational buying

2   define the dimensions of organizational buying

3   discuss the nature and marketing implications of who buys, how organizations buy and the choice criteria used to evaluate products

4   explain the influences on organizational buying behaviour—the buy class, product type and purchase importance—and discuss their marketing implications

5   describe the developments in purchasing practice: just-in-time, centralized and e-procurement, reverse marketing and leasing

6   discuss the nature of relationship marketing and how to build customer relationships

7   describe the development of buyer–seller relationships

Organizational buying involves purchasing products and services to meet the needs of manufacturers, resellers, government and public sector, and other types of organizations. There are three types of organizational markets:

1 *industrial market* consisting of companies that buy products and services to help them produce other goods and services. Industrial goods include raw materials, components and capital goods such as machinery.

2 *reseller market* comprises organizations that buy products and services to resell. Mail-order companies, retailers and online retailers are examples of resellers.

3 *government market* consists of government agencies that buy products and services to help them carry out their activities—e.g. purchases for local authorities and defence.

Business-to-business marketing (as it is sometimes called) places a similar emphasis on understanding of buying behaviour to that of consumer marketing. However, as the implications of making an incorrect buying decision tend to be greater in organizational markets than consumer ones, professional buyers and procurement specialists proceed with caution. They are much less likely to make an impulse purchase or buy on a whim. Consequently, marketing mangers need to develop an understanding of buyer behaviour and the structure of the buying group. A key challenge is to be able to satisfy diverse requirements in a single offering. A product that gives engineers the performance characteristics they demand, production managers the delivery reliability they need, purchasing managers the value for money they seek and shop floor workers the ease of installation they desire, is likely to be highly successful. This complexity of organizational buying makes marketing an extremely interesting task.

This chapter examines characteristics of organizational buying and marketing before examining some of the dimensions of buying identified in Chapter 4: who buys, how they buy and what choice criteria they use. The chapter concludes by exploring developments in purchasing practice—just-in-time purchasing, centralized purchasing, e-procurement and reverse marketing.

Characteristics of Organizational Buying

Nature and size of customers

Typically the number of customers in organizational markets is small. The Pareto rule often applies, with 80 per cent of output being sold to 20 per cent of customers, who may number fewer than 12. The reseller market is a case in point where, in Europe, most countries have a small number of supermarkets dominating the grocery trade. In the industrial market the same situation is often found. For example, in the computer manufacturing industry Apple, Acer, Lenovo, Hewlett Packard, Dell and Nintendo are the dominant global players. Clearly the importance of key customers is paramount. Consequently, when Microsoft decided to move to IBM for the processor that drives the Xbox 360, this was a major blow to Intel, which hitherto had powered almost everything that Microsoft had ever made.[1] The jet aircraft industry is even more concentrated, with only two key players: Airbus and Boeing. The implications are that the importance of a small number of large customers makes it sensible for suppliers to invest heavily in developing long-term collaborative relationships. Dedicated sales and marketing teams under the title of 'key account management' are usually employed to service such large accounts. Supply is usually direct, dispensing with the services of intermediaries as large order sizes make it economical to deal directly with the manufacturer. Face-to-face meetings are important when negotiating large contracts but the Web is also widely used; Airbus has a supplier portal which it uses to support its purchasing processes.[2]

Complexity of buying

Often, organizational purchases, notably those that involve large sums of money and that are new to the company, involve many people at different levels of the organization. The managing director, product engineers, production managers, purchasing managers and operatives may influence the decision as to which expensive machine to purchase. The sales task may be to influence as many of these people as possible and may involve multilevel selling by means of a sales team, rather than an individual salesperson.[3]

Economic and technical choice criteria

Although organizational buyers, being people, are affected by emotional factors, such as like or dislike of a salesperson, organizational buying decisions are often made on economic and technical criteria. This is because organizational buyers have to justify their decisions to other members of their organization.[4] Also, the formalization of the buying function through the establishment of purchasing departments leads to the use of economic rather than emotional choice criteria. As purchasing becomes more sophisticated, economic criteria came to the fore with techniques such as life-cycle cost, total cost of ownership and value-in-use analysis. Fleet buyers, for example, calculate life-cycle costs including purchase price, and running and maintenance costs when considering which company car to buy.

Risks

Industrial markets are characterized by a contract being agreed before the product is made. Further, the product itself may be highly technical and the seller may be faced with unforeseen problems once work has started. Thus, Scott-Lithgow won an order to build an oil rig for BP, but the price proved uneconomic given the nature of the problems associated with its construction. In the government market, a £12 billion upgrade of the UK's National Health Service IT systems ran over budget, fell behind schedule by four years and saw the departure of two of the programme's four main contractors.[5]

Buying to specific requirements

Because of the large sums of money involved organizational buyers sometimes draw up product specifications and ask suppliers to design their products to meet them. Services, too, are often conducted to specific customer requirements, marketing research and advertising services being examples. This is much less a feature of consumer marketing, where a product offering may be developed to meet a need of a market segment but, beyond that, meeting individual needs would prove uneconomic.

Reciprocal buying

Because an industrial buyer may be in a powerful negotiating position with a seller, it may be possible to demand concessions in return for placing an order. In some situations, buyers may demand that sellers buy some of their products in return for securing the order. For example, in negotiating to buy computers a company like Volvo might persuade a supplier to buy a fleet of Volvo company cars.

Derived demand

The demand for many organizational goods is derived from the demand for consumer goods. If the demand for compact discs increases, the demand for the raw materials and machinery used to make the discs will also expand. Clearly raw material and machinery suppliers would be wise to monitor consumer trends and buying characteristics as well as their immediate organizational customers. A further factor based upon the derived demand issue is the tendency for demand for some industrial goods and services to be more volatile than that for consumer goods and services. For example, a small fall in demand for compact discs may mean the complete cessation of orders for the machinery to make them. Similarly a small increase in demand if manufacturers are working at full capacity may mean a massive increase in demand for machinery as investment to meet the extra demand is made. This is known as the *accelerator principle*.[6]

Negotiations

Because of the existence of professional buyers and sellers, and the size and complexity of organizational buying, negotiation is often important. Thus, supermarkets will negotiate with manufacturers about price since their buying power allows them to obtain discounts. Car manufacturers will negotiate attractive prices from tyre manufacturers such as Pirelli and Michelin since the replacement brand may be dependent upon the tyre fitted to the new car. The supplier's list price may be regarded as the starting point for negotiation and the profit margin ultimately achieved will be heavily influenced by the negotiating skills of the seller. The implication is that sales and marketing personnel need to be conversant with negotiating skills and tactics.

The Dimensions of Organizational Buying Behaviour

As with consumer behaviour, the dimensions of organizational buying behaviour cover who buys, how they buy, the choice criteria used, and where and when they buy. We will examine the first three of these issues in detail.

Who buys?

An important point to understand in organizational buying is that the buyer, or purchasing officer, is often not the only person that influences the decision, or actually has the authority to make the ultimate decision. Rather, the decision is in the hands of a **decision-making unit** (DMU), or *buying centre* as it is sometimes called. This is not necessarily a fixed entity. Members of the DMU may change as the decision-making process continues. Thus, a managing director may be involved in the decision that new equipment should be purchased, but not in the decision as to which manufacturer to buy it from. Six roles have been identified in the structure of the DMU, as follows.[7]

1 *Initiators*: those who begin the purchase process: e.g. maintenance managers.
2 *Users*: those who actually use the product: e.g. welders.
3 *Deciders*: those who have authority to select the supplier/model: e.g. production managers.
4 *Influencers*: those who provide information and add decision criteria throughout the process: e.g. accountants.
5 *Buyers*: those who have authority to execute the contractual arrangements: e.g. purchasing officer.
6 *Gatekeepers*: those who control the flow of information: e.g. secretaries who may allow or prevent access to a DMU member, or a buyer whose agreement must be sought before a supplier can contact other members of the DMU.

A key point to realize is that the DMU resides within the buying organization. External influences, such as the salespeople of supplying companies, are not therefore part of the DMU: a DMU is customer not supplier based. Consequently a decision-making unit is defined as a group of people within a buying organization who are involved in the buying decision.

For very important decisions the structure of the DMU will be complex, involving numerous people within the buying organization. The marketing task is to identify and reach the key members in order to convince them of the product's worth. Often communicating only to the purchasing officer will be insufficient, as this person may be only a minor influence on supplier choice. Relationship management (discussed later in this chapter) is of key importance in many organizational markets.

When the problem to be solved is highly technical, suppliers may work with engineers in the buying organization in order to solve problems and secure the order. One example where this approach was highly successful involved a small company that won a large order from a major car company thanks to its ability to work with the car company in solving the technical problems associated with the development of an exhaust gas recirculation valve.[8] In this case the small company's policy was to work with the major company's engineers and to

Go to the website to determine the message Hewlett-Packard wants to give its corporate customers. www.mcgraw-hill.co.uk/ textbooks/jobber

keep the purchasing department out of the decision until the last possible moment, by which time it alone would be qualified to supply the part.

Often organizational purchases are made in committees where the salesperson will not be present. The salesperson's task is to identify a person from within the decision-making unit who is a positive advocate and champion of the supplier's product. This person (or 'coach') should be given all the information needed to win the arguments that may take place within the decision-making unit. For example, even though the advocate may be a technical person, he or she should be given the financial information that may be necessary to justify buying the most technologically superior product.

Where DMU members are inaccessible to salespeople, advertising, the Internet or direct marketing tools may be used as alternatives.

The relatively low cost of direct mail and email campaigns makes them tempting alternatives to personal visits or telephone calls. Setting up a website can also be relatively inexpensive once the initial set-up costs have been met. However, wrongly targeted direct mail, a poorly designed website or a badly executed email campaign can cause customer annoyance and tarnish the image of the company and brand. Business-to-business companies are turning to integrated marketing communications as a means of using the strengths of a variety of media to target business customers. Integrated marketing communications is a concept that sees companies coordinate their marketing communications tools to deliver a clear, consistent, credible and competitive message about the organization and its products.

Mini Case 5.1 B2B Buying and the Importance of Understanding the Benefits

Chris Ashworth is founder of Competitive Advantage, a marketing consultancy which helps businesses in the construction industry with their marketing strategies and planning. He has over 30 years' sales and marketing experience in the construction industry and is also involved in running training programmes for the Builders Merchants Federation.

The construction industry is important to the British economy as it produces 9 per cent of GDP but this industry like many others has suffered during the recession, and for 2012 gloomy forecasts predicted a 3.6 per cent downturn. Chris is eager to help businesses through this tough trading period and says that 'cutting prices is one way to give your customers better value but it's far better to focus on the relevant benefits'. Buying and selling in the construction industry tends to involve complex procurement processes, so Chris advises his clients that it is important to understand the needs of all of the members of the DMU and get to the heart of the buying decision in order to discover the desired benefits and outcomes of the purchasing decision. Getting involved in this way can deliver dividends in terms of relationship building and discovering competitors' weaknesses—for example, extended delivery times, poor after-sales service. However, it is important to recognize that undertaking successful procurement negotiations requires the seller not only to understand the benefits which the client is seeking (both functional and emotional) but also to understand how to deliver *value*. According to Chris, value consists of benefits and costs and, in order to get the balance right between these two, it is important to:

1 understand the different needs of the DMU and how your product can meet these requirements
2 present the relevant benefit to each member of the DMU to demonstrate the *value* on offer
3 seek opportunities to differentiate and create extra value by adding needed services.

Questions:

1 Explain the different needs of each member of an organization's DMU and describe how they might impact on the final buying decision.
2 Suggest ways in which an organization in the construction industry can build lasting relationships between buyer and seller. Illustrate your answer with examples.

Based on: Competitive Advantage (2012);[9] Leading Edge (2012);[10] CIM (2012)[11]

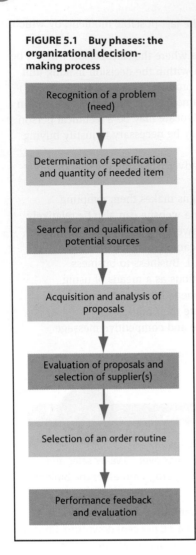

FIGURE 5.1   Buy phases: the organizational decision-making process

Recognition of a problem (need)

↓

Determination of specification and quantity of needed item

↓

Search for and qualification of potential sources

↓

Acquisition and analysis of proposals

↓

Evaluation of proposals and selection of supplier(s)

↓

Selection of an order routine

↓

Performance feedback and evaluation

Go to the website to compare how Microsoft targets individual and corporate customers. **www.mcgraw-hill.co.uk/ textbooks/jobber**

How they buy

Figure 5.1 describes the **decision-making process** for an organizational product.[12] The exact nature of the process will depend on the buying situation. In some situations some stages will be omitted. For example, in a routine rebuy situation the purchasing officer is unlikely to pass through the third, fourth and fifth stages (search for suppliers, and analysis and evaluation of their proposals). These stages will be bypassed, as the buyer, recognizing a need—perhaps shortage of stationery—routinely reorders from an existing supplier. In general, the more complex the decision and the more expensive the item, the more likely it is that each stage will be passed through and that the process will take more time.

Recognition of a problem (need)

Needs and problems may be recognized through either *internal or external factors*.[13] An example of an internal factor would be the realization of under-capacity leading to the decision to purchase plant or equipment. Thus, internal recognition leads to active behaviour (internal/active). Some problems that are recognized internally may not be acted upon. This condition may be termed internal/passive. A production manager may realize that there is a problem with a machine but, given more pressing problems, decides to put up with it.

Other potential problems may not be recognized internally, and become problems only because of external cues. Production managers may be quite satisfied with their production process until they are made aware of another, more efficient, method.

Clearly, these different problems have important implications for marketing and sales. The internal/passive condition implies that there is an opportunity for a salesperson, having identified the condition, to highlight the problem by careful analysis of cost inefficiencies and other symptoms, so that the problem is perceived to be pressing and in need of solution (internal/active). The internal/active situation requires the supplier to demonstrate a differential advantage of its products over those of the competition. In this situation problem stimulation is unnecessary, but where internal recognition is absent, the marketer can provide the necessary external cues. A fork-lift truck sales representative might stimulate problem recognition by showing how the truck can save the customer money, due to lower maintenance costs, and lead to more efficient use of warehouse space through higher lifting capabilities. Advertising or direct mail could also be used to good effect.

Determination of specification and quantity of needed item

At this stage of the decision-making process the DMU will draw up a description of what is required. For example, it might decide that five web servers are required to meet certain specifications. The ability of marketers to influence the specification can give their company an advantage at later stages of the process. By persuading the buying company to specify features that only the marketer's own product possesses, the sale may be virtually closed at this stage. This is the process of setting up *lock-out criteria*. Marketing in Action 5.1 explains the powerful effect a lock-out criterion has had on the market for diesel locomotives.

Search for and qualification of potential sources

A great deal of variation in the degree of search takes place in industrial buying. Generally speaking, the cheaper and less important the item, and the more information the buyer possesses, the less search takes place. Marketers can use advertising to ensure that their brands are in the buyers' awareness set and are, therefore, considered when evaluating alternatives.

Marketing in Action 5.1 Diesel Lock-out

The major player in the European diesel locomotive market is Electro-Motive Diesel (EMD), a former North American subsidiary of General Motors, which has sold 650 of its Class 66 diesel locomotives to European freight train operators since 1998. In the USA, however, General Electric (GE) is the market leader with about 70 per cent market share. This apparent paradox is explained by GE failing to meet a European lock-out criterion that does not apply in the USA. Until recently GE has not manufactured a locomotive small enough to pass under the low bridges and through the tunnels of the European rail system. EMD's Class 66 is able to fit on networks in nearly all of continental Europe and operates in 10 European countries.

This situation has now changed with the launch of GE's PowerHaul locomotive, which can fit the European system. Now that the lock-out criterion has been overcome, PowerHaul is threatening EMD's market share because, at the 'Evaluation of proposals and selection of supplier(s)' decision-making stage, it possesses competitive advantages on key choice criteria. One is technical (an ability to accelerate freight trains faster than the Class 66) and the other economic (better fuel economy). GE is now winning orders from European operators such as Freightliner, the UK's second-largest freight operator. The PowerHaul has now enabled GE to enter not only European markets but also Turkey, the Middle East and North Africa.

This story demonstrates the importance of lock-out criteria and shows how the nature of choice criteria can differ between Stages 2 and 5 of the organizational decision-making process.

Based on: GE Transportation (2012);[14] Wright (2008)[15,16]

Acquisition and analysis of proposals

Having found a number of companies that, perhaps through their technical expertise and general reputation, are considered to be qualified to supply the product, proposals will be called for and analysis of them undertaken.

Evaluation of proposals and selection of supplier(s)

Each proposal will be evaluated in the light of the choice criteria deemed to be more important to each DMU member. It is important to realize that various members may use different criteria when judging proposals. Although this may cause problems, the outcome of this procedure is the selection of a supplier or suppliers.

Selection of an order routine

Next, the details of payment and delivery are drawn up. Usually this is conducted by the purchasing officer. In some buying decisions—when delivery is an important consideration in selecting a supplier—this stage is merged into the acquisition and evaluation stages.

Performance feedback and evaluation

This may be formal, where a purchasing department draws up an evaluation form for user departments to complete, or informal through everyday conversations.

The implications of all this are that sales and marketing strategy can affect a sale through influencing need recognition, through the design of product specifications, and by clearly presenting the advantages of the product or service over that of competition in terms that are relevant to DMU members. By early involvement, a company can benefit through the process of *creeping commitment*, whereby the buying organization becomes increasingly committed to one supplier through its involvement in the process and the technical assistance it provides.

Choice criteria

This aspect of industrial buyer behaviour refers to the criteria used by members of the DMU to evaluate supplier proposals. These criteria are likely to be determined by the performance criteria used to evaluate the members themselves.[17] Thus, purchasing managers who are

We focus on automating Marriott's global invoice process. So they don't have to.

Xerox digitized and standardized the invoice process for Marriott Hotels & Resorts®. Now their 11 million invoices take less time to manage, and less space to archive. Which gives Marriott more time to focus on serving their customers.

RealBusiness.com

Ready For Real Business **xerox**

⬆**EXHIBIT 5.1   This advert by Xerox shows the role its technology plays in automating the invoice process with the Marriott hotel chain.**

judged by the extent to which they reduce purchase expenditure are likely to be more cost conscious than production engineers, who are evaluated in terms of the technical efficiency of the production process they design.

As with consumers, organizational buying is characterized by *technical, economic, social* (organizational) and *personal criteria.* Key considerations may be, for plant and equipment, return on investment, while for materials and components parts they may be cost savings, together with delivery reliability, quality and technical assistance. Because of the high costs associated with production downtime, a key concern of many purchasing departments is the long-run development of the organization's supply system. Personal factors may also be important, particularly when suppliers' product offerings are essentially similar. In this situation the final decision may rest upon the relative liking for the supplier's salesperson. Exhibit 5.1 illustrates the importance of economic (cost saving in time and storage space), technical (streamlined digitized processes leading to improved performance) and personal (risk reduction through increased customer focus) taking the choice criteria.

Customers' choice criteria can change in different regions of the world. For example, Xerox is generally known as a company that provides solutions for creating documents, printers and copiers and is so well known that it is a recognized household name. Xerox aims to shift the positioning of its brand to increase recognition of the service element of its global business[18] as this creates around 50 per cent of their business. In the West, when choosing a printer, a consumer considers the print quality and how easy the machine is to network and update. In eastern Europe other choice criteria prevail. Networking and servicing are not issues that are considered very much; rather, value for money is the key. The consumer attitude is: 'I can buy a Xerox, or I can buy a Canon and a car.' The marketing task for Xerox is to reduce the consumer's price sensitivity by stressing its reliability, quality, after-sales service, wide range of suppliers and medium- to long-term value for money.[19]

What are the range of motives that key players in organizations use to compare supplier offerings? Economic considerations play a part because commercial firms have profit objectives and work within budgetary constraints. Emotional factors should not be ignored, however, as decisions are made by people who do not suddenly lose their personalities, personal likes and dislikes and prejudices simply because they are at work. Let us examine a number of important technical and economic motives (quality, price and life-cycle costs, and continuity of supply) and then some organizational and personal factors (perceived risk, office politics, and personal liking/disliking).

Quality

The emergence of **total quality management** as a key aspect of organizational life reflects the importance of quality in evaluating suppliers' products and services. Many buying organizations are unwilling to trade quality for price. For example, the success of Intel was not based on price but reliable, ever-faster microprocessors for PCs and servers.[20] In particular, buyers are looking for consistency of product or service quality so that end products (e.g. motor cars) are reliable, inspection costs are reduced and production processes run smoothly. They are installing just-in-time delivery systems, which rely upon incoming supplies being quality guaranteed.

Price and life-cycle costs

For materials and components of similar specification and quality, price becomes a key consideration. For standard items—e.g., ball-bearings, transistors, carrier bags—price may be critical to making a sale given that a number of suppliers can meet delivery and specification requirements. The power of large buying organizations also means that they have the power to squeeze suppliers for tighter terms. For example, Marks & Spencer, in its drive to reduce costs, demanded a 10 per cent cut in all suppliers' prices.[21] To remain competitive when Tesco launched its 'Price Drop' initiative, many other supermarkets demanded reductions from their suppliers. Waitrose entered negotiations for a 5 per cent reduction from its ambient food suppliers to enable a new price-led marketing strategy '1000s of ways to great value'.[22] However, it should not be forgotten that price is only one component of cost for many buying organizations. Increasingly buyers take into account **life-cycle costs**, which may include productivity savings, maintenance costs and residual values as well as initial purchase price when evaluating products. Marketers can use life-cycle costs analysis to break into an account. By calculating life-cycle costs with a buyer, new perceptions of value may be achieved.

Continuity of supply

Another major cost to a company is disruption of a production run. Delays of this kind can mean costly machine downtime and even lost sales. Continuity of supply is, therefore, a prime consideration in many purchase situations. Companies that perform badly on this criterion lose out even if the price is competitive because a small percentage price edge does not compare with the costs of unreliable delivery. Supplier companies that can guarantee deliveries and realize their promises can achieve a significant differential advantage in the marketplace. Organizational customers are demanding close relationships with *accredited suppliers* that can guarantee reliable supply, perhaps on a just-in-time basis.

Perceived risk

Perceived risk can come in two forms: *functional risk* such as uncertainty with respect to product or supplier performance, and *psychological risk* such as criticism from work colleagues.[23] This latter risk—fear of upsetting the boss, losing status, being ridiculed by others in the department, or, indeed, losing one's job—can play a determining role in purchase decisions. Buyers often reduce uncertainty by gathering information about competing suppliers, checking the opinions of important others in the buying company, buying only from familiar and/or reputable suppliers and by spreading risk through multiple sourcing. Renault reduces perceived risk by communicating its reputation, by showing the popularity of its vans (see Exhibit 5.2).

Office politics

Political factions within the buying company may also influence the outcome of a purchase decision. Interdepartmental conflict may manifest itself in the formation of competing camps over the purchase of a product or service. Because department X favours supplier 1, department Y automatically favours supplier 2. The outcome not only has purchasing implications but also political implications for the departments and individuals concerned.

Personal liking/disliking

A buyer may personally like one salesperson more than another and this may influence supplier choice, particularly when competing products are very similar. Even when supplier selection is on the basis of competitive bidding, it is known for purchasers to help salespeople they like to be competitive.[24] Obviously perception is important in all organizational purchases, since how someone behaves depends upon the perception of the situation. One buyer may perceive a salesperson as being honest, truthful and likeable while another may not. As with consumer behaviour, three selective processes may be at work on buyers.

➡EXHIBIT 5.2 Fans
show their appreciation
and emotional
connections with
Renault vans.

RENAULT VANS
4 MILLIONS FANS IN EUROPE

1 *Selective attention*: only certain information sources may be sought.
2 *Selective distortion*: information from those sources may be distorted.
3 *Selective retention*: only some information may be remembered.

In general, people tend to distort, avoid and forget messages that are substantially different from their existing beliefs and attitudes.

Implications

The implications of understanding the content of the decision are that appeals may need to change when communicating to different DMU members: discussion with a production engineer may centre on the technical superiority of the product offering, while much more emphasis on cost factors may prove effective when talking to the purchasing officer. Orange, the mobile phone operator, recognized the need to change communication when talking to different members of the DMU in business-to-business markets. When talking to information technologists, Orange talks technology because that is what they expect. However, for non-technical people, such as accountants and users of the equipment, the message is kept much simpler and focuses on how more effective phone use can boost productivity.[25] Furthermore, the criteria used by buying organizations change over time as circumstances change. Price may be relatively unimportant to a company when trying to solve a highly visible technical problem, and the order will be placed with the supplier that provides the necessary technical assistance. Later, after the problem has been solved and other suppliers become qualified, price may be of crucial significance.

Influences on Organizational Buying Behaviour

Figure 5.2 shows the three factors that influence how organizations buy, who buys and the choice criteria they use: the buy class, the product type and the importance of purchase.[26]

The buy class

Organizational purchases may be distinguished between a new task, a straight rebuy and a modified rebuy.[27] A **new task** occurs when the need for the product has not arisen previously

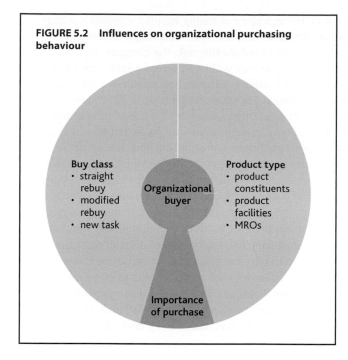

FIGURE 5.2   Influences on organizational purchasing behaviour

Buy class
- straight rebuy
- modified rebuy
- new task

Organizational buyer

Product type
- product constituents
- product facilities
- MROs

Importance of purchase

RUN
like never before.

If you could do anything with your business, what would you do with it? Where would you run with it? Whatever your vision is, SAP can help you make it real. Accelerate change. Seize opportunity wherever and whenever you find it. Unlock insights instantly. From fine-tuning your business to transforming it entirely, SAP can help you run in entirely new ways.

Run like never before at sap.com/runbetter

RUN BETTER. **SAP**

⬆ **EXHIBIT 5.3   SAP emphasizes the speed and efficiency of its business management network solutions.**

so that there is little or no relevant experience in the company, and a great deal of information is required. A **straight rebuy** occurs where an organization buys previously purchased items from suppliers already judged acceptable. Routine purchasing procedures are set up to facilitate straight rebuys. The **modified rebuy** lies between the two extremes. A regular requirement for the type of product exists, and the buying alternatives are known, but sufficient change (e.g. a delivery problem) has occurred to require some alteration to the normal supply procedure.

The buy classes affect organizational buying in the following ways. First, the membership of the DMU changes. For a straight rebuy possibly only the purchasing officer is involved, whereas for a new buy senior management, engineers, production managers and purchasing officers may be involved. Modified rebuys often involve engineers, production managers and purchasing officers, but senior management, except when the purchase is critical to the company, is unlikely to be involved. Second, the decision-making process may be much longer as the buy class changes from a straight rebuy to a modified rebuy and to a new task. Third, in terms of influencing DMU members, they are likely to be much more receptive to new task and modified rebuy situations than straight rebuys. In the latter case, the purchasing manager has already solved the purchasing problem and has other problems to deal with. So why make it a problem again?

The first implication of this buy class analysis is that there are big gains to be made if a company can enter the new task at the start of the decision-making process. By providing information and helping with any technical problems that can arise, the company may be able to create goodwill and creeping commitment, which secures the order when the final decision is made. The second implication is that since the decision process is likely to be long, and many people are involved in the new task, supplier companies need to invest heavily in sales personnel for a considerable period of time. Some firms employ missionary sales teams, comprising their best salespeople, to help secure big new-task orders.

Companies in straight rebuy situations must ensure that no change occurs when they are in the position of the supplier. Regular contact to ensure that the customer has no complaints may be necessary, and the buyer may be encouraged to use automatic reordering systems. For the out-supplier (i.e. a new potential supplier) the task can be difficult unless poor service or some other factor has caused the buyer to become dissatisfied with the present supplier. The obvious objective of the out-supplier in this situation is to change the buy class from a straight rebuy to a modified rebuy. Price alone may not be enough since changing supplier represents a large personal risk to the purchasing officer. The new supplier's products might be less reliable, and delivery might be unpredictable. In order to reduce this risk, the company may offer delivery guarantees with penalty clauses and be very willing to accept a small (perhaps uneconomic) order at first in order to gain a foothold. Supplier acquisition of a total quality management (TQM) standard such as EM29000, ISO9000 and ISP9001 or BS5750 may also have the effect of reducing perceived buyer risk. Other tactics are the use of testimonials from satisfied customers, and demonstrations. Many straight rebuys are organized on a contract basis, and buyers may be more receptive to listening to non-suppliers prior to contract renewal.

Value analysis and life-cycle cost calculations are other methods of moving purchases from a straight rebuy to a modified rebuy situation. **Value analysis**, which can be conducted by either supplier or buyer, is a method of cost reduction in which components are examined to see if they can be made more cheaply. The items are studied to identify unnecessary costs that do not add to the reliability or functionality of the product. By redesigning, standardizing or manufacturing by less expensive means, a supplier may be able to offer a product of comparable quality at lower cost. Simple redesigns like changing a curved edge to a straight one may have dramatic cost implications.[28] Life-cycle cost analysis seeks to move the cost focus from the initial purchase price to the total cost of owning and using a product. There are three types of life-cycle costs: purchase price, start-up costs and post-purchase costs.[29] Start-up costs would include installation, lost production and training costs. Post-purchase costs include operating (e.g. fuel, operator wages), maintenance, repair and inventory costs. Against these costs would be placed residual values (e.g. trade-in values of cars). Life-cycle cost appeals can be powerful motivators. For example, if the out-supplier can convince the customer organization that its product has significantly lower post-purchase costs than the in-supplier's, despite a slightly higher purchase price, it may win the order. This is because it will be delivering a higher economic value to the customer. This can be a powerful competitive advantage and, at the same time, justify the premium price.

The product type

Products can be classified according to four types: materials, components, plant and equipment, and MROs (maintenance repair and operation), as follows:

1 materials to be used in the production process: e.g. aluminium
2 components to be incorporated in the finished product: e.g. headlights
3 plant and equipment: e.g. bulldozer
4 products and services for maintenance repair and operation (MRO): e.g. spanners, welding equipment and lubricants.

This classification is based upon a customer perspective—how the product is used—and may be employed to identify differences in organizational buyer behaviour. First, the people who take part in the decision-making process tend to change according to product type. For example, senior management tend to get involved in the purchase of plant and equipment or, occasionally, when new materials are purchased if the change is of fundamental importance to company operations—for example, if a move from aluminium to plastic is being considered. Rarely do they involve themselves in component or MRO supply. Similarly, design engineers tend to be involved in buying components and materials but not normally MRO and plant equipment. Second, the decision-making process tends to be slower and more complex as product type moves from:

MRO → components → materials → plant and equipment

For MRO items, *blanket contracts* rather than periodic purchase orders are increasingly being used. The supplier agrees to resupply the buyer on agreed price terms over a period of time. Stock is held by the seller and orders are automatically printed out by the buyer's computer when stock falls below a minimum level. This has the advantage to the supplying company of effectively blocking the effort of the competitors for long periods of time.

Classification of suppliers' offerings by product type gives clues as to who is likely to be influenced in the purchase decision. The marketing task is then to confirm this in particular situations and attempt to reach those people involved. A company selling MROs is likely to be wasting effort attempting to communicate with design engineers, whereas attempts to reach operating management are likely to prove fruitful.

The importance of purchase

A purchase is likely to be perceived as being important to the buying organization when it involves large sums of money, when the cost of making the wrong decision—for example, in production downtime—is high and when there is considerable uncertainty about the outcome of alternative offerings. In such situations, many people at different organizational levels are likely to be involved in the decision and the process will be long, with extensive search and analysis of information. Thus, extensive marketing effort is likely to be required, but great opportunities present themselves to those sales teams that work with buying organizations to convince them that their offering has the best payoff; this may involve acceptance trials: for example, private diesel manufacturers supply railway companies with prototypes for testing, engineering support and testimonials from other users. Additionally, guarantees of delivery dates and after-sales service may be necessary when buyer uncertainty regarding these factors is high. An example of the time and effort that may be required to win very important purchases is the order secured by GEC to supply £250 million worth of equipment for China's largest nuclear power station. The contract was won after six years of negotiation, 33 GEC missions to China and 4000 person-days of work.

....

Developments in Purchasing Practice

Several trends have taken place within the purchasing function that have marketing implications for supplier firms. The advent of just-in-time purchasing and the increased tendency towards centralized purchasing, e-procurement, reverse marketing, leasing and outsourcing have all changed the nature of purchasing and altered the way in which suppliers compete.

Just-in-time purchasing

The just-in-time concept aims to minimize stocks by organizing a supply system that provides materials and components as they are required.[30] Stockholding costs are significantly reduced or eliminated, thus profits are increased. Furthermore, since the holding of stocks is a hedge against machine breakdowns, faulty parts and human error they may be seen as a cushion that acts as a disincentive to management to eliminate such inefficiencies.

Just-in-time (JIT) practices are also associated with improved quality. Suppliers are evaluated on their ability to provide high-quality products. The effect of this is that suppliers may place more emphasis on product quality. Buyers are encouraged to specify only essential product characteristics, which means that suppliers have more discretion in product design and manufacturing methods. Also, the emphasis is on the supplier certifying quality—which means that quality inspection at the buyer company is reduced and overall costs are minimized, since quality control at source is more effective than further down the supply chain.

The total effects of JIT can be enormous. Purchasing, inventory and inspection costs can be reduced, product design can be improved, delivery streamlined, production downtime reduced, and the quality of the finished item enhanced.

However, the implementation of JIT requires integration into both purchasing and production operations. Since the system requires the delivery of the exact amount of materials or components to the production line as they are required, delivery schedules must be very reliable and suppliers must be prepared to make deliveries on a regular basis, perhaps even daily. Lead times for ordering must be short and the number of defects very low. An attraction for suppliers is that it is usual for long-term purchasing agreements to be drawn up. The marketing implication of the JIT concept is that to be competitive in many industrial markets—for example, motor cars—suppliers must be able to meet the requirements of this fast-growing system.

An example of a company that employs just-in-time is the Nissan car assembly plant at Sunderland in the UK. Nissan has adopted what it terms synchronous supply: parts are delivered only minutes before they are needed. For example, carpets are delivered by Sommer Allibert, a French supplier, from its facility close to the Nissan assembly line in sequence for fitting to the correct model. Only 42 minutes elapse between the carpet being ordered and fitted to the car. The stockholding of carpets for the Nissan Micra is now only 10 minutes. Just-in-time practices do carry risks, however, if labour stability cannot be guaranteed. Renault discovered this to its cost when a strike at its engine and gearbox plant caused its entire French and Belgian car production lines to close in only 10 days.

Marketing in Action 5.2 The Milk Run at the Hitachi Transit System

The European headquarters for the Hitachi Transport System (HTS) is in Waardenburg, 60 km south of Amsterdam. This is part of a global transportation system that employs nearly 30, 000 people, operating 120 warehouses in 18 countries. Originally, the transportation system grew to support the in-house needs of Hitachi's manufacturing operation but it is now a logistics solution provider for many other companies. The location of Waardenburg means there are links to major road systems, giving access to routes across Europe, and is relatively close to Schipol airport and the port of Rotterdam. It also links with (HTS) hubs in the UK, France, Italy and Spain. The benefits of HTS are shared warehousing and logistics resources and facilities, which bring the benefits of economies of scale, lower cost and greater flexibility enabling more companies to enjoy the benefits of JIT. HTS operates a *milk run* method to collect goods from factories and deliver to customers using a cross-docking centre, which consolidates deliveries and cuts down the need for multiple deliveries.

Based on: Hitachi (2012)[31]

Centralized purchasing

Where several operating units within a company have common requirements, and where there is an opportunity to strengthen a negotiating position by bulk buying, centralized purchasing is an attractive option. Centralization encourages purchasing specialists to concentrate their energies on a small group of products, thus enabling them to develop an extensive knowledge of cost factors and the operation of suppliers.[32] The move from local to centralized buying has important marketing implications. Localized buying tends to focus on short-term cost and profit considerations, whereas centralized purchasing places more emphasis on long-term supply relationships. Outside influences—for example, engineers— play a greater role in supplier choice in local purchasing organizations since less specialized buyers often lack the expertise and status to question the recommendations of technical people. The type of purchasing organization can therefore give clues to suppliers regarding the important people in the decision-making unit and their respective power positions.

E-procurement

While many people relate the Internet with consumers shopping online, the reality is that the volume of trade carried out online between businesses through online e-procurements is much greater.

Modern e-procurement systems enable companies to fulfil a range of activities and processes associated with the purchasing function: tendering, awarding contracts, establishing contractual agreements, and ordering.[33] To action these processes, companies not only create their own websites but also develop extranets for buyers to send out requests for bids to suppliers. Online purchasing systems can take various formats:

- *Catalogue sites*: companies can order items through electronic catalogues.
- *Vertical markets*: companies buying industrial products such as steel, chemicals or plastic, or buying services such as logistics (distribution) or media can use specialized websites (called *e-hubs*). For instance, Plastics.com permits thousands of plastics buyers to search for the lowest prices from thousands of plastics sellers.
- *Auction sites*: suppliers can place industrial products on auction sites where purchasers can bid for them.
- *Exchange* (or spot) markets: many commodities are sold on electronic exchange markets where prices can change by the minute. For example, Title Transfer Facility provides an online marketplace where gas energy can be traded instantly.
- *Buying alliances*: companies in the same market for products join together to gain bigger discounts on higher volumes.

E-commerce portals and hubs are creating information portals and ecosystems which are facilitating greater communication within and across industries. Covisint[34] is such a system that brings together companies in healthcare and manufacturing industries, streamlining processes and improving organizational performance.

The benefits of such systems are: a reduction of procurement costs, more rapid supply, greater agility when responding to changes in marketing environment, better connectivity with new suppliers, and improvements in reliability, streamlined information processing and closer working relationships between suppliers and customers. There are potential savings to be made. For example, United Technologies expected to pay around $25 million for an order for printed circuit boards. Through e-procurement the company attracted 34 bids from suppliers and paid $14 million, a saving of $10 million, or 40 per cent. However, the ability to source large numbers of suppliers and handle large quantities of goods can have further implications for logistics management. Read Digital Marketing 5.1. to find out more.

Digital Marketing 5.1 Managing E-tail Logistics in the Grocery Sector

The supply chain has been transformed in the retail industry by digital technology. The movement of goods and the flow of information between retailers and their suppliers are critical to operational success and whereas retailers used to be 'passive recipients of products, allocated to stores by manufacturers in anticipation of demand', now they are in control and manage supplies in response to customer demand. ASOS sells over 20,000 branded and own-label products through its online e-commerce operation. Digital systems and bar code technologies are enabling ASOS to offer 'a much wider product range than its high-street competitors'. Lean and agile supply chains which support large retail operations manage the purchasing, processing and movement of vast quantities of products so that individual items are in the right place at the right time to satisfy customer needs. Online shopping is on the increase but it creates operational and logistical challenges, especially for grocery retailers. A typical online grocery order consists of '60–80 items, across three temperature regimes picking from a total range of 10,000–25,000 products within 12–24 hours for delivery to customers within one to two hour time slots'.

Supermarket retailers have made significant investment in technology to manage the complexities associated with receiving products from thousands of suppliers, picking and delivering orders to millions of consumer orders. Ocado, the online-only grocery retailer, makes extensive use of digital technology to enable its business to operate. To manage its complex online operations, Ocado has developed in-house software and uses state-of-the-art gaming software to visualize and identify problems with the aim of streamlining operations in its automated warehouse and national supply chain. The IT team is pushing the boundaries in every aspect of the business with online and mobile developing apps for all the latest platforms, e.g., Android and iPad.

To learn more about Ocado and its use of technology visit http://www.ocadotechnology.com/

Based on: Ellis-Chadwick (2011);[35] Fernie et al. (2010)[36]

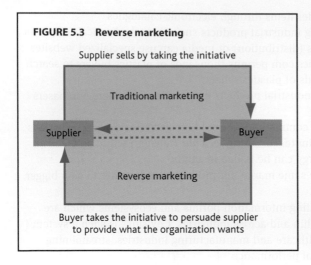

FIGURE 5.3 Reverse marketing

Supplier sells by taking the initiative

Traditional marketing

Supplier — Buyer

Reverse marketing

Buyer takes the initiative to persuade supplier
to provide what the organization wants

Reverse marketing

The traditional view of marketing is that supplier firms will actively seek the requirements of customers and attempt to meet those needs better than the competition. This model places the initiative with the supplier. Purchasers could assume a passive dimension relying on their suppliers' sensitivity to their needs, and on technological capabilities to provide them with solutions to their problems. However, this trusting relationship is at odds with a new corporate purchasing situation that developed during the 1980s and is becoming increasingly popular. Purchasing is taking on a more proactive, aggressive stance in acquiring the products and services needed to compete. This process, whereby the buyer attempts to persuade the supplier to provide exactly what the organization wants, is called **reverse marketing**.[37]

ICI, an international supplier of chemicals, uses reverse marketing very effectively to target suppliers with a customized list of requirements concerning delivery times, delivery success rates and how often sales visits should occur. Figure 5.3 shows the difference between the traditional model and this new concept.

The essence of reverse marketing is that the purchaser takes the initiative by approaching new or existing suppliers and persuading them to meet their supply requirements. The growth of reverse marketing presents two key benefits to those suppliers willing to listen to the buyer's proposition and carefully consider its merits. First, it provides the opportunity to develop a stronger and longer-lasting relationship with the customer and, second, it may be a source of new product opportunities that may be developed to a broader customer base later on.

Leasing

A lease is a contract by which the owner of an asset (e.g. a car) grants the right to another party to use the asset for a period of time in exchange for payment of rent.[38] The benefits to the customer are that a leasing arrangement avoids the need to pay the cash purchase price of the product or service, is a hedge against fast product obsolescence, may have tax advantages, avoids the problem of equipment disposal and, with certain types of leasing contract, avoids some maintenance costs. These benefits need to be weighed against the costs of leasing, which may be higher than outright buying.

There are two main types of leases: financial (or full payment) leases and operating leases (sometimes called *rental agreements*). A *financial lease* is a longer-term arrangement that is fully amortized over the term of the contract. Lease payments, in total, usually exceed the purchase price of the item. The terms and conditions of the lease vary according to convention and competitive conditions. Sometimes the supplier will agree to pay maintenance costs over the leasing period. This is common when leasing photocopiers, for example. The lessee may also be given the option of buying the equipment at the end of the period. An *operating lease* is for a shorter period of time, is cancellable and is not completely amortized.[39] Operating lease rates are usually higher than financial lease rates since they run for a shorter term. When equipment is required intermittently, this form of acquisition can be attractive because it avoids the need to let plant lie idle. Many types of equipment, such as diggers, bulldozers and skips, may be available for short-term hire, as may storage facilities.

Leasing may be advantageous to suppliers because it provides customer benefits that may differentiate product and service offerings. As such it may attract customers who might otherwise find the product unaffordable or uneconomic. The importance of leasing in such industries as cars, photocopiers and data processing has led an increasing number of companies to employ leasing consultants to work with customers on leasing arrangements and benefits. A crucial marketing decision is the setting of leasing rates. These should be set with the following factors in mind:

1 the desired relative attractiveness of leasing vs buying (the supplier may wish to promote/discourage buying compared with leasing)
2 the net present value of lease payments vs outright purchase
3 the tax advantages of leasing vs buying to the customer
4 the rates being charged by competitors
5 the perceived advantages of spreading payments to customers
6 any other perceived customer benefits, e.g. maintenance and insurance costs being assumed by the supplier.

Outsourcing

Outsourcing is a booming business. From cleaning and Internet security to aircraft assembly, jobs are being outsourced. In the UK about 10 per cent of the workforce is engaged in 'outsourced' jobs.[40] As a business model outsourcing can be very effective, as firms are contracted to do jobs they specialize in, leaving the business to get on with the core activities they are best at doing. Data centres and network computing are often outsourced to specialist providers. E.On contracted HP and TSystems to take over its network and telecommunication services in a $1.4 billion deal, which allowed E.On to hand over the parts of the business it was struggling with, in order to concentrate on its core business processes.[41] In Europe IT and business processes outsourcing is on the increase[42] despite a global downturn. However, while outsourcing offers many potential benefits, contracts and specifications must be clearly defined at the outset as things can go wrong and when they do there can be major problems. When Boeing, the USA's largest aircraft manufacturer, decided to outsource parts of the Dreamline operation, major problems arose when subcontractors failed to deliver on time, parts of the aircraft did not fit together and the result was an over-budget and over-schedule project, which cost Boeing billions of dollars.

Whichever purchasing innovations firms use, central to success is the relationship between buyers and suppliers. The next section explores relationship management.

Relationship Management

Four types of relationship have been identified.[43] The first two are market relationships between suppliers and customers. They make up the core of relationship marketing and are externally orientated. The first of these is classic market relationships concerning supplier–customer, supplier–customer–competitor and the physical distribution network. These types of relationship are discussed in this chapter. The second type is special market relationships such as the customer as a member of a loyalty programme and the interaction in the service encounter. These concepts are examined further in the services marketing and direct marketing communications chapters (Chapters 10 and 16). The third type of relationship concerns the economy and society in general. Examples of such relationships are mega-marketing (lobbying, public opinion and political power), mega-alliances (the European Union, which forms a stage for marketing) and social relationships (friendships and ethnic bonds). These issues are covered in the marketing environment and consumer behaviour chapters (Chapters 3 and 4). Finally, nano-relationships concern the internal operations of an organization, such as relationships between internal customers, internal markets, divisions and business areas inside organizations. Such relationships are discussed within the managing products (portfolio planning) and marketing implementation organization and control chapters (Chapters 11 and 22).

Managing relationships is a key ingredient in successful organizational marketing. **Relationship marketing** concerns the shifting from activities of attracting customers to activities concerned with current customers and how to retain them. Customer retention is critical, since small changes in retention rates have significant effects on future revenues.[44] At its core is the maintenance of relations between a company and its suppliers, channel intermediaries, the public and its customers.

The key idea is to create customer loyalty so that a stable, mutually profitable and long-term relationship is developed.[45] The idea of relationship marketing implies at least two essential conditions. First, a relationship is a mutually rewarding connection between the parties so that they expect to obtain benefits from it. Second, the parties have a commitment to the relationship over time and are, therefore, willing to make adaptations to their own behaviour to maintain its continuity.[46] A critical central feature of relationship marketing is the role that trust plays in creating satisfaction between parties in the relationship. Building trust is a very effective way to increase satisfaction and commitment to long-term relationships.[47] It can also help weaker partners in a business relationship to gain power over time in their dealings with more powerful companies.[48]

Applying ethical standards to relationships with business partners can also assist in relationship building and improve the reputation of whole business networks.[49]

The discussion of reverse marketing has given examples of buyers adopting a proactive stance in their dealings with suppliers, and has introduced the importance of buyer–seller relationships in marketing between organizations. The Industrial Marketing and Purchasing (IMP) Group developed the **interaction approach** to explain the complexity of buyer–seller relationships.[50] This approach views these relationships as taking place between two active parties. Thus, reverse marketing is one manifestation of the interaction perspective. Both parties may be involved in adaptations to their own process or product technologies to accommodate each other, and changes in the activities of one party are unlikely without consideration of or consultation with the other party. For example, Airbus consulted FedEx about the design of the A380 cargo plane so that it met the latter's requirement for delivering parcels and other goods.[51]

In such circumstances a key objective of business-to-business markets will be to manage customer relationships. This means considering not only formal organizational arrangements such as the use of distributors, salespeople and sales subsidiaries, but also the informal network consisting of the personal contacts and relationships between supplier and customer staff. Marks & Spencer's senior directors meet the boards of each of its major suppliers twice a year for frank discussions. When Marks & Spencer personnel visit a supplier, it is referred to as a 'royal visit'. Factories may be repainted, new uniforms issued and machinery cleaned: this reflects the exacting standards that the company demands from its suppliers and the power it wields in its relationship with them.[52]

The development of technology is facilitating the improvement of buyer–seller relationships through e-commerce hubs and supplier portals, which streamline the procurement process. Read the research to find out more about CRM.

Read the Research 5.1 CRM in Business-to-Business Markets

In business-to-business (B2B) marketing, the most important markets are often international. Despite globalization, these markets still have cross-national differences. Calls for the adoption of worldwide standards of business conduct have been ignored and these national differences make it difficult to establish common ground. This research explores the relationship between the buyer and supplier in four countries and the results may well have future implications for global account manager training.

Michelle D. Steward, Felicia N. Morgan, Lawrence A. Crosby and Ajith Kumar (2010) Exploring Cross-National Differences in Organizational Buyers' Normative Expectations of Supplier Performance, Journal of International Marketing, American Marketing Association, 18(1), 23–40.

Companies operating in today's competitive environment have started to view customer relationship management (CRM) as a strategic tool that can be leveraged to satisfy and retain their customers, rather than as an information technology investment.

In this paper, the authors discuss the importance of CRM systems in complex and simple selling settings and examine how CRM is implemented in both contexts.

Michael Ahearne, Adam Rapp, Babu John Mariadoss and Shankar Ganesan (2012) Challenges of CRM Implementation in Business-to-Business Markets: a Contingency Perspective, Journal of Personal Selling & Sales Management, 32(1), 117–30.

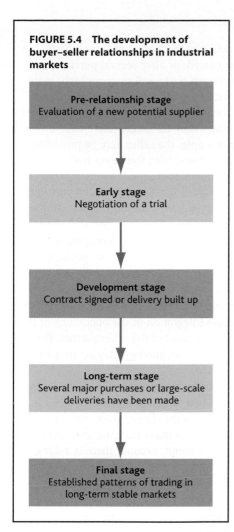

FIGURE 5.4   The development of buyer–seller relationships in industrial markets

Pre-relationship stage
Evaluation of a new potential supplier

Early stage
Negotiation of a trial

Development stage
Contract signed or delivery built up

Long-term stage
Several major purchases or large-scale deliveries have been made

Final stage
Established patterns of trading in long-term stable markets

A key aspect of the work of the IMP Group is an understanding of how relationships are established and developed over time. Ford[53] has modelled the development of buyer–seller relationships as a five-stage process (see Fig. 5.4).

Stage 1: the pre-relationship stage

Something has caused the customer to evaluate a potential new supplier. Perhaps a price rise or a decline in service standards of the current supplier has triggered the need to consider a change. The customer will be concerned about the perceived risk of change and the distance that is perceived to exist between itself and the potential supplier. Distance has five dimensions, as follows.

1   *Social distance*: the extent to which both the individuals and organizations in a relationship are unfamiliar with each other's ways of working.
2   *Cultural distance*: the degree to which the norms and values, or working methods, between two companies differ because of their separate national characteristics.
3   *Technological distance*: the differences between the two companies' product and process technologies.
4   *Time distance*: the time that must elapse between establishing contact or placing an order, and the actual transfer of the product or service involved.
5   *Geographical distance*: the physical distance between the two companies.

Stage 2: the early stage

At this stage, potential suppliers are in contact with buyers to negotiate trial deliveries for frequently purchased supplies or components, or to develop a specification for a capital good purchase. Much uncertainty will exist and the supplier will be working to reduce perceived risk of change. The reputation of the potential supplier is likely to be important and the lack of social relationships may mean a lack of trust on the part of both supplier and buyer. The supplier may believe that it is being used as a source of information and that the buyer has no intention of placing an order. The buyer may fear that the supplier is promising things it cannot deliver in order to make a sale. Both companies will have little or no evidence on which to judge their partner's commitment to the relationship.

Stage 3: the development stage

This stage occurs as deliveries of frequently purchased products increase, or after contract signing for major capital purchases. The development stage is marked by increasing experience between the companies of the operations of each other's organizations, and greater knowledge of each other's norms and values. As this occurs, uncertainty and distance reduce. A key element in the evaluation of a supplier or customer at this stage of their relationship depends on perceptions of the degree of commitment to its development. Commitment can be shown by:

- reducing social distance through familiarization with each other's way of working
- making formal adaptations that are contractually agreed methods of meeting the needs of the other company by incurring costs or by management involvement
- making informal adaptations beyond the terms of the contract to cope with particular issues and problems that arise as the relationship develops.

This stage is characterized by an increasing level of business between the companies. Many of the difficulties experienced in the early stages of the relationship are overcome through the processes at work in the development stage.

Stage 4: the long-term stage

By this stage both companies share mutual dependence. It is reached after large-scale deliveries of continuously purchased products have occurred, or after several purchases of major capital products. Experience of the operations of each party and trust are high, with the accompanying low levels of uncertainty and distance. The reduction in uncertainty can cause problems in that routine ways of dealing with the partner may cease to be questioned by this stage. This can happen even though these routines may no longer relate well to either party's needs. This is called 'institutionalization'. For example, the seller may be providing greater product variety (and incurring higher production costs) than the buyer really needs. Since no one questions the arrangements, these inefficiencies continue. Institutionalized practices may make a supplier appear less responsive to a customer or exploit the customer by taking advantage of its lack of awareness of changes in market conditions (for example, by not passing on cost savings) or by accepting annual price rises without question. Strong personal relationships will have developed between individuals in the two companies and mutual problem-solving and informal adaptations will occur. In extreme cases, problems arising from 'side changing' can arise where individuals act in the interests of the other company and against their own on the strength of their personal allegiances.

Extensive formal adaptations resulting from successive contracts and agreements narrow the technological distance between the companies. Close integration of the operations of the companies is motivated by cost reductions and increased control of the other partner. For example, automatic reordering systems based on information technology may act as a barrier to the entry of other supplier companies.

Commitment to the relationship will have been shown by the extensive adaptations that have occurred. However, the supplier has to be aware of two difficulties. First, the need to demonstrate commitment to a customer must be balanced by the danger of becoming too dependent on that customer. The supplier may feel the need to make the customer feel it is important yet does not wield too much power in the relationship. Second, there is a danger that the customer's perception of a supplier's commitment to the relationship is lower than it actually is. This is because the peak of investment of resources has taken place before the long-term stage has been reached. And so, ironically, when a supplier is at its most committed to a long-term and important customer, it may appear less committed than during the development stage.

Stage 5: the final stage

This stage is reached in stable markets over long time periods. The institutionalization process that started during the long-term stage continues to the point where the conduct of business may be based upon industry codes of practice, which may stipulate the right way to do business. Often, attempts to break out of such institutionalized patterns of trading will be met by sanctions from other trading partners.

This model of how buyer–seller relationships develop highlights some of the dangers that can occur during the process. Furthermore, suppliers can segment their customers according to the stage of development. Each stage requires differing actions based on the differing requirements of customers. The market for a supplier can be seen as a network of relationships. Each must be assessed according to the opportunity it represents, the threats posed by competitive challenges and the costs of developing the relationship. The marketing task is the establishment, development and maintenance of these relationships. They also need to be managed strategically. Decisions need to be made regarding the relative importance of a portfolio of relationships, and resources allocated to each of them based on their stage of development and likely return.

The reality of organizational marketing is that many suppliers and buying organizations have been conducting business between themselves for many years. Marks & Spencer has trading relationships with suppliers that stretch back almost 100 years. Such long-term relationships can have significant advantages for both buyer and seller. Risk is reduced for buyers as they get to know people in the supplier organization, and know whom to contact when problems arise. Communication is thus improved and joint problem-solving and design management can take place. Sellers gain through closer knowledge of buyer requirements, and by gaining the trust of the buyer an effective barrier to entry for competing firms may be established. Ocado, with its online grocery operation knows only too well how important it is to foster relationships; its partner organizations include Amazon, LoveFilm and Boden.[54] The concept of sharing information and resources has become more open as more firms adopt online technologies. *Open innovation* is a term used by Henry Chesbrough, a leading professor in innovation, to describe how firms use external and internal ideas to leverage advantage from widely distributed knowledge.[55]

Closer relationships in organizational markets are inevitable as changing technology, shorter product life-cycles and increased foreign competition place marketing and purchasing departments in key strategic roles. Buyers are increasingly treating trusted suppliers as *strategic partners*, sharing information and drawing on their expertise when developing cost-efficient, quality-based new products. The marketing implication is that successful organizational marketing is more than the traditional manipulation of the 4-Ps (product, price, promotion and place). Its foundation rests upon the skilful handling of customer relationships. This has led some companies to appoint customer relationship managers to oversee the partnership and act in a communicational and coordinated role to ensure customer satisfaction. Still more companies have reorganized their salesforces to reflect the importance of managing key customer relationships effectively. This process is called key or national account management. It should be noted, however, that strategic partnerships and key/national account management may not be suitable for all companies. For example, small companies may not be able to afford the resources necessary to make such processes work.[56]

The term 'national account' is generally used to refer to large and important customers that may have centralized purchasing departments that buy or coordinate buying for decentralized, geographically dispersed business units. Selling to such firms involves:

- obtaining acceptance of the company's products at the buyer's headquarters
- negotiating long-term supply contracts
- maintaining favourable buyer–seller relationships at various levels in the buying organization
- establishing first-class customer service.

This depth of selling activity frequently calls for the expertise of a range of personnel in the supplying company in addition to the salesperson. Many companies serving national accounts employ team selling.

Team selling involves the combined efforts of salespeople, product specialists, engineers, sales managers and even directors if the buyer's decision-making unit includes personnel of equivalent rank. Team selling provides a method of responding to the various commercial, technical and psychological requirements of large buying organizations. Such cross-functional selling teams have the ability to increase an organization's competitive advantage, and are employed by such companies as Bayer, Procter & Gamble, Xerox, ABB and Kraft Foods.[57]

Companies are increasingly structuring both external and internal staff on the basis of specific responsibility for accounts. Examples of such companies are those in the electronics industry, where internal desk staff are teamed up with outside staff around key customers. An in-depth understanding of the buyer's decision-making unit is developed by the salesperson being able to develop a relationship with a large number of individual decision-makers. In this way, marketing staff can be kept informed of customer requirements, enabling them to improve products and services, and plan effective communications.

Where companies offer similar high levels of product quality, the quality of an ongoing relationship becomes a means of gaining a competitive advantage. Putting resources into the development and continuation of a relationship with customers is most appropriate where purchases involve a high level of risk, where a stream of product and service benefits is produced and consumed over a period of time or where the costs associated with repeat purchase can be reduced by close relationships.[58] The success of the German machine tool industry is attributable not only to excellent product quality but also its capability and willingness to engage in long-term relationship building through first-rate after-sales service.[59]

How to Build Relationships

A key decision that marketers have to make is the degree of effort to put into relationship building.[60] Some organizations' customers may desire more distant contact because they prefer to buy on price and do not perceive major benefits accruing to closer ties. A supplier that attempts a relationship-building programme may be wasting resources in this situation. However, in most situations there is some potential benefit to be gained from relationship development. Indeed, as Digital Marketing 5.2 describes, there has been a movement towards the establishment of buyer–supplier partnerships and a concomitant reduction in the number of accredited suppliers.

Digital Marketing 5.2 Business-to-Business: Relationships in the Cloud

The ability to blend technology with customer requirements is an important success factor for many business-to-business companies, but managing customer relationships effectively is equally important. Increasingly, suppliers have been focusing on improving customer relationships through the application of digital technologies. The companies which achieve this successfully are using CRM as a method of differentiating themselves from their rivals. Increasingly, technology is facilitating relationship development and in doing so providing more services. For example, e-commerce hubs provide a powerful glue that unifies databases and CRM applications across organizations into a single smart information system, which facilitates the expansion of trading partnerships.

Dell Computers Corporation, for example, has saved millions of dollars by using Web services to improve coordination between its factories and its parts suppliers. Inventories have been significantly reduced and speed of delivery accelerated. Furthermore, Dell has streamlined part of its procurement operation with Ariba Buyer, a dynamic trading network that supports leading e-procurement solutions and facilitates collaborative business-to-business commerce. Ariba's commerce cloud links together over 730,000 companies in various industries. Furthermore, it helps businesses develop more effective *inter-enterprise* commerce online. In a typical day over 500 million dollars worth of goods are traded, 100,000 transactions completed, saving participating companies over 60 million dollars in supply costs and significantly reducing the processing costs associated with invoicing. Implementing the Ariba system has enabled Dell to reduce the requisition cycle by 62 per cent, saving time and eliminating 61 per cent of operational costs associated with MRO purchasing. This system ensures that 40,000 Dell employees are supplied with everything from software to security services.

Based on: Ariba (2012);[61] Dell (2012)[62]

Some features of close partnership relationships are that the parties adapt their processes and products to achieve a better match with each other, and share information and experience, which reduces insecurity and uncertainty. Sharing information and experience demonstrates commitment, leading to trust and a better atmosphere for future business.[63] Many companies are using the Internet to allow their customers to share information as well as to facilitate e-commerce. For example, John Deere, the agricultural machinery manufacturer, uses social media sites (e.g. Facebook and Twitter) to communicate with farmers with similar interests around the world.

Effective relationship building is a means to competitive advantage and is especially powerful since it is embedded within the culture of the organization and is therefore difficult for competitors to copy.[64] A relationship-orientated culture is, therefore, necessary for the successful implementation of the following range of customer services, which can be provided by a supplier—at zero or nominal cost to the customer—with the aim of helping the latter to carry out its operations.

Technical support

This can take the form of research and development cooperation, before-sales or after-sales service, and providing training to the customer's staff. The supplier is thus enhancing the customer's know-how and productivity.

Expertise

Suppliers can provide expertise to their customers. Examples include the offer of design and engineering consultancies, and dual selling, where the customer's salesforce is supplemented by the supplier. The customer benefits through acquiring extra skills at low cost.

Resource support

Suppliers can support the resource base of customers by extending credit facilities, giving low-interest loans, agreeing to cooperative promotion and accepting reciprocal buying practices where the supplier agrees to buy goods from the customer. The net effect of all of these activities is a reduced financial burden for the customer.

Service levels

Suppliers can improve their relationships with customers by improving the level of service offered to them. This can involve providing more reliable delivery, fast or just-in-time delivery, setting up computerized reorder systems, offering fast, accurate quotes and reducing defect levels. In so doing the customer gains by lower inventory costs, smoother production runs and lower warranty costs. By creating systems that link the customer to the supplier— for example, through recorder systems or just-in-time delivery—*switching costs* may be built in, making it more expensive to change supplier.[65]

Advances in technology are providing opportunities to improve service levels. The use of electronic data interchange (EDI) and the Internet offers the potential to enhance service provision.

Risk reduction

This may involve free demonstrations, the offer of products for trial at zero or low cost to the customer, product and delivery guarantees, preventative maintenance contracts, swift complaint handling and proactive follow-ups. These activities are designed to provide customers with reassurance.

When you have read this chapter

log on to the Online Learning Centre at **www.mcgraw-hill.co.uk/textbooks/jobber** to explore chapter-by-chapter test questions, links and further online study tools for marketing.

Review

1 **The characteristics of organizational buying**
- The characteristics are based on the nature and size of customers, the complexity of buying, the use of economic and technical choice criteria, the risky nature of selling and buying, buying to specific requirements, reciprocal buying, derived demand and negotiations.

2 **The dimensions of organizational buying**
- The dimensions are who buys, how they buy, the choice criteria used, and where and when they buy.

3 **The nature and marketing implications of who buys, how organizations buy and the choice criteria used to evaluate products**
- Who buys: there are six roles in the decision-making unit—initiators, users, deciders, influencers, buyers and gatekeepers. Marketers need to identify who plays each role, target communication at them and develop products to satisfy their needs.
- How organizations buy: the decision-making process has up to seven stages—recognition of problem (need), determination of specification and quantity of needed item, search for and qualification of potential sources, acquisition and analysis of proposals, evaluation of proposals and selection of supplier(s), selection of an order routine, and performance feedback and evaluation. Marketers can influence need recognition and gain competitive advantage by entering the process early.
- Choice criteria can be technical, economic, social (organizational) and personal. Marketers need to understand the choice criteria of the different members of the decision-making unit and target communications accordingly. Other marketing mix decisions such as product design will also depend on an understanding of choice criteria. Choice criteria can change over time necessitating a change in the marketing mix.

4 **The influences on organizational buying behaviour—the buy class, product type and purchase importance—and their marketing implications**
- The buy class consists of three types: new task, straight rebuy and modified rebuy. For new task, there can be large gains for suppliers entering the decision process early, but heavy investment is usually needed. For straight rebuys, the in-supplier should build a defensible position to keep out new potential suppliers. For out-suppliers, a key task is to reduce the risk of change for the buyers so that a modified rebuy will result.
- Product types consist of materials, components, plant and equipment, and maintenance items. Marketers need to recognize that the people who take part in the purchase decision usually change according to product type, and channel communications accordingly.
- The importance of purchase depends on the costs involved and the uncertainty (risk) regarding the decision. For very important decisions, heavy investment is likely to be required on the part of suppliers, and risk-reduction strategies (e.g. guarantees) may be needed to reduce uncertainty.

5 **The developments in purchasing practice: just-in-time and centralized purchasing, reverse marketing and leasing**
- Just-in-time practices aim to minimize stocks by organizing a supply system that provides materials and components as they are required. Potential gains are reduced purchasing, inventory and inspection costs, improved product design, streamlined delivery, reduced production downtime and improved quality.
- Centralized purchasing encourages purchasing specialists to concentrate on a small group of products. This often increases the power of the purchasing department and results in a move to long-term relationships with suppliers.
- Reverse marketing places the initiative with the buyer, who attempts to persuade the supplier to produce exactly what the buyer wants. Suppliers need to be responsive to buyers and provide them with an opportunity to build long-term relationships and develop new products.
- Leasing may give financial benefits to customers and may attract customers that otherwise could not afford the product.
- Outsourcing enables firms to focus on their core business process while using contracted firms to provide peripheral services and support. Firms need to ensure that contracts and arrangements are correct to prevent mistakes.

6 **The nature of relationship marketing and how to build customer relationships**
- Relationship marketing concerns the shift from activities associated with attracting customers to activities concerned with current customers and how to retain them. A key element is the building of trust between buyers and sellers.
- Relationship building can be enhanced by the provision of customer services including giving technical support, expertise, resource support, improving service levels and using risk-reduction strategies.

7 **The development of buyer–seller relationships**
- Relationships are established and developed through a five-stage process: pre-relationship stage, early stage, development stage, long-term stage and final stage.
- The pre-relationship stage is characterized by customer concern about the risk of change and the distance between itself and the potential supplier.
- The early stage is characterized by potential suppliers attempting to reduce risk of change and to build trust.
- The development stage is characterized by the reduction of uncertainty and distance.
- The long-term stage is characterized by shared mutual dependence and high levels of commitment.
- The final stage is characterized by industry codes of practice that stipulate 'the right way to do business'. Processes have become 'institutionalized'.
- Each stage requires different actions by suppliers based on the different requirements of customers.

Key Terms

decision-making process the stages that organizations and people pass through when purchasing a physical product or service

decision-making unit (DMU) a group of people within an organization who are involved in the buying decision (also known as the buying centre)

interaction approach an approach to buyer–seller relations that treats the relationships as taking place between two active parties

just-in-time (JIT) this concept aims to minimize stocks by organizing a supply system that provides materials and components as they are required

life-cycle costs all the components of costs associated with buying, owning and using a physical product or service

modified rebuy where a regular requirement for the type of product exists and the buying alternatives are known but sufficient change (e.g. a delivery problem) has occurred to require some alteration to the normal supply procedure

new task refers to the first-time purchase of a product or input by an organization

relationship marketing the process of creating, maintaining and enhancing strong relationships with customers and other stakeholders

reverse marketing the process whereby the buyer attempts to persuade the supplier to provide exactly what the organization wants

straight rebuy refers to a purchase by an organization from a previously approved supplier of a previously purchased item

team selling the use of the combined efforts of salespeople, product specialists, engineers, sales managers and even directors to sell products

total quality management the set of programmes designed to constantly improve the quality of physical products, services and processes

value analysis a method of cost reduction in which components are examined to see if they can be made more cheaply

Study Questions

1 What are the six roles that form the decision-making unit (DMU) for the purpose of an organizational purchase? What are the marketing implications of the DMU?

2 Why do the choice criteria used by different members of the DMU often change with the varying roles?

3 What are creeping commitment and lockout criteria? Why are they important factors in the choice of supplier?

4 Explain the difference between a straight rebuy, a modified rebuy and a new task purchasing situation. What implications do these concepts have for the marketing of industrial products?

5 Why is relationship management important in many supplier–customer interactions? How can suppliers build close relationships with organizational customers?

6 Explain the meaning of reverse marketing. What implications does it have for suppliers?

References

1. Naughton, J. (2005) Is Apple Right to Cosy up to the Enemy?, *Observer*, 12 June, 6.
2. Airbus (2012) Airbus for suppliers, http://www.airbus.com/tools/airbusfor/suppliers/ (accessed February 2012).
3. Corey, E. R. (1991) *Industrial Marketing: Cases and Concepts*, Englewood Cliffs, NJ: Prentice-Hall.
4. Jobber, D. and G. Lancaster (2009) *Selling and Sales Management*, London: Pitman, 27.
5. Wray, R. (2008) Second Contractor Drops Out of £12bn NHS Computer Upgrade, *Guardian*, 29 May, 26.
6. Bishop, W. S., J. L. Graham and M. H. Jones (1984) Volatility of Derived Demand in Industrial Markets and its Management Implications, *Journal of Marketing*, Fall, 95–103.
7. Webster, F. E. and Y. Wind (1972) *Organizational Buying Behaviour*, Englewood Cliffs, NJ: Prentice-Hall, 78–80. The sixth role of initiator was added by Bonoma, T. V. (1982) Major Sales: Who Really does the Buying, *Harvard Business Review*, May–June, 111–19.
8. Cline, C. E. and B. P. Shapiro (1978) *Cumberland Metal Industries (A): Case Study*, Boston, Mass: Harvard Business School.
9. Competitive Advantage Consultancy Limited, About us, http://www.cadvantage.co.uk/resources/articles/main-articles.aspx (accessed February 2012).
10. Leading edge (2012) Construction Market Research, http://www.lead-edge.co.uk./
11. CIM (2012) Construction sector set to feel the pinch in 2012, *Chartered Institute of Marketing, Construction Industry Group*, http://www.cimcig.org/news.php?id=855.
12. Robinson, P. J., C. W. Faris and Y. Wind (1967) *Industrial Buying and Creative Marketing*, Boston, Mass: Allyn & Bacon.
13. Jobber and Lancaster (2009) op. cit., 35.
14. GE Transportation (2012) Eco-minded PowerHaul leads the way into global markets, http://www.getransportation.com/rail/rail-blog/eco-minded-powerhaul-leads-the-way-into-global-markets.html.
15. Wright, R. (2008) GE Challenges EMD Dominance, *Financial Times*, 23 September, 29.
16. Wright, R. (2008) EMD Fighting to Regain Ground, *Financial Times*, Rail Industry Special Report, 23 September, 3.
17. Draper, A. (1994) Organisational Buyers as Workers: The Key to their Behaviour, *European Journal of Marketing* 28(11), 50–62.
18. Snoad, L. (2012) Taking personal control of the mission redefinition, *Marketing Week*, 26 January, 16–19.
19. Parker, D. (1996) The X Files, *Marketing Week*, 8 March, 73–4.
20. Edwards, C. (2006) Inside Intel, *Business Week*, 9 January, 43–8.
21. Walsh, F. (2006) M&S Tightens Screw on Suppliers, *Guardian*, 4 March, 27.
22. Heagarty, R (2011) Waitrose demands a 5 per cent cut from suppliers, *The Grocer*, 10 October, http://www.thegrocer.co.uk/companies/waitrose-demands-a-5-cut-from-suppliers/221572.article.
23. For a discussion of the components of risk see Stone, R. N. and K. Gronhaug (1993) Perceived Risk: Further Considerations for the Marketing Discipline, *European Journal of Marketing* 27(3), 39–50.
24. Jobber, D. (1994) What Makes Organisations Buy, in Hart, N. (ed.) *Effective Industrial Marketing*, London: Kogan Page, 100–18.
25. Mazur, L. (2002) Increasing Momentum, *Marketing Business*, June, 16–19.
26. Cardozo, R. N. (1980) Situational Segmentation of Industrial Markets, *European Journal of Marketing* 14(5/6), 264–76.
27. Robinson, Faris and Wind (1967) op. cit.
28. Lee, L. and D. W. Dobler (1977) *Purchasing and Materials Management: Text and Cases*, New York: McGraw-Hill, 265.
29. Forbis, J. L. and N. T. Mehta (1981) Value-Based Strategies for Industrial Products, *Business Horizons*, May–June, 32–42.
30. Hutt, M. D. and T. W. Speh (2006) *Business Marketing Management*, New York: Dryden Press.
31. Hitachi Transportation System (2012) Downsizing logistics space within factories and reduce parts/devices, http://www.hitachi-hb.co.jp/english/jirei/case_08.html (accessed 12 February 2012).
32. Brierty, E. G., R. W. Eckles and R. R. Reeder (1998) *Business Marketing*, Englewood Cliffs, NJ: Prentice-Hall, 105.
33. Doherty, N. F., D. McConnell and F. Ellis-Chadwick (2010) Exploring the Uptake and Application of Electronic Procurement to Central and Local Government 2010, *Fourth International Conference on Research Challenges in Information Science Proceedings* (RCIS), Nice, France, 19–21 May, 453–62.
34. Covisint, http://www.covisint.com.
35. Ellis-Chadwick, F. E. (2011), *Retail Planning and Supply Chain Management*, Buckingham: The Open University, 5.
36. Fernie, J., L. Sparks and A. C. McKinnon (2010) Retail Logistics in the UK: Past present and Future, *International Journal of Retail Distribution & Management*, 38(11/12), 894–914.
37. Blenkhorn, D. L. and P. M. Banting (1991) How Reverse Marketing Changes Buyer–Seller's Roles, *Industrial Marketing Management* 20, 185–91.
38. Anderson, F. and W. Lazer (1978) Industrial Lease Marketing, *Journal of Marketing* 42 (January), 71–9.
39. Morris, M. H. (1988) *Industrial and Organisation Marketing*, Columbus, OH: Merrill, 323.
40. *The Economist* (2011) Outsourcing is sometimes more hassle than its worth, 30 July, 62.
41. Ovum, E.On's IT outsourcing deal augurs further activity in utilities in 2011, http://ovum.com/2010/12/22/e-ons-it-outsourcing-deal-augurs-further-activity-in-utilities-in-2011/.
42. Heath, N. (2011) Megadeals are out and multisourcing is in as Europe's outsourcing spend rises. *Silicon.com*, http://www.silicon.

com/technology/it-services/2011/07/27/megadeals-are-out-and-multisourcing-is-in-as-europes-outsourcing-spend-rises-39747743/ (accessed February 2012).

43. Gummerson, E. (1996) Relationship Marketing and Imaginary Organisations: A Synthesis, *European Journal of Marketing* 30(2), 33–44.

44. Andreassen, T. W. (1995) Small, High Cost Countries' Strategy for Attracting MNC's Global Investments, *International Journal of Public Sector Management* 8(3), 110–18.

45. Ravald, A. and C. Grönroos (1996) The Value Concept and Relationship Marketing, *European Journal of Marketing* 30(2), 19–30.

46. Takala, T. and O. Uusitalo (1996) An Alternative View of Relationship Marketing: A Framework for Ethical Analysis, *European Journal of Marketing* 30(2), 45–60.

47. Geyskens, I., J.-B. E. M. Steenkamp and N. Kumar (1998) Generalizations About Trust in Marketing Channel Relationships Using Meta-Analysis, *International Journal of Research in Marketing* 15, 223–48; Selnes, F. (1998) Antecedents and Consequences of Trust and Satisfaction in Buyer–Seller Relationships, *European Journal of Marketing* 32(3/4), 305–22; and Vlaga, W. and A. Eggert (2006) Relationship Value and Relationship Quality, *European Journal of Marketing* 40(3/4), 311–27.

48. Narayandas, D. and V. K. Rangan (2004) Building and Sustaining Buyer–Seller Relationships in Mature Industrial Markets, *Journal of Marketing*, 68 (July), 63–77.

49. Lindfelt, L.-L. and J.-Å. Törnroos (2006) Ethics and Value Creation in Business Research: Comparing Two Approaches, *European Journal of Marketing* 40(3/4), 328–51.

50. See e.g. Ford, D. (1980) The Development of Buyer–Seller Relationships in Industrial Markets, *European Journal of Marketing* 14(5/6), 339–53; Hakansson, H. (1982) *International Marketing and Purchasing of Industrial Goods: An Interaction Approach*, New York: Wiley; Turnbull, P. W. and M. T. Cunningham (1981) *International Marketing and Purchasing*, London: Macmillan; Turnbull, P. W. and J. P. Valla (1986) *Strategies for Industrial Marketing*, London: Croom-Helm.

51. Foust, D. (2006) Taking Off Like 'A Rocket Ship', *Business Week*, 3 April, 76.

52. Thornhill, J. and A. Rawsthorn (1992) Why Sparks are Flying, *Financial Times*, 8 January, 12.

53. Ford (1980) op. cit.

54. Gray, R (2011) Delivering the goods, *The Marketer*, November, 24–7.

55. Chesbrough, H. W. (2003) *Open Innovation: The new imperative for creating and profiting from technology*, Boston: Harvard Business School Press, p. xxiv.

56. Sharland, A. (2001) The Negotiation Process as a Predictor of Relationship Outcomes in International Buyer–Seller Arrangements, *Industrial Marketing Management*, 30, 551–9.

57. Arnett, D. B., B. A. Macy and J. B. Wilcox (2005) The Role of Core Selling Teams in Supplier Teams in Supplier–Buyer Relationships, *Journal of Personal Selling and Sales Management* 25(1), 27–42.

58. See Lovelock, C. H. (1983) Classifying Services to Gain Strategic Marketing Insight, *Journal of Marketing* 47, Summer, 9–20; Wray, B., A. Palmer and D. Bejou (1994) Using Neural Network Analysis to Evaluate Buyer–Seller Relationships, *European Journal of Marketing* 28(10), 32–48.

59. See Shaw, V. (1994) The Marketing Strategies of British and German Companies, *European Journal of Marketing* 28(7), 30–43; Meissner, H. G. (1986) A Structural Comparison of Japanese and German Marketing Strategies, *Irish Marketing Review* 1, Spring, 21–31.

60. Jackson, B. B. (1985) Build Customer Relationships that Last, *Harvard Business Review*, Nov–Dec, 120–5.

61. Ariba, About us, http://www.ariba.com/about/.

62. Dell Streamlines Indirect Procurement with Ariba Buyer, *Power Solutions* 12–13, http://ftp.dell.com/app/ps-della.pdf.

63. Zineldin, M. (1998) Towards an Ecological Collaborative Relationship Management: A 'Co-operative Perspective', *European Journal of Marketing* 32(11/12), 1138–64.

64. See O'Driscoll, A. (2006) Reflection on Contemporary Issues in Relationship Marketing: Evidence from a Longitudinal Case Study in the Building Materials Industry, *Journal of Marketing Management* 22(1/2), 111–34; and Winklhofer, H., A. Pressey and N. Tzokas (2006) A Cultural Perspective of Relationship Orientation: Using Organisational Culture to Support a Supply Relationship Orientation, *Journal of Marketing Management* 22(1/2), 169–94.

65. Jackson (1985) op. cit., 127.

Trading Television Formats is Big Business
Do You Want to Be a Millionaire?

What do the programmes *Pointless, Million Pound Drop* and *Who Wants to be a Millionaire* have in common? They are all television quiz shows, with a presenter and teams of contestants. What separates them from each other is that each show has its own unique format, which includes the particular style of questions, special effects, the setting, the staging and lighting effects. Indeed every aspect of a show, which makes it different, is part of the format offer that can be licensed and sold on to production companies and broadcasters. Television formats are not restricted to quiz shows. *Come Dine with Me* and *Dinner Date* are examples of programmes with a culinary flavour, while *The X Factor* and *The Voice* create a showcase for performers to demonstrate their vocal skills. These types of shows involve ordinary non-professional people and are a particularly popular format. The genre has become known as 'reality television'. *Big Brother* is an example of a very popular show that attracted large viewing audiences. It offered an unusual twist to a basic contest format. The style of this show was voyeuristic and followed the lives of individuals living in the big brother house. The genre also includes documentary-style programmes, sometimes called 'fly-on-the-wall' or 'factual TV': for example, *Airport* and *Traffic Cops*. Indeed, format creators are willing to explore every aspect of life in order to find the next big idea.

New formats are not always instant hits. *Take Me*, a dating show where 30 single women compete for the attention of a potential soulmate, was conceived in France but was never seen by French audiences. Fremantle Media bought the concept and sold it into Australia, with the title *Take Out*, where it failed to attract sufficient viewers. However, with a new name at the show's next destination, Japan, it secured the success needed to become aired across the globe. The format was then sold into Netherlands, Denmark, Finland, Indonesia, Spain and Sweden and the UK, where it is a prime-time TV show regularly watched by 5 million viewers.

Whether you are interested in watching this flirtatious frolic or not, this programme is an example of a successful format. The setting involves the male contestant arriving on stage in the love lift and then 'the doors open and our man bursts out onto a set that's a cross between Barbie's dream house

and Dumbo's drunken adventure, with a haze of pink and purple fluorescent lights'. This quote helps to conjure up an image of the setting, the staging, the lighting and special effects, which help to distinguish the show from other dating programmes and add value to the franchise when the format is sold on.

Reality television has become very popular and successful shows are sold globally. *Big Brother*, *The Apprentice*, *Dancing with the Stars* are examples of shows which are aired on a global stage. TV formats are ostensibly products, which are traded in business-to-business markets. The contractual side of selling television formats is complex. The TV format includes the original concept and all of the associated production elements and branding, which can then be sold by licence. This means that television networks, broadcasters and producers can make versions of the show which suit the tastes of their national viewing audience. The selling of television formats has created an international market. Broadcasters are keen to buy format-style programmes as they represent a lower risk, the idea generally already having been proved in another part of the world.

The international TV and media market

London has become a popular centre for global production companies: for example All3Media, Shine, Fremantle and

Celador are large companies based there. Robert Clark, president of worldwide entertainment at Fremantle Media, which had revenues of €1.18 billion last year, says the chemistry between production companies and big broadcasters is a factor in the success of UK formats, as is the fact that English is the *lingua franca* of the TV world. And there is a more basic reason in that British production companies are good at making British formats travel.

But formats are not just created and sold in London. MIPTV is an annual exhibition, which attracts international broadcasters, producers and media buyers to Cannes, France to see showcases of the latest shows. Thousands of new and existing TV formats are showcased and traded at this event. Many popular shows have been launched here.

TV formats are very similar to other perhaps more recognizable brands, which are sold through franchising and licensing: for example, McDonald's, Pizza Hut, Starbucks. Licences are linked to territories and the more successful the format, the more territories it is likely to cover. A study of global formats prepared by Fremantle found that Wipeout—the game show that turns contestants into human pinballs as they navigate a giant obstacle course (known as *Total Wipeout* in the UK)—covers 22 international territories. It took the top slot from Fuji TV and Fremantle Media's contortionist gameshow *Hole in the Wall*, newly bought by 13 territories last year. Versions of Fremantle's *Britain's Got Talent* were sold to nine new countries, while *Take Me Out* was sold to five. In the league table of countries selling shows, the US dropped to third (13 per cent), behind the Netherlands (18 per cent) and Britain (41 per cent), while the surge in popularity of gameshows (accounting for a third of 2008 and 2009 titles) pushed Japan up into fourth.

Come Dine with Me, for example, has led to the production of thousands of episodes, which have been aired in over 20 countries including Croatia, Estonia, Slovakia, Turkey and Germany. The lifestyle channel in Australia was so keen on the series that they commissioned a second series before showing the first series. Global sales have earned ITV Studios, the creators of the format, in excess of £57 million and boosted the studio's international production revenue by 41 per cent last year. Tobi de Graaff, the director of global TV distribution at ITV, cautions that it is important when selling internationally to be aware of which aspects of a format create a successful programme but also to be aware of the different cultures of a particular viewing audience. It is important for a show like *Come Dine with Me* to 'feel extremely home-grown and natural'. Examples of different cultural slants are that in

the German version the focus is on serious cooking, while the Spanish version needed tweaks when dinner guests were uniformly complimentary about their hosts' cooking.

So the next time you settle on the sofa and watch a new TV show—which by the time it has ended you find yourself thinking 'Why did I bother to watch?'—remember, the show's producers may have got air time to test out a new format, which they intend to sell onto the global stage rather than be top of the ratings in their home market.

References

Brook, S. (2010) Britain leads the way in selling global TV formats, *Guardian*, http://www.guardian.co.uk/media/2010/apr/05/britain-tv-formats, sales, 5 April.

Hubert, A. (2012) Take me out: backstage with Paddy McGuinness and the girls, *Guardian*, http://www.guardian.co.uk/tv-and-radio/2012/jan/07/take-me-out-paddy-mcguinness.

Questions

1 Discuss the extent to which the organizational buying decision process is applicable to the buying of television formats.

2 Imagine you are going to the MIPTV exhibition in Cannes to buy new television formats for your television station. Make a list of the criteria you would use to guide your purchasing.

3 Many production companies and broadcasters have their headquarters in London. Suggest why it might be beneficial to be located in a particular area.

4 Suggest why the exhibition in Cannes provides a good marketplace for selling TV formats.

5 Digital technology has arguably made it easier to create video production. Using the concept of customer relationship management suggest what challenges a newcomer might have when trying to enter the world of television formats.

This case was prepared by Fiona Ellis-Chadwick, Senior Lecturer in Marketing, The Open University.

Sleeping with the Enemy?

The Delicate Art of Managing Different Roles at Ericsson's Purchasing Unit

Background

Ericsson was founded by Lars Magnus Ericsson as a telegraph equipment repair shop in Stockholm in 1876. Today, Ericsson is a Multinational Enterprise (MNE), a worldwide provider of telecommunication and data communication systems and in 2011 the fifth largest software company in the world. Ericsson's customers are amongst the world's ten largest mobile operators and approximately forty per cent of all mobile phone calls around the world are made through Ericsson's network systems. Ericsson has offices and operations in more than 175 countries with headquarters in Stockholm.

Over the past decade Ericsson has gone through a transformation from primarily being a production-oriented manufacturing firm in the capital goods industry, towards a customer-oriented solution provider. This shift in focus has significantly impacted on Ericsson's buying processes. This case looks at the issues Ericsson faced during the complex transformation period and highlights several challenges that need to be managed from a buying perspective.

Changes in the buying process

Previously, Ericsson, like many of its competitors, focused on the production of packaged systems and products, which were then sold to their global customers (mobile telecommunication operators—for example, Vodaphone or Orange). From a buying perspective the preferences and choice criteria used in buying decisions were well known. However, with an increased requirement for customization, the impact on the purchasing process is fewer certainties and increasingly buyers are looking for customized solutions. In response, Ericsson has adopted a more consultative approach which means purchasing decisions are made together with the customer. A further impact from adopting a customized approach is that Ericsson's suppliers vary depending on specific contracts and the services provided by suppliers. Therefore, not only choice criteria but also supply chain roles change from one business contract to the other. Suppliers of certain services in one project may very well become customers in another, or even competitors, offering the same solution. This often creates tricky situations for the co-workers in the buying department at Ericsson. To illustrate this delicate situation,

a tender of a customized solution and support project is here outlined.

The story of a purchaser's dilemmas

In January 2010 the Swedish mobile operator TeliaSonera sent out a tender for a customized solution, which involved three steps: 1) a request for information, 2) a request for proposal, and 3) a request for quote, detailing the set of products and services needed in the project. This brief was sent to four world-leading service providers: Hewlett Packard (HP), Oracle, Ericsson and Accenture. Each company competed in the tender process to become the prime integrator of the total solution.

After a long and thorough review of all service solution offerings, HP won the tender and their team took on the decision-making role as the prime integrator. As HP did not have a telecom system in its product portfolio, it turned to Ericsson to source the telecom system. This meant Ericsson switching from competitor to customer and partner with HP. In order to meet HP's requirements, Ericsson had in turn to source services, software tools and consultancy work. These services came from HP and another former competitor, Accenture. Ericsson also sourced the database and the operating system from Oracle, and a number of best-of-breed products from several small and large suppliers.

This case highlights how roles can change during the buying process. The complexity of the business deal leads the prime integrator to cooperate with the former competitors in the tender process in order to fulfil contract agreements. The companies go from being fierce competitors during the tender process to achieving different roles in the supplier chain as HP set up the ecosystem of suppliers upstream and downstream, forcing them to cooperate and create trustful relationships with each other. The purchasing unit at HP had, in other words, to approach the other competitors in the tender process to close the deal with the customer. Ericsson, on the other hand, became a supplier of telecom system to HP but still had to turn to HP to buy services, software tools and consultancy work. The supply chain is, therefore, no longer a chain from the supplier to the customer, but rather a reciprocal network of firms taking different roles in different situations—sometimes the role of a supplier and sometimes the role of a customer, or a competitor. These different interactions have to be managed by the purchasing department in their negotiation with the suppliers. This dilemma is expressed by the management team of the operations and sourcing departments and illustrated with the following quotations:

> 'The flexibility is much larger, which leads to the question, "Are we competitors or partners?" We are not one thing or another, we are everything.'
>
> Director of Sourcing, Ericsson

> 'It requires a lot from the organization when it is always changing, changing, changing. One day we are the customer, next day we are competitors, partners or the supplier.'
>
> Head of Operations and Support, Ericsson

> 'You need to have the capability to work short-term in a long-term relationship. In this space you do not get married with your supplier.'
>
> Director of Sourcing, Ericsson

Cooperation and competition in the supply network

The shift from product-orientated manufacturing business to collaborative service solution provider means Ericsson has had to rethink its business logic. The traditional roles of customers (the mobile network operators), competitors (other suppliers of network solutions) and suppliers (delivering technical components to the networks) are blurred and constantly changing. There is potential tension between competitors and suppliers (working on the same business contract) and the different firms are often competing with each other as well as cooperating. This can create a two-horned dilemma: on one horn is cooperation, which relies on generating a relationship based on trust, commitment and the sharing of information and knowledge. However, on the other horn is competition, which often generates relationships based on hostility, fighting to be best in class and opportunism. Ericsson's approach is to manage the multiple-role approach by stressing the importance of trust in order to make the relationship successful. The Director of Sourcing has said:

> Trust is usually where things go right or wrong. This trust comes from the fact that you know what we are doing, why we are doing it and what we are trying to achieve.

Trust becomes crucial in a relationship where a partner also might be a competitor. However, firms cannot on one hand put too much trust in their partner relationships as it may lead to a vulnerable and risky situation. On the other hand, Ericsson needs to share sufficient information with competing partners in order for the relationship to be productive and beneficial. According to Ericsson's Strategic Sourcing Manager, achieving a balance is a challenge and can create problems:

> We have situations where we have been holding back, not sharing enough information with our supplier who we also meet in competition, due to the risk involved, which led to the problem that the supplier either could not optimize their technical solution or give us the best pricing in tenders for a larger system integration business.

Ericsson is adapting to a changing marketing environment and shifting buyer requirements. It has recognized the importance of making changes but equally it has found there are many challenges to accommodate when trying to create collaborative working partnerships with many different types of organizations.

Definitions

Prime integrator The firm providing the complete solution and setting up the network of suppliers in interaction with the customer. As a prime integrator, the firm can influence which other firms should be involved in the development of the specific solution, unless the customer has some specific demands and wants to influence the set-up of suppliers.

Solution provider Provider of (in this case) an IT or telecommunication system.

Best-of-breed product Suppliers with best-of-breed products are often companies that have pioneered a segment and have developed most of the features of their products.

Questions

1. Discuss how the transition from product orientation to marketing orientation has affected the complexity of buying at Ericsson.

2. What consequences might this new way of doing business have for the organization of the internal buying unit at Ericsson?

3. Imagine you were the Sourcing Director at Ericsson: how would you manage the relationship with the other firms in the network of suppliers, competitors and customers?

4. What are the biggest challenges for a service provider when the roles in the network are constantly changing?

This case was prepared by Marlene Johansson, Lecturer in Marketing, and Helena Renström, Assistant Professor, Umeå School of Business and Economics, Sweden.

CHAPTER 6

Understanding marketing ethics and corporate social responsibility

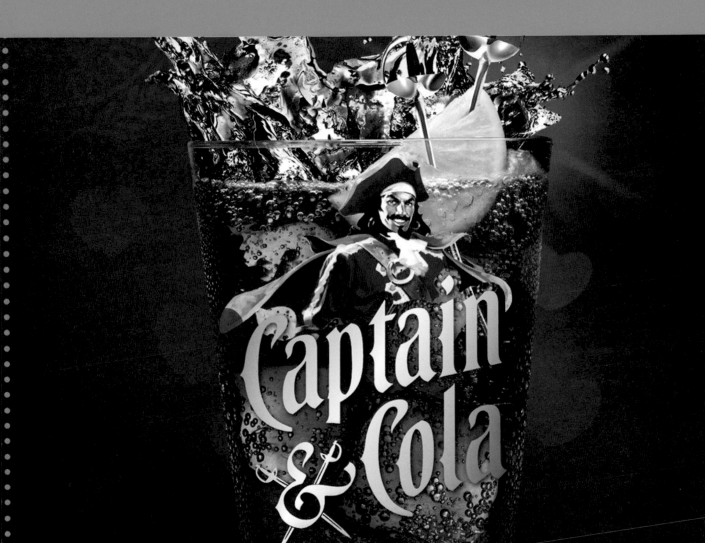

> *We know what the future looks like . . . we know that water will be very scarce, we know that energy prices will be much higher, we know sanitation will be ghastly in increasingly crowded urban areas.*
>
> **GAVIN NEATH, UNILEVER'S HEAD OF SUSTAINABILITY[1]**

> *We decided to go further because the environmental and social challenges the world faces are getting tougher.*
>
> **ADAM ELMAN, M&S HEAD OF PLAN A[2]**

LEARNING OBJECTIVES

After reading this chapter, you should be able to:

1 explain the meaning of ethics, and business and marketing ethics

2 describe ethical issues in marketing

3 discuss business, societal, and legal and regulatory responses to ethical concerns

4 explain the stakeholder theory of the firm

5 discuss the nature of corporate social responsibility

6 describe the dimensions of corporate social responsibility

7 discuss the arguments for and against corporate social responsibility programmes

Corporate Social Responsibility (CSR) and operating in an ethical way is becoming increasingly important in the modern world. Globally, companies are taking CSR seriously and responding positively: for example, TNT (Netherlands logistics firm) has 50 people on standby to respond within 48 hours to world emergencies; IBM's (USA computer corporation) philanthropic spending involves deploying staff to work on worthy projects in the developing world; Novo Nordisk (Danish manufacturer of insulin) introduced the 'triple bottom line' (striving to act in a financially, environmentally and socially responsible way) into its articles of association. It believes that having the ethos anchored so firmly makes the company more alert to both risks and opportunities.

Positive responses can benefit an organization's market position but, equally, unethical behaviour can lead to bad publicity and have a negative effect on customers' willingness to buy. Examples which have had a negative influence include: BA (price fixing), BAE Systems (bribery), BP and Shell (oil spills in USA and Nigeria), Wal-Mart (allegations of poor employee relations), McDonald's (health concerns), Coca-Cola (marketing positioning of Dasani in the UK) and Procter & Gamble (Sunny D, the drink found to turn children yellow). These examples bear witness to the importance of business and marketing ethics, not only in their own right but also for the well-being of the organizations themselves.

Consequently, organizations are now reflecting on and defining their standards of ethical behaviour. They should also use these standards as the basis for designing corporate social responsibility strategies that take account of how their actions might affect society and the environment. This requires an analysis of how decisions affect the wider community beyond the narrow interests of shareholders.

This chapter follows naturally from the discussion in Chapter 3 of the marketing environment (e.g. social/cultural, ecological/physical and technological) by discussing the meaning of marketing ethics and specific associated issues, which might affect how organizations operate and respond. This chapter focuses on organizational responses in the shape of corporate social responsibility programmes; the nature and dimensions of corporate social responsibility; and an analysis of the arguments for and against the establishment of such programmes. Finally, the chapter will conclude with a summary of some of the key issues in marketing ethics and corporate social responsibility.

Marketing Ethics

Underpinning the idea of corporate social responsibility and shaping its implementation is the concept of ethics. **Ethics** are the moral principles and values that govern the actions and decisions of an individual or group.[3] They involve *values* about right and wrong conduct. **Business ethics** are the moral principles and values that guide a firm's behaviour. Until recently, for many companies business ethics consisted mainly of compliance-based, legally driven codes and training that outlined in detail what employees could or could not do regarding such areas as conflicts of interest or improper use of company assets. Now, an increasing number of companies are designing value-based ethical programmes that are consistent across global operations. The aim is to provide employees with an in-depth understanding of ethical issues that will help them to make the correct decisions when faced with new ethical situations and challenges.[4]

Marketing Ethics and Corporate Social Responsibility in Action 6.1 discusses how Marks & Spencer has embedded ethical standards into its business.

Marketing ethics are the moral principles and values that guide behaviour within the field of marketing, and cover issues such as product safety, truthfulness in marketing communications, honesty in relationships with customers and distributors, pricing issues and the impact of marketing decisions on the environment and society. There can be a distinction between the legality and ethicality of marketing decisions. Ethics concern personal moral principles and values, while laws reflect society's principles and standards that are enforceable in the courts.

Not all unethical practices are illegal. For example, it is not illegal to include genetically modified (GM) ingredients in products sold in supermarkets. However, some organizations, such as Greenpeace, believe it is unethical to sell GM products when their effect on health

Marketing Ethics and Corporate Social Responsibility in Action 6.1
Doing the *Right Thing* at Marks & Spencer

Marks & Spencer set the green agenda for retailers when it launched its five-year eco-programme, known as 'Plan A' (there is no plan B). They have extended the original deadline from 2012 to 2015 and the number of commitments the company aims to achieve from 100 to 180. M&S has achieved '95 of the original commitments, 77 are on plan, 7 are behind and one (biodiesel) is on hold'. The extended plan A is set out under seven pillars:

1. involve the customers: e.g. more sustainable products
2. make plan A 'how we do business': e.g. create culture of innovation on sustainability
3. climate change: e.g. reduce carbon footprint
4. waste: e.g. no more operational waste to be sent to landfill sites
5. natural resources: e.g. recycle consumables, sustainable construction
6. fair partner: e.g. ensure workforces and suppliers benefit and earn a living wage
7. health and well-being: e.g. facilitate behaviour change through labelling.

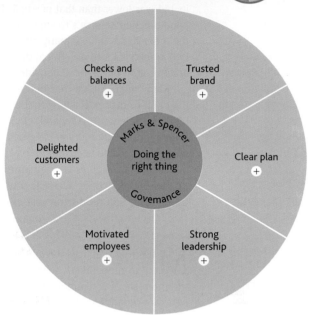

The progress of the 20 objectives set under the seven pillars is monitored continually. For example, the company has helped 15,000 children in Uganda receive a better education; it is saving 55,000 tonnes of CO_2 per year, it has recycled 48 million clothes hangers; it is tripling sales of organic food; and it has converted over 20 million garments to Fairtrade cotton. M&S has also proved through the implementation of plan A that sustainability works throughout the business as both employees and suppliers are engaged in a variety of initiatives.

Plan A is not only ethically worthy, it also makes good business sense. M&S market research has found that British consumers fall into four broad segments:

1. the *crusaders* (or *dark greens*) are passionately green and will make every attempt to shop for environmentally friendly goods and services (11 per cent)
2. the *light greens* want green consumption but want it to be easy (27 per cent)
3. the *vaguely concerned* are interested in green issues but do not see how they can make a difference (38 per cent)
4. the *uninterested* do not care about green issues (24 per cent).

In M&S's view these results represent an opportunity: three-quarters of British consumers are interested in green issues to some degree and in response they have adapted products to be more sustainable, encouraging consumers to live in a way that has a less negative impact on the environment. By taking the lead in green issues, M&S is appealing to the majority of its target market and many perceive the company to be the best at benefiting society and the environment.

Based on: Barnett (2011);[5] Marks & Spencer (2012);[6] The Economist (2008);[7] Bokaie (2008);[8] Franklin (2008)[9]

has not been scientifically proven. Such concerns have led some supermarket chains to withdraw GM ingredients from their own-brand products. Nor was it illegal for Google to launch a self-censored search engine that prevents access to 'sensitive' subjects in China, yet the action has been criticized on ethical grounds.[10]

Ethical principles reflect the cultural values and norms of society. Norms guide what ought to be done in a particular situation. For example, being truthful is regarded as good. This societal norm may influence marketing behaviour. Hence—since it is good to be truthful—deceptive, untruthful advertising should be avoided. Often, unethical behaviour may be clear-cut but, in other cases, deciding what is ethical is highly debatable. Ethical dilemmas arise when two principles or values conflict. For example, Ben & Jerry's, the US ice cream firm, was a leading member of the Social Venture Network in San Francisco, a group that promotes ethical standards in business. A consortium, Meadowbrook Lane Capital, was part of this group and was formed to raise enough capital to make Ben & Jerry's a private company again. However, its bid was lower than that of Anglo-Dutch food multinational Unilever NV. Arguably, on the one hand, for Ben & Jerry's to stick to its ethical beliefs it should accept the Meadowbrook bid. On the other hand, the company also had to perform financially in the interests of its shareholders. Ben & Jerry's faced an ethical dilemma; one of its values and preferences inhibited the achievement of financial considerations. Ultimately, they accepted the Unilever bid.[11]

Many ethical dilemmas derive from the conflict between the desire to increase profits and the wish to make decisions that are ethically justified. For example, the decision by Google to launch a self-censored search engine in China was driven by the need to be competitive in a huge market where it was lagging behind competitors. In order to secure a deal in China, Microsoft accepted censorship by the government in its agreement with Baidu (China's largest search engine).[12] Companies do seek to address such conflicts: for example, Nike and Reebok monitor their overseas production of sports goods to ensure that no child labour is used, while still producing cost-efficient ranges.

Ethical Issues in Marketing

Marketing practices have been criticized by consumers, consumer groups and environmentalists, who complain that marketing managers have been guilty of harming the interests of consumers, society and the environment. These ethical concerns are analysed by examining issues specific to the marketing mix; this is followed by consideration of general societal, environmental and political issues (see Fig. 6.1).

Ethical issues relating to marketing mix effects on consumers

Ethical concerns impinge on all aspects of the marketing mix. The rest of this section gives examples for product, price, promotion and place. Further specific examples are given in later chapters.

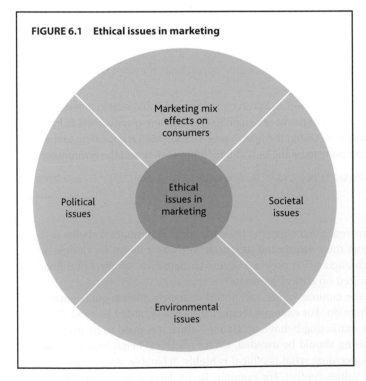

FIGURE 6.1   Ethical issues in marketing

Product: product safety

The tobacco, food and drinks industries have attracted criticism in recent years regarding the potential harm their products may cause to consumers. Tobacco companies have been criticized for marketing cigarettes, which cause lung cancer. On the one hand, the food industry has been criticized for marketing products that have high levels of fat, which can lead to obesity and, in the drinks industry, concern has been expressed over the marketing to children of sugar-rich fizzy drinks, which cause tooth decay and can also lead to obesity. Concern over Sunny D's high level of sugar forced Procter & Gamble to withdraw the drink's original formulation from the market, and the lack of success of its relaunch persuaded P&G to sell the brand six years after its original launch.[13] Pressure from consumers has prompted MacDonald's, the world's largest fast-food retailer, to diversify its product ranges by adding healthier options to its menus. On the other hand, the industry has also argued that business and government are taking steps to reduce the harmful effects of products, with bans on tobacco promotion escalating across Europe and the creation of bodies such as the Food Standards Agency, the independent food safety body set up to protect public health and consumer interests in relation to food in the UK, and the Portman Group, the industry-sponsored organization that oversees the UK's alcoholic drinks industry. Most European countries have similar organizations, which are also able to provide advice to industry.

Pricing: price fixing

An anti-competitive practice associated with marketing is price fixing, where two or more firms collude to force up the price of products. EU competition policy provides a legal framework that is designed to prevent firms from carrying out this practice. For example, the European Commission has fined three chemical groups (Hoechst, Atofina and Akzo-Nobel) £153 million for fixing the market for monochloroacetic acid, a widely used household and industrial chemical.[14] National laws also ban price fixing, as is illustrated by BA's £121 million fine from the UK's Office of Fair Trading for fixing long-haul fuel surcharges, and its £148 million fine from the USA's Department of Justice for colluding over cargo and long-haul surcharges.[15] Price fixing is considered unethical because it interferes with the consumer's freedom of choice and raises prices artificially.

Supporters of marketing claim that price fixing is the exception rather than the rule, however, and while it should not be conducted most industries are highly competitive with prices reflecting what consumers are willing to pay.

Promotion

Misleading advertising: this can take the form of exaggerated claims or concealed facts. A claim that a diet product was capable of one kilogramme weight loss per week when in reality much less was the case is an example of an exaggerated claim. When Coca-Cola launched its bottled water brand Dasani in the UK, it concealed the fact that it was made from Sidcup tap water. Consumers were enraged and felt they'd been cheated. A damaging media frenzy followed; also traces of bromate (a possible carcinogen) were found in the water. Coca-Cola withdrew tens of thousands of bottles and shortly afterwards the brand was withdrawn from the UK altogether and the planned launch into Europe was scrapped. Advertising can conceal facts and may give a misleading impression to consumers, as when a food brand is advertised as healthy because it contains added vitamins without pointing out its high sugar and fat content. Making such misleading claims is known as 'greenwashing'.

Marketers argue that in most European countries advertising is tightly regulated, minimizing opportunities for advertisers to mislead. For example, the UK's Advertising Standards Authority censured GlaxoSmithKline for making the unfounded claim that drinking Horlicks could make children taller, stronger and more intelligent. EU law states that 'nutritional and health claims which encourage consumers to purchase a product, but are false, misleading, or not scientifically proven are prohibited'.[16] They also point out that high-profile scandals that meet with consumer and media disapproval are a major deterrent to marketers who may be contemplating making similar mistakes.

Deceptive selling: salespeople can face great temptation to deceive in order to close a sale. The deception may take the form of exaggeration, lying or withholding important information. Examples of malpractice include financial services salespeople that mis-sold pension plans by exaggerating the expected returns, a media-driven scandal that resulted in millions of pounds worth of compensation being awarded to the victims. To counter this behaviour, an increasing number of companies provide ethical training in personal selling to communicate to staff how to behave appropriately.

Direct marketing's invasion of privacy: the issue of the unethical practice of entering names and addresses onto a database without the consumer's permission has caused concern. Some consumers fear that the act of subscribing to a magazine or a website or buying products by direct mail will result in the inconvenience of receiving streams of unsolicited direct mail or *spam* (the online equivalent to junk mail). Regulation in Europe by bodies such as the Direct

Marketing Association (UK) and governments aim to ensure that consumers are protected and their data is only used and stored legally. Online consumers are given various options to *opt in* or *opt out* of non-essential data collection and subsequent promotional mailings.

The use of promotional inducements to the trade: manufacturers promote their products and aim to outperform the competition. Consequently, they sometimes offer inducements to retailers to place special emphasis on particular products. For the consumer a salesperson might try to sell the particular product to earn extra bonuses. This practice is considered unethical by some groups as there can be overemphasis on the particular products. Defenders of the practice claim that consumers are able to determine their own needs and make informed decisions.

Place: slotting allowances

A slotting allowance is a fee paid by a manufacturer to a retailer in exchange for an agreement to place a product on the retailer's shelves. The importance of gaining distribution and the growing power of retailers means that slotting allowances are commonplace in the supermarket trade. They may be considered unethical since they distort competition, favouring large suppliers that can afford to pay them over small suppliers who may in reality be producing superior products.

Marketers argue they are only responding to the realities of the marketplace (i.e. the immense power of some retailers) and claim the blame should rest with the purchasing practices of those retailers that demand payment for display space, rather than the marketing profession who are often powerless to resist such pressures.

General societal, environmental and political issues

Broadly speaking, these issues focus on concerns that marketing practices promote too much materialism and put too much emphasis on the short term. Additionally too little emphasis is placed on the long-term environmental consequences. A political concern is that the power of global companies fuelled by massive marketing budgets works against the interests of consumers and society.

Societal concerns

Two societal concerns are marketing's promotion of materialism and its emphasis on short-term issues.

Materialism is an ethical concern associated with an overemphasis on material possessions. Critics argue that people judge themselves and are judged by others not by who they are but by what they own and marketers use this trait to drive consumption. For example, status symbols such as expensive houses, cars, second homes, yachts, high-tech gadgets and designer clothing are marketed as representations of success and social worth. Such conspicuous consumption is fuelled by the advertising industry, which equates materialism and success with happiness, desirability and social worth. Materialism is not considered natural by the critics but a phenomenon created by business, to drive sales and deliver high profit margins. Such companies devote large marketing expenditures to these types of brands.

Supporters of marketing argue that sociological studies of tribes in Africa, who have never been influenced by marketing's pervasive and persuasive powers, also display signs of materialism. For example, in some tribes people use the number of cows owned as a symbol of status and power. They argue that desire for status is a natural state of mind, with marketing simply promoting the kinds of possessions that may be regarded as indicators of status and success.

Short-termism: marketing is accused of putting the short-term interests of consumers before the consumers' and society's long-term interests. As we have seen when discussing product safety, marketers supply and promote products that can have long-term adverse health repercussions for consumers. Cigarettes may aid short-term relaxation but they have harmful long-term health effects for both smokers and those people forced to breathe in their smoke. Fatty food may be tasty but it may also lead to obesity and heart problems. Too much salt and sugar in food and drinks may enhance the taste but also lead to long-term health problems. Alcohol may remove inhibitions and help to create a convivial atmosphere but may also lead to dependency and liver problems.

Marketers need to act responsibly in response to these issues. For example, Coca-Cola has reduced the sugar levels in some of its fizzy drinks and stopped advertising them in television programmes targeting the under-12s.[17] Marks & Spencer has also moved to reduce salt in its food, including a 15 per cent reduction of salt in its sandwiches.[18] Government and self-regulation is also required to limit individual companies' scope for neglecting the longer-term effects of their actions.

Environmental concerns

Marketers' desire to satisfy consumers' wants may also conflict with the interests of the environment. Businesses may want the cheapest ingredients and components in their products, whereas environmentalists favour more expensive materials that are biodegradable or recyclable. Marketers may favour large packaging that gains the attention of consumers in stores, whereas environmentalists favour smaller pack sizes and refill packs. As consumer awareness of the impact of climate change and use of non-renewable resources grows, perceptions are changing and companies that are seen to be taking a serious approach towards sustainability can gain commercial advantage over those that do not take positive action.[19]

Governments have also taken positive actions in an attempt to reconcile business and environmental interests, for example with car scrappage schemes that aim to cut pollution and stimulate demand for new cars. So the politically and economically desirable option would be to create incentive structures for the advancement of innovation in the area of energy-efficient

cars, which could reduce emissions and maintain a healthy automotive industry. For example, the French government introduced a car scrappage scheme of €1000 for consumers who exchange their old cars for fuel-efficient models; the result was improved sales. Prompted by European regulations, manufacturers in the automotive industry are continually fostering innovations that aim to meet carbon reduction targets.[20] However, environmentalists have questioned the benefits of such schemes, saying new cars might be operationally greener but efficiency gains tend to be offset by the carbon footprint involved in the manufacture of a new car. They would prefer governments to invest in increasing access and improving the efficiency of public transport. For different reasons, consumers are also yet to be convinced *en masse to* adopt fuel-efficient cars. Manufacturers have to work harder to counter consumer resistance to switch from their 'gas guzzling' vehicles to more fuel-efficient alternatives. Read Mini Case 6.1 to find out more.

Increasingly, marketing managers are developing corporate social responsibility strategies that take account of the external impacts of their decisions on society and the environment. See Exhibit 6.1 for an example of fuel-efficient and less polluting cars.

THE BIG TURN ON

100 DAYS TO GO
100% ELECTRIC
DRIVING

LEAF

⬆ **EXHIBIT 6.1** Nissan focuses on alternative fuels when advertising its leading environmentally friendly, affordable cars.

Mini Case 6.1 Hybrid and Electric Cars

In Europe the adoption of electric and hybrid cars is low compared to Japan and the USA, but manufacturers are looking for new ways to boost sales. Toyota anticipates introducing ten new models into Europe to boost sales to 1 million vehicles by 2014.[21] Research suggests there are important choice criteria consumers consider when buying new cars.

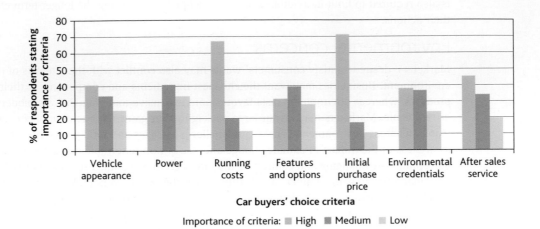

Car buyers' choice criteria

Importance of criteria: ■ High ■ Medium ■ Low

The graph shows that initial outlay to buy the car and running costs are the two most influential criteria followed by after-sales service and then vehicle appearance. Interestingly, features of the vehicle and power are much lower in terms of importance, in the new car-buying decision.

Therefore, while Toyota, Honda, Nissan and other manufacturers are introducing cars with new power options, there are other issues to address to encourage the wider adoption of more fuel-efficient cars. The marketing director at Honda UK feels that electric and hybrid cars will have to have significantly lower prices to increase consumer uptake. He feels that, even though consumers will benefit immediately from the lower running costs of hybrid and electric cars, it is still likely to take up to ten years before they will get any payback. The key trigger is lowering the price of the initial outlay.

Consequently, in order to increase the number of adopters of hybrid or electric cars, manufacturers will have to find ways to communicate the benefits to consumers, and reduce the initial purchase price; governments will need to find ways to improve the quality of the road infrastructure as electric cars in particular need very good road surfaces to run efficiently; consumers will have to achieve a greater understanding and ultimately willingness to adopt before there is likely to be a significant uplift in the number of more fuel-efficient cars on the roads of Europe.

Questions:

1   Price is often an indicator of quality and to lower the price can suggests an inferior product. However, the marketing director at Honda feels that the initial price of electric and hybrid cars should be low to encourage an increase in sales. Suggest other methods (apart from price) that you might use to market these cars.

2   Discuss what governments can do—apart from improving the roads—to ensure more 'environmentally friendly' motoring.

Based on: Barnett (2011)[22]

The politics of globalization

A third ethical concern is the growth of globalization. This is the move by companies to operate in more than one country and is usually a term applied to large multinational corporations that exert considerable power in their host countries. It is the abuse of such

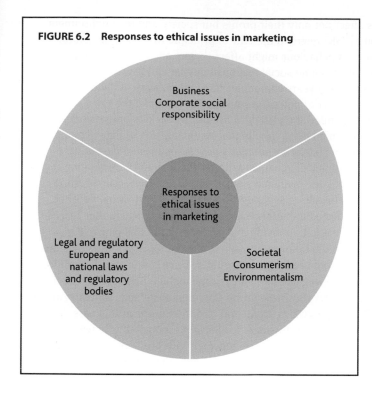

FIGURE 6.2   Responses to ethical issues in marketing

Business
Corporate social
responsibility

Responses to
ethical issues
in marketing

Legal and regulatory
European and
national laws
and regulatory
bodies

Societal
Consumerism
Environmentalism

power that is of ethical concern. Backed as they are by huge marketing expenditures and global mega-brands, concern is expressed over their influence over consumers, governments and suppliers. Critics argue that their size and huge budgets mean that it is hard for smaller rivals to compete, thus reducing consumer choice. The impact on employment and the economy means that governments vie with each other to attract global organizations to their country. Finally, their purchasing power means that they can negotiate very low prices from suppliers in the developing world.

Supporters of global companies argue that their size and global reach mean that they benefit from economies of scale in production and marketing (making them more efficient and, therefore, in a better position to charge low prices to consumers) and in R&D, enabling them to develop better-quality products and make technological breakthroughs—for example, in the area of healthcare. They further claim that their attraction to governments is evidence of the value they provide to host nations. Regarding their ability to negotiate down prices from developing-world suppliers, global organizations need to recognize their responsibilities to their supplier stakeholders. This is happening as more of them adopt corporate responsibility programmes and global corporations recognize the marketing potential of Fair Trade products (such as Nestlé, which markets Partners' Blend, a Fair Trade coffee).

Having discussed the major ethical issues relating to marketing, in the next section we will explore business, societal, and legal and regulatory responses to these concerns (see Fig. 6.2).

Business responses to ethical issues in marketing: corporate social responsibility

Business has taken action to address ethical concerns in marketing and other functional areas by adopting the philosophy of corporate social responsibility (CSR). Over the past ten years CSR has become increasingly important and commands the attention of executives around the world. It would be difficult to find a recent annual report of any large multinational company that does not talk proudly of its efforts to improve society and safeguard the environment.[23] We shall now examine the idea in depth by exploring the nature and dimensions of CSR and assessing the arguments for and against its adoption.

Corporate Social Responsibility

Corporate social irresponsibility can have painful consequences for organizations. The case of Siemens illustrates the negative fallout that can follow. Accused of paying bribes to win lucrative overseas telecoms and power contracts, Siemens was fined £523 million by the US Department of Justice, and £180 million by a court in its home town of Munich. A further £354 million was paid to settle a case in Munich over the failure of its former board to fulfil its supervisory duties. The total cost to Siemens, a symbol of German engineering excellence, was £2.25 billion, including lawyers' and accountants' fees, plus the loss of its reputation and that of former senior executives.[24]

The fallout from this and other cases raises the issue of how harmful corporate social irresponsibility can be to companies and wider society. As a result companies are increasingly examining how their actions affect not only their profits but society and the environment. Corporate social responsibility (CSR) refers to the ethical principle that an organization should be accountable for how its behaviour might affect society and the environment.

Commentators have claimed corporate social responsibility is 'an idea whose time has come'[25] but CSR is not new. For many years companies have been aware of the obligations of being an employer and a consumer of natural resources. For example, the town of Bourneville was created by the founder of Cadbury to house the workers of that company.[26] Nevertheless, there is little doubt that CSR is now higher on the agenda of many companies than it was in the past. Most multinational corporations now have a senior executive, often with a staff at his/her disposal, specifically charged with developing and coordinating the CSR function.[27] Furthermore, most large companies engage in corporate social reporting within their annual financial statements, as separate printed reports and/or on websites. The importance of CSR is also reflected in membership organizations, which offer services to members, such as providing information, lobbying and promoting the CSR cause. For example, the UK-based Business in the Community (www.bitc.org.uk) has a membership of over 700 companies, and includes in its activities cause-related marketing and the promotion of CSR internationally. Other notable organizations in Europe include Business and Society Belgium, Finnish Business and Society, Business in the Community Ireland, Samenleving and Bedrijf (Netherlands), CSR Europe (www.csreurope.org) and the European Business Ethics Network (www.eben-net.org). In the USA, Business for Social Responsibility (www.bsr.org) has grown into a major global organization.[28] These, together with pressure groups such as Greenpeace and ASH (Action on Smoking and Health), highlight the belief that organizations should consider a wider perspective regarding their activities and objectives than a narrow focus on short-term profits. However, it is not straightforward to determine the best course of action for future sustainability. Read Marketing in Action 6.1 to find out more.

Marketing in Action 6.1 IKEA Delivers Sustainable Cotton and Timber Products to Millions of its Customers

For marketing managers sustainability is possibly the biggest challenge of the twenty-first century. Not only are there issues of what to reduce, but there is also the problem of understanding the real impact of any action. The 2008/9 economic recession is said to have dampened interest in sustainable issues amongst consumers as their concerns were on keeping their jobs rather than saving the planet. However, research by Trucost, a company that helps its clients understand the real cost of their organization's operations and helps plan for a better-resourced future across the value chain, suggested in a report on green business in 2012 that environmental sustainability is at the top of most companies' agendas.

Trucost measures the financial impact of environmental issues for 4300 of the world's largest companies, and this information helps them to understand which actions are likely to bring the greatest dividends and reduce the impact on the environment.

Trucost has helped Greenbiz, a leading source of news, opinion and best practice, to provide clear and concise information for businesses that are developing their environmental and sustainability policies and business practices. GreenBiz analyses data and information from Trucost and then disseminates news of good practice through its website and blogs. IKEA is an example of a company constantly reviewing its practices across the supply chain in order to ensure it provides sustainability on a large scale. According to Steve Howard, IKEA's Chief Sustainability Officer, the company is 'using IWay, a code of conduct that specifies environmental and social requirements for sourcing and distributing products, which is bringing sustainable and affordable cotton and timber products to millions of consumers around the world.'

http://www.trucost.com/published-research/75/state-of-green-business-2012
http://www.greenbiz.com/about-greenbiz

Based on: Jeffries (2011);[29] Trucost (2012);[30] Greenbiz.com (2012); King (2012)[31]

CSR is based on the **stakeholder theory** of the firm, which contends that companies are not managed purely in the interests of their shareholders alone. Rather, there is a range of groups (stakeholders) that have a legitimate interest in the company as well.[32] Following this theory, a **stakeholder** of a company is an individual or group that either:

- is harmed by, or benefits, from the company *or*
- whose rights can be violated, or have to be respected, by the company.[33]

Other groups, besides shareholders who typically would be considered stakeholders, are communities associated with the company, employees, customers of the company's products, and suppliers (see Fig. 6.3). The key point is that stakeholder theory holds that the company has obligations not only to shareholders but to other parties that are affected by its activities. We shall return to the notion of stakeholders when we explore the dimensions of CSR later in this chapter.

The nature of corporate social responsibility

A useful way of examining the nature of CSR is Carroll's four-part model of corporate social responsibility.[34] Carroll views CSR as a multilayered concept that can be divided into four interrelated responsibilities: economic, legal, ethical and philanthropic. The presentation of these responsibilities is in the form of layers within a pyramid and the full achievement of CSR occurs only when all four layers are met consecutively (see Fig. 6.4).

Economic responsibilities

Carroll recognized that the principal role of a firm was to produce goods and services that people wanted and to be as profitable as possible in so doing. Economic responsibilities include maintaining a strong competitive position, operating at high levels of efficiency and effectiveness, and aiming for consistently high levels of profitability. Without the achievement of economic responsibilities, the other three are redundant since the firm would go out of business. Economic success is the *sine qua non* of CSR.

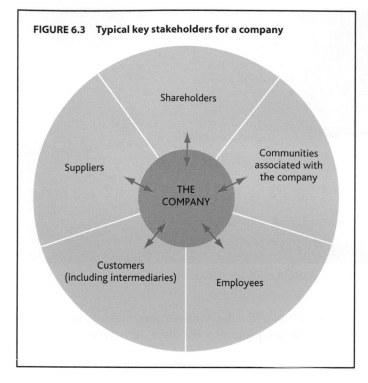

FIGURE 6.3   Typical key stakeholders for a company

Shareholders

Communities associated with the company

Suppliers

THE COMPANY

Customers (including intermediaries)

Employees

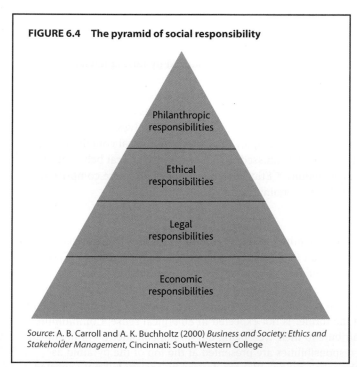

FIGURE 6.4   The pyramid of social responsibility

Philanthropic responsibilities

Ethical responsibilities

Legal responsibilities

Economic responsibilities

Source: A. B. Carroll and A. K. Buchholtz (2000) *Business and Society: Ethics and Stakeholder Management*, Cincinnati: South-Western College

Legal responsibilities

Companies must pursue their economic responsibilities within the framework of the law. Laws reflect society's principles and standards that are enforceable in the courts. Occasionally, the drive to maximize profits can conflict with the law—as with Microsoft, which has faced heavy financial penalties both in Europe and the USA for anti-competitive

⬆ EXHIBIT 6.2   McDonald's seed-bombing extends the reach of the golden arches.

behaviour (for example, bundling Media Player into the Windows operating system, thereby squeezing out competitors' software). Like economic responsibilities, the meeting of legal responsibilities is a requirement of CSR.

Ethical responsibilities

Although the establishment of laws may be founded on ethical considerations, as we have seen there can be important distinctions, as with the selling of genetically modified (GM) products, which may raise ethical questions and yet be lawful. The same could be said of the meat production industry, where 90 per cent of pork is produced by raising female pigs in metal cages, so small that the pregnant sow can hardly move. This practice is not currently illegal but thought by many to be inhumane.[35] Ethical responsibilities mean that companies should perform in a manner consistent with the principles and values of society and prevent ethical norms being compromised in order to achieve corporate objectives. Companies such as BP draw up codes of ethical conduct and employ teams to govern legal compliance and business ethics (252 BP employees were dismissed in one year for unethical behaviour in a drive to weed out bribery and corruption).[36] Ethical responsibilities therefore comprise what is expected by society over and above economic and legal requirements.

Philanthropic responsibilities

Go to the website to consider the ethical and CSR issues of McDonald's Olympics advertising campaign. www.mcgraw-hill.co.uk/ textbooks/jobber

At the top of the pyramid are the philanthropic responsibilities of firms. These are corporate actions that meet society's expectation that businesses be good corporate citizens. This includes promoting human welfare or goodwill, such as making charitable donations, the building of leisure facilities or even homes for employees and their families, arts and sports sponsorship, and support for local schools.[37] The key difference between philanthropic and ethical responsibilities is that the former is not expected in an ethical sense. Communities may desire companies to contribute to their well-being but do not consider them unethical if they do not. Philanthropic responsibilities are presented at the top of the pyramid as they represent the 'icing on the cake': actions that are desired by society but not expected or required. Warren Buffet, one of the world's richest men, made a record-breaking 37-billion-dollar donation to the Gates foundation. The foundation, set up by former head of Microsoft Bill Gates and his wife, aims to give every life across the planet equal value, through philanthropic donations that support global, development and health programmes.[38]

A strength of the four-part model of CSR is its realism in recognizing that, without the fulfilment of economic responsibilities, a company would not have the capability to engage in

TABLE 6.1 Dimensions of corporate social responsibility

Dimension	Key issues	Marketing response
Physical environment	Combating global warming Pollution control Conservation of energy and scarce resources Use of environmentally friendly ingredients and components Recycling and non-wasteful packaging	Sustainable marketing
Social (community involvement)	Support for the local community Support for the wider community	Societal marketing Cause-related marketing
Consumer	Product safety (including the avoidance of harmful long-term effects) Avoidance of price fixing Honesty in communications Respecting privacy	Societal marketing
Supply chain	Fair trading standard-setting for supplies (e.g. human rights, labour standards and environmental responsibility)	Fair trade marketing
Employee relations	Fair pay Equal opportunities Training and motivation Information provision (e.g. on career paths, recruitment policies and training opportunities)	Internal marketing

ethical and/or philanthropic activities. However, to gain a deeper understanding of the scope of CSR activities it is necessary to explore its dimensions as well as its responsibilities.

The dimensions of corporate social responsibility

CSR has four layers of responsibility: economic, legal, ethical and philanthropic. By examining the dimensions of CSR an insight into where those responsibilities may be discharged can be gained. CSR dimensions are based on four key stakeholders who are the individuals or groups affected by a company's activities, plus the physical environment that equally can be affected by its activities such as pollution or usage of scarce natural resources.[39] Table 6.1 outlines the CSR dimensions, lists associated key issues and describes marketing responses for each dimension. Please note the key issues relating to each CSR dimension are not all exclusively marketing related. For example, pollution control at a chemical plant is a production-related issue, standard setting for supplies is a procurement-related topic, and the setting of fair pay is a human resources issue. Nevertheless, for most of the issues listed in Table 6.1 marketing practices can affect outcomes. For example, car design can affect pollution levels and the rate at which oil reserves are depleted, and the creation of healthy-eating brands can improve consumers' diets through the reduction in fat, sugar and salt levels.

Physical environment

Key issues in the physical environment, such as the use of environmentally friendly ingredients and components, recycling and non-wasteful packaging and pollution control, were introduced in Chapter 3. Marketers' response to these issues can be summarized under the term 'sustainable marketing'. Environmental sustainability means to maintain or prolong the physical environment. It involves action towards the use of renewable rather than finite raw materials, and the minimization and eventual elimination of polluting effluents and toxic or hazardous wastes. **Sustainable marketing** contributes to this goal by focusing on environmental issues and reducing environmental damage by creating, producing and delivering sustainable solutions while continuing to satisfy customers and other stakeholders. As 3M describes it: 'business will need to accept a moral imperative towards planetary ecological problems'.[40]

Since marketing operates at the interface between the organization and its environment, it is uniquely positioned to lead the move towards more sustainable products and strategies. Typically, companies will move through several stages (see Fig. 6.5). To facilitate the process, marketing as a function needs to address a range of questions from the strategic to the tactical. Key questions are as follows.[41]

- Have the effects of sustainability issues on company activities been analysed as part of the marketing planning process?
- Has the company conducted marketing research into the probable impacts on the organization of sustainability issues?
- Can the company modify existing products, services or processes to take account of sustainability considerations, or will innovations be required?
- Is the firm developing positive links with environmental groups?
- Do communications strategies accurately emphasize environmental considerations?

Responding positively to environmental issues is important in order to protect and sustain brands. Market-leading brands are always susceptible to attack by media and/or pressure groups following any environmental incident. It is, therefore, sensible to build into brand strategies sustainability issues to nurture and maintain brand trust.

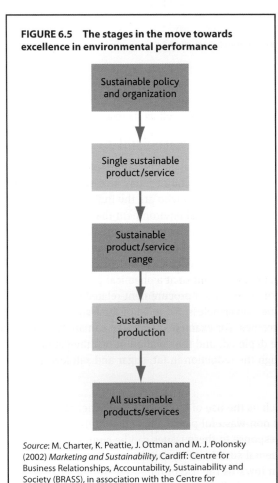

FIGURE 6.5 The stages in the move towards excellence in environmental performance

Source: M. Charter, K. Peattie, J. Ottman and M. J. Polonsky (2002) *Marketing and Sustainability*, Cardiff: Centre for Business Relationships, Accountability, Sustainability and Society (BRASS), in association with the Centre for Sustainable Design

Environmental issues can be a source of threats to organizations, but they can also provide opportunities. Toyota has responded to environmental trends by successfully launching the Toyota Prius hybrid car, which supplements normal fuel with an electric-powered engine. The electric engine starts the car and operates at low speeds using a battery. At higher speeds the Prius automatically switches to a normal engine and fuel. This saves on fuel and is less polluting. The success of the Prius has led many of its rivals, including Honda, to launch similar hybrid cars, and to the development of electric cars powered by lithium-ion batteries. Renault has invested 4 billion euros in a range of 100 per cent electric vans and cars. According to Renault's marketing the ZE Kangoo Van puts an end to all the myths about driving electric cars and gives the motorist energy-efficient driving.

The production of biofuel has risen dramatically as companies have seized the opportunity to replace petrol. For example, BP has invested £284 million in biofuels. However, opposition from environmentalists may hamper further development. They fear that carbon-absorbing rainforest in countries such as Brazil is being depleted to make way for fuel crops such as soya and palm, and that such crops are displacing land use for food, forcing up prices.[42] Detergent companies like Unilever have also embraced sustainable marketing by producing concentrated soap powder that both helps the environment and improves profitability. Environmental damage is reduced because the product requires less plastic, less water, less space for transportation, fewer chemicals and less packaging.[43] Procter & Gamble has also promoted the benefit of low-temperature washing with its award-winning Ariel 'Turn to 30' campaign, which raised awareness of the impact of washing temperatures on emissions.[44]

Marketing Ethics and Corporate Social Responsibility in Action 6.2
GE Ecomagination and the Smart Grid: Saving Energy

GE, the US-based multinational, continues to develop its green credentials through its Ecomagination programme. The aim is to build innovative solutions for today's environmental challenges while driving economic growth. Since the start of the programme GE has invested 5 billion dollars, and the resulting technology and products have generated over 70 billion dollars in revenue. Consequently, GE has decided to double its investment over the next three years (until 2015). More specific examples of developments from the programme are compact fluorescent lighting, smart appliances, battery technology, wind turbines and fuel-efficient aircraft engines. Jeffrey Immett, GE's chief executive, is so convinced that clean technologies are the future that he has made his new mantra 'green is green', equating the green of the environment with the green of the US dollar.

To qualify for Ecomagination branding, products must 'significantly and measurably' improve customers' environmental and operating performance. Already the company produces the GEnx aero engine, which powers the Airbus 350 and Boeing 787 and is 15 per cent more energy efficient than its predecessors, and the compact florescent light bulb that saves 70–80 per cent of energy compared to ordinary light bulbs. ClimateWell in Stockholm has developed energy-efficient solar hot water systems and is in partnership with GE to provide energy for GE home appliances.[45]

GE is not only aiming to cut its carbon emission but its investment in the *smart grid* is upgrading the existing energy infrastructure, making it more fuel efficient. The smart grid uses energy meters that are sensitive to times and temperatures and consequently can help reduce energy consumption in homes, businesses and on the road. GE's commitment to CO_2 reduction has enabled a massive saving of 52.4 billion pounds of CO_2 through the use of the smart technology.

Based on: GE Ecomagination (2012);[46] The Economist (2005);[47] Harvey (2005);[48] Caulkin (2006);[49] The Economist (2008)[50]

The giant US corporation GE has also embraced the environment as a source of opportunity, as Marketing Ethics and Corporate Social Responsibility 6.2 describes.

Social and consumer dimensions

Social concerns that business has sought to address are the need to support local and wider communities. Consumer concerns include the effect of business activities on product safety, including the avoidance of harmful long-term effects, the avoidance of price fixing, honesty in communications, and respecting privacy. Although social and consumer dimensions of CSR are distinct as their key issues differ, the two dimensions are analysed together as marketing's major response—societal marketing—embraces both. Whereas sustainable marketing focuses on the physical environment, societal marketing relates to marketing's direct effect on people, both in the form of consumers and society in general.

Societal marketing takes into account consumers' and society's wider interests rather than their short-term consumption. One aim of societal marketing is to consider consumers' needs and long-term welfare and society's long-term welfare as keys to satisfying organization objectives and responsibilities. It aims to rectify potential conflicts between consumers' short-term needs—for example, fast food that may contain high levels of fat, sugar and salt—and their long-term health. In the face of intense media pressure, including the hit film *Super Size Me*, which records a film-maker's descent into serious illness while living on a McDonald's-only diet, the company has introduced healthy-eating options including salads and mineral water (instead of the ubiquitous cola). While cynics may view this as a public relations exercise, the response of McDonald's may be regarded as a move towards implementing societal marketing principles. Kraft is another company responding to consumers' demands for healthier foods by cutting fat in its Philadelphia Lite soft cheese and cutting salt in its Dairylea product line by over 30 per cent.[51] Societal marketing also means that those activities that are not in consumers' or society's short- and long-term interests—such as price fixing, dishonest communications and invasions of privacy—are avoided and training is given to employees to lay out the boundaries of acceptable behaviour.

A further aspect of societal marketing is in providing support for local and wider communities. One is a company that produces various products from bottled water, eggs and toilet tissue to condoms, and uses the profits to fund social projects in Africa that are improving health and welfare for communities (see Ad Insight).[52] Other charitable donations (Wal-Mart, for example, historically has made huge donations to charities) or partnerships with charities or causes are called **cause-related marketing**. This is a commercial activity in which businesses and charities or causes form a partnership with each other to market an image or product for their mutual benefit. As consumers increasingly demand accountability and responsibility from businesses, companies such as Procter & Gamble, Unilever, Tesco, IBM, British Gas and Orange have all incorporated major cause-related marketing programmes. Typical activities include sponsoring events such as Comic Relief (Procter & Gamble and Unilever), raising money and resources for schools (Tesco and IBM), tackling social problems such as fuel poverty (British Gas) and sponsoring the arts (Orange).

A set of cause-related marketing principles has been developed by Business in the Community, as listed below.[53]

1   Integrity: behaving honestly and ethically.
2   Transparency: misleading information could cast doubt on the equity of the partnership.
3   Sincerity: consumers need to be convinced about the strength and depth of a cause-related marketing partnership.
4   Mutual respect: the partner and its values must be appreciated and respected.
5   Partnership: each partner needs to recognize the opportunities and threats the relationship presents.
6   Mutual benefit: for the relationship to be sustainable, both sides must benefit.

Cause-related marketing works well when the business and charity have a similar target audience. For example, Nambarrie Tea Company, a Northern Ireland winner of the annual Business in the Community award for excellence in cause-related marketing, chose to sponsor the breast cancer agency Action Cancer. The company and the charity targeted women aged 16–60. In a two-month period, Nambarrie released 100,000 specially designed packs promoting its sponsorship of Action Cancer and covered media costs for a TV advertising campaign. This generated income of over £200,000.[54]

Critics of societal marketing view it as a short-term public relations exercise that cynically manipulates a company's stakeholders. Supporters argue that the stakeholder principle suggests that it is in a company's long-term interests to support the long-run concerns of consumers and society, resulting in a win-win situation.

By combining sustainable and societal marketing initiatives, organizations become better prepared to meet the requirements of triple bottom-line reporting, which takes into account not only financial matters but also environmental and social issues. In 2011 Electrolux was

Go to the website to see how One makes a difference for people living in Africa.
www.mcgraw-hill.co.uk/ textbooks/jobber

⬆ EXHIBIT 6.3   Electrolux uses recycled plastics in its new products.

voted one of the world's most ethical companies and sustainability is at the heart of the business strategy. The Ethisphere Institute (a think tank devoted to sharing of best practices in business ethics and CSR) publishes world rankings of the most ethical companies, and its director said in 2011, that 'each year, the competition gets more intense' as companies vie to be the awarded the honour of being the most ethical.

Supply chain

Unfair trading arises when large buyers exert their power on small commodity producers to force prices to very low levels. This can bring severe economic hardship to the producers, who may be situated in countries of the developing world. Many of the growers of such products as coffee, tea and cocoa live in poverty and face hardship in the form of poor working conditions, health problems and prices that fail to provide a living wage. Fair trade seeks to improve the prospects of suppliers through ethical trading, including the guaranteeing of minimum prices.

Fair trade marketing is the development, promotion and selling of fair trade brands and the positioning of organizations on the basis of a fair trade ethos. Companies are increasingly realizing that many consumers care about how suppliers in countries of the developing world are treated, and wish to support them by buying fair trade brands, often at a price premium. For example, Cafédirect, a fair trade company and brand, was launched to protect coffee growers from the volatility in world coffee prices. Minimum prices for coffee beans are paid, which are pegged above market fluctuations, and business support and development programmes are provided. The popularity of fair trade brands has prompted Nestlé to launch its own fair trade coffee, Partners' Blend, and Marks & Spencer has launched a range of fair trade clothing, which benefits Indian cotton farmers through a price that includes a premium that can be invested in their communities.[55] Supermarkets are supporting fair trade products, with the Co-op stocking only own-label fair trade tea, coffee and chocolates, and Sainsbury's selling only fair trade bananas. Coffee bar chains such as Costa Coffee and Pret A Manger offer fair trade varieties. FMCG food manufacturers also support the spread of fair trade products and they have been acquiring ethical brands to facilitate access to these markets— for example, Unilever's acquisition of Ben & Jerry's, which is a brand that supports local farmers and all of the ingredients in its ice creams are certified as fair trade (see Ad insight). Kraft Foods, the multinational food and beverage corporation, expanded its product portfolio with the acquisition of Green & Black's, the organic chocolate brand. From its independent origins this brand has taken a 95 per cent share of the organic chocolate market, and since 2009—with redesigned packaging—it is gaining market share in the mainstream chocolate market. Fair trade marketing can also be based on the positioning of companies on a fair trade ethos. The Body Shop has for many years operated a 'Trade Not Aid' programme, which assists small-scale, indigenous communities in improving their standard of living through fair prices to suppliers.[56]

The success of fair trade marketing is based upon consumers being willing to try and repeat-buy fair trade brands and organizations developing genuine fair trade programmes.

Go to the website to see how EcoSwim is using the environment as part of its CSR strategy.
www.mcgraw-hill.co.uk/ textbooks/jobber

⬆EXHIBIT 6.4   **Clipper coffee redesigned its packaging to create a more contemporary look and feel to these products.**

Consumers will not put up with organizations that use such schemes as an ethical veneer. Corporate Watch (www.corporatewatch.org) and Greenpeace (www.greenpeace.org) provide examples of dubious practice by companies that consumers can boycott or campaign against in the press.[57]

Employee relations

Poor employee relations can have harmful marketing consequences. For example, Wal-Mart has suffered from years of allegations regarding low pay and sexually discriminatory hiring and employment practices, a situation it is seeking to address.[58] Bad publicity can deter ethically aware consumers from buying from companies that suffer such criticism. While most employee relations issues are the province of the human resources function, marketing can play a role through internal marketing programmes. **Internal marketing** is the development, training and motivation of employees designed to enhance their performance in providing customer satisfaction. The idea began in service organizations such as hotels and restaurants where staff are in daily communication with customers, but has spread to all sectors in reflection of the need for all employees who come into contact with customers to be trained in how to deal with such issues as giving help, dealing with complaints and treating customers respectfully. Such training avoids, as far as possible, employee–customer arguments and conflict, which not only improves customer satisfaction but is good for staff morale, reduces stress levels and aids staff retention. Digital Marketing 6.1 describes how such an approach can be applied within a digital environment.

Arguments for and against corporate social responsibility programmes

Not every observer believes that profit-orientated organizations should undertake CSR programmes. First, the arguments against will be examined.

CSR is misguided

In 1970 the Nobel Prize-winning economist Milton Friedman published a seminal article arguing that it was managers' responsibility to generate profits for their shareholders. To act in any other way was a betrayal of this special responsibility. He saw addressing social problems as being the province of governments not company managers. He did not believe, therefore, that managers should spend other people's money on some perceived social benefit, and thought that to do so was misguided.[59]

CSR is too costly

Spending in the USA on CSR activities is in excess of $3 billion and while Europe does not match this figure, spending there is vast too.[60] This brings with it the lost opportunity to spend the money on other priorities, such as research and development.

CSR encourages consumer cynicism

Many consumers regard CSR initiatives as little more than public relations exercises. Corporate brands delegate tasks to 'ethics officers' who in turn outsource the task of delivering the organization's values to consultants.[61] Senior management then takes up the minimum number of initiatives that it believes places the company in an acceptable light among its stakeholders, without really embracing the ideas and ideals associated with those values.

CSR does not improve profitability

Accused of artificially upgrading its oil reserve figures by a fifth to help boost financial bonuses to staff, Shell was fined £84 million by the SEC in the USA and the Financial

Digital Marketing 6.1 Employees Win Company Awards

Corporate social responsibility (CSR) has many dimensions, one of which is employee relations: successful staff training programmes can have a significant impact on a company's overall effectiveness. Happy Computers is a company that has an enviable reputation and has won many industry and service excellence awards. The computer training company believes that learning should be fun. The training programmes bring together technical expertise and excellent training skills. The training is based on the following ideas:

- tell me and I will forget
- show me and I will remember
- involve me and I will understand.

Henry Stewart and Cathy Busani founded the company in 1990 in response to their clients asking for help to create *great* workplaces. At Happy, there is a relatively small workforce of 45 employees, and a unique approach to CSR training. It has won numerous awards for innovative approaches to training, customer service and the quality of the working environment. Cathy is managing director of Happy Ltd and is responsible for Happy employees. She has been rated one of the best bosses in the UK in two separate national awards programmes. She is passionate about valuing people and the role they play in creating truly great places to work. The company achieves its success by applying some straightforward principles:

- transparency is important throughout (e.g. employees at the top or bottom of the scale are all aware of pay information)
- belief in the ability of the individual—members of the Happy team hold a fundamental belief that all people (with no exceptions) are born with enormous intelligence and tremendous eagerness to learn
- celebrate mistakes as part of the culture to engender learning and development—Happy believes that if you do not make mistakes you are not actively learning; it believes that you should enable an employee's natural learning abilities and delight in new possibilities to allow them to come to the fore
- create a feelgood environment as individuals work to their best ability when they feel good about themselves; Happy has created a workplace where people are trusted to make the key decisions about their work
- share information—as Francis Bacon said, 'knowledge is power'; Happy's management team takes the view that information is required to make informed decisions and to enable individuals to take responsibility and full ownership of their jobs. As more companies turn to e-learning Happy Computers has been finding additional ways to help. Learnfizz is one of Happy's products designed to 'find, organize and share the best free learning on the web'.

Applying these principles has enabled Happy to do more than win awards and it has zero recruitment costs. This is due to its employee-focused working environment, high staff morale and demand from potential employees desiring to work for this unique organization.

Based on: www.happy.co.uk (2012)

Services Authority in the UK. The scandal led to the dismissal of its chairman and two other senior executives. More damage to the company's image was done by the FSA's accusation that Shell had engaged in 'unprecedented misconduct', and comments from oil experts that it was a corporate scandal of 'historic proportions'.[62] Critics of CSR point out that, despite the bad publicity and tarnished corporate reputation, Shell's profitability was not harmed since it generated record profits just a few years after the scandal. Further, an academic review of 167 studies over 35 years concluded that although there was a positive association between companies' social and financial performance, the link was weak. It would seem that the companies are not richly rewarded for CSR. However, neither does CSR appear to harm profits, and there is the potential for smarter forms of CSR to produce better returns in the future.[63]

There are also arguments *for* CSR programmes, which help explain their current popularity.

CSR leads to enhanced brand/corporate image and reputation

A strong reputation in environmental and social responsibility can help a company build trust and enhance the image of its brands. For example, BP has also taken steps to reduce harmful emissions. Orange has enhanced its image through sponsorship of the arts. This approach can help when a company is faced with media criticism or regulatory scrutiny. Also if a company is moving to a new area or new market, or opening a new site such as a distribution centre, store or factory, it helps to be seen as trustworthy and a 'good neighbour'.[64]

CSR provides marketing opportunities

Environmental and social responsibility has created new markets for business-to-business and consumer goods and services. For example, GE is expanding its marketing of 'clean' technological goods to companies, and Cafédirect, Green & Black's, Innocent drinks and the Body Shop have built their businesses on corporate social responsibility ideals. Market segments have emerged based on 'green' credentials that provide targeting opportunities. One segment—known as ethical hardcores or dark greens—research companies and their practices thoroughly before buying their products. They view ethical consumerism as a way of life, whatever the sacrifice. A second segment—known as ethical lites or light greens—do their bit but do not have the time to research products or companies thoroughly.[65] They are happy to recycle newspapers, plastics and other material from their homes and buy ethical brands, provided there is not too much of a price premium.

CSR can reduce operating costs

Far from increasing operating costs, as is often assumed, better environmental management systems can improve efficiency by reducing waste, increasing energy efficiency and, in some cases, selling recycled materials.[66] For example, DuPont uses 7 per cent less energy than it did in 1990, despite producing 30 per cent more goods, thereby saving $2 billion, including savings of at least $10 million per year by using renewable sources.[67]

CSR increases organizations' ability to attract and retain employees

Many employees are attracted to employers who are active in social issues. For example, membership of Netimpact.org, a network of socially conscious MBA graduates, rose from 4000 in 2002 to over 10,000 in 2009, and some companies, such as salesforce.com (an Internet-based services company), have a policy of good corporate citizenship (staff are encouraged to devote time, at the company's expense, to charitable works) that they believe helps to attract, retain and motivate employees.[68]

CSR is a form of risk management

There are real penalties for companies that are not environmentally or socially responsible. The media criticisms of such companies as Nike (child labour in the developed world), BNFL (toxic discharges in the Irish Sea), Enron and Royal Bank of Scotland (financial scandals) and News of the World (phone hacking) have shown the harm that can arise from being perceived as irresponsible. CSR, then, can be employed as a form of risk management, which reduces the chances of being the subject of the next corporate scandal to hit the headlines.

CSR improves access to capital

Organizations that are committed to CSR have access to socially responsible investment (SRI), whereby investors take into account considerations such as a company's environmental and socially responsible activities. These can be assessed using indices such as Business in the Community's Corporate Responsibility Index and the FTSE4Good Index.[69]

Currently the strengths of the arguments for CSR programmes are driving companies increasingly towards the adoption of socially and environmentally responsible strategies.

Societal Responses to Ethical Issues in Marketing

S ocietal responses to ethical issues in marketing take three forms: consumerism, environmentalism and ethical consumption.

Consumerism

Consumerism takes the form of organized action against business practices that are not in the interests of consumers. Organized action is taken through the **consumer movement**, which is an organized collection of groups and organizations whose objective is to protect the rights of consumers.

The consumer movement seeks to protect consumers' rights, which include the right to expect the product to be safe, for it to perform as expected and for communications for the product to be truthful and not mislead. Pressure from consumer groups in Europe has resulted in prohibitions on tobacco advertising, improvements in car safety, reductions in the levels of fat, sugar and salt in foods, restrictions on advertising alcohol to teenagers and the forcing of financial services companies to display true interest charges (the annual percentage rate, or APR) on advertisements for credit facilities. Further successes include unit pricing (stating the cost per unit of a brand), and ingredient labelling (stating the ingredients that go into a brand).

The consumer movement often takes the form of consumer associations, which campaign for consumers and provide product information on a comparative basis allowing consumers to make informed choices. These have been very successful in establishing themselves as credible and authoritative organizations and are seen as trusted providers of information to help consumer choice. Their actions help to improve consumer power when dealing with organizations. While consumerism focuses on improving the balance between consumer and organizational power, and protecting the rights of consumers in consumption decisions, environmentalism is broader in scope with its focus on the physical environment.

Environmentalism

Environmentalism is the organized movement of groups and organizations to protect and improve the physical environment. Their concerns are: production and consumption of products which lead to global warming, pollution, the destruction of natural resources such as oil and forests, and non-biodegradable waste. They believe producers and consumers should take account not only of short-term profits and satisfaction but the cost to the environment of their actions. They wish to maximize environmental quality, which is the satisfaction of individual needs in a manner that will yield the maximum benefits to the individual while minimizing the effects on people and natural resources.[70]

Environmentalists support the concept of environmental sustainability and pressure companies to adopt strategies that promote its objectives. Environmental sustainability means 'to maintain or prolong environmental health'. Pressure groups such as Greenpeace and Friends of the Earth have been successful in persuading organizations to produce 'greener' products such as cadmium-free batteries, ozone-safe aerosols, recycled toilet tissue and packaging, catalytic converters, lead-free petrol, unbleached tea bags and cruelty-free cosmetics. Other environmental groups have successfully changed company practices. For example, UPM-Kymmene, Finland's largest paper and pulp company based in over 16 countries, has to ensure that the replanting of trees matches felling. This is the result of environmentalist action. Major electrical manufacturers like Philips and Electrolux incorporate environmental considerations systematically in new product development and have strict guidelines covering the integration of environmental considerations into product design and development.[71]

Environmentalists have concerns about how business activity affects the environment. This means they constantly pressurize organizations to deal with issues like controlling carbon emissions; reducing global warming; eliminating harmful pollutants; using recycled and recyclable materials in products. The overarching aim is to maintain a sustainable environment for future generations.

Ethical consumption

Consumerism and environmentalism are organized movements designed to protect society and the environment from the harmful effects of production and consumption. However, consumers also act in an individual way to protect society and the environment through engaging in ethical consumption. **Ethical consumption** occurs when individual consumers, when making purchase decisions, take into account not only personal interests but also the interests of society and the environment. Examples include the boycotting of products and companies that have poor records regarding social and environmental concerns, the buying of non-animal-tested products, choosing fair trade or organic products, avoiding products made by sweatshop or child labour and the purchasing of products that are made from recycled materials.[72]

As discussed earlier, consumers and businesses respond differently to ethical consumption. Some are very passionate about living and operating in a manner that does not impact on the environment, while others are not and many are somewhere in between these two extremes. Marketing managers must understand their target audiences, individual values, attitudes and motivations and align these with societal values if they are to develop successful marketing strategies.

Read the Research 6.1 **Environmental Sustainability**

Green marketing has been with us for more than 20 years and has influenced commercial organizations, policy makers and researchers. At the centre of the hub is the general public and how as consumers they respond to climate change and sustainability issues. This study surveys 1000 UK consumers to ascertain via 15 sustainability-related activities what they regard as green or normal.

The results suggest some practical marketing activities that can be adopted to reposition green activities into normal ones.

Ruth Rettie, Kevin Burchell and Debra Riley (2012) Normalising green behaviours: A new approach to sustainability marketing,
Journal of Marketing Management, 28(3–4), 420–44.

Every company should have a clear idea of why it is involved in corporate social responsibility (CSR) and the expected outcomes. Many companies preach and practise, but their efforts often lack an overall strategy that dilutes their effectiveness. This article offers some practical solutions on how to build such a strategy.

http://hbswk.hbs.edu/item/6994.html

Legal and Regulatory Responses to Ethical Issues in Marketing

European countries are bound by several layers of laws and regulatory bodies that restrict company actions and encourage the use of ethical practices, as described below.

- **EU competition laws and regulatory bodies that seek to ban anti-competitive practices**: these regulations have teeth and have resulted in fines on such companies as Microsoft (product bundling), AstraZeneca (blocking generic copies of its ulcer drug), and Hoechst, Atofina and Akzo Nobel (price fixing) imposed by the European Commission, a body set up to enforce EU competition and consumer law.
- **EU laws and regulatory bodies that aim to protect the rights of consumers**: consumers' rights are also protected by EU regulatory bodies and regulations. For example, consumers' interests regarding food safety are protected by the European Food Standards Authority, and the right to compensation for air travellers whose flights are overbooked, cancelled or delayed is covered by EU rules.
- **National laws covering consumer rights and protection, and competition regulation supported by government-backed regulatory bodies**: legislation at national level is also

designed to prevent marketing and business malpractice. For example, the Financial Services Authority fined Shell £17 million under UK market abuse laws and the Securities and Exchange Commission fined the same company $120 million for breaches of SEC rules and US laws.

- **Voluntary bodies set up by industries to create and enforce codes of practice**: industries often prefer self-regulation to the imposition of laws by government. For example, most European countries are self-regulating with regard to advertising standards through the drawing up and enforcement of codes of practice.

Marketers in Europe have great freedom in which to practise their profession. Business-imposed, societal and legal constraints on their actions not only make good sense from a long-term social and environmental perspective, they make good long-run commercial sense, too.

Online LearningCentre

When you have read this chapter

log on to the Online Learning Centre at **www.mcgraw-hill.co.uk/textbooks/jobber** to explore chapter-by-chapter test questions, links and further online study tools for marketing.

Review

1 **The meaning of ethics, and business and marketing ethics**
- Ethics are the moral principles and values that govern the actions and decisions of an individual or group.
- Business ethics are the moral principles and values that guide a firm's behaviour.
- Marketing ethics are the moral principles and values that guide behaviour within the field of marketing.

2 **Ethical issues in marketing**
- Ethical issues in marketing relate to concerns about how the marketing mix is applied to consumers, and more general societal, environmental and political issues. Specific examples include: product safety, price fixing, misleading advertising, deceptive selling, invasion of privacy through direct and Internet marketing activities, and the use of promotional and slotting allowances.
- Societal concerns focus on materialism and short-termism; environmental concerns focus on the impact of marketing decisions on the environment; and political concerns focus on the power that global companies can exert on consumers, governments and suppliers.

3 **Business, societal, and legal and regulatory responses to ethical concerns**
- The main response from businesses has been the adoption of corporate social responsibility as a philosophy guiding decisions and actions.
- Societal responses take the form of consumerism, environmentalism and ethical consumption.
- Legal and regulatory responses are the enactment of laws at European and national levels to protect the consumer and to outlaw anti-competitive business practices, and the establishment of regulatory bodies to enforce those laws. Many industries have also established organizations to apply self-regulation through the drawing up and enforcement of codes of practice.

4 **The stakeholder theory of the firm**
- Corporate social responsibility is based on the stakeholder theory of the firm, which contends that companies have multiple stakeholders, not just shareholders, to whom they hold a responsibility. These include communities associated with the company, employees, customers (including intermediaries) and suppliers.

5 **The nature of corporate social responsibility**
- Corporate social responsibility refers to the ethical principle that an organization should be accountable for how its behaviour might affect society and the environment.
- Organizations have responsibilities to ensure: economic performance meets stakeholder requirements; operational practices do not break the law; ethical principles are consistent with values of society. Additionally, an organization has a responsibility to be a good corporate citizen: e.g. supporting good causes and making philanthropic donations.

6 **The dimensions of corporate social responsibility**
- Corporate social responsibility involves five dimensions of organizational activity: the physical environment, social, consumer, supply chain, and employee relations.
- Marketing's response to each dimension involves responding to relevant issues, for example:
  - *physical environment issues*—combating global warming. By applying business practices which create, produce and deliver sustainable solutions to environmental problems while continuing to satisfy customers and other stakeholders.
  - *societal and consumer issues*—community support and attention to product safety. This is an example of societal marketing, as it takes account of consumers' and society's wider interests rather than just their short-term consumption. Societal welfare is also enhanced by cause-related marketing, which is the commercial activity by which businesses and charities form a partnership to market an image or product for mutual benefit.
  - *supply chain issues*—low prices to producers in the developing world, applying fair trade marketing, which is the development, promotion and selling of fair trade brands and the positioning of organizations on the basis of a fair trade ethos.
  - *employee relations issues*—training and motivation. This is referred to as internal marketing, which is the development, training and motivation of employees designed to enhance their performance in providing customer satisfaction.

7 **Arguments for and against corporate social responsibility**
- Arguments against are that CSR is misguided and too costly.
- Arguments for are that CSR leads to enhanced brand/corporate image and reputation, provides marketing opportunities, reduces operating costs, increases an organization's ability to attract and retain employees, is a form of risk reduction, and improves access to capital.

Key Terms

business ethics the moral principles and values that guide a firm's behaviour

cause-related marketing a commercial activity by which businesses and charities or causes form a partnership with each other to market an image or product for mutual benefit

consumer movement an organized collection of groups and organizations whose objective it is to protect the rights of consumers

environmentalism the organized movement of groups and organizations to protect and improve the physical environment

ethical consumption the taking of purchase decisions not only on the basis of personal interests but also on the basis of the interests of society and the environment

ethics the moral principles and values that govern the actions and decisions of an individual or group

fair trade marketing the development, promotion and selling of fair trade brands and the positioning of organizations on the basis of a fair trade ethos

internal marketing training, motivating and communicating with staff to cause them to work effectively in providing customer satisfaction; more recently the term has been expanded to include marketing to all staff, with the aim of achieving the acceptance of marketing ideas and plans

marketing ethics the moral principles and values that guide behaviour within the field of marketing

societal marketing focuses on consumers' needs and long-term welfare as keys to satisfying organizational objectives and responsibilities by taking into account consumers' and societies' wider interests rather than just their short-term consumption

stakeholder an individual or group that either (i) is harmed by or benefits from the company, or (ii) whose rights can be violated or have to be respected by the company

stakeholder theory this contends that companies are not managed purely in the interests of their shareholders

alone but a broader group including communities associated with the company, employees, customers and suppliers

sustainable marketing focuses on reducing environmental damage by creating, producing and delivering sustainable solutions while continuing to satisfy customers and other stakeholders

Study Questions

1 What is 'marketing ethics'? To what extent do you believe marketing practices to be unethical and how might unethical practices in marketing be restricted?

2 What are the key responsibilities of corporate social responsibility and to what extent do you believe businesses should accept them?

3 Describe the five dimensions of corporate social responsibility. Evaluate marketing's response to the issues underlying each dimension.

4 What is meant by 'consumerism' and 'environmentalism'? To what extent do you believe these movements have achieved their goals of protecting consumers, society and the environment?

5 Evaluate the contention that if ethical consumption was the norm there would be no need to legislate to protect consumers.

6 Discuss the differences in meaning of sustainability and Corporate Social Responsibility.

References

1. *The Economist* (2011) November, 78, http://www.economist.com/node/21538083.
2. http://www.guardian.co.uk/sustainable-business/staff-plan-worlds-sustainable-retailer.
3. Berkowitz, E. N., R. A. Kerin, S. W. Hartley and W. Rudelius (2004) *Marketing*, Boston, MA: McGraw-Hill.
4. Business for Social Responsibility Issue Briefs (2003) Overview of Business Ethics, www.bsr.org.
5. Barnett, M. (2011) The only way is ethics, *Marketing Week* August, 22.
6. Marks & Spencer (2012) Plan A, http://plana.marksandspencer.com.
7. *The Economist* (2008) The Good Consumer, Special Report on Corporate Social Responsibility, 19 January, 16.
8. Bokaie, J. (2008) Behind the Ethical Rhetoric, *Marketing*, 21 May, 14.
9. Franklin, D. (2008) Just Good Business, *The Economist*, Special Report on Corporate Social Responsibility, 19 January, 1.
10. Naughton, J. (2006) Google's Founding Principles Fall at Great Firewall of China, *Observer*, Business and Media, 29 January, 10.
11. Reed, C. (2000) Ethics Frozen Out in the Ben & Jerry Ice Cream War, *Observer*, 13 February, 3; *The Economist* (2000) Slipping Slopes, 15 April, 85.
12. Arthur, C. (2011) Microsoft accepts censorship in Chinese search engine deal, *Guardian*, 5 July, 16.
13. Choveke, M. (2006) Can Anything Rescue Sunny D?, *Marketing Week*, 26 February, 7.
14. Milner, M. (2005) Brussels Inquiry Could Land BT with Huge Tax Bill, *Guardian*, 20 January, 20.
15. Milmo, D. (2007) BA Fined £270m and Now Faces £300m Lawsuit, *Guardian*, 2 August, 1.
16. O'Flaherty, K. (2008) Brands Behaving Badly, *Marketing Week*, 30 October, 20–1.
17. Devaney, P. (2005) Who Cares Wins, But is There a Hidden Agenda?, *Marketing Week*, 28 April, 34–5.
18. Milmo, S. (2006) M&S Boosts Ethical Image With Fairtrade Clothing, *Guardian*, 30 January, 21.
19. Barnett (2011) op. cit.
20. Everitt, P. (2009) Car Scrappage Schemes are Not a Motor Industry Green Scam, Guardian.co.uk, 19 March 2009, www.guardian.co.uk/commentisfree/2009/mar/19/paul-everitt-response (retrieved 3 April 2009)
21. Kim, C-R (2011) http://www.reuters.com/article/2011/02/28/us-autoshow-toyota-idUSTRE71R7GM20110228 (accessed February 2012).
22. Barnett, M. (2011) Driving home the benefits of green wheels, *Marketing Week*, 7 April, 24–6.
23. Crook, C. (2005) The Good Company, *The Economist*, 22 January, 3–4.

24. Gow, D. (2008) Record US Fine Ends Siemens Bribery Scandal, *Guardian*, 16 December, 24.

25. Moon, J. (2002) Corporate Social Responsibility: An Overview, in *The International Directory of Corporate Philanthropy*, London: Europa Books.

26. Moon (2002) op. cit.

27. Crook (2005) op. cit.

28. Moon (2002) op. cit.

29. Jeffries, E. (2011) A clearer footprint, *Marketing*, 19 October, 26–27.

30. Trucost (2012) State of Green Business 2012, http://www.trucost.com/published-research/75/state-of-green-business-2012.

31. King, H. (2012) Ikea's Steve Howard on bringing sustainability to the masses, Greenbiz.com, http://www.greenbiz.com/blog/2012/02/23/ikeas-cso-steve-howard-bringing-sustainability-masses.

32. Donaldson, T. and L. E. Preston (1995) The Stakeholder Theory of the Corporation: Concepts, Evidence, and Implications, *Academy of Management Review* 20(1), 15–91.

33. Crane, A. and D. Matten (2004) *Business Ethics: A European Perspective*, Oxford: Oxford University Press.

34. See Carroll, A. B. and A. K. Buchholtz (2000) *Business and Society: Ethics and Stakeholder Management*, Cincinnati: South-Western College; and Carroll, A. B. (1991) The Pyramid of Corporate Social Responsibility: Toward the Moral Management of Organizational Stakeholders, *Business Horizons*, July/August, 39–48.

35. Gunther, M. (2012) A big push to move meat production terrible to just bad, 23 February, http://www.greenbiz.com/topic/food--agriculture?page=2.

36. Boxell, J. and F. Harvey (2005) BP Sacked 252 in Corruption Drive, *Financial Times*, 12 April, 22.

37. Crane and Matten (2004) op. cit.

38. Gates Foundation 2012 Programs and Partnerships, http://www.gatesfoundation.org/programs/Pages/overview.aspx.

39. See Maignan, I. and O. C. Ferrell (2004) Corporate Social Responsibility and Marketing: An Integrated Framework, *Journal of the Academy of Marketing Science* 32(1), 3–19; and Fukukawa, K. and J. Moon (2004) A Japanese Model of Corporate Social Responsibility: A Study of Online Reporting, *Journal of Corporate Citizenship* 16, Winter, 45–59.

40. Charter, M., K. Peattie, J. Ottman and M. J. Polonsky (2002) *Marketing and Sustainability*, Cardiff: Centre for Business Relationships, Accountability, Sustainability and Society (BRASS) in association with the Centre for Sustainable Design.

41. Charter, Peattie, Ottman and Polonsky (2002) op. cit.

42. Macalister, T. (2008) Undercut and Under Fire: UK Biofuel Feels Heat From All Sides, *Guardian*, 1 April, 28.

43. Skapinker, M. (2008) Taking a Hard Line On Soft Soap, *Financial Times*, 7 July, 16.

44. Murphy, C. (2008) Green Gold, *The Marketer*, September, 30–3.

45. Ecomagination (2012) The winning partners, http://challenge.ecomagination.com/ct/e.bix?c = ideas.

46. Lombardi, C. (2010) GE to invest $10 billion in Ecomagination initiative, http://news.cnet.com/8301-11128_3-20008698-54.html (accessed February 2012).

47. *The Economist* (2005) A Lean, Clean Electric Machine, 10 December, 79–81.

48. Harvey, F. (2005) GE Looks Out For a Cleaner Profit, *Financial Times*, 1 July, 13.

49. Caulkin, S. (2006) GE Decides it's Best to Look after the Greenhouse, *Observer*, 8 January, 8.

50. *The Economist* (2008) A Change in Climate, Special Report on Corporate Social Responsibility, 19 January, 14–18.

51. Clarke, B. (2008) Good Marketing Beats Regulation, *The Marketer*, March, 15.

52. Costa, M. L. (2011) One man's vision, *Marketing Week*, 5 May, 18–21.

53. Anderson, P. (1999) Give and Take, *Marketing Week*, 26 August, 39–41.

54. Anderson (1999) op. cit.

55. Milmo (2006) op. cit.

56. Crane and Matten (2004) op. cit.

57. CIM Insight Team (2005) Fair Trade?, *The Marketer*, January, 6–8.

58. Devaney (2005) op. cit.

59. Friedman, M. (1970) The Social Responsibility of Business is to Increase the Profits, *New York Times Magazine*, 13 September, 8.

60. Grow, B., S. Hamm and L. Lee (2005) The Rebate Over Doing Good, *The Economist*, 5/12 September, 78–80.

61. Plender, J. and A. Persaud (2005) Good Ethics Means More Than Ticking Boxes, *Financial Times*, 23 August, 10.

62. Milner, M. (2004) Shell Fined £84m Over Reserves Scandal, *Guardian*, 30 July, 16.

63. The results of the study were reported in Franklin (2008) op. cit., 10.

64. Sclater, I. (2005) Thank Goodness for Success, *The Marketer*, January, 11–13.

65. Parkinson, C. (2005) Make the Most of Your Ethics, *Marketing Week*, 9 June, 30–1.

66. Sclater (2005) op. cit.

67. Aston, A. and B. Helm (2005) The Race Against Climate Change, *Business Week*, 12/19 December, 85–93.

68. See Grow, Hamm and Lee (2005) op. cit. and *The Economist* (2005) A Union of Concerned Executives, 22 January, 7–12.

69. Sclater (2005) op. cit.

70. Charter, Peattie, Ottman and Polonsky (2002) op. cit.

71. Charter, Peattie, Ottman and Polonsky (2002) op. cit.

72. Crane and Matten (2004) op. cit.

"Today corporate social responsibility goes far beyond the old philanthropy of the past—donating money to good causes at the end of the financial year—and is instead an all-year-round responsibility that companies accept for the environment around them, for the best working practices, for their engagement in their local communities and for their recognition that brand names depend not only on quality, price and uniqueness but on how, cumulatively, they interact with companies' workforces, communities and environments. Now we need to move towards a challenging measure of corporate responsibility, where we judge results not just by the input but by its outcomes: the difference we make to the world in which we live, and the contribution we make to poverty reduction."

Gordon Brown, former British Prime Minister
(*Corporate Social responsibility: A Government Update*, first published May 2004, Department of Trade and Industry)

This quote from Gordon Brown could have been written for Britain's leading CSR (corporate social responsibility) retailer, The Co-op. Over the past few years it has won numerous awards, from most responsible retailer four years on the bounce to the 2012 *Which?* energy award.

How did it all start? It was in Rochdale 168 years ago, when a group of everyday people founded a new kind of business. This revolution was called 'The Co-operative', based on democratic principles, owned by its customers and reinvesting in the community it served. Today it's grown to become a part of daily life, with over 5,000 stores and branches across the UK.

The Co-operative has always had a purpose beyond profit, going back to its founding fathers. It aims to be transparent and publishes 'warts and all' reports on topics from salt in food to animal welfare.

In 2011 it launched a groundbreaking new plan with one clear goal: to be the most socially responsible business in the UK. As Group Chief Executive Peter Marks says:

Our ambition is to build a better society and this plan will stimulate and reinforce the unique benefit of the consumer co-operative model.

At a time when UK society is picking up the pieces from a recession exacerbated by corporate greed and

speculation, we are seeking to show that there is another way. The plc model is not the only game in town. It is possible for business to embrace the efficiencies of the market economy and also the need for robust legislation to ensure that progress is sustainable and just.

Key targets set out in the plan include the following

Democratic control and reward

- Continue to set new standards for openness and honesty globally, and seek to utilize new technology to enhance consumers' abilities to make ethical choices

- Continue a profit-sharing scheme with their members that is amongst the broadest and most generous of any major UK business

- Aim to have 20 million members by 2020 and to be opened up to the under 16s as soon as legally possible

- Encourage ethical consumerism through engagement with members and extra share of profit from 2012.

Ethical finance

The Co-operative Bank has withheld over £1 billion of funding from business activities that its customers say are unethical.

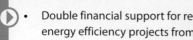

- Double financial support for renewable energy and energy efficiency projects from £400 million to £1 billion by 2013
- Continue to tackle global poverty via their £25m microfinance fund support
- Continue to take a lead on financial inclusion and champion financial literacy among young people
- Encourage primary pension scheme to operate a Responsible Investment Policy that is amongst the most comprehensive of private sector schemes in the UK.

Protecting the environment

- Having reduced its own operational carbon emissions by 20 per cent since 2006, the target will now increase to 35 per cent by 2017—the most progressive of any major UK business
- They will enhance their pesticides policy further, and seek to ban chemicals such as endosulfan and paraquat
- Leading biodiversity work in areas such as wood and fish to be matched with new targets on palm oil and soya
- On top of the 15 per cent weight reductions achieved in packaging, they will reduce the environmental impact by a further 10 per cent by 2012 and increase carrier bag reduction target to 75 per cent by 2013
- The construction by 2012 of a head office that will set new standards in sustainable design, construction and operation in the UK.

Building a fairer and better society

- Co-operative enterprise will be more heavily supported through the investment of £11 million by 2013 and the launch of a new £20 million international Co-operative Development Loan Fund
- The Co-operative's community investment, already amongst the most generous in the UK, will be expanded to include £5 million a year to help tackle poverty around their stores and branches
- The Co-operative will spearhead a cultural shift in youth perception and opportunity through a £30 million programme that will support an Apprenticeship Academy, a Green Schools programme and the creation of 200 Co-operative Schools by 2013.

Tackling global poverty

- Going forward, if it can be Fairtrade, it will be Fairtrade. By 2013 some 90 per cent of the primary commodities sourced from the developing world will be certified to Fairtrade standards. Furthermore, The Co-operative will develop a unique range of projects and initiatives that benefit producers and take them beyond Fairtrade
- Invest £8 million per annum to help tackle global poverty through cooperative support initiatives.

Responsible retailing

- Continue to target salt, saturated fat and sugar reductions in key products whilst maintaining food safety and product quality
- At least 30 per cent of own-brand food products that carry Traffic Lights will be healthy and a minimum of 30 per cent of food promotions will be for healthy offerings
- Ensure that Healthier Choice products are no more expensive than standard equivalent lines
- The nutritional content of Simply Value products will be at least as good as standard equivalent lines.

Respecting animal welfare

- Continue to ensure that shoppers operating on a variety of budgets have the opportunity to support higher baseline animal welfare standards, and that all shell eggs and egg ingredients in own-brand products are at least free-range
- Continue to pursue higher welfare standards across our meat and fish, converting our own-brand salmon to Freedom Food standard in 2012
- Continue to take a lead on the issue of animal testing of cosmetic and household products.

The plan encourages all stakeholders to get involved in a variety of ways, from sending messages to the UK government to offer greater support for smallholder farmers and cooperatives, to offering a microloan of £15 and changing a life. The aim is to inspire more people to change the world.

Leading environmentalist Jonathan Porritt believes this is a new benchmark for others to measure against.

What's the advantage?

Building a reputation as an ethical and responsible business sets you apart from the competition. This differentiation appeals to more thoughtful customers and helps build loyalty, particularly among those who insist on ethical retailing.

Also, it helps in recruitment and employee retention, as well as generating positive publicity throughout the communications networks. However, that is not enough. The company must continue to make profits to enable it to carry out such an ambitious plan. So how is the Co-op doing?

The group produced results for 2011 as expected, with sales up 1 per cent and profits by 0.5 per cent. This is against the backdrop of the severely challenging UK economic downturn.

In raising the bar across key areas like the environment, ethical finance, global poverty, animal welfare, social fairness, health and community enterprise, The Co-operative is demonstrating that the quiet revolution that began in Rochdale in 1844 is still as relevant as ever.

References

http://www.co-operative.coop/corporate/Press/Press-releases/Headline-news/Join-The-Revolution/

http://www.co-operative.coop/Corporate/CSR/Our_Ethical_Plan_2012-2014.pdf

http://www.co-operative.coop/corporate/sustainability/Downloads/

Questions

1. Using the key targets set out in The Co-operative plan as a benchmark, select one of the following supermarkets: Tesco, Asda, Sainsbury's or Morrison's to use as a comparator. Use the Internet as a resource.

2. Companies have been accused of 'green washing', which is a light-touch approach for developing a CSR policy. Suggest the difficulties you may encounter when following a fully committed CSR plan like The Co-op.

3. Many organizations criticize CSR because they don't see business delivering on its promises. Argue the case for the benefits of CSR.

This article was written by Brian Searle, Lecturer in Marketing, Loughborough University.

Nestlé vs Greenpeace

Giving the Rainforest a Break

Context

Across the world, people have become more aware of the detrimental consequences of their activities on the environment. In such a context customers increasingly try to consume sustainable, natural or organic products to protect both their health and the environment.

Accompanying this movement, the authorities have intensified public health campaigns to foster the importance of healthy lifestyles and eating habits. For instance, the UK government has launched the 'Change 4 Life' public health campaign, promoting the importance of eating healthily. This campaign was organized with the cooperation of three supermarket chains who have granted discounted prices on fruit, vegetables and fish. The French Health Ministry and the French Agency for Health Products keep developing campaigns to inform consumers of the potential risks of some food ingredients (e.g. trans-fats, hydrogenated fats, preservatives, palm oil, etc.).
At the same time, public awareness concerning ecological agriculture and food manufacturing gives rise to more coercive laws to preserve the environment. Thus, the European Union has set up a strategy 'to stop the decline of endangered species and habitats by 2020' (http://europa.eu/pol/env/index_en.htm) that has resulted in much new European legislation.

Therefore, manufacturers and retailers face many external pressures. Consequently, they have to convince their consumers that they have actually developed healthier substitutes for controversial food constituents, and that their production processes respect the environment. In such a context, Nestlé faced a dramatic crisis that brought it into conflict with Greenpeace in 2010.

In March 2010 Greenpeace published a report called *Caught Red-Handed: How Nestlé's Use of Palm Oil is Having a Devastating Impact on Rainforest, the Climate and Orang-utans*. This report explained that Nestlé, one of the world's largest food and beverage companies, is 'a major buyer of palm oil and its use is growing'. Indeed, between 2007 and 2010 Nestlé's consumption of palm oil had risen from 170,000 to 320,000 tons. However, Nestlé defended its position by stating that this corresponded to less than 1 per cent of the world's palm oil production, and that it was still less than the 500,000 tons used for biofuel production in the UK and Germany.

Greenpeace's report denounced the disastrous social, environmental and ecological outcomes of palm oil production, which is the main human activity that contributes to deforesting the Indonesian rainforest. At a social level local communities are affected by the development of conflicts over land rights and resources disputes (people claiming their rights to some parts of the land, so that they can benefit from the expansion of palm oil plantations). At the environmental and ecological levels deforestation will lead to the extinction of orang-utans and the destruction of many plant and animal species. First, orang-utans only live in the Indonesian tropical rainforests of Borneo and Sumatra. Thus, deforestation deprives them of their natural source of food and habitat, and forces them to eat young palm plants, leading plantation workers to kill them. Second, given that two-thirds of terrestrial plant and animal species are found in forests, deforestation raises dramatic concerns for their survival.

To illustrate this situation and increase public awareness, Greenpeace also released a short video called *Have a Break* (based on the slogan 'Have a break, have a KitKat', KitKat being one of Nestlé's brands) on YouTube. It shows a clerk who wants to eat a KitKat, but does not notice that instead he unpacks and eats the finger of an orang-utan, and finishes covered with blood.[1] Within a few days, this video had been viewed around 1 million times.

Moreover, palm oil consumption also comes with dangers for human health—a fact that is not stated in Greenpeace's report. Indeed, palm oil contains a high level of saturated fat, which can lead to cardiovascular diseases. It also enables the manufacturer to keep food prices relatively low, as it is much cheaper than other sources of oil (for instance, in October 2010, one ton of palm oil cost $930, while sunflower oil was $1300).

Reactions to the campaign

The Greenpeace campaign was not welcome in Indonesia, because it is the world's biggest producer of palm oil with 3 million people working in this industry.

Nestlé's response to this campaign was not positive either. The company had long promoted an ethical way of doing business and had developed a project called 'Creating Shared Value', which had been managed by Nestlé's former CEO and president of the board of directors himself, Peter Brabeck. Presented in April 2009, it implied 'that the objectives of the company and those of the environment it evolves into are aligned'. At this time, Brabeck explained also that 'Nestlé's social and environmental actions are never imposed from the outside; they are initiated by the company itself, for the own good of its shareholders and its different kinds of stakeholders'. To that extent, Nestlé had announced in January 2010 that the chocolate and sugar of KitKat would come from Fair Trade cultures. However, the Greenpeace campaign was apparently revealing a discrepancy between the image that Nestlé wanted to promote and some realities of the way that the firm was doing business. As a consequence, consumers from all over the world immediately reacted on the firm's Facebook page. They posted highly critical messages, and some even transformed the KitKat logo into 'Killer'. More than 120,000 emails were sent to Nestlé's CEO (Paul Burke) to demand that Nestlé stop destroying the Indonesian rainforest by using palm oil.

Things got worse as Nestlé's first reaction was to delete the negative posts from its Facebook page. They adopted classic communication relying on press releases and demanded that the video be removed from YouTube. Unfortunately for them it was too late, as it had been reposted by people all over the world. In addition, Greenpeace immediately reposted it on other platforms, such as Vimeo, Facebook and Twitter. This only irritated consumers even more and increased the visibility of Greenpeace's campaign, with many traditional media (newspapers, TV, radio) mentioning

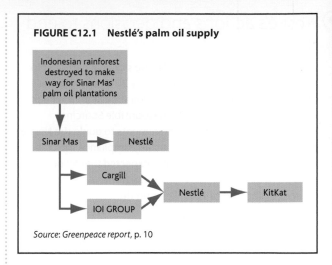

FIGURE C12.1   Nestlé's palm oil supply

Source: Greenpeace report, p. 10

this issue and emphasizing the negative outcomes of palm oil consumption.

A few days later Nestlé changed its tactics. First, the firm officially apologized on its Facebook page and changed its PR firm. Second, it announced a major change in its existing supply chain (Figure C12.1), severing any direct contract with Sinar Mas, the Indonesian producer that was accused of breaking Indonesian forestry laws and regulations. Nevertheless, Nestlé kept buying palm oil from Cargill, an intermediary that was still buying palm oil from Sinar Mas. Eventually, Nestlé announced that it intended to 'use only certified palm oil by 2015, when there will be enough available quantities'. Such an announcement was aligned with the conclusions of the 190+ participants (including Nestlé) in the Roundtable on Sustainable Palm Oil[2] (RSPO), organized on 25 March 2010. Among those, the World Wide Fund (WWF) claimed that it was urgent that firms increased their production of sustainable certified palm oil, which necessitates that palm trees be planted on non-wooded areas and respect diverse social and environmental requirements.

A turbulent shareholders' meeting

To make sure that Nestlé would take the appropriate action,[3] Greenpeace undertook additional action. First, on 15 April 2010 some Greenpeace activists unfolded a banner on the firm's German headquarters, calling for a break for the orang-utans. Below the banner, a giant screen displayed hundreds of messages posted on Twitter by people who demanded that Nestlé stop buying palm oil. The following day 30 members of Greenpeace unexpectedly participated in Nestlé's shareholders meeting in Lausanne (Switzerland), disguised as orang-utans, while two others entered through the roof and disclosed a similar banner in front of the company's management board and the 2640 shareholders who were there.

▶ Nestlé's actions and decisions to end the crisis

As a result of this whole crisis, Nestlé signed a partnership with The Forest Trust (TFT) on 17 May 2010, an NGO that promotes sustainable forestry exploitation. With the help of TFT, 'Nestlé has defined the Responsible Sourcing Guidelines, a set of critical requirements to guide the Nestlé procurement process and to ensure compliance with the Nestlé Supplier Code'. Nestlé also expected that 50 per cent of its palm oil purchases would come from sustainable sources by the end of 2011, keeping the 100 per cent objective by 2015. All the actions taken by Nestlé relative to palm oil can now be followed on a dedicated webpage of the firm's website called 'Update on deforestation and palm oil'.[4]

The Swiss group also announced in late 2011 that most of its recipes were under major revision to improve the nutritional qualities of its products. Thus, these would contain less sugar, salt and fat. At the same time, in November 2011, RSPO delivered a very good grade (8/10) to Nestlé to reward it for its efforts in managing its palm oil supplies.

References

1 http://www.youtube.com/watch?v=VaJjPRwExO8&feature=player_embedded#!

2 'RSPO is a not-for-profit association that unites stakeholders from seven sectors of the palm oil industry—oil palm producers, palm oil processors or traders, consumer goods manufacturers, retailers, banks and investors, environmental or nature conservation NGOs and social or developmental NGOs—to develop and implement global standards for sustainable palm oil' (source: http://www.rspo.org/page/9).

3 Greenpeace had already warned Nestlé of the devastating impact on the Indonesian rainforest, but considered that the Swiss group had not reacted. This is why the NGO eventually published its report and put the video online.

4 http://www.nestle.com/Media/Statements/Pages/Update-on-deforestation-and-palm-oil.aspx

Questions

1 Identify the different stakeholders that are involved in this case study.

2 What ethical marketing issues are raised in this case study?

3 What responses were given to these ethical issues?

4 As exemplified by the problems met by Nestlé, what dimensions of corporate social responsibility are at stake?

5 How did social media influence Nestlé's response to the issues raised by Greenpeace? What can be learnt from this?

This case was written by Loïc Plé, Associate Professor, IÉSEG School of Management, France. It is intended to be used as a basis for class discussion rather than to illustrate either effective or ineffective handling of a management situation.

CHAPTER 7

Marketing research and information systems

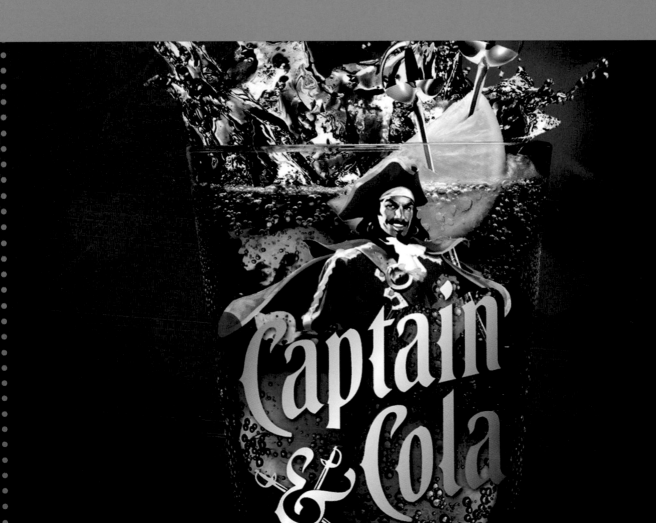

> **Knowledge is power.**
> MACHIAVELLI

> **Never knowingly undersold.**
> JOHN SPEDAN LEWIS[1]

LEARNING OBJECTIVES

After reading this chapter, you should be able to:

1 discuss the nature and purpose of marketing information systems, and the role of marketing research within such systems

2 identify the types of marketing research

3 describe the approaches to conducting marketing research

4 describe the stages in the marketing research process

5 explain how to prepare a research brief and proposal

6 discuss the role of different research methods

7 discuss approaches to research design decisions: sampling, survey method and questionnaire design issues

8 explain the processes involved with interpreting and presenting data and writing reports

9 distinguish between qualitative and quantitative research

10 discuss the ethical issues that arise in marketing research

What kinds of people buy my products? What do they value? Where do they buy? What kinds of new products would they like to see on the market? Answering these questions is the key to informed marketing decision-making. Managers can develop knowledge about their customers and the marketing environment through informal and formal channels. Informal discussions with customers at exhibitions or through sales calls can provide valuable information about their requirements, competitor activities and future happenings in the industry. However, this approach is likely to fail to provide in-depth market knowledge. Therefore, a more formal approach is needed to supply information systematically to managers.

This chapter focuses on this formal method of information provision, by describing marketing information systems and their relationship with marketing research. Then we look at the process of marketing research and its uses. Next, the essential differences between qualitative and quantitative research are explored. Finally, we will examine the influences on information systems and marketing research use.

Marketing information system design is important since the quality of a marketing information system has been shown to have an impact on the effectiveness of decision-making[2] and as use of these systems becomes more widespread, previous piecemeal systems are replaced by integrated customer relationship management systems, which are able to provide a unified view of the customer.[3]

Marketing Information Systems

A marketing information system has been defined as:[4]

A system in which marketing information is formally gathered, stored, analysed and distributed to managers in accord with their informational needs on a regular planned basis.

The system is built on an understanding of the information needs of marketing management, and supplies that information when, where and how the manager requires it. Data are derived from the marketing environment and transferred into information that marketing managers can use in their decision-making. The difference between data and information is as follows.

- **Data** are the most basic form of knowledge, e.g. the brand of butter sold to a particular customer in a certain town; this statistic is of little worth in itself but may become meaningful when combined with other data.
- **Information** is a combination of data that provide decision-relevant knowledge, e.g. the brand preferences of customers in a certain age category in a particular geographic region.

An insight into the nature of marketing information systems (MkIS) is given in Figure 7.1. The MkIS comprises four elements: internal continuous data, internal ad hoc data, environmental scanning, and marketing research.

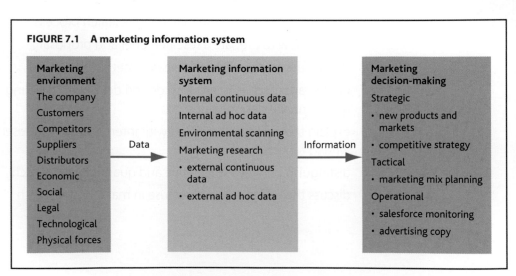

FIGURE 7.1   A marketing information system

Marketing environment	Marketing information system	Marketing decision-making
The company	Internal continuous data	Strategic
Customers	Internal ad hoc data	• new products and markets
Competitors	Environmental scanning	
Suppliers	Marketing research	• competitive strategy
Distributors	• external continuous data	Tactical
Economic		• marketing mix planning
Social	• external ad hoc data	Operational
Legal		• salesforce monitoring
Technological		• advertising copy
Physical forces		

Data → (Marketing information system) → Information

Internal continuous data

Companies possess an enormous amount of marketing and financial data that may never be used for marketing decision-making unless organized by means of an MkIS. One advantage of setting up an MkIS is the conversion of financial data and a range of other data into a form usable by marketing management. Traditionally, profitability figures have been calculated for accounting and financial reporting purposes. This has led to two problems. First, the figures may be too aggregated (e.g. profitability by division (SBU)) to be of much use for marketing decisions at a product level, and, second, arbitrary allocations of marketing expenditures to products may obscure their real profitability.

The setting up of an MkIS may stimulate the provision of information that marketing managers can use: e.g. profitability of a particular product, customer or distribution channel, or even the profitability of a particular product to an individual customer. Widespread integration of information systems across businesses provides great insight into customers and provides more informed decision-making. Read Marketing in Action 7.1 to find out how stationery distributor Viking was targeting the *wrong* customers.

Marketing in Action 7.1 Viking Targets the Wrong Customers

One of the fundamental principles of marketing is understanding and satisfying customer needs, so for Viking Direct (part of Office Depot), a global company and one of the world's largest suppliers of office stationery, targeting the wrong customer had serious implications for its promotion strategy. Viking operates in the UK in Leicester, London and Manchester and claims to sell more office products than any other company. Through the website Viking sells writing materials, office equipment, warehouse and cleaning supplies. However, when the company streamlined its information systems in order to improve customer insight, they discovered that the stereo-typical '35-year-old female secretary' was not the primary buyer as previously thought. New survey data revealed that middle-aged men were more likely to be the primary stationery buyers. This shift occurred in part because the economic recession led to many men 'leaving the corporate world to start their own business'. The data anlaysis also revealed that not only were men buying the stationery but they were older than previously thought and were working in smaller companies. As a result of this new customer insight Viking Direct changed its marketing materials and sales initiatives and Tony Dobbs (Head of CRM) developed a loyalty ladder for driving sales using motivational triggers such as relevance of product, ease of ordering, delivery, price and fulfilment.

Based on: Viking Direct (2012);[5] Costa (2011)[6]

Another application of the MkIS concept to internal continuous data is within the area of salesforce management. As part of the sales management function, many salesforces are monitored by means of recording sales achieved, number of calls made, size of orders, number of new accounts opened, etc. This can be recorded in total or broken down by product or customer/customer type. The establishment of an MkIS where these data are stored and analysed over time can provide information on salesforce effectiveness. For example, a fall-off in performance of a salesperson can quickly be identified and remedial action taken.

Internal ad hoc data

Company data can also be used for a specific (ad hoc) purpose. For example, management may look at how sales have reacted to a price increase or a change in advertising copy. Although this could be part of a continuous monitoring programme, specific one-off analyses are inevitably required from time to time. Capturing the data on the MkIS allows specific analyses to be conducted when needed.

Environmental scanning

The environmental scanning procedures discussed in Chapter 3 also form part of the MkIS and this includes environmental analysis—whereby the economic, social, political, legal, technological and ecological/physical forces are monitored. These forces can be difficult to monitor due to their amorphous nature but are important as they can shape the context within which the company, suppliers, distributors and the competition do business as in the case of Viking Direct. Environmental scanning provides an early warning system for the forces that may impact on a company's products and markets in the future.[7] In this way, scanning enables an organization to act on, rather than react to, opportunities and threats. The focus is on the longer-term perspective, allowing a company to be in the position to plan ahead and information from data analysis provides a major input into such strategic decisions as which future products to develop and market to enter, and the formulation of a competitive strategy (e.g. to attack or defend against competition).

Marketing research

While environmental scanning focuses on the longer term, **marketing research** considers the more immediate situation and is primarily concerned with providing information about markets and customer reactions to various product, price, distribution and promotion decisions.[8] As such, marketing research is a key part of the MkIS because it makes a major contribution to marketing mix planning.

There are two main types of external marketing research:

1 *External continuous data sources* include television audience monitoring and consumer panels where household purchases are recorded over time. Loyalty cards are also a source of continuous data, providing information on customer purchasing patterns and responses to promotions. The growth of e-commerce has led to new forms of continuous data collection.

2 *External ad hoc data* are often gathered by means of surveys into specific marketing issues, including usage and attitude studies, advertising and product testing, and corporate image research. More traditional forms of market research—telephone interviews and face-to-face attitude surveys—are being replaced by email surveys and online panel polls. The Internet is being used not only for gathering qualitative survey data, but also for gathering qualitative data through real-time audio and online video discussions. Social media are also providing access to an innovative form of digital discussion groups, and companies are analysing online conversations to find out what their consumers really think about their products.[9] The rest of this chapter will examine the process of marketing research and the factors that affect the use of research information.

. . . .

The Importance of Marketing Research

The importance of marketing research was highlighted in a study of the factors that were significant in the selection of an industrial goods supplier.[10] The company, as part of its marketing audit (see Chapter 2), wanted to know what were the main considerations its customers took into account when deciding to do business with it or its competitors. Before conducting marketing research, it asked its marketing staff; they said that the two main factors were price and product quality. Next the sales staff were asked the same question and their response was that customers mainly considered company reputation and quick response to customer needs (see Table 7.1). When marketing research was carried out, however, the results were very different. Customers explained that, to them, the key issues were technical support services and prompt delivery. Clearly the viewpoints within and outside the company were at odds with each other. The lesson is that it is dangerous to rely solely on the internal views of managers. Only when this company really understood what its customers wanted could it put into action marketing initiatives that improved technical and delivery services. The result was improved customer satisfaction, which led to increased sales and profits.

Marketing research has been used by an increasing range of types of organizations, from political parties to community groups. Furthermore, not only are organizations making more use of technology, but the technology itself is also enabling more insightful analysis.

Go to the website and consider how Nectar's advert might expand Sainsbury's customer database.
www.mcgraw-hill.co.uk/
textbooks/jobber

TABLE 7.1   Factors in the selection of a manufacturer*

Factor	Users	Salespeople	Marketing
Reputation	5	1	4
Credit	9	11	9
Sales reps	8	5	7
Technical support services	1	3	6
Literature	11	10	11
Prompt delivery	2	4	5
Quick response to customer needs	3	2	3
Price	6	6	1
Personal relationships	10	7	8
Complete product line	7	9	10
Product quality	4	8	2

*Factors are rated in order of importance from 1 to 11.

Source: Kotler, P., W. McGregor and W. Rodgers (1977) The Marketing Audit Comes of Age, *Sloan Management Review*, Winter, 30. Reprinted with permission. Copyright © 1977 by the Sloan Management Review Association. All rights reserved.

The market research industry is penetrating deeper into the psyche of individual consumers. Read the research to find out more about how individuals with mental health problems can contribute to greater consumer insight.

Read the Research 7.1   Customer Insights

Quite often people with mental health problems are excluded from society.

Like all of us they are consumers and like sharing their views on products and services.

In this article the author, a qualitative researcher, discusses ways to access this group and offers practical solutions to removing potential barriers to help minimize any possible distress.

Ruth Stevenson (2011) Welcoming people with mental health problems into mainstream market research,
International Journal of Market Research 53(6), 737–48.

Marketing research findings are important. JCDecaux, one of the world's largest outdoor advertising agencies, has found that rail travel provides an important arena for brands to interact with customers. In 2011, according to JCDecaux's market research, 8.8 million passengers (a third of whom were business travellers) used Eurostar.[11] JCDecaux's vision for outdoor is helping many leading brands to make for a greater impact with outdoor advertising.

Approaches to Conducting Marketing Research

Depending on the situation facing a company, particularly the resources allocated to marketing research, there are several ways of carrying out marketing research:

In-house—personally

Where a company has marketing staff but a low or non-existent marketing research budget, the only option may be for marketing staff to carry out the marketing research task themselves.

Where sample sizes are small and there are suitable skilled staff available, this option may be feasible. However, training in research techniques may be necessary. A disadvantage of doing research in-house is the possibility that responses will be biased through respondents' awareness of who is asking the questions. An organization conducting its own research must make that fact known, in order to comply with market research ethics codes.[12]

In-house—using a market research department

By hiring a marketing research executive, a company would benefit from professional specialist skills. It could be possible for the executive to design, implement and present marketing research surveys to marketing management. If the outside services of a marketing research agency are used, the executive would act as the link between company and agency.

Using a market research department and a marketing research agency

Where the design of the study can be done in-company but interviewing by internal staff is not possible, the fieldwork could be conducted by a marketing research agency. These organizations provide a wide range of services, which include fieldwork services; indeed, some specialize in fieldwork only. One possibility would be for the survey design, questionnaire design and analysis of results to be done in-company but the administration of the questionnaire to be handled by fieldwork staff employed by the marketing research agency.

Using the full services of a marketing research agency

Where resources permit, a company (client) could use the full range of skills offered by marketing research agencies. The company would brief the agency about its marketing research requirements and the agency would conduct the research. A complete service would mean that the agency would:
- prepare a research proposal stating the survey design and costs
- conduct exploratory research
- design the questionnaire
- select the sample
- choose the survey method (telephone, postal or face to face)
- conduct the interviewing
- analyse and interpret the results
- prepare a report
- make a presentation.

However, there is a growing problem for companies wishing to carry out market research—the volume of data available. Companies now not only have data from specific market research initiatives, they also have a massive amount from digital sources. This growing agglomeration of data is becoming known as 'big data', and the companies which are likely to benefit are those that can work out how to get the best out of the complex and unstructured sources of data. Read Marketing in Action 7.2 to find out how GlaxoSmithKline are addressing some of the issues.

Go to the website and identify what benefits Costa Coffee customers look for in their coffee.
www.mcgraw-hill.co.uk/textbooks/jobber

Types of Marketing Research

A major distinction is between **ad hoc research** and **continuous research**.

Ad hoc research

An *ad hoc study* focuses on a specific marketing problem and collects data at one point in time from one sample of respondents. Examples of ad hoc studies are usage and attitude surveys, product and concept tests, advertising development and evaluation studies, corporate image surveys, and customer satisfaction surveys. Ad hoc surveys are either custom-designed or omnibus studies.

Marketing in Action 7.2 Big Data

GlaxoSmithKline (GSK) is a company attempting to make use of *big data*. GSK is a very large, multinational, pharmaceutical company with a wide portfolio of brands stretching from prescription medicines like Amoxil and Betnovate cream to consumer healthcare brands including Aquafresh, Beechams, Horlicks, Nicorette, Ribena, Sensodyne, Valda. Market research comes in many guises at GSK because of the nature of the business: carrying out clinical trials and research activities associated with bringing healthcare products to market. However, when it comes to the analysis of consumer data, the company has invested in its market research operation to ensure that collection and dissemination of findings happens at a company-wide level. GSK has experts in every area of the business who concentrate on specific market research problems.

As an organization, however, it is felt that the most useful information is generated when these experts work together on common goals gathering data from a large complex data source including: internal data and online sources; weblogs, social media, web and smartphone analytics, where consumers provide signals about what they are thinking at a given point in time. More specifically, GSK is working with Occam, a company which provides data management services to help its clients reach a better understanding of their own customers. Ultimately, GSK aims to build relationships with over a million of its customers through social media, and to use these relationships as a base for market research and for multichannel marketing. Data collection takes place when customers are directed to targeted offers and promotions for particular brand websites, where external data are integrated with existing internal data. The process involves tracking a particular brand, analysing what customer are saying and thinking specifically about the brand, but also looking at everything else they are talking about (in areas of public access) in order to build a consumer profile. GSK then employs internal data management and processing analysts to make sense of the data, and uses the information to inform its marketing strategy and planning at both strategic and tactical levels.

Based on: Occam (2012);[13] *GSK (2012);*[14] *Hemsley (2011)*[15]

Custom-designed studies

Custom-designed studies are based on the specific needs of the client. The research design is based on the research brief given to the marketing research agency or internal marketing researcher. Because they are tailor-made, such surveys can be expensive.

Omnibus studies

The alternative is to use an **omnibus survey** in which space is bought on questionnaires for face-to-face or telephone interviews. The interview may cover many topics as the questionnaire space is bought by a number of clients who benefit from cost sharing. Usually the type of information sought is relatively simple (e.g. awareness levels and ownership data). Often the survey will be based on demographically balanced samples of 1000–2000 adults: for example, Ipsos UK, which covers Britain, France, Germany, Italy and Spain, takes a snapshot of consumer opinion using i-omnibus (online) capibus (weekly face-to-face survey). However, there are more specialist surveys covering the markets for children and young adults: for example, the Dubit Youth Omnibus,[16] which uses an Informer Panel made up of 37,000 young people aged 11–24. See Exhibit 7.1 for an example of how Dubit Research carries out omnibus surveys.

Continuous research

Continuous research gathers information from external sources on an ongoing basis. Major types of continuous research are consumer panels, retail audits, television viewership panels, marketing databases, customer relationship management systems and website analysis.

Consumer panels

Consumer panels are formed by recruiting large numbers of households, which provide information on their purchases over time. For example, a grocery panel would record the

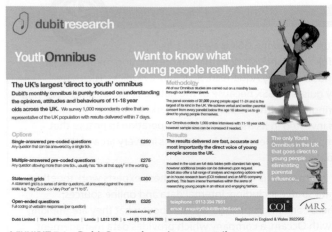

↑EXHIBIT 7.1   Dubit Research carries out omnibus surveys.

brands, pack sizes, prices and stores used for a wide range of supermarket brands. The most usual method of data collection is the use of diaries, which panel members fill in with details of purchases and return to the survey organization on a weekly basis. However, nowadays more digital and online technology is involved in the data collection process. By using the same households over a period of time, measures of brand loyalty and switching can be achieved, together with a demographic profile of the type of person who buys particular brands. Taylor Nelson Sofres (TNS) specializes in consumer research and uses consumer panels in Europe, North and South America and Asia. TNS provides consumer insight with a network of consumer panels that use innovative methods of continuous data collection from households around the world, and which are equipped with the latest technology to record price, place of purchase and selected brand. TNS has also applied the consumer panel principle to generate forward-looking rather than retrospective data in its Ideation panel sessions. Online face-to-face sessions using web cams are set up to gather consumers' *top of the mind* data. What they have found is that different data collection solutions lead to different solutions. So, if a company is looking for ideas on how to improve the performance of its marketing mix, ideation is a way to get inside the minds of the consumer.

Retail audits

Retail audits are a second type of continuous research. By gaining the cooperation of retail outlets (e.g. supermarkets) sales of brands can be measured by means of laser scans of barcodes on packaging, which are read at the checkout. Although brand loyalty and switching cannot be measured, retail audits can provide accurate assessment of sales achieved by store. Nielsen produces retail trend information based on in-store scanning on a regular basis. From this research the company is able to produce vital information that can be used to predict future behaviour. For example, retailers globally are facing increasing challenges to get consumers to visit their stores; private label brands are putting pressure on proprietary brands: for example, in the UK grocery sector 55 per cent of packaged grocery items are own-label.[17]

Television viewership panels

Television viewership panels measure audience sizes. In the UK a panel is selected from private homes from each ITV and BBC region and one panel member represents about 5000 of the UK population. All ages, demographics and lifestyles are included in the panel sample. The survey is carried out on a continuous basis using various data-collection techniques such as interviews, and online meters which are capable of monitoring television viewing (and recording) behaviour. In the household of a panel member the electronic equipment registers who is watching the television, what they are watching, when channels are changed and when the viewer leaves the room (plus a great deal more viewing data). Every night between 2 a.m. and 6 a.m. the viewing data are automatically downloaded and then analysed. The Broadcasters' Audience Research Board (BARB) collects and collates[18] viewing data which show how particular television programmes have performed. The viewing figures provide data on the weekly share of programmes and channels as well as minute-by-minute analysis. This means that commercial breaks can be allocated *ratings points* (the proportion of the target audience watching), which are the currency by which television advertising is bought and judged.

Marketing databases

Companies collect data on customers on an ongoing basis. The data are stored on marketing databases, which contain each customer's name, address, telephone number, past transactions and, sometimes, demographic and lifestyle data. Information on the types of purchase, frequency of purchase, purchase value and responsiveness to promotional offers may be held.

Retailers are encouraging the collection of such data by introducing loyalty card schemes such as the Nectar card, which allows customers to collect points that can be redeemed for cashback or gifts at various store groups, including Sainsbury's, Argos, eBay, O2, Dell, Amazon and British Gas. Boots operates its own loyalty card, called Advantage, as do many other brands.

⬆EXHIBIT 7.2   Loyalty cards are used by many retailers as a source of continuous data.

Operationally, a loyalty card is swiped through the cash machine at the checkout, and cardholder information is stored on the card with name and address, so that purchasing data including expenditure per visit, types of brands purchased, how often the customer shops and when, and at which branch, can be linked to individuals. Tesco's clubcard is another example of a store loyalty card, which is used to gather consumer behaviour data, and this information is analysed and used to produce personalized marketing and sales promotion initiatives. See Exhibit 7.2 for examples of loyalty cards and think about how the message on the card positions each card slightly differently: for example, Nectar, Starbucks and Boots messages suggest a reward and/or a treat, but Tesco's message is about saving money.

Customer relationship management systems

Customer relationship management (CRM) is built on the foundation of relationship management, which has been around since the 1920s. CRM is considered to be vitally important to building long-term relationships and effective marketing strategies with business clients and consumers. For CRM systems to perform effectively, there is a need to bring together data generated at different stages (e.g., customer acquisition, retention and relationship development). In the past[19] a potential problem with marketing databases was that a company had many separate databases created in different departments. For example, the sales department may have an account management database containing information on customers, while call centre staff may use a different database created at a different time and also containing information on customers. This fragmented approach has led to problems, so now more companies are taking an integrated approach towards data management with data captured and made accessible through one system. Additionally, data are collected, stored, analysed and used to provide information to customer-contact staff in a form that corresponds to the way they work and the way customers want to access the company (e.g. via the salesforce, telephone, email or websites). Many companies that are investing in this approach are creating competitive advantage as they are able to garner greater customer insight.[20]

Website analysis

Continuous data can also be provided by analysing consumers' use of websites. From a website or email marketing letter it is possible to generate a vast amount of user data—for example, the most frequently accessed item on a web page, how long each visitor stays on the page and when products are purchased. Technical information can also be gathered—for example, how well the site loads and downloads, whether it ranks within the top three pages of major search engines, and the number of links from other sites. Google Analytics is an example of a set of tools which can be used to analyse website performance. Read Mini Case 7.1 to find out more about how analytics can help and how data capture is changing.

Mini Case 7.1 Does Google Track our Every Move?

Website analysis enables the assessment of site performance and helps to identify key areas for improvement such as web pages on a site which are rarely visited, or features on the home page which are rarely clicked. In other words, marketing managers can summarize the actions of visitors to their websites by analysing statistically users' data. Google Analytics provides a range of statistics such as bounce rates, unique visitors, page views, average time a user spends on a particular site. Understanding website performance can be important for CRM strategies by helping identify areas for improvement that might increase customer acquisition, conversion, retention and enjoyment during website visits. For example, a website might include personalized recommendations for loyal customers or introduce interactive tools to help with product selection.

Sophisticated analytical tools and software applications mean that all eyes are on the consumer, but marketing managers should be aware that consumers are becoming increasingly unwilling to hand over their personal data, especially online. In the past, retailers and consumer-facing brand websites have been able to entice consumers into signing up to newsletters, surveys and other data capture devices by offering a small incentive such as discount vouchers for handing over their personal details. However, some consumers are increasingly reluctant to knowingly hand over personal information. In fact, research has found that consumers now expect more free information from brand websites than ever before. Sectors yet to experience this trend are insurance, charities and some alcoholic drink brands, where consumers are signing up and handing over personal details in record numbers.

Paradoxically, it is perhaps the increase in our ability to analyse data and make more meaningful interpretation that is making collecting data from some consumers harder. Part of the problem is that consumers are concerned about online security and identity fraud. Google is doing little to alleviate these fears as it integrates more data collection methods into its search engine and links together with social media, encouraging consumers to unwittingly divulge more and more personal details. As one of the Internet giants, Google provides a very efficient information search engine for 90 per cent of users in Europe. Nevertheless, it has been rebuked by the European Commissioner for Justice over what are seen as weak protection policies for personal data. Some EU member states were concerned because Google has made changes that mean it can pool data about registered users, how they use the Web, make video searches, find map directions, browse the Web and which adverts they click. This pooling of data means no stone is left unturned, and Google can capture data on every aspect of an individual's life and build personalized profiles which it can then use for its lucrative Adwords, pay-for-search advertising.

The Market Research Society (MRS)'s code of conduct advocates maintaining anonymity for any opinions deduced from analysing online content, but the tools that are facilitating the analyses are emerging faster than the MRS can produce control measures. This means that consumer profiles can become very transparent, and this information can be used for marketing initiatives. For instance, before you receive your next email marketing message, the time of day you are most likely to open and respond to the message will have been analysed, the contents of the mailing may have been personalized to suit your preferences and sophisticated software will be ready to monitor your next move. If you access the Web using a smartphone, someone somewhere may have read your electronic diary and know when you are free next week, and already be planning which marketing initiatives you are going to receive.

Questions:

Having read this vignette, try to answer the following questions:

1 Give an example of an online marketing campaign that targets consumers.
2 Suggest the broad types of consumer data a digital marketer might need to carry out the campaign.
3 From your own experience provide detailed examples of companies which are using these types of campaigns.

Based on: Chaffey and Ellis-Chadwick (2012);[21] Cowlett (2011);[22] Arthur (2012);[23] Costa (2011)[24]

Stages in the Marketing Research Process

This section presents a useful framework for understanding the main steps in the marketing research process, shown in Figure 7.2. This 'map' highlights what is involved in a major marketing research study covering both qualitative and quantitative research. This process is used by marketing research practitioners and can form the structure for a student marketing research project.

Research planning

Decisions made at the research planning stage will fundamentally affect what is done later so planning is required prior to any data collection. A commercial marketing research project is likely to involve marketing management at the client company, internal marketing research staff and, usually, research staff at an outside marketing research agency. The following discussion provides a generic view of the commercial marketing research process (see Figure 7.2).

Initial contact

The start of the process is usually the realization that a marketing problem (e.g. a new product or advertising decision) requires information to help find a solution. Marketing management may contact internal marketing research staff or an outside agency. Let us assume that the research requires the assistance of a marketing research agency. A meeting will be arranged to discuss the nature of the problem and the client's research needs.

Research brief

At the meeting, the client will explain the marketing problem and outline the research objectives. The marketing problem might be to attract new customers to a product line, and the research objectives could be to identify groups of customers (market segments) that might have a use for the product, and the characteristics of the product that appeal to them most.[25] The key point is that clients should not only tell research agencies what they want to understand but what the research will be used for.[26]

Other information that should be provided for the research agency includes the following.[27]

1 *Background information*: the product's history and the competitive situation.
2 *Sources of information*: the client may have a list of industries that might be potential users of the product. This helps the researchers to define the scope of the research.
3 *The scale of the project*: is the client looking for a 'cheap and cheerful' job or a major study? This has implications for the research design and survey costs.
4 *The timetable*: when is the information required?

The client should produce a specific written **research brief**. This may be given to the research agency prior to the meeting and perhaps modified as a result of it, but, without fail, should be in the hands of the agency before it produces its *research proposal*. The research brief should state the client's requirements and should be in written form to minimize misunderstandings. In the event of a dispute later in the process, the research brief (and proposal) form the benchmark against which any grievances can be settled.

Commissioning good research is similar to buying any other product or service. If marketing management can agree on why the research is needed, what it will be used for, when it is needed and how much they are willing to pay for it, they are likely to make a good buy. Four suggestions for buying good research are as follows.

1 *Define terms clearly*. For example, if market share information is required, the term 'market' should clearly be defined.

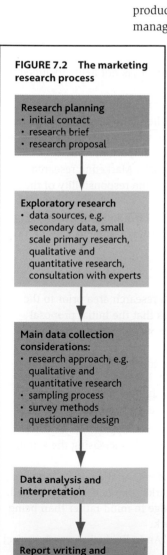

FIGURE 7.2   The marketing research process

Research planning
- initial contact
- research brief
- research proposal

Exploratory research
- data sources, e.g. secondary data, small scale primary research, qualitative and quantitative research, consultation with experts

Main data collection considerations:
- research approach, e.g. qualitative and quantitative research
- sampling process
- survey methods
- questionnaire design

Data analysis and interpretation

Report writing and presentation

2 *Beware of researchers who bend research problems* so that they can use their favourite technique. They may be specialists in a particular research-gathering method (e.g. group discussion) or statistical technique (e.g. factor or cluster analysis) and look for ways of using these methods no matter what research problem they face. This can lead to irrelevant information and unnecessary expense.

3 *Do not be put off by seemingly naïve researchers* who ask what appear to be simple questions, particularly if they are new to the client's industry.

4 *Brief two or three agencies*. The extra time involved should be rewarded by better feedback on how to tackle the research problem and a better priced quote.

Research proposal

The **research proposal** defines what the marketing research agency promises to do for its client, and how much it will cost. Like the research brief, the proposal should be written to avoid misunderstandings. A client should expect the following to be included:

1 *A statement of objectives*: to demonstrate an understanding of the client's marketing and research problems.

2 *What will be done*: an unambiguous description of the research design, including the survey method, the type of sample, the sample size and how the fieldwork will be controlled.

3 *Timetable*: if and when a report will be produced.

4 *Costs*: how much the research will cost and what, specifically, is/is not being included in those costs.

When assessing proposals a client might usefully check the following points.

1 *Beware of vagueness*: if the proposal is vague, assume that the report is also likely to be vague. If the agency does not state what is going to be done, why, who is doing it and when, assume that it is not clear in its own mind about these important issues.

2 *Beware of jargon*: there is no excuse for jargon-ridden proposals. Marketing research terminology can be explained in non-expert language, so it is the responsibility of the agency to make the proposal understandable to the client.

3 *Beware of what is missing*: assume that anything not specified will not be provided. For example, if no mention of a presentation is made in the proposal, assume it will not take place. Any doubts, ask the agency.

Exploratory research

Exploratory research involves the preliminary exploration of a research area prior to the main data-collection stage. The discussion that follows assumes that the initial proposal has been accepted and that exploratory research is to be carried out as the basis for survey design.

A major purpose of exploratory research is to guard against the sins of omission and admission.[28]

- *Sin of omission*: not researching a topic in enough detail, or failing to provide sufficient respondents in a group to allow meaningful analysis.
- *Sin of admission*: collecting data that are irrelevant to the marketing problem, or using too many groups for analysis purposes and thereby unnecessarily increasing the sample size.

Exploratory research techniques allow the researcher to understand the people who are to be interviewed in the main data-collection stage, and the market that is being researched. The main survey stage can thus be designed with this knowledge in mind rather than being based on the researcher's ill-informed prejudices and guesswork.

Figure 7.3 displays the four exploratory research activities. An individual research project may involve all or some of them.

Please note that qualitative and quantitative research methods may be used at both the exploratory and main data collection stage and it will be the market research project

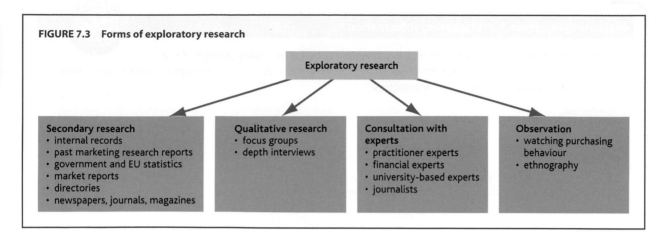

FIGURE 7.3 **Forms of exploratory research**

Exploratory research

Secondary research
- internal records
- past marketing research reports
- government and EU statistics
- market reports
- directories
- newspapers, journals, magazines

Qualitative research
- focus groups
- depth interviews

Consultation with experts
- practitioner experts
- financial experts
- university-based experts
- journalists

Observation
- watching purchasing behaviour
- ethnography

manager's responsibility to determine which methods will be the best methods to meet the research objectives.

Secondary research

Secondary research is so called because the data come to the researcher 'second-hand' (other people have compiled the data). When the researcher actively collects new data—for example, by interviewing respondents—this is called primary research (discussed in the next section).

Secondary data comes from sources such as internal company records, reports and previous research carried out for the company. External sources of secondary data include government and European Union statistics; publishers of reports and directories on markets, countries and industries; trade associations; banks; and newspapers, magazines and journals. The Internet provides access to rich sources of secondary information. Websites like Trendwatching (www.trendwatching.com) specialize in identifying emerging global consumer and marketing trends. Some online sources are free to access, others are paid-for services: for example, IDC, Gartner and Experian have an Internet presence and provide various types of information. Companies that specialize in providing secondary information also provide electronic content either by subscription or by selling individual reports. For example, a visit to Mintel (www.mintel.com) can provide hundreds of industry-specific reports such as Do-It-Yourself Retailing, Home Shopping and Gluten-free Foods in a range of European countries and the USA. A word of caution when using online resources (especially free information): remember to verify the authenticity of the data; be critical of the findings and establish the origin of the data.

In the European Union there are many secondary sources of data. Marketing in Action 7.3 lists some of the major sources of marketing information classified by research questions.

Secondary research should be carried out before primary research. Without the former, an expensive primary research survey might be commissioned to provide information that is already available from secondary sources. Furthermore, directories such as *Kompass* can be invaluable when selecting a sample in a business-to-business marketing research project.

Primary research methods

Each ad hoc marketing research project may be different. This is in order to fit the particular requirements and resources of various clients. For example, one study may focus on **qualitative research** using small numbers of respondents, while another may be largely **quantitative research**, involving interviewing hundreds or thousands of consumers. Therefore, it is important to take care to ensure that the data collection method is suitable and best able to meet the objectives of the market research activity.

Marketing in Action 7.3 Marketing Information

There are many sources of marketing information. This table provides examples of some of the main companies and online databases, which could provide information for specific industries, market competitors, economic trends statistics and abstracts and indices.

Is there a survey of the industry?

Euromonitor International	http://www.euromonitor.com	Produces 17,000 reports each year on 27 industries and 200 sub-categories and thousands of company reports in 80 countries
Business Insight Reports	http://www.business-insights.com	Full text reports available online in the sectors of healthcare, financial services, consumer goods, energy, and e-commerce and technology
Keynote Reports	http://www.keynote.co.uk	Provides market intelligence in the UK including reports on market trends and company performance
Marketline Business Information Centre	http://www.marketlineinfo.com/index.htm	Overview of over 10,000 company profiles and 3000 industry profiles in over 50 countries, as well as 100 country profiles

How large is the market and where is it located?

Euromonitor International	http://www.euromonitor.com	Data and statistics on European and international markets
Mintel Reports	http://www.mintel.com	Market analysis and intelligence
WARC	http://www.warc.com	Comprehensive marketing information service, provides access to reports, forecasts, journal articles and case studies
Regional Trends	http://data.gov.uk/dataset/regional_trends	Economic and social statistics for UK regions

Who are the competitors?

Kompass	http://gb.kompass.com	Global business-to-business and product information database
Fame	http://www.bvdinfo.com	Comprehensive information on companies in the UK and Ireland For further international information services see Amadeus, BankScope, Orbis and Isis
CAROL	http://www.carol.co.uk	Company annual reports
D & B Worldwide network	http://www.dnb.co.uk/international-data.asp	International database of company information

What are the trends?

Euromonitor International	http://www.euromonitor.com	Produces 17,000 reports each year on 27 industries and 200 sub-categories and thousands of company reports in 80 countries.
Economic and Social Data Service	http://www.esds.ac.uk	Provides access to data collections showing economic and social trends data
Eurostat	http://epp.eurostat.ec.europa.eu/portal/page/portal/eurostat/home/	Provides access to European statistics and series of publications that provide a detailed picture of the EU

Abstracts and indices		
Web of knowledge	http://wok.mimas.ac.uk/	Comprehensive research database including journals, article citations and conference papers
Science Direct	http://www.sciencedirect.com/	Full text scientific articles from journals and books
Zetoc	http://zetoc.mimas.ac.uk/	Comprehensive research database including journals, article citations and conference papers
Statistics		
Eurostat	http://epp.eurostat.ec.europa.eu/ portal/page/portal/eurostat/home/	Provides access to European statistics and series of publications that provide a detailed picture of the EU
ONS	http://www.ons.gov.uk/ons/index. html	Provides access to UK statistics and series of publications that provide a detailed picture of the EU

Note: some of these sites require passwords, which can be obtained from libraries.
Source: the author thanks Reshma Khan and Neil Jukes of Bradford University School of Management Library for their help in compiling this list.

Qualitative research

Qualitative research has been defined as 'the analysis and understanding of patterned conduct and social process of society'.[29] The main forms of qualitative research used in market research which help us to understand the complex patterns of human behaviour are: group discussions; **in-depth interviews** and **ethnography**, which involve bringing together personal encounters, life events and understandings into a more meaningful context.[30] Qualitative research aims to establish customers' attitudes, values, behaviour and beliefs and aims to understand consumers in a way that traditional methods of interviewing people using questionnaires cannot. Qualitative research seeks to understand the 'why' and 'how' of consumer behaviour.[31] The key differences between qualitative and quantitative research are explored later in this chapter.

Focus groups involve unstructured or semi-structured discussions between a *moderator*, or group leader, who is often a psychologist, and a group of consumers. The moderator has a list of areas to cover within the topic but allows the group considerable freedom to discuss the issues that are important to them. The topics might be organic foods, men's cosmetics, motor sports or activity holiday pursuits. By arranging groups of 6–12 people to discuss their beliefs, attitudes, motivation, behaviour and preferences, a good deal of knowledge may be gained about the consumer. This can be helpful when planning questionnaires, which can then be designed to focus on what is important to the respondent (as opposed to the researcher) and worded in language that the respondent uses and understands.

A further advantage of the focus group is that the findings may provide rich insights into consumer motivations and behaviour because of the group dynamics where group members 'feed off' each other and reveal ideas that would not have arisen on a one-to-one basis. Such findings may be used as food for thought for marketers, without the need for quantitative follow-up.

The weaknesses of the focus group are that interpretation of the results is highly subjective, the quality of the results depends heavily on the skills of the moderator, sample size is usually small, making generalization to wider populations difficult, and there exists the danger that the results might be biased by the presence of 'research groupies', who enjoy taking part in focus groups and return again and again. Such people sometimes even take on different identities, skewing survey results, and have led the Association of Qualitative Research Practitioners to introduce a rule which says that focus group participants have to provide proof of identity each time they attend a group.[32]

Technology is having an impact on such face-to-face discussion settings and high-tech labs can be used which allow participants to be observed through two-way glass, enabling the client organization to view the focus group session live. Online focus groups are also becoming popular and this method can reduce costs and create more opportunities to interact with customer groups. Also, research has found that, in some cases, participants are more honest in online discussion than when face to face in person. There are limitations: non-verbal communications, eye movements and interaction between participants can be missed.[33]

Internet communities and social media sites can provide access to 'communities of interests', which can take the form of chat rooms or websites dedicated to specific interests or issues. These are useful forums for conducting focus groups, or at least identifying suitable participants. Questions can be posed to participants who are not under time pressure to respond. This can lead to richer insights since they can think deeply about questions put to them online. Another advantage is that they can comprise people located all over the world at minimal cost.

In-depth interviews involve the interviewing of consumers individually for perhaps one or two hours about a topic. The aims are broadly similar to those of group discussion but are used when the presence of other people could inhibit honest answers and viewpoints, when the topic requires individual treatment, as when discussing an individual's decision-making process, and where the organization of a group is not feasible (for example, it might prove impossible to arrange for six busy purchasing managers to come together for a group discussion).

Care has to be taken when interpreting the results of qualitative research in that the findings are usually based on small sample sizes, and the more interesting or surprising viewpoints may be disproportionately reported. This is particularly significant when qualitative research is not followed by a quantitative study.

Qualitative research accounts for more than 10 per cent of all European expenditure on marketing research, of which the largest proportion is spent on group discussions, followed by in-depth interviews and then other qualitative techniques accounting for a small percentage of the spend.[34]

Consultation with experts

Qualitative research is based on discussions and interviews with actual and potential buyers of a brand or service. However, consultation with experts involves interviewing people who may not form part of the target market but who, nevertheless, can provide important marketing-related insights. Many industries have their experts in universities, financial institutions and the press, who may be willing to share their knowledge. They can provide invaluable background information, and can be useful for predicting future trends and developments.

Observation

Observation can also help in exploratory research when the product field is unfamiliar. Watching people buy wine in a supermarket or paint in a DIY store may provide useful background knowledge when planning a survey in these markets, for example. Another form of observational research that focuses on employee performance is *mystery shopping*. The 'shopper' acts like any other customer in visiting a store, but is trained to ask particular questions, and to assess performance on such criteria as service time, friendliness and product knowledge. The objective is to identify service weaknesses and strengths, and to provide input into staff training.

Ethnography

Ethnography is a form of observation that involves detailed and prolonged observation of (in the context of this book) consumers. Its origins are in social anthropology, where researchers live in a studied society for months or years. Consumer researchers usually make their observations more quickly and use a range of methods, including direct observations, interviews and video and audio recordings.[35]

This method of data collection has become popular as it connects important personal experiences to specific contexts[36] and enables researchers to get closer to consumers in order to understand their behaviour in new and more detailed ways. Such research investigates how people behave in their own environment and interact with the world around them. Unlike focus groups, where consumers are brought to the researcher, ethnography takes the researcher to the consumer. Advocates of this form of research argue that focus groups only provide part of the story and do not yield the kinds of 'consumer insights' that ethnography can.

One company that has embraced ethnographic research is Procter & Gamble. Twenty families in the UK and a further 20 in Italy were chosen to take part in a study that involved the recording of their daily household behaviour by video camera. The idea was that by studying people who buy P&G products—such as Max Factor cosmetics, Ariel washing powder and Pampers nappies—the company could gain valuable insights into people's consumer habits. The findings have had implications for its approach to product design, packaging and promotion. For example, it was ethnographic research which revealed that the nappy was not as important as P&G had previously thought. New mothers were more interested in information and knowledge than nappies. Using these consumer insights, P&G launched Pampers.com, an online community for mothers that attracts over 650,000 users across Europe. P&G has also used ethnographic research in China. It observed low-income consumers doing their washing and found that they were prepared to do the extra hand washing needed to compensate for water hardness. P&G's response was to launch a cut-price version of its China Tide detergent without water softener.[37] A P&G spokesman pointed out that ethnography will not replace other forms of research and that ethical issues concerning privacy are dealt with by getting full permission beforehand and giving the families complete editorial control over what is eventually shown to the marketing team.

Kenco's marketing team also used ethnography to help them dig deeper into how people used their product. They videoed people to understand what was most important in a coffee shop experience. Kenco found that, while its own focus was on the coffee beans, a range of other things were just as important to consumers, including the crockery in which the coffee was served. The video project had the added advantage of being much more interesting when presenting the findings to management. Watching consumers talk was much more vivid than watching a PowerPoint presentation.[38]

The objective of ethnographic research is to bridge the gap between what people say they do and what they actually do. Its usefulness is reflected in the fact that companies such as Nokia, Toyota, Land Rover, Intel, Van den Berghs, Adidas and Nike have used this genre of research. It has been used in the technology field to understand how electronic products are really used. The findings showed that people will use technology in ways its inventors never imagined. For example, one family used broadband technology to pipe sound from the local mosque into their home. Another had two Sony PlayStations: one to play games on, the other for only playing CDs. Of 10 families studied, two left their televisions on all day even when they went out—something they were unlikely to admit to in a focus group.

The objective of the exploratory research stage in the marketing research process is not to form conclusions but to get better acquainted with the market and its customers. This allows the researcher to base the next stage, which involves wider data collection on *informed assumptions* rather than guesswork.

The main data-collection stage

Following careful exploratory research, the design of the main data-collection procedures will be made. In Figure 7.4 the assumption is that quantitative research methods are the most appropriate. However, in some situations, it may be better to extend the use of qualitative research methods used at the exploratory stage of a project. In either case it is important for the project manager to select the data collection methods which are most likely to achieve the research objectives.

At the main data-collection stage two alternative approaches are descriptive and experimental research.

Assuming the main data-collection stage requires interviewing, the research design will be based on the following factors:

- who and how many people to interview (the sampling process)
- how to interview them (the survey method)
- what questions to ask (questionnaire design).

Figure 7.4 displays the two types and three research design methods associated with the main quantitative data-collection stage. These research approaches and methods will now be examined.

Descriptive research

Descriptive research may be undertaken to describe consumers' beliefs, attitudes, preferences, behaviour, etc. For example, a survey into advertising effectiveness might measure awareness of the brand, recall of the advertisement and knowledge about its content.

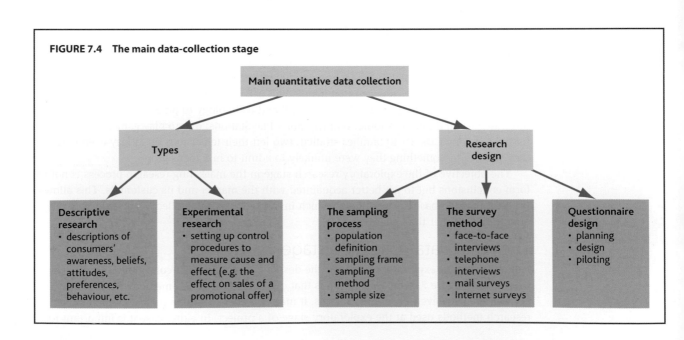

FIGURE 7.4 The main data-collection stage

Main quantitative data collection

Types — Research design

Descriptive research
- descriptions of consumers' awareness, beliefs, attitudes, preferences, behaviour, etc.

Experimental research
- setting up control procedures to measure cause and effect (e.g. the effect on sales of a promotional offer)

The sampling process
- population definition
- sampling frame
- sampling method
- sample size

The survey method
- face-to-face interviews
- telephone interviews
- mail surveys
- Internet surveys

Questionnaire design
- planning
- design
- piloting

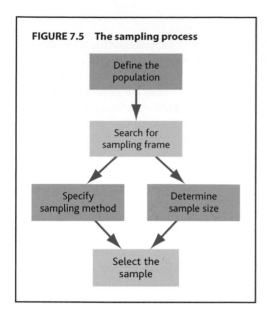

FIGURE 7.5 The sampling process

Define the population

↓

Search for sampling frame

↓

Specify sampling method | Determine sample size

↓

Select the sample

Experimental research

The aim of experimental research is to establish cause and effect. **Experimental research** involves the setting-up of control procedures to isolate the impact of a factor (e.g. a money-off sales promotion) on a dependent variable (e.g. sales). The key to successful experimental design is the elimination of other explanations of changes in the dependent variable. One way of doing this is to use random sampling. For example, the sales promotion might be applied in a random selection of stores with the remaining stores selling the brand without the money-off offer. Statistical significance testing can be used to test whether differences in sales are likely to be caused by the sales promotion or are simply random variations. The effects of other influences on sales are assumed to impact randomly on both the sales promotion and the no promotion alternatives.

The sampling process

Figure 7.5 outlines the **sampling process**. It begins by *defining the population*—that is, the group that forms the subject of study in a particular survey. The survey objective will be to provide results that are representative of this group. Sampling planners, for example, must ask questions like: 'Do we interview all people over the age of 18 or restrict it to those of the population aged 18–60?', 'Do we interview purchasing managers in all textile companies or only those that employ more than 200 people?'

Once the population has been defined, the next step is to search for a *sampling frame*—that is, a list or other record of the chosen population from which a sample can be selected. Examples include a register of electors, or the *Kompass* directory of companies. The result determines whether a random or non-random sample can be chosen. A random sample requires an accurate sampling frame; without one, the researcher is restricted to non-random methods.

Three major *sampling methods* are simple random sampling, stratified random sampling and quota sampling. It is also important to determine *sample size*.

- With simple random sampling, each individual (or company) in the sampling frame is given a number, and numbers are drawn at random (by chance) until the sample is complete. The sample is random because everyone on the list has an equal chance of selection.
- With stratified random sampling, the population is broken down into groups (e.g. by company size or industry) and a random sample is drawn (as above) for each group. This ensures that each group is represented in the sample.
- With quota sampling, a sampling frame does not exist but the percentage of the population that falls in various groupings (e.g. gender, social class, age) is known. The sample is constructed by asking interviewers to select individuals on the basis of these percentages: e.g. roughly 50:50 females to males. This is a non-random method since not everyone has an equal chance of selection, but it is much less expensive than random methods when the population is widely dispersed.
- Sample size is a further key consideration when attempting to generate a representative sample. Clearly, the larger the sample size the more likely it will represent the population. Statistical theory allows the calculation of sampling error (i.e. the error caused by not interviewing everyone in the population) for various sample sizes. In practice, the number of people interviewed is based on a balance between sampling error and cost considerations. Fortunately sample sizes of around 1000 (or fewer) can provide measurements that have tolerable error levels when representing populations counted in their millions.

The survey method

There are four options when choosing a *survey method*: face-to-face interviews, telephone interviews, mail surveys or Internet surveys. Each method has its own strengths and limitations; Table 7.2 gives an overview of these.

A major advantage of *face-to-face interviews* is that response rates are generally higher than for telephone interviews or mail surveys.[39] Seemingly the personal element in the contact makes refusal less likely. This is an important factor when considering how representative of the population the sample is and when using experimental designs. Testing the effectiveness of a stimulus would normally be conducted by face-to-face interview rather than a mail survey where high non-response rates and the lack of control over who completes the questionnaire would invalidate the results. Face-to-face interviews are more versatile than telephone and mail surveys.

The use of many open-ended questions on a mail survey would lower response rates,[40] and time restrictions for a telephone interview limit their use. Probing is easier with face-to-face interviews. Two types of probes are *clarifying probes* (e.g. 'Can you explain what you mean by . . . ?'), which help the interviewer understand exactly what the interviewee is saying, and *exploratory probes*, which stimulate the interviewee to give a full answer (e.g. 'Are there any other reasons why . . . ?'). A certain degree of probing can be achieved with a telephone interview, but time pressure and the less personalized situation will inevitably limit its use. Visual aids (e.g. a drawing of a new product concept) can be used where clearly they cannot with a telephone interview.

However, face-to-face interviews have their drawbacks. They are more expensive than telephone and mail questionnaires. Telephone and mail surveys are cheaper because the cost of contacting respondents is much less expensive, unless the population is very concentrated (face-to-face interviewing of students on a business studies course, for instance, would be relatively inexpensive). The presence of an interviewer can cause bias (e.g. socially desirable answers) and lead to the misreporting of sensitive information. For example, O'Dell found that only 17 per cent of respondents admitted borrowing money from a bank in a face-to-face interview compared to 42 per cent in a comparable mail survey.[41]

TABLE 7.2   A comparison of face-to-face, telephone, mail and Internet surveys

	Face to face	Telephone	Mail	Internet
Questionnaire				
Use of open-ended questions	High	Medium	Low	Low
Ability to probe	High	Medium	Low	Low
Use of visual aids	High	Poor	High	High
Sensitive questions	Medium	Low	High	Low
Resources				
Cost	High	Medium	Low	Low
Sampling				
Widely dispersed populations	Low	Medium	High	High
Response rates	High	Medium	Low	Low
Experimental control	High	Medium	Low	Low
Interviewing				
Control of who completes questionnaire	High	High	Low	Low/high
Interviewer bias	Possible	Possible	Low	Low

TABLE 7.3 Methods of improving mail survey response rates	
Activity	**Effect on response rate**
Prior notification by mail	Increase in consumer research, but not for commercial populations
Prior notification by telephone	Increased response rate
Monetary and non-monetary incentives	Increased response rate
Type of postage	Higher response rates for stamped return envelopes
Personalization	The effect varies: it cannot be assumed that personalization always increases response
Granting anonymity to respondents	Higher response rate when issue is sensitive
Coloured questionnaire	No effect on response rate
Deadline	No effect on response rate
Types of question	Closed-ended questions get higher response than open-ended
Follow-ups	Follow-up telephone calls and mailing increase response rates

In some ways *telephone interviews* are a halfway house between face-to-face and mail surveys. They generally have a higher response rate than mail questionnaires but lower than face-to-face interviews; their cost is usually less than face-to-face but higher than for mail surveys; and they allow a degree of flexibility when interviewing. However, the use of visual aids is not possible and there are limits to the number of questions that can be asked before respondents either terminate the interview or give quick (invalid) answers to speed up the process. The use of computer-aided telephone interviewing (CATI) is common. Centrally located interviewers read questions from a computer monitor and input answers via the keyboard. *Routing* through the questionnaire is computer-controlled, helping the process of interviewing.

Mail surveys, given a reasonable response rate, are normally the least expensive of the first three options. A low research budget, combined with a widely dispersed population, may mean that there is no alternative to the mail survey. However, the major problem is the potential of low response rates and the accompanying danger of an unrepresentative sample. Much research has focused on ways of improving response rates to mail surveys and Table 7.3 gives a summary of the results.[42]

Mail questionnaires must be fully structured, so there is no opportunity to probe further. Control over who completes the questionnaire is low; for example, a marketing manager may pass the questionnaire to a subordinate for completion. However, visual aids can be supplied with the questionnaire and because of self-completion, interviewer bias is low although there may still be a source effect (e.g. whether the questionnaire was sent from a commercial or non-commercial source).

Using the Internet as a survey tool

The Internet is a growing medium for conducting survey research. With **Internet surveys**, the questionnaire is administered by email, on a website by registering key words, or appears in banner advertising on search engines such as Yahoo! or Google, which drive people to the questionnaire. Internet surveys have grown in popularity to such an extent that they now account for a significant proportion of all the qualitative data collected in Europe and the USA. There are now many bespoke online survey and poll companies e.g. Survey monkey (http://www.surveymonkey.com/), eSurveysPro (http://www.esurveyspro.com) and EZpolls (http://www.ezpolls.com/), which provide survey tools, and methods of analysis.

The major advantages of the Internet as a marketing research platform are cost savings made on printing and postal charges, which are eliminated, making it even cheaper than mail surveys;[43] speed of delivery[44] and response; flexibility of content—visual aids such as video and graphics can be used, as well as audio input; automated digital data collection; data sets are readily available in digital format for analysis. Another strength of the Internet survey is its ability to cover global populations at low cost. However, sampling problems can arise because of the skewed nature of Internet users, if the online target populations are from younger and more affluent groups in society, although this issue is becoming less important as the global Internet user population increases.

In summary, it is suggested that Internet surveys are 'faster, easier, cheaper and better'. However, research has found that the benefits do not come in equal quantities when compared with other survey tools. For example:

- *Faster* Internet surveys are faster to distribute than mail surveys but telephone surveys can provide the most instantaneous response.
- *Easier* Internet surveys may be easier to compile and use but this will be subjective as it depends on the technological literacy of those involved.
- *Cheaper* in terms of sample size this may be true, as the larger the sample the greater the cost for the other methods of data collection, but there can be significant up-front costs involved in setting up an Internet survey and accessing the desired target respondents.
- *Better* Internet surveys need to ensure the validity of response in order to tick this box.

An absence of accurate contact lists remains a problem when using email to survey populations. Even when lists can be found, researchers need to tread very carefully as 'spamming'—sending junk mail—is seen as very offensive by most email users and messages may be blocked by firewalls and therefore never get to the recipient's mail box.

A possible way to reap the benefits and counter the problems associated with Internet surveys is to use a mixed method approach, which allows for different modes of data collection to be used to address validity issues. The use of two methods will, however, slow up the survey process and increase the costs, but it should ensure greater validity in the findings, which is one of the fundamentals when using survey data to make strategic and tactical marketing decisions.[45] To find out more about online surveys read Digital Marketing 7.1.

➡ **EXHIBIT 7.3** Oxfam illustrate the benefits of making donations by using images like this one of children playing in clean water.

Digital Marketing 7.1 Is Market Research in Crisis? Improving Online Surveys

Online market research is facing significant problems; individuals are less likely to tolerate email marketing initiatives and the likelihood of giving an email address to a brand has fallen from 67 per cent to 45 per cent in less than a year. Response rates from Internet surveys have fallen by more than 50 per cent in the past five years, and the pool of willing respondents has shrunk significantly and, even though globally the number of Internet users is increasing, there is a lack of fresh participants. Part of the reason for this lack of willingness is that taking part in an online survey is deemed to be 'boring', since people don't want to tick endless boxes and grids. Perhaps an even more significant consequence of this apathy is that, as respondents lose interest, the validity of their responses also decreases. They click any option to get to the end of the survey to reap any rewards the survey originator has offered as an incentive for completion. This too is a problem. The Direct Marketing Association found that incentives to participate (which have proved effective in the past to increase response rates) are producing fewer results on a year-on-year basis. For example, discounts and money-off vouchers are losing their appeal—only free shipping seems to attract consumers to handing over their data.

Questions are being raised about whether *market research is in a state of limbo*. So, what can companies wishing to interact with their customers do in the future to improve data collection and response rates?

The key seems to be 1) to find ways to engage consumer interest, and 2) to find ways to develop an ongoing '*conversation*' with potential recipients.

Engaging consumer interest can be achieved online by getting marketing managers to think about surveys as creative communications, using suitable imagery, animations, colours and design. Additionally, do not forget the *warm-up*, as this is important (this technique is widely used in focus groups, and pays dividends as participants are more ready to talk when it comes to the important questions). The marketing manager responsible for surveys should think of ways to make the introductory text engaging. Many online surveys are set up to force the respondent into answering certain questions, but this technique has been found to be counterproductive and also annoys respondents. Rather than forcing the respondent to answer an open-ended question before they can move to the next question, show them a good example of what someone else has written. Perhaps by reframing surveys, making them more interactive and introducing an element of fun it may be possible to turn the tables and increase respondents' willingness to participate in online surveys.

Joining the conversation can be a challenge, but marketing managers who are successfully engaging their customers' interest have the benefit of some advice: for example, Hendrick's Gin has increased the size of its marketing database significantly by creating a *good first impression* and then engaging customers in the *conversation* before asking for their personal details. To achieve this, Hendrick's have set up a website named 'the Curiositorium', which invites Web visitors to join in interactive activities and share their details while enjoying the website. For the marketing director at Be Wiser motor insurance the key to success lies in carefully protecting the use of personal data. In the motor insurance industry a great deal of personal information is required in order to complete a quotation, so getting customers' trust is paramount. Head of relationship marketing at Oxfam says permission-based email marketing in the charity sector is different, so when it comes to collecting personal data, the challenge is to get people to want to opt in to the conversation. They do this by showing potential donors what a difference their money is making (see Exhibit 7.3). For example, in the case of a humanitarian crisis they say something like: 'If you give us your email address we can keep you informed on how things are developing in that area using films and slides'. Oxfam has some very compelling stories to keep the conversation going and thereby retain the interest and engagement of their donors.

Based on: Pulestone (2011);[46] *Costa (2011)*[47]

Questionnaire design

Three conditions are necessary to get a true response to a question:

1 respondents must *understand* the question
2 respondents must be *able to provide* the information
3 respondents must be *willing to answer*.

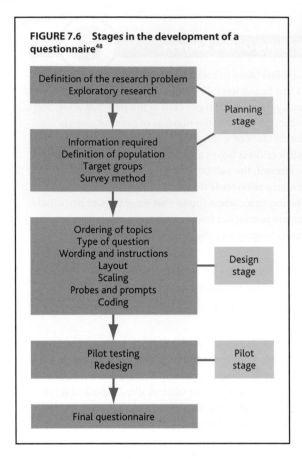

FIGURE 7.6 Stages in the development of a questionnaire[48]

Definition of the research problem
Exploratory research

Information required
Definition of population
Target groups
Survey method

Planning stage

Ordering of topics
Type of question
Wording and instructions
Layout
Scaling
Probes and prompts
Coding

Design stage

Pilot testing
Redesign

Pilot stage

Final questionnaire

Researchers must remember these conditions when designing questionnaires. Questions need to be phrased in language the respondent understands and is able to interpret.

Equally, researchers must not ask about issues that respondents cannot remember or that are outside their experience. For example, it would be invalid to ask about attitudes towards a brand of which the respondent is unaware. Finally, researchers need to consider the best way to elicit sensitive or personal information. As we have already seen, willingness to provide such information depends on the survey method employed.

Figure 7.6 shows the three stages in the development of the questionnaire: planning, design and pilot.

The *planning stage* involves the types of decision discussed so far in this chapter. It provides a firm foundation for designing a questionnaire that provides relevant information for the marketing problem that is being addressed.

The *design stage* involves a number of interrelated issues, as described below.

1 *Ordering of topics*: an effective questionnaire has a logical flow. It is sensible to start with easy-to-answer questions. This helps to build the confidence of respondents and allows them to relax. Respondents are often anxious at the beginning of an interview, concerned that they might show their ignorance. Other rules of thumb are simply common sense: for example, it would be logical to ask awareness questions before attitude measurement questions, and not vice versa. Unaided awareness questions must be asked before aided ones. Classificatory questions that ask for personal information such as age and occupation are usually asked last.

2 *Types of question*: closed-ended questions specify the range of answers that will be recorded. If there are only two possible answers (e.g. 'Did you visit a cinema within the last seven days?' YES/NO) the question is *dichotomous* (either/or). If there are more than two possible answers, then the question is *multiple choice* (e.g. 'Which, if any, of the following cinemas have you visited within the last seven days?' ODEON, SHOWCASE, CINEWORLD, NONE). *Open-ended questions* allow respondents to answer the question in their own words (e.g. 'What did you like about the cinema you visited?'). The interviewer then writes the answer in a space on the questionnaire.

3 *Wording and instructions*: great care needs to be taken in the wording of questions. Questionnaire designers need to guard against ambiguity, leading questions, asking two questions in one and using unfamiliar words. Table 7.4 gives some examples of poorly worded questions and suggests remedies. Instructions should be printed in capital letters or underlined so that they are easily distinguishable from questions.

4 *Layout*: the questionnaire should not appear cluttered. In mail questionnaires, it is a mistake to squeeze too many questions on to one page so that the questionnaire length (in pages) is shortened. Response is more likely to be lower if the questionnaire appears heavy than if its page length is extended.[49]

5 *Scaling*: careful exploratory research may allow attitudes and beliefs to be measured by means of scales. Respondents are given lists of statements (e.g. 'My company's marketing information system allows me to make better decisions') followed by a choice of five positions on a scale ranging from 'strongly agree' to 'strongly disagree'. Furthermore, computer advances are enabling the measurement of emotions using avatars (pictorial representations of people), as Digital Marketing 7.3 explains.

TABLE 7.4 Poorly worded questions and how to avoid them

Question	Problem and solution
What type of wine do you prefer?	'Type' is ambiguous; respondents; could say 'French', 'red', 'claret', depending on their interpretation. Showing the respondent a list and asking 'from this list . . .' would avoid the problem
Do you think that prices are cheaper at Asda than at Aldi?	Leading question favouring Asda; a better question would be 'Do you think that prices at Asda are higher, lower or about the same as at Aldi?' Names should be reversed for half of the sample
Which is more powerful and kind to your hands: Ariel or Bold?	Two questions in one: Ariel may be more powerful but Bold may be kinder to the hands. Ask the two questions separately
Do you find it paradoxical that X lasts longer and yet is cheaper than Y?	Unfamiliar word: a study has shown that less than a quarter of the population understand such words as paradoxical, chronological or facility. Test understanding before use

6 *Probes and prompts*: probes seek to explore or clarify what a respondent has said. Following a question about awareness of brand names, the *exploratory probe* 'Any others?' would seek to identify further names. Sometimes respondents use vague words or phrases like 'I like going on holiday because it is nice.' A *clarifying probe* such as, 'In what way is it nice?' would seek a more meaningful response. *Prompts*, on the other hand, aid responses to a question. For example, in an aided-recall question, a list of brand names would be provided for the respondent.

7 *Coding*: by using closed questions the interviewer merely has to ring the code number next to the respondent's choice of answer. In computer-assisted telephone interviewing and with the increasing use of laptop computers for face-to-face interviewing, the appropriate code number can be keyed directly into the computer's memory. Such questionnaires are *pre-coded*, making the process of interviewing and data analysis much simpler. Open-ended questions, however, require the interviewer to write down the answer verbatim. This necessitates *post-coding*, whereby answers are categorized after the interview. This can be a time-consuming and laborious task.

Once the preliminary questionnaire has been designed, it should be piloted with a representative sub-sample, to test for faults. The *pilot stage* is not the same as exploratory research. Exploratory research helps to decide upon the research design whereas piloting tests the questionnaire design and helps to estimate costs. Face-to-face piloting, where respondents are asked to answer questions and comment on any problems concerning a questionnaire read out by an interviewer, is preferable to impersonal piloting, where the questionnaire is given to respondents for self-completion and they are asked to write down any problems found.[50] If desired, several kinds of question on the same topic can be asked in order to assess the effects of the wording on respondents.[51] Once the pilot work proves satisfactory the final questionnaire can be administered to the chosen sample.

Data analysis and interpretation

Quantitative analysis of questionnaire data will invariably be carried out by computer. Basic marketing analyses can be carried out using such software-analysis packages as SNAP or more sophisticated analyses can be conducted using a package such as SPSS. Sophisticated software is being developed to enable better and more accurate analysis of increasingly complex data sets.

Basic analysis may be at the descriptive level (e.g. means, standard deviations and frequency tables) or on a comparative basis (e.g. cross tabulations and t-tests). More sophisticated analysis may search for relationships (e.g. regression analysis), group respondents (e.g. cluster analysis) or establish cause and effect (e.g. analysis of variance techniques used on experimental data). Computer-aided analysis of marketing research data is not limited to quantitative data. The analysis of vast volumes of qualitative data can be

Digital Marketing 7.2 Emotional Measurement and Social Contagion

Traditional scaling measurement techniques have been found to be wanting when it comes to capturing emotions accurately. However, better computer graphics are allowing pictorial representation of data. For example, Conquest, a London-based market research agency, has developed Metaphorix, a tool that uses avatars (pictorial representations of themselves) to test consumers' reactions to brands and advertising. Respondents can express warmth, excitement, empathy, proximity and happiness by moving their avatar around. For instance, consumers can express happiness by manipulating the avatar to jump in the air, or emotional proximity by cuddling up on a sofa or maintaining maximum distance (see illustration).

By using an avatar to project their feelings about a brand, respondents can get beyond the limitations of traditional scaling and questioning. This has been found to be particularly useful among groups such as young men, who find it hard to express their emotions.

To illustrate its use, the agency tested the highly successful Cadbury gorilla commercial, once with conventional advertising testing (word-based) and again with avatars. In the standard tests, the advertisement did well, but not exceptionally well. In the avatar-based tests it performed outstandingly. Conquest argues that, often, consumers cannot put into words how they feel. By taking words out of the equation, avatars make it easier for people to express extremes of emotion spontaneously.

Conquest has built on the success of the Metaphorix concept and developed infeXious. The underlying aim is to create 'socially contagious viral campaigns that spread around the globe'. The problem is how to answer the question 'what makes a message become a social contagion?' The team at Conquest decided they needed something more than just a measure of emotional engagement. They proposed that if a message is powerful enough it will be copied and distributed to others. So they created infeXious which is a means of measuring 'energy' using animated message boards and key words, which relate to buzz, numiosity (the extent to which ideas and/or products will be awe-inspiring—e.g., iPad, Google), belonging, momentum, excitement and empathy. Conquest claims that developing infeXious has enabled it to develop a 'blueprint for contagiousness', which involves looking at the extent to which a product, say, offers excitement, energy tribalism, numiosity. infeXious has been tested on examples of advertising and found that *engaging* advertising does not necessarily lead to *contagious* advertising. However, the rewards of developing socially contagious marketing are that the messages and ideas can become widespread for very low cost.

Using Metaphorix, respondents can express their feelings about brands by moving the avatar on the left of the sofa in relation to the one on the right (the brand).

To find out more visit the Conquest web site and hear more about infeXious.
http://www.conquestuk.com/podcast/podcast.html
http://www.conquestuk.com/index.php
http://www.infexiousuk.com/

Based on: Clegg (2008);[52] Cowlett (2008)[53]

aided by the use of software packages NVIVO or NUD*IST, where data can be filed, accessed and organized in more sophisticated ways than manual analysis.

Great care is required when interpreting marketing research results. One common failing is to infer cause and effect when only association has been established. For example, establishing a relationship that sales rise when advertising levels increase does not necessarily mean that raising advertising expenditure will lead to an increase in sales. Other marketing variables—for example, salesforce effect—may have increased at the same time as the increase in advertising, or the advertising budget may have been dependent on sales levels. Either explanation would invalidate the claim that advertising causes sales to rise.

A second cautionary note concerns the interpretation of means and percentages. Given that a sample has been taken, any mean or percentage is an estimate subject to *sampling error*—that is, the error in an estimate due to taking a sample rather than interviewing the entire population. A market research survey which estimates that 50 per cent of males but only 45 per cent of females smoke does not necessarily suggest that smoking is more prevalent among males. Given the sampling error associated with each estimate, the true conclusion might be that there is no difference between males and females. Statistical hypothesis testing allows sample differences to be evaluated in the light of sampling error to establish whether they are likely to be real differences (statistically significant) or likely to be a result of taking a sample (rather than interviewing the entire population).

Report writing and presentation

Crouch suggests that the key elements in a research report are as follows:[54]
1 title page
2 list of contents
3 preface (outline of agreed brief, statement of objectives, scope and methods of research)
4 summary of conclusions and recommendations
5 previous related research (how previous research has had a bearing on this research)
6 research method
7 research findings
8 conclusions
9 appendices.

Sections 1–4 provide a concise description of the nature and outcomes of the research for busy managers. Sections 5–9 provide the level of detail necessary if any particular issue (e.g. the basis of a finding, or the analytical technique used) needs checking. The report should be written in language the reader will understand; jargon should be avoided.

Software packages such as PowerPoint considerably ease the production of pie charts, histograms, graphs, and so on, for use in the report or for presentational purposes (such as the production of acetates for overhead projection). Clients are increasingly asking for live discussions in which ideas are thought about and the implications for marketing decisions discussed. Some agencies recommend the use of workshops, following the presentation of results, to encourage this kind of discussion.[55]

The Essential Differences between Qualitative and Quantitative Research

An important distinction in marketing research is that between qualitative and quantitative research. Earlier in this chapter we discussed qualitative and quantitative research as elements in the marketing research process. Qualitative research usually precedes quantitative research and forms the basis for an understanding of consumers that can aid planning questionnaires, which can then be designed to focus on what is important to the consumer, and worded in language that consumers use and understand. However, when the objectives of the research are to gain rich, in-depth insights into consumer motivations, attitudes and behaviour the study may be based on qualitative research alone without the quantitative follow-up. Whichever approach is taken there are a number of essential differences between these two key primary data-gathering methods that mean the skills required vary. Indeed many market research practitioners specialize in one or the other approach. These differences relate to focus, research purpose and outcome, research means and operation, data capture, sampling, analysis and reporting.

Focus

The focus for qualitative research is on verbal data based on statements made by respondents—for example, 'The thing I most like about the iPod is the convenience that comes from being able to store thousands of songs on a small, portable music player'. By contrast, quantitative research focuses on numerical data (e.g. whether the respondent owns or does not own an iPod).

Research purpose and outcome

The purpose of qualitative research is to provide rich, in-depth insights into consumer behaviour, particularly how consumers behave and why they do so. Through focus groups and depth interviews a greater degree of insight may be achieved than asking questions using a structured questionnaire since the former is more flexible and allows a longer period of time to be spent exploring a given issue. The purpose of quantitative research is to provide information that can be generalized across the study population. While at times quantitative research results may be more superficial, the researcher can be more confident that the results are applicable to a broad section of consumers.

Research means and operation

The two major means by which qualitative data are gathered are the focus group and the depth interview, whereas quantitative data is gathered using a structured questionnaire. Typically a qualitative interviewer will have a list of topics to discuss but will have the freedom to vary the precise questions asked and the length of time devoted to a particular topic, depending on the circumstances that arise during the discussion or interview. For example, if a respondent makes an interesting or novel comment, the interviewer may decide to ask a series of probing questions to investigate the issue in more depth. The questions asked in a qualitative study may, therefore, depend on the answers given by a respondent to some degree. In quantitative research there is much less flexibility. Although a structured questionnaire can provide the means for varying questions through the use of filter questions (for example, 'If the answer to question 6 is yes, go to question 7, if no go to question 10'), there is much less flexibility to vary the questions at the discretion of the interviewer.

Data capture

In qualitative research the data are usually audio recorded (and occasionally video recorded), whereas in quantitative research the data are captured on a structured questionnaire typically by means of pre-coded response categories (e.g. Yes or No). Audio recording in qualitative research means that the data require post-coding, either manually or with the assistance of a software package such as NUD*IST (see the section on 'Data analysis and interpretation', above).

Sampling

The higher cost per respondent and the focus on insight rather than statistical precision mean that qualitative studies are associated with smaller samples than quantitative research. A typical study using focus groups might involve six groups of eight people per group, or one using depth interviews might be based on 15 people. Quantitative studies involve hundreds or thousands of people. For example, studies of voting intentions use samples in excess of 1000 respondents.

Analysis

Qualitative research is based on content analysis of respondent statements taken from audio recordings, whereas quantitative studies are statistical analyses of pre-coded responses from structured questionnaires. Content analysis of vast amounts of verbal data gathered by means of qualitative techniques may be enabled using computer packages such as NUD*IST (again, see above). Statistical analysis of quantitative data is invariably carried out using a computer.

TABLE 7.5 The essential differences between qualitative and quantitative research

	Qualitative research	Quantitative research
Focus	Verbal data	Numerical data
Research purpose and outcome	Rich, in-depth insights	Broad generalizations
Research means	Focus groups or depth interviews	Structured questionnaires
Operation	High flexibility in data collection	Low flexibility in data collection
Data capture	Audio recording requiring post-coding	Pre-coded response categories on structured questionnaire
Sampling	Small samples	Large samples
Analysis	Content analysis of respondent statements from audio recording	Statistical analysis of pre-coded responses from a structured questionnaire
Reporting	Underlying themes illustrated by quotes from respondents; summary statements ('most respondents stated . . .'; 'some thought . . .')	Statistical, e.g. percentages, tables, graphs, statistical inferences and estimates

Reporting

A qualitative report looks very different to one based on quantitative research. The former is verbal, typically using quotes from respondents to provide evidence to support underlying themes. Summary statements (for example 'most respondents stated . . .', or 'some respondents thought . . .') are used rather than precise statistical estimates. Such reporting is sometimes considered more vivid than quantitative research reports that rely on statistical reporting (for example, using percentages, tables, graphs, statistical inferences and estimates, etc.). In both cases, careful interpretation of the information is required.

Table 7.5 provides a summary of the key differences between qualitative and quantitative research.

Ethical Issues in Marketing Research

Despite these good intentions of benefiting customers and sellers, there are four ethical concerns about marketing research:

Intrusions on privacy

Many consumers recognize the positive role marketing research plays in the provision of goods and services but some resent the intrusive nature of marketing research surveys. Most consumer surveys ask for classificatory data such as age, occupation and income. While most surveys ask respondents to indicate an age and income band rather than request specifics, some people feel that this is an intrusion on privacy. Other people object to receiving unsolicited telephone calls or mail surveys, dislike being stopped in the street to be asked to complete a face-to-face survey and resent unsolicited online surveys and email questionnaires. The right of individuals to privacy is incorporated in the guidelines of many research associations. For example, a code of conduct of the European Society for Opinion and Marketing Research (ESOMAR) states that 'no information which could be used to identify informants, either directly or indirectly, shall be revealed other than to research personnel within the researchers' own organization who require this knowledge for the administration and checking of interviews and data processing'.[56] Under no circumstances should the information from a survey combined with the address/telephone number of the respondent be supplied to a salesperson.

Misuse of marketing research findings

When marketing research findings are to be used in an advertising campaign or as part of a sales pitch the results could be manipulated and show a bias in favour of the desired outcome. Respondents could be chosen who are more likely to give a favourable response. For example, a study comparing a domestic versus foreign brand of car could be biased by only choosing people that own domestic-made cars.

Another potential source of bias in the use of marketing research findings is where the client explicitly or implicitly communicates to the researcher the preferred research result, whereas most marketing researchers accept the need for objective studies where there is room for more than one interpretation of study findings. However, in the long term it is in everyone's interest to produce *accurate* findings as these are likely to be used for marketing planning decision-making. Using misinformation can prove to be very risky.

Competitive information gathering

The modern marketing concept stresses the need to understand both customers and competitors in order to build a competitive advantage. However, the methods that may be required to gather competitor intelligence can raise ethical questions. Questionable practices include using student projects to gather information without the student revealing the sponsor of the research, pretending to be a potential supplier who is conducting a telephone survey to understand the market, posing as a potential customer at an exhibition, bribing a competitor's employee to pass on proprietary information, and covert surveillance such as through the use of hidden cameras and phone hacking. Procter & Gamble were embarrassed by a scandal that arose when it emerged that the company had hired 'corporate intelligence agents', who searched through bins outside Unilever's Chicago new-product development headquarters in an attempt to spy on the company's plans for the haircare market.[57] Fortunately, competitive information gathering does not depend exclusively on such methods, since much useful information can be gathered by reading trade journals and newspapers, searching the Internet, analysing databases and acquiring financial statements.

Selling under the guise of marketing research

This practice, commonly known as 'sugging', is a real danger to the reputation of marketing research. Despite the fact that it is usually practised by unscrupulous selling companies who use marketing research as a means of gaining compliance to their requests to ask people questions, rather than by bona fide marketing research agencies, it is the marketing research industry that suffers from its aftermath. Usually, the questions begin innocently enough but quickly move on to the real purpose of the exercise. Often this is to qualify leads and ask whether they would be interested in buying the product or have a salesperson call.

In Europe ESOMAR encourages research agencies to adopt codes of practice to prevent this sort of behaviour and national bodies such as the Market Research Society in the UK draw up strict guidelines. However, the problem remains that the organizations that practise sugging are unlikely to be members of such bodies. The ultimate deterrent is the realization on the part of 'suggers' that the method is no longer effective.

Online **LearningCentre**

When you have read this chapter

log on to the Online Learning Centre at **www.mcgraw-hill.co.uk/textbooks/jobber** to explore chapter-by-chapter test questions, links and further online study tools for marketing.

Review

(1) **The nature and purpose of marketing information systems, and the role of marketing research within such systems**
- A marketing information system provides the information required for marketing decision-making and comprises internal continuous data, internal ad hoc data and environmental scanning.
- Marketing research is one component of a marketing information system and is primarily concerned with the provision of information about markets and the reaction of these to various product, price, distribution and promotion decisions.

(2) **The types of marketing research**
- There are two types of marketing research, which are ad hoc research (custom-designed and omnibus studies) and continuous research (consumer panels, retail audits, television viewership panels, marketing databases, customer relationship management systems and website analysis).

(3) **The approaches to conducting marketing research**
- The options are to do it yourself personally, do it yourself using a marketing research department, do it yourself using a fieldwork agency, or use the full services of a marketing research agency.

(4) **The stages in the marketing research process**
- The stages in the marketing research process are research planning (research brief and proposal), exploratory research (secondary research, qualitative research, consultation with experts, and observation), the main (quantitative) data-collection stage (descriptive and experimental research, sampling, survey method, questionnaire design), data analysis and interpretation, and report writing and presentation.

(5) **How to prepare a research brief and proposal**
- A research brief should explain the marketing problem and outline the research objectives. Other useful information would be background information, possible sources of information, the proposed scale of the project and a timetable.
- A research proposal should provide a statement of objectives, what will be done (research design), a timetable and costs.

(6) **The nature and role of exploratory research**
- Exploratory research involves the preliminary exploration of a research area prior to the quantitative data-collection stage. Its major purpose is to avoid the sins of omission and admission. By providing an understanding of the people who are to be interviewed later, the quantitative survey is more likely to collect valid and reliable information.
- It comprises secondary research, qualitative research, consultation with experts and observation.

(7) **Quantitative research design decisions: sampling, survey method and questionnaire design issues**
- Sampling decisions cover who and how many people to interview. The stages are population definition, sampling frame search, sampling method specification, sample size determination and sample selection.
- Survey method decisions relate to how to interview people. The options are face to face, telephone, mail and the Internet.
- Questionnaire design decisions cover what questions to ask. Questionnaires should be planned, designed and piloted before administering to the main sample.

(8) **Analysis and interpretation of data**
- Qualitative data analysis can be facilitated by software packages such as NUD*IST.
- Quantitative data analysis is conducted by software packages such as SPSS.
- Care should be taken when interpreting marketing research results. One common failing is inferring cause and effect when only association has been established.

9 **Report writing and presentation**
- The contents of a marketing research report should be title page, list of contents, preface, summary, previous related research, research method, research findings, conclusions and appendices.
- Software packages such as PowerPoint can be used to make professional presentations.

10 **The distinguishing features between qualitative and quantitative research**
(*Qualitative research features precede those of quantitative research in the following list*)
- Focus: verbal data vs numerical data.
- Research purpose and outcome: rich, in-depth insights vs broad generalizations.
- Research means: focus groups or depth interviews vs structured questionnaires.
- Operation: high flexibility in data collection vs low flexibility in data collection.
- Data capture: audio recording requiring post-coding vs pre-coded response categories on structured questionnaire.
- Sampling: small samples vs large samples.
- Analysis: content analysis of respondent statements from audio recording vs statistical analysis of pre-coded responses from a structured questionnaire.
- Reporting: underlying themes illustrated by quotes from respondents and summary statements vs statistical.

11 **The factors that affect the usage of marketing information systems and marketing research reports**
- Usage of marketing information systems has been shown to be higher when the system is sophisticated and confers prestige to its users, other departments view it as a threat, there is pressure from top management to use the system and users are more involved.
- Usage of marketing research is higher if results conform to the client's prior beliefs, the research is technically competent, the presentation of results is clear, the findings are politically acceptable and the status quo is not challenged.

12 **Ethical issues in marketing research**
- These are potential problems relating to intrusions on privacy, misuse of marketing research findings, competitive information gathering, and selling under the guise of marketing research.

Key Terms

ad hoc research a research project that focuses on a specific problem, collecting data at one point in time with one sample of respondents

consumer panel household consumers who provide information on their purchases over time

continuous research repeated interviewing of the same sample of people

data the most basic form of knowledge, the result of observations

descriptive research research undertaken to describe customers' beliefs, attitudes, preferences and behaviour

ethnography a form of qualitative research which involves detailed and prolonged observation of consumers in the situations which inform their buying behaviour

experimental research research undertaken in order to establish cause and effect

exploratory research the preliminary exploration of a research area prior to the main data-collection stage

focus group a group normally of six to twelve consumers brought together for a discussion focusing on an aspect of a company's marketing

in-depth interviews the interviewing of consumers individually for perhaps one or two hours, with the aim of understanding their attitudes, values, behaviour and/or beliefs

information combinations of data that provide decision-relevant knowledge

Internet surveys various methods of gathering qualitative (and in some cases quantitive) data using email or Web-based surveys.

marketing information system a system in which marketing information is formally gathered, stored, analysed and distributed to managers in accordance with their informational needs on a regular, planned basis

marketing research the gathering of data and information on the market

omnibus survey a regular survey, usually operated by a marketing research specialist company, which asks questions of respondents for several clients on the same questionnaire

qualitative research exploratory research that aims to understand consumers' attitudes, values, behaviour and beliefs

quantitative research a structured study of small or large samples using a predetermined list of questions or criteria

research brief a written document stating the client's requirements

research proposal a document defining what the marketing research agency promises to do for its client and how much it will cost

retail audit a type of continuous research tracking the sales of products through retail outlets

sampling process a term used in research to denote the selection of a sub-set of the total population in order to interview them

secondary research data that have already been collected by another researcher for another purpose

Study Questions

1. What are the essential differences between a marketing information system and marketing research?

2. What are secondary and primary data? Why should secondary data be collected before primary data?

3. What is the difference between a research brief and proposal? What advice would you give a marketing research agency when making a research proposal?

4. Mail surveys should be used only as a last resort. Do you agree?

5. Discuss the problems facing market research as a method of generating information about consumer behaviour.

6. Why are marketing research reports more likely to be used if they conform to the prior beliefs of the client? Does this raise any ethical questions regarding the interpretation and presentation of findings?

7. What are the strengths and limitations of using the Internet as a data-collection instrument?

References

1. Motto from 1925 of the John Lewis Partnership, in *Partnership for all* (1948), Ch 29. In *The Oxford Dictionary of Quotations*, A. Partington (ed.) (1996) p. 420.
2. Van Bruggen, A., A. Smidts and B. Wierenga (1996) The Impact of the Quality of a Marketing Decision Support System: An Experimental Study, *International Journal of Research in Marketing* 13, 331–43.
3. Daniels, E., H. Wilson and M. McDonald (2003) Towards a map of marketing information systems: an inductive study, *European Journal of Marketing*, 37(5/6), 821–47.
4. Jobber, D. and C. Rainbow (1977) A Study of the Development and Implementation of Marketing Information Systems in British Industry, *Journal of the Marketing Research Society* 19(3), 104–11.
5. Viking Direct, http://www.viking-direct.co.uk/specialLinks.do;jsessionid=0000iLL4HvfFivp2SWXHkkxKk2P:130mjq8ku?ID=rb_company_info.
6. Costa, M. (2011) All roads to improvement start at insight, *Marketing Week*, 19 May, 31.
7. Jain, S. C. and G. T. Haley (2009) *Marketing: Planning and Strategy*, USA: South Western Publishing.
8. Moutinho, L. and M. Evans (1992) *Applied Marketing Research*, Wokingham: Addison-Wesley, 5.
9. Manning, J. (2011) Online Research insights, *The Marketer*, June, 42–3.
10. Kotler, P., W. Gregor and W. Rodgers (1977) The Marketing Audit Comes of Age, *Sloan Management Review*, Winter, 25–42.
11. http://www.jcdecaux.co.uk/news/?id=372 Action stations visions for the future of rail advertising, 2 March 2012.
12. Bainbridge, J. (2008) How to conduct effective research, *The Marketer*, May.
13. Occam DM Ltd (2012) http://www.occam-dm.com/how-we-help.
14. GlaxoSmithKline plc (2012) http://www.gsk.com/.
15. Hemsley, S. (2011) Embracing the elephant in the room, *Marketing Week*, October, 39–43.
16. Dubit Ltd (2012) http://www.dubitresearch.com/.
17. Nielsen (2012) Retailing, http://www.acnielsen.co.uk/industry/retailing.shtml.

18. BARB (2012) Television Measurement Service, http://www.barb.co.uk/about/tv-measurement?_s = 4.

19. Soliman, H. S. (2011) Customer relationship management and its relationship to the marketing performance, *International Journal of Business and Social Science* 2(10), 166–82.

20. Hemsley (2011) op. cit.

21. Chaffey, D. and F. E. Ellis-Chadwick (2012) *Digital Marketing: Strategy, Implementation and Practice*, 5th edn, Harlow: Pearson, 576–9.

22. Cowlett, M. (2011) A Social Insight, *Marketing*, 31–3.

23. Arthur, C. (2012) Search giant 'sneaking' citizens' privacy away warns EU justice chief, *Guardian*, 2 March, 18–19.

24. Costa, M. L. (2011) Don't let your customers fade from view, *Marketing Week*, 23 June, 27–30.

25. Crouch, S. and M. Housden (2003) *Marketing Research for Managers*, Oxford: Butterworth-Heinemann, 253.

26. Dye, P. (2008) Share The Knowledge, *Marketing*, 19 March, 33–4.

27. Crouch and Housden (2003) op. cit., 260.

28. Wright, L. T. and M. Crimp (2003) *The Marketing Research Process*, London: Prentice-Hall.

29. Denzin, N. K. and Y. S. Lincoln (eds) (2000) *The Handbook of Qualitative Research*, 2nd edn, Thousand Oaks CA: Sage Publications, 11.

30. Tedlock, B. (2000) Ethnography and ethnographic representation, in *The Handbook of Qualitative Research*, Denzin, N. K. and Y. S. Lincoln (eds), 2nd edn, Thousand Oaks CA: Sage Publications, 455–86.

31. Clegg, A. (2001) Policy and Opinion, *Marketing Week*, 27 September, 63–5.

32. Flack, J. (2002) Not So Honest Joe, *Marketing Week*, 26 September, 43.

33. Manning, J. (2011) Online Research Insights, *The Marketer* June, 42–3.

34. ESOMAR (2005) *Industry Study on 2004*, ESOMAR World Research Report.

35. Peter, J. P., J. C. Olson, and K. G. Grunert (1999) *Consumer Behaviour and Marketing Strategy*, Maidenhead: McGraw-Hill.

36. Tedlock (2000) op. cit.

37. ESOMAR (2005) op. cit.

38. Taylor, D. (2008) New Year, New Insight, *The Marketer*, February, 13.

39. Yu, J. and H. Cooper (1983) A Quantitative Review of Research Design Effects on Response Rates to Questionnaires, *Journal of Marketing Research* 20, February, 156–64.

40. Falthzik, A. and S. J. Carroll (1971) Rate of Return for Close v Open-ended Questions in a Mail Survey of Industrial Organisations, *Psychological Reports* 29, 1121–2.

41. O'Dell, W. F. (1962) Personal Interviews or Mail Panels, *Journal of Marketing* 26, 34–9.

42. See Kanuk, L. and C. Berenson (1975) Mail Surveys and Response Rates: A Literature Review, *Journal of Marketing Research* 12 (November), 440–53; Jobber, D. (1986) Improving Response Rates to Industrial Mail Surveys, *Industrial Marketing Management* 15, 183–95; Jobber, D. and D. O'Reilly (1998) Industrial Mail Surveys: A Methodological Update, *Industrial Marketing Management* 27, 95–107.

43. Schonlau, M., R. D. Fricker Jr. and M. N. Elliott (2002) *Conducting research surveys via e-mail and the web*, Santa Monica, CA: RAND.

44. Gigliotti, L. M. (2011) Comparision of an Internet Versus Mail Survey: A Case Study, *Human Dimensions of Wildlife* 16(1), 55–62.

45. Gigliotti (2011) op. cit.

46. Pulestone, J. (2011) Online Research: Now & Next 2011 (Warc), *International Journal of Marketing Research* 53(4), 557–60.

47. Costa (2011) op. cit.

48. See Kotler et al. (1977) op. cit.

49. Jobber, D. (1985) Questionnaire Design and Mail Survey Response Rates, *European Research* 13(3), 124–9.

50. Reynolds, N. and A. Diamantopoulos (1998) The Effect of Pretest Method on Error Detection Rates: Experimental Evidence, *European Journal of Marketing* 32(5/6), 480–98.

51. Sigman, A. (2001) The Lie Detectors, *Campaign*, 15 June, 29.

52. Clegg, A. (2008) Virtual Worlds are the Reality, *Marketing Week*, 3 July, 27–31.

53. Cowlett, M. (2008) Market Research Leagues, *Marketing*, 3 September, 30–9.

54. Crouch and Housden (2003) op. cit.

55. Dye, P. (2008) Share the Knowledge, *Marketing*, 19 March, 33.

56. Schlegelmilch, B. (1998) *Marketing Ethics: An International Perspective*, London: International Thomson Business Press.

57. Benady, D. (2001) Burst Bubbles, *Marketing Week*, 22 November, 25–6.

Apple's MP3 players hardly need an introduction. The full version of the iPod (the classic) has the capacity to store thousands of music tracks thanks to its large memory (160 Gb), and a well-designed navigation system that allows individual tracks to be accessed with ease. The iPod shuffle, in contrast, has less memory (4 Gb) and limited features, but is the smallest and cheapest of Apple's MP3 players. In between, Apple offers the iPod nano, with a multi-touch navigation system, but more limited storage capacity (8 or 16 Gb) than the classic. Critically, though, Apple has squeezed the iPod nano into a business-card-sized package. A more recent addition to the range is the iPod touch with a multi-touch display (8, 32 or 64 Gb). The iPod 'package' also allows consumer access to Apple's iTunes with a huge range of easily downloaded tracks. This site alone accounts for 70–80 per cent of legal music downloads. The elegant design of the iPod hardware and its navigation system, and access to iTunes, has resulted in a US market share of 74 per cent for Apple in this product category, and a Japanese market share of 45 per cent.

A multitude of accessories increase the spending associated with the iPod. Some of these accessories protect the basic product (insurance and protective cases), some are aimed at increasing convenience to the consumer (worldwide chargers, cables that reduce music download times); others extend where the iPod can be used (car and home stereo connectors, armbands, volume booster); while yet others are aimed at increasing either the quality of the basic equipment (headphone upgrades) or the functionality of the iPod (digital camera connectors, equipment allowing dictation to be taken). Toys that dance when music is played and speakers are also available.

The iPod is not just important because of the revenue it generates for Apple; it is also important to Apple in other ways as 10–20 per cent of PC users who have an iPod go on to buy a Mac. This 'halo' effect has been noted by shareholders and has boosted Apple's share price. Yet, despite its current success, Apple cannot afford to count on the iPod's current phenomenal performance in the market. Consumers have questioned the value for money of the iPod shuffle, and the quality of the iPod nano's screen. Competitors are encroaching on iTunes by setting up alternative music download sites with extensive playlists. They also fear increased competition from mobile handset manufacturers.

Consequently, Apple is interested in learning more about how consumers view the iPod. In particular, it wants to know about three areas.

1   What are the ownership and usage patterns of the different iPod models? Do consumers own multiple models and use them on different occasions, or do they just have one? Which is bought first?

2   Which features do consumers find most useful? Do different age groups use different features? How are accessories used and when do consumers buy them?

3   What are consumers' attitudes towards the iPod? Do they see it as a style/image icon, or do they look at it as a functional product?

An initial draft of the questions to be included on a questionnaire has been written with these objectives in mind (see overleaf). Apple is considering two different ways to collect data. The first idea is to sample from its customer database. After dividing the database into owners of the iPod classic, the iPod nano, the iPod shuffle and the iPod touch, Apple would mail 500 questionnaires at a time to each group. When the responses were returned, it would look at who responded from each group, and then select more customers from each group to mail the questionnaires to. This process would be repeated until it managed to get 1000 responses from each group that reflected the demographic characteristics of the owners of the iPod classic, nano, shuffle and touch.

The second way Apple is considering collecting data is to set up an online questionnaire on the iTunes website. This

●

would appear to every 25th visitor to the site, inviting them to contribute. The questionnaire would remain available until 3000 responses had been achieved.

Proposed questions

1 Which of the following Apple products do you own? (tick all that apply)

iPod ☐
iPod nano ☐
iPod shuffle ☐
iPod touch ☐

2 When do you use your iPod? (tick all that apply)

When commuting/travelling ☐
When working/studying ☐
When shopping ☐
When at the gym ☐
When jogging ☐

3 Which accessories for the iPod do you own? (tick all that apply)

Protective case ☐
Insurance cover ☐
Worldwide charger ☐
Upgraded headphones ☐
Car stereo adaptor ☐
Digital camera connector ☐
Toy ☐
Armbands ☐
Speakers ☐

Please indicate the extent to which you agree/disagree with each of the following statements.

4 The iPod's design is ahead of its time.

Strongly agree ☐
Agree ☐
Neither agree nor disagree ☐
Disagree ☐
Strongly disagree ☐

5 The technical features of the iPod are miles ahead of other companies' MP3 players.

Strongly agree ☐
Agree ☐
Neither agree nor disagree ☐
Disagree ☐
Strongly disagree ☐

6 iTunes makes it easy for me to find music I like.

Strongly agree ☐
Agree ☐
Neither agree nor disagree ☐
Disagree ☐
Strongly disagree ☐

7 I show off my iPod whenever I get the opportunity.

Strongly agree ☐
Agree ☐
Neither agree nor disagree ☐
Disagree ☐
Strongly disagree ☐

8 Music is a very important part of my life.

Strongly agree ☐
Agree ☐
Neither agree nor disagree ☐
Disagree ☐
Strongly disagree ☐

9 It is easy to find the track I want on my iPod.

Strongly agree ☐
Agree ☐
Neither agree nor disagree ☐
Disagree ☐
Strongly disagree ☐

10 I am able to find new artists I like using iTunes.

Strongly agree ☐
Agree ☐
Neither agree nor disagree ☐
Disagree ☐
Strongly disagree ☐

11 I talk about my iPod to anyone who will listen.

Strongly agree ☐
Agree ☐
Neither agree nor disagree ☐
Disagree ☐
Strongly disagree ☐

12 Having an iPod impresses people I meet.

Strongly agree ☐
Agree ☐
Neither agree nor disagree ☐
Disagree ☐
Strongly disagree ☐

13 I enjoy watching films a great deal.

Strongly agree ☐
Agree ☐
Neither agree nor disagree ☐
Disagree ☐
Strongly disagree ☐

14 The iPod has better memory than other MP3 players.

Strongly agree ☐
Agree ☐
Neither agree nor disagree ☐
Disagree ☐
Strongly disagree ☐

15 What is your income? _____

16 What is your occupation? _____

17 Gender (please circle) Male/Female

Questions

1 Will the proposed questions in the questionnaire answer Apple's questions? Outline any problems and suggest solutions.

2 Assess the expertise required, and costs associated with, the two proposed survey methods. Which design would you recommend and why?

3 Assess the strengths and weaknesses of the two proposed sampling methods. Which would you recommend and why?

This case was written by Nina Reynolds, Professor of Marketing, University of Southampton, and Sheena MacArthur, Senior Lecturer in Marketing, Glasgow Caledonian University.

Market Force

Retail Eyes UK is the UK's leading research agency, providing customized solutions to its clients that focus on mystery shopping, retail audits, social media monitoring and online customer surveys. The company offers customer experience improvement programmes across a variety of sectors by combining innovative approaches and new technologies. Its international scale and experience enable it to benefit from the most up-to-date technologies and research expertise in the market. The latter are sources of differentiation in an industry populated by several competitors all stating that they offer 'the best service' to their clients. In September 2011, Retail Eyes became part of Market Force, creating the world's largest customer intelligence agency.

Marketers are increasingly using innovative ways to better understand customers and to reach them more effectively. To enhance their understanding of customers' needs and effectively design marketing strategies, marketers need to deeply analyse the elements influencing customers' buying experiences. In fact, the quality of customer experience in a retailer's shop is one of the most cost-effective methods of differentiating competing retailers. Moreover, customers generally do not complain when they receive poor service; they simply go to shop elsewhere. Therefore, it is fundamental to monitor the quality of customer service in order to make an early identification of any strengths or weaknesses. As a result, mystery shopping has become popular among marketers since it is a powerful technique to evaluate company's customer service (i.e. staff attitude and appearance, product knowledge). Mystery shoppers are defined as: 'individuals trained to experience and measure any customer service process, by acting as potential customers and in some way reporting back on their experience in a detailed and objective way' (Market Research Society, 2003). Mystery shoppers are normal people who play the role of real customers and get a monetary reward in exchange for auditing retailers. In doing this, they must not reveal their identities. They buy products, ask questions, identify problems and finally they write reports helping companies to identify training needs or to evaluate training programmes, but also to boost staff morale through incentives.

Retail Eyes commenced business in the UK in 2003 and grew rapidly at a time when competing research companies nationwide were struggling to maintain revenues. In 2010

the company saw an increased turnover of 31 per cent, making it one of the largest customer experience agencies in the UK. The company worked for several major retailers and service providers in various sectors throughout the UK, undertaking over 200,000 mystery visits per year. Clients include Subway, HMV, O2, William Hill, BAA, Intercontinental Hotel Group, JD Sports Fashion plc, Pret A Manger, Lloyds Pharmacy, Thomas Cook, and JD Wetherspoon. In 2009 the company was ranked 27th according to *Marketing*'s market research league table and 57th in the *Sunday Times* Tech Track 100 fastest-growing technology companies.

The company's key promise is to open the eyes of retailers in order that they understand who their real customers are. Mystery shopping programmes are used to identify the key touch-points in the customers' journey that may lead to sales' improvement, customer advocacy and higher profits. This type of research can provide both customer and competitor intelligence. Mystery shoppers often follow a prescribed evaluation form in order to anonymously assess a specific business against specific criteria. Further, the evaluation may take into consideration various aspects of the retailer's business (or of a product) comprising the simple factual observation of points of sale or services, focusing especially on courtesy and preparation of the salesforce, cleanliness, waiting time, response time, commercial signage, the state of the equipment in use, adherence to the company's standards and others. The evaluation might go further to making a purchase or enquiry as an actual or potential customer. Moreover, from the report, the company will know if their training is working, or if their staff need different or additional training.

Today, the traditional customer research methodologies (i.e. surveys) used by retailers and other operators are considered primitive as they often provide unreliable and generic results and customer knowledge that is deemed to be outdated. By contrast, mystery shopping is a market research technique providing accurate findings in the short term. Market Force's mystery shoppers provide real-time, consistent and updated knowledge on a specific retailer. This is fundamental in an economy in which customers' tastes, preferences and needs can change quickly. Accordingly, Market Force recommends its mystery shoppers to return their reports as soon as possible after completing each assignment (normally the same day or the day after at the latest). Increasingly, the company uses software (re:view™) enabling clients to access all results in genuine real-time, 24 hours per day, 7 days a week so they can monitor and analyse the latest results as they occur.

Another problem with traditional surveys is that the results are often biased according to the availability and willingness of a certain population. Market Force has tried to overcome this problem by increasing the number of mystery shoppers available for each assignment. The company may choose among more than 250,000 'real' mystery shoppers, whose ages range from 16 to 96 years old, with several interests and hobbies and who represent potential customers to its clients. The quantity and heterogeneity of this sample differentiates Market Force from other research agencies that often employ a small team of professional shoppers to conduct an evaluation of pre-scripted situations. According to Simon Boydell, Marketing Manager for Market Force: 'It is great to see an increased interest into the world of mystery shopping—consumers are becoming aware that not only can they get paid to go shopping, eat out at a restaurant or stay the night in a hotel, but they will be providing valuable feedback to assist retailers in providing a more enjoyable shopping experience for everyone.'

In addition, it is not difficult to become a mystery shopper. Mystery shoppers are generally asked to fill in a form in which they are asked about their socio-demographic data. They may be asked to audit a retailer in different ways, either personally at the business establishment through observation or visits, or impersonally through other media such as Internet, mail/fax or telephone. The completion of the final report requires good observational skills, reliability, accuracy, objectivity, honesty and professionalism. Also, it is

normal practice that any organization using mystery shoppers advise their staff that they will be used periodically to check their service delivery performance.

There are a number of usual stages involved in conducting a piece of mystery shopping research. The first step consists of identifying the clients' target market and qualifying the company's database of mystery customers. Then, suitable candidates are selected from a vast community of shoppers in order to assess the business in a natural setting. Matching the right mystery shopper to the right situation is very critical to provide accurate feedback.

According to Tim Ogle, founder and marketing director of Market Force: 'There is nothing more valuable than understanding how real customers perceive a business.'

Market Force aims to differentiate itself from its competitors by ensuring that its mystery shoppers do not have to simply tick the box of simple questions like: did employees wear a name badge? Did they smile when they took your money? Did they say 'would you like anything else like that'? Rather they are more focused in getting the whole picture by collecting additional qualitative data. In doing so, they aim to provide customers with more detailed feedback.

The company's business activities are based on an online reporting system enabling mystery shoppers registered with the company to easily select tasks and to provide feedback on their mystery shopping experience. Another innovation in the service offered by Market Force comes from the use of a tablet PC instead of paper and pencil to complete compliance-led audits. The introduction of this innovation has helped the company to speed up and secure the audit process; increasingly, mystery shoppers can also integrate digital photography and video as part of the audit process. Videos are useful to reinforce the message and to show more clearly some of the aspects of the service. Thanks to its leading-edge technology, Retail Eyes then provides its clients fast and easy access to information in virtually any format.

The emergence of online reviews

Market Force and other market research companies offering mystery shopping programmes have currently to face the emergence of customers' reviews on the Internet. Online reviews are any positive or negative statement made by potential, actual or former customers about a product or company that is made available via the Internet. They may represent a substitute to mystery shopping reports; therefore, they constitute a real threat to the business. The use of online reviews is constantly growing among customers: for example, TripAdvisor.com enables customers to publish reviews on travel products and services. In

January 2005 this website hosted 1 million reviews and opinions, while today it hosts over 20 million monthly visitors, 15 million registered members and over 30 million reviews and opinions. The growth of this and other websites such as Epinions.com and booking.com suggests that those reviews are widely used and the sources are perceived as reliable and credible among both customers and companies. This has enticed marketers to encourage consumers to post product reviews on retailers' websites. Therefore, retailers can start to analyse the comments and reviews available before conducting a mystery shopping audit or they can encourage customers to directly publish reviews on the company's website or send them by email.

Questions

1. Analyse under which conditions a retailer decides to use a mystery shopping research technique.

2. Identify a set of typical research questions to be answered by a mystery shopper.

3. Discuss the advantages and disadvantages of the mystery shopping technique compared to other market research methods.

4. Discuss the innovations introduced by Market Force in their mystery shopping programmes.

This case was prepared by Dr Raffaele Filieri, Lecturer in Marketing, Newcastle Business School, Northumbria University from published sources as a basis for class discussion rather than to illustrate either effective or ineffective management.

CHAPTER 8

Market segmentation and positioning

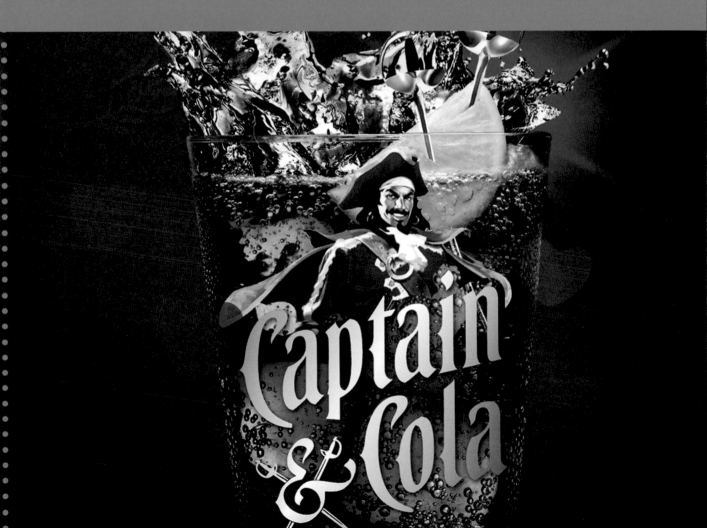

> *Finding the most revealing way to segment a market is more an art than a science. . . . Any useful segmentation scheme will be based around the needs of customers and should be effective in revealing new business opportunities.*
>
> PETER DOYLE, *Value-Based Marketing*

LEARNING OBJECTIVES

After reading this chapter, you should be able to:

1 define the concepts of market segmentation and target marketing, and discuss their use in developing marketing strategy

2 discuss the methods of segmenting consumer and organizational markets

3 identify the factors that can be used to evaluate market segments

4 distinguish between the four target marketing strategies—undifferentiated, differentiated, focused and customized marketing

5 discuss online target markets

6 define the concept of positioning and discuss the keys to successful positioning

7 discuss positioning and repositioning strategies

Few products or services satisfy all customers in a market. Not all customers want or are prepared to pay for the same things. British Airways, KLM and SAS are airlines which recognize different groups of travellers and cater for their needs accordingly. Business and pleasure travellers are different in terms of their price sensitivity and the level of service required. In the watch market the type of person that buys a Swatch fashion watch is different from the type of person who buys an 18-carat gold Rolex: their reasons for purchase are different (fashion vs status) and the type of watch they want is different in terms of appearance and materials. Therefore, to implement the marketing concept and satisfy customer needs, product and service offerings need to be tailored to meet the diverse requirements of different customer groups.

The technique used by marketers to get to grips with the diverse nature of markets is called **market segmentation**. Market segmentation may be defined as 'the identification of individuals or organizations with similar characteristics that have significant implications for the determination of marketing strategy'.

Market segmentation involves dividing a diverse market into a number of smaller, more similar, sub-markets. The objective is to identify groups of customers with similar requirements so that they can be served effectively while being of a sufficient size for the product or service to be supplied efficiently. Usually, in consumer markets, it is not possible to create a marketing mix that satisfies every individual's particular requirements exactly. Market segmentation, by grouping together customers with *similar* needs, provides a commercially viable method of serving these customers and is at the heart of strategic marketing.

For the process of market segmentation and targeting to be implemented successfully all relevant people in the organization should be made aware of the reasons for segmentation and its importance, and be involved in the process as much as is practicable. By gaining involvement, staff will be more committed to the results, leading to better implementation in the later stages.

Why Bother to Segment Markets?

Why go to the trouble of segmenting markets? What are the gains to be made? Figure 8.1 identifies four benefits, which will now be discussed.

Target market selection

Market segmentation provides the basis for the *selection of target markets*. A *target market* is a chosen segment of market that a company has decided to serve. As customers in the target market segment have similar characteristics, a single marketing mix strategy can be developed to match those requirements. Creative segmentation may result in the identification of new segments that have not been served adequately hitherto and may form attractive target markets to attack. For example, Carphone Warehouse, Europe's biggest independent mobile phone retailer,[1] was originally based on the founder Charles Dunstone's realization that a key market segment—self-employed tradesmen, such as builders, plumbers and roofers—was not being catered for. The main suppliers were targeting large corporate clients. His vision was to be the first to allow customers to visit a shop and browse through available mobile

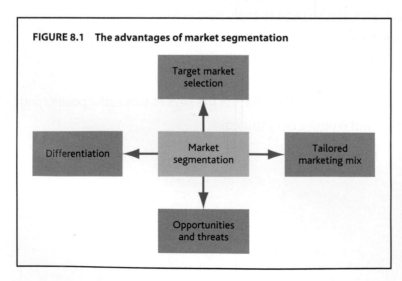

FIGURE 8.1   The advantages of market segmentation

phones. His staff were trained to help customers decide which combination of rental and call charges best met their needs.[2] Later in this chapter we will explore methods of segmenting markets so that new insight may be gained.

Tailored marketing mix

Market segmentation allows the grouping of customers based upon similarities (e.g. benefits sought) that are important when designing marketing strategies. Consequently this allows marketers to understand in-depth the requirements of a segment and *tailor a marketing mix package* that meets their needs. For example, the BMW 3 series saloon car that targets middle managers is a completely different design to the BMW X5 4x4, which is targeted at well-off couples with children. This is a fundamental step in the implementation of the marketing concept: segmentation promotes the notion of customer satisfaction by viewing markets as diverse sets of needs that must be understood and met by suppliers.

Differentiation

Market segmentation allows the development of **differential marketing strategies**. By breaking a market into its constituent sub-segments a company may differentiate its offerings between segments (if it chooses to target more than one segment), and within each segment it can differentiate its offering from the competition. By creating a differential advantage over the competition, a company is giving the customer a reason to buy from it rather than the competition. For example, competition in the smartphone market for business customers is intense. BlackBerry (previously the most successful phone in business markets) has lost ground to the iPhone, with its easy-to-use icon-based user interface, and Samsung Galaxy, which uses the Android platform and offers many high-tech features.[3]

Opportunities and threats

Market segmentation is useful when attempting to spot *opportunities and threats*. Markets are rarely static. As customers become more affluent, seek new experiences and develop new values, new segments emerge. The company that first spots a new and under-served market segment and meets its needs better than the competition can benefit from increasing sales and profit growth. The success of Next, the UK clothing retailer, was founded on identifying a new market segment: working women who wanted smart fashionable clothing at affordable prices. Similarly the neglect of a market segment can pose a threat if competition use it as a gateway to market entry. The Japanese manufacturers exploited British companies' lack of interest in the low-powered motorcycle segment, and the reluctance of US motor car producers to make small cars allowed Japanese companies to swiftly achieve market-wide penetration. The point is that market segments need to be protected from competitors. Otherwise there is a threat that new entrants might establish a foothold and grow market share in the poorly served segment of a market.

The Process of Market Segmentation and Target Marketing

The selection of a target market or markets is a three-step process (see Figure 8.2):

1   *understanding the requirements and characteristics of the individuals and/or organizations* that comprise the market. Marketing research can be used here.
2   *grouping according to these requirements and characteristics into segments* that have implications for developing marketing strategies. Note a market can be segmented in various ways depending on the choice of criteria. For example, the market for cars could be segmented by: type of buyer (individual or organizational), major benefit sought in a car (e.g. functionality or status), family size (empty nester vs family with children). There are no rules about how a market should be segmented. Using a new criterion, or using a combination of well-known criteria in a novel way, may give fresh insights into a market.

FIGURE 8.2   The process of market segmentation and target marketing

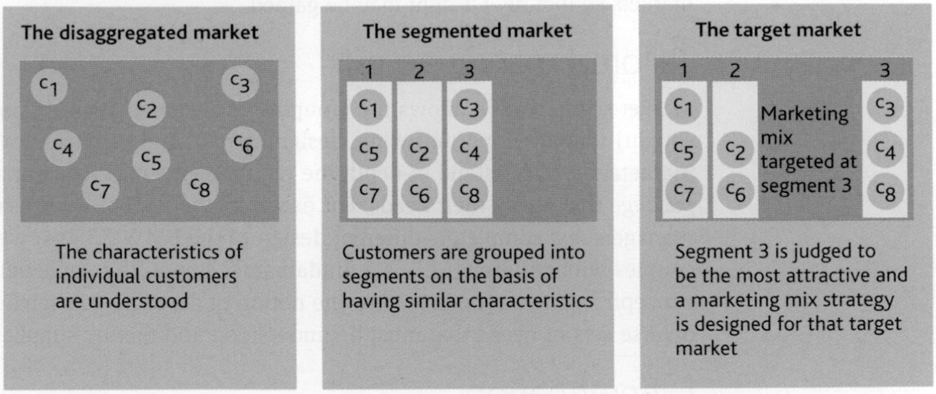

The disaggregated market	The segmented market	The target market
c_1 c_3 c_2 c_4 c_6 c_5 c_7 c_8	1 2 3 c_1 c_3 c_5 c_2 c_4 c_7 c_6 c_8	1 2 3 c_1 Marketing c_3 c_5 c_2 mix c_4 targeted at c_7 c_6 segment 3 c_8
The characteristics of individual customers are understood	Customers are grouped into segments on the basis of having similar characteristics	Segment 3 is judged to be the most attractive and a marketing mix strategy is designed for that target market

For example, Apple was the first to recognize that young consumers not only wanted mobile music, but also access to thousands of songs (via iTunes) that they could download to their mobile music player.

3   *choosing market segment(s) to target.* A marketing mix can then be developed, based on a deep understanding of target-market customers' needs and values. The aim is to design a mix that is distinctive from competitors' offerings. This theme of creating a *differential advantage* will be discussed in more detail when we examine how to position a product in the marketplace.

Segmenting Consumer Markets

Markets can be segmented in many ways. Segmentation variables are the criteria that are used for dividing a market into segments. When examining criteria, the marketer is trying to identify good predictors of differences in buyer behaviour. There is an array of options and no single, prescribed way of segmenting a market.[4] Now let's look at possible ways of segmenting consumer markets before we explore how to segment organizational markets.

There are three broad groups of consumer segmentation criteria: 1) *behavioural*, 2) *psychographic*, and 3) *profile* variables. Since the purpose of segmentation is to identify differences in behaviour that have implications for marketing decisions, *behavioural variables* such as benefits sought from the product and buying patterns may be considered the ultimate bases for segmentation. Psychographic variables are used when researchers believe that purchasing behaviour is correlated with the personality or lifestyle of consumers: consumers with different personalities or lifestyles have varying product or service preferences and may respond differently to marketing mix offerings. Having found these differences, the marketer needs to describe the people who exhibit them, and this is where profile variables such as socio-economic group or geographic location are valuable.[5] For example, a marketer may see whether there are groups of people who value low calories in soft drinks and then attempt to profile them in terms of their age, socio-economic groupings, and so on.

In practice, however, segmentation may not follow this logical sequence. Often, profile variables will be identified first and then the segments so described will be examined to see if they show different behavioural responses. Age or income groups are frequently used as a basis for identifying market segments, and marketing managers examine groups of individuals to see if they show different attitudes and requirements towards particular products and initiatives. For example, Abercrombie & Fitch have found their market to be 25-year-olds with attitude,[6] and in technology markets 18–24-year-olds are much more likely to use QR codes on their phones than 55-year-olds.[7] Figure 8.3 shows the major

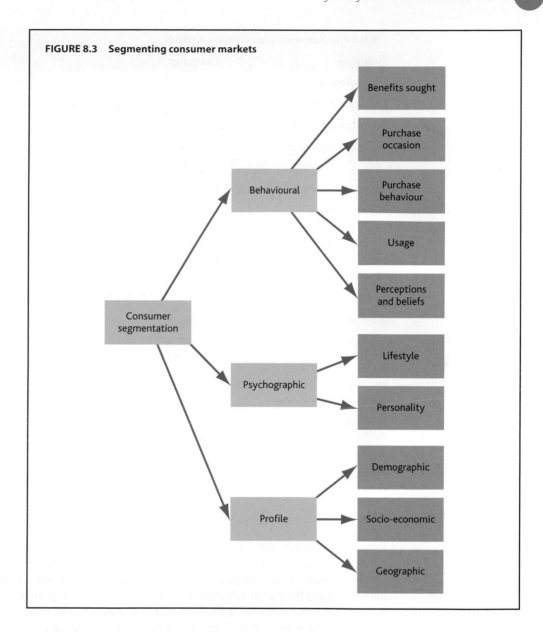

FIGURE 8.3 Segmenting consumer markets

segmentation variables used in consumer markets and Table 8.1 describes each of these variables in greater detail.

Behavioural segmentation

The key behavioural bases for segmenting consumer markets are benefits sought; purchase occasion; purchase behaviour; usage; and perceptions, beliefs and values. Each will now be discussed.

Benefits sought

This segmentation criterion can be applied when the people in a market seek different benefits from a product. For example, the fruit drink market could be segmented by benefits sought. Table 8.2 shows such a breakdown with examples of the brands targeting each segment. **Benefit segmentation** provides an understanding of why people buy in a market and can aid the identification of opportunities. For example, the Lego Group focuses predominantly on toys for boys, with its packs of building bricks designed to assemble helicopters, trains,

TABLE 8.1   Consumer segmentation methods

Variable	Examples
Behavioural	
Benefits sought	Convenience, status, performance, price
Purchase occasion	Self-buy, gift, special occasions, eating occasions
Purchase behaviour	Solus buying, brand switching, innovators
Usage	Heavy, light
Perceptions, beliefs and values	Favourable, unfavourable
Psychographic	
Lifestyle	Trendsetters, conservatives, sophisticates
Personality	Extroverts, introverts, aggressive, submissive
Profile	
Age	Under 12, 12–18, 19–25, 26–35, 36–49, 50–64, 65+
Gender	Female, male
Life-cycle	Young single, young couples, young parents, middle-aged empty nesters, retired
Social class	Upper middle, middle, skilled working, unwaged
Terminal education age	16, 18, 21 years
Income	Income breakdown according to study objectives and income levels per country
Geographic	North vs south, urban vs rural, country
Geodemographic	Upwardly mobile young families living in larger owner-occupied houses; older people living in small houses; European regions based on language, income, age profile and location

rockets and 'warrior-themed' product ranges. Playing with Lego bricks delivers educational benefits—e.g. spatial awareness, mathematical and fine motor skills through play.[8]

On the basis of psychological research across Europe, Sampson has shown how the benefits sought from a car can predict car and motor accessory/consumables buying.[9]

- *Pleasure seekers*: driving is all about pleasure (freedom, enjoyment and well-being).
- *Image seekers*: driving is all about self-image. The car provides feelings of power, prestige, status and self-enhancement. Driving is important too, but secondary.
- *Functionality seekers*: driving is only a means of getting from A to B. They enjoy the convenience afforded by the car rather than the act of driving.

Many markets are segmented on the basis of price sensitivity. Often a market will be characterized by a segment of customers who value the benefit of low price and another that values high quality or service and is prepared to pay more for that benefit. In the grocery market, the UK market leader, Tesco, has developed two product ranges, Tesco Value and Tesco Finest, to cater for both market segments, while Sainsbury's has over 1000 products in its 'Taste the difference' range for premium quality products, which have enabled the supermarket chain to capture market share and drive sales growth[10] (see Ad Insight). Also, in the tyre market, Michelin uses its own brand to target the quality (higher mileage) segment, while marketing its BF Goodrich and Kleber brands to price-sensitive buyers.

TABLE 8.2   Benefit segmentation in the fruit drink market

Benefits sought	Products favoured
Extra energy	Robinson's Barley Water
Vitamins	Ribena
Natural	Pure orange juice
Low calories	'Diet' squash
Low cost	Supermarket own-label

It was the failure of established airlines to cater for the price-sensitive market segment that allowed the so-called 'no-frills' airlines, easyJet and Ryanair, to grow so rapidly.

Intel also used benefit segmentation to define segments in the desktop computer market. It identified three segments of end user: 'basic PC users', who required limited power but were price sensitive; 'mainstream performance seekers', who wanted more power and were prepared to pay more for it; and 'enthusiasts', for whom computing power was vital and who were prepared to pay premium prices for it. Intel developed a range of microprocessors, each with differing price levels to target each of the three segments.[11] In the laptop market it identified two segments: the value segment, which was price sensitive, was served with the Celeron microprocessor; the quality segment, which was much less price sensitive, was targeted with the more expensive Centrino mobile technology brand, which delivered enhanced performance, extended battery life, integrated wireless technology and thinner, lighter designs.[12]

Benefit segmentation is a fundamental method of segmentation because the objective of marketing is to provide customers with benefits they value. Knowing the various benefits people value is therefore a basic prerequisite of understanding markets. Benefit segmentation provides the framework for classifying individuals based upon this knowledge. Profile analyses can then be performed to identify the type of people (e.g. by age, gender, socio-economic grouping) in each benefit segment so that targeting can take place.

Go to the website to find out how Dove uses psychographic variables to promote its beauty products. www.mcgraw-hill.co.uk/textbooks/jobber

Purchase occasion

Customers can be distinguished according to the occasions when they purchase a product. For example, a product (e.g. tyres) or service (e.g. plumbing) may be purchased as a result of an emergency or as a routine unpressurized buy. Price sensitivity, for example, is likely to be much lower in an emergency buying situation. Some products (e.g. mobile phones) may be bought as gifts or as self-purchases. These differing occasions can have implications for marketing mix and targeting decisions. If it is found that the gift market is concentrated at Christmas, advertising budgets will be concentrated in the pre-Christmas period. Package design may differ for the gift vs personal-buy segment also. Many brands of chocolates are targeted at the gift segment of the confectionery market, e.g. Thorntons (UK), Bonnat (France), Ritter Sport (Germany).

Segmentation by purchase occasion is also relevant in the grocery market. Tesco, the UK's leading supermarket, has provided three store formats according to the occasions when consumers purchase groceries. For the weekly shop there are Tesco Superstores offering a wide range of food (and non-food) items; and for convenience purchases, a more restricted range of food products is offered by Tesco Metro shops in central urban locations and Tesco Express shops next to petrol stations.

Often special occasions such as Easter and Christmas are associated with higher prices. For example, the prices of chocolate Easter eggs fall dramatically after Easter Sunday. Also marketers have to be aware that the price of a gift can be too low to make it acceptable as a present. Gift occasions, then, pose very interesting marketing problems and opportunities. Eating occasions also provide targeting opportunities. For example, McDonald's and other fast-food outlets offer breakfast meals in addition to their normal lunchtime and evening food.

Purchase behaviour

Differences in purchase behaviour can be based on the time of purchase relative to the launch of the product or on patterns of purchase. When a new product is launched, a key task is to identify the innovator segment of the market. These people (or organizations) may have distinct characteristics that allow communication to be targeted specifically at them (e.g. young, middle class). Innovators are more likely to be willing to buy the product soon after launch. Other segments of the market may need more time to assess the benefits, and delay purchase until after the innovators have taken the early risks of purchase. Only when the credential had been established among these 'innovators' is the brand moved to a wider target audience. For example, the number of electric cars is still relatively low and prices are typically high and as yet this type of car still has to appeal to a wide audience.

The degree of *brand loyalty* in a market may also be a useful basis for segmenting customers. Solus buyers are totally brand loyal, buying only one brand in the product group, such as a person who buys only Ariel washing powder. Most customers brand-switch; some may have a tendency to buy Ariel but also buy two or three other brands (e.g. Persil, Fairy); others might show no loyalty to any individual brand but switch brands on the basis of special offers (e.g. money-off) or because they are variety seekers who look to buy a different brand each time. By profiling the characteristics of each group, a company can target each segment accordingly. By knowing the type of person (e.g. by age, socio-economic group, media habits) who is brand loyal, a company can channel persuasive communications to defend this segment. By knowing the characteristics and shopping habits of the offer seekers, sales promotions can be targeted correctly.

In the consumer durables market, brand loyalty can be used as a segment variable to good purpose. For example, Volkswagen has divided its customers into first-time buyers, replacement buyers (model-loyal replacers and company-loyal replacers) and switch replacers. These segments are used to measure performance and market trends, and for forecasting purposes.[13]

A recent trend in consumer services sectors has been towards biographics. This is the linking of actual purchase behaviour to individuals. The growth in retailer loyalty schemes has provided a mechanism for gathering behavioural data. Customers are given cards that are swiped through an electronic machine at the checkout so that points can be accumulated towards discounts and vouchers. The more loyal the shopper, the higher the number of points gained. The retailer benefits by knowing the purchasing behaviour of named individuals. Such biographic data can be used to segment and target customers very precisely. For example, it would be easy to identify a group of customers that are 'ground coffee' purchasers and target them through direct marketing initiatives. Analysis of such data allows retailers to stock products in each of their stores that are most relevant to their customers' age, lifestyle and expenditure. Examples of loyalty schemes include Tesco Club Card, Boots Advantage Card, Costa Coffee's Coffee Club Card.

Usage

Customers can also be segmented on the basis of heavy users, light users and non-users of a product category. The profiling of heavy users allows this group to receive most marketing attention (particularly promotion efforts) on the assumption that creating brand loyalty among these people will pay heavy dividends. Sometimes the 80:20 rule applies, where about 80 per cent of a product's sales come from 20 per cent of its customers. Beer is a market where this rule often applies.[14] However, information technology has increased access to and knowledge of niche markets and the 'long tail' is a term used to reflect the increase in interest in niche products[15] by marketers. Brands are increasingly developed to target niche market segments. For example, as populations are aging there is more demand of specialist healthcare products and Ford is adding healthcare technology to its cars so it can access niche segments—i.e. the electrocardiogram (ECG) seat that measures the heart rate of the driver automatically.[16] Microsoft's Xbox Kinect gaming device is used by surgeons as a means of streamlining communications while performing operations. Marketing managers need to be aware that selecting heavy-user segments can deliver benefits in terms of volume of potential sales, but analysing the light-user segments can provide insights that can deliver advantages over the competition. Target Group Index Europa is a good source of consumer product usage and provides actionable marketing information on adults 15+.[17]

Segmenting by *use* highlights an important issue in market segmentation. Individuals' may buy product offerings that appear to appeal to different people in the market.[18] For example, the same person may buy shredded wheat and cornflakes, cheap wine and chateau-bottled wine, and an economy-class and a business-class air ticket. Critics argue that markets are not made up of segments with different requirements because buyers of one brand buy other brands as well. However, the fact that an individual may purchase two completely different product offerings does not in itself imply the absence of meaningful segments.[19] The purchases may reflect different use occasions, purchases for different family members or for variety. For example, the purchase of shredded wheat and cornflakes may reflect variety-seeking behaviour or purchases for different family members. Cheap wine may be bought to accompany a regular family meal whereas the chateau-bottled wine for a special dinner party. Finally, someone may purchase an economy-class air ticket when going on holiday and a business-class ticket when on a business trip. Both the wine and air-ticket examples reflect purchasing behaviour that is dependent on use occasion.

The key issue to remember is that market segmentation concerns the grouping of individuals or organizations with similar characteristics that have implications for the determination of marketing strategy. The fact that an individual may have differing requirements at different points in time (e.g. use occasions) does not mean that segmentation is not warranted. For example, it is still worthwhile targeting business people through the media they read to sell business-class tickets, and charging a higher price, and the leisure traveller through different media with a lower price to sell economy flights. The fact that there will be some overlap on an individual basis does not deny the sense in formulating a different marketing strategy for each of the two segments.

Perceptions, attitudes, beliefs and values

The final behavioural base for segmenting consumer markets is by studying perceptions, attitudes, beliefs and values. This is classified as a behaviour variable because perceptions, attitudes, beliefs and values are often strongly linked to behaviour. Consumers are grouped by identifying those people who view the products in a market in a similar way (perceptual segmentation) and have similar beliefs (belief segmentation). These kinds of segmentation analyses provide an understanding of how groups of customers view the marketplace. To the extent that their perceptions and beliefs are different, opportunities to target specific groups more effectively may arise.

Attitudes towards products and services can prove fruitful as a basis for segmenting a market. Research in the UK found that 71 per cent of the population said they were middle class but this very large section of the population represented a wide spectrum of incomes, wealth and attitudes. Six distinct *tribes* were identified (see Table 8.3) which shows how tribal variations produce different attitudes towards brand preferences.

Car manufacturers use belief segmentation to segment the market and target specific groups. For example, Toyota aimed to attract a new generation of car buyers in Europe with

TABLE 8.3   Middle-class tribes

Tribe name	Income (average household)	Brand preferences Like	Brand preferences Dislike	Proportion of the populations
Squeezed strugglers	£29, 556	Gillette, ITV	National Trust Sainsbury's	2.7 million adults (6% of population)
Bargain hunters	£33, 241	eBay, Muller	John Lewis Sainsbury's	8.1 million adults (17% of population)
Daily Mail disciplinarians	£36, 305	British Airways	L'Oréal Channel 4	7 million adults (15% of populations)
Comfortable greens	£36, 428	Fair Trade Green & Black's	Asda, Coca-Cola	6 million adults (13% of populations)
Deserving downtimers	£46, 897	John Lewis Channel 4	easy Jet, Coca-Cola	3.8 million adults (8% of populations)
Urban networkers	£41, 485	Apple, Pizza Express	None: this tribe are pro all brands	5.9 million adults (12% of populations)

Based on Chorley and Rentoul (2011).[20]

its Yaris model. In targeting 20–30-year-olds, Toyota used direct marketing to persuade this group that these cars are fun, entertaining and enjoyable to own. The new models have added attributes such as touch-screen, multimedia systems and other gadgets to attract the attention of the target group.[21]

Values-based segmentation is based on the principles and standards that people use to judge what is important in life. Values are relatively consistent and underpin behaviour. Values form the basis of attitudes and lifestyles, which in turn manifest as behaviour. Marketers have recognized the importance of identifying the values that trigger purchase for many years, but now it is possible to link value groups to profiling systems that make targeting feasible (see the section below on 'Combining segmentation variables').

Psychographic segmentation

Psychographic segmentation involves grouping people according to their lifestyle and personality characteristics.

Lifestyle

This form of segmentation attempts to group people according to their way of living, as reflected in their activities, interests and opinions. As we saw in Chapter 4, marketing researchers attempt to identify groups of people with similar patterns of living. The question that arises with lifestyle segmentation is the extent to which general lifestyle patterns are predictive of purchasing behaviour in specific markets.[22] Nevertheless, **lifestyle segmentation** has proved popular among advertising agencies, which have attempted to relate brands (e.g. Hugo Boss) to a particular lifestyle (e.g. aspirational). In television, Sky has used lifestyle segmentation to target special interest groups including sports enthusiasts (Sky Sports), film lovers (Sky Movies) and news followers (Sky News).

Personality

The idea that brand choice may be related to personality is intuitively appealing. However, the usefulness of personality as a segmentation variable is likely to depend on the product category. Buyer and brand personalities are likely to match where brand choice is a direct manifestation of personal values but for most fast-moving consumer goods (e.g. detergents, tea, cereals), the reality is that people buy a repertoire of brands.[23] Personality (and lifestyle) segmentation is more likely to work when brand choice is a reflection of self-expression; the brand becomes a *badge* that makes public an aspect of personality: 'I choose this brand to say this about me and this is how I would like you to see me.' It is not surprising, then, that successful personality segmentation has been found in the areas of cosmetics, alcoholic drinks and cigarettes.[24]

Profile segmentation

Profile segmentation variables allow consumer groups to be classified in such a way that they can be reached by the communications media (e.g. advertising, direct mail). Even if behaviour and/or psychographic segmentation have successfully distinguished between buyer preferences, there is often a need to analyse the resulting segments in terms of profile variables such as age and socio-economic group to communicate to them. The reason is that readership and viewership profiles of newspapers, magazines and television programmes tend to be expressed in that way.

We shall now examine a number of demographic, socio-economic and geographic segmentation variables.

Demographic variables

The demographic variables we shall look at are age, gender and life-cycle.

- *Age* has been used to segment many consumer markets.[25] For example, children receive their own television programmes; cereals, computer games and confectionery are other examples of markets where products are formulated with children in mind. The sweeter tooth of children is reflected in sugared cereal brands targeted at children (e.g. Kellogg's Frosties). L'Oréal targets the over-50s with its Age Perfect and Revitalift brands while Vodafone targets 35–55-year-olds with an easy-to-use, no-frills mobile phone that offers the uncomplicated functionality that many in this segment group value.[26]

Age is not only widely used for segmenting product markets but is also used as a segmentation variable in services. The holiday market is heavily age segmented with offerings targeted at the under-30s and the over-60s segments, for example. This reflects the differing requirements of these age groups when on holiday.

Mini Case 8.1 explores some the issues associated with using age as a segmentation variable.

Despite the latest challenges raised by using age as a segmentation variable many companies covet the youth segment, who are major purchasers of items such as clothing, consumer electronics, drinks, personal care products and magazines. One popular way to communicate with these segments is through digital media communications. Digital Marketing 8.1 explores some of the issues relating to understanding this key market segment.

- *Gender* also offers much for the marketing manager planning their segmentation strategy. Differing tastes and customs between men and women are reflected in specialist products aimed at these market segments. Magazines, clothing, hairdressing and cosmetics are product categories that have used segmentation based on gender.

- The classic family *life-cycle* stages were described in Chapter 4. To briefly recap: disposable income and purchase requirements may vary according to life-cycle stage (e.g. young single vs married with two children). Consumer durable purchases may be dependent on life-cycle stage, with young couples without children being a prime target market for furnishings and appliances as they set up home. The use of life-cycle analysis may give better precision than age in segmenting markets because family responsibilities and the presence of children may have a greater bearing than age on what people buy. The consumption pattern of a single 28-year-old is likely to be very different from that of a married 28-year-old with three children. Car manufacturers use life-cycle variables to inform then determine the benefits that drivers are looking for: e.g. small family cars, family cars. In 2011 *What Car?*, Britain's car buyers guide, rated Volkswagen Golf 1.4 Match 5-door as the best small family car, while Ford Mondeo 2.0 Zetec won the best family car. But manufacturers also consider other variables like carbon emissions and high performance, which also enables them to access particular segments.

Go to the website to compare how car manufacturers highlight different benefits depending on the target segment of each car.
www.mcgraw-hill.co.uk/textbooks/jobber

Based upon population census data, 'People UK' is arranged in eight life stages—starting out, young with toddlers, young families, singles/couples/no kids, middle-aged families, empty nesters, retired couples, and older singles. Produced by CACI, the system is particularly useful for targeted mailing because it can be applied to everyone on the UK electoral roll. People are classified according to the neighbourhood in which they live.[27] The methodology is described a little later in this section, when we discuss the ACORN geodemographic system.

Socio-economic variables

Socio-economic variables include social class, terminal education age and income. Here we shall look at social class as a predictor of buyer behaviour. *Social class* is measured in varying ways across Europe: in the UK occupation is used,

⬆ EXHIBIT 8.1   'Old Ladies Rebellion', created by Fanny Karst for women over 60.[28]

Mini Case 8.1 Age

Personality-based profiles and ageist stereotyping are becoming less effective as a segmentation strategy as boundaries between segments blur and attitudes morph. For example, a rebellious person who is a keen media consumer and interested in the latest innovations could be a teenager, but these days this description more aptly fits the 'baby boomer'. Interestingly, baby boomers (born between 1946 and 1964) are the *original* teenagers and are as equally likely to use Skype as their 15–24-year-old counterparts; they feel more up-to-date than today's youngsters and very eager to use new communication technology. However, the boomers are often missed by marketers who prefer to use age to discriminate and so target the 18–34 market segment.

Perhaps it is not surprising that marketers are getting it wrong when using age as a segmentation variable. In Europe young people seem to be different ages up to a point where they become 'old people', but even this distinction lacks precision. In the UK you are an old person at 59; youth ends at 35 and middle age spans the 24 years in between. In Greece youth does not end until you are 52 and old age does not start until you reach 67, leaving just 15 years to be middle-aged. Moreover, stereotype groupings of old and young have often been defined using measures of competence with the 'old' regularly being placed in the low competence group.

However, wherever the lines are drawn between young and old, marketers need to take care not to alienate the 'old people' as they account for a rapidly growing and increasingly wealthy market segment. Furthermore, analysis suggests that the median age in Europe will increase from 37 to 52 by 2050 and in Britain the government is increasing the minimum retirement age (by 2046 it could be 68), so the trend is set to continue and grow in the future.

Marketers need to be aware that attitudes and preferences change as we age: for example, the desire for sweet tastes dwindles and is replaced by a preference for dryer, sharper and more sophisticated flavours, while responsibilities tend to increase with age as marriage, children and property ownership come along. Some new and existing brands are taking advantage of the potential opportunities afforded by targeting the 'old people'. Old Ladies Rebellion is a new fashion label created by Fanny Karst for over-60 women, and existing companies from Marks & Spencer to Avia Motor Insurance specifically aim to develop their customer base amongst the 50 somethings.

How to communicate with the 'old people' is another consideration. New media are proving to be effective in communicating with this market segment: for example, women over 55 are the fastest-growing user segment on Facebook and they are the most unlikely to reply to direct mailing. More consumers (of all ages) are turning to the Web to find pre-purchase information and compare what is offer online before taking a decision where and from whom to buy.

The reality is that the world is changing rapidly, and using stereotypes and easily accessible demographic variables such as age is likely to prove ineffective as consumers grow older. A possible solution is to take a more rounded view by seeking to identify how customers interact with brands and examining the different channels through which they connect with a brand.

Questions:

1   Think of a segmentation classification for the 'old people', which would enable you to access this target group more precisely.
2   Discuss the implications for the life-cycle stage model discussed in Chapter 4.
3   Make a list of the brands which might profitably target the 'old people'.

Based on Edwards (2011);[29] *Handley (2011);*[30] *Hilpern (2011)*[31]

whereas in other European centres a combination of variables is used. Like the demographic variables discussed earlier, social class is relatively easy to measure, and is used for creating media readership and viewership profiles. However, as shown in Table 8.1, social class can be multi-layered and consequently may be more difficult to identify. Furthermore, many people who hold similar occupations have very dissimilar lifestyles, values and purchasing patterns. Nevertheless, social class has proved useful in discriminating between owning a dishwasher, having central heating, and privatization share ownership, for example, and therefore should not be discounted as a segmentation variable.[32]

Digital Marketing 8.1   Understanding Generation 'C'

Every few years marketers identify an upcoming generation to target: for example, Generation X, Y, @ and even a group called *Digital Natives*. The up-and-coming group of interest to marketers is Generation C, where 'C' stands for 'Content'.

To target Generation C there is no point in using age as a segmentation variable as with the previous examples. Generation C is the group of customers who, rather than being consumers of content, are in fact the creators of content or *prosumers* as they have been called.

Highly sophisticated digital devices enable consumers to produce content—for example, high resolution stills, videos, audio tracks, music and much more. Furthermore, individuals of all ages and backgrounds are creating such content. This content can then be disseminated via platforms such as YouTube and Vimeo (video platform); Audioboo and SoundCloud (audio platform); and Pintrest (photograph platform). Spreading content on a global scale has never been easier. Indeed, YouTube estimated an hour of video content was added to their servers every minute from sources across the planet. Admittedly, the vast proportion of this content might be trivial and remain unnoticed, but marketers realize that some content created by private individuals is a more compelling proposition than high-budget communication messages made by professionals.

From the marketer's perspective, there is increasing interest in engaging customers in the creation of website and social media content. There are potential commercial advantages as consumer-generated content reveals hidden preferences, which traditional consumers would not share usually with marketers. For example, the rise in popularity of 'unboxing', where a person films the unwrapping and initial operation of a new purchase (invariably a newly released piece of technology) shows how important content made by users is in the process of selling. This also gives the seller great insight into what the buyer finds difficult and what they enjoy about a particular product. Increasingly marketers are engaging consumers in the product development process, working together to produce finely tuned market offerings.

Based on: Kimmel (2010)[33]

http://trendwatching.com/trends/GENERATION_C.htm
http://www.independent.co.uk/life-style/gadgets-and-tech/features/unboxing-the-new-geek-porn-1333955.html

Geographic variables

The final set of segmentation variables is based on geographic differences. A marketer can use pure geographic segmentation or a hybrid of geographic and demographic variables called *geodemographics*.

The *geographic* segmentation method is useful where there are geographic locational differences in consumption patterns and preferences. For example, variations in food preferences may form the basis of geographic segments: France, Spain and Italy are oil-based cooking markets, while Germany and the UK are margarine and butter orientated.[34] Differences in national advertising expectations may also form geographic segments for communicational purposes. Germans expect a great deal of factual information in their advertisements, to an extent that would bore French or British audiences. France, with its more relaxed attitude to nudity, broadcasts commercials that would be banned in the UK. In the highly competitive Asian car market both Honda and Toyota have launched their first 'Asia-specific' cars, designed and marketed solely for Asian consumers, but they face emerging competitors—for example, Tata Motors in India, a company manufacturing cars specifically for the home market (e.g. Nano, a small, affordable, reliable car[35] for Indian families).

Geodemographic: in countries that produce population census data the potential for classifying consumers on the combined basis of location and certain demographic (and socio-economic) information exists. Households are classified into groups according to a wide range of factors, depending on what is asked for on census returns. In the UK variables such as age, social status, family size, ethnic background, joint income, type of housing and car ownership are used to group small geographic areas (known as *enumeration districts*) into segments that share similar characteristics. The two best-known geodemographic systems in the UK are ACORN and MOSAIC. Both use census data (and in MOSAIC's case Experian's consumer segmentation database) and classify postcodes (15 addresses) into one of their categories so that households can be targeted by direct mail.

ACORN segments households into five categories: wealthy achievers, urban prosperity, comfortably off, moderate means and hard pressed. Each is subdivided into types. For example, 'wealthy achievers' are broken down into wealthy executives, affluent greys and flourishing families.

MOSAIC groups households into 11 categories: symbols of success, happy families, suburban comfort, ties of community, urban intelligence, welfare borderline, municipal dependency, blue-collar enterprise, twilight subsistence, grey perspectives and rural isolation. Like ACORN, MOSAIC subdivides each category into types. For example, 'symbols of success' are broken down into global connections, cultural leadership, corporate chieftains, golden empty nesters, provincial privilege, high technologists and semi-rural seclusion.

On an international level, MOSAIC Global is available in 18 countries, including most of western Europe. Based on the assumption that the world's cities share common patterns of residential segregation, it uses 14 distinct types of residential neighbourhood, each with a characteristic set of values, motivations and consumer preferences.[36]

Such information has been used to select recipients of direct mail campaigns, to identify the best locations for stores and to find the best poster sites. This is possible because consumers in each group can be identified by means of their postcodes. Another area where census data are employed is in buying advertising spots on television. Agencies depend upon information from viewership panels, which record their viewing habits so that advertisers have an insight into who watches what. Census analyses are combined with viewership data via the postcodes of panellists.[37] This means that advertisers who wish to reach a particular geodemographic group can discover the type of programme they prefer to watch and buy television spots accordingly.

A major strength of geodemographics is to link buyer behaviour to customer groups. Buying habits can be determined by large-scale syndicated surveys (for example, TGI and MORI Financial Services) or from panel data (for example, the grocery and toiletries markets are covered by TNS Superpanel). By 'geocoding' respondents, those ACORN groups most likely to purchase a product or brand can be determined. This can be useful for branch location since many service providers use a country-wide branch network and need to match the market segments to which they most appeal to the type of customer in their catchment area. Merchandise mix decisions of retailers can also be affected by customer profile data. Media selections can be made more precise by linking buying habits to geodemographic data.[38]

Combining segmentation variables

We have seen that there is a wide range of variables that can be used to segment consumer markets. Often a combination of variables will be used to identify groups of consumers that respond in the same way to marketing mix strategies.

Research companies are also combining lifestyle and values-based segmentation schemes with geodemographic data. For example, CACI's Census Lifestyle system classifies segments using lifestyle and geodemographic data. Also, CCN has produced Consumer Surveys, which combines social value groups with geodemographic data. In both cases the link to geodemographic data, which contain household address information, means that targeting of people with similar lifestyles or values is feasible. Flexibility and creativity are the hallmarks of effective segmentation analyses but marketing managers must also be prepared for segmenting online markets. See Read the Research 8.1.

Influences of digital technology on segmentation variables[39]

According to research,[40] online consumer markets can be identified by considering demographic variables and behavioural and psychographic variables, which have implications for segmentation. While there is a similarity between categories of variables on- and offline, each group of variables has different characteristics in the virtual world. For

Read the Research 8.1 Online Segments

This practitioner article looks at the ways in which segmentation has now become generally accepted within the telecommunications industry. The central question has moved on from whether segmentation should be done at all, to what is the right sort of segmentation for a particular business.

The article concludes that advanced use of segmentation allows each customer to be part of a micro-segment, which allows for precise targeting, with knowledge of what the retention and value drivers are for each customer.

Judy Bayer (2010) Customer segmentation in the telecommunications industry, Journal of Database Marketing & Customer Strategy Management *17, 247–56.*

The widespread growth of e-commerce has provided retailers with a powerful marketing channel. This can reach consumers on a global scale and is technology enabled. However, consumers are less able to directly assess product characteristics because they can't feel, touch, inspect, or sample.

This results in a diminished capacity to judge a product's quality prior to purchase. By looking at the extrinsic cues given out by websites, does the website quality affect consumers' perceptions of product quality? Find out by reading this article.

John D. Wells, Joseph S. Valacich, Traci J. Hess (2011) What signal are you sending? How website quality influences perceptions of quality and purchase intensions, MIS Quarterly *35(2), 373–96.*

example, research suggests that in terms of their personal profiles—age, gender, education, salary, etc.—Internet shoppers are likely to be similar to their offline counterparts.[41] However, it is still possible to distinguish the most enthusiastic and profitable Internet shoppers on the basis of their perceptions, beliefs and behaviours. For example, it has recently been found that the Internet is a favourite channel for the compulsive shopper, as consumers are able to 'buy unobserved', 'without contact with other shoppers', and in so doing, 'experience strong positive feelings during the purchase episode'.

Furthermore, the demographic variables which have significant implication for online targeting are those found to remain static throughout an individual's lifetime, or to evolve slowly over time—such as education, race, age,[42] gender[43] and lifestyle.[44]

Important psychographic and behavioural variables are those which shape the consumer's perceptions, beliefs and attitudes that might influence their online behaviour, and in particular their intention to shop or engage with an online offer. Online behavioural characteristics—such as knowledge, attitude, innovativeness and risk aversion—have been found to have significant implications when segmenting online markets and when considering a consumer's likelihood to shop online. For example, it has been found that consumers who are primarily motivated by convenience were more likely to make purchases online, while those who value physical social interactions were found to be less interested.[45,46] Moreover, a study of Internet shoppers from six countries (developing and developed) found a surprisingly high degree of homogeneity in their characteristics and habits.[47] It concluded that Internet shoppers share 'their desire for convenience, are more impulsive, have more favourable attitudes towards direct marketing and advertising, are wealthier, and are heavier users of both email and the Internet'.

Now examine Read the Research 8.1 and discover more about other factors which are likely to influence the potential consumers' perceptions, and confidence, online.

Segmenting Organizational Markets

While the consumer goods marketer is interested in grouping individuals into marketing-relevant segments, the business-to-business marketer profiles organizations and organizational buyers. The organizational market can be segmented on several factors broadly classified into two major categories: macrosegmentation and microsegmentation.[48]

Macrosegmentation focuses on the characteristics of the buying organization, such as size, industry and geographic location. **Microsegmentation** requires a more detailed level of market knowledge as it concerns the characteristics of decision-making within each macrosegment, based on such factors as choice criteria, decision-making unit structure, decision-making process, buy class, purchasing organization and organizational innovativeness. Often organizational markets are first grouped on a macrosegment basis and then finer sub-segments are identified through microsegmentation.[49]

Figure 8.4 shows how this two-stage process works. The choice of the appropriate macrosegmentation and microsegmentation criteria is based on the marketer's evaluation of which criteria are most useful in predicting buyer behaviour differences that have implications for developing marketing strategies. Figure 8.5 shows the criteria that can be used.

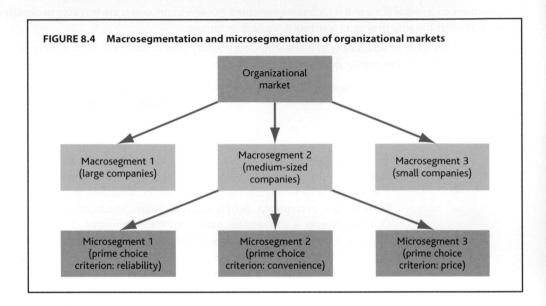

FIGURE 8.4 **Macrosegmentation and microsegmentation of organizational markets**

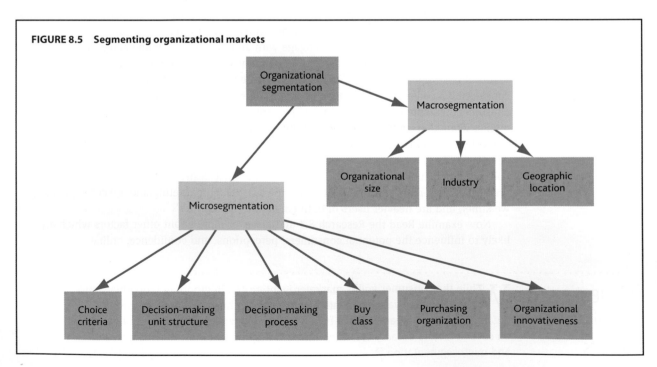

FIGURE 8.5 **Segmenting organizational markets**

Macrosegmentation

The key macrosegmentation criteria of organizational size, industry and geographic location will now be discussed.

Organizational size

The size of buying organizations may be used to segment markets. Large organizations differ from medium-sized and small organizations in having greater order potential, more formalized buying and management processes, increased specialization of function, and special needs (e.g. quantity discounts). The result is that they may form important target market segments and require tailored marketing mix strategies. For example, the salesforce may need to be organized on a key account basis, where a dedicated sales team is used to service important industrial accounts. List pricing of products and services may need to take into account the inevitable demand for volume discounts from large purchasers, and the salesforce team will need to be well versed in the art of negotiation.

Industry

Another common macrosegmentation variable is industry sector. Different industries may have unique requirements from products. For example, software application suppliers like Oracle and SAP can market their products to various sectors such as banking, manufacturing, healthcare and education, each of which has unique needs in terms of software programs, servicing, price and purchasing practice. By understanding each industry's needs in depth, a more effective marketing mix can be designed. In some instances further segmentation may be required. For example, the education sector may be further divided into primary, secondary and further education as their product and service requirements may differ.

Geographic location

Regional variations in purchasing practice and needs may imply the use of geographic location as a basis for differentiating marketing strategies. The purchasing practices and expectations of companies in central and eastern Europe are likely to differ markedly from those in western Europe. Their more bureaucratic structures may imply a fundamentally different approach to doing business that needs to be recognized by companies attempting to enter these emerging industrial markets. In Chapter 3 we saw how different cultural factors affect the purchasing practices in European countries. These differences, in effect, imply regional segments since marketing needs to reflect these variations.

Microsegmentation

Marketers may find it useful to divide each macrosegment into smaller microsegments on the basis of the buyer's choice criteria, decision-making unit structure, decision-making process, buy class, purchasing organization, and organizational innovativeness.

Choice criteria

This factor segments the organizational market on the basis of the key choice criteria used by buyers when evaluating supplier offering. One group of customers may rate price as the key choice criterion, another segment may favour productivity, while a third segment may be service orientated. These varying preferences mean that marketing and sales strategies need to be adapted to cater for each segment's needs. Three different marketing mixes would be needed to cover the three segments, and salespeople would have to stress different benefits when talking to customers in each segment. Variations in key choice criteria can be powerful predictors of buyer behaviour. For example, Moriarty found differences in choice criteria in the computer market.[50] One segment used software support and breadth of product line as key criteria and bought IBM equipment. Another segment was more concerned with price and the willingness of suppliers to negotiate lower prices; these buyers favoured non-IBM

THE RIGHT TIRE CHANGES EVERYTHING

Michelin makes some of the most fuel efficient,* longest lasting tires. Plus they offer more security with their incredible stopping power. See how the right tire changes everything at **michelinman.com/righttire**.

*Based on comparative rolling resistance testing. Copyright ©2009 Michelin North America, Inc. All rights reserved. The Michelin Man is a registered trademark owned by Michelin North America, Inc.

MICHELIN
A better way forward

⬆ **EXHIBIT 8.2   This advert explains how Michelin tyres offer better economic value and safety than its rivals.**

machines. An important choice criterion for business customers is economic value to the customer, which takes into account not only price, but also other costs. The advertisement for Michelin HydroEdge Green X tyres targets business people, explaining that when longevity and fuel efficiency are taken into account, Michelin tyres are better value than the competition.

Decision-making unit structure

Another way of segmenting organizational markets is based on decision-making unit (DMU) composition: members of the DMU and its size may vary between buying organizations. As discussed in Chapter 5, the DMU consists of all those people in a buying organization who have an effect on supplier choice. One segment might be characterized by the influence of top management on the decision; another by the role played by engineers; and a third segment might comprise organizations where the purchasing manager plays the key role. DMU size can also vary considerably: one segment might feature large, complex units, while another might comprise single-member DMUs.

Decision-making process

As we saw in Chapter 5, the decision-making process can take a long time or be relatively short in duration. The length of time is often correlated with DMU composition. Long processes are associated with large DMUs. Where the decision time is long, high levels of marketing expenditure may be needed, with considerable effort placed on personal selling. Much less effort is needed when the buy process is relatively short and where, perhaps, only the purchasing manager is involved.

Buy class

Organizational purchases can be categorized into straight rebuy, modified rebuy and new task. As we discussed in Chapter 4, the buy class affects the length of the decision-making process, the complexity of the DMU and the number of choice criteria that are used in supplier selection. It can therefore be used as a predictor of different forms of buyer behaviour, and hence is useful as a segmentation variable.

Purchasing organization

Decentralized versus centralized purchasing is another microsegmentation variable because of its influence on the purchase decision.[51] Centralized purchasing is associated with purchasing specialists who become experts in buying a range of products. Specialization means that they become more familiar with cost factors, and the strengths and weaknesses of suppliers, than decentralized generalists. Furthermore, the opportunity for volume buying means that their power base to demand price concessions from suppliers is enhanced. They have also been found to have greater power within the DMU vis-à-vis technical people, like engineers, than decentralized buyers, who often lack the specialist expertise and status to challenge their preferences. For these reasons, the purchasing organization provides a good base for distinguishing between buyer behaviour and can have implications for marketing activities. For example, the centralized purchasing segment could be served by a national account salesforce, whereas the decentralized purchasing segment might be covered by territory representatives.

Organizational innovativeness

A key segmentation variable when launching new products is the degree of innovativeness of potential buyers. In Chapter 10 we will discuss some general characteristics of innovator firms but marketers need to identify the specific characteristics of the innovator segment since these are the companies that should be targeted first when new products are launched. Follower firms may be willing to buy the product but only after the innovators have approved it. Although categorized here as a microsegmentation variable it should be borne in mind that organizational size (a macrosegmentation variable) may be a predictor of innovativeness too.

Table 8.4 summarizes the methods of segmenting organizational markets, and provides examples of how each variable can be used to form segments.

TABLE 8.4 Organizational segmentation methods	
Variable	**Examples**
Macrosegmentation	
Organizational size	Large, medium, small
Industry	Engineering, textiles, banking
Geographic location	Local, national, European, global
Microsegmentation	
Choice criteria	Economic value, delivery, price, service
Decision-making unit structure	Complex, simple
Decision-making process	Long, short
Buy class	Straight rebuy, modified rebuy, new task
Purchasing organization	Centralized, decentralized
Organizational innovativeness	Innovator, follower, laggard

Target Marketing

Market segmentation is a means to an end: *target marketing*. This is the choice of specific segments to serve and is a key element in marketing strategy. A firm needs to evaluate the segments and decide which ones to serve. For example, CNN targets its news programmes to what are known as 'influentials'. This is why CNN has, globally, focused so much of its distribution effort into gaining access to hotel rooms. Business people know that wherever they are in the world they can see international news on CNN in their hotel. Eurosport uses a similar targeting approach and provides plenty of coverage of upmarket sports such as golf and tennis for viewers in Europe. In high-tech markets Apple's introduction of the iPad enabled the company to gain a stronghold in corporate markets for its multi-touch devices. When Coca-Cola targeted consumer markets in China it[52] gave its soft drinks brand a makeover, including a new name (see Exhibit 8.3) and a strap-line which, when translated from Mandarin, becomes 'delicious happiness'. Entering markets can be costly, especially when products need to be altered, so it is important to take care in selecting those target markets that will meet marketing objectives. Accordingly, first we examine how to evaluate potential market segments, and then consider how to make a balanced choice about which markets to serve.

Evaluating market segments

When evaluating market segments, a company should examine two broad issues: market attractiveness and the company's capability to compete in the segment. Market attractiveness can be assessed by looking at market factors, competitive factors, and political, social and

↑EXHIBIT 8.3   Coca-Cola targeted consumer markets in China with a new image and strap-line.

environmental factors.[53] Figures 8.6 and 8.7 illustrate the factors that need to be examined when evaluating market segments.

Market factors

Segment size: generally, large-sized segments are more attractive than small ones since sales potential is greater, and the chance of achieving economies of scale is improved. However, large segments are often highly competitive since other companies are realizing their attraction, too. Furthermore, smaller companies may not have the resources to compete in large segments, and so may find smaller segments more attractive.

Segment growth rate: growing segments are usually regarded as more attractive than stagnant or declining segments, as new business opportunities will be greater. However, growth markets are often associated with heavy competition (e.g. in the mobile computing market, tablet computers, ultra netbooks and smartphones are three high-growth markets that are highly competitive). Therefore, an analysis of growth rate should always be accompanied by an examination of the state of competition.

Segment profitability: the potential to make profits is an important factor in market attractiveness.

Price sensitivity: in segments where customers are price sensitive there is a danger of profit margins being eroded by price competition. Low price-sensitive segments are usually more attractive since margins can be maintained. Competition may be based more on quality and other non-price factors.

Bargaining power of customers: both end and intermediate customers (e.g. distributors) can reduce the attraction of a market segment if they can exert high bargaining pressure on suppliers. The result is usually a reduction in profit margins as customers (e.g. supermarket chains) negotiate lower prices in return for placing large orders.

Bargaining power of suppliers: a company must assess not only the negotiating muscle of its customers but also its potential suppliers in the new segment. Where supply is in the hands of a few dominant companies, the segment will be less attractive than when served by a large number of competing suppliers.

Barriers to market segment entry: for companies considering entering a new segment there may be substantial entry barriers that reduce its attractiveness. Barriers can take the form of the high marketing expenditures necessary to compete, patents, or high switching costs for customers. However, if a company judges that it can afford or overcome barriers to entry, their existence may raise segment attractiveness if the company judges that the barriers will deter new rivals from entering.

Barriers to market segment exit: a segment may be regarded as less attractive if there are high barriers to exit. Exit barriers may take the form of specialized production facilities that cannot easily be liquidated, or agreements to provide spare parts to customers. Their presence may make exit extremely expensive and therefore segment entry more risky.

Competitive factors

Nature of competition: segments that are characterized by strong aggressive competition are less attractive than where competition is weak. The weakness of European and North American car manufacturers made the Japanese entry into a seemingly highly competitive (in terms of number of manufacturers) market segment relatively easy. The quality of the competition is far more significant than the number of companies operating in a market segment.

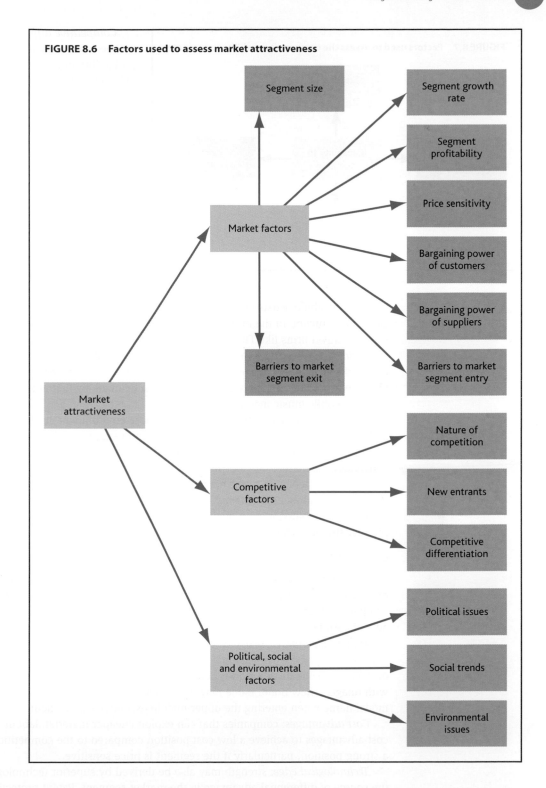

FIGURE 8.6 **Factors used to assess market attractiveness**

New entrants: a segment may seem superficially attractive because of the lack of current competition, but care must be taken to assess the dynamics of the market. A judgement must be made regarding the likelihood of new entrants, possibly with new technology, which might change the rules of the competitive game (e.g. Google changed the rules in the search engine market).

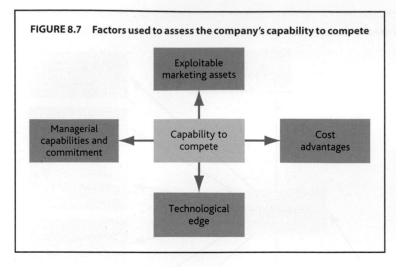

FIGURE 8.7 **Factors used to assess the company's capability to compete**

Competitive differentiation: segments will be more attractive if there is a real probability of creating a differentiated offering that customers value. This judgement is dependent on identifying unserved customer requirements, and the capability of the company to meet them.

Political, social and environmental factors

Political issues: political forces can open up new market segments (e.g. the deregulation of telecommunications in the UK paved the way for private companies to enter consumer and organizational segments of that market). Alternatively, the attraction of entering new geographic segments may be reduced if political instability exists or is forecast: for example, unrest in Tunisia, Egypt and Morocco caused a reduction in the number of tourists travelling to such regions and a downturn in sales for travel firms like Thomas Cook.[54]

Social trends: changes in society need to be assessed to measure their likely impact on the market segment. Changes in society can give rise to latent market segments, under-served by current products and services. Big gains can be made by first entrants (e.g. Apple's entry into the mobile music market with iTunes).

Environmental issues: the trend towards more environmentally friendly products has affected market attractiveness both positively and negatively. The Body Shop took the opportunity afforded by the movement against animal testing of cosmetics and toiletries; conversely the market for CFCs has declined in the face of scientific evidence linking their emission with depletion of the ozone layer.

In organizational markets individual customers may be evaluated on such criteria as sales volume, profitability, growth potential, financial strength and their fit with market and product strategy. Their allocation to a segment will be based on these factors.

Capability

Against the market attractiveness factors must be placed the firm's *capability to serve the market segment*. The market segment may be attractive but outside the resources of the company. Capability may be assessed by analysing exploitable marketing assets, cost advantages, technological edge, and managerial capabilities and commitment.

Exploitable marketing assets: does the market segment allow the firm to exploit its current marketing strengths? For example, is segment entry consonant with the image of its brands, or does it provide distribution synergies? However, where new segment entry is inconsistent with image, a new brand name may be created. For example, Toyota developed the Lexus model name when entering the upper-middle executive car segment.

Cost advantages: companies that can exploit cheaper material, labour or technological cost advantages to achieve a low cost position compared to the competition may be in a strong position, particularly if the segment is price sensitive.

Technological edge: strength may also be derived by superior technology, which is the source of differential advantage in the market segment. Patent protection (e.g. in pharmaceuticals) can form the basis of a strong defensible position, leading to high profitability. For some companies, segment entry may be deferred if they do not possess the resources to invest in technological leadership.

Managerial capabilities and commitment: a segment may look attractive but a realistic assessment of managerial capabilities and skills may lead to rejection of entry. The technical

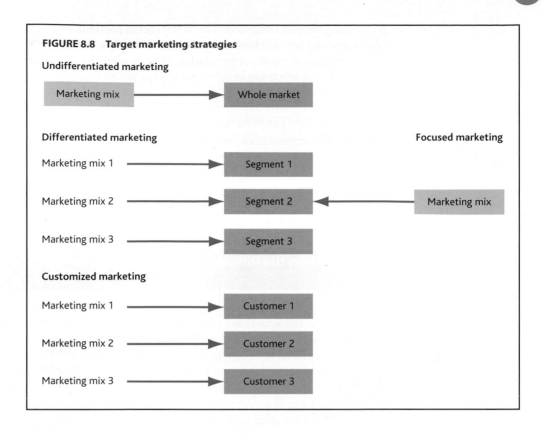

FIGURE 8.8 Target marketing strategies

and judgemental skills of management may be insufficient to compete against strong competitors. Furthermore, the segment needs to be assessed from the viewpoint of managerial objectives. Successful marketing depends on implementation. Without the commitment of management, segment entry will fail on the altar of neglect.

Target marketing strategies

The purpose of evaluating market segments is to choose one or more segments to enter. Target market selection is the choice of which and how many market segments in which to compete. There are four generic **target marketing** strategies from which to choose: undifferentiated marketing, differentiated marketing, focused marketing, and customized marketing (see Fig. 8.8). Each option will now be examined.

Undifferentiated marketing

Occasionally, a market analysis will show no strong differences in customer characteristics that have implications for marketing strategy. Alternatively, the cost in developing a separate market mix for separate segments may outweigh the potential gains of meeting customer needs more exactly. Under these circumstances a company may decide to develop a single marketing mix for the whole market. This absence of segmentation is called **undifferentiated marketing**. Unfortunately this strategy can occur by default. For example, companies that lack a marketing orientation may practise undifferentiated marketing through lack of customer knowledge. Furthermore, undifferentiated marketing is more convenient for managers since they have to develop only a single product. Finding out that customers have diverse needs that can be met only by products with different characteristics means that managers have to go to the trouble and expense of developing new products, designing new promotional campaigns, training the salesforce to sell the new products and developing new distribution channels. Moving into new segments also means that salespeople have to start prospecting for new customers. This is not such a pleasant activity as calling on existing customers who are well known and liked.

The process of market segmentation, then, is normally the motivator to move such companies from practising undifferentiated marketing to one of the next three target marketing strategies.

Differentiated marketing

When market segmentation reveals several potential targets, specific marketing mixes can be developed to appeal to all or some of the segments. This is called **differentiated marketing**. For example, airlines design different marketing mixes for first-class and economy passengers, including varying prices, service levels, quality of food, in-cabin comfort and waiting areas at

---

Marketing in Action 8.1 Companies Use Different Brands to Meet the Needs of their Various Target Markets

Market segmentation is a creative act that relies upon a clear understanding of the groups of customers that make up a particular target market. The actual basis of segmentation will vary by market sector. However, large corporations frequently aim to ensure their product portfolios offer a mix of product ranges and brands that meet the needs of different market segments. For example, Tesco differentiates its various offers by channel choice and store format. The weekly shopper tends to look for a store where they can purchase all of their needs in one location, while the convenience shopper is looking for a limited range of products and is prepared to pay a slightly higher price and select from a limited range of products as the store is very conveniently located, often within walking distance of the consumer's home. The online shopper often wants a mix of both convenience and range, but is prepared to wait for their shopping to be delivered. Each of these shoppers is looking for a different type of convenience.

By utilizing three distinct brands Tesco is able to target different target segments, extend its reach and protect its market share from competitors:

Tesco Stores   →   targets weekly shoppers
Tesco Express   →   targets convenience shoppers
Tesco.com   →   targets online shoppers

Sky has also differentiated some of its product offerings to target specific segments:

Sky Sports   →   targets sports enthusiasts
Sky Movies   →   targets film lovers
Sky News   →   targets news followers
Sky Atlantic   →   targets drama lovers

Airlines apply similar principles. For example, United Airlines is based in North America and is one of the world's largest airlines, operating a fleet of over 700 aircraft. The airline serves many target markets, catering for domestic and commercial customers and operates internal, transcontinental, and transatlantic routes. On all United Airlines flights passengers are offered a choice of classes:

First class   →   targets top business executives
Business class   →   targets senior managers
Economy class   →   targets other business travellers, and domestic travellers

All of these companies—whether they be retail or broadcast orientated, or travel related—have recognized that market segmentation can lead to higher rates of satisfaction of consumer needs than producing a single offering and hoping it will meet it all the diverse expectations of a given market.

Based on: United Airlines (2012);[55] Rose (2008);[56] Smith (2008);[57] Jack (2009)[58]

airports. A differentiated target marketing strategy exploits the differences between marketing segments by designing a specific marketing mix for each segment. Marketing in Action 8.1 describes how Tesco and Sky have designed different products to cater for the segments that exist in their markets.

One potential disadvantage of a differentiated compared to an undifferentiated marketing strategy is the loss of cost economies. However, the use of flexible manufacturing systems can minimize such problems.

Focused marketing

The identification of several segments in a market does not imply that a company should serve all of them. Some may be unattractive or out of line with business strengths. Perhaps the most sensible route would be to serve just one of the market segments. When a company develops a single marketing mix aimed at one target market (*niche*) it is practising **focused marketing**. This strategy is particularly appropriate for companies with limited resources. Small companies may stretch their resources too far by competing in more than one segment. Focused marketing allows research and development expenditure to be concentrated on meeting the needs of one set of customers, and managerial activities can be devoted to understanding and catering for their needs. Large organizations may not be interested in serving the needs of this one segment, or their energies may be so dissipated across the whole market that they pay insufficient attention to their requirements.

An example of focused marketing in the consumer market is given by Bang & Olufsen, the Danish audio electronics firm. It targets upmarket consumers who value self-development, pleasure and open-mindedness, with its stylish television and music systems. B&O describes its positioning as 'high quality but we are not Rolls-Royce—more BMW'. The company places emphasis on distinctive design, good quality and simplicity of use. Focused targeting means that B&O defies the conventional wisdom that a small manufacturer could not make profits marketing consumer electronics in Denmark.[59]

Another form of focused marketing is to target a particular age group. For example, Saga targets the over-50s. Originally a specialist holiday company, it has broadened its range of products marketed to this age group to include financial services such as a share-dealing service.[60]

One form of focused marketing is to concentrate efforts on the relatively small percentage of customers that account for a disproportionately large share of sales of a product (the heavy buyers). For example, in some markets 20 per cent of customers account for 80 per cent of sales. Some companies aim at such a segment because it is so superficially attractive. Unfortunately, they may be committing the *majority fallacy*.[61] The majority fallacy is the name given to the blind pursuit of the largest, most easily identified, market segment. It is a fallacy because that segment is the one that everyone in the past has recognized as the best segment and, therefore, it attracts the most intense competition. The result is likely to be high marketing expenditures, price cutting and low profitability. A more sensible strategy may be to target a small, seemingly less attractive, segment rather than choose the same customers that everyone else is after.

Customized marketing

In some markets the requirements of individual customers are unique and their purchasing power sufficient to make designing a separate marketing mix for each customer viable. Segmentation at this disaggregated level leads to the use of **customized marketing**. Many service providers, such as advertising and marketing research agencies, architects and solicitors, vary their offerings on a customer-to-customer basis. They will discuss face to face with each customer their requirements and tailor their services accordingly. Customized marketing is also found within organizational markets because of the high value of orders and the special needs of customers. Locomotive manufacturers will design and build products to specifications given to them by individual rail transport providers. Customized marketing is often associated with close relationships between supplier and customer in these circumstances because the value of the order justifies large marketing and sales efforts being focused on each buyer.

A fascinating development in marketing in recent years has been the introduction of *mass customization* in consumer markets. This is the marketing of highly individual products on a mass scale. Car companies such as Audi, BMW, Mercedes and Renault have the capacity to build to order where cars are manufactured only when there is an order specification from a customer. Dell Computers will also build customized products, often ordered on the Internet. Such flexible manufacturing processes allow customers to specify their own individual products from an extensive range of optional equipment.[62] For example, promotional material for the BMW Mini claims that there is only a 1 in 10,000 chance that any two Minis are the same. Even trainers can be customized, with both Nike and Adidas offering this service.[63]

Customized marketing is also possible on the Internet, with customers being treated differently on an individual basis.

Positioning

So far our discussion has taken us through market segmentation and on to target market selection. The next step in developing an effective marketing strategy is to clearly position a product or service offering in the marketplace. Figure 8.9 summarizes the key tasks involved, and shows where **positioning** fits into the process.

Positioning is the choice of:

- *target market*—*where* we want to compete
- *differential advantage*—*how* we wish to compete.

Both of these elements of positioning should be considered in conjunction with customer needs.

The objective is to create and maintain a distinctive place in the market for a company and/or its products.

Target market selection, then, has accomplished part of the positioning job already. But to compete successfully in a target market involves providing the customer with a differential advantage. This requires giving the target customer something better than the competition is offering. Creating a differential advantage will be discussed in detail in Chapter 19. Briefly, it involves using the marketing mix to create something special for the customer. Product differentiation may result from added features that give customers benefits that rivals cannot match. Promotional differentiation may stem from unique, valued images created by advertising, or superior service provided by salespeople. Distribution differentiation may arise through making the buy situation more convenient for customers. Finally, price differentiation may involve giving superior value for money through lower prices.

A landmark book by Ries and Trout suggested that marketers are involved in a battle for the minds of target customers.[64] Successful positioning is often associated with products possessing favourable connotations in the minds of customers. For example, Samsung is associated with high-technology, reliable and fashionable mobile phones. These add up to a differential advantage in the minds of its target customers whether they be in London, Amsterdam or Moscow. Similarly, the success of Cillit Bang has been based on its positioning should be Cillit as the most powerful and versatile household cleaner on the market. Such positioning is hard won and relies on four factors, as shown in Figure 8.10.

1 *Clarity*: the positioning idea must be clear in terms of both target market and differential advantage. Complicated positioning statements are unlikely to be remembered. Simple messages such as 'BMW: the ultimate driving machine', Wal-Mart's 'Low prices, always' and Stella Artois' 'Reassuringly expensive' are clear and memorable.

2 *Consistency*: people are bombarded with messages daily. To break through this noise a consistent message is required. Confusion will arise if this year we position on 'quality of

FIGURE 8.9   Key tasks in positioning

1. Market segmentation
2. Target market   } Positioning
3. Differential advantage

Where and *how* we compete

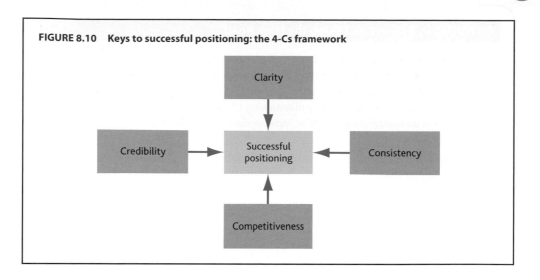

FIGURE 8.10   Keys to successful positioning: the 4-Cs framework

service', then next year we change it to 'superior product performance'. Two examples of brands that have benefited from a consistent message being communicated to their target customers are Gillette ('The best a man can get') and L'Oréal ('Because you're worth it'). Both receive high recall when consumers are researched because of the consistent use of a simple message over many years.

↑ EXHIBIT 8.4   L'Oréal appeals to its target audience by identifying their problems and providing solutions which match consumers' preferences.

3 *Credibility*: the differential advantage that is chosen must be credible in the minds of the target customer. Ford found that its brand image was not compatible with the marketing of upmarket cars. It was this lack of credibility that led it to purchase Jaguar, Land Rover, Volvo and Aston Martin. Unfortunately, as consumers became aware of their new owner the credibility of the original brands suffered, and Jaguar, Land Rover and Aston Martin were subsequently sold. Toyota's lack of credibility as an upmarket brand caused it to use 'Lexus' rather than 'Toyota Lexus' as the brand name for its top-of-the-range cars. Honda has followed a similar strategy using the Acura brand name for its luxury models. These examples clearly show the importance of credibility when positioning brands.

4 *Competitiveness*: the differential advantage should have a competitive edge. It should offer something of value to the customer that the competition is failing to supply. For example, the success of the iPod was based on the differential advantage of seamless downloading of music from a dedicated music store, iTunes, to a mobile player that produced better sound quality than its rivals.

Marketing in Action 8.2 describes how Michelin has used positioning to become the market leader in tyres.

Marketing in Action 8.2 Taking the High Road

Michelin is a company that has used the 4-Cs framework to achieve market leadership in the tyre market. It has achieved *clarity* by sending a single message—'higher mileage from a brand you can trust'—to justify its premium prices. The brand is supported by the 'Michelin Man' logo, which is instantly recognizable and memorable. *Consistency* is achieved by maintaining the same positioning for decades. The positioning is *credible* because drivers do notice the extra miles: independent tests show that Michelin tyres last 20 to 25 per cent longer than their competitors.

This adds up to a differential advantage because drivers value the extra mileage, which means overall costs are no higher than buying a rival's tyre and the inconvenience of changing tyres is less. Trust is vital because of the safety implications of tyres. Michelin is therefore highly *competitive* in its consumer and business target markets, which has meant that it is both the highest-priced product on the market and has the highest market share.

Based on: Rudloff (2008)[65]

Perceptual mapping

A useful tool for determining the position of a brand in the marketplace is the *perceptual map*. This is a visual representation of consumer perceptions of the brand and its competitors using attributes (dimensions) that are important to consumers. The key steps in developing a perceptual map are as follows.

1 Identify a set of competing brands.
2 Identify important attributes that consumers use when choosing between brands, using qualitative research (e.g. group discussions).
3 Conduct quantitative marketing research where consumers score each brand on all key attributes.
4 Plot brands on a two-dimensional map(s).

Figure 8.11 shows a perceptual map for seven supermarket chains. Qualitative marketing research has shown that consumers evaluate supermarkets on two key dimensions: price and width of product range. Quantitative marketing research is then carried out using scales that measure consumers' perception of each supermarket on these dimensions. Average scores are then plotted on a perceptual map.

The results show that the supermarkets are grouped into two clusters: the high price, wide product range group; and the low price, narrow price range group. These are indicative of two market segments and show that supermarkets C and D are close rivals, as measured by consumers' perceptions, and have very distinct perceptual positions in the marketplace compared with E, F and G. Perceptual maps are useful in considering strategic moves. For example, an opportunity may exist to create a differential advantage based on a combination of wide product range and low prices (as shown by the theoretical position at X).

Perceptual maps can also be valuable in identifying the strengths and weaknesses of brands as perceived by consumers. Such findings can be very revealing to managers, whose own perceptions may be very different from those of consumers. Consumers can also be asked to score their ideal position on each of the attributes so that actual and ideal positions can be compared.

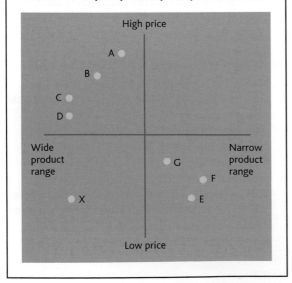

FIGURE 8.11   A perceptual map of supermarket chains

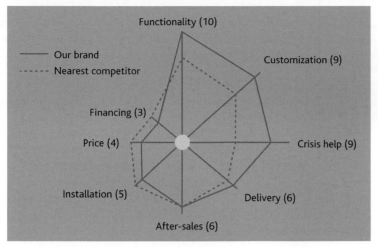

FIGURE 8.12   A spidergram positioning map for the robotic systems market

- —— Our brand
- - - - - Nearest competitor

Functionality (10)
Customization (9)
Crisis help (9)
Delivery (6)
After-sales (6)
Installation (5)
Price (4)
Financing (3)

Spidergram analysis

An alternative approach to perceptual mapping for the purpose of understanding the position of a brand in the marketplace is spidergram analysis.[66] Like perceptual mapping it provides a visual representation of consumer perceptions of the brand and its competitors using attributes (dimensions) that are important to consumers when evaluating those brands. However, spidergram analysis also asks consumers to rate the importance of the attributes, and their relative importance is represented visually by the length of the spoke on the spidergram. The key steps are as follows.

1   Identify a set of competing brands.
2   Identify important attributes that consumers use when choosing between brands, using qualitative research (e.g. group discussions).
3   Conduct quantitative marketing research where consumers:
    (i) rate the importance of each attribute in their choice between brands on a 10-point scale
    (ii) score each brand on all key attributes on a 10-point scale.
4   Plot brands on a spidergram.

Figure 8.12 shows a spidergram positioning map for the robotic systems market. The length of each spoke is proportional to the importance ratings of each attribute. Functionality is considered an essential attribute and has received a score of 10; the least important attribute is financing, scoring only 3. Each spoke is divided into 10 sections and each brand's score is plotted on each attribute. Our brand has received higher perceptual scores than its nearest competitor for functionality, customization, crisis help and delivery. Our brand and its nearest competitor are similarly rated for after-sales service; but, for installation, price and financing, our nearest competitor is rated more highly. Since our company is rated more highly on those attributes that are more important to consumers it is likely that our brand has a larger market share than its nearest competitor.

Like perceptual maps, spidergram analysis is valuable in identifying how consumers (as opposed to managers) perceive the strengths and weaknesses of competing brands. It provides a visual portrayal of the positions of brands along multiple dimensions. Spidergram software is available from the Aliah Corporation, USA, which permits the simultaneous analysis of up to six brands.

Repositioning

Occasionally a product or service will need to be repositioned because of changing customer tastes or poor sales performance. **Repositioning** involves changing the target markets, the differential advantage, or both. A useful framework for analysing repositioning options is given in Figure 8.13. Using product differentiation and target market as the key variables, four generic repositioning strategies are shown.

Image repositioning

The first option is to keep product and target market the same but to change the image of the product. In markets where products act as a form of self-expression, the product may be acceptable in functional terms but fail because it lacks the required image. Many

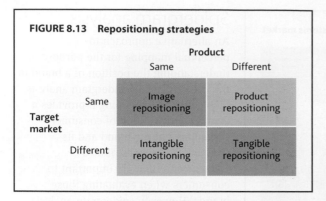

FIGURE 8.13 **Repositioning strategies**

	Product Same	Product Different
Target market Same	Image repositioning	Product repositioning
Target market Different	Intangible repositioning	Tangible repositioning

organizations—from retailers like Marks & Spencer with its Plan A programme, to low-cost airlines like Ryanair[67] to giant industrial corporations like BASF, the German chemical company—have changed their image by altering business practices in order to be perceived as sustainable and environmentally friendly.

Product repositioning

With this strategy the product is changed while the target market remains the same. For example, IBM has used product repositioning very successfully by moving away from the manufacture of computers (IBM sold its PC division to Lenovo) to the provision of software and services to essentially the same type of business customers. An example of product repositioning in services is the successful rebranding of Talk Radio, a generalist speech-based radio station, as talkSPORT. The target market of 25–44-year-old males remains the same, but the product has changed its focus to sport.[68]

Intangible repositioning

This strategy involves targeting a different market segment with the same product. Lucozade, a carbonated drink, was initially targeted by Beecham's Foods at sick children. Marketing research found that mothers were drinking it as a midday pick-me-up and the brand was consequently repositioned to aim at this new segment. Subsequently the energy-giving attributes of Lucozade were used to appeal to a wider target market—young adults—by means of advertisements featuring well-known athletes and footballers. The history of Lucozade shows how a combination of repositioning strategies over time has been necessary for successful brand building.

Pharmaceutical companies practise intangible repositioning when patents on their prescription drugs expire. Rather than fight against generic competition by price-cutting in the prescription segment, they often switch to the over-the-counter (OTC) sector where they can fight by investing in brand equity. Market leaders benefit by being able to claim 'the product most often prescribed by doctors'. An example is Tagamet, SmithKline Beecham's indigestion drug which, by switching to the OTC sector, was able to transfer to the new segment the value the consumer associated with the brand name developed through doctors' prescriptions.[69]

An example of intangible repositioning in international markets is given by Wagner, a German supplier of paint guns. In Europe such guns are bought by professional painters, but in the USA the same products are targeted at the consumer market as people use them to paint the interiors of their own homes and outside surfaces such as fences.[70]

Tangible repositioning

When both product and target market are changed, a company is practising tangible repositioning. For example, a company may decide to move upmarket or downmarket by introducing a new range of products to meet the needs of the new target customers. Highly successful tangible repositioning was undertaken by Samsung Electronics, which was once an unfocused manufacturer of cheap undifferentiated televisions and microwaves selling to all age groups and is now a premium-priced flat-screen television and mobile handset brand focused on, as we have seen, the 'high-life seeker' segment of the market—consumers who are willing to adopt technology early and pay a high price for it.[71]

Mercedes-Benz found it necessary to use tangible and product repositioning in the face of Japanese competition. Tangible repositioning took the form of developing new products (e.g. a city car) to appeal to new target customers. Product repositioning was also required in its current market segments to bring down the cost of development and manufacture in the face of lower-priced rivals such as Toyota's Lexus.

When you have read this chapter

log on to the Online Learning Centre at **www.mcgraw-hill.co.uk/textbooks/jobber** to explore chapter-by-chapter test questions, links and further online study tools for marketing.

Review

1 **The concepts of market segmentation and target marketing, and their use in developing marketing strategy**
- Market segmentation is the identification of individuals or organizations with similar characteristics that have significant implications for the determination of marketing strategy.
- Its use aids target market selection, the ability to design a tailored marketing mix, the development of differential marketing strategies, and the identification of opportunities and threats.
- Target marketing is the choice of specific segment(s) to serve. It concerns the decision where to compete.
- Its use is focusing company resources on those segments it is best able to serve in terms of company resources and segment attractiveness. Once chosen, a tailored marketing mix that creates a differential advantage can be designed based on an in-depth understanding of target customers.

2 **The methods of segmenting consumer and organizational markets**
- Consumer markets can be segmented by behavioural (benefits sought, purchase occasion, purchase behaviour, usage, and perceptions and beliefs), psychographic (lifestyle and personality), and profile (demographic, socio-economic and geographic) methods.
- Online markets are growing and consideration of how demographic, behavioural and psychographic variables are affected by the online environment is required.
- Organizational markets can be segmented by macrosegmentation (organizational size, industry and geographic location) and microsegmentation (choice criteria, decision-making unit structure, decision-making process, buy class, purchasing organization, and organizational effectiveness) methods.

3 **The factors that can be used to evaluate market segments**
- Two broad issues should be used: market attractiveness and the company's capability to compete.
- Market attractiveness can be assessed by examining market factors (segment size, segment growth rate, price sensitivity, bargaining power of customers, bargaining power of suppliers, barriers to market segment entry and barriers to market segment exit), competitive factors (nature of competition, the likelihood of new entrants, and competitive differentiation), and political, social and environmental factors (political issues, social trends and environmental issues).
- Capability to compete can be assessed by analysing exploitable marketing assets, cost advantages, technological edge, and managerial capabilities and commitments.

4 **Four target market strategies: undifferentiated, differentiated, focused and customized marketing**
- Undifferentiated marketing occurs where a company does not segment but applies a single marketing mix to the whole market.
- Differentiated marketing occurs where a company segments the market and applies separate marketing mixes to appeal to all or some of the segments (target markets).
- Focused marketing occurs where a company segments the market and develops one specific marketing mix to one segment (target market).
- Customized marketing occurs where a company designs a separate marketing mix for each customer.

5 **The concept of positioning and the keys to successful positioning**
- There are two aspects of positioning: the choice of target market (where to compete) and the creation of a differential advantage (how to compete).
- The objective is to create and maintain a distinctive place in the market for a company and/or its products.
- The four keys to successful positioning are: clarity, consistency, credibility and competitiveness.

6 **Positioning and repositioning strategies**
- A useful tool for determining the position of a brand in the marketplace is the perceptual map.
- Positioning strategy should be based on a clear choice of target market based on market segment attractiveness and company capability, and the creation of a differential advantage (based on an understanding of the attributes—choice criteria—that consumers use when choosing between brands).
- Repositioning strategies can be based on changes to the product and/or target market. Four strategies are image repositioning, product repositioning, intangible repositioning and tangible repositioning.

Key Terms

benefit segmentation the grouping of people based on the different benefits they seek from a product

customized marketing the market coverage strategy where a company decides to target individual customers and develops separate marketing mixes for each

differential marketing strategies market coverage strategies where a company decides to target several market segments and develops separate marketing mixes for each

differentiated marketing a market coverage strategy where a company decides to target several market segments and develops separate marketing mixes for each

focused marketing a market coverage strategy where a company decides to target one market segment with a single marketing mix

lifestyle segmentation the grouping of people according to their pattern of living as expressed in their activities, interests and opinions

macrosegmentation the segmentation of organizational markets by size, industry and location

market segmentation the process of identifying individuals or organizations with similar characteristics

that have significant implications for the determination of marketing strategy

microsegmentation segmentation according to choice criteria, DMU structure, decision-making process, buy class, purchasing structure and organizational innovativeness

positioning the choice of target market (where the company wishes to compete) and differential advantage (how the company wishes to compete)

profile segmentation the grouping of people in terms of profile variables, such as age and socio-economic group, so that marketers can communicate to them

psychographic segmentation the grouping of people according to their lifestyle and personality characteristics

repositioning changing the target market or differential advantage, or both

target marketing the choice of which market segment(s) to serve with a tailored marketing mix

undifferentiated marketing a market coverage strategy where a company decides to ignore market segment differences and develops a single marketing mix for the whole market

Study Questions

1 What are the advantages of market segmentation? Can you see any advantages of mass marketing, i.e. treating a market as homogeneous and marketing to the whole market with one marketing mix?

2 Choose a market you are familiar with and use benefit segmentation to identify market segments. What are the likely profiles of the resulting segments?

3 In what kind of markets is psychographic segmentation likely to prove useful? Why?

4 How might segmentation be of use when marketing in Europe?

5 Explain how you might select segmentation variables when aiming to access online markets.

6 One way of segmenting organizational markets is to begin with macrosegmentation variables and then develop sub-segments using microsegmentation criteria. Does this seem sensible to you? Are there any circumstances where the process should be reversed?

7 Why is *buy class* a potentially useful method of segmenting organizational markets? (Use both this chapter and Chapter 5 when answering this question.)

8 What is the majority fallacy? Why should it be taken into account when evaluating market segments?

9 What is the difference between positioning and repositioning? Choose three products and services and describe how they are positioned in the marketplace: i.e. what is their target market and differential advantage?

References

1. Carphone Warehouse says pre-pay phones down sharply (2012) http://www.bbc.co.uk/news/business-16696717, 24 January.
2. Steiner, R. (1999) How Mobile Phones Came to the Masses, *Sunday Times*, 31 October, 6.
3. Whittaker, Z. (2011) iPhone most popular business phone; BlackBerry loses vital street-cred, http://www.zdnet.com/blog/btl/iphone-most-popular-business-phone-blackberry-loses-vital-street-cred/63766, 17 November.
4. Wind, Y. (1978) Issues and Advances in Segmentation Research, *Journal of Marketing Research*, August, 317–37.
5. Van Raaij, W. F. and T. M. M. Verhallen (1994) Domain-specific Market Segmentation, *European Journal of Marketing* 28(10), 49–66.
6. Ritson, M. (2011) Know when to shut the door on your customer, *Marketing Week*, 25 August, 50.
7. Hilpern, K. (2011) An Ageless Strategy, *The Marketer*, November/December, 28–31.
8. Wieners, B. (2011) Lego is for girls, *Bloomberg Business Week*, 19 December, 68–73.
9. Sampson, P. (1992) People are People the World Over: The Case for Psychological Market Segmentation, *Marketing and Research Today*, November, 236–44.
10. Cattermole, G. (2012) Sainsbury's boosted by Christmas food sales growth, http://www.guardian.co.uk/business/2012/jan/11/sainsburys-christmas-food-sales.
11. Fifield, P. (2005) The People Puzzle, *The Marketer*, 12 April, 6–9.
12. Aaker, D. (2004) *Brand Portfolio Strategy*, New York: The Free Press.
13. Hooley, G. J., J. Saunders, N. Piercy and B. Nicoulaud (2012) *Marketing Strategy and Competitive Positioning: The Key to Market Success*, Hemel Hempstead: Prentice-Hall, 148.
14. Cook, V. J. Jr and W. A. Mindak (1984) A Search for Constants: The 'Heavy-User' Revisited!, *Journal of Consumer Marketing* 1(4), 79–81.
15. Brynjolfsson, E., Yu (J.) Hu and D. Simester (2011) Goodbye Pareto Principle, Hello Long Tail: the effect of search costs on the concentration of product sales, *Management Science* 57(8), 1373–86.
16. Barnett, M. (2011) Hi-tech healthcare, *Marketing Week*, 30 June, 14–17.
17. Kantar Media (2012) TGI Europa, http://kantarmedia-tgigb.com/tgi-surveys/tgi-europa/.
18. O'Shaughnessy, J. (1995) *Competitive Marketing: A Strategic Approach*, London: Routledge.
19. Ehrenberg, A. S. C. and G. J. Goodhardt (1978) *Market Segmentation*, New York: J. Walter Thompson.
20. Chorley, M. and J. Rentoul (2011) Seven in 10 of us belong to middle class Britain, *The Independent on Sunday*, 20 March, 13–17.
21. Brownsell, A. (2011) Toyota targets young drivers in £7.5m push, *Marketing Magazine*, 10 August, 3.
22. Sampson (1992) op. cit.
23. Lannon, J. (1991) Developing Brand Strategies across Borders, *Marketing and Research Today*, August, 160–8.
24. Young, S. (1972) The Dynamics of Measuring Unchange, in Haley, R. I. (ed.) *Attitude Research in Transition*, Chicago: American Marketing Association, 61–82.
25. Tynan, A. C. and J. Drayton (1987) Market Segmentation, *Journal of Marketing Management* 2(3), 301–35.
26. Simms, J. (2005) Strategising Simplicity, *Marketing*, 25 May, 15.
27. Chisnall, P. (2005) *Marketing Research*, Maidenhead: McGraw-Hill.
28. http://garconniere.tumblr.com/post/222865576/old-ladies-rebellion-the-definition-of-bad-ass.
29. Edwards, H. (2011) Sixty is the new old, *Marketing Magazine*, 9 November, 19.
30. Handley, L. (2011) Original teenagers kick segmentation into touch, *Marketing Week*, 1 December, 18–19.
31. Hilpern, K. (2011) An ageless strategy, *The Marketer*, November/December, 28–31.
32. O'Brien, S. and R. Ford (1988) Can We at Last Say Goodbye to Social Class?, *Journal of the Market Research Society* 30(3), 289–332.
33. Kimmel, A. J. (2010) *Connecting with consumers: marketing for new marketplaces realties*, Oxford University Press, 15–19.
34. Kossoff, J. (1988) Europe: Up for Sale, *New Statesman and Society*, 7 October, 43–4.
35. Tata Motors (2009) The story of the Nano, http://www.tatanano.com.
36. Chisnall (2005) op. cit.
37. Garrett, A. (1992) Stats, Lies and Stereotypes, *Observer*, 13 December, 26.
38. Mitchell, V.-W. and P. J. McGoldrick (1994) The Role of Geodemographics in Segmenting and Targeting Consumer Markets: A Delphi Study, *European Journal of Marketing* 28(5), 54–72.

39. Doherty, N. F. and F. Ellis-Chadwick (2010) Evaluating the role of electronic commerce in transforming the retail sector, *The International Review of Retail, Distribution and Consumer Research* 20(4), 375–378.

40. Doherty, N. F. and F. Ellis-Chadwick (2010) Internet retailing: the past, the present and the future, *International Journal of Retail & Distribution Management* 38, 11/12, 943–65.

41. Jayawardhena, C., L. T. Wright and C. Dennis (2007) Consumers online: intentions, orientations and segmentation, *International Journal of Retail & Distribution Management* 35(6), 512–26.

42. Hoffman, D. L., T. P. Novak and A. Schlosser (2003) The evolution of the digital divide: how gaps in internet access may impact electronic commerce, in C. Steinfield (ed.) *New Directions in Research on E-Commerce*, West Lafayette, IN: Purdue University Press, 245–292.

43. Slyke, C. V., C. L. Comunale and F. Belanger (2002) Gender differences in perceptions of Web-based shopping, *Communications of the ACM* 45(7), 82–86.

44. Shui, E. and J. Dawson (2004) Comparing the Impacts of Technology and National Culture on Online Usage and Purchase from a Four-Country Perspective, *Journal of Retailing and Consumer Services* 11(6), 385–94.

45. Swaminathan, V., E. Lepkowska-White and B. P. Rao (1999) Browsers or buyers in cyberspace? An investigation of factors influencing electronic exchange, *Journal of Computer-Mediated Communication* 5(2), 1–19.

46. Kukar-Kinney, M., N. M. Ridgway and K. B. Monroe (2009) The relationship between consumers' tendencies to buy compulsively and their motivations to shop and buy on the internet, *Journal of Retailing* 85(3), 298.

47. Brashear, T. G., V. Kashyap, M. D. Musante and N. Donthu (2009) A profile of the internet shopper: evidence from six countries, *Journal of Marketing Theory and Practice* 17(3), 267–81.

48. See Wind, Y. and R. N. Cardozo (1974) Industrial Market Segmentation, *Industrial Marketing Management* 3, 153–66; R. E. Plank (1985) A Critical Review of Industrial Market Segmentation, *Industrial Marketing Management* 14, 79–91.

49. Wind and Cardozo (1974) op. cit.

50. Moriarty, R. T. (1983) *Industrial Buying Behaviour*, Lexington, Mass: Lexington Books.

51. Corey, R. (1978) *The Organisational Context of Industrial Buying Behavior*, Cambridge, MA: Marketing Science Institute, 6–12.

52. Muller, R. (2011) Target China, *The Marketer*, July/August, 32–5.

53. See Abell, D. F. and J. S. Hammond (1979) *Strategic Market Planning: Problems and Analytical Approaches*, Hemel Hempstead: Prentice-Hall; G. S. Day (1986) *Analysis for Strategic Market Decisions*, New York: West; Hooley, Saunders, Piercy and Nicoulaud (2012) op. cit.

54. Moore, J. (2011) No fly-by-night firm but Thomas Cook can't afford to trip up in appeal to lenders, *The Independent*, 23 November, http://www.independent.co.uk/news/business/comment/james-moore-no-flybynight-firm-but-thomas-cook-cant-afford-to-trip-up-in-appeal-to-lenders-6266321.html.

55. United Airlines (2012) www.united.com.

56. Rose, S. (2008) There Are Plenty of Reasons Why Britain Still Loves M&S, *Guardian*, 25 January, 41.

57. Smith, G. (2008) On The Road, *Guardian Weekend*, 21 June, 99.

58. Jack, L. (2009) Cleaning Up Its Act, *Marketing Week*, 12 February, 21.

59. Gapper, J. (2005) When High Fidelity Becomes High Fashion, *Financial Times*, 20 December, 11.

60. *The Observer* (2000) Saga, Dealing in Satisfaction, 19 March, 29.

61. Zikmund, W. G. and M. D'Amico (1999) *Marketing*, St Paul, MN: West, 249.

62. *The Economist* (2001) A Long March, 14 July, 79–82.

63. Benady, D. (2003) King Customer, *Marketing Week*, 8 May, 24–7.

64. Ries, A. and J. Trout (2001) *Positioning: The Battle for your Mind*, New York: Warner.

65. Rudloff, T. (2008) On The Road, *The Marketer*, April, 24.

66. The author is indebted to Professor David Shipley, Trinity College, University of Dublin, for material used in this description of spidergram analysis.

67. Eletheriou-Smith, L.-M. (2011) Ryanair signal brand U-turn with eco-claims, *Marketing*, 27 July, 1.

68. Brech, P. (2000) MacKenzie Plans Sports Revolution, *Marketing*, 20 January, 9.

69. Platford, R. (1997) Fast Track to Approval, *Financial Times*, 24 April, 27.

70. Bolfo, B. (2005) The Art of Selling One Product in Two Markets, *Financial Times*, 10 August, 11.

71. Pesola, M. (2005) Samsung plays to the young generation, *Financial Times*, 29 March, 11.

Utilization of Loyalty Card Data for Segmentation

Morelli's Story

With 100 years of trading in Northern Ireland, selling ice cream is by no means new to the Morelli family. Morelli's award-winning ice cream business has a unique heritage, symbolizing a long history of migration, romance, war, and strong Italian family values. First established in 1911 with a café parlour in Coleraine, by 1914 the business had quickly blossomed, expanding to meet demand with similar premises opening in Portstewart and Portrush on the north coast of Ireland. The years of achievement rolled on, and by 2001 four generations of the Morelli family had successfully developed and passed on an ever-growing selection of their award-winning ice creams. However, Morelli's success was inextricably linked to the ice cream parlours and the goal to develop the brand as a take-home ice cream was yet to be achieved.

TABLE C15.1   Overview of Morelli's ice cream business

Overview of Morelli's Ice Cream	
Category	• Artisan Italian ice-cream specialist.
Established	• Morelli's has been making ice cream in Ireland since 1911.
History	• Originally from Frosinone, near Rome, Peter Morelli came to Northern Ireland at the end of the 19th century. • In 1911, six years after he began selling the ice cream from a handcart around the seaside town of Portstewart, County Londonderry, he opened the first Italian ice cream parlour. • Another branch of the family also set up a Morelli outlet at Broadstairs in Kent, which now operates the Morelli Gelato parlour in the prestigious Harrods store in Knightsbridge, London.
Unique selling proposition	• Family-owned and family-run business. • Secret family recipe. • Synonymous with high-quality scoop ice cream.
Wholesale and retail market outlets	• Family-owned ice cream parlours (Portrush and Portstewart). • Three franchise stores (Newcastle, Co. Down; Lisburn Road, Belfast; Letterkenny, Co. Donegal). • Hotels, restaurants, cinemas and service sector in NI/UK. • Retail: Tesco, Mace, Supervalu, Spar and Costcutter.
Product portfolio	• Over 80 sumptuous and innovative flavours using only the finest Italian natural flavours, pastes and fruit extracts. Additional ingredients are sourced from all over the world.
Awards won	• Great Taste Awards 2011: 1 Star for Morelli's Double Cream Vanilla Ice Cream; 1 Star for Morelli's Cheesecake Ice Cream with Blueberries and Biscuit Crumb • 2009 National Ice Cream Competition: Silver Challenge Cup in the Dairy Artisan category, a diploma in the Champion of Champions flavour for Vanilla, Diplomas of Merit in the Ice Cream Open, Chocolate and Raspberry Ripple categories, Diploma in the Pistachio flavour category.

Source: http://www.morellisofportstewart.co.uk

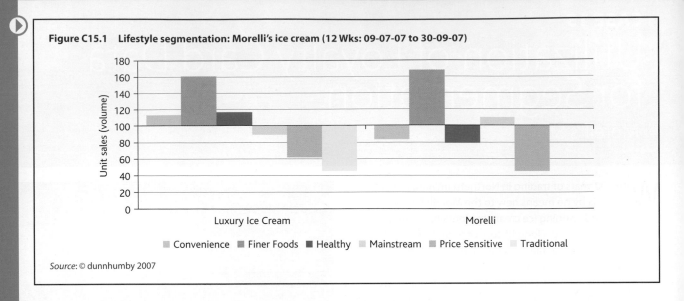

Figure C15.1   Lifestyle segmentation: Morelli's ice cream (12 Wks: 09-07-07 to 30-09-07)

Source: © dunnhumby 2007

Retail to wholesale

In 1997 Arnaldo Morelli, the fourth generation of the Morelli family to run the business, saw an opportunity to develop the wholesale side of the business. The expansion of wholesale trade enabled Morelli's to maintain sales volume year round while appealing to consumers across Northern Ireland.

> In the winter time we do a lot of carton sales for theatres, and schools we supply as well. So those sales are probably better in the winter time, and in the summer time those sales would probably go down because there's not as many people indoors, so the sales in the scoop shops would increase. So different segments of the market would go down in the winter and the other side would go up in the winter time, so it works both ways.
>
> (Arnaldo Morelli)

Morelli-branded, take-home tubs were introduced into Tesco stores across Northern Ireland in 2006. With distinctive product attributes, a strong business heritage and the Italian family brand name, the scope for opportunity within the competitive take-home ice cream category at Tesco is relatively vast. Yet, the challenge faced by Arnaldo Morelli in 2006 was also vast, as Morelli's strived to meet the needs and wants of both the new customer, Tesco, and the new consumer, the Tesco shopper. Morelli's had to re-evaluate their pricing strategy within Tesco, decide on core product flavours to stock and assess the appropriateness of promotions, all in order to build a strong awareness of the brand as a take-home product, and to gain a loyal consumer base, while trying to compete successfully for share of the consumer's wallet, and for maintenance of their shelf position within the retailer, with good sales and no product wastage.

In order to address these challenges, Morelli was among the first companies in Northern Ireland to gain free consumer insight into Tesco's loyalty card data. This data has been managed by leading marketing consultancy firm dunnhumby Ltd since 1995,[1] who are responsible for translating billions of data points from Tesco customers' shopping baskets every week into detailed insight into shopper behaviour and lifestyles[2] (See Table C15.2).

Getting to know the consumer

In 2007 dunnhumby data identified that the type of Tesco shopper most likely to buy Morelli's ice cream in a take-home pack fell into the Older Families and Younger Families lifestages category. The data also identified that Morelli's had a stronger appeal amongst Finer Foods and Traditional shoppers[3] than luxury ice cream and under-performed amongst Healthy shoppers,[4] confirming indulgence status (see analysis below).

On the strength of this lifestyle insight, Arnaldo decided to develop brand loyalty amongst the Finer Foods shopper, recognizing that this segment was a key target group for Morelli's to increase sales and maintain this in the long term.

> . . . the more I looked at the dunnhumby data, it showed me that the people who are buying our ice cream aren't the people who want a bargain . . . so that really told me that I don't really want to be on promotion . . . I want to try and establish our ice cream with customers who will be loyal to our brand.
>
> (Arnaldo Morelli)

Evolving nature of the consumer

In 2009 the lifestyles segmentation was updated from the existing 2007 profile in order to meet the significant

Table C15.2   Lifestyle segmentation (2007)[5]

Lifestyle Segment	Shoppers (%)	Key Characteristics
Finer Foods	16	Affluent shoppers who enjoy luxury products and premium brands and who typically like to cook from scratch.
Convenience	22	11% affluent shoppers who are time poor but food rich.
		11% mid-market shoppers who can't cook and won't cook.
Mainstream	25	Mainstream shoppers typically purchase mid-price brands and driven by kids' choice.
Healthy	10	Mainstream shoppers who typically count the calories and make healthy choices.
Traditional	11	Less affluent shoppers who shop for value and who typically like to cook from scratch.
Price Sensitive	16	Price-conscious shoppers likely to be on a lower income, stretching the budget and in search of the cheapest products.

Figure C15.2   Updated Lifestyles 2009[6]

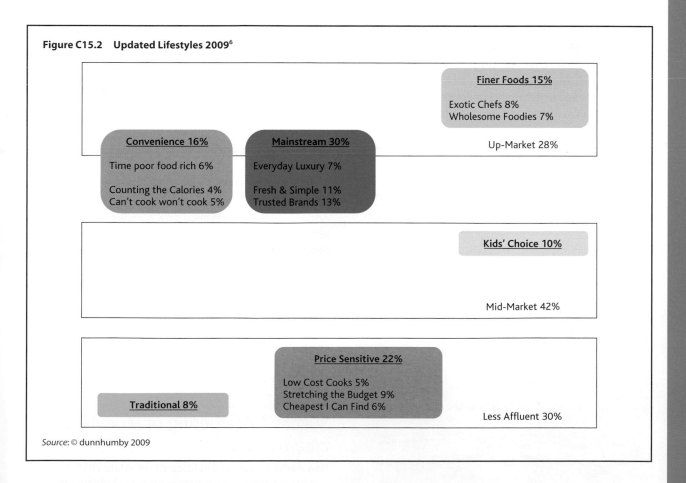

Source: © dunnhumby 2009

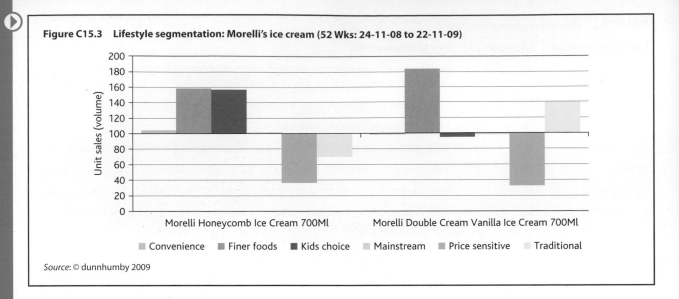

Figure C15.3   Lifestyle segmentation: Morelli's ice cream (52 Wks: 24-11-08 to 22-11-09)

Legend: ■ Convenience   ■ Finer foods   ■ Kids choice   ■ Mainstream   ■ Price sensitive   ■ Traditional

Source: © dunnhumby 2009

changes within the economy, Tesco and the Tesco shopper group itself. The Tesco shopper had changed over the five years, and dunnhumby decided to replace less significant lifestyles and move certain lifestyles into more detailed lifestyle groups. The growth in the number of price sensitive customers needed reflecting, and more detail was placed on the mainstream customer as it was the largest proportion of Tesco's customers.

Comprising 10 per cent of the Tesco market, a Kid's Choice shopper is strongly influenced by their children, shops frequently and takes advantage of promotions. With this new change in lifestyle segmentation, Arnaldo required further insight into the Morelli products to remain in tune with the consumer lifestyle segmentation.

Insight into Morelli's lifestyle segmentation

Lifestyle segmentation analysis completed on the two types of Morelli offerings within Tesco Northern Ireland (after the update in lifestyle segmentation in 2009) revealed

extremely informative insight as a result of the new Kid's Choice segmentation (see analysis below).

The result of this report illustrated the demand for Morelli Honeycomb Ice Cream was driven by both the Finer Foods and Kids Choice lifestyle, but under-performed in Traditional shoppers. Although the Finer Foods and Traditional shopper over-performed in Morelli Double Cream Vanilla Ice Cream, the demand from Kids Choice shoppers was less significant. By understanding actual lifestyles for each product, Arnaldo Morelli received in-depth understanding of consumer lifestyle segmentation to aid further business developments.

Armed with this dunnhumby data, Morelli's worked to redesign their packaging in order to address issues of functionality, to reinforce brand authenticity and, most important, to develop brand loyalty amongst their desired target group: Finer Foods and Traditional shoppers. This was also an opportunity for Morelli's to develop new packaging alongside their new website, in order to sell their amazing family story. After generations of successfully engaging and winning the support of consumers through their parlours, Morelli's wanted to be able to share their story with a wider consumer base within their family homes.

Successful targeting of Morelli ice cream in store

New packaging arrived in Tesco stores in late 2010. It would take almost a year before Arnaldo could be sure whether the new packaging and focused positioning of the product had successfully achieved in gaining loyalty amongst the Finer Foods and Traditional shopper (see analysis below).

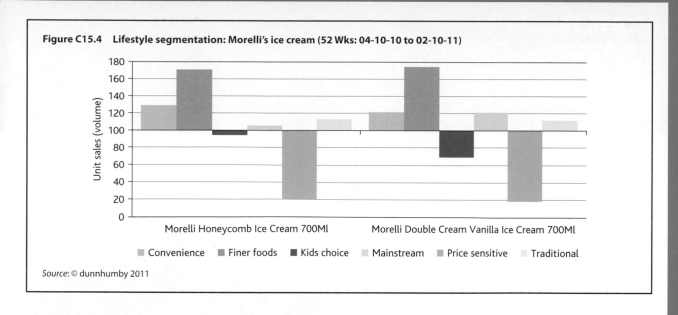

Figure C15.4   Lifestyle segmentation: Morelli's ice cream (52 Wks: 04-10-10 to 02-10-11)

Source: © dunnhumby 2011

This report illustrated the change in consumer purchasing for the Morelli Honeycomb Ice Cream from the Kid's Choice shopper to the Traditional shopper. This change is aligned with the more focused targeting by Morelli's in developing brand loyalty amongst the Finer Foods and Traditional shoppers who value heritage and quality over price.

Where to next?

Dunnhumby continues to be a key business tool as Morelli's moves forward to meet new challenges in their 100th year in business. With insight and experience built on a century of selling ice cream on the north coast of Ireland, and today gaining insight into real consumer purchasing behaviour through the most up-to-date market information from dunnhumby, Morelli's remains informed within the ice cream market.

> As an owner/manager the dunnhumby data has been invaluable. The information has allowed me to make key informed decisions in areas such as new packaging development, target markets and simply getting to know my customers better.
>
> (Arnaldo Morelli, 2011)

Arnaldo Morelli feels confident in the future of the business and in his role of ensuring that there will be many more Morelli generations to come!

References

1   Humby, C., Hunt, T. and Phillips, T. (2007) *Scoring Points: How Tesco continues to win customer loyalty*, 2nd edition, Kogan Page London & Philadelphia, 51–6.

2   Anstead, J., Samuel, J. and Crofton, A. (2008) dunnhumby— A Retailer's Secret Weapon, Citigroup Global Market, *Feeders Digest* 60, 6–25.

3   Stronger appeal demonstrated on the Y-axis of 100 to 180.

4   Under-performance demonstrated on the X-axis of 100 to 0.

5   Dunnhumby (2009) Quick Guide—What's Changing with Lifestyles? (December).

6   Dunnhumby (2009) Quick Guide—What's Changing with Lifestyles? (December).

Questions

1   What key challenges did Morelli's face in bringing their product to retail?

2   How does segmentation benefit the marketing strategy of Morelli's Ice Cream?

3   Develop a consumer segmentation basis for Morelli's Ice Cream.

This case was written by Dr Christina Donnelly, Lecturer in Marketing, NUI Maynooth and Dr Gillian Armstrong, Head of Department of Accounting, Business and Management Research Institute, University of Ulster.

Mercedes-Benz
'The Best or Nothing'

Mercedes-Benz is the most valuable premium automotive brand worldwide and Europe's most valuable brand overall. Mercedes-Benz is renowned for exciting premium automobiles that set standards in the areas of design, safety, comfort, perceived value, reliability and environmental compatibility. Mercedes-Benz has maintained its position as a market leader in the luxury car market by engaging in a very successful segmentation, target marketing and positioning strategy. However, this strategy presents a new challenge to Mercedes-Benz, as it recognizes the importance of targeting a younger generation of consumers with a range of new compact models, to drive the long term success of the company.

Background of Mercedes-Benz

Mercedes-Benz is widely renowned as the inventor of the motor car when, in 1886, Carl Benz registered his 'vehicle powered by a gas engine' with the German Imperial Patent Office. The '35 hp' of 1900/1901 was the first vehicle to sport the Mercedes brand name and went down in history as the first modern-day motor car. The Mercedes star used to symbolize motorization on land, on water and in the air can now be found as a badge on every Mercedes-Benz, and became a registered trademark in 1923. From an early date Mercedes-Benz thus established its claim as the leader in the fields of technology and design. From the world's first series production diesel passenger car (Mercedes-Benz 260 D (W 138), 1936), the body with 'crumple zones' (Mercedes-Benz 220 series (W 111 model series), 1959), and the market launch of the anti-lock brake system (Mercedes-Benz S-Class (116 model series), 1978), through to the first airbag in a series production vehicle (Mercedes-Benz S-Class (W 126), 1981) and the first lithium-ion battery in a series production car (Mercedes-Benz S 400 Hybrid, 2009): the inventor of the motor car has shaped its development more diversely and enduringly than any other automotive manufacturer. It was Carl Benz who said: 'The love of inventing never dies'. And it was Gottlieb Daimler who came up with the famous maxim 'The best or nothing'. Mercedes-Benz has remained true to these guiding principles for more than 125 years.

The Daimler-Chrysler merger in May 1998 placed the company into the economic stratosphere of Ford and GM. The products currently supplied by the Mercedes-Benz Cars division range from the high-quality small cars of the smart

brand to the premium automobiles of the Mercedes-Benz brand and to the Maybach luxury sedans. The main country of manufacture is Germany, but the division also has production facilities in the USA, China, France, South Africa, India, Vietnam and Indonesia. Worldwide, Mercedes-Benz Cars has 17 production sites at present. In the year 2011 Daimler generated revenue of €106.5 billion. The individual division of Mercedes-Benz Cars contributed 52 per cent to this total, and employed a total workforce of more than 271,000 people. The most important markets for Mercedes-Benz Cars in 2011 were Germany with 21 per cent of unit sales, the other markets of Western Europe (24 per cent), the USA (18 per cent) and China (16 per cent). The Mercedes-Benz Cars division set a new record with sales of 1,381,400 vehicles in 2011 (2010: 1,276,800). With their 'Mercedes-Benz 2020' growth strategy, Mercedes-Benz Cars division strives to occupy the leading role for premium automobiles in terms of unit sales. Mercedes-Benz intends to sell 1.6 million cars of the Mercedes-Benz brand in 2015 and to sell more cars than any other premium manufacturer in 2020. 'The best or nothing' slogan serves as an incentive to consolidate top position for the Mercedes-Benz brand in all the functions of Mercedes-Benz Cars.

Luxury car industry

Global demand for motor vehicles continued to grow during 2011, although at significantly more moderate rates than in the previous year. After a good start to 2011, growth of the global car market slowed down significantly towards the middle of the year. Car sales were dampened considerably by supply bottlenecks due to the natural disaster in Japan, high oil prices, rising inflation rates and not least the worsening debt crisis in Europe and the USA. The Daimler Group's revenue increased in 2011 by 9 per cent to €106.5 billion. Revenue grew at Mercedes-Benz Cars by 7 per cent to €57.4 billion. In the second half of the year demand revived faster than expected, so that worldwide registrations of new cars surpassed the prior-year number by about 5 per cent, reaching a new record.

Regional differences in market developments were still very pronounced. The US market continued its recovery with growth of a good 10 per cent, but was still at a comparatively low level. Due to the negative impact of the worsening sovereign-debt crisis, car sales in Western Europe fell slightly once again (−1 per cent). While the German market expanded significantly (+9 per cent), demand in the other volume markets of Western Europe declined, in some cases by double-digit percentages. The Chinese market expanded by almost 10 per cent, despite the expiry of state customer incentives at the beginning of the year. Demand in the premium and luxury segments, which are especially important for Daimler, increased at above-average rates, so the Chinese market continued to gain importance, in particular for the German premium manufacturers. However, growth in demand for cars in India weakened significantly to about 5 per cent.

The strongest growth of all regions was in Eastern Europe, thanks mainly to the booming Russian market, which once again expanded by almost 40 per cent. In the luxury segment Mercedes-Benz sold 80,700 vehicles (2010: 80,400). Mercedes-Benz expects the new generation of the SL and compact cars will boost unit sales from 2012. Growth in global automotive demand will mainly take place in the markets outside Europe, North America and Japan in the coming years, particularly in the BRIC countries. In the medium term, Mercedes-Benz anticipates significant growth in worldwide demand for automobiles and above-average growth in the premium car segment.

Challenges for Mercedes-Benz

Mercedes-Benz faces a number of significant challenges in the luxury market. Competitors such as Audi and BMW have followed an aggressive product expansion strategy in the last decade and taken luxury into smaller market segments (like the VW Golf-sized BMW 1-series and the new Mini rival Audi A1). Crucially, these moves have attracted new, younger customers to their brands without undermining their premium-to-luxury brand cachet. This represents the greatest challenge for Mercedes-Benz. Mercedes-Benz is faced with building relevance among a younger audience. A new generation of affluent consumers is needed to

generate a vital source of business in both established and emerging markets. Currently, Mercedes-Benz owners are some of the oldest in their luxury competitive set with a median age of 54 years. They also have a lower concentration of Gen Y and Gen X consumers as a percentage of current owners. Mercedes-Benz benefits from high brand awareness and admiration amongst these younger generations; however, they do not feel that it is a brand for them. Unfortunately, many younger consumers see Mercedes-Benz as an older status symbol. A large majority view Mercedes-Benz as the car choice of their predecessors and parents. In a 2010 Dwell study of New Affluents, Mercedes-Benz was ranked as #2 in an overall brand rating, with 68 per cent of respondents classifying their opinion of the brand as 'excellent' or 'very good'. However, when it comes to consideration for next auto purchase amongst the same survey group, Mercedes-Benz is ranked #8, with only 21 per cent citing Mercedes-Benz as a brand they would consider.

Mercedes-Benz now needs to build interest, relevance and aspiration among consumers in the 25–44-year-old segment, in order to drive long-term growth. Mercedes-Benz is in jeopardy of being passed by competitors such as BMW and Audi who have been faster to embrace this younger segment. Similarly, Mercedes-Benz has been characterized as having a more 'male' identity and the brand still sells the majority of their cars to men. The opportunity of increasing their presence in the female segment has been identified as an area for development, but the company still appears to have difficulty in attracting new female customers. The positioning strategy that has been so successful is in danger of causing Mercedes-Benz to stall with a new generation of consumers.

Moving towards a new segment

Mercedes-Benz Benz is planning to transform the company through marketing and design as it looks to target a younger audience (25–44-year-old age bracket) with its 'Best or Nothing' campaign. Mercedes-Benz hopes its brand repositioning will help the automotive giant attract younger, affluent consumers and meet an ambitious 1.6 million unit sales target. This younger consumer segment is defined by Mercedes-Benz as 'Progressive Premium World' consisting of young, modern and open-minded men and women in the medium to high salary sector with a high level of education. They normally live in urban environments, identifying themselves as technology-oriented early adopters and digital natives. Mercedes-Benz' marketing strategy (particularly in the USA) was centred on the safety, luxury, and precision engineering of its cars. Mercedes-Benz recognises that its buying audience is very different to its communications audience. Due to increased competition in the luxury car industry and changing consumer attitudes about the Mercedes-Benz Benz brand, that strategy has changed. Now their marketing strategy is more lifestyle-oriented and is focused more on presenting the more fun-loving, approachable, and energetic side of Mercedes-Benz Benz. The evolution of Mercedes-Benz's Benz marketing strategy can be directly connected to the expansion of its target market, which now includes persons 25–35 years old as well as its initial targets—the baby boomers. In order to provide superior customer value to its target market, Mercedes-Benz Benz has found it necessary to expand its product line, provide more competitive prices, increase communications with its target market, maintain accessibility to consumers, and continue its excellent customer service. With a total of five new compact models (instead of the current two model series), Mercedes-Benz is seeking to address the expectations and lifestyle of a dynamically growing customer group. 2011 saw the launch of the new B-Class. The launch of the new A-Class is set for 2012 while plans are in place for the release of a compact coupe, compact SUV and another model.

To begin building relationships with this younger audience, Mercedes turned to social media as a platform to connect and engage with this digitally savvy, connected audience. In May 2010, Mercedes-Benz launched Stars Insight, designed to gain valuable insights into the needs and desires of one of their new and most important customer-target groups: 20- to 45-year-old compact car drivers. The decision to target younger consumers has been reinforced through Mercedes-Benz's decision to integrate Siri into its A-Class electronics system through a programme called the 'Drive Kit Plus'. Having already introduced the possibility of posting Facebook status updates for their latest vehicles, this programme will work in conjunction with Mercedes-Benz's Digital DriveStyle App to translate the iPhone's screen onto the in-car system screen. This partnership also makes them the first carmaker to integrate Apple's flagship technology into a vehicle's electronic platform. Coming pre-installed with popular apps such as Facebook, Twitter, and Aupeo Personal Radio, drivers will be able to post status updates, send text messages, listen to music and change radio

channels. There will also be a navigation system from Garmin, which will show real-time traffic information, as well as a new 'Car Finder' feature, allowing users to find their way back to their car if they're having trouble locating it. The company also remains heavily invested in Formula 1 sponsorship through McLaren-Mercedes and the Mercedes teams.

Conclusion

Mercedes-Benz's intention to actively target the younger consumer segment represents a considerable shift in the brand's marketing strategy. Mercedes-Benz has recognized the importance of this consumer segment to the long term success of the company. Initial indications are that the younger consumer segment has reacted positively to the move by Mercedes-Benz. However, with major competitors such as Audi and BMW already established in these segments it remains to be seen whether Mercedes-Benz can become a leader in this particular segment and what effect the change in positioning strategy will have on its current customer base.

Questions

1 Evaluate the alternative bases that Mercedes-Benz might use to segment its market. Which base would you recommend and why?

2 Discuss the key factors contributing to the success of Mercedes-Benz's positioning strategy.

3 Identify the factors that could potentially be used by Mercedes-Benz to assess the attractiveness of a particular market segment.

4 Critically evaluate the decision to reposition Mercedes-Benz towards a younger consumer segment.

This case was prepared by David Cosgrave, Teaching Assistant, Department of Marketing and Management, University of Limerick.

PART 3
Marketing Mix Decisions

SHOWCASE

A new Marketing Showcase video featuring an interview with Innocent's Head of Creative is available to lecturers for presentation and class discussion.

CHAPTER 9

Branding and corporate identity management

> *The first lesson of branding is memorability It is very difficult to buy something you can't remember.*
> **JOHN HEGARTY, CREATIVE DIRECTOR, BBH**[1]

LEARNING OBJECTIVES

After reading this chapter, you should be able to:

1 define the concepts of product, brand, product line and product mix
2 distinguish between manufacturer and own-label brands
3 distinguish between a core and augmented product (the brand)
4 explain why strong brands are important
5 define brand equity, the components of customer-based and proprietary-based brand equity and brand valuation
6 explain how to build strong brands
7 distinguish between family, individual and combined brand names, and discuss the characteristics of an effective brand name
8 discuss why companies rebrand and explain how to manage the process
9 discuss the concepts of brand extension and stretching, and their uses and limitations
10 describe the two major forms of co-branding, and their advantages and risks
11 discuss the arguments for and against global and pan-European branding, and the strategic options for building such brands
12 define and discuss the dimensions of corporate identity
13 describe how to manage corporate identity programmes
14 discuss ethical issues concerning products

The core element in the marketing mix is the company's product because this provides the functional requirements sought by customers. Marketing managers develop their products into brands that help to create a unique position (see Chapter 8) in the minds of customers. Brand superiority leads to high sales, the ability to charge price premiums and the power to resist distributor power. Firms attempt to retain their current customers through brand loyalty. Loyal customers are typically less price sensitive, and the presence of a loyal customer base provides the firm with valuable time to respond to competitive actions.[2] The management of products and brands is therefore a key factor in marketing success.

This chapter will explore the nature of branding and product, the importance of strong brands, how successful brands are built and how brand equity is created. Then we explore a series of key branding decisions: brand name strategies and choices, rebranding, brand extension and stretching, and co-branding. Next, issues relating to global and pan-European branding are analysed. The chapter concludes by exploring corporate identity management and ethical issues associated with branding.

Products, Services and Brands

A product is anything that is capable of satisfying customer needs. For example, a Granny Smith eating apple, a pair of Nike trainers, a Ford Focus car, or a haircut by Toni & Guy are all capable of satisfying different needs from hunger, through clothing, transportation and self-image. However, we often distinguish between products and services, with products being tangible (e.g. a sandwich) and services mainly intangible (e.g. a haircut). Consequently, it is logical to include services within the definition of the product but to be aware there are differences. Hence, there are *physical products* such as a watch, a car or a wind turbine, or *service products* such as insurance or banking. All of these products satisfy customer needs—for example, a wind turbine provides sustainable power and insurance reduces financial risk. The principles discussed in this chapter apply equally to physical and service products. However, because there are special considerations associated with service products (e.g. intangibility), and as service industries (e.g. restaurants, tourism, banking, and the public sector) are an important and growing sector in most developed countries, Chapter 10 is dedicated to examining service products and services marketing in detail.

Branding is the process by which companies distinguish their product offerings from the competition. By developing a distinctive name, packaging and design, a **brand** is created. Most brands are supported by logos—for example, the Nike 'swoosh' and the prancing horse of Ferrari. By developing an individual identity, branding permits customers to develop associations with the brand (e.g. prestige, style, low cost) and eases the purchase decision.[3] The marketing task is to ensure positive associations between the chosen positioning objectives (see Chapter 8), the product and the brand.

Branding affects perceptions. In blind product testing consumers often fail to distinguish between brands in each product category and often cannot correctly identify what they perceive to be their favourite brand (read more about Diet Pepsi and Diet Coke in Marketing in Action 9.1).

The word 'brand' is derived from the Old Norse word 'brandr', which means 'to burn' as brands were and still are the means by which livestock owners mark their animals to identify ownership.[4] This definition is still pertinent today, as modern branding aims to permanently capture a part of the buyer's mind,[5] with the aim that they always choose a particular brand.

The Product Line and Product Mix

Brands are not often developed in isolation. They normally fall within a company's product line and mix. A **product line** is a group of brands that are closely related in terms of their functions and the benefits they provide (e.g. Dell's range of personal computers, Samsung or Philips Consumer Electronics line of television sets). The *depth* of the product line depends upon the pattern of customer requirements (e.g. the number of segments to be found in the market), the product depth being offered by competitors, and company resources. For example, although customers may require wide product variations, a small company may decide to focus on a narrow product line serving only sub-segments of the market.

A **product mix** is the total set of brands marketed in a company: the sum of the product lines offered. Thus, the *width* of the product mix can be gauged by the number of product lines an organization offers. Philips, for example, offers a wide product mix comprising the brands found within its product lines of television, audio equipment, DVD players, digital cameras, and so on. Other companies have a much narrower product mix comprising just one product line, such as Aston Martin, which produces high-performance cars.

The management of brands and product lines is a key element of product strategy. First, we shall examine the major decisions involved in managing brands—namely the type of brand to market (manufacturer vs own-label), how to build brands, brand name strategies, brand extension and stretching, and the brand acquisition decision. Then we shall look at how to manage brands and product lines over time using the product life-cycle concept. Finally, we discuss managing brand and product line portfolios.

Brand Types

The two alternatives regarding brand type are manufacturer and own-label brands. **Manufacturer brands** are created by producers and bear their own chosen brand name. The responsibility for marketing the brand lies in the hands of the producer. Examples include Kellogg's Cornflakes, Gillette Sensor razors and Norton Anti-virus software. The value of the brand lies with the producer and, by building major brands, producers can gain distribution and customer loyalty.

A fundamental distinction that needs to be made is between category, brands and variants (see Fig. 9.1). A category (or product field) is divided into brands, which in turn may be divided into variants based on flavour, formulation or other feature.[6] For example, Heinz Tomato Soup is the tomato variant of the Heinz brand of the category 'soup'. In recent years several products have emerged which have become category-creating products: for example, the iPod, Yakult probiotic drinks, Spanx body-shaping underwear and Twitter.[7]

Own-label brands (sometimes called *distributor brands*) are created and owned by distributors. Own-label branding, if associated with tight quality control of suppliers, can provide consistent high value for customers, and be a source of retail power as suppliers vie to fill excess productive capacity with manufacturing products for own-label branding. The power of low-price supermarket own-label brands has focused many producers of manufacturer brands to introduce so-called **fighter brands** (i.e. their own low-price alternative). Not all own-label brands come with a low price tag, however. An example is Tesco Finest, a premium-priced own-label brand that has overtaken Kellogg's as the UK's biggest grocery brand.[8]

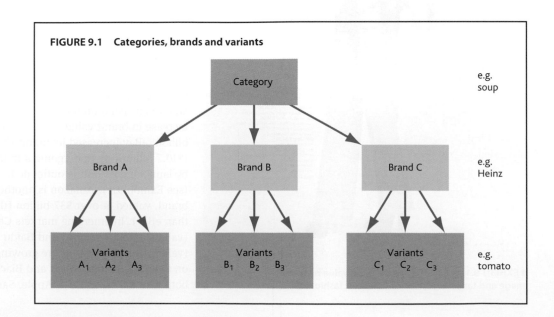

FIGURE 9.1   Categories, brands and variants

Fighter brands are not just low-price alternatives, but are generally developed as part of a competitive strategy to protect market share from predatory competitors. Examples include Qantas launching Jetstar to fight the entry of Virgin Blue into Australian airspace. Intel introduced the Intel Celeron both to protect its premium market produce, the Pentium, and to fight off its cheaper competitors.

A major decision that producers have to face is whether to agree to supply own-label products for distributors. The danger is that, should customers find out, they may believe that there is no difference between the manufacturer brand and its own-label equivalent. This led some companies, such as Kellogg's, to refuse to supply own-label products for many years. For other producers, supplying own-label goods may be a means of filling excess capacity and generating extra income from the high sales volumes contracted with distributors.

Why Strong Brands are Important

Apple, Google, IBM, China Mobile and General Electric are world leading brands valued at over $50 billion[9] and customers are prepared to pay for the assurances they offer. Strong brands, typically product category leaders, are important to both companies and consumers. Companies benefit because strong brands add value to companies, positively affect consumer perceptions of brands, act as a barrier to competition, improve profits and provide a base for brand extensions. Consumers gain because strong brands act as a form of quality certification and create trust. We now look at each of these factors in turn.

Company value

The financial value of companies can be greatly enhanced by the possession of strong brands. For example, Nestlé paid £2.5 billion for Rowntree, a UK confectionery manufacturer, a sum that was six times its balance sheet value. Nestlé was not so much interested in Rowntree's manufacturing base as its brands—such as KitKat, Quality Street, After Eight and Polo—which were major brands with brand-building potential. Procter & Gamble paid £31 billion for Gillette. Again Gillette's brands were valued at a far higher level than its physical assets. While Gillette's balance sheet mentioned only physical, tangible assets of £4 billion, its brands were worth £10 billion: Gillette £4 billion; Duracell £2.5 billion; Oral B £2 billion; Braun £1.5 billion. The balance consisted of the value of Gillette's distributor and supplier relationships (£10 billion) and its patents (£7 billion).[10] Strong branding enhances company value and brand makeovers or a slide in company performance can seriously affect valuations. For example, American Express refreshed its image, products and rewards scheme, and the additional spend on marketing contributed to an increase in brand value of 23 per cent to over $17 billion; eBay increased its brand value by 15 per cent ($10.7 billion) by undergoing a transformation driven by launching its online outlet dedicated to fashion (see Exhibit 9.1). Amazon is another very successful brand, valued at over $37 billion (three times more than eBay). In emerging markets China Mobile (valued at $57.3 billion) and Baidu search engine (valued at $22.6 billion) are growing rapidly. Brands on the slide include Nokia and BlackBerry, who have both lost market share to Apple, Samsung and other

↑ EXHIBIT 9.1 eBay extends its brand value by transforming its image and targeting specific audiences: fashion buyers.

more 'hip' smartphones. Financial brands currently losing value are Santander, the giant Spanish banking group (largely due to difficulties in the national economy), and Barclays and HSBC who have also experienced a downturn in their valuations.[11]

Consumer perceptions and preferences

Strong brand names can have positive effects on consumer perceptions and preferences. Marketing in Action 9.1 describes evidence from the soft drinks and car markets, which shows how strong brands can influence perception and preference. Clearly, the strength of Diet Coke and Toyota as powerful brand names influenced perception and preference in both markets.

Marketing in Action 9.1   Strong Brand Names Affect Consumer Perceptions and Preferences

Two matched samples of consumers were asked to taste Diet Coke, the market leader in diet colas, and Diet Pepsi. The first group tasted the drinks 'blind' (i.e. the brand identities were concealed) and were asked to state a preference. The procedure was repeated for the second group, except that the test was 'open' (i.e. the brand identities were shown). The results are presented below.

	Blind %	Open %
Prefer Diet Pepsi	51	23
Prefer Diet Coke	44	65
Equal/can't say	5	12

This test clearly shows the power of strong brand names in influencing perceptions and preferences towards Diet Coke. Advances in neuroscience may go some way to explaining the results. A re-creation of the test produced identical results, but this time the tasters were wired to a brain scanner. When the consumers tasted the drinks blind there was a flurry of activity in the part of the brain that is stimulated by taste. However, when the consumers were told which brand they were drinking, it was the part of the brain associated with higher thinking that was activated during tasting.

A second example comes from the car industry. A joint venture between Toyota and General Motors (GM) resulted in two virtually identical cars being produced from the same manufacturing plant in the USA. One was branded the Toyota Corolla, and the other GM's Chevrolet Prizm. Although the production costs were the same, the Toyota was priced higher than the Chevrolet Prizm. Despite the price difference, the Toyota achieved twice the market share of its near identical twin. The reason was that the Toyota brand enjoyed an excellent reputation for reliable cars whereas GM's reputation had been tarnished by a succession of unreliable cars. Despite the fact that the cars were virtually the same, consumers' perceptions and preferences were strongly affected by the brand names attached to each model.

Based on: De Chernatony and McDonald (2003);[12] Doyle and Stern (2006);[13] Valantine (2009)[14]

Barrier to competition

The impact of the strong, positive perceptions held by consumers about top brands means it is difficult for new brands to compete (even if the new brand performs well on blind taste testing). As we have seen, this may be insufficient to knock the market leader off the top spot. This is one of the reasons Virgin Coke failed to dent Coca-Cola's domination of the cola market. The reputation of strong brands, then, may be a powerful barrier to competition.

High profits

Strong, market-leading brands are rarely the cheapest. Brands such as Heinz, Kellogg's, Coca-Cola, Mercedes, Apple, Michelin and Microsoft are all associated with premium prices. This is because their superior brand equity means that consumers receive added value over their less powerful

⬆**EXHIBIT 9.2** **The strong Lego brand provided a foundation for its Bionicle toys.**

rivals. Strong brands also achieve distribution more readily, economies of scale, and are in a better position to resist retailer demands for price discounts. These forces feed through to profitability. A major study of the factors that lead to high profitability (the Profit Impact of Marketing Strategy project) shows that return on investment is related to a brand's share of the market: bigger brands yield higher returns than smaller brands.[15] For example, brands with a market share of 40 per cent generate, on average, three times the return on investment of brands with only 10 per cent market share. These findings are supported by research into net profit margins for US food brands. The category leader's average return was 18 per cent, number two achieved 6 per cent, number three returned 1 per cent, while the number four position was associated with a −6 per cent net profit margin.[16] Another study of hand tool manufacturers in the USA produced similar results with the market leader achieving 24 per cent, number two 4 per cent, number three 0.1 per cent and number four −4 per cent net profit margin.[17]

Base for brand extensions

A strong brand provides the foundation for leveraging positive perceptions and goodwill from the core brand to brand extensions. Examples include Diet Coke, Pepsi Max, Lucozade Sport, Smirnoff Ice, Marmite XO and Lego Bionicle (see Exhibit 9.2). The new brand benefits from the added value that the brand equity of the core brand bestows on the extension. There is a full discussion of brand extensions later in this chapter.

Quality certification

Strong brands also benefit consumers in that they provide quality certification, which can aid decision-making. The following example illustrates the lengths consumers will go to when using strong brands as a form of quality certification. Hyundai cars were not noted for their quality. Chung Ju-Yung, founder of the car company in South Korea, used to count clapped-out deserted cars as a measure of his brand's performance. So long as there were more Hyundais abandoned on the roadside than his competitors he was convinced the company was doing well. Things are very different today and the launch of the Prada Genesis cars from the Hyundai stable shows how the brand has changed. Hyundai joined with the Italian designer fashion house Prada to produce an exclusive, high-quality version of their Genesis range. Buyers in the Gulf and China are the main target audience. While this model will not significantly increase annual revenues it is a clear indication and informal certification of the quality of the brand. For online brands consumer trust is of paramount importance.[18] VeriSign produces formal certification for online brands to indicate security of an e-commerce website. In the case of Hyundai, Prada is acting as an intangible form of quality certification, whereas VeriSign certificates are highly tangible.

Trust

Consumers tend to trust strong brands. The Henley Forecasting Centre found that consumers are increasingly turning to 'trusted guides' to manage choice. A key 'trusted guide' is the brand name and its perceptual associations. Furthermore, in tough economic circumstances, trust has been found to be a discriminating factor when consumers are deciding what to buy. While consumers are making greater use of the Web and comparison sites to gather information, ultimately the belief that a brand will deliver on its promises is a deal breaker when everything else is equal. For example, Aviva and the AA both offer motor insurance in this highly competitive consumer market. Price is still a strong discriminating factor in this market but motorists are looking for something extra. Market research found that, if all motor insurance companies were offering exactly the same rate and terms, consumers' favourite brand would be the AA as it is most trusted to deliver on its brand promises.[19] Arguably, the AA has risen to this position in the minds of its target audiences by increasing its media spend and subsequently improving brand awareness. When consumers stop trusting a brand, the fallout can be catastrophic and history has revealed many notable examples. Gerald Ratner destroyed his chain of high street jewellery stores when he repeatedly spoke about the poor quality of the merchandise at public speaking engagements; Sunny Delight, Procter & Gamble's highly successful children's fruit drink, fell from grace instantly once it was revealed that drinking too much could turn children yellow; when Coca-Cola launched its Dasani bottled water in the UK, all went well until consumers were made aware it was actually bottled tap water. In each of these examples consumers lost trust in the brands because they felt they had been cheated and, while the brands made every attempt to recover, consumers were not willing to forget.

Europe's most trusted brands by product categories are shown in Table 9.1.

TABLE 9.1   Most trusted brands in Europe

Product category	Brands
Cars	VW, Toyota
Kitchen appliances	Miele, Whirlpool, Bosch, Philips, Electrolux
Personal computers	HP, Dell, Acer
Mobile phones	Nokia, Samsung
Holiday company	TUI, Club Med, Aurinkomatkat, Neckermann, Ving
Mobile phone service provider	Orange, T-Mobile, Proximus, Vodafone
Vitamins	Centrum Multi-tabs, Davitamon
Cosmetics	Nivea, Avon, Yves Rocher
Soap powder	Ariel, Persil, Dash, OMO
Breakfast cereals	Kellogg's, Nestlé, Emco

Source: based on the Readers Digest Trusted Brands 2012 report
http://www.rdtrustedbrands.com/brands.shtml

Brand Equity

Strong brands are rich in a property called brand equity. **Brand equity** is a measure of the strength of a brand in the marketplace by adding tangible value to a company through the resulting sales and profits. There are two types of brand equity: customer-based and proprietary-based brand equity. Customer-based brand equity resides in the minds of consumers and consists of brand awareness and brand image. Proprietary-based brand equity is based on assets that are attributable to the company, and consists of patents and channel relationships.

Customer-based brand equity

Marketing in Action 9.1 discussed how the strength of the Diet Coke brand name reversed consumer preferences when compared to Diet Pepsi, and how the strong reputation of Toyota meant that it could charge a higher price and still sell more than an identical car carrying GM's Chevrolet badge. This is explained by Diet Coke possessing higher brand equity than Diet Pepsi, and the Toyota brand holding more brand equity than the Chevrolet marque. This type of brand equity resides in the minds of consumers who hold more favourable perceptions and associations towards Diet Coke and Toyota than their rivals, and is called *customer-based brand equity*.

Customer-based brand equity is defined as the differential effect that brand knowledge has on consumer response to the marketing of that brand.[20] A brand has positive customer-based brand equity when consumers react more favourably to a product when the brand is identified than when it is not (e.g. the Diet Coke vs Diet Pepsi product test). Positive, customer-based brand equity is likely to result in high customer loyalty, low price sensitivity, a high willingness for customers to visit more than one outlet in order to purchase the brand and a strong base for brand extensions. On the other hand, negative customer-based brand equity occurs when consumers react less favourably towards the brand when it is identified than when it is not.

There are two sources of customer-based brand equity: brand awareness and brand image (see Fig. 9.2).

Brand awareness

Brand awareness is related to brand equity in two ways. First, by raising brand awareness, the likelihood that the brand will enter a consumer's evoked set (those brands that a consumer seriously considers before making a purchase) is increased since awareness is a pre-condition of evaluation of a brand. Second, in low-involvement situations, as we saw in Chapter 4 on understanding consumer behaviour, a purchase may follow awareness of a brand with little information processing since the purchase is of low importance or low price. In both these cases, increasing brand awareness can lead to higher sales and profits and

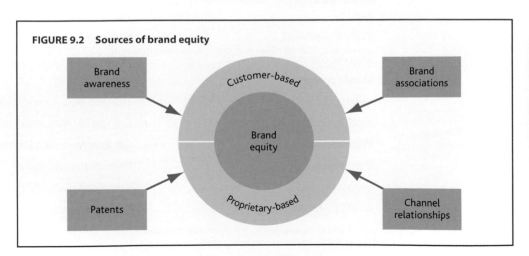

FIGURE 9.2 **Sources of brand equity**

hence increased brand equity. The global brand awareness of brands like Coca-Cola, Philips, Google, Facebook, Apple, Samsung and Nokia is a major contributor to their brand equity.

Brand image

Brand equity can also be increased by creating a strong brand image. A positive brand image is formed by generating strong, favourable and unique associations to the brand in the memory.[21] A brand image is created through the use of all elements of the marketing mix. The brand image of a car, for example, is influenced by product quality (associating it with perceptions of comfort, reliability, durability, and so on), promotion (an integrated marketing communications campaign may imbue the car with high-status connotations), price (a competitive price may confer associations with value for money), and place (a smart modern dealership may associate the car with efficient after-sales service). Advertising is often employed to create a brand image. A positive brand image, then, increases the likelihood of purchase and hence brand equity. The brands listed in Table 9.1 gain brand equity through their image of being trustworthy.

As we have seen, the value attributable to the customer-based brand equity associated with the Gillette brands (Gillette, Duracell, Oral B and Braun) when acquired by Procter & Gamble was £10 billion.[22]

In an attempt to maintain their brand image, some companies are embarking on offset schemes where, for example, air passengers are offered the option of offsetting their air miles with a fee that is invested in forest regeneration. However, the merits of such schemes need to be scrutinized carefully. Supermarkets have successfully encouraged shoppers to reduce the use of carrier bags by charging for bags or giving increased loyalty points for using your own bags. But brands need to ensure that any ecological impact claims are well founded.

Proprietary-based brand equity

Proprietary-based brand equity is derived from company attributes that deliver value to the brand. These can be found in many aspects of corporate activity but the two main sources are patents and channel relationships.

Patents

As we shall see later when discussing brand valuation, a common method is to calculate the value of a brand by taking into account future profits and discounting them to the present day. Patents give greater certainty to future revenue streams by protecting a brand from competitive threat over the lifetime of the patent. Brand equity, therefore, falls towards the end of this period. For example, the value of many pharmaceutical brands falls as their patents expire because of the launch of low-priced generic competitors. As we have seen, the value of Gillette's patents when the company was acquired by P&G was estimated at £7 billion.[23]

Channel relationships

Experience, knowledge and close relationships with distributors and suppliers can enhance the value of company brands. For example, one of the attractions of Gillette to Procter & Gamble was its complementary global distribution strengths. Gillette has strengths in India and Brazil, whereas P&G is strong in China, Russia, Japan and Turkey. This allows Gillette to push P&G brands in India and Brazil, and P&G to use its existing strong channel relationships in China, Russia, Japan and Turkey to distribute Gillette brands.[24] It is reported that the value of Gillette's channel relationships to P&G was estimated at £10 billion.[25]

Brand valuation is a difficult task. It is the process of estimating the financial value of an individual or corporate brand. A widely cited list of the top 100 global brands by financial value is produced by the Interbrand Corporation; part of this is reproduced later in this chapter. Interbrand bases its calculations on the present value of a brand after discounting future profits, rather like the way financial analysts value other assets. Its procedure is as follows:[26]

1 An estimate is made of the percentage of a company's revenue that can be credited to a brand. For some companies, the brand may be the entire company, as with McDonald's, or just a part, as with Nescafé.

2 A five-year projection of the brand's profits is made. Management consultants and banks help with these calculations.

3 The risk associated with the profit projections is assessed, taking into account such factors as market leadership, stability and global reach (the ability to cross both geographic and cultural borders).

4 A discount rate is calculated based on risk (high risk equals high discount rate), which is used to discount brand profits to arrive at a net present value.

Although Interbrand's approach does not give estimates of the value of brands in the future (something that would be useful to investors), it does provide a picture of the value of brands in any one year. In 2010, ISO 10668—the international standard framework—which sets out a standardized approach to valuing brands was introduced. The aim is to make it easier to determine the value of brands.[27] Calculating the value of brand equity is an important task since it indicates the rewards that can be reaped from marketing investments.

. . . .

Brand Building

The importance of strong brands means that brand building is an essential marketing activity. Successful brand building can reap benefits in terms of premium prices, achieving distribution more readily, and sustaining high and stable sales and profits through brand loyalty.[28]

A brand is created by augmenting a **core product** with distinctive values that distinguish it from the competition. To understand the notion of brand values we first need to understand the difference between features and benefits. A feature is an aspect of a brand that may or may not confer a customer benefit. For example, adding fluoride (*feature*) to a toothpaste confers the customer *benefits* of added protection against tooth decay and decreased dental charges. Not all features necessarily confer benefits to all users. For example, Microsoft Office is a bundle of software programs. However, for a user who only wishes to use the word processor, the spreadsheet and PowerPoint software confer no benefits.

Core benefits derive from the core product (see Fig. 9.3). Toothpaste, for example, cleans teeth and therefore protects against tooth decay. But all toothpastes achieve that. Branding allows marketers to create added values that distinguish one brand from another. Successful brands are those that create a set of brand values that are superior to other rival brands. So brand building involves a deep understanding of both the functional (e.g. ease of use) and emotional (e.g. confidence) values that customers use when choosing between brands, and the ability to combine them in a unique way to create an augmented *product* that customers prefer. This unique, **augmented product** is what marketers call the *brand*. The success of the Swatch brand was founded on the recognition that watches could be marketed as fashion items to younger age groups. By using colour and design, Swatch successfully augmented a basic product—a watch—to create appeal for its target market. Swatch combined functional and emotional values to create a successful brand. Focusing on functional values alone is rarely sufficient, as Ford discovered with its Mondeo model. Its engineers concentrated on functional attributes such as build and ride quality, fuel economy and luggage space. Exterior body design was dull, however (leading to it being referred to as the 'Blandeo'), and resulted in the car lacking the (emotional) excitement necessary to compete effectively.[29]

Figure 9.3 shows how products can be augmented. Singapore Airlines has augmented its brand by providing superior *service*. *The Times* provides superior service to its readers by being the only UK newspaper to employ an ocean correspondent (see Exhibit 9.3 below). Kia has differentiated its cars by offering seven-year *guarantees* (warranties) when most of its competitors offer only three years. Nivea was the first to differentiate its sunblock brand by the use of innovative *packaging* that allowed it to be sprayed onto the body. Bang & Olufsen has differentiated its brand using quality and design. Panasonic augments its televisions

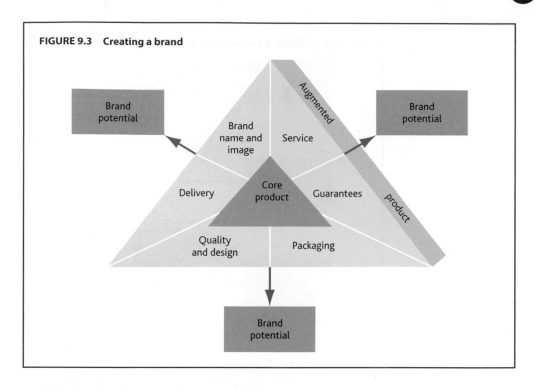

FIGURE 9.3 Creating a brand

through enhanced picture quality. The iPod has created a differential advantage by augmenting its brand through *delivery* by creating a highly efficient means of downloading music from Apple's iTunes music store. Apple has followed this success by creating its apps (applications) store for its iPhone, which allows anyone to create and sell an application, providing efficient *delivery* of extra *services* to customers. Finally, BMW has augmented its brand by its *image*, embodied in its 'The ultimate driving machine' strap-line, which differentiates it from the competition.

Managing brands involves a constant search for ways of achieving the full brand potential. To do so usually means the creation of major global brands. Leading brands such as Apple, Google, Coca-Cola, Microsoft, IBM, General Electric, AT&T and China Mobile have

⬆ EXHIBIT 9.3 *The Times* newspaper brand is augmented by providing a superior service to readers who care about the environment.

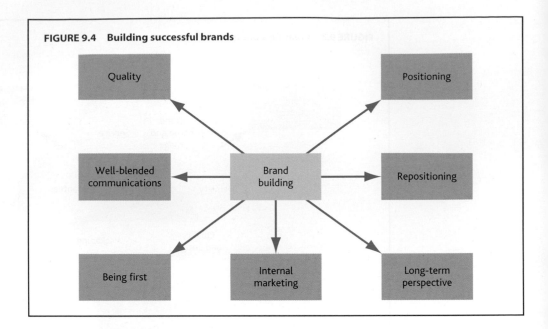

FIGURE 9.4   Building successful brands

achieved this. But how are successful brands built? A combination of some or all of seven factors can be important.[30] These are shown in Figure 9.4 and described below.

Quality

It is vital to build quality into the core product: a major reason for brand failure is the inability to get the basics right. Marketing a computer that overheats, a vacuum cleaner that does not pick up dirt effectively or a garden fork that breaks is courting disaster. The core product must achieve the basic functional requirements expected of it. A major study of factors that affect success has shown statistically that higher-quality brands achieve greater market share and higher profitability than their inferior rivals.[31] Total quality management techniques (see Chapter 5) are increasingly being employed to raise quality standards. Product quality improvements have been shown to be driven mainly by market pull (changing customer tastes and expectations), organizational push (changes in the technical potential and resources of a company) and competitor actions.[32]

Top companies such as Canon, BBC, Apple, Guinness, FedEx, Bosch, Intel, Toyota and Google understand the importance of quality in the brand-building process. Their success has been based on high-quality foundations. Once a brand is associated with quality, it forms a formidable barrier for competitors to overcome.

Positioning

Creating a unique position in the marketplace involves a careful choice of target market and establishing a clear differential advantage in the minds of those people. This can be achieved through brand names and image, service, design, guarantees, packaging and delivery. In today's highly competitive global marketplace, unique positioning will normally rely on combinations of these factors. For example, the success of BMW is founded on a quality, well-designed product, targeted at distinct customer segments and supported by a carefully nurtured exclusive brand name and image. No matter which factors are given highest priority, positioning should be founded on the 4-Cs framework discussed in Chapter 8, on market segmentation and positioning. These are clarity, consistency, credibility and competitiveness. Often the essence of the 4-Cs is used in a brand's positioning statement. For example, Audi—*Vorsprung durch Technik* (which means 'advancement through technology') or DHL—Excellence. Simply Delivered.

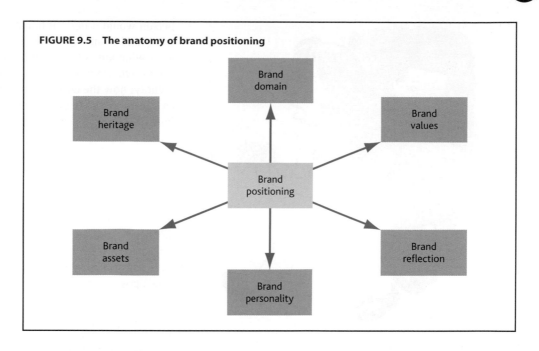

FIGURE 9.5 The anatomy of brand positioning

An analytical framework that can be used to dissect the current position of a brand in the marketplace and form the basis of a new brand positioning strategy is given in Figure 9.5. The strength of a brand's position in the marketplace is built on six elements: **brand domain, brand heritage, brand values, brand assets, brand personality** and **brand reflection**. The first element, brand domain, corresponds to the choice of target market (where the brand competes); the other five elements provide avenues for creating a clear differential advantage with these target consumers. Each will now be explained.

1   *Brand domain*: the brand's target market: i.e. where it competes in the marketplace. For example, the brand domain for Marmite is the general consumer market, while the domain for the more flavour-intensive Marmite XO is for a specialist target audience of extreme marmite lovers.

2   *Brand heritage*: the background to the brand and its culture. How it has achieved success (and failure) over its life. Brand heritage can form an extremely useful platform to build on. For example, Rose Marie Bravo built on the upmarket heritage of the Burberry brand and, by modernizing its image, created a powerful brand that saw the fortunes of the company escalate. The advertisement for Persil uses the brand's '100 years' heritage to support its reliability, toughness and gentleness.

3   *Brand values*: the core *values* and characteristics of the brand. For example, the brand values of Berghaus are high-performance outdoor clothing and the spirit of adventure, for Lycra they are comfort and fit, for Absolut Vodka purity and fun, and for Audi sophistication and progression. Ethical values for brands and companies are important. For example, Ecover, innocent smoothies, Green & Black's chocolate and Cafédirect coffee all combine strong brand values with ethical credentials.

4   *Brand assets*: what makes the brand distinctive from other competing brands, such as symbols, features, images and relationships. For example, Puma uses its namesake as its symbol that distinguishes it from other brands; the Dyson yellow bagless vacuum cleaner is a feature that distinguishes it from traditional vacuum cleaners. Nivea's 'feeling closer' strapline and distinctive blue colour captures the image of the brand, and the close relationship with customers developed by IBM over many years is a major brand asset for the company.

5   *Brand personality*: the character of the brand described in terms of other entities, such as people, animals or objects. Marketing researchers ask consumers to describe brands in these terms. For example, they might be asked 'If brand X were a person what kind of

For a
century,
the nation's
mums have
been relying,
on us to help them
with the washing. They
know that no one is better
at removing even the toughest stains
from the whitest of white dresses than Persil.
And no one is gentler on the delicate skin of the little
girls wearing them.

PERSIL *Tough but gentle for 100 years*

⬆ **EXHIBIT 9.4** Heritage can be used in advertisements to position brands in the marketplace, as this illustration featuring Persil shows.

person would it be?', 'If brand X were an animal what kind of animal would it be?' or 'If brand X were a car what kind of car would it be?'

6 *Brand reflection*: how the brand relates to self-identity; how the customer perceives him/herself as a result of buying/using the brand. The branding illustration visualizes how people use brands to reflect and project their self-identity. The importance of brand reflection is apparent in the demand for aspirational brands such as Gucci handbags, Cartier or Rolex watches, and Mercedes cars.

By analysing each element, brand managers can form an accurate portrait of how brands are positioned in the marketplace. From there, thought can be given to whether and how the brand can be repositioned to improve performance. Nostalgia is increasingly being used as a positioning concept, as Marketing in Action 9.2 discusses.

Repositioning

As markets change and opportunities arise, repositioning may be needed to build brands from their initial base. Skoda was repositioned from a downmarket car brand of dubious quality to a mid-market brand whose quality has led to several awards, and significant sales and profit growth. Samsung successfully repositioned from being perceived as a producer of cheap televisions and microwave ovens to being regarded as a 'cool' youth brand producing mobile phones and flat-screen televisions for the 'techno savvy'. Nokia also built its brand by repositioning from being a paper manufacturer to market leader in terms of its volume of mobile phone sales. See Mini Case 9.1 to find out more about repositioning a brand.

Marketing in Action 9.2 Retro Chic

In recent years there has been a spate of marketing activity intended to tap into consumer fondness for a bygone age. This can take the form of retro styling in such product categories as coffee makers, radios, refrigerators, telephones and cars. The car industry, in particular, has mixed nostalgia with progress through the successful launches of the updated Mini, VW Beetle, Fiat 500 and the 1950s-designed Chrysler PT Cruiser.

In confectionery, too, companies have attempted to link in to consumers' desire to connect with the past, with the relaunch of the Cadbury Wispa bar, Orangina returning in its iconic glass bottle and Nestlé bringing back the Drifter bar.

The number of car brands launching models in white has snowballed to meet the rise in consumer demand for the retro colour, last popular in the 1980s. The biggest-selling white car is the Mini, encouraging other manufacturers like BMW, Nissan, Toyota, Honda, Seat and Citroën to offer models in the same colour. Other sectors use the retro style. Shabby chic (a term coined by *The World of Interiors* magazine in the 1980s) styling, for example, is increasingly used by interior designers, furniture manufacturers and fabric designers to create an antique and/or vintage look and feel. From distressed tables to washed-out, bleached jeans shabby chic continues to influence product design and style.

Using nostalgia as a positioning concept makes sense as brands attempt to evoke feelings of comfort, authenticity and sanctuary in a world beset by economic and security concerns.

Based on: Brownsell (2008);[33] Gray (2008);[34] Nettleton and Lovell (2008);[35] Wikipedia (2012)[36]

Mini Case 9.1 Keep Off the Grass at the National Trust

The UK, like many other parts of Europe, abounds with historic houses, parks and gardens, sites of interest and natural beauty. The National Trust is a British organization responsible for managing over 300 such properties and a quarter of a million hectares of grounds. The National Trust had a brand positioning problem as many individuals associated the organization with the prohibitory phrase 'Keep off the grass'. The stuffy, old-fashioned image may even have been deterring the core target audience—the 50 somethings—from visiting sites and becoming National Trust members. To reposition the brand, a strategy was launched that aimed to target three groups: 1) *Explorer families*—ABC1s looking for a day out as family, and some educational time; 2) *Out and about*—individuals and groups looking for outdoor relaxation and adventure; and 3) *Curious minds*—people who like discovering new things.

The repositioning brand strategy had a budget in excess of £1 million, and the main aim was to encourage the target segments to see 'the Trust' as 'the gateway to a wide variety of experiences for all ages'. An integrated marketing communication campaign (discussed in Chapter 14) using outdoor advertising (30 per cent of the budget), press advertising (35 per cent), website advertising (25 per cent) and radio (10 per cent) was used to spread the message and change perceptions.

The campaign images showed intended target audiences in various settings, enjoying the benefits the Trust has to offer. Radio adverts featured tweeting songbirds and squeals of delight from happy children. The aim was to position the brand as a place to relax and enjoy time with friends and family.

The campaign worked; during the year there was an increase of 16 per cent in visitor numbers to National Trust properties, which translates into nearly 18 million individual visits, and the membership total grew by 600,000 to a total of nearly 4 million.

In the future the aim is to make greater use of social media to engage younger audiences and become a bigger part in everyone's daily life. The targets for 2020 are to have 5 million members.

Questions:

1 In which brand domain is the National Trust competing? Suggest some relevant examples.
2 Describe the brand heritage of the National Trust.
3 Define the brand values of the Trust and develop its brand personality.
4 Compare this personality with those of three European budget airlines.

Based on: McMeeken (2012)[37]

Well-blended communications

Brand positioning is based on customer perception. To create a clear position in the minds of a target audience requires considerable thought and effort regarding advertising, selling and other promotional activities. Awareness needs to be built, the brand personality projected and favourable attitudes reinforced. Integrated marketing communications, combining the strengths of traditional and digital media, is often used to promote such successful brands as Coca-Cola, Virgin Atlantic, Hertz car hire, Marmite and Birds Eye.

These themes need to be reinforced by salespeople, public relations and sales promotion campaigns.

Marketers can make their brands more noticeable through attractive display or package design, and also through generating customer familiarity with brand names, brand logos and a brand's visual appearance. A well-blended communications strategy is necessary to achieve these objectives.[38]

Being first

Research has shown that pioneer brands are more likely to be successful than follower brands.[39] Being first gives a brand the opportunity to create a clear position in the minds of target customers before the competition enters the market. It also gives the pioneer the opportunity to build customer and distributor loyalty. Nevertheless, being first into a market with a unique marketing proposition does not guarantee success; it requires sustained marketing effort and the strength to withstand competitor attacks. Being first into a niche market, as achieved by the iPhone, usually guarantees short-term profits, but the acid test arrives when competitors (sometimes with greater resources) enter with similar products. Another problem arises when pioneer brands have a competitive disadvantage compared with those using earlier technology. For example, the pioneers of 3G mobile phone handset technology failed to achieve success, because the handsets were bulkier and less reliable than those built on 2G technology.[40] However, this also created space for Apple and Samsung to develop 3G smartphones like the iPhone and Galaxy, which have come to dominate the market. Being first into a market can also bring the potential advantages of technological leadership, cost advantages through the experience curve effect, the acquisition and control of scarce resources and the creation of switching costs to later entrants (for example, the costs of switching from one computer system to another may be considerable).[41] Hewlett Packard (touch pad), RIM (BlackBerry Playbook) and Dell were late entrants into the tablet computer market. Companies are, therefore, speeding up their new product development (NPD) processes, even if it means being over budget.[42] A McKinsey & Co study showed that being 50 per cent over NPD budget and on time can lead to a 4 per cent reduction in profits. However, being on budget and six months late to launch can lead to a 33 per cent reduction in profits.[43]

Being first does not necessarily mean pioneering the technology. Bigger returns may come to those who are first to enter the mass market: for example, the Apple iPad. Microsoft had introduced the tablet PC in 2000 but did not successfully launch the product in the mass market, whereas Apple seized the opportunity in 2010 to capture the market.

Long-term perspective

Brand building is a long-term activity and can take many years to achieve. There are many demands on people's attention so generating awareness, communicating brand values and building customer loyalty requires significant commitment. Management should constantly evaluate brand investment to ensure they establish and maintain the desired position of a brand in the marketplace. Unfortunately, it can be tempting to cut back on expenditure in the short term. Cutting the marketing communication spend by half a million euros may immediately cut costs and increase profits. Conversely, for a well-established brand, sales are unlikely to fall substantially in the short term because of the effects of past advertising. The result is higher short-term profits. This may be an attractive proposition for managers who are often in charge of a brand for less than two years. One way of overcoming this danger is to measure brand manager (and brand) performance by measuring brand equity in terms of awareness levels, brand associations and intentions to buy, and being vigilant in resisting short-term actions, which may cause harm.

Companies also need to be prepared to suffer losses when marketing brands in entirely new markets. For example, Tesco withstood significant losses in the USA with its Fresh and Easy chain of supermarkets, but its aim was to see a return on its investment in the near future. BSkyB was also prepared to incur losses while building its Sky satellite television brand for several years before recording its current high profits. Perhaps the most significant new market investment was Amazon. Jeff Bezos launched Amazon in 1995, and continued to invest in building the brand for a further six years before his online book store made a profit.[44]

Internal marketing

Many brands are corporate in the sense that the marketing focus is on building the company brand.[45] This is particularly the case in services, with banks, supermarkets, insurance companies, airlines and restaurant chains attempting to build awareness and loyalty to the services they offer. A key feature in the success of such efforts is internal marketing—that is, training and communicating with internal staff. Training of staff is crucial because service companies rely on face-to-face contact between service provider (e.g. waiter) and service user (e.g. diner). Also, brand strategies must be communicated to staff so that they understand the company ethos on which the company brand is built. Investment in staff training is required to achieve the service levels required for the brand strategy. Top service companies like Federal Express, IBM and Singapore Airlines make training a central element of their company brand-building plans.

Besides incorporating the above factors into brand-building plans, it can be useful to examine the reasons for brand failure so that they can be avoided. Marking in Action 9.3 discusses some of the reasons for failure.

Marketing in Action 9.3 Why Do Some Brands Fail?

Brands live in an unforgiving, harsh environment. Their survival depends on many factors, and their demise can be swift when they are not met. Here are some reasons that explain why brands have disappeared from the marketplace.

- *Failure to live up to the taste test*: Mars' Banjo artificial chocolate and its low-fat chocolate bar Flyte, Jordans' cereal bar, and Nabisco's Snackwell's low-fat, low-sugar biscuits and cakes failed the taste test. The lesson is that healthy snacks need to taste delicious too.
- *Outgunned by a more powerful rival*: KP's Brannigans crisps were popular until PepsiCo acquired Walkers and decided to invest heavily in technical and product innovation, raw materials and, especially, marketing. The result was that Brannigans floundered while Walkers became brand leader.
- *Unsustainable novelty value*: Pot Noodle, Space Dust and alcopops all found life difficult after their initial novelty value wore off.
- *Manufacturer neglect or impatience*: Cadbury's Fuse bar, Biarritz chocolates and Unilever's Radion clothing detergent suffered because of neglect. Although the Fuse bar did well in research and on launch, Cadbury failed to invest in advertising and promotion, and eventually discontinued the line.
- *Changes in consumer motivations*: Sunny Delight was initially very successful but as consumers became more health conscious its high sugar content brought about its demise.
- *Losing the war*: technology battles often have only one winner. For example, Sony's Betamax video format was beaten by JVC's VHS, and Sony's Blu-Ray DVD killed off the Toshiba-backed HD DVD format, largely because the former gained the support of most of the Hollywood film studios.
- *Lack of core competencies*: Tesco has launched a series of standalone brands—e.g. Chokablock ice cream. While Tesco has been very successful at launching new brands like Tesco Finest and Tesco Value which are brand extensions bearing the corporate brand name, the new ice cream has no such affiliation to help it become established. Tesco is not a leading ice cream manufacturer so does not undermine the credibility of competing brands like Carte D'Or, Häagen-Dazs or Ben & Jerry's. Only time will tell if Chokablock will become a successful brand.

Based on: Ritson (2011);[46] *Simms (2008)*[47]

Key Branding Decisions

Besides the branding decisions so far discussed, marketers face four further key branding decisions: brand name strategies and choices, rebranding, brand extension and stretching, and co-branding.

Brand name strategies and choices

Another key decision area is the choice of brand name. Three brand name strategies can be identified: family, individual and combination.

Family brand names

A **family brand name** is used for all products (e.g. Philips, Microsoft, Heinz, Procter & Gamble, Samsung—see Exhibit 9.5). The goodwill attached to the family brand name

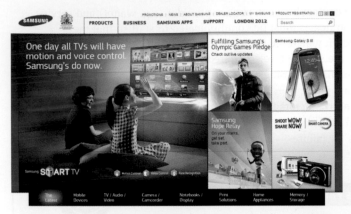

⬆EXHIBIT 9.5 Samsung uses a family brand name for all its products.

benefits all brands, and the use of the name in advertising helps the promotion of all of the brands carrying the family name. The risk is that if one of the brands receives unfavourable publicity or is unsuccessful, the reputation of the whole range of brands can be tarnished. This is also called *umbrella branding*. Some companies create umbrella brands for part of their brand portfolios to give coherence to their range of products. For example, Lego created the umbrella brand of Duplo for its range of bricks and toys targeting small children.

Individual brand names

An **individual brand name** does not identify a brand with a particular company (e.g. Procter & Gamble does not use the company name on brands such as Ariel, Fairy Liquid, Daz and Pampers). This may be necessary when it is believed that each brand requires a separate, unrelated identity. Toyota also abandoned its family brand name when it launched its upmarket executive car, which was simply called the Lexus. In some instances the use of a family brand name when moving into a new market segment may harm the image of the new product line. The same can be true when brands make acquisitions. For example, when Coca-Cola acquired Innocent,

---

Digital Marketing 9.1 The Rise and Rise of Apple as a Brand

The death of Steve Jobs, co-founder, Chairman and CEO of Apple, at the end of 2011 caused many to sit back and look at the future of one of the planet's biggest brands and biggest revenue generators. As a brand, Apple creates both love and hate in equal measure along with hotly contested debate between detractors and fans alike.

What's clear is that nothing short of continuous major success coincided with Jobs' return to Apple in 1997 and its his second career at Apple that provided the iMac, the iPod, iTunes, the iPhone and ultimately the iPad. What seems to be the reason for Apple's subsequent success?

The first is focusing on value away from price. Apple computers were expensive but they also became desirable—linked with a certain aspirational lifestyle that seemed to coincide with Apple's design ethos—in such a way that they became appliances that were pleasurable to own in their own right.

Add to that a distinct move away from the reliance on the desktop computer with the introduction of the iPod and iTunes. Apple's decision to make a version of iTunes for Windows was regarded as a masterstroke, giving non-Apple (i.e. Windows) users a chance of Apple technology ownership. The iPod clearly signalled Apple's move away from reliance on the computing market, with iTunes indicating that content rather than physical technology would be a key part of its future. And the use of white earphones (unique at the time) advertised to others that despite the iPod being hidden from view, it was clearly an Apple iPod that was being used and contributed to the vicarious tribalism attributed to Apple product ownership.

The subsequent introductions of iPod Touch, iPhone (signifying Apple's move into a completely new market) and ultimately the iPad are all signifiers of a constant move away from its computing roots. While all of the subsequent product lines are more expensive than their competitive counterparts (emphasizing the permanent link with aspiration), sales are enormous. At the time of writing Apple does not own the highest market share for iPhone, yet it generates the highest return. Its computing line generates comparatively only a small amount of income.

It's difficult to predict Apple's future. For many it is the brand more than product with which people want to share their values. Some commentators argue that the brand was/is bigger than Jobs and that the design ethos in the products came from a group of people rather than simply from him. Whatever happens, it is a huge example of the power of a single person with a vision and a single brand.

Prepared by David Bird.

the reputation of the latter was damaged as it was viewed as selling out to a large corporation[48] and setting aside its ethical brand principles. BMW also chose not to attach its family brand name to the Mini since it would have detracted from the car's sense of 'Britishness'.

Combination brand names

A **combination brand name** combines family and individual brand names to capitalize on the reputation of the company, while allowing the individual brands to be distinguished and identified. For example, in the Microsoft family, Microsoft Windows 8, MSN (Microsoft Network), Internet Explorer 9, Xbox, Connect, Bing, Windows Live and Windows Mobile are some of the company's most successful brands.[49] Read Digital Marketing 9.1 to learn more about Apple's brands.

Criteria for choosing brand names

The choice of brand name should be carefully thought out, since names convey images. For example, the brand name Pepsi Max was chosen for Pepsi's diet cola targeted at men, as it conveyed a masculine image in a product category that was associated with women. So, one criterion for deciding on a good brand name is that it evokes *positive associations*.

A second criterion is that the brand name should be easy to *pronounce and remember*. Short names such as Esso, Shell, Daz, Ariel, Orange and Mini fall into this category. There are exceptions to this general rule, as in the case of Häagen-Dazs, which was designed to sound European in the USA where it was first launched. A brand name may suggest *product benefits*, such as Right Guard (deodorant), Head & Shoulders (anti-dandruff shampoo), MacBook Air (light computer), or express what the brand is offering in a *distinctive way* such as Toys 'Я' Us. Technological products may benefit from *numerical* brand naming (e.g. Airbus 380, Aston Martin DB9) or *alphanumeric* brand names (e.g. Audi A4, Samsung F400). This also overcomes the need to change brand names when marketing in different countries.

The question of brand *transferability* is another brand name consideration. With the growth of global brands, names increasingly need to be able to cross geographical boundaries. Companies that do not check the meaning of a brand name in other languages can be caught out, as when General Motors launched its Nova car in Spain only to discover later that the word meant 'it does not go' in Spanish. The lesson is that brand names must be researched for cultural meaning before being introduced into a new geographic market. One advantage of non-meaningful names such as Diageo and Exxon is that they transfer well across national boundaries.

Specialist companies have established themselves as brand name consultants. Market research is used to test associations, memorability, pronunciation and preferences. Legal advice is important so that a brand name *does not infringe an existing brand name*. Table 9.2 summarizes the issues that are important when choosing a brand name.

Brand names can also be categorized, as shown in Table 9.3.

TABLE 9.2 **Brand name considerations**	
A good brand name should:	
1.	evoke positive associations
2.	be easy to pronounce and remember
3.	suggest product benefits
4.	be distinctive
5.	use numerals or alphanumerics when emphasizing technology
6.	be transferable
7.	not infringe an existing registered brand name

TABLE 9.3 Brand name categories

People	Adidas, McDonald's, Chanel, Heinz, Marriott, Louis Vuitton
Places	Singapore Airlines, Deutsche Bank, Air France
Descriptive	T-Mobile, Body Shop, Federal Express, Airbus, Weetabix
Abstract	KitKat, Kodak, Prozac, IKEA
Evocative	iPod, Orange, Apple, Häagen-Dazs, Dove
Brand extensions	Diet Coke, Pepsi Max, Lucozade Sport
Foreign meanings	Lego (from 'play well' in Danish)

Read the Research 9.1 Brand Relevance

The new paradigm is to make your offering so innovative that competitors become irrelevant because they don't have a 'must have' feature. David Aaker in his article shows you how to identify the 'must haves', and offers some good real-world examples from a range of top brands to identify this. The article goes on to explore the differences between brand preference and brand relevance competition and shows why winning the brand relevance battle should be an investment priority.

David A. Aaker (2012) Win the Brand Relevance Battle and then Build Competitor Barriers, California Management Review *54(2), 43–57.*

This article focuses on the management of the overall importance of brands for consumer decision-making. The main construct is brand relevance in category, or BRiC, and looks across categories and countries including the United Kingdom and United States.

The authors develop this framework and test it with 5700 consumers and demonstrate how it varies across 20 product categories and five countries.

Marc Fischer, Franziska Völckner and Henrik Sattler (2010) How Important Are Brands? A Cross-Category, Cross-Country Study, Journal of Marketing Research *47(5), 823–39.*

Rebranding

The act of changing a brand name is called **rebranding**. It can occur at the product level (e.g. Treets to M&Ms) and the corporate level (e.g. One2One to T-Mobile). Table 9.4 gives some examples of name changes. Rebranding is risky and the decision should not be taken

TABLE 9.4 Brand name changes

Product level		Corporate level	
Old name	**New name**	**Old name**	**New name**
Treets/Bonitos	M&Ms	One2One	T-Mobile
Marathon	Snickers	BT Wireless	O_2
Jif/Cif/Vif/Vim	Cif	Grand Metropolitan/Guinness	Diageo
Raider	Twix	Airmiles	Avios
Virgin One	The One Account	Airtours	MyTravel
Wanadoo	Orange	Ciba-Geigy/Sandoz	Novartis
ntl	Virgin	Andersen Consulting	Accenture
		Norwich Union	Aviva

lightly. Abandoning a well-known and, for some, favourite brand runs the risk of customer confusion and resentment, and loss of market share. When Coca-Cola was rebranded (and reformulated) as New Coke, negative customer reaction forced the company to withdraw the new brand and reinstate the original one.[50] Previously, the UK Post Office tried to rebrand as Consignia but this initiative was met with objections from consumers, employees and the media, so the decision was reversed and the Royal Mail Group established as the corporate brand name. Airmiles, the travel rewards programme, rebranded using the name Avios. The change was brought about by the merger between British Airways and International Airlines Group. The merger enabled a complete facelift for the points scheme, bringing more flexibility and greater opportunities for gathering points. The Avios brand was co-created with Interbrand and launched within an IMC communication campaign using social media, digital and PR initiatives together with print, outdoor and television advertising.[51]

Go to the website to see the Avios Anything Can Fly advert and the challenges faced while making it. www.mcgraw-hill.co.uk/textbooks/jobber

Why rebrand?

Despite such well-publicized problems, rebranding is a common activity. The reasons are as follows.[52]

Merger or acquisition

When a merger or acquisition takes place a new name may be chosen to identify the new company. Sometimes a combination of the original corporate names may be chosen (e.g. when Glaxo Wellcome and SmithKline Beecham formed GlaxoSmithKline), a completely new name may be preferred (e.g. when Grand Metropolitan and Guinness became Diageo) or the stronger corporate brand name may be chosen (e.g. when Nestlé acquired Rowntree Mackintosh).

Desire to create a new image/position in the marketplace

Some brand names are associated with negative or old-fashioned images. The move by BT Wireless to drop its corporate brand name was because it had acquired an old-fashioned, bureaucratic image. The new brand name, O_2, was chosen because it sounded scientific and modern, and because focus groups saw their mobile phones as an essential part of their lives (like oxygen).[53] The negative image of the cable television company ntl, caused by poor service, was part of the reason for buying Virgin Mobile, which allows it to use the Virgin brand under licence across its consumer businesses.[54] Similar motivations were behind the rebranding of Andersen Consulting to Accenture. Image considerations were also prominent when, after the acquisition of Orange, France Telecom decided to drop its Wanadoo brand in favour of Orange. Also the negative association of the word 'fried' in Kentucky Fried Chicken stimulated the move to change the name to KFC.

The sale or acquisition of parts of a business

The sale of the agricultural equipment operations of the farm equipment maker International Harvester prompted the need to change its name to Navistar. The acquisition of the Virgin One financial services brand by the Royal Bank of Scotland from the Virgin Group necessitated the dropping of the Virgin name. The new brand is called The One Account.

Corporate strategy changes

When a company diversifies out of its original product category, the original corporate brand name may be considered too limiting. This is why Esso (Standard Oil) changed its name to Exxon as its product portfolio extended beyond oil. Also British Steel has become Corus (now owned by Tata Steel) as the company widens its products beyond steel.

Brand familiarity

Sometimes the name of a major product brand owned by a company becomes so familiar to customers that it supersedes the corporate brand. In these circumstances the company may decide to discard the unfamiliar name in favour of the familiar. That is why Consolidated Foods became Sara Lee and BSN became Danone.

International marketing considerations

A major driver for rebranding is the desire to harmonize a brand name across national boundaries in order to create a global brand. This was the motivation for the change of the Marathon chocolate bar name in the UK to Snickers, which was used in continental Europe, the dropping of the Treets and Bonitos names in favour of M&Ms, the move from Raider to Twix chocolate bars, the consolidation of the Unilever cleaning agent Jif/Cif/Vif/Vim to Cif, Norwich Union to Aviva, and the One2One brand in the UK to T-Mobile, which is used by its parent company Deutsche Telecom in Germany. Companies may also change brand names to discourage parallel importing. When sales of a premium-priced brand in some countries are threatened by reimports of the same brand from countries where the brand is sold at lower prices, rebranding may be used to differentiate the product. This is why the Italian cleaning agent Viakal was rebranded in some European countries as Antikal.

Legal problems

A brand name may contravene an existing legal restriction on its use. For example, the Yves St Laurent perfume brand Champagne required a name change because the brand name was protected for use only with the sparkling wine from the Champagne region of France.

Managing the rebranding process

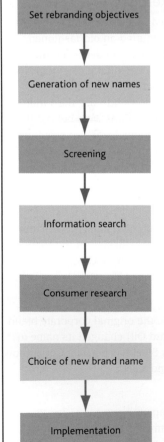

FIGURE 9.6   The rebranding process

- Set rebranding objectives
- Generation of new names
- Screening
- Information search
- Consumer research
- Choice of new brand name
- Implementation

Rebranding is usually an expensive, time-consuming and risky activity, and should only be undertaken when there is a clear marketing and financial case in its favour and a strong marketing plan in place to support its implementation.[55] Management should recognize that a rebranding exercise cannot of itself rectify more deep-seated marketing problems.

Once the decision to rebrand has been made, two key decisions remain: choosing the new name and implementing the name change.

Choosing the new brand name

The issues discussed earlier in this chapter regarding choosing brand names are relevant when changing an existing name. These are that the new brand name should evoke positive associations, be easy to pronounce and remember, suggest positive benefits, be distinctive, be transferable, not infringe an existing registered brand name, and consideration should be given to the use of numerals when emphasizing technology. These issues should form the basis of the first step, setting the rebranding objectives (see Fig. 9.6). For example, a key objective of the new name might be that it should be easily remembered, evoke positive associations and be transferable across national boundaries.

The second step is to generate as many brand names as possible. Potential sources of names include consumers, employees, distributors, specialist brand name consultants and advertising agencies.

The third step is to screen the names to remove any with obvious flaws, such as those that are difficult to pronounce, too close to an existing name, have adverse double meanings and do not fit with the rebranding objectives. The objective is to reduce the names to a shortlist of around 6–12. For the fourth step, an information search is carried out to check that each name does not infringe on an existing registered brand name in each country where the brand is, or may be, marketed.

The fifth step is to test the remaining names through consumer research. The key criteria, such as memorability, associations and distinctiveness, chosen in step one (rebranding objectives) will be used to assess the performance of the new names. Finally, management will assess the virtues of each of the shortlisted brand names and come to a conclusion about which one should be chosen and registered.

Implementing the name change

Name changes can meet considerable resistance from consumers, employees and distributors. All three groups can feel that their loyalty to a brand has been betrayed. Attention also has to be paid to the media and financial institutions, particularly for corporate name changes. Careful consideration is required to change a name and all interested parties should be involved in the process and understand the logic underlying the change. Implementing a brand name change requires attention to five key issues:[56]

1 *Coordination*: name change requires harmonious working between the company departments and those groups most involved—marketing, production, the salesforce, logistics and general management. All must work together to avoid problems and solve any that may arise.

2 *Communication*: all stakeholders—for example, customers, employees and investors— need to be targeted with communications that notify them early and with a full explanation. When the chocolate bar known as Raider in continental Europe changed its name to Twix, which was the name used everywhere else, consumers in Europe were informed by a massive advertising campaign (two years' advertising budget was spent in three weeks). Retailers were told of the name change well in advance by a salesforce whose top priority was the Twix brand. Trial was encouraged by promotional activities at retail outlets. The result was a highly successful name change and the creation of a global brand.

3 *Understanding what the consumer identifies with the brand*: consumer research is required to understand what consumers identify as the key characteristics of the brand. Shell made the mistake of failing to include the new colour (yellow) of the rebranded Shell Helix Standard (from Puissance 7) in its advertising, which stressed only the name change from Puissance 7 in France. Unfortunately customers, when looking for their favourite brand of oil, paid most attention to the colour of the can, so they could not find their usual brown can of Puissance 7 and did not realize it was now in a yellow can and had a new and unfamiliar name. The lesson is that rebranding means making sure target audiences are informed of all of the brand changes.

4 *Providing assistance to distributors/retailers*: to avoid confusion at distributors/retailers, manufacturers should avoid double-stocking of the old and new brand and ensure barcodes and product management systems are updated. Mars management took great care to ensure that on the day of the transfer from Raider to Twix, no stocks of Raider would be found in the shops, even if this meant buying back stock.

5 *Speed of change*: consideration should be given to whether the change should be immediate (as with Twix) or subject to a transitional phase where, for example, the old name is retained (perhaps in small letters) on the packaging after the rebrand (the Philips name was retained on all Whirlpool household appliances, which were branded Philips Whirlpool in Europe for seven years after the companies joined to form the world's largest household appliance group). Old names are retained during a transitional period when the old name has high awareness and positive associations among consumers. Retaining an old brand name following a takeover may be wise for political reasons, as when Nestlé retained the Rowntree name on its brands for a few years after its takeover of the UK confectionery company.

Brand Extension and Stretching

A **brand extension** is the use of an established brand name on a new brand within the same broad market or product category. For example, the Anadin brand name has been extended to related brands: Anadin Extra, Maximum Strength, Soluble, Paracetamol and Ibuprofen. The Lucozade brand has undergone a very successful brand extension with the introduction of Lucozade Sport, with isotonic properties that help to rehydrate people more quickly than other drinks, and replace the minerals lost through perspiration. Coca-Cola has

TABLE 9.5 Brand extensions and stretching

Brand (line) extensions	Brand stretching
Anadin brand name used for Anadin Extra, Maximum Strength, Soluble, Paracetamol and Ibuprofen	Dyson, from vacuum cleaners to hand dryers and bladeless room fans
McDonald's launched McCafé, a coffee house style food chain	Yamaha (pianos) brand name used on motor cycles, hi-fi, skis, pianos and summerhouses
Lucozade extends to Lucozade Sport, Energy, Hydroactive and Carbo Gel	Jimmy Choo, the luxury shoemaker, has moved into bags, men's fragrances, jewellery and clothing
McCain Chips extended its range with Home Chips (Authentic), Oven Chips (Healthier), French Fries, ready baked jacket potatoes, micro chips	Mont Blanc (pen specialist) has moved into watches, jewellery and glasses

Go to the website to see how Hyundai and Kia are using brand stretching. www.mcgraw-hill.co.uk/textbooks/jobber

extended its Coke brand into Diet Coke, and its variant form: Diet Coke with cherry. Google has also extended its core brand with many variants including Google Plus, Google Answers, Google Maps, Google Street View, Google Book Search, Google Scholar. These are examples of *line* extensions. An extreme form of brand extension is known as brand stretching. **Brand stretching** is when an established brand name is used for brands in unrelated markets or product categories, such as the use of the Yamaha pianos brand name on hi-fi equipment, skis and motorcycles. Menswear designer fashion brands like Paul Smith, Ted Baker and Tommy Hilfiger have also been extended from clothing to fragrances, footwear and home furnishings. Table 9.5 gives some examples of brand extensions and stretching.

Some companies have used brand extensions and stretching very successfully. Richard Branson's Virgin company is a classic example. Beginning in 1970 as Virgin Records, the company grew through Virgin Music (music publishing), Megastores (music retailing), Radio, Vodka, Cola, Atlantic Airways (long-haul routes), Express (short-haul routes), Rail, Money (insurance, credit cards, mortgages etc.), One (one-stop online banking), Media (digital TV, broadband, phone and mobile), Healthcare and many more. The Virgin Group has over 400 subsidiaries. Another spectacular success was when Gabrielle Coco Chanel stretched her clothing brand to perfume. Chanel No. 5 became the world's best-selling perfume, allowing women who could not afford Chanel fashion clothing to share the aura of the brand.[57] Apple has also stretched its brand from computers (Macintosh) to mobile music players (iPod), smartphones (iPhone), tablet computers (iPad) and interactive tv (iTV name subject to negotiation in the UK).

Brand extension is an important marketing tactic. Two key advantages of brand extension in releasing new products are that it reduces risk and is less costly than alternative launch strategies.[58] Both distributors and consumers may perceive less risk if the new brand comes with an established brand name. Distributors may be reassured about the 'saleability' of the new brand and therefore be more willing to stock it. Consumers appear to attribute the quality associations they have of the original brand to the new one.[59] An established name enhances consumer interest and willingness to try the new brand.[60] Consumer attitudes towards brand extensions are more favourable when the perceived quality of the parent brand is high.[61] For example, Yakult Light is an extension of the Yakult brand.

Launch costs can also be reduced by using brand extension. Since the established brand name is already well known, the task of building awareness of the new brand is eased. Consequently, advertising, selling and promotional costs are reduced. Furthermore, there is the likelihood of achieving advertising economies of scale since advertisements for the original brand and its extensions reinforce each other.[62]

A further advantage of brand extensions is that the introduction of the extension can benefit the core brand because of the effects of the accompanying marketing expenditure. Sales of the core brand can rise due to the enhancement of consumers' perception of brand values and image through increased communication.[63]

However, these arguments can be taken too far. Brand extensions that offer no functional, psychological or price advantage over rival brands often fail.[64] Consumers shop around, and brand extensions that fail to meet expectations will be rejected. There is also the danger that marketing management under-funds the launch believing that the spin-off effects from the original brand name will compensate. This can lead to low awareness and trial. *Cannibalization*, which refers to a situation where the new brand gains sales at the expense of the established brand, can also occur. For example, additional flavour extensions of the Absolut Vodka brand were found to cannibalize sales of existing ones, leading to a refocus on the original brand.[65] Further, brand extension has been criticized as leading to a managerial focus on minor modifications, packaging changes and advertising rather than the development of real innovations.[66] There is also the danger that bad publicity for one brand affects the reputation of other brands under the same name. The Virgin brand name was in danger of being tarnished at one time by the poor punctuality of its trains under the Virgin Trains brand. Massive investment in new locomotives and rolling stock cured the problem.[67] However, research has shown that the danger of the brand extension damaging the reputation of the core brand is much greater when the brand is extended within its original line (as in the Anadin example) than when the brand is stretched into new product categories. For example, if Tag Heuer's mobile phone (the Meridiist) is unsuccessful, the damage to Tag Heuer's brand equity in its original category of watches is far less than if it produced a new line of watches that kept bad time.[68]

A major test of any brand extension opportunity is to ask if the new brand concept is compatible with the values inherent in the core brand. Brand extensions, therefore, are not viable when a new brand is being developed for a target group that holds different values and aspirations from those in the original market segment. When this occurs, the use of the brand extension tactic would detract from the new brand. The answer is to develop a separate brand name, as with Toyota's Lexus, and Seiko with its Pulsar brand developed for the lower-priced mass market for watches.

Finally, management needs to guard against the loss of credibility if a brand name is extended too far. This is particularly relevant when brand stretching. The use of the Pierre Cardin name for such disparate products as clothing, toiletries and cosmetics has diluted the brand name's credibility.[69]

Brand extensions are likely to be successful if they make sense to the consumer. If the values and aspirations of the new target segment(s) match those of the original segment, and the qualities of the brand name are likewise highly prized, then success is likely. The prime example is Marks & Spencer, which successfully extended from clothing to food based on its core values of quality and reliability.

Co-Branding

There are two major forms of co-branding: **product-based co-branding** and **communications-based co-branding** (see Fig. 9.7).

Product-based co-branding

Product-based co-branding involves the linking of two or more existing brands from different companies or business units to form a product in which the brand names are visible to consumers. There are two variants: parallel and ingredient co-branding. **Parallel co-branding** occurs when two or more independent brands join forces to produce a combined brand. An example is Häagen-Dazs ice cream and Baileys liqueur combining to form Häagen-Dazs with Baileys flavour ice cream. For example, BlackBerry (RIM) partnered with Sky in the Sky

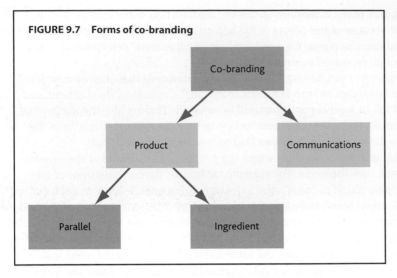

FIGURE 9.7   Forms of co-branding

Atlantic channel, and both brand names appear together on the channel communications; Siemens and Porsche Design, which produce a range of kettles, toasters and coffee machines under the Siemens Porsche co-brand; and Senseo Douwe Egberts coffee pods, created for use in the Philips Senseo coffee machine.[70]

Ingredient co-branding is found when one supplier explicitly chooses to position its brand as an ingredient of a product. Intel is an ingredient brand. It markets itself as a key component (ingredient) of computers. The ingredient co-brand is formed by the combination of the ingredient brand and the manufacturer brand—for example, Hewlett-Packard or Sony. Usually the names and logos of both brands appear on the computer. Although Baileys liqueur may at first sight seem to be an ingredient brand, it is not since its main market positioning is as an independent brand (a liqueur) not as an ingredient of ice cream.[71] Figure 9.8 shows the distinction between parallel and ingredient co-branding.

The advantages of product-based co-branding are as follows.

Added value and differentiation

The co-branding alliance of two or more brands can capture multiple sources of brand equity, and therefore add value and provide a point of differentiation. For example, Hyundai's Prada Genesis. Another example is the alliance between Nike and Lego's 'Bionicle' action heroes to form 'Bionicle by Nike' trainers. The Bionicle brand adds value and differentiates the

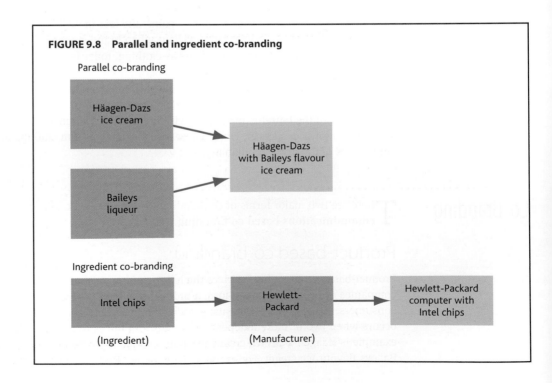

FIGURE 9.8   Parallel and ingredient co-branding

co-brand from other trainers.[72] Target (mass-market USA retailer) has joined with the Italian designer Missoni to introduce a range of 400 fashion garments.[73]

If co-branding is going to work, there needs to be certain contrasts between the brands so that joining together brings synergistic benefits. In the case of Target the Missoni design flare adds value and enables the retailer to associate more closely with premium brands. For Missoni, the biggest benefit is creating brand awareness in North America. Both companies cater for different audiences, so strong co-branding can again deliver added benefits by giving access to new customers. The potential benefits of successful co-branding are better integrated communication, organizational learning, increased brand equity and improved profits.

Positioning

A co-brand can position a product for a particular target market. The Target and Missoni co-branding partnership is a good example. Positioning was a key factor in the Senseo Douwe Egberts co-brand since the co-brand name clearly positions the coffee pods as being targeted at owners of the Philips Senseo coffee machine.

Reduction of cost of product introduction

Co-branding can reduce the cost of product introduction since two well-known brands are combined, accelerating awareness, acceptance and adoption.[74]

There are also risks involved in product-based co-branding, as described below.

Loss of control

Given that the co-brand is managed by two different companies (or at the very least different strategic business units of the same company) each company loses a degree of control over decision-making. There is potential for disagreement, misunderstanding and conflict. However, when BMW produced a limited edition of its Mini and came together with Puma interiors, both companies benefited. The major advantage for the Mini team was learning how different design teams approached the challenge of using leather to furnish their cars. For Puma the benefits were associated with brand-centric communications and greater awareness of the quality of their work.[75]

Brand equity loss

Poor performance of the co-brand could have negative effects on the original brands. In particular, each or either of the original brands' image could be tarnished.

Communications-based co-branding

Communications-based co-branding involves the linking of two or more existing brands from different companies or business units for the purposes of joint communication. This type of co-branding can take the form of recommendation. For example, Ariel and Whirlpool launched a co-branded advertising campaign where Ariel was endorsed by Whirlpool.[76] In a separate co-branding campaign Whirlpool endorsed Finish Powerball dishwasher tablets. A second variant is when an alliance is formed to stimulate awareness and interest, and to provide promotional opportunities. A deal between McDonald's and Disney gave McDonald's exclusive global rights to display and promote material relating to new Disney movies in its stores. Disney gained from the awareness and interest that such promotional material provides, and McDonald's benefited from the in-store interest and the promotional opportunities, such as competitions and free gifts (e.g. plastic replicas of film characters), the alliance provides. Communications-based co-branding can also result from sponsorship, where the sponsor's brand name appears on the product being sponsored. An example is Shell's sponsorship of the Ferrari Formula One motor racing team. As part of the deal the Shell brand name appears on Ferrari cars.

The advantages of communications-based co-branding are as follows.

Endorsement opportunities

As we have seen, Whirlpool and Ariel engaged in mutual endorsement in their advertising campaign. Endorsement may also be one-way: Shell gains by being associated with the highly successful international motor racing brand, Ferrari.

Cost benefits

One of the parties in the co-brand may provide resources to the other. Shell's deal with Ferrari demands that Shell pays huge sums of money, which helps Ferrari support the costs of motor racing. Also, joint advertising alliances mean that costs can be shared.

Awareness and interest gains

The McDonald's/Disney alliance means that new Disney movies are promoted in McDonald's outlets, enhancing awareness and interest.

Promotional opportunities

As we have discussed, McDonald's gained by the in-store promotional opportunities afforded by its co-branding alliance with Disney.

The risks involved in communications-based co-branding are similar to those of product-based co-branding.

Loss of control

Each party to the co-branding activity loses some of its control to the partner. For example, in joint advertising there could be conflicts arising from differences of opinion regarding creative content and the emphasis given to each brand in the advertising.

Brand equity loss

No one wants to be associated with failure. Poor performance of one brand could tarnish the image of the other. For example, an unsuccessful Disney movie prominently promoted in McDonald's outlets could rebound on the latter. Conversely, bad publicity for McDonald's might harm the Disney brand by association. Indeed, the Disney/McDonald's partnership was terminated by Disney, amid rumours that it did not want to be associated with a brand that had received unfavourable publicity about unhealthy eating.[77]

Some examples of product and communications-based co-brands are given in Table 9.6.

TABLE 9.6 Co-branding examples
Parallel co-brands
Häagen-Dazs and Baileys Cream Liqueur form Häagen-Dazs with Baileys flavour ice cream
Target retail and Missoni
Nike and Lego Bionicle form 'Bionicle by Nike' trainers
Siemens and Porsche Design form Siemens Porsche toasters, kettles and coffee machines
Philips Senseo and Douwe Egberts form Senseo Douwe Egberts coffee pods
Ingredient co-brands
Intel as component in Hewlett-Packard computers
Gore-tex in Berghaus and Northface waterproof jackets
Scotchgard as stain protector in fabrics
Communications-based co-brands
Ariel and Whirlpool: joint advertising campaign
Bosch dishwashers and Finish power ball
Shell and Ferrari: sponsorship

Global and Pan-European Branding

Global branding is the achievement of brand penetration worldwide. Table 9.7 lists the brands that have achieved this to become top global brands. The USA dominates the world market by owning the top ten global brands.

Europe too is home to other highly respected and well-known brands (see Table 9.8).

Levitt, a champion of global branding, argues that intensified competition and technological developments will force companies to operate globally, ignoring superficial national differences.[78] Globally consumers seek reliable, quality products at a low price, and the marketing task is to offer the same products and services in the same way, thereby achieving enormous global economies of scale. Levitt's position is that the new commercial reality is the emergence of global markets for standardized products and services on a previously unimagined scale. The engine behind this trend are the twin forces of customer convergence of tastes and needs, and the prospect of global efficiencies in production, procurement, marketing, and research and development. Asian economies are being successful in achieving these kinds of economies to produce high-quality, competitively priced global brands (e.g. Japan Toyota, Honda, Sony and Canon).

TABLE 9.7 Top global brands

Brand	Brand value ($ millions)	Country of ownership
1. Coca-Cola	71,861	USA
2. IBM	69,905	USA
3. Microsoft	59,087	USA
4. Google	55,317	USA
5. GE	42,808	USA
6. McDonald's	35,593	USA
7. Intel	35,217	USA
8. Apple	33,492	USA
9. Disney	29,018	USA
10. Hewlett-Packard	28,018	USA

Source: based on Interbrand Report (2011) Top Global Brands,
http://www.interbrand.com/en/best-global-brands/best-global-brands-2008/best-global-brands-2011.aspx

TABLE 9.8 Top brands in Europe

Brand	Brand value ($ millions)	Country of ownership
Mercedes-Benz (world rank 12)	27,445	Germany
Nokia (world rank 14)	25,071	Finland
Louis Vuitton (world rank 16)	23,172	France
H&M (world rank 21)	16,459	Sweden
Nescafé (world rank 30)	12,115	Switzerland
HSBC (world rank 32)	11,792	United Kingdom
Gucci (world rank 39)	8,763	Italy
Philips (world rank 41)	8,658	Netherlands
Zara (world rank 44)	8,065	Spain

Source: based on Interbrand Report (2011) Top Global Brands,
http://www.interbrand.com/en/best-global-brands/best-global-brands-2008/best-global-brands-2011.aspx.

The creation of global brands also speeds up a brand's time to market by reducing time-consuming local modifications. The perception that a brand is global has also been found to affect positively consumers' belief that the brand is prestigious and of high quality.[79]

In Europe the promise of pan-European branding has caused leading manufacturers to seek to extend their market coverage and to build their portfolio of brands. Nestlé has widened its brand portfolio by the acquisition of such companies as Rowntree (confectionery) and Buitoni-Perugina (pasta and chocolate), and has formed a joint venture (Cereal Partners) with the US giant General Mills to challenge Kellogg's in the European breakfast cereal market. Mars has replaced its Treets and Bonitos brands with M&Ms, and changed the name of its third largest UK brand, Marathon, to the Snickers name used in the rest of Europe.

Some global successes, such as Coca-Cola, BMW, Gucci and McDonald's, can be noted, but national varieties in taste and consumption patterns will ensure that such achievements in the future will be limited. For example, the fact that the French eat four times more yoghurt than the British, and the British buy eight times more chocolate than the Italians reflects the kinds of national differences that will affect the marketing strategies of manufacturers.[80] Indeed, many so-called global brands are not standardized, claim the 'local' marketers. For example, Coca-Cola in Scandinavia tastes different from that in Greece, and Nescafé has many different varieties of its classic instant coffee blend, the aim being to suit local tastes.

The last example gives a clue to answering the dilemma facing companies that are considering building global brands. The question is not whether brands can be built on a global scale (clearly they can) but which parts of the brand can be standardized and which must be varied across countries. A useful way of looking at this decision is to separate out the elements that comprise the brand, as shown in Figure 9.9. Can brand name and image, advertising, service, guarantees, packaging, quality and design, and delivery be standardized or not?

Gillette's global success with its Sensor, Fusion and Mach 3 razors was based on a highly standardized approach: the product, brand name, the message 'The best a man can get', advertising visuals and packaging were standardized; only the voice-overs in the advertisement were changed to cater for 26 languages across Europe, the USA and Japan.

Lever Brothers found that, for detergent products, brand image and packaging could be standardized but the brand name, communications execution and brand formulation needed to vary across countries.[81] For example, its fabric conditioner used a cuddly teddy bear across countries but was named differently in Germany (Kuschelweich), France (Cajoline), Italy (Coccolini), Spain (Mimosin), the USA (Snuggle) and Japan (Fa-Fa). Brand image and packaging were the same but the name and formulation (fragrance, phosphate levels and additives) differed between countries.

In other circumstances, the brand form and additions may remain the same across countries but the brand communications may need to be modified. For example, a BMW car may be positioned as having an exclusive image, but what Dutch and Italian car buyers consider are the qualities that amount to

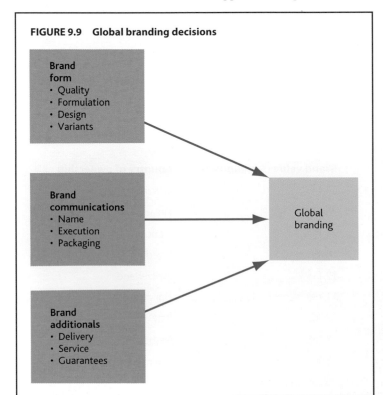

FIGURE 9.9 Global branding decisions

Brand form
- Quality
- Formulation
- Design
- Variants

Brand communications
- Name
- Execution
- Packaging

Brand additionals
- Delivery
- Service
- Guarantees

Global branding

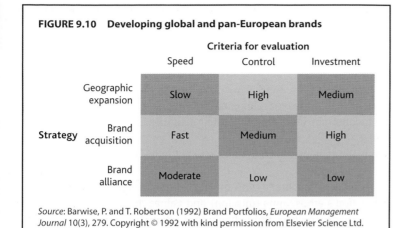

FIGURE 9.10   Developing global and pan-European brands

	Criteria for evaluation		
	Speed	Control	Investment
Strategy — Geographic expansion	Slow	High	Medium
Strategy — Brand acquisition	Fast	Medium	High
Strategy — Brand alliance	Moderate	Low	Low

Source: Barwise, P. and T. Robertson (1992) Brand Portfolios, *European Management Journal* 10(3), 279. Copyright © 1992 with kind permission from Elsevier Science Ltd.

exclusiveness are very different.[82] Consequently, differing advertising appeals would be needed to communicate the concept of exclusiveness in these countries.

Much activity has taken place over recent years to achieve global and pan-European brand positions. There are three major ways of doing this, as outlined below.[83]

1 *Geographic extension:* taking present brands into the geographic markets.
2 *Brand acquisition:* purchasing brands.
3 *Brand alliance:* joint venture or partnerships to market brands in national or cross-national markets.

Managers need to evaluate the strengths and weaknesses of each option, and Figure 9.10 summarizes these using as criteria speed of market penetration, control of operations and the level of investment required. Brand acquisition gives the fastest method of developing global brands. For example, Unilever's acquisition of Fabergé, Elizabeth Arden and Calvin Klein immediately made it a major player in fragrances, cosmetics and skincare. Brand alliance usually gives moderate speed. For example, the use of the Nestlé name for the Cereal Partners (General Mills and Nestlé) alliance's breakfast cereals (e.g. Cheerios, Shreddies and Shredded Wheat) in Europe helped retailer and consumer acceptance. Geographic extension is likely to be the slowest unless the company is already a major global player with massive resources, as brand building from scratch is a time-consuming process. Many brands are attempting to enter the rapidly expanding markets in China, with varying success. For example, B&Q and Best Buy have opened and then closed stores but Tesco and Bosch are succeeding. Bosch attributes its success to understanding the needs of the market. The company has been trading in China for over a century using the name Bo Shi and develops specific products for the local markets—e.g. power tools.[84]

However, geographic extension provides a high degree of control since companies can choose which brands to globalize, and plan their global extensions. Brand acquisition gives a moderate degree of control although many may prove hard to integrate with in-house brands. Brand alliance fosters the lowest degree of control, as strategy and resource allocation will need to be negotiated with the partner.

Finally, brand acquisitions are likely to incur the highest level of investment. For example, Nestlé paid £2.5 billion for Rowntree, a figure that was over five times its net asset value and P&G paid £10 billion for brands owned by Gillette (Gillette, Duracell, Oral B and Braun). Geographic extension is likely to be more expensive than brand alliance since, in the latter case, costs are shared, and one partner may benefit from the expertise and distribution capabilities of the other. For example, in the Cereal Partners' alliance, General Mills gained access to Nestlé's expertise and distribution system in Europe. Although the specifics of each situation need to be carefully analysed, Figure 9.10 provides a framework for assessing the strategic alternatives when developing global and pan-European brands.

Corporate Identity Management

Managers also need to be aware of the importance of the corporate brand as represented by its corporate identity. **Corporate identity** represents the ethos, aims and values of an organization, presenting a sense of its individuality, which helps to differentiate it from its competitors. A key ingredient is visual cohesion, which is necessary to ensure that all corporate communications are consistent with each other and results in a corporate image that defines values and character. The objective is to establish a favourable reputation with an organization's stakeholders, which it is hoped will be translated into a greater likelihood of purchasing the organization's goods and services, and working for and investing in the organization.[85]

Corporate identity management has emerged as a key activity of senior marketing and corporate management because of the following developments.[86]

- Mergers, acquisitions and alliances have led to many new or significantly changed companies that require new identities (e.g. Diageo).
- Some existing companies have undertaken 'reimaging' by changing the reality of their activities and/or via their communications to make their activities/image more technology orientated (e.g. O_2).
- The emergence of dotcom and new media companies created many new company identities.

Corporate identity management is concerned with the conception, development and communication of an organization's ethos, aims (mission) and values. Its orientation is strategic and is based on a company's culture and behaviour. It differs from traditional brand marketing directed towards consumers or organizational purchases since it is concerned with all of an organization's stakeholders and the wide-ranging way in which an organization communicates. If managed well, it can affect organizational performance by attracting and retaining customers, increasing the likelihood of creating beneficial strategic alliances, recruiting high-quality staff, being well positioned in financial markets, maintaining strong media relations and strengthening staff identification with the company.[87]

An example of the successful use of corporate identity management is Arcadis, an infrastructural engineering company with its headquarters in the Netherlands but with operations all over the world. A strong corporate identity was particularly important to give a sense of unity to a company that had grown largely through acquisition. The company believes that its identity, which brings with it a set of specific values, has produced benefits both for internal staff and external customers.[88]

Not all corporate identity activities are successful, however. An example is the repainting of British Airways' tail fins. Originally, all BA tail fins were the colour of the Union Jack, symbolizing its British heritage. In an attempt at global repositioning, most of them were repainted using the colours of the national emblems of many overseas countries. The move allegedly backfired as passengers, especially business people, disliked the excessive variety in tail-fin design.[89]

Dimensions of corporate identity

A corporate identity can be broken down into five dimensions or identity types, namely actual identity, communicated identity, conceived identity, ideal identity and desired identity. This framework is called the AC^2ID test and is shown in Figure 9.11. By analysing each dimension a company can test the effectiveness of its corporate identity.[90]

Each of these five dimensions will now be explained.

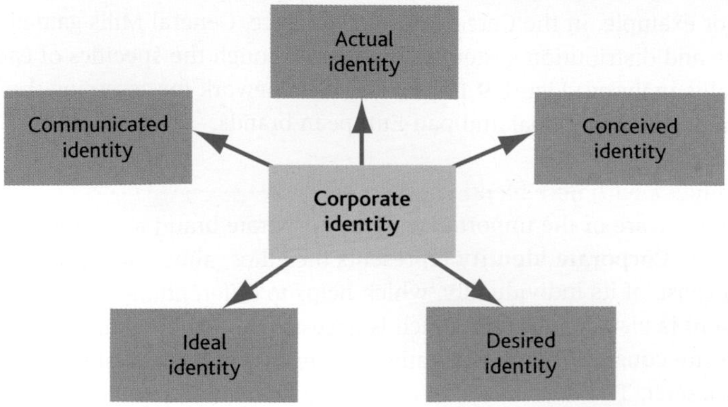

Actual identity

This represents the reality of the organization and describes what the organization is. It includes the type and quality of the products offered by the organization, the values and behaviour of staff, and the performance of the company. It is influenced by the nature of the corporate ownership, the leadership style of management, the organization structure and management policies, and the structure of the industry.

FIGURE 9.11   The five dimensions of corporate identity (the AC^2ID test)

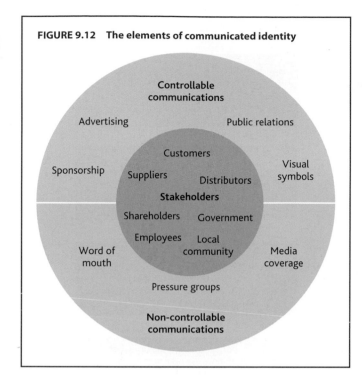

FIGURE 9.12   The elements of communicated identity

Controllable communications

Advertising

Public relations

Customers

Suppliers

Distributors

Visual symbols

Stakeholders

Shareholders   Government

Employees   Local community

Sponsorship

Word of mouth

Media coverage

Pressure groups

Non-controllable communications

Communicated identity

This is the identity the organization reveals through its 'controllable' corporate communications programme. Typically, communicational tools such as advertising, public relations, sponsorship and visual symbols (corporate names, logos, signs, letterheads, use of colour and design, and word font) are used to present an identity to stakeholders.

Additionally, communicated identity may derive from 'non-controllable' communications such as word of mouth, media coverage and pressure groups such as Greenpeace. Figure 9.12 illustrates the elements of communicated identity.

Conceived identity

This refers to the perceptions of the organization held by relevant stakeholders such as customers, suppliers, distributors, shareholders, government, employees and the local community where the company operates. It reflects the corporate image and reputation held by these groups.

Ideal identity

This represents the optimum (best) positioning of the organization in its market or markets. It is normally based on a strategic analysis of the organization's capabilities and prospects in the light of its macro- and microenvironment.

Desired identity

This lives in the hearts and minds of corporate leaders. It is their vision for the organization. This can differ from the ideal identity, which is based on research and analysis. Desired identity is likely to be based on a chief executive's vision, which is influenced more by personality and ego than rational assessment of the organization's strategic position in the marketplace.

Companies, therefore, have multiple identities, and a lack of fit between any two or more of the identities can cause problems that may weaken the company. For example, corporate communications (communicated identity) may be at odds with reality (actual identity); corporate performance and behaviour (actual identity) may fall short of the expectations of key stakeholders (conceived identity); and what is communicated to stakeholders (communicated identity) may differ from what stakeholders perceive (conceived identity).

The AC^{2}ID test, then, is a useful framework for assisting companies in researching, analysing and managing corporate identities. The next section explains how it can be used to do this.

Managing corporate identity programmes

Using the AC^{2}ID test to conduct a corporate identity audit has five stages, known as the REDS^2 AC^{2}ID Test Process.[91] This results in the identification of a strategy to resolve any gaps between the five identity dimensions. The stages are as described below.

Reveal the five identities

Each of the five identity types is audited. Actual identity is audited by measuring such elements as internal staff values, performance of products and services, and management style. Communicated identity is examined by researching such factors as the communications

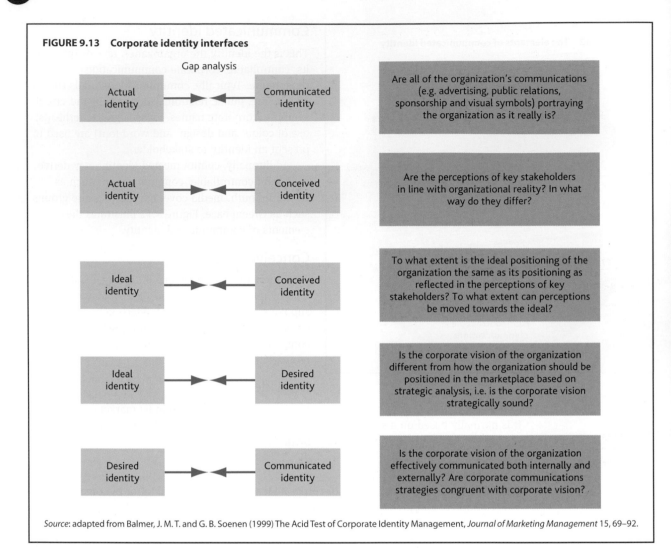

FIGURE 9.13   **Corporate identity interfaces**

Gap analysis

| Actual identity → ← Communicated identity | Are all of the organization's communications (e.g. advertising, public relations, sponsorship and visual symbols) portraying the organization as it really is? |

| Actual identity → ← Conceived identity | Are the perceptions of key stakeholders in line with organizational reality? In what way do they differ? |

| Ideal identity → ← Conceived identity | To what extent is the ideal positioning of the organization the same as its positioning as reflected in the perceptions of key stakeholders? To what extent can perceptions be moved towards the ideal? |

| Ideal identity → ← Desired identity | Is the corporate vision of the organization different from how the organization should be positioned in the marketplace based on strategic analysis, i.e. is the corporate vision strategically sound? |

| Desired identity → ← Communicated identity | Is the corporate vision of the organization effectively communicated both internally and externally? Are corporate communications strategies congruent with corporate vision? |

Source: adapted from Balmer, J. M. T. and G. B. Soenen (1999) The Acid Test of Corporate Identity Management, *Journal of Marketing Management* 15, 69–92.

sent out from the organization and media commentary. Conceived identity is measured by such elements as the corporate image and reputation as perceived by the various stakeholder groups. Ideal identity is audited by measuring such factors as the optimum product features and performance, the optimum set of internal staff values and the optimum management style. Finally, desired identity is examined by researching the vision held by senior management, especially the chief executive.

Examine the 10 identity interfaces

Each identity dimension is then compared to the others so that any gaps (misalignments) can be identified. The 10 identity interfaces can be used as a checklist of potential problem areas. To illustrate this stage, Figure 9.13 shows five interfaces and the kinds of questions that should be asked.

Diagnose the situation

The questions posed at the previous stage form the foundation for diagnosing the situation. This involves providing answers to the following questions.

- What are the problems?
- What are their nature?
- What are the implications?

Select the interfaces for attention

Which interfaces should be brought into alignment? Account should be taken of the priorities and the feasibility of the required action.

Strategic choice

What kind of strategies are required to create the corporate identity change needed to bring the interfaces into alignment? Options include reality change (including culture change), modifications to communications strategies, strategic repositioning (including moving into new technologies) and changes in corporation vision and mission.

The REDS[2] AC[2]ID Test Process, then, encourages management to address the following five questions.[92]

1 What is our current corporate identity?
2 What image is communicated by formal and informal communications?
3 What would be the ideal identity for the organization to acquire in the light of the organization's capabilities and in the light of its micro- and macroenvironment?
4 What corporate identity would senior managers wish their organization to have?
5 How can this required corporate identity be achieved?

As such it provides a practical framework for corporate identity management. It is simple, memorable, logical and operational and, therefore, is a useful tool for managers responsible for corporate branding, corporate communications and corporate identity.[93]

Ethical Issues and Anti-branding

Three major ethical issues relate to products:

1 *Product safety* is a major concern particularly in relation to consumables. Genetically modified products have attracted the attention of pressure groups such as Greenpeace who have spoken out about the dangers of genetic modification. People are sharply divided as to whether GM products are safe. Although plant breeders have for thousands of years been tampering with the genes of plants through traditional crosspollination of plants of the same species, genetic modification goes one step further as it allows scientists to cross the species barrier.

   Concerns about product safety also relate to tobacco (lung cancer), the levels of fat, sugar and salt in foods (obesity and heart problems), and sugar in soft drinks (obesity and tooth decay). Such issues have led to bans on tobacco advertising, the setting up of independent bodies to protect consumers' interests in the food and drinks industries, and reductions in the levels of fat, sugar and salt in many food and drink brands, particularly the level of sugar in food and soft drinks consumed by children. For example, Nestlé has reduced the level of sugar in its cereals targeted at children and reformulated its Rowntree range of children's sweets to make them free of artificial flavours and colours.[94]

2 *Planned obsolescence.* Many products are not designed to last a long time. From the producer's point of view this is sensible as it creates a repeat purchase situation. Hence, cars rust, clothes wear out and fashion items are replaced by the latest styles. Consumers accept that nothing lasts for ever, but the issue concerns what is an acceptable length of time before replacement is necessary. One driving force is competition. To quell the Japanese invasion, car manufacturers such as Ford and Volkswagen have made the body shells of their cars much more rust-resistant than before. Furthermore, it has to be recognized that many consumers welcome the chance to buy new clothes, new appliances with the latest features and the latest model of car. Critics argue that planned obsolescence reduces consumers' 'right to choose' since some consumers may be quite content to drive an old car so long as its body shell is free from rust and the car functions well. As we have noted, the forces of competition may act to deter the excesses of planned obsolescence.

3   *Deceptive packaging.* This can occur when a product appears in an oversized package to create the impression that the consumer is buying more than is the case. This is known as 'slack' packaging[95] and has the potential to deceive when the packaging is opaque. Products such as soap powders and breakfast cereals have the potential to suffer from 'slack' packaging. A second area where packaging may be deceptive is through misleading labelling, for example the failure of a package to state that the product contains genetically modified soya beans. This relates to the consumer's 'right to be informed', and can include the stating on labels of ingredients (including flavouring and colourants), nutritional contents and country of origin. Nevertheless, labelling can be misleading. For example, in the UK, 'country of origin' is only the last country where the product was 'significantly changed'. So oil pressed from Greek olives in France can be labelled 'French' and foreign imports that are packed in the UK can be labelled 'produce of the UK'. Consumers should be wary of loose terminology. For example, smoked bacon may well have received its 'smoked flavour' from a synthetic liquid solution, 'farm fresh eggs' are likely to be un-date-marked eggs of indeterminate age laid by battery hens, and 'farmhouse cheese' may not come from farmhouses but from industrial factories.[96]

The use of loose language and meaningless terms in the UK food and drink industry has been criticized by the Food Standards Agency (FSA). A list of offending words has been drawn up, which includes fresh, natural, pure, traditional and original.

Recommendations regarding when it is reasonable to use certain words have been drawn up. For example, 'authentic' should only be used to emphasize the geographic origin of a product and 'homemade' should be restricted to the preparation of the recipe on the premises and must involve 'some degree of fundamental culinary preparation'. The FSA has also expressed concern about the use of meaningless phrases such as 'natural goodness' and 'country-style' and recommended that they should not be used.[97]

Anti-branding and developing economies

Critics of branding accuse the practice of concentrating power and wealth in the hands of companies and economies that are already rich and powerful, whereas poor countries have to compete on price. A vociferous critic of branding is Naomi Klein,[98] who claims that branding concentrates power in the hands of the already rich and powerful, who exploit the labour force of developing countries by supporting the paying of low wages while charging high prices for their products.[99] Supporters of branding claim that it is not branding's fault that poor countries suffer from low wages and that by sourcing from those countries their economies benefit. They also point out that the companies accused of being the worst offenders, such as Nike and Gap, have taken steps to introduce ethical sourcing policies that apply when dealing with the developing world.

Arguably, such anti-brand feelings are on the increase. Powerful brands are being deconstructed by vociferous online consumers, who are voicing their opinions about brands and brand meaning via social networks, blogs and other online forums. The Internet is liberating consumers by giving them power through debate and discourse.

Consumers are making more and more use of the Internet, and instead of being passive consumers they are becoming increasingly active participants. Anti-branding websites appear high up in search listings and such sites are surviving. Expert brand-haters (rather than just moaners and complainers) are being viewed as serious sources of information for the discerning customer who likes to review and evaluate many sources of information before making a purchase decision. Websites, blogs and social media are proving to be ideal platforms for such communications.

Research has also found that there is an increasingly significant relationship between ' . . . consumer-generated anti-branding activities and brand value'. Furthermore, there has been a rise in the amount of anti-brand online content. Consequently, 'Consumers have total control of branding messages most of the time in such anti-branding spaces. Online anti-branding spaces, where the anti-branders deliver their messages in ways that conform to the consumers' points of view, gain more sympathy and credibility with most consumers.'

From the brand perspective, there is value in understanding consumer/buyer concerns and issues and seeking to identify ways to address the criticism from the increasingly powerful consumer.[100]

When you have read this chapter

log on to the Online Learning Centre at **www.mcgraw-hill.co.uk/textbooks/jobber** to explore chapter-by-chapter test questions, links and further online study tools for marketing.

Review

1 **The concept of a product, brand, product line and product mix**
- A product is anything that is capable of satisfying customer needs.
- A brand is a distinctive product offering created by the use of a name, symbol, design, packaging, or some combination of these, intended to differentiate it from its competitors.
- A product line is a group of brands that are closely related in terms of the functions and benefits they provide.
- A product mix is the total set of products marketed by a company.

2 **The difference between manufacturer and own-label brands**
- Manufacturer brands are created by producers and bear their chosen brand name, whereas own-label brands are created and owned by distributors (e.g. supermarkets).

3 **The difference between a core and an augmented product (the brand)**
- A core product is anything that provides the central benefits required by customers (e.g. toothpaste cleans teeth). The augmented product is produced by adding extra functional and/or emotional values to the core product, and combining them in a unique way to form a brand.

4 **Why strong brands are important**
Strong brands are important because they:
- enhance company value
- positively affect consumer perceptions and preferences
- act as a barrier to competition because of their impact on consumer perceptions and preferences
- produce high profits through premium prices and high market share
- provide the foundation for brand extensions
- act as a form of quality certification, which aids consumers' decision-making process
- build trust among consumers.

5 **Brand equity, its components and the concept of brand valuation**
- Brand equity is a measure of the strength of a brand in the marketplace by adding tangible value to a company through the resulting sales and profits.
- It is composed of customer-based brand equity, which is the differential effect that brand knowledge has on consumer response to the marketing of that brand, and proprietary-based brand equity, which is derived from company attributes that deliver value to the brand.
- Sources of customer-based brand equity are brand awareness and brand image.
- Sources of proprietary-based brand equity are patents and channel relationships.
- Brand valuation is the process of estimating the financial value of an individual or corporate brand.

6 **How to build strong brands**
Strong brands can be built by:
- building quality into the core product
- creating a unique position in the marketplace based on an analysis of brand domain, brand heritage, brand values, brand assets, brand personality and brand reflection
- repositioning to take advantage of new opportunities
- using well-blended communications to create a clear position in the minds of the target audience
- being first into the market with a unique marketing proposition
- taking a long-term perspective
- using internal marketing to train staff in essential skills and to communicate brand strategies so that they understand the company ethos on which the company brand is built.

7 **The differences between family, individual and combined brand names, and the characteristics of an effective brand name**
- A family brand name is one that is used for all products in a range (e.g. Nescafé); an individual brand name does not identify a brand with a particular company (e.g. Procter & Gamble does not appear with Daz); a *combination brand name* combines family and individual brand names (e.g. Microsoft Windows).
- The characteristics of an effective brand name are that it should evoke positive associations, be easy to pronounce and remember, suggest product benefits, be distinctive, use numerics or alphanumerics when emphasizing technology, be transferable and not infringe on existing registered brand names.

8 **Why companies rebrand, and how to manage the process**
- Companies rebrand to create a new identity after merger or acquisition, to create a new image/position in the marketplace, following the sale or acquisition of parts of a business where the old name is no longer appropriate, following corporate strategy changes where the old name is considered too limiting, to reflect the fact that a major product brand is more familiar to consumers than the old corporate brand, for international marketing reasons (e.g. name harmonization across national borders), consolidation of brands within a national boundary, and in response to legal problems (e.g. restrictions on its use).
- Managing the rebranding process involves choosing the new brand name and implementing the name change.
- Choosing the new brand name has six stages: setting rebranding objectives, generation of new names, screening to remove any with obvious flaws, information search to identify any infringements of existing brand names, consumer research, and choice of new brand name.
- Implementing the name change requires attention to five key issues: coordination among departments and groups; communication to consumers, employees and distributors; discovering what consumers identify with the brand so that communications can incorporate all relevant aspects of the brand; provision of assistance to distributors/retailers so that the change takes place smoothly; and care over the speed of changeover.

9 **The concepts of brand extension and stretching, their uses and limitations**
- A brand extension is the use of an established brand name on a new brand within the same broad market or product category; brand stretching occurs when an established brand is used for brands in unrelated markets or product categories.
- Their advantages are that they reduce perceived risk of purchase on the part of distributors and consumers, the use of the established brand name raises consumers' willingness to try the new brand, the positive associations of the core brand should rub off onto the brand extension, the awareness of the core brand lowers advertising and other marketing costs, and the introduction of the extension can raise sales of the core brand due to the enhancement of consumers' perception of brand values and image through increased communication.
- The limitations are that poor performance of the brand extension could rebound on the core brand, the brand may lose credibility if stretched too far, sales of the extension may cannibalize sales of the core brand and the use of a brand extension strategy may encourage a focus on minor brand modifications rather than true innovation.

10 **The two major forms of co-branding, and their advantages and risks**
- The two major forms are product-based (parallel and ingredient) co-branding and communications-based co-branding.
- The advantages of product-based co-branding are added value and differentiation, the enhanced ability to position a brand for a particular target market, and the reduction of the cost of product introduction.

- The risks of product-based co-branding are loss of control and potential brand equity loss if poor performance of the co-brand rebounds on the original brands.
- The advantages of communications-based co-branding are endorsement opportunities, cost benefits, awareness and interest gains, and promotional opportunities.
- The risks of communications-based co-branding are loss of control, and potential brand equity loss.

11 **The arguments for and against global and pan-European branding, and the strategic options for building such brands**
- The arguments 'for' are that intensified global competition and technological developments, customer convergence of tastes and needs, and the prospect of global efficiencies of scale will encourage companies to create global brands.
- The arguments 'against' are that national varieties in taste and consumption patterns will limit the development of global brands.
- The strategic options are geographic extension, brand acquisition and brand alliances.

12 **The dimensions of corporate identity**
There are five dimensions (the AC^{2}ID test):
- actual identity represents the reality of the organization and describes what the organization is.
- communicated identity is what is revealed through the organization's 'controllable' corporate communications programme and through 'non-controllable' communication such as word of mouth.
- conceived identity refers to the perceptions of the organization held by relevant stakeholders.
- ideal identity represents the organization's best positioning in its market(s).
- desired identity is what lives in the hearts and minds of corporate leaders, in particular the chief executive's vision.

13 **The management of corporate identity programmes**
This involves conducting an audit based on the REDS^2 AC^{2}ID Test Process to:
- reveal the five identities
- examine the 10 identity interfaces
- diagnose the situation
- select the interfaces for attention
- address strategic choice.

14 **Ethical issues concerning products**
- These are product safety, planned obsolescence, deceptive packaging, anti-branding and developing economies.

Key Terms

augmented product the core product plus extra functional and/or emotional values combined in a unique way to form a brand

brand a distinctive product offering created by the use of a name, symbol, design, packaging, or some combination of these, intended to differentiate it from its competitors

brand assets the distinctive features of a brand

brand domain the brand's target market

brand equity a measure of the strength of a brand in the marketplace by adding tangible value to a company through the resulting sales and profits

brand extension the use of an established brand name on a new brand within the same broad market or product category

brand heritage the background to the brand and its culture

brand personality the character of a brand described in terms of other entities such as people, animals and objects

brand reflection the relationship of the brand to self-identity

brand stretching the use of an established brand name for brands in unrelated markets or product categories

brand valuation the process of estimating the financial value of an individual or corporate brand

brand values the core values and characteristics of a brand

combination brand name a combination of family and individual brand names

communications-based co-branding the linking of two or more existing brands from different companies or business units for the purposes of joint communication

core product anything that provides the central benefits required by customers

corporate identity the ethos, aims and values of an organization, presenting a sense of its individuality, which helps to differentiate it from its competitors

customer-based brand equity the differential effect that brand knowledge has on consumer response to the marketing of that brand

family brand name a brand name used for all products in a range

fighter brands low-cost manufacturers' brands introduced to combat own-label brands

global branding achievement of brand penetration worldwide

individual brand name a brand name that does not identify a brand with a particular company

ingredient co-branding the explicit positioning of a supplier's brand as an ingredient of a product

manufacturer brands brands that are created by producers and bear their chosen brand name

own-label brands brands created and owned by distributors or retailers

parallel co-branding the joining of two or more independent brands to produce a combined brand

product-based co-branding the linking of two or more existing brands from different companies or business units to form a product in which the brand names are visible to consumers

product line a group of brands that are closely related in terms of the functions and benefits they provide

product mix the total set of products marketed by a company

proprietary-based brand equity is derived from company attributes that deliver value to the brand

rebranding the changing of a brand or corporate name

Study Questions

1. Why do companies develop core products into brands?

2. Suppose you were the marketing director of a medium-sized bank. How would you tackle the job of building the company brand?

3. Think of five brand names. To what extent do they meet the criteria of good brand naming as laid out in Table 9.2? Do any of the names legitimately break these guidelines?

4. Do you think that there will be a large increase in the number of pan-European brands over the next 10 years or not? Justify your answer.

5. What are the strategic options for pan-European brand building? What are the advantages and disadvantages of each option?

6. Why do companies rebrand product and corporate names? What is necessary for successful implementation of the rebranding process?

7. What are the two main forms of co-branding? What are their advantages and risks?

8. Describe the five dimensions of corporate identity. How can an analysis of these dimensions and their interfaces aid the management of corporate identity?

9. Discuss the major ethical concerns relating to products.

References

1. Hegarty, J.(2011) *Hegarty on advertising: turning intelligence into magic*, London: Thames & Hudson, 21.

2. DeKimpe, M. C., J.-B. E. M. Steenkamp, M. Mellens and P. Vanden Abeele (1997) Decline and Variability in Brand Loyalty, *International Journal of Research in Marketing* 14, 405–20.

3. De Chernatony, L. (1991) Formulating Brand Strategy, *European Management Journal* 9(2), 194–200.

4. Keller, K. L. (2008) *Strategic Brand Management*, New Jersey: Pearson.

5. Hegarty, J. (2011) *Hegarty on advertising: turning intelligence into magic*, London: Thames & Hudson, 39.

6. East, R. (1997) *Consumer Behaviour*, Hemel Hempstead: Prentice-Hall Europe.

7. Carter, M. (2011) 21st century alchemy, *The Marketer*, April, 28–32.

8. Bokaie, J. (2007) Too Much of a Good Thing, *Marketing*, 30 April, 15.

9. Costa, M. (2011) Brand value is jewel in the crown for marketers, *Marketing Week*, 12 May, 12–14.

10. Fisk, P. (2005) Proving Marketing's Worth, *Marketing*, 31 March, 27.

11. Costa (2011) op. cit.

12. De Chernatony, L. and M. H. B. McDonald (2003) *Creating Powerful Brands*, Oxford: Butterworth-Heinemann.

13. Doyle, P. and P. Stern (2006) *Marketing Management and Strategy*, Hemel Hempstead: Prentice-Hall.

14. Valantine, M. (2009) It's All in the Mind, *Marketing Week*, 2 April, 29.

15. Buzzell, R. and B. Gale (1987) *The PIMS Principles*, London: Collier Macmillan.

16. Reyner, M. (1996) Is Advertising the Answer?, *Admap*, September, 23–6.

17. Shipley, D. (2004) private papers.

18. Oliver, C. (2011) Hyundai shifts gear with move to quality, *Financial Times*, 19 May, 22.

19. Barnett, M. (2012) Brands build trust through media spend, *Marketing Week*, 23 February, 14–16.

20. Keller (2008) op. cit.

21. Keller (2008) op. cit.

22. Fisk (2005) op. cit.

23. Fisk (2005) op. cit.

24. Mitchell, A. (2005) P&G Scales Up Global Ambitions, *Marketing Week*, 3 February, 24–7.

25. Fisk (2005) op. cit.

26. Berner, R. and D. Kiley (2005) Global Brands, *Business Week*, 5/12 September, 54–61.

27. Mortimer, R. (2011) Getting the measure of brand valuation, *Marketing Week*, 24 August, 3.

28. Ehrenberg, A. S. C., G. J. Goodhardt and T. P. Barwise (1990) Double Jeopardy Revisited, *Journal of Marketing* 54 (July), 82–91.

29. MacIntosh, J. (2005) Ford Takes its Image Problem to the Garage, *Financial Times*, 27 September, 17.

30. See S. King (1991) Brand Building in the 1990s, *Journal of Marketing Management* 7(1), 3–14; and P. Doyle (1989) Building Successful Brands: The Strategic Options, *Journal of Marketing Management* 5(1), 77–95.

31. Buzzell and Gale (1987) op. cit.

32. Lemmink, J. and H. Kaspar (1994) Competitive Reactions to Product Quality Improvements in Industrial Markets, *European Journal of Marketing* 28(12), 50–68.

33. Brownsell, A. (2008) Marques Tap into White-Car Orders, *Marketing*, 3 September, 8.

34. Gray, R. (2008) The Good Old Days, *The Marketer*, July/August, 28–31.

35. Nettleton, K. and C. Lovell (2008) Why are Nostalgia Brands Returning?, *Campaign*, 30 May, 10.

36. Wikipedia (2012) http://en.wikipedia.org/wiki/Shabby_chic.

37. McMeeken, R. (2012) A fresh start, *The Marketer*, March/April, 22–4.

38. Pieters, R. and L. Warlop (1999) Visual Attention During Brand Choice: The Impact of Time Pressure and Task Motivation, *International Journal of Research in Marketing* 16, 1–16.

39. For example, Urban, G. L., T. Carter, S. Gaskin and Z. Mucha (1986) Market Share Rewards to Pioneering Brands: An Empirical Analysis and Strategic Implications, *Management Science* 32 (June), 645–59, showed that for frequently purchased consumer goods the second firm in the market could expect only 71 per cent of the market share of the pioneer and the third only 58 per cent of the pioneer's share. Also Lambkin, M. (1992) Pioneering New Markets: A Comparison of Market Share Winners and Losers, *International Journal of Research in Marketing* 9(1), 5–22, found that those pioneers that invest heavily from the start in building large production scale, in securing wide distribution and in promoting their products achieve the strongest competitive position and earn the highest long-term returns. For a useful summary and further evidence see Denstaulli, J. M., R. Lines and K. Grønhaug (2005) First Mover Advantage in the Discount Grocery Industry, *European Journal of Marketing* 39(7/8), 872–84.

40. Lester, R. (2005) 3 Sets Sights on Big Four, *Marketing Week*, 27 October, 26–7.

41. Leibernan, M. B. and D. B. Montgomery (1988) First Mover Advantage, *Strategic Management Journal* 9, 41–56.

42. Oakley, P. (1996) High-tech NPD Success through Faster Overseas Launch, *European Journal of Marketing* 30(8), 75–81.

43. Reinertsen, R. G. (1983) Whodunit? The Search for the New Product Killers, *Electronic Business*, 9 July, 62–6.

44. Gale Encyclopedia of E-commerce (2002), http://www.encyclopedia.com/topic/Jeffrey_Bezos.aspx.

45. King (1991) op. cit.

46. Ritson, M. (2011) Stick to running your supermarkets Tesco, *Marketing Week*, 23 June, 74.

47. Simms, J. (2008) Here Today, Gone Tomorrow, *Marketing*, 19 March, 17.

48. Barda, T. (2010) Reforming reputation, *The Marketer*, November, 32.

49. Shearman, S. (2011) Microsoft reboots, *Marketing*, 7 September, 14.

50. Benady, D. (2002) The Trouble with Facelifts, *Marketing Week*, 6 June, 21–3.

51. Johnson, B. (2011) Airmiles rebrands as Avios to meet global strategic aims, 1 September, http://www.marketingweek.co.uk/airmiles-rebrands-as-avios-to-meet-global-strategic-aims/3029731.article.

52. See Keller (2008) op. cit.; Riezebos, R. (2003) *Brand Management*, Harlow: Pearson Education.

53. Thurtle, G. (2002) Papering Over the Cracks, *Marketing Week*, 7 March, 25–7.

54. Wray, R. (2006) NTL Buys Virgin Mobile and Prepares to Battle with BSkyB, *The Guardian*, 5 April, 23.

55. Keller (2008) op. cit.

56. Kapferer, J.-N. (2008) *The New Strategic Brand Management*, London: Kogan Page.

57. BBC4 (2009) *Reputations: The Life of Gabrielle Coco Chanel*, 29 January.

58. Sharp, B. M. (1990) The Marketing Value of Brand Extension, *Marketing Intelligence and Planning* 9(7), 9–13.

59. Aaker, D. A. and K. L. Keller (1990) Consumer Evaluation of Brand Extensions, *Journal of Marketing* 54 (January), 27–41.

60. Aaker, D. A. (1990) Brand Extensions: The Good, the Bad and the Ugly, *Sloan Management Review*, Summer, 47–56.

61. Bottomley, P. A. and J. R. Doyle (1996) The Formation of Attitudes towards Brand Extensions: Testing and Generalising Aaker and Keller's Model, *International Journal of Research in Marketing* 13, 365–77.

62. Roberts, C. J. and G. M. McDonald (1989) Alternative Naming Strategies: Family versus Individual Brand Names, *Management Decision* 27(6), 31–7.

63. Grime, I., A. Diamantopoulos and G. Smith (2002) Consumer Evaluations of Extensions and their Effects on the Core Brand: Key Issues and Research Propositions, *European Journal of Marketing* 36(11/12), 1415–38.

64. Saunders, J. (1990) Brands and Valuations, *International Journal of Advertising* 9, 95–110.

65. Bokaie, J. (2008) Absolut Scales Back Flavoured Roll-Outs, *Marketing*, 13 August, 8.

66. Bennett, R. C. and R. G. Cooper (1981) The Misuse of the Marketing Concept: An American Tragedy, *Business Horizons*, Nov.–Dec., 51–61.

67. Sharp (1990) op. cit.

68. See Ritson, M. (2008) Build an Extension Outside Home Turf, *Marketing*, 25 June, 21; K. Keller and S. Sood (2003) Brand Equity Dilution, *Sloan Management Review* 45(1), 12–15.

69. Aaker (1990) op. cit.

70. Tomkins, R. (2005) A Desire for Pairings Leads Brands on a Wild Goose Chase, *Financial Times*, 29 November, 13.

71. Riezebos, R. (2003) *Brand Management*, Harlow: Pearson Education.

72. Chandiramani, R. (2002) Lego Strikes Deal with Nike for Kid's 'Bionicle' Trainers, *Marketing*, 7 November, 1.

73. Ritson, M. (2011) Opposites attract higher brand equity, *Marketing Week*, 22 September, 62.

74. Keller (2008) op. cit.

75. Ritson (2011) op. cit.

76. Kapferer (2008) op. cit.

77. Hickman, M. (2006) Disney Drops McDonald's Amid Health Fears, *Independent*, 10 May, 24.

78. Levitt, T. (1983) The Globalisation of Marketing, *Harvard Business Review*, May–June, 92–102.

79. Steenkamp, J.-B. E. M., R. Batra and D. L. Alden (2003) How Perceived Brand Globalness Creates Brand Value, *Journal of International Business Studies* 34(1), 53–65.

80. Barwise, P. and T. Robertson (1992) Brand Portfolios, *European Management Journal* 10(3), 277–85.

81. Halliburton, C. and R. Hünerberg (1993) Pan-European Marketing— Myth or Reality, *Proceedings of the European Marketing Academy Conference*, Barcelona, May, 490–518.

82. Kern, H., H. Wagner and R. Hassis (1990) European Aspects of a Global Brand: The BMW Case, *Marketing and Research Today*, February, 47–57.

83. Barwise and Robertson (1992) op. cit.

84. Costa, M. (2011) Heading East? *Marketing Week*, 7 April, 16–20.

85. Riel, C. B. M. and J. M. T. Balmer (1997) Corporate Identity: The Concept, its Measurement and Management, *European Journal of Marketing* 31(5/6), 340–55.

86. Balmer, J. M. T. and S. A. Greyser (2002) Managing the Multiple Identities of the Corporation, *California Management Review* 44(3), 72–86.

87. Balmer, J. M. T. and S. A. Greyser (2003) *Revealing the Corporation*, London: Routledge.

88. Gander, P. (2000) Image Bank, *Marketing Week*, 16 March, 43–4.

89. Martin, M. and I. Heath (1989) BA Redesign was Global Failure, *Marketing*, 2 December, 21.

90. Balmer and Greyser (2003) op. cit. (The term 'AC^{2}ID test' was trademarked by J. M. T. Balmer in 1999.)

91. See Balmer, J. M. T. and G. B. Soenen (1999) The ACID Test of Corporate Identity Management, *Journal of Marketing Management* 15, 69–92; Balmer and Greyser (2003) op. cit. The REDS^2 Acid Test Process was trademarked by J. M. T. Balmer in 1999.

92. Balmer and Soenen (1999) op. cit.

93. Davies, G. with R. Chun, R. V. Da Silva and S. Roper (2003) *Corporate Reputation and Competitiveness*, London: Routledge. This study provides empirical evidence of a link between corporate identity/image, customer and employee satisfaction, and financial performance.

94. Sweenier, M. (2005) Nestlé Takes 'Healthier' Line in Rowntree Revamp, *Marketing*, 21 March, 1.

95. Smith, N. C. (1995) Marketing Strategies for the Ethics Era, *Sloan Management Review*, Summer, 85–97. See also T. W. Dunfee, N. C. Smith and W. T. Ross Jr (1999) Social Contracts and Marketing Ethics, *Journal of Marketing* 63 (July), 14–32.

96. Young, R. (1999) First Read the Label, Then Add a Pinch of Salt, *The Times*, 30 November, 2–4.

97. *Marketing Week* (2001) An End to the Packet Racket, 2 August, 3; and Benady, D. (2001) Will They Eat Their Words? *Marketing Week*, 2 August, 24–6.

98. Klein, N. (2000) *No Logo. Taking Aim at the Brand Bullies*, London: HarperCollins.

99. Klein (2000) op. cit.

100. Kucuk, S. U. (2010) Negative Double Jeopardy revisited: A longitudinal analysis, *Journal of Brand Management* 18(2), 150–8.

iPhone
Design is Everything

Background: design is everything

Apple is a company that is good at creating markets. The iPod revolutionized popular youth culture and turned out to be the biggest trend in music markets since the launch of the Sony Walkman. In addition to changing the way we listen to music, the iPod helped secure Apple's future. Steve Jobs, chief executive of Apple, was the visionary leader who strongly influenced the development of products like the iMac, the iPod and more recently iPad. Reportedly, his guiding mantra for success is being able to *focus* and say 'no' to a product unless he feels it has world-beating qualities. Arguably, design is fundamental to the success of Apple products, and the iPhone's phenomenal success was no exception. The icon-based, touch-screen telephone handset is a symbol of Steve Job's guiding principles and he has been quoted as saying 'most people make the mistake of thinking design is just a veneer', but at Apple designers are interested in how a design works for the user as well as what a product looks and feels like. Furthermore, this approach has contributed to Apple's strong brand positioning and brand image.

The launch of the iPhone

In 2007 at the Macworld Expo, Steve Jobs launched the iPhone, and at the time of its launch it was unlike any other smartphone on the market. In terms of design, the iPhone is different from MP3 players and traditional mobile phones as there are no buttons for dialling phone numbers, or scroll wheels to select music, videos or pictures. The iPhone operates solely through its 3.5-inch 480 × 320 touchscreen, supports wireless technology, could be synchronized with other Apple products like the Mac address book and Apple's Safari browser, and has all the functionality of a video iPod. Additional innovations include a soft keyboard and the ability to change the screen content. At its launch, the phone was sold at a premium price: US$499 for the 4-gigabit (GB) version and US$599 for the 8GB. By July 2007 the iPhone had captured 1.8 per cent of the US mobile phone market, which was nearly double the sales goal set for the period, and was reported to be the best-selling mobile model on the market.

Like its predecessor, the iPod, the iPhone has some unique features, which gave the product distinctive qualities. The touchscreen was a breakthrough in the mobile phone industry as it was a blank slate, which enabled the writing of mobile software free from constraints. This feature created much excitement in the world of mobile phone software development. Indeed, the iPhone was being heralded as the next platform for software development after the personal computer and the World Wide Web. The iPhone enabled its users to be connected to the Internet wherever they were situated and carry out many activities from making a phone call, checking the weather, shopping, playing a game or trading stocks.

Development of the smartphone market

The success of Apple's iPhone attracted many competitors, each of which aimed to deliver the product features and benefits desired by the target audiences. Some of the stronger competitors included:

* The BlackBerry, produced by Research In Motion (RIM), the Canadian handset manufacturer, which was a device that offered a range of functions, and had been upgraded to offer full touchscreen functionality to rival the iPhone and The Storm, which was a similar size to the iPhone and offered better screen resolution, GPS and turn-by-turn navigation software, which is a feature missing from the early iPhone. The BlackBerry was

particularly popular with business users, perhaps due to its capacity for sending emails in a user-friendly manner.

- Nokia's 5800XpressMusic touchscreen handset was produced in direct response to the iPhone. The launch of the phone was timed to coincide with the Christmas market and, at a price of £129.95, it was aimed at parents who are concerned about their children downloading illegal music files. The phone comes with a package that allows unlimited access to 5 million music tracks from large and independent music companies.

- T-Mobile's G1 smartphone, powered by Google's open source operating system Android, was launched in autumn 2008. The handset has a small slide-out keyboard. In comparison with the iPhone, this offer lacked the aesthetic design features, but the mini-keyboard had the potential to appeal to users who need to send emails and text messages while on the move, even though its small size made it difficult to use.

- ZTE, the Chinese telecoms equipment manufacturer that produced low-cost handsets, was taking market share from all the major players. ZTE's VF 1231 smartphone was developed especially for Vodafone, and based on Windows Mobile platform. ZTE entered the market as it decided that owning a smartphone was no longer a luxury item. The phone has an attractive design that offers a range of features at very low prices, and is based on the latest operating systems. ZTE has made a significant investment in the development of smartphones in recent years.

Apple's response to the competition

This influx of imitators of the iPhone had an impact on the price of smartphones and streamlined the functionality of handsets, driving prices down and introducing various augmented features. Apple responded to the competitors by changing its original business model of selling at relatively high retail prices. In the US market the iPhone 3G sold for $199 with a two-year AT&T service contract, which is half the price of the original iPhone. The iPhone 3G offered software upgrades to owners of the original iPhone, and the introduction of an App Store which enabled owners to download free programs for every aspect of daily life (e.g. Apps for going out, Apps for around the house, Apps for managing money).

Since the launch of the original iPhone, there have been four generations of the phone and each new generation has added new benefits in addition to the standard features of portable media player, Internet client, web browsing, text and voice mail. For example, the 3GS added the 3G cellular network and a video camera as a standard feature and also new software enabled users to cut and paste text in any application, manipulate the on-screen keyboard to suit the user's preferences, and there is a range of other add-ons (e.g. games and e-books), which can be purchased through the App Store. The iPhone 4S, released in the autumn of 2011, included a front- and rear-facing camera, face time video calling and Siri, which is a voice control system. With each new generation improvements have also been made to the standard features: for example, faster processing speeds, higher-resolution display.

In the future one of the key challenges for Apple is how to constantly create added value, which distinguishes the brand from its competitors.

Convergence and the blurring of boundaries

Competition is making the new generation of mobile phones accessible to more consumers and business customers. Remember, high-tech markets are highly dynamic and the next big thing is always just around the corner. As media (video and audio) content becomes increasingly networked, available over a range of different platforms, there will be increasing demand for high-speed connectivity. Widespread adoption of the Internet and broadband connectivity has made the 365-day, 24×7 culture a reality, and users globally have come to expect instantaneous access to everything, from their emails to their favourite television programmes.

Apple has made significant inroads into the video distribution and online aggregation arena, through the iTunes online store. Users are encouraged to choose from a library of TV shows for use on its iPod. While the service is attractive, it is unlikely in its current form to challenge traditional methods of television viewing. However, Apple TV is allowing the company to move into the traditional television marketplace, and recent partnerships between Google's YouTube and Apple show how quickly the competitive landscape can change. As Apple continues to invest in developing strong content partnerships it could potentially create an alternative method for accessing television and other broadcast content through mobile devices.

Apple has its eye on other markets, too; the iPhone can be used as a navigation device, and can be coupled with a driving kit for easy use in a vehicle. Apple's developers are working hard to create totally innovative uses for the iPhone—for example, real-time remote monitoring of intensive-care patients, and many other, less serious, entertainment applications. It seems that, for the time being at least, Apple's focus on producing well-designed and innovative products with world-beating qualities will enable the company not only to lead the smartphone market but will also help the company create new markets for the future.

References

Based on: Allison, K. (2008) Apple Unveils iPhone Grand Plan, *Financial Times*, 10 March, 23; Wray, R. (2008) Nokia Challenges iPhone with Touch Screen and Unlimited Music, *Guardian*, 3 October, 31; Burrows, P. (2009) The Real Potential of Apple's iPhone, *Business Week*, 26 January, 74–6; Furness (2009)

Questions

1 Make a list of the range of features offered by a smartphone and then consider how many different devices you might use to achieve the same level of functionality in your daily life.

2 How do the new features of the 4S iPhone provide superior customer benefits compared to the earlier model?

3 Explain how smartphones are changing our daily lives and business activities.

This case was written by Fiona Ellis-Chadwick, Senior Lecturer in Marketing, The Open University.

Burberry
Reinventing the Brand

It is called 'doing a Gucci' after Domenico De Sole and Tom Ford's stunning success at turning nearly bankrupt Gucci Group into a £7 billion (€10 billion) (market capitalization) fashion powerhouse. Since 1997, when she took over, Rose Marie Bravo's makeover of the 143-year-old Burberry brand followed the same path.

The Burberry story began in 1856 when Thomas Burberry opened his first gentlemen's outfitters. By the First World War business was booming as Burberry won the contract to supply trenchcoats to the British army. Its reputation grew when it proved its contribution to the national cause. The Burberry check was introduced in the 1920s and became fashionable among the British middle to upper classes. Later, when it was worn by Humphrey Bogart in *Casablanca* and Audrey Hepburn in *Breakfast at Tiffany's*, the Burberry trenchcoat gained widespread appeal.

Bought by Great Universal Stores in 1955, the brand's huge popularity from the 1940s to the 1970s had waned by the 1980s. A less deferential society no longer yearned to dress like the upper classes, and the Burberry brand's cachet fell in the UK. This was partially offset by a surge in sales to the newly rich Japanese and other Asians after they discovered its famous (and trademarked) tan, black/red and white check pattern. By the mid-1990s the Far East accounted for an unbalanced 75 per cent of Burberry sales. British and American consumers began to regard it as an Asian brand and rather staid. Furthermore, distribution was focused on small shops with few big fashion chains and upmarket stores like Harrods stocking the brand. In the USA stores like Barney's, Neiman Marcus and Saks only sold Burberry raincoats, not the higher profit margin accessories (e.g. handbags, belts, scarves and wraps).

Change of strategy

These problems resulted in profit falls in the 1990s culminating in a £37 million (€53 million) drop in profits to £25 million (€36 million) in 1997. This prompted some serious managerial rethinking and the recruitment of American Rose Marie Bravo as a new chief executive. Responsible for the turnaround of the US store chain Saks Fifth Avenue, she had the necessary experience to make the radical changes required at Burberry.

One of her first moves was to appoint young designer Roberto Menichetti to overhaul the clothes range. His challenge was to redesign Burberry's raincoats and other traditional products to keep them fresh and attractive to new generations of younger consumers. Furthermore, he sought to extend the Burberry image to a new range of products. The Burberry brand name began to appear on such products as children's clothes, personal products, watches, blue jeans, bikinis, home-wares and shoes in order to attract new customers and broaden the company's sales base. Commenting on Menichetti, Bravo said, 'Coming in, I had studied Hermes and Gucci and other great brands, and it struck me that even during the periods when they had dipped a bit, they never lost the essence of whatever made those brands sing. And I thought, "This man will retain what's good and move us forward".'

Design was further strengthened in 2001 with the appointment of Christopher Bailey (from Gucci) as Burberry's creative director. He created Burberry 'classics with a twist' (for example, recasting the classic trenchcoat in hot pink). Bailey's job was to design clothes that met Bravo's vision of heritage and classic, but young, modern, hip and fashionable.

A second element of her strategy was to bring in advertising agency Baron & Baron and celebrity photographer Mario Testino to shoot ads featuring models Kate Moss and Stella Tennant. Other celebrities, such as the Beckhams, Callum Best, Elizabeth Jagger, Nicole Appleton and Jarvis Cocker, also featured in Burberry advertising. The focus was to emphasize the new credentials of the Burberry brand without casting off its classic roots. Getting key celebrities to don the Burberry check in its advertising was highly important in achieving this. Bravo once remarked that the famous picture of Kate Moss in a Burberry check bra cut the average age of its customers by 30 years.

A third strand in Bravo's strategy was to sort out distribution. Unprofitable shops were closed and an emphasis placed on flagship stores in cosmopolitan cities. Prestige UK retailers including Harvey Nichols were selected to stock exclusive ranges. Bravo commented, 'We were selling in 20 small shops in Knightsbridge alone, but we weren't in Harrods.' Also, stores that were selling only raincoats were persuaded to stock high-margin accessories as well. Burberry accessories increased from 20 per cent to 25 per cent of turnover. This was part of a wider focus on gifts—the more affordable side of luxury that can drive heavy footfall through the stores. As Bravo said, 'Burberry has to be thought of as a gift store. Customers have to feel they can go into Burberry and buy gifts at various price points.'

International expansion was also high on Bravo's priority list. A succession of new stores were opened, including flagship stores in London, New York and Barcelona. The New York store on 57th Street was the realization of a personal dream for Bravo, whose vision was to replace the store the company had been running in Manhattan for almost 25 years with one that was bigger, better and far more profitable. It is the biggest Burberry store worldwide and has a number of Burberry 'firsts': a lavish gift department, a large area for accessories, private shopping and an in-store Mad Hatters tea room. It also offers a service called Art of the Trench where customers can get made-to-measure trenchcoats customized by allowing them to pick their own lining, collar, checks and tartan. The Barcelona store was regarded as vital in helping to reposition the Burberry brand in Spain. Prior to its opening the brand was slightly less fashionable and sold at slightly lower prices than in the UK. The opening of the Barcelona store saw the London product being displayed for the first time as Burberry moved towards one global offering. Besides the USA and Spain, Burberry's third priority country was Japan since it was an enormous market for the company already.

The results of this activity were astonishing. Profits soared to £162 million (€227 million) by 2005, a six-fold increase since she took over, and in 2002 Great Universal Stores floated one-third of Burberry, its subsidiary, on the stock market, raising £275 million (€396 million). Then, in December 2005 it demerged Burberry completely, allocating Burberry stores to GUS shareholders in proportion to their holdings in a deal worth £1.4 billion (€2.0 billion).

Burberry did face problems, however. One was the weeding-out of grey-market goods, which were offered cheaply in Asia only to be diverted back to western markets at discounts. Not only were sales affected but brand image could be tarnished. Like Dior before it, Burberry was willing to spend the necessary money to try to eliminate this activity. Another problem was that of copycats which infringed its trademark. Burberry claim to spend about £2 million (€2.8 million) a year fighting counterfeits, running advertisements in trade publications and sending letters to trade groups, textile manufacturers and retailers reminding them about its trademark rights. It uses an Internet-monitoring service to help pick up online discussion about counterfeits. It also works with Customs officials and local police forces to seize fakes and sue infringers.

The fondness with which so-called 'chavs' regarded the Burberry check was a third problem. One observer defined a chav as a young, white, under-educated underclass obsessed with brands and unsuitable jewellery. One product with which chavs became particularly associated was the Burberry baseball cap. They were also associated with violence, particularly at football matches. The sight of football hooligans appearing in the media adorned in beige and black check was not one appreciated at Burberry HQ. In response, the company stopped producing the infamous cap and shifted emphasis to other non-check lines, including its Prorsum line of luxury clothing designed by Christopher Bailey.

A fourth problem arose in 2005 with the announcement that Bravo had decided to step down as chief executive. The woman who had built Burberry into an ultra-fashionable major global brand would need to be replaced. Her successor is Angela Ahrendts, who was recruited from the US clothing company Liz Claiborne, which owns such brands as DKNY jeans and Juicy Couture. After a period of working together, Ahrendts took the helm in July 2006 with Bravo taking the newly created role of vice-chairperson, a part-time executive position.

Ms Ahrendts made changes to the Burberry product line by making the check more subtle and using it mainly in linings and discreet areas of garments. She also placed greater emphasis on higher margin accessories such as handbags and perfumes, and top-of-the-range fashion. She has continued to use British celebrities such as Agnes Deyne and Emma Watson to represent the brand. Burberry also opened stores in emerging markets such as China, India, Russia, the Middle East and eastern Europe. In 2008 Burberry's first standalone children's-wear store in Hong Kong was opened, and in 2011 the company bought out its Chinese franchise partner in order to tighten its rein on its global image. It has also built up its presence in the US with the opening of its new headquarters in New York and further store openings.

She also improved efficiency by installing new IT systems and replacing 21 scattered distribution centres with three regional hubs in the US. Her attention has also been placed on better sourcing in an effort to improve margins.

Major investments in digital marketing have been made with digital representing 60 per cent of the marketing budget. Burberry has over 8 million Facebook fans who can watch most of its catwalk shows live and purchase Burberry products direct from its virtual store.

These activities meant that Burberry proved remarkably resilient during the economic downturn, particularly helped by demand from middle classes in emerging markets. By 2011/12 sales had risen to £1.9 billion with profits of £376 million. Ms Ahrendts saw menswear and male accessories such as bags and scarves as key to Burberry's next chapter of expansion. In 2012 its first standalone menswear store next to its branch in Knightsbridge, London was opened.

References

Based on: Heller, R. (2000) A British Gucci, *Forbes*, 3 April, 84–6; Voyle, S. (2002) Looking Beyond the Traditional Trenchcoat, *Financial Times*, 12 November, 12; White, E. (2003) Protecting the Real Plaid from a Lineup of Fakes, *Wall Street Journal*, 7 May; Barton, B. and N. Pratley (2004) The Two Faces of Burberry, *Guardian* G2, 15 April, 2–3; Barns, E. (2005) Are Advertisers Wise to Chase the Chav Pound?, *Campaign*, 24 March, 18; Callan, E. (2006) Burberry Seeks to Offer Luxury in US Midwest, *Financial Times*, 7 July, 1; Walsh, F. (2006) Burberry Chief Turns on Charm with 19 per cent Growth in Retail Sales, *Guardian*, 13 July, 28; Kollewe, J. and G. Wearden (2008) Burberry Sees Profits Rise While Laura Ashley Suffers, *Guardian*, 29 May, 26; Gumbel, P. (2008) The Luxury Market Loses Its Lustre, *Fortune*, 22 August, 27; Wardell, J. (2009) Burberry Makes Loss For Year, *Business Week*, 19 May, 64; Wood, Z. (2010) Burberry Buys Out Chinese Partner to Unify the Brand, *Guardian*, 17 July, 33; Ritson, M. (2011) Burberry Offers a Lesson in Consistency, *Marketing Week*, 2 June, 54; Barrett, C. and T. Bradshaw (2011) Burberry in Step with Digital Age, *Financial Times*, 1 September, 16; Leroux, M. and S. Thompson (2012) Burberry Banks on the Ascent of (Fashionable) Man, *The Times*, 24 May, 43.

Questions

1 How were the clothes bearing the Burberry name augmented to create a brand before the 1980s?

2 What elements of the brand-building factors discussed in this chapter have been used by Burberry to rebuild its brand?

3 What problems might arise in trying to build Burberry into a global brand?

4 What are the dangers inherent in Burberry's strategy since 1997?

This case was written by David Jobber, Professor of Marketing, University of Bradford.

CHAPTER 10

Services marketing

> **There are no such things as service industries. There are only industries whose service components are greater or less than those of other industries. Everybody is in service.**
> **LEVITT (1972)**

> **It is not so much the products you sell that guarantee success but the service you provide to customers.**
> **LUKE JOHNSON, ENTREPRENEUR**

LEARNING OBJECTIVES

After reading this chapter, you should be able to:

1   describe the nature and special characteristics of services
2   describe the activity sectors in the services industry
3   explain how customer relationships should be managed
4   explain how to manage service quality, productivity and staff
5   explain how to position a service organization and brand
6   discuss the services marketing mix
7   describe the nature and special characteristics of non-profit marketing

This chapter discusses the marketing of services. Throughout this text we adopt the stance that physical products and service products are equally important in terms of the marketing requirements. Furthermore, it is essential to be aware of how principles of marketing apply to services. In addition to the 4-Ps the marketing of services requires understanding of the services marketing mix. Furthermore, it is important to be aware of how superior value is created in the service industries by bringing together a company and its customers in the value creation process.[1] This approach has been called service *dominant logic* and it focuses marketers' attention on the creation of value and the importance of relationships in contrast to the traditional model of marketing, which has the exchange of manufactured goods as its dominant logic. From this point of view marketers should think about how best to manage and co-create value with customers. This means developing long-term relationships that are mutually beneficial.[2]

Services become increasingly valuable to industrialized economies as advances in technology lead to the development of sophisticated products that require more design, production and maintenance services. Other reasons for the rising contribution of services to the global economy are growth in per capita income. This gives citizens a greater percentage of their income to spend on non-essentials such as restaurant meals, national and international travel, which are all service-intensive products. Greater discretionary income increases demand for financial services such as investment trusts and personal pensions. It is not just in the consumer sector where there is an increase in demand for services. In industrial sectors the trend towards outsourcing means that manufacturers are buying in services. Often it is more efficient for a firm to use external expertise to manage distribution, warehousing and catering, leaving time to focus on its core competencies. Deregulation has also increased the level of competition in certain service industries (e.g. telecommunications, television, airlines) and this has also been a driver of expansion of services.

To give you an idea of the growing significance of services industry, in Europe it accounts for over 73 per cent of GDP compared to 25 per cent from industrial manufacturing and 2 per cent from agriculture. Moreover, the dominance of services can be seen globally. See Table 10.1.

The service sector in the UK dominates the economy, contributing nearly 78 per cent of GDP. There are discretely different sub-sectors within the sector (see Table 10.2).

In addition, public administration, and other services industries, which include work carried out in private households, and employed persons contribute to the service economy.

TABLE 10.1 Contribution of industrial, agricultural and service industry sectors to GDP can be divided into sectors

Country	GDP (Purchasing Power Parity)	Industrial sector (%)	Agricultural sector (%)	Services sector (%)
USA	14.6 trillion	22.1	1.1	76.8
China	10.9 trillion	46.9	10.2	43.0
Japan	4.3 trillion	24.9	1.4	73.8
India	4.06 trillion	26.3	18.5	55.2
Germany	2.9 trillion	27.8	0.9	71.3
Russia	2.2 trillion	36.8	4.0	59.1
United Kingdom	2.173 trillion	21.8	0.7	77.5
Brazil	2.172 trillion	26.8	5.8	67.4
France	2.145 trillion	18.5	2.0	79.5
Italy	1.77 trillion	25.3	1.9	72.8

Source: CIA World Facts Book (2012).

TABLE 10.2   The UK service industry sectors

Sector	Areas of activity	Leading companies
Creative industries	Advertising, software design, Web services, film industry, theatres, TV & radio, publishing, music	BBC, Tiger Aspect, Sky, Channel 4
Government services	Education, health and social work	NHS Direct
Financial and business services	Banking	HSBC, Barclays Bank, Admiral insurance, Aviva
Hotels and restaurants	Tourism, fastfood, pubs, leisure clubs	Intercontinental Hotels, Thomas Cook, Whitbread, Greene King
Property management	Real estate, renting, computer related	
Transport, storage and communications	Land, air transport, business services, post and telecoms	Vodaphone, Virgin, T-mobile, Orange, British Airways
Retailing	Motor, wholesale, supermarkets	Tesco, Morrisons, Marks & Spencer, Asda, Next
Non-profit	Alleviation of hunger, protection of animals	Oxfam, RSPCA

The Service Industries

The sectors which make up the service industries vary in what they do and the services they offer. In this section we briefly consider each of the areas of activity highlighted in Table 10.2. The basic premise in each of the sectors is that businesses engage in economic activity, which involves using particular knowledge, skills and expertise in the production of specialist services as opposed to manufacturing products (e.g. car production), growing produce (e.g. farming) or extracting minerals (e.g. mining). We will explore this idea in more detail in the next section when discussing the physical goods–service continuum model.

Creative industries

This sector relies on developing services based on creative skills: for example, creatives (advertising), writers, fashion designers, artists, musicians, television producers. Creative industries are enjoying a period of growth and in the UK around 2.2 million people work in this sector.[3] Software development and electronic publishing are the most active parts of the sector—in economic terms—followed by publishing, advertising, architecture, music and the visual arts, film, TV & radio and design. Creative industries generate distinctive and authentic 'products' which are difficult to replicate. So creative labour 'is geared to the production of original or distinctive commodities that are primarily aesthetic and/or symbolic—expressive rather than utilitarian and functional'.[4] Bill Gates (Microsoft), Steve Jobs (Apple), J. K. Rowling (writer), Jamie Oliver (celebrity chef), Damien Rice (singer/songwriter) are all examples of successful individuals who began and developed their careers in the creative industries. Increasingly, creative people understand the importance of leveraging market advantage from their skills and talents. In the past commercial values and artistic autonomy were seen as being in opposition. But now 'the very best artists are also some of the most effective entrepreneurs'.[5]

⬆ **EXHIBIT 10.1   Canary Wharf financial services centre in London, UK.**

Furthermore, it is important to remember that creative skills are also at the centre of product innovation, and a firm's innovation in the design area can contribute significantly to its overall level of performance.[6]

Government services

The public sector in many countries around the world involves the provision and delivery of services by the government for the country's citizens. The sector typically includes education, health, social care, police, defence and transport. This is a highly complex part of the service industry and processes are central to much of the activity which takes place. For example, maintaining relationships with suppliers is important to ongoing success of procurement processes. E-procurement has been widely adopted as a means of reducing operational cost while maintaining organizational standards. However, while is is arguably easy to measure the process procurement performance (especially since the advent of e-procurement systems) it is more difficult to monitor the process of, say, a patient being taken into hospital, as the individual circumstances can vary considerably—as can the outcome depending on the patient's health at presentation at the hospital (or point of care). This sector also tends to have less clear goals, which makes setting objectives complex. Another complexity which is arguably unique to this sector is the involvement of politics. In the UK the National Health Service is often subject to public scrutiny through the media.[7] Nevertheless, marketing has an important role to play, and organizations from councils to hospitals can use the marketing mix in their strategy and planning. For example, Directgov is a digital service provided to help UK citizens find helpful information and access to services. It is important to note that much of the marketing activity in this sector is concerned with customer satisfaction despite the lack of direct competition.[8]

Financial services

In this sector of the industry, banking and insurance are the key areas of activity. The focus of the industry is financial management, which includes investment, and the lending of money, insurance issues, and pensions. This industry sector serves both large corporations and individuals. Investment banking typically provides services to corporate clients. We have mentioned mergers and acquisitions and takeovers earlier, and these activities are likely to be handled by investment banks that provide the required skill sets to handle the moves. Commercial banks handle deposits and loans for companies and individuals. In the UK the financial services sector employs 1 million people and contributes around 12 per cent to GDP. The City of London is a centre of excellence for financial expertise and has attracted many leading financial organizations to locate part of their businesses there. This sector of the services industry plays a significant part in the economic well-being of local and global economies.

Hospitality, travel and tourism

This part of the sector is very diverse. Under this heading we are primarily thinking about the providers of travel and hospitality services rather than the transportation element, which is covered separately. Hospitality is made up of many facets, from pubs, restaurants and hotels, to theme parks and special-interest activities like wine-tasting events. The hospitality industry caters for the needs of business and individuals alike. From a marketing perspective, an important point to be aware of is that many of the services offered in this part of the sector are highly perishable. In other words, the vacancy rate in a hotel is an important determinant of its likely success. If the rate is high and there are many empty rooms, the business is performing poorly. The same is true of the travel industry. Service suppliers such as travel agents and operators both on- and offline are constantly aiming to fill their holidays and tours. Sales promotions are widely used to sell available places. Travelling for pleasure has been on the increase for many years. While it used to be an activity associated with the rich, package holidays and more recently low-cost air travel have made foreign travel accessible to more consumers. This sector also includes business travel.

Property management

As with other parts of the sectors, a range of activities are involved and, although provided primarily for business-to-business markets, there is a part of the sector which provides services for the individual. Property management includes handling day-to-day management of clients, maintenance and repairs, and this can mean handling residential or commercial properties.

Transport, storage and communications

This part of the sector covers rail, road, water and air transportation, and communications services for both individuals and businesses. Communication services include postal and telecommunications services.

Retailing

Retailing is an important element of the service industry: it is the activity involved in the sale of products to the ultimate consumer. Retailing is a major employer of the European Union's workforce. Again this is a very diverse industry, and retailers make use of every aspect of the product and services marketing mix. In order to deliver the service expectations of their customers, retailers have to ensure they have the right products in the right place and at the right time, which has implications for purchasing and logistics (discussed in detail in Chapter 17). One of the key functions of retailing is to 'break-bulk so that consumers can buy goods in small quantities to satisfy their needs'.[9] Consumer decision-making involves not only the choice of product and brand, but also of retail outlet. Most retailing is conducted in stores such as supermarkets, catalogue shops and departmental stores, but non-store retailing such as mail order and automatic vending also accounts for a large amount of sales. Retailing provides an important service to customers, making products available when and where customers want to buy them. Many large retailers exert enormous power in the distribution chain because of the vast quantities of goods they buy from manufacturers. The purchasing power of retailers has meant that manufacturers have to maintain high service levels and good buyer–supplier relationships.

Non-profit organizations

Non-profit organizations also contribute to service sector activity, the key difference being that these organizations attempt to achieve some objective other than profit. This does not mean they are uninterested in income, as they have to generate cash to survive. However, their primary goal is non-economic—for example, to provide cultural enrichment (an orchestra), to protect birds and animals (Royal Society for the Protection of Birds, Royal Society for the Prevention of Cruelty to Animals), to alleviate hunger (Oxfam), to provide education (schools and universities), to foster community activities (community association), and to supply healthcare (hospitals) and public services (local authorities). Their worth and standing is not dependent on the profits they generate.

Marketing is of growing importance to many non-profit organizations because of the need to generate funds in an increasingly competitive arena. Even organizations that rely on government-sponsored grants need to show how their work is of benefit to society: they must meet the needs of their customers. Many non-profit organizations rely on membership fees or donations, which means that communication to individuals and organizations is required, and they must be persuaded to join or make a donation. This requires marketing skills, which are increasingly being applied. Such is the case with political parties, which use marketing techniques to attract members (and the fees their allegiance brings) and votes at elections.

In this section, we have briefly introduced the different areas of activity in the services industry. Next, we shall examine the nature of services as these principles guide much of the management activity in all of the above.

The Nature of Services

Cowell states that 'what is significant about services is the relative dominance of *intangible attributes* in the make-up of the 'service product'. Services are a special kind of product. They may require special understanding and special marketing efforts.[10] Pure services do not result in ownership, although they may be linked to a physical good. For example, a machine (physical good) may be sold with a one-year maintenance contract (service).

Many offerings, however, contain a combination of the tangible and intangible. For example, a marketing research study would provide a report (physical good) that represents the outcome of a number of service activities (discussions with client, designing the research strategy, interviewing respondents and analysing the results). This distinction between physical and service offerings can, therefore, best be understood as a matter of degree rather than in absolute terms. Figure 10.1 shows a physical goods–service continuum, with the position of each offering dependent upon its ratio of tangible/intangible elements. At the pure goods end of the scale is clothing, as the purchase of a skirt or socks is not normally accompanied by a service. Carpet purchases may involve an element of service if they require professional laying. Machinery purchase may involve more service elements in the form of installation and maintenance. Software design is positioned on the service side of the continuum since the value of the product is dependent on design expertise rather than the cost of the physical product (disk). Marketing research is similarly services based, as discussed earlier. Finally, psychotherapy may be regarded as a pure service since the client receives nothing tangible from the transaction.

Drawing a line between goods and services is difficult. Indeed, it has been argued that any such attempt to do so misses the point. Vargo and Lusch[11] suggest the marketers' 'love affair' with products is over and has been superseded by a new 'service-aligned ethos'. This means that managers should make services central to their activities rather than the product. Ultimately, in this model the product becomes a 'keepsake' of the service experience and the customer is a 'co-creator of value'. Vargo and Lusch's[12] paper has been influential in the marketing literature but the terminology has been hotly debated by academics.[13] Nevertheless, their work sets out a model, which suggests that marketing can serve as a framework for integrating marketing and supply chain management (SCM) practices in a manner, which enables the 'target user/consumer' to take part in the creation process.[14]

We have already touched on one characteristic of services that distinguishes them from physical goods: intangibility. There are, in fact, four key distinguishing characteristics: intangibility, inseparability, variability and perishability (see Fig. 10.2).

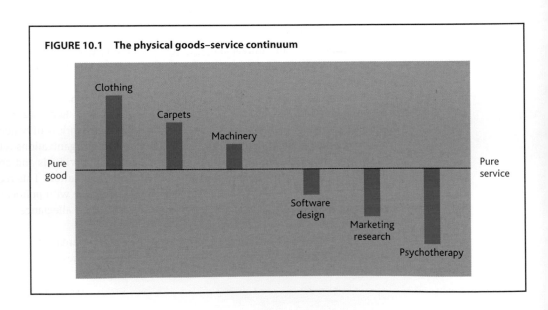

FIGURE 10.1   The physical goods–service continuum

re·search
(noun) ¹ the
study of m

Read the Research 10.1 **Service Dominant Logic**

Service dominant logic challenges the status quo of marketing thinking by putting service rather than the production of goods at the heart of business activity.

Stephen L. Vargo and Robert F. Lusch (2004) Evolving to a New Dominant Logic for Marketing,
Journal of Marketing 68(1), 1–17.

In 2004 Stephen Vargo and Robert Lusch proposed that marketing had changed significantly during past decades and consequently should be viewed from a different perspective. These authors suggested that rather than looking at marketing using a logic based on tangible resources and the economic exchange process, more attention should be given to intangible resources, relationships and co-creation of value. This paper sets out the key ideas of service dominant logic and in doing so has sparked off a controversial academic debate.

Stephen Brown and Anthony Patterson (2009) Harry Potter and the Service-Dominant Logic of Marketing: a cautionary tale,
Journal of Marketing Management 25(5–6), 519–33.

This paper contributes to the discussion of the empirical validity of the service dominate logic (SDL) theory by using the Harry Potter phenomenon as the basis of a qualitative study. Stephen Brown and Anthony Patterson suggest that SDL can be applied to the Potter marketing phenomenon if the reading of the book translates into *use value* and fans become *co-creators of value*. However, they are somewhat sceptical about the extent to which SLD offers a clear lens through which to gain greater marketing management insights.

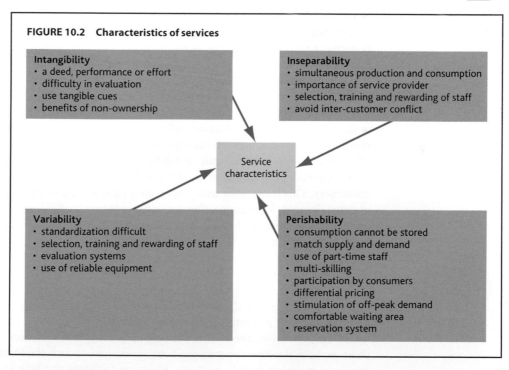

FIGURE 10.2   Characteristics of services

Intangibility

Pure services cannot be seen, tasted, touched, or smelled before they are bought—that is, they are intangible. Rather a **service** is *a deed, performance or effort*, not an object, device or thing.[15] This may mean that a customer finds difficulty in evaluating a service before purchase. For example, it is virtually impossible to judge how enjoyable a holiday will be before taking it because the holiday cannot be shown to a customer before consumption.

For some services, their **intangibility** leads to *difficulty in evaluation* after consumption. For example, it is not easy to judge how thorough a car service has been immediately afterwards: there is no way of telling if everything that should have been checked has been checked.

The challenge for the service provider is to *use tangible cues* to service quality. For example, a holiday firm may show pictures of the holiday destination, display testimonials from satisfied holidaymakers and provide details in a brochure of the kinds of entertainment available. A garage may provide a checklist of items that are required to be carried out in a service, and an indication that they have been completed.

The task is to provide evidence of service quality. McDonald's does this by controlling the physical settings of its restaurants and by using its 'golden arches' as a branding cue. By having a consistent offering, the company has effectively dealt with the difficulties that consumers have in evaluating the quality of a service. Standard menus and ordering procedures have also ensured uniform and easy access for customers, while allowing quality control.[16]

Intangibility also means that the customer cannot own a service. Payment is for use or performance. For example, a car may be hired or a medical operation performed. Service organizations sometimes stress the *benefits of non-ownership* such as lower capital costs and the spreading of payment charges.

Inseparability

Unlike physical goods, services have **inseparability**—that is, they have *simultaneous production and consumption*. For example, a haircut, a holiday and a rock concert are produced and consumed at the same time. This contrasts with a physical good, which is produced, stored and distributed through intermediaries before being bought and consumed. This illustrates the *importance of the service provider*, which is an integral part of the satisfaction gained by the consumer. How service providers conduct themselves may have a crucial bearing on repeat business over and above the technical efficiency of the service task. For example, how courteous and friendly the service provider is may play a large part in the customer's perception of the service experience. The service must be provided not only at the right time and in the right place but also in the right way.[17]

Often, in the customer's eyes, the airline cabin crew member *is* the company. Consequently, the *selection, training and rewarding of staff* who are the frontline service people are of fundamental importance in the achievement of high standards of service quality. This notion of the inseparability of production and consumption gave rise to the idea of relationship marketing in services. In such circumstances, managing buyer–seller interaction is central to effective marketing and can only be fulfilled in a relationship with the customer.[18]

Furthermore, the consumption of the service may take place in the presence of other consumers. This is apparent with restaurant meals, air, rail or coach travel, and many forms of entertainment, for example. Consequently, enjoyment of the service is dependent not only on the service provided, but also on other consumers. Therefore service providers need to identify possible sources of nuisance (e.g. noise, smoke, queue jumping) and make adequate provision to *avoid inter-customer conflict*. For example, a restaurant layout should provide reasonable space between tables so that the potential for conflict is minimized.

Marketing managers should not underestimate the role played by customers in aiding other customers in their decision-making. A study into service interactions in IKEA stores found that almost all customer–employee exchanges related to customer concerns about 'place' (e.g. 'Can you direct me to the pick-up point?') and 'function' (e.g. 'How does this chair work?'). However, interactions between customers took the form of opinions on the quality of materials used in products, advice on bed sizes and how to move around the in-store restaurant. Many customers appeared to display a degree of product knowledge or expertise bordering on that of contact personnel.[19]

Variability

Service quality may be subject to considerable **variability**, which makes standardization difficult. Two restaurants within the same chain may have variable service owing to the capabilities of their respective managers and staff. Quality variations among physical products may be subject to tighter controls through centralized production, automation and quality checking before dispatch. Services, however, are often conducted at multiple locations, by people who may vary in their attitudes (and tiredness), and are subject to simultaneous production and consumption. The last characteristic means that a service fault (e.g. rudeness) cannot be quality checked and corrected between production and consumption, unlike a physical product such as misaligned car windscreen wipers.

The potential for variability in service quality emphasizes the need for rigorous selection, training, and rewarding of staff in service organizations. Training should emphasize the standards expected of personnel when dealing with customers. *Evaluation systems* should be developed that allow customers to report on their experiences with staff.

Service standardization is a related method of tackling the variability problem. The *use of reliable equipment* rather than people can also help in standardization—for example, the supply of drinks via vending machines or cash through bank machines. However, great care needs to be taken regarding equipment reliability and efficiency. For example, bank cash machines have been heavily criticized for being unreliable and running out of money at weekends.

Perishability

The fourth characteristic of services is their **perishability** in the sense that *consumption cannot be stored* for the future. A hotel room or an airline seat that is not occupied today represents lost income that cannot be gained tomorrow. If a physical good is not sold, it can be stored for sale later. Therefore it is important to *match supply and demand* for services. For example, if a hotel has high weekday occupancy but is virtually empty at weekends, a key marketing task is to provide incentives for weekend use. This might involve offering weekend discounts, or linking hotel use with leisure activities such as golf, fishing or hiking.

Service providers also have the problem of catering for peak demand when supply may be insufficient. A physical goods provider may build up inventory in slack periods for sale during peak demand. Service providers do not have this option. Consequently, alternative methods need to be considered. For example, supply flexibility can be varied through the *use of part-time staff* during peak periods. *Multi-skilling* means that employees may be trained in many tasks. Supermarket staff can be trained to fill shelves and work at the checkout at peak periods. *Participation by consumers* may be encouraged in production (e.g. self-service breakfasts in hotels) and in avoiding queues (e.g. self-service checkouts in supermarkets). Demand may be smoothed through *differential pricing* to encourage customers to visit during off-peak periods (for example, lower-priced cinema and theatre seats for afternoon performances). *Stimulation of off-peak demand* can be achieved by special events (e.g. spa breaks or gourmet weekends for hotels). If delay is unavoidable then another option is to make it more acceptable—for example, by providing a comfortable waiting area with seating and free refreshments. Finally, a *reservation system*, as commonly used in restaurants, hair salons and theatres, can be used to control peak demand and assist time substitution.

Managing Services

Four key aspects of managing services are managing customer relationships, managing service quality, managing service productivity, managing service staff and positioning services.

Managing customer relationships

Relationship marketing in services has attracted much attention in recent years as organizations focus their efforts on retaining existing customers rather than only attracting new ones. It is not a new concept, however, since the idea of a company earning customer loyalty was well known to the earliest merchants, who had the following saying: 'As a merchant, you'd better have a friend in every town.'[20] Relationship marketing involves the shifting from activities concerned with attracting customers to activities focused on current customers and how to retain them. Although the idea can be applied to many industries it is particularly important in services since there is often direct contact between service provider and customer—for example, client/agency relationship in the advertising industry, hotel staff and guests. The quality of the relationship that develops will often determine its length. Not all service encounters have the potential for a long-term relationship, however. For example, a passenger at an international airport who needs road transportation will probably never meet the taxi driver again, and the choice of taxi supplier will be dependent on the passenger's position in the queue rather than free choice. In this case the exchange—cash for journey—is a pure transaction: the driver knows that it is unlikely that there will ever be a repeat purchase.[21] Organizations, therefore, need to decide when the practice of relationship marketing is most applicable. The following conditions suggest potential areas for the use of relationship marketing activities:[22]

- where there is an ongoing or periodic desire for the service by the customer: e.g. insurance or theatre service versus funeral service
- where the customer controls the selection of a service provider: e.g. selecting a hotel versus entering the first taxi in an airport waiting line
- where the customer has alternatives from which to choose: e.g. selecting a restaurant versus buying water from the only utility company service in a community.

Having established the applicability of relationship marketing to services, we will now explore the benefits of relationship marketing to organizations and customers, and the customer retention strategies used to build relationships and tie customers closer to service firms.

Benefits for the organization

There are six benefits to service organizations in developing and maintaining strong customer relationships.[23]

1 *Increased purchases*: which help to develop trust between the company and the customer as they become more and more satisfied with the quality of services provided by the supplier.

2 *Lower cost*: the start-up costs associated with attracting new customers are likely to be far higher than the cost of retaining existing customers. Start-up costs will include the time of making repeat calls in an effort to persuade a prospect to open an account, the advertising and promotional costs associated with making prospects aware of the company and its service offering, the operating costs of setting up accounts and systems, and the time costs of establishing bonds between the supplier and customer in the early stages of the relationship. Furthermore, costs associated with solving early teething problems and queries are likely to fall as the customer becomes accustomed to using the service.

3 *Lifetime value of a customer*: the lifetime value of a customer is the profit made on a customer's purchases over the lifetime of that customer. If a customer spends £80 in a supermarket per week, resulting in £8 profit, uses the supermarket 45 times a year over 30 years, the lifetime value of that customer is £10,800. Thus, a bad service experience early on in this relationship, which results in the customer defecting to the competition, would be very expensive to the supermarket, especially when the costs of bad word of mouth are added, as this may deter other customers from using the store.

4 *Sustainable competitive advantage*: the intangible aspects of a relationship are not easily copied by the competition. For example, the friendships and high levels of trust that can develop as the relationship matures can be extremely difficult for competitors to replicate. This means that the extra value to customers that derives from the relationship can be a source of sustainable competitive advantage for suppliers.[24]

5 *Word of mouth*: word of mouth is very important in services due to their intangible nature, which makes them difficult to evaluate prior to purchase. In these circumstances, potential purchasers often look to others who have experienced the service (e.g. a hotel) for personal recommendation. A firm that has a large number of loyal customers is more likely to benefit from word of mouth than another without such a resource.

6 *Employee satisfaction and retention*: satisfied, loyal customers benefit employees in providing a set of mutually beneficial relationships and less hassle. This raises employees' job satisfaction and lowers job turnover. Employees can spend time improving existing relationships rather than desperately seeking new customers. This sets up a virtuous circle of satisfied customers, leading to happy employees that raises customer satisfaction even higher.

The net result of these six benefits of developing customer relationships is high profits. A study has shown across a variety of service industries that profits climb steeply when a firm lowers its customer defection rate.[25] Firms could improve profits from 25 to 85 per cent (depending on the industry) by reducing customer defections by just 5 per cent. The reasons are that loyal customers generate more revenue for more years and the costs of maintaining existing customers are lower than the costs of acquiring new ones. An analysis of a credit card company revealed that improving the defection rate from 10 to 20 years increased the lifetime value of a customer from $135 to $300.

Benefits for the customer

Entering into a long-term relationship can also reap the following four benefits for the customer.

1 *Risk and stress reduction*: since the intangible nature of services makes them difficult to evaluate before purchase, relationship marketing can benefit the customer as well as the firm. This is particularly so for services that are personally important, variable in quality, complex and/or subject to high-involvement buying.[26] Such purchases are potentially high risk in that making the wrong choice has severe negative consequences for the buyer. Banking, insurance, motor servicing and hairstyling are examples of services that exhibit some or all of the characteristics—importance, variability, complexity and high involvement—that would cause many customers to seek an ongoing relationship with a trusted service provider. Such a relationship reduces consumer stress as the relationship becomes predictable, initial problems are solved, special needs are accommodated and the consumer learns what to expect. After a period of time, the consumer begins to trust the service provider, can count on a consistent level of quality service and feels comfortable in the relationship.[27]

2 *Higher-quality service*: experiencing a long-term relationship with a service provider can also result in higher levels of service. This is because the service provider becomes knowledgeable about the customer's requirements. For example, doctors get to know the medical history of their patients, and hairstylists learn about the preferences of their clients. Knowledge of the customer built up over a series of service encounters facilitates the tailoring or customizing of the service to each customer's special needs.

3 *Avoidance of switching costs*: maintaining a relationship with a service supplier avoids the costs associated with switching to a new provider. Once a service provider knows a customer's preferences and special needs, and has tailored services to suit them, to change would mean educating a new provider and accepting the possibility of mistakes being made until the new provider has learnt to accommodate them. This results in both time and psychological costs to the customer. Bitner suggests that a major cost of relocating to a new geographic location is the need to establish relationships with unfamiliar service providers such as banks, schools, doctors and hairdressers.[28]

4 *Social and status benefits*: customers can also reap social and status benefits from a continuing relationship with a supplier. Since many service encounters are also social encounters, repeated contact can assume personal as well as professional dimensions. In such circumstances, service customers may develop relationships resembling personal friendships. For example, hairdressers often serve as personal confidantes, and restaurant managers may get to know some of their customers personally. Such personal relationships can feed one's ego (status) as when a hotel customer commented, 'When employees remember and recognize you as a regular customer you feel really good.'[29]

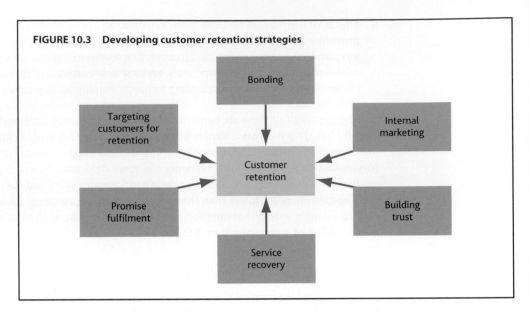

FIGURE 10.3 Developing customer retention strategies

Developing customer retention strategies

The benefits of developing long-term relationships with customers mean that it is worthwhile for services organizations to consider designing customer retention strategies. This involves the targeting of customers for retention, bonding, internal marketing, promise fulfilment, building of trust and service recovery (see Fig. 10.3), as described below.

1   *Targeting customers for retention*: not all customers are worthy of relationship building. Some may be habitual brand switchers, perhaps responding to the lowest deal currently on offer; others may not generate sufficient revenue to justify the expense of acquiring them and maintaining the relationship; and, finally, some customers may be so troublesome, and their attitudes and behaviour cause so much disruption to the service provider, that the costs of servicing them outweigh the benefits. Firms need, therefore, to identify those customers with whom they wish to engage in a long-term relationship, those for whom a transactional marketing approach is better suited, and those with whom they would prefer not to do business. This is the classical market segmentation and targeting approach discussed in Chapter 8. The characteristics of those customers that are candidates for a relationship marketing approach are high-value, frequent-use, loyalty-prone customers for whom the actual and potential service offerings that can be supplied by the firm have high utility.

    Targeting customers for retention involves the analysis of loyalty and defection-prone customers. Service suppliers need to understand why customers stay or leave, what creates value for them, and their profile. Decisions can then be made regarding which types of customer defector they wish to try to save (e.g. price or service defectors) and the nature of the value-adding strategy that meets their needs, while at the same time maintaining bonds with loyalty-prone customers.[30]

2   *Bonding*: retention strategies vary in the degree to which they bond the parties together. One framework that illustrates this idea distinguishes between three levels of retention strategy based on the types of bond used to cement the relationship.[31]

    • *Level 1*: at this level the bond is primarily through financial incentives, for example, higher discounts on prices for larger-volume purchases or frequent-flyer or loyalty points resulting in lower future prices. The problem is that the potential for a sustainable competitive advantage is low because price incentives are easy for competitors to copy even if they take the guise of frequent-flyer or loyalty points. Most airlines and supermarkets compete in this way and consumers have learnt to join more than one scheme, thus negating the desired effect.

- *Level 2*: this higher level of bonding relies on more than just price incentives, and consequently raises the potential for a sustainable competitive advantage. Level 2 retention strategies build long-term relationships through social as well as financial bonds, capitalizing on the fact that many service encounters are also social encounters. Customers become clients, the relationship becomes personalized and the service customized. Characteristics of this type of relationship include frequent communication with customers, providing community of service through the same person or people employed by the service provider, providing personal treatment like sending cards, and enhancing the core service with educational or entertainment activities such as seminars or visits to sporting events. Some hotels keep records of their guests' personal preferences, such as their favourite newspaper and alcoholic drink. This builds a special bond between the hotel and their customers, who feel they are being treated as individuals.

  Other companies form social relationships with their customers by forming clubs—for example, Harley-Davidson has created the Harley Owners Group, fostering camaraderie among its membership and a strong bond with the motorbike, and Nokia has established a club for its mobile phone customers for similar reasons.

- *Level 3*: this top level of bonding is formed by financial, social and structural bonds. Structural bonds tie service providers to their customers through providing solutions to customers' problems that are designed into the service delivery system. For example, logistics companies often supply their clients with equipment that ties them into their systems. When combined with financial and social bonds, structural bonds can create a formidable barrier against competitor inroads and provide the basis for a sustainable competitive advantage.

3 *Internal marketing*: a fundamental basis for customer retention is high-quality service delivery. This depends on high-quality performance from employees since the service product is a performance and the performers are employees.[32] Internal marketing concerns training, communicating to and motivating internal staff. Staff need to be trained to be technically competent at their job as well as to be able to handle service encounters with customers. To do this well, they must be motivated and understand what is expected of them. Service staff act as 'part-time marketers' since their actions can directly affect customer satisfaction and retention.[33] They are critical in the 'moments of truth' when they and customers come into contact in a service situation.

   A key focus of an internal marketing programme should be employee selection and retention. Service companies that suffer high rates of job turnover are continually employing new, inexperienced staff to handle customer service encounters. Employees that have worked for the company for years know more about the business and have had the opportunity to build relationships with customers. By selecting the right people and managing them in such a way that they stay loyal to the service organization, higher levels of customer retention can be achieved through the build-up of trust and personal knowledge gained through long-term contact with customers.

4 *Promise fulfilment*: the fulfilment of promises is a cornerstone for maintaining service relationships. This implies three key activities: *making* realistic promises initially, and *keeping* those promises during service delivery by *enabling* staff and service systems to deliver on promises made.[34]

   Making promises is done through normal marketing communications channels such as advertising, selling and promotion, as well as the specific service cues that set expectations such as the dress of the service staff, and the design and décor of the establishment. It is important not to over-promise with marketing communications or the result will be disappointment, and consequently customer dissatisfaction and defection. The promise should be credible and realistic. Some companies adhere to the adage 'under-promise and over-deliver'.

A necessary condition for promises to be kept is the enabling of staff and service systems to deliver on the promises made. This means staff must have the skills, competences, tools, systems and enthusiasm to deliver. Some of these issues have been looked at in the earlier discussion of internal marketing, and are dependent on the correct recruitment, training and rewarding of staff, and on providing them with the right equipment and systems to do their jobs.

The final activity associated with promise fulfilment is the keeping of promises. This relies on service staff or technology such as the downloading of software via the Internet. The keeping of promises occurs when the customer and the service provider interact: the 'moment of truth' mentioned earlier. Research has shown that customers judge employees on their ability to deliver the service right the first time, their ability to recover if things go wrong, how well they deal with special requests, and on their spontaneous actions and attitudes.[35] These are clearly key dimensions that must play a part in a training programme and should be borne in mind when selecting and rewarding service staff; not all service encounters are equal in importance, however. Research conducted on behalf of Marriott hotels has shown that events occurring early in a service encounter affect customer loyalty the most. On the basis of these findings Marriott developed its 'First 10 Minutes' strategy. It is hardly surprising that first impressions are so important since before then the customer has had no direct contact with the service provider and will be uncertain of the outcome.

Finally, we need to recognize that the keeping of promises does not depend solely on service staff and technology. Because service delivery is often in a group setting (e.g. a meal with friends or family in a restaurant, watching a film or travelling by air) the quality of the experience can be as dependent on the behaviour of other customers as that of the service provider. Lovelock, Vandermerwe and Lewis label the problem customers 'jaycustomers'.[36] These are people who act in a thoughtless or abusive way, causing problems for the organization, its employees and other customers. One particular kind of jaycustomer is the belligerent person who shouts abuse and threats at service staff because of some service malfunction. Staff need to be trained to develop the self-confidence and assertiveness required to deal with such situations, and to practise this using role-play exercises. If possible, the jaycustomer should be moved away from other customer contact to minimize the discomfort of the latter. Finally, where the service employee does not have the authority to resolve the problem, more senior staff should be approached to settle the dispute.

5 *Building trust*: customer retention relies heavily on building trust. This is particularly so for service firms since the intangibility of services means that they are difficult to evaluate before buying and experiencing them (indeed some, such as car servicing, are hard to evaluate after purchasing them). Purchasing a service for the first time can leave the customer with a feeling of uncertainty and vulnerability, particularly when the service is personally important, variable in quality, complex and subject to high-involvement purchasing. It is not surprising that customers who have developed trust in a supplier in these circumstances are unlikely to switch to a new supplier and undergo the uncomfortable feelings of uncertainty and vulnerability all over again.

Companies that wish to build up their trustworthiness should keep in touch with their customers by regular two-way communication to develop feelings of closeness and openness; provide guarantees to symbolize the confidence they feel in their service delivery as well as reducing their customers' perceived risk of purchase; and operate a policy of fairness and high standards of conduct with their customers.[37]

6 *Service recovery*: service recovery strategies should be designed to solve the problem and restore the customers' trust in the firm, and to improve the service system so that the problem does not recur in the future.[38] They are crucial because the inability to recover service failures and mistakes loses customers both directly and through their tendency to tell other actual and potential customers about their negative experiences.

The first ingredient in a service recovery strategy is to set up a tracking system to identify system failures. Customers should be encouraged to report service problems since it is those customers that do not complain that are least likely to purchase again. Systems should be established to monitor complaints, follow up on service experiences by telephone calling, and to use suggestion boxes for both service staff and customers.

Second, staff should be trained and empowered to respond to service complaints. This is important because research has shown that the successful resolution of a complaint can cause customers to feel more positive about the firm than before the service failure. If a second problem occurs, though, this effect (called the 'recovery paradox') disappears.[39] The first response from a service provider to a genuine complaint is to apologize. Often this will take the heat out of the situation and lead to a spirit of cooperation rather than recrimination. The next step is to attempt to solve the problem quickly. Marriott hotels facilitate this process by empowering frontline employees to solve customers' problems quickly, even though this may mean expense to the hotel, and without recourse to seeking approval from higher authority. Other key elements in service recovery are to appear pleasant, helpful and attentive, show concern for the customer and be flexible. Regarding problem resolution, service staff should provide information about the problem, take action and should appear to put themselves out to solve the problem.[40]

Finally, a service recovery strategy should encourage learning so that service recovery problems are identified and corrected. Service staff should be motivated to report problems and solutions so that recurrent failures are identified and fixed. In this way, an effective service recovery system can lead to improved customer service, satisfaction and higher customer-retention levels.

Managing service quality

Intuitively, it makes sense to suggest that improving service quality will increase customer satisfaction, leading to higher sales and profits. Indeed, it has been shown that companies that are rated higher on service quality perform better in terms of market share growth and profitability.[41] Yet, for many companies, high standards of service quality remain elusive.

There are four causes of poor perceived quality (see Fig. 10.4). These are the barriers that separate the perception of service quality from what customers expect.[42]

Barriers to the matching of expected and perceived service levels

Misconception barrier: this arises from management's misunderstanding of what the customer expects. Lack of marketing research may lead managers to misconceive the important service attributes that customers use when evaluating a service, and the way in which customers use attributes in evaluation. For example, a restaurant manager may believe that shortening the gap between courses may improve customer satisfaction, when the customer actually values a pause between eating.

Inadequate resources barrier: managers may understand customer expectations but be unwilling to provide the resources necessary to meet them. This may arise because of a cost reduction or productivity focus, or simply because of the inconvenience it may cause.

Inadequate delivery barrier: managers may understand customer expectations and supply adequate resources but fail to select, train and reward staff adequately, resulting in poor or inconsistent service. This may manifest itself in poor communication skills, inappropriate dress, and unwillingness to solve customer problems.

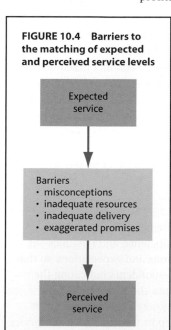

FIGURE 10.4 Barriers to the matching of expected and perceived service levels

Exaggerated promises barrier: even when customer understanding, resources and staff management are in place, a gap between customer expectations and perceptions can still arise through exaggerated promises. Advertising and selling messages that build expectations to a pitch that cannot be fulfilled may leave customers disappointed even when receiving good service. For example, a tourist brochure that claims a hotel is 'just a few minutes from the sea' may lead to disappointment if the walk takes 10 minutes.

Meeting customer expectations

A key to providing service quality is the understanding and meeting of *customer expectations*. To do so requires a clear picture of the criteria used to form these expectations, recognizing that consumers of services value not only the *outcome* of the service encounter but also the *experience* of taking part in it. For example, an evaluation of a haircut depends not only on the quality of the cut but also the experience of having a haircut. Clearly, a hairdresser needs not only technical skills but also the ability to communicate in an interesting and polite manner. Meeting and exceeding customers' expectations is even more important as good and bad experiences can easily be shared via blogs, social networking sites and websites. For example, the tripadvisor.com website publishes the experiences of customers when using hotels and airlines around the world.[43] Ten criteria may be used when evaluating the outcome and experience of a service encounter.[44]

1 *Access*: is the service provided at convenient locations and times with little waiting?
2 *Reliability*: is the service consistent and dependable?
3 *Credibility*: can customers trust the service company and its staff?
4 *Security*: can the service be used without risk?
5 *Understanding the customer*: does it appear that the service provider understands customer expectations?
6 *Responsiveness*: how quickly do service staff respond to customer problems, requests and questions?
7 *Courtesy*: do service staff act in a friendly and polite manner?
8 *Competence*: do service staff have the required skills and knowledge?
9 *Communication*: is the service described clearly and accurately?
10 *Tangibles*: how well managed is the tangible evidence of the service (e.g. staff appearance, décor, layout)?

These criteria form a useful checklist for service providers wishing to understand how their customers judge them. A self-analysis may show areas that need improvement, but the most reliable approach is to check that customers use these criteria and to conduct marketing research to compare performance against competition. Where service quality is dependent on a succession of service encounters (for example, a hotel stay may encompass the check-in, the room itself, the restaurant, breakfast and check-out), each should be measured in terms of their impact on total satisfaction so that corrective actions can be taken.[45] Questionnaires have now been developed that allow the measurement of perceived customer satisfaction at distinct stages of the service-delivery process (for example, the stages encountered while visiting a museum).[46]

Measuring service quality

A scale called *SERVQUAL* has been developed to aid the measurement of *service quality*.[47] Based on five criteria—reliability, responsiveness, courtesy, competence and tangibles—it is a multiple-item scale that aims to measure customer perceptions and expectations so that gaps can be identified. The scale is simple to administer with respondents indicating their strength of agreement or disagreement with a series of statements about service quality using a Likert scale. Service quality can also be measured by *mystery shoppers*, who visit retail outlets as normal consumers. Their job is to assess and report the quality of the service they receive.[48]

TABLE 10.3 Marketing and operations' views on operational issues

Operational issues	Typical operations goals	Common marketing concerns
Productivity improvement	Reduce unit cost of production	Strategies may cause decline in service quality
Standardization versus customization	Keep costs low and quality consistent: simplify operations tasks; recruit low-cost employees	Consumers may seek variety, prefer customization to match segmented needs
Batch vs unit processing	Seek economies of scale, consistency, efficient use of capacity	Customers may be forced to wait, feel 'one of a crowd', be turned off by other customers
Facilities layout and design	Control costs; improve efficiency by ensuring proximity of operationally related tasks; enhance safety and security	Customers may be confused, shunted around unnecessarily, find facility unattractive and inconvenient
Job design	Minimize error, waste and fraud; make efficient use of technology; simplify task for standardization	Operationally orientated employees with narrow roles may be unresponsive to customer needs
Management of capacity	Keep costs down by avoiding wasteful under-utilization of resources	Service may be unavailable when needed; quality may be compromised during high-demand periods
Management of queues	Optimize use of available capacity by planning for average throughput; maintain customer order, discipline	Customers may be bored and frustrated during wait, see firm as unresponsive

Source: Lovelock, C. (1992) Seeking Synergy in Service Operations: Seven Things Marketers Need to Know about Service Operations, *European Management Journal* 10(1), 22–9. Reprinted with permission from Elsevier Science Ltd.

Managing service productivity

Productivity is a measure of the relationship between an input and an output. For example, if more people can be served (output) using the same number of staff (input), productivity per employee has risen. Clearly there can be conflict between improving service productivity (efficiency) and raising service quality (effectiveness). For example, a doctor who reduces consultation time per patient or a university that increases tutorial group size raise productivity at the risk of lowering service quality. Table 10.3 shows how typical operational goals that seek to minimize costs can cause marketing concerns. Marketers need to understand why operations managers have such goals, and operations managers need to recognize the implications of their actions for customer satisfaction.[49]

Clearly a balance must be struck between productivity and service quality. At some point quality gains become so expensive that they are not worthwhile. However, there are ways of improving productivity without compromising quality. Technology, obtaining customer involvement in production of the service, and balancing supply and demand are three methods of achieving this.

Technology

Technology can be used to improve productivity and service quality. For example, airport X-ray surveillance equipment raises the throughput of passengers (productivity) and speeds the process of checking-in (service quality). Automatic cash dispensers in banks increase the number of transactions per period (productivity) while reducing customer waiting time (service quality). Automatic vending machines increase the number of drinks sold per establishment (productivity) while improving accessibility for customers (service quality). Computerization can also raise productivity and service quality. For example, Direct Line, owned by the Royal Bank of Scotland, is based on computer software that produces a motor insurance quote instantaneously. Callers are asked for a few details (such as how old they are, where they live, what car they drive and number of years since their last claim) and this is keyed into the computer, which automatically produces a quotation.[50]

Retailers have benefited from electronic point of sale (EPOS) and electronic data interchange (EDI). Timely and detailed sales information can aid buying decisions and provide retail buyers with a negotiating advantage over suppliers. Other benefits from this technology include better labour scheduling, and stock and distribution systems.

Customer involvement in production

The inseparability between production and consumption provides an opportunity to raise both productivity and service quality. For example, self-service breakfast bars and petrol stations improve productivity per employee and reduce customer waiting time (service quality). The effectiveness of this tactic relies heavily on customer expectations, and on managing transition periods. It should be used when there is a clear advantage to customers in their involvement in production. In other instances, reducing customer service may reduce satisfaction. For example, a hotel that expected its customers to service their own rooms would need a persuasive communications programme to convince customers that the lack of service was reflected in cheaper rates.

Balancing supply and demand

Because services cannot be stored, balancing supply and demand is a key determinant of productivity. Hotels or aircraft that are less than half full incur low productivity. If in the next period, the hotel or airline is faced with excess demand, the unused space in the previous period cannot be used to meet it. The combined result is low productivity and customer dissatisfaction (low service quality). By smoothing demand or increasing the flexibility of supply, both productivity and service quality can be achieved.

Smoothing demand can be achieved through differential pricing and stimulating off-peak demand (e.g. weekend breaks). Increasing supply flexibility may be increased by using part-time employees, multi-skilling and encouraging customers to service themselves.

Managing service staff

Many services involve a high degree of contact between service staff and customers. This is true for such service industries as healthcare, banking, catering and education. The quality of the service experience is therefore heavily dependent on staff–customer interpersonal relationships. John Carlzon, the head of Scandinavian Airlines System (SAS), called these meetings *moments of truth*. He explained that SAS faced 65,000 moments of truth per day and that the outcomes determined the success of the company.

Research on customer loyalty in the service industry showed that only 14 per cent of customers who stopped patronizing service businesses did so because they were dissatisfied with the quality of what they had bought. More than two-thirds stopped buying because they found service staff indifferent or unhelpful.[51] Clearly, the way in which service personnel treat their customers is fundamental to success in the service industry.

Also, frontline staff are important sources of customer and competitor information and, if properly motivated, can provide crucial inputs in the development of new service products.[52] For example, discussions with customers may generate ideas for new services that customers would value if available on the market.

In order for service employees to be in the frame of mind to treat customers well, they need to feel that their company is treating them well. In companies where staff have a high regard for the human resources policy, customers also have a positive opinion of the service they receive.

The *selection of suitable people* is the starting point of the process. Personality differences mean that it is not everyone who can fill a service role. The nature of the job needs to be defined and the appropriate personality characteristics needed to perform effectively outlined. Once selected, training is required to familiarize recruits with the job requirements and the culture of the organization. Orientation is the process by which a company helps new recruits understand the organization and its culture. Folklore is often used to show how employees have made outstanding contributions to the company. Training needs to continue when required, particularly when service staff face change. Inadequate training can be disastrous, as when the opening of Heathrow Terminal 5 descended into chaos, partly through service staff not knowing where they should go.[53] *Socialization* allows the recruit to experience the culture and tasks of the organization. Usually, the aim is creative individualism, whereby the recruit accepts all of the key behavioural norms but is encouraged to display initiative and innovation in dealing with problems. Thus, standards of behaviour are internalized, but the creative abilities of the individual are not subjugated to the need to conform.

Service quality may also be affected by the degree to which staff are *empowered*, or given the authority to satisfy customers and deal with their problems. For example, each member of staff of Marriott hotels is allowed to spend up to £1000 on their own initiative to solve customer problems. The company uses some of the situations that have arisen where employees have acted decisively to solve a customer problem in their advertising. The advantage is quicker response times since staff do not have to consult with their supervisors before dealing with a problem.[54] However, empowerment programmes need to recognize the increased responsibility thrust on employees. Not everyone will welcome this, and reward systems need to be thought through (e.g. higher pay or status).

Pret A Manger empowers staff in a different way. Following application and interview, prospective job candidates are paid to work for one day in a Pret store. The people working in that store then make the final decision as to whether the candidate is taken on. This empowers staff and ensures that only staff with the right attitude are employed.[55]

Maintaining a motivated workforce in the face of irate customers, faulty support systems and the boredom that accompanies some service jobs is a demanding task. The motivational factors discussed when examining salesforce management are equally relevant here and include recognition of achievement, role clarity, opportunities for advancement, the interest value of the job, monetary rewards, and setting challenging but achievable targets. Some service companies (e.g. Holiday Inn) give employee-of-the-month awards as recognition of outstanding service. A key factor in avoiding demotivation is to monitor support systems so that staff work with efficient equipment and facilities to help them carry out their job.

Service evaluation is also important in managing staff. Customer feedback is essential to maintaining high standards of service quality. McDonald's continually monitors quality, service, cleanliness and value (QSCV), and if a franchisee fails to meet these standards they are dropped. The results of customer research should be fed back to employees so that they can relate their performance standards to customer satisfaction. Enlightened companies tie financial incentives to the results of such surveys.

Positioning services

Positioning is the process of establishing and keeping a distinctive place in the market for a company and its products. Most successful service firms differentiate themselves from the competition on attributes that their target customers value highly. They develop service concepts that are highly valued, and communicate to target customers so that they accurately perceive the position of the service. For example, Credit Suisse Financial Products positions itself as a specialist in risk management products and services, an area whose image was tarnished during the credit crunch.

The positioning task entails two decisions:

1 choice of target market (where to compete)
2 creation of a differential advantage (how to compete).

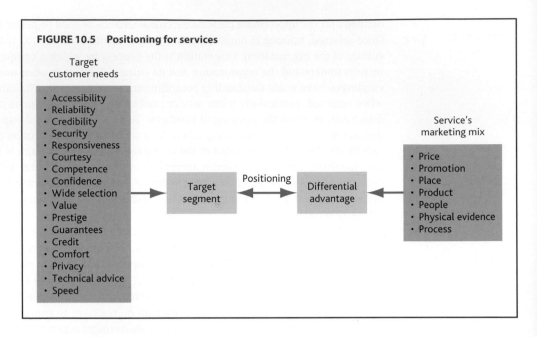

FIGURE 10.5 Positioning for services

Target customer needs
- Accessibility
- Reliability
- Credibility
- Security
- Responsiveness
- Courtesy
- Competence
- Confidence
- Wide selection
- Value
- Prestige
- Guarantees
- Credit
- Comfort
- Privacy
- Technical advice
- Speed

Target segment

Positioning

Differential advantage

Service's marketing mix
- Price
- Promotion
- Place
- Product
- People
- Physical evidence
- Process

These decisions are common to both physical products and services. Creating a differential advantage is based on understanding the target customers' requirements better than the competition. Figure 10.5 shows the relationship between *target customer needs* and the *services marketing mix*. On the left of the figure is an array of factors (choice criteria) that customers may use to judge a service. How well a service firm satisfies those criteria depends on its marketing mix (on the right of the figure). Marketing research can be useful in identifying important choice criteria but care needs to be taken in such studies. Asking customers which are the most important factors when buying a service may give misleading results. For example, the most important factor when travelling by air may be safety. However, this does not mean that customers use safety as a choice criterion when deciding which airline to use. If all major airlines are perceived as being similar in terms of safety, other less important factors like the quality of in-flight meals and service may be the crucial attributes used in decision-making.

Target marketing

The basis of target marketing is market segmentation. A market is analysed to identify groups of potential customers with similar needs and price sensitivities. The potential of each of these segments is assessed on such factors as size, growth rate, degree of competition, price sensitivity, and the fit between its requirements and the company's capabilities.

Note that the most attractive markets are often not the biggest, however, as these may have been identified earlier and will already have attracted a high level of competition. There may, however, be pockets of customers who are underserved by companies that are compromising their marketing mix by trying to serve too wide a customer base. The identification of such customers is a prime opportunity during segmentation analysis. Target marketing allows service firms to tailor their marketing mix to the specific requirements of groups of customers more effectively than trying to cater for diverse needs. For example, the airline Lufthansa has targeted first-class passengers by opening the world's first dedicated terminal to them at Frankfurt airport. Help with parking the car is available, a personal assistant is on hand throughout and check-in is swift. Individual offices, rest rooms, and a dining and cigar room are available while executives await their flight. To travel to the aircraft, passengers are chauffeur-driven in a Mercedes S-class or Porsche Cayenne.[56]

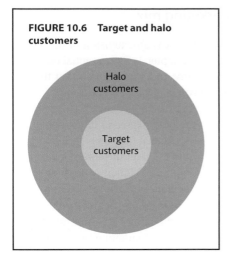

FIGURE 10.6   Target and halo customers

Halo customers

Target customers

Marketing managers also need to consider those potential customers that are not directly targeted but may find the service mix attractive. Those customers that are at the periphery of the target market are called **halo customers** and can make a substantial difference between success and failure (see Fig. 10.6). For example, Topshop, a UK clothing retailer targeting 16–24-year-olds, was very successful in attracting this group to its shops, but financial performance was marred by the lack of interest from its halo customers: those who fell outside this age bracket but nevertheless may have found Topshop's clothing to their taste. Launching into a new target market may require trials to test the innovation and refine the concept. For example, when KFC was considering moving into the breakfast segment of the fast-food market it ran trials in selected outlets before the full launch.[57]

Differential advantage

Understanding customer needs will be the basis of the design of a new service concept that is different from competitive offerings, is highly valued by target customers, and therefore creates a differential advantage. It will be based on the creative use of marketing-mix elements, resulting in such benefits as more reliable or faster delivery, greater convenience, more comfort, higher-quality work, higher prestige or other issues (listed on the left of Fig. 10.5). Marketing in Action 10.1 describes how small hotel chains have differentiated themselves from larger chains, which themselves are launching new boutique brands to bring a different experience to consumers.

Marketing in Action 10.1 Boutique Hotels: Small is Beautiful

For some travellers the reassurance of a global hotel chain with many standardized features is highly valued so that they know what to expect. For others, though, such chains are regarded as bland and boring. This segment is looking for a different experience, something that the Eton Collection, a small UK boutique hotel company, provides with individually designed hotels, personalized service and packages with partners like Harvey Nichols, the Tate and the British Museum. Franklin Hotels, a small boutique chain of hotels, also offers a different experience. Its success is built on building the 'wow' factor into service, something that traditionally big corporate chains have found hard to create.

Their success has not gone unnoticed, however. Larger chains have responded by launching their own boutique brands. For example, Hilton has launched Denizen Hotels, a new premium lifestyle brand. Denizen appeals across generations, with a fusion of styles from boutique ideas such as chandeliers to technology spaces and hubs where customers can relax. The concept is to create an engaging personality rather than dull corporate blandishments. The chain is not a simple-minded crib of its smaller rivals: its design is partly based on marketing research exploring the views and opinions of 4500 people. In this way, the chain is hoping to create a differential advantage of its own.

Based on: Roberts (2009)[58]

Research can indicate which choice criteria are more or less valued by customers, and how customers rate the service provider's performance on each.[59] Figure 10.7 shows three possible outcomes: *underperformance* results from performing poorly on highly valued choice criteria; *overkill* arises when the service provider excels at things of little consequence to customers; and the *target area* is where the supplier performs well on criteria that are of high value to customers and less well on less valued criteria. Differentiation is achieved in those areas that are of most importance, while resources are not wasted improving service quality levels in areas that are unimportant to customers. The result is the achievement of both effectiveness and efficiency in the service operation.

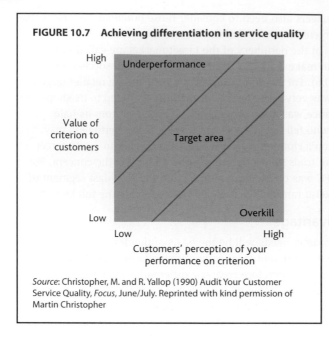

FIGURE 10.7 Achieving differentiation in service quality

Source: Christopher, M. and R. Yallop (1990) Audit Your Customer Service Quality, *Focus*, June/July. Reprinted with kind permission of Martin Christopher

The services marketing mix

The **services marketing mix** is an extension of the 4-Ps framework introduced in Chapter 1. The essential elements of *product*, *promotion*, *price* and *place* remain, but three additional variables—*people, physical evidence* and *process*—are included to produce a 7-Ps mix.[60] The need for the extension is due to the high degree of direct contact between the firm and the customer, the highly visible nature of the service assembly process, and the simultaneity of production and consumption. While it is possible to discuss people, physical evidence and process within the original 4-Ps framework (for example, people could be considered part of the product offering) the extension allows a more thorough analysis of the marketing ingredients necessary for successful services marketing. Each element of the marketing mix will now be examined.

Product: physical products can be inspected and tried before buying, but pure services are intangible; you cannot go to a showroom to see a marketing research report or medical operation that you are considering. This means that service customers suffer higher perceived risk in their decision-making and that the three elements of the extended marketing mix—people, physical evidence and process—are crucial in influencing the customer's perception of service quality. These will be discussed later.

The *brand name* of a service can also influence the perception of a service. Four characteristics of successful brand names are as follows.[61]

1 *Distinctiveness*: it immediately identifies the services provider and differentiates it from the competition.
2 *Relevance*: it communicates the nature of the service and the service benefit.
3 *Memorability*: it is easily understood and remembered.
4 *Flexibility*: it not only expresses the service organization's current business but is also broad enough to cover foreseeable new ventures.

Go to the website to see how Visa advertises its services. www.mcgraw-hill.co.uk/ textbooks/jobber

Examples of effective brand names are: Visa, which suggests internationality; Travelodge, which implies travel accommodation; and Virgin Atlantic, which associates the airline with flights to and from North America.

Although trial of some services is impossible, for others it can be achieved. For example, some hotels invite key decision-makers of social clubs (for example, social secretaries of pensioner groups) to visit their hotels free of charge to sample the facilities and service. The hotels hope that they will recommend a group visit to their members. Service providers such as hotels are constantly seeking ways of differentiating themselves from their competitors. For example, Marriott has invested heavily in new super-comfortable beds and bedding to gain an advantage over its competitors.

The quality of the physical product is also used as a differentiator by airlines—for example, stainless-steel rather than plastic cutlery, more leg room, personal television screens showing up-to-date movies and, for first-class long-haul passengers, more comfortable beds. Service companies need to reassess their product offerings to keep up with changing consumer tastes. For example, to appeal to a generation of young people who spend a lot of time playing computer games, Disneyland has designed attractions that offer theme park guests the chance to 'get interactive', and is experimenting with mobile phones and other handheld electronic devices to add interactive appeal.[62]

Promotion: the intangible element of a service may be difficult to communicate. For example, it may be difficult to represent courtesy, hard work and customer care in an advertisement. Once again, the answer is to use *tangible cues* that will help customers understand and judge the service. A hotel can show its buildings, swimming pool, friendly

Go to the website to see how HSBC's advert makes its services tangible.
www.mcgraw-hill.co.uk/
textbooks/jobber

staff and happy customers. An investment company can provide tangible evidence of past performance. Testimonials from satisfied customers can also be used to communicate services benefits. Netto, the Danish-based supermarket chain, used testimonials from six customers in its UK advertising to explain the advantages of shopping there.

Advertising can be used to communicate and reinforce the image of a service. For example, store image can enhance customer satisfaction and build store loyalty.[63] Advertising can also be used to create awareness of the benefits consumers can expect from the service provider, as the advertisement for HSBC shows. Promotions can be used to provide value-based offerings such as the Marks & Spencer 'Dine in for £10' and Sainsbury's 'Feed a Family for a Fiver' campaigns.

New media can also be used to promote services. For example, some online retailers use targeted email to encourage customers to visit their sites. The travel and leisure retailer Lastminute.com sends more than two million emails to customers every week with content tailored to fit the recipient's age and lifestyle.[64] Online retailers Amazon and eBay also use email to send regular messages to their customers about products and special offers. Traditional methods are also used, however. For example, eBay uses direct mail to tell businesses about the benefits of using its site to sell goods.[65]

Personal selling can also be effective in services marketing because of the high perceived risk inherent in many service purchases. For example, a salesperson can explain the details of a personal pension plan or investment opportunity, answer questions and provide reassurance.

Because of the high perceived risk inherent in buying services, salespeople should develop lists of satisfied customers to use in reference selling. Also salespeople need to be trained to ask for referrals. Customers should be asked if they know of other people or organizations that might benefit from the service. The customer can then be used as an entrée and point of reference when approaching and selling to the new prospect.

Word of mouth is critical to success for services because of their experiential nature. For example, talking to people that have visited a resort or hotel is more convincing than reading holiday brochures. Promotion, therefore, must acknowledge the dominant role of personal influence in the choice process and stimulate word of mouth communication. Cowell suggests four approaches, as follows.[66]

1 Persuading satisfied customers to inform others of their satisfaction (e.g. American Express rewards customers that introduce others to its service).
2 Developing materials that customers can pass on to others.
3 Targeting opinion leaders in advertising campaigns.
4 Encouraging potential customers to talk to current customers (e.g. open days at universities).

⬆ EXHIBIT 10.2   Sainsbury's advertises its capacity to provide quality at an affordable price.

Viral communications—sometimes called electronic word of mouth—can also be used to promote services. This may take the form of an email sent to a target audience, who are encouraged to spread the word among their friends by passing the message on electronically.

Communication should also be targeted at employees because of their importance in creating and maintaining service quality. Internal communications can define management expectations of staff, reinforce the need to delight the customer and explain the rewards that follow from giving excellent service. External communications that depict service quality can also influence internal staff if they include employees and show how they take exceptional care of their customers.

Care should be taken not to exaggerate promises in promotional material since this may build up unachievable expectations. For example, Delta Airlines used the advertising slogan 'Delta is ready when you are'. This caused problems because it built up customers' expectations that the airline would always be ready—an impossible task. This led Delta to change its slogan to the more realistic 'We love to fly and it shows'.[67]

The unethical promotion of service products has caused problems in some sectors. A study of senior managers in UK insurance companies revealed an awareness of a range of ethical problems. The design of commission systems which may encourage bias towards products that provide greater returns to the salesperson, and the promotion of inappropriate products were of particular concern.[68]

Price: price is a key marketing tool, for three reasons. First, as it is often difficult to evaluate a service before purchase, price may act as an indicator of perceived quality. For example, in a travel brochure the price charged by hotels may be used to indicate their quality. Some companies expect a management consultant to charge high fees, otherwise they cannot be particularly good. Second, price is an important tool in controlling demand: matching demand and supply is critical in services because they cannot be stored. Creative use of pricing can help to smooth demand. Third, a key segmentation variable with services is price sensitivity. Some customers may be willing to pay a much higher price than others. Time is often used to segment price-sensitive and price-insensitive customers. For example, the price of international air travel is often dependent on length of stay. Travellers from Europe to the USA will pay a lot less if they stay a minimum of six nights (including Saturday). Airlines know that customers who stay for less than that are likely to be business people who are willing and able to pay a higher price.

Many companies do not take full advantage of the opportunities to use price creatively in the marketing of their services. For example, in the business-to-business services sector, one study found that firms 'generally lack a customer orientation in pricing; emphasize formula-based approaches that are cost-orientated; are very inflexible in their pricing schemes; do not develop price differentials based on elasticity of different market segments; and rarely attempt to measure customer price sensitivity'.[69] An exception is the budget hotel chain, Travelodge. The company has adopted a demand-led online pricing system similar to that pioneered by easyJet and Ryanair. Rooms are often priced cheaply to begin with, but the price rises as the hotel becomes fully booked.[70]

Some services, such as accounting and management consultancy, charge their customers fees. A strategy needs to be thought out concerning fees. How far can fees be flexible to secure or retain particular

Who loves flying you to the place you actually booked?

Ryanair
"Barcelona" = Girona
"Paris" = Beauvais
"Milan" = Bergamo
"Venice" = Treviso

easyJet
Barcelona = Barcelona
Paris = Paris
Milan = Milan
Venice = Venice

Get on board the love plane now!

easyJet.com
Flights · Hotels · Cars · Holidays

⬆ **EXHIBIT 10.3** easyJet aims to differentiate its service from that of Ryanair.

customers? How will the fee level compare to that of the competition? Will there be an incentive built in to the fee structure for continuity, forward commitment or the use of the full range of services on offer? Five pricing techniques may be used when setting fee levels.

1 *Offset*: low fee for core service but recouping with add-ons.
2 *Inducement*: low fee to attract new customers or to help retain existing customers.
3 *Diversionary*: low basic fees on selected services to develop the image of value for money across the whole range of services.
4 *Guarantee*: full fee payable on achievement of agreed results.
5 *Predatory*: competition's fees undercut to remove them from the market; high fees charged later.

The Internet is making price transparency a reality. This has caused problems for premium-price service companies such as Avis. In the face of online holiday companies offering cheap holidays and car rental deals, and the ease with which consumers can compare prices, Avis has had to reduce prices, thereby depressing profitability.[71]

Place: distribution channels for services are usually more direct than for many physical goods. Because services are intangible, the services marketer is less concerned with storage, the production and consumption is often simultaneous, and the personal nature of services means that direct contact with the service provider (or at best its agent) is desirable. Agents are used when the individual service provider cannot offer a sufficiently wide selection for customers. Consequently, agents are often used for the marketing of travel, insurance and entertainment. However, the advent of the Internet means that direct dealings with the service provider are becoming more frequent.

Growth for many service companies means opening new facilities in new locations. Whereas producers of physical goods can expand production at one site to serve the needs of a geographically spread market, the simultaneous production and consumption of hotel, banking, catering, retailing and accounting services, for example, means that expansion often means following a multi-site strategy. The evaluation of store locations is therefore a critical skill for services marketers. Much of the success of top European supermarket chains has been due to their ability to choose profitable new sites for their retailing operations.

Service companies are also employing multi-channel strategies to make their products widely available. For example, the retailer Next uses bricks-and-mortar stores and the Next Directory mail-order channel, as well as an online business.[72] Consumers are increasingly buying services through the Internet. This can often mean lower prices and, in some cases, faster service.

People: because of the simultaneity of production and consumption in services, the firm's personnel occupy a key position in influencing customer perceptions of product quality.[73] In fact, service quality is inseparable from the quality of the service provider. Without courteous, efficient and motivated staff, service organizations will lose customers. A survey has shown that one in six consumers have been put off making a purchase because of the way they were treated by staff.[74] An important marketing task, then, is to set standards to improve the quality of service provided by employees and monitor their performance. Without training and control, employees tend to be variable in their performance, leading to variable service quality.

Training is crucial so that employees understand the appropriate forms of behaviour. British Airways trains its flight attendants to identify and categorize different personality types of passengers, and to modify their behaviour accordingly. Staff (e.g. waiters) need to know how much discretion they have to talk informally to customers, and to control their own behaviour so that they are not intrusive, noisy or immature. They also need to be trained to adopt a warm and caring attitude to customers. This has been shown to be linked to customers' perceptions of likeability and service perception, as well as loyalty to the service provider.[75] Finally, they need to adopt a customer-first attitude rather than putting their own convenience and enjoyment before that of their customers. This is not to say that staff should not enjoy their work. As Ross Urquhart, managing director of brand experience consultancy RPM, puts it:

> When people enjoy their work it is clear from their body language and the tone of their voice. They give off positive messages about their employer and will go the extra mile for their clients too. The company brand enjoys a very real boost as a result.[76]

⬆EXHIBIT 10.4 The iconic Singapore girl is used in Singapore Airlines' advertising to illustrate the company's passion for service quality.

Marketing should also examine the role played by customers in the service environment and seek to eliminate harmful interactions. For example, the enjoyment of a restaurant meal or air travel will very much depend on the actions of other customers. At Christmas, restaurants are often in demand by groups of work colleagues for staff parties. These can be rowdy affairs that can detract from the pleasure of regular patrons. This situation needs to be managed, perhaps by segregating the two types of customer in some way.

Physical evidence: this is the environment in which the service is delivered, and any tangible goods that facilitate the performance and communication of the service. Customers look for clues to the likely quality of a service by inspecting the tangible evidence. For example, prospective customers may gaze through a restaurant window to check the appearance of the waiters, the décor and furnishings. The ambience of a retail store is highly dependent on décor, and colour can play an important role in establishing mood because colour has meaning. For example, black signifies strength and power, whereas green suggests mildness. The interior of jet aircraft is pastel-coloured to promote a feeling of calmness, whereas many nightclubs are brightly coloured, with flashing lights to give a sense of excitement.

The layout of a service operation can be a compromise between operations' need for efficiency, and marketing's desire to serve the customer effectively. For example, the temptation to squeeze in an extra table at a restaurant or extra seating in an aircraft may be at the expense of customer comfort.

Process: this describes the procedures, mechanisms and flow of activities by which a service is acquired. Process decisions radically affect how a service is delivered to customers. For example, a self-service cafeteria is very different from a restaurant. Marketing managers need to know if self-service is acceptable (or indeed desirable). Queuing may provide an opportunity to create a differential advantage by reduction/elimination, or making the time spent waiting more enjoyable. Certainly, waiting for service is a common experience for customers and is a strong determinant of overall satisfaction with the service and customer loyalty. Research has shown that an attractive waiting environment can prevent customers becoming irritated or bored very quickly, even though they may have to wait a long time. Both appraisal of the wait and satisfaction with the service improved when the attractiveness of the waiting environment (measured by atmosphere, cleanliness, spaciousness and climate) was rated higher.[77] Providing a more effective service (shorter queues) may be at odds with operations as the remedy may be to employ more staff.

Reducing delivery time—for example, the time between ordering a meal and receiving it—can also improve service quality. As discussed earlier, this need not necessarily cost more if customers can be persuaded to become involved in the production process, as successfully reflected in the growth of self-service breakfast bars in hotels.

Finally, Berry suggests seven guidelines when implementing a positioning strategy.[78]

1 Ensure that *marketing* happens at all levels, from the marketing department to where the service is provided.
2 Consider introducing *flexibility* in providing the service; when feasible, customize the service to the needs of customers.
3 Recruit *high-quality staff*, treat them well and communicate clearly to them; their attitudes and behaviour are the key to service quality and differentiation.
4 Attempt to market to *existing customers* to increase their use of the service, or to take up new service products.
5 Set up a *quick-response facility* to customer problems and complaints.
6 Employ *new technology* to provide better services at lower cost.
7 Use *branding* to clearly differentiate service offerings from those of the competition in the minds of target customers.

Non-Profit Organizations

Non-profit organizations are not driven by creating surplus profits but they still generate sufficient cash to survive and have different goals: for example to provide cultural enrichment (Hallé orchestra), to protect nature (Royal Society for the Protection of Birds), and to alleviate hunger (Oxfam).

Marketing is of growing importance to many non-profit organizations as they need to generate funds in an increasingly competitive environment. Even organizations that rely on government-sponsored grants need to show how their work is of benefit to society: they must meet the needs of their customers. Many non-profit organizations rely on membership fees or donations, which means that communication to individuals and organizations is required, and they must be persuaded to join or make a donation. This requires marketing skills, which are increasingly being applied. Such is the case with political parties, which use marketing techniques to attract members (and the fees their allegiance brings) and votes at elections.[79]

Non-profit characteristics

Despite the growing use of marketing in the non-profit sector it is important to be aware of the characteristics which distinguish this form of marketing from that of profit-orientated marketing organizations.[80]

Education vs meeting current needs

Some non-profit organizations see their role as not only meeting the current needs of their customers but also educating them in terms of new ideas and issues, cultural development and social awareness.

Multiple publics

Most non-profit organizations serve several groups, or publics (discussed further in Chapter 15 under the topic of Public Relations). The two broad groups are *donors*, who may be individuals, trusts, companies or government bodies, and *clients*, who include audiences, patients and beneficiaries.[81] Non-profit organizations need to adopt marketing as a coherent philosophy for managing multiple public relationships[82] and in doing so satify the needs of donors and clients.

Measurement of success and conflicting objectives

Profit-orientated organizations' success is ultimately measured in financial terms. For non-profit organizations measuring success is not so easy, and decision-making is therefore complex in non-profit-orientated organizations.

Public scrutiny

While all organizations are subject to public scrutiny, public-sector, non-profit organizations are closely monitored. The reason is that they are publicly funded from taxes.

Marketing procedures for non-profit organizations

Despite needing to taking into account these characteristics, marketing procedures relevant to profit-orientated companies can largely be applied to non-profit organizations. Target marketing, differentiation and marketing-mix decisions need to be made. For example, when target marketing for political parties, potential voters are segmented according to their propensity to vote (obtainable from electoral registers) and the likelihood that they will vote for a particular party (obtainable from door-to-door canvassing returns). Resources can then be channelled to the segments most likely to switch votes in the forthcoming election, via direct mail and doorstep visits.[83]

Developing a marketing mix

Non-profit organizations often use *event marketing*. Events including dinners, dances, coffee mornings, book sales, sponsored walks and theatrical shows are organized to raise funds. Not all events are designed to raise funds for the sponsoring organization. For example, the BBC hosts the Comic Relief and Children in Need *telethons* to raise money for worthy causes.

Like most services, distribution systems for many non-profit organizations are short, with production and consumption taking place almost simultaneously. Such organizations have to think carefully about how to deliver their services to accommodate the convenience that customers require. For example, the Hallé Orchestra is based in Manchester but over half of its performances are in other towns or cities. Some non-profit organizations have their own retail outlets. For example, Oxfam, an organization that seeks to reduce poverty and suffering around the world through fundraising and issue-awareness campaigns, has 750 shops around the UK that sell donated second-hand clothing, books, music and household items.

Many non-profit organizations are adept at using all aspects of the promotion mix to further their objectives. For example, print media and direct mail have been widely used to elicit donations for major disasters: for example, famine relief in Africa, victims of the tsunami in Japan. Advertising is widely used by charities such as Oxfam and Barnados to create awareness of issues and raise funds so they can continue to provide services. Public relations has an important role to play in generating positive word-of-mouth communications and to confirm the non-profit identity of the charity.

When you have read this chapter

Review

1   **The nature and special characteristics of services**
- Services are a special kind of product that may require special understanding and special marketing efforts because of their special characteristics.
- The key characteristics of pure services are intangibility (they cannot be touched, tasted or smelled); inseparability (production and consumption takes place at the same time, e.g. a haircut); variability (service quality may vary, making standardization difficult); and perishability (consumption cannot be stored, e.g. a hotel room).

2   **Managing customer relationships**
- Relationship marketing involves shifting from activities concerned with attracting new customers to activities focused on retaining existing customers.
- The benefits to the organization are increased purchases, lower costs, maximizing lifetime value of customers, sustainable competitive advantage, gaining word of mouth, and improved employee satisfaction and retention.
- The benefits to the customer are risk and stress reduction, higher-quality service, avoidance of switching costs, and social and status advantages.
- Customer retention strategies are targeting customers worthy of retention, bonding, internal marketing, promise fulfilment, building of trust, and service recovery.

3   **Managing service quality, productivity and staff**
- Two key service quality concepts are customer expectations and perceptions. Customers may be disappointed with service quality if their service perceptions fail to meet their expectations. This may result because of four barriers: the misconception barrier (management's misunderstanding of what the customer expects); the inadequate resources barrier (management provides inadequate resources); inadequate delivery barrier (management fails to select, train and adequately reward staff); and the exaggerated promises barrier (management causes expectations to be too high because of exaggerated promises).
- Service quality can be measured using a scale called SERVQUAL, which is based on five criteria: reliability, responsiveness, courtesy, competence and tangibles (e.g. quality of restaurant décor).
- Service productivity can be improved without reducing service quality by using technology (e.g. automatic cash dispensers); customer involvement in production (e.g. self-service petrol stations); and balancing supply and demand (e.g. differential pricing to smooth demand).
- Staff are critical in service operations because they are often in contact with customers. The starting point is the selection of suitable people, socialization allows the recruit to experience the culture and tasks of the organization, empowerment gives them the authority to solve customer problems, they need to be trained and motivated, and evaluation is required so that staff understand how their performance standards relate to customer satisfaction.

4   **How to position a service organization or brand**
- Positioning involves the choice of target market (where to compete) and the creation of a differential advantage (how to compete). These decisions are common to both physical products and services. However, because of the special characteristics of services, it is useful for the services marketer to consider not only the classical 4-Ps marketing mix but also an additional 3-Ps—people, physical evidence and process—when deciding how to meet customer needs and create a differential advantage.

5   **The services marketing mix**
- The services marketing mix consists of 7-Ps: product, price, place, promotion, people (important because of the high customer contact characteristic of services), physical evidence (important because customers look for cues to the likely quality of a service by inspecting the physical evidence, e.g. décor), and process (because the process of supplying a service affects perceived service quality).

6 **The nature and special characteristics of non-profit marketing**
- Non-profit organizations attempt to achieve some other objective than profit. For example, an orchestra's primary objective may be cultural enrichment. Non-profit organizations are still interested in income as they have to generate cash to survive.
- Their special characteristics are that they may wish to pursue educational objectives as well as meeting the current needs of customers; they often serve multiple publics—for example, donors (e.g. the government) and clients (e.g. audiences); the difficulty of measuring success given multiple, sometimes conflicting objectives; and the close public scrutiny of public-sector organizations because of their funding from taxes.

Key Terms

exaggerated promises barrier a barrier to the matching of expected and perceived service levels caused by the unwarranted building up of expectations by exaggerated promises

halo customers customers that are not directly targeted but may find the product attractive

inadequate delivery barrier a barrier to the matching of expected and perceived service levels caused by the failure of the service provider to select, train and reward staff adequately, resulting in poor or inconsistent delivery of service

inadequate resources barrier a barrier to the matching of expected and perceived service levels caused by the unwillingness of service providers to provide the necessary resources

inseparability a characteristic of services, namely that their production cannot be separated from their consumption

intangibility a characteristic of services, namely that they cannot be touched, seen, tasted or smelled

misconception barrier a failure by marketers to understand what customers really value about their service

perishability a characteristic of services, namely that the capacity of a service business, such as a hotel room, cannot be stored—if it is not occupied, this is lost income that cannot be recovered

service any deed, performance or effort carried out for the customer

services marketing mix product, place, price, promotion, people, process and physical evidence (the '7-Ps')

variability a characteristic of services, namely that, being delivered by people, the standard of their performance is open to variation

Study Questions

1 To what extent is the marketing of services the same as the marketing of physical goods? Discuss.

2 What are the barriers that can separate expected from perceived service? What must service providers do to eliminate these barriers?

3 Discuss the role of service staff in the creation of a quality service. Can you give examples from your own experience of good and bad service encounters?

4 Identify and evaluate how supermarkets can differentiate themselves from their competitors. Choose three supermarkets and evaluate their success at differentiation.

5 Discuss the problems of providing high-quality service in retailing in central and eastern Europe.

6 Discuss the benefits to organizations and customers of developing and maintaining strong customer relationships.

References

1. Karpen, I., L. Bove and B. Lukas (2012) Linking service-dominant logic and strategic business practice: A conceptual model of a service-dominant orientation, *Journal of Service Research* 15(1), 21–38; DOI: 10.1177/1094670511425697.
2. Karpen, Bove and Lukas (2012) op. cit.
3. DCMS (2010) *Creative industries economic estimates statistical bulletin*, London: DCMS, http://www.culture.gov.uk/images/research/CIEE_Full_Release_Dec2010.pdf.
4. Hirsch, P. (1972) Processing fads and fashions: an organization set analysis of culture industry systems, *American Journal of Sociology*, 77, 639–659. In M. Banksa and D. Hesmondhalgh (2009) Looking for work in creative industries policy, *International Journal of Cultural Policy* 15(4), 415–430.
5. Arts Council (2004) Market matters: the dynamics of the contemporary art market, London: Arts Council.
6. Rubera, G. and A. Kirca (2012) Firm Innovativeness and Its Performance Outcomes: A Meta-Analytic Review and Theoretical Integration *Journal of Marketing* 76(May), 130–47.
7. Collinson, S. (2012) Why is the public sector so complex? http://flipchartfairytales.wordpress.com/2012/03/19/why-is-the-public-sector-so-complex/.
8. *Marketing in the public sector*, ftp://ftp.pearsonedema.com/HPE_Samples/SampleChapters/9780273708094.pdf.
9. Ellis-Chadwick, F. (2011) *B22 An introduction to retail management and marketing: Book 1 What is retailing?* The Open University, 7.
10. Cowell, D. (1995) *The Marketing of Services*, London: Heinemann, 35.
11. Vargo, S. L. and R. F. Lusch (2006) 'Service-Dominant Logic: What It Is, What It Is Not, What It Might Be,' in R. F. Lusch and S. L. Vargo (eds), *The Service-Dominant Logic of Marketing: Dialog, Debate, and Directions*, Armonk: M.E. Sharpe, 43–56.
12. Vargo and Lusch (2006) op. cit.
13. Brown, S. and A. Patterson (2009) Harry Potter and the Service-Dominant Logic of marketing: a cautionary tale, *Journal of Marketing Management* 25(5–6), 519–33.
14. Lusch, R. F., S. L. Vargo and M. Tanniru (2010) Service, value networks and learning, *Journal of the Academy of Marketing Science* 38, 19–31.
15. Berry, L. L. (1980) Services Marketing is Different, *Business Horizons*, May–June, 24–9.
16. Edgett, S. and S. Parkinson (1993) Marketing for Services Industries: A Review, *Service Industries Journal* 13(3), 19–39.
17. Berry (1980) op. cit.
18. Aijo, T. S. (1996) The Theoretical and Philosophical Underpinnings of Relationship Marketing, *European Journal of Marketing* 30(2), 8–18; Grönroos, C. (1990) *Services Management and Marketing: Managing the Moments of Truth in Service Competition*, Lexington, MA: Lexington Books.
19. Baron, S., K. Harris and B. J. Davies (1996) Oral Participation in Retail Service Delivery: A Comparison of the Roles of Contact Personnel and Customers, *European Journal of Marketing* 30(9), 75–90.
20. Grönroos, C. (1994) From Marketing Mix to Relationship Marketing: Towards a Paradigm Shift in Marketing, *Management Decision* 32(2), 4–20.
21. Egan, C. (1997) Relationship Management, in Jobber, D. (ed.) *The CIM Handbook of Selling and Sales Strategy*, Oxford: Butterworth-Heinemann, 55–88. See also Coviello, N. E., R. J. Brodie, P. J. Danaker and W. J. Johnson (2002) How Firms Relate to Their Markets: An Empirical Examination of Contemporary Marketing Practices, *Journal of Marketing* 66, July, 33–46.
22. Berry, L. L. (1995) Relationship Marketing, in Payne, A., M. Christopher, M. Clark and H. Peck (eds) *Relationship Marketing for Competitive Advantage*, Oxford: Butterworth-Heinemann, 65–74.
23. Zeithaml, V. A., M. J. Bitner, and D. D. Gremier (2005) *Services Marketing*, New York: McGraw-Hill, 174–8.
24. Roberts, K., S. Varki and R. Brodie (2003) Measuring the Quality of Relationships in Consumer Services: An Empirical Study, *European Journal of Marketing* 37(1/2), 169–96.
25. Reichheld, F. F. and W. E. Sasser Jr (1990) Zero Defections: Quality Comes to Services, *Harvard Business Review*, Sept.–Oct., 105–11.
26. Berry, L. L. (1995) Relationship Marketing of Services—Growing Interest, Emerging Perspectives, *Journal of the Academy of Marketing Science* 23(4), 236–45.
27. Bitner, M. J. (1995) Building Service Relationships: It's All About Promises, *Journal of the Academy of Marketing Science* 23(4), 246–51.
28. Bitner (1995) op. cit.
29. Parasuraman, A., L. L. Berry and V. A. Zeithaml (1991) Understanding Customer Expectations of Service, *Sloan Management Review*, Spring, 39–48.
30. Berry (1995) op. cit.
31. Berry, L. L. and A. Parasuraman (1991) *Marketing Services*, New York: Free Press, 136–42.
32. Berry (1995) op. cit.
33. Gummesson, E. (1987) The New Marketing–Developing Long-term Interactive Relationships, *Long Range Planning* 20, 10–20.
34. Bitner (1995) op. cit.
35. See Bitner, M. J., B. H. Booms and M. S. Tetreault (1990) The Service Encounter: Diagnosing Favourable and Unfavourable Incidents, *Journal of Marketing* 43, January, 71–84; Bitner, M. J., B. H. Booms and L. A. Mohr (1994) Critical Service Encounters: The Employee's View, *Journal of Marketing* 58, October, 95–106.
36. Lovelock, C. H., S. Vandermerwe and B. Lewis (1999) *Services Marketing—A European Perspective*, New York: Prentice-Hall, 176.
37. Berry (1995) op. cit.
38. Kasper, H., P. van Helsdingen and M. Gabbott (2006) *Services Marketing Management*, Chichester: Wiley, 528.
39. Maxham III, J. G. and R. G. Netemeyer (2002) A Longitudinal Study of Complaining Customers' Evaluations of Multiple Service Failures and Recovery Efforts, *Journal of Marketing* 66, October, 57–71.
40. Johnson, R. (1995) Service Failure and Recovery: Impact, Attributes and Process, in Swartz, T. A., D. E. Bowen and S. W. Brown (eds) *Advances in Services Marketing and Management* 4, 52–65.
41. Buzzell, R. D. and B. T. Gale (1987) *The PIMS Principles: Linking Strategy to Performance*, New York: Free Press, 103–34.
42. Parasuraman, A., V. A. Zeithaml and L. L. Berry (1985) A Conceptual Model of Service Quality and its Implications for Future Research, *Journal of Marketing*, Fall, 41–50.
43. Johnson, L. (2008) The Incalculable Appeal of Good Service, *Financial Times*, 26 March, 16.
44. Parasuraman, Zeithaml and Berry (1985) op. cit.
45. Danaher, P. J. and J. Mattson (1994) Customer Satisfaction during the Service Delivery Process, *European Journal of Marketing* 28(5), 5–16.
46. De Ruyter, K., M. Wetzels, J. Lemmink and J. Mattsson (1997) The Dynamics of the Service Delivery Process: A Value-Based Approach, *International Journal of Research in Marketing* 14, 231–43.
47. Zeithaml, V. A., A. Parasuraman and L. L. Berry (1988) SERVQUAL: A Multiple Item Scale for Measuring Consumer Perceptions of Service Quality, *Journal of Retailing* 64(1), 13–37.
48. Sherwood, B. (2008) An Eye For The Next Opportunity, *Financial Times*, 17 September, 16.
49. Lovelock, C. (1992) Seeking Synergy in Service Operations: Seven Things Marketers Need to Know about Service Operations, *European Management Journal* 10(1), 22–9.

50. Mudie, P. and A. Cottam (1997) *The Management and Marketing of Services*, Oxford: Butterworth-Heinemann, 211.

51. Schlesinger, L. A. and J. L. Heskett (1991) The Service-Driven Service Company, *Harvard Business Review*, Sept.–Oct., 71–81.

52. Lievens, A. and R. K. Moenaert (2000) Communication Flows During Financial Service Innovation, *European Journal of Marketing* 34(9/10), 1078–110.

53. Jones, A. (2008) Shambolic But Totally Predictable, *Guardian*, 28 March, 3.

54. Bowen, D. E. and L. L. Lawler (1992) Empowerment: Why, What, How and When, *Sloan Management Review*, Spring, 31–9.

55. Hiscock, J. (2002) The Brand Insiders, *Marketing*, 23 May, 24–5.

56. Milne, R. (2004) High Fliers Get a Champagne Check-in, *Financial Times*, 23 November, 12.

57. Charles, G. (2008) KFC Launches Breakfast Menu, *Marketing*, 7 May, 1.

58. Roberts, J. (2009) When the Big Go Boutique, *Marketing Week*, 19 March, 12–16.

59. Christopher, M. and R. Yallop (1990) Audit your Customer Service Quality, *Focus*, June–July, 1–6.

60. Booms, B. H. and M. J. Bitner (1981) Marketing Strategies and Organisation Structures for Service Firms, in Donnelly, J. H. and W. R. George (eds) *Marketing of Services*, Chicago: American Marketing Association, 47–51.

61. Berry, L. L., E. E. Lefkowith and T. Clark (1980) In Services: What's in a Name?, *Harvard Business Review*, Sept.–Oct., 28–30.

62. Garrahan, M. (2005) The Ride of a Lifetime, *Financial Times*, 18 August, 19.

63. Bloemer, J. and K. de Ruyter (1998) On the Relationship Between Store Image, Store Satisfaction and Store Loyalty, *European Journal of Marketing* 32(5/6), 499–513.

64. Cole, G. (2003) Window Shopping, *Financial Times IT Review*, 5 February, 4.

65. Parry, C. (2005) Consumers and E-tail Begin to Click, *Marketing Week*, 14 April.

66. Cowell, D. (1995) op. cit.

67. Sellers, P. (1988) How to Handle Customers' Gripes, *Fortune* 118 (October), 100.

68. Diacon, S. R. and C. T. Ennew (1996) Ethical Issues in Insurance Marketing in the UK, *European Journal of Marketing* 30(5), 67–80.

69. Morris, M. H. and D. Fuller (1989) Pricing an Industrial Service, *Industrial Marketing Management* 18, 139–46.

70. Fernandez, J. (2009) Sparking a Hotel Price War, *Marketing Week*, 12 March, 22–3.

71. Davoudi, S. (2005) From Brand Leader to Struggler in Eight Years, *Financial Times*, 17 June, 24.

72. Jack, L. (2008) Painful Times for the Next Generation, *Marketing Week*, 27 November, 8.

73. Rafiq, M. and P. K. Ahmed (1992) The Marketing Mix Reconsidered, *Proceedings of the Annual Conference of the Marketing Education Group*, Salford, 439–51.

74. Wilkinson, A. (2002) Employees can get the Message Across, *Marketing Week*, 3 October, 20.

75. Lemmink, J. and J. Mattsson (1998) Warmth During Non-Productive Retail Encounters: The Hidden Side of Productivity, *International Journal of Research in Marketing* 15, 505–17.

76. Sumner-Smith, D. (2001) A Winning Strategy, *Marketing Business*, May, 26–8.

77. Pruyn, A. and A. Smidts (1998) Effects of Waiting on the Satisfaction with the Service: Beyond Objective Times Measures, *International Journal of Research in Marketing* 15, 321–34.

78. Berry, L. L. (1987) Big Ideas in Services Marketing, *Journal of Services Marketing*, Fall, 5–9.

79. See Lock, A. and P. Harris (1996) Political Marketing—Vive La Difference, *European Journal of Marketing* 30(10/11), 21–31; Butler, P. and N. Collins (1996) Strategic Analysis in Political Markets, *European Journal of Marketing* 30(10/11), 32–44.

80. Bennett, P. D. (1988) *Marketing*, New York: McGraw-Hill, 690–2.

81. Shapiro, B. (1992) Marketing for Non-Profit Organisations, *Harvard Business Review*, Sept.–Oct., 123–32.

82. Balabanis, G., R. E. Stables and H. C. Phillips (1997) Market Orientation in the Top 200 British Charity Organisations and its Impact on their Performance, *European Journal of Marketing* 31(8), 583–603.

83. For an in-depth examination of political marketing, see Butler, P. and N. Collins (1994) Political Marketing: Structure and Process, *European Journal of Marketing* 28(1), 19–34.

Sandals Resorts International (SRI)
Positioning Services

The hospitality and tourism industry is very diverse and there are many opportunities for service providers to devise highly targeted offers. This case explores how Sandals Resorts International has built a successful hotel brand by providing very specialized services.

Gordon 'Butch' Stewart bought his first hotel in 1981, invested $4 million in renovation costs and gave it the name Sandals Montego Bay. Now, Sandals Resorts International (SRI) employs 10,000 people and operates 13 couples-only and 6 family-oriented resorts under the brand names Sandals and Beaches, respectively, as well as 4 private villas (private homes of Butch Stewart) and a private island. These all-inclusive resorts are located on some of the best beaches in Jamaica, Antigua, St Lucia, Bahamas and Turks and Caicos.

Stewart believes in 'giving customers more than they expect or think they need', a philosophy that guided him in his earlier entrepreneurial days in the air-conditioning business and in the ensuing Sandals years. Therefore, although classified an all-inclusive resort, Sandals successfully separated itself from the rest of the hospitality industry by offering more than the other all-inclusive resorts. Some of their 'Ultra All-inclusive®' offers included special packages for weddings and honeymoons, access to private offshore islands at selected resorts, themed gourmet restaurants, nightly entertainment, unlimited scuba diving and water sports, top golf courses at some resorts, airport transfers, tips, gratuities and hotel taxes.

Their upgraded Luxury Inclusive® offer adds free Martha Stewart weddings and house wines by Beringer Vineyards. In addition, up to 16 restaurants per resort are available, serving a variety of cuisines, such as Asian, Thai, Sushi, Japanese Teppanyaki, West Indian, Jamasian, Fusion, Mediterranean, Italian, Classic French, English Pub, TexMex and Southwestern. And for those who want more, some suites come with a personal butler service from butlers trained by the Guild of Professional English Butlers. Although the Luxury Included® offer is quite comprehensive, there are even more additional services that guests can purchase, for example, spa treatments and off-property adventure tours.

Both brands share the amenities listed above; however, they each serve their guests in different ways. Sandals provide couples with the 'perfect romantic getaway'. They assert that 'love is all you need' and boast that there is no other resort in the world that is completely dedicated to two people in love. Couples can enjoy plush king-size beds in all rooms and suites, intimate ambience at all romantic spa resorts, plenty of secluded spots for romance, and gourmet dining with candlelit tables for two. In Jamaica and St Lucia, Sandals offers its pioneering 'stay at 1, play at all' feature, where couples can freely transfer to any other Sandals resorts in that island and enjoy the facilities of the other resorts.

The Beaches brand serves 'everyone'—families, friends, couples and groups. The first, Beaches Negril, was opened in 1997 as a family-oriented resort offering the same amenities as Sandals. Now it serves guests wanting to stay there for a variety of reasons, such as family reunions, corporate retreats and girlfriends/guys getaway. Accommodation includes luxury suites for up to eight people and private beachside bungalows. In addition to the Luxury Included® offer above, Beaches has entertainment for all ages. Some of these are Sesame Street programmes, Kids Camps with certified nannies, Pirate Islands, Kinect for Xbox 360® Game Garage, night club for teens and adults (Liquid at Beaches) and the Scratch DJ Academy®. There is also the Caribbean's only Surf Simulator at Beaches Turks and Caicos.

Understanding the customer experience and providing consistently high levels of service across all the resorts is important to everyone at the Sandals resorts. At the heart of the company's operation is a business intelligence system, which enables Joanne Pearson, the Director of Corporate Reporting at Sandals International resorts, to have the 'right tools' to carry out the analysis that is needed to not only ensure that customers are completely satisfied but also that the company operates profitably. The system gathers data on a daily basis and close attention is paid to key performance indicators such as occupancy rates, staffing levels, food costs and spend-per-room. Daily management reports enable the team to monitor performance and take immediate action if any issues are detected.

In addition to the emphasis on exceeding guests' expectations, SRI invests substantially in their employees, whom they call 'team members', through the Sandals Corporate University (SCU). Each team member is specially selected and trained to carry out his/her role and continually encouraged to personally develop. The SCU ensures they understand that they are as important as their guests. This is fundamental to a successful service organisation because happy team members give excellent service resulting in happy, loyal guests.

SRI also has a strong commitment to society and through its Sandals Foundation makes investments to support the development of local communities. Resort founder Gordon Stewart is only too aware of the importance of the communities and the Caribbean and the role they play in making the resorts a success. There are three core elements to the foundation: the community, education and the environment. By working with the community the foundation aims to tackle social issues relating to violence, poverty, unemployment and healthcare and community programmes have succeeded in 'giving people chance to change their lives'. Through education initiatives, the foundation aims to provide scholarship and learning for thousands of students in the Caribbean of all ages and across all aspects of life. For example, in Montego Bay, parenting workshops raise awareness of the importance of education and lifelong learning. At the Green Island primary school in Jamaica, an oral hygiene project aims to reduce tooth decay amongst the island population. Children are encouraged to eat fewer sweets and brush their teeth several times a day. At the Sandals Cricket Academy over 500 cricketers have been trained since its launch in 2001 and the academy has won awards for sports development in the region. Preserving the environment is very important and the foundation increasingly is taking a leadership role in environmental programmes in both the public and private sector. At the Boscobel marine sanctuary, ecologists are working to protect coral and fish stocks and also engage local community fishermen to raise awareness of behaviour, which is damaging the fragile underwater environment. At the resort in Grande Antigua, tree planting is an initiative aimed to combat global warming. Throughout the Sandals operations, every day is a 'clean up the beach day' not just on World Ocean days. Teams from Sandals resorts work with local communities and fishermen to gather garbage and debris from the beaches.

Over the past 30 years SRI has been consistently rewarded for its emphasis on people. They receive high satisfaction levels from guests and more than half return, their employees are happy and remain loyal and they hold numerous awards from the hospitality sector. Furthermore, Gordon 'Butch' Stewart's original vision of providing high levels of customer satisfaction has gone much further than just developing a successful hospitality brand; it has provided economic and community development and made a significant contribution to helping societies in the Caribbean have a more sustainable way of living.

Sources

Brown, P., S. Hassan and R. Teare (2011) The Sandals philosophy: exceeding guest expectations—now and in the future, *Worldwide Hospitality and Tourism Themes* 3(1), 8–13.

Funding Universe (2004) Sandals Resorts International [webpage] Available at: file:///Users/deneisedadd/Desktop/OU:abdi/Literature%20Review/Case%20Studies/Sandals%20Resorts%20International%20--%20Company%20History.webarchive (accessed 12 January 2012).

Pike, J. (2011) Sandals' Success Story, *Travel Agent*, Questex Media Group, 25 July, 19–21.

Travel Agent (2011) Through the years with Sandals, *Travel Agent*, Questex Media Group, 25 July, 32.

Sandals Resorts International websites—sandals.com and beaches.com.

Aptech Computer Systems (2012) Sandals Resorts International optimizes profitably with big data http://www.hotelnewsresource.com/article63403Sandals_Resorts_International_Optimizes_Profitably_with_Big_Data.html 16 May.

Sandals Foundation (2012) News, http://www.sandalsfoundation.org/news/improving-dental-care-in-jamaican-children.html (accessed 30 June).

Questions

1 Explain how the characteristics of a service apply to SRI.

2 Customer retention is at the centre of relationship management. Suggest why SRI has been successful in encouraging over half its customers to return.

3 Discuss why it is beneficial to an organization like Sandals to develop and maintain strong customer relationships.

4 Imagine you are responsible for developing the customer retention strategy at one of SRI's resorts. Devise a strategy for a specific target audience.

5 Managing service quality successfully can increase customer satisfaction and lead to higher profitability. At SRI resorts meeting customer expectations is a key priority. Suggest what measures the management team needs to have in place to ensure customer perceptions of service quality remain high.

This case was prepared by Deneise Dadd, The Open University.

Marketing Care
A Healthy Challenge?

Background

The market

The population of the UK is ageing. The improvements in living standards and healthcare in the UK have resulted in people living longer with average life expectancy now 77.2 years for males and 81.5 years for women (Office for National Statistics, 2008). There are now more pensioners, classified as people over 65 years of age, than under-16-year-olds for the first time, and by 2033 23 per cent of the population will be pensioners. The fastest growing population group are those aged 85 years and over, and this age group is forecast to double to 3.2 million people in 2033, representing 5 per cent of the total population (Office for National Statistics, 2009). An ageing population inevitably results in an increased need for private care services to support elderly people to live independently. This type of care is known as *domiciliary care*. Dementia associated with ageing is also increasing; currently 820,000 people in Britain are thought to suffer from dementia and it is estimated that 1.7 million will be suffering from the disease by 2051 (Dementia, UK). Other people requiring home care support are those with disabilities, both physical and learning. One and half million individuals in the UK have a learning disability with 58,000 supported by daily care services (Mencap, 2011). There are currently 29,000 adults with learning disabilities living with elderly parents, many of whom are too old or frail to continue to act as carers.

Recent UK government policy has recognized the need to reduce demand for residential care by introducing a series of initiatives to support independent living: that is, rather than people moving into care homes, they are supported in their own homes (DOH, 2010). These reforms will focus on increased patient choice in that patients will be able to make decisions with their GP about the type of treatment that is best for them and they will also have more control and choice over where they are treated and who they are treated by. Councils will have a much greater leadership role in local health services in that they will be responsible for local health care priorities, joining up health and care services and ensuring they meet the needs of their local communities. This new direction for adult social care is an agenda that puts personalized services and outcomes at the heart of the vision.

Indeed, Mintel (2009) predicts that the UK market for domiciliary care is just under £55 billion and the market has grown on average between 2 and 4 per cent each year (Mintel, 2009). Domiciliary care is provided either informally by family members or friends, local authorities, the NHS community or private care companies. Mintel (2009) anticipates that the private sector will grow marginally more than the overall market due to local authorities sourcing domiciliary care from private companies. The private domiciliary market is dominated by a number of large franchised national chains, regionally based small- and medium-sized enterprises (SMEs) and individuals. The demand for domiciliary care obviously attracts market entrants, keen to capitalize on market trends.

Small business marketing

The number of SMEs prevalent in the domiciliary care sector is set to rise and, given the competitive nature of the industry, the care services offered by an SME need to be marketed effectively. Although marketing is practised by small firms, the type and amount of activity small businesses undertake differs between sectors and is certainly different from the marketing practised by large firms. Small business marketing is different owing to the small businesses' unique characteristics: their budgetary and other resource constraints and the influence of the owner manager. Management culture with SMEs tends to be more innovative and entrepreneurial. SME owners/

managers are often in charge of all the decision-making and operational issues of the firms. This has an impact on SMEs in managing the businesses on a day-to-day basis, making it difficult for them to adopt a more planned, strategic approach and instead focusing on tactical aspects. SME owners/managers lack a theoretical grounding in marketing and, instead, rely on networking, relationship marketing, word of mouth and their entrepreneurialism. If, added to this mix, is the nature of the domiciliary care market in terms of the level of trust, reliability and safety that is required, this raises particular marketing challenges.

Marketing domiciliary services

In addition to the size of the business having an impact upon how care services are marketed, it is important to understand how the marketing of services such as domiciliary care is different from the marketing of goods. The characteristics of services, such as their intangibility, the nature of their simultaneous production, distribution and consumption and the requirement for customer participation in the service, makes the assessment of a service delivery more complex to measure (Grönroos, 2000; Svensson, 2006). In domiciliary services deciding on who the customer is can be complex, with the purchaser not necessarily being the consumer of the service. Services are often evaluated through interactions between the service provider and the service user and are reliant on attributes such as trust, assurance and empathy (Parasuraman et al., 1988). Service encounters in the domiciliary market means evaluation of care can be difficult to independently evaluate, with issues of confidentiality providing a further ethical dimension. Care can be seen by potential entrepreneurs as a 'me-too' product and individuals can set themselves up as carers or as providers of home care support. Without appropriate standards of care being practised this issue could reverberate around the market. Moreover, recent work (Baron, 2008; Stone, 2009) has called for the elderly voice to come to the fore in marketing decisions.

The case company

'Home Support' is a small company, which provides domiciliary services to the elderly and disabled. This includes helping clients with dressing and personal grooming, food preparation and feeding, washing and ironing, collecting medication and offering companionship services such as accompanying clients on days out. It was established in 2008 by a single owner, Rosemary King, and currently provides services on a local basis. It has a current turnover of £0.5 million and employs 49 personnel. There are three main customers for 'Home Support': local social services who commission specific care packages for people requiring support, the general public who wish to access home support on an individual basis and self-help groups who require services on behalf of their members. Home Support's business proposition is high quality of care provision and excellent customer service. It has rigorous staff recruitment and training procedures in place and prides itself on providing a high level of customer service to both existing and potential customers. It works with bodies such as the local Chamber of Commerce and is undertaking accreditation for the Investor in People Award and the Information Standards Board. It was recently awarded a local 'best new small company' award, which has generated positive public relations (PR) and additional business for the company. There are a number of competitors in the local domiciliary services market in which Home Support is operating: national franchised chains, small local providers and companies of similar scale to Home Support but who operate on a cost rather than a quality proposition. Home Support currently holds a 2-star care rating award by the Care Quality Commission (2009) which implies that the company is offering a good standard of care.

The rapid growth of Home Support has prompted Rosemary to review the long term future of the business. Changes in population statistics in terms of increases in life expectancy and the associated growth of age related diseases such as dementia suggest this is a market with potential for expansion. In addition, social services are increasingly turning to the private sector to provide localized care and support to enable people to live independently in older age. Consequently, the next step for Home Support has been identified as regional expansion of the business and to help achieve this expansion, Rosemary needs to develop a marketing communication plan that can be replicated and delivered as the company develops into new regional areas.

Home Support currently undertakes a number of marketing activities including a website, an information leaflet and internal and external PR. Current marketing activities provide information around the service offer rather than actively promote the company. Rosemary does not use search engine optimization for the website, and information packs are used primarily for distribution to social services. Rosemary perceives that most of the current 'marketing' which is undertaken for Home Support is the communication with her customers and, in particular, social services. New business is driven through acquiring new contracts with social services or through positive word of mouth from existing customers. Rosemary perceives that she delivers the 'marketing' activity in Home Support through her personal interaction with key customers and the high level of customer service which the company delivers. As she herself explains, 'We know for a fact that we do it so differently . . . that really helps us stand out in the market place.' One of Rosemary's concerns about expansion is that she will be personally unable to carry out this function in other regional locations. 'The biggest issue is how we roll it out because there is not a "me" in every region.'

Currently there is no specific marketing budget and activities are decided on an opportunity-by-opportunity basis. Rosemary herself manages any marketing activity, although PR and website support is bought in externally on an ad hoc basis. Marketing activities are not specifically monitored although a customer database is maintained. The website provides details about the company and its services, but Rosemary is of the view that most of her business is generated through direct interaction with potential customers and as she sees it: 'The website does very little compared to what we get from face to face. It's all word of mouth and if we get a referral in, rather than just fax a response, we offer to go and talk it through with the customer and that sort of interaction influences sales and marketing and everything else.'

Rosemary has identified a number of barriers around the development of a formal marketing communication plan for Home Support. A major concern of hers is the perception that marketing is expensive and unnecessary and uses investment that could be ploughed into the quality of care provision. In discussions around marketing, Rosemary has concerns that marketing can be perceived negatively particularly amongst her key customers. 'It's a social services enterprise and if we were seen to be spending a lot of money on marketing . . . if we went overboard with huge press releases etc they would perceive that was where the money was going and not on the quality of the care

provision.' Other barriers to marketing are time and expertise. Although Rosemary has some background in sales, she is responsible for running the business and her focus is on meeting customer needs, recruiting and training staff and running the day-to-day business. The small management team she employs are from home care backgrounds and have no expertise or experience in marketing. The new regional office for Home Support is scheduled to open within the next six months and Rosemary needs a marketing communication plan in place before the opening. The clock is ticking . . .

Questions

1   **What marketing communication activities would you propose for Home Support?**

2   **How best can Rosemary support the development of marketing in her business?**

3   **What marketing challenges are there for an SME operating in a service market?**

4   **Consider the ethical dimensions that arise when marketing a domiciliary care company.**

Source: 'Home Support' is a pseudonym for an SME in which research has been undertaken by the authors.

This case was prepared by Clare Brindley, Professor of Marketing and Entrepreneurship, Dr Carley Foster, Reader, Dr Sheilagh Resnick, Senior Lecturer in Services Marketing, Nottingham Trent University, and Dr Ranis Cheng, University of Sheffield Management School.

CHAPTER 11

Managing products: product life-cycle, portfolio planning and product growth strategies

nothing but fruit

Here to save the peckish

> *Nothing can last for ever*
> *Though the sun shines gold*
> *It must plunge into the sea*
> *The moon has also disappeared*
> *Which but now so brightly gleamed.*
> **GRAFFITO, POMPEII**

LEARNING OBJECTIVES

After reading this chapter, you should be able to:

1 describe the concept of the product life-cycle

2 discuss the uses and limitations of the product life-cycle

3 describe the concept of product portfolio planning

4 explain the Boston Consulting Group Growth-Share Matrix, its uses and the criticisms of it

5 explain the General Electric Market Attractiveness–Competitive Position Model, its uses and the criticisms of it

6 discuss the contribution of product portfolio management

7 discuss product strategies for growth

This chapter examines the application of analytical tools used in the area of strategic product planning beginning with the product life-cycle. This section also considers the implication for managing brands over a period of time. The next key topic area is managing brand and product line portfolios. Many companies handle numerous products and serve multiple markets segments. Consequently, managers need to address the question of where to place investment for product growth and where and when to withdraw resources. Such questions are considered in the second part of this chapter. Finally, the topic of product strategies for growth is explored.

Managing Product Lines and Brands Over Time: the Product Life-Cycle

No matter how wide the product mix, both product lines and individual brands need to be managed over time. A useful tool for conceptualizing the changes that may take place during the time that a product is on the market is called the **product life-cycle**. It is quite flexible and can be applied to both brands and product lines.[1] For simplicity, in the rest of this chapter, brands and product lines will be referred to as products. We shall now look at the product life-cycle, before discussing its uses and limitations.

The classic product life-cycle has four stages (see Fig. 11.1): introduction, growth, maturity and decline.

Introduction

When first introduced on to the market a product's sales growth is typically low, and losses are incurred because of heavy development and promotional costs. Companies will be monitoring the speed of product adoption and, if this is disappointing, may terminate the product at this stage.

All leading companies, such as Canon, IBM, Mercedes, Intel and Apple, invest heavily in new product development to create products that confer new features and benefits for consumers. Because of this heavy investment, high promotional expenditures and low sales, losses are often suffered during product introduction. Nokian Tyres has made a long-term investment in product research and innovations. Their expertise in heavy tyres manufacturing has made them a world-leading specialist manufacturer. They also invest in communicating the benefits of their products.[2]

Growth

This stage is characterized by a period of faster sales and profit growth. Sales growth is fuelled by rapid market acceptance and, for many products, repeat purchasing. Profits may

Go to the website to see how Nokian Tyres uses its features in its advertising.
www.mcgraw-hill.co.uk/textbooks/jobber

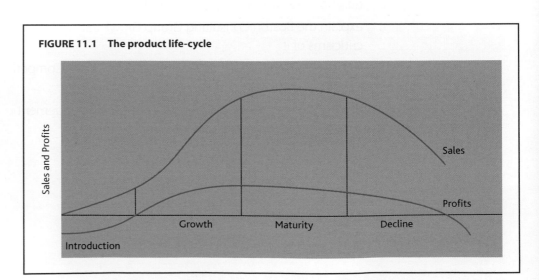

FIGURE 11.1 The product life-cycle

⬆ EXHIBIT 11.1   Samsung reminds its customers there are no limits with new products in its Galaxy range.

begin to decline towards the latter stages of growth as new rivals enter the market, attracted by fast sales growth and high profit potential. The tablet computer market is an example of this. Apple introduced the iPad in 2010 and the rapid sales growth was mirrored by a vast increase in competitors such as Samsung Galaxy Tab, BlackBerry Playbook, Hewlett-Packard TouchPad. The smartphones market developed as technology innovation enabled mobile computing to be integrated into modern handsets. During the growth stage many rival technology companies entered the market with operating systems for the new type of phones, including Apple iOS, Google Android, Microsoft's Windows, Nokia Symbian. The end of the growth period is often associated with *competitive shakeout*, when weaker suppliers cease production. Technology markets are particularly susceptible. Read Digital Marketing 11.1 to find out about the winners and losers in the dot-com bubble.

⬆ EXHIBIT 11.2   Heinz differentiated its canned beans using the slogan Beanz Meanz Heinz and this campaign enabled Heinz to fend off competitors for decades.

Maturity

Eventually sales peak and flatten as saturation occurs, hastening competitive shakeout. The survivors battle for market share by employing product improvements, advertising and sales promotional offers, dealer discounts and price cutting; the result is a strain on profit margins particularly for follower brands. The need for effective brand building is acutely recognized during maturity as brand leaders are in the strongest position to resist the pressure on profit margins.[3] Heinz have been advertising their brand of beans for over 40 years. The manufacturer differentiated the brand using the slogan Beanz Meanz Heinz. Investment in this iconic advertising campaign enabled Heinz to fend off competitors and stimulate sales in a mature market.

Digital Marketing 11.1 The Dot-Com Bubble Winners and Losers

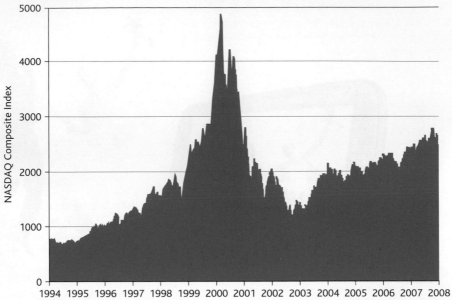

The size of the Internet economy started to grow rapidly from 1996. Between 1999 and 2001 there was a period of intense growth in the value of technology stocks. Forrester Research estimated the total Internet economy was worth US$15 billion, and by 2000 revenues from online consumer spending in the US alone were estimated at US$45 billion (Boston Consulting Group, 2001). Predictions about the growth of online markets and the rapidly rising share prices got everyone excited. This was a rapid growth market. But there were very few Internet-savvy businesses offering stocks for sale. Investors scrambled to buy Internet stocks. The high demand and low level of supply created a trading frenzy, which stimulated exponential market growth (see image). In the retail sector, predictions suggested that 'by the year 2005 it (the Internet) would capture between 8 and 30 per cent of the UK retail market', leaving high streets looking like ghost towns. Extreme examples of increases in valuations and personal gains for the entrepreneurs (dot.com millionaires) helped to drive the growth even more. For example, Xcelera.com, developed by Norwegian Alexander Vik, saw its stock soar from a few pennies to over $200 a share in less than a year, giving the company a market capitalization of $3.8 billion. Indeed, in 2000 there were 63 dot-com millionaires on the *Sunday Times* rich list but by 2001 this was down to just 26. The bubble burst and many innovative companies—which had rushed to move online—collapsed almost overnight. There were some notable winners and losers.

Winners:
- Google
- Amazon
- Lastminute.com
- eBay

Losers:
- Boo.com (spent $180 million in six months trying to create a global fashion store, but went into bankruptcy in 2000)
- America Online (AOL) (merged with Time Warner)
- Geocities.com (bought out by Yahoo!)
- Webvan (filed for bankruptcy in 2001)
- Startups.com (failed in 2002)
- FreeInternet.com (filed for bankruptcy in October 2000)
- Pets.com (pet supplies retailer filed for bankruptcy in 2000)

Based on: Doherty et al. (2003);[4] *Ellis-Chadwick et al. (2002);*[5] *Boston Consulting Group (2001);*[6] *Pavitt (1997);*[7] *Wikipedia (2012);*[8] *Virzi (2000);*[9] *Hudson (2010)*[10]

Decline

Sales and profits fall during the decline stage as new technology or changes in consumer tastes work to reduce demand for the product. For example, Sony lost out when the market for cathode-ray TVs went into decline following the development of flat-screen TVs. The technological advance resulted in Samsung and Panasonic overtaking Sony in sales of televisions.[11] Suppliers may decide to cease production completely or reduce product depth. Promotional and product development budgets may be slashed and marginal distributors dropped as suppliers seek to maintain (or increase) profit margins. Advertising may be used to defend against rivals and prevent the sales of a brand from falling into decline.

Uses of the Product Life-Cycle

The product life-cycle (PLC) concept is useful for product management in several ways.

Product termination

First, the PLC emphasizes the fact that nothing lasts for ever. There is a danger that management may fall in love with certain products. Maybe a company was founded on the success of a particular product; perhaps the product champion of a past success is now the chief executive. Under such circumstances there can be emotional ties with the product that can transcend normal commercial considerations. The PLC underlines the fact that companies have to face the fact that products need to be terminated and new products developed to replace them. Without this sequence a company may find itself with a group of products all in the decline stage of their PLC.

Growth projections

The second use of the PLC concept is to warn against the dangers of assuming that growth will continue for ever. Swept along by growing order books, management can fall into the trap of believing that the heady days of rising sales and profits will continue for ever. The PLC reminds managers that growth will end, and suggests a need for caution when planning investment in new production facilities.

Marketing objectives and strategies over the PLC

The PLC emphasizes the need to review marketing objectives and strategies as products pass through the various stages. Changes in market and competitive conditions between the PLC stages suggest that marketing strategies should be adapted to meet them. Table 11.1 shows a set of stylized marketing responses to each stage. Note these are broad generalizations and serve to emphasize the need to review marketing objectives and strategies in the light of environmental change.

Introduction

The strategic marketing objective is to build sales by expanding the market for the product. The brand objective will be to create product (as well as brand) awareness so that customers will become familiar with generic product benefits.

The product is likely to be fairly basic, with an emphasis on reliability and functionality rather than special features to appeal to different customer groups. For example, the introduction of the netbook when desktop computers were the de facto machine for all our computing needs. Then the laptop arrived which was a mobile equivalent. Generally, these machines were expensive, heavy and suffered from poor battery life. So there was a gap in the market for target audiences which wanted lighter machines to last longer while on the move. The netbook was able to fill this gap. Fairly basic models were offered, providing mobile computing and Internet access at affordable prices (e.g. Asus, Acer, Samsung). The

TABLE 11.1 Marketing objectives and strategies over the product life-cycle

	Introduction	Growth	Maturity	Decline
Strategic marketing objective	Build	Build	Hold	Harvest/manage for cash/divest
Strategic focus	Expand market	Penetration	Protect share/innovation	Productivity
Brand objective	Product awareness/trial	Brand preference	Brand loyalty	Brand exploitation
Products	Basic	Differentiated	Differentiated	Rationalized
Promotion	Creating awareness/trial	Creating awareness/ trial/repeat purchase	Maintaining awareness/ repeat purchase	Cut/eliminated
Price	High	Lower	Lowest	Rising
Distribution	Patchy	Wider	Intensive	Selective

functionality was basic, and the processor speed and memory fairly limited compared to their desktop and laptop counterparts.

Promotion will support the brand objectives by gaining awareness for the brand and product type, and stimulating trial. Advertising has been found to be more effective in the beginning of the life of a product than in later stages.[12] Typically price will be high because of the heavy development costs and the low level of competition. Distribution will be patchy as some dealers are wary of stocking the new product until it has proved to be successful in the marketplace.

Growth

The strategic marketing objective during the growth phase is to build sales and market share. The strategic focus will be to penetrate the market by building brand preference. To accomplish this task the product will be redesigned to create differentiation, and promotion will stress the functional and/or psychological benefits that accrue from the differentiation. The netbook market has moved on, and now the ultra netbook (or ultra portable notebooks) provide more sophisticated features. These machines are small laptop computers, which have been designed to be light to transport, have good battery life and have much of the functionality of larger computers (e.g. Apple Macbook Air, Asus UX31E, X53TA). Awareness and trial to acquire new customers are still important, but promotion will begin to focus on repeat purchasers. As development costs are defrayed and competition increases, prices will fall. Rising consumer demand and increased salesforce effort will widen distribution.

Maturity

As sales peak and stabilize, the strategic marketing objective will be to hold on to profits and sales by protecting market share rather than embarking on costly competitive challenges. Since sales gains can only be at the expense of competition, strong challenges are likely to be resisted and lead to costly promotional or price wars. Brand objectives now focus on maintaining brand loyalty and customer retention, and promotion will defend the brand, stimulating repeat purchase by maintaining brand awareness and values. For all but the brand leader, competition may erode prices and profit margins, while distribution will peak in line with sales.

A key focus will be innovation to extend the maturity stage or, preferably, inject growth. This may take the form of innovative promotional campaigns, product improvements, and extensions and technological innovation. Ways of increasing usage and reducing repeat purchase periods of the product will also be sought. Digital Marketing 11.2

Digital Marketing 11.2 Mobile Marketing in a Mature Market

Technological innovations at the maturity stage of the product life-cycle can inject growth. This has happened in the mobile phone market with the launch of smartphones (e.g. iPhone, Samsung Galaxy and BlackBerry). These handsets extend the services available via a mobile from the basic features by allowing fast access to the Internet and emails, apps and many other features.

Perhaps a key driver of the growth of the smartphone markets is that the feature mobile phone market has reached saturation. In the USA sales of smartphones are set to overtake sales of feature phones, which go beyond making basic calls but stop short of being a smartphone.

This means that makers of mobile feature phones now operate in a mature market. No longer can profits be fuelled by explosive growth; instead attention has turned to competing for a dwindling number of customers. In classic product life-cycle style, this has meant a move from customer acquisition to retention, attempts to increase usage rates and lowering repeat purchase periods. It has also resulted in a period of falling prices and rationalization as all players—including Nokia, the market leader—have significantly reduced costs.

Nevertheless, mobile phones have become part of everyday life, particularly in the youth market where 15–24-year-olds are avid users of their mobiles for texting, videoing and accessing social networks, so there are still opportunities for makers of feature phones especially in emerging economies. However, consumers are very clear about what they are looking for from their phones. In Brazil and India price is most important, whereas in Russia it's design and style, while in China the form and shape of the phone are as important as price.

The word 'maturity' may conjure up images of tranquillity, but for incumbent companies, competitive and economic forces mean that they face a demanding and volatile marketplace. Nokia holds on to its lead in the mobile phone market, followed by Samsung, Apple, LG, and ZTE. But competition is fierce and there is intense rivalry among the leading players. Nokia is trying to maintain its share of the mature feature phone market, while Samsung, Apple and others are building their share of the smartphone market.

Based on: Neilsen (2012);[13] IDC (2012);[14] Deere and Kilby (2005);[15] Lester (2005);[16] Odell (2006);[17] Wray (2006)[18]

shows how mobile phone manufacturers and operators are seeking to revitalize sales in a mature market.

Decline

The conventional advice to companies managing products in the decline stage of the product life cycle is to harvest or divest. A harvest strategy would result in the raising of prices while slashing marketing expenditures in an effort to boost profit margins. The strategic focus, therefore, is to improve marketing productivity rather than holding or building sales. The brand loyalty that has been built up over the years is in effect being exploited to create profits that can be used elsewhere in the company (e.g. new products). Product development will cease, the product line will be cut to the bare minimum of brands and promotional expenditure cut, possibly to zero. Distribution costs will be analysed with a view to selecting only the most profitable outlets. The Internet will be examined to explore its potential as a low-cost promotional and distribution vehicle.

Divestment may take the form of selling products to other companies, or, if there are no willing buyers, product elimination. The strategy is to extract any residual value in the products where possible, and to free up managerial time and resources to be redirected at more attractive products and opportunities. Occasionally, products are harvested and then divested. For example, Beecham harvested and then sold Brylcreem to the Health and Personal Care division of Sara Lee at a time when it was unfashionable for males to use hair cream. It proved a fortunate purchase as hair gel became fashionable and Sara Lee had the marketing expertise to reposition the brand in that market. However, the whole healthcare division was sold to Unilever in 2009[19] and it is now developing sales of Brylcreem in India.[20]

Two other strategies that can be applied at the decline stage are 1) industry revitalization, and 2) pursuit of a profitable survivor strategy.

Industry revitalization: some products go into decline not because they are inherently unpopular but because of lack of investment. For example, years of under-investment in cinemas meant the facilities were often dilapidated and the programming offered limited choice of films. However, one company saw this scenario as a marketing opportunity. Showcase Cinemas was launched, offering a choice of around 12 films in modern purpose-built premises near large conurbations. This completely changed the experience of going to the cinema, resulting in revitalization of the industry and growth in cinema attendances and profits. Thus, the classic PLC prescription of harvesting in the decline stage was rejected by a company that was willing to invest in order to reposition cinemas as an attractive means of offering evening entertainment.

Profitable survivor strategy: another alternative to harvesting or divestment is called the *profitable survivor strategy*.[21] This involves deciding to become the sole survivor in a declining market. This may involve being willing to incur losses while competitors drop out, or if it is thought that this process is likely to be lengthy and slow, to accelerate it by:

- further reducing the attractiveness of the market by such actions as price cuts or increases in promotional expenditures
- buying competitors (which may be offered at a low price due to the unattractive markets they operate in) or their product lines that compete in the same market
- agreeing to take over competitors' contracts (e.g. supplying spare parts or service contracts) in exchange for their agreement to drop out of the market.

Once in the position of sole supplier, the survivor can reap the rewards of a monopolist by raising prices and resuming profitable operations.

Product planning

The PLC emphasizes the need for *product planning*. We have already discussed the need to replace old products with new. The PLC also stresses the need to analyse the balance of products that a company markets from the point of view of the PLC stages. A company with all of its products in the mature stage may be generating profits today, but as it enters the decline stage, profits may fall and the company become unprofitable. A balanced range of product is better, i.e. some products in the mature stage, some in the growth stage, and prospects of new product launches in the near future. The growth products would replace the mature products as the latter enter decline, and the new product successes would eventually become the growth products of the future. The PLC is, then, a stimulus to thinking about products as an interrelated set of profit-bearing assets that need to be managed as a group. We shall return to this theme when discussing product portfolio analysis later in this chapter.

The dangers of overpowering

The PLC concept highlights the dangers of overpowering. A company that introduces a new-to-the-world product may find itself in a very powerful position early in its PLC. Assuming that the new product confers unique benefits to customers there is an opportunity to charge a very high price during this period of monopoly supply. However, unless the product is patent-protected this strategy can turn sour when competition enters during the growth phase (as predicted by the PLC concept). This situation arose for the small components manufacturer that was the first to solve the technical problems associated with developing a seal in an exhaust recirculation valve used to reduce pollution in car emissions. The company took advantage of its monopoly supply position to charge very high prices to Ford. The strategy rebounded when competition entered and Ford discovered it had been overcharged.[22] Had the small manufacturer been aware of the predictions of the PLC concept it may have anticipated competitive entry during the growth phase, and charged a lower price during introduction and early growth. This would have enabled it to begin a relationship-building exercise with Ford, possibly leading to greater returns in the long run.

Limitations of the Product Life-Cycle

The product life-cycle is an aid to thinking about marketing decisions, but it needs to be handled with care. Management needs to be aware of the limitations of the PLC so that it is not misled by its prescriptions.

Fads and classics

Not all products follow the classic S-shaped curve. The sales of some products 'rise like a rocket then fall like a stick'. This is normal for *fad* products such as hula hoops (popularized in the 1950s), 'pet rocks' (1970s), Pokemon cards (1990s), Zumba classes (2010s).

Other products (and brands) appear to defy entering the decline stage. For example, classic confectionery products and brands such as Mars bars, Cadbury's Milk Tray and Toblerone have survived for decades in the mature stage of the PLC. Nevertheless, research has shown that the classic S-shaped curve does apply to a wide range of products, including grocery food products, and pharmaceuticals.[23]

Marketing effects

The PLC is the *result* of marketing activities not the cause. One school of thought argues that the PLC is not simply a fact of life—unlike living organisms—but is simply a pattern of sales that reflects marketing activity.[24] Clearly, sales of a product may flatten or fall simply because it has not received enough marketing attention, or has had insufficient product redesign or promotional support. Using the PLC, argue the critics, may lead to inappropriate action (e.g. harvesting or dropping the product) when the correct response should be increased marketing support (e.g. product replacement, positioning reinforcement or repositioning).

Unpredictability

The duration of the PLC stages is unpredictable. The PLC outlines the four stages that a product passes through without defining their duration. Clearly this limits its use as a forecasting tool since it is not possible to predict when maturity or decline will begin. The exception to this problem is when it is possible to identify a comparator product that serves as a template for predicting the length of each stage. Two sources of comparator products exist: first, countries where the same product has already been on the market for some time; second, where similar products are in the mature or decline stages of their life-cycle but are thought to resemble the new product in terms of consumer acceptance. In practice, the use of comparator products is fraught with problems. For example, the economic and social conditions of countries may be so different that simplistic exploitation of the PLC from one country to another may be invalid; the use of similar products may offer inaccurate predictions in the face of ever-shortening product life-cycles.

Misleading objective and strategy prescriptions

The stylized marketing objectives and strategy prescriptions may be misleading. Even if a product could accurately be classified as being in a PLC stage, and sales are not simply a result of marketing activities, critics argue that the stylized marketing objectives and strategy prescriptions can be misleading. For example, there can be circumstances where the appropriate marketing objective in the growth stage is to harvest (e.g. in the face of intense competition), in the mature stage to build (e.g. when a distinct, defensive differential advantage can be developed), and in the decline stage to build (e.g. when there is an opportunity to dominate).

As was discussed earlier, the classic PLC advice concerning strategy in the decline stage is to harvest or divest, but other strategies—industry revitalization or the profitable survivor strategy—can be employed if the right conditions apply.

A summary of the usefulness of the product life-cycle concept

Like many marketing tools, the product life-cycle should not be viewed as a panacea to marketing thinking and decision-making but as an aid to managerial judgement. By emphasizing the changes that are likely to occur as a product is marketed over time, the concept is a valuable stimulus to strategic thinking. Yet as a prescriptive tool it is blunt. Marketing management must monitor the real-life changes that are happening in the marketplace before setting precise objectives and strategies. Digital Marketing 11.3 offers insight into the digital world and the PLC.

Digital Marketing 11.3 The Permanent Beta

Companies finding the traditional product development life-cycle is taking too long before a product can reach market have now adopted the 'Permanent Beta'. While some traditional products still require a formal development process, particularly where safety, warranty or legality is concerned (e.g. cars, airplanes, electrical goods), services and digital products can be released ahead of their final version.

There are potential advantages to early product release:
* *Encourages evangelism*—early adopters can experience early versions of software or services and then provide feedback and reviews on design and performance. Evangelist users often communicate with other potential adopters and this can spread excitement, which encourages wider adoption.
* *Allows for errors*—in a freemium economy model (products are provided free of charge—e.g. Google Search, Internet Explorer web browzer) mistakes can be made and customers are far more forgiving of a service that does not work—as expected—if they are not paying. Again users are more inclined to provide feedback—passively in the form of usage statistics and data and actively as engaged users who want to contribute to the production of something special. Companies can then experience an early-to-market introduction of a service and respond early to the feedback. Companies such as Dropbox do this regularly for new features in their Cloud storage service to see how they work for a broad range of customers. Because many businesses regard their products as constantly evolving, it makes sense for them to be described as in a state of permanent beta.

However there are also drawbacks to the permanent beta concept:
* *Questionable reliability*—Google found that it could not convince businesses to take its Gmail and Google Docs services seriously, because businesses did not know how reliable those services were for mission-critical and key operation. In fact, Google's history for ending the life-cycle of products in permanent beta made many suspicious and reluctant to commit to a particular product, and it was only when Google took many products 'out of permanent beta' that there was increased uptake by business users.
* *Lack of permanence*—while there may be benefits from continual developments, this can also be troublesome as continual investment in training of how to use products might be required.

Permanent beta has implications for product management insofar as the whole concept of product development becomes highly fluid and constantly evolving. For the marketing manager this means changing planning horizons between pre-launch activity, launch and eventual divestment.

See also:
http://www.entrepreneur.com/blog/223099
http://www.eweek.com/c/a/Cloud-Computing/Google-Apps-End-Their-State-of-Permanent-Beta-870262/

Read the Research 11.1 Managing Product Developments

Today many corporations suffer from brand proliferation, a phenomenon in which companies keep producing more and more brands without giving strategic consideration to how these additions affect their overall brand portfolio. Unilever's strategy a few years ago was to shed brands in order to grow. The purpose of this research is to contribute to the understanding of brand-portfolio management by adopting a case study approach with L'Oréal. Its major focus is on L'Oréal's brand-portfolio strategy and how it can create competitive advantage.

Claude Chailan (2010) From an aggregate to a brand network: a study of the brand portfolio at L'Oréal,
Journal of Marketing Management 26(1–2), 74–89.

Managing Brand and Product Line Portfolios

So far in this chapter we have treated the management of products as distinct and independent entities. However, many companies are multi-product, serving multiple markets and segments. Some of these products will be strong, others weak. Some will require investment to finance their growth, others will generate more cash than they need. Somehow companies must decide how to distribute their limited resources among the competing needs of products so as to achieve the best performance for the company as a whole. Specifically within a product line, management needs to decide which brands to invest in or hold, or from which to withdraw support. Similarly within the product mix, decisions regarding which product lines to build or hold, or from which to withdraw support, need to be taken. Canon, for example, took the strategic decision to focus on its profitable products—mainly copiers, printers and cameras—while divesting personal computers, typewriters and liquid crystal displays.[25] Managers who focus on individual products often miss the bigger picture that helps ensure the company's entire portfolio of products fits together coherently rather than being a loose confederation of offerings that has emerged out of a series of uncoordinated historical decisions.[26] Philips found itself in this position, marketing a sprawling set of products, namely semiconductors, consumer electronics, medical equipment, lighting and small electrical appliances.[27] In an attempt to bring coherence to its product lines, Philips has responded by selling its semiconductor business to focus on consumer lifestyle (consumer electronics and domestic appliances), healthcare and lighting.

Clearly, these are strategic decisions since they shape where and with what brands/product lines a company competes and how its resources should be deployed. Furthermore these decisions are complex because many factors (e.g. current and future sales and profit potential, cash flow) can affect the outcome. The process of managing groups of brands and product lines is called **portfolio planning**.

Key decisions regarding portfolio planning involve decisions regarding the choice of which brands/product lines to build, hold, harvest or divest. Marketing in Action 11.1 discusses several companies' approach to portfolio planning.

↑EXHIBIT 11.3   Cadbury's Twirl has been marketed for many years but product redesign shown in this advert aims to stimulate growth.

Marketing in Action 11.1 Portfolio Planning to the Core

The composition of a company's product portfolio is a vital strategic issue for marketers. Few companies have the luxury of starting with a clean sheet and creating a well-balanced set of products. An assessment of the strengths and weaknesses of the current portfolio is, therefore, necessary before taking the strategic decisions of which ones to build, hold, harvest or divest.

Major multinationals, like Nestlé, Kraft Foods, Procter & Gamble, GE, IBM and Unilever, constantly review their product portfolios to achieve their strategic objectives. The trend has been to focus on core brands and product categories, and to divest minor, peripheral brands.

Nestlé, for example, has sold Crosse & Blackwell, whose portfolio of brands includes Branston Pickle, Gale's Honey and Sun-Pat Peanut Butter, to Premier International Foods as it focuses on key product categories where it can establish and maintain leadership. The focus is on the core categories of beverages, confectionery, chilled dairy, milks and nutrition. In line with this strategy Nestlé has acquired the Ski and Munch Bunch dairy brands from Northern Foods, propelling it into the number-two position behind Müller in the chilled dairy market.

Kraft Foods has many globally recognized food brands in its product portfolio. Internationally, it has a mixed portfolio, with 49 per cent of its business in North America, 23 per cent in Europe and 28 per cent in developing markets. Of these businesses, the largest concentration is in the confectionery sector (28 per cent), followed by biscuits (22 per cent), beverages (18 per cent), cheese (14 per cent), convenience meals (10 per cent) and grocery (8 per cent). These holdings in its portfolio make Kraft Foods the second largest food company in the world and in order to maintain this position, the product portfolio is constantly reviewed, as 80 per cent of its revenues come from products that are market leaders in their categories. In 2008 Kraft acquired LU, a global biscuit business, but got rid of Post, its cereal food operation. In 2010 Cadbury's was added to the portfolio to help build its dominance in the confectionery sector in Europe, while DiGiono, its pizza business, was divested as convenience foods account for only a small part of the portfolio.

This trend is not confined to the grocery business, however. For example, Adidas sold its ski and surf equipment firm Salomon to Amer Sports Corporation so that it could focus on its core strength in the athletic footwear and apparel market as well as the growing golf category. IBM sold its PC division to Lenovo to concentrate on software and services.

Philips rationalized its product portfolio, selling its semiconductor business to focus on consumer lifestyle, healthcare and lighting. Its mission is to centre on health and well-being, and it has invested in healthcare, moving away from its medical imaging business and into patient monitoring and home healthcare. One example is its acquisition of Respironics, a medical equipment maker specialising in sleep therapy. It sees healthcare as a growth market as people live longer.

One advantage of this strategy is to enable maximum firepower to be put behind core brands.

Based on: Kraft Foods (2012);[28] Mason (2002);[29] Tomlinson (2005);[30] Milner (2006);[31] Steen (2008)[32]

Go to the website and consider how the imagery in the advert helps promote the Twirl.
www.mcgraw-hill.co.uk/
textbooks/jobber

Two methods for managing products are widely discussed in management literature: 1) Boston Consulting Group Growth-Share Matrix, and 2) General Electric Market Attractiveness–Competitive Position portfolio evaluation models. Like the product life-cycle these are very flexible tools and can be used at both the brand and product line levels. Indeed, corporate planners can also use them when making resource allocation decisions at the strategic business unit level.

The Boston Consulting Group Growth-Share Matrix

A leading management consultancy, the Boston Consulting Group (BCG), developed the well-known BCG Growth-Share Matrix (see Fig. 11.2). The matrix allows portfolios of products to be depicted in a 2 × 2 box, the axes of which are based on market growth rate and relative market share. The analysis is based upon cash flow (rather than profits) and its key assumptions are:

- market growth has an adverse effect on cash flow because of the investment in such assets as manufacturing facilities, equipment and marketing needed to finance growth
- market share has a positive effect on cash flow as profits are related to market share.

The following discussion will be based on an analysis at the product line level.

Market growth rate forms the vertical axis and indicates the annual growth rate of the market in which each product line operates. In Figure 11.2 it is shown as 0–15 per cent although a different range could be used, depending on economic conditions, for example. In this example the dividing line between high and low growth rates is considered to be 7 per cent. Market growth rate is used as a proxy for market attractiveness.

Relative market share is shown on the horizontal axis and refers to the market share of each product relative to its largest competitor. It acts as a proxy for competitive strength. The division between high and low market share is 1. Above this figure a product line has a market share greater than its largest competitor. For example, if our product had a market share of 40 per cent and our largest competitor's share was 30 per cent this would be indicated as 1.33 on the horizontal axis. Below 1 we have a share less than the largest competitor. For example, if our share was 20 per cent and the largest competitor had a share of 40 per cent our score would be 0.5.

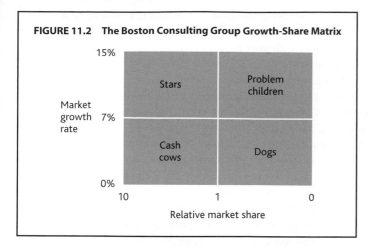

FIGURE 11.2 The Boston Consulting Group Growth-Share Matrix

The Boston Consulting Group argued that cash flow is dependent on the box in which a product falls. Note that cash flow is not the same as profitability. Profits add to cash flow but heavy investment in such assets as manufacturing facilities, equipment and marketing expenditure can mean that a company can make profits and yet have a negative cash flow.

Stars are likely to be profitable because they are market leaders but require substantial investment to finance growth (e.g. new production facilities) and to meet competitive challenges. Overall cash flow is therefore likely to be roughly in balance. *Problem children* are products in high-growth markets, which cause a drain on cash flow, but these are low-share products; consequently they are unlikely to be profitable. Overall, then, they are big cash users. *Cash cows* are market leaders in mature (low-growth) markets. High market share leads to high profitability and low market growth means that investment in new production facilities is minimal. This leads to a large positive cash flow. *Dogs* also operate in low-growth markets but have low market share. Except for some products near the dividing line between cash cows and dogs (sometimes called *cash dogs*) most dogs produce low or negative cash flows. Relating to their position in the product life-cycle, they are the also-rans in mature or declining markets.

What are the strategic implications of the BCG analysis? It can be used for setting strategic objectives and for maintaining a balanced product portfolio.

Guidelines for setting strategic objectives

Having plotted the position of each product on the matrix, a company can begin to think about setting the appropriate strategic objective for each line. As you may recall from Chapter 2, there are four possible strategic objectives: build, hold, harvest and divest. Figure 11.3 shows how each relates to the star, problem children, cash cow and dog categories. However, it should be emphasized that

FIGURE 11.3 Strategic objectives and the 'Boston box'

Stars	Problem children
Build sales and/or market share	*Build* selectively
Invest to maintain/increase leadership position	Focus on defendable *niche* where dominance can be achieved
Repel competitive challenges	*Harvest* or *divest* the rest
Cash cows	**Dogs**
Hold sales and/or market share	*Harvest* or
Defend position	*Divest* or
Use excess cash to support stars, selected problem children and new product development	Focus on defendable niche

the BCG matrix provides guidelines for strategic thinking and should not be seen as a replacement for managerial judgement.

- *Stars*: these are the market leaders in high-growth markets. They are already successful and the prospects for further growth are good. As we have seen when discussing brand building, market leaders tend to have the highest profitability so the appropriate strategic objective is to build sales and/or market share. Resources should be invested to maintain/increase the leadership position. Competitive challenges should be repelled. These are the cash cows of the future and need to be protected.

- *Problem children*: as we have seen these are cash drains because they have low profitability and need investment to keep up with market growth. They are called problem children because management has to consider whether it is sensible to continue the required investment. The company faces a fundamental choice: to increase investment (*build*) to attempt to turn the problem child into a star, or to withdraw support by either *harvesting* (raising price while lowering marketing expenditure) or *divesting* (dropping or selling it). In a few cases, a third option may be viable: to find a small market segment (*niche*) where dominance can be achieved. Unilever, for example, identified its speciality chemicals business as a problem child. It realized that it had to invest heavily or exit. Its decision was to sell and invest the billions raised in predicted future winners such as personal care, dental products and fragrances.[33]

- *Cash cows*: the high profitability and low investment associated with high market share in low-growth markets mean that cash cows should be defended. Consequently the appropriate strategic objective is to *hold* sales and market share. The excess cash that is generated should be used to fund stars, problem children that are being built, and research and development for new products.

- *Dogs*: dogs are weak products that compete in low-growth markets. They are the also-rans that have failed to achieve market dominance during the growth phase and are floundering in maturity. For those products that achieve second or third position in the marketplace (*cash dogs*) a small positive cash flow may result, and for a few others it may be possible to reposition the product into a defendable *niche*. (The problem with using the niche strategy is lack of economies of scale compared with bigger rivals, as MG Rover found.) But for the bulk of dogs the appropriate strategic objective is to *harvest* to generate a positive cash flow for a time, or to *divest*, which allows resources and managerial time to be focused elsewhere.

Maintaining a balanced product portfolio

Once all of the company's products have been plotted, it is easy to see how many stars, problem children, cash cows and dogs are in the portfolio. Figure 11.4 shows a product portfolio that is unbalanced. The company possesses only one star and the small circle indicates that sales revenue generated from the star is small. Similarly the two cash cows are also low revenue earners. In contrast, the company owns four dogs and four problem children. The portfolio is unbalanced because there are too many problem children and dogs, and not enough stars and cash cows. What many companies in this situation do is to spread what little surplus cash is available equally between the products in the growth markets.[34] To do so would leave each with barely enough money to maintain market share, leading to a vicious circle of decline.

The BCG remedy would be to conduct a detailed competitive assessment of the four problem children and select one or two for investment. The rest should be harvested (and the cash channelled to those that are

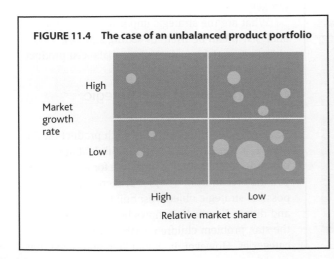

FIGURE 11.4 The case of an unbalanced product portfolio

Market growth rate — High / Low

Relative market share — High / Low

being built) or divested. The aim is to build the existing star (which will be the cash cow of the future) and to build the market share of the chosen problem children so that they attain star status.

The dogs also need to be analysed. One of them (the large circle) is a large revenue earner, which despite low profits may be making a substantial contribution to overheads. Another product (on the left) appears to be in the cash dog situation. But for the other two, the most sensible strategic objective may be to harvest or divest.

Criticisms of the BCG Growth-Share Matrix

The simplicity, ease of use and importance of the issues tackled by the BCG Matrix saw its adoption by a host of North American and European companies that wanted to get a handle on the complexities of strategic resource allocation. But the tool has also attracted a litany of criticism.[35] The following list draws together many of the points raised by its critics.

1 The assumption that cash flow will be determined by a product's position in the matrix is weak. For example, some stars will show a healthy positive cash flow (e.g. IBM PCs during the growth phase of the PC market) as will some dogs in markets where competitive activity is low.

2 The preoccupation of focusing on market share and market growth rates distracts managerial attention from the fundamental principle in marketing: attaining a sustainable competitive advantage.

3 Treating the market growth rate as a proxy for market attractiveness, and market share as an indicator of competitive strength is oversimplistic. There are many other factors that have to be taken into account when measuring market attractiveness (e.g. market size, strengths and weaknesses of competitors) and competitive strengths (e.g. exploitable marketing assets, potential cost advantages), besides market growth rates and market share.

4 Since the position of a product in the matrix depends on market share, this can lead to an unhealthy preoccupation with market share gain. In some circumstances this objective makes sense (for example, brand building) but when competitive retaliation is likely the costs of share building may outweigh the gains.

5 The matrix ignores interdependencies between products. For example, a dog may need to be marketed because it complements a star or a cash cow. For example, the dog may be a spare part for a star or a cash cow. Alternatively, customers and distributors may value dealing with a company that supplies a full product line. For these reasons, dropping products because they fall into a particular box may be naive.

6 The classic BCG Matrix prescription is to build stars because they will become the cash cows of the future. However, some products have a very short product life-cycle, in which case the appropriate strategy should be to maximize profits and cash flow while in the star category (e.g. fashion goods).

7 Marketing objectives and strategy are heavily dependent on an assessment of what competitors are likely to do. How will they react if we lower or raise prices when implementing a build or harvest strategy, for example? This is not considered in the matrix.

8 The matrix assumes that products are self-funding. For example, selected problem children are built using cash generated by cash cows. But this ignores capital markets, which may mean that a wider range of projects can be undertaken so long as they have positive net present values of their future cash flows.

9 The matrix is vague regarding the definition of 'market'. Should we take the whole market (e.g. for confectionery) or just the market segment that we operate in (e.g. expensive boxed chocolates)? The matrix is also vague when defining the dividing line between high- and low-growth markets. A chemical company that tends to generate in lower-growth markets might use 3 per cent, whereas a leisure goods company whose markets on average experience much higher rates of growth might use 10 per cent. Also, over

what period do we define market growth? These issues question the theoretical soundness of the underlying concepts, and allow managers to manipulate the figures so that their products fall in the right boxes.

10 The matrix was based on cash flow but perhaps profitability (e.g. return on investment) is a better criterion for allocating resources.

11 The matrix lacks precision in identifying which problem children to build, harvest or drop.

General Electric Market Attractiveness–Competitive Position model

As we have already noted, the BCG Matrix enjoyed tremendous success as management grappled with the complex issue of strategic resource allocation. Stimulated by this success and some of the weaknesses of the model (particularly the criticism of its oversimplicity) McKinsey & Co developed a more wide-ranging Market Attractiveness–Competitive Position (MA–CP) model in conjunction with General Electric (GE) in the USA.

Market attractiveness criteria

Instead of market growth alone, a range of market attractiveness criteria were used, such as:
- market size
- market growth rate
- beatable rivals
- market entry barriers
- social, political and legal factors.

Competitive strength criteria

Similarly, instead of using only market share as a measure of competitive strength, a number of factors were used, such as:
- market share
- reputation
- distribution capability
- market knowledge
- service quality
- innovation capability
- cost advantages.

Assessing market attractiveness and competitive strength

Management is allowed to decide which criteria are applicable for their products. This gives the MA–CP model flexibility. Having decided the criteria, management's next task is to agree upon a weighting system for each set of criteria, with those factors that are more important having a higher weighting. Table 11.2 shows a set of weights for market attractiveness. Management has decided that the key factors that should be used to assess market attractiveness are market size, market growth rate, beatable rivals and market entry barriers. Ten points are then shared between these four factors depending on their relative importance in assessing market attractiveness. Market size (weighting = 4.0) is considered the most important factor and market entry barriers (1.5) the least important of the four factors.

Next, management assesses the particular market for the product under examination on each of the four factors on a scale of 1 to 10. The market is rated very highly on size (rating = 9.0), it possesses beatable rivals (8.0), its growth rate is also rated highly (7.0) and there are some market barriers, although they are not particularly high (6.0). By multiplying each weighting by its corresponding rating, and then summing, a total score indicating the overall attractiveness of the particular market for the product under examination is obtained. In this case, the market attractiveness for the product achieves an overall score of 79 per cent.

TABLE 11.2   An example of market attractiveness assessment

Market factors	Relative importance weightings (10 points shared)	Factor ratings (scale 1–10)	Factor scores (weightings × ratings)
Market size	4.0	9.0	36
Market growth rate	2.0	7.0	14
Beatable rivals	2.5	8.0	20
Market entry barriers	1.5	6.0	9
			79%

TABLE 11.3   An example of competitive strength assessment

Strengths needed for success	Relative importance weightings (10 points shared)	Factor ratings (scale 1–10)	Factor scores (weightings × ratings)
Market share	2.5	8.0	20
Distribution capability	1.0	7.0	7
Service quality	2.0	5.0	10
Innovation capability	3.0	9.0	27
Cost advantages	1.5	8.0	12
			76%

Competitive strength assessment begins by selecting the strengths that are needed to compete in the market. Table 11.3 shows that market share, distribution capability, service quality, innovation capability, and cost advantages were the factors considered to be needed for success. Management then assigns a weight by sharing 10 points between each of these strengths according to their relative importance in achieving success. Innovation capability (weighting = 3.0) is regarded as the most important strength required to compete effectively. Distribution capability (1.0) is considered the least important of the five factors. The company's capabilities on each of the required strengths are rated on a scale of 1 to 10. Company capabilities are rated very highly on innovation capability (rating = 9.0), market share (8.0) and cost advantages (8.0), highly on distribution capability (7.0) but service quality (5.0) is mediocre. By multiplying each weighting by its corresponding rating, and then summing, a total score indicating the overall competitive strength of the company is obtained. In this example, the competitive strength of the company achieves an overall score of 76 per cent.

The market attractiveness and competitive strength scores for the product under appraisal can now be plotted on the MA–CP matrix (see Fig. 11.5). The process is repeated for each product under investigation so that their relative positions on the MA–CP matrix

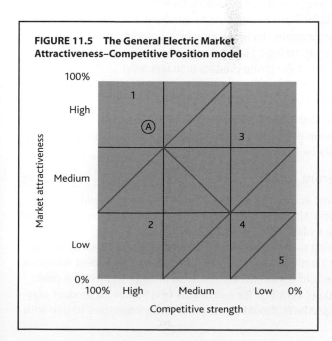

FIGURE 11.5   The General Electric Market Attractiveness–Competitive Position model

can be established. Each product position is given by a circle, the size of which is in proportion to its sales.

Setting strategic objectives

The model is shown in Figure 11.5. Like the BCG Matrix the recommendations for setting strategic objectives are dependent on the product's position on the grid. Five zones are shown in Figure 11.5. The strategic objectives associated with each zone are as follows.[36]

- *Zone 1*: build—manage for sales and market share growth as the market is attractive and competitive strengths are high (equivalent to star products).
- *Zone 2*: hold—manage for profits consistent with maintaining market share as the market is not particularly attractive but competitive strengths are high (equivalent to cash cows).
- *Zone 3*: build/hold/harvest—this is the question-mark zone. Where competitors are weak or passive, a build strategy will be used. In the face of strong competitors a hold strategy may be appropriate, or harvesting where commitment to the product/market is lower (similar to problem children).
- *Zone 4*: harvest—manage for cash as both market attractiveness and competitive strengths are fairly low.
- *Zone 5*: divest—improve short-term cash yield by dropping or selling the product (equivalent to dog products).

In the example shown in Figure 11.5, the circle labelled A indicates the position of the product, which shows that it falls within zone 1 as it operates in an attractive market and its competitive strengths are high. This would suggest a build strategy that probably involves investing in raising service quality levels, which were found to be relatively weak.

Criticisms of the GE portfolio model

The proponents of the GE portfolio model argue that the analysis is much richer than BCG analysis—thanks to more factors being taken into account—and flexible. These are substantial advantages and the model is widely used, with companies such as BP, IBM, Honda, Nissan, Philips, Centrica, Mitsubishi and GE employing it to aid their strategic thinking. Critics argue, however, that it is harder to use than the BCG Matrix since it requires managerial agreement on which factors to use, their weightings and scoring. Furthermore, its flexibility provides a lot of opportunity for managerial bias to enter the analysis whereby product managers argue for factors and weightings that show their products in a good light (zone 1). This last point suggests that the analysis should be conducted at a managerial level higher than that being assessed. For example, decisions on which product lines to be built, held, and so on, should be taken at the strategic business unit level, and allocations of resources to brands should be decided at the group product manager level.

The contribution of product portfolio planning

Despite the limitations of the BCG and the GE portfolio evaluation models, both have made a contribution to the practice of portfolio planning. We shall now discuss this contribution and suggest how the models can usefully be incorporated into product strategy.

Different products and different roles

The models emphasize the important strategic point that *different products should have different roles* in the product portfolio. Hedley points out that some companies believe that all product lines and brands should be treated equally—that is, set the same profit requirements.[37] The portfolio planning models stress that this should not necessarily be the case, and may be harmful in many situations. For example, to ask for a 20 per cent return on investment (ROI) for a star may result in under-investment in an attempt to meet the profit requirement. On the other hand, 20 per cent ROI for a cash cow or a harvested product may be too low. The implication is that products should be set profitability objectives in line with the strategic objective decisions.

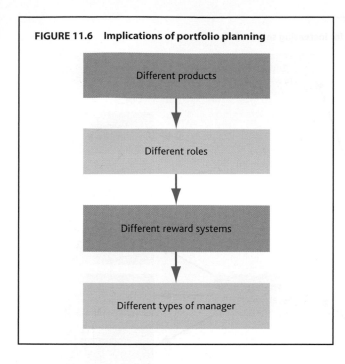

FIGURE 11.6   Implications of portfolio planning

Different products

↓

Different roles

↓

Different reward systems

↓

Different types of manager

Different reward systems and types of manager

By stressing the need to set different strategic objectives for different products, the models, by implication, support the notion that *different reward systems and types of manager* should be linked to them. For example, managers of products being built should be marketing led, and rewarded for improving sales and market share. Conversely, managers of harvested (and to some extent cash cow) products should be more cost orientated, and rewarded by profit and cash flow achievement (see Fig. 11.6).

Aid to managerial judgement

Managers may find it useful to plot their products on both the BCG and GE portfolio grids as an initial step in pulling together the complex issues involved in product portfolio planning. This can help them get a handle on the situation and issues to be resolved. The models can then act as an *aid to managerial judgement* without in any way supplanting that judgement. Managers should feel free to bring into the discussion any other factors they feel are not adequately covered by the models. The models can therefore be seen as an aid to strategic thinking in multi-product, multi-market companies.

Product Strategies for Growth

The emphasis in product portfolio analysis is on managing an *existing* set of products in such a way as to maximize their strengths, but companies also need to look to new products and markets for future growth. The Dyson DC08 vacuum cleaner is an example of a new product that is an addition to an existing line.

A useful way of looking at growth opportunities is the Ansoff Matrix, as shown in Figure 11.7.[38] By combining present and new products, and present and new markets into a 2 × 2 matrix, four product strategies for growth are revealed. Although the Ansoff Matrix does not prescribe when each strategy should be employed, it is a useful framework for thinking about the ways in which growth can be achieved through product strategy.

Figure 11.8 shows how the Ansoff Matrix can be used to implement a growth strategy. The most basic method of gaining **market penetration** in existing markets with current products is by *winning competitors' customers*. This may be achieved by more effective use of promotion or distribution, or by cutting prices. Increasing promotional expenditure is a method of winning competitors' customers and market penetration. Greggs, the UK's largest retail food brand, with more shops than McDonald's and Subway, made a significant investment in digital promotion by using Facebook to find out what its 20,000 customers thought about the brand. 11,000 replied and the information gathered from this promotional initiative was used to deliver a 7.5 per cent increase in annual turnover.[39] Another way of gaining market penetration is to *buy competitors*. An example is the Morrisons supermarket chain, which bought Safeway, a competitor, in order to

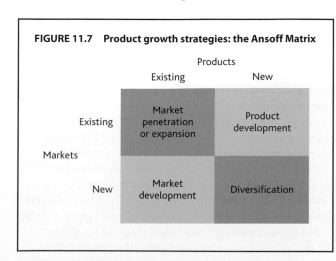

FIGURE 11.7   Product growth strategies: the Ansoff Matrix

	Products	
	Existing	New
Markets Existing	Market penetration or expansion	Product development
New	Market development	Diversification

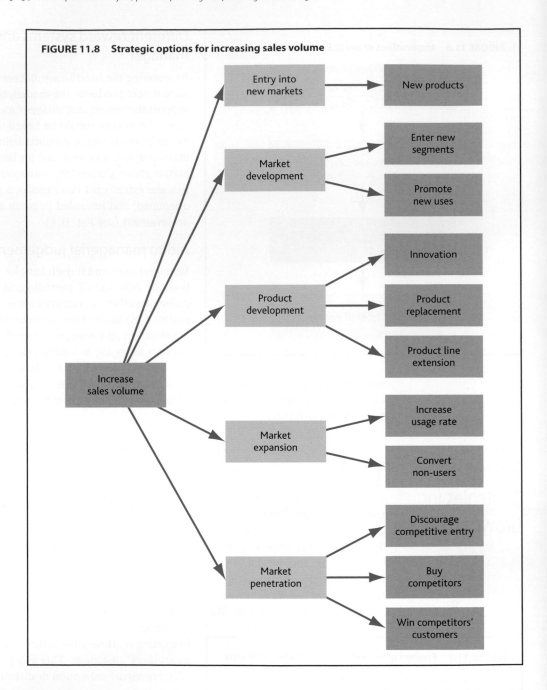

FIGURE 11.8   Strategic options for increasing sales volume

gain market penetration. This achieves an immediate increase in market share and sales volume. To protect the penetration already gained in a market, a business may consider methods of *discouraging competitive entry*. *Barriers* can be created by cost advantages (lower labour costs, access to raw materials, economies of scale), highly differentiated products, high switching costs (the costs of changing from existing supplier to a new supplier, for example), high marketing expenditures and displaying aggressive tendencies to retaliate.

A company may attempt **market expansion** in a market that it already serves by converting *non-users to users* of its product. This can be an attractive option in new markets when non-users form a sizeable segment and may be willing to try the product given suitable inducements. Lapsed users can also be targeted. Kellogg's has targeted lapsed breakfast cereal users (fathers) who rediscover the pleasure of eating cornflakes when feeding their children. Market expansion can also be achieved by *increasing usage rate*. Kellogg's has also

THE NEW ŠKODA YETI.
WINNER OF THE EURO NCAP SAFETY TEST.

⬆ **EXHIBIT 11.4** Skoda has successfully repositioned itself in the car market through investment in product development and development of product features.

Go to the website and road test the Yeti with Jeremy Clarkson, then identify the product features that make this a successful brand in Skoda's portfolio.
www.mcgraw-hill.co.uk/ textbooks/jobber

tried to increase the usage (eating) rate of its cornflakes by promoting eating in the evening as well as at breakfast. Affordability and improving sustainability market expansion have also been found to aid market expansion.[40]

The **product development** option involves the development of new products for existing markets.[41] One variant is to *extend existing product lines* to give current customers greater choice. For example, the original iPod has been followed by the launches of the iPod nano, shuffle and touch, giving its target market of young music lovers greater choice in terms of size, capacity and price. When new features are added (with an accompanying price rise) trading up may occur, with customers buying the enhanced-value product on repurchase. However, when the new products are cheaper than the original (as is the case with the iPod) the danger is cannibalization of sales of the core product. *Product replacement* activities involve the replacement of old brands/models with new ones. This is common in the car market and often involves an upgrading of the old model with a new (more expensive) replacement. For Skoda and Fiat, product replacement has been essential to their survival, as Mini Case 11.1 describes. A final option is the replacement of an old product with a fundamentally different one, often based on technology change. The business thus replaces an old product with an *innovation* (although both may be marketed side by side for a time). Microsoft operating systems are a classic example of replacement products being introduced but the older products continue to be marketed and supported: for example, Windows Vista (released in 2006) was superseded by Windows 7 in 2009[42] and in 2012 Windows 8 should be released.

Mini Case 11.1 Product Development at Skoda and Fiat

Once decried for its poor design, quality and performance, Skoda has successfully repositioned itself in the car market through investment in product development. The brand's astonishing renaissance is reflected in its position as a top-five car brand for 12 consecutive years in the JD Power Survey of Customer Satisfaction. The brand continues to invest in innovation and product development and winning innovation awards. The Skoda Yeti even won acclaim in the 4x4 market from BBC TV's *Top Gear's* Jeremy Clarkson, the hard-talking presenter.

Hoping to emulate Skoda's turnaround is Fiat. For many years, the Fiat brand performed poorly in the same survey because of poor reliability. Further hampered by its tendency to make ugly cars, the company became one of Europe's worst-performing car companies. This has begun to change with the appointment of Sergio Marchionne, who told his designers and engineers to make cars that people would want to be seen driving. All the designers were put under one roof and told to give up the wilful eccentricity that had led to some notably ugly cars. Development was speeded up by going further with virtual engineering than any other car maker. This allowed the elimination of the 'prototype' stage of new car development, and cut the time from design to production to 18 months, providing a vital speed advantage over competitors.

The result has been a succession of stylish new models like the Fiat Bravo and 500, which have restored Fiat's fortunes. By implementing an effective product replacement strategy, Mr Marchionne has revived a sleeping giant of the European car industry.

Questions:

1 Renault, another central European car manufacture, has started to instigate radical change to enable it to compete in this highly competitive jungle. Outline its plans for the future.
2 What strategy are they currently adopting, and how is it going to change in the near future?

Based on: Top Gear (2011);[43] The Economist (2008);[44] Love (2008)[45]

Market development entails the promotion of *new uses of existing products to new customers*, or the marketing of *existing products (and their current uses) to new market segments*. The promotion of new uses accounted for the growth in sales of nylon, which was first marketed as a replacement for silk in parachutes but expanded into shirts, carpets, tyres, etc. Tesco, the UK supermarket chain, practised market development by marketing existing grocery products, which were sold in large out-of-town supermarkets and superstores, to a new market segment—convenience shoppers—by opening smaller grocery shops in town centres and next to petrol stations. Market development through entering new segments could involve the search for overseas opportunities. Andy Thornton Ltd, an interior design business, successfully increased sales by entering Scandinavia and Germany, two geographic segments that provided new expansion opportunities for its services. The growth of overseas markets in China, India, Russia and eastern Europe is providing major market development opportunities for companies such as BP, Vodafone, Wal-Mart, Carrefour and Nokia.[46] When Wagner, the German manufacturer of spray guns for painting, expanded to the USA in search of market development it found that it had to refocus on an entirely different market segment. In Europe it sells its products to professional painters but in the USA its products are bought by people who use spray guns in their own homes to paint interiors and outside surfaces such as fences.[47]

The **entry into new markets (diversification)** option concerns the development of *new products for new markets*. This is the most risky option, especially when the entry strategy is not based on the *core competences* of the business. However, it can also be the most rewarding, as exemplified by Honda's move from motorcycles to cars (based on its core competences in engines), and Apple Computer's launch of the iPod mobile music player, which can download music via a computer (based on its core competences in computer electronics). This was followed by its highly successful diversification into smartphones (the iPhone) based on its new-found competences in mobile communication and tablet computers with the iPad. It is the lure of such rewards that has tempted the Internet networking equipment maker Cisco to venture into consumer electronics, and Intel, which manufactures microprocessors that power personal computers, to diversify into platforms combining silicon and software, which has led to new devices and technologies in consumer electronics, wireless communications and healthcare.[48]

Online **LearningCentre**

When you have read this chapter

log on to the Online Learning Centre at **www.mcgraw-hill.co.uk/textbooks/jobber** to explore chapter-by-chapter test questions, links and further online study tools for marketing.

Review

1 **The concept of the product life-cycle**
   - A four-stage cycle in the life of a product illustrated as sales and profit curves, the four stages being introduction, growth, maturity and decline. It is quite flexible and can be applied to both brands and product lines.

2 **The uses and limitations of the product life-cycle**
   - Its uses are that it emphasizes the need to terminate old and develop new products, warns against the danger of assuming growth will last for ever, stresses the need to review marketing objectives and strategies as products pass through the four stages, emphasizes the need to maintain a balanced set of products across the four stages, and warns against the damages of overpowering (setting too high prices early in the cycle when competition is low).

- The limitations are that it is wrong to assume that all products follow the classic S-shaped curve and it is misleading to believe that the product life-cycle sales curve is a fact of life; it depends on marketing activity. The duration of the stages are unpredictable, limiting its use as a forecasting tool, and the stylized marketing objectives and strategy prescriptions associated with each stage may be misleading in particular cases.
- Overall it is a valuable stimulus to strategic thinking but as a prescriptive tool it is blunt.

3 **The concept of product portfolio planning**

- This is the process of managing products as groups (portfolios) rather than separate, distinct and independent entities.
- The emphasis is on deciding which products to build, hold, harvest and divest (i.e. resource allocation).

4 **The Boston Consulting Group Growth-Share Matrix, its uses and associated criticisms**

- The matrix allows portfolios of products to be depicted in a 2×2 box, the axes of which are based on market growth rate (proxy for market attractiveness) and relative market share (proxy for competitive strength).
- Cash flow from a product is assumed to depend on the box in which a product falls.
- Stars are likely to have cash flow balance; problem children cause a drain on cash flow; cash cows generate large positive cash flow; and dogs usually produce low or negative cash flow.
- Its uses are that the matrix provides guidelines for setting strategic objectives (for example, stars should be built; problem children built selectively, harvested or divested; cash cows held; and dogs harvested or divested), and emphasizes the need to maintain a balanced portfolio with the cash generated by the cash cows being used to fund those being built.
- The criticisms are: the assumption that cash flow is determined by a product's position in the matrix is weak; it distracts management from focusing on sustainable competitive advantage; treating market growth rate and market share as proxies for market attractiveness and competitive strength is oversimplistic; it can lead to an unhealthy preoccupation with market share; it ignores interdependencies between products; building stars may be inappropriate; competitor reactions are ignored; the assumption that products are self-funding ignores capital markets; the theoretical soundness of some of the underlying concepts (e.g. market definition) is questionable; cash flow may not be the best criteria for allocating resources; and the matrix lacks precision in identifying which problem children to build, harvest or divest.

5 **The General Electric Market Attractiveness–Competitive Position model, its uses and associated criticisms**

- The model is based on market attractiveness (e.g. market size, market growth rate, strength of competition) and competitive strength (e.g. market share, potential to develop a differential advantage, cost advantages). By weighting the criteria and scoring products, these can be positioned on a matrix.
- Its advantages over the 'Boston Box' are that more criteria than just market growth rate and market share are used to determine the position of products in the matrix, and it is more flexible.
- Its uses are that the matrix provides guidelines for setting strategic objectives based upon a product's position in the matrix, and that the analysis is much richer than that of the Boston Box because more factors are being taken into account, leading to better resource allocation decisions.
- The criticisms are that it is harder to use than the Boston Box, and its flexibility can provide an opportunity for managerial bias.

6 **The contribution of portfolio planning**

- The models emphasize the important strategic point that different products should have different roles in a product portfolio, and different reward systems and managers should be linked to them.
- The models can be useful as an aid to managerial judgement and strategic thinking, but should not supplant that judgement and thinking.

7 **Product strategies for growth**

- A useful way of looking at growth opportunities is offered by the Ansoff Matrix as it is a practical framework for thinking about how growth can be achieved through product strategy.
- It comprises four general approaches to sales growth: market penetration/expansion, product development, market development and diversification.

- Market penetration and expansion are strategies relating to growing existing products in existing markets. Market penetration depends on winning competitors' customers or buying competitors (thereby increasing market share). Defence of increased penetration may be through discouraging competitive entry. Market expansion may be through converting non-users to users or increasing usage rate. Although market share may not increase, sales growth is achieved through increasing market size.
- Product development is a strategy for developing new products for existing markets. It has three variants: extending existing product lines (brand extensions) to give current customers greater choice; product replacement (updates of old products); and innovation (developing fundamentally different products).
- Market development is a strategy for taking existing products and marketing them in new markets. This may be through the promotion of new uses of existing products to new customers, or the marketing of existing products to new market segments (e.g. overseas markets).
- Diversification (entry into new markets) is a strategy for developing new products for new markets. It is the most risky of the four growth strategies but also potentially the most rewarding.

Key Terms

entry into new markets (diversification) the entry into new markets by new products

market development to take current products and market them in new markets

market expansion the attempt to increase the size of a market by converting non-users to users of the product and by increasing usage rates

market penetration to continue to grow sales by marketing an existing product in an existing market

portfolio planning managing groups of brands and product lines

product development increasing sales by improving present products or developing new products for current markets

product life-cycle a four-stage cycle in the life of a product illustrated as sales and profits curves, the four stages being introduction, growth, maturity and decline

Study Questions

1. To what extent can the product life-cycle help to inform marketing management decision-making? Discuss.

2. Evaluate the usefulness of the BCG Matrix. Do you believe that it has a role to play in portfolio planning?

3. What is the difference between product and market development in the Ansoff Matrix? Give examples of each form of product growth strategy.

4. How does the GE Matrix differ from the BCG Matrix? What are the strengths and weaknesses of the GE Matrix?

5. Evaluate the contribution of product portfolio planning models to product strategy.

6. Suggest possible advantages of actively managing a company's product portfolios.

7. Suggest how product portfolio planning might be affected by changing forces in the marketing environment.

References

1. Polli, R. and V. Cook (1969) Validity of the Product Life Cycle, *Journal of Business*, October, 385–400.
2. Nokian (2012) http://www.nokianheavytyres.com/innovativeness_int.
3. Doyle, P. (1989) Building Successful Brands: The Strategic Options, *Journal of Marketing Management* 5(1), 77–95.
4. Doherty, N. F., F. E. Ellis-Chadwick and C. A. Hart (2003) An analysis of the factors affecting the adoption of the Internet in the UK retail sector, *Journal of Business Research* 56, 887–97.
5. Ellis-Chadwick, F., N. Doherty and C. Hart (2002) Signs of change? A longitudinal study of Internet adoption in the UK retail sector, *Journal of Retailing and Consumer Services* 9, 71–80.
6. Boston Consulting Group (2001) On-line Retail Market in North America to reach $65 billion in 2001, http://www.beg.com.
7. Pavitt, D. (1997) Retailing and the super highway: the future of the electronic home shopping industry, *International Journal of Retail & Distribution Management*, 25(1), 38–43.
8. http://en.wikipedia.org/wiki/Dot-com_bubble.
9. Virzi, A. M. (2000) Billionaire builds wealth at Internet speed, *Forbes.com*, http://www.forbes.com/2000/06/30/feat.html.
10. Hudson, A. (2010) Whatever happened to the dotcom millionaires? http://news.bbc.co.uk/1/hi/technology/8505260.stm.
11. Gapper, J. (2006) Sony is Scoring Low at its Close Game, *Financial Times*, 6 November, 17.
12. Vakratsas, D. and T. Ambler (1999) How Advertising Works: What Do We Really Know? *Journal of Marketing* 63, January, 26–43.
13. Nielsen (2012) Mobile Youth Around the World, http://www.nielsen.com/content/dam/corporate/us/en/reports-downloads/2010%20Reports/Nielsen-Mobile-Youth-Around-The-World-Dec-2010.pdf.
14. IDC (2012) Worldwide mobile phone market maintains its growth trajectory in the Fourth Quarter despite soft demand in the feature phone market http://www.idc.com/getdoc.jsp?containerId=prUS23297412, 1 February.
15. Deere, G. and N. Kilby (2005) White Heat or Lukewarm, *Marketing Week*, 18 August, 34–5.
16. Lester, R. (2005) 3 Sets Sights on Big Four, *Marketing Week*, 27 October, 26–7.
17. Odell, M. (2006) Mobile Television May Be the Answer, *FT Digital Business*, 13 February, 1.
18. Wray, R. (2006) Falling Prices Bring Nokia Handsets Below £70, *Guardian*, 27 January, 22.
19. Beckett, A. (2012) Unilever complete Sara Lee deal, *The Grocer*, http://www.thegrocer.co.uk/companies/unilever-completes-sara-lee-deal/214444.article 6 December.
20. McDougall, A. (2012) Unilever steps up Brylcreem ops in India as expansion march continues, http://www.cosmeticsdesign-europe.com/Business-Financial/Unilever-steps-up-Brylcreem-ops-in-India-as-expansion-march-continues.
21. Aaker, D. (2007) *Strategic Marketing Management*, New York: Wiley.
22. Cline, C. E. and B. P. Shapiro (1979) *Cumberland Metal Industries (A): Case Study*, Cambridge, Mass: Harvard Business School.
23. Polli and Cook (1969) op. cit.
24. Dhalia, N. K. and S. Yuspeh (1976) Forget the Product Life Cycle Concept, *Harvard Business Review*, Jan.–Feb., 102–12.
25. Rowley, I. and H. Tashiro (2005) Can Canon Keep Printing Money? *Business Week*, 5/12 September, 18–20.
26. Shah, R. (2002) Managing a Portfolio to Unlock Real Potential, *Financial Times*, 21 August, 13.
27. Marsh, P. and I. Bickerton (2005) Stewardship of a Sprawling Empire, *Financial Times*, 18 November, 13.
28. Kraft Foods (2012) http://www.kraftfoodscompany.com/assets/pdf/kraft_foods_fact_sheet.pdf.
29. Mason, T. (2002) Nestlé Sells Big Brands in Core Strategy Focus, *Marketing*, 7 February, 5.
30. Tomlinson, H. (2005) Adidas Sells Ski and Surf Group for £329m, *Guardian*, 3 May, 5.
31. Milner, M. (2006) £1.2bn Sale of Schweppes' European Drinks Business Agreed, *Guardian*, 22 November, 26.
32. Steen, M. (2008) Reinventing the Philips Brand, *Financial Times*, 27 March, 18.
33. Brierley, D. (1997) Spring-Cleaning a Statistical Wonderland, *European*, 20–26 February, 28.
34. Hedley, B. (1977) Boston Consulting Group Approach to the Business Portfolio, *Long Range Planning*, February, 9–15.
35. See, e.g. Day, G. S. and R. Wensley (1983) Marketing Theory with a Strategic Orientation, *Journal of Marketing*, Fall, 79–89; Haspslagh, P. (1982) Portfolio Planning: Uses and Limits, *Harvard Business Review*, Jan.–Feb., 58–73; Wensley, R. (1981) Strategic Marketing: Betas, Boxes and Basics, *Journal of Marketing*, Summer, 173–83.
36. Hofer, C. and D. Schendel (1978) *Strategy Formulation: Analytical Concepts*, St Paul, MN: West.
37. Hedley (1977) op. cit.
38. Ansoff, H. L. (1957) Strategies for Diversification, *Harvard Business Review*, Sept.–Oct., 114.
39. Handley, L. (2012) Greggs finds ingredient for growth on Facebook, *Marketing Week*, 1 March, 15–18.
27. Webb, T. (2008) Apple's Guru Calls a New Tune, *Observer*, 15 June, 6.
40. Banga, V. V. and S. L. Joshib (2010) Market expansion strategy–performance relationship, *Journal of Strategic Marketing* 18(1), 57–75.
41. Ansoff, I. (1957) Strategies for Diversification, *Harvard Business Review*, Sept.–Oct., 113–24.
42. Windows (2012) A history of Windows, http://windows.microsoft.com/en-US/windows/history.
43. TopGear (2011) http://www.youtube.com/watch?v=E7kEJ-pHkWA.
44. *The Economist* (2008) Rebirth of a Carmaker, 26 April, 91–93.
45. Love, M. (2008) Promise to Do My Best, *Observer Magazine*, 25 May, 75.
46. *The Economist* (2008) Face Value, 31 May, 86.
47. Bolfo, B. (2005) The Art of Selling One Product to Two Markets, *Financial Times*, 10 August, 11.
48. See Palmer, M. (2006) Cisco Lays Plans to Expand into Home Electronics, *Financial Times*, 16 January, 21; and Edwards, C. (2006) Inside Intel, *Business Week*, 9 January, 43.

Unilever's Quest for Growth

In February 2000, when Niall FitzGerald, chairman of Unilever, rose in front of his shareholders to reveal his plans for the most comprehensive restructuring and strategy review to hit the company in over 100 years, there was a sharp intake of breath. His four-year 'Path to Growth' strategy was to see 1200 of its 1600 consumer brands axed to concentrate marketing muscle behind 400 high-growth brands. All brands that were not among the top two sellers in their market segment would be dropped either immediately or over a period of time.

Buyers would be sought for those that were to be divested immediately, the rest would be harvested (milked) and the cash generated ploughed into support for the 400 big brands. This would mean £450 million (€648 million) of extra marketing expenditure put behind such global brands as Magnum ice cream, Dove soap, Knorr soup and Lipton's tea. Local successes such as Persil washing powder and Colman's mustard in the UK would also be supported heavily. The promise was to increase profit margins from 11 to 16 per cent and to achieve target annual growth rates of between 4.5 and 5 per cent from its 400 top brands. Brands scheduled to be harvested or divested included Timotei shampoo, Brut deodorant, Radion washing powder, Harmony hairspray, Pear's soap and Jif lemon.

The analysis that Unilever had done revealed that only a quarter of Unilever's brands provided 90 per cent of its turnover and that disposing of the other three quarters would lead to a more efficient supply chain and reduced costs of £1 billion (€1.44 billion) over three years. As FitzGerald explained, 'We were doing too many things. We had too many brands in too many places. Many were just not big enough to move the needle so we had to focus and simplify. That simplification would allow us to take cost out of the business.'

Not everyone was convinced. There were £3.5 billion (€5 billion) of restructuring costs (bigger than most companies' market capitalizations) and the prospect of 25,000 jobs going. The exercise would require a highly effective internal communications programme to obtain buy-in from Unilever staff.

By the end of 2002 FitzGerald could claim considerable achievements. Cost savings of over £450 million (€648 million) had already been banked and margins had moved from 11 to 15 per cent. The top 400 leading brands accounted for 88 per cent of sales and achieved an

average growth rate of 4.5 per cent. Three businesses had also been bought. Bestfoods, the US foods giant, brought the Hellman's mayonnaise, Knorr soups and Skippy peanut butter brands into the Unilever portfolio; the acquisition of Ben & Jerry's gave the company one of two major brands in the premium ice cream sector; and Slimfast provided major penetration of the diet food market.

Unilever was also busy dropping or selling off Elizabeth Arden, Batchelor's soups, Oxo, Knight's Castille soap, Frish toilet cleaner and Stergene handwashing liquid. Some of Unilever's unwanted brands have been bought by small companies. For example, Buck UK bought Unilever's Sqezy—the washing-up liquid formerly marketed as 'easy, peasy, lemon Sqezy'. Also, Unilever sold its Harmony hairspray and Stergene fabric conditioner brands to Lornamead. Others such as Oxo and Bachelors were sold to larger companies—in this case Campbell Grocery Products.

A number of brand extensions were also planned in 2002, most notably in the Bertolli olive oil, Dove soap, Knorr soup, Lynx (Axe) male grooming and Slimfast diet food brands. The Lynx (Axe) men's deodorant was launched in the USA, and three new flavours of Hellman's mayonnaise and an Asian side-dishes range were introduced.

The result of all this activity was that Unilever posted a 16 per cent increase in 2002 profits: that is, £1.5 billion compared to £1.3 billion (€2.1 billion compared to €1.9 billion) in 2001. Sales of its top 400 brands grew

5.4 per cent, above the company's target of 4.5 and 5 per cent. The company invested £5.1 billion (€7.3 billion) in advertising and promotion, up 8.5 per cent on the 2001 level.

During 2003 Unilever earmarked an additional 20 per cent of marketing investment in its global ice cream portfolio over the next three years. The ice cream group has a remarkable global brand portfolio. For example, in the UK Unilever owns Walls; in France, it bought Miko; in Portugal it owns Ola; and in Sweden it owns GB Glace. Over Europe as a whole Unilever owns and operates more than 12 different ice cream brands, each with its own strong heritage and relationships with customers. Unilever has retained the names of its national brands while replacing original brand symbols with a single heart-shaped logo.

Unfortunately the successes of the early years were followed by two years of performance below expectations leading to the departure of Mr FitzGerald in May 2004. Poor sales and profit performance was blamed on poor organizational structure, lack of innovation and poor advertising. Poor structure stemmed from Unilever's Anglo-Dutch heritage which resulted in joint chairmen—one for the Dutch arm and one for the UK—and no chief executive. The company was run by two boards and separate headquarters in London and Rotterdam. Consequently, decision-making was cumbersome and slow with the ever-present threat of conflict between the two groups compounding the problems. The group was also divided into divisions—health and personal products, food, and frozen foods. These were regarded as fiefdoms under which separate management teams managed their products separately in each country.

Following Mr FitzGerald's departure, Unilever carried out a strategic review under its joint chairmen, Patrick Cescau in the UK and Antony Burgmans in the Netherlands. Mr Cescau, the driving force behind the review, became Unilever's chief executive with Mr Burgmans becoming non-executive chairman. The board was unified and headquarters were centralized in London. These changes gave Mr Cescau the autonomy to push through the reform needed to get Unilever back on track. Under the slogan 'One Unilever' he dismantled the fiefdoms which were merged to form one executive team covering all divisions and nationalities, resulting in the loss of almost a fifth of senior management. A cull of about 30,000 jobs took place and some loss-making factories were closed to cut costs.

Mr Cescau also changed focus from Path to Growth's fixation on profit margins to boosting market share. This meant price reductions and the introduction of cheaper product ranges to complement the premium priced brands. The Magnum ice cream brand was complemented in this way, for example.

He also sold Unilever's cosmetics and fragrances arm Unilever Cosmetics International to Coty International for £438m (€613m) in a move which allowed it to focus on its core categories of food, cleaning and personal care brands such as Ben & Jerry's ice cream, Knorr soups, Flora margarine, Cif cleaning products, Persil detergents, Dove personal care products, Sunsilk shampoos and Lynx (Axe) men's deodorants. This was quickly followed by the sale of its frozen-food division (Birds Eye) to Permira, a venture capitalist, for £1.2 billion (€1.7 billion). At the time of the sale, Birds Eye was the number one food brand in the UK with a turnover of £500 million (€700 million) a year and profits of around £50 million (€70 million). It was also the UK's second-biggest supermarket brand after Walker's crisps. Unilever also sold its North American detergents business in 2008 to a private equity firm.

A greater emphasis was placed on emerging markets such as China, India, Brazil, Russia, Africa, and central and eastern Europe. Advertising budgets in western Europe were tightened to fund extra investment in these growth markets. In line with this strategy, Inmarko, Russia's largest ice cream brand, was acquired in 2008. By 2009 emerging markets accounted for around 50 per cent of Unilever's sales revenue.

Another change in strategy was to adopt a more standardized approach to global marketing. The company moved from autonomous localized initiatives to the roll-out of innovation and marketing programmes on a global basis. Power was taken away from country managers and given to global marketing teams to oversee the development and marketing of new products. Brand marketing was split into two divisions: the brand development team and brand building. The brand development team devise a global strategy for each brand including innovation. A package of recommendations is then created, usually in conjunction with two key countries. This is then sent to brand building teams in each country and they 'make it happen' within local markets.

Mr Cescau has also invested in 'healthy living' brands to capitalize on the trend towards health and well-being. For example, a number of 'healthy' sauces and soups under the Knorr brand were launched with no artificial flavours or colourings, reflecting Unilever's 'vitality' positioning.

In 2008 Mr Cescau stepped down as chief executive after achieving what most commentators regard as a fairly successful period at the helm, transforming the company from a lumbering, regionally driven bureaucracy into a more streamlined, globally managed business. However, Unilever's performance did not match that of Reckitt Benckiser, maker of the Cillit Bang cleaner, whose strategy was to launch brands such as stain removers targeting niche markets that avoided direct head-to-head competition with Procter & Gamble and Unilever.

His successor was Paul Polman, a former P&G and Nestlé man, breaking with an 80-year-old tradition of appointing insiders. Faced with a recession, Mr Polman embarked on a cost-cutting programme, including a freeze on management salaries and travel budget cuts of 30 per cent (replacing travel with teleconferencing), designed to achieve £45m (€50m) savings. A job-cutting and factory closure programme that began in 2007 was accelerated, and a global procurement officer was recruited to seek savings by using the company's vast scale to obtain better prices. Acquisitions were also made, including the purchase of Toni & Guy and Alberto Culver (both haircare), and Sara Lee's personal care business. The Russian personal care group Kalina was also bought in 2011. By 2012 emerging markets accounted for over half of Unilever's sales revenue. The impact of its brand portfolio strategy is reflected in the fact that 75 per cent of sales are now made from its top 25 brands.

References

Jack, L. (2009) The Soaps, the Glory and the Universal Truths in Marketing, *Marketing Week*, 23 April, 20–4.

Kilby, N. (2005) Coty Scents Growth Potential in Unilever Cosmetics, *Marketing Week*, 26 May, 11.

Kilby, N. (2006) Permira Aims to Make Birds Eye Cooler than Chilled, *Marketing Week*, 7 September, 10.

Lucas, L. (2011) Unilever 'On Front Foot' but Full-Year Margins Disappoint, *Financial Times*, 4 November, 22.

Mortished, C. (2009) Unilever Chief Paul Polman Ditches Pay Rises and Targets, *The Times*, 6 February, 18.

Ritson, M. (2003) Unilever Goes with its 'Heart' to Make Global Brand of Local Ices, *Marketing*, 1 May, 18.

Ritson, M. (2012) Bereft of Stars, Premier's Plan Will Flop, *Marketing Week*, 26 January, 58.

Wiggins, J. (2008) Unilever Hangs on to European Laundry List, *Financial Times*, 29 July, 18.

Wiggins, J. (2008) Unilever Buys Russia's Inmarko Ice Cream, *Financial Times*, 5 February, 21.

Wiggins, J. (2009) Unilever Looks to the Silver Lining, *Financial Times*, 6 February, 19.

Questions

1. What were the advantages to Unilever of reducing the size of its brand portfolio? What were the risks?

2. To what extent does it appear that Unilever followed (i) the BCG Growth-Share Matrix, and (ii) the General Electric Market Attractiveness-Competitive Position Model approaches to portfolio planning?

3. What are the attractions to small companies of buying marginal Unilever brands? What are the dangers of doing so?

4. Comment on Unilever's approach to the global marketing of its brands.

5. Why did the sale of Bird's Eye and its North American detergent business make strategic sense for Unilever?

This case was prepared by David Jobber, Professor of Marketing, University of Bradford.

Intel Inside Out
The Search for Growth

Intel is one of the most famous business-to-business brand names in the world, and with sales of over $54 billion, profits of $13 billion and 80 per cent share of the market for microprocessors that power PCs, it is also one of the most successful. The foundation for its success was the development and marketing of microprocessors for PCs and servers. By investing billions in ever-faster processors Intel has become the dominant force in this industry, with efficient plants that can produce more processors in a day than some rivals can in a year. The combination of low-cost production and ever faster chips was a powerful concoction that none of its rivals could match.

Much of the credit for Intel's success goes to Andy Grove, its former chief executive, who took the decision to leave the unprofitable memory chip business in order to focus on microprocessors for the fast-growing personal computer market, a move that enabled Intel to bury the competition. Intel's products were supported by powerful branding using the Pentium brand name and 'Intel inside' strap-line, bringing consumer awareness of a product hidden from sight in the heart of a computer. Intel's strategy was to work with Microsoft to appeal to PC industry giants such as Dell, HP, IBM and Compaq to be the first choice for microprocessors.

Under Grove, engineers dominated and the culture at Intel was summarized by his motto: 'Only the paranoid survive'. Managers often engaged in 'constructive confrontation', otherwise known as shouting at each other. Under Grove's successor, Craig R. Barrett, the company continued its successful path to ever greater sales and profits.

Times they are a 'changin'

By 2005 the market for microprocessors was changing. Growth in PC demand was slowing as markets became saturated. No longer could Intel rely on double-digit market growth to fuel its sales and profit trajectory. Another change was occurring within Intel itself. A new chief executive, Paul Otellini, was at the helm. A non-engineer, Otellini joined Intel in 1974 straight out of business school at the University of California at Berkeley. A close working associate of Grove, who continued as chairman until 2005 after his departure as CEO in 1998, Otellini has a marketing background. Among his successes was the Centrino brand. When Otellini was

head of product planning, he decided, against the wishes of Intel engineers, that rather than launch yet another fast processor, he would bundle it with a relatively new wireless Internet technology called WiFi. The combination enabled consumers to connect from their laptop to the Internet from such places as airport lounges and coffee shops. Supported by a $300 million marketing campaign, Centrino laptops caught on, revitalizing the PC market while encouraging consumers to purchase higher margin products. Since launch, over $6 billion worth of Centrino chips have been sold.

Intel was also faced with an energetic British competitor, Advanced Micro Devices, which had slowly been gaining ground in the battle of the microchip. A major competitive weapon of AMD was price, which prompted Intel to develop the low-priced Celeron microprocessor. AMD stole a march on Intel by being the first to launch a 64-bit chip, which held the competitive advantages of having greater power and lower power consumption. By 2005 AMD had increased its market share to 15 per cent of the PC microprocessor market and held 26 per cent of the market for the microprocessors that drive servers where lower power consumption was highly valued. Even more impressive was its 48 per cent share of the growing multi-core processor market, where two or more chips are put on to a single sliver of silicon. Such products consume less power, enabling laptops to run longer before recharge, and enhance performance without generating more heat, which was a problem with single chips. Using less power is especially important for business-to-business customers. For example,

Google claimed that it cost more to run its computers than to buy them. A landmark came in 2005 when Dell, hitherto an Intel stronghold, moved to AMD chips for its servers. Its decision was influenced by the competitive advantage its rivals HP, Toshiba and Gateway were getting by using the more powerful AMD chips in their consumer and business systems, particularly servers.

A change of strategy

The promotion of Otellini to chief executive heralded a change in strategic direction for Intel. The changing technological, competitive and market landscape was reflected in his desire to move the company away from its dependence on single microprocessor chips for the PC market. First, Intel developed new dual-core chips for laptops (using the Core brand name), which place two microprocessors on one sliver of silicon. This allowed laptops to run for five to ten hours rather than three to four, which was typical before.

Second, Intel focused on 'complete technology platforms' rather than individual microprocessors. *Platformization*, as Intel calls it, means bundling a range of chips and the software needed to tie them all together, offering different features such as security, video, audio and wireless capabilities in a combination to suit a particular target market. This is recognition of the fact that computer manufacturers value the opportunity to buy a complete package of chips from one manufacturer rather than assemble components from several suppliers. It also means that Intel sells more components, and so takes a larger slice of the selling price of each PC. Whereas Intel can handle the process in-house, AMD requires partners to develop platforms.

Otellini also announced plans to broaden Intel's target markets. Rather than focus only on PC manufacturers, Intel intends to be a major technological player in home entertainment, wireless communications and healthcare. In home entertainment, Otellini's vision is for the PC to be the central connection to individual entertainment devices. The company developed the Viiv multicore chip, which allowed PCs to connect to DVD players, TVs, stereo systems, and so on, so that consumers can move digital content around the home. This meant that Viiv computers could act as an all-in-one DVD player, games console, CD player and television, and enable downloads of movies, music and games, which could then be moved around the home. Viiv was chosen as the chip to power Windows Media Centre PCs.

In targeting wireless communications, Intel is hoping to make a breakthrough in an area where it has traditionally been weak. Hitherto, Intel's focus on PC microprocessors meant that investment in chips for mobile communications was considered secondary. Intel launched in 2008 the Atom, an ultra-small energy-efficient chip. The Atom allowed Intel to compete in the market for mobile internet devices (MIDs, bigger than smartphones), netbooks (very small laptops) and nettops (cheap, stripped-down desktop PCs). By 2009, the Atom chip was found at the heart of most netbooks. However, the market for netbooks has faded with the rise of tablets, most notably the Apple iPad. In response Intel is championing a new category of mobile computers called Ultrabooks. Powered by second-generation Core chips these ultra-thin, ultra-responsive devices are designed to take over from netbooks and challenge tablets.

Despite its successes in the PC and server markets, Intel's impact in the growing smartphone and tablets markets has been poor with AMD the market leader with 90 per cent market share. This may change from 2012 when Intel and Google signed an alliance so that Android-based smartphones and tablets could be powered by Intel chips. Intel has also developed a chip based on 3D technology aimed to generate the power efficiency needed with these devices. Already Intel chips are powering Motorola (which is Google-owned) and Lenovo smartphones. Otellini is also hoping for breakthrough innovations in healthcare. His vision is for digital technology to help healthcare professionals. Ethnographers are employed to understand the problems of the elderly and people with specific diseases such as Alzheimer's. Intel is developing sensors that can communicate with computer networks, enabling care-givers to monitor the health of the elderly remotely. One benefit of this would be to allow elderly people to remain in their own homes.

In line with his strategy, Otellini reorganized Intel into platform-specific divisions: digital home (for consumer PCs and home entertainment), corporate (business PCs and servers), mobility (laptops and mobile devices) and healthcare, and scattered the processor engineers among them. New product development was also reorganized. In the past engineers worked on ever faster chips and marketers were asked to sell them. Now new products are developed by teams of people: chip engineers, software developers and marketers all work together to design attractive new products. The type of person Intel hires has changed too. They include ethnographers, sociologists and software developers. Ethnographers, for example, are researching how people in emerging markets like China and India use technology.

Eric Kim, chief marketing officer, was recruited from Samsung and was widely credited with raising its brand awareness and image as a leading consumer electronics company. Among his first marketing initiatives was the rebranding of the Core family of microprocessors to simplify a range that had become too unwieldy and confusing. The names—the Core i3, Core i5 and Core i7—described the basic, mid-range and high-end features of the Core line, respectively. Intel has also become corporate technological partner with BMW, which sees its chips powering operations across BMW dealerships, the company and its cars. The partnership also makes Intel a major sponsor of BMW's Sauber Formula One motor racing team. The male-dominated F1 audience, with its keen interest in technology, is a core target market for Intel.

Not everyone at Intel was happy about the reorganization and the increased emphasis on marketing, however. Before Otellini's elevation to CEO anyone not working for the core PC business was considered a second-class citizen, and many high-level engineers working on PC products feel they have lost their star status. Some regard marketing as little more than gloss and glitz, and others have left to join rivals such as AMD. The competition is also critical of Intel's practice of offering volume-based rebates to computer manufacturers, which they claim acts as a barrier to entry. This has led to a record £950m (€1.03m) fine imposed by the European Commission for anticompetitive behaviour.

References

Based on: Kilby, N. (2006) Intel's Power Drive, *Marketing Week*, 5 January, 21; Edwards, C. (2006) AMD: Chipping Away at Intel's Lead, *Business Week*, 12 June, 72–3; *The Economist* (2008) Battlechips, 7 June, 76–7; Baldwin, C. (2009) Intel, AMD Take Battle To New Ultra-Thin Laptops, *reuters.com*, 19 June; Edwards, C. (2009) Intel Tries to Invest Its Way Out of a Rut, *Business Week*, 27 April, 44–6; Chipperfield, E. (2009) A Pocket Laptop to Be Reckoned With, *The Times*, 7 June, 28; Shiels, M. (2009) Intel and Nokia Band Together, www.news.bbc.co.uk; Nuttall, C. (2011) Intel Raises Stakes for Rivals as it Hails Revolution in 3D chips, *Financial Times*, 5 May, 1; Nuttall, C. (2011) Intel and Google Sign Android Alliance, *Financial Times*, 14 September, 26; Nuttall, C. and R. Kwong (2011) Intel Unveils Vision for Laptops as it Fends off Tablet Rivals, *Financial Times*, 1 June, 21; Garside, J. and C. Arthur (2012) Intel Chips Away at ARM's Control of Mobile Market, *Guardian*, 12 January, 30.

Questions

1 Interpret Intel's move from its reliance on microprocessors for PCs into home entertainment, healthcare and mobile communications using (i) the product life-cycle, (ii) the BCG, and (iii) the General Electric Market Attractiveness–Competitive Position models.

2 Locate each of Intel's moves (products and markets) since Otellini became CEO in the Ansoff product growth matrix. Justify your answer.

3 How has the corporate culture changed since Otellini became CEO? Support your answer with examples.

4 What challenges does Intel face as it moves into home entertainment, healthcare and mobile communications?

This case was prepared by David Jobber, Professor of Marketing, University of Bradford.

CHAPTER
12

Developing new products

> **Design is a funny word. Some people think design means how it looks. But of course, if you dig deeper, it's really how it works.**
> **STEVE JOBS**[1]

> **You learn more from failure . . . but the key is to fail early, fail cheaply, and not to make the same mistake twice.**
> **A. G. LAFLEY, CEO, PROCTER & GAMBLE**

LEARNING OBJECTIVES

After reading this chapter, you should be able to:

1 define the different types of new products that can be launched
2 describe how to create and nurture an innovative culture
3 discuss the organizational options that apply to new product development
4 identify the methods of reducing time to market
5 explain how marketing and R&D staff can work together effectively
6 describe the stages in the new product development process
7 explain how to stimulate the corporate imagination
8 discuss the six key principles of managing product teams
9 describe the innovation categories and their marketing implications
10 discuss the key ingredients in commercializing technology quickly and effectively

The life-blood of corporate success is bringing new products to the marketplace. Changing customer tastes, technological advances and competitive pressures mean that companies cannot afford to rely on past product success. Instead they have to work on new product development programmes and nurture an innovation climate to lay the foundations for new product success.

New product development is a risky activity as most new products fail. But, as we shall see, new product development should not be judged in terms of the percentage of failures. To do so could stifle the spirit of innovation. The acid test is the number of successes. Failure has to be tolerated; it is endemic in the whole process of developing new products.

To fully understand new product development, we need to distinguish between invention and innovation. **Invention** is the discovery of new ideas and methods. **Innovation** occurs when an invention is commercialized by bringing it to market. Not all countries have the same capacity for invention. The UK has a history of being inventive from the steam engine, the bicycle, to the television, the computer, and the jet engine. The Japanese, are equally inventive but also have the ability to successfully market products by constantly seeking to improve and develop using a process called *Kaizen* (sometimes *Kaisan*).[2] The classic example is the Sony Walkman, which was not an invention in the sense that it was fundamentally new; rather its success (over 75 million have been sold worldwide) was based on the innovative marketing of existing technologies. In Scandinavia many businesses were built on a local invention. For example, Tetra Pak was founded by a person who conceived of 'pouring milk into a paper bag'. Lego bricks have revolutionized toys, Gambro invented a machine that can take the place of kidneys, and the invention of a new way to deliver furniture was central to the development of IKEA. In these cases, the key was not just the invention but the capability to innovate by bringing the product successfully to market.[3]

The USA is a major source of innovation. The Internet is dominated by US companies such as Apple, Amazon, Google, eBay and, as Table 12.1 shows, US companies occupy six out of the top 10 places in a survey of the world's most innovative companies.[4]

A key point to remember is that the focus of innovation should be on providing new solutions that better meet customer needs. Innovative solutions often do not require major breakthroughs in technology. For example, the growth of Starbucks was not fuelled by technological breakthroughs but by redefining what city-centre coffee drinking meant, and Ryanair has built its success by creating a different consumer appeal from that of traditional airlines, based on low prices and strict cost control. The Body Shop's success was based on the modern woman's concern for the environment, and Dell became the most profitable computer company by becoming the first to market computers directly to its customers.[5]

Because many innovations fail, it is important to understand the key success factors. Research found the key success factors in innovation involve the following:[6]

- *Creating and delivering added value*. Innovations that produce large improvements in value perform much better than those that fail to deliver improved benefits. Radical innovation has greater potential for enhancing marketing performance but is inherently more risky than incremental innovations which deliver small improvements.
- *Speed to market counts*. The most successful new products tend to be those that are launched quickly. There are two reasons for this. First, delay increases the risk of others getting to market first; second, consumer priorities may change.
- *A product's inferior perceived value cannot be compensated for with high communications spending*. High expenditures on advertising and promotion only have a significant effect on performance where the product is already perceived to have high consumer value. High expenditures for inferior products actually worsen the performance: advertising makes bad products fail quicker.

In this chapter we shall ask the question 'What is a new product?' and examine three key issues in new product development: 1) organization, 2) developing an innovation culture, 3) new product development process. Then we examine the strategies involved in product replacement and the most common form of new product development. Finally, we look at the

TABLE 12.1   The world's most innovative companies

Company	Headquarters—industrial sector	Innovative products
Apple	USA—Technology and telecommunication	iTV, iPad, iPhone, MacBook Pro, MacBook Air
Google	USA—Technology and telecommunication	Google search, Maps, Google+, Gmail
Microsoft	USA—Technology and telecommunication	Microsoft Office, Windows 7 operating system, Bing, Microsoft SQL, Xbox
IBM	USA—Technology and telecommunication	PureSystems, SmartCloud computing
Toyota	Japan—Automotive	Yaris Hybrid, Prius, Hybrid synergy drive, electric vehicles
Amazon.com	USA—Retail	Online book and retail store, Kindle, MP3 player, Web services
LG Electronics	South Korea—Consumer electronics	Televisions, mobile phones, digital signage
BYD	China—Automotive industry	Manufacturer of cars and rechargeable batteries
General Electric Company	USA—Industrial goods and manufacturing	Jet engines for the airline industry, GE90 and GEnx engines, wind turbines
Sony	Japan—Consumer products	Bravia, televisions and cinema systems, Vaio computing, PlayStation, memory cards
Samsung	South Korea—Consumer products	Televisions, computers, netbooks, smartphones
Intel	USA—Technology and telecommunication	Microprocessors, Pentium, Desktop Board, Xeon processors, server chipsets, ethernet controllers

Source: a 2010 survey of 2700 senior executives by the Boston Consulting Group, reported in *Business Week* by Andrew *et al.* (2010).[7]

consumer adoption process, which is how people learn about new products, try them, and adopt or reject them. Throughout this chapter reference will be made to research that highlights the success factors in new product development.

What is a New Product?

Some new products are so fundamentally different from products that already exist that they reshape markets and competition: for example, satellite navigation systems, which have created a new market for digital navigation devices and reduced the sale of printed road maps significantly. Publisher HarperCollins said sales of maps and atlases declined from £13.5 million in 2006 to £9.7 million in 2010.[8]

At the other extreme, a shampoo that is different from existing products only by means of its brand name, fragrance, packaging and colour is also a new product. In fact, four broad categories of new product exist.[9]

1   *Product replacements*: these account for about 45 per cent of all new product launches, and include revisions and improvements to existing products, e.g. repositioning (existing products such as Lucozade Sport being positioned as a 'body fuel' to access new market segments) and cost reductions (existing products being reformulated or redesigned to cost less to produce). Dyson releases new products based on improvement to an existing product. Its new vacuum cleaner has an innovative ball to improve manoeuverability, is smaller and more flexible than previous models.

2 *Additions to existing lines*: these account for about 25 per cent of new product launches and take the form of new products that add to a company's existing product lines. This produces greater product depth. Chocolate Weetabix is an extension which enables the well-known cereal brand to compete with chocolate cereals. Another example is the addition to the Crest toothpaste brand of Crest Pro-health whitening toothpaste.

3 *New product lines*: these total around 20 per cent of new product launches, and represent a move into a new market. For example, in Europe Volvic introduced the 'touch of flavour' range of bottled waters and Evian brought out a facial spray—both targeted at different target audiences. This strategy widens a company's product mix.

4 *New-to-the-world products*: these total around 10 per cent of new product launches, and create entirely new markets. For example, ultra netbooks, tablet computers, smartphones and the Internet have created new markets because of the highly valued customer benefits they provide.

Clearly the degree of risk and reward varies according to the new product category. New-to-the-world products normally carry the highest risk since it is often very difficult to predict consumer reaction. Often, market research will be unreliable in predicting demand as people do not really understand the full benefits of the product until it is on the market and they get the chance to experience them. Furthermore, it may take time for the products to be accepted. For example, the Sony Walkman was initially rejected by marketing research since the concept of being seen in a public place wearing earphones was alien to most people. After launch, however, this behaviour was gradually accepted by younger age groups, who valued the benefit of listening to music when on a train or bus, walking down the street, and so on. At the other extreme, adding a brand variation to an existing product line lacks significant risk but is also unlikely to proffer significant returns.

Effective new product development is based on creating and nurturing an innovative culture, organizing effectively for new product development and managing the new product development process. We shall now examine these three issues.

Creating and Nurturing an Innovative Culture

The foundation for successful new product development is the creation of a corporate culture that promotes and rewards innovation. Unfortunately many marketing managers regard their company's corporate culture as a key constraint to innovation.[10] Managers, therefore, need to pay more attention to creating a culture that encourages innovation. Figure 12.1 shows the kinds of attitudes and actions that can foster an innovative culture. People in organizations observe those actions that are likely to lead to success or punishment. The surest way to kill innovative spirit is to conspicuously punish those people who are prepared to create and champion new product ideas through to communication when things go wrong, and to reward those people who are content to manage the status quo. Such actions will breed the attitude 'Why should I take the risk of failing when by carrying on as before I will probably be rewarded?' Research has shown that those companies that have supportive attitudes to rewards and risk, and a tolerant attitude towards failure, are more likely to innovate successfully.[11] Read Marketing in Action 12.1 to find out more.

An innovation culture can also be nurtured by senior management visibly supporting new product development in general, and high-profile projects in particular.[12] British Rail's attempt to develop the ill-fated Advanced Passenger Train (APT), which involved new technology, was hampered by the lack of this kind of support. Consequently, individual managers took a subjective view on whether they were for or against the project. Beside sending clear messages about the role and importance of new product development, senior management should reinforce their words by allowing time off from their usual duties to people who wish to develop their own ideas, make available funds and resources for projects, and make themselves accessible when difficult decisions need to be taken.[13]

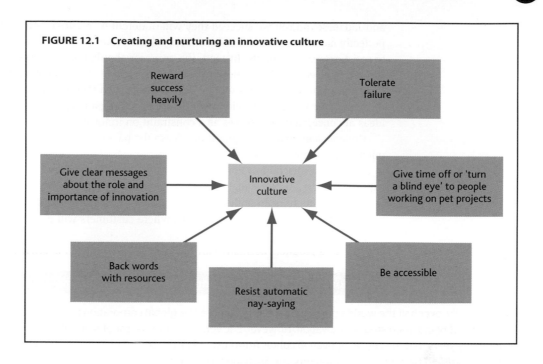

FIGURE 12.1 Creating and nurturing an innovative culture

Marketing in Action 12.1 Investing in Innovation at 3M

3M produces innovative products for many different industrial sectors, from healthcare to transport. With over $30 billion in global sales and operations in more than 65 countries the company has had a constant stream of innovation in its hundred-year history. Innovations which have helped the company grow are: waterproof sandpaper, Scotch pressure-sensitive tape, Cellophane tape, Scotchgard fabric protector, Post-it notes, Privacy Plus filter, optical film for LCD televisions and Scotch-Brite cleaning products. Indeed, there are over 55,000 products in the company's portfolio.

3M has an innovative culture, set in place by former CEO William McKnight. He believed that if the company was going to continue to grow and make the innovative products then it needed to employ the right employees and then give them freedom to explore and to get things wrong. 3M has a programme known as the '15 Percent Time', which allows employees to use part of their time at work to develop their own ideas and, although it may take years to bear fruit, the results of this programme have been some of the company's most innovative products, including the Scotch® Brand Tapes, Post-it® Notes, Scotchgard™ Fabric Protector and silicon adhesive systems for transdermal drug delivery.

Innovation development is well organized across the world. 3M has a global science and technical community which fosters a culture of cooperation, communication and cross-pollination of ideas. There are rewards for innovators and scientists and managers alike can progress up the career ladder. 3M also invests in supporting education and development beyond the walls of the business in order to promote industry standards and develop national workforces.

Based on: 3M (2012);[14] Kovacs (2012)[15]

Google also supports new product development, allowing employees 20 per cent of their work time to spend on individual projects. Gmail, Google News and Google+ are three products that have resulted.[16]

Finally, management at all levels should resist the temptation of automatic 'nay-saying'. Whenever a new idea is suggested the tendency of the listener is to think of the negatives. For example, when Nokia made a move into mobile phones from heavy industrial manufacturing just imagine what the management might have said. 'We know nothing about the mobile phone business', 'We are not strong enough to compete against the Americans and Japanese' and 'If we succeed they will undercut us on price.' All these might have been perfectly natural responses but would only demotivate the proposer. The correct response is to resist expressing doubts. Instead, the proposer should be encouraged to take the idea further, to research and develop it (which is obviously what happened in this case). This does not mean that all ideas will be developed as each will be scrutinized and have to pass through many stages of development before becoming a reality. The point is that stifling new ideas at conception only serves as a constraint on innovation.

Creative leadership is required to release the passions, imagination and energy needed for outstanding innovation. Such leadership encourages staff to reject the status quo and operate in a productive discomfort zone, has a clear vision of the future, provides support for exploration (e.g. Apple, Google, General Electric, Toyota).

Arguably, there is an underlying assumption that all innovation by commercial, profit-based businesses is for affluent markets, where customers will eventually pay for the

Mini Case 12.1 Frugal Innovations: From Clay Fridges to Cardboard Splints

Historically, over half the world's population has been ignored by global corporations as a segment capable of being interested in innovation. However, Eric von Hippel, professor of technological innovation, has argued for many years that the key to innovation comes from customers, not corporate thinking and everyone has *needs* which can be satisfied by new products and services. Sustained global recession has affected many areas of business, and governments around the world have taken to using austerity as a watchword for managing national and regional affairs. This shift in emphasis has profound implications for marketers. For example, the engineers in India won the day with the Tata Nano when Renault-Nissan asked its engineers in France, India and Japan to come up with some cost-saving ideas. The Haier Group, a Chinese consumer electronic manufacturer, has undercut western competitors by producing goods from air conditioners and washing machines to wine coolers, often at half the cost. The result has been that Haier has taken significant percentages of US and European markets. However, the shift towards frugal innovation is more far-reaching than just producing goods for western markets more cheaply. According to Pralad and Mashelkar, a form of new product development, called *frugal innovations* or *reverse innovations*, are those which are specifically engineered to meet the needs of developing countries.

In the developing world there are various champions of frugal innovations, such as Anil Gupta who is an academic at one of India's top business schools, the Indian Institute of Management, and is a champion of individuals who are deemed to be 'knowledge-rich yet economically poor'. Anil believes that there is a solution to world poverty but it requires a different approach: a bottom-up one. He established the Honey Bee Network in the 1980s with the aim of nurturing innovation, knowledge and creativity at a grassroots level. This initiative has led to the development of a village-to-government approach towards innovation. There are *innovation* scouts who go to rural villages in India looking for potential products to develop. Mansukhbhai Prajapati is an example of a successful entrepreneur who has emerged out of this initiative. He developed the Mitti cool brands which includes clay pans, pressure cookers and non-electric refrigerators which are making a difference to local communities' health through better-kept and better-cooked food.

Jugaad is an example of a company that began creating products from recycled material in 1997 through a Delhi-based children's home, which organized work for disadvantaged children. '*Jugaad*' is a unique Hindi word which refers to the practice of getting required results by using whatever limited resources are available. People Tree (a retailer) provided outlets and supported Jugaad until it became an independent brand in 2004. This creative manufacturer now provides employment, training and helps its workforce to become independent entrepreneurs.

The Tata Nano may not have changed the world, but frugal innovation will!

Questions:

1   What are 'frugal' innovations and how might they change the world?
2   If you work for a large multi-national, how would you incorporate frugal innovations into your marketing strategy?

Based on: Day (2012);[17] The Economist (2012);[18] Jugaad (2012);[19] Kadri (2010);[20] Duggan (2012);[21] Honey Bee (2012);[22] Prahalad and Mashelkar (2010)[23]

research, development and marketing of new products and deliver surplus profits by paying high prices for such goods and services. On the one hand, perhaps this is a reasonable assumption as over half the world's population survives on less than 2.50 dollars a day and therefore are deemed to be uninterested in or unable to purchase innovative products.[24] On the other hand, is it a classic example of marketing myopia as suggested by Theodore Levitt in the 1960s,[25] whereby companies are short-sighted about growth opportunities in the market? Read Mini Case 12.1 to find out more about how a shift towards frugal innovation is creating innovative products for billions of underserved consumers.

Organizing Effectively for New Product Development

The second building block of successful innovation is an appropriate organization structure. Most companies use one or a combination of the following methods: project teams, product and brand managers, new product departments and new product committees. Read Marketing in Action 12.2 to find out more about how Toyota manages innovation.

Project teams

Project teams involve the bringing together of staff from such areas as R&D, engineering, manufacturing, finance and marketing to work on a new product development project. Research has shown that assigning the responsibility of new product development to such cross-functional teams has a positive effect on new product performance.[26] Specialized skills are combined to form an effective team to develop the new product concept. Furthermore, if the members of the team remain stable for the duration of a project there is greater potential to: foster better decision-making; engender shared responsibility; leverage advantage from the collective expertise. Ultimately, this approach helps develop better new product advantage. Working together in stable teams can also help to avoid 'tunnel vision and inflexibility in problem solving' up to a certain point.

Slotegraaf and Atuahene-Gima (2011)[27] discuss how stable teams benefit from better decision-making. However, a key challenge associated with developing a new product is that innovation requires the conversion of knowledge into something tangible, and the stability of a product team can help the process. However, there is a certain point where the benefits begin to diminish. So, long-term stability beyond a particular project may be less successful. GE, 3M, Google and many of today's large corporations support their staff in working together to develop future products.

Marketing in Action 12.2 Toyota Leading the Way in Sustainable Mobility

Toyota is a company which prides itself on being innovative. In 1997 it launched the Prius, a car which uses a combination of petrol and electricity. This car has become the world's best-selling hybrid vehicle and makes use of cutting-edge *green* technology. Toyota's approach towards organization has influenced management thinking for many decades. The company attributes its success to commitment to quality, innovation, aspiring to exceed expectations and smiling! Toyota has devised a tree metaphor to symbolize its vision of 'roots to fruits'. The tree was chosen as it represents natural strength, longevity, growth and ongoing development.

More specifically, the roots represent Toyota's management principles, which are driven by the belief that everything should grow from a good foundation. The roots support the trunk of the tree, which signifies the strength and stability of the organization's operations. 'From the trunk, the branches lead to the 12 tenets that make up the Toyota vision—the "fruits" of the tree. The tree allows all of this imagery to be connected together, a metaphor for how closely we at Toyota work together to achieve success'.

The final and perhaps most important element of the Toyota metaphor is the physical environment, which represents the importance of Toyota's customers and the planet.

Product and brand managers

Product and brand management entails the assignment of product managers to product lines (or groups of brands within a product line) and/or brand managers to individual brands. These managers are then responsible for their success and have the task of coordinating functional areas (e.g. production, sales, advertising and marketing research). They are also often responsible for new product development, including the creation of new product ideas, improving existing products and brand extensions. They may be supported by a team of assistant brand managers and a dedicated marketing researcher. In some companies a new product development manager may help product and brand managers in the task of generating and testing new product concepts. This form of organization is common in the high-volume, relatively low-value products such as groceries, toiletries and the drinks industries.

New product departments and committees

The review of new product projects is normally in the hands of high-ranking functional managers, who listen to progress reports and decide whether further funds should be assigned to a project. They may also be charged with deciding new product strategies and priorities. No matter whether the underlying structure is venture team, product and brand management or new product department, a new products committee often oversees the process and services to give projects a high corporate profile through the stature of its membership.

The importance of teamwork

Whichever method (or combination of methods) is used, effective cross-functional teamwork is crucial for success[28] and there has to be effective communication and teamwork between R&D and marketing.[29] Although all functional relationships are important during new product development, the cultural differences between R&D and marketing are potentially the most harmful and difficult to resolve. The challenge is to prevent technical people developing only things that interest them professionally, and to get them to understand the realities of the marketplace.

The role of marketing directors

A study by Gupta and Wileman asked marketing directors of technology-based companies what they believed they could do to improve their relationship with R&D and achieve greater integration of effort.[30] Six major suggestions were made by the marketing directors.

1 *Encourage teamwork*: marketing should work with R&D to establish clear, mutually agreed project priorities to reduce the incidence of pet projects. Marketing, R&D and senior management should hold regular joint project review meetings.

2 *Improve the provision of marketing information to R&D*: one of the major causes of R&D rejecting input from marketing was the lack of quality and timely information. Many marketing directors admitted that they could do a better job of providing such information to R&D. They also believed that the use of information would be enhanced if R&D personnel were made part of the marketing research team so that the questions on their minds could be incorporated into studies. They also felt that such a move would improve the credibility and trust between marketing and R&D.

3 *Take R&D people out of the lab*: marketing should encourage R&D staff to be more customer aware by inviting them to attend trade shows, take part in customer visits and prepare customer materials.

4 *Develop informal relationships with R&D*: they noted that there were often important personality and value differences between the two groups, which could cause conflict as well as being a stimulus to creativity. More effort could be made to break down these barriers by greater socializing, going to lunch together, and sitting with each other at seminars and presentations.

5 *Learn about technology*: the marketing directors believed that improving their 'technological savvy' would help them communicate more effectively with R&D people, understand

various product design trade-offs, and comprehend the capabilities and limits of technology to create competitive advantages and provide solutions to customer problems.

6 *Formalize the product development process*: they noted that marketing people were often preoccupied with present products to the neglect of new products, and that the new product development process was far too unstructured. They advocated a more formal process, including formal new project initiation, status reports and review procedures, and a formal requirement that involvement in the process was an important part of marketing personnel's jobs.

The role of senior management

The study also focused on marketing directors' opinions of what senior management could do to help improve the marketing/R&D relationship. We have already noted, when discussing how to create an innovative culture, the crucial role that senior management staff play in creating the conditions for a thriving new product programme. Marketing directors mentioned six major ways in which senior management could play a part in fostering better relations.

1 *Make organizational design changes*: senior management should locate marketing and R&D near to each other to encourage communication and the development of informal relationships. They should clarify the roles of marketing and R&D in developing new products and reduce the number of approvals required for small changes in a project, which would give both R&D and marketing greater authority and responsibility.

2 *Show a personal interest in new product development*: organizational design changes should be backed up by more overt commitment and interest in innovation through early involvement in the product development process, attending product planning and review meetings, and helping to coordinate product development plans.

3 *Provide strategic direction*: many marketing directors felt that senior management could provide more strategic vision regarding new product/market priorities. They also needed to be more long term with their strategic thinking.

4 *Encourage teamwork*: senior management should encourage, or even demand, teamwork between marketing and R&D. Specifically, they should require joint R&D/marketing discussions, joint planning and budgeting, joint marketing research and joint reporting to them.

5 *Increase resources*: *some* marketing directors pointed to the need to increase resources to foster product development activities. The alternative was to reduce the number of projects. Resources should also be provided for seminars, workshops and training programmes for R&D and marketing people. The objective of these programmes would be to develop a better understanding of the roles, constraints and pressures of each group.

6 *Understand marketing's importance*: marketing directors complained of senior management's lack of understanding of marketing's role in new product development and the value of marketing in general. They felt that senior management should insist that marketing becomes involved with R&D in product development much earlier in the process so that the needs of customers are more prominent.

This research has provided valuable insights into how companies should manage the marketing/R&D relationship. It is important that companies organize themselves effectively since cross-functional teamwork and communication has proved to be a significant predictor of successful innovation in a number of studies.[31]

Managing the New Product Development Process

There are three inescapable facts about new product development: it is expensive, risky, and time-consuming. For example, Gillette spent in excess of £100 million over more than 10 years developing its Sensor razor brand. The new product concept was to develop a non-disposable shaver that would use new technology to produce a shaver that would follow the contours of a man's face, giving an excellent shave (through two spring-mounted, platinum-hardened, chromium blades) with fewer cuts. This made commercial sense since shaving systems are more profitable than disposable razors and allow more opportunity for creating a differential advantage. Had the brand failed, Gillette's position in the shaving market could have been damaged irreparably. Nike is another company that invests heavily in new product development to maintain its lead in the specialist sports shoe market.

Managing the process of new product development is an important factor in reducing cost, time and risk. Studies have shown that having a formal process with review points, clear new product goals and a strong marketing orientation underlying the process leads to greater success whether the product is a physical good or a service.[32]

An eight-step new product development process to provide these characteristics is shown in Figure 12.2 and consists of setting new product strategy, idea generation, screening, concept testing, business analysis, product development, market testing and commercialization. Although the reality of new product development may resemble organizational chaos, the discipline imposed by the activities carried out at each stage leads to a greater likelihood of developing a product that not only works, but also confers customer benefits. We should note, however, that new products pass through each stage at varying speeds: some may dwell at a stage for a long period while others may pass through very quickly.[33]

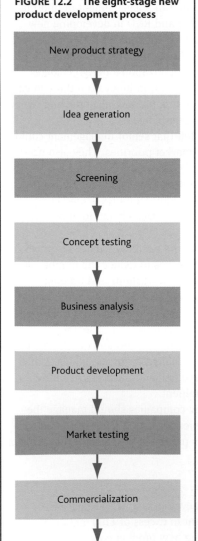

FIGURE 12.2   The eight-stage new product development process

New product strategy

Idea generation

Screening

Concept testing

Business analysis

Product development

Market testing

Commercialization

New products

New product strategy

As we have already seen, marketing directors value strategic guidance from senior management about their vision and priorities for new product development. By providing clear guidelines about which products/markets the company is interested in serving, senior management staff can provide a focus for the areas in which idea generation should take place. Also, by outlining their objectives (e.g. market share gain, profitability, technological leadership) for new products they can provide indicators for the screening criteria that should be used to evaluate those ideas. A key issue in new product strategy is where to allocate resources. A company may have several divisions and a multitude of product lines. Where should funds be invested? Marketing in Action 12.3 discusses how Hewlett-Packard tackles this question.

Idea generation

One of the benefits of developing an innovative corporate culture is that it sparks the imagination. The objective is to motivate the search for ideas so that salespeople, engineers, top management, marketers and other employees are all alert to new opportunities. Interestingly, questioning Nobel Prize winners about the time and circumstances when they had the important germ of an idea that led them to great scientific discovery revealed that it can occur at the most unexpected time: just before going to sleep, on waking up in the morning, at a place of worship. The common factor seems to be a period of quiet contemplation, uninterrupted by the bustle of everyday life and work.

Successful new product ideas are not necessarily based on technological innovation. Often they are based on novel applications of existing technology (e.g. Velcro poppers on disposable nappies). The iPhone created a need for a place to buy 'portable music' which led to the development of the iTunes store. The novelty in this case is that, unlike its competitors, LimeWire and Napster, the iTunes store legally sells copyright music.

Marketing in Action 12.3 Investing in New Product Development the Hewlett-Packard Way

For many years business leaders have tried to grapple with the question of how much money to invest in R&D when the payoff could take 10 years. Even more vexing is the problem of where to allocate scarce funds. Many expert observers believe that Hewlett-Packard has produced the gold standard for resource allocation.

HP's method is simplicity itself. It uses a metric called 'R&D productivity'. It measures R&D spending as a percentage of gross margin for each product line. A standard desktop computer with low margins would normally get a low allocation of funds, perhaps leading to one or two innovative features. A high-end laptop with fat margins would get a high allocation, leading to enough innovative features to differentiate it from its rivals.

To determine the appropriate R&D level, HP calculates three-year projections of expected gross margins. Where it sees an opportunity to raise margins, investment funds follow. For example, HP saw an opportunity for a premium-priced desktop computer with touchscreen technology. It believed that such a feature would make a desktop easier for families with children to use. The result was R&D investment that led to the first touchscreen, all-in-one desktop. The TouchSmart PC, which is sold in the USA for $2000, has helped boost HP's profits and sales.

HP allocates a bigger percentage of its overall budget to game-changing types of technologies—such as multitouch technology and gesture-based controls, which allow users to point at their computers to launch a music or photo program—that create differentiation and lead to high gross profit margins. By linking R&D expenditure to current and projected gross margins, HP has developed one of the most quantitative approaches to new product development budget allocation in the world.

Based on: Edwards (2008);[34] Edwards (2009)[35]

The sources of new product ideas can be internal to the company: scientists, engineers, marketers, salespeople and designers (as at 3M). Some companies use **brainstorming** as a technique to stimulate the creation of ideas, and use financial incentives to persuade people to put forward the ideas they have had. At Royal Dutch Shell, virtual teams meet via the Internet to share ideas. These sessions have generated many ideas for ways to reduce paperwork to using sophisticated laser sensors to find oil.[36]

Hamel and Prahalad's prediction—that global competitive battles will be won by those companies that have the corporate imagination to build and dominate fundamentally new markets[37]—has been proved right especially in high-tech markets.

Often fundamentally new products/markets are created by small businesses that are willing to invent new business models or radically redesign existing models. Sources of new product ideas can also be external to the company. Examining competitors' products may provide clues to product improvements. Competitors' new product plans can be gleaned by training the salesforce to ask distributors about new activities. Distributors can also be a source of new product ideas directly, since they deal with customers and have an interest in selling improved products.

Another source of externally generated new product ideas is the millions of scientists, engineers and other companies globally. By collaborating with them, a firm can gain access to innovative solutions. Procter & Gamble leads the way by using online networks to get in touch with thousands of experts, as Digital Marketing 12.1 explains.

A major source of good ideas is consumers themselves. Their needs may not be satisfied by existing products and they may be genuinely interested in providing ideas that lead to product improvement. Sometimes traditional marketing research techniques such as focus groups can be useful. Researching blogs and online social community sites can reveal ideas for new products, and insights into the strengths and weaknesses of existing products, which can lead to improved product replacements.

Digital Marketing 12.1 Connect + Develop

Anyone anywhere can connect with Procter & Gamble through the Web and share ideas. Procter & Gamble taps in to a vast well of expertise through its Connect + Develop programme. It practises open innovation, which is a means of accessing externally developed intellectual property, while allowing its internally developed assets and know-how to be used by others. This two-way process has led to innovation in such areas as technology, engineering, marketing, packaging, design and business services.

Bounce, the world's first dryer-aided softener was created by an independent Canadian inventor. By working together, this innovative product was patented and licensed and sold throughout the world. The Internet has enabled the creation of Connect + Develop hubs joining together innovators as far and wide as China, Japan, Europe, North and South America.

The consumer is at the heart of innovation, and Bruce Brown, Chief Technology Officer for P&G, invites all innovators to submit their ideas. Through Connect + Develop, P&G actively seeks collaboration with external partners to generate and develop new product ideas. As Nabil Sakkab, global leader of its fabric and homecare research and development, commented, 'I pay 7000 scientists to work for me at P&G but there are 1.5 million scientists out there who do not work for P&G. I want to make my R&D department 1,507,000 strong.' This attempt to 'unsource' ideas is working: 45 per cent of the new ideas he is working on have come from outside the company. Across P&G as a whole external collaboration plays a key role in nearly 50 per cent of its products.

An example is the launch of Pringle Prints in North America. The product is a line of potato crisps printed with entertaining pictures and words, and was developed in record time and at a fraction of the usual cost. Instead of looking internally for solutions to the problem of how to print images on crisps, P&G searched its global networks of individuals and institutions. It discovered a small bakery in Italy, owned by a university professor who had invented an ink-jet method of printing edible images on cakes and biscuits. P&G adapted the method for crisps and the result was double-digit growth for its North American Pringles business.

Based on: Procter & Gamble (2012);[38] Huston and Sakkab (2006);[39] Mitchell (2005)[40]

Other companies require a less traditional approach. Procter & Gamble, for example, has used ethnographic research to observe consumers using its products, in order to develop new and improved products. Philips employs anthropologists and cognitive psychologists to gather insights into the needs and expectations of consumers around the world. It conducts 'culture scan' research into shorter-term social, cultural and aesthetic trends, and 'strategic futures' research into trends over a five- to seven-year period. The findings play a major role in which products should be brought to market and how they should be designed.[41]

In organizational markets, keeping in close contact with customers who are innovators and market leaders in their own marketplace is likely to be a fruitful source of new product ideas.[42] These *lead customers* are likely to recognize required improvements ahead of other customers as they have advanced needs and are likely to face problems before other product users. For example, GE's healthcare division researches 'luminaries', who tend to be well-published doctors and research scientists from leading medical institutions. Up to 25 luminaries are brought together at regular medical advisory board sessions to discuss developments in GE's technology. GE then shares some of its advanced technology with a subset of these people. The result is a stream of new products that emerge from collaboration with these groups. Marketing research can play a role in providing feedback when the product line is familiar to customers. For example, the original idea for Hewlett-Packard's successful launch of its Desk-Jet printer came from marketing research, which revealed that personal computer users would value a relatively slow-speed printer that approached the quality of a laser printer but sold at less than half the price.[43] However, for radically new products customers may be unable to articulate their requirements and so conventional marketing research may be ineffective as a source of ideas. In this situation, as can be seen in Marketing in Action 12.4, companies need to be proactive in their search for new markets rather than rely on customer suggestions.[44]

Go to the website and compare approaches used by Diet Coke, Philadelphia Cheese and Kenco Coffee to commercialize product innovation.
www.mcgraw-hill.co.uk/ textbooks/jobber

Marketing in Action 12.4 **Creating Radical Innovation**

Many new products are incremental, such as Diet Coke from Coca-Cola or Persil detergent tablets from Unilever; others fundamentally change the nature of a market and may be based on technological breakthroughs such as the development of mobile phones or the invention of new business models such as Dell selling customized computers direct to consumers or Starbucks' reinvention of city-centre coffee drinking. Radical innovation is risky but can bring huge rewards, creating new markets and destroying old ones. The focus is on making the competition irrelevant by creating a leap in value for customers, and entry into new and uncontested market space.

Avoiding an incremental approach to new product development involves a sharpening of the corporate imagination to become more alive to new market opportunities. Five factors can aid this development.

1   *Escaping the tyranny of served markets*: looking outside markets that are currently served can be assisted by defining core competences and looking at products/markets that lie between existing business units. For example, Motorola's core competences in wireless technology led it to look beyond current products/markets (e.g. mobile phones) and towards global positioning satellite receivers. Looking for white space between business units led Kodak to envisage a market for storing and viewing photographs.

2   *Searching for innovative product concepts*: this can be aided by viewing markets as a set of customer needs and product functionalities. This has led to adding an important function to an existing product (e.g. Yamaha's electronic piano), creating a new way to deliver an existing function (e.g. electronic notepads), or creating a new functionality (e.g. the Internet).

3   *Weakening traditional price–performance assumptions*: traditional price–performance assumptions should be questioned. For example, it was Sony and JVC that questioned the price tag of £25,000 on early video recorders. They gave their engineers the freedom and the technology to design a video recorder that cost less than £500.

4   *Leading customers*: a problem with developing truly innovative products is that customers rarely ask for them. Successful innovating companies lead customers by imagining unarticulated needs rather than simply following them. They gain insights into incipient needs by talking in-depth to and observing closely a market's most sophisticated and demanding customers. For example, Yamaha set up a facility in London where Europe's most talented musicians could experiment with state-of-the-art musical hardware. The objective was not only to understand the customer but also to convey to the customer what might be possible technologically.

5   *Building a radical innovation hub*: a hub is a group of people who encourage and oversee innovation. It includes idea hunters, idea gatherers, internal venture capitalists, members of project evaluation committees, members of overseeing boards and experienced entrepreneurs. The hub's prime function is to nurture hunters and gatherers from all over the company to foster a stream of innovative ideas. At the centre of each project is a product champion who takes risks, breaks the rules, energizes and rescues, and re-energizes the project.

The attitudes and practices within innovative firms are also important and help create a culture that assists in driving radical innovation. Attitudes include a tolerance for risk-taking and a future market focus that encourages managers to seek customer needs through strategic futures research. Key practices are the empowerment of product champions, which encourages them (supported by resources) to explore research and build on promising, but uncertain, future technologies, and the use of generous financial and non-financial (e.g. recognition and autonomy) rewards for innovative employees.

Based on: Moosmayer et al. (2011);[45] Hamel and Prahalad (1991);[46] Hamel (1999);[47] Leifer et al. (2001);[48] Hunt (2002);[49] Bartram (2004);[50] Tellis et al. (2009)[51]

Screening

Having developed new product ideas, they need to be screened to evaluate their commercial worth. Some companies use formal checklists to help them judge whether the product idea should be rejected or accepted for further evaluation. This ensures that no important criterion is overlooked. Criteria may be used that measure the attractiveness of the market for the proposed product, the fit between the product and company objectives, and the capability of the company to produce and market the product.

Concept testing

Once the product idea has been accepted as worthy of further investigation, it can be framed into a specific concept for testing with potential customers. In many instances the basic product idea will be expanded into several product concepts, each of which can be compared by testing with target customers. For example, a study into the acceptability of a new service—a proposed audit of software development procedures that would lead to the award of a quality assurance certificate—was expressed in eight service concepts depending on which parts of the development procedure would be audited (e.g. understanding customer needs, documentation, benchmarking, and so on). Each concept was evaluated by potential buyers of the software to gauge which were the most important aspects of software development that should be audited.[52] **Concept testing** thus allows the views of customers to enter the new product development process at an early stage.

Group discussion can also be used to develop and test product concepts. The concept may be described verbally or pictorially so that the major features are understood. Potential customers can then state whether they perceive any benefits accruing from the features. A questionnaire is used to ascertain the extent of liking/disliking what is liked/disliked, the kind of person/organization that might buy the product, how/where/when/how often the product would be used, its price acceptability, and how likely they would be to buy the product.

Online marketing research is being used increasingly to test concepts, partly because of its relatively low cost. Companies such as Lego, BA, Philips, O_2 and P&G have set up their own community websites where they can test consumers' reactions to new product concepts. Online images as well as words can be used to describe the new concepts. Firms without their own community sites use research agencies such as YouGov and Toluna, which specialize in conducting online research and have access to panels that can be used to test new concepts.[53]

Considerable ingenuity is needed to research new concepts. For example, research into a new tea shop/tea bar concept avoided the mistake of asking people about it 'cold' (unprepared). This would have resulted in consumers saying negative things like 'only grannies like tea shops' or 'tea isn't fashionable like coffee is'. Instead, in order to establish the tea bar concept as contemporary in feel, a cuttings file of 'articles' about it in fashionable areas such as Soho and Brighton was produced and shown to participants before the market research session took place. Because they felt that the tea bar chain was already up and running and that it was contemporary, the participants became very enthusiastic about it. The research had successfully conveyed the correct concept to the participants and, therefore, their responses were more valid than if they had been asked about their reaction to the concept without the associated image.[54]

This example illustrates the use of a scenario to help the participant in the research visualize the new product concept. The scenario method is of particular use when researching radical innovation concepts that, if launched, produce new-to-the-world products. Traditional marketing research methods rely on asking target consumers what they want, or asking them to rate the attractiveness of new product concepts. This can lead to less radical innovations being favoured because of the concept of *functional fixedness*, which is the tendency for people to evaluate new products in terms of what they already know. New products are evaluated by consumers in terms of already existing products and technologies rather than considering their needs in future situations. This can lead consumers to favour conventional new product concepts that are most likely the ones they already know.

The scenario method overcomes this problem by describing the new product in the context of a future technological and market setting. Usually a short story is told in which a potential consumer uses the new product in a future setting. The scenario can also be accompanied by visual material that shows various design features of the product and its future environment. By portraying the new product concept in a new environment, scenarios help consumers to evaluate new products outside the usage situations that are familiar to them, and encourage them to imagine what it would be like to use the product portrayed. The result is that judgements of radical innovations are less likely to suffer from the consumer's normal frame of reference, on the basis of which more conservative options are usually favoured.[55]

Often the last question (buying intentions) is a key factor in judging whether any of the concepts are worth pursuing further. In the grocery and toiletries industries, for example, companies (and their marketing research agencies) often use *action standards* (e.g. more than 70 per cent of respondents must say they intend to buy) based on past experience to judge new product concepts. Concept testing allows a relatively inexpensive judgement to be made by customers before embarking on a costly product development programme. Although not foolproof, obvious non-starters can be eliminated early on in the process.

Business analysis

Based on the results of the concept test and considerable managerial judgement, estimates of sales, costs and profits will be made. This is the **business analysis** stage. In order to produce sensible figures a marketing analysis will need to be undertaken. This will identify the target market, its size and projected product acceptance over a number of years. Consideration will be given to various prices and the implications for sales revenue (and profits) discussed. By setting a tentative price this analysis will provide sales revenue estimates.

Costs will also need to be estimated. If the new product is similar to existing products (e.g. a brand extension) it should be fairly easy to produce accurate cost estimates. For radical product concepts, costings may be nothing more than informal 'guesstimates'.

Break-even analysis, where the quantity needed to be sold to cover costs is calculated, may be used to establish whether the project is financially feasible. *Sensitivity analysis*, in which variations from given assumptions about price, cost and customer acceptance, for example, are checked to see how they impact on sales revenue and profits, can also prove useful at this stage. Optimistic, most likely and pessimistic scenarios can be drawn up to estimate the degree of risk attached to the project.

If the product concept appears commercially feasible, this process will result in marketing and product development budgets being established based on what appears to be necessary to gain customer awareness and trial, and the work required to turn the concept into a marketable product.

Read Digital Marketing 12.2 to find out how 3D printers can turn ideas into reality.

Product development

At this stage the new product concept is developed into a physical product. As we have seen, the trend is to move from a situation where this is the sole responsibility of the R&D and/or engineering department. Multi-disciplinary project teams are established with the task of bringing the product to the marketplace. A study by Wheelwright and Clark lays out six key principles for the effective management of such teams.[56]

1 *Mission*: senior management must agree to a clear mission through a project charter that lays out broad objectives.
2 *Organization*: the appointment of a heavyweight project leader and a core team consisting of one member from each primary function in the company. Core members should not occupy a similar position on another team.
3 *Project plan*: creation by the project leader and core team of a contract book, which includes a work plan, resource requirements and objectives against which it is willing to be evaluated.
4 *Project leadership*: heavyweight leaders not only lead, manage and evaluate other members of the core team, they also act as product champions. They spend time talking to project contributors inside and outside the company, as well as customers and distributors, so that the team keeps in touch with the market.

Digital Marketing 12.2 3D Printers

3D technology is now commercially available. Televisions, games and cameras offer the opportunity to see images in a new dimension. Globally, it is estimated by 2016 the market for 3D technology will be in the region of nearly $230 billion. Gaming and animation is expected to dominate the market. However, perhaps the most radical 3D innovation to date is the 3D printer: manufacturing on your desktop. 3D printers create the images from computer screens just like the one you can see in the image. A three-dimensional form can be created layer by layer. According to Lisa Harouni, we are about to witness 'an industrial revolution in the digital age'. This type of technology is not new. It has been around for about 20 years but it is only now that the bespoke products built on demand are beginning to find a niche (but growing) market. There are advantages to this form of bespoke manufacturing: it is very localized and significantly reduces carbon footprints and there is less waste too.

Currently, this technology is only being used in very limited ways—for example, to produce body parts and medical devices, but it is more efficient and significantly lower in price than the methods used previously. So, in the future we may be able to download physical goods like car parts, phone covers and even chocolates in a similar way to which we download music, software and movies today.

Based on: Rowan (2011)[57]

5 *Responsibilities*: all core members share responsibility for the overall success of the project as well as their own functional responsibilities.

6 *Executive sponsorship*: an executive sponsor in senior management is required to act as a channel for communication with top management and to act as coach and mentor for the project and its leader.

The aim is to integrate the skills of designers, engineers, production, finance and marketing specialists so that product development is quicker, less costly and results in a high-quality product that delights customers. For example, the practice of **simultaneous engineering** means that designers and production engineers work together rather than passing the project from one stage of development to another once the first department's work is finished. Costs are controlled by a method called *target costing*. Target costs are worked out on the basis of target prices in the marketplace, and given as engineering/design and production targets.

Cutting time to market by reducing the length of the product development stage is a key marketing factor in many industries. This process, known as *virtual engineering*, has been used by Fiat, which, when designing its Bravo and 500, chose to rely solely on computer simulations rather than take the traditional route of making prototypes. This cut design-to-production time from 26 to 18 months.[58] In addition, three-dimensional CAD system designs can be shared with suppliers and customers. For example, Boeing engages customers such as British Airways and United Airlines in an online design process that allows them to engage in debates over alternative cabin layouts.

There are two reasons why product development is being accelerated. First, markets such as personal computers, digital cameras, laptops and cars change so fast that to be slow means running the risk of being out of date before the product is launched. Second, cutting time to market can lead to competitive advantage. This may be short-lived but is still valuable while it lasts. For example, Zara: being consistently the fastest to market gives it a competitive advantage in the fashion industry.

Marketing has an important role to play in the product development stage. R&D and engineering may focus on the functional aspects of the product, whereas seemingly trivial factors may have an important bearing on customer choice. For example, the foam that appears when washing-up liquid is added to water has no functional value: a washing-up liquid could be produced that cleans just as effectively but does not produce bubbles. However, the customer sees the foam as a visual cue that indicates the power of the washing-up liquid. Therefore, to market a brand that did not produce bubbles would have a negative outcome. Marketing needs to keep the project team aware of such psychological factors when developing the new product. Marketing staff need to make sure that the project team members understand and communicate the important attributes that customers are looking for in the product.

In the grocery market, marketing will usually brief R&D staff on the product concept, and the latter will be charged with the job of turning the concept into reality. For example, Yoplait, the French market leader in fruit yoghurts, found through marketing research that a yoghurt concept based on the following attributes could be a winner:

- top-of-the-range dessert
- position on a health–leisure scale at the far end of the pleasure range—the ultimate taste sensation
- a fruit yoghurt that is extremely thick and creamy.

This was the brief given to the Yoplait research and development team that had the task of coming up with recipes for the new yoghurt and the best way of manufacturing it. Its job was to experiment with different cream/fruit combinations to produce the right product—one that matched the product concept—and to do it quickly. Time to market was crucial in this fast-moving industry. To help them, Yoplait employed a panel of expert tasters to try out the new recipes and evaluate them in terms of texture, sweetness, acidity, colour, smell, consistency and size of the fruit.

Product testing focuses on the functional aspects of the product and on consumer acceptance. Functional tests are carried out in the laboratory and out in the field to check such aspects as safety, performance and shelf life. For example, a car's braking system must be efficient, a jet engine must be capable of generating a certain level of thrust and a food package must be capable of keeping its contents fresh. Product testing of software products by users is crucially important in removing any 'bugs' that have not been picked up by internal testers. For example, Google releases new products as 'betas' (unfinished versions) so that users can check for problems and suggest improvements.[59]

Digital Marketing 12.3 Beta Testing

Besides conforming to basic functional standards, products need to be tested with consumers to check acceptability in use. For consumer goods this often takes the form of in-house product placement. *Paired companion tests* are used when a new product is used alongside a rival, so that respondents have a benchmark against which to judge the new offering. Alternatively two (or more) new product variants may be tested alongside one another. A questionnaire is administered at the end of the test, which gathers overall preference information as well as comparisons on specific attributes. For example, two soups might be compared on taste, colour, smell and richness. In *monadic placement tests* only the new product is given to users for trial. Although no specific rival is used in the test, in practice users may make comparisons with previously bought products, market leaders or competitive products that are quickly making an impact on the market.

Another way of providing customer input into development is through *product clinics*. For example, prototype cars and trucks are regularly researched by inviting prospective drivers to such clinics where they can sit in the vehicle, and comment on its design, comfort and proposed features. In organizational markets, products may be placed with customers free of charge or at below cost to check out the performance characteristics.

Market testing

So far in the development process, potential customers have been asked if they intend to buy the product but have never been placed in the position of having to pay for it. **Market testing** takes measurement of customer acceptance one crucial step further than product testing by forcing consumers to 'put their money where their mouth is'. The basic idea is to launch the new product in a limited way so that consumer response in the marketplace can be assessed. Two major methods are used: the simulated market test and test marketing.

The *simulated market test* can take a number of forms, but the principle is to set up a realistic market situation in which a sample of consumers chooses to buy goods from a range provided by the organizing company, usually a marketing research company. For example, a sample of consumers may be recruited to buy their groceries from a mobile supermarket that visits them once a week. They are provided with a magazine in which advertisements and sales promotions for the new product can appear. This method allows measurement of key success indicators such as *penetration* (the proportion of consumers that buy the new product at least once) and *repeat purchase* (the rate at which purchasers buy again) to be made. If penetration is high but repeat purchase low, buyers can be asked why they rejected the product after trial. Simulated market tests are therefore useful as a preliminary to test marketing by spotting problems, such as in packaging and product formulation, that can be rectified before test market launch. They can also be useful in eliminating new products that perform so badly compared to competition in the marketplace that test marketing is not justified. Indeed, as techniques associated with simulated market tests become more sophisticated and distributors increasingly refuse to cooperate in test marketing, they have become an attractive alternative to a full test market.[60]

Test marketing involves the launch of the new product in one or a few geographical areas chosen to be representative of its intended market. Towns or television areas are chosen in which the new product is sold into distribution outlets so that performance can be gauged face to face with rival products. Test marketing is the acid test of new product development since the product is being promoted as it would during a national launch, and consumers are being asked to choose it against competitor products as they would if the new product went national. It is a more realistic test than the simulated market test and therefore gives more accurate sales penetration and repeat purchasing estimates. By projecting test marketing results to the full market, an assessment of the new product's likely success can be made.

Test marketing does have a number of potential problems. Test towns and areas may not be representative of the national market, and thus sales projections may be inaccurate. Competitors may invalidate the test market by giving distributors incentives to stock their product, thereby denying the new product shelf space. Also, test marketing needs to run over a long enough period to measure the repeat purchase rate for the product, since this is a crucial indicator of success for many products (e.g. groceries and toiletries). This can mean a delay in national launch stretching to many months or even years. In the meantime, more aggressive competitors can launch a rival product nationally and therefore gain market pioneer advantages. A final practical problem is gaining the cooperation of distributors. In some instances, supermarket chains refuse to take part in test marketing activities or charge a hefty fee for the service.

The advantages of test marketing are that the information it provides facilitates the 'go/no go' national launch decision, and the effectiveness of the marketing mix elements—price, product formulation/packaging, promotion and distribution—can be checked for effectiveness. Sometimes a number of test areas are used with different marketing mix combinations to predict the most successful launch strategy. Its purpose therefore is to reduce the risk of a costly and embarrassing national launch mistake.

Although commonly associated with fast-moving consumer goods, service companies use test marketing to check new service offerings. Indeed, when they control the supply chain, as is the case with banks and restaurants, they are in an ideal situation to do so. Companies selling to organizations can also benefit from test marketing when their products have short repeat purchase periods (e.g. adhesives and abrasives). For very expensive equipment, however, test marketing is usually impractical, although as we have seen product development with lead users is to be recommended.

On a global scale, many international companies roll out products (e.g. cars and consumer electronics) from one country to another. In so doing they are gaining some of the benefits of test marketing in that lessons learned early on can be applied to later launches.

Commercialization

In this section we shall examine four issues: a general approach to developing a commercialization strategy for a new product, specific options for product replacement strategies, success factors when commercializing technology, and reacting to competitors' new product introductions.

Developing a commercialization strategy for a new product

An effective commercialization strategy relies upon marketing management making clear choices regarding the target market (where it wishes to compete), and the development of a marketing strategy that provides a differential advantage (how it wishes to compete). These two factors define the new product positioning strategy, as discussed in Chapter 8.

A useful starting point for choosing a target market is an understanding of the **diffusion of innovation process**.[61] This explains how a new product spreads throughout a market over time. Particularly important is the notion that not all people or organizations who make up the market will be in the same state of readiness to buy the new product when it is launched. In other words, different actors in the market will have varying degrees of innovativeness—that is, their willingness to try something new. Figure 12.3 shows the diffusion *of innovation* curve which categorizes people or organizations according to how soon they are willing to adopt the innovation.

The curve shows that those actors (*innovators* and *early adopters*) who were willing to buy the new product soon after launch are likely to form a minor part of the total number of actors who will eventually be willing to buy it. As the new product is accepted and approved by these customers, and the decision to buy the new product therefore becomes less risky, so the people that make up the bulk of the market, comprising the *early and late majority*, begin to try the product themselves. Finally, after the product has gained full market acceptance, a group suitably described as the *laggards* adopt the product. By the time the laggards have begun buying the product, the innovators and early adopters have probably moved on to something new.

This diffusion of innovation categories has a crucial role to play in the choice of target market. The key is to understand the characteristics of the innovator and early adopter categories and target them at launch. Simply thinking about the kinds of people or organizations that are more likely to buy a new product early after launch may suffice. If not, marketing research can help. To stimulate the thinking process, Rogers suggests the following broad characteristics for each category.[62]

- *Innovators*: these are often venturesome and like to be different; they are willing to take a chance with an untried product. In consumer markets they tend to be younger, better educated, more confident

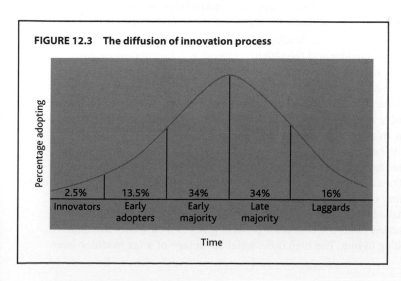

FIGURE 12.3 The diffusion of innovation process

Percentage adopting

| 2.5% | 13.5% | 34% | 34% | 16% |
| Innovators | Early adopters | Early majority | Late majority | Laggards |

Time

and more financially affluent, and consequently can afford to take a chance on buying something new. In organizational markets, they tend to be larger and more profitable companies if the innovation is costly, and have more progressive, better-educated management. They may themselves have a good track record in bringing out new products and may have been the first to adopt innovations in the past. As such they may be easy to identify.

- *Early adopters*: these are not quite so venturesome; they need the comfort of knowing someone else has taken the early risk. But they soon follow their lead. They still tend to have similar characteristics to the innovator group, since they need affluence and self-confidence to buy a product that has not yet gained market acceptance. They, together with the innovators, can be seen as opinion leaders who strongly influence other people's views on the product. As such, they have a major bearing on the success of the product. One way of looking at the early adopters is that they filter the products accepted by the innovator group and popularize them, leading to acceptance by the majority of buyers in the market.[63]

Go to the website to see how Samsung's Galaxy Nexus smartphone advert targets early adopters.
www.mcgraw-hill.co.uk/
textbooks/jobber

- *Early and late majorities*: these form the bulk of the customers in the market. The early majority are usually deliberate and cautious in their approach to buying products. They like to see products prove themselves on the market before they are willing to part with cash for them. The late majority are even more cautious, and possibly sceptical of new products. They are willing to adopt only after the majority of people or organizations have tried the products. Social pressure may be the driving force moving them to purchase.
- *Laggards*: these are tradition-bound people. The innovation needs to be perceived almost as a traditional product before they will consider buying it. In consumer markets they are often the older and less well-educated members of the population.

These categories, then, can provide a basis for segmenting the market for an innovative product (see Chapter 8) and for target market selection.[64] For example, Samsung Electronics directs much of its marketing effort towards the innovator/early adopter segments by targeting what it calls 'high-life seekers'—consumers who adopt technology early and are prepared to pay a premium price for it.[65] Note that the diffusion curve can be linked to the product life-cycle, which was discussed in Chapter 11. At introduction, innovators buy the product, followed by early adopters as the product enters the growth phase. Growth is fuelled by the early and late majority, and stable sales during the maturity phase may be due to repurchasing by these groups. Laggards may enter the market during late maturity or even decline. Thus promotion designed to stimulate trial may need to be modified as the nature of new buyers changes over time.

The second key decision for commercialization is the choice of marketing strategy to establish a differential advantage. Understanding the requirements of customers (in particular, the innovator and early adopter groups) is crucial to this process and should have taken place earlier in the new product development process. The design of the marketing mix will depend on this understanding and the rate of adoption will be affected by such decisions. For example, advertising, promotion and sales efforts can generate awareness and reduce the customer's search costs, sales promotional incentives can encourage trial, and educating users in product benefits and applications has been found to speed the adoption process.[66] The innovative Philips MRI scanner is an example of a company tapping in to the needs of customers in an attempt to create a differential advantage.

As we have seen, the characteristics of customers affect the rate of adoption of an innovation, and marketing's job is to identify and target those with a high willingness to adopt upon launch. The characteristics of the product being launched also affect the diffusion rate and have marketing strategy implications (see Fig. 12.4).

First, its differential advantage compared to existing products affects the speed of adoption. The more added customer benefits a product gives to a customer the more customers will be willing to buy. The high differential advantage of a fax machine over

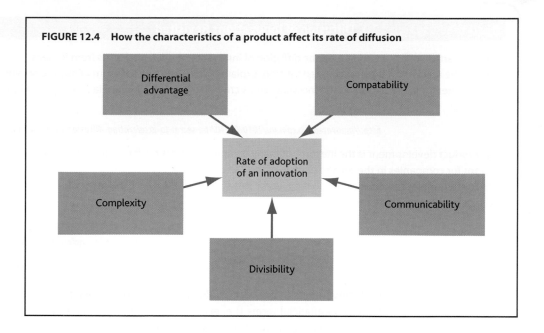

FIGURE 12.4   How the characteristics of a product affect its rate of diffusion

sending telegrams (e.g. convenience) or letters (e.g. speed) meant fast adoption. In turn, the convenience of email over fax has meant rapid adoption. The differential advantage can be psychological. More recently, the adoption of the iPad can be explained by high functional (mobile email and Internet access) and psychological (status symbol among business people) benefits.

Second, there is the innovation's *compatibility* with consumers' values, experiences, lifestyles and behaviours. The congruence between mobile phones and the lifestyles of many young people helped their diffusion. The iPod's rapid diffusion was also aided by such compatibility. The new product also needs to be compatible with consumers' behaviour. If its adoption depends on significant behaviour change, failure or prolonged diffusion may result. For example, the unsuccessful Dvorak typing keyboard was supposed to modestly increase typing speed, but at the behavioural cost of having to 'unlearn' the QWERTY keyboard. Although the telephone is now part of our everyday lives, diffusion was slow because its adoption required significant behaviour change.[67] The diffusion of e-books has also been slow, partly because people value the tactility and aesthetics of books rather than reading from an electronic screen.

A third factor affecting diffusion rate is the innovation's *complexity*. Products that are difficult to understand or use may take longer to be adopted. For example, Apple launched its Macintosh computer backed by the proposition that existing computers were too complex to gain widespread adoption. By making its model more user friendly, it gained fast adoption among the large segment of the population that was repelled by the complexity of using computers.

Fourth, an innovation's *divisibility* also affects its speed of diffusion. Divisibility refers to the degree to which the product can be tried on a limited basis. Inexpensive products can be tried without risk of heavy financial loss. The rapid diffusion of Google was aided by the fact that its functionality could be accessed free of charge.

The final product characteristic that affects the rate of diffusion of an innovation is its *communicability*. Adoption is likely to be faster if the benefits and applications of the innovation can be readily observed or described to target customers. If product benefits are long term or difficult to quantify, then diffusion may take longer. For example, Skoda's attempt to produce more reliable cars took time to communicate, as buyers' acceptance of this claim depended on their long-term experience of driving the cars. In service industries,

This short article offers an update on the diffusion of innovation model. It takes us from Roger's work on the model to a new 'accelerated' version, explaining the 16% rule (the sum of innovators and early adopters). Finally, it looks at the message, and a critique of the way the media mix is generally used to launch a product.

http://innovateordie.com.au/2010/05/10/the-secret-to-accelerating-diffusion-of-innovation-the-16-rule-explained/.

New product development is the life force of many companies. The oft quoted 'innovate or die' couldn't be more relevant for companies in the second decade of the 21ˢᵗ century. Most companies do have an idea-to-launch process such as stage-gate. The question is: do they work? This study looks at 211 companies and finds out what the best practice may be.

Robert G. Cooper and Scott J. Edgett (2012) Best Practices in the Idea-to-Launch Process and Its Governance,
Research Technology Management, March–April, 43–54.

marketing innovations like providing more staff to improve the quality of service are hard to quantify in financial terms (i.e. extra revenue generated) and therefore have a low adoption rate by the management of some companies. The marketing implications are that marketing management must not assume that what is obvious to them will be clear to customers. They need to devise a communications strategy that allows potential customers to become aware of the innovation, and understand and be convinced of its benefits.

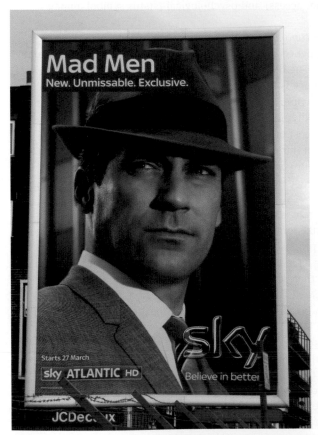

↑EXHIBIT 12.1 Sky revitalized viewer interest by relaunching its channels with new brand names, e.g. Sky Atlantic.

Product replacement strategies

As we found at the start of this chapter, product replacement is the most common form of new product introduction. A study of the marketing strategies used to position *product replacements* in the marketplace found eight approaches based on a combination of product change and other marketing modifications (i.e. marketing mix and target market changes).[68] Figure 12.5 shows the eight replacement strategies used by companies.

1 *Facelift*: minor product change with little or no change to the rest of the marketing mix or target market. Cars are often given facelifts midway through their life-cycle by undergoing minor styling alterations, for example. Japanese companies constantly facelift current electronic products such as cameras, flat screen televisions, netbook computers and smartphones by changing product features, a process known as **product churning**.

2 *Inconspicuous technological substitution*: a major technological change with little or no alteration of the other elements of the marketing mix. The technological change is not brought to the consumer's attention, a strategy often used by washing powder manufacturers, where the improved performance rather than the technological change is brought to the consumers' attention (e.g. Skip intelligent liquid).

3 *Remerchandising*: a modification of name, promotion, price, packaging and/or distribution, while maintaining the basic product. For example, Suchards Terry's All Gold chocolates.

4 *Relaunch*: both the product and other marketing mix elements are changed. Relaunches are common in the car industry where, every four to five years, a model is replaced with an upgraded version. Sky has relaunched Sky 1, 2 and 3 channels as Sky Atlantic, Sky Living and Sky HD (see Exhibit 12.1).

5 *Conspicuous technological substitution*: a major technological change is accompanied by heavy promotional and other mix changes to stimulate awareness and trial. An example is the replacement of the Rover Mini with the BMW Mini, which, despite remaining faithful to the character of the original, is technologically a fundamentally different car.

6 *Intangible repositioning*: the basic product is retained but other mix elements and target customers change. Diageo has retained the product (Piat D'Or wine) but is targeting a new audience of 45–50-year-old female wine drinkers. New packaging is designed to give clearer branding and shelf appeal.[69]

7 *Tangible repositioning*: both the product and target market change. Skoda is an example of the product being significantly improved to appeal to a more upmarket, wealthier target market.

8 *Neo-innovation*: a fundamental technology change accompanied by target market and mix changes. For example, Nokia practised neo-innovation when it moved from a conglomerate operating in such industries as paper, chemicals and rubber to being a marketer of mobile phones.

Companies, therefore, face an array of replacement options with varying degrees of risk. Figure 12.5 categorizes these options and provides an aid to strategic thinking when considering how to replace products in the marketplace.

Commercializing technology

Superior commercialization of technology has been, and will continue to be, a key success factor in many industries. Some companies, such as Canon, Sony, and Philips, already have the capability to bring sophisticated high-tech products to market faster than other companies that treat the commercialization process in a less disciplined manner. For example, Canon spends heavily on R&D (8 per cent of sales revenues) to maintain its leadership in the laser printer market by fast introduction of innovations such as colour improvements and to develop new products such as LED TVs, which can produce the wide viewing angle and deep colours of a cathode-ray TV but are as thin as a liquid-crystal or plasma screen.[70] Consistently beating the competition has been found to rest on four capabilities: being faster to market, supplying a wider range of markets, executing a larger number of product launches, and using a wider breadth of technologies.[71]

Many major market innovations appear in practice to be technologically driven: a technology seeking a market application rather than a market opportunity seeking a technology.[72] Marketing's input in such situations is to provide the insight as to how the technology may provide customer benefits within a prescribed target market. For example, as we have already discussed, traditional marketing research techniques have only a limited role to play when using technology to create new markets: people find it difficult to articulate their views on subjects that are unfamiliar, and acceptance may come only over time (the diffusion of innovation). Indeed, the price the customer will be asked to pay is usually unclear during the early stage of technological development.

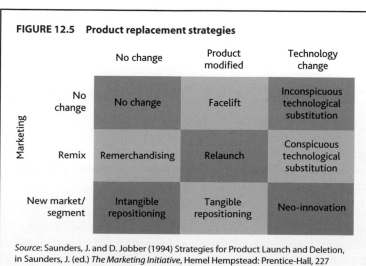

FIGURE 12.5　Product replacement strategies

	No change	Product modified	Technology change
No change	No change	Facelift	Inconspicuous technological substitution
Remix	Remerchandising	Relaunch	Conspicuous technological substitution
New market/ segment	Intangible repositioning	Tangible repositioning	Neo-innovation

(Marketing)

Source: Saunders, J. and D. Jobber (1994) Strategies for Product Launch and Deletion, in Saunders, J. (ed.) *The Marketing Initiative*, Hemel Hempstead: Prentice-Hall, 227

A combination of these factors may have been responsible for the first-ever forecast for computers, which predicted worldwide sales of 10 units.

The marketing of technological innovations, therefore, calls for a blend of technology and marketing. The basic marketing question, 'What potential benefits over existing products is this product likely to provide?', needs to be asked constantly during product development.

Furthermore the following lessons from the diffusion of innovation curve need to be remembered.

- The innovator/early adopter segments need to be identified and targeted initially.
- Initial sales are likely to be low: these groups are relatively small.
- Patience is required as the diffusion of an innovation takes time as people/organizations originally resistant to it learn of its benefits and begin to adopt it.
- The target group and message will need to be modified over time as new categories of customer enter the market.

Competitive Reaction to New Product Introductions

Go to the website to see how Sony promoted its Bravia LCD TV and learn about the creative ideas behind the advert.
www.mcgraw-hill.co.uk/ textbooks/jobber

Ｎew product launches may be in response to new product entries by competitors. Research suggests that when confronted with a new product entry by a competitor, incumbent firms should respond quickly with a limited set of marketing mix elements. Managers should rapidly decide which ones (product, promotion, price and place) are likely to have the most impact, and concentrate their efforts on them.[73]

Competitors' reaction times to the introduction of a new product have been found to depend on four factors.[74] First, response is faster in high-growth markets. Given the importance of such markets, competitors will feel the need to take action speedily in response to a new entrant. Second, response is dependent on the market shares held by the introducing firm and its competitors. Response time is slower when the introducing firm has higher market share and faster for those competitors who have higher market share. Third, response time is faster in markets characterized by frequent product changes. Finally, it is not surprising to find that response time is related to the time needed to develop the new product.

When you have read this chapter

log on to the Online Learning Centre at **www.mcgraw-hill.co.uk/textbooks/jobber** to explore chapter-by-chapter test questions, links and further online study tools for marketing.

Review

①   **The different types of new product that can be launched**
- There are four types of new product that can be launched: product replacements, additions to existing lines, new product lines and new-to-the-world products.

②   **How to create and nurture an innovative culture**
- Creating and nurturing an innovative culture can be achieved by rewarding success heavily, tolerating a certain degree of failure, senior management sending clear messages about the role and importance of innovation, their words being supported by allowing staff time off to develop their own ideas, making available resources and being accessible when difficult decisions need to be taken, and resisting automatic nay-saying.

3 The organizational options applying to new product development
- The options are project teams, product and brand managers, and new product departments and committees. Whichever method is used, effective cross-functional teamwork is essential for success.

4 Methods of reducing time to market
- A key method of reducing time to market is the process of simultaneous engineering. Design and production engineers, together with other staff, work together as a team rather than sequentially.
- Consumer goods companies are bringing together teams of brand and marketing managers, external design, advertising and research agency staff to develop simultaneously the brand and launch strategies.

5 How marketing and R&D staff can work together effectively
- A study by Gupta and Wileman suggests that marketing and R&D can better work together when teamwork is encouraged, there is an improvement in the provision of marketing information to R&D, R&D people are encouraged to be more customer aware, informal relationships between marketing and R&D are developed, marketing is encouraged to learn about technology, and a formal process of product development is implemented. Senior management staff have an important role to play by locating marketing and R&D close to each other, showing a personal interest in new product development, providing strategic direction, encouraging teamwork, increasing the resources devoted to new product development and enhancing their understanding of the importance of marketing in new product development.

6 The stages in the new product development process
- A formal process with review points, clear new product goals and a strong marketing orientation underlying the process leads to greater success.
- The stages are new product strategy (senior management should set objectives and priorities), idea generation (sources include customers, competitors, distributors, salespeople, engineers and marketers), screening (to evaluate their commercial worth), concept testing (to allow the views of target customers to enter the process early), product development (where the concept is developed into a physical product for testing), market testing (where the new product is tested in the marketplace) and commercialization (where the new product is launched).

7 How to stimulate the corporate imagination
- Four ways of stimulating the corporate imagination are: to encourage management to escape the tyranny of served markets by exploring how core competences can be exploited in new markets; to search for innovative product concepts—for example, by creating a new way to deliver an existing function (e.g. the electronic notepad); questioning traditional price–performance assumptions and giving engineers the resources to develop cheaper new products; and gaining insights by observing closely the market's most sophisticated and demanding customers.

8 The six key principles of managing product teams
- These are the agreement of the mission, effective organization, development of a project plan, strong leadership, shared responsibilities, and the establishment of an executive sponsor in senior management.

9 The diffusion of innovation categories and their marketing implications
- The categories are innovators, early adopters, early and late majorities, and laggards.
- The marketing implications are that the categories can be used as a basis for segmentation and targeting (initially the innovator/early adopters should be targeted). As the product is bought by different categories, so the marketing mix may need to change.
- The speed of adoption can be affected by marketing activities—for example, advertising to create awareness, sales promotion to stimulate trial, and educating users in product benefits and applications.
- The nature of the innovation itself can also affect adoption—that is, the strength of its differential advantage, its compatibility with people's values, experiences, lifestyles and behaviours, its complexity, its divisibility and its communicability.

10 The key ingredients in commercializing technology quickly and effectively
- The key ingredients are the ability of technologists and marketing people to work together effectively, simultaneous engineering, constantly asking the question 'What benefits over existing products is this new product likely to provide?', and remembering lessons from the diffusion of innovation curve (i.e. target the innovator/early adopter segments first).

Key Terms

brainstorming the technique where a group of people generate ideas without initial evaluation; only when the list of ideas is complete is each idea then evaluated

business analysis a review of the projected sales, costs and profits for a new product to establish whether these factors satisfy company objectives

concept testing testing new product ideas with potential customers

diffusion of innovation process the process by which a new product spreads throughout a market over time

innovation the commercialization of an invention by bringing it to market

invention the discovery of new methods and ideas

market testing the limited launch of a new product to test sales potential

product churning a continuous and rapid spiral of new product introductions

project teams the bringing together of staff from such areas as R&D, engineering, manufacturing, finance and marketing to work on a project such as new product development

simultaneous engineering the involvement of manufacturing and product development engineers in the same development team in an effort to reduce development time

test marketing the launch of a new product in one or a few geographic areas chosen to be representative of the intended market

Study Questions

1. Try to think of an unsatisfied need that you feel could be solved by the introduction of a new product. How would you set about testing your idea to examine its commercial potential?

2. How would you go about evaluating the idea?

3. What are the advantages and disadvantages of test marketing? In what circumstances should you be reluctant to use test marketing?

4. Your company has developed a new range of Thai curry sauce, intended to compete with the market leader. How would you conduct product tests for your new line?

5. What are the particular problems associated with commercializing technology? What are the key factors for success?

6. Discuss how marketing and R&D can form effective teams to develop new products.

References

1. Steve Jobs. (n.d.). BrainyQuote.com, http://www.brainyquote.com/quotes/quotes/s/stevejobs416926.html (retrieved 13 April 2012).
2. Pearson, D. (1993) Invent, Innovate and Improve, *Marketing*, 8 April, 15.
3. Richard, H. (1996) Why Competitiveness is a Dirty Word in Scandinavia, *European*, 6–12 June, 24.
4. McGregor, J. (2006) The World's Most Innovative Companies, *Business Week*, 24 April, 63–76.
5. Doyle, P. (1997) From the Top, *Guardian*, 2 August, 17.
6. A study conducted by Kashami, K. and T. Clayton, reported in Murphy, D. (2000) Innovate or Die, *Marketing Business*, May, 16–18.
7. Andrew, J., J. Manget, D. Michael, A. Taylor and H. Zablit (2010) Innovation 2010: A return of prominence—and the emergence of a new world order, Boston Consulting group, http://www.bcg.de/documents/file42620.pdf April.
8. Geoghegan, J. (2011) Satnavs and smartphones put traditional maps on the road to nowhere as sales drop massively, The Mail online, http://www.dailymail.co.uk/sciencetech/article-2033227/Satnavs-smart-phones-traditional-maps-road-sales-drop-massively.html#ixzz1rwFKziSX, 3 September.
9. Booz, Allen and Hamilton (1982) *New Products Management for the 1980s*, New York: Booz, Allen and Hamilton, Inc.

10. Matthews, V. (2002) Caution Versus Creativity, *Financial Times*, 17 June, 12.

11. See Gupta, A. K. and D. Wileman (1990) Improving R&D/Marketing Relations: R&D Perspective, *R&D Management* 20(4), 277–90; Koshler, R. (1991) Produkt—Innovation as management als Erfolgsfaktor, in Mueller-Boehling, D. *et al.* (eds) *Innovations— und Technologiemanagement*, Stuttgart: C. E. Poeschel Verlagi; Shrivastava, P. and W. E. Souder (1987) The Strategic Management of Technological Innovation: A Review and a Model, *Journal of Management Studies* 24(1), 24–41.

12. See Booz, Allen and Hamilton (1982) op. cit.; Maidique, M. A. and B. J. Zirger (1984) A Study of Success and Failure in Product Innovation: The Case of the US Electronics Industry, *IEEE Transactions in Engineering Management*, EM-31 (November), 192–203.

13. See Bergen, S. A., R. Miyajima and C. P. McLaughlin (1988) The R&D/Production Interface in Four Developed Countries, *R&D Management* 18(3), 201–16; Hegarty, W. H. and R. C. Hoffman (1990) Product/Market Innovations: A Study of Top Management Involvement among Four Cultures, *Journal of Product Innovation Management* 7, 186–99; Cooper, R. G. (1979) The Dimensions of Industrial New Product Success and Failure, *Journal of Marketing* 43 (Summer), 93–103; Johne, A. and P. Snelson (1988) Auditing Product Innovation Activities in Manufacturing Firms, *R&D Management* 18(3), 227–33.

14. 3M (2012) Who we are, http://solutions.3m.co.uk/wps/portal/3M/en_GB/about-3M/information/about/us/.

15. Kovacs, J. (2012) 3M and NJATC Join Forces to Develop Online Curriculum for All IBEW/NECA Electrical Workers, Press release, 10 April, Market Watch, *Wall Street Journal*.

16. *The Marketers* (2008) Marketing Greats, May, 7.

17. Day, P. (2012), http://www.bbc.co.uk/programmes/b01gvtjj.

18. *The Economist* (2012) Asian Innovation, http://www.economist.com/node/21551028, 24 March.

19. Jugaad (2012) http://www.jugaad.org/?page_id=2.

20. Kadri, M. (2010) Finding innovation in every corner, http://changeobserver.designobserver.com/feature/finding-innovation-in-every-corner/12691/, 2 August.

21. Duggan, M. (2012) Frugal innovation, http://knowinnovation.com/frugal-innovation/

22. http://www.sristi.org/hbnew/.

23. Prahalad, C. K. and R. A. Mashelkar (2010) Innovation's Holy Grail, *Harvard Business Review*, July–August.

24. Shah, A. (2012) Causes of poverty, http://www.globalissues.org/issue/2/causes-of-poverty, 8 April.

25. Levitt, T. (1960) Marketing Myopia, *Harvard Business Review*, July–August.

26. Joshi, A. W. and S. Sharma (2004) Customer Knowledge Development: Antecedents and Impact on New Product Performance, *Journal of Marketing*, 68 (October), 47–9.

27. Slotegraaf, R. J. and K. Atuahene-Gima (2011) Product Development Team Stability and New Product Advantage: The Role of Decision-Making Processes, *Journal of Marketing* 75(1), 96–108.

28. See Hise, R. T., L. O'Neal, A. Parasuraman and J. U. McNeal (1990) Marketing/R&D Interaction in New Product Development: Implications for New Product Success Rates, *Journal of Product Innovation Management* 7, 142–55; Johne and Snelson (1988) op. cit.; Walsh, W. J. (1990) Get the Whole Organisation Behind New Product Development, *Research in Technological Management*, Nov.–Dec., 32–6.

29. Fred, D. (1991) Learning the Ropes: My Life as a Product Champion, *Harvard Business Review*, Sept.–Oct, 46–56.

30. Gupta, A. K. and D. Wileman (1991) Improving R&D/Marketing Relations in Technology Based Companies: Marketing's Perspective, *Journal of Marketing Management* 7(1), 25–46.

31. See Dwyer, L. M. (1990) Factors Affecting the Proficient Management of Product Innovation, *International Journal of Technological Management* 5(6), 721–30; Gupta and Wileman (1990) op. cit.; Adler, P. S., H. E. Riggs and S. C. Wheelwright (1989) Product Development Know-How, *Sloan Management Review* 4, 7–17.

32. Brentani, U. de (1991) Success Factors in Developing New Business Services, *European Journal of Marketing* 15(2), 33–59; Johne, A. and C. Storey (1998) New Source Development: A Review of the Literature and Annotated Bibliography, *European Journal of Marketing* 32(3/4), 184–251.

33. Cooper, R. G. and E. J. Kleinschmidt (1986) An Investigation into the New Product Process: Steps, Deficiencies and Impact, *Journal of Product Innovation Management*, June, 71–85.

34. Edwards, C. (2008) How HP Got the Wow! Back, *Business Week*, 22 December, 60–1.

35. Edwards, C. (2009) The Return on Research, *Business Week*, 23/30 March, 45.

36. Viklund, A. (n.d.) Brainstorming, http://teamvirtute.wordpress.com/promotingcreativity/brainstorming/.

37. Hamel, G. and C. K. Prahalad (1991) Corporate Imagination and Expeditionary Marketing, *Harvard Business Review*, July–August, 81–92.

38. Procter & Gamble (2012) Connect + develop, http://www.pg.com/connect_develop/index.shtml.

39. Huston, L. and N. Sakkab (2006) Connect and Develop: Inside Procter & Gamble's New Model for Innovation, *Harvard Business Review* 84(3), 58–72.

40. Mitchell, A. (2005) After Some Innovation? Perhaps You Just Need to Ask Around, *Marketing Week*, 16 June, 28–9.

41. Tomkins, R. (2005) Products that Aim Straight for Your Heart, *Financial Times*, 29 April, 13.

42. Parkinson, S. T. (1982) The Role of the User in Successful New Product Development, *R&D Management* 12, 123–31.

43. Nevens, T. M., G. L. Summe and B. Uttal (1990) Commercializing Technology: What the Best Companies Do, *Harvard Business Review*, May–June, 154–63.

44. Johne, A. (1992) Don't Let Your Customers Lead You Astray in Developing New Products, *European Management Journal* 10(1), 80–4.

45. Moosmayer, D. C. and A. Koehn (2011) The moderating role of managers' uncertainty avoidance values on the performance impact of radical and incremental innovation, *International Journal of Business Research* 11(6), 32–39.

46. Hamel, G. and C. K. Prahalad (1991) Corporate Imagination and Expeditionary Marketing, *Harvard Business Review*, July–August, 81–92.

47. Hamel, G. (1999) Bringing Silicon Valley Inside, *Harvard Business Review*, Sept.–Oct., 71–84.

48. Leifer, R. G., C. O'Connor and M. Rice (2001) Implementing Radical Innovation in Mature Firms: The Role of Hubs, *Academy of Management Executives* 15(3), 61–70.

49. Hunt, J. W. (2002) Crucibles of Innovation, *Financial Times*, 18 January, 18.

50. Bartram, P. (2004) Why the Competition Doesn't Matter, *The Marketer*, April, 18–21.

51. Tellis, G., J. C. Prabhu and R. K. Chandy (2009) Radical Innovation Across Nations: The Preeminence of Corporate Culture, *Journal of Marketing* 73(1), 3–23.

52. Jobber, D., J. Saunders, G. Hooley, B. Gilding and J. Hatton-Smooker (1989) Assessing the Value of a Quality Assurance Certificate for Software: An Exploratory Investigation, *MIS Quarterly*, March, 19–31.

53. Valentine, M. (2009) Research Extends Beyond the Lab, *Marketing Week*, 5 March, 27–8.

54. Matthews, V. (2002) Caution Versus Creativity, *Financial Times*, 17 June, 12.

55. The author is indebted to Dr Dirk Snelders of Delft University, Netherlands, for supplying material on the scenario method.

For further reading see Burt, G. and K. van der Heijden (2003) First Steps: Towards Purposeful Activities in Scenario Thinking and Future Studies, *Futures*, 35, 1011–26; Carroll, J. M. (2000) Scenario-based Design: A Brief History and Rationale, in Eastman C., M. McCracken and W. Newsletter (eds), *Knowing and Learning to Design: Cognitive Perspectives in Design Education*, Amsterdam: Elsevier; Tauber, E. M. (1974) How Marketing Research Discourages Major Innovation, *Business Horizons*, 17 (June), 22–6; and Ulwick, A. W. (2002) Turn Customer Input Into Innovation, *Harvard Business Review*, (January), 91–7.

56. Wheelwright, S. and K. Clark (1992) *Revolutionizing Product Development*, New York: Free Press.

57. Rowan, D. (2011) 3D printing—an industrial revolution in the digital age? *IWired*, 9 May, http://www.wired.com/epicenter/2011/05/3d-printing-an-industrial-revolution-in-the-digital-age/.

58. *The Economist* (2008) Rebirth of a Carmaker, 26 April, 91–3.

59. Jarvis, J. (2009) The Foresight of Google, *Media Guardian*, 9 February, 8.

60. Chisnall, P. (2005) *Marketing Research*, Maidenhead: McGraw-Hill.

61. Rogers, E. M. (2003) *Diffusion of Innovations*, New York: Free Press.

62. Rogers (2003) op. cit.

63. Zinkmund, W. G. and M. D'Amico (1999) *Marketing*, St Paul, MN: West.

64. Easingwood, C. and C. Beard (1989) High Technology Launch Strategies in the UK, *Industrial Marketing Management* 18, 125–38.

65. Pesola, M. (2005) Samsung Plays to the Young Generation, *Financial Times*, 29 March, 11.

66. See Mahajan, V., E. Muller and R. Kerin (1987) Introduction Strategy for New Product with Positive and Negative Word-of-Mouth, *Management Science* 30, 1389–404; Robertson, T. S. and H. Gatignon (1986) Competitive Effects on Technology Diffusion, *Journal of Marketing* 50 (July), 1–12; Tzokas, N. and M. Saren (1992) Innovation Diffusion: The Emerging Role of Suppliers Versus the Traditional Dominance of Buyers, *Journal of Marketing Management* 8(1), 69–80.

67. Gourville, J. (2006) The Curse of Innovation: Why Innovative Products Fail, MSI Report No. 05-117.

68. Saunders, J. and D. Jobber (1994) Product Replacement Strategies: Occurrence and Concurrence, *Journal of Product Innovation Management* (November).

69. Fox, P. (2010) Piat d'Or launches first Sauvignon Blanc, http://www.talkingretail.com/products/drinks-news/piat-dor-launches-first-sauvignon-blanc, 1 July.

70. Harding, R. (2008) Canon to Launch Radical TV, *Financial Times*, 2 December, 25.

71. Nevens, Summe and Uttal (1990) op. cit.

72. Brown, R. (1991) Managing the 'S' Curves of Innovation, *Journal of Marketing Management* 7(2), 189–202.

73. Gatignon, H., T. S. Robertson and A. J. Fein (1997) Incumbent Defence Strategies Against New Product Entry, *International Journal of Research in Marketing* 14, 163–76.

74. Bowman, D. and H. Gatignon (1995) Determinants of Competitor Response Time to a New Product Introduction, *Journal of Marketing Research* 33, February, 42–53.

UGG Australia

Fad of the Season to Fashion Staple of the Decade,
Establishing an International Fashion Brand

Background

The ubiquitous sheepskin boot was originally developed by the surfing community in Australia during the 1960s and 1970s. The style was designed from widely available sheepskin to create a soft, warm boot that could be worn after a session in the surf during the winter months. In essence its origins were a functional, slip-on boot that offered practicality, warmth and an alternative to the flip-flop.

By the end of the 1970s an entrepreneurial Australian surfer had introduced the generic UGG boot to the shores of California. With a growing surf culture and alternative lifestyle seekers, the UGG boot met with increasing popularity. Through the 1980s and early 1990s sales of the product grew through limited distribution in surf shops and speciality lifestyle boutiques along the west coast of America. In 1995 lifestyle footwear company Deckers Outdoor Corporation bought the 'name' and distribution rights for the USA, and 'UGG Australia' was born.

At the introductory stage of the brand's life-cycle there was one basic boot style, a simple design with a sheepskin upper and a flat rubber sole. There were three or four natural colour options—chestnut, brown and sand—and it was manufactured in Australia and New Zealand. By 1998 the product line comprised two boots, four slippers and a few casual shoes. The product was designed, developed and sold in California by a team of entrepreneurial innovators, not fashion followers but people looking for a job that would support their passion for surfing. The ethos of the product was authenticity and a free spirit. Its target market was like-minded individuals who also enjoyed the laid-back Californian surf lifestyle. In 1999 66 per cent of the company's sales were in California alone.

Developing the brand

By 1998 Deckers had started to cultivate an ambitious strategy for growth using the foundation stone of the humble sheepskin boot. When the company established the brand in 1995, they required a product that they could sell alongside their sandals to generate sales revenue during the winter months. They soon saw a momentum building around a niche product and developed a plan to establish an international brand and reposition its focus on to the

luxury footwear sector. During the late 1990s the most crucial repositioning took place, as they reviewed distribution, developed new product lines and, most important, integrated a powerful marketing and communication campaign.

The product was originally distributed through wholesale accounts into selective surf shops and independent retailers. The boot was an additional sale to the surf boards and hardware but soon attracted a broader clientele than surfers. This type of limited distribution added to the exclusive and sometimes elusive availability of the product. Lack of stock and limited access added certain kudos to those who were in the know. This type of distribution appealed to the early adopters in Californian fashion circles, such as stylists, journalists and fashion PRs many of whom worked in the media and film industry. These fashion influencers held sway with the Hollywood elite and celebrities such as Pamela Anderson, Gwyneth Paltrow and Kate Moss who quickly adopted the boots, the images of which were rapidly circulated through the global communications network of Internet and magazines. This type of celebrity seeding led to a further strategy which included key media personalities such as TV's Oprah Winfrey endorsing the UGG boot in 2000 in her 'Oprah's Favourite Things' section. This operated on two levels: the glamorous, luxury LA lifestyle as personified by Pamela Anderson et al.

and the sophisticated comfort and durability endorsed by Oprah.

Deckers pride themselves on finding niche products and turning them into global brands and in 2005 recruited a new CEO, Angel Martinez, and one of his remits was to push the UGG Australia brand further. Martinez brought strong leadership and a definitive vision for Deckers. UGG Australia was a well-established name in the fashion and footwear sector; they did not discount and so had a strong regular price business. For retailers, they offered high gross margins and strong brand recognition. Their wholesale clients, such as Nordstrom in the USA, were well-established and reputable retailers who offered a high-end distribution route. Their consumers were loyal and enjoyed comfort and quality coupled with brand recognition. This was evidenced over a ten-year period when sales rose from $19.2 million in 2001 to $1.2 billion in 2011. The company had an exciting brand and was cash rich; this put them in a strong position to gain wider appeal.

Design and global production

Growing international recognition of UGG Australia brought its own challenges for the product design team, who were based in California. In order to meet a growing global demand and increase speed to market, alternative manufacturing facilities were needed. The boots were originally made and exported from Australia but by 2005 the majority of production shifted to China. This did not seem to dent the image of the brand. If anything its status was elevated through strong endorsements and up-market retailers; furthermore, the customer still believed its provenance to be Australian. Deckers did not own any production facilities and with such strong brand awareness, contracting out manufacturing to Chinese factories left UGG vulnerable to counterfeiting. The boots are relatively easy to imitate and lesser-quality sheepskin from China and synthetic imitations were readily available. A global campaign was launched by the brand to combat the problem. This included rigorously filing law suits against offenders and partnering with regional distributors to enforce plans consistently. They also developed a system of adding unique coding to each new season's merchandise which helps all stakeholders identify counterfeit product.

Coinciding with this growing global awareness, Deckers challenged the use of the word 'UGG' by existing Australian manufacturers of the generic sheepskin boot, claiming that they alone should be able to use the word 'UGG' exclusively. The Australian manufacturers, many of whom had been making the sheepskin boot for 20 or 30 years eventually won the right to use the generic word in their marketing within Australia only. However this has a wider impact on international and online sales, which have been rigorously policed by Deckers' legal team.

In order to maintain their market share and sustain growth in the footwear sector UGG Australia started to expand their product offer beyond the 'classic' boot. From 2005 they developed bi-annual seasonal collections to drive sales orders through the traditionally lean summer months. This type of diversification also offered alternative styles; however, the 'classic' has always generated the majority of orders. The style, offered in a tall or short version, has seen many reincarnations over the years but has stayed fundamentally the same. It is available in core colours and seasonal variations such as raisin in 2007. Different uppers have been developed, the 'cardi' a woollen knitted style proved popular for several seasons, and the 'bailey button' is a simple inclusion of a button to the split at the side. In all, the design team has to reinvent the same product every season. Additions to the existing womenswear line over the years have included suede wedges, sheepskin lined sandals and slippers. New product lines such as accessories offer sheepskin handbags, the children's wear collection comprises mini-versions of the classic style, and most recently the mini 'bailey button' style has proved popular. In 2011 the brand introduced a women's premium footwear range called the 'UGG Collection' made in Italy.

Other issues facing the production and design team have been apparent shortages of raw materials during 2011. Sheepskin is the key component used and pressure on the supply due to natural weather extremes in Australia (drought and floods) has put a strain on the output. As a result the team has to look for alternative materials and substitutes for the classic boot. Lack of availability of sheepskin and rising production costs in China have also affected the margins.

In spite of offering a men's collection since 2000 sales were poor, at times less than 1 per cent of turnover. Men simply did not want to wear the iconic effeminate boot, despite the fact that its original purpose had been for surfers. In 2011 the company tried to reignite the market with a new collection and an expensive promotional campaign fronted by US sports star Tom Brady. Initial sales suggest that men are purchasing the product: however, the best-selling 'rockville' biker style boot is very different from its slouchy sheepskin sister.

President of UGG Australia, Connie Rishwain oversees the in-house design team which is managed by Leah Larson, who in 2012 was appointed to a new role as Creative Director for the brand. They also rely on freelance designers and collaborations in product areas that they are less familiar with. For example, LA-based designer Rozae Nichols developed an outwear collection in 2008. In 2011 UGG and luxury footwear brand Jimmy Choo collaborated and

to the Dragons' Den and wanted around £80,000 for a 15 per cent investment in his business, but was unsuccessful. His idea was in the form of a brush, which worked differently—by 'flicking and teasing hair apart' rather than by pulling the bristles through the hair. Nevertheless, this proved to be a successful idea and from a small manufacturing base in Oxford (with much publicity from Shaun's appearance on the show) Shaun was able to grow his business and make the Tangle Teezer into a top-selling hair brush. (Find out more about the Tangle Teezer at http://www.tangleteezer.com/.)

Developing a commercialization strategy

Before making an investment the Dragons intensely question the entrepreneurs about why they need the money, how it will be spent and why the idea is going to work. Many of the entrepreneurs fail to convince the Dragons to invest, sometimes due to lack of market potential, lack of compatibility with potential customer values, or the presence of high risk. Ultimately, the success of an innovation relies heavily on developing a commercialization strategy that identifies the right target market and marketing strategy that can monetize the differential advantage offered by the product. The diffusion of the innovation process helps to explain how innovative products spread through market over time, and this model highlights the importance of the concept 'readiness'. In other words, if sufficient customers in a particular target market are not willing to try a product, then it is likely to fail. So, innovative entrepreneurs need to understand the extent to which their target customers are willing to try something new. Their willingness is also likely to be affected by the characteristics of the product and the extent to which it offers advantage over existing market offers. Ultimately, the characteristics of the product will affect its rate of diffusion over time.

Questions

Reggae Reggae Sauce, the Kymera Wand and Tangle Teezer are three examples of innovations which have successfully been commercialized. Imagine you are responsible for new product development and wish to seek investment in the Den for a new product idea but you want to get some ideas of how other innovations have been successful before developing your own commercialization strategy and the pitch for the Dragons.

1 Use the characteristics of a product which are likely to affect its rate of diffusion (see Figure 12.4 earlier in the chapter) to determine why Reggae Reggae Sauce, the Kymera Wand and Tangle Teezer have been successfully accepted by their target markets.

2 Select one of these products and then suggest which of its characteristics offer the greatest potential for communicating the benefits of the product to the target audience.

3 Sketch out a new product idea and then write an executive summary, which gives an outline of the product, the problem(s) it will solve and explain your passion and commitment to making this innovation work.

This case was written by Fiona Ellis-Chadwick, Senior Lecturer in Marketing, The Open University.

CHAPTER 13

Pricing strategy

> **Everything is worth what its purchasers will pay for it.**
> **SYRUS**

> **There are two fools in every market.**
> **One charges too little; the other charges too much.**
> **RUSSIAN PROVERB**

LEARNING OBJECTIVES

After reading this chapter, you should be able to:

1 explain the economist's approach to price determination

2 distinguish between full cost and direct cost pricing

3 discuss your understanding of going-rate pricing and competitive bidding

4 explain the advantages of marketing-orientated pricing over cost and competitor-orientated pricing

5 discuss the factors that affect price setting when using a marketing-orientated approach

6 identify when and how to initiate price increases and cuts

7 identify when and when not to follow competitor-initiated price increases and cuts; when to follow quickly and when to follow slowly

8 discuss ethical issues in pricing

Price is the odd-one-out of the marketing mix, because it is the revenue earner. The price of a product is what the company gets back in return for all the effort that is put into producing and marketing the product. The other three elements of the marketing mix—product, promotion and place—are costs. Therefore, no matter how good the product, how creative the promotion or how efficient the distribution, unless price covers costs the company will make a loss. Therefore, managers need to understand how to set prices, because both undercharging (lost margin) and overcharging (lost sales) can have dramatic effects on profitability.

One of the key factors that marketing managers need to remember is that price is just one element of the marketing mix. Price should not be set in isolation; it should be blended with product, promotion and place to form a coherent mix that provides superior customer value. The sales of many products, particularly those that are a form of self-expression—such as drinks, cars, perfume and clothing—could suffer from prices that are too low. As we shall see, price is an important part of positioning strategy since it often sends quality cues to customers.

Understanding how to set prices is an important aspect of marketing decision-making, not least because of changes in the competitive arena that many believe will act to drive down prices in many countries. Since price is a major determinant of profitability, developing a coherent pricing strategy assumes major significance.

Many people's introduction to the issue of pricing is a course in economics. We will now consider, very briefly, some of the ideas discussed by economists when considering price.

Economists' Approach to Pricing

Although a full discussion of the approach taken by economists to pricing is beyond the scope of this chapter, the following gives a flavour of some of the important concepts relating to price. The discussion will focus on demand since this is of fundamental importance in pricing. Economists talk of the *demand curve* to conceptualize the relationship between the quantity demanded and different price levels. Figure 13.1 shows a typical demand curve. At a price of P_1, demand is Q_1. As price drops so demand rises. Thus at P_2 demand increases to Q_2. For some products, a given fall in price leads to a large increase in demand. The demand for such products is said to be *price elastic*. For other products, a given fall in price leads to only a small increase in demand. The demand for these products is described as *price inelastic*. Clearly it is useful to know the price elasticity of demand. When faced with elastic demand, marketers know that a price drop may stimulate much greater demand for their products. Conversely, when faced with inelastic demand, marketers know that a price drop will not increase demand appreciably.

An obvious practical problem facing marketers who wish to use demand curve analysis is plotting demand curves accurately. There is no one demand curve that relates price to demand in real life. Each demand curve is based on a set of assumptions regarding other factors such as advertising expenditure, salesforce effectiveness, distribution intensity and the price of competing products, which also affect demand. For the purposes of Figure 13.1, these have been held constant at a particular level so that one unique curve can be plotted. A second problem regarding the demand curve relates to the estimation of the position of the curve even when other influences are held constant. Some companies conduct experiments to estimate likely demand at various price levels. However, it is not always feasible to do so since they may rely on the cooperation of retailers who may refuse or demand unrealistically high fees. Second, it is

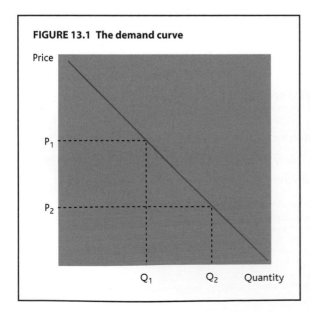

FIGURE 13.1 The demand curve

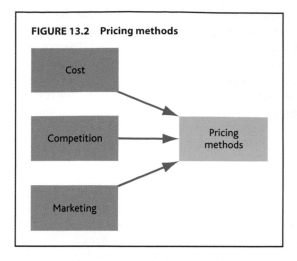

FIGURE 13.2   Pricing methods

very difficult to implement a fully controlled field experiment. Where different regions of the country are involved, differences in income levels, variations in local tastes and preferences, and differences in the level of competitor activities may confound the results. The reality is that while the demand curve is a useful conceptual tool for thinking about pricing issues, in practice its application is limited. In truth, traditional economic theory was not developed as a management tool but as an explanation of market behaviour. Managers therefore turn to other methods of setting prices and it is these methods we shall discuss in this chapter.

Shapiro and Jackson identified three methods used by managers to set prices (see Fig. 13.2).[1] The first reflects a strong internal orientation and is based on costs. The second is to use competitor-orientated pricing where the major emphasis is on competitor activities. The final approach is called marketing-orientated pricing as it focuses on the value that customers place on a product in the marketplace and its marketing strategy. In this chapter we shall examine each of these approaches and draw out their strengths and limitations. We shall also discuss how to initiate and respond to price changes.

Cost-Orientated Pricing

Companies often use cost-orientated methods when setting prices.[2] Two methods are normally used: full cost pricing and direct (or marginal) cost pricing.

Full cost pricing

Full cost pricing can best be explained by using a simple example (see Table 13.1). Imagine that you are given the task of pricing a new product (a memory card) and the cost figures given in Table 13.1 apply. Direct costs such as labour and materials work out at £10 per unit. As output increases, more people and materials will be needed and so total costs increase. Fixed costs (or overheads) per year are calculated at £1,000,000. These costs (such as office and manufacturing facilities) do not change as output increases. They have to be paid whether 10 or 1 million memory cards are produced.

Having calculated the relevant costs, the next step is to estimate how many memory cards we are likely to sell. We believe that we produce good-quality memory cards and therefore sales should be 100,000 in the first year. Therefore, total (full) cost per unit is £20 and, using the company's traditional 10 per cent mark-up, a price of £22 is set.

TABLE 13.1 Full cost pricing			
Year 1		**Year 2**	
Direct costs (per unit)	= £10	Expected sales	= 50,000
Fixed costs	= £1,000,000		
Expected sales	= 100,000		
Cost per unit		**Cost per unit**	
Direct costs	= £10	Direct costs	= £10
Fixed costs (1,000,000 ÷ 100,000)	= £10	Fixed costs (1,000,000 ÷ 50,000)	= £20
Full costs	= £20	Full costs	= £30
Mark-up (10%)	= £2	Mark-up (10%)	= £3
Price (cost plus mark-up)	= £22	**Price** (cost plus mark-up)	= £33

In order to appreciate the problem of using full cost pricing, let us assume that the sales estimate of 100,000 is not reached by the end of the year. Because of poor economic conditions or as a result of setting the price too high, only 50,000 units are sold. The company believes that this level of sales is likely to be achieved next year. What happens to price? Table 13.1 gives the answer: it is raised because cost per unit goes up. This is because fixed costs (£1,000,000) are divided by a smaller expected sales volume (50,000). The result is a price rise in response to poor sales figures. This is clearly nonsense and yet can happen if full cost pricing is followed blindly. A major European technology company priced one of its main product lines in this way, and suffered a downward spiral of sales as prices were raised each year with disastrous consequences.

The first problem with full cost pricing, then, is that it leads to an increase in price as sales fall. Second, the procedure is illogical because a sales estimate is made *before* a price is set. Third, it focuses on internal costs rather than customers' willingness to pay. Finally, there may be a technical problem in allocating overheads in multi-product firms.[3]

However, inasmuch as the method forces managers to calculate costs, it does give an indication of the minimum price necessary to make a profit. Once direct and fixed costs have been measured *break-even analysis* can be used to estimate the sales volume needed to balance revenue and costs at different price levels. Therefore, the procedure of calculating full costs is useful when other pricing methods are used since full costs may act as a constraint. If they cannot be covered then it may not be worthwhile launching the product.

Direct cost pricing

In certain circumstances, companies may use **direct cost pricing** (sometimes called *marginal cost pricing*). This involves the calculation of only those costs that are likely to rise as output increases. In the example shown in Table 13.1 direct cost per unit is £10. As output increases, so total costs will increase by £10 per unit. Like full cost pricing, direct cost pricing includes a mark-up (in this case 10 per cent) giving a price of £11.

The obvious problem is that this price does not cover full costs and so the company would be making a loss selling a product at this low price. However, there are situations where selling at a price above direct costs but below full cost makes sense. Suppose a company is operating at below capacity and the sales director receives a call from a buyer who is willing to place an order for 50,000 memory cards but will pay only £11 per unit. If, in management's judgement, to refuse the order will mean machinery lying idle, a strong case for accepting the order can be made since the £1 per unit (£50,000) over direct costs is making a contribution to fixed costs that would not be made if the order was turned down. The decision is not without risk, however. The danger is that customers who are paying a higher price become aware of the £11 price and demand a similar deal.

Direct cost pricing is useful for services marketing—for example, where seats in aircraft or rooms in hotels cannot be stored; if they are unused at any time the revenue is lost. In such situations, pricing to cover direct costs plus a contribution to overheads can make sense. As with the previous example, the risk is that customers who have paid the higher price find out and complain.

Direct costs, then, indicate the lowest price at which it is sensible to take business if the alternative is to let machinery (or seats or rooms) lie idle. Also, direct cost pricing does not suffer from the 'price up as demand down' problem that was found with full cost pricing, as it does not take account of fixed costs in the price calculation. Finally, it avoids the problem of allocating overhead charges found with full cost pricing for the same reason. However, when business is buoyant it gives no indication of the correct price because it does not take into account customers' willingness to pay. Nor can it be used in the long term as, at some point, fixed costs must be covered to make a profit. Nevertheless, as a short-term expedient or tactical device, direct cost pricing does have a role to play in reducing the impact of excess capacity.

Competitor-Orientated Pricing

A second approach to pricing is to focus on competitors rather than costs when setting prices. This can take two forms: **going-rate pricing** and **competitive bidding**.

Going-rate pricing

In situations where there is no product differentiation—for example, a certain grade of coffee bean—a producer may have to take the going rate for the product. This accords most directly to the economist's notion of perfect competition. To the marketing manager it is anathema. A fundamental marketing principle is the creation of a differential advantage, which enables companies to build monopoly positions around their products. This allows a degree of price discretion dependent upon how much customers value the differential advantage. Even for what appear to be commodity markets, creative thinking can lead to the formation of a differential advantage on which a premium price can be built. A case in point was Austin-Trumans, a steel stockholder, which stocked the same kind of basic steels held by many other stockholders. Faced with a commodity product, Austin-Trumans attempted to differentiate on delivery. It guaranteed that it would deliver on time or pay back 10 per cent of the price to the buyer. So important was delivery to buyers (and so unreliable were many of Austin-Trumans' rivals) that buyers were willing to pay a 5 per cent price premium for this guarantee. The result was that Austin-Trumans were consistently the most profitable company in its sector for a number of years. This example shows how companies can use the creation of a differential advantage to move away from going-rate pricing.

Competitive bidding

Many contracts are won or lost on the basis of competitive bidding. The most usual process is the drawing up of detailed specifications for a product and putting the contract out to tender. Potential suppliers quote a price that is confidential to themselves and the buyer (sealed bids). All other things being equal, the buyer will select the supplier that quotes the lowest price. A major focus for suppliers, therefore, is the likely bid prices of competitors.

Statistical models have been developed by management scientists to add a little science to the art of competitive bidding.[4] Most use the concept of *expected profit* where:

Expected profit = Profit × Probability of winning

It is clearly a notional figure based on actual profit (bid price – costs) and the probability of the bid price being successful. Table 13.2 gives a simple example of how such a competitive bidding model might be used. Based on past experience the bidder believes that the successful bid will fall in the range of £2000–£2500. As price is increased so profits will rise (full costs = £2000) and the probability of winning will fall. The bidder uses past experience to estimate the probability of each price level being successful. In this example the probability ranges from 0.10 to 0.99. By multiplying profit and probability an expected profit

TABLE 13.2   Competitive bidding using the expected profit criterion

Bid price (£)	Profit	Probability	Expected profit
2000	0	0.99	0
2100	100	0.90	90
2200	200	0.80	160*
2300	300	0.40	120
2400	400	0.20	80
2500	500	0.10	50

*Based on the expected profit criterion, recommended bid price is £2200.

figure can be calculated for each bid price. Expected profit peaks at £160, which corresponds to a bid price of £2200. Consequently this is the price at which the bid will be made.

Unfortunately this simple model suffers from a number of limitations. First, it may be difficult, if not impossible, for managers to express their views on the likelihood of a price being successful in precise statistical probability terms. Note that if the probability of the £2200 bid was recorded as 0.70 rather than 0.80, and likewise the £2300 bid was recorded as 0.50 rather than 0.40, the recommended bid price would move from £2200 (expected profit £140) to £2300 (expected profit £150). Clearly the outcome of the analysis can be dependent on small changes in the probability figures. Second, use of the expected profit criterion is limited to situations where the bidder can play the percentage game over the medium to long term. In circumstances where companies are desperate to win an order, they may decide to trade off profit for an improved chance of winning. In the extreme case of a company fighting for survival, a more sensible bid strategy might be to price at below full cost (£2000) and simply make a contribution to fixed costs, as we discussed above under direct cost pricing.

Clearly the use of competitive bidding models is restricted in practice. However, successful bidding depends on having an efficient competitor information system. One Scandinavian ball-bearing manufacturer, which relied heavily on effective bid pricing, installed a system that was dependent on salespeople feeding into its computer-based information system details of past successful and unsuccessful bids. The salespeople were trained to elicit successful bid prices from buyers, and then to enter them into a customer database that recorded order specifications, quantities and the successful bid price.

Because not all buyers were reliable when giving their salespeople information (sometimes it was in their interest to quote a lower successful bid price than actually occurred), competitors' successful bid prices were graded as category A (totally reliable—the salesperson had seen documentation supporting the bid price or it came from a totally trustworthy source), category B (probably reliable—no documentary evidence but the source was normally reliable) or category C (slightly dubious—the source may be reporting a lower than actual price to persuade us to bid very low next time). Although not as scientific as the competitive bidding model, this system, built up over time, provides a very effective database that salespeople can use as a starting point when they are next asked to bid by a customer.

Marketing-Orientated Pricing

Marketing-orientated pricing is more difficult than cost-orientated or competitor-orientated pricing because it takes a much wider range of factors into account. In all, 10 factors need to be considered when adopting a marketing-orientated approach—these are shown in Figure 13.3.

Marketing strategy

The price of a product should be set in line with *marketing strategy*. The danger is that price is viewed in isolation (as with full cost pricing) with no reference to other marketing decisions such as positioning, strategic objectives, promotion, distribution and product benefits. The result is an inconsistent mess that makes no sense in the marketplace and causes customer confusion.

The way around this problem is to recognize that the pricing decision is dependent on other earlier decisions in the marketing planning process (see Chapter 2). For new products, price will depend on positioning strategy, and for existing products price will be affected by strategic objectives. First, we shall examine the setting of prices for new products. Second, we shall consider the pricing of existing products.

Pricing new products

In this section we shall explore the way in which positioning strategy affects price, launch strategies based upon skimming and penetration pricing, and the factors that affect the decision to charge a high or low price.

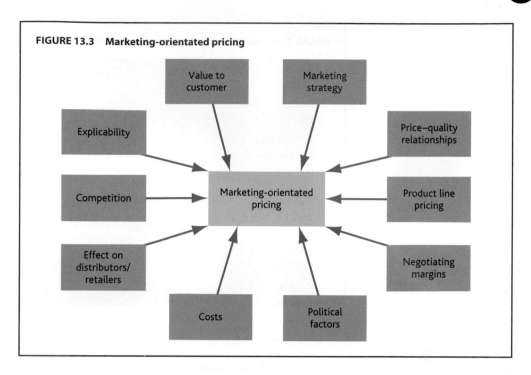

FIGURE 13.3 Marketing-orientated pricing

Positioning strategy: a key decision that marketing management faces when launching new products is **positioning strategy**. This in turn will have a major influence on price. As discussed in Chapter 8, product positioning involves the choice of target market and the creation of a differential advantage. Each of these factors can have an enormous impact on price.

When strategy is being set for a new product, marketing management is often faced with an array of potential target markets. In each, the product's differential advantage (value) may differ. For example, when calculators were developed commercially for the first time, three distinct segments existed: S1 (engineers and scientists who placed a high value on calculators because their jobs involved a lot of complex calculations); S2 (accountants and bankers who also placed a high value on a calculator because of the nature of their jobs, although not as high as S1); and S3 (the general public, who made up the largest segment but placed a much lower value on the benefits of calculators).[5]

Clearly the choice of target market had a massive impact on the price that could be charged. If engineers/scientists were targeted, a high price could be set, reflecting the large differential advantage of the calculator to them. For accountants/bankers the price would have to be slightly lower, and for the general public a much lower price would be needed. In the event, the S1 segment was chosen and the price set high (around £250/€360). Over time, price was reduced to draw into the market segments S2 and S3 (and a further segment, S4, when exam regulations were changed to allow schoolchildren to use calculators). Much later, when Casio entered the market, it targeted the general public with calculators priced at less than £10. The development of the market for calculators, based upon targeting increasingly price-sensitive market segments, is shown in Figure 13.4.

Two implications follow from this discussion. First, for new products, marketing management must decide on a target market and on the value that people in that segment place on the product (the extent of its differential advantage): only then can a market-based price be set which reflects that value. Second, where multiple segments appear attractive, modified versions of the product should be designed and priced differently, not according to differences in costs, but in line with the respective values that each target market places on the product.

Launch strategies: price should also be blended with other elements of the marketing mix. Figure 13.5 shows four marketing strategies based on combinations of price and promotion.

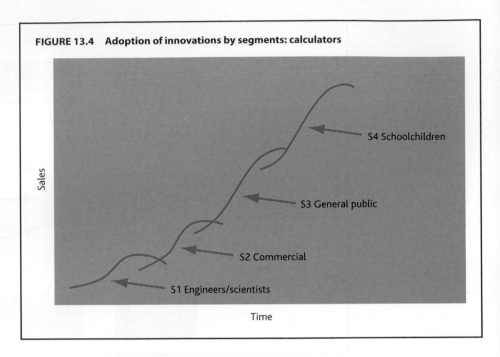

FIGURE 13.4   Adoption of innovations by segments: calculators

Similar matrices could also be developed for product and distribution, but for illustrative purposes promotion will be used here.

A combination of high price and high promotion expenditure is called a *rapid skimming strategy*. The high price provides high margin returns on investment and the heavy promotion creates high levels of product awareness and knowledge. Nike usually employs a rapid skimming strategy when it launches new ranges of trainers. Coca-Cola also employs rapid skimming strategies. A *slow skimming strategy* combines high price with low levels of promotional expenditure. High prices mean big profit margins, but high levels of promotion are believed to be unnecessary, perhaps because word of mouth is more important and the product is already well known (e.g. Rolls-Royce) or because heavy promotion is thought to be incompatible with product image.

Companies that combine low prices with heavy promotional expenditure are practising a *rapid penetration strategy*. The aim is to gain market share rapidly, perhaps at the expense of a rapid skimmer. For example, no-frills airlines such as easyJet and Ryanair have successfully attacked British Airways by adopting a rapid penetration strategy. Direct Line is an example of a company that challenged traditional UK insurance companies with great success by using heavy promotion and a low charge for its insurance policies. Supermarkets also use a rapid penetration strategy with low prices heavily promoted. For example, Tesco uses the strap-lines 'price drop' and 'Every little helps'; Asda uses 'permanently low prices forever', 'price guarantee 10 per cent lower than other supermarkets'; Aldi uses 'Like brands, only cheaper'.

Finally, a *slow penetration strategy* combines a low price with low promotional expenditure. Own-label brands use this strategy: promotion is not necessary to gain distribution, and low promotional expenditure helps to maintain high profit margins for these brands. The supermarket chains Netto and Lidl adopt a slow penetration strategy. The low promotional expenditures help to promote the low cost base necessary to support their low prices. This price/promotion framework is

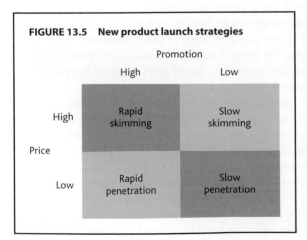

FIGURE 13.5   New product launch strategies

	Promotion	
	High	Low
Price High	Rapid skimming	Slow skimming
Price Low	Rapid penetration	Slow penetration

Go to the website and see how Aldi uses humour to promote its pricing strategy. www.mcgraw-hill.co.uk/textbooks/jobber

▲EXHIBIT 13.1   Aldi invests in television advertising to penetrate the market with its low-priced offers.

useful in thinking about marketing strategies at launch.

A major question remains, however: when is it sensible to use a *high price (skimming) strategy* and when should a *low price (penetration)* strategy be used?[6] To answer this question we need to understand the characteristics of market segments that can bear a high price. These characteristics are shown in Table 13.3. The more that each of these characteristics is present, the more likely that a high price can be charged.[7]

The first characteristic is that the market segment should place a *high value on the product*, based on the customer benefits it provides. Calculators provided high functional value to engineers and scientists, other products (for example, perfumes and clothing) may rely more on psychological value where brand image is crucial (for example, Chanel perfume or Gucci shoes). Second, high prices are more likely to be viable where *customers have a high ability to pay*. *Cash rich segments* in organizational markets often correlate with profitability. For example, the financial services sector and the textile industry in Europe may place similar values on marketing consultancy skills but in general the former has more ability to pay.

In certain markets the *consumer of the product is different from the bill payer*. This distinction may form the basis of a high-price market segment. Rail travel is often segmented by price sensitivity. Early-morning, long-distance trips are more expensive than midday journeys since the former are usually made by business people and sometimes the company they are working for will pay for their travel.

The fourth characteristic of high-price segments is *lack of competition* among supplying companies. The extreme case is a monopoly where customers have only one supplier from which to buy. When customers have no, or very little, choice of supply, the power to determine price is largely in the hands of suppliers. This means that high prices can be charged if suppliers so wish.

The fifth characteristic of high price segments is *excess demand*. When demand exceeds supply there is the potential to charge high prices. For example, when the demand for gold/petrol/cocoa exceeds supply the price of gold/petrol/cocoa usually rises.

The next situation where customers are likely to be less price sensitive is where there is *high pressure to buy*. For example, in an emergency situation where a vital part is required to repair a machine that is needed to fulfil a major order, the customer may be willing to pay a high price if a supplier can guarantee quick delivery.

The final situation where high prices can be charged is where there are high *switching costs*. Buyers may have made investments in dealing with a supplier that they would have to make again if they switched suppliers. Production, logistical or marketing operations may be geared to using the equipment of a particular supplier (e.g. computer systems). Customers may have invested heavily in product-specific training that would have to be repeated if they chose to switch. These factors are likely to make customers less sensitive to the price charged by existing suppliers in such circumstances.

The task of the marketing manager is to evaluate the chosen target market for a new product using the checklist provided in Table 13.3. It is unlikely that all seven conditions will apply and so judgement is still required. But the more these characteristics are found in the target market, the greater the chances that a high price can be charged.

TABLE 13.3   Characteristics of high-price market segments

1 Product provides high value
2 Customers have high ability to pay
3 Consumer and bill payer are different
4 Lack of competition
5 Excess demand
6 High pressure to buy
7 Switching costs

Table 13.4 lists the conditions when a *low price (penetration) strategy* should be used. The first situation is when an analysis of the market segment using the previous checklist reveals that a low price is the *only feasible alternative*. For example, a product that has no differential advantage launched on to a market where customers are not cash rich, pay for themselves, have little pressure to buy and have many suppliers to choose from has no basis for charging a price premium. At best it could take the going-rate price but, more likely, would be launched using a penetration (low-price) strategy, otherwise there would be no incentive for consumers to switch from their usual brand. The power of consumers to force down prices is nowhere greater than on the Internet.

Digital Marketing 13.1 Online Pricing

Increasingly businesses are developing multichannel strategies in order to give their customers more opportunities to interact with brands. In the early days of consumer adoption of the Internet, price was used to drive customers to buy online. Heavily discounted prices were attractive to certain target audiences, who were happy to forgo any perceived risks of buying online to benefit from lower prices. However, it is becoming more difficult to justify on- and offline pricing policies, especially in consumer markets. Low-cost airlines sell the majority of their products online and penalize consumers with higher prices if they do not buy online. However, for companies selling tangible goods, it is becoming harder to legitimize differential online pricing. Part of the reason for this change is that the Internet provides increased price transparency and, as more and more consumers gain confidence to shop online, there is less need for a price differential. Indeed, differences in pricing can act as a disincentive to shopping online. Dixons Retail, operating the brands of Currys, PC World, PIXmania.com, Gigantti, Lefdal, Elkjop, UniEuro and other well-known brands in Europe, is not a newcomer to the world of multichannel retailing. The business has now adopted a strategy whereby customers can buy at the same price regardless of the channel they choose to make a purchase. This is part of its business strategy to put the customer at the heart of everything the company does.

Based on: Chaffey and Ellis-Chadwick (2012)[8]

There are, however, more positive reasons for using a low-price strategy. A company may wish to gain *market penetration* or *domination* by pricing its products aggressively. This requires a market containing at least one segment of price-sensitive consumers. Direct Line priced its insurance policies aggressively to challenge traditional insurance companies and is now market leader for home and motor insurance in the UK. Tesco, the UK supermarket chain, has also become the market leader through charging low prices for good-quality products. The importance of having a sizeable segment of price-sensitive customers is illustrated in Marketing in Action 13.1.

Penetration pricing for market presence is sometimes followed by price increases once market share has reached a satisfactory level. Tata cars has followed this approach with the Nano, partly as a strategic move and partly in response to increased production costs.

Low prices may also be charged to increase output and so bring down costs through the *experience curve effect*. Research has shown that, for many products, costs decline by around 20 per cent when production doubles.[9] Cost economies are achieved by learning how to produce the product more effectively through better production processes and improvements in skill levels. Economies of scale through, for example, the use of more cost-effective machines at higher output levels also act to lower costs as production rises. Marketing costs per unit of output may also fall as production rises. For example, an advertising expenditure of £1 million represents 1 per cent of revenue when sales are £100 million, but rises to 10 per cent of revenue when sales are only £10 million. Therefore, a company may choose to price aggressively to become the largest

TABLE 13.4 Conditions for charging a low price

1	Only feasible alternative
2	Market penetration or domination
3	Experience curve effect/low costs
4	Make money later
5	Make money elsewhere
6	Barrier to entry
7	Predation

Marketing in Action 13.1 Tata Nano: The Lowest-Priced Car in the World?

Henry Ford famously used a low-price penetration strategy to bring affordable cars to the general public in the USA, employing the now legendary strap-line 'You can have any colour of car you want, so long as it is black'. Now other car-making entrepreneurs seem to be following a similar strategy.

Tata Motors of India launched a low-priced, small 'people's car' priced at the equivalent of around £1450. The car is the dream of company chairman Ratan Tata, whose idea is to market a vehicle that would bridge the gap between cars and motor scooters for 3 million people a year in India. 'Families who presently all ride through the heat and dust on a two-wheeler will have an alternative in the form of a car for the first time,' said Ravi Kant, managing director of Tata Motors.

The new model's price is kept low by employing a small-capacity engine, keeping its size small, using more plastic than steel, and swapping high-tech glue for traditional welding. At £1450 it is less than half the price of the next cheapest car in India. With an enormous market segment of people on low incomes, the demand for this vehicle is high. Indeed, the first 100,000 Nanos were sold through a lottery system as demand outstripped supply. But, despite the tremendous opportunity, mistakes were made in production and the car has been positioned as a 'poor person's car' and sales volume is down.

However, rival Indian carmaker Baja has launched its RE60. The vehicle is very fuel efficient and environmentally friendly. The RE60 is positioned as a solution to the growing transport problem in India's major cities and priced low to target Nano's market share.

Based on: BBC News (2012);[10,11] *Mishra (2012);*[12] *Ramesh (2006);*[13] *Hutton (2008)*[14]

producer and, if the experience curve holds, the lowest-cost supplier. Intel has taken full advantage of the cost economies that come with being the dominant market leader in the microprocessor market, with over 80 per cent share and the investment of billions of dollars in hyper-productive plants that can produce more processors in a day than some of its rivals can produce in a year.[15] This has given it the option of achieving higher profit margins than its competitors or charging low prices, as it did with its top-performing Pentium processor; prices dropped by 57 per cent in a six-week period in a move designed to hurt its major rival AMD.[16] Indeed, *low costs* through ruthless cost-cutting may be necessary to achieve profits

Go to the website and compare how Tesco and Asda supermarkets use pricing strategies to promote their brands.
www.mcgraw-hill.co.uk/ textbooks/jobber

using low-price strategies. For example, the German supermarket chain Lidl keeps costs low by displaying products on racks and in the packaging in which they are delivered, and by keeping advertising and promotional expenditure to a minimum. Interestingly, its strategy is different in Germany, where it has much greater market penetration. Its scale economies allow it to maintain low costs even though its advertising expenditure is much higher.

A low-price strategy can also make sense when the objective is to *make money later*. Two circumstances can provoke this action. First, the sale of the basic product may be followed by profitable after-sales service and/or spare parts. For example, the sale of an aero-engine at cost may be worthwhile if substantial profits can be made on the later sale of spare parts.

Two companies that have successfully applied this strategy are Hewlett-Packard and Gillette. Hewlett-Packard printers are sold at a low price to consumers but replacement ink cartridges are expensive, which is where it makes large profits. Gillette follows a similar strategy, pricing its razors competitively but charging a high price for replacement blades. Its razors account for 5 per cent of the razor division's profits, while blades account for 95 per cent.[17] Sony and Microsoft have also sold their games consoles at a loss, making money on the subsequent sales of games.

Second, the price sensitivity of customers may change over time as circumstances change. For example digital cameras were highly priced initially, then prices began to fall as more competitors entered the market. Prices then fell further as mobile phones and smartphones incorporated highly sophisticated cameras as part of a bundle of features.

Marketers also charge low prices to *make money elsewhere*. For example, retailers often use loss leaders, which are advertised in an attempt to attract customers into their stores and to create a low-cost image. Supermarkets, much to the annoyance of traditional petrol retailers, use petrol as a loss leader to attract motorists to their stores.[18] Manufacturers selling a range of products to organizations may accept low prices on some goods in order to be perceived by customers as a full-range supplier. In both cases, sales of other higher-priced and more profitable products benefit.

Low prices can also act as a *barrier to entry*. A company may weigh the longer-term benefits of deterring competition by accepting low margins to be greater than the short-term advantages of a high-price, high-margin strategy, which may attract rivals into its market.

Finally, low prices may be charged in an attempt to put other companies out of business; this is known as *predation*. However, this approach is rarely used because it can cause harmful price wars and in many countries is considered as an anti-competitive practice.

An alternative strategy to charging permanently low prices is to run sales promotions (e.g. temporary price cuts or bulk-buy offers). Some advantages of using a permanently low-price strategy (sometimes known as 'everyday low prices') are:

- price is perceived as honest, as consumers see consistently low prices, which suggests a fair profit margin; using a promotion may imply that the original price was high—big enough for temporary price reductions
- there is no need for expensive promotional advertising to gain awareness of promotional offers
- the danger of getting into costly promotional battles with rivals is reduced.

Some advantages of varying price levels by the use of sales promotions (sometimes known as 'hi-lo pricing') are:

- sales events and promotions create excitement that can generate extra store traffic
- sales promotions attract 'promotion junkies' who form a segment of consumers that have high price awareness and respond to promotions
- sales promotions have a proven record of increasing short-term sales.

Pricing existing products

The pricing of existing products should also be set within the context of strategy. Specifically, the *strategic objective* for each product will have a major bearing on pricing strategy. As with new products, price should not be set in isolation, but should be consistent with strategic objectives. Four strategic objectives are relevant to pricing: build, hold, harvest and reposition.

- *Build objective*: for price-sensitive markets, a build objective for a product implies a *price lower than the competition*. If the competition raises its prices we would be slow to match it. For price-insensitive markets, the best pricing strategy becomes less clear-cut. Price in these circumstances will be dependent on the overall positioning strategy thought appropriate for the product.

- *Hold objective*: where the strategic objective is to hold sales and/or market share, the appropriate pricing strategy is to maintain or match *price* relative to the competition. This has implications for price changes: if competition reduces prices then our prices would match this price fall.

- *Harvest objective*: a harvest objective implies the maintenance or raising of profit margins even though sales and/or market share are falling. The implication for pricing strategy would be to set *premium prices*. For products that are being harvested, there would be much greater reluctance to match price cuts than for products that were being built or held. On the other hand, price increases would swiftly be matched.

- *Reposition objective*: changing market circumstances and product fortunes may necessitate the repositioning of an existing product. This may involve a price change, the direction and magnitude of which will be dependent on the new positioning strategy for the production. As discussed under 'product replacement strategies' (Chapter 12), Skoda's repositioning involved better quality and a higher price.

The above examples show how developing clear strategic objectives helps the setting of price and clarifies appropriate reaction to competitive price changes. Price setting, then, is much more sophisticated than simply asking 'How much can I get for this product?' The process starts by asking more fundamental questions like 'How is this product going to be positioned in the marketplace?' and 'What is the appropriate strategic objective for this product?' Only after these questions have been answered can price sensibly be determined.

Value to the customer

A second marketing consideration when setting prices is estimating a product's value to the customer. Already when discussing marketing strategy its importance has been outlined: price should be accurately keyed to the value to the customer. In brief, the more value a product gives compared to that of the competition, the higher the price that can be charged. In this section we shall explore a number of ways of estimating value to the customer. This is critical because of the close relationship between value and price. Three methods of estimating value will now be discussed: trade-off analysis, experimentation and economic value to the customer analysis.

Trade-off analysis

Trade-off analysis (otherwise known as *conjoint analysis*) measures the trade-off between price and other product features so that their effects on product preference can be established.[19] Respondents are not asked direct questions about price; instead product profiles consisting of product features and price are described and respondents are asked to name their preferred profile. From their answers, the effect of price and other product features can be measured using a computer model. The following is a brief description of the procedure.

The first step is to identify the most important product features (attributes) and benefits that are expected to be gained as a result of buying the product. Product profiles are then built using these attributes (including price) and respondents are asked to choose which product they would buy from pairs of product profiles. Statistical analysis allows the computation of *preference contributions* that permit the preference for attributes to be compared. For example, if the analysis was for a business-to-business product, trade-off analysis might show that improving delivery time from one week to one day is worth a price increase of 5 per cent. In addition, the relative importance of each of the product attributes, including price, can be calculated. By translating these results into market share and profit figures for the proposed new product the optimal price can be found.

This technique has been used to price a wide range of industrial and consumer products and services, and can be used to answer such questions as the following:[20]

1   What is the value of a product feature including improving service levels in price terms?
2   What happens to market share if price changes?
3   What is the value of a brand name in terms of price?
4   What is the effect on our market share of competitive price changes?
5   How do these effects vary across European countries?

Experimentation

A limitation of trade-off analysis is that respondents are not asked to back up their preferences with cash expenditure. Consequently, what they say they prefer may not be reflected in actual purchase when they are asked to part with their money. *Experimental pricing research* attempts to overcome this drawback by placing a product on sale at different locations with varying prices.

The major alternatives are to use a controlled store experiment or test marketing. In a *controlled store experiment* a number of stores are paid to vary the price levels of the product under test. Suppose 100 supermarkets are being used to test two price levels of a brand of coffee; 50 stores would be chosen at random (perhaps after controlling for region and size) and allocated the lower price, the rest would use the higher price. By comparing sales levels and profit contributions between the two groups of stores the most profitable price would be established. A variant of this procedure would test price differences between the test brand and major rival brands. For example, in half the stores a price differential of 2p may be compared with 4p. In practice, considerable sums need to be paid to supermarkets to obtain approval to run such tests, and the implementation of the price levels needs to be monitored carefully to ensure that the stores do sell at the specified prices.

Test marketing can be used to compare the effectiveness of varying prices so long as more than one area is chosen. For example, the same product could be sold in two areas using an identical promotional campaign but with different prices between areas. A more sophisticated design could measure the four combinations of high/low price and high/low promotional expenditure if four areas were chosen. Obviously, the areas would need to be matched (or differences allowed for) in terms of target customer profile so that the result would be comparable. The test needs to be long enough so that trial and repeat purchase at each price can be measured. This is likely to be between 6 and 12 months for products whose purchase cycle lasts more than a few weeks.

A potential problem of using test marketing to measure price effects is competitor activity designed to invalidate the test results. For example, competitors could run special promotions in the test areas to make sales levels atypical if they discovered the purpose and location of the test marketing activities. Alternatively, they may decide not to react at all. If they know that a pricing experiment is taking place and that syndicated consumer panel data are being used to measure the results they may simply monitor the results since competitors will be receiving the same data as the testing company.[21] By estimating how successful each price has been, they are in a good position to know how to react when a price is set nationally.

Economic value to the customer analysis

Experimentation is more usual when pricing consumer products. However, industrial markets have a powerful tool at their disposal when setting the price of their products: **economic value to the customer (EVC)** analysis. Many organizational purchases are motivated by economic value considerations since reducing costs and increasing revenue are prime objectives of many companies. If a company can produce an offering that has a high EVC, it can set a high price and yet still offer superior value compared to the competition. A high EVC may be because the product generates more revenue for the buyer than competition or because its

Pricing on the Internet has received a lot of research attention in recent years. Quite often that research was to determine whether price dispersion still existed on the Internet where shopping search engines and price comparison websites could make pricing information from all vendors much more transparent.

This study investigates whether online retailer reputation can influence their pricing strategy, and thus provide an explanation for online price dispersion.

Wenhong Luo and Q. B. Chung (2010) Retailer Reputation and Online Pricing Strategy,
Journal of Computer Information Systems, Summer, 50–56.

Price discrimination is the practice of charging different customers different prices for the same product. Many people consider price discrimination unfair, but economists argue that in many cases price discrimination is more likely to lead to greater welfare than is the uniform pricing alternative. This article shows that there are many situations in which it is necessary to engage in differential pricing in order to make the provision of a product possible.

Juan M. Elegido (2011) The Ethics of Price Discrimination, Business Ethics Quarterly 21(4), 633–60.

operating costs (such as maintenance, operation or start-up costs) are lower over its lifetime. The Lexus was marketed using the latter approach, with the tag-line 'Lowest Cost of Ownership' based on its decent fuel economy, durability and resale value. Lexus salespeople were trained to provide the financial evidence to justify the claim.[22] Microsoft also used EVC analysis to defend its Windows platform against the threat from the lower-cost Linux operating system. Microsoft commissioned independent tests that showed how the total lifetime cost of open-source operating systems could exceed the costs of Windows despite their lower purchase price.[23] EVC analysis is usually particularly revealing when applied to products whose purchase price represents a small proportion of the lifetime costs to the customer.[24]

Figure 13.6 illustrates the calculation of EVC and how it can be used in price setting.

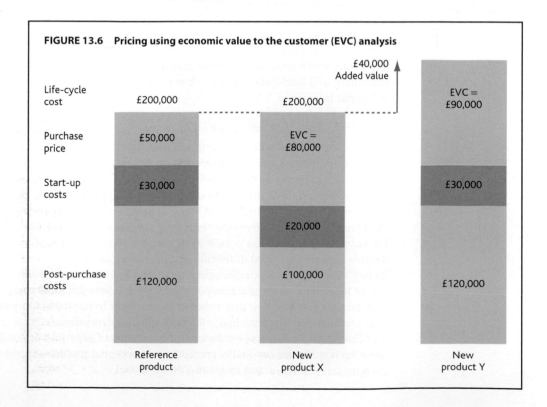

FIGURE 13.6 Pricing using economic value to the customer (EVC) analysis

A reference product is chosen (often the market leader) with which to compare costs. In the example, the market leader is selling a machine tool for £50,000. However, this is only part of a customer's life-cycle costs. In addition, £30,000 start-up costs (installation, lost production and operator training) and £120,000 post-purchase costs (operator, power and maintenance) are incurred. The total life-cycle costs are, therefore, £200,000.

Our new machine tool (product X) has a different customer cost profile. Technological advances have reduced start-up costs to £20,000 and post-purchase costs to £100,000. Therefore, total costs are reduced by £30,000 and the EVC our new product offers is £80,000 (£200,000 − £120,000). Thus, the EVC figure is the amount a customer would have to pay to make the total life-cycle costs of the new and reference products the same. If the new machine tool was priced at £80,000 this would be the case. Below this price there would be an economic incentive for customers to buy the new machine tool.

EVC analysis is clearly a powerful tool for price setting since it establishes the upper economic limit for price. Management then has to use judgement regarding how much incentive to give the customer to buy the new product and how much of a price premium to charge. A price of £60,000 would give customers a £20,000 lifetime cost saving incentive while establishing a £10,000 price premium over the reference product. In general, the more entrenched the market leader, the more loyal its customer base and the less well known the newcomer, the higher the cost saving incentive needs to be.

In the second example shown in Figure 13.6 the new machine tool (product Y) does not affect costs but raises the customer's revenues. For example, faster operation may result in more output, or greater precision may enhance product quality leading to higher prices. This product is estimated to give £40,000 extra profit contribution over the reference product because of higher revenues. Its EVC is, therefore, £90,000 indicating the highest price the customer should be willing to pay. Once more, marketing management has to decide how much incentive to give to customers and how much of a price premium to charge.

EVC analysis can be useful in target market selection since different customers may have varying EVC levels. A decision may be made to target the market segment that has the highest EVC figure since for these customers the product has the greatest differential advantage. The implementation of an EVC-based pricing strategy relies on a well-trained salesforce, which is capable of explaining sophisticated economic value calculations to customers, and field-based evidence that the estimates of cost savings and revenue increases will occur in practice.

Price–quality relationships

A third consideration when adopting a marketing-orientated approach to pricing is the relationship between price and perceived quality. Many people use price as an indicator of quality. This is particularly the case for products where objective measurement of quality is not possible, such as drinks and perfume. But the effect is also to be found with consumer durables and industrial products. A study of price and quality perceptions of cars, for example, found that higher-priced cars were perceived to possess (unjustified) high quality.[25] For example, the Seat Leon is built using many of the same components as the Audi A3, but the two cars are perceived differently, with the latter often being perceived to be of higher quality. Also sales of a branded agricultural fertilizer rose after the price was raised above that of its generic competitors despite the fact that it was the same compound. Interviews with farmers revealed that they believed the fertilizer to improve crop yield compared with rival products. Clearly price had influenced quality perceptions.

Mini Case 13.1 discusses some interesting results of experiments conducted to investigate the influence of price on quality perceptions. A potential problem, therefore, is that, by charging a low price, brand image may be tarnished.

Go to the website to see the creative approach used by American Airlines to differentiate its business and first class services. www.mcgraw-hill.co.uk/ textbooks/jobber

Mini Case 13.1 Does Price Really Influence Perceptions of Quality?

The question of the influence of price on quality perceptions has interested marketing managers for decades. Two experiments have investigated this issue. The first was a study into the effect of the price of placebos (dummy pills) on the killing of pain. Both pills were identical (a sugar compound) but patients that took the $2.50 placebo judged it better at killing pain than those that took one costing only 10 cents.

In the second experiment 20 occasional red wine drinkers were asked to taste a Cabernet Sauvignon marked with a $5 price tag and one with a $45 price label. However, both came from the same $5 bottle. The higher-priced wine was selected as tasting superior by most of the drinkers. To explain the results, neuroscience was called upon. In a second experiment, the drinkers were asked to drink again while wired up to a brain scanner. When they drank the 'more expensive' wine, the part of the brain associated with pleasure became more active than when the 'less expensive' wine was drunk. Clearly, the higher price caused the drinkers to experience more pleasure, even if the product itself was no different.

Question:

1   As a marketer, how could you use this information to promote lower-priced goods against competitors selling higher-priced goods? Use further examples to justify your argument.

Based on: The Guardian (2008);[26] *Rangel, O'Doherty and Shiv (2008);*[27] *Ritson (2008)*[28]

Product line pricing

Marketing-orientated companies also need to take account of where the price of a new product fits into its existing product line. For example, when Apple developed the iPod nano it had to carefully price-position the device against the original iPod mobile music player. Given that some potential buyers of the original iPod might now buy the nano, pricing it too cheaply could have resulted in lower overall profits for Apple.

Some companies prefer to extend their product lines rather than reduce the price of existing brands in the face of price competition. They launch cut-price fighter brands to compete with the low-price rivals. This has the advantage of maintaining the image and profit margins of existing brands (see Marketing in Action 13.2).

By producing a range of brands at different price points, companies can cover the varying price sensitivities of customers and encourage them to trade up to the more expensive, higher-margin brands.

Explicability

The capability of salespeople to explain a high price to customers may constrain price flexibility. In markets where customers demand economic justification of prices, the inability to produce cost and/or revenue arguments may mean that high prices cannot be set. In other circumstances the customer may reject a price that does not seem to reflect the cost of producing the product. For example, sales of an industrial chemical compound that repaired grooves in drive-shafts suffered because many customers believed that the price of £500 did not reflect the cost of producing the compound. Only when the salesforce explained that the premium price was needed to cover high research and development expenditure did customers accept that the price was not exploitative.

Competition

Competition factors are important determinants of price. At the very least, competitive prices should be taken into account; yet it is a fact of commercial life that many companies do not know what the competition is charging for its products.

Marketing in Action 13.2 Fighter Branding

Successful brands sometimes find that they are attacked by low-priced rivals. One option is to reduce price in order to improve the benefit–cost to buy ratio. This may defend sales volume but at the cost of lowering margins. It also means that consumers who are still prepared to pay the higher price are purchasing the brand at a discount. A better alternative may be to maintain the price of the existing brand and compete by launching a lower-priced fighter brand. This means that the image and profit margins of the original brand are maintained and the new brand may raise overall sales revenue by attracting price-sensitive consumers. The danger is that the fighter brand may cannibalize sales of the original brand.

Apple found itself being attacked by low-priced competitors in the mobile music player and desktop computer markets. The company chose a fighter brand strategy in both cases. The iPod shuffle, originally retailing at £49 compared to £219 for the iPod, was launched to compete with low-price MP3 players, and the Mac mini computer was introduced to compete against cheaper PCs entering the market from companies like China's Lenovo.

Bosch also found itself at a disadvantage compared to low-price white goods competitors. Fearing that the brand would lose its premium positioning if it price-discounted, the company has launched Viva, aimed at price-conscious consumers who are looking for no-frills white goods. This means that the Bosch brand can maintain its upmarket image and price, while the company can compete on price using the Viva range of white goods.

The launch of the Celeron microchip by Intel is another example of successful fighter branding. Instead of cutting the price of its flagship Pentium chip, Intel responded to cheap rival chips by creating the Celeron chip, which involved no additional design or tooling costs as it was based on the Pentium design (some co-processor capabilities were simply turned off) and so could be sold at a low price, targeting home and small business computers.

Some supermarkets use fighter branding to minimize the impact of heavy discounters like Netto, Aldi and Lidl. For example, Tesco created its Value brand for this purpose, and Sainsbury's has its Basics range of groceries.

Based on: Parry (2005);[29] Nagle and Hogan (2006);[30] Ritson (2008);[31] Jobber and Fahy (2009)[32]

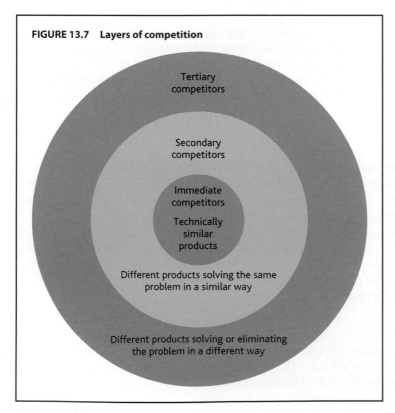

FIGURE 13.7 Layers of competition

Tertiary competitors

Secondary competitors

Immediate competitors

Technically similar products

Different products solving the same problem in a similar way

Different products solving or eliminating the problem in a different way

Care has to be taken when defining competition. When asked to name competitors, many marketing managers list companies that supply technically similar products. For example, a paint manufacturer will name other paint manufacturers. However, as Figure 13.7 illustrates, this is only one layer of competition. A second layer consists of dissimilar products solving the same problem in a similar way. Polyurethane varnish manufacturers would fall into this category. A third level of competition would come from products solving the problem (or eliminating it) in a dissimilar way. Since window frames are often painted, PVC double glazing manufacturers would form competition at this level.

This analysis is not simply academic, as the effects of price changes can be misleading if these three layers of competition are not taken into consideration. For example, if all paint manufacturers raised their prices simultaneously, they might believe that overall sales would not be dramatically affected if they mistakenly defined competition as technically similar products. The reality is, however, that such price collusion would make polyurethane varnish and, over a longer period, PVC double glazing more attractive to customers. The implication is that companies must take into account all three levels of competition when setting and changing prices.

In Europe a potential competitive threat is the development of **parallel importing**, which is the practice of importing goods from low-priced markets into high-priced ones by distributors. This produces the novel effect of a brand competing with itself (on price). For example, a pharmaceutical company might sell its drugs in a developing country at a low price only to discover that its discounted drugs have been purchased by distributors in another country where it is in direct competition with the same product sold for higher prices by the same firm. Manufacturers can lose out on this activity. First, it lowers average selling prices and, therefore, reduces profit margins. Second, manufacturers lose control over where and to whom their products are sold. This can damage brand image (compounded by the price drop) as the product range is sold in retail outlets that are incompatible with the brand's position in the marketplace. Finally, the relationship between manufacturers and their traditional distributors can be damaged as the latter see their sales decline in favour of their price-cutting rivals.[33] Levi Strauss sought to prevent the parallel importing of cut-price Levi 501 jeans by Tesco, a UK supermarket chain. Tesco had been selling 501s, purchased cheaply in the USA, for £27.99, compared to £50 in Levi's authorized shops. Levi Strauss won the case, which was heard at the European Court of Justice, arguing that its premium brand reputation was in danger of being damaged by this activity.[34]

Negotiating margins

In some markets customers expect a price reduction. Price paid is therefore very different from list price. In the car market, for example, customers expect to pay less than the asking price in return for a cash sale. For organizational customers, Marn and Rosiello describe the difference between list price and realized or transaction price as the **price waterfall**.[35] The difference can be accounted for by order-size discounts, competitive discounts (a discretionary discount negotiated before the order is taken), a fast payment discount, an annual volume bonus and promotional allowances.

Managing this price waterfall is a key element in achieving a satisfactory transaction price. Marketing-orientated companies recognize that such discounting may be a fact of commercial life and build in *negotiating margins* that allow prices to fall from list price levels but still permit profitable transaction prices to be achieved.

Effect on distributors/retailers

When products are sold through intermediaries such as distributors or retailers, the list price to the customer must reflect the margins required by them. When Müller yoghurt was first launched in the UK, a major factor in gaining distribution in a mature market was the fact that its high price allowed attractive profit margins for the supermarket chains. Conversely, the implementation of a penetration pricing strategy may be hampered if distributors refuse to stock the product because the profit per unit sold is less than that for competitive products.

The implication is that pricing strategy is dependent on understanding not only the ultimate customer but also the needs of the distributors and retailers who form the link between them and the manufacturer. If their needs cannot be accommodated, product launch may not be viable or a different distribution system (for example, direct selling) may be required.

Political factors

High prices can be a contentious public issue, which may invoke government intervention. Where price is out of line with manufacturing costs, political pressure may act to force down prices. The European Commission and national bodies such as the Competition Commission have been active in discouraging anti-competitive practices such as price-fixing. Indeed, the establishment of the single European market was a result of the desire to raise competitive pressures and thereby reduce prices throughout the European Union.

Companies need to take great care that their pricing strategies are not seen to be against the public interest. Ofcom, the independent regulator for the UK communications industries, provides advice to help consumers and businesses make informed choices when selecting communication products. Exploitation of a monopoly position may bring short-term profits but incur the backlash of a public inquiry into pricing practices.

Costs

The final consideration that should be borne in mind when setting prices is costs. This may seem in contradiction to the outward-looking marketing-orientated approach but, in reality, costs do enter the pricing equation. The secret is to consider costs alongside all of the other considerations discussed under marketing-orientated price setting rather than in isolation. In this way costs act as a constraint: if the market will not bear the full cost of producing and marketing the product it should not be launched.

What should be avoided is the blind reference to costs when setting prices. Simply because one product costs less to make than another does not imply that its price should be less.

Initiating Price Changes

Our discussion of pricing strategy so far has looked at the factors that affect it. By taking into account the 10 marketing-orientated factors, managers can judge the correct level at which to set prices. But in a highly competitive world, pricing is dynamic: managers need to know when and how to raise or lower prices, and whether or not to react to competitors' price moves. First, we shall discuss initiating price changes, before analysing how to react to competitors' price changes.

Three key issues associated with initiating price changes are the *circumstances* that may lead a company to raise or lower prices, the *tactics* that can be used, and *estimating competitor reaction*. Table 13.5 illustrates the major points relevant to each of these considerations.

Circumstances

A price increase may be justified as a result of marketing research (for example, trade-off analysis or experimentation) which reveals that customers place a higher *value* on the product than is reflected in its price. *Rising costs*, and hence reduced profit margins, may also stimulate price rises. Another factor that leads to price increases is *excess demand*. A company that

TABLE 13.5   Initiating price changes

	Increases	**Cuts**
Circumstances	Value greater than price Rising costs Excess demand Harvest objective	Value less than price Excess supply Build objective Price war unlikely
Tactics	Price jump Staged price increases Escalator clauses Price unbundling Lower discounts	Price fall Staged price reductions Fighter brands Price bundling Higher discounts
Estimating competitor reaction	Strategic objectives Self-interest Competitive situation Past experience Statements of intent	

cannot supply the demand created by its customers may choose to raise prices in an effort to balance demand and supply. This can be an attractive option as profit margins are automatically widened. The final circumstance when companies may decide to raise prices is when embarking on a *harvest objective*. Prices are raised to increase margins even though sales may fall.

Correspondingly, price cuts may be provoked by the discovery that price is high compared to the *value* that customers place on the product, *falling costs* (and the desire to bring down costs further through the experience curve effect), and where there is *excess supply* leading to excess capacity. A further circumstance that may lead to price falls is the adoption of a *build objective*. When customers are thought to be price sensitive, price cutting may be used to build sales and market share. The final circumstance that might lead to price cuts is the desire to *pre-empt competitive entry* into a market. Proactive price cuts—before the new competitor enters—are painful to implement because they incur short-term profit sacrifices but immediately reduce the attractiveness of the market to the potential entrant and reduce the risk of customer annoyance if prices are reduced only after competitive entry.

Tactics

Price increases and cuts can be implemented in many ways. The most direct is the *price jump* or *fall*, which increases or decreases the price by the full amount in one go. A price jump avoids prolonging the pain of a price increase over a long period but may raise the visibility of the price increase to customers. Using *staged price increases* might make the price rise more palatable but runs the risk of a company being charged with 'always raising its prices'. A *one-stage price fall* can have a high-impact dramatic effect that can be heavily promoted, but also has an immediate impact on profit margins. *Staged price reductions* have a less dramatic effect but may be used when a price cut is believed to be necessary but the amount necessary to stimulate sales is unclear. Small cuts may be initiated as a learning process that proceeds until the desired effect on sales has been achieved.

Price can also be raised by using *escalator clauses*. The contracts for some organizational purchases are drawn up before the product has been made. Constructing the product—for example, a new defence system or motorway—may take a number of years. An escalator clause in the contract allows the supplier to stipulate price increases in line with a specified index—for example, increases in industry wage rates or the cost of living.

Price unbundling is another tactic that effectively raises prices. Many product offerings actually consist of a set of products for which an overall price is set (for example, computer hardware and software). Price unbundling allows each element in the offering to be priced separately in such a way that the total price is raised. A variant on this process is charging for services that were previously included in the product's price. For example, manufacturers of mainframe computers have the option of unbundling installation and training services, and charging for them separately.

A final tactic is to maintain the list price but *lower discounts* to customers. In periods of heavy demand for new cars, dealers lower the cash discount given to customers, for example. Quantity discounts can also be manipulated to raise the transaction price to customers. The percentage discount per quantity can be lowered, or the quantity that qualifies for a particular percentage discount can be raised.

Companies that are contemplating a price cut have three options besides a direct price fall. A company defending a premium-priced brand that is under attack from a cut-price competitor may choose to maintain its price while introducing a *fighter brand*. The established brand keeps its premium-price position while the fighter brand competes with the rival for price-sensitive customers. Where a number of products and services that tend to be bought together are priced separately, *price bundling* can be used to effectively lower price. For example, televisions can be offered with 'free three-year repair warranties' or cars offered with 'free labour at first service'. Finally, *discount terms* can be made more attractive by increasing the percentage or lowering the qualifying levels. However, giving higher discounts over too long a period of time can be risky, as General Motors found to disastrous effect.

By pursuing a four-year price discounting strategy in the USA in the face of poor sales, it provoked a price war with Ford and Chrysler, caused consumers to focus on price rather than value offered by the product, and reduced profits.[36]

Estimating competitor reaction

A key factor in the price change decision is the extent of competitor reaction. A price rise that no competitor follows may turn customers away, while a price cut that is met by the competition may reduce industry profitability. Four factors affect the extent of competitor reaction: their strategic objectives, what is in their self-interest, the competitive situation at the time of the price change, and past experience.

Companies should try to gauge their *competitors' strategic objectives* for their products. By observing pricing and promotional behaviour, talking to distributors and even hiring their personnel, estimates of whether competitor products are being built, held or harvested can be made. This is crucial information: the competitors' response to our price increase or cut will depend upon it. They are more likely to follow our price increase if their strategic objective is to hold or harvest. If they are intent on building market share, they are more likely to resist following our price increase. Conversely, they are more likely to follow our price cuts if they are building or holding, and more likely to ignore our price cuts if they are harvesting.

Self-interest is also important when estimating competitor reactions. Managers initiating price changes should try to place themselves in the position of their competitors. What reaction is in their best interests? This may depend on the circumstances of the price change. For example, if price is raised in response to a general rise in cost inflation, the competition is more likely to follow than if price is raised because of the implementation of a harvest objective. Price may also depend upon the *competitive situation*. For example, if the competition has excess capacity, a price cut is more likely to be matched than if this is not the case. Similarly, a price rise is more likely to be followed if the competition is faced with excess demand.

Competitor reaction can also be judged by looking at their reactions to previous price changes. While *past experience* is not always a reliable guide, it may provide insights into the way in which competitors view price changes and the likely responses they might make. Past experience may be supplemented by *statements of intent*. For example, when T-Mobile dropped the price of its Flext brand, Vodafone immediately responded to prevent T-Mobile gaining market share, and its chief executive stated publicly, 'If anyone thinks that just by dropping prices they will take share from us, I will respond. I will compete, so they won't be getting an advantage on pure price.' Such declarations leave competitors in no doubt about Vodafone's reaction to further price falls.[37]

Reacting to Competitors' Price Changes

When competitors initiate price changes, companies need to analyse their appropriate reactions. Three issues are relevant here: when to follow, when to ignore, and the tactics required if the price change is to be followed. Table 13.6 summarizes the main considerations.

When to follow

Competitive price increases are more likely to be followed when they are due to general *rising cost* levels, or industry-wide *excess demand*. In these circumstances the initial pressure to raise prices is the same on all parties. Following a price rise is also more likely when customers are relatively *price insensitive*, which means that the follower will not gain much advantage by resisting the price increase. Where *brand image is consistent* with high prices, a company is more likely to follow a competitor's price rise as to do so would be consistent with the brand's positioning strategy. Finally, a price rise is more likely to be followed when a company is pursuing a *harvest or hold objective* because, in both cases, the emphasis is more on profit margin than sales/market share gain.

TABLE 13.6   Reacting to competitors' price changes

	Increases	Cuts
When to follow	Rising costs Excess demand Price-insensitive customers Price rise compatible with brand image Harvest or hold objective	Falling costs Excess supply Price-sensitive customers Price fall compatible with brand image Build or hold objective
When to ignore	Stable or falling costs Excess supply Price-sensitive customers Price rise incompatible with brand image Build objective	Rising costs Excess demand Price-insensitive customers Price fall incompatible with brand image Harvest objective
Tactics: – quick response – slow response	Margin improvement urgent Gains to be made by being customer's friend	Offset competitive threat High customer loyalty

Price cuts are likely to be followed when they are stimulated by general *falling costs* or *excess supply*. Falling costs allow all companies to cut prices while maintaining margins, and excess supply means that a company is unlikely to allow a rival to make sales gains at its expense. Price cuts will also be followed in *price-sensitive markets* since allowing one company to cut price without retaliation would mean large sales gains for the price cutter. The image of the company can also affect reaction to price cuts. Some companies position themselves as low-price manufacturers or retail outlets. In such circumstances they would be less likely to allow a price reduction by a competitor to go unchallenged for to do so would be *incompatible with their brand image*. Finally, price cuts are likely to be followed when the company has a *build* or *hold strategic objective*. In such circumstances an aggressive price move by a competitor would be followed to prevent sales/market share loss. In the case of a build objective, response may be more dramatic with a price fall exceeding the initial competitive move.

When to ignore

The circumstances associated with companies not reacting to a competitive price move are in most cases simply the opposite of the above. Price increases are likely to be ignored when *costs are stable or falling*, which means that there are no cost pressures forcing a general price rise. In the situation of *excess supply* companies may view a price rise as making the initiator less competitive, and therefore allow the price rise to take place unchallenged, particularly when customers are *price sensitive*. Companies occupying low-price positions may regard a price rise in response to a price increase from a rival to be *incompatible with their brand image*. Finally, companies pursuing a *build objective* may allow a competitor's price rise to go unmatched in order to gain sales and market share.

Price cuts are likely to be ignored in conditions of *rising costs*, *excess demand* and when servicing *price-insensitive customers*. Premium price positioners may be reluctant to follow competitors' price cuts for to do so would be *incompatible with brand image*. Lastly, price cuts may be resisted by companies using a *harvest objective*.

Tactics

When a company decides to follow a price change it can do so quickly or slowly. A *quick price reaction* is likely when there is an urgent need to *improve profit margins*. Here the competitor's price increase will be welcomed as an opportunity to achieve this objective.

Conversely, a *slow reaction* may be desirable when an *image of being the customer's friend* is being sought. The first company to announce a price increase is often seen as the high-price supplier. Some companies have mastered the art of playing the low-cost supplier by never initiating price increases and following competitors' increases slowly.[38] The key to this tactic is timing the response: too quickly and customers do not notice; too slowly and profit is foregone. The optimum period can be found only by experience but, during it, salespeople should be told to stress to customers that the company is doing everything it can to hold prices for as long as possible.

A *quick response* to a competitor's price fall will happen to ward off a *competitive threat*. In the face of undesirable sales/market share erosion, fast action is needed to nullify potential competitor gains. However, reaction will be slow when a company has a *loyal customer base* willing to accept higher prices for a period so long as they can rely on price parity over the longer term.

Ethical Issues in Pricing

Key issues regarding ethical issues in pricing are price fixing, predatory pricing, deceptive pricing, penetration pricing and obesity, price discrimination and product dumping.

Price fixing

One of the driving forces towards lower prices is competition. Therefore, it can be in the interests of producers to agree among themselves not to compete on price. This is an act of collusion and is banned in many countries and regions, including the EU. Article 83 of the Treaty of Rome is designed to ban practices preventing, restricting or distorting competition, except where these contribute to efficiency without inhibiting consumers' fair share of the benefit. Groups of companies that collude are said to be acting as a cartel and these are by no means easy to uncover.

Cartels push up prices and are outlawed by the European Commission. It has had several notable successes in unearthing and heavily fining price-fixing cartels. One of its most famous success stories is the uncovering of the illicit cartel among 33 of Europe's top chemical companies from the UK, France, Germany, Belgium, Italy, Spain, the Netherlands, Finland, Norway and Austria. Through collusion, they were able to sustain levels of profitability for low-density polyethylene and PVC in the face of severe overcapacity. Quotas were set to limit companies' attempts to gain market share through price competition. Prices were fixed to harmonize the differences between countries to discourage customers from shopping around for the cheapest deals.

Opponents of price fixing claim that it is unethical because it restrains the consumer's freedom of choice and interferes with each firm's interest in offering high-quality products at the best price. Proponents argue that under harsh economic conditions price fixing is necessary to ensure a fair profit for the industry and to avoid price wars that might lead to bankruptcies and unemployment.

Predatory pricing

This refers to the situation where a firm cuts its prices with the aim of driving out the competition. The firm is content to incur losses with the intent that high profits will be generated through higher prices once the competition is eliminated.

Deceptive pricing

This occurs when consumers are misled by the price deals offered by companies. Two examples are misleading price comparisons. Misleading price comparisons occur when a store sets artificially high prices for a short time so that much lower 'sale' prices can be claimed later. The purpose is to deceive the customer into believing they are being offered bargains. Some countries, such as the UK and Germany, have laws that state the minimum period over which the regular price should be charged before it can be used as a reference price in a sale.

Penetration pricing and obesity

A controversial issue is the question of the ethics of charging low prices for fatty food targeting young people. Critics claim that, by doing so, fast-food companies encourage obesity. Others claim that such companies cannot be blamed when consumers are made well aware by the media of the consequences of eating fatty foods.

Price discrimination

This occurs when a supplier offers a better price for the same product to one buyer and not to another, resulting in an unfair competitive advantage. Price discrimination can be justified when the cost of supplying different customers varies, where the price differences reflect differences in the level of competition and where different volumes are purchased.

Product dumping

This involves the export of products at much lower prices than charged in the domestic market, sometimes below the cost of production. Products are 'dumped' for a variety of reasons. First, unsold stocks may be exported at a low price rather than risk lowering prices in the home market. Second, products may be manufactured for sale overseas at low prices to fill otherwise unused production capacity. Finally, products that are regarded as unsafe at home may be dumped in countries that do not have such stringent safety rules. For example, the US Consumer Product Safety Commission ruled that three-wheel cycles were dangerous. Many companies responded by selling their inventories at low prices in other countries.[39]

When you have read this chapter

log on to the Online Learning Centre at **www.mcgraw-hill.co.uk/textbooks/jobber** to explore chapter-by-chapter test questions, links and further online study tools for marketing.

Review

1 **The economist's approach to price determination**
- The economist's approach to pricing was developed as an explanation of market behaviour and focuses on demand and supply. There are limitations in applying this approach in practice, which means that marketers turn to other methods in business.

2 **The differences between full cost and direct cost pricing**
- Full cost pricing takes into account both fixed and direct costs. Direct cost pricing takes into account only direct costs such as labour and materials.
- Both methods suffer from the problem that they are internally orientated methods. Direct cost pricing can be useful when the corporate objective is survival and there is a desperate need to fill capacity.

3 **An understanding of going-rate pricing and competitive bidding**
- Going-rate pricing is setting price levels at the rate generally applicable in the market, focusing on competitors' offerings and prices rather than on company costs. Marketers try to avoid going-rate pricing by creating a differential advantage.
- Competitive bidding involves the drawing up of detailed specifications for a product and putting the contract out to tender. Potential suppliers bid for the order with price an important choice criterion. Competitive bidding models have been developed to help the bidding process but they have severe limitations.

4 **The advantages of marketing-orientated pricing over cost-orientated and competitor-orientated pricing methods**
- Marketing-orientated pricing takes into account a much wider range of factors that are relevant to the setting of prices. Although costs and competition are still taken into account, marketers will take a much more customer-orientated view of pricing, including customers' willingness to pay as reflected in the perceived value of the product. Marketers will also evaluate the target market of the product to establish the price sensitivity of customers. This will be affected by such factors as the degree of competition, the degree of excess demand, and the ability of target customers to pay a high price. A full list of factors that marketers take into account is given in point 5 below.

5 **The factors that affect price setting when using a marketing-orientated approach**
- A marketing-orientated approach involves the analysis of marketing strategy, value to the customer, price–quality relationships, explicability, product line pricing, competition, negotiating margins, effect on distributors/retailers, political factors and costs.

6 **When and how to initiate price increases and cuts**
- Initiating price increases is likely to be carried out when value is greater than price, in the face of rising costs, when there is excess demand and where a harvest objective is being followed.
- Tactics are a price jump, staged price increases, escalator clauses, price unbundling and lower discounts.
- Initiating price cuts is likely to be carried out when value is less than price, when there is excess supply, where a build objective is being followed, where a price war is unlikely and when there is a desire to pre-empt competitive entry.
- Tactics are a price fall, staged price reductions, the use of fighter brands, price bundling and higher discounts.

7 **When and when not to follow competitor-initiated price increases and cuts; when to follow quickly and when to follow slowly**
- Competitor-initiated price increases should be followed when there are rising costs, excess demand, price-insensitive customers, where the price rise is compatible with brand image and where a harvest or hold objective is being followed.
- Competitor-initiated price increases should not be followed when costs are stable or falling, with excess supply, with price-sensitive customers, where the price rise is incompatible with brand image and where a build objective is being followed.
- The price increase should be followed quickly when the need for margin improvement is urgent, and slowly when there are gains to be made by being seen to be the customer's friend.
- Competitor-initiated price cuts should be followed when there are falling costs, excess supply, price-sensitive customers, where the price cut is compatible with brand image, and where a build or hold objective is being followed.
- Competitor-initiated price cuts should not be followed when there are rising costs, excess demand, price-insensitive customers, where the price fall is incompatible with brand image and where a harvest objective is being followed.
- The price cut should be followed quickly when there is a need to offset a competitive threat, and slowly where there is high customer loyalty.

8 **Ethical issues in pricing**
- There are potential problems relating to price fixing, predatory pricing, deceptive pricing, price discrimination and product dumping.

Key Terms

competitive bidding drawing up detailed specifications for a product and putting the contract out to tender

direct cost pricing the calculation of only those costs that are likely to rise as output increases

economic value to the customer (EVC) the amount a customer would have to pay to make the total life-cycle costs of a new and a reference product the same

full cost pricing pricing so as to include all costs and based on certain sales volume assumptions

going-rate pricing pricing at the rate generally applicable in the market, focusing on competitors' offerings rather than on company costs

marketing-orientated pricing an approach to pricing that takes a range of marketing factors into account when setting prices

parallel importing when importers buy products from distributors in one country and sell them in another to distributors who are not part of the manufacturer's normal distribution; caused by big price differences for the same product between different countries

positioning strategy the choice of target market (*where* the company wishes to compete) and differential advantage (*how* the company wishes to compete)

price unbundling pricing each element in the offering so that the price of the total product package is raised

price waterfall the difference between list price and realized or transaction price

trade-off analysis a measure of the trade-off customers make between price and other product features so that their effects on product preference can be established

Study Questions

1 Accountants are always interested in profit margins; sales managers want low prices to help promote sales; and marketing managers are interested in high prices to establish premium positions in the marketplace. To what extent do you agree with this statement in relation to the setting of prices?

2 You are the marketing manager of a company that is about to launch an electric car. What factors should you take into consideration when pricing this product?

3 Why is value to the customer a more logical approach to setting prices than cost of production? What role can costs play in the setting of prices?

4 Discuss the advantages and disadvantages of experimentation in assessing customers' willingness to pay.

5 What is economic value to the customer analysis? Under what conditions can it play an important role in price setting?

6 Under intense cost-inflationary pressure you are considering a price increase. What other considerations would you take into account before initiating the price rise?

7 You are the marketing manager of a range of premium-priced all-weather tyres. A competitor has launched a cut-price alternative that possesses 90 per cent of the effectiveness of your product. If you do not react, you estimate that you will lose 30 per cent of sales. What are your strategic pricing options? What would you do?

8 The only reason that companies set low prices is that their products are undifferentiated. Discuss.

References

1. Shapiro, B. P. and B. B. Jackson (1978) Industrial Pricing to Meet Customer Needs, *Harvard Business Review*, Nov.–Dec., 119–27.

2. See Shipley, D. (1981) Pricing Objectives in British Manufacturing Industry, *Journal of Industrial Economics* 29 (June), 429–43; Jobber, D. and G. J. Hooley (1987) Pricing Behaviour in the UK Manufacturing and Service Industries, *Managerial and Decision Economics* 8, 167–71.

3. Christopher, M. (1982) Value-in-Use Pricing, *European Journal of Marketing* 16(5), 35–46.

4. Edelman, F. (1965) Art and Science of Competitive Bidding, *Harvard Business Review*, July–August, 53–66.

5. Brown, R. (1991) The S-Curves of Innovation, *Journal of Marketing Management* 7(2), 189–202.

6. Jobber, D. and D. Shipley (1998) Marketing-orientated Pricing Strategies, *Journal of General Management* 23(4), 19–34.

7. Jobber, D. and D. Shipley (2012) Marketing-orientated Pricing: Understanding and Applying Factors that Discriminate Between Successful High and Low Pricing Strategies, *European Journal of Marketing* 46(11/12).

8. Chaffey, D. and F. E. Ellis-Chadwick (2012) *Digital Marketing: Strategy, Implementation and Practice*, 5th edn, Harlow: Pearson, 278–87.

9. Abell, D. F. and J. S. Hammond (1979) *Strategic Marketing Planning*, Englewood Cliffs, NJ: Prentice-Hall.

10. BBC News (2012) India car boss Ratan Tata admits Tata Nano 'mistakes', http://www.bbc.co.uk/news/world-asia-india-16427707, 5 January.

11. BBC News (2012) India carmaker Bajaj unveils Tata Nano rival, the RE60, http://www.bbc.co.uk/news/world-asia-16391248, 3 January.

12. Mishra, A. (2012) Bajaj RE60—Is it a car? *Forbes India*, 3 January.

13. Ramesh, R. (2006) Indian Motor Maker Gives the Go-Ahead for £1200 'People's Car', *The Guardian*, 20 May, 26.

14. Hutton, R. (2008) Tata Takes Lead with Small Cars, *The Sunday Times*, 14 December, 6.

15. Edwards, C. (2006) Inside Intel, *Business Week*, 9 January, 43–8.

16. Popovich, K. (2002) Intel to Cut Chip Pricing by 57 per cent, *eWeek*, 4 January, 16.

17. Nagle, T. T. and J. E. Hogan (2006) *The Strategy and Tactics of Pricing*, New Jersey: Pearson Education.

18. Eastham, J. (2002) Prices Down, Numbers Up, *Marketing Week*, 20 June, 22–5.

19. Kucher, E. and H. Simon (1987) Durchbruch bei der Preisentscheidung: Conjoint-Measurement, eine neue Technik zur Gewinnoptimierung, *Harvard Manager* 3, 36–60.

20. Cattin, P. and D. R. Wittink (1989) Commercial Use of Conjoint Analysis: An Update, *Journal of Marketing*, July, 91–6.

21. Moutinho, L. and M. Evans (1992) *Applied Marketing Research*, Wokingham: Addison-Wesley, 161.

22. Helm, B. (2008) How to Sell Luxury to Penny-Pinchers, *Business Week*, 10 November, 60.

23. Nagle and Hogan (2006) op. cit.

24. Forbis, J. L. and N. T. Mehta (1979) *Economic Value to the Customer*, McKinsey Staff Paper, Chicago: McKinsey & Co., Inc., February, 1–10.

25. Erickson, G. M. and J. K. Johansson (1985) The Role of Price in Multi-Attribute Product Evaluations, *Journal of Consumer Research*, September, 195–9.

26. *The Guardian* (2008) In Praise of Placebos, 5 March, 36.

27. Rangel, A., J. O'Doherty and B. Shiv (2008) *Marketing Actions Can Modulate Neural Representations of Experienced Pleasantness*, Stanford University Working Paper.

28. Ritson, M. (2008) Why Brands Are at a Premium, *Marketing*, 30 April, 19.

29. Parry, C. (2005) A Fridge Too Far for BSH?, *Marketing Week*, 16 June, 31.

30. Nagle and Hogan (2006) op. cit.

31. Ritson, M. (2008) Tesco Take Fight to Aldi, *Marketing*, 29 October, 20.

32. Jobber, D. and J. Fahy (2009) *Foundations of Marketing*, Maidenhead: McGraw-Hill.

33. Ghauri, P. N. and P. R. Cateora (2005) *International Marketing*, Maidenhead: McGraw-Hill.

34. Osborn, A. (2001) Levi's Wins Fight to Halt Tesco Price Cuts, *The Guardian*, 21 November, 13.

35. Marn, M. V. and R. L. Rosiello (1992) Managing Price, Gaining Profit, *Harvard Business Review*, Sept.–Oct., 84–94.

36. Simon, B. (2005) Detroit Giants Count Cost of Four Year Price War, *Financial Times*, 19 March, 29.

37. Ritson, M. (2008) Mobile Brands Make Poor Call on Value, *Marketing*, 23 January, 21.

38. Ross, E. B. (1984) Making Money with Proactive Pricing, *Harvard Business Review*, Nov.–Dec., 145–55.

39. Schlegelmilch, B. (1998) *Marketing Ethics: An International Perspective*, London: International Thomson Business Press.

The story behind the success of Europe's no-frills airlines began in the USA. Southwest Airlines, a Texas-based carrier, was the first to successfully exploit the deregulation of American skies in 1978. Since then the airline has operated a no-frills, low-fare business model involving no free meals or coffee, only peanuts. The attraction is fares set at about one-fifth of those of the mainstream airlines. Its fleet is made up entirely of one type of aircraft, the Boeing 737, to keep costs down by reducing pilot training and maintenance costs. It flies between secondary airports, which are sometimes over an hour's drive from city centres.

An essential component in the Southwest Airlines approach is fast turnaround times from uncongested airports, which can be as short as 20 minutes with no seat allocation for passengers and cabin crews doing the cleaning. This means that aircraft can be used for 15 hours per day. In comparison, conventional airlines that run a 'hub and spoke' network fly aircraft for only half that length of time, as aircraft must wait to connect with incoming flights. Southwest Airlines has embraced Internet transactions to cut paperwork and administrative costs, and has rejected corporate acquisitions in favour of organic growth. The result has been a continual stream of profits (unlike other American airlines) and a business that attracts nearly 65 million passengers a year.

In Europe Southwest Airlines' approach and success has been mirrored by easyJet and Ryanair, who have pioneered low-fare, no-frills flying. Growth has been spectacular with both airlines consistently recording annual increases in passenger numbers of 15–20 per cent although this has slowed in recent years.

The growth in the low-cost sector has been fuelled by the burgeoning market for short-haul city breaks, the desire of more adventurous holidaymakers to arrange their own vacation packages, and their wish to own holiday homes in warm, sunny climates. These factors, together with the drive by business to trim back on travel costs, have fuelled growth in passenger numbers.

Marketing strategy at easyJet

A key element in the success of easyJet has been its approach to pricing. The conventional method of selling airline seats was to start selling at a certain price and then

lower it if sales were too low. What Stelios Haji-Ioannou, owner of easyJet, pioneered was the opposite: the start was a low headline price that grabbed attention, then it was raised according to demand. Customers are never told how soon or by how much the price will be changed. This system, called *yield management*, is designed to allow airline seats to be priced according to supply and demand, and achieve high seat occupancy. This reflects the fact that a particular seat on a specific flight cannot be stored for resale: if it is empty, the revenue is lost.

For the customer the result has been fares much lower than those offered by conventional airlines such as BA and Lufthansa, and, to be profitable, easyJet has needed to control costs strictly. Following the example of Southwest Airlines, it has achieved this through simplicity (using one aircraft type), productivity (fast turnaround times to achieve high aircraft use) and direct distribution (using the Internet for upfront payment and low administrative charges). Also, onboard costs are reduced by not providing free drinks or meals to passengers.

Although easyJet operates out of secondary airports such as Luton in the UK, it is increasingly using mainstream airports such as Gatwick in a direct attempt to take passengers from more conventional rivals such as BA. Its approach is to fly to relatively few destinations but with a higher frequency on each route. This provides a barrier to entry, and the higher frequency attracts high-volume business travellers who prize schedule over price and are, therefore, willing to pay a little more for the service (the average easyJet seat price is reported to be higher than that of Ryanair). EasyJet also offers flexible fares that are attractive to business travellers as they allow free date changes. One in five of easyJet's passengers are business customers. The airline also derives revenue from the sale of onboard food and drinks, check-in charges, priority boarding fees, car hire and hotel bookings.

In 2002 easyJet bought the rival Go airline for £374 million (€523.6 million), a price lower than expected by many analysts. For easyJet, the deal was about creating a route network that stretched across Europe. With the exception of domestic routes, the two airlines had few destinations in common. easyJet's top routes include Amsterdam, Geneva and Paris, while Go took holidaymakers to Faro, Bologna and Bilbao. There was overlap on only a handful of destinations, both flying to Barcelona, Nice, Majorca and Malaga. Furthermore, the UK bases of the two airlines were complementary, with easyJet operating from Luton, Gatwick and Liverpool, while Go operated from Stansted, Bristol and East Midlands airports. At the time the combined companies were about the same size as Ryanair in terms of passenger numbers. The takeover alone gave easyJet scale and increased buying power, a factor that was important when it decided to abandon its policy of using only Boeing 737s by buying a fleet of aircraft from Airbus in 2002 at a knockdown price.

In 2007 easyJet bought GB Airways in a £103 million deal that allowed easyJet to expand operations at London Gatwick airport and also establish a base at Manchester airport.

Under its entrepreneurial leader, Stelios, the easyJet group moved into other areas, such as car hire, Internet cafés and cruises, using the same low-price model. Another venture was the setting up of easyCinema to challenge the established cinema chains. The motivation was the half-empty cinema auditoria Stelios saw when visiting conventional cinemas. He could not understand why price was not varied according to demand (by day and by film). Although some cinemas did reduce prices midweek, their pricing policies were not considered flexible enough compared to pricing using yield management. Also, he argued, why pay the same to see a blockbuster as a flop? And why is the price of the blockbuster the same on the opening night as it is six weeks later? What he proposed was an infinite number of prices depending on supply and demand, following his success in the airline business.

The easyCinema formula worked as follows. The pricing structure began at 20 pence (less than €0.30). People logged on to easyCinema.com where they found three options. First, they could select the movie they most wanted to see, the dates when they could see it and at what prices; second, they could select the day on which they wanted to

visit the cinema, what films were showing and at what prices; and third they could come to the site with a budget of, say, £1 (€1.44), and find all the movies that could be seen for £1 or less. Bookings could be made up to two weeks in advance. As with aircraft seats, the likelihood was that, the earlier the booking was made, the cheaper the seat would be. Also, after examining costs, Stelios decided not to install food and drink stands, saying, 'If ya want popcorn, go to a popcorn vendor. For movies come to easyCinema'. Staff costs were also reduced since there were no tickets. Booking was done through the website, and a membership card was printed out that admitted visitors to the cinema via a turnstile. Finally, no advertising for unrelated products (e.g. the local curry house) prior to the movie showing was allowed. The first easyCinema was opened in Milton Keynes with a view to expanding the business across the UK. In 2006, however, three years after its opening, it closed, and the plan to transform the movie business was abandoned in the face of meagre audiences.

In 2002 Mr Haji-Ioannou stood down as chairman to take on the role of non-executive director. He remains the largest shareholder, and in 2008 became embroiled in a dispute with the board, believing that their plans for expansion were too ambitious in the light of a looming recession.

Marketing strategy at Ryanair

Ryanair is run by Michael O'Leary, who is famous for his outspoken views and controversial advertising campaigns. Like easyJet, Ryanair has followed the Southwest Airlines business model but, if anything, has been more ruthless on cost-cutting. It provides cheap point-to-point flying from secondary airports, rather than shadowing and undercutting the major carriers as easyJet increasingly does. Sometimes the airports can be 60 miles from the real destination: for Frankfurt read Hahn, for Hamburg read Lübeck, for Stockholm read Vesteraas or Skavsta, and for Brussels read Charleroi. Ryanair has kept to its single-aircraft policy, the Boeing 737, which it bought second-hand and cheaply, reducing maintenance, spares and crew training. Its new fleet of 737–800s were purchased at record low prices at the bottom of the market. They offer 45 per cent more seats at lower operating costs and the same number of crew. Ryanair has continued this policy with the purchase of a further 70 Boeings in 2005 at an even lower price. In 2009 it entered negotiations with Boeing and Airbus over the purchase of up to 300 short-haul jets and announced plans to become a transatlantic carrier. In the event, Ryanair continued its policy of buying only one type of aircraft. By 2011 it operated over 300 Boeing 737s.

Turnaround times at airports are fast, to keep more aircraft in the air, and online booking has slashed sales and distribution costs. Ryanair.com has become the largest travel website in Europe, selling more than 2 million seats per month. Ryanair's focus on cost reduction has resulted in profit margins about double those of easyJet despite the latter's higher prices. Some of the cost savings are passed on to the customers in the form of lower fares (the plan is an average fall in fare levels of 5 per cent per year) to make Ryanair even more attractive to its target market: the leisure customer. By contrast, easyJet has increasingly targeted business passengers. Ryanair is the only European airline to record profits for each of the last 16 years. Even during the recession it continued to make a small operating profit despite soaring fuel prices. An important part of its revenue comes from the sale of onboard food and drinks, charges for passengers checking in rather than doing so online, priority boarding and for putting luggage in the hold, and income from car hire and hotel bookings. It plans to reduce the number of toilets from three to one in each of its aircraft, allowing it to put in extra seats.

Ryanair has also been on the acquisition trail by buying Buzz, the budget division of KLM Royal Dutch Airlines, for £15.8 million (€23 million). Loss-making Buzz was immediately given the Ryanair cost-cutting treatment, including the loss of 440 jobs and new contracts for pilots, which raised pay but meant longer flying hours. Half of Buzz's routes were axed, but Ryanair still intended to increase passenger load from 2 million to 3 million through lower prices—£31.50 (€45) versus £56 (€81) previously—and more frequent flying along the retained routes.

Competitive response

The stellar growth in low-cost flying has attracted new entrants such as Flybe, bmibaby and Jet2 in the UK, and TUIfly, Goodjet and Transavia elsewhere in western Europe. There are now over 50 no-frills airlines operating in Europe. Traditional airlines have also responded. For example, Air France, Lufthansa and BA have cut prices on many of their European flights in an attempt to stem the flow to the low-price carriers.

BA has embarked on an aggressive strategy of slashing prices from Heathrow and Gatwick to almost all its European short-haul destinations. Fares to places such as Berlin, Paris and Barcelona have been cut by up to 50 per cent. Unlike the low-cost carriers, BA still offers its traditional service benefits, including free food and drinks, on all flights and, unlike Ryanair, which charges £6, there are no charges for checking in luggage. The strategy of competitive fares, in-flight extras and the convenience and flight transfers offered by Heathrow and Gatwick is designed to win large numbers of passengers from no-frills operators. In support of the strategy, BA's former chief executive, Willie Walsh, whose nickname—The Slasher—was earned during his time at Aer Lingus, cut 600 managerial jobs and announced a

further 1000 job losses at the airline's call centres and travel shops in 2006.

Ryanair's reaction was to claim that BA's prices were still more expensive than its own after the cuts, and pointed out that, unlike BA and many other carriers, it had not introduced a fuel surcharge. It also claimed better punctuality—90 per cent flights arriving on time compared to BA's 74 per cent—and a significantly lower missing bags ratio: 0.5 per 1000 passengers against 17.7 for BA.

Customer service

The need to trim costs to the bone has meant that some customers have been dissatisfied with the service provided by both no-frills airlines. For example, the need for fast turnaround times at airports has meant that customers who check in late are usually refused entry. Where lateness is the fault of another travel provider, such as a rail company, customers have been known to complain bitterly about entry refusal. Fast turnaround times also mean that there is little slack should a flight be delayed, with a knock-on effect on other flights.

Another problem is the reluctance of the no-frills airlines to pay compensation. For example, when easyJet cancelled a flight after it admitted it had no crew to fly the aircraft, it offered a refund of the ticket price but no compensation for the other costs, such as the lost hotel deposit and car parking fees incurred by one of its customers. Ryanair, similarly, was reported to have said, 'We never offer compensation, food or hotel vouchers'. Ryanair also experienced teething problems with lost and delayed luggage after switching baggage contractors, and in the past has appeared reluctant to pay compensation with respect to lost luggage.

Questions

1 How do easyJet and Ryanair achieve success using low-price strategies?

2 What are the advantages and risks associated with low-price strategies?

3 To what extent do the conditions for charging low prices discussed in this chapter hold for easyJet and Ryanair?

4 Why did the low-price, no-frills business model fail with easyCinema?

This case was prepared by David Jobber, Professor of Marketing, University of Bradford.
It is based on a large number of published sources.

Limited Range Discounters
In a Recession Discounters are Booming

In the wake of the credit crisis, discount retailers have been surging ahead. Grocery retailers like Aldi and Lidl are proving formidable competitors. Non-grocery retailers like fixed-price stores (e.g. Poundland) are exploring new markets. Value fashion brands like New Look and Primark are booming, while online buying clubs (e.g. Vente Privée) and daily deal sites (e.g. Groupon) are garnering larger customer bases. There is a huge appetite among customers for value for money. Discounters are powering ahead with their expansion plans throughout Europe and beyond. Their formula of low prices and offering a limited assortment of products on their shelves appears to be a winning pan-European formula for retailing. The retailing concept was pioneered by German hard discounter Aldi, and has now been successfully duplicated by other discounters such as the German Lidl and Danish Netto chains. In Germany over 90 per cent of the German population lives within 15 minutes of an Aldi store.

These 'Limited Range Discounters' (LRDs) believe that success can be achieved through offering good-quality products at low prices, and stocking minimal assortments that match consumers' basic needs, such as staple items that consumers buy regularly. Success is achieved through the generation of high volumes, their ability to communicate to consumers, their price gaps with traditional retailers, and placing costs at the forefront of all their business activities. Their continued success has led to dramatic changes within the retail sector, leaving manufacturers with difficult decisions as to how to supply these LRDs effectively, while not damaging their brands, and relations with other retailers. So who are these LRDs, and how do they operate?

In the UK the discounters are experiencing 9% year-on-year growth, triple the growth rates of traditional stores. Aldi alone achieved 18.8% growth thanks to new store openings. Countries like Norway (40%) and Germany (38%) have high levels of discounter activity, whereas countries like the UK (6%) and Ireland (8%) have very low levels. Hard discounters have four central planks in their operating philosophies. First, they stock a very limited product assortment (around 1000 stock-keeping units), whereas a traditional store may have 25,000 different product variants. These are typically fast moving, high stock rotation items. Usually, a shopper is offered only one type of brand from a category. Second,

these stores are very simple in layout, design and operation. They require lean management, and very few employees to operate. A hard discounter will typically have longer queues, which people bear for greater savings. Third, the retailers have a low cost and highly efficient supply chain infrastructure, utilising large regional distribution centres to service their retail outlets. Last and most importantly, these stores operate on the principle of EDLP or Every Day Low Prices.

Competition between discounters is rife. Price wars are common between these retailers. However, if they stock similar products they typically stock different size variants and at different prices, to avoid direct confrontation where possible. Their success has led traditional supermarkets to introduce cheaper brand ranges such as Tesco Value in an attempt to deter customers from switching. Some consumers view these discounters as too frugal and downmarket to give them their custom. LRD's decision to locate in socially deprived areas has contributed to this image even further, although this is changing. Open pallets, lack of assortment, and lack of extra value added services alienate some shoppers. However in Germany, where many of these discounters initially emerged, wealthy Mercedes' drivers typically frequent these retailers.

Netto is operated by Dansk Supermarked which, in turn, is owned by A.P. Moeller-Maersk Group. It is Denmark's' most successful discounter, having roughly 9 per cent of the

Danish grocery retail market. From these origins it has become one of Denmark's most recognized and respected brands. Netto proclaims that it is part of Europe's largest buying group and passes on these savings to customers. Netto stores resemble large warehouses, with items stocked on pallets. High-quality merchandise presentation is not top of the agenda for Netto: costs are. Stores are run with very few employees, and the stores do not accept credit cards so as not to incur any transaction charges. A large proportion of Netto produce is well-known retail brands (stocking brands such as Coca-Cola, Nescafé, Persil, etc.) stocked at discount prices. The company takes advantage of large bulk buying and supplier discounts. On the downside, customers may be faced with longer queues, no master butcher is available, and favourite brands may not be in stock if no promotion is available that week. In addition, the company does stock Netto's own-branded products. This formula made it appealing for many customers, who wanted their favourite brands. The first Netto store opened in 1981 in Denmark. Since then the company has rolled out in other international countries such as Germany in 1990, the UK in 1990, and Sweden in 2002. It successfully entered the Swedish market through a 50:50 joint venture with leading Swedish retailer ICA, and other markets like Germany through joint ventures. It was created by Dansk Supermarked, Denmark's leading supermarket retailer, as a response to Aldi entering the Danish marketplace. Netto sold its UK stores to industry rival Asda in 2010 for £778 million.

Aldi is completely privately owned by the secretive Albrecht family. Its owners are now one of Europe's wealthiest families. The name originated from Albrecht Discount. It pioneered the hard discounter market. The Aldi Group from its German base has two main divisions: Aldi Nord and Aldi Sud. Both operate independently and have clearly defined operating markets and different own-label brands, but both cooperate in terms of pricing and assortment decisions. Aldi Sud is responsible for Southern Germany, and Austria, and English-speaking countries, while Aldi Nord is responsible for all other non-German-speaking European countries. Aldi has saturation coverage within the German market, and possesses limited growth opportunities. Every German is within a 15–20-minute drive to an Aldi outlet. As a result the chain has grown aggressively abroad.

The emphasis within Aldi is on efficiency and productivity. Each store is responsible for its own revenues and cost base. Costs are kept to an absolute minimum. By having a basic store layout and design, low staff numbers, non-expensive in-store storage displays, and a limited number of products on shelves, it keeps costs to a absolute minimum, which other retailers find hard to compete against. It does not accept credit cards in almost all of its stores. It has built up a reputation among its loyal consumer based on the strength of the quality of its product offering. Products are strenuously tested for quality and are only allocated to stores once they are proved to be fast movers. The company has also moved into selling an organic range of produce. Aldi sources products from leading food manufacturers, and sells them under the Aldi own-label brand. Its sheer size enables Aldi to save through bulk buys, and through strong price negotiation with suppliers. The company now sells products that are specific to a particular country in a bid to attract local customers. Through its scale it can then source country-specific products suitable for market needs. If it still does not have the necessary scale, it will import brands into

TABLE C26.1   LRDs: A profile—A comparison of Netto, Lidl and Aldi

Netto	Lidl	Aldi
Owned by Danske Supermarked, Part of A. P. Moller-Maersk Group Owned by Edeka in Germany	Owned by Schwarz Group, Privately owned	Owned by Albrecht Family, Privately owned
Stores in Denmark—400 Stores in Germany—293 Stores in Sweden—107 Stores in Poland—157 Total No. of Stores—1,151	Stores in the UK—580 Stores in Sweden—151 Stores in Germany—3,000 Stores in France—1,600 Stores in Ireland—140 Total No. of Stores—6,120	Stores in the UK—458 Stores in Denmark—242 Stores in Germany—4,242 Stores in USA—1,016 Stores in Ireland—61 Total No. of Stores—8,877
Data not available	Sales of over €21 billion	Sales of over €45 billion
Stocks around 3,500 products	Stocks up to 1,600 products	Stocks around 1,000 products
Stocks favoured brands, a strong selling point	A third of products are branded items	Over 90% are private label
Typical store size—1,100 sq metres	Typical store size—1000 sq metres	Typical store size—760 sq metres

that country. Aldi utilizes huge regional distribution centres to service up to 50 outlets at a time. Goods are brought into the store on pallets, and are gradually emptied by consumers before being replenished with another new pallet. The company is famous for its frugality and thriftiness at all levels of its operations, utilizing a strong, decentralized operation with the focus on simplicity.

The first Lidl discount outlet opened in 1973. It originated as a clone of the successful Aldi format, but has since evolved into having its own strong brand identity. Like Aldi, Lidl has grown rapidly by expanding its international operations. It is privately owned by the Schwarz Group, who are notoriously secretive about its operations. The group owns a suite of different retailing divisions such as hypermarkets, traditional supermarkets, and discounters. The company is still number 2 in its domestic German market, but it has been pursuing a rapid internationalization strategy, hoping to achieve over 70 per cent of its revenues from overseas markets. Its scope of operations is limited to Europe, unlike Aldi which also owns stores in the USA and Australia. The company uses a rapid property acquisition programme, and establishes large regional distribution centres to service these new markets. The majority of its stores in international markets are non-unionized; however, in some markets it has appeased local interests by allowing trade union activity.

One of the biggest weapons in the armoury of discounters is their 'one-off' specials. These promotions typically entail the sale at substantial discount of a non-food item (e.g. a personal computer, gardening or DIY equipment, etc.). These specials are promoted on a weekly basis through local press advertising, and leaflet drops. They act as a major inducement and increase footfall to these stores. These heavily discounted items are allocated to stores, where there are only a handful of units per store. This creates a weekly sale frenzy at these stores. The biggest problem with 'one-off specials' is that it is very hard to estimate demand and, if a special proves unpopular, the stores are left with unsold stock, which can create logistical difficulties and contributes to costs.

One of the main reasons behind their success and apparent unstoppable growth is their store location strategy. Each of these discounter stores is substantially smaller in size than a typical traditional supermarket. In addition, they require smaller property sites, and ancillary works such as car parking and special entry and exit points. This has allowed the LRDs to obtain planning permission at a much faster rate than typical retailers and with enhanced likelihood of success. In France Lidl achieved rapid growth rates through store adaptation of their business formula, which overcame strict planning laws, through having higher shelves, smaller aisles, and lower product assortments.

The LRDs are continually evolving with some offering instore bakeries, and premium regional products to bolster their brand. In addition, Aldi has signed up several celebrity chefs as endorsers for their brands. The middle tier of supermarkets are under pressure from the discounters, as their operating philosophies of large assortments places them at a cost disadvantage. The discounters themselves are facing a number of new challenges with the likes of Tesco testing discount outlets in Eastern Europe, and Asda testing discount store concepts. This is a similar strategy to that carried out by continental retailers in response to the threat of discounters. However, in some overseas markets market share has plateaued after the initial success of the discounters. Shoppers are still drawn to their traditional supermarket retailers because of the attraction of wide choice, one-stop shopping and the availability of low-price product ranges. However, LRDs are here to stay, and leave both retailers and suppliers with difficult decisions to face—how do we compete? And how do we supply?

Questions

1. Discuss the strengths and weaknesses associated with the Limited Range Discounter format.

2. What are the advantages associated with the EDLP concept versus Hi-Lo pricing for retailers?

3. How should branded manufacturers respond with their pricing strategies if they want to supply a Limited Range Discounter while simultaneously supplying traditional retailers?

This case was written by Dr Conor Carroll, Lecturer in Marketing, University of Limerick. Copyright © Conor Carroll (2012). The material in the case has been drawn from a variety of published sources.

CHACTER 14

Integrated marketing communications

Probably the most powerful form of communication we have at our disposal is story telling. It has been incorporated by virtually every civilization into their culture. It is the simplest, most memorable device we have for engaging, learning, entertaining and persuading.

JOHN HEGARTY[1]

LEARNING OBJECTIVES

After reading this chapter, you should be able to:

1 explain how to develop an IMC strategy and set relevant communication objectives
2 describe the elements of integrated marketing communications
3 explain the distinction between mass and direct communications
4 discuss the promotional communication mix
5 explain the key characteristics of each of the main media channels
6 consider the implications for planning communications for different audiences and contexts

Good communications are the lifeblood of successful market-orientated companies and their brands, but creating good communications presents many challenges. As discussed in Chapter 9, all companies need to communicate what they stand for and the benefits they have on offer if they are to earn their customers' trust. Trust is at the core of a brand's very existence.[2] However, the way businesses communicate with their audiences is constantly evolving. Currently, digital technology is reshaping both the tools and the media through which we communicate. There are also more channels and opportunities for a customer to engage with a brand. In the UK alone over 500 television channels compete to catch the attention of consumers; around the world tens of millions of company websites provide product and marketing information to stimulate buyer behaviour. Social media are used by individuals and companies as a means of extending their communication networks. This increase in the number of opportunities to communicate has created a greater need for coordination of all of an organization's communications activities. Additionally, to manage the challenges of the changing communication environment and the proliferation of channels, organizations wishing to promote themselves also have to understand which communications tools to use in which situations. They must also consider operational issues associated with the management of promotional campaigns and assess whether to place responsibility for communication campaigns with an internal department or to employ external specialist communication agencies. For example, in large manufacturing organizations producing fast-moving consumer goods (FMCG) (e.g. Kraft Foods, Unilever, Procter & Gamble), promotional activity might involve various types of communication tools, such as personal selling, advertising, sales promotion and public relations. Organizations of this size tend to have the resources for all these activities to be controlled internally under the umbrella of the marketing function. For example, personal selling strategies can be decided by the sales management team, advertising and sales promotion initiatives by the marketing communications team, and a publicity event by the public relations department. The danger of a piecemeal approach to communication planning is that messages sent to the target audience are all slightly different, which means overall they can become blurred at best and conflicting at worst. This can happen if the advertising department creates messages that aim to convey that a brand is of high quality, while at the same time the sales team are using heavy discounting and money-off sales promotions. The result will be that customers will not know what to think about the brand. Mixed messages can seriously damage the public's perception of a brand.

Finding solutions to these challenges has been a driver of changes in the communication environment which have led to the **Integrated Marketing Communications** (IMC) school of thought. This delivers many potential benefits through integration, but also significant challenges for marketing managers.

This chapter will focus on IMC, and how brand message, the tools and the media channels can be managed to develop into coordinated communication strategies, which maximize the efficiency and effectiveness of the promotional element of the marketing mix.

The chapter begins with a consideration of the drivers of IMC, then looks at the planning process and how to develop a communication strategy. Next we explore the elements of IMC including the principles of communication and the importance of the message, the communication tools and their characteristics, and then we briefly introduce the media channels, touch on the people involved in communications and finally consider communication contexts: business-to-business (B2B) and business-to-consumer (B2C). Chapter 15 focuses in detail on mass communications tools by examining advertising, the media, sales promotions and public relations (PR). Chapter 16 discusses direct communications tools: personal selling and sales management, direct marketing, and customer relationship management, while Chapter 18 explores the tools and channels of digital marketing and social media.

Integrated Marketing Communications Approach

The IMC school of thought aims to move the emphasis of communications away from a step-by-step, linear, transactional process to an ongoing relational dialogue. Another fundamental shift is to move away from transactional communications to make communications customer-centred by capturing and using the reality of how individuals and businesses engage and come into contact with communications. The debate over IMC continues in Read the Research 14.1.

The transactional approach means promotional campaigns are designed to meet specific communication objectives such as creating awareness or stimulating action, using separate communications tools. Rarely are there any linkages between the messages carried by each tool. For example, Heinz had a long-running television advertising campaign for their baked beans, which aimed to position the product as a quality brand. However, at times they also used sales promotions techniques (e.g. multi-pack four cans for the price of three) to combat supermarket value brands being sold at a few pence per can, although there were no explicit links between the television advertising campaign and the sales portions initiatives. By contrast Marks & Spencer sought to understand its customer's situation and used this as a way of building relationships during the global economic recession. They used television advertising to position the brand as a provider of premium-quality food, using the strap-line 'this is not just any food, this is M&S food'. Then they linked to this positioning with sales promotions campaigns on- and offline. The sales promotions initiative 'Dine in for two £20' (see Exhibit 14.1) focused on adding value rather than cutting the price of its foods. The aim of the campaign was for the customer to associate M&S products with 'treats', albeit at a value-for-money price level. Furthermore, the brand was able to connect to other audiences seeking quality and value.

IMC campaigns seek to rationalize the approach to communications. By focusing on developing relational and coordinated communication strategies, it becomes possible to bring together communication tools, techniques, messages and media channels favoured by a particular target audience.[3] For example, in his bid to become President of the USA Barack Obama established a position his opponents could not match by synchronizing all the elements of communications: 'The message and media were at one with each other. Its message championed change with a medium that represented change (digital channels and social media) and the brand, Obama, embodied change.'[4]

It is difficult to pinpoint exactly when this change in communication planning took place. However, IMC began to be accepted as a valid approach for communications in the early 1990s. Duncan and Everett commented that the new customer-focused, technology-driven communications were an *orchestration, whole egg, seamless communication* approach[5] and Schultz referred to it as 'the process of developing and implementing various forms of persuasive communication programs with customers and prospects over time'.[6] From the mid 1990s IMC adoption has become increasingly widespread and now IMC means:

integrating all useable promotional tools and appropriate media to deliver synergistic communication campaigns.

In other, words, promotional campaigns select the most appropriate tools and channels which can be used in harmony with one another to maximize communication effectiveness so that the sum is greater than the individual parts.

The principles of IMC are that organizations coordinate their use of marketing communications tools, branding, images, logos and CRM strategies to deliver a clear, consistent, credible and competitive

⬆ **EXHIBIT 14.1**　M&S uses sales promotions techniques to drive sales in periods of recession.

↑EXHIBIT 14.2   Volkswagen uses a creative campaign featuring dogs and a *Star Wars* movie theme to grab attention for its IMC campaign.

message about the organization and its products. The objective is to position products and organizations clearly and distinctively in the marketplace by providing target audiences with multiple opportunities to see, hear, read and/or interact with consistent marketing messages. As we discussed in Chapter 8, successful positioning is associated with products and services being favourably positioned in the minds of target audiences. 'A brand is the most valuable piece of real estate in the world: a corner of someone's mind.'[7] IMC facilitates the positioning process by sending out consistent messages through all of the components of the promotional mix, and in doing so reinforces the core message.

Go to the website to see Volkswagen's 'The Dog Strikes Back' commercial.
www.mcgraw-hill.co.uk/ textbooks/jobber

Drivers of IMC

Currently, advances in communication technology account for many changes taking place in the industry, but there are other key drivers that help to explain why more organizations are adopting the IMC approach:

- *Organizational drivers* focus on the benefits IMC can bring from an operational perspective— for example, streamlining communications activities, creating opportunities for increased profits through efficiency gains. Many organizations are faced with having to show greater accountability in the communication budget, and more measurable outcomes. IMC creates opportunities to create competitive advantage through coordinated brand development, and across an organization can deliver improved productivity and greater focus.
- *Target-market-based drivers* focus on changes which are affecting the delivery of communication messages. For example, the cost and availability of media channels is changing. Audiences are becoming more fragmented, and organizations are using different media and different timings to grab the attention of their audiences. Technology-enabled communications are used more frequently as target audiences' skills and communication literacy are increasing.
- *Communication drivers* focus on the potential benefits associated with the delivery of the message: for example, increased effectiveness of the message, through constant reinforcement of the core ideas, consistent product and brand communication across a range of touch points; less confusion over the meaning of the message; opportunities to build brand reputation and position clearly a product, brand or company.[8]

For marketing managers, achieving high levels of consistency across a range of communications is challenging. On the one hand, well-planned IMC campaigns can contribute to the development of competitive advantage, building stronger relationships between a brand and its stakeholders, improved consistency and clearer positioning of brands in the minds of customer. This approach can also be a source of further advantages insofar as there are opportunities to:

- *reduce costs* by standardizing communication messages across a selected promotional mix
- *create synergies* between the use of communication tools: for example, television advertising can be linked to in-store sales promotions and social media. So, members of a target audience receive a consistent message wherever they 'touch' an IMC campaign
- *reinforce competitive advantage* by creating a more consistent communication experience for customers. IMC campaigns potentially garner greater advantage than isolated campaigns: for example, VW's campaign at the Super Bowl clearly demonstrated its creativity and reinforced its brand messages.[9]

Digital Marketing 14.1 VW at the Super Bowl—The Dog Strikes Back

Volkswagen, the German car manufacturer, has won many industry awards for its advertising campaigns and has always been keen to make use of creative imagery and innovative technologies to communicate with its target markets. VW America launched a campaign that aimed to grab the attention of Super Bowl fans. The Super Bowl national league football final in the USA is a high-profile event, and advertisers vie for air time as there can be in excess of 90 million viewers. At the event commercial messages feature strongly as advertisers generate interest before the event, with a variety of pre-launch teaser campaigns in order to create interest among consumers. The final on 5 February 2012 was no different, with many advertisers including Fiat, M&Ms, Best Buy, Chevrolet, Doritos, Coca-Cola and many others showing creative and engaging commercials. VW launched a television commercial, with Bolt, the canine star of the commercial who is down at heel, having let himself go, become overweight and inactive. Bolt realizes he has a problem when he cannot get through the dog flap. He starts on a testing exercise regime and diets, and by the end of the commercial he is back to full active fitness. The message for the campaign is being back and 'better than ever', the car is the Beetle.

In mid-January, as part of its multifaceted communication campaign, VW launched a viral campaign using Twitter, Facebook and YouTube. The Bark side online advertising teaser campaign proved popular and received over half a million views across social networks in a single week, building up anticipation for the launch of the new advert at the NFL game on 5 February. Online viewers could see not only the teaser campaign, where a chorus of dogs bark the theme tune to *Star Wars*, but could also view a short film on the making of the commercial. Using TV and social media, VW wanted to remind its target markets just how good its cars are and that they are the best choice in motoring. Each part of the campaign delivered a consistent message and created multiple opportunities to engage the interest of the target audience.

Based on: Hall (2012)[10]

On the other hand, however, organizations might have to change management structures and organizational culture to accommodate IMC, creativity can be stifled and, if campaigns go wrong, they can do on a grander scale and have greater potential to damage a brand's reputation. Furthermore, other potential disadvantages of adopting an IMC approach are:

- *requires greater management commitment* throughout the development and implementation of an IMC campaign.
- *requires increased agency commitment* with the integration of all of the stages across a number of platforms, media and promotional tools, leading to a need for more involvement from all agencies involved.
- *encourages uniformity* since increased commitment from management and agencies can lead to demand for uniformity and might stifle creativity.[11]

Managers should consider the advantages and disadvantages not only when deciding whether to adopt an IMC approach but also when developing and planning IMC campaigns.[12]

Planning for Integrated Marketing Communications

So far we have discovered there are many drivers which are now encouraging wider uptake of IMC as a framework for planning and managing communication campaigns and initiatives. We have, however, also identified a number of management considerations and challenges to be taken up if a brand is to maximize the potential advantages and avoid the disadvantages of adopting an IMC approach. A framework for applying an integrated marketing communications approach is given in Figure 14.1.

Marketing strategy and situation analysis

IMC is a framework for planning the use of the promotional mix. Therefore, it is important to remember that the objectives, the brand positioning statement, and more come from the

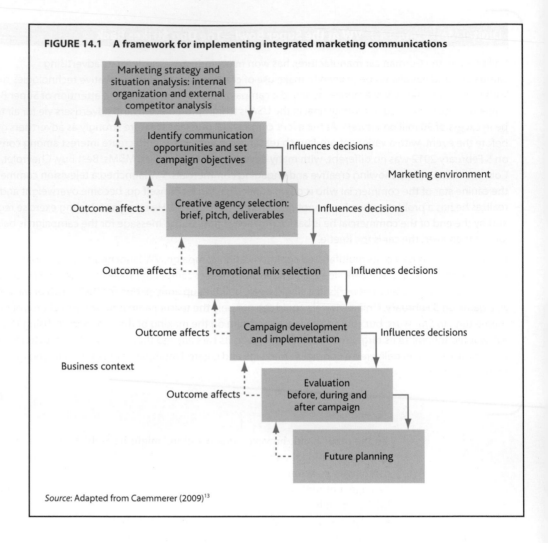

FIGURE 14.1   A framework for implementing integrated marketing communications

Marketing strategy and situation analysis: internal organization and external competitor analysis

Identify communication opportunities and set campaign objectives — Influences decisions

Marketing environment

Outcome affects ···› Creative agency selection: brief, pitch, deliverables — Influences decisions

Outcome affects ···› Promotional mix selection — Influences decisions

Outcome affects ···› Campaign development and implementation — Influences decisions

Business context

Outcome affects ···› Evaluation before, during and after campaign

Future planning

Source: Adapted from Caemmerer (2009)[13]

marketing strategy (see Chapter 2 for more details). Opportunities identified from the marketing situation analysis and the target market analysis should be captured in order to enable use of promotions to contribute to the creation of differential advantage. This initial stage in the planning framework serves to ensure integration between the marketing strategy and promotional mix selection. The analysis should also clarify the overarching objectives which guide the campaign, in the manner of Renault, wishing to enter new markets in Germany and position its products as the safest cars available. The promotional mix decisions depend on the marketing strategy, competitive positioning and the target market. For example, target market definition will lead to an understanding of the needs of the target audiences and how they can be reached by different promotional tools and media channels. Furthermore, differential advantage will affect message decisions.

IMC campaign objectives

Once issues from the marketing strategy and situation analysis have been decided, communication objectives will be set and promotional options selected (e.g. advertising, direct marketing and personal selling) to form a brand-led approach. However, it should be noted that among practitioners there is some debate over which comes first—the marketing and brand strategy or the objectives for the communication campaign (further discussion of these issues and specific communication objectives appears in Chapters 15, 16 and 18). See Marketing in Action 14.1 to find out more about campaign objectives.

Marketing in Action 14.1 Are Your Customers Interested in What You Want to Achieve?

In just over a decade the communications industry has been reshaped by digital communications. There has been a fundamental shift in the ways communication messages are disseminated among target audiences. However, while everything is arguably in place to deliver fully integrated, seamless communication campaigns, in the digital age many marketing departments lag behind. Often new media is used as an 'add on' to existing campaign strategies rather than being fully integrated. Both approaches are laden with potential risk, especially if they set objectives that do not necessarily contribute to the marketing strategy. Yet it is perhaps no surprise that large corporations have rushed to use social media as part of their integrated campaigns. There are rarely any criticisms of this rapidly growing social phenomenon. For example, a large brand like Cadbury's has much to lose if things go wrong. In a recent campaign, they invested £50 million to promote Cadbury's role as the official treat provider for the Olympics. The spots and stripes campaign used advertising on television, PR, sponsorship and social media to encourage consumers to become interactive with their chosen Olympic team. A few months into the campaign, the results were not as expected. Facebook pages attracted disappointing numbers of 'likes' and Twitter activity was relatively low.

Nevertheless, Cadbury's pioneering approach has highlighted that social media need to be applied with caution. Communication objectives need to be clear. For Cadbury, if the goal was to increase Facebook followers, they achieved only moderate success. However, had the objective been to build brand awareness or increase sales, they most probably failed. Social media can be a distraction rather than a benefit and it should be remembered that consumers adopt this technology on a voluntary basis. While it may be cool to 'engage your consumers in conversation', what happens when they would rather chat with friends about how their parents are interfering in their daily lives than talk to *you* about what you have to say about the benefits of your brand!

Based on: Ritson (2011);[14] *Ritson (2011);*[15] *Bendaby (2011)*[16]

So how do companies decide on communication objectives for integrated campaigns?

There are benefits to following the top-down, market-strategy-driven, brand-led approach as it means the marketing team are aware of what is required to position the brand and can tailor communications accordingly. This approach means that campaigns are coordinated and efficient. However, sometimes marketing managers actually use[17] their large IMC budgets to determine the shape of the campaign. In other words, they select promotional tools which are affordable, desirable or in-vogue with only a limited consideration of what the IMC campaign objectives actually are. This approach means that campaigns can become disjointed and inefficient, and the outcome can be that they perform poorly and achieve little for the brand when driven by the promotional tools rather than the marketing and branding strategy.

Consider British Airways' Olympics campaign, where they used celebrity chef, Heston Blumental, actor Richard E. Grant and artist Tracy Emin holding a paper airplane while standing in front of a half-finished sports stadium. The campaign used print and digital channels and was a sales promotion contest, to identify *aspiring chefs, scriptwriters and artists*. These elements of the BA campaign seemed to lack coherence and be driven by a desire to use social media and celebrity endorsements rather than to produce a campaign which contributed to the overall positioning of the brand in the minds of the target audiences—unlike competitors Cathay Pacific and Singapore Airlines, which have very specific objectives and constantly remind travellers of the quality of their brands.

The key point to be aware of is this: clear objectives are imperative for IMC if it is to be considered as a valid and achievable framework for planning communications. (Specific communication objectives for each of the tools are discussed in Chapters 15, 16 and 18.)

Creative agency selection

Once the objectives are set, the next step is to select creative **agencies** (which includes using internal teams and departments) to develop a communication brief and determine the

WE CAN
HELP
YOUR
TALENT
FLY.

If there's one secret
that the greatest chefs
share, it's that they've
all had the chance to
learn from the masters.

To celebrate our
partnership with the
London 2012 Olympic
Games we're giving
one budding chef the
chance to create a menu,
with inspiration from
Heston Blumenthal,
to be served on our
planes next summer.

It's an opportunity that
could make a career.
Apply at ba.com/greatbritons
Entries close 27 July 2011.

BRITISH AIRWAYS

⬆ EXHIBIT 14.3 British Airways focused on its partnership with the London Olympic Games during summer 2012.

deliverables. Once the creative brief has been developed, creative agencies will be selected to pitch for the campaign. It should be noted that often communications are developed by the internal marketing team, but there should still be a briefing document as this sets down on a single page the core requirement of the campaign, which act as a guide for everyone in terms of the message, target audiences, the tone, the budget and the deliverables. Agencies and/or internal departments will prepare a pitch for the client that will show how their ideas and use of the communication budget will meet the client's requirements. Marketing managers must decide how to determine whether an agency can deliver on its promises. This has always been an issue, but it is a problem that has become increasingly difficult to solve in the digital age. Agencies are not opposed to claiming they offer a full range of services when, in fact, they are not able to deliver seamless integration across all of the communication tools[18] (the issue of agency selection is revisited in Chapters 15 and 18).

In the past, selection of the agencies that will produce the required elements of the campaign was considered to be in the advertising domain. This is no longer the case as a full service agency should offer the capacity to provide all of the promotional tools. Some agencies (e.g. BBH advertising agency) do offer a complete service across all of the communication tools. However, there are specialist agencies with particular expertise (e.g. Fever PR, an agency specializing in public relations on- and offline), or an internal company team. Once the agency selection is complete the creative teams, account managers and other service providers will work together to produce each of the elements of the campaign. Media schedulers will be involved in making sure that any media requirements are available and fulfilled. A Gantt chart or similar project management timetable will be set out as a guide to make sure that each of the elements of the campaign is ready at the prescribed time. Timing is very important to IMC campaigns, especially as different tools might be required to fulfil different functions as happened in the VW America campaign, where the Dogs Bite Back viral campaign preceded the launch of the new VW beetle advert at the NFL final.

The advantage of using one agency is better communication, but using several agencies gives clients more flexibility regarding the choice of the best agencies to handle each media type.[19] However, using several agencies can lead to conflict regarding who is paid for what and who takes charge. Suppose an integrated campaign is mainly direct marketing, but includes an online game, created by a digital specialist who also thinks of the main campaign strap-line. Which agency has contributed more to the campaign and which deserves the greater financial reward?[20] Such questions can create conflict between agencies, and problems for clients.

The chosen integrated communication strategy will be executed and subsequently evaluated in the light of the set objectives. An example of a successful integrated marketing communications campaign is the Dove campaign 'Real women, real curves'. The campaign used a combination of advertising, public relations and in-store marketing to portray the aspirational image the brand needed.[21] Please note, integrated marketing communications is not restricted to consumer markets. Furthermore, relationships between clients and agencies are fundamental to the success of communication initiatives. (Client–agency relationships are covered in detail in Chapter 15.)

The promotional mix

The communication objectives can help to determine which communication tools to include in a campaign.[22] Furthermore, the creative pitch enables an agency to make suggestions about which tools are the most likely to achieve the campaign objectives set by the client. Ultimately, the client (the company commissioning the campaign) decides which tools to use, which creative message and combination of agencies represent the best value, and which are likely to achieve their communication aims.

Campaign development and implementation

At this stage the promotional mix decision is finalized and the message and creative execution confirmed. Other major decisions taken at this stage are the media channel selection, planning and scheduling. The media decision will affect the budget. For example, television advertising reaches a large television audience but can be expensive, whereas print media advertising using regional newspapers can be a relatively low-cost option but will not have the same reach. The relative merits of media channels are discussed later in the chapter and in Chapter 15.

Evaluation

Following the implementation, each of the elements of the campaign will be evaluated to assess overall effectiveness. Evaluation should take place at all stages of the campaign, including pre-testing, tracking studies and post-testing. This approach can help to assess the effectiveness and efficiency of the IMC campaign.[23] Measurements are taken to determine the extent to which campaigns have achieved communication objectives, and whether it is moving target audiences in the planned direction. Evaluation also feeds into future planning.

Future planning

After the implementation of an IMC campaign each of the elements should be reviewed. Findings from the review should be fed back and recorded to inform the development of future campaigns. Throughout the campaign information should be fed back. While the planning framework shows a linear process which moves from one stage to another, in reality the process is rather more iterative with information and learning influencing and informing developments at every stage of the process.

This section has examined the IMC planning process. The next section looks at the elements which underpin the IMC planning process and are fundamental to its successful application: the message, the tools, the media channels, and the contexts. For further insights into IMC read more in Read the Research 14.1.

Read the Research 14.1[24] **Rethinking Communications**

Although it would appear that IMC has become widely accepted among marketers, clients and agencies, in their 2010 paper, 'Managing Dynamism of IMC Anarchy to Order', Mishra and Muralie contest this view and suggest that in some quarters of management it is considered something of a fad. They examine some of the conflicts surrounding IMC and the ways used to evaluate and measure its success. The authors then go on to suggest a two-way approach where integration and measurement takes place, for example at the client / agency level and the consumer / customer end.

Mishra and Muralie (2010) Managing Dynamism of IMC Anarchy to Order, Journal of Marketing Communications, *6(2), 29–36.*

Elements of Integrated Marketing Communications

To survive, organizations need to communicate with their customers; marketing messages tell buyers about the meaning of a brand and the benefits it can deliver. Arguably 50 years ago, delivering a message to a particular target audience was relatively straightforward; there was a small number of commercial television and radio channels, and a few well-known printed publications, which a marketer might use to get the messages across. Now the communications environment has changed, however; it is more complex, integrated and universal. There are more interconnections between the core elements of communications to consider when planning an IMC campaign. The core elements are: the message, which is used to position a product, brand and/or an organization in the minds of the customer; the tools, the six key methods which provide the means of achieving communication objectives; the media, which are the channels that carry the message to the audience; the people, who collectively are responsible for creating, planning, managing and implementing the communication campaign; and the context, the setting in which communication takes place (see Table 14.1).

TABLE 14.1   Core elements of IMC

Elements	Examples
The message	Rational, emotional
The tools	Advertising, personal selling, sales promotions, digital promotions, direct marketing, public relations
The media channels	Broadcast, print, Internet, mobile, outdoor
The people	Account managers, clients, agencies, schedulers, planners, Web service providers
The context	Industrial, consumer, public sector

The message

In this section we explore the function of the **message** and how it might be communicated to target audiences using both simple and complex processes.

At the heart of communications is the message. Messages are very important as they not only transfer information from a message sender to its recipient but can also determine the nature of a relationship, establish credibility,[25] set the tone for a *conversation* and cross tangible and intangible boundaries. Effective messages can become so powerful that they can be heard around the globe, when used with suitable media channels. For example, when Bob Geldof, the Irish rock star, wanted to communicate the message that millions of people in Africa were dying of starvation, he decided to use a rock concert to get the message across to young audiences around the world. His core message was famine relief for Africa. The rock concert was Live Aid. This concert was transmitted from the UK and the USA on live television. Bob's message brought together a global audience, united music and youth and spread the message of famine relief to a 400 million television viewers, in over 50 countries.[26]

In marketing, messages take on a special meaning—they are not mercurial asides between individuals, or unplanned, off-the-cuff remarks, but are carefully planned and crafted. Messages play an important role in positioning. To create effective messages, marketers need to consider the credibility of the message and its source.[27] For a target audience to engage with a marketing message, it has to be attractive and interesting, the source (the sender of the message) has to be perceived as credible and believable to have the power to deliver the message promise. The next step is to establish suitable brand messages to communicate with target audiences.

As discussed earlier, product (Chapter 9) and service (Chapter 10) brands are distinctive market offerings which can be easily identified by target audiences for whom they deliver a parcel of benefits. During the development of a brand, its quality, value, features, name, design, packaging are determined. These features of the brand can then be used in crafting marketing messages.

Marketing messages take many forms: for example, emotional and rational appeals that are designed to stimulate different responses such as fear, humour, action. In Chapters 4 and 5 we discovered how consumers react to both emotional and factual stimuli, whereas business buyers respond to more rational, information-based messages.

Information-based messages

Go to the website to watch the iPhone 4S advert. What messages is Apple trying to give consumers?
www.mcgraw-hill.co.uk/textbooks/jobber

Sometimes companies wish to provide their customers with information that will enable them to make an informed decision about the brands they choose. For example, insurance company Aviva informed its target audience that it has been sponsoring the British Olympic teams since 1999. The television commercial showed the sports men and women whom the company has supported in their quest to succeed in winning medals for their country. The commercial provides much factual information. Another example is the iPhone 4S: the message showed all different generations from young to old, using the phone, on the move and in a whole range of lifestyle situations—from a young girl asking questions, to a person locked out of their home looking for a locksmith and a jogger filling in his diary while on the run. This style of message delivery is sometimes referred to as a *slice of life*.

Emotional messages

Go to the website to see the Cravendale cats advert.
www.mcgraw-hill.co.uk/textbooks/jobber

Sometimes messages are designed to stimulate a response, which might connect with the target audience through a particular emotion. For example, Cravendale's award-winning advert 'cats with thumbs'. This commercial uses a humorous appeal to encourage target audiences to buy milk. Messages which shock are often used to attract not only the attention of the target audiences but also the wider media.

In Chapter 15 we explore messages in more detail and how to create different types of message appeals—informative, interactive or actionable. Now we are going to consider how the message is delivered through the communication process.

The communication process: simple and complex

While messages are at the heart of the process, the actual way we communicate is also very important. In this section we examine the elements of the simple communication model which shows how a message is transferred from one person to another. Then we consider how messages are spread within and across communities.

A simple model of the *communication process* is shown in Figure 14.2. The *source* (or communicator) *encodes* a message by translating the idea to be communicated into a symbol consisting of words, pictures and numbers. Some advertisements attempt to encode a message using the minimum of words, while others provide extensive detail. We explore message content later in this section. The message is *transmitted* through media such as television or posters, which are selected for their ability to reach the desired target audience in the desired way. Communication requirements may affect the choice of media. For example, if the encoded message requires the product to be demonstrated, the Internet, television and cinema may be preferred to posters and the printed publications. *Noise*— distractions and distortions during the communication process—may prevent transmission to some of the target audience. A television advertisement may not reach a member of the household because of conversation or the telephone ringing. Similarly a press advertisement may not be noticed because of editorial competing for attention.

When a *receiver* sees or hears the message, it is *decoded*. This is the process by which the receiver interprets the symbols transmitted by the source. The aim is for the receiver's decoding to coincide with the source's encoding process. The receiver thus interprets the message in the way intended by the source. Messages that rely on words more than pictures can also be decoded differently. For example, a message such as 'the most advanced washing machine in the world' may be accepted by some receivers but rejected by others.

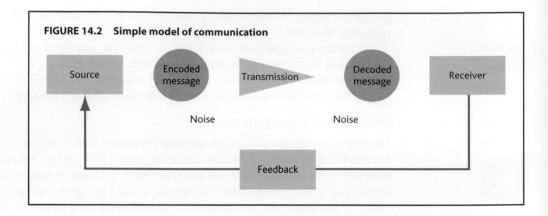

FIGURE 14.2 **Simple model of communication**

Communicators need to understand their targets before encoding messages so that they are credible. Otherwise the response may be disbelief and rejection. In a personal selling situation, *feedback* from buyer to salesperson may be immediate, as when objections are raised or a sale is concluded. For other types of marketing such as advertising and sales promotion, feedback may rely on marketing research to estimate reactions to commercials, and increases in sales due to incentives.

An important point to recognize in the communication process is the sophistication of receivers and how they can play different roles in the wider dissemination of the message.

The simple model of communication explains the basic concepts and transmission of a message from sender to receiver, but the communication of a message rarely takes place in such isolation. Message receivers interact with one another and consequently they can act as a conduit to spread messages further afield. There are also other levels of complexity to consider; different message recipients play different roles in the wider diffusion of messages. Katz and Lazarfield[28] found that some individuals were able to exert greater influence than others. These opinion leaders[29]—as they have become known—enjoy higher status within social groups and their views are considered more highly by other members of the social/ peer group. Opinion leaders play an important role in the communication process as 'they are receptive to new ideas' and are happy to try and buy new products and services.[30] *Opinion formers are individuals who are able to exert personal influence because of authority, education or status associated with the objects of the communication process.*[31] The influence of opinion formers is also important in the communication process. For example, Jeremy Clarkson, presenter of the popular motoring television series *Top Gear*, is an opinion former. The series reviews and demonstrates different motor vehicles, exploring features and aspects of many different cars, and offers informative opinions. A theatre critic writing reviews in a local or national newspaper or blogging online could also be considered as an opinion former.

The simple model of communication suggests that communications are unidirectional, passing from sender to receiver, and in the past this model has been used to explain the spread of many mass-marketing campaigns. But the world of communications has become highly complicated. There are many different ways for individuals and companies to communicate and interact. Indeed, the boundaries between the pillars of the marketing mix are becoming eroded as products and communications come closer together. Read Marketing in Action 14.2 to find out more about how this is happening at British Airways.

In a multichannel world, where message receivers gather information from multiple points such as websites, apps, a multitude of television channels, printed publications and, perhaps more importantly, each other, a more complex model is needed to understand how communication messages are disseminated. Figure 14.3 shows the complexity of communication networks.

Figure 14.3 shows how complex two-way linkages can form between target audiences, opinion formers and leaders, the media (television, radio, Internet), digital sources of influence (e.g. websites, social media), and personal sources of information (experiences). The

Marketing in Action 14.2 The British Airways App

New technology speeds up communications and enables interactions, but at the same time it is eroding the boundaries between the message, the media, the channel and the product.

In the airline industry, technology has facilitated many advances, which have implications for marketing communications: for example, the British Airways mobile app. This technological device supplies travellers with all their own personalized travel information for their next flight directly to a mobile phone (most smartphones). The app allows travellers to check in for their flight, download their boarding pass to the phone, and check departure and arrivals information, which are all elements of the service product (the flight). However, the app also allows travellers to check up on their loyalty points (a marketing communication device) and also carries the BA brand logo. Furthermore, thanks to the nature of airline travel (with respect to security and passenger information), BA knows exactly who the app is sending information to, which means this is also a highly targeted means of communication, and also streamlines the process the traveller engages with when consuming the service product (the flight).

British Airways (BA) is an icon global airline company, which wants all of its customers from business class to economy to perceive the company as offering high levels of quality, safety and reliability in the air travel business. BA flies to most parts of the world and carries tens of millions of passengers a year. The company designs and communicates messages, which it hopes help to position the brand in the minds of its passengers and wider target audiences. In addition to the app, BA uses many different channels to carry its messages, including television, magazine and newspaper adverts, in-flight magazines, the company website, email marketing campaigns and the AVIOS loyalty scheme. So the marketing communication team has to ensure the right messages are being sent every step of the way on the relationship with its customers. The BA app shows the highly challenging and complex communication environment.

Based on: BA.com (2012); Highlife (2012)

implications for developing IMC campaigns are that multiple two-way integrated communications become formal and informal. This means message senders need to use multiple methods and channels to ensure messages are being received by the intended target audience. For instance, a website selling innovative products (digital source) may provide information that may then be picked up by a journalist (opinion former) who does a review for a special interest magazine

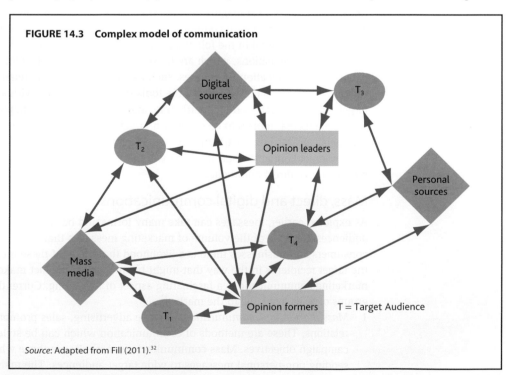

FIGURE 14.3   Complex model of communication

Source: Adapted from Fill (2011).[32]

↑EXHIBIT 14.4 Levi's told a compelling story, which significantly boosted sales of its 501 jeans.

(mass media) which is read by the local computer expert (opinion leader) who informs her friends (target audience). The communication message potentially is the central core of a conversation between multiple participants. Read more about how conversations and storytelling can help to spread a message in Mini Case 14.1.

The increasing complexity of communications channels, the shift towards informal away from formal lines of communications and the growing importance of digital and mobile channels and media are blurring the divisions between communication tools, sales channels and the media. Research[33] into the use of digital technology in the retail sector has highlighted that for this industry the Internet is a channel which facilitates communications, interactions and sales. For example, Dixons Retail uses SMS to send messages to its customers, informing them of the latest offers but also uses this channel to provide product delivery information. Additionally, the company's brand websites are used for sales, communications and aftersales care. For the customer, the message, the media and the channel work seamlessly together, while for the company the main point is that the basic premise of their messages has not changed but the opportunities to leverage advantage through greater functionality and extended touch points of the message have increased significantly.

The tools

In this section we explore the promotional communication tools which deliver the message to the target audiences. We also examine their key characteristics and the impact on selection of tools to use for IMC campaigns. In addition to this brief section introducing the tools, each element of the promotional communication mix, and how they can be used in campaigns, is covered in more detail in the following chapters. Three chapters cover specific tools: Chapter 15 mass communications, which are those tools that reach wide audiences using non-personal communication techniques, such as advertising, public relations, sales promotions; Chapter 16 direct communications, the tools that communicate with specific members of the target audience, such as direct marketing, and personal selling; Chapter 18 digital promotions and social media, tools that connect with target audiences through digital and mobile channels, such as buzz marketing and email marketing.

Before looking at the specific tools we briefly consider the division of tools into the groups: mass, direct and digital.

Mass, direct and digital communications

As explored earlier, messages can take many forms and be communicated to various audiences. Because of the volume of marketing messages that are currently aimed at consumers and businesses there is a likelihood that many of these messages will not reach the target recipients in the way that might be intended. This fact makes the study of marketing communications a fascinating aspect of marketing. Currently, there are three major groups of tools available to the marketer.

1   *Mass marketing communications* include advertising, sales promotions and public relations. These are methods of communication which can be styled to meet IMC campaign objectives. Mass communications methods are those which primarily involve sending non-personal messages to wide target audiences. The main media for mass

Mini Case 14.1   Conversations, Storytelling and Happy Endings

Conversations

When Owen Baxter and Geoffrey Lewis (executives of the then failing Hush Puppy brand of shoes) had a conversation with a New York stylist, they were told that 'Hush Puppies had suddenly become hip in the clubs and downtown bars of Manhattan and that there were resale shops in the Village in Soho where the shoes (Hush Puppies) were being sold'.[34] Reportedly, what followed was that the shoes were chosen by fashion buyers to feature in their new ranges, and the basset hound (symbol for the brand) was used by a Los Angeles designer on his store in Hollywood. The sales of Hush Puppies quadrupled year on year and so the brand that was on its way out was not only saved but became a staple item in every young trendy American's wardrobe. In this tale the informal communication network enabled the message to be filtered back from the target audience (youngsters in East Village Manhattan), to the opinion leaders (fashion designers and stylists), eventually to more formal traditional mass media communication channels.

Storytelling

Storytelling is part of our daily lives and helps us to make sense of the complex world around us. Often we become part of the story, and brands utilize storytelling as a platform for developing meaning. John Hegarty, Creative Director of Bartle, Bogle & Hegarty (BBH), is one of the world's advertising aficionados and he advocates that storytelling is probably the most powerful form of communication as it can be used very effectively to make brands memorable (see quote at opening of chapter). However, he suggests messages and stories need to be created for the screen-based culture (television, computers, mobile phones), which is now so prevalent in modern society. To be successful in the screen-based world of communications, it is important to get the balance right between visuals and words. In many of the highly successful Levi's 501 jeans commercials the story is a visual narrative. For example, in the 1985 classic advert, set in a 1950s launderette, Nick Kamen (the leading character) walks into the launderette wearing sunglasses, which he proceeds to remove. He then fills the washing machine with soap powder, removes his top and Levi's and then, wearing just his boxer shorts, sits down to read a magazine while he waits for his jeans to be washed. The slogan shown on screen at the end of the commercial 'Levi's 501 the original shrink-to-fit jeans' neatly brings the tale to an end. Another tip from William Goldman, award-winning novelist and screenwriter is 'come in late, leave early'. What this means is that the scriptwriter should leave space for the target audience to fill in some of the gaps and should not over-explain. Scripts for commercials do tend to be brief and give the creative director space to tell the story visually. According to John Hegarty, 'Great writing and storytelling also has to understand the principle of input and out-take. For example, 'If I want to make you think I'm funny, I don't tell you that I'm really funny, I tell you a joke. You laugh and think, Wow, that guy is really funny.' He also explains that communicators should inspire people to do something rather than merely give them instructions and should never forget that 'a brand is an agglomeration of stories linked together by a vision'.

Happy endings

Creating successful communication messages is a challenge for marketing managers and identifying opportunities to stimulate meaningful conversations or create a story that *captures the hearts and minds* of the target audience is difficult. Furthermore, the attitude of the recipient will be influenced by whether they are favourably disposed towards advertising in general or not, as this will affect the effectiveness of the communication message. Despite these challenges, manufactures of generic products like butter, milk, tea and toilet rolls have frequently been successful in ticking all the boxes and creating messages with the best happy endings in the communication industry by developing stories involving animals.

Recently, the award-winning 'Cravendale Cats with Thumbs' campaign proved so popular with target audiences that the company initiated a cats with thumbs roadshow providing more opportunities to engage with the brand.

In 1972 the likeable Labrador puppy first appeared in Andrex toilet-roll commercials and proved so successful that it has since appeared in over 130 campaigns. The puppies feature on the products and the website, and over the years the slogans have evolved from 'soft strong and very long' through 'tuggable, huggable softness' to 'Be kind to your behind'. The loveable puppies continue to make the brand memorable, and deliver happy endings all round for Andrex and its customers.

There are many other examples of products that have successfully used animals in their campaign stories: Kerrygold butter with its cows; PG Tips tea and its chimpanzees; Cesar dog food with a white west highland terrier; and the Felix cat food brand that uses the iconic black and white cartoon cat. From shoes to car commercials animals score highly on the likeability scale and are usually a safe bet for delivering a happy ending that captures the imagination of the target audience and delivers a good ROI for the brand.

Questions:

1   How does the interactional model of communication work for Hush Puppies?
2   Explain more fully why coming in late and leaving early might be a valid approach for developing communication messages. Give examples of commercials which take this approach.
3   Why do certain brands use animals in their campaigns?

Based on: Gladwell (2000); Hegarty (2011); Mehta (2000);[35] Fill (2011); Cordiner (2009)[36]

communications are broadcast, print and digital. Mass communications are sometimes criticized because their impart is difficult to measure—particularly advertising and PR—therefore it can be difficult to value the return on investment.

2   *Direct marketing communications* include personal selling, exhibitions and direct marketing. These are also methods of communications which can be styled to meet IMC campaign objectives, but the main difference is that direct communications can be personalized, highly specific and tend to be used to target narrow or niche audiences. These tools rarely use broadcast or print media to deliver the message. Direct communications are also easier to measure than mass communications. The measurement aspect has been a key driver in the increase in the use of these tools in recent years.

3   *Digital promotions and social media communications* include, websites, email marketing, buzz marketing and social media. Digital communications can also be styled to meet IMC campaign objectives, but are more difficult to categorize because of their flexibility. For example, a company website can accommodate many aspects and elements of IMC.[37] The British Broadcasting Corporation (BBC) uses its websites as a communication channel, an information resource, a media player and a sales channel. Digital communications can reach wide, narrow and individual target audiences. These forms of communication are the most measurable: sophisticated analytics and metric programs provide a wealth of data ranging from what a website user downloads to the time of day they open and read their email messages.

The rest of this section introduces the individual tools, which make up the promotional mix and considers their impact for IMC campaigns.

The challenge for marketing managers responsible for communications is selecting the *right* mix of tools and then the media channels to deliver the message. The promotional communication mix is a key element in any IMC campaign. The reason is that the mix provides the means by which the message achieves campaign objectives and determines the style used to craft the message. There are six major components of the mix: advertising, personal selling, direct marketing, digital promotions, sales promotion and public relations.

1   **Advertising**: any paid form of non-personal communication of ideas or products in the prime media: i.e. television, the press, outdoor, cinema, radio and the Internet.

2   **Personal selling**: oral communication with prospective purchasers with the intention of making a sale.

3   **Direct marketing**: the distribution of products, information and promotional benefits to target consumers through interactive communication in a way that allows response to be measured.

4   **Digital promotions**: the promotion of products to consumers and businesses through digital media channels.

5   **Sales promotion**: incentives to consumers or the trade that are designed to stimulate purchases.

6   **Public relations**: to educate and inform an organization's publics through the media without paying for the time or space directly.

In addition, product placement, sponsorship and exhibitions are also used to communicate with target audiences, and create corporate identity and branding.

These tools are covered in Chapters 15 and 16 respectively.

In order to develop an IMC campaign, the marketing manager must make a choice of the promotional blend needed to communicate to the target audience. Each of the six major promotional tools has its own strengths and limitations and these are summarized in Table 14.2. Marketers will carefully weigh these factors against communication objectives to decide the amount of resources to channel into each tool. Usually, five considerations will have a major impact on the choice of the promotional mix.

1   *Resource availability and the cost of promotional tools*: to conduct a national advertising campaign may require several million pounds. If resources are not available, cheaper tools such as sales promotion or public relations may have to be used.

TABLE 14.2   Key characteristics of the core tools of the promotional mix

Advertising

- Good for awareness building because it can reach a wide audience quickly
- Repetition means that a brand positioning concept can be communicated effectively; TV is particularly strong but the level of use is changing due to the Internet
- Can be used to aid the sales effort, to legitimize a company and its products
- Impersonal, lacks flexibility and questions cannot be answered
- Limited capability to close the sale

Personal selling

- Interactive: questions can be answered and objectives overcome
- Adaptable: presentations can be changed depending on customer needs
- Complex arguments can be developed
- Relationships can be built because of its personal nature
- Provides the opportunity to close the sale
- Sales calls are costly

Direct marketing

- Individual targeting of consumers most likely to respond to an appeal
- Communication can be personalized
- Short-term effectiveness can easily be measured
- A continuous relationship can be built through periodic contact
- Activities are less visible to competitors
- Response rates are often low
- Poorly targeted direct marketing activities cause consumer annoyance

Digital promotions

- Global reach to consumers and businesses at a comparatively low cost
- Highly measurable
- Interactive enables a dialogue between companies and their customers and suppliers
- Highly adaptable as messages, prices, products and content can be changed rapidly
- Highly flexible, can be used to create sales and communication channel
- Highly targeted and can be personalized
- Convenient form of access to product and company information and purchasing
- Avoids the necessity of negotiating and arguing with salespeople
- High cost of development of websites
- Poses security issues and risk of intrusion

Sales promotion

- Incentives provide a quick boost to sales
- Effects may be only short term
- Excessive use of some incentives (e.g. money off) may damage brand image

Public relations

- Highly credible as message comes from a third party
- Higher readership than advertisements in trade and technical publications
- Loss of control: a press release may or may not be used, and its content may be distorted

2   *Market size and concentration*: if a market is small and concentrated then personal selling may be feasible, but for mass markets that are geographically dispersed selling to the ultimate customer would not be cost effective. In such circumstances advertising, digital promotion or direct marketing may be the correct choice.

3   *Customer information needs*: if a complex technical argument is required, personal selling may be preferred. If all that is required is the appropriate brand image, advertising may be more sensible.

4   *Product characteristics*: because of the above arguments, business-to-business companies tend to spend more on personal selling than advertising, whereas consumer goods companies tend to do the reverse.

5   *Push versus pull strategies*: a push strategy involves an attempt to sell into channel intermediaries (e.g. retailers) and is dependent on personal selling and trade promotions. A pull strategy bypasses intermediaries to communicate to consumers directly. The resultant consumer demand persuades intermediaries to stock the product. Advertising and consumer promotions are more likely to be used.

Two points need to be stressed. First, marketing communications is not the exclusive province of the promotional mix. All of the marketing mix communicates to target customers. The product itself communicates quality; price may be used by consumers as an indicator of quality, and the choice of distribution channel will affect customer exposure to the product. Secondly, effective communication is not a one-way producer-to-consumer flow. Producers need to understand the needs and motivation of their target audience before they can talk to them in a meaningful way. For example, marketing research may be used to understand large consumer segments before designing an IMC campaign, and salespeople may ask questions of buyers to unfold their particular circumstances, problems and needs before making a sales presentation. Furthermore, through the Internet and the Web members of the target audience can freely express their views and opinions, through customer feedback, reviews, blogs and social media.

Marketing in Action 14.3   What do Sausage, Sushi and Crispbreads Have in Common? Renault's IMC Campaign Has the Answer

When Renault was looking to expand its market share into Germany, the Director of Marketing Communications and his team took advantage of primary and secondary data. They used tracking studies carried out by GfK (www.gfk.com) and readership surveys in leading car magazines such as *Auto* and *Motor und Sport*,[38] to capture changing consumer attitudes towards car brands. Following this analysis the Renault Communications Director decided to attack the main German competitors directly by positioning their cars closer to Mercedes, Audi and BMW, improving perceptions of safety and desirability of the Renault products. The objective of the IMC campaign was to raise awareness, so one of the key challenges was to decide on the promotional mix. The core message for the campaign was *Die sichersten Autos kommen aus Frankreich* (The safest cars come from France). Renault sent the brief (outline of the communication details) to various communication agencies—advertising, public relations and direct marketing—for them to suggest creative ideas that could communicate the message. German agency Nordpol + Hamburg (http://www.nordpol.com/) suggested a mix of cinema and television advertising, supported by a viral marketing initiative and a new website, as well as print media. These tools were chosen to give widespread reach, grab attention and provide a source of detailed information to enable potential customers to find out about the safety record of Renault cars against other leading German, Japanese and Swedish manufacturers. To reinforce the central message of safety, a TV commercial showed national food items (rather than cars) being tested in a crash test situation. To represent Germany, a huge frankfurter squashed into the barrier and exploded, an enormous sushi roll (Japan) and giant crispbread (Sweden) suffered the same fate, but when it was the turn of the French bread, it bounced back from the barrier with very limited damage, as it was able to absorb the impact of the crash. The message was reinforced with the slogan *Die sichersten Autos kommen aus Frankreich Renault* appearing at the end of the commercial.

Once the creative side was decided on, the media channels were selected—cinema, radio and the Internet—as a good media mix whose elements would complement each other. The cinema advert was supported by a viral email marketing campaign. Post-campaign evaluation and analysis revealed that consumer attitudes were changing as a result of seeing the campaign.

The crash concept proved very successful, and Renault continued to use the idea in follow-up commercials for a number of years including creating a ballet with eight different Renault models.

Based on: Caemmerer (2009)

Developing a successful IMC campaign involves careful planning and implementation, topics which are discussed in more detail later in the chapter. However, at the start of a campaign, companies should ensure they have completed a situation analysis and have identified communication opportunities before selecting the communication mix. Read Marketing in Action 14.3 to find out how Renault used an IMC campaign to enter German markets.

Furthermore, communication mix decisions should not be taken in isolation. Marketers need to consider the complete communication package by selecting tools which create a suitable blend with other components of the promotional campaign mix. The aim is to ensure that a clear and consistent message is received by target audiences. The media channel which carries the message is a further consideration. In the past media decisions were mainly associated with advertising, but now other tools can be involved in media selection. For example, sales promotions can appear on broadcast, outdoor media, in-store, or delivered via email. Direct marketing uses the Internet, mail services, mobile, and even personal selling is now possible via the Web. Public relations messages can also involve similar media selection as they can be sent via the Internet and through mobile messaging.

The Renault IMC campaign highlights how combining tools and media to deliver a consistent message can be effective in generating the interest of a wide audience and eventually changing the attitudes of target consumers.

Media channels

This section introduces the channels which carry the message using the selected communication tool to the target audience. There used to be a joke among media people that the client's attitude to their part in advertising was 'Ten minutes to go before lunch. Just enough time to discuss media.'[39] However, as media costs have risen and brands become more targeted, and the choice of media channels has increased, this attitude has disappeared. Table 14.3 shows the different media channels available to marketing communication managers.

Arguably, before the Internet was available commercially (pre-1989), media decisions were clear cut. They involved deciding which **media class** (e.g. broadcast, print), and which media vehicle (the specific newspaper) would carry the message. Print was the most widely used media, followed by television. However, since the commercialization of the Internet the whole media world has changed. The Internet now accounts for more of the communication budget spend than any other single media (e.g. television, newspapers, radio, outdoor). The reason for its increasing popularity is bound up in its flexibility. The Internet (the Web and associated technology) can act not only as a multimedia channel, offering marketing communication managers the opportunity to send video, audio and text-based messages, but also creates an environment for advertising, sales promotions, direct marketing, personal selling and public relations. Consequently, Internet digital technologies now accommodate almost every aspect of the communication and media mix. The technology also adds

TABLE 14.3 Media channels	
Media channel	**Type**
Broadcast	Television, radio
Print	Newspapers, magazines, fanzines
Digital	Websites, intranets, portals, email, interactiveTV
Social	Online communities, blogs
Outdoor	Billboards, street furniture, transport, guerrilla
Indoor	Point of sale, in-store posters, window and shelf displays, ambient
Cinema	Multiplex, Imax, outdoor

innovative ways to communicate with messages to a target audience, for example animation, interaction, social communities and crowd-sourcing (discussed further in Chapter 18).

Currently, organizations use various media channels to carry their message. Probably the key media decision is which forms of **media channel** to use (for example, broadcast, print, digital).

Media channel choice

When considering which media channel the media planner faces the choice of using television, press, cinema, outdoor, radio, the Internet or some combination of media classes. Various considerations will be taken into account: *creative factors* may have a major bearing on the decision. The key question that needs to be addressed is 'Does the medium allow the communication objectives to be realized?' For example, if the objective is to position the brand as having a high-status aspirational personality, television would be better than posters. However, if the communication objective is to remind the target audience of a brand's existence, a poster campaign may suffice. Each medium possesses its own set of creative qualities and limitations, as described below.

Broadcast television: advertisers can demonstrate the product in action. For example, a lawnmower can be shown to cut grass efficiently, or the ease of application of a paint can be demonstrated. The capability of television to combine colour, movement and sound (unlike the press, posters and radio) means that it is often used when building brand image and introducing new products. It is easier to create an atmosphere using television than other media that lack its versatility. Advertisements can be repeated over a short time period, but it is a transitory medium (unless the commercial is video recorded). Traditionally, viewers could not refer back to the advertisement once it has been broadcast (unlike the press); however, with the advent of YouTube and other online video platforms adverts can be viewed repeatedly.

Despite the increase in popularity of television commercials online a potential threat to mainstream television advertising is digital recording devices (e.g. DVD recorders, digi boxes like Sky+, FreeSat), which can store up to over 100 hours of programmes, allowing the viewer to record their choice of programmes, watch when convenient and skip through the adverts, bringing about a fall in television advertising effectiveness.

Digital television technology means that signals can be compressed, allowing more to be sent to the viewer. The result is the escalation of the number of channels that can be received. The extra 'bandwidth' created by digital technology is likely to reduce costs, enabling small players to broadcast to small target audiences such as small geographical areas and special interest groups (e.g. shoppers). Also, digital technology allows the development of interactive services, promoting the potential for home shopping.[40]

Television programmes can now be watched via a computer with the development of such online services as the BBC's iPlayer and iTVPlayer. Following the success of YouTube companies have found that setting up their own-brand TV channel is proving to be very successful for fostering consumer engagement. Marks & Spencer has launched a channel and claims it improves the length of time that customers remain on its website. The men's clothing company Thomas Pink has a TV channel which aims to replicate the in-store experience.[41] Car manufacturers Audi and Land Rover also have their own dedicated Internet television channels. Audi has found that potential car buyers return 12 times during the decision-making process and the channel features several streams of video-on-demand content: sport, lifestyle, behind the scenes, on the road, adventure, people, culture, places. (Press and media vehicles are discussed in more detail in Chapter 15, section on Advertising.)

Broadcast radio: this is creatively limited to sound and thus may be better suited to communicating factual information (for example, a special price reduction) than attempting to create a brand image. The nature of the audience changes during the day (for example, motorists during rush hours) and so a measure of targeting is possible. Production costs are relatively low. The arrival of digital radio has increased the number of radio stations available, and marginally improved sound quality. Digital radios have screen displays, which allow websites and telephone numbers to be run at the same time as an advertisement is being played.[42] Radio listening may rise with the growth of the Internet as people listen to the radio while surfing and because radio listening through web browsers is fast becoming a reality.[43]

Press: factual information can be presented in a press advertisement (e.g. specific features of a washing machine, car or computer) and the readers are in control of how long they take to absorb the information. Allied to this advantage is the possibility of re-examination of the advertisement at a later date. But print media lacks movement and sound, and advertisements in newspapers and magazines compete with editorial for the reader's attention. However, the boundaries are blurring and the introduction of the iPad and other tablet computers is enabling print publications to be delivered digitally and in doing so they are able to carry multimedia content.(Press and media vehicles are discussed in more detail in Chapter 15, section on Advertising.)

Digital: this medium allows global reach at relatively low cost. The number of website visits, clicks on advertisements and products purchased can be measured. Interactivity between supplier and consumer is possible either by website-based communication or email. Direct sales are possible, which is driving the growth of e-business in such areas as hotels, travel and information technology. Advertising content can be changed quickly and easily. Catalogues and price lists can be amended rapidly, and a dialogue between companies and their customers and suppliers can be established. The fastest form of advertising is the placing of sponsored links to websites on search engines. Google and Yahoo! are the market leaders in so-called 'paid search' or 'pay-per-click' advertising. The basic idea is that advertisers bid in an online auction for the right to have their link displayed next to the results for specific search terms, such as 'used cars' or 'digital cameras', and then pay only when an Internet surfer actually clicks on that link (hence 'pay-per-click'). An advantage to the advertiser is that the consumer has already expressed interest and intent—first by typing in the search term and then by clicking on the advertiser's link—and, therefore, is more likely to make a purchase than someone passively watching an advertisement on television or looking at one in a newspaper.[44] Internet-based advertising is on the increase and now accounts for more of the media spend than any other form of media-based advertising. (Digital marketing, social media and the Internet are discussed in greater detail in Chapter 18.)

Social media: messages can be straightforward and direct but the way messages are transmitted through social media communities can be highly complex and multilayered. To make creative use of this media, it is important to understand the concept of social capital and how power is attached to particular members of the online community.[45] Such communities provide an area for digital conversations, where members of the community can feel a sense of belonging.[46] For example, Facebook enables its millions of users to start conversations with their friends, and share thoughts, pictures and conversations with like-minded people around most parts of the globe. This type of media can act as a conduit to access homogeneous groups of individuals, but commercial organizations which use this type of space to carry their messages should be aware that social media can be many things to many people—from a community to a publishing space to entertainment and social commerce arena—and consequently great care needs to be taken to ensure the content and tone of the message is in keeping with the expectations of the chosen target community.[47] For example, Mumsnet.com is an online community for parents seeking help and advice on bringing up children. Many issues have been debated within this community from the sexualization of children to the growth in occurrence of childhood diabetes. (Social media is discussed in greater detail in Chapter 18.)

Outdoor: simplicity is required in the creative work associated with outdoor advertising because many people (for example, car drivers) will have the opportunity only to glance at a poster. Like the press it is largely a visual media and is often used as a support medium alongside television, Internet or press campaign because of its creative limitations. However, it is an effective medium for carrying messages which remind target audiences of issues and

↑EXHIBIT 14.5 Thames Reach makes use of thought-provoking posters as part of an IMC campaign.[48]

products (see the Thames Reach poster, which was used in a campaign for a homelessness charity). In conjunction with its poster campaigns, Thames Reach's Communication Director also used print media. Poster campaigns can be created with a limited promotions budget but can be used to good effect. Probably the most effective use of outdoor advertising was done by Bennetton's creative director Olivera Toscani. With a series of highly controversial poster campaigns Toscani led the brand from being a medium-sized European brand into a global one. In 2011, to gain attention for its 'Unhate campaign'—which aims to break down cultural barriers—a series of thought-provoking images carrying the Benetton logo have appeared on billboards around the world. Often outdoor advertising sites are sold as a package targeting specific audiences. For example, targeting supermarket shoppers can be realized by buying a retail package where advertisers can buy space close to supermarket stores; if business people are the target, it is possible to buy a package of sites at major airports.[49]

Technology is helping outdoor advertising to gain a bigger share of advertising in the prime media. Backlit and scrolling sites are gradually replacing more traditional glued posters. Digital technology is allowing animated posters, whose content alters during the day, and high-definition-quality moving images. For outdoor advertising the keyword is simplicity. An ad has, on average, just six seconds to get a message across, which has led to the golden rule 'no more than seven words on a poster'.[50] Piccadilly Circus in London is an ideal place for outdoor messages as millions of pedestrians and drivers pass by every week. The Piccadilly Lights complex carries static and animated adverts, and messages can be changed according to the time of day (see Exhibit 14.7).

Guerrilla is potentially a controversial way to use outdoor media. The aim is often to deliver conmmunication messages through unexpected means and in ways that almost 'ambush' the consumer to gain attention.[51] One of the most effective guerrilla marketing campaigns was that used by Carlsberg in the UK which also employed its well-known positioning slogan 'Carlsberg don't do . . . but if they did it would probably be the best . . . in the world'. The company dropped £50,000 worth of £5 and £10 notes all over London on which were stickers containing the slogan—'Carlsberg don't do litter but if they did, it would probably be the best litter in the world'. For a small investment, the brand received enormous publicity. Another

⬆EXHIBIT 14.6   Benetton aims to capture attention through its use of controversial poster campaigns.

example is when DSL55 launched its first London store aimed at young skateboarders. It employed people to place stickers showing the company's winged angel at locations where the target audience might be, for example, close to skateboard parks, on street furniture, lamp posts, etc. To use this form of media, communicators must be prepared to connect with their target audience in a very unusual, unconventional, surprising and often illegal manner. This is not mainstream media and is often used when the communication budget is small.

Indoor media includes in-store point of purchase materials, packaging, window display signs, on-shelf display. This form of media is used predominantly by retailers and consumer-facing service providers, but may also be used at transit stations, within shopping malls, at entertainment and sports arenas. This type of media is increasingly using digital technology to deliver highly creative messages. For example, East Midlands Airport has a cut-out figure of a member of the airport service staff, and a moving image is projected on to the face of the model, informing passengers how to streamline their journey through the airport.

In addition, both outdoor and indoor media can apply techniques called *ambient media*. This is a non-traditional form of media and is often used to take the target audience by surprise. Ambient advertising generally refers to the established outdoor categories such as billboards,[52] bus signs, or the point-of-sale or in-store posters found at checkouts. Advertising that appears on shopping bags, on petrol pump nozzles, on balloons or on banners towed by airplanes, on street pavements, on overhead lockers on an aircraft, and so on are also classed as ambient. Ambient media are only limited by the advertiser's imagination.

Cinema: advertisements can benefit from colour, movement and sound, and exposure is high, due to the captive nature of the audience. Repetition may be difficult to achieve given the fact that people visit cinemas intermittently, but the nature of the audience is predictable, usually between 15 and 25 years of age. However, the age range has widened in recent years with the success of family films such as the *Harry Potter* and *Shrek* series. This has led companies like Disney to purchase 60-second slots before family feature films. Following the success of the BMW Mini, which used cinema extensively, other car manufacturers such as Volkswagen, Toyota, Citroën and Ford have used cinema to target young audiences.[53]

The creative opportunities afforded by the media channel can add to the richness of the message. Other considerations when selecting media are the **media type** (newspaper, website, poster), the **media vehicle decision** (e.g. a particular newspaper, *The Times*, *Le Monde*) and **media planning** (the media buying, scheduling, timing, frequency). These issues are covered in detail in Chapter 15.

The People

Managing communications involves complex decision-making. There are also many challenges involved in bringing together teams and departments in an integrated manner to satisfy the marketing objectives of the audiences, while engaging the attention of target audiences. Research proposes a two-stage approach: the first stage is the client / agency level, the second stage is target audience level.[54] Consequently, there are three types of people to consider: the customer, the client and the agency.

Customers vary from single individuals, to families and groups to business customers and global corporations. Consequently, their motivations, interests, spending power and needs vary considerably. Nevertheless, it is becoming increasingly important to ensure that any company (the client) wishing to communicate does so by understanding its customers' needs and how they engage with communications.

Clients can come in many different shapes and sizes from large corporate clients, with multimillion-dollar communication budgets to spend in promoting a wide portfolio of products and building brands (e.g. Unilever, Kraft Foods, GE, Mercedes) to small independent companies planning their first website.

Agencies which develop communications also vary considerably in terms of what they have to offer. Agencies generally provide account management and liaison with the client, the creative teams and production of the communication campaigns. They also plan the media and can be responsible for research. Types of agencies include: full service, creative boutiques, specialized agencies, digital agencies and Web service providers.

The client is generally the originator of communication initiatives and is also likely to make key decisions, and ultimately be responsible for the planning approach—target market selection (the customer), financial resources and agency selection. Corporate marketing is where decisions are made about a company's image and corporate identity. Again the client (the company) will strongly influence communication decisions. Selection of the marketing communication mix and media coordination is where the agency can become much more influential in the decision-making process and is likely to be responsible for the management of these elements of IMC. Ensuring consistency of the message is really the responsibility of both the client and the agency and they need to ensure that, whatever form the IMC campaign takes, it should deliver a consistent message throughout to the target audiences (the customer).

Office politics can occur, especially when there are clashes between advertising creatives who, say, have radical ideas to take a brand forward with the latest of a series of television commercials, and brand executives with very conservative values, who want to protect a brand's traditional target markets. Other difficult situations can arise when IMC strategies call for a shift in expenditure from advertising to direct or digital promotion. Other problems surround the specialist nature of different communication disciplines

⬆ **EXHIBIT 14.7** The Piccadilly Lights complex carries static and animated adverts, and messages can be changed according to the time of day to suit the advertiser's requirements.

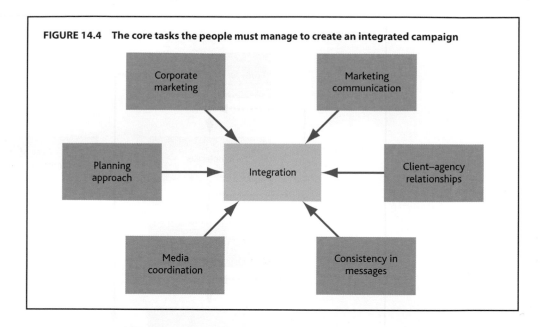

FIGURE 14.4   **The core tasks the people must manage to create an integrated campaign**

that can narrow people's minds to such an extent that they fail to understand how some marketing objectives can be better achieved by using a different communications technique.[55]

However, to be successful, issues and problems must be overcome and this is often achieved by appointing a senior level communications officer to oversee all of the company's communications activities. A Director of Marketing Communications is likely to be responsible for deciding the extent to which each of the components of the promotional mix is used to achieve business and marketing objectives. The person needs to be a visionary and someone with passion, who has the communications ability to persuade everyone of the benefits of an integrated approach to marketing communications.[56]

Client and agency relationships are discussed in more detail in Chapter 15 and types of digital agencies and Web service providers in Chapter 18. Figure 14.4 shows the core tasks that people must manage to create an integrated campaign. For further insight into management issues relating to IMC see Read the Research 14.1.

The contexts

In this chapter we have explored the changing nature of the communication environment, looked at the drivers for the adoption of an IMC approach, considered the processes associated with developing a campaign, and examined important elements which form the core constituents of an IMC campaign. In this final section we look at the different contexts for IMC campaigns: namely, business-to-consumer, business-to-business settings and corporate profile.

There are three main contexts which define the target audience and nature of IMC campaigns. These contexts determine the focus, strategy and the actions which a campaign aims to achieve. The three contexts are:

1   Pull-positioning strategies aim to encourage consumers and end-user business customers to make a purchase, thereby pulling goods through the supply chain from the manufacturer to the retailer (or final purchase point in the supply chain) (see Fig. 14.5).

In a pull-positioning strategy messages tend to be designed to create awareness, and *stimulate action among members of the **target audience***. The underlying idea is that target audiences expect the product to be available when they wish to make a purchase. Many consumer brands use pre-announcement, and give launch dates to stimulate interest and excitement. For example, Apple gives launch dates for its new products and latest versions of existing products. This raises anticipation, excitement and creates pre-sale demand. High-tech shoppers and Apple aficionados form queues at Apple stores and stockists on

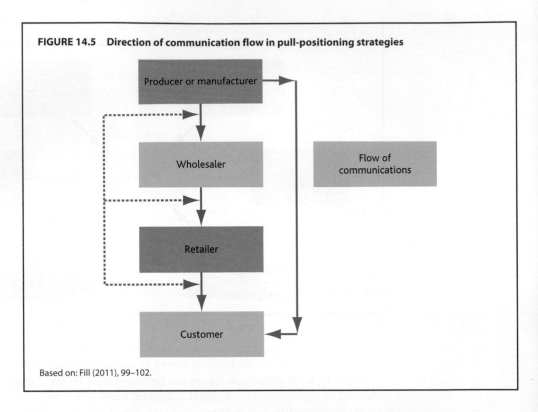

FIGURE 14.5 Direction of communication flow in pull-positioning strategies

Producer or manufacturer

Wholesaler

Retailer

Customer

Flow of communications

Based on: Fill (2011), 99–102.

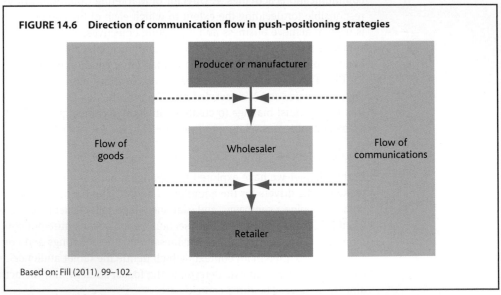

FIGURE 14.6 Direction of communication flow in push-positioning strategies

Flow of goods

Producer or manufacturer

Wholesaler

Retailer

Flow of communications

Based on: Fill (2011), 99–102.

the launch date hoping to be able to make a purchase of the latest iPhone or iPad. The pull strategy also enables Apple to encourage its stockists (e.g. PC World, Giganten, Ledfal, Electro World) to have stock available in-store to meet consumer demand.

2 Push-positioning strategies aim to *move goods through the supply chain*. The target audiences for this type of communications initiatives are channel intermediaries. Often communication objectives aim to build relationships between channel intermediaries and influence trade partners to take stock, allocate shelf space and also help to develop trade partners' awareness of product features and benefits.[57] Push communications also tend to take place in a channel network moving goods from one point to another (see Fig. 14.6).

This strategy is widely used between businesses, and the most prevalent communication tools are personal selling and trade promotions (see Chapter 15 for further details). For example, Costco is a large intermediary in the retail supply chain. It supplies both trade and retail customers with FMCG top brands (e.g. Heinz, Coca-Cola, Gillette, Colgate), white goods (e.g. Beko, Bosch), small electrical (e.g. Breville), electric kettles and fresh foods from various producers. Each of the suppliers engages in push communications designed to ensure that Costco continues to stock its ranges. Manufacturers also work together with Costco to increase purchases using a range of techniques from tastings to bonus packs.

3 Profile-positioning strategies aim to *develop the image and identity of an organization*. In addition to consumer and business target audiences there are many other stakeholders that might be interested in an organization: for example, investors, the local community, the media, trade unions, pressure groups, employees. Perceptions and views of such stakeholders are increasingly important, and this has given rise to greater use of IMC campaigns to raise corporate reputations. Public relations, sponsorship, lobbying, **media relations** and internal communications are examples of the methods which are used in this instance to develop a corporate profile (further discussion of these methods is in Chapters 15 and 22).

Online
LearningCentre

When you have read this chapter

log on to the Online Learning Centre at **www.mcgraw-hill.co.uk/textbooks/jobber** to explore chapter-by-chapter test questions, links and further online study tools for marketing.

Review

1 The elements of integrated marketing communication campaigns
- These include the message, the tools, the media channel and the context applied in a coordinated campaign designed to create multiple opportunities to engage with the target audience.

2 The value of integrated marketing communications
- Integrated marketing communications is the concept by which companies coordinate their marketing communications tools to deliver a clear, consistent, credible and competitive message about the organization and its products.
- Its achievement can be hampered by office politics, and a high-ranking communications officer may be needed to see through its successful implementation.
- Its philosophy has led to the rise in media-neutral planning, which is the process of solving communications problems through an unbiased evaluation of all media.

3 How IMC campaigns are organized
- Planning campaigns develop from a situation analysis, which should aid a company in identifying communication opportunities. Following on from this is agency selection, the briefing process and setting out the deliverables that an agency will produce. The next stage in the process is the development of the campaign and its implementation. The penultimate stage is evaluation of the effectiveness of all of the elements of the campaign. The final stage is future planning.

4 **Elements of IMC**
- The core elements are: the messages, which are used to position a product, brand and/or an organization in the minds of the customer; the tools, the six key methods which provide the methods of achieving communication objectives; the media, which are the channels that carry the message to the audience; the people, who collectively are responsible for creating, planning, managing and implementing the communication campaign; and the context, the setting in which communication takes place.

5 **The message**
- At the heart of communications is the message. Messages are very important as they not only transfer information from a message sender to its recipient, but can also determine the nature of a relationship, establish credibility,[58] set the tone for a *conversation* and cross tangible and intangible boundaries. Effective messages can become so powerful that they can be heard around the globe, when used with suitable media channels.

6 **The communication process**
- The communication process begins with the source encoding a message that is transmitted through media to the receiver who decodes. Noise (e.g. distractions) may prevent the message reaching the receiver. Feedback may be direct when talking to a salesperson or through marketing research. The communication process: the simple model explains the basic elements of the communication model whereas the complex model explains how communication messages pass by formal and informal messages between message senders and different types of message recipients.

7 **The factors that affect the choice of the promotional mix for IMC campaigns**
- These are resource availability and the cost of promotional tools, market size and concentration, customer information needs, product characteristics and push versus pull strategies.

8 **The key characteristics of the major promotional tools**
- Advertising: strong for awareness building, brand positioning, company and brand legitimization, but it is impersonal and inflexible, and has only a limited ability to close a sale.
- Personal selling: strong for interactivity, adaptability, the delivery of complex arguments, relationship building and the closing of the sale, but is costly.
- Direct marketing: strong for individual targeting, personalization, measurement, relationship building through periodic contact, low visibility to competitors, but response rates are often low and can cause annoyance.
- Digital marketing: strong for global reach, measurement, establishing a dialogue, quick changes to catalogues and prices, convenience and avoids arguments with salespeople, but impersonal and requires consumers to visit website.
- Sales promotion: strong on providing immediate incentive to buy but effects may be short term and can damage brand image.
- Public relations: strong on credibility, high readership but loss of control.

9 **The media channels**
- When considering which media channel the media planner faces the choice of using television, the press, cinema, outdoor, radio, the Internet or some combination of media classes. Various considerations will be taken into account: *creative factors* may have a major bearing on the decision. The key question that needs to be addressed is 'Does the medium allow the communication objectives to be realized?'

10 **The people**
- Managing communications involves complex decision-making. There are also many challenges involved in bringing together teams and departments in an integrated manner to satisfy the marketing objectives of the audiences, while engaging the attention of target audiences.
- Research proposes a two-stage approach: the first stage is the client / agency level, the second stage is target audience level.[59] Consequently, there are three types of people to consider: the customer, the client and the agency.

11 **The contexts**
- There are three main contexts, which define the target audience and nature of IMC campaigns. These contexts determine the focus, strategy and the actions which a campaign aims to achieve.

Key Terms

advertising any paid form of non-personal communication of ideas or products in the prime media: i.e. television, the press, posters, cinema and radio, the Internet and direct marketing

agency an organization that specializes in providing services such as media selection, creative work, production and campaign planning to clients

digital promotion the promotion of products to consumers and businesses through electronic media

direct marketing (1) acquiring and retaining customers without the use of an intermediary; (2) the distribution of products, information and promotional benefits to target consumers through interactive communication in a way that allows response to be measured

integrated marketing communications the concept that companies coordinate their marketing communications tools to deliver a clear, consistent, credible and competitive message about the organization and its products

media channel the means used to transmit a message, including spoken words, print, radio, television or the Internet. Also called the *medium*

media class decision the choice of prime media: i.e. the press, cinema, television, posters, radio, or some combination of these

media planning an advertising strategy most commonly employed to target consumers using a variety of informational outlets. Media planning is generally conducted by a professional media planning or advertising agency and typically finds the most appropriate media outlets to reach the target market

media relations the communication of a product or business by placing information about it in the media without paying for time or space directly

media type (also referred to as a *content type*) is a general category of data content, such as: application (executable program), audio content, an image, a text message, a video stream, and so forth

media vehicle decision the choice of the particular newspaper, magazine, television spot, poster site, etc.

message the use of words, symbols and illustrations to communicate to a target audience using prime media

personal selling oral communication with prospective purchasers with the intention of making a sale

public relations the management of communications and relationships to establish goodwill and mutual understanding between an organization and its public

sales promotion incentives to customers or the trade that are designed to stimulate purchase

target audience the group of people at which an advertisement or message is aimed

Study Questions

1. Compare the possible use of advertising and personal selling in an IMC campaign.

2. Discuss how communication messages can be used to build a brand.

3. Explain the difference between mass and direct communications.

4. Explain the consideration a company might use to help with the selection of the promotional mix.

5. Media class decisions should always be based on creative considerations, while media vehicle decisions should be determined solely by cost per thousand calculations. Do you agree?

6. Outline the stages in the IMC planning framework.

7. Discuss the drivers of an IMC and suggest possible limitations when developing a pan-European campaign.

8. Discuss the advantages and disadvantages of adopting an IMC approach towards communication planning.

References

1. Hegarty J. (2011) *Hegarty on advertising: turning intelligence into magic*, London: Thames & Hudson, 95.
2. Hegarty (2011) op. cit., 42.
3. Fill, C. (2011) *Essentials of Marketing Communications*, London: Prentice Hall, 7–8.
4. Hegarty (2011) op. cit., 113.
5. Duncan, T. and S. Everett, (1993) Client perceptions of integrated communications, *Journal of Advertising Research*, 3(3), 30–39.
6. Schultz, D. (1993) Integrated marketing communications: maybe definition is in the point of view, *Marketing News*, 18 January, 17.
7. Hegarty (2011) op. cit., 39.
8. Based on Fill (2011) op. cit., 117.
9. Fill (2011) op. cit., 118.
10. Hall, B. (2012) Campaign Viral Chart: 'the bark side' rises for VW, *Campaign.co.uk*, 27 January, http://www.campaignlive.co.uk/news/1114282/Campaign-Viral-Chart-the-bark-side-rises-VW/?DCMP=ILC-SEARCH.
11. Fill (2011) op. cit., 118.
12. Fill (2011) op. cit., 118.
13. Caemmerer, B. (2009) The planning and implementation of integrated marketing communications, *Marketing Intelligence & Planning* 27(9), 524–38.
14. Ritson, M. (2011) What if your customers are silent? *Marketing Week*, 14 April, 70.
15. Ritson, M. (2011) Marketers put the cart before the horse, *Marketing Week*, 30 June, 68.
16. Bendaby, D. (2011) Marketers divided on the merits of integration, *Pitch Agency Reputation Survey*, 40.
17. Ritson (2011) op. cit., June, 68.
18. Bendaby (2011) op. cit.
19. Weissberg, T. (2008) One Message, Many Media, *Marketing Week*, 18 September, 31–4.
20. Bidlake, S. (2008) Goodwill to All Agencies, *Campaign*, 5 December, 3.
21. *Marketing* (2005) Marketing Communications Awards, June, 21.
22. Caemmerer (2009) op. cit., 528.
23. Sherwood, P. K., R. E. Stevens and W. E. Warren (1989) Periodic and continuous tracking studies: matching methodology with objectives, *Marketing Intelligence and Planning*, 7(1/2), 11–14.
24. Fill (2011) op. cit., 117.
25. Fill (2011) op. cit., 376.
26. Hegarty (2011) op. cit., 170–71.
27. Kelman, H. (1961) Process of opinion change, *Public Opinion Quarterly*, 25(spring), 57–78.
28. Katz, E. and P. F. Lazarfield (1955) *Personal Influence*, Glencoe, Il: Free Press.
29. Rogers, E. (1983) *Diffusion of innovations*, 3rd edn, New York: Free Press.
30. Fill (2011) op. cit., 45–47.
31. Fill (2011) op. cit., 45–47.
32. Fill (2011) op. cit., 41.
33. Doherty, N. F., F. E. Ellis-Chadwick and C. A. Hart (1999) Cyber retailing: the potential in the UK: the potential of the Internet as a retail channel, *International Journal of Retail & Distribution Management* 27(1).
34. Gladwell, M. (2000) *The Tipping Point*, London: Abacus, 3–5.
35. Mehta, A. (2000) Advertising Attitudes and Advertising Effectiveness, *Journal of Advertising Research*, May/June, 67–72.
36. Cordiner R. (2009) Set free your core native: the brand as a storyteller, *Admap*, October.
37. Chaffey, D. and F. E. Ellis-Chadwick (2012) *Digital Marketing: Strategy, Implementation and Practice*, 5th edn, Harlow: Pearson.
38. Caemmerer, B. (2009) The planning and implementation of integrated marketing communications, *Marketing Intelligence and Planning* 27(4), 524–38.
39. Syedain, H. (1992) Taking the Expert Approach to Media, *Marketing*, 4 June, 20–1.
40. Ellis-Chadwick, F., N. F. Doherty and L. Anastasakis (2007) E-strategy in the UK retail grocery sector: a resource-based analysis, *Managing Service Quality* 17(6), 702–27.
41. Smith, N. (2012) Own-branded TV channel boosts consumer engagement, *Marketing Week*, January.
42. Hicks, R. (2005) Special Report: Radio, *Campaign*, 4 November, 26.
43. Croft, M. (1999) Listeners Keep Radio On Air, *Marketing Week*, 8 July, 30–1.
44. *The Economist* (2005) Pay Per Sale, 1 October, 73.
45. Coleman, S. (1988) Social capital in the creation of human capital, *The American Journal of Sociology* 94, 95–120.
46. Tuten, T. L. and M. R. Solomon (2013) *Social media marketing*, Harlow: Pearson, 86.
47. Tuten and Solomon (2013) op. cit.
48. http://www.thirdsector.co.uk/news/1050651/Case-Study-Thames-Reach---persistent-campaign-worked/?DCMP=ILC-SEARCH.
49. Tomkins, R. (1999) Reaching New Heights of Success, *Financial Times*, 28 May, 16.
50. Fitzsimmonds, C. (2008) Outdoor's Digital Future, *Campaign*, 18 July, 24–5.
51. Fahy, J. and D. Jobber (2012) *Foundations of Marketing*, London: McGraw-Hill Education, 242–3.
52. Fahy and Jobber (2012) op. cit.
53. Donnelly, A. (2008) Big Screen Draw, *Marketing*, 9 July, 19.
54. Mishra, S. and S. Muralie (2010) Managing dynamism of IMC Anarchy to order, *Journal of Marketing & Communications*, 6(2), 29–37.
55. Murgatroyd, L. (2004) All together now, *Marketing Business*, March, 39.
56. Eagle, L. and P. J. Kitchen (2000) Brand Communications and Corporate Cultures, *European Journal of Marketing*, 35(5/6), 667–86.
57. Fill (2011) op. cit., 101.
58. Fill (2011) op. cit., 376.
59. Mishra and Muralie (2010) op. cit.

The Budweiser Ice Cold Index App

'The Hotter the Day, the Less You Pay'

Irish people have always been fascinated by the weather, but this interest reached new heights during the summer of 2011 with the launch of the Budweiser Ice Cold Index. The centrepiece was an innovative free phone app, which could be downloaded on most smart and standard phones. This app utilized cutting-edge, mobile-vouchering technology, that matched real Irish temperatures to the offer Irish consumers received off their pints of Budweiser Ice Cold. Only available to people who downloaded the Budweiser Ice Cold Index app between April and September 2011, this promotion offered Irish consumers special deals based on the temperature in their towns and cities.

A user could check the app to see what the daily temperature and resultant offer was in their region. If the temperature rose above 20°C, consumers were offered a free pint. The app also offered €2 off when the temperature reached 18°C or 19°C outdoors, with €1 off when the temperature reached 16°C or 17°C. Simply put: 'the hotter the day, the less you pay'. The app issued the user with a code that could be redeemed at any one of the 2500 participating pubs across Ireland between 1 p.m. and 11.59 p.m. on that day. The app even showed the user the nearest participating pub on a map!

By using daily weather feeds and linking discounts at the bar directly to the weather, Budweiser was not just talking to consumers, but making them an active part of the campaign by encouraging them to download and engage with the app before passing it on to friends. To celebrate the launch of the Index, everyone who downloaded the app initially enjoyed a free pint of Budweiser Ice Cold free, regardless of the weather!

The birth of Budweiser Ice Cold

Budweiser is a relatively new brand in the Irish market and in Ireland is sold by Diageo under licence from Anheuser Busch. Although it has been sold in the US for the past 150 years, it was only launched in the Irish market in the late 1980s. After its initial launch, Budweiser enjoyed a massive growth trajectory and went from having no distribution and no market share to become the number one lager in the Irish market. However, from 2000 onwards Budweiser sales began to slip. Budweiser realized they needed to emphasize the brand's uniqueness as one of the coldest beers on the market and its being the leader in refreshment. This led to the birth of Budweiser Ice Cold.

Budweiser Ice Cold was launched in Ireland in March 2009 as a new variant of Budweiser to drive volume during peak summer months and to attract 18–34-year-old drinkers to the brand. Budweiser Ice Cold is the same liquid as Budweiser, but is just served at a colder temperature. The brand quickly became the market leader in refreshment, outscoring Carlsberg, Heineken, Bulmers, Miller, Coors Light and Corona Extra on 'refreshment' in taste tests among trialists of the product. Budweiser Ice Cold has transformed Budweiser's draught performance in the Irish market, and the brand has seen a steady increase in sales since its launch. Subsequent TV campaigns did a good job at raising awareness, but struggled to turn that awareness into trial among advocates of competitor brands.

Launching the Budweiser Ice Cold Index

In an effort to build on the successful sales of Budweiser Ice Cold and to convert awareness into trial in the Irish market, Budweiser set themselves a target to increase the growth in the Budweiser Ice Cold trial rate among 18–34-year-olds (their target market)! In order to achieve this, a number of clear objectives were identified. First, Budweiser wanted to effect a behaviour change and drive trial in an innovative way. Their research had shown that only one-third of 18–34-year-olds in Ireland had tried Budweiser Ice Cold, but that 88 per cent of those who did would consider it in the future. The focus was now on trying to increase the brand's drinker base and to drive trial of the brand. Second, Diageo wanted to drive Budweiser Ice Cold's summer refreshment credentials. They wanted Budweiser Ice Cold to be viewed as the summertime lager of choice and as an intrinsic part of the nation's summertime culture (the ice cream of the lager market!).

Diageo wanted to develop a campaign that would connect with their target market who were heavy users of social media. The concept of the Budweiser Ice Cold Index was developed by DDB UK and it was one that instantly grabbed Diageo's attention. However, in order to make the Index work, Budweiser needed some means of distributing vouchers to consumers. Postal vouchers, printable email vouchers, newspaper vouchers or promotional staff voucher distribution were all seen as problematic.

Mobile phone vouchering was seen as a viable distribution option, although one that hadn't been used in Ireland in the past. The feeling was that the time was right for such an approach as smartphone usage was on the increase. However, the implementation implications of using mobile vouchering were huge and after almost 18 months development work, the Budweiser Ice Cold Index was launched in April 2011. It was greeted with much enthusiasm by the Irish public and was generally hailed as an exciting approach to drinks promotion. According to Christopher Wooff, Senior Brand Manager at Budweiser, 'Budweiser Ice Cold Index is an innovative concept, which we feel will excite consumers and we are thrilled to be the first brand to bring mobile vouchering to the Irish on-trade.'

An integrated campaign

The Budweiser Ice Cold brand team were faced with three important communication tasks for this campaign: they needed to educate the public on how to use the Index, they needed to facilitate a compelling brand experience via digital media and events and they wanted to celebrate Budweiser Ice Cold's superior refreshment credentials.

It was important to choose the right creative message that would have the flexibility to work through the line from advertising to events to Facebook and would stay true to Budweiser's brand values of optimism, celebration and anticipation. A spokesperson was used for the campaign—a 'cool' American weatherman called 'Scott Campbell'. He was used as a mouthpiece for the campaign to do everything from explaining how to use the voucher to providing temperature updates. It gave Budweiser a voice to have a conversation digitally on social networking sites throughout the summer, and it was also a character Budweiser could use to interact and engage with effectively at experiential events. The use of a brand spokesperson was a proven success model that had been used across the drinks category and beyond for brands such as Old Spice, Captain Morgan and Stella Artois. Choosing the 'right' kind of weatherman was extremely important to the success of the campaign. Budweiser wanted him to be aspirational, approachable, consistent with Budweiser's personality, sense of celebration and optimism and consistent with current culture. He had to be someone who was interesting and entertaining enough to gain social currency with the target audience. Scott Campbell promoted the Index across all media from TV to Twitter and kept people up-to-date with the campaign's development. Through targeted media relations and digital media, Budweiser built Scott Campbell's profile to make him one of the most recognizable celebrities in Ireland.

Budweiser used both consumer-generated and brand-generated communication for this integrated campaign. In terms of brand-generated communication, they developed the app itself, a Budweiser Ice Cold Index microsite, in-pub point-of-sales material, trade and technical Index launches and an award-winning advertising campaign. Three different TV ads ('beach', 'pool' and 'golf') were developed. Scott Campbell appeared in all three explaining the concept behind the Budweiser Ice Cold Index and providing consumers with details on its use. This TV advertising campaign was supported by outdoor, radio and digital advertising. Digital advertising on YouTube and Facebook drove online traffic to download the app. This advertising campaign proved beneficial in raising public awareness of the Index and was only the third Irish advertising campaign ever to win at the Cannes Lions International Festival of Creativity.

However, they also felt that it was important for consumers to converse, create, amplify and connect and consumer-generated promotion would facilitate this. Facebook, Twitter and blogs played an important role in the communication strategy. The Facebook page providing in-depth consumer information which consumers could access if required was pivotal in handling consumer technical queries. Scott Campbell provided strong content for the Index Facebook page and the Index temperature updates created good daily content for the page. The fan numbers and interactions on the Facebook page highlight its massive success. Facebook fans exploded by over 600 per cent during the Index, from 5000 in April 2011 to almost 40,000 by September 2011! Twitter also played an important role in the campaign as Scott Campbell's Twitter feed drove brand interaction and affinity. Users were prompted to tweet on redemption of the vouchers, with a hashtag tracking redemptions.

Challenges

When implementing the campaign, Budweiser were faced with certain challenges. The summer of 2011 was the worst summer Ireland had witnessed over the last 50 years and this limited the number of weather vouchers used. However, Diageo felt that it was still essential to drive trial whatever the weather and they introduced 'free pint Fridays', weekly bonus vouchers, whatever the weather. This helped to significantly increase download and redemption rates, despite the bad weather. Diageo also extended the campaign into September, which allowed the Irish public to avail themselves of vouchers for longer than was initially promised.

Achieving publican engagement with this campaign was also an issue. Some smaller, local publicans were not very technically savvy and it was a challenge for Diageo to get them on board. Promoting public engagement with the campaign was also an issue. This was the first time Irish consumers had the opportunity to use a mobile-phone vouchering app like this. Some consumers weren't familiar with how to download an app, and even those who went to the trouble of downloading the app didn't always use the vouchers offered.

Despite these challenges, the Budweiser Ice Cold Index campaign has been hugely beneficial for Diageo. Although the final results of the campaign have yet to be made public, initial results suggest that the campaign has been a huge success for Budweiser Ice Cold. By the end of the summer, the increase in the number of males drinking Budweiser in the past four weeks was growing faster than for any other mainstream beer brand in Ireland. Initially launched in just 1500 pubs across Ireland, Budweiser Ice Cold's distribution has grown and it is now distributed in over 2700 pubs nationwide (about 25–30 per cent of Irish pubs). The campaign generated enormous awareness for the brand, both on- and off-line. It received extensive TV and press coverage, and was the most talked-about drinks campaign of that summer 2011. Diageo used an innovative approach for this campaign. It remains to be seen how Diageo will build on the success of the Budweiser Ice Cold Index campaign in the future.

Questions

1   **Evaluate Diageo's integrated campaign for the launch of the Budweiser Ice Cold Index in Ireland. What were the key objectives of this campaign?**

2   **Why did Diageo choose to use mobile vouchering for this campaign instead of other voucher distribution methods? Comment on the challenges associated with the use of this innovative voucher distribution method.**

3   **View all three Budweiser Ice Cold ads on YouTube ('beach', 'pool' and 'golf'). Why do you think Diageo chose to use Scott Campbell as the spokesperson for this campaign? Do you think he appeals to the 18–34-year-old target market? Why?**

This case was written by Marie O'Dwyer, Lecturer in Marketing, Waterford Institute of Technology, Ireland. Special thanks to Christopher Wooff, Senior Brand Manager, Diageo Ireland for his generosity in providing information to assist in the writing of this case study.

Comparethemarket.com

'Simples'

Comparethemarket.com has been offering an online price comparison service for consumers since 2006. The company, which is owned by the BGL Group, has grown rapidly over the past three years, and is one of the UK's leading price comparison websites. This success is largely due to its hard-to-avoid but phenomenally effective advertising campaigns. Comparethemarket.com has embraced a totally integrated and symbiotic communications plan that links together above-the-line media (mainly TV and radio), digital (Comparethemeerkat.com and search) and social media (Twitter and Facebook). The success of this integrated marketing communication campaign is largely due to a new cult advertising hero—Aleksandr Orlov. Aleksandr Orlov, the new face of Comparethemarket.com, is an entrepreneur from Moscow. He is in his mid-40s, about two-and-a-half feet tall and, most important, he is a meerkat!

Background of the campaign

Comparethemarket.com is a price comparison website operating in the insurance industry in the UK. The insurance comparison market in the UK is notoriously crowded, competitive and undifferentiated. It's also a very low-interest category, even though consumers could save hundreds of pounds on insurance costs by switching providers. Comparethemarket.com was a small player in this category where market share is king. In a category where market share is determined by spend, Comparethemarket.com were fourth in a category of four. Comparethemarket.com were being heavily outspent on generic Google search terms, such as 'car insurance' and 'compare insurance'. Similarly, they were one of the last entrants to an already crowded market, had no clear point of difference and a cumbersome brand name that no one could remember. In a market where name familiarity is key, research demonstrated that Comparethemarket.com had a long unmemorable name and that their identity and name were very similar to their nearest (bigger spending) competitor GoCompare. In research Compare.com (which doesn't exist) was as well remembered as Comparethemarket.com. People would describe GoCompare's ads and site and attribute them to Comparethemarket.com (and visa versa). This similarity enhanced the challenge faced by Comparethemarket.com in having no single feature on which they could build a point of differentiation to capture market share.

A good summary of the battle within the category is 'to spend more than the competition on communicating the generic benefit'. Not surprisingly the ads were perceived by consumers to all be the same—computer screens, cars with stars and price-saving claims. The four major players shared around 1500 TV spots a day. The benefits being communicated to consumers were the same. By increasingly focusing on 'differentiating' claims in advertising, all the sites increasingly blended into one. As a result, despite what this new category did for consumers, few seemed to like it much and consumers couldn't differentiate rationally between them. This lack of differentiation reinforced the necessity to spend heavily on search terms. If comparison sites want to keep costs down, they have to get people to type in their brand name directly. Google charges less if people search by brand name, they charge more if they search for something generic: i.e. car insurance. In order to close the gap on the market leaders, Moneysupermarketcom, Confused.com and GoCompare.com, creating affection for Comparethemarket.com was crucial. To create affection for a price comparison site would require Comparethemarket.com to shatter the conventions of marketing communications within the industry.

Outmanoeuvred in a crowded market overflowing with rational messages Comparethemarket.com recognised the need to create love for the brand. The only thing that distinguished Comparethemarket.com from the competition was the word 'market'. It was felt that by drawing attention to the word 'market', Comparethemarket. com would be able to create space between their site and the competition. Comparethemarket.com turned to the agency VCCP to deliver such a campaign. VCCP's planning process started with an insight about the way people use Google. The majority of consumers find a price comparison site through Google, so it was essential for VCCP to think about the key words consumers were typing in if they wanted them to come to Comparethemarket.com, rather than any of its competitors.

The footnote of the creative brief from Comparethemarket. com asked the creatives if they could find a way of sidestepping the high cost per click on the word 'market' (which is over £5). They asked the creatives if they might be able to find a way of introducing a cheaper term or phrase into their advertising that could exist alongside the word 'market'. The emphasis was to make the word 'market' famous as many other companies used the word 'compare' in their brand names. In exploring this idea it found that cost per click on the word 'meerkat' was in the region of 5p (market was £5). By learning from other communication successes (Cadbury's Gorilla) and applying them to the forgotten rules of the insurance market (a brand icon) they were able to create affection and stand out for the differentiated part of their name (market). This discovery was the starting point for the creation of Aleksandr Orlov, a loveable but complex character who is desperately frustrated by the confusion between Comparethemarket. com and Comparethemeerkat.com. For Aleksandr to be successful Comparethemarket.com needed to create layers to his character, in order to generate continued warmth and affection towards the brand.

Comparethemeerkat.com

Aleksandr Orlov is a very successful business meerkat. He is the founder of Comparethemeerkat.com, the world's premier meerkat comparison website. Aleksandr's website allows his customers to key in a few details, such as the size of meerkat you are looking for, your hobbies and your preferred meerkat location. The bane of Aleksandr's life is a company called Comparethemarket.com, a UK-based insurance price comparison website. The problem is that its name sounds very much like that of Aleksandr's site, so people come to his website wanting to compare cheap car insurance instead of wanting to compare meerkats. It is taking up his time and valuable bandwidth and distracting him from his everyday business. Aleksandr has decided to launch an advertising campaign to clear up 'meerkat/ market' confusion once and for all. You see, it is really quite simple. Or, as Aleksandr would say, 'simples'. The Comparethemeerkat.com website (where you can compare thousands of meerkats) built by Aleksandr, Sergei (his trusty

IT manager) and the integrated team at VCCP captured the imagination of consumers in initial research. Historically, many great insurance brands had been built on affection and salience embodied in an icon. Admiral, Churchill, Hastings all developed warm iconic personalities with which to become famous. The comparison site category however, had been slow to embrace this type of marketing communications. Instead marketers in this category seemed keen to communicate a revolutionary product and moved away from unfashionable conventions. Comparethemarket. com recognized that Aleksandr's character was the key to capture market share and developed an integrated marketing communications plan.

Each communications platform was carefully considered and used for a specific purpose within the advertising campaign strategy for Comparethemarket.com. Traditional communication allowed mass reach and awareness, developing the lovable character of Aleksandr. TV advertising was the catalyst, without which the other components would not have worked as effectively. The digital focus was spent on developing Aleksandr's official comparison website, Comparethemeerkat.com, and ensuring that engagement levels were high. Social media were at the very heart of the campaign in order to create and facilitate conversations about Aleksandr Orlov, Comparethemeerkat.com and Comparethemarket.com, primarily on Facebook and Twitter. Facebook was designed to be the place for Aleksandr's community to engage, create and connect together. Comparethemarket.com are using the space to upload content, pictures, videos and notes on a weekly basis. They use Facebook to encourage consumer uploads of meerkat suggestions (which are being fed into version two of the website), meerkat photos and ideas for new marketing launches (toys, ringtones etc). Aleksandr is the first UK advertising character to have his own Twitter account. He is an active and engaged participant in the Twittersphere, sharing links, photos (like the user generated content one of Aleks and Stephen Fry stuck in a lift together!) and his daily thoughts. He is also committed to answering specific questions that his fans tweet him. Twitter was also used to find real people to appear as part of his new Testimonials page on his website. Social media was also used to introduce the campaign's second execution where Comparethemeerkat's bespectacled IT manager Sergei was created and discussed through posts on Twitter and Facebook.

Campaign results

The campaign is ongoing, but this new approach to marketing the car insurance category seems to be paying off for Comparethemarket.com. The love people have for Aleksandr Orlov has had an outstanding impact on the fortunes of the brand. Return on investment for this integrated communications campaign can be proven by robust figures. The campaign achieved all of its twelve-month objectives in nine weeks. In the first five months, there was a 100 per cent increase in traffic to Comparethemarket.com. Cost-per-visit has been reduced by 75 per cent. The campaign has also seen a 100 per cent increase in insurance quotes. Market share has tripled and 5.5 million people have visited Comparethemeerket.com since its creation in 2009, of which 21 per cent go through to Comparethemarket.com. Softer metrics, such as spontaneous brand awareness, have seen the brand rise from fourth to first in the sector. Social media conversations about car insurance were monitored before the campaign broke and found that 15 per cent were about Comparethemarket.com. Now the firm accounts for 55 per cent of UK conversations about car insurance. Aleksandr now has 814,000 fans on Facebook, making it the most popular branded fan site in the UK (Aleksandr's closest rival is Marmite, with 238,000 fans). These have created and uploaded almost 1000 meerkat-inspired photos, left 8370 wall posts and watched his videos. Aleksandr has received 311 offers of marriage, 256 offers of adoption, and there are at least 20 active petitions from fans demanding Aleksandr merchandise including toys, ringtones and iPhone meerkat comparison applications. There is also a popular discussion board on which one topic is whether Aleksandr could be persuaded to stand for Prime Minister in the UK. The *Daily Telegraph* newspaper reported that Aleksandr Orlov is even more popular than real-world celebrities such as football superstar Wayne Rooney and singer Cheryl Cole combined. Aleksandr is being followed by almost 21,000 people on Twitter. This number of followers to a branded advertising campaign is unprecedented. To put it into context, Vinnie, the Fox's Biscuit panda character, is followed by 643. A Twitter influence model developed by *Marketing* magazine/JCPR discovered that Aleksandr is more influential on Twitter than London Mayor Boris Johnson and US Secretary of State Hillary Clinton. For Comparethemarket.com, the campaign has significantly impacted on their human resources. Job applications have increased dramatically and staff morale is at an all-time high. Finally, the campaign has also brought about a major change for their competitors in terms of their search strategy. The success of the campaign means that competitors of Comparethemarket.com are now forced to actively target the keyword 'meerkat'.

Conclusion

Comparethemarket.com and VCCP have been heralded as modern communications visionaries for the success of the current campaign. Comparethemeerkat.com is a very good example of modern integrated marketing communications planning. The idea at the heart of the campaign is totally consistent, but they have incorporated dispersed fragments of the brand narratives across multiple platforms. Comparethemarket.com have revolutionised the conventions of the marketing communications in the insurance comparison industry and it is up to competitors to see if they can regain the leadership position in the market despite the presence of Aleksandr Orlov.

Questions

1. Discuss the potential advantages and disadvantages of implementing an integrated marketing communications campaign. What were the key success factors for the Comparethemarket.com campaign?

2. Outline the factors which would have impacted on the choice of promotional mix used by Comparethemarket.com.

3. Evaluate the importance of the meerkat character to the brand's identity. Discuss the importance of social media as a tool in the creation of Aleksandr's message.

This case was written by David Cosgrave, Teaching Assistant, Department of Marketing and Management, University of Limerick.

CHAPTER 15

Mass marketing communications

nothing but fruit

Here to save the peckish

> *All of us professionally who use the mass media are the shapers of society. We can vulgarize that society. We can brutalize it. Or we can help lift it on to a higher level.*
>
> **WILLIAM BERNBACH**[1]

LEARNING OBJECTIVES

After reading this chapter, you should be able to:

1 explain the role of each of the tools in the mass communication promotional mix

2 discuss how advertising works and how to develop an advertising strategy

3 discuss the reasons for the growth of product placement

4 define public relations, key objectives, targets and characteristics

5 describe the guidelines to use when writing a press release

6 discuss the objectives and methods of sponsorship

7 explain how to select and evaluate a potential sponsored event

8 identify the major sales promotion types, including objectives

9 explain how to evaluate sales promotion

10 describe trade promotions

11 discuss ethical issues in mass marketing communications

Wider use of communications has placed the emphasis on developing integrated communications campaigns, using different communication methods. As discussed in Chapter 14, mass marketing communications primarily involve sending non-personal messages to wide target audiences. These key tools are the focus of this chapter and are discussed in the following order: advertising and product placement, public relations and sponsorship, and sales promotions. The chapter also explores the main media channels, building on coverage of the topics in the previous chapter and looking specifically at media vehicle selection.

Mass communication methods enable wide dispersion of product, brand and company messages. The simple and complex communication processes explain how messages spread. Mass communication tools provide the focus, style and tone of the message. This is then delivered to the target audience by a variety of media channels. Each aspect shapes the communication message and impacts on how it might be received. For example, television commercials sometimes seek to irritate the target audience to get their attention. Gocompare.com (see Exhibit 15.1), Webuyanycar.com, L'Oréal Elvive and Danone's Activia are some of the most irritating according to the latest research.[2] In other instances print adverts often present rational and logical arguments to encourage target audiences to make a buying decision: for example, the Halifax reward account. According to the Halifax's message, 'it's the little things in life that make the difference'[3] and therefore the advert asks the reader to switch bank accounts for the reward of £5 per month. Other mass communication tools also add more opportunities to vary and shape the message. For instance, in the case of PR, stories in the media and events provide a source of public information and experience, which can raise awareness and educate various publics (target audiences) about a brand and its corporate image. It should be noted that the use of PR is on the increase as corporate reputations are increasingly at the heart of a company's competitive advantage. Sales promotions are often used to elicit action and this technique is used widely from selling FMCGs to car finance. For example, Vauxhall offered prospective new car buyers the opportunity of flexible finance at 0 per cent APR plus lifetime warranty (limited to 100,000 miles) in return for buying an Astra GTC Sport, 1.4 16v VVT Turbo during March 2012.[4] These examples help to highlight various theories, which seek to explain how mass communications might work.

Broadly speaking, advertising and PR raise awareness, while sales promotion is used to stimulate action. But each tool has much more to offer a marketing manager planning an IMC campaign. These tools are now explored in more detail.

⬆ **EXHIBIT 15.1** The Gocompare campaign has been named the 'most irritating ad' in the UK two years running.[5]

Advertising

What is advertising? How does it work? When should it be used and how can we evaluate its effectiveness? These questions, asked about advertising, have tormented academics and practitioners alike and filled thousands of pages of hundreds of publications. Yet still there are no definitive answers. Hegarty says success comes from the big idea.[6] For Sorrell it is all about the capacity to deliver ROI.[7] Jones explains how it can persuade,[8] while Ehrenburg suggests a weaker response.[9] And just when you think you might have some answers, throw into the debate *disruptive* technology like the Internet. Here, newcomers to the world of business, like college students Page and Brin (Google) and Zuckerberg (Facebook), have created new environments that are part of the networks that encase the planet and operate at the speed of light. Furthermore, the Internet, the Web and social networks are rapidly changing the way we communicate and the content of our messages which we use to influence others. At this point, the likelihood of getting conclusive answers about how advertising works in the modern world arguably becomes more unlikely.

⬆EXHIBIT 15.2 **Lucozade used an unknown band to connect with its target audiences.**

Go to the website to see the inspiration and energy that went into the making of the Lucozade advert.
www.mcgraw-hill.co.uk/ textbooks/jobber

So, what can we achieve in this short section on advertising? We start with the basics: strong and weak theories of advertising, which seek to explain the principle of how advertising works. Then we look at the practicalities: identify the different objectives which create a platform for using advertising, look at campaign planning, media decisions, and client–agency relationships. Furthermore, throughout this section, we use practitioner examples to provide evidence of the difficulties and possible solutions for the simple questions raised at the start.

Advertising: the basics

Advertising messages rely on mass media to deliver communications messages. Uses and gratifications theory suggests that the mass media constitute a resource on which audiences draw to satisfy various needs. Its assumptions are:

- the audience is active and their consumption of mass media is largely directed by their needs
- the initiative in linking need satisfaction with media choice lies mainly with the individual
- the media compete with other sources of need satisfaction
- the gratifications sought from the media include diversion and entertainment as well as information.[10]

Research suggests that people use advertising for at least seven kinds of satisfaction: namely product information, entertainment, risk reduction, added value, past purchase reassurance, vicarious experience and involvement.[11] Vicarious experience is the opportunity to experience situations or lifestyles to which an individual would not otherwise have access. Involvement refers to the pleasure of participation in the puzzles or jokes contained in some advertisements. Research among a group of young adults aged 18–24 added other uses of advertising, including escapism, ego enhancement (demonstrating their intelligence by understanding the advertisement) and checking out the opposite sex.[12] Uses and gratifications theory identifies the link between advertising, the media and the motivations of message receivers.

For example, when Lucozade wanted to communicate with its target audiences, it recruited an unknown band (James Cleaver Quintet) and sent them with their friends, spectators and a camera crew rolling down the hill on skateboards (see Exhibit 15.2).

In essence the television commercial supports the research as it provides entertainment. Through the Web, target audiences can derive further satisfaction by engaging directly with the adverts (see Ad Insight). The brand message provides further gratification by telling its users what to expect when they buy the brand.

These linkages give us some clues to why advertising appears on different media and also why the Internet has become such a popular medium for messages which invite engagement. But we need to know more about how advertising works.

Strong and Weak Theories of How Advertising Works

For many years there has been considerable debate about how advertising works. The consensus is that there can be no single all-embracing theory that explains how all advertising works because it has varied tasks.[13] For example, advertising that attempts to make an instant sale by incorporating a return coupon that can be used to order a product is very different from corporate image advertising that is designed to reinforce attitudes.

The competing views on how advertising works have been termed the **strong theory of advertising** and the **weak theory of advertising**.[14] The strong theory has its base in the USA and is shown on the left-hand side of Figure 15.1. A person passes through the stages of awareness, interest, desire and action (AIDA). According to this theory, advertising is strong enough to increase people's knowledge and change people's attitudes, and as a consequence

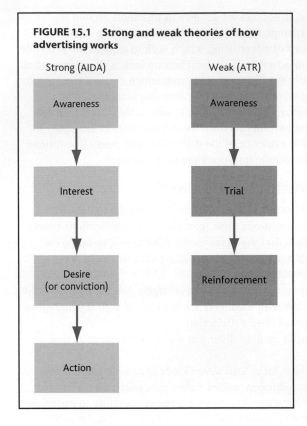

FIGURE 15.1 Strong and weak theories of how advertising works

Strong (AIDA)

Awareness → Interest → Desire (or conviction) → Action

Weak (ATR)

Awareness → Trial → Reinforcement

is capable of persuading people who had not previously bought a brand to buy it. It is therefore a conversion theory of advertising: non-buyers are converted to buyers. Advertising is assumed to be a powerful influence on consumers.

This model has been criticized on two grounds.[15] First, for many types of product there is little evidence that consumers experience a strong desire before action (buying the brand). For example, in the case of an inexpensive product, a brand might be bought on a trial basis without any strong conviction that it is superior to competing brands. Second, the model is criticized because it is limited to the conversion of a non-buyer to a buyer. It ignores what happens after action (i.e. first purchase). Yet in most mature markets advertising is designed to affect people who have already bought the brand at least once.

The major alternative to the strong advertising theory is shown on the right-hand side of Figure 15.1. The steps in this model are awareness, trial and reinforcement (ATR). The ATR model, which has received support in Europe, suggests that advertising is a much less powerful influence than the strong theory would suggest. As Ehrenberg explains, 'advertising can first arouse awareness and interest, nudge some customers towards a doubting first trial purchase (with the emphasis on trial, as in "maybe I'll try it") and then provide some reassurance and reinforcement after that first purchase. I see no need for any strong AIDA-like Desire or Conviction before the first purchase is made.'[16] His work in fast-moving consumer goods (FMCG) markets has shown that loyalty to one brand is rare. Most consumers purchase a selection of brands. The proportions of total purchases represented by the different brands show little variation over time, and new brands join the selection only in exceptional circumstances. A major objective of advertising in such circumstances is to defend brands. It does not work to increase sales by bringing new buyers to the brand advertised. Its main function is to retain existing buyers, and sometimes to increase the frequency with which they buy the brand.[17] Therefore, the target is existing buyers who are fairly well disposed to the brand (otherwise they would not buy it), and advertising is designed to reinforce these favourable perceptions so they continue to buy it.[18]

As we saw when discussing consumer behaviour, level of involvement has an important role in determining how people make purchasing decisions. Jones suggests that involvement may also explain when the strong and weak theories apply.[19] For high-involvement decisions such as the purchase of expensive consumer durables, mail order or financial services, the decision-making process is studied with many alternatives considered and an extensive information search undertaken. Advertising, therefore, is more likely to follow the strong theory either by creating a strong desire to purchase (as with mail order) or by convincing people that they should find out more about the brand (for example, by visiting a showroom). Since the purchase is expensive it is likely that a strong desire (or conviction) is required before purchase takes place.

However, for low-involvement purchase decisions (such as low-cost packaged goods) people are less likely to consider a wide range of brands thoroughly before purchase and it is here that the weak theory of advertising almost certainly applies. Advertising is mainly intended to keep consumers doing what they already do by providing reassurance and reinforcement. Advertising repetition will be important in maintaining awareness and keeping the brand on the consumer's selection of brands from which individual purchases will be chosen.

Advertising: the Practicalities of Developing a Strategy

Advertising is one element of the marketing mix and decisions regarding advertising expenditure should not be taken in isolation. Marketing strategy needs to be taken into account. In particular, competitive positioning needs to be considered: what is the target market and what differential advantage does the product possess? Target market definition allows the *details of the audience* to be identified through segmentation variables: both in consumer and industrial markets (e.g. 16–19-year-old women, or fashion buyers in the retail industry). More specifically, for example, Asus is a leading manufacturer of computer hardware, such as high-performance motherboards. It targets gamers (age 20+ males) who are looking for intense action from their selected products, and Asus uses knowledge of its customers to develop advertising which grabs the attention of its target audiences. The target selection process also helps focus on the differential advantage and the features and benefits of the product to stress in the advertising. Figure 15.2 shows the major decisions that need to be taken when developing advertising strategy.

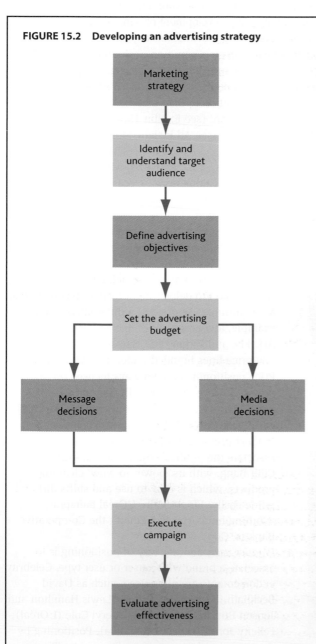

FIGURE 15.2 Developing an advertising strategy

- Marketing strategy
- Identify and understand target audience
- Define advertising objectives
- Set the advertising budget
- Message decisions
- Media decisions
- Execute campaign
- Evaluate advertising effectiveness

Identify and understand the target audience

The **target audience** is the group of people at which the advertisement is aimed. In consumer markets it may be defined in terms of socioeconomic group, age, gender, location, buying frequency (e.g. heavy vs. light buyers) and/or lifestyle. In organizational markets, it may be defined in terms of role (e.g. purchasing manager, managing director) and industry type.

Once the target audience has been identified, it needs to be understood. Buyer motives and choice criteria need to be analysed. Choice criteria are those factors buyers use to evaluate competing products. Understanding criteria in line with the needs of the target audience is vital: it has fundamental implications for message and media decisions.

Define advertising objectives

Advertising is used to achieve various objectives including stimulating sales and increasing profits. To deliver operational value from using advertising it is important to set clear communication *objectives*. Advertising can create awareness, stimulate trial, position products in customers' minds, correct misconceptions, remind and reinforce, and provide support for the sales force. Each objective will now be discussed.

Create awareness

Advertising can create awareness of a company, a brand, a website, an event, or something of interest to target audiences. It can even alert buyers to a solution to a problem. For example, Colgate toothpaste can stop plaque, bad breath, tooth and gum decay; More-than car insurance protects from disruption in car drivers' lives; Yell.com can help find anything including a 'Day V Lately' transmix CD. It is widely agreed (in principle) that advertising can help to legitimize a company, its products, brands and sales teams in the minds of the target audience. In doing so it can also improve acceptance of what a company has on offer. Brand awareness is considered as a precondition of purchase and can be achieved through advertising.

Stimulate trial

Advertising can create interest and stimulate trial. The sale of some products suffers because of lack of trial. Perhaps marketing research has shown that, once consumers try the product, acceptance is high but for some reason only a small proportion of the target group has actually bought the product. In such circumstances, advertising focuses on stimulating trial. For example, Walls sausage adverts, created by Saatchi & Saatchi, use a surreal advert, with a talking dog called Alan and a man thanking his wife for serving his favourite meaty snack for his tea.[20]

Position products in customers' minds

Advertising copy and visuals have a major role to play in positioning brands in the minds of the target audience.[21] Creative positioning involves the development or reinforcement of an image or set of associations for a brand. There are seven ways in which this objective can be achieved.[22]

Go to the website to see how T-mobile uses humour and music to convey the product characteristics and customer benefits.
www.mcgraw-hill.co.uk/textbooks/jobber

1   *Product characteristics and customer benefits*: this is a common positioning strategy. For example: Ford Focus uses its high-tech features and characteristics, e.g. self-parking, eco-boost, low-speed safety system, traffic sign recognition, to portray its car's benefits to the user and this is summed up in the statement 'Start more than a car'; Old Spice aftershave offers its users the opportunity to 'smell like a man' (see Exhibit 15.3); T-mobile offers a compelling message about how 'life's for sharing' (see Ad Insight); Corsodyl toothpaste prevents gum disease.

Another tactic used for positioning is being first, e.g. Sky News, which claims the number one position by its claim to be 'first for breaking news'. Occasionally two or more attributes are used, as with Ecover laundry liquid (cleans clothes with its non-biological product and is good for the environment as it uses less packaging and fewer transport miles). L'Oréal Men Expert helps fight five signs of skin fatigue (see Exhibit 15.4).

2   *Price*: this positioning approach focuses on price as a weapon to deliver higher value to consumers. Many airlines use price as a differentiator: for example, low-cost airlines like EasyJet, Jet2, ArkeFly, and Virgin Blue. Sainsbury's promotes low-price lines branded under its 'basics' range. Price positioning is not always focused on low prices, however. Occasionally a brand is positioned based on its high price, as is the case with Stella Artois ('reassuringly expensive').

3   *Product use*: another positioning method is to associate the product with a use. An example is Cillit Bang, with its 'power to wow' cleaning products, which is easy to use and shifts dirt and grime easily; Elnett Satin, L'Oréal hairspray, 'Nothing holds you like Elnett'; the Co-operative Bank is 'Good with money'.

4   *Product user*: another way of positioning is to associate a brand with a user or user type. Celebrity endorsements are often used, such as David Beckham (Burger King, H&M), Lewis Hamilton and Jensen Button (Santander), Cheryl Cole (L'Oréal), Felicity Jones (Dolce & Gabbana). Positioning by user type has been successfully used by *The Economist* (intelligent, knowledgeable).

⬆ **EXHIBIT 15.3**   This Old Spice advert features product characteristics and customer benefits to position the brand in the minds of consumers.

HYDRA ENERGETIC
ICE COOL EYE ROLL-ON

TARGET
BAGS + DARK CIRCLES

• HELP REVIVE TIRED LOOKING EYES
• WITH VITAMIN C + CAFFEINE

"DON'T LET YOUR
EYES BETRAY YOU"

GERARD BUTLER, Actor

L'ORÉAL
menexpert

↑ EXHIBIT 15.4 L'Oréal appeals to its target audience by identifying their problems and providing solutions which match consumer preferences.

Go to the website to find out about advertising standards and codes of practice.
www.mcgraw-hill.co.uk/textbooks/jobber

5 *Product class*: some products can benefit by positioning themselves within a product class. For example, Red Mountain coffee positioned itself within the ground coffee class with the tag-line 'Ground coffee taste without the grind' and a margarine called 'I Can't Believe It's Not Butter' was positioned within the butter class by virtue of its name and advertising; and of course the classic Beanz Meanz Heinz.

6 *Symbols*: the use of symbols to position brands in the marketplace has been achieved by Michelin (Michelin Man), McDonald's (golden arches) and Apple (black and white apple logo). The use of symbols is particularly effective when the symbol reflects a quality desired in the brand, as with the Andrex puppy (softness).

7 *Competition*: positioning against well-entrenched competitors can be effective since their image in the marketplace can be used as a reference point. For example, Subaru positioned against Volvo by claiming 'Volvo has built a reputation for surviving accidents. Subaru has built a reputation for avoiding them', based on ABS for better braking and four-wheel drive for better traction. Dyson positions itself against the competition by claiming that, unlike those of its rivals, its vacuum cleaners do not lose suction thanks to Dyson's patented technology. Adidas positions its products against other brands of trainers (e.g., Nike). In the Steadicam campaign a runner in the desert is wearing Nike trainers but the cameraman, carrying a 50lb camera and filming the event, is wearing Adidas. The message is that Adidas trainers offer better performance and enable users to remain fresh and lively even after an extreme run. Positioning against competitors can be effective when consumers base their purchase decision on facts. Hence, a well-adjusted statement claiming a factual advantage against a key competitor can be highly successful. However, research has shown that, if used inappropriately, it can tarnish the image of the brand that is using the technique. There is also the risk of legal action, as when Ryanair was (unsuccessfully) sued by British Airways over its advertisement headlined 'Expensive ba****ds', which compared the airlines' prices on certain routes.[23]

Not all slogans are used for their intended purpose. Read Marketing in Action 15.1 to find how to Keep Calm and Carry on.

Correct misconceptions

A fourth objective of advertising can be to correct misconceptions that consumers hold against brands. For example, McCain's, the market leader in the UK for oven chips, ran a successful advertising campaign claiming that oven chips contained 40 per cent less fat than home-cooked chips. However, marketing research showed that consumers still believed that their oven chips contained 30 per cent fat. A new campaign was designed to correct this misconception by stating that they contained only 5 per cent fat. Advertising cosmetic surgery has become increasingly commonplace. Service providers are keen to dispel fears, and often use advertising as a way of conveying the message that cosmetic procedures and treatments are safe. However, in the UK the Advertising Standards Authority (ASA) has often ruled against such advertising, on the grounds of it being misleading, exaggerated or breaching social responsibility.

Marketing in Action 15.1 Keep Calm and Carry On

Successful advertising slogans (sometimes referred to as strap-lines) are short, memorable phrases. They can focus on a particular aspect of a product or service and can be long lasting. Or they may be created for a single campaign. They are not a new phenomenon. The iconic Keep Calm and Carry On[24] poster was originally designed for the British government to be used in the advent of an invasion, and the message aimed to encourage the nation to be positive and to boost moral. However, the poster was never used officially. The 2.5 million copies were held in reserve and remained largely unseen by the British public until 2000.

Stuart Manley, owner of Barter Books, a second-hand book shop in Alnwick,[25] Northumberland, found a copy of the poster and had it framed for his wife, who liked it so much she displayed it by the side of the shop checkout. The bookshop is unusual insofar as it allows its customers to *barter* for goods as well as making cash purchases. But more notably, it has become famous for finding the poster.

Since their discovery of the Keep Calm and Carry On poster, millions of copies have been sold worldwide. The posters can be seen in places far and wide, from Buckingham Palace, the US Embassy in Belgium, to David Beckham's chest (on a T-shirt). The slogan appears on mugs, jewellery, baby clothes, T-shirts, travel bags and screen savers.

Simple, timeless and succinct, this slogan has longevity. Although not used for its intended purpose, the slogan eschews common values and brings people together in a common goal and, according to Alain Samson (Social Psychologist at the London School of Economics), 'The words are also particularly positive, reassuring, in a period of uncertainty, anxiety, even perhaps of cynicism'.

Based on: Wikipedia (2012); Barter Books (2012);[26] Henley (2009)[27]

⬆**EXHIBIT 15.5 Guinness uses a thought-provoking campaign to maintain top-of-mind awareness among its target audiences.**

Remind and reinforce

Once a clear position in the minds of the target audience has been established, the objective of advertising may be to remind consumers of the brand's existence and to reinforce its image. For many leading brands in mature markets, such as Coca-Cola, Heinz Beans or Nestlé's Kit Kat, the objective of their advertising is to maintain top-of-mind awareness and favourable associations. Given their strong market position, a major advertising task is to defend against competitive inroads, thus maintaining high sales, market share and profits. Guinness has managed to maintain its brand for over 250 years making it one of the world's most successful alcoholic drink brands.

Provide support for the sales force

Advertising can provide invaluable support for the sales force by identifying warm prospects and communicating with otherwise unreachable members of a decision-making unit. Some business-to-business advertising contains return coupons that potential customers can send to the advertiser indicating a degree of interest in the product.

Set the advertising budget

The achievement of any of the previous objectives will depend upon the size of the budget and how effectively it is spent. There are various methods of setting budgets which are discussed in more detail later in this section. These are the percentage of sales, affordability, matching competition, and the objective and task methods.

Message decisions

This section builds on our earlier discussion of the message (see Chapter 14) and explores how messages can be tailored to suit the advertiser's need and the target audience's behaviour. Advertising messages should clearly communicate with the target audience, be important to them, communicate benefits and aim to secure competitive advantage. This is why an understanding of the motives and choice criteria of the target audience is essential for effective advertising. Without this knowledge a campaign could be built upon an advertising platform that is irrelevant to its audience.

An **advertising message** translates the platform into words, symbols and illustrations that are attractive and meaningful to the target audience (see Marketing in Action 15.2).

Humour is another powerful weapon in advertising, associating the brand with a feeling of warmth (see Exhibit 15.6). Humour can be used in various media as discussed earlier in the T-mobile television advert.

Television messages also need to be built on a strong advertising platform. Because television commercials are usually 30 seconds or less in duration, most communicate only one major selling appeal—sometimes called the *single-minded proposition*—which is the single most motivating and differentiating thing that can be said about the brand.[28]

Television advertising often uses one of three creative approaches.[29] First, the *benefits* approach, where the advertisement suggests a reason for the customer to buy (customer benefit). For example, WeightWatchers advertises the benefits of losing weight. The second approach is more subtle: no overt benefit is mentioned. Instead, the intention is to *involve* the viewer. An example of involvement advertising was the commercial for Heinz Spaghetti in which a young couple's son tells them that the tomato on his plate is the sun, the triangles

⬆ Exhibit 15.6   Fedex uses a humorous visual appeal to demonstrate the ease with which the company can move parcels around Europe.

Marketing in Action 15.2 Pioneering Messages Can Create Meaningful Campaigns

According to John Caples (a top direct response copywriter), using the right message is important. He suggested there can be significant benefits: 'I have seen one ad actually sell not twice as much, not three times as much but 19 times as much as another. Both ads occupied the same space. Both were run in the same publication. Both had photographic illustrations. Both had carefully written copy. The difference was that one used the *right* appeal and the other used the *wrong* appeal.'

In the 1970s the Health Education Council ran a poster campaign (see http://www.fpa.org.uk/aboutus/fpahistory/ourfirst80years) which got the message and balances *right* between the images and the copy and achieved great impact. The campaign brief was to raise awareness of the issues of contraception and get young men to accept greater responsibility. The poster of the pregnant man was highly successful: it not only changed attitudes towards contraception among the target audience of young men, but it also helped to change wider societal attitudes towards sex education.

The HEC poster proved to be particularly powerful, and its success lies in the dramatization of reality, the message and the copywriting. So, the key challenge is how to get the entire element right. Here are some useful pointers for print advertisements based on guidance from David Ogilvy (anonymously quoted as the 'father of advertising'):

The message:

> The appeal (benefit) should be important to the target audience, written in language it can understand, be specific to the target audience's needs and should provide supporting evidence (as required).

The advert (complete, with image, headline and body copy) should contain:

- a *headline* which aims to achieve one of the following: promise a benefit; deliver news; tell a significant story; identify a problem; cite a satisfied customer review.
- *body copy* (if required—additional copy supporting and flowing from the headline) should adhere to the following rules:
  - (a) only use long copy if it is relevant to the needs of the target audience
  - (b) avoid long paragraphs and sentences
  - (c) maximize the use of white space, break up text to avoid it looking heavy to read
  - (d) use coupons as a device for providing company contact details. Alternatively, website and other contact details should appear at the end of the body copy.
- *images*. These can affect comprehension and add to the complexity of developing messages which the target audience can understand. Therefore it is important to get the *right* balance between the emotional content and the informational content.

Increasingly, adverts which can be interpreted by a global target audience are becoming important. Images can provide instant access to the message idea. But it is important to ensure that the visual imagery is as clear and uncluttered as the headline and the body copy.

Remember, most people when reading a press advertisement read the headline but not the body copy and then use associated imagery to help with their interpretation of the message. Simple visuals can convey powerful messages and reinforce brand identity.

Based on: Hegarty (2011);[30] Ogilvy (1987);[31] Pieters et al. (2010)[32]

of toast are the mountains, and the Heinz Spaghetti is the sea. When the father enters into the game and asks 'So that's the boat then?', the boy responds witheringly 'No, it's a sausage'. The third type of creative approach attempts to register the brand as significant in the market, and is called *salience advertising*. The assumption is that advertising that stands out as being different will cause the brand to stand out as different. For example, Cillit Bang uses the name of the brand, the colours associated with the brand and the style of its television adverts to stand out. Shock advertising is arguably an extreme form of salient advertising. Research[33] suggests that shock adverts take the audience by surprise because they do not conform to social norms. For example: FCUK (connotation of vulgar language); Pot Noodle ran an advertising campaign called the 'slag of all snacks', which was ultimately banned (sexual innuendo).[34] Advertisers using shock advertising should take extra care to ensure that the messages do not alienate the target audience. Benetton's Death campaign resulted in a social outcry culminating in the loss of its coveted franchise with the leading US department store chain Sears. Barnardo's, the children's charity, is known for its use of shock advertising to stimulate a response from its target audiences. In one campaign the life story of Michael, a vulnerable child, is told in reverse. The reasonable, smiling face of the 25-year-old Michael regresses as the viewer hears about what he has been through since a very early age. The strap-line 'It doesn't have to end how it began' is the trigger to encourage the target audience to make a donation and support the charity so that more vulnerable children may benefit (see Ad Insight).

Television advertising is also often used to build a brand personality. The *brand personality* is the message that the advertisement seeks to convey.

Go to the website to see the Barnados advert 'It doesn't have to end how it began'. www.mcgraw-hill.co.uk/textbooks/jobber

Media decisions

There used to be a joke among media people that the client's attitude to their part in advertising was 'Ten minutes to go before lunch. Just enough time to discuss media.' As media costs have risen and brands become more sharply targeted, this attitude has disappeared. Two key media decisions are:

1 the **media class decision** (e.g. television versus the press)
2 the **media vehicle decision** (e.g. a particular newspaper or magazine).

The media class decision

The selection of media channels has already been discussed in Chapter 14. Table 15.1 lists the media options and the following discussion has explored some of the benefits and limitations of each of the media options. In this section we build on the discussions in the previous chapter by exploring the decisions facing the media planner. The media planner faces the choice of using television, the press, cinema, outdoor, radio, the Internet or some combination of media classes. Television advertising is often used to convey the desired emotional response and the print media to supply objective information. In low-involvement situations, such as with the choice of drinks and convenience foods, humour is sometimes used to create a feeling of warmth about a brand and even regular exposure to a brand name over time can generate the desired feeling of warmth.[35] Interestingly, different media are perceived with different levels of 'trustworthiness': for example, television, print and cinema advertising is generally seen as more trusted than outdoor, online and direct mail.[36] Consequently, selecting media can be complex and there are five considerations to be taken into account.

1 *Creative factors.* The key question that needs to be addressed is 'Does the medium allow the communication objectives to be realized?' For example, if the objective is to position the brand as having a high-status aspirational personality, television would be better than posters. However, if the communication objective is to remind the target audience of a brand's existence, a poster campaign may suffice. Outdoor media are becoming more

TABLE 15.1	Definition of an opportunity to see (OTS)
Television	Presence in room with set switched on at turn of clock minute to relevant channel, provided that presence in room with set on is for at least 15 consecutive seconds
Press	Read or looked at any issue (for at least two minutes) within the publication period (for example, for weeklies, within the last seven days)
Posters	Traffic past site (including pedestrians)
Cinema	Actual cinema admissions

dynamic thanks to technological advancements, which means many of the benefits of television can be conveyed to outdoor adverts. J. C. Decaux is an example of a company making use of new technology to bring outdoor advertising to life (see http://www.jcdecaux.co.uk).

2 *Size of the advertising budget.* Some media are naturally more expensive than others. For example, £500,000 may be sufficient for a national poster campaign but woefully inadequate for national television. Advertisers with less than £3 million to spend on a national campaign may decide that television advertising is not feasible.

3 *Relative cost per opportunity to see.* The target audience may be reached much more cheaply using one medium rather than another. However, the calculation of opportunity to see differs according to media class, making comparisons difficult. For example, in the UK, an opportunity to see for the press is defined as 'read or looked at any issue of the publication for at least two minutes', whereas for posters it is 'traffic past site'.

4 *Competitive activity.* The key decision is whether to compete in the same medium or to seek to dominate an alternative medium. Deciding to compete in the same medium may be appropriate if it is seen as the most effective one by the competition, so that to ignore it would be to hand the competition a massive communication advantage. Domination of an alternative medium may be sensible for third or fourth players in a product market who cannot match the advertising budgets of the big two competitors. Supposing the major players were using television, the third or fourth competitor might choose the press or the Internet where it could dominate, achieving higher impact than if it followed the competition into television.

5 *Views of the retail trade* (for example, supermarket buyers). These may influence the choice of media class. Advertising expenditure is often used by salespeople to convince the retail trade to increase shelf space for existing brands and to stock new brands. Since distribution is a key success factor in these markets, the views of retailers will be important. For example, if it is known that supermarkets favour television advertising in a certain product market, the selling impact on the trade of £3 million spent on television may be viewed as greater than the equivalent spend of 50:50 between television and the press.

Sometimes a combination of media classes is used in an advertising campaign to take advantage of their relative strengths and weaknesses. For example, a new car launch might use television to gain awareness and project the desired image, the Internet to foster engagement, the press to supply more technical information and later in the campaign outdoor media posters may be used as a support medium to remind and reinforce earlier messages.

The media vehicle decision

Media vehicle decision concerns the choice of the particular newspaper, magazine, television spot, poster site, etc. Although creative considerations still play a part, *cost per thousand calculations* is more dominant. This requires readership and viewership figures. In the UK readership figures are produced by the National Readership Survey, based on over 36,000 interviews per year. Viewership is measured by the Broadcasters' Audience Research Board (BARB), which produces weekly reports based on a panel of 5100 households equipped with metered television sets. Poster research is conducted by an organization called Postar (Poster Audience Research). It provides information on not only the number of people who pass but also the number of people who are likely to see a particular site.[37] Cinema audiences are monitored by Cinema and Video Industry Audience Research (CAVIAR), and radio audiences are measured by Radio Joint Audience Research (RAJAR). Table 15.1 shows how a viewer or reader is measured in terms of opportunity to see (OTS). Read more in Marketing in Action 15.3.

Media buying is a specialized skill and many thousands of pounds can be saved off rate card prices by powerful media buyers. Media buying is now largely done through media independents, but many of the world's top media buying operations are associated with global marketing companies such as WPP and GroupM (media agency). Buying power enables agencies to acquire and retain clients because advertisers believe that the media

Marketing in Action 15.3   Media Buying Challenges Facing Digital Companies

The problem with buying from television channels is that generally space is sold based on the broad audience profiles. So, for a dot-com company like e-harmony there is very little way of knowing whether the company's target audience of 'singles' are watching particular commercial breaks, even though technology is changing the way advertising is measured. For example, since the first digital set-top boxes were launched there has been the possibility of using them to collect data. They have memory and there is a return path. Return path panels have become an increasingly important part of television measurement around the world. Sky started developing SkyView, the first panel of its kind in the world, back in 2003 and began using the data in 2006. Sky's panel of 33,000 Sky Digital Homes is a unique research tool, combining viewing behaviour with actual brand-purchasing data.[38]

Nevertheless, marketers still have concerns about the lack of detailed information from BARB, the power struggles between broadcasters and the general lack of information about viewing audiences.

Based on: Barnett (2011)[39]

houses with the biggest budgets buy cheapest. This means that media buyers need to be of a sufficient size to attract global clients.[40] However, the Internet provides a platform for access to a media channel, which does not require high-powered media buyers. YouTube is an environment for video content and the way it is being used to upload personal and commercial messages is changing the way we communicate. The Internet has created an opportunity for advertisers small and large to access global audiences.[41]

Execute campaign

Once the advertisements have been produced and the media selected, they are sent to the relevant media for publication or transmission. A key organizational issue is to ensure that the right advertisements reach the right media at the right time. Each media vehicle has its own deadlines after which publication or transmission may not be possible.

Evaluate advertising effectiveness

All marketing communications, not just advertising, should be evaluated to determine a) whether the message and the tools that are to be used to deliver the campaign are likely to be effective; and b) the impact and effectiveness of the campaign once it has been released.[42] This means pre-testing (before the campaign) and post-testing (during and after the campaign).

What should be measured depends on whatever the advertising is trying to achieve. As we have already seen, advertising objectives include gaining awareness, trial, positioning, correcting misconceptions, reminding and providing support for the sales force (for example, by identifying warm prospects). By setting targets for each objective, advertising research can assess whether objectives have been achieved. For example, a campaign might have the objective of increasing awareness from 10 to 20 per cent, or of raising beliefs that the product is the 'best value brand on the market' from 15 to 25 per cent of the target consumers.

If advertising objectives are couched in sales or market share terms, campaign evaluation methods should monitor the sales or market share effects of the advertising. If trade objectives are important, distribution and stock levels of wholesalers and/or retailers, and perhaps their awareness and attitudes, could be measured. Each tool has different methods of evaluation. In the rest of this section we focus on advertising research methods by looking at pre- and post-testing.

Pre-testing before the campaign is part of the creative process. Adverts can be tested at various stages of development from testing the concept to finished adverts (before they are released):

• *Concept testing* is part of the development of the advertising campaign and helps the creative team to identify the ideas that are most likely to be effective. This method works by showing the target audience a rough outline of the ideas, for example storyboards, photographs. The advantages are that a variety of ideas can be tested prior to further development. Limitations of this approach are that it takes place in an artificial setting and this must be considered when evaluating the results.

- *Focus groups*—a small number of target audience members are brought together to discuss ideas and relevant topics. There will be a moderator who is experienced in interviewing who uses the gathering to probe thoughts and emotions. The advantages are that this is a relatively low-cost approach, which can reveal in-depth information about target audience preferences but the results can lack objectivity and be potentially biased.

- *Consumer juries*—a representative group (from the target audiences) are asked to judge a set of 'mock-ups' of the final advert. Again, there is potential for bias emerging as the 'halo effect' can occur if one aspect of the advert is rated as good. This can transfer to other elements and members of the jury sometimes become less objective.

- *Readability tests* are used for testing finished print-based adverts. This method enables testing comprehension of the words used in the copy.

- *Dummy vehicles* are created so members of the target audience encounter the advert in a 'live' setting. For example, dummy magazines can be produced with all the features of the regular magazine or paper but also the adverts being tested. The publications are then distributed, and the sample readers are asked questions at a later date to determine the effectiveness of the advert. The advantages are that the advert is placed in a real setting but on the downside the target audience members in the test are still aware and may respond in a biased manner.

- *Theatre tests* are used for evaluating finished adverts which are to be delivered by broadcast media. Members of the target audience are invited to view the advert and afterwards they are asked to evaluate what they have seen. The advantage of this method is that it is the completed advert is being tested. Criticisms are again that there is potential for bias and the setting is artificial.[43]

Post-testing is carried out after the release of the advert and can be used to assess its effectiveness throughout and when the campaign is over. Checking how well an advertising campaign has performed provides information for future campaigns. A key advantage of post-testing is that it is carried out in the 'live' environment. Methods of post-testing include:

- *Inquiry tests* that measure the number of direct inquiries and responses resulting from the advertising, which may include completed coupons or requests for more information. This method has become more widely used with the rise in the use of direct marketing.

- *Recall tests* are designed to measure the impact of adverts on the target audience. Recall tests usually rely on responses from many members of the target audience who are interviewed within a short time after seeing the advert. This form of measurement is considered to be reasonably accurate (e.g. each time an advert is tested the results are the same). However, the ability of recall tests to predict sales is generally considered to be low (bringing the validity of this method into question). Despite these issues recall testing is widely used especially to evaluate television advertising and can also be used for press advertisements.

- *Recognition tests* are based on memory and the ability of members of the target audience to reprocess information in an advert. This is one of the main methods used for measuring magazine readership. The reliability of the recognition test is high and much better than recall tests.[44]

- *Likeability* has been found to be a very powerful predictor of sales.[45] The problem with likeability is it is difficult to measure. For example, if one person says 'I like the advert a lot' how does this compare with a person who says 'I like the advert a little'. For each person the evaluation will have a different meaning and relevance, and will stimulate different levels of interest.

- *Financial analysis* requires the cost of the resources to be evaluated, which includes the media spend. This is usually carried out continuously and acts as an early warning system if costs are spiralling out of control. Financial control and accountability of the advertising spend have become increasingly important in recent years.

In response to criticisms and the inherent weaknesses of pre- and post-testing methods, sophisticated techniques of evaluation have been developed. Read Digital Marketing 15.1 to find out more about physiological testing.

Would you be more careful if it was you that got pregnant?

It's a lot easier for a man to have a baby than for a woman.
She's the one who has to hump it around for nine months.
She's the one who has to grin and bear it. Backache,
morning sickness and all.
It's not a lot of fun being pregnant, if you don't want the
baby. It's not a lot of fun being an unwanted baby, either.
The Health Education Council
Anyone married or single, can get advice on contraception, from their local family planning clinic.

Do you want a cigarette more than you want your baby?

When a pregnant woman smokes she puts her unborn baby's life at risk.
Every time she inhales, she poisons her baby's bloodstream with nicotine
and carbon monoxide.
Smoking can restrict your baby's growth inside the womb. It can make him
underdeveloped and underweight at birth.
It can even kill him.
In just one year, in Britain alone, over 1,500 babies might not have died if
their mothers had given up smoking when they were pregnant.
If you give up smoking when you're pregnant your baby
will be as healthy as if you'd never smoked. **The Health Education Council**

Digital Marketing 15.1 Using Technology to Test our Emotions and Physical Reactions

In the past, self-reporting measures have been used to collect data on emotional responses, for example, verbal and visual reporting and ratings used in pre- and post-testing. However, while these methods provide immediate measurement of emotional responses and are relatively easy to administer, they suffer from bias and are often criticized for lacking validity. Recently, remote (autonomic) measures and techniques have been developed to analyse facial expressions (smiling, frowning) and physiological reactions (eye movements, blushing, sweating).

Eyetracking is a process that measures the movement of the eyes and is becoming widely used in advertising research. Feng-GUI is a group of artificial vision scientists and interactive designers, who specialize in attention analysis and have developed highly sophisticated methods to track viewers' gaze when looking at websites. This high-tech approach uses heatmaps to track human vision and find out where and how people look at adverts. These techniques are able to detect what we look at in the first five seconds of exposure to visuals.

Following our eyes is not the only form of physiological measurement used in advertising. To consider how to measure a range of physiological reactions, it is important to recognize that they are intertwined with our emotions. Furthermore, emotions vary considerably: low-order emotions are spontaneous and uncontrollable emotions relating to pleasure and arousal (type 1 emotion). When Type 1 emotions are triggered more attention will be given to brands which can satisfy such emotions—for example, Häagen-Dazs ice cream, which was positioned as a brand that could deliver sensual pleasure rather than being positioned against other ice creams on taste or price (see image). High-order emotions (Type 2) involve more complex cognitive processing, and somewhere in between are emotions like fear, anger and happiness.

Sophisticated technology can now detect activity in the nervous systems (galvanic skin responses), and measure facial expressions (electromyography), brain activity (electroencephalographs) and heart rates. These measures have the advantage of telling advertisers about the emotional responses they might get from their adverts in real time.

Based on Fill (2009);[46] Feng-Gui (2012);[47] Poels and Dewitte (2006);[48] Rossiter and Bellman (2005);[49] Hegarty (2011)[50]

Read the Research 15.1 Communication Tools

For many years, media buyers have wanted detailed audience information of what happens during the commercial break in television during particular programmes. Simply, these metrics are the currency for negotiation between the two parties, on the type of show and level of attention.

This article sets out to answer some of those questions and uses specific television programmes as an illustration.

Robert J. Kent and David A. Schweidel (2011) Journal of Advertising Research, *December 1, 586–93.*

This article checks out the state of health of public relations (PR) in the UK in the first decade of the 21st century. It looks at PR from two perspectives: PR practitioners and CEOs. The UK is second only to the USA in terms of use of PR (originators of PR in the 1920s), and concludes that the profession is in good health and continues to grow. However, it still doesn't have universal approval among senior managers, although there is tacit acknowledgement that it does contribute to organizational success.

Anne Gregory (2011) The state of the public relations profession in the UK: A review of the first decade of the twenty-first century, Corporate Communications: An International Journal *16(2), 89–104.*

Does regular use of sales promotion have a negative impact on brand image, particularly over the long term? This paper tries to answer this question through analysis and discussion in the premium brand sector of FMCG.

This interesting piece of research concludes that by not focusing purely on price, but using the sales promotion tool creatively, you can make it a useful addition to your strategic communications plan, therefore enhancing rather than damaging the company's image.

Danijela Mandić (2009) Trziste / Market *21(2), 235–46.*

Organizing for Campaign Development

There are various options when developing an advertising campaign and this will be largely dependent on the resources, skills and capabilities of the company wishing to develop the campaign. In principle, campaigns may be developed:

- *in cooperation* with people from the media. For example, advertising copy may be written by company staff but the artwork and layout of the advertisement may be done by the newspaper or magazine.
- *in-house* by the advertising department staffed with copy-writers, media buyers and production personnel.
- *in cooperation with an **advertising agency***. Larger agencies offer a full service, comprising creative, media planning and buying, planning and strategy development, market research and production.

In reality, given the growing complexity of communication campaigns and wider use of media platforms, companies wishing to advertise use a combination of approaches. Central to the success of any campaign is the relationship between clients and agencies. Key figures in the development of a campaign are account directors and executives, who liaise with client companies and coordinate the work of the other departments on behalf of their clients. Because agencies work for many clients, they have a wide range of experience and can provide an objective outsider's view of what is required, and how problems can be solved.

When an advertiser uses an agency, managing the relationship is of critical importance. Therefore, a company should aim to find the type of agency which best suits its needs. Types of agencies include: *full service agencies*, which offer strategic planning, research, creative development, brand building, media buying and scheduling and a full range of expertise across all of the communication tools; *boutiques or creative shops*, which provide specialist services: for example, copywriting, creative content development expertise; smaller agencies are often chosen for their ability to develop specialist creative ideas; digital agencies (and/or web service providers) can offer an extensive range for Web-based and mobile services such as content development, blogging, online PR, buzz marketing, social media, and search engine optimization (SEO). The Internet and mobile and digital marketing have extended the range of choice of agencies and these issues are discussed in more detail in Chapter 18.

The formal part of an agency selection is the pitching process, where the client produces a creative brief and the agency prepares a pitch to demonstrate how it will meet that brief. However, the communication industry is a 'people' business and therefore it is critically important to get the relationships right, in order to develop trust and commitment that will see the campaign through to a successful conclusion. Read Mini Case 15.1 to find out more about client and agency relationships.

Mini Case 15.1 Managing the Client–Agency Relationship

Strong relationships between clients (advertisers) and their agencies can provide the platform for effective advertising. A survey of clients and agencies focused on those issues that were causing problems in achieving this desired state.

Many clients demanded that agencies become more involved in their business, with comments like 'they need to spend more time understanding our challenges and goals' and 'they need to take more notice of the client's view with regard to creative work'. Clearly, clients were looking for agencies to spend more time and attention on understanding their business objectives before beginning the creative process.

The importance of the early stages of the advertising development process was also emphasized by agencies. Some complained about having to deal with junior people at the briefing stage who had not been trained to write a clear brief. This was critical, because unless clients get the briefing stage right, things will inevitably go wrong further down the line. This problem was connected to the lack of accessibility of senior marketing staff because they have too much other work to do. This means that briefing is left in the hands of junior staff, who have the power to say 'no' but not 'yes'. This can be very frustrating for agencies. One agency complained about not enough 'ear time' with a senior member of his client's marketing team: 'he is too busy and there is too big an experience gap between him and his team'. Two further consequences of this were insufficient access to business objectives and strategy and an inability to provide constructive feedback on their proposals.

One issue that can spoil client–agency relationships is client conflict. This occurs when an advertising agency wins a new account from a rival to an existing client, or when an agency is taken over by an agency that holds the account of a rival. Both of these scenarios have happened to Procter & Gamble. Media planning agency Zenith Optimedia won the L'Oréal account, causing potential client conflict with its existing P&G account. P&G was also concerned when its advertising agency Grey Global was acquired by the WPP Group, which counts arch-rival Unilever among its client base. Such situations can end relationships or, as was the case with WPP, the client's fears may be assuaged if it is satisfied that separate agency networks will be working for the two clients.

Research into relationships with Web and Internet agencies indicates that firms will be more successful if they build long-term, mutually supportive relationships with their customers. However, in order to work together, both parties rely on making agreements that are dependent on high levels of trust and commitment. Furthermore, the need for understanding how to build successful relationships in highly complex and challenging online trading environments is not only important but critical for the success of digital campaigns.

Three key factors are critical in managing client relationships. First, the agency should be client-centric. This means understanding the client's market and business, and how both are changing. There can be a tendency for such an understanding to dwindle over time. To combat this, agencies should invite clients to talk about their business. Second, agencies should not neglect personal contact. With digital communication the easy option, it can be tempting to communicate remotely. However, face-to-face contact is critical as it is difficult to build and maintain a business relationship purely through email. Finally, the strength of the relationship needs to be checked regularly. The presumption that everything is fine because nobody has complained is a dangerous path to follow.

Questions:

1   How can the client help improve the client–agency relationship?
2   Why should the agency always question a brief?

Based on: Vize et al. (2011);[51] *Morgan and Hunt (1994);*[52] *Rauyruen and Miller (2007);*[53] *Curtis (2002);*[54] *Curtis (2002);*[55] *Singh (2005);*[56] *Rhind-Tutt (2009)*[57]

Agency selection

As with buying any product, agency selection begins by defining requirements, which can vary considerably depending on whether the advertising is for a discount grocery store, a new car or a luxury designer fashion brand, for example. While grocery retailer Lidl might communicate clear messages about pricing, BMW and Gucci are brands that give great priority to the creative talents of prospective agencies.

Consequently, agency selection involves: defining advertising objectives and creative message requirements in order to brief potential agencies; creating a list of possible agencies; arranging for agencies to pitch their creative ideas; analysing each agency's offer; selecting and contracting the preferred agency.

Once an agency has been selected and the contract agreed, it is important to brief the agency carefully, giving much relevant information about the company developing the campaign: for example, product history in terms of past sales, market share, previous campaigns; product features and benefits; target audiences—who they are, their motives and choice criteria. In addition, communication objectives and timetable for delivery and launch of the campaign should be clearly stated and agreed, and the budget set, as this might affect choice of media.

Agency remuneration (payment) systems

According to the IPA, the changing media environment, digital technologies and the multiple service requirements of clients has had an impact on the way agencies are paid. The rest of this section discusses the industry guidelines on agency remunerations in the UK.[58]

Before deciding how to pay its chosen agency(ies) the client should follow these ten steps:

1 negotiate the scope of the work (which the client determines)
2 agree on the tenure—in other words the period the agency is to be employed
3 establish the territory—regional, national, global
4 set out a work plan showing the scope of the costs, people hours and how the client and agency will work together
5 compare the work plan with the available budget from the client's marketing plan. If there is a shortfall, revise the work plan for the agency.
6 agree on the level of remuneration (and desired profit margins)
7 client and agency to determine the goals, and the key performance indicators
8 determine how much the client will pay the agency
9 determine how performance is to be evaluated and the timing of the review
10 finalize the terms of the contract.

This may seem a rather long list but client–agency relationships often break down over some of these details. Therefore, if the terms and details are agreed in advance there is less opportunity for conflict. Table 15.2 shows the main methods of agency remuneration and provides brief descriptions of what is involved.

Product Placement

Product placement is the deliberate placing of products and/or their logos in movies, television programmes, songs and video games, usually in return for money. For example, Steven Spielberg's sci-fi film *Minority Report* featured more than 15 major brands, including Gap, Nokia, Pepsi, Guinness, Lexus and Amex, with their logos appearing on video billboards throughout the film. These product placements earned Dreamworks and 20th Century Fox US$25 million, which went some way towards reducing the US$102 million production costs of the film. Similarly, when the hip-hop artist Busta Rhymes had a smash hit with 'Pass the Courvoisier', US sales of the cognac rose by 14 per cent in volume and 11 per cent in value. Allied Domecq, the brand's owner, claims it did not pay for the plug, but McDonald's is more upfront, offering hip-hop artists US$5 each time they mention Big Mac in a song. The value

TABLE 15.2 Agency remuneration

Method of remuneration	Description	Advantages	Disadvantages
1. Retainer fee	Fees now account for the majority of agency agreements. This type of fee is usually paid in advance, on a monthly basis. Fees usually cover estimated cost. Likely to have payment by results element in the fee structure. This is the main method of agency remuneration.	Agency knows what the income will be in the coming trading period. Aids cash-flow forecasts. Client similarly knows the costs. Encourages media-neutral planning.	Scope of the work has to be clearly defined or the fee scheme cannot work accurately. Can be less accountable than an output-based system. Not directly linked to performance. Time-consuming to negotiate contracts.
2. Project fee	Worked out on a single project basis. Usually short-term project. Often used for PR and sales promotions. Normally higher fee than a retainer fee.	Ideal for top-up. Easy to control. Reflects specific client needs. Suits IMC or niche service approach.	Too short-term focus can result in lack of agency confidence. Difficult to include performance incentives.
3. Variable fee based on actual time spent	More suited to direct marketing, sales promotions and PR. Fees are based on the actual time spent on the job. Fees are calculated after the event.	Relatively easy to administer. Reflects client's needs and allows for some flexibility. Allows an agency to get a return on clearly defined process and actual deliverables.	Limited scope of advance budgeting. Can suffer from accountability problems and the agency may spend more time on task than required.
4. Scale fee and bonus	Client pays a 'salary' to the agency, i.e. a fixed percentage of sales (or of the annual marketing budget).	Good for FMCG where sales are the main KPI. Remuneration is linked to client success rather than hours worked. Based on what the marketing communication achieves. Agency benefits according to increase in the volume of activity.	Difficult if not working with FMCG, especially in the services industry. Less directly accountable than other methods. Can be unfair on the agency if the company performs poorly. Some forms of communication are directly related to sales.
5. Consultancy and concept fees	One-off fees agreed to cover the cost of developing the creative campaign.	Attractive option for client wanting to buy licence of rights to a concept.	Measurement of time commitment difficult to evaluate. Intellectual rights and wider use of concept beyond the client can cause conflict.
8. Commission fee	Worked out based on the fee earned from the media owner. Historically 15 per cent, when the agencies provided the media. But now 84 per cent of media agreements are with independent agencies.	Simple to work out commission rate according to level of service. Easy to administer. Client and agency are focused on quality rather than price. Commission acts as a form of payment by results.	Based on volume of spend not scope of the work. Volume-based and works for digital agencies and other forms of communications which do not use media. Commission is paid by the media owner. Cancellations can cause problems.

Source: Su Johnstone, Creative Development and Production.

of product placement deals in the USA grew from $174 million in 1974 to an estimated US$7.6 billion in 2009.

This technique has been used in the USA for some time. However, in Europe there have been restrictions preventing product placement until now when the rules are being gradually relaxed. Since 2011 paid-for product placement has been allowed in UK television programmes. The new rules for product placement are more stringent than in the USA. Tobacco, alcohol, gambling, medicines, baby milk and any foods which are high in fat, salt or sugar are not permitted. Furthermore, the product is not allowed to distort the editorial content or affect its independence. On the plus side, UK broadcasters are now able to access the revenue generated by the product placement. In the future many interesting relationships/issues may develop between advertisers and programme makers.[59]

Product placement has grown significantly in recent years, for the following reasons: media fragmentation means it is increasingly hard to reach mass markets; the brand can benefit from the positive associations it gains from being in a film or television show; many consumers do not realize that the brand has been product-placed; repetition of the movie or television show means that the brand is seen again and again; careful choice of movie or television show means that certain segments can be targeted; and promotional and merchandising opportunities can be generated on the show's website. For example, the clothes and accessories worn by actresses in popular television shows like *Sex and the City* and *Desperate Housewives* have been in great demand from viewers and some have quickly sold out. Show producers are increasingly looking at the merchandising opportunities that their shows can present, and manufacturers are happy to pay handsomely. Reportedly, the company that makes the the Nescafé Dolce Gusto Melody II coffeemaker, which retails for about $130 in the United States, paid £100,000 ($162,000) to feature on *This Morning*, the UK breakfast-time programme, for a three-month period.[60]

Technological developments in the online gaming sector allow for different products to be placed in games at different times of the day or in different geographic locations, expanding the marketing possibilities available to companies. For example, Blizzard Entertainment, a video game developer, is looking to recruit a specialist who can work with consumer brands so real products can be licensed and then appear in Blizzard's next generation of games.[61]

While product placement is becoming very popular, it is important to remember that there are risks involved. If the movie or television show fails to take off, it can tarnish the image of the brand and reduce its potential exposure. Even when a movie is highly successful, there may still be issues which prevent brands from wanting to be involved. For example, Danny Boyle in his film *Slumdog Millionaire* was not allowed to use Mercedes-Benz products in a slum setting[62] and all images of the brand had to be removed from the film.

Furthermore, audiences can become annoyed by blatant product placement, damaging the image, and brand owners may not have complete control over how their brand is portrayed. Also, the popularity of product placement is fast giving rise to claims that it constitutes deceptive advertising. Lobby groups in the USA claim that one of the difficulties with product placement is that it can't be controlled by the consumer in the way the traditional advertising breaks can, through zapping, and they want it restricted.

Product placement is subject to the same kinds of analysis as all the other promotional techniques described in this chapter. For example, in the James Bond movie *Die Another Day*, the Ford Motor Company had three of its car brands 'starring' in the film: an Aston Martin Vanquish, a Thunderbird and a Jaguar XKR. Movie-goers were interviewed both before and after seeing the film to see if their opinions of the brands had changed. In addition, the product placement was part of an integrated campaign including public relations and advertising, which ensured that even people who had not seen the film were aware of Ford's association with it. During the film's peak viewing periods in the USA and UK, Ford's research found that the number of times its name appeared in the media increased by 34 per cent and that Ford corporate messages appeared in 29 per cent of the Bond-related coverage.[63,64,65,66,67]

Public Relations and Sponsorship

In a 365-day, 24/7 interconnected global society, every move a company makes can be shared. Intended and unintended messages about a product, a brand or a company can appear online. This means corporate reputation is constantly in the spotlight and this change in emphasis has meant a rise in importance of public relations (PR).[68]

A company is dependent on many groups if it is to be successful. The marketing concept focuses on customers and distributors, but the needs and interests of other groups are also important, such as employees, shareholders, the local community, the media, government and pressure groups. **Public relations** is concerned with all of these groups and may be defined as:

> . . . the management of communications and relationships to establish goodwill and mutual understanding between an organization and its public.

Public relations is therefore wider ranging than marketing, which focuses on markets, distribution channels and customers. By communicating to other groups, public relations creates an environment in which it is easier to conduct marketing.[69] These publics are shown in Figure 15.3.

Public relations activities include media relations, lobbying, corporate advertising and sponsorship.[70] PR can accomplish many objectives, as outlined below.[71]

1 *Prestige and reputation*: it can foster prestige and reputation, which can help companies to sell products, attract and keep good employees, and promote favourable community and government relations.
2 *Promotion of products*: the desire to buy a product can be helped by the unobtrusive things that people read and see in the press, radio and television. Awareness and interest in products and companies can be generated.
3 *Dealing with issues and opportunities*: the ability to handle social and environmental issues to the mutual benefit of all parties involved.
4 *Goodwill of customers*: ensuring that customers are presented with useful information, are treated well and have their complaints dealt with fairly and speedily.

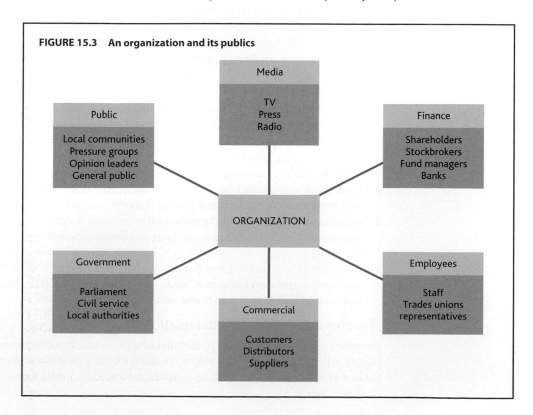

FIGURE 15.3   An organization and its publics

Media
TV
Press
Radio

Public
Local communities
Pressure groups
Opinion leaders
General public

Finance
Shareholders
Stockbrokers
Fund managers
Banks

ORGANIZATION

Government
Parliament
Civil service
Local authorities

Employees
Staff
Trades unions
representatives

Commercial
Customers
Distributors
Suppliers

5 *Goodwill of employees*: promoting the sense of identification and satisfaction of employees with their company. Activities such as internal newsletters, recreation activities, and awards for service and achievement can be used.

6 *Overcoming misconceptions*: managing misconceptions about a company so that unfounded opinions do not damage its operations.

7 *Goodwill of suppliers and distributors*: building a reputation as a good customer (for suppliers) and a reliable supplier (for distributors).

8 *Goodwill of government*: influencing the opinions of public officials and politicians so that they feel the company operates in the public interest.

9 *Dealing with unfavourable press coverage*: responding quickly, accurately and effectively to negative publicity such as an oil spill or an air disaster.

10 *Attracting and keeping good employees*: creating and maintaining respectability in the eyes of the public so that the best personnel are attracted to work for the company.

Public relations can take two basic models. In the first model communication messages flow one way—for example, a company's press agent produces favourable information in the form of press releases and media events. A variation of this approach is to disseminate information which presents a more balanced view (including positive and negative information). This is sometimes referred to as a *public information model*.[72]

The second model focuses on two-way communications so feedback from target audiences is of paramount importance. There are a further two derivations of this model:

• *Two-way asymmetric*. In this model power is not equally distributed between the stakeholders and the organization. The purpose of this form of PR is to influence attitudes and behaviour through persuasion.[73]

• *Two-way symmetric*. This model aims to be mutually rewarding as power is dispersed equally between the organization and its stakeholders. Communication flow is reciprocal. Some organizations use PR as a means of mediating relationships between the organization and its various stakeholders.

In the highly connected, multichannel media world it is difficult to isolate the various forms of PR and therefore there is a tendency for these models to coexist.[74] The remainder of this section on PR examines the different methods and techniques including: media relations, lobbying, corporate advertising, crisis communications, and sponsorship.

Media relations

A major element of public relations is media relations, which includes press releases, press conferences and interviews, and publicity. Media relations can be defined as communication about a product or organization by the placing of news about it in the media without paying for the time or space directly.

Three key tasks of a media relations department are:[75]

1 responding to requests from the media—although a passive service function, it requires well-organized information and prompt responses to media requests

2 supplying the media with information on events and occurrences relevant to the organization—this requires general internal communication channels and knowledge of the media

3 stimulating the media to carry the information and viewpoint of the organization—this requires creative development of ideas, developing close relationships with media people and understanding their needs and motivations.

The characteristics of media relations

Information dissemination may be through news releases, news conferences, interviews, feature articles, photo calls and public speaking (at conferences and seminars, for example). No matter which method is used to carry the information, media relations has five important characteristics.

TABLE 15.3   Potentially newsworthy topics

Being or doing something first

Marketing issues

New products

Innovative research

Large orders/export contracts

Changes to the marketing mix: e.g. price

Rebranding

Production issues

Productivity achievements

Employment changes

Capital investments

Financial issues

Financial statements

Acquisitions

Sales/profit achievements

Personal issues

Training awards

Winners of company contests

Promotions/new appointments

Success stories

Visits by famous people

General issues

Conferences/seminars/exhibitions

Anniversaries of significant events

1   *The message has high credibility*: the message has higher credibility than advertising because it appears to the reader to have been written independently (by a media person) rather than by an advertiser.

2   *No direct media costs*: since space or time in the media is not bought, there is no direct media cost. However, this is not to say that it is cost-free. Someone has to write the news release, take part in the interview or organize the news conference. This may be organized internally, by a press officer or media relations department, or externally, by a public relations agency.

3   *Lose control of publication*: unlike advertising, there is no guarantee that the news item will be published. This decision is taken out of the control of the organization and into the hands of an editor. A key factor in this decision is whether the item is judged to be newsworthy. Table 15.3 lists a number of potentially newsworthy topics.

4   *Lose control of content*: there is no way of ensuring that the viewpoint expressed by the news supplier is reflected in the published article. For example, a news release might point to an increase in capital expenditure to deal with pollution, but this might be used negatively (for example, saying the increase is inadequate).

5   *Lose control of timing*: an advertising campaign can be coordinated to achieve maximum impact. The timing of the publication of news items, however, cannot be controlled. For example, a news item publicizing a forthcoming conference to encourage attendance could appear in a publication after the event has taken place or, at least, too late to have any practical effect on attendance.

Writing news releases

Perhaps the most popular method of disseminating information to the media is through the news release. By following a few simple guidelines (as outlined below), the writer can produce news releases that please editors and therefore stand a greater chance of being used.[76]

- *The headline*: make the headline factual and avoid the use of flamboyant, flowery language that might irritate editors. The headline should briefly introduce the story: 'British Airways and Iberia sign merger agreement'; 'Apple to unveil new iPhone'.
- *Opening paragraph*: this should be a brief summary of the whole release. If this is the only part of the news release that is published the writer will have succeeded in getting across the essential message.
- *Organizing the copy*: the less important ideas should be placed towards the end of the news release. The further down the paragraph, the more chance of its being cut by an editor.
- *Copy content*: like headlines, copy should be factual not fanciful. An example of bad copy would be 'We are proud to announce that Virgin Airlines, the world's most innovative airline, will fly exotic and exciting new routes in India'. Instead, this should read 'New routes to India will be flown by Virgin Airlines'. Whenever possible, statements should be backed up by facts. For example: 'Shetland wind farm plans by Viking Energy approved by Scottish government',[77] 'Sony Develops "IPELA Engine", Capable of an Industry-First 130db Wide Dynamic Range in Full HD Quality'.[78]
- *Length*: news releases should be as short as possible. Most are written on one page, some are merely one paragraph. The viewpoint that long releases should be sent to editors so that they can cut out the parts they do not want is a fallacy. Editors' self-interest is that their job should be made as easy as possible; the less work they have to do amending copy the greater the chances of its publication.

- *Layout*: the release should contain short paragraphs with plenty of *white space* to make it appear easy to read. There should be good-sized margins on both sides, and the copy should be double-spaced so that amendments and printing instructions can be inserted by the editor. When a story runs to a second or third page, 'more' should be typed in the bottom right-hand corner and succeeding pages numbered with the headline repeated in the top left-hand corner.
- *Embargoes* must be clearly stated for date of release of sensitive information.

Media relations can be a powerful tool for creating awareness and strengthening the reputation of organizations. The trick is to motivate everyone in an organization to look for newsworthy stories and events, not simply to rely on the media relations department to initiate them. All forms of public relations should be part of an integrated communications strategy so that they reinforce the messages consumers receive from other communication methods.

As explained earlier, media relations can result in a loss of control, and negative articles and media releases can be generated by other parties,[79] which raise doubts about an organization's stability, such as 'Sony doubles forecast of annual loss to $6.4bn'.[80] To counter negative press and also build confidence among stakeholders, companies can engage in different forms of publicity events. Such events may focus on:

- *the product* and take the form of demonstrations, book signings, product launch events. For example, the *Harry Potter* series of books and films used such events extensively to create a sense of anticipation and excitement.
- *corporate profile events*—open days, factory visits, donations, educational events.
- *community events*—activities, events and contributions which benefit local communities, such as funding development of facilities, which benefit the local people (play areas, gardens, computers for schools).

Lobbying

Go to the website to see the Co-operative's new plan for becoming the most socially responsible business in the UK. www.mcgraw-hill.co.uk/textbooks/jobber

Lobbying is a mechanism for influencing government decision-making. When new laws are being created, or old ones adapted, organizations and industries often need representation to ensure their views are heard. Research suggests that lobbying is part of PR because it involves members of the organization and its stakeholders in persuading and negotiating with governments.[81] For example, The Co-operative Group has founded its business on strong ethical values and principles. However, the company is not satisfied with just operating ethically; it also wishes to take an active part in shaping agendas and has lobbied the government on a number of measures ranging from use of safer chemicals to mandatory social reporting and curtailing trade in 'conflict diamonds'.[82] Read more in Marketing in Action 15.4.

Marketing in Action 15.4 The Co-operative is Lobbying against Tar Sands to Protect the Environment

Lobbying is a form of monitoring which aims to sway public policy and ensure it accommodates public interest (or at the very least the interest of the group of lobbyists). The Co-operative has always been a revolutionary organization right from the early days. In 1844, in Rochdale, a group of people got together and formed a new type of business which they called 'The Co-operative'. Since then the business has always had the benefit of the local community at the heart of the business. It has lobbied the government and retail industry bodies and brought about many positive changes, from honest food labelling, to fair-trade goods.

The latest campaign trail for the Co-operative is clean energy. It is calling for a stop to tar sand developments. These are developments which can destroy virgin forests, produce toxic waste and pollute air and water. Tar sands exploration is being developed in Canada where the deposits represent the second largest reserve of fuel after Saudi Arabia.

Based on: Fill (2011);[83] The Co-operative (2012)[84]

Corporate advertising

Corporate advertising is a form of public relations advertising designed to promote the company as a whole rather than a particular product or service. The objectives of this form of advertising are typically to inform and build awareness of, or sometimes to defend, a particular position adopted by a company.[85] This form of advertising tends to aim to be distinctive and portray the professionalism and credibility of an organization. Corporate advertising should aim to be consistent and adopt a long-term approach which aligns to the marketing strategy and corporate mission. It may be used for various tasks including:

- to manage the reputation of an organization (e.g., Royal Bank of Scotland, British Airways, BP)
- to substantiate a company's position in a takeover bid (e.g., Cadburys and Kraft Foods)
- to recruit employees (e.g., BBC, Met Office, Barclays Bank)
- to inform of management restructuring or changes (e.g., Apple, Tesco)
- to inform and reassure customers (e.g., Toyota).[86]

This type of communication is used by organizations to disclose information to various different stakeholders. See Ad Insight to view how BP used corporate advertising to keep in touch and inform the American people on progress on the Gulf coast following the Deepwater Horizon accident.[87]

Go to the website to see how BP used corporate advertising during the Deepwater Horizon incident in the Gulf of Mexico.
www.mcgraw-hill.co.uk/textbooks/jobber

Sponsorship

Sponsorship has been defined by Sleight as:[88]

> . . . a business relationship between a provider of funds, resources or services and an individual, event or organization which offers in return some rights and association that may be used for commercial advantage.

Potential sponsors have a wide range of entities and activities from which to choose, including sports, arts, community activities, teams, tournaments, individual personalities or events, competitions, fairs and shows. Sports sponsorship is by far the most popular sponsorship medium as it can offer high visibility through extensive television press coverage, the ability to attract a broad cross-section of the community and to service specific niches, and the capacity to break down cultural barriers.[89]

Sponsorship can achieve a number of communicational objectives—but there are also risks, as outlined below.[90]

- The Festina cycling team was thrown out of the Tour de France following the arrest of the team's masseur. French customs officials had discovered performance-enhancing drugs in his car four days before the start of the race.
- Team Philips' £4 million catamaran broke its hull shortly after the start of The Race, a non-stop, around-the-world yacht race. The sponsor's plight was not helped by having Philips' strap-line 'Let's make things better' emblazoned on the boat.
- When Zanussi sponsored Real Madrid its sales plummeted in Barcelona.[91]

Companies should be clear about their reasons for spending money on sponsorship. The four principal objectives of sponsorship are to gain publicity, create entertainment opportunities, improve community relations and create promotional opportunities.

Gaining publicity

Sponsorship provides ample opportunities to create publicity in the news media. Worldwide events such as major golf, football and tennis tournaments supply the platform for global media coverage. Sponsorship of such events can provide brand exposure to millions of people. Some events, such as athletics championships, have mass audience appeal, while others such as golf have a more upmarket profile. Rolex supports more than 150 sporting events around the world exposing the brand name to its more upmarket customer segment. Budweiser's sponsorship of the FA cup has given it exposure to

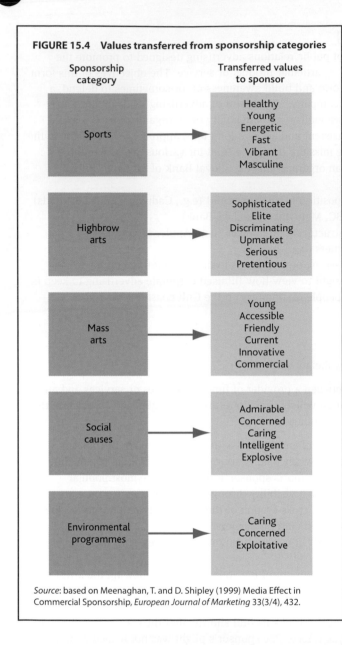

FIGURE 15.4   Values transferred from sponsorship categories

Sponsorship category	Transferred values to sponsor
Sports	Healthy Young Energetic Fast Vibrant Masculine
Highbrow arts	Sophisticated Elite Discriminating Upmarket Serious Pretentious
Mass arts	Young Accessible Friendly Current Innovative Commercial
Social causes	Admirable Concerned Caring Intelligent Explosive
Environmental programmes	Caring Concerned Exploitative

Source: based on Meenaghan, T. and D. Shipley (1999) Media Effect in Commercial Sponsorship, *European Journal of Marketing* 33(3/4), 432.

the young male demographic.[92] Many companies sponsor large events like the Olympic Games, for example: for London 2012, Olympic partners included Adidas, British Airways, BP, BMW, Lloyds TSB, Panasonic, Omega and Acer.

The publicity opportunities of sponsorship can produce major *awareness* shifts. For example, Canon's European sponsorship of fashion weeks in London, Milan and Paris raised awareness of the brand name. Canon carefully selects activities to sponsor which align with its values of 'living and working together for a common good',[93] such as WWF (environment), European Red Cross (social responsibility), the Canon Foundation (education) and Canon Pro Golf series (sport).

Sponsorship can also be used to position brands in the marketplace. Tag Heuer's sponsorship of the McLaren motor racing team was designed to position the watch brand as exciting, sporty and international.[94]

Creating entertainment opportunities

A major objective of much sponsorship is to create entertainment opportunities for customers and the trade. Sponsorship of music, the performing arts and sports events can be particularly effective. For example, Rolex supports classical concerts and the arts (e.g. the Royal Opera House in London and the Tate Gallery). Vodafone's sponsorship of the Ghana music awards in 2012 supported a live event aired in London. Brit Insurance sponsored the England Cricket team. Often sports personalities are invited to join the sponsor's guests. Attendance at sponsored events can also be used to reward successful employees.

Figure 15.4 shows some broad values conferred on the sponsor from five sponsorship categories. They point out that these are composite views. Values may depend on a specific activity or event—for example, football versus tennis.

Improving community relations

Sponsorship of schools—for example, by providing low-cost personal computers—and supporting community programmes can foster a socially responsible, caring reputation for a company. A survey in the Republic of Ireland found that developing community relations was the most usual sponsorship objective for both industrial and consumer companies.[95]

Creating promotional opportunities

Sponsored events provide an ideal opportunity to promote company brands. Sweatshirts, bags, pens, etc., carrying the company logo and the name of the event can be sold to a captive audience. Where the brand can be consumed during the event (e.g. Stella Artois at the Cannes Film Festival) this provides an opportunity for customers to sample the brand perhaps for the first time.

Sponsorship can also improve the effectiveness of other promotional vehicles. For example, responses to the direct marketing materials issued by the Visa credit card organization and featuring its sponsorship of the Olympic Games were 17 per cent higher than for a control group to whom the sponsorship images were not transmitted.[96]

Expenditure on sponsorship

Six factors account for the growth of sponsorship:

1   restrictive government policies on tobacco and alcohol advertising
2   escalating costs of media advertising
3   increased leisure activities and sporting events
4   the proven record of sponsorship
5   greater media coverage of sponsored events
6   the reduced efficiencies of traditional media advertising (e.g. clutter, and zapping between television programmes).

Although most money is spent on **event sponsorship**, such as a sports or arts event, of increasing importance is **broadcast sponsorship** where a television or radio programme is the focus. An example of event sponsorship is the sponsorship of music designed to target the youth market, as Figure 15.4 illustrates.

Broadcast sponsorship of programmes can extend into the sharing of production costs. This is attractive to broadcasters, who face increasing costs of programming, and sponsors, who gain a greater degree of influence in negotiations with broadcasters. BlackBerry signed up for a two-year deal as sponsor for a whole channel: Sky Atlantic. In this exclusive deal no other brand can sponsor content on the channel. Panasonic sponsors Sky movies in a similarly exclusive deal.[97] The benefits for both companies are ongoing, cheaper advertising, and the rights to exploit the programme, its characters and actors for promotional purposes. Another growth area is that of **team sponsorship**, such as the sponsorship of a football, cricket or motor racing team. For example, Emirates sponsors Arsenal Football Club.

Selection and evaluation of an event or programme to sponsor

Selection of an event or programme to sponsor should be undertaken by answering a series of questions.

- *Communications objectives*: What are we trying to achieve? Are we looking for awareness or image, improvement in community relations or entertainment opportunities? Does the personality of the event match the desired brand image?
- *Target market*: Who are we trying to reach? Is it the trade or final customers? How does the profile of our customer base match the likely audience of the sponsored event or programme?
- *Risk*: What are the associated risks? What are the chances that the event or programme might attract adverse publicity (e.g. football hooliganism tainting the image of the sport and, by implication, the sponsor)? To what extent would termination of the sponsorship contract attract bad publicity (e.g. mean the closing of a theatre)?
- *Promotional opportunities*: What are the potential sales promotion and publicity opportunities?
- *Past record*: If the event or programme has been sponsored before, what were the results? Why did the previous sponsor withdraw?
- *Cost*: Does the sponsorship opportunity represent value for money?

The evaluation process should lead to a clear idea of why an event or programme is being sponsored. Understanding *sponsorship objectives* is the first step in evaluating sponsorship's success. For major sponsorship deals, evaluation is likely to be more formal and involve the measurement of *media coverage and name mentions/sightings* using a specialist monitoring agency. However, the reality is that evaluation of this tool is often neglected. A survey into the evaluation of football sponsorship found that while two-thirds of companies evaluated their sponsorship activities few went beyond the basic measurement of media coverage.[98]

Sales Promotion

Sales promotions are incentives to consumers or the trade that are designed to stimulate purchase. Examples include money off and free gifts (consumer promotions), discounts and sales force competitions (trade promotions).

A vast amount of money is spent on sales promotion. Peattie and Peattie explain the growth in sales promotion as follows.[99]

- *Increased impulse purchasing*: the retail response to greater consumer impulse purchasing is to demand more sales promotions from manufacturers.
- *Sales promotions are becoming respectable*: through the use of promotions by market leaders and the increasing professionalism of the sales promotion agencies.
- *The rising cost of advertising and advertising clutter*: these factors erode advertising's cost effectiveness.
- *Shortening time horizons*: the attraction of the fast sales boost of a sales promotion is raised by greater rivalry and shortening product life-cycles.
- *Competitor activities*: in some markets, sales promotions are used so often that all competitors are forced to follow suit.[100]
- *Measurability*: measuring the impact of sales promotions is easier than for advertising since their effect is more direct and, usually, short term. The use of electronic point-of-sale (EPOS) scanner information makes measurement easier.

The effects of sales promotion

Sales promotion is often used to provide a short, sharp shock to sales. In this sense it may be regarded as a short-term tactical device. Figure 15.5 shows a typical sales pattern. The sales promotion boosts sales during the promotion period because of the incentive effect. This is followed by a small fall in sales to below normal level because some consumers will have stocked up on the product during the promotion. The long-term sales effect of the promotion could be positive, neutral or negative. If the promotion has attracted new buyers, who find that they like the brand, repeat purchases from them may give rise to a positive long-term effect.[101] Alternatively, if the promotion (e.g. money off) has devalued the brand in the eyes of consumers, the effect may be negative.[102] Where the promotion has caused consumers to buy the brand only because of its incentive value, with no effect on underlying preferences, the long-term effect may be neutral.[103] An international study of leading grocery brands has shown that the most likely long-term effect of a price promotion for an existing brand is neutral. Such promotions tend to attract existing buyers of the brand rather than new buyers during the promotional period.[104]

Go to the website to see Staples' promotions on office supplies.
www.mcgraw-hill.co.uk/ textbooks/jobber

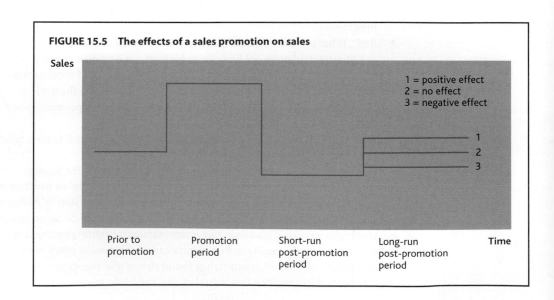

FIGURE 15.5   The effects of a sales promotion on sales

Sales

1 = positive effect
2 = no effect
3 = negative effect

Prior to promotion   Promotion period   Short-run post-promotion period   Long-run post-promotion period   **Time**

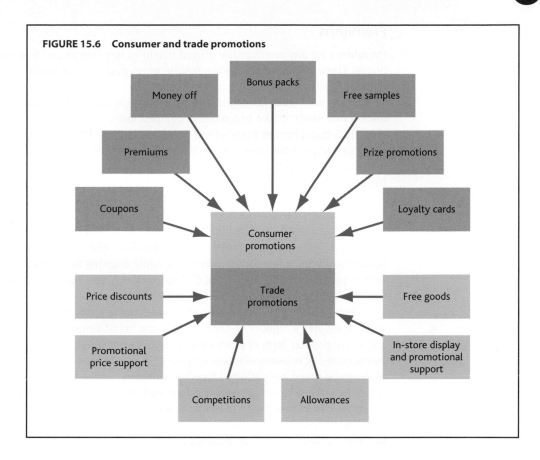

FIGURE 15.6   Consumer and trade promotions

Major sales promotion types

Sales promotions can be directed at the consumer or the trade (see Fig. 15.6). Major consumer sales promotion types are money off, bonus packs, premiums, free samples, coupons, prize promotions and loyalty cards. A sizeable proportion of sales promotions are directed at the trade, including price discounts, free goods, competitions, allowances, promotional price support, and in-store display and promotional support.

The following sections examine the main types of *consumer promotions*.

Money off

Money-off promotions provide direct value to the customer, and therefore an unambiguous incentive to purchase. They have a proven track record of stimulating short-term sales increases and encouraging trial.[105] However, price reductions can easily be matched by the competition and if used frequently can devalue brand image. Consumer response may be 'If the brand is that good why do they need to keep reducing the price?' A variant on the normal money-off promotion is the *value pack*. With value packs, the consumer pays a higher price for the larger pack, but the per-unit price (e.g. per gram or per tablet) is less.

Bonus packs

These give *added value* by giving consumers extra quantity at no additional cost. **Bonus packs** are often used in the drinks, confectionery and detergent markets. For example, cans of lager may be sold on the basis of '12.5 per cent extra free!' Because the price is not lowered, this form of promotion runs less risk of devaluing brand image. Extra value is given by raising quantity rather than cutting price. With some product groups, this encourages buyers to consume more. For example, a Mars bar will be eaten or a can of lager drunk whether there is extra quantity or not.

Premiums

Premiums are any merchandise offered free or at low cost as an incentive to purchase a brand. There are four major forms: free in- or on-pack gifts; free-in-the-mail offers; self-liquidating offers; buy-one-get-one-free offers.

Free in- or on-pack gifts: gifts may be given away free with brands. For example, Innocent offered free seeds, linked to a series of competitions.

FMCG manufacturer brands from Lucozade and PG Tips to Garnier deodorants use premiums to promote sales. This technique is widely used in the cosmetics industry as an incentive to purchase more high-priced items. Clinique, Estee Lauder and L'Occitane frequently have offers which provide free gifts when the customer spends over a certain amount of money.

Occasionally the gift is a free sample of one brand that is banded to another brand (*branded pack offer*). The free sample may be a new variety or flavour that benefits by getting trial. In other cases the brands are linked, as when Nestlé promoted its Cappuccino brand by offering a free KitKat to be eaten while drinking the coffee, and Cadbury ran a similar promotion with a packet of Cadbury's Chocolate Chip Cookies attached to its Cadbury's Chocolate Break, a milk chocolate drink.

When two or more items are banded together the promotion is called a *multibuy* and can involve a number of items of the same brand being offered together. Multibuys are a very popular form of promotion. They are frequently used to protect market share by encouraging consumers to stock up on a particular brand when two or more items of the same brand are packaged together. However, unlike price reductions, they do not encourage trial because consumers do not bulk buy a brand they have not tried before. When multibuys take the form of two different brands, range trial can be generated. For example, a manufacturer of a branded coffee launching a new brand of tea could band the two brands together, thus leveraging the strength of the coffee brand to gain trial of the new tea brand.[106]

Free-in-the-mail offers: this sort of promotion involves the collection of packet tops or labels, which are sent in the mail as proof of purchase to claim a free gift or money-off voucher: Kellogg's Fruit 'n Fibre has been promoted by such an offer.

Gifts can be quite valuable because redemption rates can be low (less than 10 per cent redemption is not unusual). This is because of *slippage*: consumers collect labels with a view to mailing them but never collect the requisite number.

Self-liquidating offers: these are similar to free-in-the-mail offers except that consumers are asked to pay a sum of money to cover the costs of the merchandise plus administration and postage charges. The consumer benefits by getting the goods at below normal cost because the manufacturer passes on the advantage of bulk buying and prices at cost. The manufacturer benefits by the self-funding nature of the promotion, although there is a danger of being left with surplus stocks of the merchandise.

Buy-one-get-one-free offers: sometimes known as BOGOFs, with this type of promotion the consumer is in effect getting two items for the price of one. Wine is sometimes offered as a BOGOF promotion so that the consumer can buy two bottles of a particular brand for the price of one. The danger of running BOGOF promotions for heavily advertised brands is that they lose their premium positioning and are seen as just another brand available in bulk at discount prices.[107]

Free samples

Free samples of a brand may be delivered to the home or given out in a store. The idea is that having tried the sample a proportion of consumers will begin to buy it. For new brands or brand extensions (for example, a new shampoo or fabric conditioner) this form of promotion is an effective if expensive way of gaining consumer trial. However, sampling may be ineffective if the brand has nothing extra to offer the consumer but there may be other incentives a brand may add for free. For existing brands that have a low trial but high purchasing rate, sampling may be effective. As it would appear that many of those who try the brand like it and buy it again, raising the trial rate through free samples could have a beneficial long-term effect.

Coupons

There are three ways of couponing. Coupons can be delivered to the home, appear in magazines or newspapers, or appear on packs. *Home couponing*, after home sampling, is the best way to achieve trial for new brands.[108] *Magazine or newspaper couponing* is much cheaper than home delivery and can be used to stimulate trial, but redemption rates are much lower at around 5 per cent on average. The purpose of *on-pack couponing* is to encourage initial and repeat purchasing of the same brand, or trial of a different brand. A brand carries an on-pack coupon redeemable against the consumer's next purchase, usually for the same brand. Redemption rate is high; averaging around 40 per cent.[109] The coupon can offer a higher face value than the equivalent cost of a money-off pack since the effect of the coupon is on both initial and repeat sales. However, it is usually less effective in raising initial sales than money off because there is no immediate saving and its appeal is almost exclusively to existing consumers.[110]

Prize promotions

There are three main types of *prize promotion*: competitions, draws and games. Unlike other promotions, the cost can be established in advance and does not depend on the number of participants. *Competitions* require participants to exercise a certain degree of skill and judgement. For example, a competition to win free cinema seats might require entrants to name five films based upon stills from each. Entry is usually dependent on at least one purchase. Compared to premiums and money off, competitions offer a less immediate incentive to buy, and one that requires time and effort on the part of entrants. However, they can attract attention and interest in a brand. *Draws* make no demands on skill or judgement: the result depends on chance. For example, a supermarket may run an out-of-the-hat draw, where customers fill in their name and address on an entry card and on a certain day a draw is made. Another example of a draw is when direct mail recipients are asked to return a card on which there is a set of numbers. These are then compared against a set of winning numbers.

An example of a *game promotion* is where a newspaper encloses a series of bingo cards and customers are told that, over a period of time, sets of bingo numbers will be published. If these numbers form a line or full house on a bingo card a prize is won. Such a game encourages repeat purchase of the newspaper.

The national laws governing sales promotions in Europe vary tremendously and local legal advice should be taken before implementing a sales promotion. The UK, Ireland, Spain, Portugal, Greece, Russia and the Czech Republic have fairly relaxed laws about what can be done. Germany, Luxembourg, Austria, Norway, Switzerland and Sweden are much more restrictive. For example, in Sweden free mail-ins, free draws and money-off-next-purchase promotions, and in Norway self-liquidating offers, free draws, money-off vouchers and money-off-next-purchase, are not allowed.[111]

We will now go on to look at *trade promotions*.

Price discounts

The trade may be offered (or may demand) *discounts* in return for purchase. The concentration of buying into fewer trade outlets has placed increasing power with these organizations. This power is often translated into discounts from manufacturers. The discount may be part of a joint promotion, whereby the retailer agrees to devote extra shelf space, buy larger quantities, engage in a joint competition and/or allow in-store demonstrations. Volume discounts are given to retailers that hit sales targets.[112]

Free goods

An alternative to a price discount is to offer more merchandise at the same price. For example, the *baker's dozen* technique involves offering 13 items (or cases) for the price of 12.

Competitions

This involves a manufacturer offering financial inducements or prizes to distributors' sales forces in return for achieving sales targets for their products. Alternatively, a prize may be given to the sales force with the best sales figures.

Allowances

A manufacturer may offer an *allowance* (a sum of money) in return for retailers providing promotional facilities in-store (*display allowance*). For example, an allowance would be needed to persuade a supermarket to display cards on its shelves indicating that a brand was being sold at a special low price. An *advertising allowance* would be paid by a manufacturer to a retailer for featuring its brands in the retailer's advertising. *Listing allowances* are paid by the manufacturer to have a brand stocked.

Promotional price support

Promotional price support occurs when the manufacturer/supplier of particular goods or services works with the retailer to give money-off deals. For example, HSBC Bank had an introductory offer for its customers offering a £50 wine voucher to spend with Laithwaites Wine. This technique is often used by manufacturers and retailers.

In-store display and promotional support

Another form of trade promotion is when the manufacturer pays for in-store display and promotion. For example, a supplier could pay for a gondola-end display or a 10-second advertisement on the retailer's in-store television network.[113]

Sales promotion objectives

The most basic objective of any sales promotion is to provide extra value that encourages purchase. When targeted at consumers the intention is to stimulate **consumer pull**; when the trade is targeted **distribution push** is the objective. We will now look at specific sales promotion objectives.

Fast sales boost

Sales promotions deliver short-term sales increases, which may be required for a number of reasons: needing to reduce inventories or meet budgets prior to the end of the financial year, moving old stocks, or increasing stockholding by distributors in advance of the launch of a competitor's product.[114] Promotions that give large immediate benefits, such as money off or bonus packs, have bigger effects on sales volume than more distant promotions such as competitions or self-liquidators. However, whatever the objective for the sales promotion, it should not be used as a means of patching up more fundamental inadequacies such as inferior product performance or poor positioning.

A sales promotion that went seriously wrong was Hoover's attempt to boost sales of its washing machines, vacuum cleaners, refrigerators and tumble driers by offering two free US flight tickets for every Hoover product purchased over £100. The company was the target of much bad publicity as buyers discovered that the offer was wreathed in difficult conditions (found in the promotion's small print) and complained bitterly to Hoover and the media. In an attempt to limit the danger done to its reputation, the company announced that it would honour its offer to its customers, at an estimated cost of £20 million.

Encourage trial

Sales promotions can be highly successful by encouraging trial. If new buyers like the brand, the long-term effect of the promotion may be positive. Home sampling and home couponing are particularly effective methods of inducing trial. Promotions that simply give more product (e.g. bonus packs) are likely to be less successful since consumers will not place much value on the extra quantity until they have decided they like it.

Encourage repeat purchase

Certain promotions, by their nature, encourage repeat purchase of a brand over a period of time. Any offer that requires the collection of packet tops or labels (e.g. free mail-ins and promotions such as bingo games) is attempting to raise repeat purchase during the promotional period. Loyalty cards are designed to offer consumers an incentive to repeat purchase at a store.

Stimulate purchase of larger or more expensive packs

Promotions that are specifically linked to larger pack sizes may persuade consumers to switch from the less economical smaller packs. However, there has been a trend within the FMCG market for more concentrated products, which come in smaller packages, are more expensive but last longer and give better value for money (e.g. Ecover, 40 washes; Fairy liquid concentrated lasts 50 per cent longer). Even own-label value brands offer concentrated versions of their products (Tesco Value Bio Concentrated Liquid Wash).

Gain distribution and shelf space

Trade promotions are designed to gain distribution and shelf space. These are major promotional objectives since there is a strong relationship between sales and these two factors. Discounts, free gifts and joint promotions are methods used to encourage distributors to stock brands. Also, consumer promotions that provide sizeable extra value may also persuade distributors to stock or give extra shelf space.

Traditionally, sales promotions have been associated with achieving objectives for supermarket brands. However, their presence has spread to other sectors such as financial services, cars, IT and telecoms. There is a trend towards integrated media campaigns. For example, Fiat used a sales promotion to encourage people to visit its dealers. A direct mailing offered them the chance to compete in a racing game to win free Xbox consoles and DVDs. In the first three weeks, the campaign generated more than 1400 visits and resulted in an extra 203 cars being sold.[115]

Evaluating sales promotion

There are two types of research that can be used to evaluate sales promotions: *pre-testing research* is used to select, from a number of alternative promotional concepts, the most effective in achieving objectives; *post-testing research* is carried out to assess whether or not promotional objectives have been achieved.

Pre-testing research

Three major pre-testing methods are group discussions, hall tests and experimentation. **Group discussions** may be used with target consumers to test ideas and concepts. They can provide insights into the kinds of promotions that might be valued by them, and allow assessment of several promotional ideas so that some can be tested further and others discounted. Group discussions should be used as a preliminary rather than a conclusive tool.

Hall tests involve bringing a sample of target consumers to a room that has been hired, usually in a town or city location so that alternative promotional ideas can be tested. For example, a bonus pack, a free gift and a free-in-the-mail offer might be tested. The promotions are ranked on the basis of their incentive value. No more than eight alternatives should be tested and the promotions should be of a similar cost to the company.[116] Usually a sample of 100 to 150 is sufficient to separate the winners from the losers.

Experimentation closes the gap between what people say they value and what they actually value by measuring actual purchase behaviour in the marketplace. Usually two panels of stores are used to compare two promotional alternatives, or one promotion against no promotion (control). The two groups of stores must be chosen in such a way that they are comparable (a matched sample) so that the difference in sales is due to the two promotions rather than differences in the stores themselves. Experimentation may be used in a less sophisticated way where one or a small number of stores is used simply as a final check on promotional response before launching a promotion nationally. For service companies, the process may be even easier. Leaflets are produced to communicate the offer and are distributed to a sample of target consumers.[117] Group discussions and hall tests can be used prior to an experiment to narrow the promotional alternatives to a manageable few.

Post-testing research

After the sales promotion has been implemented, the effects must be monitored carefully. Care should be taken to check sales both during *and* after the promotion so that post-promotional sales dips can be taken into account (a *lagged effect*). In certain situations a sales fall can precede a promotion (a *lead effect*). If consumers believe a promotion to be imminent they may hold back purchases until it takes place. Alternatively, if a retail sales promotion of consumer durables (e.g. gas fires, refrigerators, televisions) is accompanied by higher commission rates for salespeople, they may delay sales until the promotional period.[118] If a lead effect is possible, sales prior to the promotion should also be monitored.

Ex-factory sales figures are usually an unreliable guide to consumer uptake at the retail level. Consequently, consumer panels and retail audits are usually employed to measure sales effects. **Consumer panel data** also reveal the types of people who responded to the sales promotion. For example, they would indicate whether any increase in sales was due to heavy buyers stocking up or new buyers trying the brand for the first time.

Retail audit data could be used to establish whether the promotion was associated with retail outlets increasing their stock levels or a rise in the number of outlets handling the brand, as well as measuring sales effects.

An attempt may also be made to assess the long-term impact of a sales promotion. However, in money promotion-prone markets—such as food, drink and toiletries—the pace of promotional activity means that it is impossible to disentangle the long-term effects of one promotion from another.

Ethical Issues in Advertising

As suggested by the quote at the start of the chapter advertising has an influence on society and subsequent behaviours. There are many controversial issues:

Advertising to children

Critics argue children are especially susceptible to persuasion and therefore need special protection from advertising. Others claim children are remarkably streetwise and can look after themselves. However, many European countries have regulations which control advertising to children. For example, in Germany advertising specific types of toys is banned and in the UK alcohol advertising is controlled.[119] In Sweden, advertising to under-12s on terrestrial television stations is banned, and in Belgium and Australia advertising within children's programmes is limited.

The UK has a code of practice to control advertisements aimed at children, which is designed to make sure advertisers avoid the misleading presentation of product information. For example, when advertising toys, accurate information about their size, price and operation should be included.[120] Pepsi and McDonald's have also introduced voluntary restrictions on their advertising to children in response to rising levels of obesity in the USA and western Europe.[121] Advertisements featuring toys, clothes and entertainment products have been criticized for promoting an acquisitive lifestyle and encouraging 'pester-power', whereby children request their parents to buy them such products, leading to family conflict. However, others point out that advertising may be only one factor in such conflict because some children's products sell well without advertising.[122]

Misleading advertising

This takes the form of exaggerated claims and concealed facts. For example, it would be unethical to claim that a car achieved 50 miles to the gallon when in reality it was only 30 miles. Nevertheless, most countries accept a certain amount of *puffery*, recognizing that consumers are intelligent and interpret the claims in such a way that they are not deceptive. In the UK the advertising slogan 'Carlsberg: probably the best lager in the world' is acceptable because of this. However, in Europe advertisers should be aware that a European directive on misleading advertising states that the burden of proof lies with the advertiser should the claims be challenged. Many industrialized countries have their own codes of practice that protect the consumer from deceptive advertising. For example, in the UK the Advertising Standards Authority (ASA) administers the British Code of Advertising Practice. It insists that advertising should be 'legal, decent, honest and truthful'.

This means that advertisers need to be very careful about the claims they make. For example, Procter & Gamble was forced to drop its claim 'Pantene Pro-V is the world's best haircare system' after Lever Fabergé complained to the ASA. A recent form of misleading advertising is 'greenwashing', where a brand is falsely attributed with green credentials. For example, the Lexus 'High performance, low emissions, zero guilt' press campaign was banned by the ASA for misleading consumers.[123]

Advertising's influence on society's values

Critics argue that advertising images have a profound effect on society. They claim that advertising promotes materialism and takes advantage of human frailties. Advertising is accused of stressing the importance of material possessions, such as the ownership of an expensive car or the latest in consumer electronics. Critics argue that this promotes the wrong values in society.

Promoting anti-social behaviour

The promotion of events that can lead to anti-social behaviour also raises ethical issues. For example, a 'promotion night' in pubs and clubs can lead to excessive drinking. Drunkenness, crime and violence may follow. In the longer term, health problems may arise.

Use of trade inducements

Retailers sometimes accept inducements from manufacturers to encourage their salespeople to push their products. This often takes the form of bonus payments to salespeople. The result is that there is an incentive for salespeople to pay special attention to those product lines that are linked to such bonuses when talking to customers. Customers may thus be subjected to pressure to buy products that do not meet their needs.

When you have read this chapter

log on to the Online Learning Centre at **www.mcgraw-hill.co.uk/textbooks/jobber** to explore chapter-by-chapter test questions, links and further online study tools for marketing.

Review

1 **The role of advertising in the promotional mix**
- Advertising is any paid form of non-personal communication of ideas or products in the prime media: i.e. television, the press, posters, cinema and radio.
- It possesses strengths and limitations, and should be combined with other promotional tools to form an integrated marketing communications campaign.

2 **The differences between strong and weak theories of how advertising works**
- The strong theory of advertising considers advertising to be a powerful influence on consumers, increasing knowledge, changing attitudes, and creating desire and conviction, and as a consequence persuading people to buy brands.
- The weak theory of advertising considers advertising to be a much less powerful influence on consumers. It suggests that advertising may arouse awareness and interest, nudge some consumers towards trial, and then provide some reassurance and reinforcement after the trial.

3 **How to develop advertising strategy: target audience analysis, objective setting, budgeting, message and media decisions, execution, and advertising evaluation**
- Advertising decisions should not be taken in isolation but should be based on a clear understanding of marketing strategy, in particular positioning. Then the steps are as follows.
- Identify and understand the target audience: the audience needs to be defined and understood in terms of its motives and choice criteria.
- Define advertising objectives: communicational objectives are to create awareness, stimulate trial, position products in consumer's minds, correct misconceptions, remind and reinforce, and provide support for the salesforce.
- Set the advertising budget: options are the percentage of sales, affordability, matching competition, and objective and task methods.
- Message decisions: messages should be important to the target audience and communicate competitive advantages.
- Media decisions: two key decisions are the choice of media (e.g. television versus the press) and media vehicle (a particular newspaper or magazine).
- Execution: care should be taken to meet publication deadlines.
- Evaluation of advertising: three key questions are what, when and how to evaluate.

4 **How campaigns are organized, including advertising agency selection and payment systems**
- An advertiser has four organizational options:
  1 advertising can be developed directly in cooperation with the media
  2 an in-house advertising department can be created
  3 a full-service advertising agency can be used
  4 a combination of in-house staff (or the full service agency) can be used for some functions and a specialist agency (media or creative) for others.
- Agency selection should begin with a clear definition of requirements. A shortlist of agencies should be drawn up and each briefed on the product and campaign. Selection will take place after each has made a presentation to the client.
- Agency payment can be by commission, fee or payment by results.

5 **The reasons for the growth in product placement and its risks**
- Product placement activity is growing because of its mass-market reach, ability to confer positive associations to brands, high credibility, message repetition, its ability to avoid advertising bans, its targeting capabilities, the opportunities it provides for new linked brands and promotions, and the ability to measure its impact on audiences.
- Its risks are that the movie or television programme may fail, tarnishing brand image; there is the possibility that the placement may not get noticed or may cause annoyance; and there is also the reduction in control, compared to advertisements, concerning how the brand will be portrayed in the movie or television programme.

6 **The objectives and targets of public relations**
- The objectives of public relations are to foster prestige and reputation, promote products, deal with issues and opportunities, enhance the goodwill of customers and employees, correct misconceptions, improve the goodwill of suppliers, distributors and government, deal with unfavourable publicity, and attract and keep good employees.
- The targets of public relations are the general public, the media, the financial community, government, commerce (including customers) and employees.

7 **The key tasks and characteristics of media relations**
- Three key tasks are: responding to requests from the media; supplying the media with information on events relevant to the organization; stimulating the media to carry the information and the viewpoint of the organization.
- The characteristics of publicity are that the message has higher credibility than advertising, there are no direct media costs and no control over what is published (content), whether the item will be published or when it will be published.

8 **The guidelines to use when writing a news release**
- The guidelines are: make the headline factual and briefly introduce the story; the opening paragraph should be a summary of the whole release; the copy should be organized by placing the less important messages towards the end; copy should be factual and backed up by evidence; the release should be short; the layout should contain short paragraphs with plenty of white space.

9 **The objectives and methods of sponsorship**
- The objectives of sponsorship are to gain publicity, create entertainment opportunities, foster favourable brand and company associations, improve community relations and create promotional opportunities.
- The two key methods of sponsorship are event sponsorship (such as a sports or arts event) and broadcast sponsorship (where a television or radio programme is sponsored).

10 **How to select and evaluate a potential sponsored event or programme**
- Selection should be based on asking what we are trying to achieve (communication objectives), who we are trying to reach (target market), what are the associated risks (e.g. adverse publicity), what are the potential promotional opportunities, what is the past record of sponsorship of the event or programme, and what are the costs.
- Evaluation should be based on measuring results in terms of sponsorship objectives (e.g. changes in awareness and attitudes). Formal evaluation involves measurement of media coverage and name mentions/sightings using a specialist monitoring agency.

11 **The growth in sales promotion**
- The reasons for growth are increased impulse purchasing, the growing respectability of sales promotions, the rising costs of advertising and advertising clutter, shortening time horizons for goal achievement, competitor activities and the fact that their sales impact is easier to measure than that of advertising.

12 **The major sales promotion types**
- Major consumer promotions are money off, bonus packs, premiums (free in- or on-pack gifts, free-in-the-mail offers, self-liquidating offers and buy-one-get-one-free offers), free samples, coupons, prize promotions (competitions, draws and games), and loyalty cards; major trade promotions are price discounts, free goods, competitions, allowances, promotional price support, and in-store display and promotional support.

13 **The objectives and evaluation of sales promotion**
- The objectives of sales promotion are to provide a fast sales boost, encourage trial, encourage repeat purchase, stimulate purchase of larger packs, and gain distribution and shelf space.
- Sales promotion can be evaluated using pre-testing research (group discussions, hall tests and experimentation) and post-testing research (consumer panel and retail audit data).

14 **Ethical issues in mass marketing communication**
- There are potential problems relating to misleading advertising, advertising's influence on society's values and advertising to children.
- There are potential problems relating to the use of trade inducements and the promotion of anti-social behaviour.

Key Terms

advertising any paid form of non-personal communication of ideas or products in the prime media, i.e. television, the press, posters, cinema and radio, the Internet and direct marketing

advertising agency an organization that specializes in providing services such as media selection, creative work, production and campaign planning to clients

advertising message the use of words, symbols and illustrations to communicate to a target audience using prime media

bonus pack giving a customer extra quantity at no additional cost

broadcast sponsorship a form of sponsorship where a television or radio programme is the focus

consumer panel data a type of continuous research where information is provided by household consumers on their purchases over time

consumer pull the targeting of consumers with communications (e.g. promotions) designed to create demand that will pull the product into the distribution chain

distribution push the targeting of channel intermediaries with communications (e.g. promotions) to push the product into the distribution chain

event sponsorship sponsorship of a sporting or other event

experimentation the application of stimuli (e.g. two price levels) to different matched groups under controlled conditions for the purpose of measuring their effect on a variable (e.g. sales)

group discussion a group, usually of six to eight consumers, brought together for a discussion focusing on an aspect of a company's marketing

hall tests bringing a sample of target consumers to a room that has been hired so that alternative marketing ideas (e.g. promotions) can be tested

media class decision the choice of prime media, i.e. the press, cinema, television, posters, radio, or some combination of these

media vehicle decision the choice of the particular newspaper, magazine, television spot, poster site, etc.

money-off promotions sales promotions that discount the normal price

premiums any merchandise offered free or at low cost as an incentive to purchase

product placement the deliberate placing of products and/or their logos in movies and television, usually in return for money

public relations the management of communications and relationships to establish goodwill and mutual understanding between an organization and its public

retail audit data used to establish whether the promotion was associated with retail outlets increasing their stock levels, a rise in the number of outlets handling the brand, as well as for measuring sales effects.

sales promotion incentives to customers or the trade that are designed to stimulate purchase

sponsorship a business relationship between a provider of funds, resources or services and an individual, event or organization that offers in return some rights and association that may be used for commercial advantage

strong theory of advertising the notion that advertising can change people's attitudes sufficiently to persuade people who have not previously bought a brand to buy it; desire and conviction precede purchase

target audience the group of people at which an advertisement or message is aimed

team sponsorship sponsorship of a team—for example, a football, cricket or motor racing team

weak theory of advertising the notion that advertising can first arouse awareness and interest, nudge some consumers towards a doubting first trial purchase and then provide some reassurance and reinforcement; desire and conviction do not precede purchase

Study Questions

1 Compare the situations where advertising and PR are more likely to feature strongly in the promotional mix.

2 Describe the strong and weak theories of how advertising works. Consider the extent to which each theory is more likely to apply to the purchase of a car, and the purchase of a bottle of water.

3 Media class decisions should always be based on creative considerations, while media vehicle decisions should be determined solely by cost per thousand calculations. Do you agree?

4 Describe the structure of a large advertising agency. Why should an advertiser prefer to use an agency rather than set up a full-service internal advertising department?

5 As a highly visible communication tool, advertising has its share of critics. What are their key concerns? How far do you agree or disagree with their arguments?

6 When you next visit a supermarket, examine three sales promotions. What types of promotion are they? What are their likely objectives?

7 Why would it be wrong to measure the sales effect of a promotion only during the promotional period? What are the likely long-term effects of a promotion?

8 Explain the difference between public relations and media relations.

9 Discuss the extent to which PR provides free advertising.

10 Discuss the main reasons for an organization becoming involved in event sponsorship.

References

1. Reinhard, K. (2006). *Response to 'Distinguished Communicator' Award*, California State University, Fullerton, http://communications.fullerton.edu/news/Faculty_news/May06_Reinhard.htm (accessed August 2006).
2. Clark, N. (2011) Memorable for irritation, *Marketing* 12 January, 24.
3. Halifax (2012) Halifax advert extra value for you, *Sunday Times*, 20 May, 5.
4. Vauxhall (2012) 'Flexible finance' advert, *Sunday Times*, 11 March, 8.
5. Clark, N. (2011) Gocompare campaign is 'most irritating ad', *Brand Republic*, http://www.brandrepublic.com/news/1048581/ 11 January.
6. Hegarty, J. (2011) *Hegarty on Advertising: Turning Intelligence into Magic*, London: Thames & Hudson, 23–4.
7. Sweney, M. (2012) WPP breaks £1bn profit barrier, *Guardian*, 1 March.
8. Jones, J. P. (1991) Over-Promise and Under-Delivery, *Marketing and Research Today*, November, 195–203.
9. Ehrenberg, A. S. C. (1992) Comments on How Advertising Works, *Marketing and Research Today*, August, 167–9.
10. Katz, E., M. Gurevitch and H. Haas (1973) On the Use of the Mass Media for Important Things, *American Sociological Review* 38, 164–81.
11. Crosier, K. (1983) Towards a Praxiology of Advertising, *International Journal of Advertising* 2, 215–32.
12. O'Donohoe, S. (1994) Advertising Uses and Gratifications, *European Journal of Marketing* 28(8/9), 52–75.
13. Wright, L. T. and M. Crimp (2003) *The Marketing Research Process*, London: Prentice-Hall, 180.

14. Jones (1991) op. cit.
15. Ehrenberg (1992) op. cit.
16. Ehrenberg (1992) op. cit.
17. Jones (1991) op. cit.
18. Dall'Olmo Riley, F., A. S. C. Ehrenberg, S. B. Castleberry, T. P. Barwise and N. R. Barnard (1997) The Variability of Attitudinal Repeat-Rates, *International Journal of Research in Marketing* 14, 437–50.
19. Jones (1991) op. cit.
20. Williams, E. (2011) The Wall's sausage dog returns, *Creative Review*, http://www.creativereview.co.uk/cr-blog/2011/may/walls-sausages-saatchi.
21. Ries, A. and J. Trout (2001) *Positioning: The Battle for your Mind*, New York: McGraw-Hill.
22. Aaker, D. A., R. Batra and J. G. Myers (1996) *Advertising Management*, New York: Prentice-Hall.
23. Grey, R. (2002) Fighting Talk, *Marketing*, 20 September, 26.
24. http://en.wikipedia.org/wiki/Keep_Calm_and_Carry_On.
25. http://en.wikipedia.org/wiki/Barter_Books.
26. http://www.keepcalmhome.com/about.htm.
27. Henley, J. (2009) What crisis? *The Guardian*, 18 March, http://www.guardian.co.uk/lifeandstyle/2009/mar/18/keep-calm-carry-on-poster.
28. Saatchi & Saatchi Compton (1985) *Preparing the Advertising Brief*, 9.
29. Hall, M. (1992) Using Advertising Frameworks: Different Research Models for Different Campaigns, *Admap*, March, 17–21.
30. Hegarty (2011) op. cit., 124–6.

31. Ogilvy, D. (1987) *Ogilvy on Advertising*, London: Pan.

32. Pieters, R., M. Wedel and R. Batra (2010) The Stopping Power of Advertising: Measures and Effects of Visual Complexity, *Journal of Marketing* 74(5), 48–60.

33. Dahl, D. W., K. D. Frankenberger and R. V. Manchanda (2003) Does it pay to shock? *Journal of Advertising Research* 43, 3 September, 268–81.

34. Whitehead, J. (2002) Pot noodle banned for calling itself the 'slag of all snacks', *Brand Republic*, http://www.brandrepublic.com/news/155509/Pot-Noodle-banned-calling-itself-slag-snacks/.

35. Elliott, R. (1997) Understanding Buyer Behaviour: Implications for Selling, in D. Jobber (ed.) *The CIM Handbook of Selling and Sales Strategy*, Oxford: Butterworth-Heinemann.

36. Barnett, M. (2011) In advertising we've a broad level of trust, *Marketing Week*, 2 May, 28–30.

37. Reid, A. (2005) Should Postar Move Faster?, *Campaign*, 21 October, 8.

38. http://www.skymedia.co.uk/Audience-insight/skyview.aspx.

39. Barnett, M. (2011) Will the picture improve for TV advertising data? *Marketing Week*, 13 October, 16–20.

40. Tomkins, R. (2001) Media Buyers Get Hitched and Attend Critical Mass, *Financial Times Creative Business*, 24 July, 2.

41. Hegarty (2011) op. cit., 185–7.

42. Fill, C. (2009) *Marketing Communications: Interactivity, communication and content*, Prentice Hall, 153.

43. Fill (2009) op. cit., 445–51.

44. Fill (2009) op. cit., 453–9.

45. Gordon, W. (1992) Ad pre-testing—hidden maps, *Admap* (June) 23–7.

46. Fill (2009) op. cit., 451–2.

47. Feng-Gui (2012) http://www.feng-gui.com/about.htm, 10 April.

48. Poels, K. and S. Dewitte (2006) How to Capture the Heart? Reviewing 20 Years of Emotion Measurement in Advertising, KUL Working Paper No. MO 0605, http://ssrn.com/paper=944401.

49. Rossiter, J. R. and S. Bellman (2005) *Marketing Communications: Theory and Applications*, Harlow: Prentice Hall.

50. Hegarty (2011) op. cit., 52.

51. Vize, R., J. Coughlan, A. Kennedy and F. Ellis-Chadwick (2011) 'B2B Relationship Quality: Conceptualisation of Relationship Quality in online B2B Retail services', *18th Recent Advances in Retailing and Services Science Conference*, The European Institute of Retailing and Services Science, San Diego USA, 12–18 July.

52. Morgan, M. R. and S. D. Hunt (1994) The Commitment-Trust Theory of Relationship Marketing, *Journal of Marketing* 58(July), 20–38.

53. Rauyruen, P. and K. E. Miller (2007) Relationship Quality as a Predictor of B2B Customer Loyalty, *Journal of Business Research* 60(1), 21–31.

54. Curtis, J. (2002) Clients Speak Out on Agencies, *Marketing*, 28 March, 22–3.

55. Curtis, J. (2002) Agencies Speak Out on Clients, *Marketing*, 4 April, 20–1.

56. Singh, S. (2005) P&G Reads the Riot Act Over Client Conflict, *Marketing Week*, 4 August, 9.

57. Rhind-Tutt, S. (2009) Put a Positive Spin on Change, *Marketing Week*, 5 February, 14.

58. Agency remunerations: A best practice guide on how to pay agencies, IPA/ISBA/MCCA/PRCA Joint Industry Guidelines.

59. Williams, A. (2011) TV product placement is here, *The Marketer*, April, 17.

60. Twilley, N. (2011) The Dawn of Product Placement: Morgan Spurlock on What the United Kingdom Can Expect Next, *Good Magazine: Lifestyle*, http://www.good.is/post/the-dawn-of-product-placement-morgan-spurlock-on-what-the-united-kingdom-can-expect-next/ 10 March.

61. Dumitrescu, A. (2012) Blizzard's Project Titan Will Have Product Placement, 25 January, *Softpedia*, http://news.softpedia.com/news/Blizzard-s-Project-Titan-Will-Have-Product-Placement-248355.shtml.

62. Wikipedia (2012) Product placement, http://en.wikipedia.org/wiki/Product_placement.

63. *Campaign* (2002) The Top Ten Product Placements in Features, 17 December, 36.

64. Tomkins, R. (2003) The Hidden Message: Life's a Pitch, and Then You Die, *Financial Times*, 24 October, 14.

65. Armstrong, S. (2005) How to Put Some Bling into Your Brand, *Irish Times*, Weekend, 30 July, 7.

66. Silverman, G. (2005) After the Break: The 'Wild West' Quest to Bring the Consumers to the Advertising, *Financial Times*, 18 May, 17.

67. Dowdy, C. (2003) Thunderbirds Are Go, *Financial Times*, Creative Business, 24 June, 10.

68. Roper, S. and C. Fill (2012) *Corporate Reputation: Brand and communication*, London: Pearson, 5.

69. White, J. (1991) *How to Understand and Manage Public Relations*, London: Business Books.

70. Fill (2009) op. cit., 256–72.

71. Lesly, P. (1998) *The Handbook of Public Relations and Communications*, Maidenhead: McGraw-Hill, 13–19.

72. Fill (2009) op. cit., 55.

73. Fill (2009) op. cit., 256.

74. Grunig, J. E. (1997) A situational theory of publics: conceptual history, recent challenges and new research, in D. Moss, T. MacManus and D. Vercic (eds), *Public Relations Research: An International Perspective*, London: International Thomson Business, 3–48.

75. Lesly (1998) op. cit.

76. Jefkins, F. (1985) Timing and Handling of Material, in W. Howard (ed.) *The Practice of Public Relations*, Oxford: Heinemann, 86–104.

77. BBC News (2012) http://www.bbc.co.uk/news/uk-scotland-north-east-orkney-shetland-17609719.

78. Sony (2012) http://www.sony.net/SonyInfo/News/Press/201203/12-037E/index.html.

79. Fill (2009) op. cit., 250, 260–1.

80. http://www.bbc.co.uk/news/business-17662059.

81. Maloney, K. (1997) Government lobby activities, in *Public relations and practice* (ed. P. J. Kitchen), London: International Thomson Press.

82. http://www.bitc.org.uk/resources/case_studies/cfs_lobbying.html.

83. Fill, C. (2011) *Essentials of Marketing Communications*, Harlow: Pearson.

84. http://www.co-operative.coop/join-the-revolution/our-plan/clean-energy-revolution/tar-sands/.

85. White, R. (2008) Corporate advertising: WARC Best Practice, www.warc.com.

86. Roper, S. and C. Fill (2012) *Corporate reputation: brand and communication*, London: Pearson, 272–75.

87. http://www.bp.com/genericarticle.do?categoryId=2012968&contentId=7072749.

88. Sleight, S. (1989) *Sponsorship: What It Is and How to Use It*, Maidenhead: McGraw-Hill, 4.

89. Bennett, R. (1999) Sports Sponsorship, Spectator Recall and False Consensus, *European Journal of Marketing* 33(3/4), 291–313.

90. Barrand, D. (2005) When Disaster Strikes, *Marketing*, 9 March, 35–6.

91. *The Marketer* (2008) Ten Clues for Keen Competition, June, 7.

92. Reynolds, J. and G. Charles (2011) A game of four brands, *Marketing*, 29 June, 14–15.

93. http://www.canon.co.uk/About_Us/Advertising_Sponsorship/Sponsorship/ (accessed 2012).

94. De Burton, S. (2004) Fancy a Touch of Star Status?, *Financial Times*, 13/14 November, 7–8.

95. Haywood, R. (1984) *All About PR*, Maidenhead: McGraw-Hill, 186.

96. Crowley, M. G. (1991) Prioritising the Sponsorship Audience, *European Journal of Marketing* 25(11), 11–21.

97. McCabe, M. (2011) BlackBerry signs up as exclusive sponsor of Sky Atlantic, *Marketing*, http://www.marketingmagazine.co.uk/news/1049758/, 18 January.

98. Thwaites, D. (1995) Professional Football Sponsorship—Profitable or Profligate?, *International Journal of Advertising* 14, 149–64.

99. Peattie, K. and S. Peattie (1993) Sales Promotion: Playing to Win?, *Journal of Marketing Management* 9, 255–69.

100. Lal, R. (1990) Manufacturer Trade Deals and Retail Price Promotion, *Journal of Marketing Research* 27(6), 428–44.

101. Rothschild, M. L. and W. C. Gaidis (1981) Behavioural Learning Theory: Its Relevance to Marketing and Promotions, *Journal of Marketing* 45, Spring, 70–8.

102. Tuck, R. T. J. and W. G. B. Harvey (1972) Do Promotions Undermine the Brand?, *Admap*, January, 30–3.

103. Brown, R. G. (1974) Sales Response to Promotions and Advertising, *Journal of Advertising Research* 14(4), 33–9.

104. Ehrenberg, A. S. C., K. Hammond and G. J. Goodhardt (1994) The After-Effects of Price-Related Consumer Promotions, *Journal of Advertising Research* 34(4), 1–10.

105. Wilson, R. (2005) Brands Need Not Pay the Price, *Marketing Week*, 7 July, 39–41.

106. Killigran, L. and R. Cook (1999) Multibuy Push May Backfire, *Marketing Week*, 16 September, 44–5.

107. Ritson, M. (2005) Cadbury's Decision to BOGOF is a Strategic Error, *Marketing*, 25 May, 24.

108. Davidson, J. H. (2003) *Offensive Marketing*, Harmondsworth: Penguin, 249–71.

109. Cummins, J. and R. Mullin (2008) *Sales Promotion*, London: Kogan Page, 79.

110. Davidson (2003) op. cit.

111. http://www.mosaicmarketing.co.uk/promowatch/2012/april/shreddies-win-1-of-75-summer-holidays-with-eurocamp.aspx.

112. Quilter, J. (2005) Aisles of Plenty, *Marketing*, 10 August, 15.

113. Quilter (2005) op. cit.

114. Cummins and Mullin (2008) op. cit.

115. McLukan, R. (2005) Branching Out, *Marketing*, 6 April, 39–40.

116. Collins, M. (1986) Research on 'Below the Line' Expenditure, in Worcester, R. and J. Downham (eds) *Consumer Market Research Handbook*, Amsterdam: North Holland, 537–50.

117. Cummins and Mullin (2008) op. cit.

118. Doyle, P. and J. Saunders (1985) The Lead Effect of Marketing Decisions, *Journal of Marketing Research* 22(1), 54–65.

119. Schlegelmilch, B. (1998) *Marketing Ethics: An International Perspective*, London: International Thomson Business Press.

120. Oates, C., M. Blades and B. Gunter (2003) Marketing to Children, *Journal of Marketing Management* 19(4), 401–10.

121. Ward, A. and J. Grant (2005) PepsiCo Admits Curbing Adverts to Children, *Financial Times*, 28 February, 23; J. Simms (2008) From Light Touch to Iron Fist, *Marketing*, 30 July, 30–3.

122. Proctor, J. and M. Richards (2002) Word-of-Mouth Marketing: Beyond Pester Power, *International Journal of Advertising and Marketing to Children* 3(3), 3–11.

123. Hudson, R. (2008) Engineered for Success, *Marketing*, 29 October, 22–3.

Toyota and Buddy

S teve Campbell (Marketing Communication Director) closed his office door and thought about the newspaper report he had received from his American colleagues. 'Toyota recall: reports of runaway cars' was the headline provided by ABC News. Others were more dramatic: '"There's no brakes . . . hold on and pray": Last words of man before he and his family died in Toyota Lexus crash'. He imagined how his colleagues would be feeling, or even the families of those affected by the situation. He thought of how it would feel if this were *his* family that had been involved. He thought of his current position as Marketing Communication Director at Toyota Motors South Africa (TMSA). Fortunately, no tragic events had been reported, but Steve was worried about how the news reports would affect Toyota owners and the general public. Toyota was such a reliable and trustworthy name in South Africa (as it was in many other parts of the world). As he travelled home, he made a decision. A marketing communication campaign was needed. But what type of campaign? What should the message be at a time like this? What did he want to achieve with the marketing campaign? What would be the best way to compile such a programme?

Background information

Based in Japan, Toyota is an international manufacturer of passenger and commercial vehicles throughout the world. Manufacturing takes places via 50 companies in 26 countries. Toyota vehicles are sold in 170 countries.

One country where Toyota has a manufacturing company is South Africa, where the motor vehicle industry is important to the local economy. Currently, the industry accounts for 7.5 per cent of the country's GDP and the total industry (including associated industries) creates approximately 36,000 jobs (both directly and indirectly). Toyota South Africa has a reputation in South Africa of producing and selling reliable, good-quality motor vehicles. Toyota has consistently been the top-selling motor vehicle manufacturer in South Africa, despite strong competition from Volkswagen South Africa.

In the midst of this positive situation for Toyota, technical problems were identified in November 2009 with the accelerator of various models. Initially the problem was identified in the United States, but by January 2010 the

necessity for a recall of Toyota vehicles in South Africa was identified. This situation had the potential to affect the trust in the brand, as well as the perceptions of quality associated with the brand, if not managed well.

The objectives of the campaign

Steve knew that building trust in a brand is part of the task of any marketing manager, and once it has been built, it is important to keep the trust. This was important with existing customers, but also with people who may be customers in the future. This would have to be one of the goals of the campaign. Not only was it a question of maintaining trust, it was also to create an emotional connection with the viewer (both existing and potential Toyota owners). That gave him another idea.

Why a dog? Why Buddy?

Underpinning the campaign that was developed to rebuild the brand and prevent brand erosion was the use of a dog ('Buddy') in an integrated marketing communication campaign. The purpose of using the dog was to 'break through the advertising clutter' which was identified in the mass media. Further, Buddy (as all dogs) shows 'reliability, honesty, loyalty and warm-heartedness', and he was the symbol selected to appeal to people from various ages and races. Selecting the type of dog was important as each breed has characteristics with which it is associated. It is suggested that boxers are 'a combination of all dogs' while still being 'careful and cautious'. Buddy is a boxer in all ways, except in his lips, which are 'human', thus making use of anthropomorphism. The breed of dog selected was required to have a flat snout so that the creative team could incorporate human lips. The campaign used both print and broadcast media, and was used to advertise all Toyota brands (Corolla, Hi-Lux, as well as the used-vehicle division). The campaign commenced on 23 September 2009, and consists of different versions which reflect different components of the Toyota business and brands.

The components of the campaign

Use of social media

When the problems with the motor cars were identified, Toyota published an open letter to the public which indicated the impact of the recall on customers and in so doing attempted to address customer concerns and apologise for the situation. This was placed in the mass media as well as on its website. The Toyota website was used so that customers could determine whether they were affected by the recall, and the actions necessary in this situation. Toyota owners could also access the official website and supply their vehicle's details. This would enable the owner to check whether the specific vehicle was affected by the recall, and Toyota could advise the owner on what the appropriate steps were to be. Blogs managed by Toyota SA were also used to discuss the situation and advise customers. An address from the Managing Director of Toyota South Africa was also placed on YouTube.

Use of mass media

Use was made of a print and television campaign in the national media. Magazines selected included those that focused on the motor enthusiast, as well as other popular magazines. The advertising was positively perceived and in the case of the television campaign, Buddy and the Corolla were #2 on the most liked advertising list for 2010, while Buddy and the Hilux were at #10.

What effect did Buddy have on the Toyota brand?

Research was conducted among both Toyota and non-Toyota owners. They were shown the storyboard for the advertisement and asked a number of questions. These included:

- *How did the advertisement make you feel about Toyota?* Among Toyota owners, 85 per cent found Toyota much more appealing (in contrast with 51 per cent of owners of other vehicles). By contrast, 31 per cent of owners of other vehicles felt that the advertisement made Toyota a little more appealing, while a further 18 per cent indicated that it didn't change their feelings about Toyota. Toyota owners were exceedingly positive towards Toyota after having seen the storyboard. Non-Toyota owners were also positive towards the brand, but not as positive as Toyota owners. The advertisement was positively perceived by all those who viewed the advertisement, affecting the perception of the brand.

- *Has the advertisement improved your perceptions of the brand?* Among Toyota owners, 93 per cent agreed strongly that the advertisement had improved their perceptions of the brand, compared with 62 per cent of owners of other vehicles. In the case of 'agree slightly', 25 per cent of owners of other cars responded in this way compared to 5 per cent of Toyota owners. This increase shows the effect of the advertisement on changes in brand perception. The effect was more pronounced among Toyota owners.

- *Thinking about this advertisement, if you were to change/replace your current vehicle, how would this advertisement affect your consideration of Toyota?* Among Toyota owners, 89 per cent indicated it would make them much more likely to consider Toyota, while 42 per cent of owners of other vehicles were much more likely to consider Toyota. A further 36 per cent of owners of other vehicles indicated that the advertisement would make them a little more likely to consider Toyota. This indicates the ability of the advertisement to change not only perceptions, but also the actions of customers.

- *Thinking about the recalling of Toyota vehicles, if you were to change/replace your current vehicle, how would this recall issue affect your consideration of Toyota?* This question was relevant as the campaign was associated with the attempt to limit any potential damage associated with the recall of Toyota motor vehicles. Among Toyota owners, 49 per cent indicated that it would make them much more likely to consider Toyota, while in the case of owners of other vehicles, 21 per cent indicated it would make them much more likely to consider Toyota. Among both groups, 12 per cent indicated that they would be a little more likely to consider Toyota. For 37 per cent of Toyota owners and 57 per cent of non-owners, the recall issue made no difference to their considering buying a Toyota.

Conclusion

Steve smiled happily. The campaign had been a great success. It had built connection and trust, and opinions of consumers were reflected in the research and the statistics. It was time to start thinking about the follow-up campaign.

References

Kruger, C. 2010. Personal interview with the author.

Kruger, C. 2010. Presentation at Southern African Institute of Management Scientists Conference 2010, Mpekweni Sun, 12–15 September 2010.

http://www.toyota-global.com/company/profile/facilities/worldwide_operations.html (accessed 15 September 2011).

http://www.southafrica.info/business/economy/sectors/automotive-overview.htm (accessed 15 September 2011).

http://business-ethics.com/2010/01/31/2123-toyota-recall-five-critical-lessons/ (accessed 15 September 2011).

http://abcnews.go.com/Blotter/RunawayToyotas/runaway-toyotas-problem-persists-recall/story?id=9618735&page=2 (accessed 21 September 2011).

http://www.dailymail.co.uk/news/article-1248177/Toyota-recall-Last-words-father-family-died-Lexus-crash.html#ixzz1YaJKrtWw (accessed 21 September 2011).

http://www.superbrands.com/za/pdfs/TOYOTA.pdf (accessed 21 September 2011).

http://www.thebrandunion.co.za/News/Detail/39/TheBrandUnionSouthAfricaSixClientsNamedNumberOne (accessed 21 September 2011).

Questions

1. Do you think Buddy was able to connect with Toyota owners and the general public?

2. What suggestions do you have for Steve concerning a follow-up campaign?

3. Was this the best way to deal with the situation facing Toyota South Africa?

4. What other strategies could also have been considered?

This case was prepared by Adele Berndt, Associate Professor, Jönköping International Business School, Sweden.

White Horse Whisky
Developing a New Advertising Strategy

Market background

United Distillers & Vintners (UDV), the brand owner of Bell's and White Horse, is seeking to recruit a new generation of young drinkers to the whisky market. It has taken the view that this can be achieved by repositioning its White Horse brand so that it shakes itself free of the old-fashioned imagery currently associated with Scotch whisky. This will involve developing a marketing strategy and advertising campaign that will change the way White Horse is perceived by young people. UDV then intends to promote Bell's in a way that continues to appeal to mainstream, older, established whisky drinkers by continuing to reflect more traditional values.

The Scotch whisky market has been in decline for over 15 years. Drinking patterns generally have moved away from traditional dark spirits (such as rum and whisky) in favour of white spirits (vodka), wine and lagers. Each generation of new drinkers has been attracted to the marketing and promotion of chilled, long, lighter drinks. Brands from exotic countries that combine genuine authenticity with exciting contemporary images have enjoyed persistent growth.

Over time the profile of whisky drinkers has gradually become older, within a base that is in itself declining (see Tables C30.1 and C30.2). The number of adults drinking whisky at least once a month has declined by around 900,000, and over half the remaining 3.9 million consumers are over 50 years old. The rate of recruitment of people in their twenties and thirties has declined over recent years.

Whisky has always been acknowledged as an 'acquired taste' that was unlikely to appeal to novice drinkers, but rather reflected a more mature palate. However, people are no

TABLE C30.2   Profile of whisky drinkers

Age	Dec. 1991 %	Dec. 2001 %	Dec. 2011 %
18–24	11	10	9
25–34	19	15	15
35–49	27	24	24
50+	44	50	52
Base 000s	4906	4626	3997

TABLE C30.1   Blended whisky market (000-litre cases)

2005	10,980
2006	10,090
2007	9,428
2008	9,659
2009	9,540
2010	8,595
2011	8,210

longer making the transition to traditional dark spirits in anything like the numbers they did historically. Consumers no longer seem motivated to rise to the challenge of drinking traditional dark spirits (although they are still interested in trying new dark spirits as the growth in malt whisky and bourbon has demonstrated).

The leading brand has consistently remained Bell's (see Table C30.3), but the total share of all the brands is

	2008 %	2009 %	2010 %	2011 %
Bell's	18.9	17.7	17.7	17.0
Teachers	7.4	7.5	6.9	6.2
Famous Grouse	13.4	12.8	12.4	12.9
White Horse	3.1	2.7	2.9	2.3
Grant's	5.3	5.3	5.1	4.8
Whyte & Mackay	4.4	4.6	4.7	4.1
Own-label	18.3	18.9	19.0	18.9
Cheapest on display	8.7	9.1	10.8	12.8

consistently being eroded by less expensive and less famous alternatives. So, in addition to operating in a market that is in overall decline, brands are losing their share of that market.

White Horse whisky is available in some off-licences and in supermarkets like Waitrose and Sainsbury's, where it is among a broad competitive set.

The current image of whisky

UDV commissioned qualitative research among 18–25-year-olds (typically still experimenting) and 25–30-year-olds (usually becoming established in their repertoire) to try and understand what the barriers to drinking whisky are and therefore how it might go about challenging these beliefs through its presentation of White Horse.

This research found that there were both product and image barriers to whisky drinking. It is believed to be a strong and overpowering spirit, with a potent bitter smell and 'rough' or 'fiery' taste that will linger unpleasantly after drinking. It is also universally described as a spirit that is very difficult to mix. Repertoires are usually restricted to 'ordinary' mixes such as ice, water, ginger and lemonade. This makes it more difficult to make whisky accessible in a more dilute form, which is typically how young people learn to acquire a taste for spirits; it is rare to be able to take them neat from the beginning.

For some, these product barriers can be seen as an initiation test, with the reward being the acknowledgement of being a 'real man'.

Current whisky imagery is seen as outdated and largely irrelevant. It elicits tired, safe old images of tartan, hills, heather and glens, lochs, bagpipers, open fires, old men drinking on their own, and so on—which are all considered to have once been targeted at their parents or grandparents. These images are not felt to reflect the more

authentic, real-life images of Scotland and its rich heritage. Films such as *Braveheart* and political moves to give Scotland greater independence are all areas of much greater interest, and offer more compelling images of the dignity and depth of Scotland's rich history.

The consumer

This research project also investigated the values of young people generally, not just with respect to whisky. The findings were as follows.

- Today's young people view balance as a necessity to a successful life. They are motivated by success in their desired careers, but the focus for them must also be on enjoyment and escapism in their spare time. They are materialistic, but in a less aggressive way than the young people of the Thatcherite 1980s. To some extent, an environmental awareness and the need to treat and respect the world we live in have softened this.

- The 1990s and 'noughties' also brought a shift towards honesty and authenticity—a move away from the contrived, lifestyle-orientated 1980s. Being true to oneself has been identified as being important. Optimism was also in evidence, as it is with many young people who have not been hardened by the reality of life.

- They appreciate quality, sincerity and unpretentiousness. This reflects a going-back-to-basics mentality. They also consider originality, intelligence and a degree of irreverence (or not taking oneself too seriously) to be particularly important. In sum, 'less is more'.

- Humour is seen to be an important vehicle for facing up to the realities of life. Humour that is self-deprecating, subtle and self-referential is particularly liked. Honesty and insight are also appreciated because it credits the viewer with some intelligence.

- The values associated with young people today are also tinged with a degree of vulnerability. The recent recession has made people recognize that jobs are not for life and that they might underachieve in their lives.

White Horse

White Horse whisky was created in 1890 by Peter Mackie, one of the best-known whisky blenders and distillers of his day. He named it after one of Edinburgh's most famous coaching inns: The White Horse Cellar. Indeed, the brand logo reflects the pub sign design. In its distinctive, modernized, squat bottle, the brand sells for £16.99 (€21.60) per litre, a price below that of Bell's (£18.49/€23.70) and Teachers (£17.79/€23), but above own-label (e.g. Waitrose at £14.99/€18.70).

Yorkshire farmers have always been particularly attached to the brand and created the very smooth and drinkable 'whisky milk'. This consists of a tumbler made up of half cold milk and half White Horse whisky—a favourite way to wind down at the end of a hard day. Alternatively, the brand mixes very well with ginger ale or orange juice.

It is many years since the brand had any advertising support, with most of UDV's effort being behind Bell's. However, it is recognized that the successful targeting of a new generation of young consumers is vital to the future of the whisky market. The recent relaxation of the voluntary code, whereby whisky brands may now be advertised on TV, represents a particular opportunity.

Marketing objective

UDV intends to relaunch White Horse whisky. Its aim is to achieve a brand share of 6 per cent in three years. It is expected that 60 per cent of the brand's consumers should be under 50 years of age by that time.

The task

Each syndicate must come up with an advertising strategy based on a budget level of £3 million (€4.2 million) in the first year of advertising. For the purpose of the exercise, in terms of media, you are asked to consider only what your strategy will be (i.e. which target audience should be reached, using which type of media and when), which is the role fulfilled by a media planner, often in conjunction with the creative agency team. You will not be asked to cost out the plan, and will not be given costings for the various media. A simple ratio is included below.

The advertising strategy must answer the following questions.

1   What are the advertising objectives?

2   Who exactly are the people the advertising must affect/ reach?

3   What is the main message the advertising must put across and what evidence can be used to support that message?

4   What do we want people to think/feel after seeing the advertising?

5   What should the style of advertising be?

6   Where should the advertising appear (i.e. TV, newspapers, magazines, posters, radio, etc.)? Which would be the primary vehicle and which the secondary support? What percentage of the £3 million (€4.2 million) would you allocate to which media and why?

Issues to consider when developing your media strategy

Today, most creative agencies use a media agency to plan and buy media. The media agency specializes both in understanding how consumers 'consume' media (and therefore which media are most effective in reaching particular audiences) and in being able to negotiate the best-value schedule from the ever-expanding selection of media opportunities. The average person in Britain today is exposed to around 2500 advertising messages a week, so optimum targeting of the media chosen and cut-through of the message displayed are essential.

Consider what target audience can achieve the advertising objectives you have decided upon; then consider what media that target might 'consume' and when might be the most propitious moment to 'approach' them in that medium. Consider both time of day as well as seasonality, and what their activities might be while viewing the medium as this will impact on their frame of mind when seeing the advertising message. You might feel that one medium is not sufficient and that you need to convey your message using a multi-layered effect (e.g. television with direct response, posters with radio, Internet banners with sales promotion, etc.). Consider where and when they can buy the brand, and how this might affect the media chosen. Most types of media are segmented (e.g. different press titles or TV programmes can reach different audiences), so consider a typical example to clarify your answer.

Think about what sort of message you wish to promote. Do you need to explain your positioning and be able to use a lot of words, or is a simple visual able to convey your message? This will dictate whether press or posters, for example, would be most appropriate.

Allow a notional 10 per cent cost for creative production for each medium that you choose.

Use your own consumption of different media to guide you in your media choice, and then consider whether someone in a different consumer age group would react differently and why.

Note

All figures in the tables in this case are indicative of a real-life situation.

The authors of the book are grateful to Ann Murray Chatterton, Director of Training and Development at the Institute of Practitioners in Advertising, for permission to publish this case. Copyright © IPA www.ipa.co.uk

CHAPTER
16

Direct marketing communications

nothing but fruit

= 2 of your
5-a-day

= 2 of your
5-a-day

innocent
pure fruit smoothie

mangoes &
passion fruits

innocent
pure fruit smoothie
strawberries
& bananas

innocent
pure fruit smoothie

strawberries
& bananas

Here to save the peckish

> **Everyone lives by selling something.**
> ROBERT LOUIS STEVENSON

> **I have travelled the length and breadth of this country and talk with the best people and I can assure you that data processing is a fad that won't outlast the year.**
> (EDITOR IN CHARGE OF PRENTICE HALL BUSINESS BOOKS 1957)

LEARNING OBJECTIVES

After reading this chapter, you should be able to:

1 discuss the key direct communication tools: personal selling, exhibitions, direct marketing

2 discuss the characteristics of modern selling and the stages in the selling process

3 consider the key issues involved in sales management

4 discuss exhibitions and trade shows in a business-to-business context

5 explain the concept of direct marketing and how to manage campaigns

6 describe the reasons for the growth in direct marketing communication activity

7 discuss the importance of database marketing and explain the nature of customer relationship management

8 describe the media used in direct marketing

9 discuss the ethical issues in direct communications

The world of communications is changing rapidly. Digital and mobile communication platforms are blurring the boundaries between communication tools and media. Websites (potentially) carry text, audio, video messages as well as acting as information sources, means of data collection and sales channels.[1] In this chapter we are going to explore elements of the promotional mix that are direct forms of communication, which generally do not require media scheduling and offer a level of personalization not afforded by the mass communication tools discussed in Chapter 15. The chapter begins with personal selling and sales management as this is the oldest, most direct and interactive form of direct communications. This is followed by exhibitions and trade fairs, and finally we explore direct marketing, the importance of database marketing and the role of customer relationship management. The chapter provides more detailed investigation of each tool, building on the foundations set down in Chapter 14 and, in doing so, provides more insight into how each of the direct communication methods might contribute to an Integrated Marketing Communication (IMC) campaign strategy.

Personal Selling and Sales Management

Personal selling is the marketing task that involves face-to-face contact with a customer. Unlike advertising, promotion, sponsorship and other forms of non-personal communication, personal selling permits a direct interaction between buyer and seller. This two-way communication means that the seller can identify the specific needs and problems of the buyer and tailor the sales presentation in the light of this knowledge. The particular concerns of the buyer can also be dealt with on a one-to-one basis.

This flexibility comes only at a cost. The cost of a car, travel expenses and sales office overheads can mean that the total annual bill for a field salesperson is often twice the level of their salary. In business-to-business marketing over 70 per cent of the marketing budget is usually spent on the salesforce. This is because of the technical nature of the products being sold, and the need to maintain close personal relationships between the selling and buying organizations.

However, the nature of the personal selling function is changing. Organizations are reducing the size of their salesforces in the face of greater buyer concentration, moves towards centralized buying, and recognition of the high costs of maintaining a field sales team. The concentration of buying power into fewer hands has also fuelled the move towards relationship management, often through key account selling. This involves the use of dedicated sales teams that service the accounts of major buyers. As the commercial director of HP Foods said:

> Twenty years ago we had between 70 and 100 salespeople. The change in the retail environment from small retailers to central warehouses and supermarkets has meant a big change in the way we communicate with our customers. Instead of sending salespeople out on the road, we now collect a large proportion of our sales by telephone or computer. We have replaced the traditional salesforce with 12 business development executives, who each have a small number of accounts dealing with customers at both national and regional levels.[2]

Selling and sales management are experiencing a period of rapid change. The next section explores the major forces at work.

Characteristics of Modern Selling

In today's competitive environment, a salesforce must have a wide range of skills to compete successfully. Gone are the days when salespeople required simple presentational and closing skills to be successful. The characteristics of the job today (illustrated in Fig. 16.1) require a wide array of skills; these will be identified in the next section. In this part of the book we discuss the characteristics of modern selling. Without such an understanding salespeople will be ill-equipped to tackle the job.

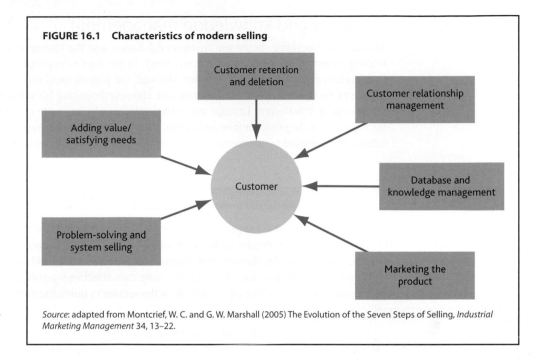

FIGURE 16.1 Characteristics of modern selling

Source: adapted from Montcrief, W. C. and G. W. Marshall (2005) The Evolution of the Seven Steps of Selling, *Industrial Marketing Management* 34, 13–22.

Customer retention and deletion

Many companies find that 80 per cent of their sales come from 20 per cent of their customers. This means that it is vital to devote considerable resources to retaining existing high-volume, high-potential and highly profitable customers. **Key account management** has become an important form of sales organization because it means that a salesperson or sales team can focus their efforts on one or a few major customers.

At the other end of the spectrum, companies are finding that some small customers actually cost the organization money. This is because servicing and distribution of products to these customers may push costs beyond the revenue generated. This may mean a change to **telemarketing** as a means of servicing their requirements and taking orders, or dropping them altogether.

Customer relationship management

The emphasis on customer retention has led to an increasing focus on **customer relationship management**. Customer relationship management requires that the salesforce focuses on the long term and not simply on closing the next sale. The emphasis should be on creating win/win situations with customers so that both parties to the interaction gain and want to continue the relationship. For major customers, relationship management may involve setting up dedicated teams to service the account and maintain all aspects of the business relationship.

The focus moves from order taking and order making to strategic customer management.[3] The challenge is to reposition sales as a core element of a firm's competitiveness, where the sales organization is closely integrated into marketing strategy and planning.[4] This process places the customer at the centre of the company's focus, with the sales organization charged with taking a strategic view of designing and implementing superior customer relationships.[5] This requires sales management to work towards the total integration of how customer relationships are designed, established, managed and sustained. For example, companies like Cisco Systems have developed sales strategies that use personal selling when the purchase is important and complicated, and the decision uncertain—usually the first sale to a customer or a new application—leaving subsequent purchases to be made via the Internet.[6]

Database and knowledge management

The modern salesforce should use customer databases, and the Internet to aid the sales task (e.g. finding customer and competitor information). In the past salespeople recorded customer information on cards and sent in orders through the post to head office. Today, technological advances such as email, mobile phones and videoconferencing have transformed the way knowledge is transferred. Laptops mean that salespeople can store customer and competitor information, make presentations and communicate with head office electronically. Furthermore, information supplied by the company, such as catalogues and price lists, can be held electronically.

Read the Research 16.1 **Multichannel Communications**

Over the last ten years, the drive to get customers to purchase via the Internet hasn't eliminated the other channels like call centres and mailed catalogues for direct retailers. As this research shows, customers will use the traditional call centre when they are not very familiar with the purchase, or perceive it to be of high risk. The findings suggest that retailers should continue to drive customers to use the more cost-effective Internet, but maintain the call centre for extended problem-solving situations. This choice will allow the retailer to guide the customer to use the most appropriate channel.

Eddie Rhee (2010) Multi-channel Management in Direct Marketing Retailing, Journal of Database Marketing & Customer Strategy Management 17, 70–77.

In today's competitive marketplace, the ability to handle and analyse large amounts of data effectively and profitably can give your organisation a competitive advantage. McKinsey interviewed three experts in their fields, Professor Erik Brynjolfsson, Jeff Hammerbacher and coach Brad Stevens. Each offered their views on a range of issues, from data analytics, productivity, profitability and harnessing 'big data' to how to use data in the sporting arena to help squads punch above their weight.

https://www.mckinseyquarterly.com/Competing_through_data_Three_experts_offer_their_game_plans_2868

Marketing the product

The modern salesperson is involved in a much broader range of activities than simply planning and making a sales presentation. Indeed, face-to-face presentations can now sometimes be substituted by information presented on Web pages and email attachments that can give the customer up-to-date information on many topics more quickly, more comprehensively and in a more time-convenient manner than many face-to-face interactions.[7] The role of the salesperson is expanding to participation in marketing activities such as product development, market development and the segmentation of markets, as well as other tasks that support or complement marketing activities, such as database management, provision and analysis of information, and assessing market segments.[8]

Problem-solving and system selling

Much of modern selling, particularly in business-to-business situations, is based upon the salesperson acting as a consultant, who works with the customer to identify problems, determine needs, and propose and implement effective solutions.[9] This approach is fundamentally different from the traditional view of the salesperson as a smooth, fast talker who breezes in to see a customer, persuades them to buy and walks away with an order. Modern selling often involves multiple calls, the use of a team-selling approach and considerable analytical skills. Further, customers are increasingly looking for a systems solution rather than the buying of an individual product. This means, for example, that to sell door handles to a company like Ford a supplier must be able to sell a door *system* that includes door handles, locking and opening devices, as well as having a thorough knowledge of door technology, and the ability to suggest to Ford solutions to problems that may arise.

Go to the website to consider how Nokia's sales staff and advertising work together. www.mcgraw-hill.co.uk/ textbooks/jobber

Satisfying needs and adding value

The modern salesperson must have the ability to identify and satisfy customer needs. Some customers do not recognize that they have a need. It is the salesperson's job in such situations to stimulate need recognition. For example, a customer may not realize that a machine in the production process has low productivity compared to newer, more technologically advanced machines. The salesperson's job will be to make the customer aware of the problem in order to convince him/her that they have a need to modernize the production process. In so doing, the salesperson will have added value to the customer's business by reducing costs, and created a win/win situation for both his/her company and the customer.

Personal Selling Skills

Many people's perception of a salesperson is of a slick, fast-talking confidence trickster devoted to forcing unwanted products on innocent customers. Personal experience will tell the reader that this is unrealistic in a world of educated consumers and professional buyers. Success in selling comes from implementing the marketing concept when face to face with customers, not denying it at the very point when the seller and buyer come into contact. The sales interview offers an unparalleled opportunity to identify individual customer needs and match behaviour to the specific customer that is encountered.[10] Salespeople have an opportunity to implement unique sales presentations tailored to individual customers and rapidly adjust messages in response to customer reactions. Indeed, research has shown that such customer-orientated selling is associated with higher levels of salesforce performance.[11]

Research has shown that, far from using high-pressure selling tactics, success is associated with:[12]

- asking questions
- providing product information, making comparisons and offering evidence to support claims
- acknowledging the viewpoint of the customer
- agreeing with the customer's perceptions
- supporting the customer
- releasing tension
- having a richer, more detailed knowledge of customers
- increased effort
- confidence in one's own abilities.

All these findings are in accord with the marketing concept.

In order to develop personal selling skills it is useful to distinguish seven phases of the selling process (see Fig. 16.2). These phases need not occur in the order shown. Objections may be raised during the presentation or negotiation, and a trial close may be attempted at any point during the presentation if buyer interest is high. Furthermore, negotiation may or may not take place, or may occur during any of the stages. As Moncrief and Marshall report:[13]

> The evolved selling process assumes that the salesperson typically will perform the various steps of the process in some form, but the steps (phases) do not occur for each sales call. Rather, they occur over time, accomplished by multiple people within the selling firm, and not necessarily in any sequence.

Each of these phases will now be discussed.

Preparation

Preparation before a sales visit can reap dividends by enhancing confidence and performance when face to face with the customer. Some situations cannot be prepared for—the unexpected question or unusual objection, for example—

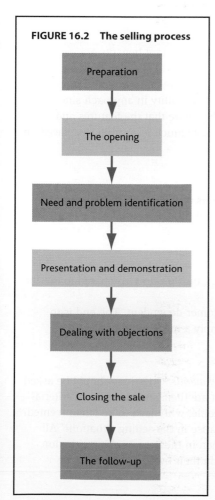

FIGURE 16.2   The selling process

Preparation

↓

The opening

↓

Need and problem identification

↓

Presentation and demonstration

↓

Dealing with objections

↓

Closing the sale

↓

The follow-up

but many customers face similar situations, and certain questions and objections will be raised repeatedly. Preparation can help the salesperson respond to these recurring situations.

Salespeople will benefit from gaining knowledge of their own products and competitors' products, sales presentation planning, setting call objectives and understanding buyer behaviour.

Product knowledge

Product knowledge means understanding both **product features** and the customer benefits that they confer. Understanding product features alone is not enough to convince customers to buy because they buy products for the benefits that the features provide, not the features in themselves. Salespeople need to ask themselves what are the benefits a certain feature provides for customers. For example, a computer mouse (product feature) provides a more convenient way of issuing commands (customer benefit) than using the keyboard. The way to turn features into benefits is to view products from the customer's angle. A by-product of this is the realization that some features may provide no customer benefit whatsoever.

Competitors' products

Knowledge of competitors' products allows their strengths to be offset against their weaknesses. For example, if a buyer claims that a competitor's product has a cost advantage, this may be offset against the superior productivity advantage of the salesperson's product. Similarly, inaccuracies in a buyer's claims can be countered. Finally, competitive knowledge allows salespeople to stress the differential advantage of their products compared to those of the competition.

Sales presentation planning

Preparation here builds confidence, raises the chances that important benefits are not forgotten, allows visual aids and demonstrations to be built into the presentation, and permits the anticipation of objections and the preparation of convincing counter-arguments. Although preparation is vital there should be room left for flexibility in approach since customers have different needs. The salesperson has to be aware that the features and benefits that should be stressed with one customer may have much less emphasis placed on them for another.

Setting call objectives

The key to setting call objectives is to phrase them in terms of what the salesperson wants the customer to do rather than what the salesperson should do. For example:

- for the customer to define what his or her needs are
- for the customer to visit a showroom
- for the customer to try the product: e.g. drive a car
- for the customer to be convinced of the cost saving of 'our' product compared to that of the competition.

This is because the success of the sales interview is customer-dependent. The end is to convince the customer; what the salesperson does is simply a means to that end.

Understanding buyer behaviour

Thought should also be given to understanding *buyer behaviour*. Questions should be asked, such as 'Who are the likely key people to talk to?' 'What are their probable choice criteria?' 'Are there any gatekeepers preventing access to some people, who need to be circumvented?' 'What are the likely opportunities and threats that may arise in the selling situation?' All of the answers to these questions need to be verified when in the actual selling situation but prior consideration can help salespeople to be clear in their own minds about the important issues.

The Internet can provide a wealth of information about the buying organization. The buyer's website, online product catalogues and blogs are useful sources of information. Customer relationship management (CRM) systems allow salespeople to access customer information held by their company via the Internet. For example, Orange, the telecommunications company, enables its field salespeople to access its CRM databases using personal digital assistants (PDAs) equipped with wireless modems.[14]

The opening

Initial impressions often affect later perceptions, and so it is important for salespeople to consider how to create a favourable initial response from customers. The following factors can positively shape first impressions.

- Be businesslike in appearance and behaviour.
- Be friendly but not over-familiar.
- Be attentive to detail, such as holding a briefcase in the hand that is not used for handshaking.
- Observe common courtesies like waiting to be asked to sit down.
- Ask if it is convenient for the customer to see you. This signals an appreciation of their needs (they may be too busy to be seen). It automatically creates a favourable impression from which to develop the sales call, but also a long-term relationship because the salesperson has earned the right to proceed to the next stage in selling: need and problem identification.
- Do not take the sales interview for granted: thank the customer for spending time with you and stress that you believe it will be worthwhile for them.

Using the Internet can help to create favourable first impressions. For example, research using online business databases can make salespeople appear highly knowledgeable about the customer's company and business.

Need and problem identification

People buy products because they have problems that give rise to needs. For example, machine unreliability (problem) causes the need to replace it with a new one (purchase). Therefore the first task is to identify the needs and problems of each customer. Only by doing so can the salesperson connect with each customer's situation. Having done so, the salesperson can select the product that best fits the customer's need and sell the appropriate benefits. It is benefits that link customer needs to product features, as in:

> Customer need → Benefit ← Product feature

In the previous example, it would be essential to convince the customer that the salesperson's machine possessed features that guaranteed machine reliability. Knowledge of competitors' products would allow salespeople to show how their machine possessed features that gave added reliability. In this way, salespeople are in an ideal situation to convince customers of a product's differential advantage. Whenever possible, factual evidence of product superiority should be shown to customers. This is much more convincing than mere claims by the salesperson.

Effective needs and problem identification requires the development of questioning and listening skills. The problem is that people are more used to making statements than asking questions. Therefore the art of asking sensible questions that produce a clear understanding of the customer's situation requires training and considerable experience. The hallmark of inexperienced salespeople is that they do all the talking; successful salespeople know how to get the customer to do most of the talking. In this way they gain the information necessary to make a sale.

David Crossland, the entrepreneur who built Airtours (now MyTravel) into one of the UK's biggest travel companies, based his success at selling holidays on his technique of 'just listening' to customers. By asking questions and listening, he picked up clues about what holidays they would prefer from what they said they liked and hated about previous trips.[15]

Presentation and demonstration

The presentation and demonstration provides the opportunity for the salesperson to convince the customer that his or her company can supply the solution to the customer's problem. It should focus on **customer benefits** rather than **product features**. These can be linked using the following phrases:

- which means that
- which results in
- which enables you to.

For example, the machine salesperson might say that the machine possesses proven technology (product feature), *which means that* the reliability of the machine (customer benefit) is guaranteed. Evidence should then be supplied to support this sales argument. Perhaps scientific tests have proved the reliability of the machine (these should be shown to the customer), satisfied customers' testimonials could be produced or a visit to a satisfied customer arranged.

In business-to-business markets, some salespeople are guilty of presenting features and failing to communicate the benefit to the business customer. For example, in telecommunications it is not enough to say how fast the line speed is. The benefit derives from the impact that the extra speed has on the customer. It could be that faster speed means reduced call costs, reduced number of lines or increased customer satisfaction.[16]

The salesperson should continue asking questions during the presentation to ensure that the customer has understood what the salesperson has said and to check that what the salesperson has mentioned really is of importance to the customer. This can be achieved by asking, say, 'Is that the kind of thing you are looking for?'

Technological advances have greatly assisted the presentation. For example, laptops allow the use of online resources such as video material, and the ability to get a response from a sales office during a presentation.[17] Access to company websites permits the carrying of masses of product information, including sound and animation.

Demonstrations allow the customer to see the product in operation. As such, some of the claims made for the product by the salesperson can be verified. Demonstrations allow the customer to be involved in the selling process through participation. They can, therefore, be instrumental in reducing the *perceived risk* of a purchase and moving the customer towards purchase.

Information technology can allow multimedia demonstrations of industrial products in the buyer's office. No longer is it always necessary for buyers to visit the supplier's site or to provide facilities to act as 'video show rooms' for salespeople wishing to demonstrate their product using video projectors.[18]

Dealing with objections

It is unusual for salespeople to close a sale without the need to overcome objections. Objections are any concerns or questions raised by the buyer.[19] While some objections are an expression of confusion, doubt or disagreement with the statements or information presented by the salesperson, objections should not always be viewed negatively since they highlight the issues that are important to the buyer.

The secret of *dealing with objections* is to handle both the substantive and emotional aspects. The substantive part is to do with the objection itself. If the customer objects to the product's price, the salesperson needs to use convincing arguments to show that the price is not too high. But it is a fact of human personality that the argument that is supported by the greater weight of evidence does not always win, since people resent being proved wrong. Therefore, salespeople need to recognize the emotional aspects of objection handling. Under no circumstances should the buyer lose face or be antagonized during this process. Two ways of minimizing this risk are to listen to the objection without interruption, and to employ the agree-and-counter technique.

The Internet can aid the creation of convincing answers to objections. The salesperson can guide buyers to the firm's website, where frequently answered questions and testimonials may be found. Potential customers might also be directed to favourable online reviews at independent websites. This improved dialogue between sellers and buyers can improve the chances of a successful sale.[20]

Listen and do not interrupt

Experienced salespeople know that the impression given to buyers by salespeople who interrupt buyers when they are raising an objection is that the salesperson believes that:

- the objection is obviously wrong
- the objection is trivial
- it is not worth the salesperson's time to let the buyer finish.

Interruption denies buyers the kind of respect they are entitled to receive and may lead to a misunderstanding of the real substance behind the objection.

The correct approach is to listen carefully, attentively and respectfully. The buyer will appreciate the fact that the salesperson is taking the problem seriously, and the salesperson will gain through having a clear and full understanding of what the problem really is.

Agree and counter

The salesperson agrees with the buyer's viewpoint before putting forward an alternative point of view. The objective is to create a climate of agreement rather than conflict, and shows that the salesperson respects the buyer's opinion, thus avoiding loss of face. For example:

Buyer: The problem with your bulldozer is that it costs more than the competition.
Salesperson: You are right, the initial cost is a little higher, but I should like to show you how the full lifetime costs of the bulldozer are much lower than the competition.

Closing the sale

Inexperienced salespeople sometimes think that an effective presentation followed by convincing objection handling should mean that the buyer will ask for the product without the seller needing to close the sale. This does occasionally happen, but more often it is necessary for the salesperson to take the initiative. This is because many buyers still have doubts in their mind that may cause them to wish to delay the decision to purchase.

If the customer puts off buying, the decision may be made when a competitor's salesperson is present, resulting in a lost sale.

Buying signals

The key to closing a sale is to look for **buying signals**. These are statements by buyers that indicate they are interested in buying. For example:

- 'That looks fine.'
- 'I like that one.'
- 'When could the product be delivered?'
- 'I think that product meets my requirements.'

These all indicate a very positive intention to buy without actually asking for the order. They provide excellent opportunities for the salesperson to ask the buyer to make a decision without appearing pushy.

Closing techniques

A variety of closing techniques can be used.

- *Simply ask for the order*: a direct question, such as 'Would you like that one?', may be all that is needed.

- *Summarize and then ask for the order*: with this approach, the salesperson reminds the buyer of the main points of the sales discussion in a manner which implies that the time for decision-making has arrived and that buying is the natural next step: 'Well, Ms Jones, we have agreed that the ZX4 model best meets your requirements of low noise and high productivity at an economical price. Would you like to place an order for this machine?'
- *Concession close*: by keeping a concession back to use in the close, a salesperson may convince an indecisive buyer to place an order: 'I am in a position to offer an extra 10 per cent discount on price if you are willing to place an order now.'
- *Action agreement*: in some situations it is inappropriate to try to close the sale. To do so would annoy the buyer because the sale is not in the hands of one person but a decision-making unit. Many organizational purchasing decisions are of this kind, and the decision may be made in committee without any salesperson being present. Alternatively, the salesperson may be talking to a specifier (such as a doctor or architect) who does not buy directly. In such circumstances, the close may be substituted by an action agreement: instead of closing the sale the salesperson attempts to achieve an action agreement with the customer. For example, in the selling of prescription drugs, either the salesperson or the doctor agrees to do something before the next meeting. The salesperson might agree to bring details of a new drug or attempt to get agreement from the doctor to read a leaflet on a drug before the next meeting. This technique has the effect of maintaining the relationship between the parties and can be used as the starting point of the discussion when they next meet.

The follow-up

Once the order is placed there could be a temptation for the salesperson to move on to other customers, neglecting the follow-up visit. However, this can be a great mistake since most companies rely on repeat business. If problems arise, customers have every right to believe that the salesperson was interested only in the order and not their complete satisfaction. By checking that there are no problems with delivery, installation, product use and training (where applicable), the follow-up can show that the salesperson really cares about the customer.

The follow-up can also be used to provide reassurance that the purchase was the right thing to do. As we discussed when analysing consumer behaviour, people often feel tense after deciding to buy an expensive product. Doubts can materialize about the wisdom of spending so much money, or whether the product best meets their needs. This anxiety, known as *cognitive dissonance*, can be minimized by the salesperson reassuring the customer about the purchase during the follow-up phase.

Websites can be helpful following the order, reminding buyers about post-purchase support resources, and salespeople can maintain an open dialogue with buyers through online user newsletters. Companies such as Dell and Xerox allow customers to log in to a secure buyer website to track the status of their orders, order products online or pay invoices.[21]

Salespeople operating in overseas markets need to be aware of the cultural nuances that shape business relationships. For example, in the West a deadline is acceptable, whereas in many Middle Eastern cultures, it would be taken as an insult. In China, salespeople need to acknowledge the importance of personalized and close business relationships, known as *guanxi*. *Guanxi* is a set of personal relationships/connections on which a person can draw to secure resources or advantage when doing business. *Guanxi* can lead to preferential treatment in the form of easy access to limited resources, increased accessibility to information and preferential credit terms. For foreigners, this means having as part of their *guanxi* network an influential person in an organization or government position. Another key issue in Chinese culture is the avoidance of 'loss of face'. Visiting salespeople should avoid creating a situation where a Chinese person might 'lose face' by finding themselves in an embarrassing situation (e.g. by displaying lack of knowledge or understanding).

In the Middle East selling may involve presentations to kings and high-ranking government officials, as Marketing in Action 16.1 explains.

Marketing in Action 16.1 Cisco's Brave New World

Cisco Systems, the networking giant, sees a major part of its future growth coming from massive construction projects in the Middle East. One example is the creation of King Abdullah Economic City (KAEC) in Saudi Arabia. By 2020 the Saudis expect 2 million people to be living in a future metropolis supported by some of the most advanced technology money can buy. All told, King Abdullah plans to build four brand new cities and upgrade the country's infrastructure at a cost of $600 billion over the coming years.

To tap in to this vast potential, Cisco hired a well-connected local person to head the business in the country. He, in turn, hired salespeople and engineers, and got Cisco involved in major government projects. For the KAEC project, senior Cisco executives played host to the King for a demonstration of Cisco technology that allowed a person elsewhere to appear on stage as a holographic image. They realize, though, that Cisco is not just selling technology (a product feature). The real benefit is that it can help countries such as Saudi Arabia to modernize their economies and become leaders in the digital age. The company argues that, by investing in the technology infrastructure Cisco sells, these governments can better educate their people, improve healthcare and boost national productivity.

To achieve this, Cisco provides consulting services to help government officials work out how best to use the Internet, and pays for training centres to produce the technicians to implement such plans. Cisco is helping the leaders of countries like Saudi Arabia imagine the future, to bring about 'country transformations' and brainstorm big ideas. One example was the call to Cisco to help with a new broadband network for Sudair City, but a Cisco executive saw the potential of the city as a hub for vast computer data centres, based on its cheap electricity rates. The electricity bill is often the biggest expense in running such centres, which are increasingly important to Internet companies such as Google and Amazon. The idea was well received and helped Cisco secure a $280 million contact to create the underlying fibre-optic network for Sudair City.

Based on: Burrows (2008)[22]

Many salespeople make the mistake of using 'self-reference' criteria when selling abroad. They assume that the values and behavioural norms that apply in their own country are equally applicable abroad. To avoid this failing, they need training in the special skills required to sell to people of different cultures.

Sales Management

In many respects, the functions of the sales manager are similar to those of other managers. Sales managers, like their production, marketing and finance counterparts, need to recruit, train, motivate and evaluate their staff. However, there are several peculiarities of the job that make effective sales management difficult and the job considerably demanding.

Problems of sales management

Geographic separation

The geographic separation between sales managers and their field salesforce creates problems of motivation, communication and control.

Repeated rejections

Salespeople may suffer repeated rejections when trying to close sales. This may cause attrition of their enthusiasm, attitudes and skills. A major role for sales managers is to provide support and renew motivation in such adverse circumstances.

The salesperson's personality vs. the realities of the job

Most people who go into sales are outgoing and gregarious. These are desirable characteristics for people who are selling to customers. However, the reality of the job is that, typically, only 30 per cent of a salesperson's time is spent face to face with customers, with travelling (50 per cent) and administration (20 per cent) contributing the rest.[23] This means

FIGURE 16.3   Marketing strategy and the management of the salesforce

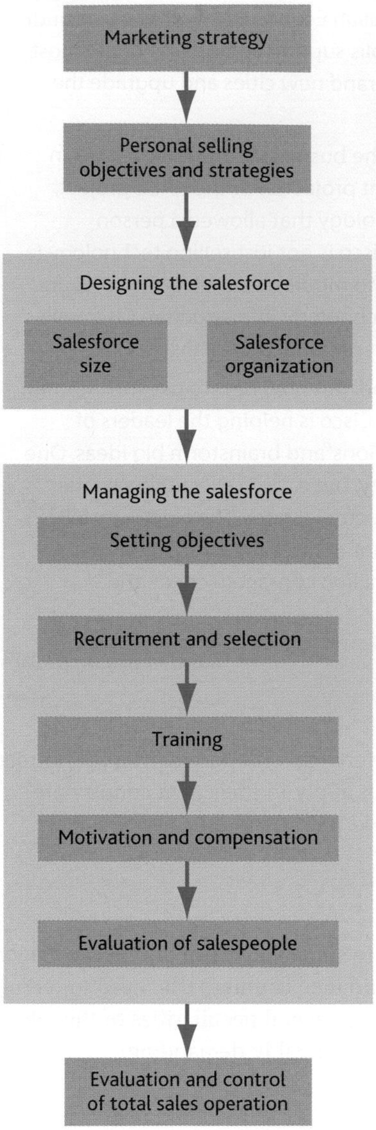

that over half of the salesperson's time is spent alone, which can cause frustration in people who enjoy the company of others.

Oversimplification of the task

Some sales managers cope with the difficulties of management by oversimplifying the task. They take the attitude that they are interested only in results. It is their job to reward those who meet sales targets and severely punish those who fail. Such an attitude ignores the contribution that sales management can make to the successful achievement of objectives. Figure 16.3 shows the functions of a sales manager and the relationship between marketing strategy and the personal selling function.

Marketing strategy

As with all parts of the marketing mix, the personal selling function is not a stand-alone element, but one that must be considered in the light of overall marketing strategy. At the product level, two major marketing considerations are choice of target market and the creation of a differential advantage. Both of these decisions affect personal selling.

Target market choice

The definition of the target market has clear implications for sales management because of its relationship to **target accounts**. Once the target market has been defined (e.g. organizations in a particular industry over a certain size), sales management can translate that specification into individual accounts to target. Salesforce resources can, therefore, be deployed to maximum effect.

Differential advantage

The creation of a differential advantage is the starting point of successful marketing strategy, but this needs to be communicated to the salesforce and embedded in a sales plan which ensures that the salesforce is able to articulate it convincingly to customers.

Two common dangers

First, the salesforce undermines the differential advantage by repeatedly giving in to customer demands for price concessions. Second, the features that underlie the differential advantage are communicated but the customer benefits are neglected. **Customer benefits** need to be communicated in terms that are meaningful to customers. This means, for example, that advantages such as higher productivity may require translation into cash savings or higher revenue for financially minded customers.

Four strategic objectives

Marketing strategy also affects the personal selling function through strategic objectives. Each objective—build, hold, harvest and divest—has implications for *sales objectives* and strategy; these are outlined in Table 16.1. Linking business or product area strategic objectives with functional area strategies is essential for the efficient allocation of resources, and effective implementation in the marketplace.[24]

Personal selling objectives and strategies

As we have seen, selling objectives and strategies are derived from marketing strategy decisions, and should be consistent with other elements of the marketing mix. Indeed, marketing strategy will determine if there is a need for a salesforce at all, or whether the

TABLE 16.1 Marketing strategy and sales management

Strategic marketing objective	Sales objective	Sales strategy
Build	Build sales volume Increase distribution Provide high service levels	High call rates on existing accounts High focus during call Call on new accounts (prospecting)
Hold	Maintain sales volume Maintain distribution Maintain service levels	Continue present call rates on current accounts Medium focus during call Call on new outlets when they appear
Harvest	Reduce selling costs Target profitable accounts Reduce service costs and inventories	Call only on profitable accounts Consider telemarketing or dropping the rest No prospecting
Divest	Clear inventory quickly	Quantity discounts to targeted accounts

Source: adapted from Strahle, W. and R. L. Spiro (1986) Linking Market Share Strategies to Salesforce Objectives, Activities and Compensation Policies, *Journal of Personal Selling & Sales Management*, August, 11–18.

selling role can be accomplished better by using some other medium, such as direct mail. Objectives define what the selling function is expected to achieve. Objectives are typically defined in terms of:

- sales volume (e.g. 5 per cent growth in sales volume)
- market share (e.g. 1 per cent increase in market share)
- profitability (e.g. maintenance of gross profit margin)
- service levels (e.g. 20 per cent increase in number of customers regarding salesperson assistance as 'good or better' in annual customer survey)
- salesforce costs (e.g. 5 per cent reduction in expenses).

Salesforce strategy defines how those objectives will be achieved. The following may be considered:

- call rates
- percentage of calls on existing vs potential accounts
- discount policy (the extent to which reductions from list prices allowed)
- percentage of resources
  - targeted at new vs existing products
  - targeted at selling vs providing after-sales service
  - targeted at field selling vs telemarketing
  - targeted at different types of customers (e.g. high vs low potential)
- improving customer and market feedback from the salesforce
- improving customer relationships.

Once sales managers have a clear idea of what they hope to achieve, and how best to set about accomplishing these objectives, they can make sensible decisions regarding salesforce design.

Designing the sales force

Two critical design decisions are those of determining salesforce size and salesforce organization.

Salesforce size

The most practical method for deciding the number of salespeople is called the *workload approach*. It is based on the calculation of the total annual calls required per year divided by the average calls per year that can be expected from one salesperson.[25] The procedure follows seven steps, as outlined below.

1 Customers are grouped into categories according to the value of goods bought, their potential for the future, and the need for prospecting.

2 The call frequency (number of calls per year to an account) is assessed for each category of customer.

3 The total required workload per year is calculated by multiplying the call frequency by the number of customers in each category and then summing for all categories.

4 The average number of calls that can be expected per salesperson per week is estimated.

5 The number of working weeks per year is calculated.

6 The average number of calls a salesperson can make per year is calculated by multiplying (4) and (5).

7 The number of salespeople required is determined by dividing the total annual calls required by the average number of calls one salesperson can make per year.

Salesforce organization

There are three basic forms of *salesforce organization*: geographic, product and customer-based structures. The strengths and weakness of each are as follows.

Geographic: the sales area is broken down into territories based on workload and potential, and a salesperson is assigned to each one to sell all of the product range. This provides a simple, unambiguous, definition of each salesperson's sales territory, and proximity to customers encourages the development of personal relationships. It is also a more cost-efficient method of organization than product- or customer-based systems. However, when products are technically different and sell in a number of diverse markets, it may be unreasonable to expect a salesperson to be knowledgeable about all products and their applications. Under such circumstances a company is likely to move to a product- or customer-based structure.

Product: product specialization is effective where a company has a diverse product range selling to different customers (or at least different people within a given organization). However, if the products sell essentially to the same customers, problems of route duplication (and, consequently, higher travel costs) and multiple calls on the same customer can arise. When applicable, product specialization allows each salesperson to be well informed about a product line, its applications and customer benefits. Hewlett-Packard uses a product-based system because of its wide product range. The salespeople are assigned to one of its three divisions: PCs, laptops and handheld devices; printers and printing; or IT solutions for large enterprises.

Customer-based: the problem of the same customer being served by product divisions of the same supplier, the complexity of buyer behaviour that requires input not only from the sales function but from other functional groups (such as engineering, finance, logistics and marketing), centralization of purchasing, and the immense value of some customers, have led many suppliers to rethink how they organize their salesforces. Companies are increasingly organizing around customers and shifting resources from product or regional divisions to customer-focused business units.[26] Salesforces can be organized along market segment, account size, or new versus existing accounts lines. First, computer firms have traditionally organized their salesforce on the basis of industry served (e.g. banking, retailing, manufacturing) in recognition of their varying needs, problems and potential applications. Specialization by these *market segments* allows salespeople to gain in-depth knowledge of customers and to be able to monitor trends in the industry that may affect demand for their products. In some industries, the applications knowledge of market-based salespeople has led them to be known as *fraternity brothers* by their customers.[27] Second, an increasing trend in many industries is towards **key account management**, which reflects the increasing concentration of buying power into fewer but larger customers. These are serviced by a key account salesforce comprising senior salespeople who develop close personal

TABLE 16.2 Distinctions between transactional selling and key account management

	Transactional selling	Key account management
Overall objective	Sales	Preferred supplier status
Sales skills	Asking questions Handling objections Closing	Building trust Negotiation Providing excellent service
Nature of relationship	Short, intermittent	Long, more intensive interaction
Salesperson goal	Closed sale	Relationship management
Nature of salesforce	One or two salespeople per customer	Many sales people, often involving multifunctional teams

relationships with customers, can handle sophisticated sales arguments and are skilled in the art of negotiation. Table 16.2 illustrates some important distinctions between traditional (transactional selling) and key account management.

A number of advantages are claimed for a key account structure.

1 *Close working relationships with the customer*: the salesperson knows who makes what decisions and who influences the various players involved in the decision. Technical specialists from the selling organization can call on technical people (e.g. engineers) in the buying organization, and salespeople can call on administrators, buyers and financial people armed with the commercial arguments for buying.

2 *Improved communication and coordination*: the customer knows that a dedicated salesperson or sales team exists so that it is clear who to contact when a problem arises.

3 *Better follow-up on sales and service*: the extra resources devoted to the key account mean that there is more time to follow up and provide service after a major sale has been made.

4 *More in-depth penetration of the DMU*: there is more time to cultivate relationships within the key account. Salespeople can *pull* the buying decision through the organization from the users, deciders and influencers to the buyer, rather than the more difficult task of pushing it through the buyer into the organization, as is done with more traditional sales approaches.

5 *Higher sales*: most companies that have adopted key account selling claim that sales have risen as a result and research has shown that supplier performance normally improves.[28]

6 *The provision of an opportunity for advancement for career salespeople*: a tiered salesforce system with key (or national) account selling at the top provides promotional opportunities for salespeople who wish to advance within the salesforce rather than enter a traditional sales-management position.

7 *Lower costs*: through joint agreement of optimum production and delivery schedules, and demand forecasting.

8 *Cooperation on research and development*: for new products and joint promotions (for example, within the fast-moving consumer goods/retail sector).

Managing the salesforce

Besides deciding personal selling objectives and strategies, and designing the salesforce, the company has to manage the salesforce. This requires setting specific salesperson objectives, recruitment and selection, training, motivation and compensation, and evaluation of salespeople. These activities have been shown to improve salesperson performance, indicating the key role sales managers play as facilitators helping salespeople to perform better.[29]

Setting objectives

In order to achieve aggregate sales objectives, individual salespeople need to have their own sales targets to achieve. Usually, targets are set in sales terms (sales quotas) but, increasingly, profit targets are being used, reflecting the need to guard against sales being bought cheaply by excessive discounting. To gain commitment to targets, consultation with individual salespeople is recommended but in the final analysis it is the sales manager's responsibility to set targets. Payment may be linked to their achievement.

Sales management may also wish to set input objectives such as the proportion of time spent developing new accounts, and the time spent introducing new products. They may also specify the number of calls expected per day, and the precise customers who should be called upon.

Recruitment and selection

The importance of recruiting high-calibre salespeople cannot be overestimated. A study into salesforce practice asked sales managers the following question: 'If you were to put your most successful salesperson into the territory of one of your average salespeople, and made no other changes, what increase in sales would you expect after, say, two years?'[30] The most commonly stated increase was 16–20 per cent, and one-fifth of all sales managers said they would expect an increase of over 30 per cent. Clearly the quality of salespeople that sales managers recruit has a substantial effect on performance.

The recruitment and selection process follows five stages:

1   preparation of the job description and personnel specification
2   identification of sources of recruitment and methods of communication
3   design of the application form and preparation of a shortlist
4   the interview
5   use of supplementary selection aids.

Training

Many sales managers believe that their salespeople can best train themselves by doing the job. This approach ignores the benefits of a training programme that provides a frame of reference in which learning can take place. Its benefits are immense, ranging from enhanced skill levels to improved motivation and greater confidence in the ability to perform well at selling, a factor that has been shown to be related to improved sales performance.[31] Indeed, the importance of training is supported by research, which has found a positive link between training and sales performance.[32] Training should include not only product knowledge but also skills development. Success at selling comes when the skills are performed automatically, without consciously thinking about them, just as a tennis player or footballer succeeds.

A training programme should include knowledge about the company (its objectives, strategies and organization), its products (features and benefits), its competitors and their products, selling procedures and techniques, work organization (including report preparation), and relationship management. Salespeople need to be trained in the management of long-term customer relationships as well as context-specific selling skills.[33] For example, the IBM consultative sales training programme emphasizes working with clients as consultants to build close relationships and to work jointly to solve problems. The core components of the programme involve people and communication skills.[34]

Lectures, films, role-playing and case studies can be used in a classroom situation to give knowledge and understanding and to develop competences. These should be followed up with in-the-field training, where skills can be practised face to face with customers. Sales managers and trainers should provide feedback to encourage on-the-job learning. In particular the sales manager needs to:

- analyse each salesperson's performance
- identify strengths and weaknesses
- communicate strengths
- gain agreement that a weakness exists
- train the salesperson in how to overcome the weakness
- monitor progress.

The heavy time constraints placed on modern salespeople mean that taking days off work to attend a traditional sales training course may not be feasible. Companies are rethinking their training models to include Web-based training and teleconferencing. Using technology to package information is an inexpensive and effective alternative to traditional programmes. This approach means that training can take place over long distances and at a time that fits in with salespeople's work patterns.

Sales managers themselves need training in the considerable range of skills that they require, including analytical, teaching, motivational and communicational skills, and the ability to organize and plan. Some of the skills are not essential to be able to sell (e.g. teaching and motivating others), hence the adage that the best salespeople do not always make the best sales managers.

Motivation and compensation

Effective motivation is based on a deep understanding of salespeople as individuals, their personalities and value systems. In one sense, sales managers do not motivate salespeople—they provide the enabling conditions in which salespeople motivate themselves. Motivation can be understood through the relationship between needs, drives and goals. Luthans stated that, 'the basic process involves needs (deprivations) which set drives in motion (deprivations with direction) to accomplish goals (anything which alleviates a need and reduces a drive)'.[35] For example, the need for more money may result in a drive to work harder in order to receive increased pay. Improving motivation is important to sales success; research has shown that high levels of motivation lead to:[36]

- increased creativity
- working smarter and a more adaptive selling approach
- working harder
- increased use of win/win negotiation tactics
- higher self-esteem
- a more relaxed attitude and a less negative emotional tone
- enhancement of relationships.

Motivation has been the subject of much research over many years. Maslow, Herzberg, Vroom, Adams and Likert, among others, have produced theories that have implications for the motivation of salespeople.[37] Some of their important findings are summarized in the list below.

- Once a need is satisfied it no longer motivates.
- Different people have different needs and values.
- Increasing the level of responsibility/job enrichment, giving recognition of achievement and providing monetary incentives work to increase motivation for some people.
- People tend to be motivated if they believe that effort will bring results, results will be rewarded and the rewards are valued.
- Elimination of disincentives (such as injustices or unfair treatment) raises motivational levels.
- There is a relationship between the performance goals of sales managers and those of the salespeople they lead.

The implication of these findings is that sales managers should:

- get to know what each salesperson values and what each one is striving for (unrealized needs)
- be willing to increase the responsibility given to salespeople in mundane jobs
- realize that training can improve motivation as well as capabilities by strengthening the link between effort and performance
- provide targets that are believed to be attainable yet provide a challenge to salespeople
- link rewards to the performance they want improved
- recognize that rewards can be both financial and non-financial (e.g. praise).

For many companies their market is the world, which means that they are faced with motivating international salesforces. Marketing in Action 16.2 discusses some of the problems involved and their solutions.

Marketing in Action 16.2 Motivating an International Salesforce

Sales managers should not assume that a motivation and compensation system that works well in their home country will work in overseas markets: the values and expectations of their foreign-based salespeople need to be understood. For example, in Europe financial incentives are often used to motivate salespeople, but in Japan and the Middle East commission is rarely used. Instead, non-financial factors such as increased responsibility or greater job security are more common. An understanding of local customs is essential. In Japan, for example, salary increases are based on seniority. Political factors can also determine the level of fringe benefits provided for employees.

Care needs to be taken over salaries paid to an overseas salesforce when it consists of a mixture of expatriates and local salespeople. Because a salary increase often accompanies an expatriate's overseas move, they may be paid more than local recruits. If this becomes common knowledge, the motivation of locally recruited salespeople may decline.

A common complaint among international salespeople is that their head office does not understand them. They often feel alone or deserted. Their motivation can be boosted through the setting of realistic sales targets, giving them full support and improving communication.

Based on: Cundif and Hilger (1988);[38] Hill et al. (1991);[39] Ghauri and Cateora (2010)[40]

Evaluation of salespeople

Salesforce evaluation provides the information necessary to check if targets are being achieved, and provides the raw information to guide training and motivation. By identifying the strengths and weaknesses of individual salespeople, training can be focused on the areas in need of development, and incentives can be aimed at weak spots such as poor prospecting performance.

Often performance will be compared to standards of performance such as sales or profit quotas, although other comparisons such as salesperson-to-salesperson or current-to-past sales are also used. Two types of performance measures are used, based on quantitative and qualitative criteria.

Quantitative measures of performance: salespeople can be assessed on input, output and hybrid criteria. Output criteria include:

- sales revenue
- profits generated
- gross profit margin
- sales per active account
- number of new accounts opened.

Input criteria include:

- number of calls
- calls per active account
- calls on new accounts (prospects)
- number of prospects visited.

Hybrid criteria are formed by combining output and input criteria, for example:

- sales revenue per call
- profit per call
- prospecting success ratio = number of new accounts opened ÷ number of prospects visited.

These quantitative measures can be compared against target figures to identify strengths and weaknesses. Many of the measures are diagnostic, pointing to reasons why a target is not being reached. For example, a poor call rate might be a cause of low sales achievement. Measuring call rate is important as call frequency has been found to have a positive effect on sales volume and customer satisfaction. Some results will merit further investigation. For example, a low prospecting success ratio should prompt an examination of why new accounts are not being opened despite the high number of prospects visited. A survey of evaluation metrics has shown that there is an increasing tendency to use profit-orientated criteria.

Qualitative measures of performance: whereas quantitative criteria will be measured with hard figures, qualitative measures rely on soft data. They are intrinsically more subjective and include assessment of:

- sales skills, e.g. questioning, making presentations
- customer relationships, e.g. how much confidence do customers have in the salesperson, and whether rapport is good
- product knowledge, e.g. how well informed is the salesperson regarding company and competitor products
- self-management, e.g. how well are calls prepared, routes organized
- cooperation and attitudes, e.g. to what extent does the salesperson show initiative, follow instructions?

An increasing number of companies are measuring their salespeople on the basis of the achievement of customer satisfaction. As Richard Harrison, a senior sales manager at IBM states, 'Our sales team is compensated based on how quickly and how efficiently they achieve customer satisfaction.'[41]

The use of quantitative and qualitative measures is interrelated. For example, a poor sales per call ratio will mean a close qualitative assessment of sales skills, customer relationships and product knowledge.

A final form of qualitative assessment does not focus on the salesperson directly but the likelihood of *winning or losing an order*. Particularly for major sales, a sales manager needs to be able to assess the chances of an order being concluded successfully in time to rectify the situation if things seem to be going astray. Unfortunately, asking salespeople directly will rarely result in an accurate answer. This is not because they are trying to deceive but because they may be deluding themselves. The answer is to ask a series of who, when, where, why and how questions to probe deeper into the situation. It also means working out acceptable and unacceptable responses. Table 16.3 provides an illustration of how such questions could be employed in connection with a major computer sale.

TABLE 16.3   Winning and losing major orders

Question	Poor (losing answer)	Good (winning answer)
Who will authorize the purchase?	The director of MIS	The director of MIS, but it requires an executive director's authorization, and we've talked it over with this person
When will they buy?	Right away. They love the new model	Before the peak processing load at the year end
Where will they be when the decision is made: in the office alone, in their boss's office, in a meeting?	What difference does that make? I think they have already decided	At a board meeting. But don't worry, the in-supplier has no one on its board and we have two good customers on it
Why will they buy from us? Why not their usual supplier?	They and I go way back. They love our new model	The next upgrade from the in-supplier is a big price increase, and ours fits right between its models. They are quite unhappy with the in-supplier about that
How will the purchase be funded?	They've lots of money, haven't they?	The payback period on reduced costs will be about 14 months and we've a leasing company willing to take part of the deal

The losing answers are thin and unconvincing. The salesperson may be convinced that the sale will be achieved but the answers show that this is unlikely. The winning answers are much more assured and credible. The sales manager can be confident that there is no need to take action.

However, with the losing answer the sales manager will need to act and the response will depend on how important the sale and the salesperson are to the company. If they both have high potential, the sales manager should work with the salesperson. He or she should be counselled so that they know why they are being helped and what they will learn from the experience. The aim is to conclude the sale and convince the salesperson that their personal development will be enhanced by the experience.

If the salesperson has high potential but not the sale, only a counselling session is needed. Care should be taken not to offend the salesperson's ego. When only the sale has high potential, the alternatives are not so pleasant. Perhaps the salesperson could be moved to a more suitable post. When neither the salesperson nor the sale has potential, the only question to ask is whether the salesperson is redeployed before or after the sale is lost.

Evaluation and control of the total sales operation

Evaluation of the total personal selling function is necessary to assess its overall contribution to marketing strategy. The results of this assessment may lead to more cost-efficient means of servicing accounts being introduced (e.g. direct mail or telemarketing), the realization that the selling function is under-resourced, or the conclusion that the traditional form of sales organization is in need of reform. One company that suspected its salesforce had become complacent moved every salesperson to a different territory. Despite having to forge new customer relationships, sales increased by a quarter in the following year.

Evaluation of the personal selling function should also include assessing the quality of its relationship with marketing and other organizational units. Salespeople that manage the external relationship with distributors (e.g. retailers) must collaborate internally with their colleagues in marketing to agree joint business objectives and to develop marketing programmes (for example, new products and promotions) that meet the needs of distributors, as well as consumers, so that they are readily adopted by them. This means that close collaboration and good working relations are essential.[42]

Personal selling enables individuals to interact and form bonds which can develop into long-term relationships that are beneficial for all parties concerned. Another element of the promotional mix which comes under the banner of direct communications is trade fairs and exhibitions, which are a platform for personal selling as well as other communication tools. Trade fairs and exhibitions are the topic in the next section.

Exhibitions and Trade Shows

Trade shows and exhibitions offer marketing managers a unique opportunity to engage with buyers, sellers and the competitors under one roof. These types of events are used in both industrial and consumer markets but are considered to be highly effective in the industrial buying process, second only to personal selling and ahead of direct mail and print advertising.[43] Indeed, exhibitions have been shown to increase the effectiveness of personal selling activities directly after the event.[44] A key role of trade fairs and exhibitions is to enable manufacturers, buyers, distributors, agents, present and future customers and media representatives to meet at a live event in a specific location.[45]

The remainder of this section will focus on business-to-business trade shows and exhibitions as this element of the promotional mix is most frequently used in this context.

Why choose exhibitions and trade fairs as part of the communication mix?

Good relationships are essential in industrial trade situations and these types of events have been found to be very useful for developing strong buyer–seller relationships.[46] Other

⬆ EXHIBIT 16.1 Who's Next 'ready to wear' international fashion exhibition.

potential benefits are: enhancing corporate identity (an issue already discussed in more detail in Chapter 15 under public relations and sponsorship); gathering market intelligence[47] about competitors and industry trends;[48] and exchanging information and news about products, innovations, promotions and new marketing strategies. Exhibitions and trade shows are an ideal arena to *show off* and demonstrate a company's new products, but this can be costly. The organizers of the Spielwarenmesse International toy fair in Nürnberg, Germany invest heavily to ensure that at the end of January each year over 2800 exhibitors and 76,000 trade visitors from 120 nations[49] visit 12 exhibition halls (each dedicated to a different type of toy-related product such as dolls, hobbies, action toys, games, educational) at the fair to see over a million different products. Each company exhibiting at the fair then has to put together their own event plan, set objectives and decide how to allocate the budget to get best value. Read Mini Case 16.1 to find out more about what is required when planning an event.

Trade fair and exhibition objectives

There are various objectives that this element of the promotional mix can achieve and in doing so contribute to an IMC strategy:
* reach an audience with a distinct interest in the market and the products on display
* create awareness and develop relationships with new prospects
* strengthen existing customer relationships
* provide product demonstrations
* determine and stimulate needs of customers
* gather competitive intelligence
* introduce a new product
* recruit dealers or distributors
* maintain/improve company image
* deal with service and other customer problems
* generate a mailing list
* make a sale.

Research suggests that it is important to consider whether objectives are selling or non-selling oriented and whether they are aimed at new or existing customers.[50] Despite the many possible objectives it has been found that the major objectives are:
* to generate leads/enquiries
* to introduce a new product or service
* because competitors are exhibiting
* to recruit dealers or distributors.

Planning for an exhibition

Success at an exhibition involves considerable pre-event planning. Clear objectives should be set, selection criteria for evaluating exhibition attendance determined, and design and promotional strategies decided. Pre-show promotions to attract visitors to the stand include direct mail, telephoning, a personal sales call before the event and an advertisement in the trade or technical press.

Mini Case 16.1 Stella McCartney at London Fashion Week

The clothing industry displays its goods at exhibitions and trade shows but probably the most famous are the week-long series of events held in leading fashion capitals around the world of which New York, Paris, Milan and London are the most outstanding. These events are a showcase for designers to highlight new trends and present their new ranges. Buyers visit runway shows and media representatives are on hand to report on what's *in* and what's *out* for next season. For the designers, one of the aims for such an event is to be outstanding and maximize press coverage. Stella McCartney 'blew the audience away during her London Fashion Week show with a mixture of illusions, magic and model acrobatics as she presented the Autumn/Winter 2012 season'. Her aim was to 'do something bold' to capture attention and she used her passion for magic to create a theme for the event. The guest list included celebrities like Kate Moss, Rihanna and Yasmin Le Bon, and everything was carefully choreographed to ensure the audience would be spellbound. A meal was followed by an acrobatic performance of dance and music. Instead of the usual runway-style presentation, the models wearing McCartney's collection were joined by male dancers from the Royal Ballet, disguised as waiters and even Stella joined in, performing a magic trick. The night, which started calmly, ended with a rock 'n' roll style finale, dancing on tables and throwing chairs in a church in London's Mayfair.

The 140 guests at the Stella McCartney event were treated to a fashion spectacular but making sure everything went smoothly on the day requires a great deal of planning.

For the marketing manager responsible for such an event, there are a number of key considerations:
- whether to outsource management of the event, and benefit by freeing up the time of in-house staff to focus on the business objectives for the event or use the in-house team and have more control over what is happening and reduce the overall costs
- how to find suitable sponsors
- identifying and selecting a suitable venue
- planning the promotional mix, setting prices
- deciding how to get the best out of the budget
- delivering value.

Imagine you were responsible for organising a trade show or an exhibition.

Questions:

1 Describe the event and the industry it is targeting.
2 Explain the methods you will use to evaluate the event.

Based on: Cavatore (2012);[51] Cartner-Morley (2012);[52] Hilpern (2011)[53]

A high degree of professionalism is required by the staff who attend the exhibition stand. The characteristics of a good exhibitor have been found to be:[54]
- exhibiting a wider range of products, particularly large items that cannot be demonstrated on a sales call
- staff always in attendance at the stand—visitors should never hear that 'the person who covers that product is not here right now'
- well-informed staff
- informative literature available
- seating area or office provided on the stand
- refreshments provided.

Evaluating an exhibition

Post-show evaluation will examine performance against objectives. This is a learning exercise that will help to judge whether the objectives were realistic, how valuable the exhibition appears to have been and how well the company was represented.

Quantitative measures include:

- the number of visitors to the stand
- the number of key influencers/decision-makers who visited the stand
- how many leads/enquiries were generated
- the cost per lead/enquiry
- the number and value of orders
- the cost per order
- the number of new distributorships opened/likely to be opened.

Other more subjective, qualitative criteria include:

- the worth of competitive intelligence
- interest generated in the new products
- the cultivation of new/existing relationships
- the value of customer query and complaint handling
- the promotion of brand values.

Sales and marketing may not always agree on the key evaluation criteria to use. For example, sales may judge the exhibition on the number of leads while marketing may prefer to judge the show on the longer-term issue of the promotion of brand values.[55]

Finally, since a major objective of many exhibitors is to stimulate leads and enquiries, mechanisms must be in place to ensure that these are followed up promptly. Furthermore, the leads generated at an exhibition can be used to build a marketing database for future direct mail campaigns. In the next section we examine direct marketing and customer relationship management.

Direct Marketing

Direct marketing is now a major component of the promotional mix and uses various media to precisely target consumers and request an immediate direct response. Originally, this communication method mainly involved direct mail and mail-order catalogues, but today's direct marketers use a wide range of media, including telemarketing, direct response advertising, the Internet and mobile devices. Direct marketing is no longer synonymous with 'junk mail', as it is a suite of communication techniques that are an integral part of the relationship marketing concept, where companies attempt to establish ongoing direct and profitable relationships with customers. As with all marketing communications, direct marketing campaigns should be integrated both within themselves and with other communication tools such as advertising, publicity and personal selling. Uncoordinated communication leads to blurred brand images, low impact and customer confusion.

Direct marketing attempts to acquire and retain customers by contacting them without the use of an intermediary and is usually designed to stimulate an immediate response from the recipient. A key advantage of direct marketing is it is easier to measure than mass-communication tools to determine the effectiveness of campaigns.

A definition of direct marketing is:

> The distribution of products, information and promotional benefits to target consumers through interactive communication in a way that allows response to be measured.

Direct marketing campaigns are not necessarily short-term, response-driven activities. More and more companies are using direct marketing to develop ongoing direct relationships with customers. Some marketers believe that the cost of attracting a new customer is five times that of retaining existing customers. Direct marketing techniques can be used effectively as part of an IMC campaign and also create further opportunities for selling more products using cross-selling and up-selling, which encourage the purchase of a wider range of products and higher value products respectively. These particular tactics are discussed in Chapter 18.

Direct marketing covers a wide array of techniques, sometime referred to as *media*. Each offers a marketing manager a set of potential benefits and limitations, which need to be considered when planning to incorporate these techniques into an IMC campaign strategy.

Table 16.4 shows the main techniques/media used for direct marketing. The Internet and the Web are important as a platform for direct marketing campaigns. How these techniques are used online and in mobile environments is discussed in more detail in Chapter 18.

TABLE 16.4 Benefits and limitations of direct communications techniques

Techniques/media	Description	Benefits	Limitations
Direct mailing	Material sent through the postal service to the recipient's home or business address with the purpose of promoting a product and/or maintaining an ongoing relationship	– relatively low cost: e.g. in business-to-business marketing, it might cost £50 to visit potential customers, £5 to telephone them but less than £1 to send out a mailing – enables specific targeting of individuals and businesses	– poor quality mailing lists, which can quickly become outdated by people moving home, changing their names, through marriage and divorce – cost of building and maintaining database – organization of the actual mailing: e.g. addressing and filling the envelopes can be costly
Email-marketing	Material sent to the recipient's email address for the purpose of promoting a product and/or maintaining an ongoing relationship, linked directly to a company website to foster further engagement with the brand and also making purchases	– relatively low cost – enables specific targeting of individuals and businesses – global reach – facilitates inclusion of multi-media and interactive features[56] – highly flexible – permission emails can help build relationships	– poor quality mailing lists, email address changes – reaching the recipient as often treated as unsolicited junk mail
Telemarketing	Makes use of telecommunications and information technologies to conduct marketing and sales activities via telephone. Can be inbound telemarketing when a prospect contacts the company by telephone, or outbound when the company calls the prospect	– versatility: e.g. telemarketing can support direct marketing, follow up sales leads, establish customer contact validate customer information – cost-effective – accountable – relative low cost – less time-intensive than personal sales calls – technology can automate process and help manage campaigns	– intrusive and is often seen as an annoyance by customers – lacks visual impact and stimulation – cost per-contact more expensive than direct mail
Direct response advertising	Appears in the prime media, e.g. the Web, television, print media but differs from standard advertising as it is designed to elicit a direct response such as an order, enquiry or request for a visit. Often a freefone telephone number is included in the advertisement and a website address	– Highly measurable in terms of performance of a campaign: e.g. Macmillan Cancer Support ran a direct response campaign to drive more callers to avail themselves of its financial and emotional support services. It's 'Good Day, Bad Day' campaign significantly increased calls to its helplines[57]	– application to certain product types can be perceived as difficult – response rates can be low

TABLE 16.4 *(cont'd)*

Techniques/media	Description	Benefits	Limitations
Catalogue marketing	The sale of products through catalogues distributed to agents and customers, by mail, at stores or online	– convenient way of selecting products at home that allows discussion between family members – can offer flexible financing solutions for consumers: e.g. credit facilities – accessibility to remote rural locations and provides valuable services, which removes the need to travel long distances to shop in stores – potential cost savings: e.g. catalogues are expensive to produce but they are a lower cost option than operating a chain of highstreet stores – unlimited displays of product as catalogues do not have any physical space restrictions – distribution can be centralized, lowering costs	– cost of catalogue production – inflexible (print versions of catalogues require regular updating, particularly when selling fashion items. This issue has been circumvented to an extent by online catalogues) – costs associated with managing the flow of goods and return products

Direct Marketing Campaigns

Overall direct marketing is growing in popularity as a communication tool in both consumer and industrial markets. In the UK sales generated by direct marketing campaigns (using all techniques) are estimated to account for around 9 per cent of total UK consumer spend and approaching £60 billion business-to-business sales. However, there is wide variation in use of different DM techniques. Use of direct marketing in the USA has increased by nearly 6 per cent in recent years but Internet and Web-based campaigns account for a significant proportion of all DM campaigns. Use of specific techniques also varies: for example, analysis of the sales generated from direct mailing between 2008 to 2012 reveal that in China and India its use is increasing, whereas in Germany, France and Russia there has been a significant decline[58] and in the USA the amount of DM activity is only less than 20 per cent compared to France, UK, Brazil and Russia.

Direct marketing is increasingly used in communication campaigns. Several factors have influenced this expansion:

- *Market and media fragmentation* has meant the effectiveness of mass-marketing techniques (e.g. using television and other broadcast media) has declined, as the requirement to reach target segments with highly individualized needs has increased. Consequently, the importance of direct marketing media which can not only target specialized niche targets but also distribute highly personalized appeals has grown. Direct response advertising is more effective since market niches can be tightly targeted.
- *Technology advances* have led to the increasing sophistication of software, allowing the generation of personalized letters and telephone scripts, and enabling direct marketers to develop highly targeted and sophisticated campaigns. Databases and data warehouses hold detailed information on individuals and businesses and, once analysed, this enhances targeting. Customer relationship management software has enabled companies to manage one-to-one relationships with huge numbers of consumers. Automated

telephone systems make it possible to handle dozens of calls simultaneously, reducing the risk of losing potential customers. Furthermore, developments in technology in telephone, cable and satellite television and the Internet have triggered the rise in home-based electronic shopping.

- *Emerging analytical techniques* mean that by using geodemographic analysis, households can be classified into a neighbourhood type—for example, 'modern private housing, young families' or 'private flats, single people'. These, in turn, can be cross-referenced with product usage, media usage and lifestyle statements to create market segments that can be targeted by direct mail (see Chapter 8 for more detailed discussion).

Marketing database

The marketing database is central to direct marketing as activities depend on customer information. A marketing database is an electronic filing cabinet containing a list of customer data—e.g. names, addresses, telephone numbers, lifestyle and transactional data. Information such as the types of purchase, frequency of purchase, purchase value and responsiveness to promotional offers may be held. By using the marketing database companies can take an interactive approach towards developing highly targeted direct communication campaigns using individually addressable marketing media and channels (such as mail, telephone and the salesforce) to provide information to a target audience.

Some key characteristics of marketing databases are that, first, they allow direct communication with customers through a variety of media, including direct mail, telemarketing and direct response advertising. Second, it usually requires the customer to respond in a way that allows the company to take action (such as contact by telephone, sending out literature or arranging sales visits). Third, it must be possible to trace the response back to the original communication.[59] Sophisticated databases provide the capability of storing and analysing large quantities of data from diverse sources and presenting information in a convenient, accessible and useful format.[60] The creation of a database relies on the systematic collection and storage of information. Table 16.5 provides examples of sources and types of data.

TABLE 16.5 Sources and types of data

Data source	Examples of data type
Company records	Purchase behaviour, name, address, telephone number
Warranty and guarantee cards	Product types
Enquiries	Clarifications of data held: e.g. an account holder at HSBC bank might enquire about a new loan, at which point credit and personal finance data will be updated
Exchanging data with other companies	Loyalty cards like Nectar gather and share information between companies in the group (e.g. American Express, Sainsbury's, BP, Ford Hertz, Viking-Direct)
Salesforce records	Account details, customer leads, past sales data
Application forms	Personal or business data
Complaints	Reasons for returns, outcomes
Responses to direct marketing activities	Sales promotions, direct marketing: e.g. timing, frequency, purchase activity
Organized events	At corporate events/conferences, business cards are often collected
Website registrations	Personal data, email addresses
Emails	Requirements, requests, qualitative data

Businesses across the globe have benefited from the use and management of data, but as information technology has continued to expand the collection and distribution of data, companies also have to deal with the information overload. Too much information can be a bad thing, research suggests; in certain situations it reduces productivity and hampers creativity. To get the best out of data and information, marketing managers need to filter and focus it and use it improve specific marketing performance.[61] For example, the department store retailer Debenhams has been using direct mail to drive sales. They found, however, that while they had lots of data, they had only limited visibility into the behaviours and preferences of their customers, which meant that instead of direct targeted campaigns, their mailings were more a form of mass communication. To rectify the situation, Debenhams invested in new data-management software, which enabled the brand to centralize its communication into a single platform.[62]

Go to the website and identify the different situations in which American Express promises to 'make things happen'.
www.mcgraw-hill.co.uk/textbooks/jobber

Typical information stored on a database

⬆EXHIBIT 16.2   Ryman's stationers gather detailed information when opening business accounts.

Figure 16.4 shows typical information that is recorded on a database. This is described in more detail below.[63]

Customer and prospect information

This provides the basic data required to access customers and prospects (e.g. name, home and email addresses, telephone number) and contains their general behavioural characteristics (e.g. psychographic and behavioural data). For organizational markets, information on key decision-makers and influencers, and the choice criteria they use would also be stored.

Transactional information

Past transactions are a key indicator of likely future transactions. Transactional data must be sufficiently detailed to allow FRAC (frequency, recency, amount and category) information to be extracted for each customer. *Frequency* refers to how often a customer buys. Both the average frequency and the trend (is the customer tending to buy more or less frequently?) is of use to the direct marketer. *Recency* measures when the customer last bought. If customers

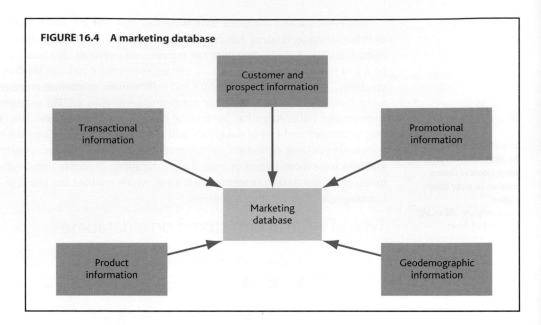

FIGURE 16.4 A marketing database

are waiting longer before they rebuy (i.e. recency is increasing) the reasons for this (e.g. less attractive offers or service problems) need to be explored. *Amount* measures how much a customer has bought and is usually recorded in value terms. Analysis of this data may reveal that 20 per cent of customers are accounting for 80 per cent of the value of transactions. Finally, *category* defines the type of product being bought. Cross-analysing category data with type of customer (e.g. geodemographics or lifestyle data) can reveal the customer profile most likely to buy a particular product. Also, promotions can be targeted at those individuals known to be interested in buying from a particular product category.

Promotional information

This covers information on what promotional campaigns have been run, who has responded to them and what the overall results were in terms of contacts, sales and profits. The database will contain information on which customers were targeted, and the media and contact strategy employed.

Product information

This information would include which products have been promoted, who responded, when and from where.

Geodemographic information

Information about the geographic areas of customers and prospects, and the social, lifestyle or business category they belong to would be stored. By including postcodes in the address of customers and employing the services of an agency that conducts geodemographic analysis (such as ACORN) a customer profile would be built up. Direct mail could then be targeted at people with similar geodemographic profiles.

The main application of marketing databases

- Developing targeted direct marketing campaigns: for example, a special offer on garden tools from a mail-order company could be targeted at those people who have purchased gardening products in the past. Another example would be a car dealer which, by holding a database of customers' names and addresses and dates of car purchase, could use direct mail to promote service offers and new model launches.

Mini Case 16.2 Using a Marketing Database in Retailing

Marketing databases offer great potential for planning and developing integrated marketing communications campaigns. Suppose a retailer wanted to increase sales and profits using a database. How might this happen? First, the retailer analyses its database to find distinct groups of customers for whom the retailer has the potential to offer superior value. The identification of these target market segments allows tailored products, services and communications to be aimed at them.

The purchasing patterns of individuals are established by means of a loyalty card programme. The scheme's main objective is to improve customer loyalty by rewarding varying shopping behaviours differently. The scheme allows customers to be tracked by frequency of visit, expenditure per visit and expenditure per product category. Loyalty schemes are not about garnering customer allegiance to a particular brand, they are an opportunity for companies to capture data, which can be used for future marketing initiatives. Retailers can gain an understanding of the types of products that are purchased together. For example, Boots, the UK retailer, uses its Advantage card loyalty scheme (which has 15 million active members) to conduct these kinds of analyses. One useful finding is that there is a link between digital photo frames and the purchase of new baby products. Because its products are organized along category lines it never occurred to the retailer to create a special offer linked to picture frames for the baby products buyer, yet these are the kinds of products new parents are likely to want.

The retailer's customers are classified into market segments based on their potential, their degree of loyalty and whether they are predominantly price- or promotion-sensitive. A different marketing strategy is devised for each group. For example, to trade up high-potential, promotionally sensitive, low-loyalty shoppers who do their main shopping elsewhere, high-value manufacturers' coupons for main shopping products are mailed every two months until the consumer is traded up to a different group. Also, high-loyalty customers can be targeted for special treatment such as receiving a customer magazine.

The Tesco Clubcard gathers a rich stream of information from many millions of Clubcard members in the UK and overseas, which is then used for example to: define segments—for example, discount-driven 'price sensitives', 'foodies', 'heavy category users' and 'brand loyalists'; test consumer response to promotions; test the effects of different prices and use of different media; and communicate more effectively with consumers. Product assortments in stores can also be fine-tuned according to the buying habits of customers. Both schemes have worked hard to tailor their rewards offered to consumers. For example, Boots launched a Health Club and a Parenting Club to offer card holders rewards relevant to their lifestyles and interests. Tesco Clubcard enables its users to collect green Clubcard points when customers use their own shopping bags.

The success of the Boots Advantage card and the Tesco Clubcard continues to prompt other retailers to launch loyalty cards: for example, Waitrose, the high-quality UK supermarket, has invested in developing a loyalty card as part of its strategy to reward customers. Rewarding customers has been found to be a highly successful strategy for improving ROI. Staples, the office and business stationery supplier, has introduced a reward card for targeting small businesses and uses the data on purchasing patterns to drive online promotional offers. Nectar is Britain's biggest loyalty card with over 18 million subscribers. It started as a joint initiative launched by its founders (Sainsbury's, BP, Barclaycard and Debenhams) and is constantly expanding its company membership in order to extend the rewards it can offer to signed-up shoppers. For example, Nectar points can be collected from Sainsbury's, eBay, Amazon, Sky and other Nectar member companies and then be used to buy goods (e.g. easyJet flights). In the early days when the technology needed to set up loyalty schemes was expensive, only the largest retailers offered loyalty cards but implementation costs have fallen dramatically, which has meant that more companies in different industries are developing such schemes. For example, Tata Group, which is India's biggest family conglomerate, has set up a loyalty scheme modelled on Nectar.

Questions:

1   Lastminute.com has launched a credit card which earns loyalty points for the customer. Suggest why last minute. com has decided to take this action.
2   Discuss the potential benefits and issues for Lastminute.com customers who sign up for the new credit/loyalty card.
3   Explain the type of data you might need to gather if you are wishing to improve customer retention.

Based on: Mitchell (2002);[64] James (2003);[65] Barnes (2005);[66] McCawley (2006);[67] Murphy (2008);[68] Finch (2009);[69] Charles (2011);[70] Clews (2011);[71] The Economist (2011)[72]

- Strengthening relationships with customers: for example, direct marketing techniques can be used strategically to improve customer retention with long-term programmes established to maximize customer lifetime value. Mini Case 16.2 shows how a database could be used by a retailer to develop customer loyalty.
- Developing an information resource for use in direct marketing campaigns.
  For this various techniques are employed:
- *Direct mail*: a database can be used to select customers for mailings.
- *Telemarketing*: a database can store telephone numbers so that customers and prospects can be contacted. Also when customers contact the company by telephone, relevant information can be stored, including when the next contact should be made.
- *Distributor management systems*: a database can be the foundation on which information is provided to distributors and their performance monitored.
- *Loyalty marketing*: highly loyal customers can be selected from the database for special treatment as a reward for their loyalty.
- *Target marketing*: other groups of individuals or businesses can be targeted as a result of analysing the database. For example, buyer behaviour information stored by supermarkets can be used to target special promotions to those individuals likely to be receptive to them. For example, a consumer promotion for organic baby foods could be sent exclusively to mothers with young babies.
- *Campaign planning*: using the database as a foundation for sending consistent and coordinated campaigns and messages to individuals and market segments.
- *Marketing evaluation*: by recording responses to marketing mix inputs (e.g. price promotions, advertising messages and product offers), it is possible to assess how effective different approaches are to varying individuals and market segments.

The marketing database is at the heart of the customer relationship management systems that use databases as the foundation for managing customer relationships. The next section discusses these systems.

Customer Relationship Management

Customer relationship management (CRM) is a term for the methodologies, technologies and e-commerce capabilities used by firms to manage customer relationships.[73] CRM software packages aid the interaction between the customer and the company, enabling the company to coordinate all of the communication effort so that the customer is presented with a unified message and image. CRM companies offer a range of information technology-based services such as call centres, data analysis and website management. The basic principle behind CRM is that company staff have a single-customer point of view of each client.[74] However, interactions between buyers and sellers are becoming increasingly complex as they are now using multiple channels to satisfy their needs. For example, an individual may buy one product in-store, then refer to a website for further product information, buy a second product online and after the product arrives, call a customer support line for after sales care. Consequently, there is a need to align all the physical *touchpoints* where a customer interacts with a company with its technical infrastructure[75] (see Fig. 16.5).

The drivers of growth of direct marketing activity are also leading to a change in how companies communicate and interact with their customers, and CRM is at the heart of many new multichannel marketing initiatives. This means as well as developing integrated communication campaigns, companies also consider the whole *journey* customers are taking from initial awareness to the final purchase and beyond. For example, Currys and PC World are the market leaders in the sale of electrical goods in the UK with an extensive range of branded and own-brand products from electric kettles to ultra netbooks. So understanding customers' behaviour and their needs at every stage in the buying process is very important. Information is gathered, analysed and fed into the marketing strategy from every *touchpoint* on the customer journey. According to Jeremy Fennel, Head of Multichannel Operations,[76] communications, store visits and online sales are all part of the multichannel journey a

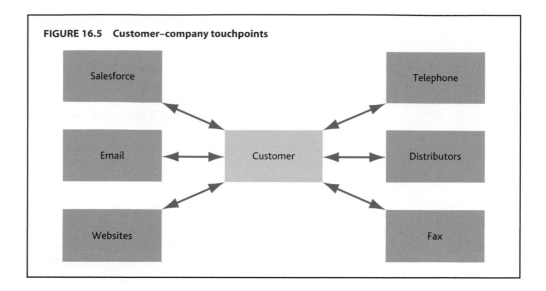

FIGURE 16.5   Customer–company touchpoints

customer takes when interacting with these brands. He also says that communications messages and cues are being sent throughout the process whether it is at the initial point of awareness of a new product through to the final purchase, say, in store. For a business with tens of thousands of different products and millions of customers making different journeys there are many challenges to overcome in order to present up-to-date timely information.

Nevertheless, CRM systems offer the opportunity to deal with challenges and bring benefits through developing and maintaining mutually beneficial relationships between buyers and sellers by seamlessly bringing together data from each touchpoint into a centrally managed system. However, this invariably means that companies need to consolidate their many databases from across the organization. The potential benefits are accurate and company-wide accessible customer information, managed staff access and integration with the marketing strategy. In other words, whenever and wherever a customer *touches* a company, frontline staff have instant access to the same data about the customer, such as his/her details and past purchases, which creates opportunities to offer the customer better service. Other ways in which CRM systems are used include:

1 *Targeting* customer and prospect groups with clearly defined propositions.
2 *Enquiry management*—this starts as soon as an individual expresses an interest and continues through qualification, lead handling and outcome reporting.
3 *Welcoming*—this covers new customers and those upgrading their relationship; it covers simple 'thank you' messages to sophisticated contact strategies.
4 *Getting to know*—customers need to be persuaded to give information about themselves; this information needs to be stored, updated and used; useful information includes attitude and satisfaction information and relationship 'health checks'.
5 *Customer development*—decisions need to be made regarding which customers to develop through higher levels of relationship management activity, and which to maintain or drop.
6 *Managing problems*—involves early problem identification, complaint handling and 'root cause' analysis to spot general issues that have potential to cause problems for many customers.
7 *Win-back*—activities include understanding reasons for loss, deciding which customers to try to win back, developing win-back programmes that give customers good reasons to return.

Getting the technology right and ensuring full integration of existing databases and management information systems can present many challenges. However, research has revealed that the following factors are associated with success:[77]

- having a customer orientation and organizing the CRM system around customers
- taking a single view of customers across departments, and designing an integrated system so that all customer-facing staff can draw information from a common database
- having the ability to manage cultural change issues that arise as a result of system development and implementation
- involving users in the CRM design process
- designing the system in such a way that it can readily be changed to meet future requirements
- having a board-level champion of the CRM project, and commitment within each of the affected departments to the benefits of taking a single view of the customer and the need for common strategies—for example, prioritizing resources on profitable customers
- creating 'quick wins' to provide positive feedback on the project programmes
- ensuring face-to-face contact (rather than by paper or email) between marketing and IT staff
- piloting the new system before full launch.

Once a company has established the structures and process required to manage customer data, it can then consider how to manage a specific direct marketing campaign.

Managing a Direct Marketing Campaign

Direct marketing can be very effective when integrated with other elements of the promotional mix and used to support a coherent *marketing strategy*. In Chapter 14 Integrated Marketing Communications it was stressed that all of the communication tools should send a consistent message and reinforce other elements of the marketing mix (product, place and price). Following this logic, messages sent out using various direct marketing media should also form a coherent whole. For example, information disseminated through advertising should be consistent with that sent out via a direct mail campaign. In the past there was sometimes a tendency for direct marketing campaigns not to use multiple contacts or multiple media. However, increased use of digital channels gives direct marketers the opportunity to use a combination of media in sequence to achieve their objectives. For example, a business-to-business company marketing a new adhesive might place a direct response advertisement in trade magazines to stimulate trial and orders. A response coupon, freefone telephone number and email address would be provided, and prospects invited to choose their most convenient method of contact. An inbound telemarketing team would be trained to receive calls and take either orders or requests for samples for trial. Another team would deal with mail and email correspondence. An outbound telemarketing team would follow up prospects judged to be of small and medium potential and the salesforce targeted at large potential customers and prospects.

Accordingly direct marketers need to understand how a product is positioned and its target market as it is crucial that messages sent out as part of a direct marketing campaign do not conflict with those communicated by other channels such as advertising or the salesforce. The integrating mechanism is a clear definition of marketing strategy. Figure 16.6 shows the steps in the management of a direct marketing campaign.

In essence the key stages in a direct marketing campaign are similar to those in a mass communication plan (as discussed in Chapter 15). However, there are certain differences at each of the stages.

Identify and understand target audience

These are the groups of people at whom the direct marketing campaign is aimed (targeting strategies described in Chapter 8). Lifestyle is often targeted, but a particularly useful method of segmentation for direct marketing purposes involves considering the following groups:

- *Competitors' customers*: all people who buy the types of product our company produces but from our competitors.
- *Prospects*: people who have not bought from our company before but qualify as potential purchasers (e.g. our customers are large companies, therefore other large companies should be targeted).

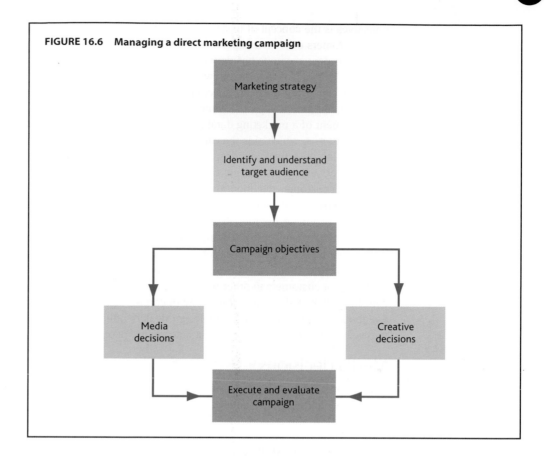

FIGURE 16.6 Managing a direct marketing campaign

- *Enquirers*: people who have contacted the organization and shown interest in one or more products but, as yet, have not bought.
- *Lapsed customers*: people who have purchased in the past but appear to have ceased buying.
- *Referrals*: people who have been recommended to the organization as potential customers.
- *Existing customers*: people who are continuing to buy.

Once a target group is identified, the marketing manager has to consider how to access the group. This may be done through existing Internet information from the CRM system and marketing database, which will provide a list of existing contacts, or may come from an external list broker. Experian is a global provider of individual and company information for direct marketing initiatives. Understanding current trends and changes in buying behaviour is important. For example, consumers have become increasingly in favour of opening direct mail letters, if they perceive the offer is relevant to them. In fact, consumers seem to have become less cynical about this form of communication and are often prompted to open the mailing to see if there are any reward vouchers or coupons.[78]

Campaign objectives

Campaign objectives vary and may focus on financial goals—sales, profits and return on investment; marketing goals—acquire or retain customers, or to generate enquiries; communication goals—create awareness or change beliefs. However, one of the benefits of direct marketing is its capacity to deliver against short-term objectives, which are easily measured and evaluated. For example, the Spanish car maker, Seat, targeted a select list of UK companies in an effort to break into the lucrative fleet car business. A combined direct mail and press campaign generated a 44 per cent increase in new car sales.[79]

Acquisition objectives can be costly as it is more expensive to attract new customers than develop and keep existing customers. So, a consideration when setting this type of campaign objectives is the concept of *lifetime value*. This measures the profits that can be expected from customers over their expected life with a company. Banks know, for example, that gaining student accounts has very high lifetime value since switching between banks is unusual. This means that the allowable marketing cost per acquisition (or how much a company can afford to spend to acquire a new customer) can be quite high. If the calculation was based on potential profits while a student, the figure would be much lower. The establishment of a marketing database can, over time, provide valuable information on buying patterns, which aids the calculation of lifetime value.

Retention objectives focus on keeping customers and can have a direct impact on profitability. A study conducted by PricewaterhouseCoopers showed that a 2 per cent increase in customer retention has the same profit impact as a 10 per cent reduction in overhead costs.[80] Customer loyalty programmes have blossomed as a result, with direct marketing playing a key role. Retention programmes are aimed at maximizing a customer's lifetime value to the company. Maintaining a long-term relationship with a customer provides the opportunity to up-sell, cross-sell and renew business. Up-selling involves the promotion of higher-value products—for example, a more expensive car. Cross-selling entails the switching of customers to other product categories, as when a music club promotes a book collection. Renewal involves the timing of communication to existing customers when they are about to repurchase. For example, car dealers often send direct mail promotional material two years after the purchase of a car, since many people change cars after that period.

Media decisions

Direct marketers have a large number of techniques and media which they can use to reach customers and prospects. Table 16.4 earlier in this chapter shows the main techniques/ media used for direct marketing and the benefits and problems of using each of them.

Creative decisions

Most direct marketing campaigns have different objectives from those of advertising. Whereas advertising usually attempts to create awareness and position the image of a brand in prospects' minds, the aim of most direct marketing is to make a sale. It is more orientated to immediate action than advertising. Recipients of direct marketing messages (particularly through direct mail) need to see a clear benefit in responding. Costa Coffee Club offers its members (in return for signing up via the website and providing personal data) five points per pound on purchases. The Costa Coffee Club has worked very well and has a positive impact on customers' frequency of consumption.[81]

Creative decisions will be captured using a creative brief, which is a document that usually contains details of specific communications objectives, product benefits, target market analysis, details of the offer being made, the message that is to be communicated and the action plan (i.e. how the campaign will be run).

Executing and evaluating the campaign

Execution of the campaign may be in-house or through the use of a specialist agency. Direct marketing activity usually has clearly defined short-term objectives against which performance can be measured. Some of the most frequently used measurements are:
- response rate (the proportion of contacts responding)
- total sales (volume and value)
- number of contacts purchasing
- sales rate (percentage of contacts purchasing)
- number of enquiries
- enquiry rate
- cost per contact

- cost per enquiry
- cost per sale
- conversion rate from enquiry to sale
- average order value
- renewal rate
- repeat purchase rate.

Direct marketers should bear in mind the longer-term effects of their activities. A campaign may seemingly be unprofitable in the short term, but when renewals and repeat purchases are taken into account the long-term value of the campaign may be highly positive.

Ethical Issues in Direct Communications

Personal selling and direct marketing methods are increasingly subject to scrutiny by industry bodies, consumer groups, governments and ultimately the national and international legal systems. Under the heading of personal selling deception, the hard sell, bribery and reciprocal buying are issues which marketing managers should plan to avoid. The implications of each of these issues are:

- *Deception*. A dilemma that, sooner or later, faces most salespeople is the choice of telling the customer the whole truth and risk losing the sale, or misleading the customer to clinch it. The deception may take the form of exaggeration, lying or withholding important information that significantly reduces the appeal of the product. Such actions should be avoided by influencing salespersons' behaviour by training, by sales management encouraging ethical behaviour, by their own actions and words, and by establishing codes of conduct for their salespeople. Nevertheless, sometimes evidence of malpractice in selling is discovered, and action taken to recompense the injured party: for example, in the financial services industry Lloyds TSB bank paid out over £500 million in compensation to customers as a result of mis-selling endowment mortgages.[82]
- *The hard sell*. Personal selling is criticized for employing high-pressure sales tactics to close a sale. Some car dealerships have been deemed unethical in using hard-sell tactics to pressure customers into making a quick decision on a complicated purchase that may involve expensive credit facilities.
- *Bribery*. This is the act of giving payment, gifts or other inducements to secure a sale. Bribes are considered unethical as they violate the principle of fairness in commercial negotiations. A major problem is that in some countries bribes are an accepted part of business life: to compete, bribes are necessary. So, organizations in such a situation face an ethical dilemma. On the one hand they will be castigated in their home country if they use bribes and this becomes public knowledge. On the other hand, without the bribe the organization could be operating at a commercial disadvantage. Taking an ethical stance may cause difficulties in the short term but in the long run the positive publicity that can follow is likely to be of greater benefit. Although there are regulations in place to outlaw bribery to foreign individuals, with the 1997 Organization for Economic Cooperation and Development Convention on Bribery being signed by 36 countries, in practice very few successful prosecutions have resulted.[83] One notable exception is the record fines imposed upon Siemens for paying bribes to win lucrative overseas telecoms and power contracts.[84]
- *Reciprocal buying*. This is where a customer only agrees to buy from a supplier if that supplier agrees to purchase something from the buying organization. This may be considered unfair to other competing suppliers, who may not agree to such an arrangement or may not be in a position to buy from the customer. Supporters of reciprocal buying argue that it is reasonable for a customer to extract the best terms of agreement from a supplier; if this means reaching agreement to sell to the supplier, then so be it. Indeed, counter-trade, where goods may be included as part of the payment for supplies, has been a feature of international selling for many years and can benefit poorer countries and companies that cannot afford to pay in cash.

Direct marketing methods also face different types of ethical issues associated with consumer concerns:

- *Poorly targeted direct mail.* Although designed to foster closer relationships in targeting of consumers, some direct mail is of little relevance to the recipient and can be a clear source of irritation and distress. As more attention is paid to the natural environment, the waste of natural resources caused by poorly directed mailshots is a questionable practice.[85]
- *Intrusive nature of telemarketing calls.* Consumers complain about the annoyance caused by unsolicited telephone calls pressuring them to buy products at inconvenient times (e.g. in the middle of eating dinner or bathing the baby).
- *Invasion of privacy.* Many consumers fear that every time they subscribe to a website, club, society or magazine, apply for a credit card, or buy anything by telephone or direct mail, their names, addresses and other information will be entered on to a database that will guarantee a flood of mail from the supplier. The direct marketing industry and governments are responding to the public concerns noted above. There is further discussion of these in Chapter 18.

Online **LearningCentre**

When you have read this chapter

log on to the Online Learning Centre at **www.mcgraw-hill.co.uk/textbooks/jobber** to explore chapter-by-chapter test questions, links and further online study tools for marketing.

Review

1 **The key direct marketing communication tools: personal selling, exhibitions, direct marketing**
- Direct communications enable a direct dialogue between buyers and sellers; moreover they do not involve the purchase of media space.
- Personal selling allows buyers and seller to communicate in a face-to-face manner, which facilitates relationship development but from a marketing management perspective is relatively costly.
- Exhibitions are an opportunity to bring together all of the buyers and sellers in a particular market under one roof and create an environment for furthering customer relationships, enhancing corporate ideas and gathering competitive information.
- Direct marketing is a means of creating a dialogue between buyers and sellers, using various techniques, such as direct mail, digital marketing, telemarketing and **catalogue marketing**.

2 **Characteristics of modern selling**
- The characteristics are customer acquisition, retention and deletion, customer relationship management, adding value and satisfying customer needs.

3 **The stages in the selling process**
- Salespeople should prepare for selling by gaining knowledge of their own and competitors' products, planning sales presentations, setting up call objectives and seeking to understand buyer behaviour.

4 **The key tasks of sales management**
- The tasks of a sales manager are to understand marketing strategy; set personal selling objectives and strategies; design the salesforce; manage the salesforce by setting objectives, organizing recruitment and training, setting reward structures and performance measures for salespeople; and evaluation and control of the total sales operation.

5 **The objectives, conduct and evaluation of exhibitions**
- Objectives of exhibitions can be classified as selling objectives to current customers (e.g. stimulate extra sales), selling objectives to potential customers (e.g. determine needs and transmit benefits), non-selling objectives to current customers (e.g. maintain image and gather competitive intelligence) and non-selling objectives to potential customers (e.g. foster image building and gather competitive intelligence).
- Staff conduct at an exhibition should ensure that there is always someone in attendance to talk to visitors, staff should be well-informed, provide informative literature and a seating area/office, and refreshments should be provided.
- Evaluation of an exhibition includes number of visitors/key influencers/decision-makers who visit the stand, number of leads/enquiries/orders/new dealerships generated and cost per lead/enquiry/order. Qualitative evaluation includes the worth of competitive intelligence, and interest generated in new products.

6 **The meaning of direct marketing**
- Direct marketing is the distribution of products, information and promotional benefits to target customers through interactive communication in a way that allows response to be measured.
- It includes such methods as direct mail, telemarketing, direct response advertising, catalogue marketing and digital media.

7 **The reasons for the growth of direct marketing activity**
- Direct marketing activity has grown because of market and media fragmentation, developments in technology, the list explosion, sophisticated analytical techniques, and coordinated marketing systems.

8 **The importance of database marketing**
- **Database marketing** is an approach to marketing communications that targets individuals using various media channels.
- Databases are central to all forms of direct marketing activity as they store customer contact and behavioural data which helps marketing strategy and planning; for example, when planning promotional campaigns designed to target very loyal customers who are to receive special treatment. Databases are useful for planning campaigns as they hold details of past customer behaviour, e.g. responses to price promotions.

9 **How to manage a direct marketing campaign**
- A direct marketing campaign should not be designed in isolation but based on a clear understanding of marketing strategy in particular positioning. Then the steps are as follows.
- Identify and understand the target audience: never sell to a stranger. Who is to be reached, their motives and choice criteria need to be understood.
- Campaign objectives: these can be expressed in financial (e.g. sales), in marketing (e.g. acquire or retain customers) or communication (e.g. change beliefs) terms.
- Media decisions: major media options are **direct mail**, telemarketing, mobile marketing, **direct response advertising**, catalogue marketing and the Internet (discussed in Chapter 18).
- Creative decisions: a creative brief will include a statement of communication objectives, product benefits (and weaknesses), target market analysis, development of the offer, communication of the message, and an action plan.
- Execute and evaluate the campaign: execution of the campaign may be in-house or through the use of a specialist agency. Evaluation should be taken against defined objectives such as total sales, number of enquiries, cost per sale and repeat purchase rate.

10 **The nature of customer relationship management**
- Customer relationship management (CRM) is the term that describes the methodologies, technologies and e-commerce capabilities used by firms to manage customer relationships.
- The basic principle behind CRM is that company staff have a single-customer point of view of each client.
- Companies can assess how well they are managing their customer relationships by examining the following areas: analysis and planning, the proposition made to each customer segment, how well information and technology are being used, how well people are being managed and supported by an effective organizational structure, the efficiency of customer-impinging processes, the effectiveness of the implementation of the customer management activity, the quality of measuring performance against plan and against competitors, and the quality of the customer experience.

- Success in CRM projects is associated with having a customer orientation, taking a single view of customers across departments, having the ability to manage cultural change, involving users in the design process, having a project champion on the board and a commitment to the benefits of CRM across affected departments, creating 'quick wins', ensuring face-to-face contact between marketing and information technology staff, and piloting the new system before launch.

11 **Ethical issues in direct communications**
- Using direct communication tools can mean marketing managers face difficult choices. Personal selling has been criticized for using bribery, the hard sell and reciprocal buying techniques in order to secure sales orders. Direct marketing tools can be seen by customers as poorly targeted, a waste of natural resources and an intrusion of privacy.

Key Terms

buying signals statements by a buyer that indicate s/he is interested in buying

campaign objectives goals set by an organization in terms of, for example, sales, profits, customers won or retained, or awareness creation

catalogue marketing the sale of products through catalogues distributed to agents and customers, usually by mail or at stores

customer benefits those things that a customer values in a product; customer benefits derive from product features

customer relationship management the methodologies, technologies and e-commerce capabilities used by firms to manage customer relationships

database marketing an interactive approach to marketing that uses individually addressable marketing media and channels to provide information to a target audience, stimulate demand and stay close to customers

direct mail material sent through the postal service to the recipient's house or business address promoting a product and/or maintaining an ongoing relationship

direct response advertising the use of the prime advertising media such as television, newspapers and magazines to elicit an order, enquiry or request for a visit

e-commerce involves all electronically mediated transactions between an organization and any third party it deals with, including exchange of information

exhibition an event that brings buyers and sellers together in a commercial setting

key account management an approach to selling that focuses resources on major customers and uses a team selling approach

product features the characteristics of a product that may or may not convey a customer benefit

salesforce evaluation the measurement of salesperson performance so that strengths and weaknesses can be identified

target accounts organizations or individuals whose custom the company wishes to obtain

telemarketing a marketing communications system whereby trained specialists use telecommunications and information technologies to conduct marketing and sales activities

trade show similar to an exhibition as it brings together buyers, sellers and competitors under one roof, but is not open to the public

Study Questions

1 Select a car with which you are familiar. Identify its features and translate them into customer benefits.

2 Imagine you are face to face with a customer for that car. Write down five objections to purchase and prepare convincing responses to them.

3 You are the new sales manager of a company selling natural ingredients to the pharmaceutical industry. Discuss how you would motivate and manage your salesforce.

4 Suggest how you might strengthen buyer–seller relationships using CRM systems.

5 From your own personal experience, do you consider salespeople to be unethical? Can you remember any sales encounters when you have been subject to unethical behaviour?

6 Explain the benefits of using exhibitions as part of a business-to-business IMC campaign.

7 Compare the strengths and weaknesses of different forms of direct marketing.

8 Define direct marketing. Identify the different forms of direct marketing. Give an example of how at least three of them can be integrated into a marketing communications campaign.

9 Discuss why databases are important for marketing communication campaigns and why. Explain the types of information that are recorded on a database.

10 What are the stages of managing a direct marketing campaign? Why is the concept of lifetime value of a customer important when designing a campaign?

References

1. Chaffey, D. and F. E. Ellis-Chadwick (2012) *Digital Marketing: Strategy, Implementation and Practice*, 5th edn, Harlow: Pearson.
2. Rines, S. (1995) Forcing Change, *Marketing Week*, 1 March, 10–13.
3. Lane, N. and N. Piercy (2004) Strategic Customer Management: Designing a Profitable Future for Your Sales Organization, *European Management Journal* 22(6), 659–68.
4. Stephens, H. (2003) 'CEO', American Marketing Association Summer Educators' Conference, The H. R. Challey Group, August, Chicago.
5. Lane and Piercy (2004) op. cit.
6. Royal, W. (2004) Death of Salesmen, *Industry Week*, 21 December.
7. Moncrief, W. C. and G. W. Marshall (2005) The Evolution of the Seven Steps of Selling, *Industrial Marketing Management* 34, 13–22.
8. Leigh, T. H. and G. W. Marshall (2001) Research Priorities in Sales Strategy and Performance, *Journal of Personal Selling and Sales Management* 21, 83–93.
9. Rackham, N. and J. DeVincentis (1999) *Rethinking the Sales Force: Redefining Selling to Create and Capture Customer Value*, New York: McGraw-Hill.
10. Weitz, B. A. (1981) Effectiveness in Sales Interactions: A Contingency Framework, *Journal of Marketing* 45, 85–103.
11. Román, S., S. Ruiz and J. L. Munuera (2002) The Effects of Sales Training on Salesforce Activity, *European Journal of Marketing* 36(11/12), 1344–66.
12. Schuster, C. P. and J. E. Danes (1986) Asking Questions: Some Characteristics of Successful Sales Encounters, *Journal of Personal Selling and Sales Management*, May, 17–27; Sujan, H., M. Sujan and J. Bettman (1998) Knowledge Structure Differences Between Effective and Less Effective Salespeople, *Journal of Marketing Research* 25, 81–6; Szymanski, D. (1988) Determinants of Selling Effectiveness: the Importance of Declarative Knowledge to the Personal Selling Concept, *Journal of Marketing* 52, 64–77; Weitz, B. A., H. Sujan and M. Sujan (1986) Knowledge, Motivation and Adaptive Behaviour: a Framework for Improving Selling Effectiveness, *Journal of Marketing* 50, 174–91; Krishnan, B. C., R. G. Netemeyer and J. S. Boles (2002) Self-efficacy, Competitiveness, and Effort as Antecedents of Salesperson Performances, *Journal of Personal Selling and Sales Management* 20(4), 285–95.
13. Moncrief and Marshall (2005) op. cit.
14. Long, M. M., T. Tellefsen and J. D. Lichtenthal (2007) Internet Integration into the Industrial Selling Process: A Step-by-Step Approach, *Industrial Marketing Management* 36, 676–89.
15. Walters, J. (2000) Journey's End For the King of the Costas, *Observer*, 19 November, 9.
16. Brooke, K. (2002) B2B and B2C Marketing is not so Different, *Marketing Business*, July/August, 39.
17. Picaville, L. (2004) Mobile CRM Helps Smith and Nephew Reps Give Hands-On Service, *CRM Magazine* 8(5), 53.
18. Long, Tellefsen and Lichtenthal (2007) op. cit.
19. See Hunt, K. A. and R. Bashaw (1999) A New Classification of Sales Resistance, *Industrial Marketing Management* 28, 109–18.
20. Long, Tellefsen and Lichtenthal (2007) op. cit.
21. Long, Tellefsen and Lichtenthal (2007) op. cit.
22. Burrows, P. (2008) Cisco's Brave New World, *Business Week*, 24 November, 57–68.
23. McDonald, M. H. B. (2002) *Marketing Plans*, London: Heinemann.
24. Strahle, W. and R. L. Spiro (1986) Linking Market Share Strategies to Salesforce Objectives, Activities and Compensation Policies, *Journal of Personal Selling and Sales Management*, August, 11–18.
25. Talley, W. J. (1961) How to Design Sales Territories, *Journal of Marketing* 25(3), 16–28.
26. Homburg, C., J. P. Workman Jr and O. Jensen (2000) Fundamental Changes in Marketing Organization: the Movement Toward a Customer-Focused Organizational Structure, *Journal of the Academy of Marketing Science* 28, 459–78.
27. Magrath, A. J. (1989) To Specialise or Not to Specialise?, *Sales and Marketing Management* 14(7), 62–8.
28. Homburg, C., J. P. Workman Jr and O. Jensen (2002) A Configurational Perspective on Key Account Management, *Journal of Marketing* 66, April, 38–60.
29. Piercy, N., D. W. Cravens and N. A. Morgan (1998) Salesforce Performance and Behaviour Based Management Processes in Business-to-Business Sales Organisations, *European Journal of Marketing* 32(1/2), 79–100.
30. PA Consultants (1979) *Salesforce Practice Today: A Basis for Improving Performance*, Cookham: Institute of Marketing.
31. Krishnan, B. C., R. G. Netemeyer and J. S. Boles (2002) Self-Efficacy, Competitiveness and Effort as Antecedents of Salesperson Performance, *Journal of Personal Selling and Sales Management* 22(4), 285–95.
32. See DeCormier, R. and D. Jobber (1993) The Counsellor Selling Method: Concepts and Constructs, *Journal of Personal Selling and Sales Management* 13(4), 39–60; Román, S., S. Ruiz and J. L. Munuera (2002) The Effects of Sales Training on Salesforce Activity, *European Journal of Marketing* 36(11/12), 1344–66.
33. Wilson, K. (1993) Managing the Industrial Salesforce in the 1990s, *Journal of Marketing Management* 9(2), 123–40.

34. Cron, W. L., G. Marshall, J. Singh, R. L. Spiro and H. Sujan (2005) Salesperson Selection, Training and Development: Trends, Implications and Research Opportunities, *Journal of Personal Selling and Sales Management* 25(2), 123–36.

35. Luthans, F. (1997) *Organizational Behaviour*, New York: McGraw-Hill.

36. See Pullins, E. B. (2001) An Exploratory Investigation of the Relationship of Sales Force Compensation and Intrinsic Motivation, *Industrial Marketing Management* 30, 403–13; and Holmes, T. L. and R. Srivastava (2002) Effects of Job Perceptions on Job Behaviours: Implications for Sales Performance, *Industrial Marketing Management* 31, 421–8.

37. See Maslow, A. H. (1954) *Motivation and Personality*, New York: Harper & Row; Herzberg, F. (1966) *Work and the Nature of Man*, Cleveland: W. Collins; Vroom, V. H. (1964) *Work and Motivation*, New York: Wiley; Adams, J. S. (1965) Inequity in Social Exchange, in Berkowitz, L. (ed.) *Advances in Experimental Social Psychology 2*, New York: Academic Press; Likert, R. (1961) *New Patterns of Sales Management*, New York: McGraw-Hill.

38. Cundiff, E. and M. T. Hilger (1988) *Marketing in the International Environment*, Englewood Cliffs, NJ: Prentice-Hall.

39. Hill, J. S., R. R. Still and U. O. Boya (1991) Managing the International Salesforce, *International Marketing Review* 8(1), 19–31.

40. Ghauri, P. N. and P. R. Cateora (2006) *International Marketing*, Maidenhead: McGraw-Hill.

41. The quotation appears in Jap, S. D. (2001) The Strategic Role of the Salesforce in Developing Customer Satisfaction Across the Relationship Lifecycle, *Journal of Personal Selling and Sales Management* 21(2), 95–108.

42. Dewsnap, B. and D. Jobber (2002) A Social Psychological Model of Relations Between Marketing and Sales, *European Journal of Marketing* 36(7/8), 874–94.

43. Parasuraman, A. (1981) The Relative Importance of Industrial Promotional Tools, *Industrial Marketing Management* 10, 277–81.

44. Smith, T. M., S. Gopalakrishna and P. M. Smith (2004) The Complementary Effect of Trade Shows on Personal Selling, *International Journal of Research in Marketing* 21(1), 61–76.

45. Fill, C. (2011) *Essentials of Marketing Communications*, Harlow: FT/Prentice Hall, 312.

46. Geigenmüller, A. (2010) The role of virtual trade fairs in relationship value creation, *Journal of Business and Industrial Marketing*, 25(4), 282–92.

47. Shipley, D. and K. S. Wong (1993) Exhibiting, strategy and implementation, *International Journal of Advertising*, 12(2), 117–30.

48. Hansen, K. (2004) Measuring Performance at Trade Shows: Scale Development and Validation, *Journal of Business Research* 54, 1–13.

49. Spielwarenmesse (2012) http://www.toyfair.de/visitors/frequent-questions/?L=1.

50. Bonoma, T. V. (1985) Get more out of your trade show, in Gumpert, D. E. (ed.) *The Marketing Renaissance*, New York: Wiley.

51. Cavatore, A. (2012) Stella McCartney's Acrobatic Show at London Fashion Week, http://www.hauteliving.com/2012/02/stella-mccartneys-acrobatic-show-at-london-fashion-week/ (accessed February 2012).

52. Cartner-Morley, J. (2012) London fashion week showcases the best of British, http://www.guardian.co.uk/fashion/2012/feb/21/london-fashion-week-best-british.

53. Hilpern, K. (2011) How to manage and market events, *The Marketer*, February, 36–9.

54. Lancaster, G. and H. Baron (1977) Exhibiting for Profit, *Industrial Management*, November, 24–7.

55. Blaskey, J. (1999) Proving Your Worth, *Marketing*, 25 February, 35–6.

56. Ellis-Chadwick, F. E. and N. F. Doherty (2012) Web advertising: the role of e-mail marketing, *Journal of Business Research* 65(6), 843–848.

57. Fahy, J. and D. Jobber (2012) *Foundations of Marketing*, Maidenhead: McGraw-Hill, 262.

58. 2011 Worldwide Direct Mail Advertising Industry Report, www.researchandmarkets.com.

59. Fletcher, K., C. Wheeler and J. Wright (1990) The Role and Status of UK Database Marketing, *Quarterly Review of Marketing*, Autumn, 7–14.

60. Linton, I. (1995) *Database Marketing: Know What Your Customer Wants*, London: Pitman.

61. Dean, D. and C. Webb (2011) Recovering from information overload, *McKinsey Quarterly*, 1, 80–88.

62. Benady, D. (2011) Redefining direct mail, *Marketing*, 16 November, 27.

63. Stone, M., D. Davies and A. Bond (1995) *Direct Hit: Direct Marketing with a Winning Edge*, London: Pitman.

64. Mitchell, A. (2002) Consumer Power Is on the Cards in Tesco Plan, *Marketing Week*, 2 May, 30–1.

65. James, M. (2003) The Quest for Fidelity, *Marketing Business*, January, 20–2.

66. Barnes, R. (2005) Nectar Readies B2B Loyalty Card Launch, *Marketing*, 19 January, 14.

67. McCawley, I. (2006) Nectar Loyalty Card Set for Global Roll-out, *Marketing Week*, 19 January, 3.

68. Murphy, C. (2008) No Such Thing as a Freebie, *The Marketer*, May, 28–31.

69. Finch, J. (2009) Tesco Sales Top £1 billion a Week, *The Guardian*, 22 April, 22.

70. Charles, G. (2011) Waitrose unveils loyalty-card programme in strategic shift, *Marketing*, 26 October, 1.

71. Clews, M.-L. (2011) The evolution of loyalty, *Marketing Week*, August, 42–3.

72. *The Economist* (2011) Spies in your wallet, 5 November.

73. Foss, B. and M. Stone (2001) *Successful Customer Relationship Marketing*, London: Kogan Page.

74. Dempsey, J. (2001) An Elusive Goal Leads to Confusion, *Financial Times Information Technology Supplement*, 17 October, 4.

75. Clatworthy, S. (2012) Bridging the gap between brand strategy and customer experience, *Managing Service Quality*, 22(2), 108–27.

76. Fennel, J. (2012) *Business Functions in Context*, Milton Keynes: Open University.

77. See Ryals, L., S. Knox and S. Maklan (2002) *Customer Relationship Management: Building the Business Case*, London: FT Prentice Hall; Wilson, H., E. Daniel and M. McDonald (2002) Factors for Success in Customer Relationship Management Systems, *Journal of Marketing Management* 18(1/2), 193–200.

78. Handley, L. (2011) Do you want to know an open secret? *Marketing Week*, 20 October, 25.

79. Fahy and Jobber (2012) op. cit., 260.

80. Murphy, J. (1997) The Art of Satisfaction, *Financial Times*, 23 April, 14.

81. Baker, R. (2012) Costa eyes loyalty scheme for vending business, *Marketing Week*, 10 January.

82. Treanor, J. (2005) Lloyds Pays Customers £150m for Endowment Mis-Selling, *The Guardian*, 13 December, 21.

83. SenGupta, R. (2006) Trouble at Home for Overseas Bribes, *Financial Times*, 2 February, 12.

84. Gow, D. (2008) Record US Fine Ends Siemens Bribery Scandal, *The Guardian*, 16 December, 24.

85. Reed, D. (2008) Making a Visible Difference, *Marketing Week*, 14 August, 27.

Charles Tyrwhitt
Bricks, Clicks and Flips

Many retailers have been slow at reinventing themselves in the age of Internet shopping and strive to combine the benefits of the two. This hasn't applied to Charles Tyrwhitt. When Nicholas Charles Tyrwhitt Wheeler first set up his mail-order shirt business in 1986 while still a student at Bristol University, he couldn't have envisaged opening his first shop 11 years later in London's Jermyn Street, home to some of the best tailors in London. Since then more stores have opened in London, Paris and New York with plans to open in Chicago, Boston, Atlanta and Houston over the next couple of years. With a turnover in excess of £105 million and 532 staff, this quality British clothes retailer for both men and women goes from strength to strength.

Strategy

Bricks, clicks and flips is a business strategy which integrates both offline (bricks) and online (clicks) and sometimes flips (physical catalogue). Charles Tyrwhitt encompasses all three. The success of this model should allay the fears of commentators who suggested the High Street is doomed because of the introduction of disintermediation into the supply chain via the Internet. The key to this success is to deliver the same experience both online and offline, as customers today have extremely high expectations. Therefore, the message and experience need to be consistent, to enhance customer loyalty.

To enable greater consistency, the website was redesigned by cxpartners. They conducted extensive research, aimed at understanding their needs. This included user research, call centre listening and store visits to find out how people buy the products, what mattered or didn't matter in the process. The result was a robust, flexible site that reflected the elegance of Charles Tyrwhitt and was easy for the customer to use. In 2011 the website won Redesign of the Year at the National eCommerce Awards, beating prestigious competition including BT and Ocado to the prize. More importantly, conversion rates on the new site had increased by 27 per cent.

Tactics

The secret is that retailers need to be more customer-centric—the ability of everyone in the company to continuously learn about customers and the market. That's why Nick Wheeler shares his email with his 1.2 million customers in his database. 'As businesses grow, and certainly in those where you have a lot of consumers, there is a tendency to see customers as a nuisance, not an asset,' he said. 'But the people who can tell you how your business is doing are your customers and the people who work in your business on the front line.' This isn't just rhetoric, as he quotes one such example. 'I had an email from a guy who wondered why we had changed the lining in one range of suits from viscose to polyester. I did not know that we had. I suspect that someone in the business had done it to save a small amount of money. I think it is wrong, because I say that we will not cut corners on quality to save money. I have taken it up with the head of technology, who is looking at how it happened, and I suspect we will change it back.'

This attention to detail has paid off, as the business has doubled in the past three years.

Competition

Two major competitors with similar turnovers of just over the £100 million mark are Thomas Pink and T. M. Lewin. Both have very different backgrounds, although they all started as gentleman's shirt retailers.

- **T. M. Lewin** was founded in 1898 when Thomas Mayes Lewin opened his first shop in Jermyn Street, St James's, London. Having traded through both World Wars, supplying the RAF and the British Army, they were taken over in 1979 by the McKenna family, and in 1980 Geoff

Quinn, the current managing director, joined the company. Today, Lewin's has over 100 stores and concessions worldwide.

- **Thomas Pink** is a retail clothing business started in London in 1984, by three Irish brothers James, Peter and John Mullen. They selected the name of Thomas Pink, as this was the name of a famous eighteenth-century London tailor who designed the iconic hunting coat worn by Masters of Foxhounds. Like its competitors it also has a flagship store in Jermyn Street, London and over 90 stores throughout the world. In 1999 it became part of the LVMH (Louis Vuitton Moet Hennessy) group.

Although they all sell similar products and target very similar audiences, their strategies are somewhat dissimilar. Both Lewin's and Pink have a large network of stores, and factors of almost five times that of Tyrwhitt's. Quite often the success or failure of a business is the control of costs. Having to maintain and pay for so many physical stores and their staffing requires larger capital expenditure than selling online. This is where Tyrwhitt has the advantage, profiting from reduced capital risk, as far more of its revenue is coming from its online operation. Competition is never stagnant and Pink's has responded by implementing the Fits.Me Virtual Fitting Room into its e-commerce operations to meet the needs of an increasing number of sophisticated e-commerce customer. However, all three are on the expansion track of opening stores overseas as they see growth of their business outside the UK.

Reflecting on his success, Nick Wheeler says, 'Business is profiting from the relatively high take-up of Internet sales in the UK,' but this growth isn't guaranteed.

What rate this will carry on growing at is difficult to say and I'm not in the business of trying to predict what it is going to be. If it carries on growing and people stop going to stores then our focus will be on the Internet, while if it stops growing our focus will be more on stores. We are in the lucky position of not having to look into a crystal ball and decide. We just follow the market.

Wheeler thinks 'the really important thing is to look at what the customer wants'.

Maybe that is the way forward, a multichannel approach where resources are swapped to cater for the ever-shifting customer preferences.

Questions

1. **Charles Tyrwhitt started as a catalogue business and developed his mailing list. Suggest what advantages this has given the company over its nearest competitors, Thomas Pink and TM Lewin.**

2. **Make a list of the number of touchpoints at which Charles Tyrwhitt can collect customer data and suggest the types of data which might be gathered.**

3. **Apply the potential benefits and limitations of direct marketing techniques to Charles Tyrwhitt.**

4. **Devise a direct marketing campaign for Charles Tyrwhitt.**

This case was prepared by Brian Searle, Lecturer at Loughborough University

Selling in China
Harnessing the Power of the *Guanxi*

China's economy has been growing at an average of 9 per cent over the past 20 years. The country possesses considerable strengths in mass manufacturing and is currently building large electronics and heavy industrial factories. The country is also investing heavily in education and training, especially in the development of engineers and scientists. While these advances mean that China poses new threats to Western companies, the country also provides opportunities. China has a population of over 1.3 billion people and they are spending their growing incomes on consumer durables such as cars, a market that has reached 3 million, mobile phones where China has the world's biggest subscriber base of over 500 million, and computers where over 200 million people browse the Internet on broadband connections. Western companies such as Microsoft, Procter & Gamble, Coca-Cola, BP and Siemens have already seen the Chinese market as an opportunity and entered it, usually with the aid of local joint-venture partners.

Although the Chinese economy undoubtedly possesses many strengths, it also has several weaknesses. First, it lacks major global brands. When business people around the world were asked to rank Chinese brands, Haier, a white-goods (refrigerators, washing machines, etc.) and home appliance manufacturer was ranked first, and Lenovo, a computer company, famous for buying IBM's personal computer division, second. Neither company is a major global player in their respective markets. Second, China suffers from the risk of social unrest—resulting from the widening gap between rich and poor, as well as from corruption. Third, the country has paid a heavy ecological price for rapid industrial and population growth, with thousands of deaths attributed to air and water pollution. Fourth, while still a low-labour cost economy, wage levels are rising fast, particularly in skilled areas, reducing its competitive advantage in this area. Finally, bureaucracy can make doing business in China difficult.

Although Western companies have made successful entries to the Chinese market, some such as Whirlpool, a US white-goods manufacturer, and Kraft, the food multinational, have made heavy losses. Overseas companies hoping to sell successfully in China need to understand a number of

realities of the market there. First, the country is very diverse: 1.3 billion people speak 100 dialects, and covering such a large geographic area the climate is very different across regions. For example, parts of the south are humid, while the north is more temperate. Also, income levels vary considerably between less affluent rural districts and richer cities.

Many Western companies enter China by means of a joint venture, but they need to be aware of the different business conditions there. In China there is no effective rule of law governing business. Bureaucracy and governmental interference can also bring difficulties. For example, Thames Water pulled out of a 20-year water treatment project in Shanghai after the government ruled that the guaranteed rate of return to investors was illegal.

A key element in Chinese business dealings is the existence of *guanxi* networks. *Guanxi* is a set of personal connections on which a person can draw to obtain resources or an advantage when doing business. Developing such a network may involve performing favours or the giving of gifts. For example, a business person may participate in a public ceremonial function or a profession could send books to a Chinese university. Favours are 'banked' and there is a reciprocal obligation to return a favour. The favour and reciprocation element of *guanxi* is called *renqing*. Two other elements are *ganqing* (feelings or affection) and *xinren* (trust). An important aspect of Chinese culture is the avoidance of 'loss of face'. This can occur when a Chinese person finds him/herself embarrassed by, for example, displaying lack of knowledge or understanding. Chinese people like to gather as much information as possible before revealing their thoughts to avoid losing face and displaying ignorance. They also value modesty and reasoning. They also regard the signing of a contract to be only the beginning of a business relationship.

Questions

1. **What are the implications of *guanxi* networks for selling in China?**

2. **An important Chinese cultural issue is the avoidance of loss of face. Discuss its implications for selling in China.**

3. **Explain the concept of self-reference criteria and its implications for selling in China.**

This case was prepared by David Jobber, Professor of Marketing, University of Bradford.

CHAPTER 17

Distribution

nothing but fruit

Here to save the peckish

LEARNING OBJECTIVES

After reading this chapter, you should be able to:

1 describe the functions and types of channels of distribution

2 explain how to determine channel strategy

3 discuss the three components of channel strategy: channel selection, intensity and integration

4 discuss the five key channel management issues: member selection, motivation, training, evaluation and conflict management

5 explain the cost–service trade-off in physical distribution

6 discuss the components of a physical distribution system: customer service, order processing, inventory control, warehousing, transportation and materials handling

7 explain how to improve customer service standards in physical distribution

8 discuss retailing and retail marketing

9 discuss ethical issues in distribution

Distribution, along with location of services, makes up the place element of the marketing mix Products need to be available in adequate quantities, in convenient locations and at times when customers want to buy them. In this chapter we examine the functions and types of distribution channels, the key decisions that determine channel strategy, how to manage channels, and issues relating to the physical flow of goods through distribution channels (physical distribution management). We also explore the relevance of place in terms of where goods are purchased by looking at the retail industry and consider the impact of the Internet on distribution by considering e-commerce. The chapter concludes by discussing ethical considerations.

Producers should consider not only the needs of their ultimate customer but also the requirement of **channel intermediaries** (the organizations which facilitate the distribution of products to customers). For example, success for Müller yoghurt in the UK was dependent on convincing a powerful retailer group (Tesco) to stock the brand. The high margins the brand supported were a key influence in Tesco's decision. Without retailer support Müller would have found it uneconomic to supply consumers with its brand. Clearly, establishing a supply chain that is efficient and meets customers' needs is vital to marketing success. This supply chain is termed a **channel of distribution**, and is the means by which products are moved from producer to the ultimate customer. To be successful, manufacturers and suppliers need to get access to their end customers and gaining distribution outlets does not come easily. Advertising to channel intermediaries is sometimes used to explain the benefits of the brand to encourage channel members to stock products.

The choice of the most effective channel of distribution is an important aspect of marketing strategy. The development of supermarkets effectively shortened the distribution channel between producer and consumer by eliminating the wholesaler. Prior to their introduction the typical distribution channel for products like food, drink, tobacco and toiletries was producer to wholesaler to retailer. The wholesaler would buy in bulk from the producer and sell smaller quantities to the retailer (typically a small grocery shop). By building up buying power, supermarkets could shorten this chain by buying direct from producers. This meant lower costs to the supermarket chain and lower prices to the consumer. The competitive effect was to drastically reduce the numbers of small grocers and wholesalers in this market. By being more efficient and meeting customers' needs better, supermarkets had created a competitive advantage for themselves.

Digital technologies are making further changes to distribution channels. In some cases from physical to virtual: for example, the distribution of music and video (downloads), airline booking (electronic ticketing), hotel reservations (electronic booking). In other cases the shift is from store to home and office purchasing—e.g. groceries (home shopping). Mobile networks permit the distribution of such products as music, video and ringtones.[2] Increasingly retailers are adopting a multichannel approach, which means they supply products and communicate with their customers, in-store, online, via mobile and through social media. In business-to-business markets customers can place orders, receive quotes and track deliveries over the Internet.

Next, we explore the functions of channel intermediaries and then examine the different types of channels that manufacturers can use to supply their products to customers.

Functions of Channel Intermediaries

The most basic question to ask when deciding channel strategy is whether to sell directly to the ultimate customer or to use channel intermediaries such as retailers and/or wholesalers. To answer this question we need to understand the functions of channel intermediaries—that is, what benefits might producers derive from their use. Their functions are to reconcile the needs of producers and customers, to improve efficiency by reducing the number of transactions or creating bulk, to improve accessibility by lowering location and time gaps between producers and consumers, and to provide specialist services to customers. Each of these functions is now examined in more detail.

Reconciling the needs of producers and consumers

Manufacturers typically produce a large quantity of a limited range of goods, whereas consumers and businesses usually want only a limited quantity of a wide range of goods.[3] The role of channel intermediaries is to reconcile these conflicting situations. For example, a manufacturer of tables sells to retailers, each of which buys from a range of manufacturers of furniture. The manufacturer can gain economies of scale by producing large quantities of tables, and selling to many companies further along the supply chain—e.g. retailers like DFS, Harvey's, The Furniture Market. Each retailer can then offer its customers a wide assortment of products offering its customers considerable choice under one roof. It is important to remember the key function of channel intermediaries is *breaking bulk*. A wholesaler may buy large quantities from a manufacturer (perhaps a container load) and then sell smaller quantities (such as by the case) to retailers. Alternatively, large retailers such as supermarkets buy large quantities from producers, and break bulk by splitting the order between outlets. In this way, producers make large quantities while consumers are offered limited quantities at the point of purchase.

Improving efficiency

Channel intermediaries can improve distribution efficiency by *reducing the number of transactions* and *creating bulk for transportation*. Figure 17.1 shows how the number of transactions between three producers and three customers is reduced by using one intermediary. Direct distribution to customers results in nine transactions, whereas the use of an intermediary cuts the number of transactions to six. Distribution (and selling) costs and effort, therefore, are reduced.

Small producers can benefit by selling to intermediaries, which then combine a large number of small purchases into bulk for transportation. Without the intermediary it may

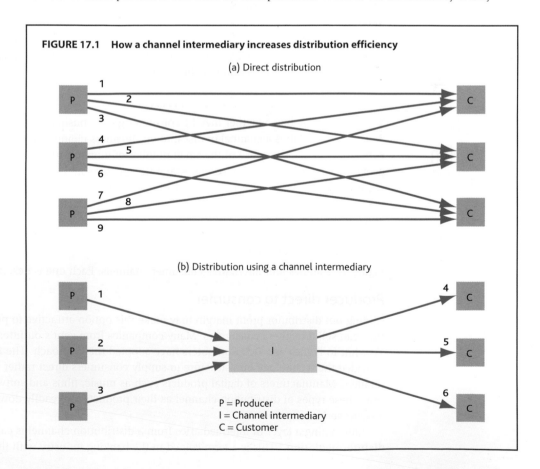

FIGURE 17.1 How a channel intermediary increases distribution efficiency

(a) Direct distribution

(b) Distribution using a channel intermediary

P = Producer
I = Channel intermediary
C = Customer

prove too costly for each small producer to meet transportation costs to the consumer. Agricultural products such as fruit and vegetables—for example, green beans from Kenya, pineapples and bananas from Central America—are grown by small producers, who sometimes benefit from this arrangement.

Improving accessibility

Two major divides that need to be bridged between producers and consumers are the location and time gaps. The *location gap* derives from the geographic separation of producers from the customers they serve. Many of the cars produced in the UK by Nissan and Toyota are exported to Europe. Car dealers in Europe provide customer access to these cars in the form of display and test drive facilities, and the opportunity to purchase locally rather than deal direct with the producer thousands of miles away. The Internet is reducing the location gap, allowing buyers to purchase without the need to visit a producer or distributor. Producers can play their part in improving accessibility by making consumers aware of the location of their distributors.

The *time gap* results from discrepancies between when a manufacturer wants to produce goods and when consumers wish to buy. For example, manufacturers of spare parts for cars may wish to run their manufacturing processes from Monday to Friday but shoppers may wish to purchase goods every day of the week. By opening at the weekend, car accessory outlets bridge the time gap between production and consumption. The Internet has facilitated 365/24/7 buying, which is streamlining communications throughout global supply chains. This is also very popular in consumer markets.

Providing specialist services

Channel intermediaries can perform specialist customer services that manufacturers may feel ill-equipped to provide themselves. Distributors may have long-standing expertise in such areas as selling, servicing and installation to customers. Producers may feel that these functions are better handled by channel intermediaries so that they can specialize in other aspects of manufacturing and marketing activity.

Types of Distribution Channel

Everything we buy, whether they be consumer goods, business-to-business goods or services, requires a channel of distribution. Business channels tend to be shorter than consumer channels because of the small number of ultimate customers, the greater geographic concentration of customers, and the greater complexity of the products that require close producer–customer liaison. Service channels also tend to be short because of the intangibility of services and the need for personal contact between the service provider and consumer.

Consumer channels

Figure 17.2 shows four alternative consumer channels. Each one is described briefly below.

Producer direct to consumer

Cutting out distributor profit margin may make this option attractive to producers as they can sell directly to consumers. Many companies from gent's outfitters Charles Tyrwhitt to iTunes and Dell Computers have adopted this approach. The Internet has provided the technology infrastructure to supply consumers direct rather than through retailers. Manufacturers of digital products such as music, films and software have benefited from these types of distribution channel as their products are readily downloadable via a customer's computer.

Eliminating a layer of intermediaries from a distribution channel is called **disintermediation**.[4] This is a term coined in the banking industry with the advent of retail

FIGURE 17.2   Distribution channels for consumer goods

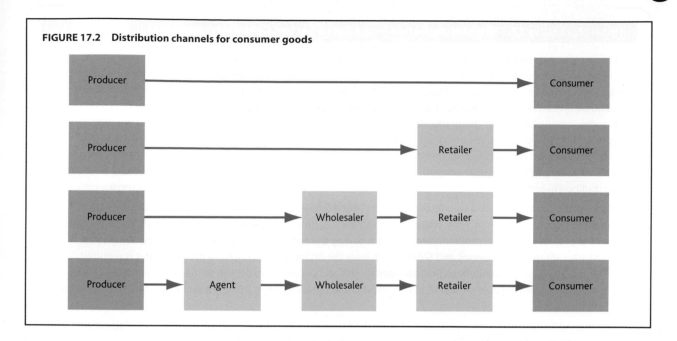

banking. The basic idea is that the 'middleman' is removed and manufacturers sell directly to consumers. Examples in other industries include airlines such as easyJet and Ryanair who have moved towards Internet bookings, eliminating the need to go through a travel agent. Dell Computers has largely eliminated retailers from the traditional PC distribution channel. The service industry has also adopted this approach. IYogi is a global supplier of computer support services. Based in India, it provides remote access computer repair and support. A broader definition of disintermediation includes the displacement of traditional channel intermediaries with new forms of distribution. For example, iTunes music stores are replacing specialist record shops in the distribution of music. Disintermediation occurs when a new type of channel intermediary or structure serves customers better than the old channels. Spotify and Last.fm provide access to almost limitless musical choice through streaming technology for a small monthly fee. YouTube provides a distribution platform for new recording artists.

At the opposite end of the spectrum is **reintermediation**. This happens when a new and additional intermediary is introduced into the supply chain. Read Digital Marketing 17.1 to find out more about reintermediation in the retail sector.

Producer to retailer to consumer

The growth in retailer size has meant that it becomes economic for producers to supply retailers directly rather than through wholesalers. Consumers then have the convenience of viewing and/or testing the product at the retail outlet. Supermarket chains such as Sainsbury's exercise considerable power over manufacturers because of their enormous buying capabilities. However, technology has created new channels to consumers. Internet retailers such as Amazon (books and consumer goods), ASOS (fashion) and Expedia (travel and hotel bookings) compete with store-based retailers supplying directly from their websites. Apple has created its own online retail store, iTunes, to supply music downloads for the iPod, and the App Store to distribute software applications to owners of the iPhone. Store-based retailers have responded by developing their own sophisticated websites selling a wide range of goods. Increasingly, these types of retailers are developing a multichannel approach, which means they can serve customer needs in-store, online and on the move via mobile communications.

Digital Marketing 17.1 Reintermediation in the Retail Sector: Cyber Intermediaries

Retailers use the Internet for different purposes ranging from a simple poster website advertising the company to a fully integrated online business operation that facilitates online sales, builds customer relationships, and acts as a portal for new business opportunities. But research has found that in general retailers tend to lack the skills and technical resources required to develop their online presence. A solution is to use Web service providers that act as 'cyber intermediaries' for designing, developing, hosting and managing their websites. Adding this extra level in the supply chain enables retailers to exploit the potential of the Internet by using third-party Web service providers, who have the technical expertise and knowledge necessary for all of the retailer's online business requirements. Many retailers are taking this action in an attempt to protect their investment in increasingly competitive and challenging online trading environments. They also try to build strong collaborative relationships with their Web service providers.

However, issues can arise which cause relationships between retailer and their digital suppliers to disintegrate. Potentially, contentious issues include ownership of intellectual property, levels of service and insufficient budget to meet the project brief. Such problems are compounded by this being a relatively young industry. Many cyber intermediaries are micro businesses and SMEs, which have the technical know-how to produce what is required online by the retailers but do not have the managerial skills and personnel expertise to manage their retail clients. Furthermore, because of increasing demand for websites and digital systems there is a skill shortage in the IT sector for able programmers.

Despite the challenges, there are a growing number of Web service providers which specialize in developing and building systems solutions for retailers who want to get online: for example, companies like CSY retail systems; citruslime and Cyber till. These companies provide services which include cloud computing, epos systems and e-commerce solutions.

Based on: Vise et al. (2010);[5] White and Daniel, (2004);[6] Doherty and Ellis-Chadwick (2010);[7] Ray and Ray (2006)[8]

Producer to wholesaler to retailer to consumer

For small retailers (e.g. confectionery, tobacco and news (CTNs), convenience stores) with limited order quantities, the use of wholesalers makes economic sense. Wholesalers can buy in bulk from producers, and sell smaller quantities to numerous retailers. The danger is that large retailers in the same market have the power to buy directly from producers and thus cut out the wholesaler. In certain cases the buying power of large retailers has meant that they can sell products to their customers cheaper than a small retailer can buy from the wholesaler. In Europe long channels involving wholesalers are common in France and Italy. In France, for example, the distribution of vehicle spare parts is dominated by small independent wholesalers.[9]

Producer to agent to wholesaler to retailer to consumer

This long channel is sometimes used by companies entering foreign markets. They may delegate the task of selling the product to an agent (who does not take title to the goods). The agent contacts wholesalers (or retailers) and receives commission on sales. Overseas sales of books are sometimes generated in this way.

Some companies use multiple channels to distribute their products. Grocery products, for example, use both producer to wholesaler to retailer (small grocers), and producer to retailer (supermarkets). The advent of the Internet has also encouraged the use of multiple channels. For example, in the tourist industry, package holidays can be booked through travel agencies or via the Internet, and hotels and flights can be booked over the telephone or by using the Internet. Such multichannel strategies allow companies to differentiate their services to take advantage of the inherent strengths of each channel.[10] Multiple channels also provide wide market coverage. For example, mobile handset manufacturers such as Nokia distribute their products through their website, service providers such as Orange, Internet retailers and supermarkets, allowing wide reach of potential customers. Sony also achieves wide

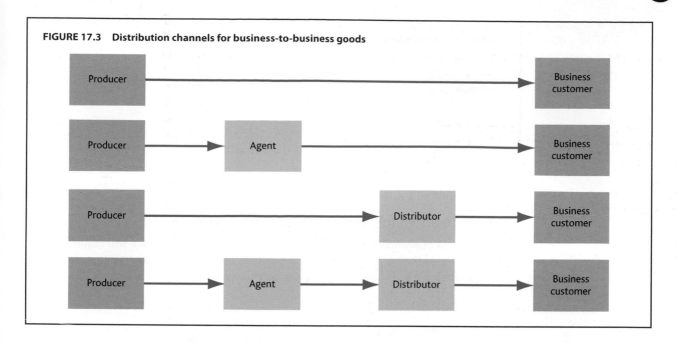

FIGURE 17.3   Distribution channels for business-to-business goods

distribution coverage by using multiple channels, including its own Sony Centres, electrical goods chain stores such as Currys/PC World, catalogue shops such as Argos and online retailers such as Amazon. In Japan distribution channels to consumers tend to be long and complex, with close relationships between channel members, a fact that has acted as a barrier to entry for foreign companies.

Business-to-business channels

Common business-to-business distribution channels are illustrated in Figure 17.3. Usually a maximum of one channel intermediary is used.

Producer to business customer

Supplying business customers directly is common for expensive industrial products such as gas turbines, diesel locomotives and aero-engines. There needs to be close liaison between supplier and customer to solve technical problems, and the size of the order makes direct selling and distribution economic.

Producer to agent to business customer

Instead of selling to business customers using their own salesforce, a business-to-business goods company could employ the services of an agent who may sell a range of goods from several suppliers (on a commission basis). This spreads selling costs and may be attractive to companies without the reserves to set up their own sales operation. The disadvantage is that there is little control over the agent, who is unlikely to devote the same amount of time selling on products compared with a dedicated sales team.

Producer to distributor to business customer

For less expensive, more frequently bought business-to-business products, distributors are used. These may have both internal and field sales staff.[11] Internal staff deal with customer-generated enquiries and order placing, order follow-up (often using the Internet) and checking inventory levels. For many goods that are routinely purchased, fully automated digital systems are used. Outside sales staff are more proactive: their practical responsibilities are to find new customers, get products specified, distribute catalogues and gather market information. The advantage to customers of using distributors is that they can buy small quantities locally.

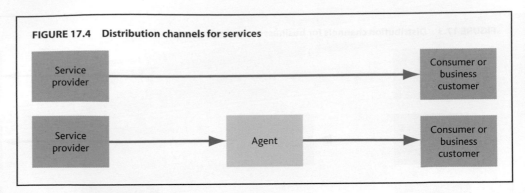

FIGURE 17.4 **Distribution channels for services**

Producer to agent to distributor to business customer

Where business customers prefer to call upon distributors, the agent's job will require selling into these intermediaries. The reason why a producer may employ an agent rather than a dedicated salesforce is usually cost based (as previously discussed).

Services channels

Distribution channels for services are usually short: either direct or using an agent. While in many situations stocks are not held, the role of the wholesaler, retailer or industrial distributor is different in service supply chains. For example in the fast food industry and beauty industries products are purchased to use in the 'production' of service deliverables, like a Big Mac burger or a manicure and painted nails. Figure 17.4 shows the two alternatives whether they be to consumer or industrial customers.

Service provider to consumer or business customer

The close personal relationships between service providers and customers often mean that service supply is direct. Examples include healthcare, office cleaning, accountancy, marketing research and law.

Service provider to agent to consumer or business customer

A channel intermediary for a service company usually takes the form of an agent. Agents are used when the service provider is geographically distant from customers, and where it is not economical for the provider to establish its own local sales team. Examples include insurance, travel, secretarial and theatrical agents.

Channel Strategy

Channel strategy decisions involve the selection of the most effective distribution channel, the most appropriate level of distribution intensity and the degree of channel integration (see Fig. 17.5). Each of these decisions will now be discussed.

Channel selection

Why does Procter & Gamble sell its brands through supermarkets rather than selling direct? Why does General Electric sell its locomotives direct to train operating companies rather than use a distributor? The answers are to be found by examining the following factors that influence *channel selection*. These influences can be grouped under market, producer, product and competitive factors.

Market factors

An important market factor is buyer behaviour: buyer expectations may dictate that the product be sold in a certain way. Buyers may prefer to buy locally and in a particular type of shop. Failure to match these expectations can have serious consequences.

Go to the website to see how Procter & Gamble uses a surreal advertising campaign based on delivery to promote its Müller yoghurts.
www.mcgraw-hill.co.uk/ textbooks/jobber

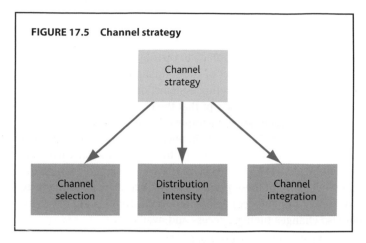

FIGURE 17.5   Channel strategy

Buyer needs regarding product information, installation and technical assistance also have to be considered. A judgement needs to be made about whether the producer or channel intermediary can best meet these needs in terms of expertise, commitment and cost. For example, products that require facilities for local servicing, such as cars, often use intermediaries to carry out the task. Where the service requirement does not involve large capital investment the producer may carry out the service. For example, suppliers of pest control Rentokil train their staff to conduct annual inspection and servicing as well as fulfilling their sales role.

The willingness of channel intermediaries to market a product is also a market-based factor that influences channel decisions. Direct distribution may be the only option if distributors refuse to handle the product. For industrial products, this may mean the recruitment of salespeople, and for consumer products direct mail may be employed to communicate to and supply customers. The profit margins demanded by wholesalers and retailers, and the commission rates expected by sales agents also affect their attractiveness as channel intermediaries. These costs need to be assessed in comparison with those of a salesforce.

The location and geographical concentration of customers also affects channel selection. The more local and clustered the customer base, the more likely direct distribution is feasible. Direct distribution is also more prevalent when buyers are few in number and buy large quantities. A large number of small customers may mean that using channel intermediaries is the only economical way of reaching them (hence supermarkets).

Producer factors

A constraint on the channel decision is when the producer lacks adequate resources to perform the functions of the channel. Producers may lack the financial and managerial resources to take on channel operations. Lack of financial resources may mean that a salesforce cannot be recruited, and sales agents and/or distributors are used instead. Producers may feel that they do not possess the customer-based skills to distribute their products and prefer to rely on intermediaries.

The product mix offered by a producer may also affect channel strategy. A wide mix of products may make direct distribution (and selling) cost-effective. Narrow or single product companies, on the other hand, may find the cost of direct distribution prohibitive unless the product is extremely expensive.

The final product influence is the desired degree of control of channel operations. The use of independent channel intermediaries reduces producer control. For example, by distributing their products through supermarkets, manufacturers lose total control of the price charged to consumers. Furthermore, there is no guarantee that new products will be stocked. Direct distribution gives producers control over such issues.

Product factors

Large complex products are often supplied direct to customers. The need for close personal contact between producer and customer, and the high prices charged, mean that direct distribution and selling is both necessary and feasible. Perishable products such as frozen food, meat and bread require relatively short channels to supply the customer with fresh stock. Finally, bulky or difficult to handle products may require direct distribution because distributors may refuse to carry them if storage or display problems arise.[12]

Competitive factors

If the competition controls traditional channels of distribution—for example, through franchise or exclusive dealing arrangements—an innovative approach to distribution may be required. Two alternatives are to recruit a salesforce to sell direct or to set up a producer-owned distribution network (see the section on vertical marketing systems, under 'Conventional marketing channels', below). Producers should not accept that the channels of distribution used by competitors are the only ways to reach target customers. Direct marketing provides opportunities to supply products in new ways. Traditional channels of distribution for personal computers through high-street retailers are being circumvented by direct marketers, who use direct response advertising to reach buyers. The emergence of the more computer-aware and experienced buyer, and the higher reliability of these products as the market reaches maturity, has meant that a local source of supply (and advice) is less important. Digitization of product not only changes the mode but also changes timings, access and availability.

Distribution intensity

The second channel strategy decision is the choice of *distribution intensity*. The three broad options are intensive, selective and exclusive distribution.

Intensive distribution

Intensive distribution aims to achieve saturation coverage of the market by using all available outlets. With many mass-market products, such as soft drinks, foods, toiletries, alcohol and newspapers, sales are a direct function of the number of outlets penetrated. This is because consumers have a range of acceptable brands from which they can choose. If a brand is not available in an outlet, an alternative is bought. The convenience aspect of purchase is paramount. New outlets may be sought that hitherto had not stocked the products, such as the sale of confectionery and grocery items at petrol stations: for example, Esso has introduced 380 On the Run stores in 13 European countries.[13] In the UK this trend has also encouraged supermarkets to locate convenience stores with a wide range of products at motorway service station, e.g. Marks & Spencer's Simply Food stores in Moto service stations and Waitrose became Welcome Break's newest food brand in its service stations (see Exhibit 17.1).[14]

Selective distribution

Market coverage may also be achieved through **selective distribution**, in which a producer uses a limited number of outlets in a geographical area to sell its products. The advantages to the producer are the opportunity to select only the best outlets to focus its efforts to build close working relationships and to train distributor staff on fewer outlets than with intensive distribution, and, if selling and distribution is direct, to reduce costs. Upmarket aspirational brands are often sold in carefully selected outlets. Retail outlets and industrial distributors like this arrangement since it reduces competition. Selective distribution is more likely to be used when buyers are willing to shop around when choosing products. This means that it is not necessary for a company to have its products available in all outlets. Products such as audio and video equipment, cameras, personal computers and cosmetics may be sold in this way.

Problems can arise when a retailer demands distribution rights but is refused by producers. This happened in the case of Superdrug, a UK discount store chain, which requested the right to sell expensive perfume but was denied by manufacturers who claimed

▲ EXHIBIT 17.1   Waitrose became Welcome Break's newest food brand in its service stations.

that the store did not have the right ambience for the sale of luxury products. Superdrug maintained that its application was refused because the chain wanted to sell perfumes for less than their recommended prices. A Monopolies and Mergers Commission investigation supported current practice. European rules allow perfume companies to confine distribution to retailers who measure up in terms of décor and staff training. Manufacturers are not permitted to refuse distribution rights on the grounds that the retailer will sell for less than the list price.[15]

Exclusive distribution

This is an extreme form of selective distribution in which only one wholesaler, retailer or industrial distributor is used in a geographic area. Cars are often sold on this basis with only one dealer operating in each town or city. This reduces a purchaser's power to negotiate prices for the same model between dealers since to buy in a neighbouring town may be inconvenient when servicing or repairs are required. It also allows very close cooperation between producer and retailer over servicing, pricing and promotion. Initially, Apple's iPhone was also subject to exclusive distribution in the UK through the mobile phone operator O_2 and retailer Carphone Warehouse.[16] The right to **exclusive distribution** may be demanded by distributors as a condition for stocking a manufacturer's product line. Similarly, producers may wish for exclusive dealing where the distributor agrees not to stock competing lines. The selection of an exclusive set of distributors can provide the basis for excellent customer service. For example, Caterpillar, the tractor manufacturer, is renowned for the quality of its exclusive dealer network. Dealers undergo rigorous selection procedures but, once accepted, are treated royally in order to make them feel part of the Caterpillar family. This is because Caterpillar recognizes the importance of dealer service in backing up its reputation for highly reliable machines.[17]

Exclusive dealing can reduce competition in ways that may be considered contrary to consumers' interests. The European Court of Justice rejected an appeal by Unilever over the issue of exclusive outlets in Germany. By supplying freezer cabinets Unilever maintained exclusivity by refusing to allow other competing ice creams into them. Also, Coca-Cola, Schweppes Beverages and Britvic's exclusive ties with the leisure trade (such as sports clubs) were broken by the Office of Fair Trading, making competitive entry easier.[18]

However, the European Court rejected an appeal by the French Leclerc supermarket group over the issue of the selective distribution system used by Yves St Laurent perfumes. The judges found that the use of selective distribution for luxury cosmetic products increased competition and that it was in the consumer's and manufacturer's interest to preserve the image of such luxury products.

Channel integration

Channel integration can range from conventional marketing channels, comprising an independent producer and channel intermediaries, through a franchise operation, to channel ownership by a producer. Producers need to consider the strengths and weaknesses of each system when setting channel strategies.

Conventional marketing channels

The independence of channel intermediaries means that the producer has little or no control over them. Arrangements such as exclusive dealing may provide a degree of control, but separation of ownership means that each party will look after its own interests. Conventional marketing channels are characterized by hard bargaining and, occasionally, conflict. For example, a retailer may believe that cutting the price of a brand is necessary to move stock, even though the producer objects because of brand image considerations.

However, separation of ownership means that each party can specialize in the function in which it has strengths: manufacturers produce, intermediaries distribute. Care needs to be taken by manufacturers to stay in touch with customers and not abdicate this responsibility to retailers.

A manufacturer that dominates a market through its size and strong brands may exercise considerable power over intermediaries even though they are independent. This power may result in an **administered vertical marketing system** where the manufacturer can command considerable cooperation from wholesalers and retailers. Major brand builders such as Procter & Gamble and Lever Brothers had traditionally held great leverage over distribution but, more recently, power has moved towards the large dominant supermarket chains through their purchasing and market power. Marks & Spencer is a clear example of a retailer controlling an administered vertical marketing system. Through its dominant market position it is capable of exerting considerable authority over its suppliers.

Franchising

A **franchise** is a legal contract in which a producer and channel intermediaries agree each member's rights and obligations. Usually, the intermediary receives marketing, managerial, technical and financial services in return for a fee. Franchise organizations such as McDonald's, Benetton, Hertz, the Body Shop and Avis combine the strengths of a large sophisticated marketing-orientated organization with the energy and motivation of a locally owned outlet. Franchising is also commonplace in the car industry, where dealers agree exclusive deals with manufacturers in return for marketing and financial backing. Although a franchise operation gives a degree of producer control, there are still areas of potential conflict. For example, the producer may be dissatisfied with the standards of service provided by the outlet, or the franchisee may believe that the franchising organization provides inadequate promotional support. Goal conflict can also arise. For example, some McDonald's franchisees were displeased with the company's rapid expansion programme, which meant that new restaurants opened within a mile of existing outlets. This led to complaints about lower profits and falling franchise resale values.[19] Also, compared with ownership, the franchise organization lacks total control over franchisees. For example, Marriott, which franchises many of its hotels, had to rely on persuasion rather than control when it asked its franchisees to spend more than $1 billion worldwide on its new bedding design.[20]

A franchise agreement provides a **contractual vertical marketing system** through the formal coordination and integration of marketing and distribution activities. Some franchise organizations exert a considerable degree of control over financial and marketing operations. For example, to become a KFC franchisee, there is a licence fee of $43,600, a monthly royalty of 6 per cent, a 5 per cent contribution to advertising plus the cost of buying and fitting out the restaurant, which can be in excess of $100,000. Additional funding is required for purchasing stock, paying for training, wages, utility bills and insurance premiums.[21]

Despite the cost of setting up and running a franchise there are compelling reasons why a producer might choose franchising as a means of distribution. Franchising allows the producer to overcome internal resource constraints by providing access to the franchisee's resources as can be seen in the KFC example. The franchisee not only pays a set-up fee but also makes an ongoing contribution through regular royalty payments. Using this method, companies can gain access to geographically dispersed areas. KFC dominates the fast food

Alone we're Delicious. Together we're Yum!®

⬆ EXHIBIT 17.2 Yum! operates franchises worldwide including KFC, Pizza Hut and Taco Bell.

Go to the website and compare how KFC uses logistics in its advertising. www.mcgraw-hill.co.uk/ textbooks/jobber

Marketing in Action 17.1 Alone We're Delicious, Together We Are Yum![22]

Yum! Brands Inc. is based in Louisville, Kentucky USA and has three highly successful brands in
its portfolio: KFC, Pizza Hut and Taco Bell. Yum! operates 3700 fast-food restaurants in China of which KFC is currently
the most profitable. Initially, Yum! took care to recruit managers who understood the local area and was also careful
to select the right joint-venture partners: Beijing Corp of animal production, processing, industry and commerce, and
Beijing Travel & Tourism Corp. The reasons for not using the franchise model to expand in the early days were because
of stringent Chinese rules and legislation. Changing economic conditions favours franchising, and there is plenty of
demand from the 600 million-strong middle-class.

Yum! aims to expand the number of outlets in this area to 20,000. The franchise approach has enabled the company to
become the most successful foreign company operating in China. The business has been so successful because it has
used local foods and management teams to build partnerships and drive expansion. If you visit a KFC in China, you can
not only buy a bucket of fried chicken, you can also have a bowl of rice porridge, with pork, pickles, mushrooms and
preserved egg.

Based on: Mellor (2011);[23] Hernandez (2011)[24]

franchise market in China, beating McDonald's to highly sought-after locations in major
Chinese cities. Read Marketing in Action 17.1 to find out more about franchising Yum! and
its successful franchise operations.

In such situations, producers may value the notion of the owner-manager who has a
vested interest in the success of the business. Although some control may still be necessary,
the franchisee benefits directly from increases in sales and profits and so has a financial
incentive to manage the business well. Finally, franchising may be a way for a producer to
access the local knowledge of the franchisee. Franchising may therefore be attractive when a
producer is expanding into new markets and where potential franchisees have access to
information that is important in penetrating such markets.

The three most common levels where franchising is used in the distribution chain are:

1 *Manufacturer and retailer*: the car industry is dominated by this arrangement. The
   manufacturer gains retail outlets for its cars and repair facilities without the capital outlay
   required by ownership.
2 *Manufacturer and wholesaler*: this is commonly used in the soft drinks industry.
   Manufacturers such as Schweppes, Coca-Cola and Pepsi grant wholesalers the right to
   make up and bottle their concentrate in line with their instructions, and to distribute the
   products within a defined geographic area.
3 *Retailer and retailer*: a frequently used method that often has its roots in a successful
   retailing operation seeking to expand geographically by means of a franchise operation,
   often with great success. Examples include McDonald's, Benetton, Pizza Hut and KFC.
   See Table 17.1 for examples of some of the top franchises.

Channel ownership

Total control over distributor activities comes with channel ownership. This establishes a
corporate vertical marketing system. By purchasing retail outlets, producers control their
purchasing, production and marketing activities. In particular, control over purchasing means
a captive outlet for the manufacturer's products. For example, channel ownership is common
in the clothing industry, with companies such as Zara and H&M owning their own chains of
retail outlets.

The advantages of control have to be weighed against the high price of acquisition and
the danger that the move into retailing will spread managerial activities too widely.
Nevertheless, corporate vertical marketing systems have operated successfully for many years
in the oil industry where companies such as Shell and BP own not only considerable
numbers of petrol stations but also the means of production.

TABLE 17.1 Examples of top franchises in Europe

Rank	Franchise name	Number of units in Europe	Industry	Origin
1.	7-Eleven	37,496	Food convenience stores	USA
2.	Subway	35,000	Food sandwich bars	USA
3.	McDonald's	32,805	Food restaurants	USA
4.	Kumon Institution of Education	26,311	Education	Japan
5.	KFC (Yum! restaurants)	22,000	Food restaurants	USA
6.	Spar	13,600	Food convenience stores	Netherlands
7.	Europcar	13,000	Auto leasing and rental	France
8.	Pizza Hut	12,700	Food restaurants	USA
9.	Burger King	12,000	Food restaurants	USA
10.	Mexx	11,000	Retail clothing	Netherlands

Source: Franchise Europe (2012) http://www.franchiseeurope.com/top500/

Channel Management

Once the key channel strategy decisions have been made, effective implementation is required. Specifically, a number of channel management issues must be addressed (see Fig. 17.6). These are the selection, motivation, training and evaluation of channel members, and managing conflict between producers and channel members.

Selection

For some producers the distribution problem is not so much channel selection as channel acceptance. The selection decision can vary depending on the size of the producer: for example, very small companies face difficulties when trying to persuade large retailers to stock their products. Selection then involves identifying candidates and developing *selection criteria*.

Identifying sources

Sources for identifying candidates include trade sources, reseller enquiries, customers of distributors and the field salesforce.[25] *Trade sources* include trade associations, exhibitions and trade publications. Talking to trade associations can lead to the supply of names of prospective distributors. Exhibitions provide a useful means of meeting and talking to

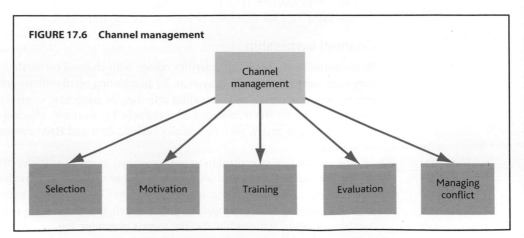

FIGURE 17.6 Channel management

Channel management → Selection, Motivation, Training, Evaluation, Managing conflict possible distributors. Sometimes channel members may be proactive in contacting a producer to express an interest in handling their products. Such *reseller enquiries* show that the possible distributor is enthusiastic about the possibility of a link. *Customers of distributors* are a useful source since they can comment on their merits and limitations. Finally, if a producer already has a *field salesforce* calling on intermediaries, salespeople are in a good position to seek out possible new distributors in their own territory.

Developing selection criteria

Common selection criteria include market, product and customer knowledge, market coverage, quality and size of the salesforce (if applicable), reputation among customers, financial standing, the extent to which competitive and complementary products are carried, managerial competence, and the degree of enthusiasm for handling the producer's lines. In practice, selection may be complex because large, well-established distributors may carry many competing lines and lack enthusiasm for more, whereas smaller distributors may be more enthusiastic and hungry for success. The top selection criteria of overseas distributors are market knowledge, enthusiasm for the contract, hunger for success, customer knowledge, and the fact that the distributor does not carry competitors' products.

Motivation

Once selected, channel members need to be motivated to agree to act as a distributor, and allocate adequate commitment and resources to the producer's lines. The key to effective motivation is to understand the needs and problems of distributors as they are linked. For example, a distributor that values financial incentives may respond more readily to high commission than one that is more concerned with having an exclusive territory. Possible motivators include financial rewards, territorial exclusivity, providing resource support (e.g. sales training, field sales assistance, provision of marketing research information, advertising and promotion support, financial assistance and management training) and developing *strong work relationships* (e.g. joint planning, assurance of long-term commitment, appreciation of effort and success, frequent interchange of views and arranging distributor conferences).

Producers should seek to develop strong long-term relationships with their distributors based on a recognition of their performance and integrated planning and operations. Jointly determined sales targets can motivate salespeople, who might receive a bonus on achievement. Targets are also useful for monitoring performance.

At the outset establishing a long-term commitment is important, especially with international partners as this can foster trust. The most popular methods cited by export managers and directors to motivate their overseas distributors were territorial exclusivity, provision of up-to-date product and company information, regular personal contact, appreciation of effort and understanding of the distributors' problems, attractive financial incentives, and provision of salespeople to support the distributors' salesforce.[26] Given overseas distributors' fears that they may be replaced, it was disappointing to note that only 40 per cent of these exporters provided assurances of a long-term business commitment to their distributors as a major motivator.

Mutual commitment between channel members is central to successful relationship marketing. Two types of commitment are affective commitment that expresses the extent to which channel members like to maintain their relationship with their partners, and calculative commitment where channel members need to maintain a relationship. Commitment is highly dependent on interdependence and trust between the parties.[27]

Training

The need to train channel members obviously depends on their internal competences. Large-market supermarket chains, for example, may regard an invitation by a manufacturer to provide marketing training as an insult. However, many smaller distributors have been found to be weak on sales management, marketing, financial management, stock control and personnel management, and may welcome producer initiatives on training.[28] From the producer's perspective, training can provide the necessary technical knowledge about a supplier company and its products, and help to build a spirit of partnership and commitment.

However, the training of overseas distributors by British exporters appears to be the exception rather than the rule.[29] When training is provided, it usually takes the form of product and company knowledge. Nevertheless when such knowledge is given it can help to build strong personal relationships and give distributors the confidence to sell those products.

Evaluation

The evaluation of channel members has an important bearing on distributor retention, training and motivation decisions. Evaluation provides the information necessary to decide which channel members to retain and which to drop. Shortfalls in distributor skills and competences may be identified through evaluation, and appropriate training programmes organized by producers. Where a lack of motivation is recognized as a problem, producers can implement plans designed to deal with the root causes of demotivation (e.g. financial incentives and/or fostering a partnership approach to business).[30]

However, the scope and frequency of evaluation may be limited where power lies with the channel member. If producers have relatively little power because they are more dependent on channel members for distribution than channel members are on individual producers for supply, in-depth evaluation and remedial action will be restricted. Channel members may be reluctant to spend time providing the producers with comprehensive information on which to base evaluation. Remedial action may be limited to tentative suggestions when producers suspect there is room for improvement.

Where manufacturer power is high, through having strong brands and many distributors from which to choose, evaluation may be more frequent and wider in scope. Channel members are more likely to comply with the manufacturer's demands for performance information and agree for their sales and marketing efforts to be monitored by the manufacturer.

Evaluation criteria include sales volume and value, profitability, level of stocks, quality and position of display, new accounts opened, selling and marketing capabilities, quality of service provided to customers, market information feedback, ability and willingness to meet commitments, attitudes and personal capability.

Although the evaluation of overseas distributors and agents is more difficult than that for their domestic counterparts, research has shown that over 90 per cent of producers carry out evaluation, usually at least once a year.[31]

Managing conflict

When producers and channel members are independent, conflict inevitably occurs from time to time. The intensity of conflict can range from occasional, minor disagreements that are quickly forgotten, to major disputes that fuel continuous bitter relationships.[32]

Sources of channel conflict

The major sources of *channel conflict* are differences in goals, differences in views on the desired product lines carried by channel members, multiple distribution channels, and inadequacies in performance.

- *Differences in goals*: most resellers attempt to maximize their own profit. This can be accomplished by improving profit margin, reducing inventory levels, increasing sales, lowering expenses and receiving greater allowances from suppliers. In contrast, producers might benefit from lower margins, greater channel inventories, higher promotional expenses and fewer allowances given to channel members. These inherent conflicts of interest mean that there are many potential areas of disagreement between producers and their channel members.
- *Differences in desired product line*: resellers that grow by adding product lines may be regarded as disloyal by their original suppliers and can cause resentment. For example, WHSmith, a UK retailer, originally specialized in books, magazines and newspapers but

has grown by adding new product lines such as computer games, DVDs and PC accessories. In Europe the growth of speciality shops selling sportswear and trainers is another source of potential conflict as the retailers with a narrow product range have a deep assortment on offer, selling a wide variety of branded sports shoes, for example. The increased competition can cause conflict with its original suppliers of these product lines since the addition of competitors' brands makes the retailer appear disloyal.[33]

- *Multiple distribution channels*: in trying to achieve market coverage, a producer may use multiple distribution channels. For example, a producer may decide to sell directly to key accounts because their size warrants a key account salesforce, and use channel intermediaries to give wide market coverage. Conflict can arise when a channel member is denied access to a lucrative order from a key account because it is being serviced directly by the producer. Disagreements can also occur when the producer owns retail outlets that compete with independent retailers that also sell the producer's brands. For example, Clarks, a footwear manufacturer, owns a chain of outlets that compete with other shoe outlets that sell Clarks' shoes.[34]

- *Inadequacies in performance*: an obvious source of conflict is when parties in the supply chain do not perform to expectations. For example, a channel member may underperform in terms of sales, level of inventory carried, customer service, standards of display and salesperson effectiveness. Producers may give poor delivery, inadequate promotional support, low profit margins, poor-quality goods and incomplete shipments. These can all be potential areas of conflict.

Avoiding and resolving conflict

How can producers and channel members avoid and resolve conflict? There are several ways of managing conflict.

- *Developing a partnership approach*: this calls for frequent interaction between producer and resellers to develop a spirit of mutual understanding and cooperation. Producers can help channel members with training, financial help and promotional support. Distributors, in turn, may agree to mutually agreed sales targets and provide extra sales resources. The objective is to build confidence in the manufacturer's products and relationships based on trust. When conflicts arise there is more chance they will be resolved in a spirit of cooperation. Organizing staff exchange programmes can be useful in allowing each party to understand the problems and tensions of the other to avoid giving rise to animosity.

- *Training in conflict handling*: staff who handle disputes need to be trained in negotiation and communication skills. They need to be able to handle high-pressure conflict situations without resorting to emotion and *blaming behaviour*. Instead, they should be able to handle such situations calmly and be able to handle concession analysis, in particular the identification of *win-win situations*. These are situations where both the producer and reseller benefit from an agreement.

- *Market partitioning*: to reduce or eliminate conflict from multiple distribution channels, producers can try to partition markets on some logical basis, such as customer size or type. This can work if channel members accept the basis for the partitioning. Alternatively, different channels can be supplied with different product lines. For example, Hallmark sells its premium greetings cards under its Hallmark brand name to upmarket department stores, and its standard cards under the Ambassador name to discount retailers.[35]

- *Improving performance*: many conflicts occur for genuine reasons. For example, poor delivery by manufacturers or inadequate sales effort by distributors can provoke frustration and anger. Rather than attempt to placate the aggrieved partner, the most effective solution is to improve performance so that the source of conflict disappears. This is the most effective way of dealing with such problems.

- *Channel ownership*: an effective but expensive way of resolving conflicting goals is to buy the other party. Since producer and channel member are under common ownership, the common objective is to maximize joint profits. Conflicts can still occur but the dominant partner is in a position to resolve them quickly. Some producers in Europe have integrated with channel intermediaries successfully. For example, over 40 per cent of household furniture is sold through producer-owned retail outlets in Italy.[36]

• *Coercion*: In some situations, conflict resolution may be dependent on coercion, where one party induces compliance through the use of force. For example, producers can threaten to withdraw supply, deliver late or withdraw financial support; channel members, on the other hand, can threaten to delist the manufacturer's products, promote competitive products and develop own-label brands. In Europe the increasing concentration of retailing into groups of very large organizations has meant that the balance of power has moved away from the manufacturers. The development of own-label brands has further strengthened the retailers' position, while giving them the double advantage of a high profit margin (because their purchase price is low) and a low price to the customer. Manufacturers' power in the supply chain is increased when they are large with high market share. By having a large and loyal customer base, manufacturers' brands become essential for distributors to stock. This increases manufacturers' negotiating power. Also by dominating a product category (e.g. Unilever and Procter & Gamble in detergents) manufacturers gain power over distributors. By using multiple channels of distribution (e.g. direct as well as through distributors) and using a wide selection of distributors, the power of any one distributor is reduced. Control over distributors can also be gained by franchising and channel ownership (where manufacturers own retail outlets).

Physical Distribution and Retailing

In the first part of this chapter we examined channel strategy, focusing on the key areas of channel management decisions. In this section we examine physical distribution decisions, and the implications for channel management and for retailing.

Physical distribution is defined as a 'set of activities concerned with the physical flows of materials, components and finished goods from producer to channel intermediaries and consumers'.

The aim is to provide intermediaries and customers with the right products, in the right quantities, in the right locations, at the right time. Physical distribution activities have been the subject of managerial attention for some time because of the potential for cost savings and improving customer service levels. Cost savings can be achieved by reducing inventory levels, using cheaper forms of transport and shipping in bulk rather than small quantities. Customer service levels can be improved by fast and reliable delivery, including just-in-time delivery, holding high inventory levels so that customers have a wide choice and the chances of stockouts are reduced, fast order processing, and ensuring products arrive in the right quantities and quality.

In the clothing industry, fast-changing fashion demands mean that companies such as H&M and Zara use extremely short lead times to create a competitive advantage over their slower, more cumbersome, rivals. Such methods used are discussed in Mini Case 17.1.

Physical distribution management concerns the balance between cost reduction and meeting customer service requirements. Trade-offs are often necessary. For example, low inventory and slow, cheaper transportation methods reduce costs but lower customer service levels and satisfaction. Determining

⬆ **EXHIBIT 17.3 Zara uses open-plan work spaces to encourage collaboration in its manufacturing units in Spain.**

Mini Case 17.1 **Managing the Supply Chain the Zara Way**

Zara, the Spanish clothing company owned by Inditex, has revolutionized the fashion industry by becoming the first global retailer to sell fashion lines designed especially for seasons in the southern as well as the northern hemisphere. Zara has a successful business model, which has enabled the retail chain to expand to over 5000 outlets and stores in Europe, South America, Oceania and Africa, so developing ranges to suit the seasons is an important part of the expansion strategy. Its key competitive advantage lies in its ability to match fashion trends that change quickly. This in turn relies on an extremely fast and responsive supply chain. While other retailers moved production to the Far East to save money, Zara knew that it could make its best-selling clothes faster in Spain.

Zara uses its stores to find out what consumers want, what styles are selling, what colours are in demand, and which items are hot sellers and which are failures. The data are fed back to Zara headquarters through a sophisticated marketing information system. At the end of each day Zara sales assistants report to the store manager using wireless headsets to communicate inventory levels. The store managers then inform the Zara design and distribution departments at headquarters about what consumers are buying, asking for and avoiding. Top-selling items are requested and low-selling items are withdrawn from shops within a week. There is a big incentive for the store managers to get it right, as up to 70 per cent of their salary is based on commission.

Garments are made in small production runs to avoid overexposure, and no item stays in the shops for more than four weeks, which encourages Zara shoppers to make repeat visits. Whereas the average high-street store in Spain expects shoppers to visit on average three times a year, Zara shoppers visit up to 17 times.

The company's designers use the feedback from the stores when preparing new designs. The fabrics are cut and dyed at Zara's own highly automated manufacturing facilities, which gives it control over this part of the supply chain. Seamstresses in 350 independently owned workshops in Spain and Portugal stitch about half of the pre-cut pieces into garments; the other half are stitched in-house. Only basic items such as T-shirts are bought from low-cost regions such as eastern Europe, Africa and Asia. Although wages are higher in Spain, Zara saves time and money on shipping.

The finished garments are sent back to Zara's headquarters with its state-of-the-art logistics centre where they are electronically tagged, quality checked and sorted into distribution lots for shipping to their destinations. Although Zara supplies every market from warehouses in Spain, it manages to get new merchandise to European stores within 24 hours, and, by flying goods via commercial airlines, to stores in the Americas and Asia in 48 hours or less.

So efficient are Zara's production and distribution systems that the average turnaround time from design to delivery is 10 to 15 days, with around 12,000 garments being marketed each year. In this way, Zara stays on top of fashion trends rather than being outpaced by the market. And, by producing smaller batches of clothing, it adds an air of exclusivity that encourages customers to shop often. As a result, the chain does not have to slash prices by 50 per cent, as rivals often do, to move mass quantities of out-of-season stock. Since Zara is more in tune with current looks, it can also charge slightly more than, for example, Gap, which it has now overtaken to become the world's largest clothing retailer.

Questions:

1   Discuss the implications of shorter product life-cycles for a clothing manufacturer like Zara and H&M.
2   Suggest why Zara doesn't just use the garment ranges developed in the winter for the northern hemisphere and then sell them on in the southern hemisphere.
3   At the opposite end of the spectrum is the 'slow fashion' movement, which advocates buying fewer clothes of better quality that will last longer and helps to save the environment. Do you think this growing trend will affect the demand for fast fashion and do fast fashion brands only appeal to the young?

Based on: The Economist (2002);[37] Roux (2002);[38] BBC (2003);[39] Mitchell (2003);[40] Jobber and Fahy (2009);[41] Capell (2008);[42] Johnson and Falstead (2011)[43]

this balance is a key marketing decision as physical distribution can be a source of competitive advantage. A useful approach is to analyse the market in terms of customer service needs and price sensitivity. The result may be the discovery of two segments:

- segment 1—low service needs, high price sensitivity
- segment 2—high service needs, low price sensitivity.

Unipart was first to exploit segment 2 in the do-it-yourself car repair and servicing market. It gave excellent customer service but charged a high price. This analysis, therefore, defined the market segment to target and the appropriate marketing mix. Alternatively, both segments could be targeted with different marketing mixes. In business-to-business markets, large companies may possess their own service facilities while smaller firms require producer or distributor service as part of the product offering and are willing to pay a higher price.

Not only are there trade-offs between physical distribution costs and customer service levels, but there are also possible conflicts between elements of the physical distribution system itself. For example, an inventory manager may favour low stocks to reduce costs, but if this leads to stock-outs this may raise costs elsewhere: the freight manager may have to accept higher costs resulting from fast freight deliveries in order to guarantee the safety of the products. A key role that the physical distribution manager would perform would be to reconcile the conflicts inherent in the system so that total costs are minimized subject to required customer service levels.

The Physical Distribution System

A system is a set of connected parts managed in such a way that overall objectives are achieved. The physical distribution system contains the following parts (see Fig. 17.7).

- *Customer service*: What level of customer service should be provided?
- *Order processing*: How should the orders be handled?
- *Inventory control*: How much inventory should be held?
- *Warehousing*: Where should the inventory be located? How many warehouses should be used?
- *Transportation*: How will the products be transported?
- *Materials handling*: How will the products be handled during transportation?

Companies like DHL, Fedex and Norbert Dentressangle provide specialist expertise in these areas. Each of the above questions will now be explored.

Customer service

Customer service standards need to be set. For example, a customer service standard might be that 90 per cent of orders are delivered within 24 hours of receipt and 100 per cent are delivered within 48 hours.

Higher customer service standards normally mean higher costs as inventory levels need to be higher. Since inventory ties up working capital, the higher the inventory level the higher the working capital charge. The physical distribution manager needs to be aware of the costs of fulfilling various customer service standards (e.g. 80, 90 and 100 per cent of orders delivered within 48 hours) and the extra customer satisfaction that results from raising standards.

In some cases customers value consistency in delivery time rather than speed. For example, a customer service standard of guaranteed delivery within five working days may be valued more than that of 60 per cent within two, 80 per cent within five or 100 per cent within seven days. Since the latter standard requires delivery at 60 per cent within two days it may require higher inventory levels than the former. Therefore, by understanding customer requirements, it may be possible to increase satisfaction while lowering costs.

Customer service standards should be given considerable attention because they may be the differentiating factor between suppliers: they may be used as a key customer choice

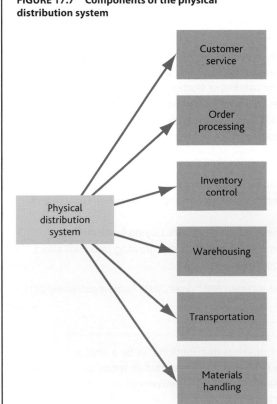

FIGURE 17.7 Components of the physical distribution system

TABLE 17.2   Methods of improving customer service standards in physical distribution

Improve product availability
Raise in-stock levels
Improve accuracy, speed and reliability of deliveries

Improve order cycle time
Shorten time between order and delivery
Improve consistency between order and delivery time

Raise information levels
Improve salesperson information on inventory
Raise information levels on order status
Be proactive in notifying customer of delays

Raise flexibility
Develop contingency plans for urgent orders
Ensure fast reaction time to unforeseen problems (e.g. stolen goods, damage in transit)

criterion. Methods of improving customer service standards in physical distribution are listed in Table 17.2. By examining ways of improving product availability and order cycle time, and raising information levels and flexibility, considerable goodwill and customer loyalty can be created. The advertisement for DHL explains how it provides excellent service, versatility and a portfolio of shipping solutions.

The Internet is providing the means of improving customer service for some distribution companies. For example, if a customer of Federal Express wants to track a package they can do so via the Internet. Creating a user-friendly way to track parcels is a win-win situation as the customer instantly knows where his parcel is and FedEx saves money as it is no longer handling as many customer telephone enquiries. The main logistical companies—FedEx, UPS and DHL—take a significant percentage of their business-to-business transactions via the Internet.

Technology has also enabled logistics to become more efficient and effective through satellite-based distribution systems. For example, Cemex, which makes ready-to-pour concrete, uses such a system to track its trucks. When customers place or change orders, trucks can be rerouted, if needed. This means that customers waste less time waiting and Cemex has become more efficient in supplying them.[44]

If there's an address, we'll find it   DHL

⬆EXHIBIT 17.4   DHL communicates its excellent service and versatility.

Order processing

Reducing time between a customer placing an order and receiving the goods may be achieved through careful analysis of the components that contribute to the order-processing time. Automated digital ordering systems and modern electronic data interchange (EDI) systems via the Internet speed up order-processing, validating customers, checking availability, issuing an order to the warehouse, invoicing the customer and updating the inventory records.

Grocery deliveries which fulfil online orders present the greatest logistical challenges. Typically online orders for tesco.com involve picking an order comprising 60–80 items, across three temperature regimes from a total range of 10–25,000 products within 12–24 hours for

Go to the website and learn about the logistics of getting salad vegetables to Tesco stores.
www.mcgraw-hill.co.uk/ textbooks/jobber

delivery to customers within one- to two-hour time-slots. For example, Tesco is currently picking and delivering an average of 250,000 such orders every week. New logistical techniques have had to be devised to support e-grocery retailing on this scale., which is highly efficient.[45]

Inventory control

Inventory levels can be a source of conflict between finance and marketing management. Since inventory represents costs, financial managers seek stock minimization; marketing management, acutely aware of the customer problems caused by stock-outs, want large inventories. In reality, a balance has to be found, particularly as inventory cost rises at an increasing rate as customer service standards near 100 per cent. This means that to always have in stock every conceivable item that a customer might order would normally be prohibitively expensive for companies marketing many items. One solution to this problem is to separate items into those that are in demand and those that are slower-moving. This is sometimes called the '80:20 rule', since for many companies 80 per cent of sales are achieved by 20 per cent of products. A high customer service standard is then set for the high-demand 20 per cent (e.g. in stock 95 per cent of the time) but a much lower standard used for those items less in demand (e.g. in stock 70 per cent of the time).

Two related *inventory decisions* are knowing when and how much to order so that stocks are replenished. As inventory for an item falls, a point is reached when new stock is required. Unless a stock-out is tolerated the *order point* will be before inventory reaches zero. This is because there will be a *lead time* between ordering and receiving inventory. The *just-in-time inventory system* (discussed in Chapter 5) is designed to reduce lead times so that the order point (the stock level at which reordering takes place), and overall inventory levels for production items, are low. The key to the just-in-time system is the maintenance of a fast and reliable lead time so that deliveries of supplies arrive shortly before they are needed.

The order point depends on three factors: the viability of the order lead time, fluctuation in customer demand, and the customer service standard. The more variable the lead time between ordering and receiving stock, and the greater the fluctuation in customer demand, the higher the order point. This is because of the uncertainty caused by the variability, leading to the need for **safety (buffer) stocks** in case lead times are unpredictably long or customer demand unusually high. Suppliers can build strong relationships with their customers through automated inventory restocking systems, as Mini Case 17.1, on Zara, describes.

Warehousing

Warehousing involves all the activities required in the storing of goods between the time they are produced and the time they are transported to the customer. These activities include breaking bulk, making up product assortments for delivery to customers, storage and loading. *Storage warehouses* hold goods for moderate or long time periods whereas *distribution centres* operate as central locations for the fast movement of goods. Retailing organizations use regional distribution centres where suppliers bring products in bulk. These shipments are broken down into loads, which are then quickly transported to retail outlets. Distribution centres are usually highly automated with computer-controlled machinery facilitating the movement of goods. A computer reads orders and controls forklift trucks that gather goods and move them to loading bays.

Warehousing strategy involves the determination of the location and the number of warehouses to be used. At one extreme is one large central warehouse to serve the entire market; at the other is a number of smaller warehouses that are based near to local markets. In Europe the removal of trade barriers between countries of the EU has reduced transportation time and costs.

This change, together with distribution focus being on regional rather than national markets, has fuelled the trend towards fewer, larger warehouses where economies of scale can reduce costs. As with most physical distribution decisions, the optimum number and location of warehouses is a balance between customer service and cost considerations. Usually the more locally based warehouses a company uses, the better the customer service but the higher the cost.

The need for greater efficiency in the supply chain has led to a new generation of warehouse management systems. In traditional warehouse systems, goods are logged in manually and time is wasted chasing paperwork and correcting errors, while stock gets mislaid and pallets mixed up. Warehouse management systems use IT to organize, optimize and, ultimately, replace the labour-intensive tasks of receiving goods and selecting items for orders. In Europe Lever Fabergé has adopted such systems to virtually eliminate errors and take advantage of such features as paperless picking via radio data terminals, advanced shipping notification and real-time order status checking. Customers can do their own order process checking, if they wish, and receive pre-delivery advice via the Internet.[46]

Transportation

Customer service ultimately depends on the ability of the physical distribution system to transport products on time and without damage. Timely delivery is even more important with wider use of the just-in-time system, distribution centres and quick response systems. Goods are moved around the world with amazing efficiency. In the UK and parts of Europe goods are sourced and delivered from over 125 different countries. Movements of goods, especially perishable goods, relies on the transportation network spanning the globe. Road, rail, air and sea transport systems are interlinked to provide streamlined and efficient logistics solutions. Companies like Maersk (one of the world's largest shipping companies), FedEx, Kuehne + Nagel, Deutche Logistics SCM (logistics and supply chain management) work together to move goods on different forms of transport. Key forms of transport include water, air, road and rail.

Water transport—moving goods by sea is an import part of the goods 'super-highway'. At any one time there are approximately 6 million containers, full of goods, being transported from one part of the world to another. Water transportation is slower but less costly. A large proportion of long-haul deliveries between Europe and the Pacific Rim is by sea transport.

Air transport—this moves goods quickly and is a solution which offers speed and long-distance capabilities. Furthermore, in a period when companies are seeking to reduce inventories, air freight can be used to supply inventories under just-in-time systems. With the growth in international trade, air freight is predicted to be a growth activity. Its major disadvantages are high cost and the need to transport goods by road to and from air terminals.

Road transport—this provides more flexibility than rail, when moving goods from supplier to, say, retailer. Furthermore, the speed of road transport in Europe has increased since the advent of the EU, with the removal of cross-border restrictions.[47] However, the growth of road transport in Europe, and particularly the UK, has received considerable criticism because of increased traffic congestion and the damage done to roads by heavy juggernauts. Nevertheless, the quote at the beginning of the chapter is about Eddie Stobart a man who 'humanized transport' and built his small family business (started in Cumbria) into one of Britain's most popular brands.[48] Eddie built up the business on a reputation of having good-looking trucks and well-dressed drivers, who acknowledge the public when a Stobart lorry is 'spotted'.

Rail transport—this is efficient at transporting large, bulky freight on land over large distances. Rail is often used to transport coal, chemicals, oil, aggregates and nuclear flasks. A problem, though, is lack of flexibility. For many companies the use of rail would mean transport by lorry to and from a rail depot. Furthermore, for small quantities the use of rail may prove uneconomic. Nevertheless, rail is more environmentally friendly than road and can be an ideal solution, especially when long, regular journeys carrying large quantities are needed.

There are some industry specific issues which distributors must adhere to when moving foodstuffs and perishables. Health authorities set rules for the movement of these products at controlled temperatures, which apply to all forms of transport. One of the biggest issues for food producers to deal with is that the moment that fresh produce is picked it is deteriorating. Some exotic foodstuffs are grown in equatorial regions, picked, processed, packaged and transported thousands of miles within a very short time frame—e.g. chopped mango and pineapple from equatorial regions are flown to the northern hemisphere.

Materials handling

Materials handling involves the activities related to the moving of products in the producer's plant, warehouses and transportation depots. Modern storage facilities are designed to allow a high level of automation. At the Dixons Retail distribution centre in Newark, a large part of goods processing is automated. In-bound goods enter on pallets and are identified and documented using scanners. At any time the logistics team know where every product is, from the smallest memory card to the largest flat-screen television. Out-bound goods are processed and picked using part automation. Individual team members responsible for picking have digital headsets which enable speedy and efficient selection of orders for stores and individual customers.

Two key developments in materials handling are unit handling and containerization. *Unit handling* achieves efficiency by combining multiple packages on to pallets that can be moved by forklift trucks. *Containerization* involves the combining of many quantities of goods (e.g. car components) into a single large container. Once sealed they can easily be transferred from one form of transport to another. For example, a container could be loaded on to a lorry and taken to a rail freight terminal to form part of a trainload of containers destined for the docks. There the container can easily be transferred to a ship for transportation to a destination thousands of miles away. Since individual items are not handled, damage in transit is reduced.

An important element in materials handling is the quality of packaging. It is necessary to evaluate not only the appearance and cost of packaging, but also the ability to repackage into larger quantities for transportation. Packages must be sturdy enough to withstand the rigours of physical distribution, such as harsh handling and stacking.

Retailing

Traditionally, retailing was considered a rather passive activity, with goods passing from the manufacturer to the wholesaler then to the retailer and, finally, to individual customers. Retailers would display available products and attempt to sell them to their customers with limited regard for what the customers wanted. However, eventually, retailers discovered that understanding what was important to the customer meant they could stock the right products, sell at the right price and ultimately *increase profits* rather than having to *push* the products they had in stock, often at reduced prices. The era of 'stack them high and sell them cheap' ended. Retailers had discovered the importance of *understanding and satisfying customer needs* and this represented an important landmark in the development and definition of modern retailing.[49] The implication of this shift towards a customer-centric operation is at the heart of many of the channel management decisions we have discussed so far in this chapter.

Retail marketing decisions

Like any modern business retailers must understand the environment they trade in and anticipate and adapt to changing environmental circumstances. We shall now explore some of the key retailing decisions necessary to prosper in today's competitive climate. These decisions are retail positioning, store location, product assortment and services, price and store atmosphere. These call for decisions to be taken against a background of rapid change in information technology.

Retailers are no strangers to information technology developments, with electronic point of sale (EPOS) systems allowing the counting of products sold, money taken and faster service at checkouts. Barcodes, UPC codes, scanners and associated technology have

Read the Research 17.1 Logistics and Channel Management

This article overviews the last 20 years of logistics in the UK, using the grocery and fashion sectors as examples. It highlights the retailers' control of the supply chain and the challenges for the future. The authors describe key macroenvironmental issues like climate change, recession and technological factors such as radio frequency identity (RFID) as future challenges that face logistics managers.

John Fernie, Leigh Sparks and Alan McKinnon (2010) Retail logistics in the UK: past, present and future, International Journal of Retail & Distribution Management, 38(11/12), 894–914.

Conflict is an unavoidable aspect of channel relationships. How you manage and prevent it from breaking out into a bitter war is important to both parties. Any research findings to help illuminate touchpoints that can initiate conflict would be useful to managers. This article focuses on how perceived unfairness acts as 'relationship poison'. Using longitudinal data from Fortune 500 companies and its channel members the results indicate that perceived unfairness has the greatest impact on channel member cooperation and flexibility.

Stephen A. Samaha, Robert W. Palmatier and Rajiv P. Dant (2011) Poisoning Relationships: Perceived Unfairness in Channels of Distribution, Journal of Marketing 75(May), 99–117.

revolutionized retail supply chains, stock management and retail operations. A further technological innovation is using the Internet to shop. Online shopping is growing as more people become accustomed to electronic payment, and have broadband access to the Internet. Read the research to find out more about the development of online retail, how it has changed the way we shop, and the implications for managing a store in a virtual world.

Retail positioning

As with all marketing decisions, **retail positioning** involves the choice of target market and differential advantage. Targeting allows retailers to tailor their marketing mix, which includes product assortment, service levels, store location, prices and promotion, to the needs of their chosen customer segment. Differentiation provides a reason to shop at one store rather than another. A useful framework for creating a differential advantage has been proposed by Davies, who suggests that innovation in retailing can come only from novelty in the process offered to the shopper, or from novelty in the product or product assortment offered to the shopper.[50] Figure 17.8 shows that differentiation can be achieved through *process innovation* or *product innovation*, or a combination of the two (*total innovation*). Online retailers have offered innovation in the process of shopping, whereas Next achieved success through product innovation (stylish clothes at affordable prices). Toys 'Я' Us is an example of both product and process innovation through providing the widest range of toys at one location (production innovation) and thereby offering convenient, one-stop shopping (process innovation). By way of contrast, Woolworths, by not offering differentiation in either of these dimensions, lost market share in toys and went out of business on the high street. The customer was offered a limited choice, no price advantage and the risk of having to shop around to be sure of finding a suitable toy. Toys 'Я' Us is now suffering from the impact of online retailers who translate their cost advantage into lower prices. Woolworths has been repositioned as an online retailer with its stores closing.[51]

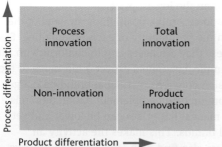

FIGURE 17.8 Retailing differentiation

Source: Davies, G. and N. Sanghavi (1993) Is the Category Killer a Significant Innovation?, ESRC Seminar: Strategic Issues in Retailing, Manchester Business School, 1–23.

Store location

Convenience is an important issue for many shoppers, and so store location can have a major bearing on sales performance. Retailers have to decide on regional coverage, the towns and cities to target within regions, and the precise location within a given town or city. Location for Ted Baker, the clothes-to-home-furnishings fashion retailer, is absolutely key as the company does not advertise. Ted Baker is at Gatwick and Heathrow airports, Bluewater and Glasgow but also in Miami, Paris and New York's Bloomingdales. Its London store sits opposite Paul Smith, the designer clothes store, in one of the city's trendiest enclaves.[52] Many retailers begin life as regional suppliers, and grow by expanding geographically. In the UK, for example, the Asda supermarket chain expanded from the north of England, while the original base for Sainsbury's was in the south of England.

The choice of town or city will depend on such factors as correspondence with the retailer's chosen target market, the level of disposable income in the catchment area, the availability of suitable sites and the level of competition. The choice of a particular site may depend on the level of existing traffic (pedestrian and/or vehicular) passing the site, parking provision, access to the outlet for delivery vehicles, the presence of competition, planning restrictions and the opportunity to form new retailing centres with other outlets. For example, an agreement between two or more non-competing retailers (e.g. Marks & Spencer and Tesco) to site outlets together out of town means greater drawing power than could be achieved individually. Having made that decision, the partners will look for suitable sites near their chosen towns or cities.

The location of stores can be greatly aided by geographic information systems (GISs), which profile geographical areas according to such variables as disposable income, family size, age and birth rates. We saw in Chapter 8, on market segmentation and positioning, how such systems can be used to segment markets. GISs allow marketers to understand the profiles of people living in specific geographic areas. Asda, the UK supermarket chain, uses GIS data as a method of finding new store locations. By understanding the number and profile of consumers living in different geographical areas, it can plan its stores (and product assortment) to be located in the right areas to serve its target market.[53]

Product assortment and services

Retailers have to decide upon the breadth of their product assortment and its depth. A supermarket, for example, may decide to widen its product assortment from food, drink and toiletries to include clothes, electrical goods and toys; this is called *scrambled merchandising*. Within each product line it can choose to stock a deep or shallow product range. Some retailers specialize in particular product rages, like Rymans the stationery retailer. Department stores, like Debenhams and House of Fraser, offer a much broader range of products including toys, cosmetics, jewellery, clothes, electrical goods and household accessories. Some retailers begin with one product line and gradually broaden their product assortment to maximize revenue per customer. For example, petrol stations broadened their product range to include motor accessories, confectionery, drinks, flowers and newspapers. A by-product of this may be to reduce customers' price sensitivity since selection of petrol station may be based on the ability to buy other products rather than the lowest price.

The choice of product assortment will be dependent on the positioning strategy of the retailer, customer expectations and, ultimately, on the profitability of each product line. Slow-moving unprofitable lines should be dropped unless they are necessary to conform with the range of products expected by customers. For example, customers expect a full range of food products in a supermarket. Another product decision concerns own-label branding. Large retailers may decide to sell a range of own-label products to complement national brands. Often the purchasing power of large retail chains means that prices can be lower and yet profit margins higher than for competing national brands. This makes the activity an attractive proposition for many retailers. Consumers also find own-label brands attractive, with many of them in the grocery field being regarded as being at least equal to, if not better than, established manufacturer brands.[54] Supermarkets have moved into this area, as has UK consumer electrical retailer Dixons Retail with its range of computer and electronic own-brand products (e.g., e-machines, computers and Advent and Logik branded products).

Marks & Spencer has moved in the opposite direction, adding 140 branded goods, such as Coca-Cola, Budweiser, Fairy Liquid, Shredded Wheat and Tetley tea, to its previously own-brand-only range of grocery products. The aim is to convert some M&S food halls into full supermarkets where shoppers do their entire weekly shop rather than merely top-up and luxury shopping.[55]

Finally, retailers need to consider the nature and degree of *customer service*. Discount stores traditionally provided little service but, as price differentials have narrowed, some have sought differentiation through service. For example, many electrical goods retailers provide a comprehensive after-sales service package for their customers. Superior customer service may make customers more tolerant of higher prices and, even where the product is standardized (as in fast-food restaurants), training employees to give individual attention to each customer can increase loyalty to the outlet.[56]

Price

For some market segments price is a key factor in store choice. Consequently, some retailers major on price as their differential advantage. This requires vigilant cost control and massive buying power. Where price is a key choice criterion, retailers who lose price competitiveness can suffer. For example, Carrefour, the world's second largest retailer after Wal-Mart, lost its reputation for low prices in France because of its focus on profit margins rather than volume. Market share plummeted in the face of intense competition from its domestic rivals, Leclerc and Auchan, and discounters such as Germany's Aldi and Lidl.[57] A recent trend is towards *everyday low prices* favoured by retailers rather than higher prices supplemented by promotions supported by manufacturers. Retailers such as B&Q, the do-it-yourself discounter, Aldi and Asda maintain that customers prefer predictable low prices rather than occasional money-off deals, three-for-the-price-of two offers and free gifts. Supermarket chains are also pressurizing suppliers to provide consistently low prices rather than temporary promotions. This action is consistent with the desire to position themselves on a low-price platform.

The importance of price competitiveness is reflected in the alliance of European food retailers called Associated Marketing Services. Retailers such as Morrisons (UK), Ahold (the Netherlands), ICA (a federation of Swedish food retailers) and Superquinn (Ireland) have joined forces to foster cooperation in the areas of purchasing and marketing of brands. Its range of activities includes own branding, joint buying, the development of joint brands and services, and the exchange of information and skills. A key aim is to reduce cost price since this accounts for 75 per cent of the sales price to customers.[58]

Some supermarkets sell *no-frills products*. These are basic commodities, such as bread, sugar and soft drinks, sold in rudimentary packaging at low prices. For example, Tesco offers its Value range of own-label products and Aldi sells its 'no-frills' own-label brands at low prices.

Retailers need to be aware of the negative consequences of setting artificial 'sales' prices. The use of retail 'sales' by outlets to promote their merchandise can lead to increasing scepticism as to their integrity, especially those that 'must end soon' but rarely do, and the 'never to be repeated' bargain offers that invariably are.[59]

Store atmosphere

This is created by the design, colour and layout of a store. Both exterior and interior design affect atmosphere. External factors include architectural design, signs, window display and use of colour, which together create an identity for a retailer and attract customers. Retailers aim to create a welcoming rather than an intimidating mood. The image that is projected should be consonant with the ethos of the shop. The Body Shop, for example, projects its environmentally caring image through the green exterior of its shops, and window displays that feature environmental issues.

Interior design also has a major impact on atmosphere. Store lighting, fixtures and fittings, and layout are important considerations. Supermarkets that have narrow aisles that contribute to congestion can project a negative image, and poorly lit showrooms can feel intimidating. Colour, sound and smell can affect mood. As we have discussed earlier in this chapter, colour has meaning and can be used to create the desired atmosphere in a store. Sometimes red-toned lighting is used in areas of impulse purchasing. For example, one stationer uses red tones at the front of its stores for impulse buys such as pens and stationery. Supermarkets often use music to create a relaxed atmosphere, whereas some boutiques use contemporary music to attract their target customers. Departmental stores often place perfume counters near the entrance, and supermarkets may use the smell of baking bread to attract their customers. Luxury car manufacturers are even said to spray their cars and showrooms with 'essence of leather' to convey the perception of luxury.

The success of Stew Leonard's supermarket in Connecticut, USA, in projecting a fun atmosphere for shoppers has attracted the attention of European retailers. Quinn's supermarket chain in Ireland has emulated its success, and other chains, such as Asda in the UK, provide a face-painting service for children at holiday times to make grocery shopping more fun.

Ethical Issues in Distribution

Five key ethical issues in distribution are the use of slotting allowances, grey markets, exclusive dealing, restrictions on supply, and fair trading.

Slotting allowances

The power shift from manufacturers to retailers in the packaged consumer goods industry has meant that slotting allowances are often demanded to take products. A slotting allowance is a fee paid to a retailer in exchange for an agreement to place a product on the retailer's shelves. Critics argue that they represent an abuse of power and work against small manufacturers who cannot afford to pay the fee. Retailers argue that they are simply charging rent for a valuable, scarce commodity: shelf space.[60]

Grey markets

These occur when a product is sold through an unauthorized distribution channel. When this occurs in international marketing the practice is called parallel importing. Usually a distributor buys goods in one country (where prices are low) and sells them in another (where prices are high) at below the going market price. This causes anger among members of the authorized distribution channel, who see their prices being undercut. Furthermore, the products may well be sold in downmarket outlets that discredit the image of the product, which has been built up by high advertising expenditures. Nevertheless, supporters of grey markets argue that they encourage price competition, increase consumer choice and promote the lowering of price differentials between countries.

Exclusive dealing

This is a restrictive arrangement whereby a manufacturer prohibits distributors that market its products from selling the products of competing suppliers. The act may restrict competition and restrict the entry of new competitors and products into a market. It may be found where a large supplier can exercise power over weaker distributors. The supplier may be genuinely concerned that anything less than an exclusive agreement will mean that insufficient effort will be made by a distributor to sell its products and that unless such an agreement is reached it may be uneconomic to supply the distributor.

Restrictions in supply

A concern of small suppliers is that the power of large manufacturers and retailers will mean that they are squeezed out of the supply chain. In the UK farmers and small grocery suppliers have joined forces to demand better treatment from large supermarket chains, which are forging exclusive deals with major manufacturers. They claim the problem is made worse by the growth of category management where retailers appoint 'category captains' from their suppliers, who act to improve the standing of the whole product category such as breakfast cereals or confectionery. The small suppliers believe this forces them out of the category altogether as category captains look after their own interests. They would like to see a system similar to that in France where about 10 per cent of shelf space is by law given to small suppliers.[61]

Fair trading

One problem of free market forces is that when small commodity producers are faced with large powerful buyers the result can be very low prices. This can bring severe economic hardship to the producers, who may be situated in countries of the developing world. In the face of a collapse in world coffee prices, a fair trading brand, Cafédirect, was launched. The company was founded on three principles: to influence positively producers' income security, to act as an example and catalyst for change, and to improve consumer understanding of fair trade values. It pays suppliers a minimum price for coffee beans, pegged above market fluctuations, and provides tailor-made business support and development programmes. The fashion industry has been the subject of fair trade criticism over the years, but several initiatives have now been launched to improve its ethical position. For example, Gap, Nike and Adidas have taken steps to improve employment and working conditions for staff in developing countries. High-profile events such as London Fashion Week attract ethical designers who wish to showcase their ethically produced designer labels. In addition, the Sustainable Action Plan for Clothing sets out a blueprint for sustainable fashion, which places emphasis on the importance of the environmental and social impact of clothing manufacturing. A positive outcome has been that big retailers like Tesco and Marks & Spencer are offering more organic and fairly traded items in their fashion ranges.

Online LearningCentre

When you have read this chapter

log on to the Online Learning Centre at **www.mcgraw-hill.co.uk/textbooks/jobber** to explore chapter-by-chapter test questions, links and further online study tools for marketing.

Review

1 **The functions and types of channels of distribution**
- The functions are to reconcile the needs of producers and consumers, improving efficiency, improving accessibility and providing specialist services.
- Four types of consumer channel are producer direct to consumer, producer to retailer to consumer, producer to wholesaler to retailer to consumer, and producer to agent to wholesaler to retailer to consumer.
- Four types of industrial channels are producer to industrial customer, producer to agent to industrial customer, producer to distributor to industrial customer, and producer to agent to distributor to industrial customer.
- Two types of service channel are service provider to consumer or industrial customer, and service provider to agent to consumer or industrial customer.

2 **How to determine channel strategy**
- Channel strategy should be determined by making decisions concerning the selection of the most effective distribution channel, the most appropriate level of distribution intensity and the correct degree of channel integration.

3 **The three components of channel strategy: channel selection, intensity and integration**

- Channel selection is influenced by market factors (buyer behaviour, ability to meet buyer needs, the willingness of channel intermediaries to market a product, the profit margins required by distributors and agents compared with the costs of direct distribution, and the location and geographic concentration of customers), producer factors (lack of resources, the width and depth of the product mix offered by a producer, and the desired level of control of channel operations), product factors (complexity, perishability, extent of bulkiness and difficulty of handling), and competitive factors (need to choose innovative channels because traditional channels are controlled by the competition or because a competitive advantage is likely to result).

- Channel intensity options are intensive distribution to achieve saturated coverage of the market by using all available outlets, selective distribution, where a limited number of outlets in a geographical area are used, and exclusive distribution, which is an extreme form of selective distribution where only one wholesaler, retailer or industrial distributor is used in a geographic area.

- Channel integration can range from conventional marketing channels (where there is separation of ownership between producer and distributor, although the manufacturer power of channel intermediaries may result in an administered vertical marketing system), franchising (where a legal contract between producers and channel intermediaries defines each party's rights and obligations, leading to a contractual marketing system) and channel ownership (where the manufacturer takes control over distributor activities through ownership, leading to a corporate vertical marketing system).

4 **The five key channel management issues: member selection, motivation, training, evaluation and conflict management**

- Selection of members involves identifying sources (the trade, reseller enquiries, customers of distributors and the field salesforce) and establishing selection criteria (market coverage, quality and size of the salesforce, reputation, financial standing, extent of competitive and complementary products, managerial competence, hunger for success, and enthusiasm).

- Motivation of distributors involves understanding the needs and problems of distributors, and methods include financial rewards, territorial exclusivity, providing resource support, the development of strong work relationships (possibly in the context of informal partnerships).

- Training may be provided where appropriate. It can provide the necessary technical knowledge about a supplier company and its products, and help to build a spirit of partnership and commitment.

- Evaluation criteria include sales volume and value, profitability, level of stocks, quality and position of display, new accounts opened, selling and marketing capabilities, quality of service, market information feedback, willingness and ability to meet commitments, attitudes and personal capability. Evaluation should be based on mutually agreed objectives.

- Conflict management sources are differences in goals, differences in desired product lines, the use of multiple distribution channels by producers, and inadequacies in performance. Conflict-handling approaches are developing a partnership approach, training in conflict handling, market partitioning, improving performance, channel ownership and coercion.

5 **The cost–customer service trade-off in physical distribution**

- Physical distribution management concerns the balance between cost reduction and meeting customer service requirements. An example of a trade-off is incompatibility between low inventory and slow, cheaper transportation methods that reduce costs, and the lower customer service levels and satisfaction that results.

6 **The components of a physical distribution system: customer service, order processing, inventory control, warehousing, transportation and materials handling**

- The system should be managed so that its components combine to achieve overall objectives. Management needs to answer a series of questions related to each component: customer service (What levels of service should be provided?); order processing (How should orders be handled?); inventory control (How much inventory should be held?); warehousing (Where should the inventory be located and how many warehouses should be used?); transportation (How will the products be transported?); materials handling (How will the products be handled during transportation?).

7 **How to improve customer service standards in physical distribution**
- Customer service standards can be raised by improving product availability (e.g. by increasing inventory levels), improving order cycle time (e.g. faster order processing), raising information levels (e.g. information on order status) and raising flexibility (e.g. fast reaction time to problems).

8 **Retailing and retail marketing**
- Retailing fulfils an essential role in the supply chain insofar as breaking bulk and enabling goods manufactured in very large quantities to be supplied to consumers in very small quantities. This process has many implications for channel management. Furthermore, marketing mix decisions, positioning and other marketing concepts have particular meaning when applied to retailing.
- Retail positioning involves the choice of target marketing and use of the marketing mix to develop differential advantage.
- Store location decisions are made using a number of variables from convenience to disposable income of a particular catchment area.
- Product assortment decisions focus on the breadth and depth of range, which enables retailers to tailor their product mix to suit particular audiences.
- Pricing is important in retailing and retailers need to ensure they manage cost control and levels of pricing effectively.
- Store atmosphere—the internal and external design, colour and store layout can all impact on consumer buying behaviour.

9 **Ethical issues in distribution**
- There are potential problems relating to slotting allowances, grey markets, exclusive dealing, restrictions on supply, and fair trading.

Key Terms

administered vertical marketing system a channel situation where a manufacturer that dominates a market through its size and strong brands may exercise considerable power over intermediaries even though they are independent

channel integration the way in which the players in the channel are linked

channel intermediaries organizations that facilitate the distribution of products to customers

channel of distribution the means by which products are moved from the producer to the ultimate consumer

channel strategy the selection of the most effective distribution channel, the most appropriate level of distribution intensity and the degree of channel integration

contractual vertical marketing system a franchise arrangement (e.g. a franchise) that ties together producers and resellers

corporate vertical marketing system a channel situation where an organization gains control of distribution through ownership

disintermediation the removal of channel partners by bypassing intermediaries and going directly from manufacturer to consumer via the Internet

exclusive distribution an extreme form of selective distribution where only one wholesaler, retailer or industrial distributor is used in a geographical area to sell the products of a supplier

franchise a legal contract in which a producer and channel intermediaries agree each other's rights and obligations; usually the intermediary receives marketing, managerial, technical and financial services in return for a fee

intensive distribution the aim of this is to provide saturation coverage of the market by using all available outlets

reintermediation the introduction of new forms of channel intermediaries, which provide sevices which link members of the supply chain: e.g. Web service providers and retailers

retail positioning the choice of target market and differential advantage for a retail outlet

safety (buffer) stocks stocks or inventory held to cover against uncertainty about resupply lead times

selective distribution the use of a limited number of outlets in a geographical area to sell the products of a supplier

Study Questions

1 What is the difference between channel decisions and physical distribution management? In what ways are they linked?

2 Of what value are channels of distribution? What functions do they perform?

3 The best way of distributing an industrial product is direct from manufacturer to customer. Discuss.

4 Why is channel selection an important decision? What factors influence choice?

5 What is meant by the partnership approach to managing distributors? What can manufacturers do to help build partnerships?

6 Describe situations that can lead to conflict between channel members. What can be done to avoid and resolve conflict?

7 Why is there usually a trade-off between customer service and physical distribution costs? What can be done to improve customer service standards in physical distribution?

8 A distributor wishes to estimate the economic order quantity for a spare part. Annual demand is 5000 units, the cost of placing an order is £5, and the cost of one spare part is £4. The per-unit annual inventory cost is 50p. Calculate the economic order quantity.

9 Unlike advertising, the area of distribution is free from ethical concerns. Discuss.

References

1. Barford, V. (2011) How did Eddie Stobart become so famous?, http://www.bbc.co.uk/news/magazine-12925163, 1 April.
2. Bunwell, S. (2005) One Channel, Many Paths, *The Mobile Channel*, supplement to *Marketing Week*, 7 June, 5.
3. Coughlan, A., E. Anderson, L. W. Stern and A. I. El-Ansany (2005) *Marketing Channels*, Englewood Cliffs, NJ: Prentice-Hall, 6.
4. Mills, J. F. and V. Camek (2004) The Risks, Threats and Opportunities of Disintermediation: A Distributor's View, *International Journal of Physical Distribution and Logistics Management* 34(9), 714–27.
5. Vize, R., J. Coughlan, A. Kennedy and F. Ellis-Chadwick (2010) B2B Relationship Quality: Do Trust and Commitment lead to Loyalty? Exploring the Factors that Influence Retailers' Loyalty with Web Solution Providers, 17th Recent Advances in Services Science Conference, European Institute of Retailing and Services Science, 2–5 July.
6. White, A. and M. E. Daniel (2004) The impact of e-marketplaces on dyadic buyer–supplier relationships: evidence from the healthcare sector, *The Journal of Enterprise Information Management* 17(6), 441–53.
7. Doherty, N. and F. Ellis-Chadwick (2010) Internet Retailing: the past, the present and the future, *International Journal of Retail & Distribution Management* 38(11/12), 943–65.
8. Ray, A. W. and J. J. Ray (2006) Strategic benefits to SMEs from third party web services: An action research analysis, *The Journal of Strategic Information Systems* 15(4), 273–91.
9. Dudley, J. W. (1990) *1992 Strategies for the Single Market*, London: Kogan Page, 327.
10. Wikström, S. (2005) From E-channel to Channel Mix and Channel Integration, *Journal of Marketing Management* 21, 725–53.
11. Narus, J. A. and J. C. Anderson (1986) Industrial Distributor Selling: The Roles of Outside and Inside Sales, *Industrial Marketing Management* 15, 55–62.
12. Rosenbloom, B. (1987) *Marketing Channels: A Management View*, Hinsdale, IL: Dryden, 160.
13. Exxon Mobil (2012) Downstream, http://www.exxonmobileurope.com/Europe-English/about_what_downstream.aspx, 22 April.
14. http://motorwayservicesonline.co.uk/Waitrose, 22 April 2012.
15. Laurance, B. (1993) MMC in Bad Odour Over Superdrug Ruling, *The Guardian*, 12 November, 18.
16. Ritson, M. (2008) iPhone Strategy: No Longer a Grey Area, *Marketing*, 11 June, 21.
17. Nagle, T. T. and J. E. Hogan (2006) *The Strategy and Tactics of Pricing*, Upper Saddle River, NJ: Pearson.
18. Meller, P. (1992) Isostar Enters the Lucozade League, *Marketing*, 2 July, 9.
19. Helmore, E. (1997) Restaurant Kings or Just Silly Burgers, *Observer*, 8 June, 5.
20. Lambert, K. (2005) Marriott Hip? Well, It's Trying, *Business Week*, 26 September, 79.
21. KFC (2012) Want to open a KFC? http://www.kfc.co.uk/our-restaurants/franchise.
22. http://www.yum.com/.
23. Mellor, W. (2011) McDonald's no match for KFC in China as Colonel rules fast food, http://www.bloomberg.com/news/2011-01-26/

mcdonald-s-no-match-for-kfc-in-china-where-colonel-sanders-rules-fast-food.html, 26 January.

24. Hernandez, H. (2011) Franchising in China, http://www.businessforum-china.com/article_detail.html?articleid=333, December.

25. Rosenbloom (1987) op. cit.

26. Shipley, D. D., D. Cook and E. Barnett (1989) Recruitment, Motivation, Training and Evaluation of Overseas Distributors, *European Journal of Marketing* 23(2), 79–93.

27. Kumar, N., L. K. Scheer and J.-B. E. M. Steenkamp (1995) The Effects of Perceived Interdependence on Dealer Attitudes, *Journal of Marketing Research* 32 (August), 248–56.

28. See Shipley, D. D. and S. Prinja (1988) The Services and Supplier Choice Influences of Industrial Distributors, *Service Industries Journal* 8(2), 176–87; Webster, F. E. (1976) The Role of the Industrial Distributor in Marketing Strategy, *Journal of Marketing* 40, 10–16.

29. Shipley, Cook and Barnett (1989) op. cit.

30. See Pegram, R. (1965) *Selecting and Evaluating Distributors*, New York: National Industrial Conference Board, 109–25; Shipley, Cook and Barnett (1989) op. cit.

31. Philpot, N. (1975) Managing the Export Function: Policies and Practice in Small and Medium Companies, *Management Survey Report No. 16*, British Institute of Management; Shipley, Cook and Barnett (1989) op. cit.

32. Magrath, A. J. and K. G. Hardy (1989) A Strategic Paradigm for Predicting Manufacturer–Reseller Conflict, *European Journal of Marketing* 23(2), 94–108.

33. Magrath and Hardy (1989) op. cit.

34. Magrath and Hardy (1989) op. cit.

35. Hardy, K. G. and A. J. Magrath (1988) Ten Ways for Manufacturers to Improve Distribution Management, *Business Horizons*, Nov.–Dec., 68.

36. Magrath and Hardy (1989) op. cit.

37. *The Economist* (2002) Chain Reaction, 2 February, 1–3.

38. Roux, C. (2002) The Reign of Spain, *The Guardian*, 28 October, 6–7.

39. BBC (2003) Store Wars: Fast Fashion, *The Money Programme*, 19 February.

40. Mitchell, A. (2003) When Push Comes to Shove, It's All About Pull, *Marketing Week*, 9 January, 26–7.

41. Jobber, D. and J. Fahy (2009) *Foundations of Marketing*, Maidenhead: McGraw-Hill.

42. Capell, K. (2008) Zara Thrives By Breaking All the Rules, *Business Week*, 20 October, 66.

43. Johnson, M. and A. Falstead (2011) Inditex breaks new ground for season in the south, *Financial Times*, May, p. 17.

44. Sawhney, M. (2005) Technology is the Secret of an Agile Advantage, *Financial Times*, 24 August, 10.

45. Fernie, J., L. Sparks and A. McKinnon (2012) Retail logistics in the UK: past, present and future, *International Journal of Retail & Distribution Management* 38(11/12), 894–914.

46. Nairn, G. (2002) More Than Just Boxing Clever, *Financial Times IT Review*, 2 October, 7.

47. Samiee, S. (1990) Strategic Considerations of the EC 1992 Plan for Small Exporters, *Business Horizons*, March–April, 48–56.

48. Childs, M. (2011) Edward Stobart, *Independent* 5 April, 8.

49. Ellis-Chadwick, F. (2011) An introdutions to retail management and marketing, *The Open University*, block 1, 8–9.

50. Davies, G. (1992) Innovation in Retailing, *Creativity and Innovation Management*, 1(4), 230.

51. Harwood, J. (2008) The Worth of Woolies, *Marketing Week*, 21 August, 20–1.

52. Ryle, S. (2002) How to Get Ahead in Advertising at No Cost, *Observer*, 1 December, 8.

53. Hayward, C. (2002) Who, Where, Win, *Marketing Week*, 12 September, 43.

54. Burt, S. (2000) The Strategic Role of Retail Brands in British Grocery Retailing, *European Journal of Marketing* 34(8), 875–90.

55. Finch, J. (2008) From Dog Food to Dentures: M&S Lets in Other Brands to Save its Bottom Line, *The Guardian*, July 5, 39.

56. Bloemer, S., K. de Ruyter and M. Wetzels (1999) Linking Perceived Service Quality and Service Loyalty: A Multi-Dimensional Perspective, *European Journal of Marketing* 33(11/12), 1082–106.

57. *The Economist* (2005) Carrefour at the Crossroads, 22 October, 79.

58. Elg, U. and U. Johansson (1996) Networking When National Boundaries Dissolve: The Swedish Food Sector, *European Journal of Marketing* 30(2), 61–74.

59. Betts, E. J. and P. J. McGoldrick (1996) Consumer Behaviour with the Retail 'Sales', *European Journal of Marketing* 30(8), 40–58.

60. Schlegelmilch, B. (1998) *Marketing Ethics: An International Perspective*, London: International Thomson Business Press.

61. McCawley, I. (2000) Small Suppliers Seek Broader Shelf Access, *Marketing Week*, 17 February, 20.

ASOS
Setting the Pace in Online Fashion

ASOS is the UK's largest online-only fashion retailer. The company has experienced phenomenal growth based on showing young shoppers how to emulate the designer looks of such celebrity magazine favourites as Kate Moss, Alexa Chung and Sienna Miller at a fraction of the cost.

ASOS was founded in 2000 by Nick Robertson. In 1996 he set up a business called Entertainment Marketing to place products in films and television programmes. By 2000 he was running a website called AsSeenOnScreen showing and selling brands that were used in films and on TV—from a pair of Oakley sunglasses worn by Tom Cruise in *Mission Impossible* to a pestle and mortar used by Jamie Oliver the *TV Chef*. But it was fashion that proved the biggest success and Robertson decided to focus on that. ASOS was born.

The company offers 50,000 branded and own-label product lines including womenswear, menswear, footwear, accessories, jewellery and beauty—a much wider range than that offered by other online rivals such as Topshop and New Look. Their key target market is women aged 18–34 with half of the online retailer's customers aged under 25. They demand new items to choose from, and ASOS provides this. Stock turnover (the speed at which items are replaced) is nine weeks, ensuring that visitors to the site are rewarded with new items on offer.

The company has its own design team and prefers to use suppliers based in Europe rather than the Far East. Between 60 and 70 per cent of its stock is made in Europe. This means that from spotting a celebrity wearing a new style of dress ASOS designers and buyers are in a position to have similar ones made and ready to sell in four weeks.

The Asos website

A major factor in the success of ASOS is its website. Visitors to the site can click on their favourite celebrity or pop star and view clothes they have been seen in. Perhaps a shopper prefers the style of Kate Moss. The cheapest way is not to visit ASOS's bricks-and-mortar competitor Topshop, but to choose a £6 ASOS Lurex vest 'in the style of' the London supermodel. At any one time on the website there are over 400 styles of dresses plus mountains of tops, trousers, shoes, bags, lingerie, swimwear and jewellery and an entire men's section, all of which is modelled by people walking on a catwalk. At the ASOS headquarters in North London, there are four studios where a pool of 30 models attempt to bring

the clothes to life and transmit the excitement of the catwalk to the consumer.

The range of brands has expanded from own-label celebrity look-a-like items to include its own luxury brand together with well-established labels such as Gap, Christian Dior, Ted Baker, Balenciaga, and YSL. The website attracts 13 million visitors a month. with around 6 million registered users and 4 million active customers (those who have bought within the past six months), who place orders worth on average £60. Women's fashion items make up the vast majority of sales. Menswear accounts for 20 per cent of sales with beauty and cosmetics a further 3 per cent.

One problem with buying online rather than in a traditional retail outlet is that returns are higher. An average catalogue company experiences about 40 per cent returns but ASOS achieves the much lower figure of 22 per cent. A key feature of ASOS's marketing tactics is to offer free delivery anywhere in the world and free returns in the UK.

Customer service

ASOS aims for fast speed of delivery and when a delay is foreseeable every effort is made to contact the customer. For example, when snow was forecast emails were sent warning customers of probable delays. When it did snow, an apology email was sent offering a delivery refund and 10 per cent off next orders. Their customer care team is available 24 hours a day. They are required to reply to customer enquiries within an hour and are assessed by the speed and quality of their reply.

Promotion

ASOS's success has provided many opportunities for PR activity in newspapers including quarterly reports on record profits and sales, and features on the reasons for their success. They avoid advertising in traditional media, preferring digital. Search engine optimization and pay-per-click advertising on women's magazine sites such as *Look* and *Grazia* help to generate traffic to their site. Social networking also plays a part in raising awareness. ASOS has the second largest UK fan group for any fashion retailer on Facebook (behind H & M). In 2011 ASOS launched a Facebook application that allows customers to make purchases from the store without having to leave the social networking site.

ASOS's largest marketing expenditure is on a print magazine which is carefully targeted to reach 500,000 active customers. It showcases well-known brands as well as its own brands, and photos are blended with editorial content to rival the standards of news-stand glossies. This is supplemented by 24-page supplements in magazines such as *Glamour* and *Cosmopolitan*, and sponsorship of the Sky Living show *America's Next Top Model*. ASOS achieves 60 per cent awareness among its target market.

New ventures

A major source of sales and profit growth has been overseas expansion with new websites being established in the USA, Germany, France, Spain, Italy and Australia.

The company has also launched a number of extensions from the core brand:

- ASOS Marketplace: this allows customers to sell their own clothes and accessories on the ASOS site—whether they are recycling their clothes for cash or opening a boutique to sell their own designs. ASOS receives commission on sales.

- Little ASOS: this site caters for babies and children aged 2 to 6 years. As well as stocking ranges from high-fashion brands such as Diesel and Tommy Hilfiger, Little ASOS offers a number of boutique and independent labels such as Cath Kidson and No Added Sugar.

- ASOS Outlet: this is the discount arm of ASOS offering end-of-line and previous season products at discounts of up to 75 per cent.

- ASOS Life: this allows customers to create their own profiles and communicate through forums, blogs and groups. The site includes a help forum that allows customers to answer each other's questions and an ideas section that lets customers submit suggestions for site improvements.

- ASOS Fashion Finder: showcases fashion trends and allows customers to research outfit building and creation. Visitors to the site are redirected to rival retailers if the product the shopper wants is not available at ASOS.

References

Finch, J. (2008) Nick Robertson: Wannabe Celebs Provide The Silver On Screen, *The Guardian*, 18 April, 31; Kollewe, J. (2008) Asos Defies Shopping Gloom by Reaching Height of Online Fashion, *The Guardian*, 18 November, 32; Barda, T. (2009) Winning Looks, *Marketer*, April, 24–7; Armstrong, L. (2009) Asos.com: As Seen On The Screens of The Fashion Savvy, *The Times*, 21 January, 26; Asos.com http://en. wikipedia.org/w/index; Costa, M. (2011) Fashion Leader Maps Out an International Future, *Marketing Week*, 16 June, 17–20; Treanor, J. (2012) Asos Managers Share £66m Bonus Pot, *The Guardian*, 25 May, 33.

Questions

1. Discuss the advantages and disadvantages of marketing fashion items online rather than through traditional retail stores.

2. To what extent does ASOS operate an integrated distribution channel system?

3. Perform a strengths, weaknesses, opportunities and threats (SWOT) analysis on ASOS.

4. On the basis of the SWOT analysis, what are your recommendations for ASOS?

This case was prepared by David Jobber, Professor of Marketing, University of Bradford.

Thorntons

Company background

Thorntons, the company whose name is synonymous with quality chocolate and confectionery, is the largest independent chocolate and confectionery company in the United Kingdom since the takeover of Cadbury by the American company Kraft.

Joseph Thornton opened his first shop in Sheffield in 1911 selling sweets. During the twentieth century the business expanded, opening other shops throughout the UK. They developed a reputation for quality confectionery, particularly in the supply of toffee as they added manufacturing to the business. In 1968 they began manufacturing for Marks & Spencer, and in 1975 their first franchised store opened in Barrow, Cumbria which allowed for further expansion across the UK. Their first significant venture into supermarkets was in 2001 when five lines gained listings in Sainsbury's. Since 1983 their main factory and distribution depot has been based in Alfreton, Derbyshire.

In 2010/11 turnover was £218 million—up from £215 million on the previous year. However, pre-tax profit fell from £6.9 million to £4.3 million for the same period. As a confectionery company the business is very seasonal, nearly 50 per cent of sales being in the Christmas and Easter periods. They are trying to reduce these seasonal variations by developing other confectionery products to offset the peaks and troughs that occur throughout the year.

Distribution

The company distributes its products through a number of different channels (see Figure C34.1).

Though sales through their own stores are currently their most important channel, these fell by nearly 9 per cent in 2010/11. Analysis of sales by individual shops found that those in top-rated retail locations performed better than the rest of the portfolio. The company is aiming to reduce the number of shops to between 180 and 200; it expects to close at least 120 shops over the next three years as their leases expire.

Sales through franchises declined by nearly 11 per cent in 2010/11, though their number actually increased, 19 new franchises being opened in this period and eight shut. New franchisees need to have a minimum of 1000 square feet of retail sales area. In addition to confectionery they sell cards and gifts and may have a café/coffee shop on the premises,

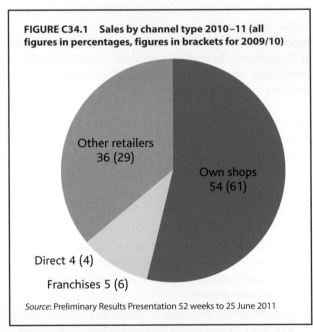

FIGURE C34.1   Sales by channel type 2010–11 (all figures in percentages, figures in brackets for 2009/10)

Other retailers 36 (29)

Own shops 54 (61)

Direct 4 (4)

Franchises 5 (6)

Source: Preliminary Results Presentation 52 weeks to 25 June 2011

95% of franchises operating next to a card or other type of gift shop. The company is currently keen to increase their number, locating franchises in busy shopping areas such as high streets or shopping malls and near other branded retailers. As they close shops they are aiming to use franchises to replace them.

Direct sales started in 1998 through Thornton Direct, their e-commerce channel. Currently they use this channel to sell the more luxurious chocolates in their range as well as flowers and hampers; these may include champagne, wine

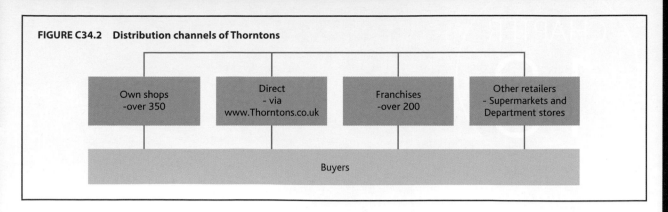

FIGURE C34.2   Distribution channels of Thorntons

| Own shops -over 350 | Direct - via www.Thorntons.co.uk | Franchises -over 200 | Other retailers - Supermarkets and Department stores |

Buyers

or whisky. Sales through this channel grew by over 4 per cent in the 2010/11 period.

Sales to other retailers grew by over 25 per cent in this period as more listings were gained; particularly strong were sales in the Easter period. It is believed to be the channel with most potential for growth as UK retailing becomes increasingly dominated by supermarkets. This is expected to replace own shops as the main channel of distribution by 2014.

References

100 years of Thorntons available at [http://www.thorntons. co.uk/c/Centenary_History_of_Thorntons.html].

Briefing Thorntons (2011) The *Sunday Times Business Section*, 13.2. p. 11.

Preliminary Results Presentation 52 weeks to 25 June 2011 by John Van Spreckelsen, Chairman available at [http:// investors.thorntons.co.uk/download/pdf/preliminary_ results_presentation_sept2011.pdf]

www.thorntons.co.uk

Questions

1. **Thorntons use a multichannel strategy. Explain this term.**

2. **Do Thorntons adopt an intensive, selective or exclusive approach to channel distribution?**

3. **What is meant by franchising? Outline the roles of the franchisor and franchisee.**

4. **Explain the advantages and disadvantage of the four channels of distribution Thorntons use.**

5. **Why might sales through electronic channels have not grown in the same way as other products such as books and DVDs?**

This case was prepared by Adrian Pritchard, Senior Lecturer in Marketing, Coventry University.

CHAPTER 18

Digital marketing and social media

" *As global competition intensifies, an organization's performance and strategic positioning will become more dependent upon its ability to successfully exploit information technologies.*
DOHERTY AND ELLIS-CHADWICK[1]

" *If an email is too complicated, the customer can feel overwhelmed or lost, which may cause them to lose focus and interest rapidly.*[2] "

LEARNING OBJECTIVES

After reading this chapter, you should be able to:

1 explain the concept of digital promotions and digital marketing

2 explain the meaning of the term 'social media'

3 identify the dimension of the digital marketing environment

4 discuss the implications of digital promotions and social media for marketing planning

5 identify and explain different digital communication tools

6 discuss social media and networking

7 discuss ethical issues in digital promotions and marketing

Digital technologies are becoming increasingly important in most sectors of economic activity. Due to high levels of interconnectivity, the Internet has been likened to the wheel and the airplane in terms of its ability to affect the future development of business and society. Consequently, the Internet has provided the impetus for many companies to rethink the role of technology, and evidence already indicates the extent of its global impact. Research on major trends in the dispersion of Internet technologies found that approximately 90 per cent of UK businesses have access to the Internet and, in companies with over 50 employees, the percentage is approaching 100 per cent.[3] The situation was found to be very similar in Australia, Canada, France, Germany, Italy, Japan, the Republic of Ireland, South Korea, Sweden and the USA. Interestingly, the report also concluded that the key measure of information and communication technologies (ICT) adoption is no longer just about connectivity and access to the Internet but rather the degree to which digital technology is being used to deliver real value for businesses. Increasingly, business adoption of technologies focuses on an expanding range of digital devices and platforms (e.g. mobile phones, wireless, and digital TV). Indeed, global system for mobile communications (GMS) has become the fastest-growing communications technology of all time. Consequently, adoption of digital technologies has profound implications for marketing planning and implementation.

The Internet is a major communications channel, providing an arena for multi-faceted communications. Vast numbers of people spend hours each day surfing the Web. Research covering 16 countries found that, on average, people spend 29 per cent of their leisure time on the Web. Overall, the Chinese spend the largest part of their leisure time online: 44 per cent compared with 28 per cent for British people. Scandinavians spend the least of their leisure time on the Internet, with Danes at 15 per cent, Swedish consumers at 18 per cent and Norwegians at 22 per cent.[4]

The Internet exploded into commercial life in the 1990s. During the same period network technology was also undergoing significant change, switching from analogue to digital circuits, and mobile phone networks and handsets were rapidly developing both in terms of sophistication and number of users. By 2000 further changes had occurred in the world of digital communications infrastructure. Suddenly there were more mobile phone subscribers than fixed-line phone users, Internet traffic exceeded voice traffic on fixed-line telephone networks at night, and wireless technologies began to be developed. Mobile phones have increased facilities for receiving multimedia content, and digital and online television have become available.

For its users the Internet and digital technologies have not only provided the means to find, buy and sell products but they have also created an environment for building communities, where like-minded people can network, socialize and be entertained. The emergence of social networking sites such as Facebook, LinkedIn, Google+ and **microblogging** sites like Twitter have had a significant impact on global society. Social networking has become pervasive throughout the world, even in China where Facebook is banned. Renren is the Chinese equivalent and this social network has 22 million[5] active users and many times more user accounts (approximately 160 million).

Social media have given a voice to masses of individuals, businesses and communities around the world. For example, in 2000 around 1.5 million users in China[6] had access to the Internet. Now, there are over 513 million users. This body represents over 50 per cent of the Internet population in Asia.[7] The change in the size of the Chinese user population is reflected in social media use. *Weibo* is a term which refers to Chinese microblogging sites and shows there is a great deal of interest in this form of online activity. Twitter has over 56 million accounts, and around 21 million users who publish each month. Weibo, however, has 140 million users, with 50 million actively blogging each month.[8] The trend for exponential growth in Internet users has spread from the USA, where its commercial use began early in the 1990, throughout Europe, to Oceania, Asia, the Middle East and Africa. Not all regions have equal levels of adoption. For instance, the world average Internet penetration per head of population is 33 per cent, but in Europe the average is 61 per cent and in Asia 26 per cent. This means there is plenty of scope for greater adoption of the Internet (and all it offers through the Web, social networks, etc.) as infrastructures and access to technology are improved, and political and social barriers and restrictions are removed.

As the use of the Internet, the Web and social media grows, a major challenge for marketers is to determine how to make best use of what the technology offers. In this chapter we focus on how this technology can be used in the IMC context. We use the terms *digital promotions* and *social media* to frame our discussions. We begin by defining these terms and then we explore the key dimensions of the digital communications environment and planning and types of digital communications; social media is then examined in detail. The chapter concludes by considering the ethical and social issues raised by digital promotions and social media.

What are Digital Promotions?

Digital technologies are able to emulate almost every aspect of marketing communications and traditional media channels and, in doing so, to span the marketing mix. However, digital promotions are more specific and are an element of the marketing communication mix. Nevertheless, the boundaries are less than clear, because digital technology is not only a means of communication but also a method of distribution. The flexibility afforded by the technology means it is highly complex. Marketers are faced with learning how to use and understand emerging technologies (e.g., social media), determining how to make strategic decisions that enable them to make best use of the technology and implementing digital

---

Marketing in Action 18.1 Digital Marketing: A Rose by Any Other Name?

The Internet, the Web and associated technologies have led to the introduction of many new words and terms which were hitherto unknown to us. The newness and variation in the use of these technologies have also meant that many of these new names can have multiple definitions. Digital marketing, for example, has been defined as:

> the application of digital technologies that form channels to market and to achieve corporate goals through meeting and exceeding customer needs better than the competition.

This is because the Web presents a fundamentally different environment for marketing activities than traditional media and conventional marketing activities. One of the unique properties of this evolving digital business environment is its capacity to facilitate many-to-many communications. As a result of the advent of this new communication model, the role of the consumer and the importance of interactive digital technologies have increased significantly. There has been a continuing debate as to how to refer to business activities that involve the use of digital technologies.

Internet marketing is another term originally used to refer to the achievement of corporate goals through meeting and exceeding customer needs better than the competition through the utilization of Internet technologies.

E-marketing is a term which refers to the use of technology (telecommunications and Internet based) to achieve marketing objectives and bring customer and supplier closer together. For instance, a company might use email to manage customer enquiries and also integrate Web-based technologies with email and other information systems, such as customer databases, in order to facilitate management of customer and supplier relationships. From a marketing perspective e-marketing can help identify and anticipate customer needs, and also provide a means to satisfy customers by providing prompt and informed responses quickly.

Perhaps the term **digital marketing** has become popular thanks to the inclusion of a wider range of digital and network communication technologies, including mobile phones and digital television, in the pursuit of marketing objectives. The widening application of digital technologies suggests that marketers should extend their thinking beyond the Internet to encompass all the platforms that permit a firm to do business electronically.

Postscript: 'What's in a name? That which we call a rose by any other name would smell as sweet.' This Shakespearean quote sums up many of the issues raised in naming technology-enabled marketing (even though taken out of its original context). The key point is that it is not what we call this new form of marketing but what it means to us and how it is used that are important.

Based on: Hoffman and Novak (1997);[9] Shakespeare (1600); Chaffey & Ellis-Chadwick (2012)[10]

marketing plans which benefit their businesses. Due to the expansive use of 'all things digital' many terms have been used to describe marketers' use of the technology. In this text digital promotions include digitally enabled communications tools—websites, email marketing, blogging, and the supporting media. See Marketing in Action 18.1 to find out more about the definition of digital marketing.

Social media

Later in the chapter we discuss **social media** in more detail and explore how it is used in marketing. However, to begin with we need a working definition—and like digital promotions—social media (in the digital world) is another complicated phenomenon, which means different things to different people. There are three separate elements to consider: *social, media* and *network*. According to Tuten and Solomon (2013) the **social element** involves thinking

> about social media as the way digital natives live a social life . . . it is all about a culture of participations; a belief in democracy, the ability to freely interact with other people, companies and organizations; open access to venues that allows users to share content from simple comments to reviews, ratings, photos, stories and more.[11]

In other words, being part of a social media network means that individuals and companies share ideas, interact with one another, work together, learn, enjoy group entertainment and even buy and sell.

Use of the word **media** also deserves separate attention because it has further meanings in the social context than those discussed in Chapter 14 (broadcast, print). In this context the technology is used to create an environment which facilitates different forms of online activity. For example:

- *social community media*, like Facebook, and LinkedIn, which enable sharing of ideas, interests, socializing and having conversations
- *social publishing media* like YouTube, pintrest, Flickr which enable signed-up members to publish and distribute editorial content, movies, audio, photos
- *social commerce media* like TripAdvisor, Groupon and Facebook, which enable buying and selling, trading, building relationships
- *social entertainment media* like come2play, Zynga[12] which enable game playing and entertainment across communities.

The final element is **network**, which in one sense can be defined by the underlying technology, which makes everything possible. For example, if you are a member of the Facebook social community, the network element is the message boards, forums and wikis, which facilitate communication and conversation. In a social publishing environment, a blog (online diary) often forms the underlying technology. In the commerce arena the technology can be: deal sites, deal aggregators and social shopping markets. Finally, virtual worlds and avatars are at the heart of social entertainment media.

However, in another sense, networks are the interconnections between the members of the community. The greater the number of members and interactions the more interesting the network becomes to all involved. In other words, social (life), media (environment) and network (interconnections—technology and human) are three elements which have come together to create the latest and fastest-growing online phenomenon.

Key Dimensions of the Digital Communication Environment

Since 1982 *digitization* has taken place and there has been a steady increase in the use of digital technologies. Products such as televisions, telephones, watches, cameras and music have changed to digital formats. As digitization spreads, the level of *connectivity* across devices, people and locations increases. For example, photographs can be shown on computer screens, shared on social networks and stored remotely in the computing cloud. The Internet connects billions of people and organizations around the world, allowing fast transfer of information. Intranets connect people within a company, facilitating communications, and extranets connect a company with its trading partners, such as suppliers

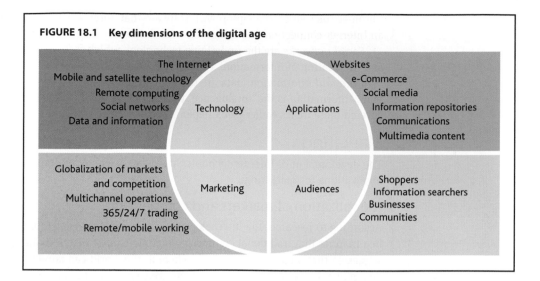

FIGURE 18.1   Key dimensions of the digital age

Technology
- The Internet
- Mobile and satellite technology
- Remote computing
- Social networks
- Data and information

Applications
- Websites
- e-Commerce
- Social media
- Information repositories
- Communications
- Multimedia content

Marketing
- Globalization of markets and competition
- Multichannel operations
- 365/24/7 trading
- Remote/mobile working

Audiences
- Shoppers
- Information searchers
- Businesses
- Communities

and distributors. In this chapter we are concerned with four dimensions of the digital age that have implications for marketing: 1) technology, 2) applications, 3) marketing, 4) audiences (see Figure 18.1).

Technology

The *Internet* is at the heart of the digital age; it has facilitated the creation of a global network of computer networks, which create the infrastructure for all online activity. Wireless networks are a growing part of the Internet and are enabling users to access the Internet remotely. *Mobile and satellite technologies* are revolutionizing the communication industry. They are widely used in logistics from the transportation industry and air traffic control to the individual shopper at home. Tesco, for example, uses mobile and satellite technology throughout the supply chain; at the shopper end there is a Tesco.app which lets you add your shopping list to a smartphone and then it will create a map to show you the shortest route to your product selection.[13] In-store Tesco's best-selling product is bananas, and there are technology systems in place to make sure the fruit is readily available on the shelves to meet customer demand. On the road there is a satellite grid system which updates managers on the distance from the store of the next bunch of bananas.[14]

One of the main drivers of this expansion of the use of digital technology is convergence, which means the bringing together into one device of the functions that were previously performed by several. For example, smartphones perform the functions of telephones, cameras, computers, audio systems and televisions.

Convergence brings the convenience of being able to carry out several tasks using just one device. Platforms are switching from analogue to digital (e.g. television) and also from fixed to wireless (e.g. telephones and computers); services are offered over multiple platforms (e.g. online television—BBC iPlayer, TV over broadband—iTV by Apple). Convergence is creating many opportunities for developing new ways to provide access to multimedia content and a range of additional services. Convergence has also prompted the development of *remote computing* and given rise to the concept of cloud computing.

We probably all have many documents, spreadsheets, business and personal files and photographs which we are saving on to an increasing array of storage devices. But the problem can be finding a particular document in its latest version. Cloud computing promises to be a solution to this problem as all documents can be stored in a single secure remote location. Google and Apple offer different ways to access cloud computing, but both are aiming to make these services more accessible. Steve Jobs said 'keeping these devices in sync is driving us crazy' when he launched Apple's iCloud service.[15] Google's solution is the

Chromebook, which is a laptop with software that automatically stores data in the cloud via an Internet connection rather than on a hard drive.

Social networks are the underlying technology which facilitate community developments and the sharing of information. This topic is covered in detail later in the chapter.

Data and information: data are the building blocks on which many of the applications are built. Information is the 'intelligence' that can be gleaned from the data. We have already covered these topics earlier (see Chapter 7).

Marketing

The development of Internet technologies and subsequent widespread adoption has profound implications for marketing.

Globalization of markets and competition

According to research, the Internet's 'global connectivity opens up new avenues for business in a manner that traditional commerce conduits cannot match'[16] and it has also been suggested that a company based anywhere in the world can launch a website to compete on a global basis, as long as its products are easily transportable or downloadable.[17] Many established brands are successfully taking advantage of these online opportunities to expand globally (e.g. Tesco, Zara, Apple). However, they inevitably face stiff competition from *virtual merchants*—global online players like Amazon, ASOS, Netflicks, and '*disintermediators*' that have cannabilized the supply chain by going straight from manufacturer to the end consumer (e.g. Dell.com). Retailers and consumer brands are likely to face growing pressure from a variety of completely new businesses, keen to get their share of the electronic market. If one thing has become very clear, from the first 15 years of Internet retailing, it is that there is always the opportunity for the innovative and dynamic company that has read the market well and has an effective business model to make a strong impact, and in so doing, grow very big and powerful, very quickly as in the case of Google, Facebook and eBay. The experiences of these organizations demonstrate that the Internet can be a very fertile environment for global expansion if organizations have good ideas, supported by an appropriate set of core competences and capabilities.[18] These discussions link to later chapters on competition (Chapters 19 and 20), and global strategy (Chapter 21).

Multichannel is becoming the de facto approach to managing online and offline operations. Many retailers have harnessed the Internet's capacity to provide information, facilitate two-way communication with customers, collect market research data, promote goods and services and ultimately to support the online ordering of merchandise, as an extremely rich and flexible new channel.[19] The Internet has given retailers a mechanism for broadening target markets, improving customer communications, extending product lines, improving cost efficiency, enhancing customer relationships and delivering customized offers[20] through their multichannel operations.[21] Carphone Warehouse is an example of a European retailer that is using the Web and mobile technology to provide multichannel assistance and drive customers to their stores. To begin with they developed the multichannel service by building a mobile-optimized website incorporating a 'click to call' feature, which allowed users to contact the call centre and make a purchase. Then they also promoted the service through mobile and Web channels and also included a link on the Carphone Warehouse main website store finder page. This enabled customers in the high street who were thinking about buying a new mobile phone to be instantly directed to the nearest store.[22] Indeed many retailers are finding that they are achieving a much higher ROI if they use their website, and mobile apps as an integral part of their businesses.[23] These discussions link to further issues associated with channel development and management in Chapter 17.

Continuous trading

The Internet never closes, 365, 24/7 trading is a reality, and companies are being pressured to manage their interface with the customers on an 'open all hours basis'. Many companies provide self-help information on their websites, which customers can access around the clock. But they also provide call centres, customer services and returns departments which provide real-time support, via the phone or online.

Remote and mobile working

Many more people are now working remotely than in the past. In the UK 13.6 per cent of the working population are working on a remote basis. A surprisingly large proportion do so from their home premises (37.5 per cent). However, the biggest group of 62.5 per cent work remotely away from home (e.g., transport drivers, sales representatives).[24] New technology is facilitating this process and making more things possible. For home workers, there are many advantages and disadvantages to consider. On the plus side, travel costs are reduced, workers can have more control over how they plan their working day, but on the negative side there can be an increase in family conflict; lack of understanding from family members about the tasks the worker has to complete and pressure on space needed to successfully carry out a job at home. There is also the loss of interaction with other members of the workforce— organization and managerial support are also only available on a remote basis. However, research has found that if there is increased social support from work for remote workers, many of the negatives of working at home are reduced.[25] Social media has been found to offer support and boost employee satisfaction, trust and productivity.[26] Leeds Metropolitan University introduced MyWellbeing to tackle absenteeism among university staff and it estimates the portal has saved the university £75,000 a year in salary costs. Aviva World (available to over 36,000 staff worldwide) is very popular and regularly receives over 7 million hits a month. Aviva encourages its staff to get involved with the business at various different levels through social media and in doing so it is enabling remote workers to feel more involved in the business. These are not isolated examples: companies from Coca-Cola, the BBC, to Sainsbury's are using social media networks and intranets to communicate, interact and ultimately improve job satisfaction and productivity.

Applications

In the early days the Internet was viewed primarily as a means to facilitate two-way communications between companies and their customers. However, very quickly the underlying technology and widespread adoption of websites became far more sophisticated and enabled more applications and uses to be introduced (see Chapter 14 for further detailed discussion of the use of digital communication in IMC strategies and Chapter 16 for discussion of direct marketing). E-commerce enabled websites to be added to the extent that they could be used to: purchase and pay for merchandise, sell and promote goods and services, collect market research data, and track orders.[27,28] Currently, the Internet provides business with a highly effective mechanism for broadening target markets, improving customer communications, extending product lines, improving cost efficiency, enhancing customer relationships and delivering customized offers.[29] Indeed, target audiences have taken to the new technology, and whether companies are trading in business to business or business to consumer markets there is an increasing range of applications being used— e-commerce, information repositories, social media, interactive communications and multimedia content delivery.

Given the Internet's potential to radically reconfigure underlying business processes and because of the highly dynamic and innovative nature of the online marketplace, it is not surprising that there has been a rapid expansion in the application of these relatively new technologies. Furthermore, it should be remembered that commercial exploitation of the Internet has far-reaching implications: technical, logistical, strategic, behavioural, social and legal. Companies wishing to take advantage of the opportunities created by the Internet need to make sure they have clear strategic goals and well-planned implementation strategies if they are to garner the best advantage from Internet-based applications (see Chapter 2 for further discussion of marketing strategy and planning).[30]

Audiences

Across the world many *shoppers, information searchers, businesses* and *communities members* are now happy to use Internet technology as part of their daily lives. For marketing managers it is, however, increasingly important to understand the target audiences, as there are significant changes taking place resulting from more and more interactions between organizations and their audiences via digital technology (for more detailed discussion of target audiences and related segmentation strategies see Chapter 8). For instance, in the consumer services sector there is an increasingly intense struggle for power between the consumer and the service provider. Sites like TripAdvisor freely allow visitors to hotels, restaurants and other places of entertainment to air their views of the service they received. However, while service providers need to take heed and be aware of what their customers are saying online, they too make use of highly sophisticated customer databases, to track and trace their customers, so that they can implement highly targeted 'one-to-one' marketing campaigns[31] and other initiatives which build strong customer relationships and deliver even more value.[32] So, on the one hand, consumer audiences have access to tools which can help them disseminate their levels of satisfaction and dissatisfaction far and wide. On the other hand, consumer service providers have a wealth of consumer-oriented data, which could enable them better to predict their customers' needs[33] and requirements and in doing so create more effective IMC campaigns. For example, Britvic set out to create a 'light touch' communication strategy, which would engage the interest of parents of 10-year-olds. So, the soft drinks company monitored online behaviour when it launched its Fruit shoot website. Once the site was established, Britvic launched its 'parents for playgrounds' campaign and monitored what people were responding to, then tailored the content to suit their interests. This is a very different approach to planning an eight-week advertising campaign with fixed content and messages.[34]

The Internet allows advertisements to be targeted on an individual basis. *Behavioural targeting* (or personalized Internet advertising) is a method of directing advertisements at consumers based on their previous online behaviour. At its most basic, it is the Amazon 'you've bought this so you might like to buy this' approach. However, more sophisticated behavioural techniques log where Internet users have been surfing online, using 'cookies'. Once this is known, advertisements on other sites appear based on that information. For example, an online user could be browsing cinema listings when a banner advertisement for bargain breaks in Rome appears—something the user had been researching a few days previously.[35] There is some evidence that consumers object to this kind of tracking of their Internet activity, with a survey revealing that 77 per cent objected to behavioural targeting.[36]

A word of warning: the EU Privacy and Electronic Communication Directive is bringing in a new set of legislation to control the use of data. For digital marketers this means rethinking how they use 'cookies'. In the past cookies (text-files that recognize users) have been seen as digital mechanisms which remember log-in details and store individual preferences. However, the EU sees cookies as a means of tracking online behaviour and potentially represents an intrusion of privacy. As a result the new legislation is being implemented to ensure that website visitors explicitly agree to the use of cookies when browsing websites.

A huge amount of research has been conducted to try to understand typical online buyer behaviour. In Chapter 4 we learnt how pre-family man uses online technology depending on life-cycle stages, cultural differences and personal priorities. Other influences identified from a body of academic research carried out during the past 20 years[37] are:

1 *Demographic variables*: personal attributes that tend to remain static throughout an individual's life time, or evolve slowly over time—such as age, gender, race, etc.—can be defined as 'demographic variables'. Key elements of a customer's demographic profile that have been found to influence their online behaviour include such variables as income, education, race, age, gender and lifestyle.[38]

2 *Psychographic and behavioural variables*: any aspect of a person's perceptions, beliefs and attitudes that might influence their online behaviour, and in particular their intention to shop. Indeed, behavioural characteristics—such as knowledge, attitude, innovativeness, risk aversion etc.—can also affect a person's intention to shop. For example, it has been found that consumers who are primarily motivated by convenience were more likely to make purchases online, while those who value social interactions were found to be less interested.[39]

3 *Personal profiles*: age, gender, education, salary. Indeed, it is important to note that Internet shoppers are no longer likely to be greatly different from their offline counterparts.[40] However, it is perhaps useful to differentiate between the most enthusiastic and profitable Internet shoppers. For example, it has recently been found that the Internet is a favourite channel for the compulsive shopper, as consumers are able to 'buy unobserved', 'without contact with other shoppers', and in so doing, 'experience strong positive feelings during the purchase episode'.[41] This study, which looked at the behaviour of Internet shoppers from six countries, including both developing and developed countries, found a surprisingly high degree of homogeneity in their characteristics and habits.[42] Internet shoppers were found to share their desire for convenience, were more impulsive, have more favourable attitudes towards direct marketing and advertising, were wealthier and were heavier users of both email and the Internet.

For marketing managers the importance is to understand the nature and behaviour of the target audience. Read Marketing in Action 18.2 to find out more about how behaviours are being translated into action via the Internet.

Marketing in Action 18.2 Know your Customer when Entering Global Markets

How to beat the buffet		
1: Fill bowl and lay carrot sticks across the top	2: Build 'walls' with cucumber slices	3: Fill tower with food of your choice

Pizza Hut has successfully expanded around the globe using joint ventures and franchising to enter new markets. However, they did not anticipate that a visit from a single consumer called Shen Horgrui, an engineer to one of the chain's many restaurants in China, would result in the closure of all of their salad bars across the country. Shen Horgrui devised a way to make the best of the Pizza hut 'one bowl, one visit' rule at the salad bar to go a very long way. He used his knowledge of maths and architecture to create a food tower, using the buffet's ingredients over a metre high. Once he had perfected the technique of building food towers, he shared the instructions online so that other diners could benefit. This proved to be very popular, so much so that Pizza Hut banned this practice and removed all its salad bars in China.

Based on: Ceurstemont, S. (2011);[43] Condliffe (2011);[44] Fernandez (2012)[45]

The dimensions of the digital age have far-reaching implications for marketers. The technology has led to the development of new routes and channels to market, and there are a myriad of new applications which are used to entice growing audiences to live part of their lives online. Existing and new companies are continually in competition for market share. To succeed, online companies should plan carefully how they are using digital technology.

Digital Promotions and Social Media Planning

This section explores the implications of digital promotions and social media for marketing planning. Digital technologies are reshaping business models, choice of promotional tools and media. In a recent study it was found digital is the 'central plank' which all communication agencies must be able to deliver. As a consequence there has been a significant shift away from more traditional communication tools and media[46] and battles are being fought over which service providers are the most adept at delivering digital communication plans. This shift in emphasis means marketers need to be aware of what they expect and how the technology can deliver their marketing objectives.

Deciding how to plan, resource, integrate, implement and monitor digital marketing activities can be guided by applying established marketing management principles and planning activities (as discussed in detail in Chapters 2 and 3). New technologies can be used to meet a range of different business objectives: sales, communications, or focus on the development and maintenance of mutually satisfying long-term relationships with customers by using digital technologies.[47] Therefore, the type of activities will determine the strategic significance of the plan and give focus to the operational context.

The formulation of the digital marketing plan is likely to be informed by four significant and interdependent elements.[48]

1 *Strategic alignment* of digital promotional activities with corporate, marketing and marketing communication strategies is important as it should ensure development of a potentially successful digital marketing plan. This process should also help define the purpose of the digital marketing activities.

2 The *value proposition* should emphasize the unique advantages created by the use of digital technologies for example, *choice* (amazon.com offers the world's widest and deepest range of books at very low prices), *convenience* (tesco.com offers round-the-clock shopping), *community* (Facebook brings people together around the world). The value proposition created through the relative advantage afforded by digital technologies should reinforce core brand values and be clearly articulated to target audiences. It will also determine the extent to which organizational change is required.

3 *Organizational change* is likely if the digital marketing plan is to be delivered successfully. A good example to consider is how retailers like Tesco and Sainsbury's have developed unique logistical solutions to support online ordering. E-commerce initiatives can involve applying a wide range of digital technologies: Internet, EDI, email, electronic payment systems, advanced telephone systems, mobile and handheld digital appliances, interactive television, self-service kiosks and smart cards. Consequently, utilizing such technologies may require significant changes to operations and working practices in order to ensure that the right skill sets (capabilities) and resources are available when required.

4 *Implementation* of the plan should be executed in a timely manner. Additionally, the success of the digital marketing plan is likely to be affected by senior management commitment, availability of appropriate resources and the appropriateness of the strategic vision that is guiding the implementation. The significance of the digital marketing plan for a company's overall strategy will also largely be dependent upon levels of technology adoption, investment and integration.

Go to the website to view eBay's value proposition.
www.mcgraw-hill.co.uk/textbooks/jobber

In addition, analysis of the environment should take place in order to determine the likely relevance of digital marketing. When assessing a target audience the following information will be useful.[49]

1 *Customer connectivity*: the proportion of the target markets that has access to relevant technologies.

2 *Customer channel usage*: how often target market participants use online channels and how they use the particular digital channel/platform (e.g. purchase or research?). For instance, for each customer segment and digital channel (e.g. Internet, interactive digital TV or mobile), a company should know the proportion of the target market that:
   - *makes use* of and has access to a particular channel
   - *browses* and, as a result, is influenced by using the channel for pre-purchase research and evaluation
   - *buys* through the particular channel.

3 *Online media consumption*: how many hours each week are spent using the Internet in comparison with traditional media such as watching TV, reading newspapers or magazines, or listening to the radio?

In addition, marketers should also consider the competition and be able to answer the following questions.

- What specific strategic resources, capabilities and competences are required for successful digital marketing?
- How well are the expectations of consumers being fulfilled by our digital marketing activities? For example, is our website easy to use? Are our email or mobile campaigns well received or regarded as intrusive?
- What is the number of visitors to our website per month? How many viewers watch our interactive television (iTV) commercials?
- What is the average length of time visitors spend on our site?
- What are the most popular pages and products? What are the least popular?
- Which product categories generate most sales?
- Conversion rates: what is the proportion of visitors who place an order? What is the proportion of recipients of email or mobile campaigns, or iTV viewers who place an order?
- Click-through rates: how many visitors arrive at our site from banner advertisements or Web links from other sites?

Findings of the internal and external analysis should feed into marketing objectives, the creation of competitive advantage and communication plans.

Implications for Marketing Planning in a Digital World

The degree to which digital marketing objectives will be defined can vary tremendously depending on the extent and time in which digital technologies have been utilized (for example, mobile phone operator Orange may set objectives that focus on customer retention, whereas Britvic sets objectives designed to foster the engagement of their target audience of parents). In general, digital marketing objectives fall within some or all of five categories.[50] Marketers must decide whether all or only some are going to drive their marketing plan.

1 *Grow sales*: through cheaper prices, wider distribution or greater product range.
2 *Add value*: through greater convenience (home shopping), improved 24/7 access, and/or more information (e.g. track orders, receive advice, read customer reviews, compare product features and benefits).
3 *Get closer to customers*: inbound by conducting online marketing research, monitoring chatrooms, **blogs** and social network sites, and tracking visits to sites; and outbound by search engine marketing, online public relations and advertising, and email and viral marketing campaigns.
4 *Save costs*: by replacing sales and telemarketing staff with online sales, order confirmation by email rather than post, online purchasing, and replacing hard copy catalogues, manuals and reports with online versions.
5 *Extend the brand online*: by raising awareness, enhance brand image and extend the brand experience.

Creating competitive advantage

Marketers have long accepted that success demands identification of some form of *competitive advantage* capable of distinguishing an organization from other firms operating in the same market sector. The unique properties of digital technologies offer opportunities to establish new forms of competitive advantage. These include highly tailored communication campaigns, which can be designed to meet very specific communication objectives. The secret of the success of most digital operations is that they have exploited digital market advantages and new technologies, in order to deliver a value proposition superior to that of their competitors. Once a company has developed an understanding of the environment, competition and target market it can then begin to decide which digital tools are likely to be most effective.

Evaluation and performance control

Evaluation and control systems need to be created that permit management to rapidly identify variance in actual performance versus forecast for all aspects of the digital marketing mix. Management also requires mechanisms that generate diagnostic guidance on the cause of any variance. To achieve this aim, control systems should focus on the measurement of key variables within the plan, such as targeted market share, customer attitudes, awareness objectives for digital promotions and distribution targets.

Web analytics are the methods used to evaluate the success of digital marketing programmes. Such techniques allow the checking of whether objectives have been achieved by recording website visitor numbers, the most popular pages and products, how long visitors spend on site, which pages they visit (clickstreams), sales, and the individual sites or search terms used by visitors to find a site. Google Analytics is an excellent analytical tool, which is free to use. Omniture and Visual Sciences also provide web analytics systems.[51]

Digital promotional tools

Once the environmental analysis is complete and the objectives set, consideration of the mix of digital promotional tools should be carried out. The Internet and the Web provide innovative options for the digital marketer: communications can be interactive, animated, personalized and instantaneous. However, the marketer needs to understand how the target customers will respond if he/she is to use this media successfully. For instance, sending personalized email marketing messages can help to build customer relationships, but the level of personalization should be appropriate to the stage of the relationship. If a company is too familiar too early in the relationship, the customer is likely to feel the company is being intrusive.[52] Nevertheless, use of digital promotional tools is on the increase.[53] In the UK spend on online advertising is now the most popular media for advertisers having overtaken the spend on television advertising. This includes social media, **mobile marketing**, video and online display advertising, all of which are increasing in terms of spend year on year.[54]

Types of digital promotional include:

Online advertising and search engine marketing

Online display advertising aims to get a target customer to act immediately by clicking on the advert. These types of adverts include banner adverts, skyscrapers and pop-ups. They may be used to elicit various responses and meet a range of communications objectives, for example, increase action, change opinions, increase recall.

Affiliate marketing is a form of online advertising in which one business rewards another for placing advertising on their website. Each time a potential customer clicks on the link through to the originator of the advert website, the third party earns revenue. This approach originated on the PC Flowers & Gifts website and this company gains several thousand affiliates through the Worldwide Web. Affiliates place a PC Flowers & Gifts advert on their Web pages and this generates a great deal of business. The third-party advertisers were paid commission on the referred business. Amazon expanded its business using a similar approach and continues to encourage everyone to advertise Amazon products through its affiliate program.

Search engine marketing involves optimization of search listings and keyword searching. For instance, if searching Yahoo! using key words such as 'jewellery shop', the search engine will provide a list of companies offering such services. Yahoo! provides its Keyword Selector to help advertisers choose

⬆ **EXHIBIT 18.1** Leading brands use Facebook to engage target audiences.

the best search term. Search engines like Yahoo! and Google generate revenue by charging each time an individual clicks on a sponsored link. The higher up the listing, the higher the price for click-through. Google sells a product called AdWords and claims:

> AdWords adverts connect you with new customers at the precise moment the customers are looking for your products or services. With Google AdWords you create your own ads, choose keywords to help Google match your adverts to your audience and you pay only when someone clicks on them.[55]

It has been argued that it is very important for advertisers to appear in the optimum position on the computer screen if they are to attract the greatest number of visitors to their online offering. By paying for a sponsored link, an advertiser gains a prominent position on the search engine's listings. The amount a company pays depends on how much it bids for keywords that Internet users seeking a particular product are likely to enter: the higher the keyword bid compared to rivals, the higher the listing. While the average

↑EXHIBIT 18.2   Photos of celebrities such as Kate Moss, Eva Longoria and Jennifer Aniston wearing their products have helped Australian footwear and accessories company, UGG, grow their markets in both the US and Europe.

cost per click is 10–20p, in some competitive industries, such as financial services, it can be as high as £3.[56]

A second method of traffic building to a particular website is known as *search engine optimization* (SEO). This involves the achievement of the highest position in the natural listings on the search engine results pages after a keyword or phrase has been entered. The position depends on a calculation made by a search engine (e.g. Google) that matches the relevant site page content with the keyword (phrase) that is typed in. Unlike sponsored search (pay-per-click) SEO does not involve payment to a search engine to achieve high rankings. What a digital marketer needs is an understanding of how to achieve high natural rankings. Search engines use 'spiders' to identify the titles, links and headings that are employed to assess relevance to keywords and phrases. It is therefore important to ensure that the website includes the keywords (phrases) that a potential visitor might use to search for a particular type of company. For example, Ragdale Hall Spa Hotel's website includes terms such as 'weekend spa break', 'spa resort' and 'health spa', because they are key phrases used by consumers when searching for that type of hotel. This has achieved high ranking for the hotel on search engine listings.[57]

However, SEO has become more of an exercise in behavioural segmentation than a technical website development exercise, and so driving the *right* type of person to a site might be more important than where it ranks for a key phrase. Google suggest that there are more than 200 separate variables that can have an effect on the where and how a website finds itself in a search result. Google has set in place changes that might see website owners 'penalized' for overzealous SEO activity. There are clearly some organizations that play the SEO game with consummate success. A search for almost any consumer product will often find

Amazon and eBay returned within the first few results, a virtue of their size and authority as sites, their high-level linking, involvement in advertising programs and sophisticated automation of the SEO process. Within the hotel sector, many specialists admire Laterooms.com for its ability to perform highly against hotel brands and other booking services. Highly competitive industries, such as the insurance business, expend huge resources to compete with other firms on Google. However, some brand names, such as GoCompare, prefer to spend that resource in pay-per-click campaigns than on SEO activity—perhaps an indication that brand awareness and a large PPC budget might be more important in some verticals than SEO.

Online video and interactive television advertising

Media-sharing sites have become increasingly popular and provide organizations and individuals with a platform on which to share visual, video and audio content. Popular platforms like YouTube and Flickr enable sharing of such content in an online environment. There are different types of content being produced depending on whether it is an individual or a business.

The growth of digital television has given rise to an increase in *interactive television (iTV) advertising*, where viewers are invited to 'press the red button' on their remote control handset to see more information about an advertised product. This form of advertising has a number of advantages from being highly measurable, which means advertisers can track the success of adverts displayed on different channels and at different times of the day. It also allows the targeting of niche audiences through specialist digital channels that focus on leisure activities such as sport, music and motoring and the provision of more in-depth information than a single television or press advertisement. For the user it is a convenient means of buying a product without having to use a telephone or computer. Apple iTV is an example of a form of interactive TV, which enables viewing, downloading and purchasing of a wide variety of films and video content.

Go to the website to learn about PC World/Curry's multichannel approach.
www.mcgraw-hill.co.uk/textbooks/jobber

Many advertisers producing high-profile television campaigns are using this form of media to extend the reach of their adverts. Often films showing how the adverts are made are also used to increase customer engagement (see Ad Insight).

Online video and interactive television advertising refers to permission-based emails sent to customers, which are a form of marketing communications that is on the increase.[58] According to Pavlov *et al.* (2008),[59] email marketing campaigns produce approximately twice the return on investment of the other main forms of online marketing such as web banners and online directory adverts. Email marketing is an important method of digital marketing communication especially for companies seeking to build and maintain closer relationships with customers. Its widespread adoption as a means of distributing promotional messages has the advantages of low set-up and distribution costs, highly targeted distribution of promotional messages such as discounts and coupons, and affordability by small and medium-sized businesses.[60]

Permission-based emails are in use because of widespread consumer complaints about unsolicited emails (known as 'spam'). Generally, permission marketing messages are sent when the receiver has given their consent to receive direct emails (in some countries, this is a legal requirement). Marketers using this form of communication find ways to encourage target audiences to 'opt in' to a firm's emailing list and in return they will receive materials that match their interests as recipients are more likely to open and read such messages.

Go to the website and see how LoveFilm is making use of digital technologies.
www.mcgraw-hill.co.uk/textbooks/jobber

Email marketing has been found to be most widely used as a call to action or for sales promotion offers. There are many techniques and tactics, which can be used to ensure the best performance for email marketing campaigns. Read the Research 18.1 tells you more.

Online newsletters are a form of email marketing, which tend to focus on a specific set of issues or interests. They can be sent at different frequencies and serve different communication objectives. For instance, when British Airways became part of IAG and switched its loyalty programme from Airmiles to Avios, it used its regular monthly newsletter to provide members of the programme with regular updates and information. When Avios was ready to launch, links to the sign-up page were provided. Newsletters are also a way to provide a direct link to a firm's Web pages.

Read the Research 18.1 Technologically Enabled Communications

Robert McDonald, CEO of Procter & Gamble, is on a mission to make his company the most technologically enabled business in the world. This insightful article from McKinsey traces the growth of digitization within the company and how to harness its power to 'touch and improve lives' better than before. No section has been spared. From improved innovation in manufacturing and lowering costs to building one-to-one relationships with all of its customers. The mission is clear and the outcome: a promise of faster growth.

With the continued exponential growth of emails dropping into our mailboxes, the e-retailers have had to devise an increasing number of tactical features to grab our attention. This research delves into how email marketers gain our attention with a range of features from animation to interaction, time of send and content length and structure. This comprehensive research lifts the lid and lets you see inside the world of the email.

Fiona Ellis-Chadwick and Neil F. Doherty (2012) Web advertising: The role of email marketing, Journal of Business Research 65(6), 843–8.

Mobile marketing refers to the creation and delivery of marketing communications messages through mobile devices (phones, smartphones or tablet computers). Early examples of mobile marketing involved sending text messages containing advertising to willing recipients. However, widespread adoption of smartphones and wireless tablet computers have increased capacity for visual content as well as text-based content. Mobile marketing is becoming increasingly popular, but not all consumers are keen to receive marketing messages via their phones. Research found that 75 per cent of consumers in the UK were happy to get offers via their handsets compared to 72 per cent in the USA, 50 per cent in France and 46 per cent in Germany.[61] Nevertheless, one of the most rapidly growing forms of mobile marketing is smartphone applications (apps) (see Digital Marketing 18.1). For example, the deodorant brand Lynx, which is targeted mainly at young males, developed two mobile phone apps designed to help young guys be more successful with girls as part of their 'Get in There' campaign. The apps were downloaded over 350,000 times.

Mobile marketing has several advantages. It is:

- *cost effective.* The cost per message is between 15p and 25p, compared with 50p to 75p per direct mail shot, including print production and postage.
- *targeted and personalized.* For example, operators like Vodafone, Virgin Mobile and Blyk offer free texts and voice calls to customers if they sign up to receive some advertising. In signing up, customers have to fill out questionnaires on their hobbies and interests.
- *interactive.* The receiver can respond to the text message, setting up the opportunity for two-way communication.
- *personal.* It enables dialogues and relationship development. Multiple retailers like Currys, PC World and Carphone Warehouse are developing ongoing 'conversations' with their customers across a range of mobile and digital media.
- *time-flexible.* Text messages can be sent at any time, giving greater flexibility when trying to reach the recipient.
- able to *engage the audience.* This is becoming known as *proximity marketing.* Messages can be sent to mobile users at nightclubs, shopping centres, festivals and universities, indeed wherever recipients are at any time of the day or night.
- *immediately available.* For example, the US consumer electronics retailer, Best Buy, sends special offers and deals to customer smartphones using a technology that pinpoints when they are entering a Best Buy store.
- *immediate and measurable.* It can assist in database development.
- the *gateway to other channels.* For example, while the majority of marketers spend less than 5 per cent of their marketing budgets on mobile marketing, smartphones are increasingly replacing other devices as the means by which users download music, films and other multimedia content, access the Web, answer their emails and navigate (e.g,

Digital Marketing 18.1 'Apps'—The New Digital Marketing Frontier

The increased use of mobile smartphones (such as iPhone, Android and Windows Phone) and tablet devices such as the iPad has led to an increase in the development and use of mobile applications—or *apps* as they are more commonly known.

The rise in apps can be attributed to two things—one is the huge processing power provided by mobile and tablet devices. The other is the relative small cost of apps when compared to traditional software costs. Mobile and tablet apps can often be free, but chargeable apps may cost no more than the price of a cup of coffee. App developers make their money not so much from the price of the app, but from the sheer volume of sales that come from a public able to afford (and not notice) the price of an app.

The environment for app use (mobile) has seen a rise in use of geolocational tools. These apps combine location awareness with particular services which can be provided to the users while they are on the move. Notable apps include FourSquare and Facebook Places (through the Facebook App) that allow users to 'check-in' at a location. A number of businesses are beginning to cotton on to the potential marketing capability of such tools and now market directly through geolocational apps to individual customers.

Check-in, originally seen as a kind of game without a goal, now has material benefits to the user. Many businesses have taken ownership of their locations and offer discounts, value-added products or unique purchases to people who have checked in. Businesses can yield publicity (both positive and negative) through the social element of location sharing.

Business uptake of geolocational app marketing has been limited, but the opportunities for place marketing combined with the social element of sharing means there could be business opportunities.

satnav apps). **QR codes** may increasingly be linked to an app store, where coupons can be downloaded for instant use.

Buzz marketing is defined as the passing of information about products and services by verbal or electronic means in an informal, person-to-person manner. It is also about identifying triggers that will prompt new conversations from target audiences. For example, in the USA Nintendo recruited suburban mothers to spread the word among their friends that the Wii was a gaming console that the whole family could enjoy together. Buzz marketing is similar to word-of-mouth marketing, long recognized as one of the most powerful forms of marketing, but it has enjoyed a renaissance due to advances in technology such as email, websites and mobile phones.

The first step in a buzz marketing campaign involves identifying and targeting 'alphas'—that is, the trendsetters that adopt new ideas and technologies early on—and the 'bees', who are the early adopters. Brand awareness then passes from these customers to others, who seek to emulate the trendsetters. In many instances, the alphas are celebrities who either directly or indirectly push certain brands. For example, the Australian footwear and accessories brand UGG became popular in the US and European markets when photographs of actresses like Sienna Miller and Cameron Diaz appeared in the media wearing the products. Celebrities may be paid to endorse products or simply popularize products through their own choice. Critical to the success of buzz marketing is that every social group, whether it is online or offline, has trendsetters. The record company, Universal, successfully promoted its boy bands Busted and McFly by targeting these trendsetters. It recruited a 'school chairman' who was given the task of spreading the word about a particular band in their school. This involved giving out flyers, putting up posters on school noticeboards and then sending back evidence that this had been done. In return, the 'chairman'—who was typically a 12- to 15-year-old schoolgirl—was rewarded with free merchandise and a chance to meet members of the band. Developments in technology have allowed the 'buzz' to spread very quickly. As we saw earlier, viral marketing is popular because of the speed with which advertising gets passed on via email. The launch of Apple's iPhone is a classic example of the power of buzz marketing. According to Nielsen's Buzz Metrics, which tracks English-language blogs, the product had more mentions than even the President of the USA around the time of its launch in January 2007, and had an entry on Wikipedia within minutes of it going on show.

Once the target audience has been identified, the next key decisions, like those for all forms of promotion, are the message and the medium. The message may take many forms, such as a funny video clip or email attachment, a blog or story, an event such as a one-off concert, and so on. For example, Diageo launched Smirnoff Raw Tea in the USA with a video clip featuring a spoof hip-hop song. The clip, entitled 'Smirnoff Tea Party', has been one of the most popular on YouTube, with over 3.5 million views. The medium used for carrying the message is frequently online but could also be through offline means such as posters or flyers. But, as with all aspects of buzz marketing, the only limitation is the imagination. For example, many individuals have used parts of their bodies or their private cars to carry commercial messages. Finally, given its novelty, evaluating the effectiveness of buzz marketing is difficult. Numbers are available regarding how many times a video clip is viewed but marketers will not be able to determine by whom.

Websites are an important part of an organization's communication strategy. The Web offers a high degree of flexibility in terms of what can be created in a website along with supporting digital technologies, which have revolutionized how organizations communicate.

Some organizations have developed highly sophisticated websites, which target various global audiences with an extensive range of product. However, others have been far more timid, developing small-scale, experimental applications: for example, the stark contrast between the reach and sophistication of Tesco.com compared to Morrison.co.uk.[62] Websites are potentially much more than a form of advertising as they can be used as an online store, an information repository, a portal or gateway for many different services. Two examples of website types are:

1 *Intermediaries websites*—which act as a portal or gateway to a variety of content. Examples are:
    * *Mainstream news media sites or portals*. These include traditional, for example, FT.com, Times, Guardian, Pureplay, Google news.
    * *Social networks*, for example, Facebook, Twitter, LinkedIn, Bebo, Tagged.
    * *Price comparison sites* (also known as aggregators), for example, Moneysupermarket, Kelkoo, Shopping.com, confused.com, mysupermarket.com.
    * *Superaffiliates*. Affiliates gain revenue from a merchant they refer traffic to by being paid commission based on a proportion of the sale or a fixed amount. They are important in e-retail markets, accounting for significant sales.
    * *Niche affiliates or bloggers*. These are often individuals but they may be important, for example, in the UK Martin Lewis of Moneysavingexpert.com receives millions of visits every month. Smaller affiliates and bloggers can be important collectively.
2 *Destination sites*. These are the sites that the marketer is trying to generate visitors for and which may be transactional sites: for example, retailers—John Lewis Partnership; financial services—Aviva.com; travel companies—ryanair.com, manufacturer's brands—Procter & Gamble.

Social Media and Social Networking

Social media and social networking are relatively new phenomena, which are shaping the way some sectors of society communicate. Digital natives,[63] keyboard warriors and serial bloggers live out parts of their lives online, in communities created at virtual meeting places like Facebook, Biip, Habbo Hotel, Pintrest or Weibo. The Internet has given us a virtual environment, which has wrapped its way around the planet and created a platform for a multitude of activities. Social networking is the most pervasive so far; it has overtaken porn as the number 1 online activity, and consequently is proving to be of great interest to marketers as a potential communication and sales channel. In comparison, it took radio nearly 40 years to reach 50 million listeners and television 13 years to reach the same number, but in just four years 50 million users had Internet access and in less than one year over 100 million

TABLE 18.1 Social media sites, their origin and users

Social network	Country of origin	User Community	Number of members in 2012 (estimated) in millions	Community of users
Facebook	USA	Youth 13+	800	Global (limitations, e.g. China, Iran, Bangladesh, Pakistan)
Renren	China	College students	160	China, Asia
LinkedIn		Business and professionals	150	Europe, Asia, South Africa
Badoo	Europe	Place to meet with friends	125	Europe and Latin America
Tagged	USA	Youth 13+ Mature users 35+	100	North America
Google Plus	USA	18+ circles of friends, place to get together online	90	Global (with some exceptions, e.g. N. Vietnam, China)
GupShup[64]	India	Youth 13+ sharing messages	50	India
Orkut	USA	School friends/college students and workmates	66	India and Brazil
Xing		For business professionals	11	Germany, Austria and Switzerland

Source: http://www.affilatenetworking.com/top-social-networking-sites/ accessed April 2012; http://en.wikipedia.org/wiki/List_of_social_networking_websites accessed April 2012.

people had a Facebook account.[65] Table 18.1 shows the examples of social media sites, their country of origin and key community users. There are many online communities, which focus on various interests from art to education, but by far the most compelling driver of community growth is socializing, and sharing information, pictures, music and video.

In reality social networks are nothing new and certainly were not invented by Tom Anderson (Myspace), Mark Zuckerberg (Facebook) or Joseph Chen (Renren). Social networks have existed almost since the beginning of human kind. They consist of people (for the purpose of this text) who are connected together by relationships, friendships or interests. In 1975 Burke and Weir[66] found that individuals prefer to turn to friends and family in times of need, and being part of a social community gives individuals a sense of purpose.[67] Sociologists suggested that a great deal of our daily lives involves relationships between *helpers* and *recipients* (of help)[68] and the nature of these relationships is at the heart of the creation of social networks.

Online social networks have spread through global societies and research provides insight into this rapid diffusion.[69] It has been found that a potential adopter of a social network that is connected to many adopters (already members of a social network) is predisposed toward becoming an adopter him/herself. In other words, if you know many people who are, say, connected to Facebook, you are more likely to become a member than if very few of your friends, family, work colleagues are members. This research also highlights the importance of word of mouth in the development of online communities. You are also more likely to join a network that already has many members than one that is new with few members. The purpose of a Web-based social network is to enable an online community to use the functionality tools of the site (e.g. Pintrest, enable the sharing of pictures and images; YouTube, the sharing of video) to share messages, ideas and content with an online community of *friends* (term used by Facebook). So, now we understand a little about why more people than ever before are connected to each other via the Internet. But who are these people, what are they actually doing online, what is the impact of virtual communities on marketing? The rest of this section explores who social media consumers are and what they are doing online. How are social media used in marketing? What is the impact of social media on social behaviour?

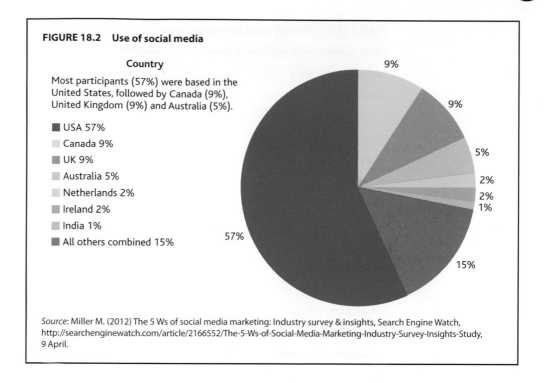

FIGURE 18.2 Use of social media

Country

Most participants (57%) were based in the United States, followed by Canada (9%), United Kingdom (9%) and Australia (5%).

■ USA 57%
□ Canada 9%
■ UK 9%
▨ Australia 5%
▨ Netherlands 2%
▨ Ireland 2%
▨ India 1%
■ All others combined 15%

Source: Miller M. (2012) The 5 Ws of social media marketing: Industry survey & insights, Search Engine Watch, http://searchenginewatch.com/article/2166552/The-5-Ws-of-Social-Media-Marketing-Industry-Survey-Insights-Study, 9 April.

Who are social media consumers?

What do Eminem, Lady Gaga, Van Diesel and Megan Fox have in common? Nearly 20 million Facebook users say they like them. As well as saying who they like, every hour Facebook users share 3 million links, tag 4 million photos, upload almost 9 million pictures and post over 30 million comments.[70] But who are the members of social network communities and which businesses are seeking to target online communities?

Research has found that over 9 per cent of marketers use social media and over three-quarters feel this environment is important to their business.[71]

Looking at demographic variables—gender, age, race, income, education and geographic location of users—helps to build a profile of online users. See Table 18.2 for demographic variables of social networking site users (in the USA) and Figure 18.3 for use of social networking sites between 2005 and 2011.

By 2012 66 per cent of adults that have access to the Internet used social networking sites. Table 18.2 shows that users are most likely to be aged between 18 and 49, as almost three-quarters of all adults in these age bands say they use one or more social networking sites. They are most likely to have some form of post-16 education and and are slightly more likely to be female than male.

Age has been a key differentiator of the users of social networks since their inception. Although the number of users over the age of 65 is increasing, those under 30 are more likely to use a social networking site than any other age group. Social media are increasingly being added to campaigns targeting younger audiences. See Digital Marketing 18.2 to see how Boots 17 adopted social media and developed a highly creative campaign.

How social media are used in marketing

Developing a plan for using social media is much the same as any other marketing planning exercise in so far as there is a requirement to understand the situation in which social media are going to be used, the needs of the target audience and their behaviour. It is also equally important to set clear objectives. This is perhaps where the planning process becomes more complicated. In order to state objectives, a company must be clear about the types of

TABLE 18.2 Who uses social networking sites?	
% of internet users within each group who use social networking sites	
All internet users	**66%**
Gender	
Men	61
Women	71*
Age	
18–29	86***
30–49	72**
50–64	50*
65+	34
Race/Ethnicity	
White, non-Hispanic	64
Black, non-Hispanic	68
Hispanic (English- and Spanish-speaking)	72
Household Income	
Less than $30,000	71*
$30,000–$49,999	69
$50,000–$74,999	60
$75,000+	69*
Education level	
Less than high school	63
High school grad	62
Some college	71*
College+	67
Geographic location	
Urban	69
Suburban	65
Rural	64

Note: *indicates statistically significant difference between rows. Extra asterisks mean differences with all rows with lower figures.

Source: Pew Research Center's Internet & American Life Project, January 20–February 19, 2012 Winter Tracking Survey. n = 1729 adult internet users ages 18 and older, including 901 cell phone interviews. Interviews were conducted in English and Spanish.

objectives that can be achieved through social media. According to Tuten and Solomon (2013),[72] companies using social media can be at different stages, which can have implications for the types of objectives they are likely to pursue:

Trial phase—at this level a company has just begun using social media and is testing what it can deliver. There is a tendency to 'play' and experiment. At this stage there is little consideration of longer-term strategic objectives, as the focus is on making use of social media platforms like Facebook, Twitter and YouTube. The types of objectives typically pursued at the level are: increasing website traffic and improving public relations.

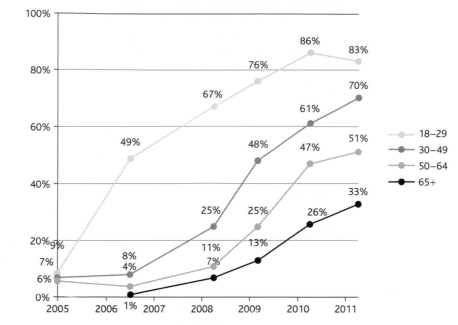

FIGURE 18.3   Social networking site use by age group, 2005–2011

The percentage of adult Internet users in each age group who use social networking sites

Note: Total n for Internet users age 65+ in 2005 was < 100, and so results for that group are not included.

Source: Pew Research Center's Internet & American Life Project surveys: February 2005, August 2006, May 2008, April 2009, May 2010, and May 2011. http://pewInternet.org/Commentary/2012/March/Pew-Internet-Social-Networking-full-detail.aspx

Digital Marketing 18.2   Mother and '17 Make-up Songs' to Share

Many brands are using social media to connect with their target audiences. Boots 17 Cosmetics is no exception. The brand has launched a social media campaign, making use of new music artists to engage the brand with its teen audiences.

The campaign created by Mother, a UK independent advertising agency, was called '17 make-up songs' and featured new bands and solo artists creating music and videos. The thinking behind the campaign was to use young musicians that the teenagers in the target audience could connect with. Each of the products launched by 17 had 'emotions' of the item of make-up explained to an artist, for the artist then to bring it to life through music.

The campaign featured a pop promotion with the launch of each new product, with press and digital ads. The aim was to drive members of the target audience to Boots 17's Facebook page. The songs were then made available through iTunes and Spotify.

A band called Summer Camp created the first song for 17's 'Magnetised Nail Polish' promotion. The title for the song was 'You Might Get Stuck On Me'. The resulting product was tailored by the consumers, who created their own customised nail polish.

Lara Purcell, head of marketing for beauty at Boots, said: '17 is a young, vibrant, sassy brand that consistently delivers exciting and innovative products.'

Based on: Eleftheeriou-Smith (2011)[73]

Transition phase—this occurs when companies are making more significant use of social media. This can be considered as a mature phase. Beall's, a US department store, began using Internet advertising in the early days to drive traffic to its website and promote sales, etc. Currently, the company makes extensive use of social media in order to engage its target audiences in conversation. The company's Facebook pages are updated several times a day and commercial fan coupons are released so they can be shared among the community. At this phase, the use of social media becomes more sophisticated and more integrated with the IMC and marketing strategy. At this level examples of objectives are: improving public relations and increasing product awareness.

Strategic phase—this occurs when an organization enters the final level. At this point the use of social media will be fully integrated across the business activities and incorporated into all levels of planning. At this level, the majority of adopters are pursuing objectives such as: increasing brand awareness, improving brand reputation and increasing website traffic.

Across all of the phases limited attention is given to objectives associated with increasing sales or reducing costs. See Mini Case 18.1 for further insight into who does have a profit motive when it comes to social media.

Once objectives have been set, the next stage in planning social media initiatives is to gather insight into target audiences by finding out which segments to target and which type of social media is the most appropriate. It is especially important to find out about their media habits, interests and online behaviour. This analysis should help to focus on the type of social media area (as discussed earlier in the chapter): for example: *social community media*, *social publishing media*, *social commerce media* or *social entertainment media*.

Each area has implications for the types of social media that the organization might employ to achieve its objectives. Figure 18.4 shows the different zones.

Social community: in this type of community individuals build personal profiles and these form the basis of what other community members can see and engage with. In addition there are indicators as to the type of presence an individual wishes to portray. For example, they can use availability indicators, mood icons, friend lists, status updates and news feeds, which can be shared with other community members (e.g. Facebook).

Social publishing: in this type of community the focus is on producing content. Written, video, audio, and in the form of blogs, microblogs, reviews, press releases, webinars, podcasts. Site examples are Twitter, YouTube and Pintrest.

Social commerce: in this type of site the community interest is shopping, developing relationships and providing support. The aim of the community is to enhance the shopping

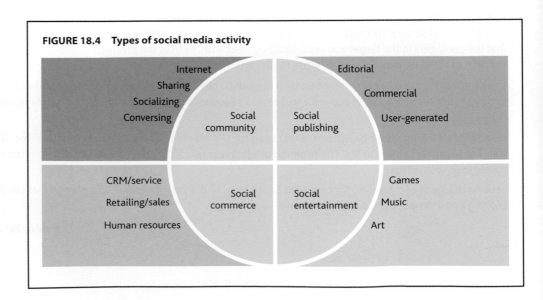

FIGURE 18.4 Types of social media activity

Google, with its sponsored links and Adword rankings has developed a financially successful model for generating advertising revenue. It is important that Google users are not averse to the sponsored links as they are able to discriminate easily between advertisers' links and generic search results. This aspect is part of the key to the success of Google's advertising revenue model. Social networks have yet to produce such a successful model that can leverage income from millions of global users.

However, Facebook is encouraging the spread of brand messages through its massive and complex community of friends. If it can successfully persuade network members to promote brands individually, Facebook may have a compelling model for making direct connections and relationships between consumers and brands. The advertising model used by Facebook is not yet as robust as Google's, but companies are spending at least some of their communication budget on social networks (particularly in the USA) and this is set to grow in the future. Twitter also allows some advertising. 'Promoted tweets' are listed at the top of tweet listings based on keyword content. Trend topics are an extension of this method, which are expensive for the advertiser as they have greater reach.

Charging a platform tax is another method of raising revenue from social networks. Facebook, LinkedIn, Twitter and Skype have devised platforms that can allow other providers to operate within their platform frameworks. For example, Facebook allows other Internet companies to run services within its platform. Zynga sells virtual goods to people who play on its free games in Cityville (a simulation game). The game is a freemium game, for which there is no charge to play, but there are options to purchase premium content. Facebook makes money by tracking users of Zynga games and charging for the number of users.

Virtual gifts—Facebook's virtual gift shop generates revenue but also uses this revenue stream for making charity donations. So, as well as a financial gain there is also an opportunity for developing brand equity.

Social networking sites have the critical mass required to make advertisements *fly* and generate significant revenues. However, there is still some caution in the world of finance about whether the promised wealth from the billions of connections provided by social networks will ever be fully delivered.

Questions:

1   Comment on the growing domination of advertising by Google and Facebook.
2   What are the advantages and disadvantages of using Facebook as an advertising medium?

Based on: Wikipedia (2012);[74] Waters (2011);[75] Kulkarni (2012);[76] Phatak (2012);[77] Bradshaw (2011)[78]

experience through referrals, ratings, reviews and sharing opinions of levels of service. Retailers are part of these communities and they seek to educate shoppers about their products and services. Site examples are Groupon, Etsy, Facebook.

Social entertainment: involves communities of like-minded individuals who play games and enjoy online entertainment. Social games include games platforms such as Sony Playstation3 and Microsoft Xbox which enable multiplayer games. Other genres of games are *simulation games* (e.g. Farmville), *action games* (e.g. Epic goal, Paradise Paint Ball), *role playing games* (e.g. Dungeons and Dragons, Tennis Mania) and *strategy games* (e.g. Word Cube, Kingdoms of Camelot). Game-based marketing means that brands take part and offer social games which have promotional marketing elements. In-game advertising is

Digital Marketing 18.3 Last Exit to Nowhere

'Last Exit to Nowhere' is a small t-shirt business selling handmade t-shirts linked to the cult movie business and is in every way a typical long-tail business. It produces a niche product that will appeal only to a small handful of people in any town, but it manages to reach out to many people across the globe.

Last Exit provides a stylish website powered by a standard e-commerce engine. It practises normal search marketing techniques to attract new customers in a fairly crowded novelty t-shirt market. What distinguishes this company is its use of social media to engage (and ultimately retain) a growing band of loyal customers.

A lively Facebook page constantly engages its followers with quirky discussions of films. Rather than a direct sale, conversations and dialogues often dwell on subjects and topics that have little to do with any of the products on sale. The Facebook page acts more like a gentle nostalgia trigger, throwing out suggestions and asking opinions. The trick is the reliance on nostalgia, which unifies (and at times divides) the fans of the page.

The Twitter account invites followers to new engagements made on the Facebook page or stimulates similar conversations in the much shorter dialogue framework Twitter permits.

Example of a Last Exit t-shirt inspired by the legendary English film director and producer Alfred Hitchcock.

Occasionally there are competitions for free products and even less often there are links to the product range—although new lines are clearly announced when they are created. Last Exit is confident that it does not have to do the hard sell. In fact there are many occasions where the customers are involved in the product design—film fans are like music fans and can have zealous knowledge of certain films and genres—and involving them in the decision as to whether a t-shirt design is 'good enough' is an important tool in their product development kit.

Based on: www.lastexittonowhere.com

also popular as well as product placement. Read Digital Marketing 18.3 to find out more about how Last Exit to Nowhere is making use of social media.

A key benefit of digital technology is that it allows companies to target very specific markets, even a market of one. This means developing plans to operate as 'micronichers', customizing communications to the needs of an individual. Broadly speaking, at this highly customized level it is crucial to know which variables are most important for the target customer. A digital marketing manager should know the key triggers for individual (targeted) customer decisions (best price, best quality, best delivery, best service, best image, best environment) as this will help to determine which digital promotions are the most significant.

Are blogs out of date?

In the early part of the twenty-first century blogging platforms appeared on a regular basis allowing individuals and (perhaps more importantly) the non-technical participants of business to publish content on the Internet for others to see and share. Many commentators, such as Robert Scoble, identified the blog as a key platform that businesses could use to engage directly with customers, sharing news and views and communicating values through what appeared to be a more human and organic approach.

With the growth of other participatory content-creation platforms, including Facebook, the question has to be asked whether blogs have simply blurred into mainstream media production—or is there still a place for something special called 'a blog'? Many corporate blogs have become part of the normal production of everyday marketing communications. Too many blogs are not written by the CEO, but by a ghost writer, and they seem less of an insight and a direct communication with customers and more of a channel to broadcast news. Celebrity bloggers seem to have moved channels, with many transforming their content into written literature or working with traditional media news outlets. Other blogs have increased in size (e.g. Mashable and BoingBoing), in terms of followers.

Platforms such as Twitter (described as a 'micro-blogging' tool) clearly take something away. Popular blogs have to some extent become social networks in their own right—which establishes 'the blog' as potentially the digital heart of a community. Marketers who identify this may find they are able to access customers directly in their channel of preference. As for the small business, a blog becomes a valuable and simple communication tool. Blogging platforms now regard themselves as content-management systems that are easy to use. The name may be changing as a result of evolution, but there are still elements that will persist for the foreseeable future.

Once the focus of the social media campaign is decided then the messages need to be shaped and the experience decided on. This is challenging for many brands and organizations as they have to determine how to engage their customers in an online social space. In the final stages of the planning activity an activation plan is defined and suggestions on how to measure performance are offered.

Measurement of social media involves looking at levels of:
* *activity*—frequency and number of blogs, and posts
* *interaction*—frequency of registrations, downloads, time spent on the site
* *performance*—customer lifetime value, lead conversion rates, ROI.[79]

Ethical Issues in Digital Marketing

Increased adoption of digital technologies within marketing has had many beneficial effects, such as increasing customer choice and convenience, and enabling smaller companies to compete in global markets across a range of digital platforms. However, there are some key ethical issues emerging as a result of increased usage of digital technologies.

The digital divide

The historical timeline of the development of Internet technologies reveals that, in the early days, it served highly specialized purposes and was used by expert technologists. Expansion and changes in the development of the World Wide Web have made Internet technology more accessible to a greater number of people, but there remains a virtual divide between the technology's 'haves' and 'have nots'. Hoffman and Novak[80] examined the extent to which the Internet has become indispensable, and found significant differences in usage based on race and educational attainment. They concluded that educational attainment is crucial if the digital divide is to be closed, and that efforts should be made to improve access for Hispanic and black populations in North America.[81]

Public and private organizations around the globe need to find creative solutions to improve Internet access for all citizens, regardless of their demographic background, as they should not be deprived of Internet access due to financial restrictions, a poor education and/or a lack of computer skills. From a commercial perspective it is also important to acknowledge that while the networks forming the Internet reach around the globe, access is far from equal and equitable.

However, mobile phones and digital television (DTV) have been more widely adopted and reach into the community. For example, mobile phone ownership is currently nearing 95 per cent of the adult population and DTV reaches 63 per cent of households.[82] The digital divide in computing might also be on the point of being bridged, with a £7 laptop being launched in India.[83]

Recent research suggests that there is a new form of digital divide forming.[84] As digital technologies become more widespread it is specific aspects of the technologies that form divisions. For example, Londoners prefer to talk rather than text, whereas in Northern Ireland more texts are sent per week than anywhere else in the UK; rural Internet users are stuck with slow connections in comparison with their urban neighbours; and three hours more television is watched per week in Scotland than anywhere else in the UK.

Social exclusion

Another ethical consideration is the fear of technological exclusion of the poorest members of society who cannot afford a computer, broadband connection, interactive television, digital radio or 3G phone and therefore cannot benefit from the vast array of products and services available, or access to information sources. For example, Prudential, the financial services company, has faced strong criticism for the way Egg, its high-interest savings bank, cut itself off from mainstream customers by offering Internet-only access, thereby creating a system that ensured it attracted only the wealthiest customers. Some utility companies, too, may be discriminating against low-income groups by offering cut-price energy only over the Internet. Conversely, many other public- and private-sector organizations throughout the European Union are committed to finding ways to support sectors of the community that are currently excluded from the growing knowledge economy. Abbey National, a UK bank, working in conjunction with the charity Age UK, has invested in free computer and Internet taster sessions for the over-50s as part of an initiative to encourage use of the Internet.

However, there is also evidence of technology delivering advantages to socially deprived sectors of society. Mobile phones have aided homeless people by allowing them to avoid the embarrassment of not having a permanent address by giving a mobile number on job applications.[85] Additionally, mobile phones are reportedly popular with people who are deaf and hard of hearing, as using the short messaging service (SMS) functions on mobiles helps people with hearing difficulties to communicate freely by sending text messages.[86]

Intrusions

Some Internet users are very wary of online shopping because of the information provided about them by cookies. These are tiny computer files that a marketer can download on to the computer of the online shoppers that visit the marketer's website, to record their visits. Cookies serve many useful functions: they remember users' passwords so individuals do not have to log on each time they revisit a site; they remember users' preferences in order to provide more relevant pages or data; they remember the contents of consumers' shopping baskets from one visit to the next. However, because they can provide a record of users' movements around the Web, cookies can give a very detailed picture of people's interests and circumstances. For example, cookies contain information provided by visitors, such as product preferences, personal data and financial information, including credit card numbers. From a marketer's point of view, cookies allow customized and personalized content for online shoppers. However, most Internet users probably do not know that this information is being collected and stored, and would object if they did. (Incidentally, online users can check if their drive contains cookies by opening any file named 'cookies'.) Some people fear that companies will use this information to build psychographic profiles that enable them to influence a customer's behaviour. Others simply object that information about them is being held without their express permission

However, there is a counter-revolution taking place. While companies have been keen to dispel fears (especially amongst consumers) and play down the extent to which technology can be used to predict behaviour, there has been a rise in the use of what might be called *consumer espionage*. Consumer brands, social networks and dedicated sites like ihateryanair.org and mumsnet have to be wary of the rise of the 'acute public analysis or outright criticism of a brand's behaviour products or service'. Viral messages can spread fast and consumer power is on the increase.[87]

E-mail is an excellent medium, but it is a mistake to use it without prior consent. It is better suited to the later stages of developing a relationship. We believe the best solution is for Internet service providers to install the protection on behalf of their customers, who shouldn't have to worry about it.[88]

Once again there are also examples of how technologies are enhancing rather than reducing an individual's privacy—for instance, texting medical results to individuals so avoiding anyone else being able to intercept the message.

Marketing to children

Another potential ethical issue is that of using the Internet to market to children. The Internet is a very popular medium with youngsters and there are ethical issues that companies need to keep in mind. For example, websites may contain advertisements. Are children being tricked by merging advertising with other website content? Are children aware that personal information that is being solicited from them may be used for future marketing purposes? Do they realize that every mouse click may be being monitored?

When you have read this chapter

log on to the Online Learning Centre at **www.mcgraw-hill.co.uk/textbooks/jobber** to explore chapter-by-chapter test questions, links and further online study tools for marketing.

Review

1 **The concept of digital marketing**
- The application of digital technologies that form channels to market (the Internet, mobile, wireless, and digital television) to achieve corporate goals through meeting and exceeding customer needs better than the competition.

2 **The concept of social media**
- Online social communities which facilitate the sharing of ideas, information, publishing documents and video content. The concept is increasingly being used by marketing managers as part of their digital promotion campaigns.

3 **Dimensions of the digital communication environment**
- There are four key dimensions to consider: technology, applications, marketing, and audiences.

4 **Digital promotions and social media planning**
- Deciding how to plan, resource, integrate, implement and monitor digital marketing activities can be guided by applying established marketing management principles and planning activities (as discussed in detail in Chapters 2 and 3). New technologies can be used to meet a range of different business objectives: sales, communications, or focus on the development and maintenance of mutually satisfying long-term relationships with customers by using digital technologies.

5 **Digital marketing objectives**
- Fall into five categories; grow sales, add value, get closer to customers, save costs, and extend the brand online. Marketing managers need to select objectives which meet their needs.

6 **Digital promotional tools**
- Types of digital promotions include online advertising, online video and interactive television advertising, mobile marketing, buzz marketing, websites and social media.

7 **Social media and social networking**
- A term used to refer to online community websites, with individuals who can become members, share ideas and interests, e.g. Facebook; publish and distribute articles and video and other multimedia content, e.g. YouTube; carry out social commerce activities like writing reviews, buying and selling, e.g. TripAdvisor; play games across communities, e.g. Zynga.

8 **Ethical issues in digital marketing**
- These are the potentially harmful effects of creating a digital divide between those with digital access and those without. The possible outcome is social exclusion of those who cannot afford digital devices. Intrusions on privacy, and marketing to children are also ethical considerations related to digital marketing.

Key Terms

blog short for weblog; a personal diary/journal on the web; information can easily be uploaded on to a website and is then available for general consumption by web users

buzz marketing the passing of information about products and services between individuals, which is sufficiently interesting to act as a trigger for the individuals to share the information with others

digital marketing the application of digital technologies that form channels to market (the Internet, mobile communications, interactive television and wireless) to achieve corporate goals through meeting and exceeding customer needs better than the competition

e-marketing a term used to refer to the use of technology (telecommunications and Internet-based) to achieve marketing objectives and bring the customer and supplier closer together

microblogging involves the posting of short messages on social media sites like Twitter and Reddit

mobile marketing the sending of text messages to mobile phones to promote products and build relationships with consumers

multichannel involves an organization that is using different channels—physical retailer stores, the Web and mobile, to enable its customers to buy, communicate, gain access to information or pay for goods and services. The organization in return provides consistent levels of service and marketing mix across all of the channels

QR codes a form of barcode which, once scanned, can link the user directly to Web content, digital adverts and other available content. They are easy to use and smartphones can read the codes

social media a term used to refer to online community websites, with individuals who can become members, share ideas and interests, e.g. Facebook; publish and distribute articles and video and other multimedia content, e.g. YouTube; carry out social commerce activities like writing reviews, buying and selling, e.g. TripAdvisor; or play games across communities, e.g. Zynga

Study Questions

1 Explain the meaning of the terms *digital promotions* and *social media*.

2 Identify the key dimensions of the digital communication environment.

3 Discuss how marketing might be affected by the dimensions of the digital communication environment.

4 Suggest how a business-to-consumer organization might use a multichannel approach. Give examples of companies using a multichannel approach.

5 Consumer behaviour is highly variable and complex. Suggest what variables a marketing manager might use to help him gain a better understanding of the company's online target audiences.

6 Discuss the key considerations when developing a digital and social media campaign.

7 Identify and explain the different types of digital promotional tools.

8 Explain social media and suggest how this growing phenomenon might be used by marketing managers.

9 Discuss the key ethical issues a marketing manager might consider when planning a social media campaign.

References

1. Doherty, N. and F. Ellis-Chadwick (2003) The Relationship between Retailers' Targeting and E-commerce Strategies: An Empirical Analysis, *Internet Research* 13(3), 170–82.
2. Ellis-Chadwick, F. and N. Doherty (2012) Web advertising: the role of email marketing, *Journal of Business Research* 65(6), 843–8.
3. DTI (2004) *Business in the Information Age: The International Benchmarking Study 2004.*
4. Pidd, H. (2009) Web Worldwide: UK Housewives Love It, Chinese Use It Most, Danes Are Least Keen, *The Guardian*, 1 January, 3.
5. Rushe, D. (2011) Renren, China's answer to Facebook, plans US float, *The Guardian*, 21 February.
6. Chaffey, D., K. Johnston, R. Mayer and F. Ellis-Chadwick (eds) (2000) *Internet Marketing: strategy, implementation and practice*, Harlow: Prentice Hall/Financial Times, 411.
7. Asia Internet Usage (2011) *Internet World Stats* http://www.Internetworldstats.com/stats3.htm#asia 31 December.
8. Kiss, J. (2011) Weibo: the Chinese twitter that dwarfs twitter, *Guardian*, http://www.guardian.co.uk/technology/pda/2011/jul/15/weibo-twitter-china 15 July.
9. Hoffman, D. and T. Novak (1997) A New Marketing Paradigm for Electronic Commerce, *The Information Society* 13, 43–54.
10. Chaffey, D. and F. E. Ellis-Chadwick (2012) *Digital Marketing: Stralegy, Implementation and Practice*, 5th edn, Harlow: Pearson, 8.
11. Tuten, T. L. and M. R. Solomon (2013) *Social Media Marketing*, Upper Saddle River NJ: Pearson, 3.
12. Tuten and Solomon (2013) op. cit., 4–7.
13. Martin, Arlene (2011) Want a 'sat nav' app to get round Tesco? Um, no thanks, *Which?*, 27 May.
14. Treeva Fenwick (2010) *Bar Code Technology, Retail Management and Marketing*, The Open University, iTunes.
15. Nuttall, C. (2011) Our future is up in the clouds, *Financial Times*, 17 June, 14.
16. Pyle, R. (1996) Electronic Commerce and the Internet, *Communications of the ACM* 39(6), 22–4.
17. Doherty, N. F. and F. Ellis-Chadwick (2010) Internet retailing: the past, the present and the future, *International Journal of Retail & Distribution Management* 38(11/12), 943–65.
18. Doherty and Ellis-Chadwick (2010) op. cit.
19. Basu, A. and S. Muylle (2003) Online support for commerce processes by web retailers, *Decision Support Systems* 34(4), 379–95.
20. Srinivasan, S., R. Anderson and P. Kishore (2002) Customer Loyalty in e-commerce: an Exploration of its Antecedents and Consequences, *Journal of Retailing* 78(1), 41–50.
21. Doherty and Ellis-Chadwick (2010) op. cit.
22. Jones, G. (2011) The Carphone Warehouse harnesses the power of the mobile medium to facilitate multi-channel assistance and drive sales, *Marketing Week*, May, 43.
23. Barnett, M. (2011) Why websites generate much more than sales, *Marketing Week*, 16 June, 22–3.
24. Mark Frary (2012) Staff may be remote but they're not out of touch, *The Times*, 1 May.
25. Wylie, E., S. Moore, L. Grunberg, E. Greenberg and P. Sikora (2010) What Influences Work-Family Conflict? The Function of Work Support and Working from Home, *Curr. Psychol.* 29, 104–120, DOI 10.1007/s12144-010-9075-9.
26. Snoad, L. (2011) The vital connection between staff and the bottom line, *Marketing Week*, 10 November, 14–18.
27. Basu and Muylle (2003) op. cit.
28. Doherty, N. F. and F. E. Ellis-Chadwick (2009) Exploring the Drivers, Scope and Perceived Success of e-Commerce Strategies in the UK Retail Sector, *European Journal of Marketing* 43(9/10), 1246–62.
29. Srinivasan, S., R. Anderson and P. Kishore (2002) Customer Loyalty in e-commerce: an Exploration of its Antecedents and Consequences, *Journal of Retailing* 78(1), 41–50.
30. Doherty, N. F. and F. Ellis-Chadwick (2010) Evaluating the role of electronic commerce in transforming the retail sector, *The International Review of Retail, Distribution and Consumer Research*, 20(4), 375–78.
31. Arora, N., X. Dreze, A. Ghose, J. D. Hess, R. Iyengar, B. Jing, Y. Joshi, V. Kumar, N. Lurie, S. Neslin, S. Sajeesh, M. Su, N. Syam, J. Thomas and Z. J. Zhang (2008) Putting One-to-One Marketing to Work: Personalization, Customization, and Choice, *Marketing Letters* 19, 305–21.
32. Kim, C. S., W. H. Zhao and K. H. Yang (2008) An Empirical Study on the Integrated Framework of e-CRM in Online Shopping: Evaluating the Relationships Among Perceived Value, Satisfaction, and Trust Based on Customers' Perspectives, *Journal of Electronic Commerce in Organizations* 6(3), 1–19.
33. Kaufman-Scarborough, C., M. Morrin, G. Petro and E. T. Bradlow (2006) Improving the Crystal Ball: Consumer Consensus and Retail Prediction Markets, Working Paper: The Wharton School of the University of Pennsylvania, April.
34. Nutley, M. (2011) Constant communication takes marketers down a beta channel, *Marketing Week*, 1 September.
35. Grant, J. (2008) Timesaver or Digital Foot in the Door?, *The Guardian*, Special Report on Internet Advertising, 3 November, 4.
36. Murphy, C. (2008) Campaigns Get Smart, *The Guardian*, Media Guardian Report on Changing Advertising, 22 September, 1.

37. Doherty and Ellis-Chadwick (2010) op. cit.
38. Hoffman, L. and T. P. Novak (1997) A New Marketing Paradigm for Electronic commerce, *The Information Society* 13, 43–54.
39. Swaminathan, V., E. Lepkowska-White and B. P. Rao (1999) Browsers or buyers in cyberspace? An investigation of factors influencing electronic exchange, *Journal of Computer-Mediated Communication* 5(2), 1–19.
40. Jayawardhena, C., L. T. Wright and C. Dennis (2007) Consumers online: intentions, orientations and segmentation, *International Journal of Retail & Distribution Management* 35(6), 512–26.
41. Kukar-Kinney, M., N. M. Ridgway and K. B. Monroe (2009) The relationship between consumers' tendencies to buy compulsively and their motivations to shop and buy on the Internet, *Journal of Retailing* 85(3), 298.
42. Brashear, T. G., V. Kashyap, M. D. Musante and N. Donthu (2009) A profile of the Internet shopper: evidence from six countries, *Journal of Marketing Theory and Practice* 17(3), 267–281.
43. Ceurstemont, S. (2011) Beat the salad bar: build the ultimate food tower, *New Scientist*, 28 December.
44. Condliffe, J. (2011) Salad-bar strategy: the battle of the buffet, *New Scientist*, http://www.newscientist.com/article/mg21228440.800-saladbar-strategy-the-battle-of-the-buffet.html?full=true, 27 December.
45. Fernandez, C. (2012) The leaning tower . . . of Pizza Hut's salad bar: Diner devises 3ft pile to get round rules at local restaurant, http://www.dailymail.co.uk/news/article-2084033/The-leaning-tower--Pizza-Huts-salad-bar-Diner-devises-3ft-pile-round-rules-local-restaurant.html, 10 January.
46. Singh, S. (2011) Pitch, *Marketing Week*, http://pitch.marketingweek.co.uk.
47. Chaffey, D. and P. R. Smith (2008) *eMarketing Excellence: Planning and Optimizing your Digital Marketing*, Oxford: Butterworth Heinemann; Payne, A. F. T. and P. Frow (2005) A Strategic Framework for Customer Relationship Marketing, *Journal of Marketing* 69(4), 161–76.
48. Doherty, N. and F. Ellis-Chadwick (2004) Strategic Thinking in the Internet Era, *British Rail Consortium [BRC] Consortium Solutions* 3, 59–63.
49. Chaffey and Ellis-Chadwick (2012) op. cit.
50. Chaffey and Smith (2008) op. cit.
51. Chaffey, D. (2008) How to Exploit Search Engines, *The Marketer*, December/January, 32–7.
52. White, T. B., D. L. Zahay, H. Thorbjørnsen and S. Shavitt (2008) Getting too Personal: Reactance to Highly Personalized Email Solicitations, *Marketing Letters* 19(1), 39–50.
53. http://searchenginewatch.com/article/2166552/The-5-Ws-of-Social-Media-Marketing-Industry-Survey-Insights-Study.
54. Sweney, M. (2012) UK advertising spending to hit £5 billion, *The Guardian* http://www.guardian.co.uk/media/2012/apr/03/uk-web-advertising-spend, 3 April.
55. Google AdWords (2006) https://adwords.google.co.uk/select/Login?sourceid=AWO&subid=UK-ET-ADS&hl-en_GB, accessed 30 April 2006.
56. Chaffey (2008) op. cit.
57. Chaffey (2008) Rise Through the Ranks, *The Marketer*, November, 51–3.
58. Kim, J. and S. J. McMillan (2008) Evaluation of Internet advertising research: a bibliometric analysis of citations from key sources, *Journal of Advertising*, 37(1), 99–112.
59. Pavlov, O. V., N. Melville and R. K. Plice (2008) Toward a sustainable email marketing infrastructure. *Journal of Business Research* 61(11), 1191–9.
60. Ellis-Chadwick and Doherty (2012) op. cit.
61. Akhtar, T. (2012) Brands search for higher level of reception, *Marketing Week*, 5 January, 18–20.
62. Doherty, N. F. and F. Ellis-Chadwick (2009) Exploring the drivers, scope and perceived success of e-commerce strategies in the UK retail sector, *European Journal of Marketing* 43(9/10), 1246–62
63. Prensky, M. (2001) Digital natives digital immigrants, *On the horizon* 9(5), 1–6.
64. http://news.yahoo.com/india-largest-social-network-sms-gupshup-expands-leadership-160250174.html.
65. Tuten and Solomon (2013) op. cit., 3.
66. Burke, R. J. and T. Weir (1975) Receiving and giving help with work and non-work related problems, *Journal of Business Administration* 6, 59–78.
67. Argyle, M. and M. Henderson (1985) *The Anatomy of Relationships and the Rules and Skills Needed to Manage Them Successfully*, London: Heinemann.
68. Amato, R. and J. Saunders (1990) Personality and social network involvement as predictors of helping behaviour in everyday life, *Social Psychology Quarterly* 53(1), 31–43.
69. Katona, Z., P. P. Zubcsek and M. Sarvary (2010) Network effects and personal influence: the diffusion of an online social network, *Journal of Marketing Research* 48(3), 425–43.
70. Kiss, J. (2011) Facebook began as a geeks hobby now it's more popular than google, *The Guardian*, 4 January, 23.
71. Miller, M. (2012) The 5 Ws of social media marketing: Industry survey & insights, Search Engine Watch, http://searchenginewatch.com/article/2166552/The-5-Ws-of-Social-Media-Marketing-Industry-Survey-Insights-Study, 9 April.
72. Tuten and Solomon (2013) op. cit., 33–41.
73. Eleftheeriou-Smith, L.-M. (2011) 17 uses cosmetics to engage with teens, http://www.marketingmagazine.co.uk/news/1103518/, 10 November.
74. Wikipedia (2112) cityvillehttp://en.wikipedia.org/wiki/CityVille.
75. Waters, R. (2011) Inflated expectations, *Financial Times*, 29 June, 24.
76. Kulkarni, A. (2012) How does Facebook make money? http://www.buzzle.com/articles/how-does-facebook-make-money.html, 9 January.
77. Phatak, O. (2012) How does Twitter make money? Buzzel.com, http://www.buzzle.com/articles/how-does-twitter-make-money.html, 15 March.
78. Bradshaw, T. (2011) Facebook set for display ad lead, *Financial Times*, 10 May, 21.
79. Tuten and Solomon (2013) op. cit. 209.
80. Hoffman, D. and T. Novak (1999) *The Growing Digital Divide: Implications for an Open Research Agenda*, eLab Owen Graduate School of Management Vanderbilt University (http://ecommerce.vanderbilt.edu/).
81. Hoffman, D. L., T. P. Novak and A. Venkatesh (2004) Has the Internet Become Indispensable?, *Communications of the ACM* 47(7), 37–42.
82. Ofcom (2005) Digital Television UK Household Penetration, www.ofcom.org.uk/media/news/2005/09/nr_20050915#content.
83. Ramesh, R. (2009) After the World's Cheapest Car, India Launches £7 Laptop, *The Guardian*, 3 February, 19.
84. Office of Communications (2005) http://www.ofcom.org.uk/.
85. Office of the Deputy Prime Minister (2005) Digital Solutions to Social Exclusion, at http://egovmonitor.com/node/3362.
86. *BBC News* (2002) Deaf Go Mobile Phone Crazy, at http://news.bbc.co.uk/1/hi/sci/tech/1808872.stm.
87. Cooper, L. (2011) Your mission is to turn spies into special agents, *Marketing Week*, 7 July, 16–19.
88. *Marketing Week* (2002) UK Consumers Have Had Enough of Spam E-Mail, 31 October, 39.

Buy4Now
Powering eCommerce Solutions

The use of the Internet as an additional sales channel offers traditional retailers opportunities to reach expanded markets while improving the efficiency of their operations.[1] Although the potential benefits of the online channel are clear, there are variations in how retailers go about creating such channels. Retailers can develop an online presence by participating in a portal,[2] by outsourcing their e-commerce function to a full-service solution provider or alternatively by developing in-house e-commerce expertise and building an online presence themselves. Whichever route is chosen, it is imperative that retailers can offer a multichannel solution (both on- and offline channels) to customers who increasingly want to shop anytime, anyplace, anywhere.[3]

Established in August 2000, Buy4Now created Ireland's first online retail portal (www.buy4now.ie) comprising leading Irish 'bricks and mortar' brands such as Superquinn, Atlantic Homecare and Arnotts. The company quickly expanded its portal services to include 20 of the country's best known retailers and over 2.5 million products. Since then the company has become Ireland's largest provider of software and services to online retailers.

The e-Commerce Solution arm of the business trades as an independent entity as the Buy4Now Technology Group (www.Buy4Now.com). The company based in Sandyford in Dublin employs 65 people, out of whom 40 work in technology development.[4] In 2010 the company announced the opening of its UK office in Hammersmith, London.[5] Buy4Now Technology Group is the company behind some of the fastest-growing and most successful e-commerce websites in Ireland and internationally. The company has a large portfolio of clients including Superquinn, 3 mobile, Roche Bros (USA), Arnotts, Woodies, Elverys Sports and RTE.

Buy4Now Technology Group provides retailers with the platform and tools needed to optimize their online business, and meet the ever-changing market requirements and expectations of the online shopping community. The group offers a combination of experienced retail consultancy with carefully chosen best-of-breed features and a powerful software as a service (SaaS) platform. The Buy4now eCommerce Suite is an offering capable of blending creativity with a functionally rich e-commerce platform which can provide retailers with all the tools necessary for a successful online business.

Buy4Now has invested millions of euros into developing this product suite, which covers all aspects of the online experience, from placing the order right through to picking and delivering, reporting, marketing and content management. In effect the Buy4Now Technology Group provides a 'one-stop shop' approach which, they suggest, takes away the pain of online retail and empowers the retailer to focus on the elements that make the difference to their business and their customers. The company is a lot more than merely a software provider, and the Buy4Now Technology Group provides a full range of services including marketing, hosting, consultancy, product database creation and a help desk for customers. The group specialises in complete end-to-end e-commerce solutions and the company is now selling 'solutions not software'[6] to the retailer.

In 2010 the Buy4Now Technology Group was contracted by Carphone Warehouse to redesign, redevelop and provide new e-commerce services for its new online store. The technology deployed offers customers of the nationwide chain a high-end, online store. The site is user friendly, interactive and gives customers another channel to communicate with, and purchase from, Carphone Warehouse. Peter Scott from Carphone Warehouse said that Carphone Warehouse was looking for 'a personalized, modern and effective e-commerce solution and the

Buy4Now software as a service is the right fit'. Speaking on the redevelopment contract, Michael Veale, CEO Buy4Now Technology Group, described Carphone Warehouse as 'a fast-moving company that requires excellent e-commerce solutions to deliver to their customers and open up new sales channels in the online market'.[7]

Later the same year the group secured a contract to design, develop and host a solution for Pamela Scott, Ireland's leading ladies fashion retailer. 'Pamela Scott realises the importance of a strong online offering going forward. As part of our multichannel offering, the site will drive sales online and in store. It will enable us to bring our excellent range and offerings to a wider audience both in Ireland and internationally,' said Robert Barron, Director of Pamela Scott.[8]

In August 2010 Buy4Now Technology Group also designed, developed and deployed a new site for Roche Bros., based on the latest Buy4Now Technology Group eGrocery software. Roche Bros. is an up-market Boston (USA)-based supermarket chain. Roche Bros. offers approximately 16,000 products to the online shopper. This large product assortment offers Bostonian online shoppers even more reason to engage with Roche Bros or to switch their grocery allegiance away from competitors.

3, the mobile network operator, is also a client of the group having selected Buy4Now as a company that could uniquely provide a complete end-to-end e-commerce solution. For 3, Buy4Now also provides additional managed services, which effectively means that all three ways a consumer may use to purchase a 3 mobile package—retail outlets, telesales and online/e-commerce channels—utilise Buy4Now software and services.

Arnotts' e-commerce solution is also powered by the Buy4Now Technology Group. Arnotts is Ireland's oldest and largest department store. With a retail area of 300,000 square feet it ranks in the top five stores in Britain and Ireland, alongside such icons of international retailing as Harrods and Selfridges. The full Buy4Now Technology Group software suite was installed into Arnotts, which enabled the company to pick, pack and process orders as efficiently as possible. With no requirement to hold stock in a warehouse facility, the Internet operations could be managed and maintained with minimum staffing and space requirements. The in-store solution allowed Arnotts to develop its online business utilizing existing resources and stock and thus minimizing the store's initial investment. Launched in 2009, the new site developed by Buy4Now Technology Group provides customers with a real multi-channel experience. Arnotts' aim is to provide the majority of its products online to help consumers to shop with them.[9] The technology deployed generated 100 per cent online revenue growth at the department store in its first year.[10]

In February 2011 Irish pet and equestrian retailer Equipet entered into contracts with the Buy4Now Technology Group to develop a complete e-commerce solution to enhance its customer and product offering. Equipet plans to take its bricks and mortar retailing to a whole new level with the new e-commerce and online marketing operation. Equipet has three physical premises within the Irish marketplace. The Buy4Now Technology Group designed and developed an e-commerce store in a complete solution contract that includes email marketing campaigns, content management, customer service, essential support and services, helpdesk and logistics. Equipet also joined the online shopping centre. Micheal Veale, CEO Buy4Now Technology Group, stated that the company will 'provide a complete multi-channel offer to Equipet' with a site that allows customers 'no matter where they are geographically, to shop for equestrian and pet products'.[11]

References

1 Xia, Y. and Zhang, Peter G. (2010) The Impact of the Online Channel on Retailers' Performances: An Empirical Evaluation, *Decision Sciences* 41(3), 517–45.
2 A portal is effectively an online shopping centre gathering together a number of retailers under one umbrella site.
3 Bagge, D. (2007) Viewpoint; Multi-channel Retailing the Route to Customer Focus, *European Retail Digest*, 57–70.
4 Buy4Now expanding its IT workforce (2010) 11 February. Access via www.businessandleadership.com
5 Expansion into the UK, *Buy4Now Technology Group Press Release*, 20 April 2010. Access via www.Buy4Now.com.
6 Presentation by Kevin Murray, Finance Director, Buy4Now Technology Group in DIT (www.dit.ie) College of Business, 26 January 2010.
7 Buy4Now Technology Group to Redevelop Carphone Warehouse Online (2010), *Buy4Now Technology Group Press Release*, 28 April 2010. Access via www.Buy4Now.com.
8 Buy4Now Technology Group Secures Pamela Scott Contract for Online Store (2010), *Buy4Now Technology Group Press Release*, 12 March 2010. Access via www.Buy4Now.com.
9 Arnotts' e-commerce success: Retailer scores with Buy4Now Solution (2011), access via http://techcentral.ie. Accessed June 2011.
10 Buy4Now Expanding its IT workforce (2010), 1 February. http://www.businessandandleadership.com
11 Retailer Equipet outsources e-commerce to Buy4Now, 1 February 2011. http://www.bizstartup.ie.

Note: Unattributed case information is sourced from www.Buy4Now.com.

Questions

1 What attracts people to buy online? What are the likely perceived drawbacks of buying online?

2 What are the benefits to the retailer of having an online presence?

3 What are the benefits to the retailer of outsourcing their e-commerce function? What are the drawbacks of such an approach to e-commerce development?

4 Why do retailers need to provide multichannel solutions for customers?

This case was prepared by Aileen Kennedy (Lecturer) and Joseph Coughlan (Lecturer), College of Business, Dublin Institute of Technology.

Google Has all the Answers?

Google helps the world to answer questions and solve problems by using its search engine, and now also offers a host of other virtual services. This case looks at how Google has created competitive advantage by using virtual information to create a new genre of advertising: search engine marketing.

Graduate students Larry Page and Sergey Brin began developing their search technology in 1996, and Google.com was launched in September 1998. By 2012 the company had grown rapidly and Google has become a global success of the digital age with a market value of over 200 billion dollars. Its rapid rise to being 'the world's biggest and best-loved search engine' can in part be attributed to the smart algorithms (mathematical instructions that computers can understand) devised by Larry and Sergey. But equally important is the value proposition (the benefits to the user) the search engine provides. Google enables its users to find relevant information quickly and easily, and delivers search results in an uncluttered format, which improves usability and increases user enjoyment online. However, in return, users of the search engine provide valuable information about their interests, lifestyles and behaviour. Indeed, Google gathers information every step of the way from when we search and browse the Web, to sending and receiving Gmail communications, to using maps to find directions. By gathering this data from its users Google is able to sell highly targeted advertising space.

In 2012 Google made some changes to make it easier for users to sign up for its additional services (e.g. Google Plus) but the company came under attack from the European Minister of Justice. Questions were raised about security of data and personal privacy because the new joining process means that Google can pool data about signed-up users across over 60 different services including Google search, YouTube, Gmail, maps, Web browsing and Blogger.

Google Technology

Google has developed sophisticated IT resources that offer distinctively better functionality and services than its competitors, and part of the company's success comes from its network of data centres based around Santa Clara, USA. It uses thousands of computer servers to provide a search capacity much greater than its competitors.

Google's search principle is straightforward: by focusing on page rankings rather than just indexing contents, the search engine is able to provide more relevant search results than its competitors (e.g. Yahoo!, AltaVista, Excite). Search tools crawl the Web, checking the content of pages without needing to understand the meaning of the content. As a result, such 'web crawlers' are unable to differentiate between relevant and irrelevant web pages when delivering search results. However, adopting a rank-ordering system, logging pages according to the number of links from other Web pages and the structure of these connections, has enabled Google to develop a quasi-intelligent search tool. To assist the ranking process, Google also checks font sizes, whether a word appears in the page title, the position on the page in which a word appears, and a range of other page characteristics, in order to give an indication of the significance of the search term within a given page.

By making creative use of information technology resources to enhance the capabilities of its search engine, Google created a search service that was quickly perceived by its users as superior to the competition. The Google brand differentiated itself from the competition by introducing the customer benefit of 'relevance' to online searching. The business continued to grow as consumers and business users increasingly turned to the Internet as a primary source of information (searching is the second most common function of the web).

In addition to its effective and efficient use of technology resources and capabilities, Google's strong market position was supported by its financial success. This was generated by the application of an e-business model that provided free-to-user search services, highly targeted and yet discreet advertising and licensing the search technology to third parties (Google currently provides search services for a number of leading search engines). It should be noted that Google continues to generate the majority of its income from advertising. Advertisers pay per click for referrals to their web pages via the Google interface using AdWords, which are search terms chosen by the advertisers and paid for at a rate determined by the popularity of the term. The cost per click varies according to the level of competition from advertisers for a particular keyword.

Competitive markets

Larry and Sergey had a good idea and implemented it in a manner that enabled the company to differentiate itself from the competition, while protecting itself by raising market entry barriers through innovative applications of its resources and capabilities. However, the marketplace is constantly changing as technologies advance and new entrants join the market. Google has responded by diversifying and providing niche search services—news, maps, alerts, blogs, videos for specific target audiences; Scholar (for academics) and Mobile (for remote users)—and the company continues to explore how new technologies can be used to provide innovative search services and products.

Google has also entered new markets:

- web browsers—Chrome, Google's first attempt at developing a Web browser, was released in September 2008; the browser is designed to be more robust than Internet Explorer, but is said not to be a threat to its Microsoft rival at the moment

- email—Gmail (Google email), a free email service, became available to the general public in 2007 and has become very popular, with over 100 million users worldwide

- mobile Internet—Google's Android phone allows owners to call their friends, surf the web and find their way around with the built-in compass as they, say, search for a restaurant or entertainment venue; the Google phone has taken market share from Apple by offering more functionality at more affordable prices.

- social media—in 2011 Google+ was introduced as a social network linking with Gmail, YouTube and Google search.

Since it was established, Google has used technology resources creatively and, in so doing, has developed superior technology-based capabilities that have enabled the company to become financially successful and stay ahead of the competition. In terms of the search market the nearest rival is Baidu with just 11.9 per cent of the market compared to Google's 75.5 per cent of desktop searches. And when it comes to mobile searching Google's share rises to 88.4 per cent, with Yahoo! accounting for just 6.6 per cent. However, in the browser markets the tables are turned. Google has just 18.9 per cent market share with its Chrome browser compared to Firefox with 20.9 per cent and Microsoft Internet Explorer's 52.9 per cent. Furthermore, Google has been challenged by Facebook and Twitter and Google+ is the company's attempt to make up lost ground. Facebook has over 900 million users, whereas Google+ has around 170 million. One of the potential advantages is that users can link across YouTube and Gmail. Bradley Horowitz, Product vice president at Google, says that introducing friction into the system, which allows sharing across applications and with external services is a unique force, which means that we are likely to see more and more apps, especially mobile ones, being developed.

References

Based on: Barney, J. B. (1991) From Resources and Sustained Competitive Advantage, *Journal of Management* 17(1), 99–120; Naughton, J. (2002) Web Masters, *Observer*, 15 December, 27; Vogelstein, F. (2002) Looking for a Dotcom Winner? Search no Further, *Fortune* 145(11), 65–8; McHugh, J. (2003) Google vs Evil, *Wired* 11(1), 130–5; Hitwise (2006) http://www.hitwise.com/news/us200508.html (accessed May 2006); Rose, F. (2006) Are You Ready for Googlevision?, *Wired* 14(5), at www.wired.com/wired/archive/14.05/google_pr.html; Brit, B. (2005) Google Moves Beyond Search, *Marketing*, September, 19.

Questions

1 How does Google differentiate itself from the competition and, in doing so, create competitive advantage?

2 Discuss whether Google will remain as market leader in the search engine market for the next decade.

3 Google established its position in the marketplace as a search engine and this enabled the company to earn significant revenues from advertising. Facebook, however, is the leading social media network, which has avoided looking to advertising as a source of revenue, but now this has changed. Suggest to what extent Facebook is likely to overtake Google in terms of advertising revenue.

This case was written by Fiona Ellis-Chadwick, Senior Lecturer in Marketing, The Open University.

PART 4
Competition and Marketing

MARKETING
SHOWCASE

A new Marketing Showcase video featuring an interview with BMW's General Manager for Marketing Communications (UK) is available to lecturers for presentation and class discussion.

CHAPTER
19

Analysing competitors and creating a competitive advantage

> *If you don't have a competitive advantage, don't compete.*
>
> **JACK WELCH, FORMER CHIEF EXECUTIVE OF GENERAL ELECTRIC**

LEARNING OBJECTIVES

After reading this chapter, you should be able to:

1 describe the determinants of industry attractiveness

2 explain how to analyse competitors

3 distinguish between differentiation and cost leader strategies

4 discuss the sources of competitive advantage

5 discuss the value chain

6 explain how to create and maintain a differential advantage

7 explain how to create and maintain a cost leadership position

Satisfying customers is central to the marketing concept, but it is not enough to guarantee success. The real question is whether a firm can satisfy customers better than the competition. For example, many car manufacturers market cars that give customer satisfaction in terms of appearance, reliability and performance. They meet the basic requirements necessary to compete. Customer choice, however, will depend on creating more value than the competition. Extra value is brought about by establishing a competitive advantage—a topic that will be examined later in this chapter.

Since corporate performance depends on both customer satisfaction and creating greater value than the competition, firms need to understand their competitors as well as their customers. By understanding its competitors, a firm can better predict their reactions to any marketing initiative that the firm might make, and exploit any weaknesses. Competitor analysis is thus crucial to the successful implementation of marketing strategy. Our discussion of competitors in this chapter begins by examining competitive industry structure, then explains how to create competitive and differential advantage and finally cost leadership.

Analysing Competitive Industry Structure

An **industry** is a group of firms that market products that are close substitutes for each other. There is more to understanding an 'industry' and how it works than the core product or service being sold. Commonly we refer to the oil, computer or retail industry. Some industries are more profitable than others. In the past the car, steel, coal and textile industries have been highly profitable, but in more recent years they have had poor profitability records, whereas recently the creative industries, (e.g. TV, publishing, web development), pharmaceuticals and soft drinks industries have enjoyed high profits. Not all of this difference can be explained by the fact that one industry provides better customer satisfaction than another. Other determinants of industry attractiveness and long-run profitability shape the rules of competition. These are the threat of entry of new competitors, the threat of substitutes, the bargaining power of buyers and of suppliers, and the rivalry between the existing competitors.[1] The intensity of these forces shapes an industry and its levels of performance. Their influence is shown diagrammatically in Figure 19.1, which is known as the Porter model of competitive industry structure. Each of the 'five forces' in turn comprises a number of elements that, together, combine to determine the strength of each force and its effect on the degree of competition. Each force is discussed below.

The threat of new entrants

New entrants can raise the level of competition in an industry, which may ultimately reduce its attractiveness. For example, Starbucks is entering the 'coffee capsules market' to take on market leaders Nespresso. Nestlé owns the Nespresso brand and has made significant investment in building the market for this product in Europe using an extensive advertising campaign fronted by Hollywood actor George Clooney, which led to a 20 per cent rise in sales. Nespresso's high levels of profitability have attracted many new entrants including Green Mountain, Côte D'Or, Jacobs and Kenco (see Exhibit 19.1).[2] The threat of new entrants depends on the barriers to entry. High entry barriers exist in some industries (e.g. pharmaceuticals), whereas other industries are much easier to enter (e.g. restaurants).

Key **entry barriers** include:

- economies of scale
- capital requirements
- switching costs
- access to distribution
- expected retaliation.

For present competitors, industry attractiveness can be increased by raising entry barriers. High promotional and R&D expenditures, and clearly communicated retaliatory actions to entry are some methods of raising barriers as in the situation with the Nespresso coffee pods.

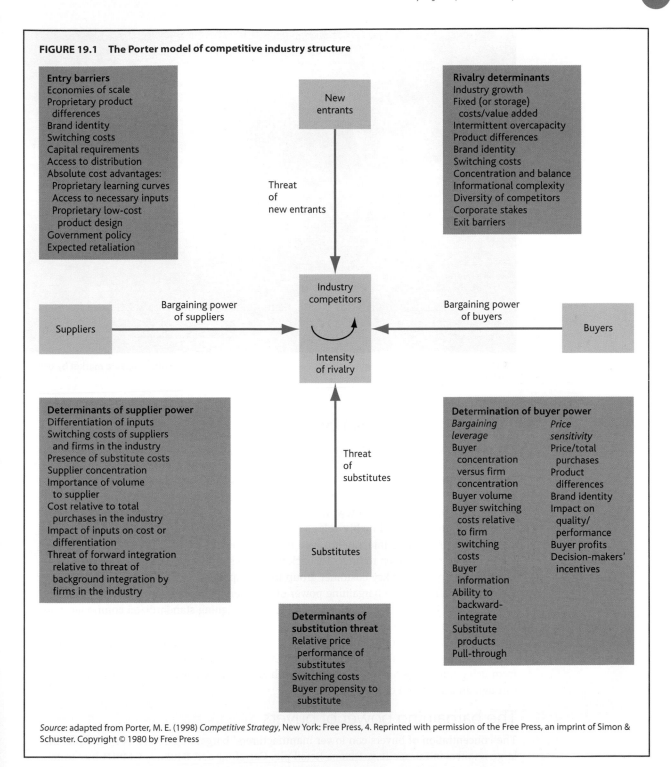

FIGURE 19.1 The Porter model of competitive industry structure

Entry barriers
Economies of scale
Proprietary product
  differences
Brand identity
Switching costs
Capital requirements
Access to distribution
Absolute cost advantages:
  Proprietary learning curves
  Access to necessary inputs
  Proprietary low-cost
  product design
Government policy
Expected retaliation

New
entrants

Threat
of
new entrants

Rivalry determinants
Industry growth
Fixed (or storage)
  costs/value added
Intermittent overcapacity
Product differences
Brand identity
Switching costs
Concentration and balance
Informational complexity
Diversity of competitors
Corporate stakes
Exit barriers

Suppliers

Bargaining power
of suppliers

Industry
competitors

Intensity
of rivalry

Bargaining power
of buyers

Buyers

Determinants of supplier power
Differentiation of inputs
Switching costs of suppliers
  and firms in the industry
Presence of substitute costs
Supplier concentration
Importance of volume
  to supplier
Cost relative to total
  purchases in the industry
Impact of inputs on cost or
  differentiation
Threat of forward integration
  relative to threat of
  background integration by
  firms in the industry

Threat
of
substitutes

Substitutes

Determination of buyer power
*Bargaining   Price
leverage   sensitivity*
Buyer   Price/total
  concentration   purchases
  versus firm   Product
  concentration   differences
Buyer volume   Brand identity
Buyer switching   Impact on
  costs relative   quality/
  to firm   performance
  switching   Buyer profits
  costs   Decision-makers'
Buyer   incentives
  information
Ability to
  backward-
  integrate
Substitute
  products
Pull-through

**Determinants of
substitution threat**
Relative price
  performance of
  substitutes
Switching costs
Buyer propensity to
  substitute

Source: adapted from Porter, M. E. (1998) *Competitive Strategy*, New York: Free Press, 4. Reprinted with permission of the Free Press, an imprint of Simon & Schuster. Copyright © 1980 by Free Press

Nestlé continues to make a significant investments in these areas. Other ways of raising barriers are by taking out patents and developing strong relationships/partnerships with suppliers and/or distributors. Some managerial actions can unwittingly lower barriers. For example, new product designs that dramatically lower manufacturing costs can ease entry for newcomers.

⬆**EXHIBIT 19.1** Nespresso aims to retain its competitive advantage in the coffee capsule market by using celebrity endorsement of the brand.

The bargaining power of suppliers

The cost of raw materials, components and intellectual skills can have a major bearing on a firm's profitability. The higher the bargaining power of suppliers, the higher these costs. For example when Apple decided to adopt Intel processors there were lengthy extensive negotiations. The bargaining power of suppliers will be high when:

- there are many buyers and few dominant suppliers
- there are differentiated highly valued products
- suppliers threaten to integrate forward into the industry
- buyers do not threaten to integrate backward into supply
- the industry is not a key customer group to the suppliers.

A firm can reduce the bargaining power of suppliers by seeking new sources of supply, threatening to integrate backward into supply, and designing standardized components so that many suppliers are capable of producing them.

Backwards integration means that a buyer (like Apple) purchases the supplier and a form of vertical integration takes place. Currently, there is speculation that Apple might switch from using Intel chips and replacing them with ARM (processor chips made by Apple, through an acquisition of PA Semi).[3]

The bargaining power of buyers

The concentration of buyers can lower manufacturers' bargaining power. For example, the large retailers in Europe (e.g. Dixons Retail plc, Carrefour and Bauhaus GMbH) buy from many suppliers in large volumes and this has increased the bargaining power. The bargaining power of buyers is greater when:

- there are few dominant buyers and many sellers
- products are standardized
- buyers threaten to integrate backwards into the industry
- suppliers do not threaten to integrate forwards into the buyer's industry
- the industry is not a key supplying group for buyers.

EXHIBIT 19.2   The design of Apple's Store in Shanghai reflects the innovativeness of its products.

Manufacturing firms in the industry can attempt to lower buyer power by increasing the number of buyers they sell to, threatening to integrate forwards into the buyer's industry and producing highly valued, differentiated products. Apple has become a leading retailer around the world with its dedicated, high-tech, Apple product stores.

Threat of substitutes

The presence of substitute products can lower industry attractiveness and profitability because these put a constraint on price levels. For example, tea and coffee are fairly close substitutes in many European countries. Raising the price of coffee, therefore, would make tea more attractive. The threat of substitute products depends on:

- buyers' willingness to substitute
- the relative price and performance of substitutes
- the costs of switching to substitutes.

The threat of substitute products can be lowered by building up switching costs, or for example, by creating a strong distinctive brand and maintaining a price differential in line with perceived customer values. If these tactics fail to deter a rival from launching a substitute product, the incumbent is faced with the following options: copy the substitute; copy but build in a differential advantage; form a strategic alliance with the rival; buy the rival; or move to a new market. For example, BlackBerry products manufacturer Research in Motion (RIM) has seen its market share plummet as adopters switch to faster touchscreen smartphones like iPhone and Samsung Galaxy.[4] Kodak has suffered a more significant decline as consumers have shifted from using film to digital cameras to capture images.

Industry competitors

The intensity of rivalry between competitors in an industry will depend on the following factors.

- *Structure of the competition*: there is more intense rivalry when there are a large number of small competitors or a few equally balanced competitors, and less rivalry when a clear market leader exists with a large cost advantage.
- *Structure of costs*: high fixed costs encourage price-cutting to fill capacity.
- *Degree of differentiation*: basic commodity products encourage rivalry, while highly differentiated products that are hard to copy are associated with less intense rivalry.
- *Switching costs*: rivalry is reduced when switching costs are high because the product is specialized, the customer has invested a lot of resources in learning how to use the product or has made tailor-made investments that are worthless with other products and suppliers. For example, a product might be customized, production, logistical or marketing operations might be geared to using the equipment of a particular supplier (e.g. computer systems), or retraining may be required as a result of a switch to another supplier.
- *Strategic objectives*: when competitors are pursuing build strategies, competition is likely to be more intense than when playing hold or harvesting strategies.
- *Exit barriers*: when barriers to leaving an industry are high due to such factors as lack of opportunities elsewhere, high vertical integration, emotional barriers or the high cost of closing down plant, rivalry will be more intense than when exit barriers are low.

Firms need to be careful not to spoil a situation of competitive stability. They need to balance their own position against the well-being of the industry as a whole. For example, an intense price or promotional war may gain a few percentage points in market share but lead to an overall fall in long-run industry profitability as competitors respond to these moves. It is sometimes better to protect industry structure than follow short-term self-interest.

A major threat to favourable industry structure is the use of a no-frills, low-price strategy by a minor player seeking positional advantage. For example, the launch of generic products in the pharmaceutical and airline industries has lowered overall profitability.

Despite meeting customers' needs with high-quality, good-value products, firms can 'compete away' the rewards. An intensive competitive environment means that the value created by firms in satisfying customer needs is given away to buyers through lower prices, dissipated through costly marketing battles (e.g. advertising wars) or passed on to powerful suppliers through higher prices for raw materials and components.

In Europe the competitive structure of industries was fundamentally changed with the advent of the single European market. The lifting of barriers to trade between countries has radically altered industry structures by affecting the underlying determinants. For example, the threat of new entrants and the growth in buyer/supplier power through acquisition or merger are fundamentally changing the competitive climate of many industries.

Competitor Analysis

The analysis of how industry structure affects long-run profitability has shown the need to understand and monitor competitors. Their actions can spoil an otherwise attractive industry, their weaknesses can be a target for exploitation, and their response to a firm's marketing initiatives can have a major impact on their success. Indeed, firms that focus on competitors' actions have been found to achieve better business performance than those who pay less attention to their competitors.[5] Competitive information can be obtained from marketing research surveys, secondary sources (e.g. the Web, trade magazines, newspaper articles), analysing competitors' products and gathering competitors' sales literature.

Competitor analysis seeks to answer five key questions.

1 Who are our competitors?
2 What are their strengths and weaknesses?
3 What are their strategic objectives and thrust?
4 What are their strategies?
5 What are their response patterns?

These issues are summarized in Figure 19.2. Each question will now be examined.

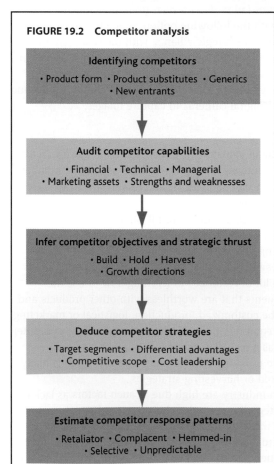

FIGURE 19.2   Competitor analysis

Identifying competitors
• Product form • Product substitutes • Generics
• New entrants

Audit competitor capabilities
• Financial • Technical • Managerial
• Marketing assets • Strengths and weaknesses

Infer competitor objectives and strategic thrust
• Build • Hold • Harvest
• Growth directions

Deduce competitor strategies
• Target segments • Differential advantages
• Competitive scope • Cost leadership

Estimate competitor response patterns
• Retaliator • Complacent • Hemmed-in
• Selective • Unpredictable

Who are our competitors?

We need to take a wide view of potential competition. Only those companies that are producing technically similar products are considered to be the competition (e.g. paint companies). We may miss other sources of competition by ignoring companies purchasing substitute products that perform a similar function (e.g. polyurethane varnish firms) and those that solve a problem or eliminate it in a dissimilar way (e.g. PVC double-glazing companies). The actions of all of these types of competitors can affect the performance of our firm and therefore should be monitored. Their responses also need to be assessed as they will determine the outcome of any competitive move that our firm may wish to make, which can result in loss of market share or being made irrelevant. Making the competition irrelevant is a strategic option discussed in Chapter 20.

The marketing environment needs to be scanned for potential entrants into the industry. These can take two forms: entrants with technically similar products and those invading the market

FIGURE 19.3   Competitor identification

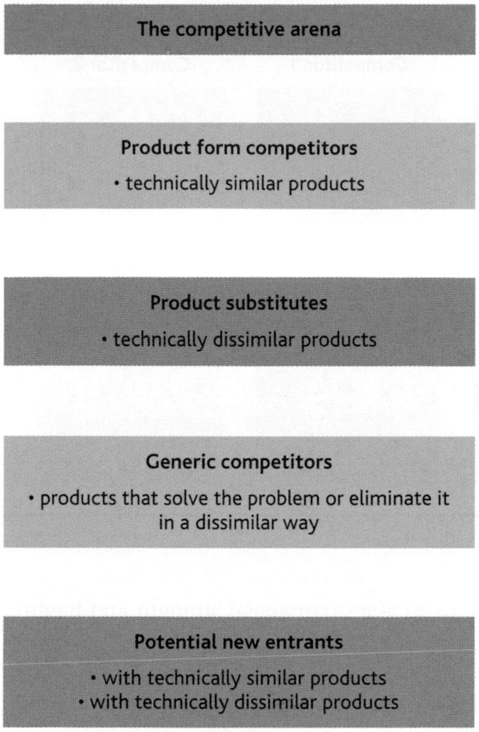

The competitive arena

Product form competitors
• technically similar products

Product substitutes
• technically dissimilar products

Generic competitors
• products that solve the problem or eliminate it in a dissimilar way

Potential new entrants
• with technically similar products • with technically dissimilar products

with substitute products. Companies with similar core competences to the present incumbents may pose the threat of entering with technically similar products. For example, Apple's skills in computer electronics provided the springboard for it to become market leader in the portable music player market with its iPod brand. The source of companies entering with substitute products may be more difficult to locate, however. A technological breakthrough may transform an industry by rendering the old product obsolete, for example the computer replacing the typewriter. In such instances it is difficult to locate the source of the substitute product well in advance. Figure 19.3 illustrates this competitive arena.

What are their strengths and weaknesses?

Having identified our competitors the next stage is to complete a **competitor audit** in order to assess their relative strengths and weaknesses. Understanding competitor strengths and weaknesses is an important prerequisite for developing a competitor strategy and identifying a competitor's vulnerabilities.

The process of assessing competitors' strengths and weaknesses may take place as part of a marketing audit (see Chapter 2). As much internal, market and customer information should be gathered as is needed. For example, financial data concerning profitability, profit margins, sales and investment levels, market data relating to price levels, market share and distribution channels used, and customer data concerning awareness of brand names, and perceptions of brand and company image, product and service quality, and selling ability may be relevant.

Not all of this information will be easily accessible. Management needs to decide the extent to which each element of information is worth pursuing. For example, a decision is required regarding how much expenditure is to be allocated to measuring customer awareness and perceptions through marketing research.

This process of data gathering needs to be managed so that information is available to compare our company with its competitors on the *key factors for success* in the industry. A three-stage process can then be used.

1 Identify key factors for success in the industry

These should be restricted to about six to eight factors otherwise the analysis becomes too diffuse.[6] Which factors to use is a matter of managerial judgement. They may be functional (such as financial strength or flexible production) or generic (for example, the ability to respond quickly to customer needs, innovativeness, or the capability to provide other sales services). Since these factors are critical for success they should be used to compare our company with its competitors.

2 Rate our company and competitors on each key success factor using a rating scale

Each company is given a score on each success factor using a rating device. This may be a scale ranging from 1 (very poor) to 5 (very good); this results in a set of company capability profiles (an example is given in Fig. 19.4). Our company is rated alongside two competitors on six key success factors. Compared with our company, competitor 1 is relatively strong regarding technical assistance to customers and access to international distribution channels, but relatively weak on product quality. Competitor 2 is relatively strong on international

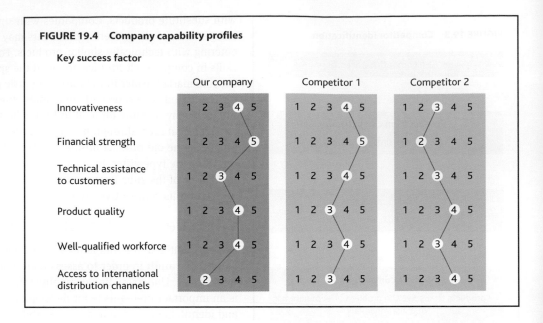

FIGURE 19.4   Company capability profiles

distribution channels but relatively weak on innovativeness, financial strength and having a well-qualified workforce.

3 Consider the implications for competitive strategy

The competitive profile analysis helps to identify possible competitive strategies. This analysis would suggest that our company should consider taking steps to improve technical assistance to customers to match or exceed competitor 1's capability on this factor. At the moment, our company enjoys a differential advantage over competitor 1 on product quality. Our strength in innovativeness should be used to maintain this differential advantage and competitor 1's moves to improve product quality should be monitored carefully.

Competitor 2 is weaker overall than competitor 1 and our company. However, it has considerable strengths in having access to international distribution channels. Given our company's weakness in this area, a strategic alliance with or take-over of competitor 2 might be sensible if our company's objective is to expand internationally. Our company's financial strength and competitor 2's financial weakness suggests that a take-over might be feasible.

What are their strategic objectives and thrust?

The third part of competitor analysis is to infer their *strategic objectives*. Companies may decide to build, hold or harvest products and strategic business units (SBUs). To briefly recap, a build objective is concerned with increasing sales and/or market share, a hold objective suggests maintaining sales and/or market share, and a harvest objective is followed when the emphasis is on maximizing short-term cash flow through slashing expenditure and raising prices whenever possible. It is useful to know what strategic objectives are being pursued by competitors because their response pattern and strategies may depend upon objectives (this topic is covered in further detail in Chapter 20).

As well as considering objectives for specific products, services and SBUs it is also worthwhile to consider a competitor's broader strategic aims. For example, strategic thrust refers to the future areas of expansion a company might be contemplating. Broadly speaking, a company can expand by penetrating existing markets more effectively with current products, launching new products in existing markets or by growing in new markets with existing or new products. Knowing the strategic thrust of competitors can help our strategic decision-making. For example, knowing that our competitors are considering expansion in

South Africa but not Europe might make expansion into Europe a more attractive strategic option for our company.

What are their strategies?

At the product service level, competitor analysis will attempt to deduce positioning strategy. This involves assessing a competitor's target market and differential advantage of its product and/or service. The marketing mix strategies (e.g. price levels, media used for promotion, and distribution channels) may indicate target market, and marketing research into customer perceptions can be used to assess relative differential advantages.

Companies and competitors should be monitored continuously for changes in positioning strategy. For example, Volvo's traditional positioning strategy, based on safety, has been modified to give more emphasis to performance and style enabling the company to compete with other high performance cars.

Strategies can also be defined in terms of competitive scope. For example, are competitors attempting to service the whole market or a few segments of a particular niche? If a niche player, is it likely that they will be content to stay in that segment or will they use it as a beachhead to move into other segments in the future? Japanese companies are renowned for their use of small niche markets as springboards for market segment expansion (e.g. the small car segments in the USA and Europe).

Competitors may use cost-leadership, focusing on cost-reducing measures rather than expensive product development and promotional strategies. (Cost leadership will be discussed in more detail later in this chapter.) If competitors are following this strategy it is more likely that they will be focusing research and development expenditure on process rather than product development in a bid to reduce manufacturing costs.

What are their response patterns?

A key consideration in making a strategic or tactical move is the likely response of competitors. Indeed, it is a major objective of competitor analysis to be able to predict competitor response to market and competitive changes. A competitor's past behaviour is also a guide to what they might do in the future. Market leaders often try to control competitor response by retaliatory action. These are called *retaliatory* competitors because they can be relied on to respond aggressively to competitive challenges. For example LoveFilm (UK company) spotted an opportunity in home film rentals and Netflix (US company) saw an opportunity to sell movies-on-demand via the internet and in a pre-emptive move LoveFilm linked with the UK's leading television channels BBC and ITV to launch its LoveFilm web-stream of TV favourites. Netflix retaliated by agreeing a similar deal and in doing so took some of the power from the 'home' side.[7]

By punishing competitor moves, market leaders can condition competitors to behave in predicted ways—for example, by not taking advantage of a price rise by the leader. As we discussed in Chapter 13, Pricing Strategy, Vodafone sought to condition competitor actions and response patterns when it responded aggressively to a cut in price of T-Mobile's Flext brand, and declared that no competitor would be allowed to gain an advantage purely on price.[8]

It is not only market leaders that retaliate aggressively. Where management is known to be assertive, and our move is likely to have a major impact on their performance, a strong response is usual.

The history, traditions and managerial personalities of competitors also have an influence on competitive response. Some markets are characterized by years of competitive stability with little serious strategic challenge to any of the incumbents. This can breed complacency, with predictably slow reaction times to new challenges. For example, innovation that offers superior customer value may be dismissed as a fad and unworthy of serious attention.

Another situation where competitors are unlikely to respond is where their previous strategies have restricted their scope for retaliation. An example of such a *hemmed-in competitor* was a major manufacturer of car number plates that were sold to car dealerships. A new company was started by an ex-employee who focused on one geographical area, supplying the same quality product but with extra discount. The national supplier could not respond since to give discount in that particular region would have meant granting the discount nationwide.

A fourth type of competitor may respond *selectively*. Because of tradition or beliefs about the relative effectiveness of marketing instruments, a competitor may respond to some competitive moves but not others. For example, extra sales promotion expenditures may be matched but advertising increases to, say, build brand awareness may be ignored. Another reason for selective response is the varying degree of visibility of marketing actions. For example, giving extra price discounts may be highly visible, but providing distributors with extra support (e.g. training, sales literature, loans) may be less discernible.

A final type of competitor is totally *unpredictable* in its response pattern. Sometimes there is a response and, at other times, there is no response. Some moves are countered aggressively; with others reaction is weak. No factors explain these differences adequately; they appear to be at the whim of management.

Interestingly, research has shown that managers tend to over-react more frequently than they under-react to competitors' marketing activities.[9]

Competitive Advantage

The key to superior performance is to gain and hold a *competitive advantage*. Firms can gain a competitive advantage through *differentiation* of their product offering, which provides superior customer value, or by managing for *lowest delivered cost*.

Competitive strategies

These two means of competitive advantage, when combined with the **competitive scope** of activities (broad vs narrow), result in four generic strategies: differentiation, cost leadership, differentiation focus, and cost focus. The differentiation and cost leadership strategies seek competitive advantage in a broad range of market or industry segments, whereas differentiation focus and cost focus strategies are confined to a narrow segment[10] (see Fig. 19.5).

Differentiation

Differentiation strategy involves the selection of one or more choice criteria that are used by many buyers in an industry. The firm then uniquely positions itself to meet these criteria. Differentiation strategies are usually associated with a premium price, and higher than average costs for the industry as the extra value to customers (e.g. higher performance) often raises costs. The aim is to differentiate in a way that leads to a price premium in excess of the cost of differentiating. Differentiation gives customers a reason to prefer one product over another and thus is central to strategic marketing thinking. Here are some examples of brands that have achieved success using a differentiation strategy.

- Nokia became market leader in mobile phones by being the first to realize that they were fashion items and to design stylish phones to differentiate the brand from its rivals.
- Toyota has built its success and reputation by targeting a broad market with highly reliable, high build quality, stylish and environmentally friendly cars, which differentiate the brand from its competitors, such as GM, Ford and Fiat.

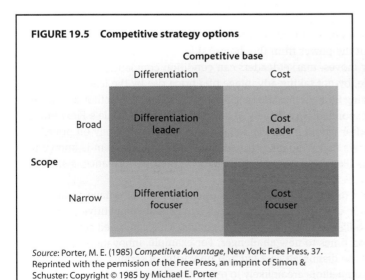

FIGURE 19.5   Competitive strategy options

Source: Porter, M. E. (1985) *Competitive Advantage*, New York: Free Press, 37. Reprinted with the permission of the Free Press, an imprint of Simon & Schuster: Copyright © 1985 by Michael E. Porter

Digital Marketing 19.1 Shopping on the Internet: Is it all about Price?

The perceived wisdom is that consumers flock to the Internet in order to get a better deal on a known branded item. In fact, many search engine marketers work with the assumption that customers are seeking the lowest price. Activity on 'comparison' sites might suggest that this is true. The existence in the UK of sites such as CompareTheMarket, MoneySupermarket and GoCompare suggests that people will indeed want to search on price. But price isn't necessarily why these insurance intermediaries have sprung up.

The move in the late 1980s and early 1990s towards direct insurance meant the disappearance of a large part of the insurance broker network through disintermediation. With a massive increase in the number of direct insurers available in the market, consumers found they were faced with too many choices and (one specific issue) they had to complete application forms for each insurer.

This led to the arrival of comparison sites, making it possible for customers to complete one form and yet still receive insurance quotations from hundreds of providers. This reintermediation is more about convenience and ease of use than price comparison (although this is sometimes touted by such sites in their marketing). Often it is about providing comparison information regarding policies and policy differences, of which price is only one small part.

Price is often cited as the reason why shoppers 'search'. But again price is only one factor. Simple availability of stock is more often favoured as well as the ability to serve niche needs and develop customized solutions for individuals. If anything, shopping on the Internet is about choice, and price is only one of the choices shoppers have to make.

So, in order to compete successfully companies need to ensure that they differentiate themselves from their competitors in a number of ways.

- Dyson differentiated its vacuum cleaners by inventing a bagless version, which outperformed its rivals by providing greater suction and convenience, and by eliminating the need to buy and install dust bags. Its vacuum cleaners are also differentiated from other brands by their distinctive design.
- Google created a differential advantage over its search engine rivals by enabling the most relevant websites to be ranked at the top of listings.

Other companies are also creating differential advantages using Internet technologies. Comparison engines bring competitors together onto one virtual platform where consumers search for the best deals. Read Digital Marketing 19.1 to find out more.

Cost leadership

This strategy involves the achievement of the lowest cost position in an industry. Many segments in the industry are served and great importance is attached to minimizing costs throughout the business So long as the price achievable for its products is around the industry average, cost leadership should result in superior performance. Thus, cost leaders often market standard products that are believed to be acceptable to customers. Heinz and United Biscuits are believed to be cost leaders in their industries. They market acceptable products at reasonable prices, which means that their low costs result in above-average profits. Wal-Mart is also a cost leader, which allows the company the option of charging lower prices than its rivals to achieve higher sales and yet achieve comparable profit margins, or to match competitors' prices and attain higher profit margins. Dell has also achieved success using a cost leadership strategy. It outsources manufacturing, sells direct to customers, does little R&D and keeps overheads to less than 10 per cent of sales. This meant that it was able to undercut Hewlett-Packard on price while achieving higher profit margins, and to force IBM out of the PC business. However, the Dell case provides an example of the dangers of a cost focus. Dell took its eye off the customer (e.g. it became the subject of many complaints about poor service) and rapidly lost market share to a rejuvenated Hewlett-Packard.

Differentiation focus

With this strategy, a firm aims to differentiate within one or a small number of target market segments. The special needs of the segment mean that there is an opportunity to differentiate the product offering from that of the competition, which may be targeting a broader group of customers. For example, some small speciality chemical companies thrive on taking orders that are too small or specialized to be of interest to their larger competitors. Differentiation focusers must be clear that the needs of their target group differ from those of the broader market (otherwise there will be no basis for differentiation) and that existing competitors are underperforming. Examples of differentiation focusers are Burberry, Bang & Olufsen, Mercedes and Ferrari; each of these markets differentiated products to one or a small number of target market segments.

Cost focus

With this strategy a firm seeks a cost advantage with one or a small number of target market segments. By dedicating itself to the segment, the cost focuser can seek economies that may be ignored or missed by broadly targeted competitors. In some instances, the competition, by trying to achieve wide market acceptance, may be over-performing (for example, by providing unwanted services) to one segment of customers. By providing a basic product offering, a cost advantage will be gained that may exceed the price discount necessary to sell it. Examples of cost focusers are easyJet and Ryanair, who focus on short-haul flights with a basic product trimmed to reduce costs. Lidl is also a cost focuser, targeting price-sensitive consumers with a narrow product line (around 300 items in stock) but with large buying power. Ibis, the no-frills hotel brand in the Accor Hotels portfolio, is another example with its focus on one market segment: price-conscious consumers.

Choosing a competitive strategy

The essence of corporate success is to choose a generic strategy and pursue it with gusto. Below-average performance is associated with the failure to achieve any of these generic strategies. The result is no competitive advantage: a *stuck-in-the-middle position* that results in lower performance than that of the cost leaders, differentiators or focusers in any market segment. An example of a company that made the mistake of moving to a stuck-in-the-middle position is Fiat. The Fiat 500 was sold in the US through a stand-alone dealership network. Dealers were required to make a heavy investment in creating an Italian feel in their showrooms. This was in preference to launching the car through the 500-strong Chrysler dealers (Chrysler acquired a stake in Fiat in 2009). The advantages of the first option were an image of exclusivity, but heavy investment was required—for example, $3 million for the showroom makeover. In the second option leveraging[11] advantage from Chrysler could have meant making use of existing sales and service infrastructures. One of the downsides was

Read the Research 19.1 Porter revisited

Porter's 5-forces is probably the most widely used model for industry analysis among business school students. Criticism from both the academic community and students has led Steen Ehlers to revisit and update the model in line with economic theory. Read the article and draw your own conclusions.

http://www.berg-marketing.dk/GIF/porterrev.pdf

Many companies strive to gain competitive advantage. One way is to use their considerable resources as a weapon in the fight for supremacy. This article applies resource-based theories to analyse the success of online retailing by leading supermarkets. Five case studies provide insights into how Tesco creates competitive advantage over its rivals, Sainsbury's, Morrisons, Asda and Waitrose.

http://oro.open.ac.uk.libezproxy.open.ac.uk/27749/1/estrategy_UK_Grocery_Retailers_[final_for_publication_300707]].doc

that the Fiat 500 had a higher ticket price than similar performing cars like the Nissan Versa or Toyota Yaris and being sold in the same location could have had a negative impact on sales. So, the Fiat 500 was, arguably, stuck in the middle and its strategy did not lead to the coverage needed to establish the brand as rapidly as it would have liked.

Firms need to understand the generic basis for their success and resist the temptation to blur strategy by making inconsistent moves. For example, a no-frills cost leader or focuser should beware the pitfalls of moving to a higher cost base (perhaps by adding expensive services). A focus strategy involves limiting sales volume. Once domination of the target segment has been achieved there may be a temptation to move into other segments in order to achieve growth with the same competitive advantage. This can be a mistake if the new segments do not value the firm's competitive advantage in the same way.

In most situations differentiation and cost leadership strategies are incompatible: differentiation is achieved through higher costs. However, there are circumstances when both can be achieved simultaneously. For example, a differentiation strategy may lead to market share domination, which lowers costs through economies of scale and learning effects; or a highly differentiated firm may pioneer a major process innovation that significantly reduces manufacturing costs leading to a cost-leadership position. When differentiation and cost leadership coincide, performance is exceptional since a premium price can be charged for a low-cost product.

Sources of competitive advantage

In order to create a differentiated or lowest cost position, a firm needs to understand the nature and location of the potential *sources of competitive advantage*. The nature of these sources are the superior skills and resources of a firm. Management benefits by analysing the superior skills and resources that are contributing, or could contribute, to competitive advantage (i.e. differentiation or lowest cost position). Their location can be aided by value chain analysis. A **value chain** is the discrete activities a firm carries out in order to perform its business.

Superior skills

Superior skills are the distinctive capabilities of key personnel that set them apart from the personnel of competing firms.[12] The benefit of superior skills is the resulting ability to perform functions more effectively than other firms. For example, Sergey Brin and Larry Page worked together to produce a search engine that outperformed its rivals. Their technical know-how enabled them to use their superior skills not only to create Google, but also to lead the company to become the world's most influential Internet search tool.

Superior resources

Superior resources are the tangible requirements for advantage that enable a firm to exercise its skills. Examples of superior resources include:
* the number of sales people in a market
* expenditure on advertising and sales promotion
* distribution infrastructure
* expenditure on R&D
* scale of and type of production facilities
* financial resources
* brand equity
* knowledge

Core competences

The distinctive nature of these skills and resources makes up a company's **core competences**. For example, Google is able to use its technical skills and vast resources to enable the company to operate a global search engine. Google's operation has grown thanks to its innovative use of technology and its data centres in the USA, Finland and Belgium.

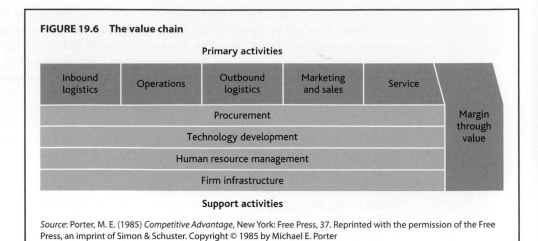

FIGURE 19.6 The value chain

Source: Porter, M. E. (1985) *Competitive Advantage*, New York: Free Press, 37. Reprinted with the permission of the Free Press, an imprint of Simon & Schuster. Copyright © 1985 by Michael E. Porter

Value chain

A useful method for locating superior skills and resources is the **value chain**.[13] All firms consist of a set of activities that are conducted to design, manufacture, market, distribute and service its products. The value chain categorizes these into primary and support activities (see Fig. 19.6). This enables the sources of costs and differentiation to be understood and located.

Primary activities include inbound physical distribution (e.g. materials handling, warehousing, inventory control), operations (e.g. manufacturing, packaging, reselling), outbound physical distribution (e.g. delivery, order processing), marketing (e.g. advertising, selling) and service (e.g. installation, repair, customer training). A key skill of Wal-Mart is its inbound logistics, which is based on real-time information systems and lets customers decide what appears in its stores. The Internet is used to inform suppliers what was sold the day before. In this way, it buys only what sells. Zara's competitive advantage relies on its marketing skills, which relate product design to fashion trends, and operational and logistical skills that get new clothing designs in stores faster than competitors.

Support activities are found within all of these primary activities, and consist of purchased inputs, technology, human resource management and the firm's infrastructure. These are not defined within a given primary activity because they can be found in all of them. Purchasing can take place within each primary activity, not just in the purchasing department; technology is relevant to all primary activities, as is human resource management; and the firm's infrastructure, which consists of general management, planning, finance, accounting and quality management, supports the entire value chain.

By examining each value-creating activity, management can look for the skills and resources that may form the basis for low cost or differentiated positions.

To the extent that skills and resources exceed (or could be developed to exceed) those of the competition, they form the key sources of competitive advantage. Not only should the skills and resources within value-creating activities be examined, the *linkages* between them should be examined too. For example, greater coordination between operations and inbound physical distribution may give rise to reduced costs through lower inventory levels.

Value chain analysis can extend to the value chains of suppliers and customers. For example, just-in-time supply could lower inventory costs; providing salesforce support to distributors could foster closer relations. Thus, by looking at the linkages between a firm's value chain and those of suppliers and customers, improvements in performance can result that can lower costs or contribute to the creation of a differentiated position.

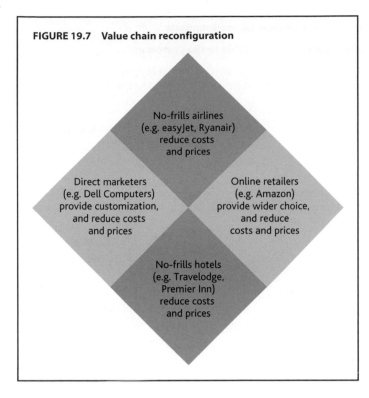

FIGURE 19.7   Value chain reconfiguration

No-frills airlines
(e.g. easyJet, Ryanair)
reduce costs
and prices

Direct marketers
(e.g. Dell Computers)
provide customization,
and reduce costs
and prices

Online retailers
(e.g. Amazon)
provide wider choice,
and reduce
costs and prices

No-frills hotels
(e.g. Travelodge,
Premier Inn)
reduce costs
and prices

Overall, the contribution of the value chain is in providing a framework for understanding the nature and location of the skills and resources that provide the basis for competitive advantage. Furthermore, the value chain provides the framework for cost analysis. Assigning operating costs and assets to value activities is the starting point of cost analysis so that improvement can be made, and cost advantages defended. For example, if a firm discovers that its cost advantage is based on superior production facilities, it should be vigilant in upgrading those facilities to maintain its position against competitors. Similarly, by understanding the sources of differentiation, a company can build on these sources and defend against competitive attack. For example, if differentiation is based on skills in product design, then management knows that sufficient investment in maintaining design superiority is required to maintain the firm's differentiated position. Also, the identification of specific sources of advantage can lead to their exploitation in new markets where customers place a similar high value on the resultant outcome. For example, Marks & Spencer's skills in clothing retailing were successfully extended to provide differentiation in food retailing. Finally, analysis of the value chain can lead to its reconfiguration to fundamentally change the way a market is served. Figure 19.7 provides some examples.

Creating a Differential Advantage

Although skills and resources are the sources of competitive advantage, they are translated into a **differential advantage** only when the customer perceives that the firm is providing value above that of the competition.[14] The creation of a differential advantage, then, comes from linking skills and resources with the key attributes (choice criteria) that customers are looking for in a product offering. However, it should be recognized that the distinguishing competing attributes in a market are not always the most important ones. For example, if customers were asked to rank safety, punctuality and onboard service in order of importance when flying, safety would undoubtedly be ranked at the top. Nevertheless, when choosing an airline, safety would rank low because most airlines are assumed to be safe. This is why airlines look to less important ways of differentiating their offerings (e.g. by giving superior onboard service).

A differential advantage can be created with any aspect of the marketing mix. Product, distribution, promotion and price are all capable of creating added customer value. The key to whether improving an aspect of marketing is worthwhile is to know whether the potential benefit provides value to the customer. Table 19.1 lists ways of creating differential advantages and their potential impact on customer value.

Product

Product performance can be enhanced by, say, raising speed, comfort and safety levels, capacity and ease of use, or improving taste or smell. For example, improving comfort levels (e.g. of a car), taste (e.g. of food), or smell (e.g. of cosmetics) can give added pleasure to consumption. Raising productivity levels of earth-moving equipment can bring higher revenue if more jobs can be done in a given period of time. Singapore Airlines has created a differential advantage based on superior service. Performance can also be improved by added

TABLE 19.1   Creating a differential advantage using the marketing mix

Marketing mix	Differential advantage	Value to the customer
Product	Performance	Lower costs; higher revenue; safety; pleasure; status; service; added functions
	Durability	Longer life; lower costs
	Reliability	Lower maintenance and production costs; higher revenue; fewer problems
	Style	Good looks; status
	Upgradability	Lower costs; prestige
	Technical assistance	Better-quality products; closer supplier–buyer relationships
	Installation	Fewer problems
Distribution	Location	Convenience; lower costs
	Quick/reliable delivery	Lower costs; fewer problems
	Distributor support	More effective selling/marketing; close buyer–seller relationships
	Delivery guarantees	Peace of mind
	Computerized reordering	Less work; lower costs
Promotion	Creative/more advertising	Superior brand personality
	Creative/more sales promotion	Direct added value
	Cooperative promotions	Lower costs
	Well-trained salesforce	Superior problem-solving and building close relationships
	Dual selling	Sales assistance; higher sales
	Fast, accurate quotes	Lower costs; fewer problems
	Free demonstrations	Lower risk of purchase
	Free or low-cost trial	Lower risk of purchase
	Fast complaint handling	Fewer problems; lower costs
Price	Lower price	Lower cost of purchase
	Credit facilities	Lower costs; better cash flow
	Low-interest loans	Lower costs; better cash flow
	Higher price	Price–quality match

functions that create extra benefits for customers. For example, Apple has enhanced the performance of its iPhone by the creation of its App Store, which allows users to access software applications from independent developers. This creates additional functions that the iPhone can carry out, such as Urbanspoon, which allows users to find the location and price range of restaurants nearby in London.

The *durability* of a product has a bearing on costs since greater durability means a longer operating life. Improving product *reliability* (i.e. lowering malfunctions or defects) can lower maintenance and production costs, raise revenues through lower downtime and reduce the hassle of using the product. Product *styling* can also give customer value through the improved looks that good style brings. This can confer status to the buyer and allow the supplier to

Go to the website to discover how Vodafone differentiates its products from the competition.
www.mcgraw-hill.co.uk/ textbooks/jobber

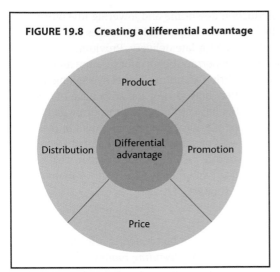

FIGURE 19.8   Creating a differential advantage

charge premium prices, as with Bang & Olufsen hi-fi equipment. Mini Case 19.1 discusses how style can be used as a differentiator.

The capacity to *upgrade* a product (to take advantage of technological advances) or to meet changing needs (e.g. extra storage space in a computer) can lower costs, and confer prestige by maintaining state-of-the-art features. The Apple MacBook Pro and MacBook Air computers demonstrate how style can be used to create a differential advantage.

Products can be augmented by the provision of *guarantees* that give customers peace of mind and lower costs should the product need repair, as well as giving *technical assistance* to customers, so that they are provided with better-quality products. Both parties benefit from closer relationships and from the provision of product *installation*, which means that customers do not incur problems in properly installing a complex piece of equipment.

Distribution

Wide distribution coverage and/or careful selection of distributor *locations* can provide convenient purchasing for customers. *Quick and/or reliable delivery* can lower buyer costs by

---

Mini Case 19.1 Using Style to Differentiate Products

Two companies that have successfully used style to differentiate their products from those of the competition are Bang & Olufsen and Audi. Bang & Olufsen has long been regarded as the style leader in audio and television equipment, and Audi has become one of the car industry's most successful luxury brands, producing some of the world's most coveted and copied cars.

Bang & Olufsen has built a worldwide reputation for quality and a fanatically loyal customer base. Its sleek, tastefully discreet designs and high standards of production have earned it elite status in the market. For decades these factors have formed the basis of its advertising and marketing strategy. The company recognizes that style needs to be displayed distinctively in retail outlets. This has led to the creation of 'concept shops' where subtle images are projected onto walls and products displayed in free-standing areas constructed from translucent walls. The company's view is that you cannot sell Bang & Olufsen equipment when it is sandwiched between a washing machine and a shelf of videos. The concept shop gives the right look to make the most of the products. The company exemplifies the importance of style and aesthetics rather than technology or low prices in buying decisions. It trades on ambience as much as sound. Bang & Olufsen's challenge is to keep the brand relevant in a world where media habits (e.g. listening to music via portable devices) are changing, and to maintain its style distinction in the face of the high-end equipment produced by Samsung and Sony.

A major element in Audi's surge in popularity has been based on style. An online survey of 800 car enthusiasts conducted for the *Financial Times* by Britain's *WhatCar* magazine revealed that Audi was the most admired car brand for design, winning 44 per cent of the poll, well ahead of Jaguar, BMW or Mercedes-Benz. Perhaps most famous for its iconic TT sports car, Audi has benefited from the sleek lines of the A4, which has made it a major challenger against the BMW 300 series. Audi's challenge is to continue to produce stylish cars as it expands its range into a number of niches, from sports utility vehicles to tiny eco-cars.

Questions:

1   Discuss what is meant by 'style' and examine whether it is a sound basis on which to develop a differentiation strategy.
2   Explain the difference between a differentiation strategy and differentiation focus strategy using luxury car brands.
3   Outline Audi's primary source of competitive advantage.

Based on: Gapper (2005);[15] Brownsell (2008);[16] Reed (2008)[17]

↑EXHIBIT 19.3   Bang & Olufsen's stylish audio and television equipment.

reducing production downtime and lowering inventory levels. Reliable delivery, in particular, reduces the frustration of waiting for late delivery. Providing distributors with *support* in the form of training and financial help can bring about more effective selling and marketing, and offers both parties the advantage of closer relationships. FedEx has continued to prosper by giving *delivery guarantees* of critical documents 'down to the hour'.[18] Working with organizational customers to introduce *computerized reordering* systems can lower their costs, reduce their workload and increase the cost for them of switching to other suppliers.

Promotion

A differential advantage can be created by the *creative use of advertising*. For example, *spending more on advertising* can also aid differentiation by creating a stronger brand personality than competitive brands. Similarly, using *more creative sales promotional methods* or simply *spending more on sales incentives* can give direct added value to customers. By engaging in *cooperative promotions* with distributors, producers can lower their costs and build goodwill.

The salesforce can also offer a means of creating a differential advantage. Particularly when products are similar, a *well-trained salesforce* can provide superior problem-solving skills for their customers.

massive delivery
of top brand surf and
swimwear is in stores **now**
always up to 60% less

BIG LABELS SMALL PRICES

T·K·maxx

↑EXHIBIT 19.4   TK Maxx uses price and quality to differentiate from its competitors

Price

Using low price as a means of gaining differential advantage can fail unless the firm enjoys a cost advantage and has the resources to fight a price war. For example, Acer has successfully challenged Dell and Hewlett-Packard in the market for the inexpensive portable computers known as 'netbook'. Its strategy is to exploit its lowest cost position, allowing it to become extremely aggressive on price.[19] Budget airlines such as Ryanair and easyJet have challenged more traditional airlines by charging low prices based on low costs.

A less obvious means of lowering the effective price to the customer is to offer *credit facilities* or *low-interest loans*. Both serve to lower the cost of purchase and improve cash flow for customers. Finally, a *high price* can be used as part of a premium positioning strategy to support brand image. Where a brand has distinct product, promotional or distributional advantages, a premium price provides consistency within the marketing mix.

This analysis of how the marketing mix can be used to develop a differential advantage has focused on how each action can be translated into value to the customer. Remember, however, that for a differential advantage to be realized, a firm needs to provide not only customer value but also value that is superior to that offered by the competition. If all firms provide distributor support in equal measure, for example, distributors may gain value, but no differential advantage will have been achieved.

Go to the website to work out UPS' differential advantage over FedEx. www.mcgraw-hill.co.uk/ textbooks/jobber

Fast reaction times

In addition to using the marketing mix to create a differential advantage, many companies are recognizing the need to create *fast reaction times* to changes in marketing trends. For example, H&M and Zara have developed fast-reaction systems so that new designs can be delivered to stores within three weeks, and top-selling items are requested and poor sellers withdrawn from shops within a week. This is made possible by sophisticated marketing information systems that feed data from stores to headquarters every day.

Scale of operations

Companies can also create a differential advantage when the scale of their operations creates value for their customers. For example, eBay has built a sustainable differential advantage by building a large participant base. As the customer value of an auction site is directly related to the size of the participant base, once eBay gained a large user base advantage it became extremely difficult for any competitor to duplicate the value that it offers.[20]

Sustaining a differential advantage

When searching for ways to achieve a differential advantage, management should pay close attention to factors that cannot easily be copied by the competition. The aim is to achieve a *sustainable differential advantage*. Competing on low price can often be copied by the competition, meaning that any advantage is short-lived. Other attempts at creating a differential advantage may also be copied by the competition. For example, when DHL challenged FedEx and UPS in the US postal delivery market, all its attempts at gaining a competitive edge were copied by its rivals. When DHL hired the US Postal Service to carry out its domestic deliveries, a move that was popular with customers, FedEx and UPS followed suit. The result was that DHL could not find a way of creating a differential advantage and was forced to exit the US market.[21] The key to achieving a long-term advantage is to focus on areas that the competition find impossible or, at the very least, very difficult to copy, including:

- patent-protected products
- strong brand personality
- close relationships with customers
- high service levels achieved by well-trained personnel
- innovative product upgrading
- creating high entry barriers (e.g. R&D or promotional expenditures)
- strong and distinctive internal processes that deliver the above and are difficult to copy
- scale (where the scale of operations provides value to the customer, e.g. eBay).[22]

Eroding a differential advantage

However, many advantages are contestable. For example, IBM's stronghold on personal computers was undermined by cheaper clones. Three mechanisms are at work that can erode a differential advantage:[23]

1 technological and environment changes that create opportunities for competitors by eroding the protective barriers (e.g. long-standing television companies are being challenged by satellite television)
2 competitors learn how to imitate the sources of the differential advantage (e.g. competitors engage in a training programme to improve service capabilities)
3 complacency leads to lack of protection of the differential advantage.

Creating Cost Leadership

Creating a cost-leadership position requires an understanding of the factors that affect costs. Porter has identified 10 major *cost drivers* that determine the behaviour of costs in the value chain (see Fig. 19.9).[24]

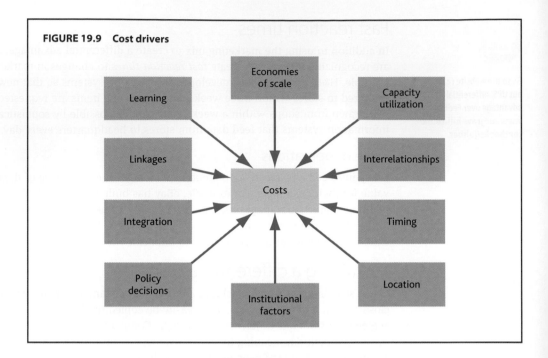

FIGURE 19.9 Cost drivers

Economies of scale

Scale economies can arise from the use of more efficient methods of production at higher volumes. For example, United Biscuits benefits from more efficient machinery that can produce biscuits more cheaply than that used by Fox's Biscuits, which operates at much lower volume. Scale economies also arise from the less-than-proportional increase in overheads as production volume increases. For example, a factory with twice the floor area of another factory is less than twice the price to build. A third scale economy results from the capacity to spread the cost of R&D and promotion over a greater sales volume. Such scale economies mean that companies such as Coca-Cola, General Electric, Intel, Microsoft and Wal-Mart have a huge advantage over their competitors. However, economies of scale do not proceed indefinitely. At some point, diseconomies of scale are likely to arise as size gives rise to overcomplexity and, possibly, personnel difficulties.

Learning

Costs can also fall as a result of the effects of learning. For example, people learn how to assemble more quickly, pack more efficiently, design products that are easier to manufacture, lay out warehouses more effectively, cut driving time and reduce inventories. The combined effect of economies of scale and learning as cumulative output increases has been termed the **experience curve**. The Boston Consulting Group has estimated that costs are reduced by approximately 15–20 per cent on average each time cumulative output doubles. This suggests that firms with greater market share will have a cost advantage through the experience curve effect, assuming all companies are operating on the same curve. However, a move towards a new manufacturing technology can lower the experience curve for adopting companies, allowing them to leap-frog more traditional firms and thereby gain a cost advantage even though cumulative output may be lower.

Capacity utilization

Since fixed costs must be paid whether a plant is manufacturing at full or zero capacity, underutilization incurs costs. The effect is to push up the cost per unit for production. The impact of capacity utilization on profitability was established by the PIMS (profit impact of marketing strategy) studies, which have shown a positive association between utilization and return on investment.[25] Changes in capacity utilization can also raise costs (e.g. through the extra costs of hiring and laying off workers). Careful production planning is required for seasonal products such as ice cream and fireworks, in order to smooth output.

Linkages

These describe how the costs of activities are affected by how other activities are performed. For example, improving quality-assurance activities can reduce after-sales service costs. In the car industry, the reduction in the number of faults on a new car reduces warranty costs. The activities of suppliers and distributors also link to affect the costs of a firm.

For example, the introduction of a just-in-time delivery system by a supplier reduces the inventory costs of a firm. Distributors can influence a firm's physical distribution costs through their warehouse location decision. To exploit such linkages, though, the firm may need considerable bargaining power. In some instances it can pay a firm to increase distributor margins or pay a fee in order to exploit linkages. For example, Seiko paid its US jewellers a fee for accepting its watches for repair and sending them to Seiko; this meant that Seiko did not need local services facilities and its overall costs fell.[26]

Interrelationships

Sharing costs with other business units is another potential cost driver. Sharing the costs of R&D, transportation, marketing and purchasing lower costs. Know-how can also be shared to reduce costs by improving the efficiency of an activity. Car manufacturers share engineering platforms and components to reduce costs. For example, Volkswagen does this across its VW, Skoda, Seat and Audi cars. Care has to be taken that the cars appearing under different brand names do not appear too similar, however, or this may detract from the appeal of the more expensive marques.[27]

Integration

Both integration and forms of integration can affect costs. For example, owning the means of physical distribution rather than using outside contractors could lower costs. Ownership may allow a producer to avoid suppliers or customers with sizeable bargaining power. De-integration can lower costs and raise flexibility. For example, by using many small clothing suppliers, Benetton is in a powerful position to keep costs low while maintaining a high degree of production flexibility.

Timing

Both first movers and late entrants have potential opportunities for lowering costs. First movers in a market can gain cost advantages: it is usually cheaper to establish a brand name in the minds of customers if there is no competition. Also, they have prime access to cheap or high-quality raw materials and locations. However, late entrants to a market have the opportunity to buy the latest technology and avoid high market development costs.

Policy decisions

Firms have a wide range of discretionary policy decisions that affect costs. Product width, level of service, channel decisions (e.g. small number of large dealers vs large number of small dealers), salesforce decisions (e.g. in-company salesforce vs sales agents) and wage levels are some of the decision areas that have a direct impact on costs. Southwest Airlines, for example, cuts costs by refusing to waste time assigning seats and does not wait for late arrivals. The overriding concern is to get the aeroplane in and out of the gate quickly so that it is in the air earning money. Southwest flies only one kind of aircraft, which also keeps costs down.[28]

Companies can also collaborate to reduce costs. For example, Vodafone has teamed up with O$_2$'s parent company, Telefónica, to share mobile network infrastructure (e.g. masts, equipment and power supply), following a similar deal between T-Mobile and 3.[29]

Ryanair accepts bookings only over the Internet, thus eliminating the need for an inbound telemarketing team and allowing e-ticketing, which cuts postage and paper costs. Other sectors, such as insurance, rail, banking, package holidays and hotels, encourage transactions over the Internet in order to reduce costs. Care must be taken, however, not to reduce costs with regard to activities that have a major bearing on customer value. For example, moving from a company-employed salesforce to sales agents may not only cut costs but also destroy supplier–customer relationships. Even high-technology companies such as Nokia and Ericsson have had to make policy decisions designed to cut costs in the face of intense competition. The problem is that, for undifferentiated companies, cost cutting alone, as General Motors found, is insufficient to ensure success.

Go to the website and analyse how Quaker Oats supports its parent company's (PepsiCo) corporate strategy. www.mcgraw-hill.co.uk/textbooks/jobber

Location

The location of plant and warehouses affects costs through different wage, physical distribution and energy costs. Dyson, for example, manufactures its vacuum cleaners in Malaysia to take advantage of low wage costs.[30] Car manufacturers such as VW, Peugeot, Citroën and Fiat have moved production to eastern Europe to take advantage of low costs.[31] Locating near customers can lower outbound distributional costs, while locating near suppliers reduces inbound distributional costs.

Institutional factors

These include government regulations, tariffs and local content rules. For example, regulations regarding the maximum size of lorries affect distribution costs.

Firms employing a cost leadership strategy will be vigilant in pruning costs. This analysis of cost drivers provides a framework for searching out new avenues for cost reduction.

When you have read this chapter

log on to the Online Learning Centre at **www.mcgraw-hill.co.uk/textbooks/jobber** to explore chapter-by-chapter test questions, links and further online study tools for marketing.

Review

1   **The determinants of industry attractiveness**
- Industry attractiveness is determined by the degree of rivalry between competitors, the threat of new entrants, the bargaining power of suppliers and buyers, and the threat of substitute products.

2   **How to analyse competitors**
- Competitor analysis should identify competitors (product from competitors, product substitutes, generic competitors and potential new entrants); audit their capabilities; analyse their objectives, strategic thrust and strategies; and estimate competitor response patterns.

3 **The difference between differentiation and cost leadership strategies**
- Differentiation strategy involves the selection of one or more choice criteria used by buyers to select suppliers/brands and uniquely positioning the supplier/brand to meet those criteria better than the competition.
- Cost leadership involves the achievement of the lowest cost position in an industry.

4 **The sources of competitive advantage**
- Competitive advantage can be achieved by creating a differential advantage or achieving the lowest cost position.
- Its sources are superior skills, superior resources, and core competences. A useful method of locating superior skills and resources is value chain analysis.

5 **The value chain**
- The value chain categorizes the value-creating activities of a firm. The value chain divides these into primary and support activities. Primary activities are in-bound physical distribution, operations, outbound physical distribution, marketing and service. Support activities are found within all of these primary activities, and consist of purchased inputs, technology, human resource management and the firm's infrastructure.
- By examining each value-creating activity, management can search for the skills and resources (and linkages) that may form the basis for low cost or differentiated positions.

6 **How to create and maintain a differential advantage**
- A differential advantage is created when the customer perceives that the firm is providing value above that of the competition.
- A differential advantage can be created using any element in the marketing mix: superior product, more effective distribution, better promotion and better value for money by lower prices. A differential advantage can also be created by developing fast reaction times to changes in marketing trends.
- A differential advantage can be maintained (sustained) through the use of patent protection, strong brand personality, close relationships with customers, high service levels based on well-trained staff, innovative product upgrading, the creation of high entry barriers (e.g. R&D or promotional expenditures), and strong and distinctive internal processes that deliver the earlier points and are difficult to copy.

7 **How to create and maintain a cost leadership position**
- Cost leadership can be created and maintained by managing cost drivers, which are economies of scale, learning effects, capacity utilization, linkages (e.g. improvements in quality assurance can reduce after-sales service costs), interrelationships (e.g. sharing costs), integration (e.g. owning the means of distribution), timing (both first movers and late entrants can have low costs), policy decisions (e.g. controlling labour costs), location, and institutional factors (e.g. government regulations).

Key Terms

competitive scope the breadth of a company's competitive challenge, e.g. broad or narrow

competitor audit a precise analysis of competitor strengths and weaknesses, objectives and strategies

core competences the principal distinctive capabilities possessed by a company—what it is really good at

differential advantage a clear performance differential over the competition on factors that are important to target customers

differentiation strategy the selection of one or more customer choice criteria and positioning the offering accordingly to achieve superior customer value

entry barriers barriers that act to prevent new firms from entering a market, e.g. the high level of investment required

experience curve the combined effect of economies of scale and learning as cumulative output increases

industry a group of companies that market products that are close substitutes for each other

value chain the set of a firm's activities that are conducted to design, manufacture, market, distribute and service its products

Study Questions

1 Using Porter's 'five forces' framework, suggest why there is intense rivalry between leading European supermarket brands.

2 For any product of your choice identify the competition using the four-layer approach discussed in this chapter.

3 Why is competitor analysis essential in today's turbulent environment? How far is it possible to predict competitor response to marketing actions?

4 Distinguish between differentiation and cost-leadership strategies. Is it possible to achieve both positions simultaneously?

5 How might Google use differential advantage to stand out from its rivals?

6 How can value chain analysis lead to superior corporate performance?

7 Using examples, discuss the impact of the advent of the single European market on competitive structure.

8 What are cost drivers? Should marketing management be concerned with them, or is their significance solely the prerogative of the accountant?

References

1. Porter, M. E. (1980) *Competitive Strategy: Techniques for Analysing Industries and Competitors*, New York: Free Press.
2. Simonian, H. and L. Lucas (2012) Starbucks takes coffee wars to Nespresso, *Financial Times* http://www.ft.com/cms/s/0/d90109a4-66ec-11e1-9e53-00144feabdc0.html, 5 March.
3. Grabham, D. (2011) ARM vs Intel: the next processor war begins http://www.techradar.com/news/phone-and-communications/mobile-phones/arm-vs-intel-the-next-processor-war-begins-920875, 11 January.
4. Garside, J. (2012) BlackBerry creators pay price for failing to keep up with Apple, *The Guardian*. 23 January, 23.
5. Noble, C. H., R. K. Sinha and A. Kumar (2002) Market Orientation and Alternative Strategic Orientations: A Longitudinal Assessment of Performance Implications, *Journal of Marketing*, 66, October, 25–39.
6. Macdonald, M. H. B. and H. Wilson (2011) *Marketing Plans*, Oxford: Butterworth Heinemann.
7. Walton, G. (2012) LoveFilm's TV revolution as it launches preemptive strike on US rival, http://www.thisismoney.co.uk/money/markets/article-2083354/, 6 January.
8. Ritson, M. (2008) Mobile Brands Make Poor Call on Value, *Marketing*, 23 January, 21.
9. Leeflang, P. H. S. and D. R. Wittink (1996) Competitive Reaction versus Consumer Response: Do Managers Over-react? *International Journal of Research in Marketing* 13, 103–19.
10. Porter (1980) op. cit.
11. Wunker, S. (2012) Fiat's Smart US launch strategy—really, HBR Blog Network http://blogs.hbr.org/cs/2012/02/fiats_smart_us_launch_strategy_really.html, 1 February.
12. Day, G. S. and R. Wensley (1988) Assessing Advantage: A Framework for Diagnosing Competitive Superiority, *Journal of Marketing* 52, April, 1–20.
13. Porter, M. E. (1985) *Competitive Advantage*, New York: Free Press.
14. For methods of calculating value in organizational markets, see

Anderson, J. C. and J. A. Narus (1998) Business Marketing: Understand What Customers Value, *Harvard Business Review*, Nov.–Dec., 53–65.
15. Gapper, J. (2005) When High Fidelity Becomes High Fashion, *Financial Times*, 20 December, 11.
16. Brownsell, A. (2008) Bang & Olufsen, *Marketing*, 28 May, 24.
17. Reed, J. (2008) Designs that Keep on Moving, *Financial Times*, 29 July, 12.
18. *Business Week* (2006) Business Week Top 50 US Companies, 3 April, 82–100.
19. Einhorn, B. (2009) Acer's Game-Changing PC Offensive, *Business Week*, 20 April, 65.
20. Nagle, T. T. and J. E. Hogan (2006) *The Strategy and Tactics of Pricing*, Upper Saddle River, NJ: Pearson.
21. *The Economist* (2008) Failure to Deliver, 15 November, 80.
22. De Chernatony, L., F. Harris and F. Dall'Olmo Riley (2000) Added Value: Its Nature, Roles and Sustainability, *European Journal of Marketing* 34(1/2), 39–56.
23. Day, G. S. (1999) *Market Driven Strategy: Processes for Creating Value*, New York: Free Press.
24. Porter (1985) op. cit.
25. Buzzell, R. D. and B. T. Gale (1987) *The PIMS Principles*, New York: Free Press.
26. Porter (1985) op. cit.
27. MacKintosh, J. (2005) Car Design in a Generalist Market, *Financial Times*, 6 December, 20.
28. McNulty, S. (2001) Short on Frills, Big on Morale, *Financial Times*, 31 October, 14.
29. Kollewe, J. (2008) Vodafone Cuts Costs by Sharing Networks with Telefónica, *The Guardian*, 24 March, 26.
30. Marsh, P. (2002) Dismay at Job Losses as Dyson Shifts Production to Malaysia, *Financial Times*, 6 February, 3.
31. Milne, R. and H. Williamson (2005) BMW Ignores Signals and Puts its Faith in Germany, *Financial Times*, 13 May, 20.

General Meltdown
Too Big to Fail

On 1 June 2009 General Motors (www.gm.com) filed for bankruptcy protection, a historic landmark event. GM has been leading the automotive business for over a century. The company owns several internationally known automotive brands, which it markets around the world. It builds nearly 9 million vehicles a year, making it an industry colossus. It is seen as the heartbeat of the American manufacturing industry. For decades it was viewed as an exemplar in the effective management, strategic thinking and organization of a modern corporation. Yet, it faced the perfect storm in 2009, as sales fell by a staggering 30 per cent. Low-cost competition is eroding its market share. It had lost its mantle as the world's largest car manufacturer to Toyota in 2007. Most alarmingly, the company has over $176 billion in liabilities, and lost a staggering $30 billion in 2008.

General Motors was the iconoclast of the American multinational corporation. The contribution of GM to American industry is gargantuan, spending $50 billion dollars a year on parts, and with a wage bill of $476 million a month. However, it has lost a colossal $88 billion since 2004, an untenable situation! At the height of the financial crisis GM had to be bailed out by the US government. The US government has invested over $862 billion in the auto industry. The company has offloaded several brands so that it can concentrate on core car models, and it will shed thousands of dealerships to make it leaner. The bankruptcy meant that original investors lost everything, as the share price collapsed. Backed by the US and Canadian governments, the company has undergone radical change. Indeed, the US government owns 32.4 per cent of the new GM. The company's sheer size and impact on American economic life meant that it was too big to countenance failure.

General Motors had a huge product portfolio, where its sells cars in nearly every single market. Under its ten different car brands it manufactured 89 different car models. The company had a truly international manufacturing presence with 11 assembly plants in Europe, 3 in Asia, 8 in South America, and 29 in North America. The company has set up a number of manufacturing centres in low-cost countries such as Mexico, India, South Africa and China. In addition, the company has grown through a series of acquisitions and alliances, which it is hoped will strengthen the brand portfolio even further. In 2000 GM gained 100 per cent control of Swedish luxury carmaker Saab. It has several joint ventures, such as with Chinese car-maker, Shanghai Automotive Industry Corporation to build a family car for the Chinese market. In 2002 it took over troubled South Korean car-maker, Daewoo. This has proved to be one of GM's remarkable success stories. Now the firm produces low-cost cars under the Chevrolet brand in 140 different international markets, using low-cost manufacturing bases. The company dropped the Daewoo brand in 2004, using the Chevrolet brand, with the aim of turning it into a global brand, and moving it away from the firm's over-reliance on the North American market.

It is attempting to strengthen its international presence by focusing on growth areas such as China. Growth there has been stellar, achieving 10 per cent quarterly sales growth. In China it operates 11 joint ventures with local companies, and employs over 35,000, selling international brands like Chevrolet, Buick and Opel, coupled with domestic Chinese automotive brands like Baojun, Jiefang, and Wuling. To get a synopsis of GM's ten main automotive brands see Table C37.1. The company uses these different brands to target different segments of the market, in different countries. In America, its uses eight different car brands: Chevrolet, GMC, Pontiac, Buick, Cadillac, Saturn, Saab and Hummer, while in Europe it sells Opel/Vauxhall, Saab and Chevrolet. In Australia it sells GM car marques under the Holden brand.

One of the biggest difficulties for the GM stable of car brands was the lack of distinction between the various car marques. Car buyers view many of the models launched by

TABLE C37.1   General Motors' main automotive brands

Current GM brands				
Chevrolet	**Cadillac**	**Buick**	**Opel/Vauxhall**	**GMC**
The Chevrolet brand is the third biggest car brand in the world. GM's most important brand. Has offering in nearly every sector of market. Focuses strongly on the SUV sector of the market. GM wants to hold onto brand. GM sells this brand in Asian and European markets. Focused on small and medium size cars, that are value for money.	The luxury car brand in the GM stable. The quintessential luxury American car brand, with an emphasis on luxury, comfort, performance, and technology. Aims to hold on to its premium brand.	A mid-tier brand, with several luxury saloon cars and SUV offerings. Criticized for lacking distinction and rationalizing its current car model portfolio. Focuses on safety, quality, and premium interiors at attainable prices. Brand has been successful in China.	The Vauxhall and Opel brands are sold in the UK, Germany and other parts of Europe. There are a wide range of cars and vans in product ranges. In 2012, both brands were facing difficulties as car sales were declining.	It focuses on producing SUVs, pickup trucks, and a range of commercial vehicles. Formerly known as GMC Truck. Sales up 12%, despite rising oil prices for SUVs.

GM brands sold or defunct			
Pontiac	**Saab**	**Hummer**	**Saturn**
Pontiac is a mid-level brand, aimed typically at a young market. Focuses on projecting an image of performance, sport and youth. Only available in North America. Sells roadsters, saloons, and SUVs. Brand was phased out, as part of restructuring.	Focused on premium market with sporty designs. Small niche brand. Sold to Swedish super luxury car maker, with support from the Swedish government. Now in receivership. Production stopped in 2011.	The former military vehicle jeep has been transformed into a highly popular and ridiculously expensive 4x4 vehicle. Launched in 1999, has earned a cache for cool. Sold for $100 million to Chinese manufacturer.	Created Saturn brand in 1990 in response to low cost Japanese imports in the sub-compact sector, using plastic body styling. Saturn is now repositioning in several different sectors such as saloons, SUV, roadsters and minivans. GM shut Saturn factories.

GM as very similar to other cars in its range. GM adopted a 'euthanasia' policy on several of its underperforming brands in an effort to quell costs, and create a stronger brand proposition. It argues that the cars sold under the various brands confuse customers, and that better returns could be gained by a coordinated branding strategy that communicated the true brand essence of each of the brands. For example, you could have bought a similar saloon car under the Pontiac, Buick, Saturn, and Chevrolet brand names with little or no discernable differences. GM suffers from the curse of sameness. Other companies have developed stronger reputations with a smaller repertoire of vehicles. Originally each of the GM brands had a strong distinctive image, with various brands focusing on different tiers of the market. For instance, Chevrolet focused on the value end, while Cadillac focused on the premium spectrum of the market. It has culled its line-up in the past in an effort to rationalize its product portfolio; it scrapped the Oldsmobile brand in 2000. This famous US car brand suffered perennially a decline in its revenue, due to a poor product offering, and the brand's lack of differentiation.

Now the company has culled its Pontiac, Saab, Saturn, and Hummer brands from its portfolio.

To put the malaise into perspective, in America the eight different brands had eight different slogans such as;

- GMC—Professional grade
- Saturn—People first
- Chevrolet—An American revolution
- Pontiac—Action
- Buick—Beyond precision
- Cadillac—Break-through
- Hummer—Like nothing else
- Saab—Born from Jets.

These slogans really highlight the past failings of GM's brand strategy.

One of the key challenges for its brand stable is the production of eco-friendly cars, in response to rising oil prices and growing environmental concerns. It launched the Chevrolet Volt in 2011, which is an electric hybrid car. However, this is not its first foray into green energy as it launched the EV11 car, an innovative electric car, in 1999.

This car was immortalized in a documentary called *Who Killed the Electric Car?* which accused oil companies, car dealers, and the car companies themselves of helping to accelerate the project's downfall. This green initiative failed to be capitalized upon by General Motors, whereas Toyota's Prius hybrid car became an instant hit. GM let this innovative technology languish, while driving ahead with its traditional product portfolio. GM focused on hydrogen-powered technology as the future for the car industry. However, this technology is years from providing a viable alternative to oil, leaving GM without any foothold in this sector. Hybrid technology, ethanol or electricity were seen as viable technologies. The sales of the Volt have failed to electrify industry pundits, despite receiving very positive reviews and awards.

Its demise

The company has been prone to difficulties throughout its history. It managed to stave off bankruptcy by 40 minutes in 1992 during a credit crunch. During that turbulent period it bounced back by slashing 21 plants and cutting 70,000 jobs, eliminating corporate bureaucracy, and improving productivity and quality. GM is heavily reliant on the North America market, where most of it problems resided. Excess capacity, diminishing margins, a rigid sales channel structure, confusing brand propositions, falling market share, labour problems and exorbitant legacy costs have all made a serious impact. Over 42 per cent of its sales come from North America, making it very susceptible to market shocks within the US market. In 2008 the Western European car market contracted by 8.4 per cent owing to the global economic recession, with some car inventories piling up due to lack of demand and consumer confidence. Key markets like Spain collapsed by 28 per cent.

In recent years the firm had focused on churning out gas-guzzling SUVs (large Sports Utility Vehicles) and pick-up trucks, diverting its attention from normal saloon cars. These vehicles at the time were much sought after by the market, and yielded higher margins. The company lost sight of developing a solid car range, while foreign competitors developed strong reputations in the sector. In the wake of rising oil prices, demand for these expensive to run SUVs has slumped, and consumers have turned to more fuel-efficient cars. With so much of GM's portfolio focused on large cars, it has been particularly susceptible to rising petrol prices. Consumers swapped their gas guzzlers for smaller cars, which destroyed the residual value of second-hand GM cars. This led to losses for GM Finance division, as cars returning from a lease were depreciating at a calamitous rate.

Its US market share is continuing to slide: where it once garnered 41 per cent of the market in 1985, it now accounts for only 24.7 per cent. In an effort to stave off the decline, the company has deployed an aggressive price-discounting strategy, which has devalued many of GM's venerable brands. It offered its cars at 'employee discount for everyone'. Sales drop when a promotion ends and consumers wait for the latest rebate or promotional offer. The company shifted away from price promotions, and focused on building brands, through lower advertised prices, more advertising expenditure and extra equipment as standard.

Key to the future survival is the efficiency and effectiveness of GM's manufacturing capabilities. GM factories have won several awards for quality processes: however, this is not reflected in the market, where consumers have poor-quality perceptions toward GM brands. Continued improvement in its manufacturing capabilities is vital, focusing on quality, efficiency and costs. For instance, it takes 34 hours to build a typical GM car, while a Toyota takes 28 hours. The company has only recently focused on harmonizing production, and sharing parts and car platforms. The new GM company has formed a partnership, with its powerful trade unions now owning 17.5 per cent of the new company, and agreeing profit-sharing incentives.

GM has been criticized for launching numerous new models under different brands, then subsequently ditching them if not proved to be a stellar success, thus creating huge levels of product churn. This is a substantial investment in terms of marketing expenditure, constantly boosting up brand recognition for these new brands. Other car-makers have several cornerstone car marques, which they frequently update with the latest technology and revamp with subtle stylistic changes. GM has increased the level of new product launches to unprecedented levels, placing the emphasis on getting newer models out to market very quickly. Also, GM had too many dealers. GM had five times more dealers than Toyota. Now it is cutting nearly a half of its dealer network. Dealer margins have slipped to 1.6 per cent. The dealership structure needs to be consolidated and to become more sustainable. Continued efforts to alter GM sales channels have been restricted due to franchised dealers' rights under US law. However, bankruptcy enables the company to make radical changes that would normally be impossible. The only way to change a dealership contract is through expensive compensation to the franchise. Over 1100 GM dealers were culled in 2009, with subsequent sizable job losses.

Its rebirth and turnaround strategy

Between 2009 and the end of 2010 GM had a total of four different CEOs. This highlights the extent of the calamity at the company. On 18 November 2010 GM emerged from bankruptcy a very different company, free from the shackles that potentially obliterated it. Now the company is headed by Daniel Akerson, a company outsider. The group has launched several initiatives in order to reverse its declining fortunes: namely, reducing exorbitant fixed costs, maximizing manufacturing capacity, and revitalizing a weak product offering through improved R&D. Manufacturing plants that are not operating at full capacity really hurt the business, especially in high-cost manufacturing countries. Previously the company had allowed autonomous R&D within divisions, but now the firm is seeking to leverage engineering expertise across its global operations. This it is hoped will improve design, reduce costs, and avoid fruitless duplication of activities. It is spending nearly $8 billion on R&D every year, which equates to approximately 5 per cent of its revenue. It also hopes to eliminate look-alike products from its portfolio, developing best in segment cars. It has culled a swath of middle managers, in a bid to eliminate bureaucracy. The company wants to radically overhaul its cost base, rationalizing powertrains, trim options, and the sheer variety of models. All of which cost money. In addition it has formed strategic alliances with rivals like French-based Peugeot-Citroën to develop cost-saving initiatives like shared vehicle platforms and shared purchasing costs.

GM is now attempting to amalgamate several brands into one sales channel. For instance, in the US it is creating dealerships where Buick and GMC are sold under the same dealership. Similarly in Europe, it is selling Vauxhall and Chevrolet (formerly Daewoo) car marques in the same dealer premises, creating strong sales propositions. Obviously developing markets like China and Brazil are the big hope for the automotive trade. This burgeoning market is a key priority for the firm. In Europe Opel/Vauxhall is still struggling. Developing cars that Chinese consumers want is critical, leveraging their relationships with local partners. The company has to have a truly global perspective. GM is developing an array of cross-over cars, supermini cars, and fuel-efficient electric cars. In 2011 GM earned over $150 billion, an 11 per cent increase on the previous year. The new GM vision is to design, build and sell the world's best vehicles. It has now regained the title as the world's largest automaker.

Questions

1. Using Porter's 'five forces' framework, discuss the competitiveness of the global automobile market.

2. Identify and discuss the weaknesses associated with General Motors' marketing strategy. (Visit its affiliated sites: www.gm.com, www.opel.com, www.vauxhall.co.uk, www.chevrolet.com.)

3. What are GM's sources of competitive advantage? Discuss how GM could achieve a differential advantage over competitors.

This case was written by Conor Carroll, Lecturer in Marketing, University of Limerick. Copyright © Conor Carroll (2012). The material in the case has been drawn from a variety of published sources and research reports.

For further reading to answer these questions visit www.acea.be

Wal-mart and Asda
Battling for Retail Success

In the spring of 1999 the shareholders of Kingfisher, the UK retail group, were smiling. They had just seen their share price rocket from around £5 (€7.2) to over £9 (€13) in less than a year with the news that Kingfisher was to take over Asda, the UK supermarket chain. Geoffrey Mulcahy, who headed Kingfisher (the owner of B&Q, Comet and Superdrug), saw the move as another step towards his ambition of being a 'world-class retailer', where the efficiencies of buying merchandise in massive quantities, managing large stores, and achieving lower prices and higher sales turnover would reap further benefits for shareholders, employees and customers alike.

Mulcahy was well aware that Wal-Mart was lurking in the wings, but all the talk was that the US retailer was cool about entering the UK market where retail competition was intense and planning restrictions made the likelihood of opening the kind of vast Supercentres it operates in the USA unlikely. All that changed one June Monday morning when he received a 7 a.m. telephone call from Archie Norman, Asda's chief executive, to say that he had 'a bit of a problem'. The 'problem' was that Asda had agreed a deal with Wal-Mart.

Wal-Mart USA

Enter any Wal-Mart store in the USA and you are struck by the sheer scale of the operation. These are stores of over 200,000 square feet in which seven UK superstores could be accommodated. Next come the 'greeters', who welcome customers into the stores, give them their card in case they need help and put a smiley sticker on them. Then come the prices where, for example, a cotton T-shirt that would sell for the equivalent of around $15 (£9.40/€13.5) in a UK department store sells for $1 (£0.60/€0.90) in Wal-Mart. The choice of products is wide ranging, from clothes via groceries and pharmaceuticals to electrical goods. Stores are well organized with the right goods always available, kept neat and clean in appearance and with goods helpfully displayed.

At the heart of the Wal-Mart operation are its systems and information technology: 1000 information technologists run a massive database; its information collection, which comprises over 65 million transactions (by item, time, price and store), drives most aspects of its business. Within 90 minutes of an item being sold, Wal-Mart's distribution

centres are organizing its replacement. Distribution is facilitated by state-of-the-art delivery tracking systems. So effective is the system that when a flu epidemic hit the USA, Wal-Mart followed its spread by monitoring flu remedy sales in its stores. It then predicted its movement from east to west so that Wal-Mart stores were adequately stocked in time for the rise in demand.

Wal-Mart also uses real-time information systems to let consumers decide what appears in its stores. The Internet is used to inform suppliers what was sold the day before. In this way, it only buys what sells.

Its relationship with its suppliers is unusual in that they are only paid when an item is sold in its stores. Not only does this help cash flow, it also ensures that the interests of manufacturer and Wal-Mart coincide. Instead of the traditional system where once the retailer had purchased stock it was essentially the retailer's problem to sell it, if the product does not sell it hurts the manufacturer's cash flow more than Wal-Mart's. Consequently, at a stroke, the supplier's and retailer's interests are focused on the same measures and rewards. There is no incentive for the supplier to try to sell Wal-Mart under-performing brands since they will suffer in the same way as the retailer if they fail to sell in the store.

Wal-Mart staff are called 'associates' and are encouraged to tell top management what they believe is wrong with their stores. They are offered share options and encouraged to put the customer first.

Wal-Mart has enjoyed phenomenal success in the USA, but faced a tough challenge by its rival, Target, which has built its business by selling similar basic consumable goods like soap at low prices, but also higher-margin, design-based items such as clothing and furnishings. The problem Wal-Mart faced was that consumers were buying groceries and toiletries at its stores but not its clothing, furnishing or electronics ranges. Target was stealing customers by positioning itself as an up-market discounter using designers such as Isaac Mizraki and stylish lifestyle advertising to attract consumers to its clothing and furnishings. Wal-Mart, by contrast, was using mundane in-store advertising focusing on low prices.

Wal-Mart's response was to commission, for the first time, a marketing research survey. Hitherto it had believed marketing research was the province of its suppliers. The survey of its customers revealed that Wal-Mart's clothing was considered dull. This led to the launch in 2005 of a more up-market fashion brand, Metro 7, targeted at the group Wal-Mart called 'selective shoppers'—those who buy groceries and toiletries but who previously would not have bought clothing. The new clothing range was backed by a change in advertising, including a spread in *Vogue* magazine and a move to lifestyle advertising, designed to appeal to what the retailer termed 'fashion-savvy' female customers with an urban lifestyle. However, Metro 7 failed, as the line was not 'hip' enough to attract fashion buyers or cheap enough to appeal to traditional Wal-Mart customers.

Wal-Mart also redesigned its electronics and furnishings departments and improved the product ranges to appeal to wealthier customers. In consumer electrics, for example, it added high-end products from Sony LCD televisions and Toshiba laptops to Apple iPods, and backed the new ranges with aggressive advertising campaigns. Departments were redesigned with wider aisles and lower shelves. Wal-Mart revamped all its stores to make them appear less dull and appeal to middle-income shoppers trading down in the recent recession.

The retailer also employed what it termed its 'win, play or show' strategy. 'Win' product categories are those where Wal-Mart can outmanoeuvre rivals with low prices on high demand products such as flat-screen TVs, including higher-end models. This has increased Wal-Mart's share of TVs while increasing margins. 'Play' applies to areas like clothing where Wal-Mart can be a player but is unlikely to dominate. Here product lines are pruned to top sellers like $20 Levi jeans while cutting back on higher-end items. 'Show' are the one-stop-shopping essentials such as hardware, which are necessary to compete in the USA with rivals like Home Depot. Here, product lines like hammers and tape measures are restricted to one or two brands.

However, Wal-Mart has been criticized for being slow to fully embrace the opportunities provided by online shopping. The company has recently embarked on a major investment programme to rectify this weakness.

Wal-Mart's overseas operations

Since 1992 Wal-Mart has moved into 16 countries, and this strategy has been the engine for most of its sales and profit growth in recent years. In Canada and Mexico it is already market leader in discount retailing. In Canada it bought Woolco in 1994, quickly added outlets, and by 1997 became market leader with 45 per cent of the discount store market—a remarkable achievement. In countries such as China and Argentina it has been surprisingly successful and international sales have grown to around 25 per cent of total revenue.

In 1998 it entered Europe with the buying of Germany's Wertkauf warehouse chain, quickly followed by the acquisition of 74 Interspar hypermarkets. It immediately closed stores, then reopened them with price cuts on 1100 items, making them 10 per cent below competitors' prices. Wal-Mart's German operation was not a success, however, because of the presence of more aggressive discounters such as Aldi. In 2006 it admitted failure by selling its 85 stores to a local rival, Metro, at a loss of £530 million (€740 million).

Wal-Mart's entry into the UK was the next step in its move into the European market. Asda was a natural target since it shared Wal-Mart's 'everyday low prices' culture. It was mainly a grocery supermarket, but also sold clothing. Its information technology systems lagged badly behind those of its UK supermarket competitors, but it has acted as 'consumer champion' by selling cosmetics and over-the-counter pharmaceuticals for cheaper prices than those charged by traditional outlets. It has also bought branded products such as jeans from abroad to sell at low prices in its stores. Wal-Mart decided to keep the Asda store name rather than rebranding it as Wal-Mart. Most of Asda's stores are located in the north of the UK.

The early signs were that the acquisition was a success with sales and profits rising. A major move was to create a speciality division that operates pharmacy, optical, jewellery, photography and shoe departments. The aim was to make store space work harder (i.e. improve sales revenue and profits per square metre). Asda has also benefited from the introduction of thousands of non-food items across a wide range of home and leisure categories. Space has been made for these extra products in existing food-dominated supermarkets by decreasing the amount of shelf space devoted to food and reducing pack sizes.

The George line of clothing was a huge success and was expanded to include a lower-priced version of the brand called Essentially George. So impressed were Wal-Mart management with the success of George clothing, that they introduced the range in their own stores. Asda took the George brand to the high street by launching standalone 10,000-square-foot clothing stores branded George, The stores carried the complete line of George-brand men's, women's and children's clothing at prices the same as those offered in the George departments in Asda supermarkets. However, in the face of competition from Primark and New Look they were only moderately successful.

Besides expanding its product lines, Asda has also focused on cutting prices, aided by its inclusion in the Wal-Mart stable, which brings it enormous buying power. For example, since the takeover, it has made 60 per cent savings on fabrics and 15 per cent on buttons. This has meant price reductions on such clothing items as jeans, ladies' tailored trousers, skirts, silk ties and baby pyjamas. In four years, the price of George jeans fell from £15 (€21.6) to £6 (€8.6).

Change of fortunes

Asda's initial success was reflected in its overtaking of Sainsbury's to become the UK's number two supermarket chain behind Tesco in 2004. Shortly afterwards, however, Asda's fortunes changed. Faced with a rampant Tesco and a resurgent Sainsbury's, the company lost market share. When Wal-Mart bought Asda the intention was to build huge, US-style hypermarkets. Unfortunately, shortly after the acquisition, UK planning rules tightened to prevent out-of-town shopping developments. Tesco, and to a lesser extent Sainsbury's, entered the smaller store market, opening outlets in town and city centres and petrol stations where planning restrictions were much less severe. Asda kept its focus on large supermarkets.

In 2005 Andy Bond was promoted internally to replace Tony de Nunzio, who left to join Dutch non-food retailer Vendex. Faced with a dominant Tesco with over 30 per cent market share, and a more aggressive Sainsbury's under the leadership of Justin King, Bond faced an enormous challenge. Helped by Asda's positioning as a cut-price, full-range supermarket Bond met with early success. Some of his key actions were as follows:

- Removed 1400 managers: 200 jobs at Asda's head office and 1200 junior managerial positions in stores were cut. Part of the savings were invested in front-line customer service staff in stores.

- Opened 17 more Asda Living stores to bring the total to 22 and developed the Living range online: these are non-food stores offering such products as furnishings, electrical goods, DVDs and beauty items. By 2015 150 Asda Living stores are planned.

- Slowed the growth of George fashion store openings and in 2010 closed all of them, citing high rental costs.

- Trialled two Asda Essentials stores: these were small-format stores to challenge Tesco Express and Sainsbury's Local convenience stores. They stocked a limited range of products, including fresh food, and were based on the French Leader Price chain, which sells fresh fruit, vegetables, meat, grocery products and cosmetics. The stores sold almost entirely Asda own-label products. After less than a year one of these trial stores was closed and Asda announced it had no plans to open any more.

- Improved the product line: healthier food sourced from local producers, and sold new products online such as contact lenses and airline tickets.

- Urged the Office of Fair Trading to open an inquiry into Tesco's land bank of 185 development sites with a view to preventing it buying land and opening stores close to existing outlets without reference to the OFT. And if an existing store was sold by one supermarket chain to another, the deal had to be scrutinized by the competition authority.

- Responded to the recent recession by selling hundreds of products for £1, offering 50p bargains, including 400g of mince, two pints of milk, a white loaf, six eggs and 2kgs of carrots, and launching a TV campaign (supported by evidence from the price comparison website moneysupermarket.com) showing how Asda was cheaper than Tesco.

- Adopted the 'less is more' strategy, which includes dropping secondary brands to concentrate on the biggest brand names.

In 2010 Mr Bond resigned from his post as chief executive to take up the role of part-time chaiman. He was replaced by Andy Clarke, formerly Asda's chief operating officer. One of his first moves was to buy the 193 UK stores off Danish discount retailer Netto. Netto stores average only 750 square metres compared with Asda's average superstore of 4,300 square metres.

References

Based on: Merrilees, B. and D. Miller (1999) Defensive Segmentation Against a Market Spoiler Rival, *Proceedings of the Academy of Marketing Conference*, Stirling, July, 1–10; Bowers, S. (2003) Hunter to Raise the Stakes, *The Guardian*, 6 January, 17; Teather, D. (2003) Asda's £360m Plan Will Create 3,900 Jobs, *The Guardian*, 19 February, 23; Troy, M. (2003) 'Buy' George! Wal-Mart's Asda Takes Fashion to UK's High Street, *DSN Retailing Today*, 23 June, 1; Finch, J. (2005) Asda to Open Hundreds of Discount Shops, *The Guardian*, 10 December, 22; Finch, J. (2005) Asda Cuts 1400 Managers in Fight to Stay No

2 Grocer, *The Guardian*, 6 July, 16; Birchall, J. (2005) What Wal-Mart Women Really Want, *Financial Times*, 10 October, 11; Birchall, J. (2005) Supermarket Sweep, *Financial Times*, 10 November, 17; Anonymous (2006) Wal-Mart Admits Defeat in Germany and Sells Stores, *The Guardian*, 24 July, 32; Palmeri, C. (2008) Wal-Mart Is Up For This Downturn, Businessweek, 30 October, 42; Finch, J. and A. Clark (2008) 70,000 Extra Customers a Week Head For Asda, *The Guardian*, 10 July, 27; Finch, J. (2009) Asda Sales Continue To Soar As 'Intelligent Offers' Pull in Record 18m Shoppers a Week, *The Guardian*, 14 August, 23; Wood, Z. and G. Wearden (2010) Asda Boss Andy Bond Stuns City by Quitting, *The Guardian*, 13 April, 24; Finch, J. and Z. Wood (2010) Asda Buys Netto for £778m in Attempt to Close Gap on Tesco, *The Guardian* 28 May, 33; Boyle, M. and D. MacMillan (2011) Wal-Mart's Rocky Path From Bricks to Clicks, *Bloomberg Business Week*, 25–31 July, 31–3; Felsted, A. (2012) Asda Goes for Growth but Tesco Pulls Back, *Financial Times*, 24 January, 18.

Questions

1. What are Wal-Mart's sources of competitive advantage? How do these sources manifest themselves in creating competitive advantage for Wal-Mart customers?

3. Does Wal-Mart's acquisition of Asda make competitive sense?

3. Why did Asda's fortunes worsen around 2004?

4. Assess the actions taken by Andy Bond and Andy Clarke to revive Asda.

This case was written by David Jobber, Professor of Marketing, University of Bradford.

CHAPTER
20

Competitive marketing strategy

Very noble social objectives, welfare, health and education, can only be met if the economy is successful and there are wealth creators.

SIR TERRY LEAHY[1]

LEARNING OBJECTIVES

After reading this chapter, you should be able to:

1. discuss the nature of competitive behaviour
2. explain how military analogies can be applied to competitive marketing strategy
3. identify the attractive conditions and strategic focus necessary to achieve the following objectives—build, hold, niche, harvest and divest
4. discuss the nature of frontal, flanking, encirclement, bypass and guerrilla attacks
5. discuss the nature of position, flanking, pre-emptive, counter-offensive and mobile defences, and strategic withdrawal

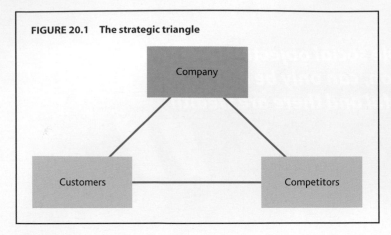

FIGURE 20.1   The strategic triangle

In many markets, competition is the driving force of change and is at the heart of a healthy economy. The quote at the beginning of the chapter by Sir Terry Leahy (former Chief Executive of Tesco PLC) is calling for recognition of the importance of thriving and surviving in a competitive marketplace. Without competition companies satisfice: they provide satisfactory levels of service but fail to excel. Where there is a conflict between improving customer satisfaction and costs, the latter often take priority since customers have little choice and cost-cutting produces tangible results. Competition, then, is good for the customer as it means that companies have to try harder or lose their customer base.

When developing marketing strategy, companies need to be aware of their own strengths and weaknesses, customer needs, and the competition. This three-pronged approach to strategy development has been termed the 'strategic triangle' and is shown in Figure 20.1. This framework recognizes that to be successful it is no longer sufficient to be good at satisfying customers' needs: companies need to be better than the competition. In Chapter 19 we discussed various ways of creating and sustaining a competitive advantage. In this chapter we shall explore the development of marketing strategies in the face of competitive activity and challenges. First, we shall look at alternative modes of competitive behaviour and then, examine when and how to achieve strategic marketing objectives.

Competitive Behaviour

Rivalry between firms does not always lead to conflict and aggressive marketing battles. **Competitive behaviour** can take five forms: conflict, competition, co-existence, cooperation and collusion.[2]

Conflict

Conflict is characterized by aggressive competition, where the objective is to drive competitors out of the marketplace. The retail industry is highly competitive and compounded by the global economic recession many businesses have been forced to close as a result of competitive conflict. For example, Dixons Retail changed the face of its business in the UK, bringing together two of its leading brands, Currys and PC World, together in one store. The new format proved a strong challenge for its rivals, Comet and Best Buy. Dixons was able to significantly increase sales of iPads, Kindles and other popular electronic goods, outselling its competitors. The outcome was that Comet was sold for £2 and Best Buy moved its operation out of the UK.[3]

Competition

The objective of competition is not to eliminate competitors from the marketplace but to perform better than them. This may take the form of trying to achieve faster sales and/or profit growth, larger size or higher market share. Competitive behaviour recognizes the limits of aggression. Competitor reaction will be an important consideration when setting strategy. Players will avoid spoiling the underlying industry structure, which is an important influence on overall profitability. For example, price wars will be avoided if competitors believe that their long-term effect will be to reduce industry profitability.

Co-existence

Three types of co-existence can occur. First, co-existence may arise because firms do not recognize their competitors owing to difficulties in defining market boundaries. For example, Waterman and Mont Blanc, makers of fine-quality and luxury writing instruments, fountain pens and propelling pencils, may ignore competition from jewellery companies since their definition may be product-based rather than market-centred (i.e. the gift market). Second, firms may not recognize other companies they believe are operating in a separate market segment. For example, Mont Blanc and Waterman are likely to ignore the actions of Mitsubishi Pencil company, which manufactures Uniball roller-ball pens, as they are operating in different market segments. Third, firms may choose to acknowledge the territories of their competitors (for example, geography, brand personality, market segment or product technology) in order to avoid harmful head-to-head competition.

Cooperation

This involves the pooling of the skills and resources of two or more firms to overcome problems and take advantage of new opportunities. A growing trend is towards **strategic alliances** where firms join together through a joint venture, licensing agreement, long-term purchasing and supply arrangements, or joint research and development contract to build a long-term competitive advantage. For example, Shell International Petroleum, Rolls-Royce and Airbus have worked in collaboration to develop alternative fuels for the A380, which has led to the use of cleaner aviation fuels. In today's global marketplace, where size is a key source of advantage, cooperation is a major type of competitive behaviour.[4]

Collusion

The final form of competitive behaviour is collusion, whereby firms come to some arrangement that inhibits competition in a market. Collusion is more likely where there are a small number of suppliers in each national market, the price of the product is a small proportion of buyer costs, where cross-national trade is restricted by tariff barriers or prohibitive transportation costs, and where buyers are able to pass on high prices to their customers. For example, in 2009 Amazon was selling e-books at around 7 euros. However, publishers were not happy as the cost of the e-book was too low and there was a worry that books would follow the fate of music, losing a lot of commercial value. In 2010 Apple entered the market with its iBook platform and agreed terms with publishers, that put Amazon in a position where it was likely to lose customers, who would switch to Apple. The US Justice Department and the European Commission decided that Apple's decision to side with the publishers was tantamount to collusion and an example of anti-competitive behaviour.

Developing Competitive Marketing Strategies

The work of such writers as Ries and Trout, and Kotler and Singh has drawn attention to the relationship between military and marketing 'warfare'.[5,6] Their work has stressed the need to develop strategies that are more than customer based. They placed the emphasis on attacking and defending against the competition, and used military analogies to guide strategic thinking. They saw competition as the enemy and thus recognized the relevance of the principles of military warfare as put forward by such writers as Sun Tzu and von Clausewitz to business.[7,8] As von Clausewitz wrote:

> Military warfare is a clash between major interests that is resolved by bloodshed—that is the only way in which it differs from other conflicts. Rather than comparing it to an art we could more accurately compare it to commerce, which is also a conflict of human interests and activities.

Indeed, military terms have been used in business and marketing for many years. Terms such as *launching a campaign*, *achieving a breakthrough*, *company division* and *strategic business unit* are common in business language. Frequently, sales and service personnel are referred to as *field forces*.[9]

In recent years, the language and the basis of competition have focused on winning—that is, 'my brand is better than your brand' and making the competition irrelevant through a battle of the brands.[10] See Read the Research 20.1 to find out more about how by expanding their brands beyond functional benefits companies like Marriot Hotels, Toyota, Starbucks and Harley-Davidson have been able to create barriers that are difficult for the competition to surmount.

The context in which we shall explore the development of competitive marketing strategy is the achievement of strategic marketing objectives. Four of these objectives have already been discussed (to *build, hold, harvest* and *divest*), to which a fifth objective—to *niche*—may be added. The discussion of each objective will focus on the *attractive conditions* that favour its adoption, and the **strategic focus**, which comprises the strategies that can be employed to achieve the objective.*

Read the Research 20.1 Mergers, Acquisitions and Strategies

A widely held view is that a strategic solution to financial distress in corporate organizations is the route of mergers and acquisitions. Organizations facing difficulties have in recent times followed or been compelled by regulators onto the path of mergers and acquisitions as the only option to liquidation. However, this article from McKinsey looks at the other side when big acquisitions really pay off.

www.mckinseyquarterly.com/When_big_acquisitions_pay_off_2801

This interesting article on the evolution of business strategy puts into chronological order some of the key models of the last 50 years. In particular it highlights Kenichi Ohmae's contribution with his strategic triangle or 3C's and goes on to discuss military theories.

http://in2eastafrica.net/the-evolution-of-business-strategy/

Build Objectives

Attractive conditions

A *build objective* is suitable in *growth markets*. Because overall market sales are growing, all players can achieve higher sales even if the market share of one competitor is falling. This is in marked contrast to mature (no growth) markets where an increase in the sales of one player has to be at the expense of the competition (zero sum game).

Some writers point out that if competitors' expectations are high in a growth market (for example, because they know that the market is growing) they may retaliate if those expectations are not met.[11] While this is true, their reaction is not likely to be as strong or protracted as in a no-growth situation. For example, if expectations have led to an expansion of plant capacity that is not fully utilized because of competitor activity, the situation is not as serious as when over-capacity exists in a no-growth market. In the former case, market growth will help fill capacity without recourse to aggressive retaliatory action, whereas, in the latter, capacity utilization will improve only at the expense of the competition.

---

*The format of this part of Chapter 20 is similar to that of 'Offensive and Defensive Marketing Strategies' in *Market Strategy and Competitive Positioning* by John Saunders, Graham Hooley and Nigel Piercy (London: Prentice-Hall). This is because the approach was developed by the author of the current text and Graham Hooley when they worked together at the University of Bradford School of Management.

A build objective also makes sense in growth markets because new users are being attracted to the product. Since these new users do not have established brand or supplier loyalty it is logical to invest resources into attracting them to our product offering. Provided the product meets their expectations, trial during the growth phase can lead to the building of goodwill and loyalty as the market matures. One company that has pursued a build objective in growth markets is Cisco Systems. The company is the world's biggest manufacturer of networking equipment and has achieved staggering growth by providing 'routers' that direct traffic around the Internet and corporate intranets. In one 15-year period the company doubled its size every year. Cisco has continued to build through acquisition and recently acquired Inseime, an R&D company, so that it can expand its provision into the datacenter market.[12,13]

A build objective is also attractive in mature (no growth) markets where there are *exploitable competitive weaknesses*. For example, Japanese car producers exploited US and European car manufacturers' weaknesses in reliability and build quality; Starbucks exploited competitive weaknesses in traditional coffee shops to build a global business; easyJet and Ryanair exploited traditional airlines' high prices on short-haul flights; and Virgin Airlines took advantage of long-haul carriers' unexceptional service levels across the Atlantic to build based on service excellence (which now includes massage for business-class passengers).

A third attractive condition for building sales and market share is when the company has *exploitable corporate strengths*. For example, Marks & Spencer's core competence lies in its capability to produce quality products, from clothes or food.

When taking on a market leader, an attractive, indeed a necessary, condition is *adequate corporate resources*. The financial muscle that usually accompanies market leadership, and the importance of the situation, mean that forceful retaliation can be expected. Google Plus has entered the social media marketplace and is taking on Facebook. Games are important to social networks. Google has invested $200 million in Zynga to bring gaming into its social network even though it is not able to have top titles like Cityville and Farmville.[14] This may turn out to be a clash of the Titans as both Google and Facebook have extensive corporate resources. While Google challenges Facebook in the social media arena, Facebook is attacking Google's dominance of the online advertising market.

Finally, a build objective is attractive when *experience curve effects* are believed to be strong. Some experience curve effects (the combined impact on costs of economies of scale and learning) are related to cumulative output: by building sales faster than the competition, a company can achieve the position of cost leader, as United Biscuits has done in the UK and Wal-Mart has achieved worldwide.

Strategic focus

A build objective can be achieved in four ways: through market expansion, winning market share from the competition, by merger or acquisition, and by forming strategic alliances.

Market expansion

This is brought about by creating new users or uses, or by increasing frequency of purchase. *New users* may be found by expanding internationally, Kellogg's developed Nutri-grain and Special K bars so that consumers could eat breakfast on the go. This means that people who are prone to skip breakfast can take their breakfast and eat it at any time of the day.

New uses—many cereal brands dropped the word 'breakfast' from their advertising so that consumers would be happy to eat these products at any time of the day. In fact, cereals are a popular bedtime snack.

Increasing frequency of use may rely on persuasive communications—for example, by persuading people to clean their teeth twice a day rather than only once. By changing the range of products and the time at which people eat their cereals Kellogg's has significantly increased the use of its leading brands—All Bran, Crunchy Nut, Frosted Flakes, Rice Krispies, Special K.

Go to the website to compare M&S advertising for its food and clothing ranges.
www.mcgraw-hill.co.uk/textbooks/jobber

Winning market share

If a market cannot be expanded, a build strategy implies gaining marketing success at the expense of the competition. Winning market share is an important goal as market share has been found to be related to profitability in many studies (see Chapter 9, Managing products: brand and corporate identity management). There are several reasons why this should be so. Market leaders are often high-price brands (examples include Coca-Cola, Kellogg's, Heinz, Nestlé, Nike and Nokia). They are also in a stronger position to resist distributor demands for trade discounts. Because of economies of scale and experience curve effects, their costs are likely to be lower than those of their smaller-volume rivals. Therefore, their profit margins should be greater than those of their competitors. Since they are market leaders by definition the unit sales volume is higher and consequently their overall profits (profit margin × sales volume) should be higher than those of their rivals. This is why companies such as GE, Unilever, Procter & Gamble and Heinz are willing to compete only in those markets where they can reach number one or two position.

In business companies seek to win market share through product, distribution, promotional innovation and penetration pricing. Kotler and Singh have identified five competitor confrontation strategies (see Fig. 20.2) designed to win sales and market share.[15]

Frontal attack involves the challenger taking on the defender head on. For example, the number two in the PC market, Hewlett-Packard, has successfully challenged the one-time market leader, Dell, using a combination of innovation and price cutting. If the defender is a market leader, the success of a head-on challenge is likely to depend on four factors.[16] First, the challenger should have a clear and sustainable *competitive advantage*. Virgin Atlantic's challenge to British Airways and American Airlines on transatlantic routes is based upon continuous service innovation. For example, it was the first to introduce in-seat video screens and the 'limo to lounge in 10 minutes' offering, which promises passengers arriving at its Upper Class Wing at Heathrow airport to speed them through check-in.[17] If the advantage is based on cost leadership this will support a low price strategy to fight the market leader.

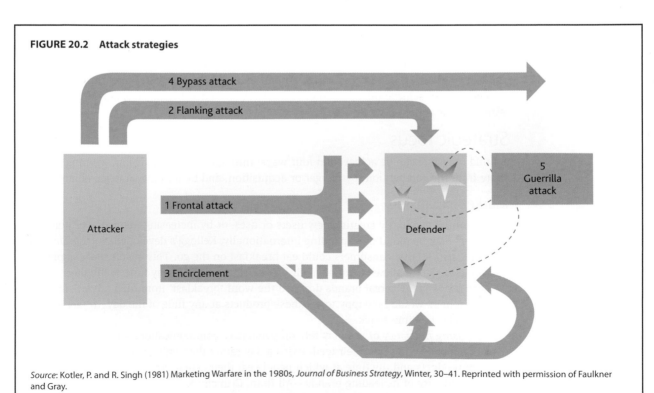

FIGURE 20.2   Attack strategies

Source: Kotler, P. and R. Singh (1981) Marketing Warfare in the 1980s, *Journal of Business Strategy*, Winter, 30–41. Reprinted with permission of Faulkner and Gray.

Ryanair is the cost leader in short-haul air travel, allowing it to undercut traditional carriers such as British Airways and Lufthansa on price. A distinct differential advantage provides the basis for superior customer value. Sustainability is necessary to delay the leader's capability to respond.

Second, the challenger should achieve proximity *in other activities*. John Deere and Caterpillar are America's biggest heavy equipment manufacturers. John Deere challenged with a machine that gave buyers productivity gains but this initiative failed because John Deere could not match Caterpillar's after-sales service.

Third, success is more likely if there is some *restriction on the leader's ability to retaliate*. Restrictions include patent protection, pride, technological lead times and the costs of retaliation. Where a differential advantage or cost leadership position is supported by *patent protection*, imitation by the market leader will be very difficult. *Pride* may hamper retaliation; the market leader refused to imitate because to do so would admit that the challenger had outsmarted the leader. This is thought to be the main reason why Nokia was slow to retaliate in the face of Samsung's advances in mobile handset design and high-tech functionality. Where the challenge is based on a technological innovation it may take the leader *time to put in place the new technology*. John Deere's challenge to Caterpillar was based on a hydrostatic drive that would take Caterpillar two to three years to install in its own machines. Furthermore, retaliation may be difficult for the market leader because of the *costs* involved. The risk of damaging brand image and lowering profit margins may also deter market leaders from responding to price challenges.

Finally, the challenger needs *adequate resources* to withstand the battle that will take place should the leader retaliate. An example of a challenge to a market leader that succeeded because most of these conditions were met was IBM's attack on Apple, once market leader in the personal computer market.[18] Initially slow into the segment, IBM developed a computer that possessed a competitive advantage over Apple based on a 16-bit processor that was faster and more powerful than Apple's 8-bit machine. IBM also persuaded software houses to develop a wide range of software that would run only on its machines. Buyers would therefore have a wider choice of software from which to choose if they bought an IBM rather than an Apple computer (a major differential advantage). IBM also managed to achieve proximity to Apple in other activities, particularly in terms of reliability and after-sales service.

Apple refused to follow IBM's route regarding software, preferring to remain distinctive (perhaps pride was a factor here). Instead it retaliated by launching the Mac based on an *ease of use differential* advantage. IBM, therefore, still held the software edge.

IBM's massive resources, based on its mainframe computer cash cows, enabled it to launch a powerful promotional campaign aimed at the business market. IBM's ability to create a differential advantage, its ability, initially, to match Apple on other activities, Apple's inability to generate as wide a range of software as IBM, and IBM's superior resources made up the platform that led to IBM overtaking Apple as market leader. However, IBM's inability to sustain its differential advantage with software as IBM clones entered the market with cheaper prices has been a major factor in its recent downturn in sales and profits, and its decision to sell its PC division to Lenovo.

Table 20.1 shows examples of companies which are regularly in head-to-head competitive confrontation.

A **flanking attack** involves attacking unguarded or weakly guarded ground. In marketing terms it means attacking geographical areas or market segments where the defender is poorly represented. For example, in the USA as major supermarket chains moved out of town, the 7-11 chain prospered by opening stores that provided the convenience of local availability and longer opening hours.

The growth in ethical consumption has provided opportunities for ethically based brands to issue a flanking attack on traditional suppliers. For example, companies such as Green & Black's (organic chocolate), Cafédirect (fair trade coffee), Innocent (smoothie drinks based

TABLE 20.1 Major marketing head to heads	
Companies	**Competitive area**
Nike vs Adidas	Footwear
Coca-Cola vs Pepsi	Soft drinks
McDonald's vs Burger King	Fast-food restaurants
Unilever vs Procter & Gamble	Fast-moving consumer goods
Apple (iPhone) vs Samsung Galaxy	Smartphones
iPad vs Samsung Galaxy Tab	Tablet computers
Apple vs Dell	Computers
Google vs Yahoo!	Search engines
Intel vs Advanced Micro Devices	Microchips
Boeing vs Airbus	Aircraft
Google Plus vs Facebook	Social network

Go to the website and suggest why Magnum Infinity is a premium brand. www.mcgraw-hill.co.uk/textbooks/jobber

on natural ingredients), Pret A Manger (sandwiches and salads made from natural ingredients free from chemicals and preservatives) and Ben & Jerry's (an ethically orientated company marketing ice cream) have all been highly successful in growing sales and profits.

The attack by Japanese companies on the European and US car markets was a flanking attack—on the small car segment—from which they have expanded into other segments including sports cars. The success of Next, the retail clothing chain, was based on spotting an underserved, emerging market segment: working women aged 25–40 who were finding it difficult to buy stylish clothes at reasonable prices.

Mars introduced ice cream chocolate bars (e.g. Mars, Snickers, Galaxy and Bounty ice cream) as a threat to Unilever's ice cream business. In response, Unilever launched a range of premium brands, including Magnum and Gino Ginelli, and took steps to defend vigorously its *shop exclusivity deals*, which prevent competitors from selling its products in shops that sell Walls ice cream, and *freezer exclusivity*, which prohibits competitors from placing their ice cream in Unilever-supplied freezer cabinets.

The advantage of a flanking attack is that it does not provoke the same kind of response as a head-on confrontation. Since the defender is not challenged in its main market segments, there is more chance that it will ignore the challenger's initial successes. If the defender dallies too long, the flank segment can be used as a beachhead from which to attack the defender in its major markets, as Japanese companies have repeatedly done.

An **encirclement attack** involves attacking the defender from all sides. Every market segment is hit with every combination of product features to completely encircle the defender. An example is Seiko, which produces over 2000 different watch designs for the worldwide market. These cover everything the customer might want in terms of fashion and features. A variant on the encirclement-attack approach is to cut off supplies to the defender. This could be achieved by the acquisition of major supply companies.

A **bypass attack** circumvents the defender's position. This type of attack changes the rules of the game, usually through technological leap-frogging as Casio did when bypassing Swiss analogue watches with digital technology. Also, the BlackBerry and iPod bypassed traditional mobile phone producers like Nokia and Motorola to create a new growth market in smartphones. A bypass attack can also be accomplished through diversification. An attacker can bypass a defender by seeking growth in new markets with new products, as Tesco and Marks & Spencer have done with their move into financial services, and Cisco is doing with its move into consumer electrical goods.[19]

A **guerrilla attack** hurts the defender with pin-pricks rather than blows. Unpredictable price discounts, sales promotions or heavy advertising in a few television regions are some of the tactics attackers can use to cause problems for defenders.

Guerrilla tactics may be the only feasible option for a small company facing a larger competitor. Such tactics allow the small company to make its presence felt without the dangers of a full-frontal attack. By being unpredictable, guerrilla activity is difficult to defend against. Nevertheless, such tactics run the risk of incurring the wrath of the defender, who may choose to retaliate with a full-frontal attack if sufficiently provoked.

Digital Marketing 20.1   Digital Guerilla Marketing Tactics

Guerilla marketing tactics offer competitors the chance to try unusual (though possibly risky) approaches to taking on other firms. Traditionally low cost, the digital guerilla marketing tactic continues the themes of unpredictability, sometimes 'leftfield creative' to which a competitor finds it difficult to respond. In the digital domain, the guerilla marketing tactic is often viral, but despite digital's apparent cost benefits, good digital guerilla marketing is thin on the ground.

Procter & Gamble's revival of the Old Spice brand, in the face of a more sophisticated male grooming population and growing male scent market, needed something to grab the attention of both the marketplace and the competitive scene. The launch of the Isaiah Mustafa 'I'm on a horse' video on YouTube, which became an overnight success with millions of views and shares, was subsequently trumped by the Fabio 'New Old Spice Guy' and the 'Mano a Mano in El Bano' videos—in which personal Twitter replies and personal video replies were played out to questions from Internet sources. As a campaign, this came into the grooming marketplace not accustomed to such ironic marketing, and accompanied a more conventional promotional strategy in stores.

Paramount Pictures' *Cloverfield* was marketed online in some highly unconventional formats. In mid 2007 pictures and apparently covert videos started appearing on key sites, including sites for fake products and Japanese conglomerates. Combined with a teaser ad shown with the *Transformers* movie, the campaign created a sense of bewilderment among potential fans and those who hadn't seen the teaser. Often cited as a guerilla campaign, it is perhaps less in keeping with the traditions of guerilla marketing because of the relative higher costs of creating the whole *Cloverfield* marketing campaign. Critics argue that it had merely taken ideas from an earlier similar campaign for *Blair Witch Project*.

Merger or acquisition

A third approach to achieving a build objective is to merge with or acquire competitors. By joining forces, costly marketing battles are avoided, and purchasing, production, financial, marketing and R&D synergies may be gained. Further, a merger can give the scale of operation that may be required to operate as an international force in the marketplace. Such potential gains are fuelling merger and acquisition activity. Read Marketing in Action 20.1.

Mergers are not without their risks, though, not least when they involve parties from different countries. Differences in culture, language, business practices, and the problems associated with restructuring may cause terminal strains. Currently, cash-rich Chinese companies are looking to strengthen their foothold in Europe by acquiring businesses. Wang Zong Nan (Chairman of the Bright Food Group, China's largest food company) is looking to buy at least three major European food manufacturers in the next few years.[20] However, he will have to ensure that he is able to deliver on his promises if he is to avoid conflict like that experienced by Chinese Overseas Engineering Company (COVEC) in Poland. COVEC won a contract in 2009 to build a 50-kilometre highway (A2) as part of Poland's infrastructure improvements for the UEFA Euro 2012 Championship. COVEC submitted a very low bid to secure the contract, but failed to complete the project citing payment issues as the cause for the delay. This left the Polish government in a very difficult position and angered officials. Radisław Sikorski, Poland's Foreign Minister, tweeted on June 7:

Marketing in Action 20.1 The International Airlines Group (IAG) Acquires BMI and Bmibaby

'International Airlines Group, the parent of British Airways, has completed the acquisition of bmi but will receive a "significant" discount after two unwanted subsidiaries were folded into the deal.'

IAG, owner of British Airways and Iberia has acquired BMI from Lufthansa. A price reduction of £172 million was needed to secure the deal due to the operating losses of BMI of around £3 million a week. The takeover should help to cut costs through cutting the size of the workforce. Staff being made redundant are largely head office personnel; their roles in the regional head office at East Midlands airport in Leicestershire are being moved to Heathrow.

Virgin Atlantic feels threatened by this move as it claims it distorts the market as IAG would have too many landing slots at Heathrow.

Based on: Milmo (2012);[21] BBC News (2012)[22]

We let them into the market of large EU investment projects, and now here's this mess. They should save their reputation.[23]

One way to avoid such conflict is to set clear objectives for mergers and acquisitions. These objectives fall within five categories, as described below.[24]

Reduce overcapacity and increase market share and efficiency: the acquiring company aims to eliminate capacity, gain market share and improve efficiency. This type of merger and acquisition is the most difficult to implement as it often occurs between two large companies that have deeply entrenched processes and values.[25]

Also, if the problems facing the acquiring company are deeper than inefficiencies, a merger designed to gain share, lower costs and reduce capacity will fail. For example, Hewlett-Packard's acquisition of Compaq sought these benefits, but failed because it did not address HP's flawed business model of low-inventory direct sales to compete with Dell and its traditional high-inventory model used when it distributed through its retail partners. In the former, the company lost out to Dell, which had greater scale and efficiency, and in the latter it failed to complete with IBM, which targeted higher-margin corporate accounts.[26]

Geographic expansion: the merger or acquisition allows both companies to expand geographically. Part of the logic behind P&G's acquisition of Gillette was based on this benefit. The deal allowed P&G to expand in India and Brazil, where Gillette had distribution strengths, and Gillette to take advantage of P&G's strengths in China, Russia, Japan and Turkey. Also, by buying Reebok, Adidas gained a strong presence in the USA, as did BP with its highly successful acquisition of Amoco. Mini Case 20.1 explains that geographic expansion of beer brands was at the heart of InBev's acquisition of Anheuser-Busch.

Product and/or market extension: the objective here is to extend a company's product line and/or its market coverage. For example, L'Oréal's purchase of Body Shop extended its product line into ethically orientated cosmetics, and hence extended its market appeal to ethically conscious consumers. Tata Motors' purchase of Jaguar and Land Rover extended its product line and allowed it to compete in the prestige car market sector.

Mini Case 20.1 InBev Buys Bud

There have to be good reasons to pay $52 billion for a company. InBev, the Brazilian-run, Belgian-located brewer, bought the US beer company Anheuser-Busch. The acquisition catapulted the combined company to the number-one position in global brewing and to one of the world's top five consumer products companies. Such scale gives it enormous negotiating power when buying hops, barley, glass and aluminium, but the major potential benefits lie in the marketing opportunities that their combined assets present.

First, Anheuser controls almost half of the American beer market, the world's most profitable. InBev's American operations are tiny, but it is big in Europe and Latin America, where A-B is hardly present. The acquisition therefore gives InBev's brands—such as Stella Artois, Skol and Becks—access to A-B's vast distribution network in the US, while InBev's strong distribution channels gives A-B brands such as Budweiser and Bud Light access to Europe and Latin America.

Second, the ownership of such strong international brands is becoming increasingly important to brewers because they are prized by consumers in fast-growing markets such as Russia and China. Also, even in mature western markets, the profit margins on leading global brands are high. For example, Heineken says that profits on its Heineken brand are twice those on its regional brands, such as Amstel, which still form about 80 per cent of sales. By buying the company that owns Budweiser and Bud Light, InBev is buying the world's number-one and number-three brands (second place is taken by China's Snow beer).

Like all mergers, there are risks. First, InBev is better known for cost cutting than brand building. For example, when it acquired Boddingtons, a UK beer brand, it cut advertising support, and its record with Stella Artois in the UK is questionable. Second, Budweiser is seen by Americans to be quintessentially American. US beer drinkers may react negatively to its new Brazilian-Belgian ownership, providing opportunities for A-B's archrival SABMiller. Third, the cultures of the two companies differ. InBev is a cost cutter and is stinting with standard industry perks like company cars and free beer. Anheuser-Busch, on the other hand, comes with expensive tastes like helicopters, two free cases of beer each month for employees, and free admission to the company's theme parks.

These issues mean that the merger is full of opportunities but the risks of failure are also present. It will take skilful management to make the merger a success.

Questions

1   Discuss the operational issues that a brand using geographic expansion might encounter.
2   Suggest what you would need to do to maximize the opportunities and reduce the risk given the wide cultural differences between Inbev and Anheuser-Busch.

Based on: The Economist (2008);[27] Foust (2008);[28] Ritson (2008);[29] Wiggins (2008)[30]

Research and development benefits: the merger or acquisition is to acquire research and development expertise and output, instead of in-house research, so that market position can be built quickly. Most of Cisco System's acquisitions fall into this category.

Exploitation of industry convergence: the company judges that a new industry is emerging and tries to establish a position by acquiring resources from existing companies. A key reason for Microsoft's purchase of Skype was to enable it to develop a consumer gateway to the digital world, which enables it to compete with Google, Facebook and Apple[31] in a converging communications industry.

Despite these potential gains, studies have shown that 65 per cent of acquisitions and mergers fail to benefit shareholders.[32] Cultural problems can arise. An extreme example is the merger of the Metal Box Company, based in the UK, with the French company Carnaud: at times the French and British directors refused even to speak to each other. More usually, the problem arises that the cultures of the two companies take so long to meld that new marketplace opportunities are missed. Second, so much emphasis may be placed on the benefits of the merger that potential negative consequences are ignored. For example, when

PepsiCo acquired fast-food operators KFC, Pizza Hut and Taco Bell, the benefits of tying these outlets to sell Pepsi rather than Coca-Cola were realized. What was not appreciated was that this gave Coca-Cola an easy entry into its competitors, such as McDonald's.

A third problem is deciding who is in charge. Mergers of equals can be dangerous because it is not always clear who is the boss. This can lead to indecision while more nimble competitors move ahead. Finally, acquisitions and mergers can lead to staff-related problems. Top managers and salespeople become recruitment targets for competitors, and redundancies damage morale.

Clearly, building through merger and acquisition is not an easy option. Before doing so, managers need to ask (i) 'What advantages will the merger bring that competitors will find difficult to match?', and (ii) 'Would the premium that is usually paid to the shareholders of the acquired company be better spent on another strategy that will build sales and market share—for example, improving customer service levels or expanding internationally?'

Forming strategic alliances

A final option for companies seeking to build is the strategic alliance. The aim is to create a long-term competitive advantage for the partners, often on a global scale. The partners typically collaborate by means of a joint venture (a jointly owned company), licensing agreements, long-term purchasing and supply arrangements, or joint R&D programmes. Strategic alliances maintain a degree of flexibility not apparent with a merger or acquisition.

A major motivation for strategic alliances is the sharing of product development costs and risks. For example, the cost of developing and creating manufacturing facilities for a new car targeted at world markets exceeds £2 billion, and developing a new drug can cost over £25 million. Sharing these costs may be the only serviceable economic option for a medium-sized manufacturer in either of these industries.

Marketing benefits can accrue too. For example, access to new markets and distribution channels can be achieved, time to market reduced, product gaps filled and product lines widened.[33] It was to take advantage of marketing opportunities in financial services that Tesco partnered a bank. Virgin Trains also required its partner T-mobile to improve the Wi-Fi service it provided customers. Furthermore, a strategic alliance can be the initial stage to a merger or acquisition, allowing each party to assess their abilities to work together effectively. Examples of companies that have successfully formed strategic alliances to build sales, market share and profits are GlaxoSmithKline and Hoffman-La Roche to market Zantac, the anti-ulcer drug, in the USA, and the alliance between European aircraft manufacturers to create the A380 aircraft.

A third reason for alliances is because mergers and acquisitions are sometimes not possible because of legal restrictions or national sensitivities. Many airline alliances, such as the multi-airline Star Alliance, led by United Airlines of the USA and Lufthansa of Germany,

TABLE 20.2 Some key strategic alliances	
Companies	**Competitive area**
Apple/O$_2$	Smartphones
British Airways/American Airlines/Iberia	Transatlantic air travel
Ericsson/China Mobile/China Unicom	Telecoms network equipment
Fiat/Chrysler	Cars
Virgin Rail/T-Mobile	Onboard wireless Internet access
Vodafone/China Mobile/Verizon Wireless	Mobile phones and other telecoms equipment
VW/Sanyo	Lithium car batteries

TABLE 20.3 Build objectives
Attractive conditions
Growth markets
Exploitable competitive weaknesses
Exploitable corporate strengths
Adequate corporate resources
Strategic focus
Market expansion
• new users
• new uses
• increasing frequency of use
Winning market share
• product innovation
• distribution innovation
• promotional innovation
• penetration pricing
• competitor confrontation
Merger or acquisition
Forming strategic alliances

are formed for this reason.[34] Finally, strategic alliances can provide production benefits. For example, BP's alliance with the Russian oil producer TNK gave BP access to Russian oil fields, while TNK gained BP's extensive resources and oil exploration skills.

A key factor in benefiting from strategic alliances is the desire and ability to learn from the alliance partner. Japanese companies have excelled at this, while European and US companies have traditionally lagged. The risk is that the alliance leaks technological and core capabilities to the partner, thereby giving away important competitive information. This one-way transfer of skills should be avoided by building barriers to capability seepage: core competences should be protected at all costs. This is easier when a company has few alliances, when only a limited part of the organization is involved, and when the relationships built up in the alliance are stable.[35]

Strategic alliances can lead to conflict, however. For example, in the TNK–BP alliance, the Russian side demanded greater control of the company, a reduction in the number of BP staff and more overseas investment, even when it meant competing with BP operations. The conflict was settled when BP agreed to an independent chief executive officer, parity between the partners at board level and international expansion.[36]

Table 20.2 lists some of the major strategic alliances of recent years.

A summary of the key attractive conditions and strategic focuses for build objectives is given in Table 20.3.

Hold Objectives

Hold objectives involve defending a company's current position against would-be attackers. The principles of defensive warfare are, therefore, relevant. Perhaps the principle that has the most relevance in business is the recognition that strong competitive moves should always be blocked. This was not missed by political parties, which, ever since Bill Clinton's successful challenge to George Bush Snr, have recognized the importance of rapid response. Learning from attacks by Republicans on Democratic candidates in earlier presidential elections, Clinton's strategists established a 24-hour-response capability to any Bush attack. As predicted, Bush attempted to position Clinton as a man of high taxes. Clinton was accused in a television advertisement of increasing taxes if elected. The advertisement featured the kinds of people who would suffer as a result of the extra tax they would have to pay. Within 24 hours Clinton ran his own advertisement quoting the *Washington Post* as stating that the Republican ad was misleading. This fast response capability was believed by the Democrats to be a major factor in Clinton's ability to maintain his opinion poll lead and emerge the victor in the election. Now all major political parties have in place a fast-response capability.

We shall now analyse the conditions that make a hold objective attractive, and the strategic focus necessary to achieve the objective.

Attractive conditions

The classic situation where a hold objective makes strategic sense is a *market leader in a mature or declining market*. This is the standard cash cow position discussed as part of the Boston Consulting Group market share/market growth rate analysis. By holding on to market leadership, a product should generate positive cash flows that can be used elsewhere in the company to build other products and invest in new product development. Holding on to market leadership per se makes sense because brand leaders enjoy the marketing benefits of bargaining power with distribution outlets, and brand image (the number one position), as well as enjoying experience curve effects that reduce costs. Furthermore, in a declining market, maintaining market leadership may result in becoming a virtual monopolist as weaker competitors withdraw.

A second situation where holding is suitable is in *growth markets when the costs of attempting to build sales and market share outweigh the benefits*. This may be the case in the face of aggressive rivals, who will respond strongly if attacked. In such circumstances it may be prudent to be content with the status quo, and avoid actions that are likely to provoke the competition.

Strategic focus

A hold objective may be achieved by monitoring the competition or by confronting the competition.

Monitoring the competition

In a market that is characterized by competitive stability, the required focus is simply to *monitor the competition*. Perhaps everyone is playing the 'good competitor' game, content with what they have, and no one is willing to destabilize the industry structure. Monitoring is necessary to check that there are no significant changes in competitor behaviour but, beyond that, no change in strategy is required.

Confronting the competition

In circumstances where rivalry is more pronounced, strategic action may be required to defend sales and market share from aggressive challenges. The principles of defensive warfare provide a framework for identifying strategic alternatives that can be used in this situation. Figure 20.3 illustrates six methods of defence derived from military strategy.[37]

Position defence involves building a fortification around one's existing territory. This reflects the philosophy that the company has good products, and all that is needed is to price them competitively and promote them effectively. This is more likely to work if the products have differential advantages that are not easily copied—for example, through patent protection. Marketing assets like brand names and reputation may also provide a strong defence against aggressors, although it can be a dangerous strategy. For example, Ever Ready's refusal to develop an alkaline battery in the face of an aggressive challenge to its market leadership by Duracell was an example of position defence. Instead it stuck with its zinc-carbon product, which had a shorter life than its alkaline rival, and invested £2 million in promotion. Only later did Ever Ready develop its own alkaline battery.[38]

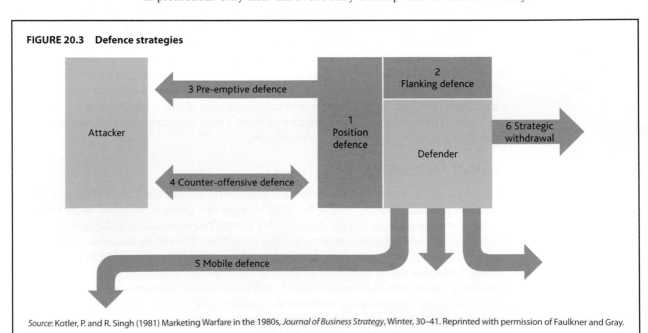

FIGURE 20.3   Defence strategies

Source: Kotler, P. and R. Singh (1981) Marketing Warfare in the 1980s, *Journal of Business Strategy*, Winter, 30–41. Reprinted with permission of Faulkner and Gray.

Land Rover and Range Rover provide another instance of an unsuccessful position defence. Believing firmly in their invincibility, they conducted little new product development. This created the opportunity for Subaru to introduce its cheaper, 'fun' four-wheel-drive vehicles. Only belatedly did Land Rover respond by developing the successful Discovery model.

Flanking defence is characterized by the defence of a hitherto unprotected market segment. The danger is that if the segment is left unprotected, it will provide a beachhead for new entrants to gain experience in the market and attack the main market later. This means that if it helps to avoid or slow down competitive inroads, it can make sense for a defender to compete in a segment that, in pure short-term profitability terms, looks unattractive. This danger has prompted Wal-Mart's defence of the small-format grocery market on the west coast of the USA. In retaliation to Tesco's entry with its Fresh & Easy stores, Wal-Mart has opened its own version under the banner 'Marketside', which also has an emphasis on fresh food.[39]

A further problem is that the defence of the segment may be half-hearted as it is not central to the main business. An example is General Motors' and Ford's weak attempts to build a small car to compete with Volkswagen and the Japanese companies. The products—the Vega and Pinto—suffered from poor build quality and unreliability, and proved ineffective in defending the exposed flank. When a flanking defence is required against successful but smaller attackers, acquisition may be an attractive option. For example, many large companies have responded to the attacks by ethically minded rivals by buying them. For example, L'Oréal has bought Body Shop, Nestlé has acquired Buxton Water, Innocent Drinks is part owned by the Coca-Cola Company and Unilever has purchased Ben & Jerry's.

Failure to defend an emerging market segment can have catastrophic consequences. For example, Distillers, which was dominant in the market for blended Scotch whisky with its Johnny Walker, Dewars and White Horse brands, ignored the growing malt whisky and white spirit segments. This preoccupation with the declining blended whisky segment resulted in disappointing performance and a successful take-over by Guinness. Exhibit 20.1 shows how the brand has defended its flanks by marketing four variants to cater for diverse consumer tastes.

⬆ EXHIBIT 20.1   Green & Black's defends its position in the organic chocolate market by supplying Milk, Dark, White and Creamy Milk brand varieties.

Pre-emptive defence follows the philosophy that the best form of defence is to attack first. This may involve continuous innovation and new product development, a situation characteristic of the camcorder market. Japanese manufacturers are caught up in a continuous spiral of product introductions (known as product *churning*). Failure to maintain this rate of change would soon lead to product obsolescence and market share collapse.

Counter-offensive defence: a defender can choose from three options when considering a counter-offensive defence. It can embark on a head-on counter-attack, hit the attacker's cash cow or encircle the attacker.

With a *head-on counter-attack* a defender matches or exceeds what the attacker has done. This may involve heavy price cutting or promotion expenditure, for example. This can be a costly operation but may be justified to deter a persistent attacker. For example, when Microsoft was challenged by Linux, which began to find favour as the operating system in netbooks, the company cut the price of a version of Windows that normally cost around $70 to $15. The result was that Linux was driven off the majority of netbooks.[40] Tesco also launched a counter-offensive against the growth of discount supermarkets (Netto, Aldi and Lidl) by introducing two cut-price ranges—Tesco Value and Discount—to discourage shoppers from switching.[41]

Alternatively, the counter-attack may be based on innovation, as when Apple counter-attacked IBM's challenge in the personal computer market by launching its successful Macintosh.

Hitting the attacker's cash cow strikes at the attacker's resource supply line. For example, when Xerox attacked IBM in the mainframe computer market, IBM counter-attacked by striking at Xerox's cash cow (the medium-range photocopier) with a limited range of low-priced copiers plus leasing arrangements that were particularly attractive to Xerox's target market (smaller businesses). The result was that Xerox sold its computer business to Honeywell, and concentrated on defending copiers.[42] As we saw in Chapter 19, on analysing competitors and creating a competitive advantage, Rotaprint hit Toshiba's cash cow (the Japanese market) as a counter-offensive defence in retaliation to Toshiba's attack in Rotaprint's home market of the USA. The result was that Toshiba withdrew from the USA.

The third strategic option is to *encircle the attacker*. This strategy was successfully employed by Heublein when its Smirnoff vodka brand was attacked by the cheaper Wolfsmidt brand in the USA. Its response was to maintain the price of Smirnoff while launching two new brands, one at the same price as Wolfsmidt and one at a lower price. This manoeuvre successfully defended Heublein's position as market leader in the vodka market.

When a company's major market is under threat a **mobile defence** may make strategic sense. The two options are diversification and market broadening. A classic example of a company using *diversification* as a form of mobile defence is Imperial Tobacco, which responded to the health threat to its cigarette business by diversifying into food and leisure markets. *Market broadening* involves broadening the business definition, as film companies like Warner Brothers did in the face of declining cinema audiences. By defining its business as entertainment provider rather than film maker, it successfully moved into television, gambling and theme parks.

A **strategic withdrawal**, or contraction defence, requires a company to define its strengths and weaknesses, and then to hold on to its strengths while divesting its weaknesses. This results in the company concentrating on its core business. An example is Diageo, which withdrew from the fast-food business by selling Burger King, and from food by selling Pillsbury to concentrate on premium drinks.[43] Nokia also practised strategic withdrawal, moving initially from a paper, rubber goods and cables group into computers, consumer electronics and telecoms, and then, very successfully, concentrating on mobile handsets, where it is market leader. IBM also practised strategic withdrawal by selling its PC division to Lenovo in a move designed to focus the company more towards high-margin services and software than manufacturing. Strategic withdrawal can also be on a geographic basis. For example, in the face of a worsening financial situation Vodafone has withdrawn from Japan.[44]

A strategic withdrawal allows a company to focus on its core competences and is often required when diversification has resulted in too wide a spread of activities away from what it does really well. Peters and Waterman termed this focus on core skills and competences *sticking to your knitting*.[45]

Table 20.4 summarizes the key points for hold objectives.

TABLE 20.4   Hold objectives
Attractive conditions
Market leader in a mature or declining market
Costs exceed benefits of building
Strategic focus
Monitoring the competition
Confronting the competition

Niche Objectives

A company may decide to pursue a market **niche objective** by pursuing a small market segment or even a segment within a segment. In doing so, it may avoid competition with companies that are serving the major market segments. However, niche-orientated companies, if successful, run the risk that larger competitors are attracted into the segment. For example, the initial success of Sock Shop, a niche provider of stylish men's socks, stimulated large department stores such as Marks & Spencer to launch their own competitive ranges.

Also the success of 'boutique' hotels has caused larger chains to copy them. For example, Hilton has launched Denizen Hotels to provide a similar experience.[46] There is also the danger of not having the support of revenue from other segments if demand falls or costs rise in the niche market. This was the case for niche operators Silverjet, Eos and MAXjet, which targeted only business-class passengers and went into liquidation following a fall in demand in the recent recession and a rise in fuel costs.

Attractive conditions

'Nicheing' may be the only feasible objective for companies with a small budget and where strong competitors are dominating the main segments. As such, it may be an attractive option for small companies that lack the resources to compete directly against the major players. However, there need to be pockets within the market that provide the opportunity for profitable operations, and in which a competitive advantage can be created. Typical circumstances where these conditions apply are when the major players are underserving a particular group of customers as they attempt to meet the needs of the majority of customers, and where the market niche is too small to be of interest to them.

Strategic focus

A key strategic tool for a niche-orientated company is *market segmentation*. Management should be vigilant in its search for underserved segments that may provide profitable opportunities. The choice will depend upon the attractiveness of the niche and the capability of the company to serve it. Once selected, effort—particularly research and development expenditure—will be focused on serving customer needs. An example is Tyrrells, which saw an opportunity to produce a better-quality potato crisp than those found in supermarkets. Targeting a segment that would be prepared to pay more, and avoiding direct competition with the market leader, Walkers crisps, its products are sold in top food halls, farm shops, delis and gastropubs.

Focused R&D expenditure gives a small company a chance to make effective use of its limited resources.[47] The emphasis should be on creating and sustaining a *differential advantage* through intimately understanding the needs of the customer group, and focusing attention on satisfying those needs better than the competition. Tyrrells differentiates by hand-cooking its potato crisps from home-grown potatoes, and processing them on the farm—hand-stirred in small batches.[48] Finally, niche operators should be wary of pursuing growth strategies by broadening their customer base. Often this will lead to a blurring of the differential advantage upon which their success has been built. Indeed, since some niche companies trade on *exclusivity*, to broaden their market base would by definition run the risk of diluting their differential advantage. The Morgan Motor Company which specializes in distinctive, high-performance sports cars, is a company that consistently pursues a niche objective. Morgan consciously *thinks small*, eschewing unsustainable growth in favour of profitability. The emphasis is on high margin not high volume. Table 20.5 summarizes this brief discussion of niche objectives.

TABLE 20.5 Niche objectives
Attractive conditions
Small budget
Strong competitors dominating major segments
Pockets existing for profitable operations
Creating a competitive advantage
Strategic focus
Market segmentation
Focused R&D
Differentiation
Thinking small

Harvest Objectives

A company embarking upon a **harvest objective** attempts to improve unit profit margins even if the result is falling sales. Although sales are falling, the aim is to make the company or product extremely profitable in the short term, generating large positive cash flows that can be used elsewhere in the business (for example, to build stars and selected problem children, or to fund new product development).

Attractive conditions

Also-ran products or companies in *mature or declining markets* (dogs) may be candidates for harvesting, since they are often losing money, and taking up valuable management time and effort.[49] Harvesting actions can move them to a profitable stance, and reduce management attention to a minimum. In *growth markets* harvesting can also make sense where the *costs of building or holding exceed the benefits*. These are problem children companies or products that have little long-term potential. Harvesting is particularly attractive if a *core of loyal customers* exists, which means that sales decline to a stable level. For example, a SmithKline Beecham hair product, Brylcreem, was harvested but sales decline was not terminal as a group of men who used the product in their adolescence continued to buy it in later life. This core of loyal customers meant it was still profitable to market Brylcreem, although R&D and marketing expenditure was minimal. More recently, Brylcreem has been repositioned as a hair gel targeting young men. Cussons Imperial Leather soap and Fry's Turkish Delight chocolate are also examples of brands that are marketed with very little promotional support. Both are long-standing brands that benefit from a core of loyal customers. A final attractive condition is where *future breadwinners exist* in the company or product portfolio to provide future sales and profit growth potential. Obviously harvesting a one-product company is likely to lead to its demise.

TABLE 20.6 **Harvest objectives**
Attractive conditions
Market is mature or declining (dog products)
In growth markets where the costs of building or holding exceed the benefits (selected problem children)
Core of loyal customers
Future breadwinners exist
Strategic focus
Eliminate R&D expenditure
Product reformulation
Rationalize product line
Cut marketing support
Consider increasing price

Strategic focus

Implementing a harvest objective begins with *eliminating research and development expenditure*. The only product change that will be contemplated is *reformulations* that reduce raw material and/or manufacturing costs. *Rationalization of the product line* to one or a few top sellers cuts costs by eliminating expensive product variants. *Marketing support is reduced* by slashing advertising and promotional budgets, while every opportunity is taken to *increase price*.

Table 20.6 summarizes the attractive conditions and strategic focus for achieving harvest objectives.

Divest Objectives

A company may decide to **divest** itself of a strategic business unit or product. In doing so it may stem the flow of cash to a poorly performing area of its business.

Attractive conditions

Divestment is often associated with *loss-making products or businesses* that are a drain on both financial and managerial resources. An example is Konica Minolta, which pulled out of the manufacture of cameras and photographic film in the face of growing losses.[50] *Low-share products or businesses in declining markets* (dogs) are prime candidates for divestment. Other areas may be considered for divestment when it is judged that the *costs of turnaround exceed the benefits*. As such, also-rans in growth markets may be divested, sometimes after harvesting has run its full course. However, care must be taken to examine interrelationships within the corporate portfolio. For example, if a product is making a loss it would still be

TABLE 20.7 Divest objectives
Attractive conditions
Loss-making products or businesses: drain on resources
Often low share in declining markets
Costs of turnaround exceed benefits
Removal will not significantly affect sales of other products
Strategic focus
Get out quickly; minimize the costs

worthwhile supporting it if its removal would *adversely affect sales of other products*. In some industrial markets, customers expect a supplier to provide a full range of products. Consequently, even though some may not be profitable, sales of the whole range may be affected if the loss makers are dropped.

Strategic focus

Because of the drain on profits and cash flow, once a decision to divest has been made, the focus should be to *get out quickly so as to minimize costs*. If a buyer can be found then some return may be realized; if not, the product will be withdrawn or the business terminated.

Table 20.7 summarizes the attractive conditions and strategic focus relating to divestment.

When you have read this chapter

log on to the Online Learning Centre at **www.mcgraw-hill.co.uk/textbooks/jobber** to explore chapter-by-chapter test questions, links and further online study tools for marketing.

Review

1 The nature of competitive behaviour
- Competitive behaviour can take five forms: conflict, competition, co-existence, cooperation and collusion.

2 Competitive marketing strategy can appear as a military initiative
- Military analogies have been used in the past to guide strategic thinking because of the need to attack and defend against competition. While the underlying thinking remains very important the language of war appears less in modern business speak.
- Attack strategies are the frontal attack, the flanking attack, encirclement, the bypass attack and the guerrilla attack.
- Defence strategies are the position defence, the flanking defence, the pre-emptive defence, the counter-offensive defence, the mobile defence, and strategic withdrawal.

3 The attractive conditions and strategic focus necessary to achieve the following objectives: build, hold, niche, harvest and divest
- Build objectives: attractive conditions are growth markets, exploitable competitive weaknesses, exploitable corporate strengths and adequate corporate resources; strategic focus is market expansion, winning market share, merger or acquisition, and forming strategic alliances.
- Hold objectives: attractive conditions are market leader in a mature or declining market, and costs exceed benefits of building; strategic focus is monitoring the competition, and confronting the competition.
- Niche objectives: attractive conditions are small budget, strong competitors dominating major segments, pockets exist for profitable operations, and opportunity to create a competitive advantage; strategic focus is market segmentation, focused R&D, differentiation and thinking small.
- Harvest objectives: attractive conditions are market is mature or declining, growth markets where the cost of building or holding exceeds the benefits, a core of loyal customers and future breadwinners exists; strategic focus is eliminate R&D expenditure, reformulate product, rationalize the product line, cut marketing expenditure and consider increasing price.

4 **The nature of frontal, flanking, encirclement, bypass and guerrilla attacks**
- Frontal attack: the challenger takes on the defender head on.
- Flanking attack: this involves attacking unguarded or weakly guarded ground (e.g. geographical areas or market segments).
- Encirclement attack: the defender is attacked from all sides (every market segment is hit with every combination of product features).
- Bypass attack: the defender's position is circumvented by, for example, technological leap-frogging or diversification.
- Guerrilla attack: the defender's life is made uncomfortable through, for example, unpredictable price discounts, sales promotions or heavy advertising in a few selected regions.

5 **The nature of position, flanking, pre-emptive, counter-offensive and mobile defences, and strategic withdrawal**
- Position defence: building a defence around existing products, usually through keen pricing and improved promotion.
- Flanking defence: defending a hitherto unprotected market segment.
- Pre-emptive defence: usually involves continuous innovation and new product development, recognizing that the best form of defence is attack.
- Counter-offensive defence: a counter-attack that takes the form of a head-on counter-attack, an attack on the attacker's cash cow or an encirclement of the attacker.
- Mobile defence: moving position by diversification or broadening the market by redefining the business.
- Strategic withdrawal: holding on to the company's strengths while divesting its weaknesses (e.g. weak strategic business units or product lines), resulting in the company focusing on its core business.

Key Terms

bypass attack circumventing the defender's position, usually through technological leap-frogging or diversification

competitive behaviour the activities of rival companies with respect to each other; this can take five forms— conflict, competition, co-existence, cooperation and collusion

counter-offensive defence a counter-attack that takes the form of a head-on counter-attack, an attack on the attacker's cash cow or an encirclement of the attacker

divest to improve short-term cash yield by dropping or selling off a product

encirclement attack attacking the defender from all sides: i.e. every market segment is hit with every combination of product features

flanking attack attacking geographical areas or market segments where the defender is poorly represented

flanking defence the defence of a hitherto unprotected market segment

frontal attack a competitive strategy where the challenger takes on the defender head on

guerrilla attack making life uncomfortable for stronger rivals through, for example, unpredictable price discounts, sales promotions or heavy advertising in a few selected regions

harvest objective the improvement of profit margins to improve cash flow even if the longer-term result is falling sales

hold objective a strategy of defending a product in order to maintain market share

mobile defence involves diversification or broadening the market by redefining the business

niche objective the strategy of targeting a small market segment

position defence building a fortification around existing products, usually through keen pricing and improved promotion

pre-emptive defence usually involves continuous innovation and new product development, recognizing that attack is the best form of defence

strategic alliance collaboration between two or more organizations through, for example, joint ventures, licensing agreements, long-term purchasing and supply arrangement, or a joint R&D contract to build a competitive advantage

strategic focus the strategies that can be employed to achieve an objective

strategic withdrawal holding on to the company's strengths while getting rid of its weaknesses

Study Questions

1 At the beginning of the chapter, Sir Terry Leahy's quote implies that competition is good for economic growth. Explain why this might be the case.

2 Imagine you are responsible for brokering a merger/acquisition between a European and Chinese company. Discuss your key priorities when bringing the companies from both countries together for the first time.

3 When Microsoft acquired Skype it did so to address technology convergence. Suggest examples of other companies which have merged as a result of technological convergence.

4 Compare and contrast the conditions conducive to building and holding sales/market share.

5 Why is a position defence risky?

6 Imagine you are the Marketing Director for Apple. Discuss the tablet computing market; suggest a competitive strategy which will enable you to protect market share for the iPad and outline the strategies you think Samsung might adopt in response to your approach.

7 A company should always attempt to harvest a product before considering divestment. Discuss.

8 In defence, it is always wise to respond to serious attacks immediately. Do you agree? Explain your answer.

References

1. Tyler, R. (2012) *The Telegraph* http://www.telegraph.co.uk/finance/yourbusiness/9141572/Sir-Terry-Leahy-on-nobility-of-making-money.html, 14 March.
2. Easton, G. and L. Araujo (1986) Networks, Bonding and Relationships in Industrial Markets, *Industrial Marketing and Purchasing* 1(1), 8–25.
3. This is money.co.uk (2012) http://www.thisismoney.co.uk/money/markets/article-2087765/Dixons-boasts-beating-rivals-Comet-Best-Buy-Xmas-despite-slide-sales.html, 17 January.
4. Airbus (2012) Alternative Fuel Sources http://www.airbus.com/innovation/eco-efficiency/operations/alternative-fuels/.
5. Ries, A. and J. Trout (2005) *Marketing Warfare*, New York: McGraw-Hill.
6. Kotler, P. and R. Singh (1981) Marketing Warfare in the 1980s, *Journal of Business Strategy*, Winter, 30–41.
7. Sun Tzu (1963) *The Art of War*, London: Oxford University Press.
8. Von Clausewitz, C. (1908) *On War*, London: Routledge & Kegan Paul.
9. Jeannet, J.-P. (1987) *Competitive Marketing Strategies in a European Context*, Lausanne: International Management Development Institute, 101.
10. Aaker, D. (2012) Win the brand relevance battle and then build competitor barriers, *The Californian Management Review* 54(2), 43–57.
11. See Aaker, D. and G. S. Day (1986) The Perils of High-Growth Markets, *Strategic Management Journal* 7, 409–21; Wensley, R. (1982) PIMS and BCG: New Horizons or False Dawn?, *Strategic Management Journal* 3, 147–58.
12. Palmer, M. (2006) Cisco Lays Plans to Expand into Home Electronics, *Financial Times*, 16 January, 21.
13. Robertson, J. (2012) Cisco invest $100 million in Insiene with option to buy, http://www.bloomberg.com/news/2012-04-19/cisco-invests-100-million-in-insieme-with-option-to-buy.html, 19 April.
14. Mitchell, J. (2011) http://www.readwriteweb.com/archives/google_plus_games_arrive_to_challenge_facebook.php, 11 August.
15. Kotler and Singh (1981) op. cit.
16. Porter, M. E. (1998) *Competitive Advantage*, New York: Free Press, 514–17.
17. Benady, D. (2008) Trouble in the Air for Virgin, *Marketing Week*, 16 November, 20–1.
18. Hooley, G., J. Saunders, N. Piercy and B. Nicoulaud (2007) *Marketing Strategy and Competitive Positioning*, London: Prentice-Hall, 224.
19. Wildstrom, S. H. (2009) Meet Cisco, the Consumer Company, *Business Week*, 4 May, 73–4.
20. Miller, J. (2011) Chinese companies embark on a shopping spree in Europe, http://online.wsjChinese companies embark i.com/article/SB10001424052748704355304576214683640225122.html, 6 June.
21. Milmo, D. (2012) International Airlines Group completes BMI Acquisition, *The Guardian*, http://www.guardian.co.uk/business/2012/apr/20/iag-bmi-acquisition-british-airways, 20 April.
22. BBC News (2011) BA-owner IAG completes BMI takeover, http://www.bbc.co.uk/news/business-17786998, 20 April.
23. Buehrer, J. (2011) Region: Chinese contractor stiffs Poland http://www.praguepost.com/news/9044-region:-chinese-contractor-stiffs-poland.html, 15 June.
24. London, S. (2001) Risks of Grasping a Tiger by the Tail, *Financial Times*, 10 September, 15.
25. Research conducted by Professor J. Bowers, Harvard Business School, and reported by London (2001) op. cit.
26. See Elgin, B. (2004) A Licence to Print Money but is the System Overloaded at HP?, *Independent on Sunday*, 15 December, 8–9; Teather, D. (2005) HP to Cut 1000 UK Jobs, *The Guardian*, 14 September, 28.
27. *The Economist* (2008) A Bid for Bud, 21 June, 91.

28. Foust, D. (2008) Looks Like a Beer Brawl, *Business Week*, 28 July, 52–3.

29. Ritson, M. (2008) InBev May Create Bud Brand Crisis, *Marketing*, 18 June, 23.

30. Wiggins, J. (2008) Thirst to Be First, *Financial Times*, 24 July, 11.

31. Grossmann, W. (2011) So why did Microsoft buy skype? http://www.guardian.co.uk/commentisfree/2011/may/12/why-did-microsoft-buy-skype, 12 May.

32. Skapinker, M. (2000) Marrying in Haste, *Financial Times*, 12 April, 22.

33. Lorenz, C. (1992) Take your Partner, *Financial Times*, 17 July, 13.

34. Skapinker, M. (2001) Tips for a Beautiful Relationship, *Financial Times*, 11 July, 14.

35. Lorenz, C. (1992) The Risks of Sleeping with the Enemy, *Financial Times*, 16 July, 11.

36. See Crooks, E. and C. Hoyos (2008) BP Pledges to Stay as Partner with Russians as TNK Dispute Ends, *Financial Times*, 5 September, 17; Macalister, T. (2008) Oligarchs to Sue TNK–BP After Failing to Agree Control of Company, *The Guardian*, 12 June, 30.

37. Kotler and Singh (1981) op. cit.

38. Urry, M. (1992) Takeover put Spark into Battery Maker, *Financial Times*, 14 April, 21.

39. Birchall, J. (2008) Wal-Mart Takes on Tesco's US Challenge, *Financial Times*, 14 January, 1.

40. Burrows, P. (2009) How Microsoft is Fighting Back (Finally), *Business Week*, 20 April, 63–4.

41. *Marketing* (2008) Is Tesco's Latest Discount Brands Range A Step Too Far?, 5 November, 24.

42. James, B. J. (1984) *Business Wargames*, London: Abacus.

43. Eastham, J. (2002) Thin Times Ahead for Burger King, *Marketing Week*, 1 August, 19–20.

44. Teather, D. (2006) Vodafone Chief Hailed as Victor in Board Battle, *The Guardian*, 14 March, 25.

45. Peters, T. J. and R. H. Waterman Jr (1995) *In Search of Excellence: Lessons from America's Best-Run Companies*, New York: Harper & Row.

46. Roberts, J. (2009) Hilton's Boutique Brands, *Marketing Week*, 19 April, 15–16.

47. Hammermesh, R. G., M. J. Anderson and J. E. Harris (1978) Strategies for Low Market Share Businesses, *Harvard Business Review* 50(3), 95–102.

48. Anonymous (2008) *Cool Brands*, Superbrands UK Ltd, sponsored supplement to *The Observer*, 20.

49. Hedley, B. (1977) Strategy and the Business Portfolio, *Long Range Planning*, February, 9–15.

50. Nakamoto, M. and A. Yee (2006) Minolta to Stop Making Cameras, *Financial Times*, 20 January, 21.

Air Wars
Airbus vs Boeing

Every day Airbus (www.airbus.com) and Boeing (www.boeing.com) fight an ongoing battle for mastery of the skies. Both these American and European giants of aviation are at loggerheads fighting for every last dollar of the commercial aircraft market. In 2011 Airbus garnered 1608 orders, while Boeing achieved 921 orders, despite a difficult trading environment, and has huge order backlogs. Airbus celebrated this much-lauded triumph over its long-time adversary; however both are cautious about the future in such a volatile market. Many of the large airline carriers are facing bankruptcy, and the market is very susceptible to environmental shocks such as the credit crunch, 9/11, the euro crisis, political upheaval in the Middle East, and any airline crash. The demand is credited with the growth in the low-cost industry, burgeoning demand in Asian markets, new models being launched, and airlines striving to have more fuel-efficient planes in the wake of rising oil prices. The industry is notoriously cyclical: in some years orders have fallen in the world aviation market to just 250 aircraft for the duopoly—for example, in 1994.

The battle for dominance has seen many peaks and troughs. Over the past few years, Airbus has emerged as the industry leader, when it supplanted Boeing. European Airbus rose to prominence due to a strong portfolio of jets, a winning formula of 'commonality', efficient manufacturing, and an excellent reputation. Airbus is the quintessential pan-European company that is the pride of the European Union, showing possible close integration between member countries. The wings are made in Wales, and shipped by barge and boat to France for assembly. Tailfins are made in Germany, while fuselage sections are flown in from Spain, in super-large transport aircraft. The company's headquarters is based in Toulouse, France, but it has a network of manufacturing centres around Europe, and global supply partners. A company called EADS, an amalgam of several European aerospace and defence manufacturing companies, controls Airbus. The integration of several European aerospace companies was the only way the necessary scale could be achieved to take on the might of American giant Boeing. The company built up much of its initial success in the mid-size jet market. Developing 'hit' products in this duopoly is tremendously important as revenues generated can be poured back into the next generation of products used in future battles. This can create a virtuous circle, leaving competitors at a distinct disadvantage. However, Boeing still dominated the large, wide-body aircraft market, reaping huge dividends. Airbus wanted a bigger slice of this market. It decided to develop the world's first double-decker jumbo jet, capable of carrying 555 passengers.

The big gamble

Developing the new A-380 double-decker super jumbo, the largest, most expensive commercial plane ever built, was a big gamble for Airbus, not only in terms of design, technology and manufacturing, but also in terms of capital resources. With so much capital tied up in the development of a new aircraft, any delays in delivery could cripple the firm. Airbus was extremely successful in the mid-size jet market, but the real profit potential lay in the wide-body, long-range jet aircraft like Boeing's iconic 747 jumbo, and its widely popular 777 series. Now at least, however, Airbus has a competitive offering that will test the dominance of the Boeing 747 in the market. The Boeing 747 has been untouched for over five decades, being conceived back in the 1960s. Now demand for 747 is diminishing due to the rising cost of oil, and a 10-year-old 747 costs $36 million. Development of the A-380 began back in 1994, with €12 billion allocated to a formal budget in 1999. Airbus promises that the A-380 will deliver 15–20 per cent lower operating costs than a 747 jumbo. This news set the aircraft industry abuzz. It announced its first customer in 2001, with Singapore Airlines committing to several orders. Other

TABLE C39.1   Airbus vs Boeing—at a glance

Airbus	Boeing
Founded in 1970	Founded in 1916
Headquarters based in Toulouse, France	Headquarters based in Chicago, USA
Employs 55,000	Employs 68,000
The company has received 11,611 orders for aircraft and has delivered more than 7270 aircraft. Airbus has consistently won market share away from arch-rival Boeing. Record number of orders in 2005.	World's largest producer of commercial and military aircraft. Produces the 7 series of commercial aircraft, weapons systems, and satellite launch systems. Three-quarters of the world's 12,000 jets are Boeing aircraft.
2011 Revenue of $22.3 billion	2011 Revenue of $36.2 billion
Orders in 2011 = 1419 new aircraft	Orders in 2011 = 921 new aircraft
Airbus has 14 different aircraft models, ranging in capacity from 100 seats to 555 seats. Its most popular plane is the short haul A-320. The plane is economical and has a moderate flight range. The A-330/340 cater for long haul routes. Airlines love Airbus's commonality feature, which reduces training costs.	The Boeing 7 series of aircraft caters for an array of different markets. The 737 jet is the world's most popular aircraft. Reliable, economic, adaptable, has a moderate range, perfect for short haul flights. The 767, the 777, and the famous jumbo 747 cater for long distance markets.
New products include its new Superjumbo the Airbus A-380, and A-350 series. The A-380 jet is the world's largest commercial jet ever built. The A-350 is a long haul mid sized plane, which boasts greater fuel economy. The A-380 launched in 2007, while the A-350 is expected to launch in 2012.	Its new product the 787 Dreamliner is its primary new focus. The 787 Dreamliner mid-size, long-range jet promises to be super efficient, using advanced materials, engines and components, which results in a 20% reduction in fuel costs per passenger. Large sales orders have already been secured. Launch is 2012. Has over 857 firm orders for the new jet.

customers like Virgin Atlantic envisaged that the new plane could accommodate bars, a beauty saloon and casinos. Its first flight of the test plane took place to much fanfare in April 2005. Despite all the hype, some industry commentators question whether there is a market for planes with 555-capacity.

The scale of the project is breathtaking, with specially built ships used for exclusively transporting sections of the plane to final assembly in Toulouse, specially widened roads to transport sections, and new airport terminals/customer delivery centres created in Toulouse to cater for the handover of the aircraft to airline customers. While Airbus garnered an impressive order book for the A-380 initially, sales quickly slowed. The company now has 253 firm orders for the plane from 19 different operators. The big question in aviation circles is: will volume in terms of capacity lead to

TABLE C39.2   The colossal Superjumbo Airbus A-380 vs the Boeing 747 Jumbo

Features	Airbus A-380	Boeing 747— Stretch Version
Capacity	555	450
Range	15,000 KM	15,000 KM
Speed	560 mph	567 mph
Purchased by	Singapore Airlines Emirates Lufthansa Qantas Virgin Atlantic	Air France British Airways Cathay Pacific Japan Airlines KLM
Cost per plane	$389.9 million	$332.9 million

TABLE C39.3   Airbus vs Boeing—plane by plane

Single aisle passenger planes	Twin aisle passenger planes
90–175 Seats Boeing 737-100 through -500 Boeing 737-600, -700, -800 Airbus A318, A319, A320	**230–340 Seats (Small)** Boeing 767, 787 Airbus A330-200 Airbus A350-800
More than 175 Seats Boeing 737-900ER Airbus A321	**340–450 Seats (Medium)** Boeing 777 Airbus A330-300, A340 Airbus A350-900, -1000
	More than 400 Seats Boeing 747-8 Airbus A380 Boeing 747

profit for airlines? Some contend that the new super-jumbo could potentially create a viable low-cost, long-haul operation, while others view the market as needing only mid-size, long-range, fuel-efficient, twin-engine jets for the global market, moving away from these super carriers. Consumers want to fly non-stop to destinations rather than through congested hub airports.

The double-decker jumbo will take years to become a core profit centre for the Airbus group. The challenge for Airbus was to build a super-jumbo at a reasonable cost, and get enough airlines interested in the project to make it viable. The firm cites 2015 as its break-even target for the project. Some of the big carriers are sitting in the wings waiting to see how things pan out, before taking a gamble. With $12 billion invested, it is huge table-stakes poker. It is hoped that it will dominate the sector for the next twenty years, like its predecessor the Boeing 747. It does not want the A-380 to be the next Concorde, which was an unmitigated commercial disaster, and yet a technological marvel. After 15 years in development the first A380 entered service in 2007 with Singapore Airlines. However, the alarm bells sounded in Toulouse when cracks appeared on some of the A380 wings, causing consternation. As a result their super jumbo fleet had to be retrofitted with extra brackets within the wings, costing an additional $332 million to Airbus. This was coupled with the dramatic failure of an A380's Rolls-Royce engine after taking off in Singapore in 2010.

Boeing bounces back

After seeing years of decline, problems with production, and the company mired in a spate of corporate ethic scandals, Boeing is now boasting a strong order book and claims to have left its troubles behind. The company was beleaguered by corporate woes such as charges of corporate espionage, harassment, and political shenanigans surrounding military contracts that have cost two CEOs their job. In 2003 the firm lost its coveted status as the world's No. 1 commercial aircraft manufacturer to Airbus. In an effort to recapture the lead, Boeing is banking on the introduction of its highly innovative 787 'Dreamliner' jet. This radical plane is made from ground-breaking materials, using lightweight yet super-strong, carbon-fibre technology. This is its first all-new aircraft in over a decade. The company is using the technology developed in the Dreamliner project in its other aircraft. Rising energy costs for airlines makes the fuel efficiency of aircraft a key selling point for the plane. This has led the Dreamliner to be a hot seller for Boeing, with sales of over 850 to 59 different customers. The jet aims to use 20 per cent less fuel, fewer emissions, and is quieter.

The success of Dreamliner led Airbus to launch the A-350, its foray into the long-range, mid-sized, fuel-efficient market,

delivery of which is estimated to be in 2017, five years behind the planned release date. Airbus has attracted 548 orders for its competing plane. Boeing for the first time has outsourced several core aspects of the plane's manufacturing, to cut down on costs and access key technology. Over 80 per cent of the plane's structure is being fabricated by external suppliers, unlike the typical 51 per cent for other Boeing aircraft. Sections of the plane are built in Japan and Italy, and are flown into the USA. Boeing is experiencing a rise in demand thanks to the popularity of its two fuel-efficient, long-range jets, in the midst of rising energy prices, the 777 and the 787. With its attention focused on the launch of its super-jumbo, Airbus failed to see the same opportunity as Boeing in the market seeking a long-range, mid-sized jet like the Dreamliner.

Like Airbus, Boeing is wrestling with production difficulties with the Dreamliner project due to delays in testing the new groundbreaking technology. These glitches have led to missed deadlines, which pushes out delivery times. Also a 57-day strike exacerbated the problem, costing Boeing $100m a day. If delivery times are not met, huge penalty clauses are invoked. Over 90 per cent of the plane's value is paid on delivery. In the late 1990s the firm tried to build too many planes, leading to overstretched production lines, and inevitable delays, resulting in penalties of $2.5 billion. The company's reputation for reliability was irrevocably damaged. Airbus won many subsequent airline orders from new business as a result. Both companies have huge production backlogs. Now Boeing is regaining the momentum, with strong sales for its ever-popular 737 series from low-cost airlines, new product development and a strong order book for the new Dreamliner. Also, the company recently launched a 'stretch' version of its 747 jumbo jet series to fight against Airbus's new super jumbo, proclaiming larger capacities and greater efficiency, although demand for these colossal traditional 747 planes is weak owing to higher operational costs.

Airbus has the ability to build planes for less, even with all the logistical complexities associated with assembly. This allows for greater flexibility in setting prices for the aircraft, which were real deal clinchers. Now Boeing has upped its game through excellent product innovation and improvements in manufacturing operations. Selling aircraft is a long and laborious process, yet the battles between Airbus and Boeing are worth billions and affect countries' balance of trade. Both firms fight bitter contests to pitch to clients, some going down to the wire with last-minute deals being cut, using an array of discounts, financing and leasing options, as well as extra training and service arrangements for clients.

Both companies receive state aid from national governments, which both largely dispute, and which gives rise to charges of unfair competition between both parties. This has led to heated debates between the US and Europe over trade subsidies. Both demand a level playing field, yet both garner lucrative tax breaks, repayable launch aid, indirect research and technological subsidies and a whole array of other state support, worth billions. The governments of Britain, France, Germany and Spain contribute money to safeguard their aerospace industry in their respective countries, and protect jobs. For instance, the new A-350 costs $4.35 billion to develop, a third of which has been sought in state aid support. The row over subsidies has nearly led to a trade war between the USA and Europe on several occasions. Commercial Aircraft Corporation of China is seen as possibly the next aviation industry rival to emerge, given the country's manufacturing prowess. Airbus has entered a joint venture with the Chinese concern to manufacture four A320 jets a year, since they realize there will be technological transfer to the Chinese. However, the initiative will lead to enhanced access in the booming Chinese market. Boeing estimates that the Asia Pacific market is estimated to grow at least 7 per cent per year up until 2030.

As with any war, the battle ebbs and flows. One thing is sure. Within such an industry this intense rivalry between Airbus and Boeing is good for the industry. Boeing has bet on medium-sized, fuel-efficient planes, while Airbus has gambled on very large super-jumbo carriers.

Questions

1. Why is the aircraft manufacturing industry dominated by only two companies? Discuss the barriers to entry that exist in the market.

2. Critically appraise Airbus's decision to enter the super-jumbo market by launching its double-decker A-380 plane.

3. Develop a competitive marketing strategy for Airbus in the wake of Boeing's success with its new 'Dreamliner' 787 jet.

This case was written by Dr Conor Carroll, Lecturer in Marketing, University of Limerick. Copyright © Conor Carroll (2012). The material in the case has been drawn from a variety of published sources.

Data Display is a manufacturing company based in County Clare in Ireland, operating from offices in Europe, Australia and North America. Even though it is located on the periphery of Europe, it has established a reputation as one of the world's leading suppliers of electronic information displays to customers such as Siemens, Warner Cinemas and London Underground. To reach this position, Data Display has had to engage in careful market analysis, the results of which have directed its strategy in a highly competitive and dynamic marketplace dominated by multinational companies. This has resulted in the company focusing on developing high-quality, state-of-the-art products and technologies, diversifying into three key industries, building strong relationships with customers who can also be competitors, and building a strong network of strategic alliances to help compete with larger competitors.

Many of Data Display's customers are international blue-chip companies, which compete for multi-million-dollar/pound/euro contracts in three different industry sectors: road, rail and cinema. For example, in the rail industry, the company has won major contracts to supply electronic signs to transport agencies worldwide, including the New York Subway, the London Underground, Seattle's Public Transport System and the Paris Metro. The signs provided by Data Display are only one part of a much bigger bid by a large multinational, and mean that the company must meet the highest international quality standards to produce systems that integrate seamlessly, and operate flawlessly, with every system it bids for.

One of the major strengths of the company is being agile enough to react to whatever the customer wants. One of the biggest advantages for Data Display is that it has an international direct salesforce, which constantly feeds the management team with the latest market trends and pertinent market intelligence. This invaluable feedback mechanism allows the firm to adapt to changing market needs, and adjust and enhance product offerings. Since it was established in 1990, Data Display has used a highly competitive marketing strategy to support its growth, to a point where it now offers an unrivalled range of technologies, which means that it can provide complete display solutions, incorporating software and hardware components, that are designed and produced in-house to meet customer requirements.

The company has an interesting relationship with its customers. The nature of the industry means that Data Display is an SME competing against much larger firms, and selling to multinational firms. It needs to close two sales to get one sale. First, it needs to sell to its customers; once it has been selected as the nominated electronic signage partner for its customer, it then becomes part of its customer's sales team and helps them to bid against their competitors for the overall project. This means that the company invests a lot of time and money in travel, meetings, tenders and prototype development, without any guarantee of achieving a sale. For example, a multinational company such as Siemens could be involved in a bid tendering for an upgrade of New York City Subway. In turn, Siemens would then look for tenders from each of its sub-suppliers for each component required in the upgrade. One of these sub-suppliers might be Data Display, which would be asked to tender for the electronic display sign section of the contract. Notably, Data Display could be in competition with Siemens itself in this part of the tender process. However, assuming that Data Display wins the tender, it then becomes part of the Siemens sales team in the bid for the overall tender from New York City subway. The overall Siemens bid is judged on many elements, some of which include the price, reputation, quality and standards of each of its sub-suppliers and their sub-suppliers. Thus, quality assurance is crucial for Data Display.

> **TABLE C40.1   Data display at a glance**

Background

Founded by Kevin Neville in 1979

Designs and manufactures customized electronic information displays

Generates nearly €20 million a year in revenue

'Europe's leading supplier of electronic information displays'

Location of Data Display

Data Display headquarters is based in the picturesque town of Ennistymon, Co. Clare. Ennistymon is a small town on Ireland's westerly seaboard; Data Display is the town's largest employer; approximately 263 km from Dublin

Location of Data Display sales offices	Clients include:
• Data Display USA	• New York Metro
• Data Display UK	• Warner Cinemas
• Data Display Ireland	• Charles De Gaulle Airport
• Data Display France	• Heathrow Express
• Data Display Netherlands	• London Underground
• Data Display Portugal	• Copenhagen Stock Exchange
• Data Display Sweden (TA Poltech)	• National Amusements
	• Seattle Light Rail

Types of product sold	Markets include:
LCD display signs	Public transport—rail and bus
Datalines	Road
Data boards	Airports
TFT displays	Banks
Reception displays	Cinemas
Advertising displays	Call centres
Ticker displays	Shopping centres
Forecourt petrol displays	Forecourt stations
Large departure boards	Hotels and conference centres
Large highway signs	Leisure parks and stadia
	Municipalities
	Banks
	Stock markets

Operating in such a remote, beautiful location has both advantages and notable drawbacks. The company has an intensely loyal and dedicated workforce, who are focused on ensuring Data Display's success, as there are limited job opportunities in a small town such as Ennistymon. The factory itself is one of the company's most powerful selling tools. Potential clients are invited to the factory, a hive of activity showcasing the plant's excellent manufacturing capability. On the downside, coordinating an international sales effort from the periphery of Europe presents unique challenges for the firm. Many commentators within Ireland see the manufacturing industry in Ireland as unsustainable due to competition from low-cost countries.

The marketplace is constantly evolving due to technology. Markets are being created in new sectors that were previously unviable and not technically feasible. For example, with outdoor advertising, the costs of installing a high-impact display suitable for advertising have fallen dramatically. Now these displays can be powered through low-cost solar energy units, and the content can be managed remotely through 3G mobile technologies. Technology advancements provide both new opportunities and threats for the business.

In order to invest its limited resources widely and not spend too much time chasing sales that won't result in a winning bid, Data Display needs to use marketing intelligence and expertise to maximize every opportunity identified, bearing in mind the investment required to close the sale and the potential profit from the deal. However, once it closes the two sales, the company becomes deeply embedded with its customer and their customer. This is highlighted on its website, where it illustrates that, 'At Data Display, we think long term regarding the relationships we have with our

FIGURE C40.1   Two of Data Display's largest markets for display devices are film information in cinemas and traffic information on roads

customers, and in relation to the products and services with which we provide them. This is why we design our electronic display solutions with long-term performance and ease of maintenance in mind, and back them up with a comprehensive range of after-sales support options.'

In looking to its positioning within a highly competitive, dynamic market, Data Display has clearly identified that low-cost competition from the Far East makes specialization and customization of its products essential. Mass-produced products from the Far East enjoy economies of scale with which Data Display cannot hope to compete on price; thus, it needs to be cost-effective for its customers, but also to provide a level of customization that makes it unattractive for its customers to purchase more cost-effective products: 'Everything we do is in a niche because otherwise we'd be up against mass markets, and if we were up against mass markets, then as a small company we can't compete.' This approach is feasible only if Data Display adopts a market-centred approach, focusing on customer needs.

To survive in this market, Data Display has spread its risk by operating across three industries: cinema, rail and road. In each of these it has competitors, none of which competes in all three markets. Data Display's success in the face of such competition can be attributed to two factors: first, its participation in different markets, each of which has its own economic cycle, so when one market is depressed Data Display concentrates on a more buoyant market; second, it has formed strategic alliances with similar companies in other countries—Australia, Estonia, France, Germany,

> **The marketplace is constantly evolving due to technology. Markets are being created in new sectors that were previously unviable and not technically feasible.**

Ireland, Israel, Italy, the Netherlands, Portugal, Spain, Sweden, the UK and the USA. These alliances mean that Data Display can mimic the business strategies and models of much larger companies; this reassures large customers, which like the reassurance of dealing with a larger rather than small company. Furthermore, having a local presence reassures customers.

Data Display is one of the longest-established manufacturers in a highly competitive market, with new entrants entering and exiting the market on a regular basis. It has survived and grown in this market based on its clear identification of its competitive advantage in a global market as being based on its commitment to customer service, in combination with its flexibility in providing the best dedicated solutions for each customer. It would be wrong to envisage Data Display as a just a simple manufacturing company, producing an array of products for industrial clients. The company is solution-driven, rather than a product company. When a potential client comes to Data Display with a problem, it develops a customized solution to that problem. For example, the firm's R&D section would develop a customized design solution for that particular customer, matching their particular specifications. Customized management software would be developed for the particular client (e.g. a cinema chain required software that would display information over the auditorium, the screens and outdoors). For example, the company has created highly customized products for its client base, with numerous value-added benefits for customers. One of its products has an inbuilt diagnostics system that will identify to a controller problems within the system, down to the exact location of a fault (e.g. one faulty LED on a display array). This type of value-added mechanism allows clients to make repairs quickly and cost effectively, causing minimal disruption. The sale of 10-year maintenance contracts for display systems is a lucrative additional revenue stream. The firm will look after the whole life-cycle cost of a display solution.

Data Display engages in a proactive approach towards its suppliers, customers, products, processes and technologies. This approach is necessary in order for Data Display to identify and successfully engage multinational companies in a highly intuitive sales process. In engaging with such multinational companies Data Display must illustrate its competences, quality benchmarking, change management skills and ability to service a world-class multinational relationship in the face of strong international low-cost competition. Data Display is successful in this domain given its strength of relationships with clients that demand excellence.

Questions

1. What is Data Display's source of competitive advantage?

2. Discuss the merits of Data Display's strategic focus in building its business.

3. Assess Data Display's relationship with its customers.

This case was written by Dr Michele O'Dwyer, Lecturer in Entrepreneurship, and Conor Carroll, Lecturer in Marketing, University of Limerick.

CHAPTER 21

Global marketing strategy

> *I want to be a good Frenchman in France and a good Italian in Italy. My strategy is to go global when I can and stay local when I must.*
>
> **ERIC JOHANNSON,**
> **FORMER PRESIDENT OF ELECTROLUX**

LEARNING OBJECTIVES

After reading this chapter, you should be able to:

1. explain why companies seek foreign markets
2. discuss the factors that influence which foreign market to enter
3. identify and discuss the range of foreign market entry strategies
4. identify the factors influencing foreign market entry strategies
5. discuss the influences on the degree of standardization or adaptation
6. discuss the special considerations involved in designing an international marketing mix
7. explain how to organize for international marketing operations

Today's managers need international marketing skills to be able to compete in an increasingly global marketplace. They require the capabilities to identify and seize opportunities that arise across the world. Failure to do so brings stagnation and decline, not only to individual companies but also to whole regions. Global expansion and exports are important to all nations and all sectors. The contribution to the economy varies by sector: for example, in 2010 the EU textile sector exported €33.8 billion of goods, whereas the automotive industry exported €132 billion.[1]

The importance of international and global marketing is reflected in the support given by governmental bodies set up to encourage and aid export activities. For example, UK Trade & Investment (UKTI) is a government body that works with UK-based businesses to help them succeed in overseas markets, whether they are trying to establish a new business or exporting to a new country. The services offered include: providing expert advice on international trade and export; taking part in trade fairs and outward trade missions; providing market intelligence; identifying international business opportunities; and helping to develop international business relationships.[2]

The purpose of this chapter is to explore four issues in developing global marketing strategies; 1) whether to go international or stay domestic; 2) the factors that impact upon the selection of countries in which to market; 3) foreign market entry strategies; 4) the options available for companies developing international marketing strategies.

Deciding Whether to Go Global or Stay Local

Many companies shy away from the prospect of competing internationally. They know their domestic market better, and they would have to come to terms with the customs, language, tariff regulations, transport systems and trading in foreign currencies. Furthermore, their products may require significant modifications to meet foreign regulations and different customer preferences. So, why do companies choose to market abroad? There are seven triggers for international expansion (see Fig. 21.1).

Saturated domestic markets

The pressure to raise sales and profits, coupled with few opportunities to expand in current domestic markets, provide one condition for international expansion. This has been a major driving force behind Tesco's expansion into Europe, Asia and the US. In 1997 less than 2 per cent of the group's profits were generated by international trade. In 2012 foreign trade accounted for 25 per cent of the profits. Many of the foreign expansion plans of European supermarket chains are fuelled by the desire to take a proven retailing formula out of their saturated domestic market into new overseas markets. Currently, many retailers, including Carrefour, Wal-mart and Tesco, are focusing on emerging markets in India, Brazil and China and looking at expansion opportunities with existing formats or new offerings. Tesco aims to make its F&F fashion label a major global brand, using a franchising model and local business partners to grow a network of stand-alone stores and in-store concessions. The retailer has already expanded into 11 countries (mainly in Europe).[3]

FIGURE 21.1 Triggers for international expansion

Saturated domestic markets
Small domestic markets
Low-growth domestic markets
Customer drivers
Competitive forces
Cost factors
Portfolio balance

↓

Internationalization

Small domestic markets

In some industries survival means broadening scope beyond small national markets to the international arena. For example, Philips, Nokia and Electrolux (electrical goods) could not compete against the strength of global competitors by servicing their small domestic market alone. For them, internationalization was not an option: it was a fundamental condition for survival.

Low-growth domestic markets

Often recession at home provides the spur to seek new marketing opportunities in more buoyant overseas economies. BMW has been exploiting the demand for luxury cars in China while its home markets in Europe are experiencing slow growth. In China sales rose by 76 per cent compared to 13 per cent in Europe. VW has also announced a significant increase in profits thanks to increase in demand in these overseas markets. Indeed China has been a key contributor to strong performances by many European car manufacturers.[4]

Customer drivers

Customer-driven factors may also affect the decision to go global. In some industries customers may expect their suppliers to have an international presence. This is increasingly common in advertising, with clients requiring their agencies to coordinate international campaigns. A second customer-orientated factor is the need to internationalize operations in response to customers expanding abroad.

Competitive forces

There is a substantial body of research which suggests that when several companies in an industry go abroad, others feel obliged to follow suit to maintain their relative size and growth rate.[5] This is particularly true in oligopolistic industries. A second competitive factor may be the desire to attack, in their own home market, an overseas competitor that has entered our domestic market. This may make strategic sense if the competitor is funding its overseas expansion from a relatively attractive home base.

Cost factors

High national labour costs, shortages of skilled workers, and rising energy charges can raise domestic costs to uneconomic levels. These factors may stimulate moves towards foreign direct investment in low-cost areas such as China, Taiwan, Korea, and central and eastern Europe. Expanding into foreign markets can also reduce costs by gaining economies of scale through an enlarged customer base.

Portfolio balance

Marketing in a variety of regions provides the opportunity to achieve portfolio balance as each region may be experiencing different growth rates. At any one time, the USA, Japan, individual European and Far Eastern countries will be enjoying varying growth rates. By marketing in a selection of countries, the problems of recession in some countries can be balanced by the opportunities for growth in others.

Deciding Which Markets to Enter

Having made the commitment to enter international territories, marketing managers require the analytical skills necessary to pick those countries and regions that are most attractive for overseas operations. Two sets of factors will govern this decision: macroenvironmental issues and microenvironmental issues. These are shown in Figure 21.2.

Macroenvironmental issues

These consist of *economic*, *socio-cultural* and *political-legal technological influences* on market choice.

Economic influences

A country's size, per capita income, stage of economic development, infrastructure, and exchange rate stability and conversion affect its attractiveness for international business expansion. Small markets may not justify setting up a distribution and marketing system to

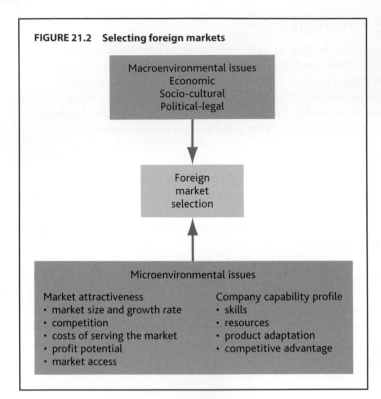

FIGURE 21.2 Selecting foreign markets

Macroenvironmental issues
Economic
Socio-cultural
Political-legal

Foreign
market
selection

Microenvironmental issues

Market attractiveness
• market size and growth rate
• competition
• costs of serving the market
• profit potential
• market access

Company capability profile
• skills
• resources
• product adaptation
• competitive advantage

supply goods and services. Low per capita income will affect the type of product that may sell in that country. The market may be very unattractive for car manufacturers but feasible for bicycle producers. Less developed countries, in the early stages of economic development, may demand inexpensive agricultural tools but not computers. Research into the decision to enter a new foreign market found that the issue that had the greatest impact was that the country had a developed economy, emphasizing the importance of economic considerations in this decision.[6]

The economic changes that have taken place globally have had varying effects on each country's attractiveness. For example, Russia has moved from being a nation on the verge of bankruptcy to a high growth economy, with GDP of about $2 trillion.[7] A key driver of change has been the shift from a centrally managed to a free market economy. Another economic consideration is a nation's infrastructure. This comprises the transportation structures (roads, railways, airports), communication systems (telephone, television, the press, radio) and energy supplies (electricity, gas, nuclear). A poor infrastructure may limit the ability to manufacture, advertise and distribute goods, and provide adequate service back-up. Some central and eastern European countries suffer because of this. In other areas of Europe infrastructure improvements are enhancing communications—for example, the ambitious, if costly, Eurotunnel that links the UK with mainland Europe, and the bridge and tunnel that connect the two main parts of Denmark.

Finally, exchange rate stability and conversion may affect market choice. A country that has an unstable exchange rate or one that is difficult to convert to hard currencies such as the dollar or euro may be considered too risky to enter.

Socio-cultural influences

Differences in socio-cultural factors between countries are often termed *psychic distance*. These are the barriers created by cultural disparities between the home country and the host country, and the problems of communication resulting from differences in social perspectives, attitudes and language.[8] This can have an important effect on selection. International marketers sometimes choose countries that are psychically similar to begin their overseas operations. This has a rationale in that barriers of language, customs and values are lower. It also means that less time and effort is required to develop successful business relationships.[9] Research looking at Swedish manufacturing firms showed that they often begin by entering new markets that are psychically close—that is, both culturally and geographically—and gained experience in these countries before expanding operations abroad into more distant markets.[10] This has also been found to be the case for service firms that move from culturally similar foreign markets into less familiar markets as their experience grows.[11] Language, in particular, has caused many well-documented problems for marketing communications in international markets. Classic communication faux pas resulting from translation errors in brand names include: General Motors car called Nova which means 'doesn't go' in Spanish; Mitsubishi had to change the name Pajero in Spanish-speaking countries because it is a slang word meaning masturbator; Toyota's MR2 is pronounced 'merde' in French which translates to excrement, while Nissan's Moco means mucus in Spanish. In addition, history, religion and culture have also been found to influence the attractiveness of a global market and competitive positioning.[12] Greater knowledge of the history of a country and the resulting culture and economic performance can assist marketing managers in developing a better understanding of the social fabric of a new market. For example, in Indian supermarkets they do not display as many varieties of individual products as Western supermarket do, e.g. bread. Careful analysis of the history of a nation and its cultural heritage can offer an insight into its business behaviour. Read the Research 21.1 explores cultural influences on global marketing strategy.

Read the Research 21.1 Cultural Influences on Global Marketing Strategies

Over the years there has been a lot of publicity about parallel importing, particularly within the pharmaceutical industry. Parallel importing occurs when products bought unofficially in foreign countries by companies or people who then sell them more cheaply than usual in their own countries. This article looks at the problem within the pharmaceutical industry, and how it has responded to changes in intellectual property rights and trade barriers within the EU.

> *Margaret Kyle (2011) Strategic Responses to Parallel Trade,* Journal of Economic Analysis & Policy Advances, 11(2), Article 2.

How do senior executives go about creating a global strategy? This is what these authors are attempting to show. With primary data from 134 companies across a wide spectrum of industries, they look at the processes through which top executive attention is channelled and structured. They develop their ideas around the linkages between a firm's operating environment, its internal organization and global outlook.

> *Cyril Bouquet and Julian Birkinshaw (2011) How Global Strategies Emerge: An Attention Perspective,* Global Strategy Journal, 1, 243–62.

Go to the website to consider how the Benetton Unhate campaign might impact on its global marketing strategy.
www.mcgraw-hill.co.uk/textbooks/jobber

Political-legal influences

Political factors which have implications for global marketing are: the general attitudes of foreign governments to imports and foreign direct investment; political stability; governmental policies; and trade barriers. Negative attitudes towards foreign firms may also discourage imports and investment because of the threat of protectionism and expropriation of assets. Positive governmental attitudes can be reflected in the willingness to grant subsidies to overseas firms to invest in a country and a willingness to cut through bureaucratic procedures to assist foreign firms and their imports. The willingness of the UK government to grant investment incentives to Japanese firms was a factor in Nissan, Honda and Toyota setting up production facilities there.

Eagerness to promote imports has not always been a feature of Japanese attitudes, however. Until recently, imports of electrical goods were hampered by the fact that each one had to be inspected by government officials. Also, their patent laws rule that patents are made public after 18 months but are not granted for four to six years. In many Western countries patents remain secret until they are granted. The Japanese system discourages high-technology firms and others that wish to protect their patents from entering Japan. Legal regulations can also act as a barrier. For example, Russian government regulations classify beer as 'perishable' even though when canned it has a shelf life of up to a year. This forces companies to refrigerate beer when it is transported, pushing up costs.[13]

Countries with a history of political instability may be avoided because of the inevitable uncertainty regarding their future. Countries such as Iraq and Lebanon have undoubtedly suffered because of their respective political situations.

Government policies can also influence market entry. For example, the Chinese government's censorship of information has been a barrier to the early entry of Google into that country, although it is now there, competing with such companies as Yahoo! and Microsoft, even though Facebook is still not welcome.

Finally, a major consideration when deciding which countries to enter will be the level of tariff barriers. Undoubtedly the threat of tariff barriers to imports to the countries of the EU has encouraged US and Japanese foreign direct investment into Europe. Within the single market the removal of trade barriers is making international trade in Europe more attractive, as not only do tariffs fall but, in addition, the need to modify products to cater for national regulations and restrictions is reduced.

Technological influences

The Internet has had a profound influence on global market expansion and we have discussed many examples throughout the book of how companies have used the Internet and associated technologies to grow market share both nationally and internationally. However, when considering the influence of technology on market entry, it is important to understand the information and communication technology (ICT) infrastructure of a nation as it is essential particularly in emerging economies for there to be a high-quality infrastructure in place. ICT is particularly important for the coordination of movement of goods, transportation, global production and for cross-border investment.[14]

Microenvironmental issues

While the macroenvironmental analysis provides indications of how attractive each country is to an international marketer, microenvironmental analysis focuses on the attractiveness of the particular market being considered, and the company capability profile.

Market attractiveness

Market attractiveness can be assessed by determining market size and growth rate, competition, costs of serving the market, profit potential and market access.

- *Market size and growth rate*: large, growing markets (other things being equal) provide attractive conditions for market entry. Research supports the notion that market growth is a more important consideration than market size.[15] It is expectations about future demand rather than existing demand that are important, particularly for foreign direct investment. It is China's enormous market size and growth rate that is attracting the UK's Tesco, France's Carrefour and Louis Vuitton, and Germany's Metro and Tengelmann.[16] Russia's large and growing market is also attracting multinationals like Unilever, PepsiCo, Kellogg's, Kraft, Nestlé, Coca-Cola and Carlsberg, which have made large-scale acquisitions in the country.[17]

- *Competition*: markets that are already served by strong, well-entrenched competitors may dampen enthusiasm for foreign market entry. However, when a competitive weakness is identified a decision to enter may be taken. For example, Tesco, the leading UK supermarket chain, spotted an opportunity on the west coast of the USA, based on Wal-Mart's weakness in the convenience sector. Tesco has entered the market based on a small store format targeting the 'top-up' shopper.[18] However, volatility of competition also appears to reduce the attractiveness of overseas markets. Highly volatile markets, with many competitors entering and leaving the market and where market concentration is high, are particularly unattractive.[19] Dixons Retail saw an opportunity in the US and bought Silo, an electronics retailer. However, it was unable to handle the ensuing competition from bigger US rivals and decided to withdraw, writing off more than £200 million in the process.[20]

- *Costs of serving the market*: two major costs of servicing foreign markets are distribution and control. As geographic distance increases, so these two costs rise. Many countries' major export markets are in neighbouring countries—such as the USA, whose largest market is Canada. Costs are also dependent on the form of market entry. Obviously, foreign direct investment is initially more expensive than using distributors. Some countries may not possess suitable low-cost entry options, making entry less attractive and more risky. Long internal distribution channels (e.g. as in Japan) can also raise costs as middlemen demand their profit margins. If direct investment is being contemplated, labour costs and the supply of skilled labour will also be a consideration. Finally, some markets may prove unattractive because of the high marketing expenditures necessary to compete in them.

- *Profit potential*: some markets may be unattractive because industry structure leaves them with poor profit potential. For example, the existence of powerful buying groups may reduce profit potential through their ability to negotiate low prices.
- *Market access*: some foreign markets may prove difficult to penetrate because of informal ties between existing suppliers and distributors. Without the capability of setting up a new distribution chain, this would mean that market access would effectively be barred. Links between suppliers and customers in organizational markets would also form a barrier. In some countries and markets, national suppliers are given preferential treatment. The German machine tool industry is a case in point, as is defence procurement in many western European countries.

Company capability profile

Company capability to serve a foreign market also needs to be assessed: this depends on skills, resources, product adaptation and competitive advantage.

- *Skills*: does the company have the necessary skills to market abroad? If not, can sales agents or distributors compensate for any shortfalls? Does the company have the necessary skills to understand the requirements of each market? For example, when VW established Volkswagen Financial Services in Milton Keynes one of the biggest concerns about locating in this operation in the UK was the availability of a workforce with the right skills. The operation is now based in Milton Keynes and employs 400 people which serve 250,000 customers.
- *Resources*: different countries may have varying market servicing costs. Does the company have the necessary financial resources to compete effectively in them? Human resources also need to be considered as some markets may demand domestically supplied personnel.
- *Product adaptation*: for some foreign markets, local preferences and regulations may require the product to be modified. Does the company have the motivation and capability to redesign the product?
- *Competitive advantage*: a key consideration in any market is the ability to create a competitive advantage. Each foreign market needs to be studied in the light of the company's current and future ability to create and sustain a competitive advantage.

Deciding How to Enter a Foreign Market

Go to the website and see how Fiat and Gucci appear together in an internal campaign to promote the Fiat 500.
www.mcgraw-hill.co.uk/textbooks/jobber

Once a firm has decided to enter a foreign market, it must choose a mode of entry—that is, select an institutional arrangement for organizing and conducting international marketing activities.

See the Ad Insight to learn more about how government agencies and agents can help with entering and buying in foreign markets.

The choice of foreign market entry strategy is likely to have a major impact on a company's performance overseas.[21] Each mode of entry has its own associated levels of commitment, risks, control and profit potential. The major options are indirect exporting, direct exporting, licensing, joint ventures, and direct investment either in new facilities or through acquisition (see Fig. 21.3).

Indirect exporting

Indirect exporting involves the use of independent organizations within the exporter's domestic market; these include the following:

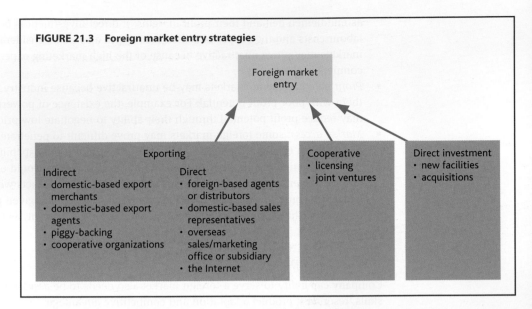

FIGURE 21.3 Foreign market entry strategies

1 *Domestic-based export merchants* who take title to the products and sell them abroad.
2 *Domestic-based export agents* who sell on behalf of the exporter but do not take title to the products; agents are usually paid by commission.
3 *Piggy-backing*, whereby the exporter uses the overseas distribution facilities of another producer.
4 *Cooperative organizations*, which act on behalf of a number of producers and are partly controlled by them; many producers of primary products, such as fruit and nuts, export through cooperative organizations.

Indirect exporting has three advantages. First, the exporting organization is domestically based, making communication easier than using foreign intermediaries. Second, investment and risk are lower than setting up one's own sales and marketing facility. Third, use can be made of the exporting organization's knowledge of selling abroad.

Direct exporting

As exporters grow more confident, they may decide to undertake their own exporting task. This will involve building up overseas contracts, undertaking marketing research, handling documentation and transportation, and designing marketing-mix strategies. **Direct exporting** modes include export through foreign-based agents or distributors (independent middlemen), a domestic-based salesforce, an overseas sales/marketing office or subsidiary, and via the Internet.

Foreign-based agents or distributors

Most companies use specialist agents or distributors in some or all of their exporting abroad. Over 60 per cent of US companies use them for some or all of their export activity, and for European firms the figure rises to over 70 per cent.[22] Agents may be *exclusive*, where the agreement is between the exporter and the agent alone; *semi-exclusive*, where the agent handles the exporter's goods along with other non-competing goods from other companies; or *non-exclusive*, where the agent handles a variety of goods, including some that may compete with the exporter's products.

Distributors, unlike agents, take title to the goods, and are paid according to the difference between the buying and selling prices rather than commission. Distributors are often appointed when after-sales service is required as they are more likely to possess the necessary resources than agents.

The advantages of both agents and distributors are that they are familiar with the local market, customs and conventions, have existing business contracts and employ foreign nationals. They have a direct incentive to sell through either commission or profit margin, but, since their remuneration is tied to sales, they may be reluctant to devote much time and effort to developing a market for a new product. Also, the amount of market feedback may be limited as the agent or distributor may see themselves as a purchasing agent for their customers rather than a selling agent for the exporter.

Overall, exporting through independent middlemen is a low-investment method of market entry although significant expenditure in marketing may be necessary. Also, it can be difficult and costly to terminate an agreement with them, which suggests that this option should be viewed with care and not seen as an easy method of market entry.

Domestic-based sales representatives

As the sales representative is a company employee, greater control of activities compared to that when using independent middlemen can be expected. A company has no control over the attention an agent or distributor gives to its products or the amount of market feedback provided, whereas it can insist that various activities be performed by its sales representatives.

Also, the use of company employees shows a commitment to the customer that the use of agents or distributors may lack. Consequently, they are often used in industrial markets, where there are only a few large customers who require close contact with suppliers, and where the size of orders justifies the expense of foreign travel. This method of market servicing is also found when selling to government buyers and retail chains, for similar reasons.

Overseas sales/marketing office or subsidiary

This option displays even greater customer commitment than using domestic-based sales representatives, although the establishment of a local office requires a greater investment. However, the exporter may be perceived as an indigenous supplier, improving its chances of market success. In some markets, where access to distribution channels is limited, selling direct through an overseas sales office may be the only feasible way of breaking into a new market. The sales office or subsidiary acts as a centre for foreign-based sales representatives, handles sales distribution and promotion, and can act as a customer service centre.

The Internet

The global reach of the Internet means that companies can now engage in exporting activities direct to customers. By creating a website, overseas customers can be made aware of a company's products and ordering can be direct. Products can be supplied straight to the customer without the need for an intermediary. The Internet is not only a channel to market but also a useful research tool.

Licensing

Licensing refers to contracts in which a foreign licensor provides a local licensee with access to one or a set of technologies or know-how in exchange for financial compensation.[23] The licensee will normally have exclusive rights to produce and market the product within an agreed area for a specific period of time in return for a *royalty* based on sales volume. A licence may relate to the use of a patent for either a product or process, copyright, trademarks and trade secrets (e.g. designs and software), and know-how (e.g. product and process specifications).

Licensing agreements allow the exporter to enter markets that otherwise may be closed for exports or other forms of market entry, without the need to make substantial capital investments in the host country. However, control of production is lost and the reputation of the licensor is dependent on the performance of the licensee. A grave danger of licensing is the loss of product and process know-how to third parties, which may become competitors once the agreement is at an end.

The need to exploit new technology simultaneously in many markets has stimulated the growth in licensing by small high-tech companies that lack the resources to set up their own sales and market offices, engage in joint ventures or conduct direct investment abroad. Licensing is also popular in R&D-intensive industries such as pharmaceuticals, chemicals and synthetic fibres, where rising research and development costs have encouraged licensing as a form of reciprocal technology exchange.

Sometimes the licensed product has to be adapted to suit local culture. For example, packaging that uses red and yellow, the colours of the Spanish flag, is seen as an offence to Spanish patriotism; in Greece purple should be avoided as it has funereal associations; and the licensing of a movie, TV show or book whose star is a cute little pig will have no prospect of success in Muslim countries, where the pig is considered an unclean animal.[24]

In Europe licensing is encouraged by the European Union (EU), which sees the mechanism as a way of offering access to new technologies to companies lacking the resources to innovate; this provides a means of technology sharing on a pan-European scale. Licensing activities have been given exemption in EU competition law (which means that companies engaged in licensing cannot be accused of anti-competitive practices), and *tied purchase* agreements, whereby licensees must buy components from the licensor, have not been ruled anti-competitive since they allow the innovating firm protection from loss of know-how to other component suppliers.

Franchising

Franchising is a form of licensing where a package of services is offered by the franchisor to the franchisee in return for payment. The two types of franchising are *product* and *trade name franchising*, the classic case of which is Coca-Cola selling its syrup together with the right to use its trademark and name to independent bottlers, and *business format franchising* where marketing approaches, operating procedures and quality control are included in the franchise package as well as the product and trade name. Business-format franchising is mainly used in service industries such as restaurants, hotels and retailing, where the franchisor exerts a high level of control in the overseas market since quality-control procedures can be established as part of the agreement. For example, McDonald's specifies precisely who should supply the ingredients for its fast-food products wherever they are sold to ensure consistency of quality in its franchise outlets.

The benefits to the franchisor are that franchising may be a way of overcoming resource constraints, as an efficient system to overcome producer–distributor management problems and as a way of gaining knowledge of new markets.[25] Franchising provides access to the franchisee's resources. For example, if the franchisor has limited financial resources, access to additional finance may be supplied by the franchisee.

Franchising may overcome producer–distributor management problems in managing geographically dispersed operations through the advantages of having owner-managers that have vested interests in the success of the business. Gaining knowledge of new markets by tapping into the franchisee's local knowledge is especially important in international markets where local culture may differ considerably between regions.

There are risks, however. Although the franchisor will attempt to gain some control of operations, the existence of multiple, geographically dispersed owner-managers makes control difficult. Service delivery may be inconsistent because of this. Conflicts can arise through dissatisfaction with the standard of service, lack of promotional support and the opening of new franchises close to existing ones, for example. This can lead to a breakdown of relationships and deteriorating performance. Also, initial financial outlays can be considerable because of expenditures on training, development, promotional and support activities.

The franchisee benefits by gaining access to the resources of the franchisor, its expertise (sometimes global) and buying power. The risks are that it may face conflicts (as discussed above) that render the relationship unviable.

Franchising is also exempt from EU competition law as it is seen as a means of achieving increased competition and efficient distribution without the need for major investment. It promotes standardization, which reaps scale economies with the possibility of some adaptation to local tastes. For example, in India McDonald's uses goat and lamb rather than pork or beef in its burgers, and Benetton allows a degree of freedom to its franchisees to stock products suitable to their particular customers.[26]

Joint ventures

Two types of joint venture are *contractual* and *equity* joint ventures. In **contractual joint ventures** no joint enterprise with a separate personality is formed. Two or more companies form a partnership to share the cost of an investment, the risks and long-term profits. The partnership may be to complete a particular project or for a longer-term cooperative effort.[27] They are found in the oil exploration, aerospace and car industries, and in co-publishing agreements.[28] An **equity joint venture** involves the creation of a new company in which foreign and local investors share ownership and control.

Joint ventures are sometimes set up in response to government conditions for market entry or because the foreign firm lacks the resources to set up production facilities alone. Also, the danger of expropriation is less when a company has a national partner than when the foreign firm is the sole owner.[29] Finding a national partner may be the only way to invest in some markets that are too competitive and saturated to leave room for a completely new operation. Many of the Japanese/US joint ventures in the USA were set up for this reason. The foreign investor benefits from the local management talent, and knowledge of local markets and regulations. Also, joint ventures allow partners to specialize in their particular areas of technological expertise in a given project. They may also be the only means of entering a country because of national laws. For example, in India overseas supermarket chains are not allowed to operate as retailers unless they can find a local partner to own and operate the store.[30] For this reason, Marks & Spencer's stores are operated by Indian retailer Planet Retail. Finally, the host firm benefits by acquiring resources from its foreign partners. For example, in Hungary host firms have gained through the rapid acquisition of marketing resources, which has enabled them to create positions of competitive advantage.[31]

There are potential problems, however. The national partner's interests relate to the local operation, while the foreign firm's concerns relate to the totality of its international operations. Particular areas of conflict can be the use made of profits (pay-out vs plough-back), product line and market coverage of the joint venture, and transfer pricing.

Equity joint ventures are common between companies from western European and eastern European countries. Western European firms gain from low-cost production and raw materials, while former eastern bloc companies acquire western technology and know-how. Eastern European governments are keen to promote joint ventures rather than wholly owned foreign direct investment in an attempt to prevent the exploitation of low-cost labour by western firms. A joint research project between French car makers and British designers led to the Renault Clio winning European Car of the Year Award.

Direct investment

This method of market entry involves investment in foreign-based assembly or manufacturing facilities. It carries the greatest commitment of capital and managerial effort. Wholly owned **direct investment** can be through the acquisition of a foreign producer (or by buying out a joint venture partner) or by building *new facilities*. Acquisition offers a quicker way into the market and usually means gaining access to a qualified labour force, national management, local knowledge, and contacts with the local market and government.

Acquisition also is a means of getting ownership of global brands. This was the motivation behind Lenovo's acquisition of IBM's PC division and Tata Motors' buying of Jaguar and Land Rover.[32] In saturated markets, acquisition may be the only feasible way of establishing a production presence in the host country.[33] However, coordination and styles of management between the foreign investor and the local management team may cause problems. Whirlpool, the US white goods (washing machines, refrigerators, etc.) manufacturer, is an example of a company that has successfully entered new international markets using acquisition. The company has successfully entered European markets through its acquisition of Philips' white goods business and its ability to develop new products that serve cross-national Euro-segments. European companies have also gained access to North American markets through acquisition. For example, ABN-Amro has built up market presence in the USA through a series of acquisitions to become the largest foreign bank in that country.[34] One company that has built a global brand through acquisitions is Vodafone, as Digital Marketing 21.1 explains.

Central and eastern Europe have been the recipients of high levels of direct investment as companies have sought to take advantage of low labour costs. Car companies, in particular, have opened production facilities there, notably VW in the Czech Republic and Slovakia; Renault in Romania, Slovakia and Turkey; and Fiat in Poland.

Wholly owned direct investment offers a greater degree of control than licensing or joint ventures, and maintains the internalization of proprietary information for manufacturers. It accomplishes the circumvention of tariff and non-tariff barriers, and lowers distribution costs compared with domestic production. A local presence means that sensitivity to customers' tastes and preferences is enhanced, and links with distributors and the host nation's government can be forged. Foreign direct investments can act as a powerful catalyst for economic change in the transition from a centrally planned economy. Foreign companies bring technology, management know-how and access to foreign markets.[35] Direct investment

---

Digital Marketing 21.1 Global Brand Building by Acquisition and Partnering

Vodafone, the mobile phone operator, has built an enviable reputation of building a global brand by acquisition. Sir Christopher Gent transformed Vodafone from an obscure British company into a global giant through a series of daring acquisitions, most famously the takeover of Mannesmann, a German telecoms company.

Arun Sarin, his successor, was supposed to be a steady hand who would fit the pieces of Vodafone's empire together and focus attention on detail and operational efficiency. While attempting to do this, however, Sarin moved strategy from developed markets where mobile phone usage was saturated to high-growth emerging markets. Acquisitions in the Czech Republic, Romania and Turkey followed this strategy, while Vodafone's ailing Japanese division was sold. His crowning glory, though, was the acquisition of Hutchison Essar, an Indian operator, enabling Vodafone to supply inexpensive handsets to the booming Indian market.

With a strong presence in the US market with its 45 per cent stake in Verizon Wireless, the leading US mobile operator, Vodafone has built a formidable global presence but has decided to focus its energies on its core markets and sold its stake in China Mobile of 3.2 per cent although continuing with its strategic alliance which involves cooperation on mobile phone technology.

In 2012 Vodafone celebrated a ten-year landmark for its partner programme, which develops relationships with local mobile network operators. Through these strategic partnership alliances Vodafone is able to offer its customers reliable connectivity when using international roaming and offer consistency of service worldwide, while expanding the company's share of global markets. Vodafone's partner markets include Asia, South America and 40 other markets. The success of its expansion programme in providing multinational business with voice and data communication and advance roaming services has enabled Vodafone to become the world's most valuable telecoms brand.

Based on: Vodafone (2012);[36] Parket (2010);[37] The Economist (2008);[38] Gapper (2008)[39]

FIGURE 21.4 Selecting a foreign market entry mode: control, resources and risk

Level	Factor: Risk of losing proprietary information	Factor: Resources	Factor: Control
High		Direct investment	Direct investment Exporting (own staff)
Medium	Licensing Joint venture	Joint venture Exporting (own staff)	Joint venture Licensing
Low	Exporting (own staff) Exporting (middlemen) Direct investment	Licensing Exporting (middlemen)	Exporting (middlemen)

TABLE 21.1 Factors affecting choice of market-entry method

External variables

Country environment

- Large market size and market growth encourage direct investment
- Barriers to imports encourage direct investment[40]
- The more the country's characteristics are rated favourable, the greater the propensity for direct investment[41]
- The higher the country's level of economic development, the greater the use of direct investment
- Government incentives encourage direct investment
- The higher the receiving company's technical capabilities, the greater the use of licensing
- Government intervention in foreign trade encourages licensing[42]
- Geocultural distance encourages independent modes: e.g. agents, distributors[43]
- Psychical distance does not favour integrated modes: e.g. own salesforce, overseas sales/marketing offices[44]
- Low market potential does not necessarily preclude direct investment for larger firms[45]

Buyer behaviour

- Piecemeal buying favours independent modes
- Project and protectionist buying encourages cooperative entry: e.g. licensing and joint ventures[46]

Internal variables

Company issues

- Lack of market information, uncertainty and perception of high investment risk lead to the use of agents and distributors[47]
- Large firm size or resources encourage higher level of commitment[48]
- Perception of high investment risk encourages joint ventures[49]
- Small firm size or resources encourages reactive exporting[50]
- Limited experience favours integrated entry modes[51]
- Service firms with little or no experience of foreign markets tend to prefer full control modes: e.g. own staff, overseas sales/marketing offices
- Service firms that expand abroad by following their clients' expansion plans tend to favour integrated modes[52]
- When investment rather than exporting is preferred, lack of market information leads to a preference for cooperative rather than integrated modes[53]

Source: Whitelock, J. and D. Jobber (1994) The Impact of Competitor Environment on Initial Market Entry in a New, Non-Domestic Market, *Proceedings of the Marketing Education Group Conference*, Coleraine, July, 1008–17.

is an expensive option, though, and the consequent risks are greater. If the venture fails, more money is lost and there is always the risk of expropriation. Furthermore, closure of plant may mean substantial redundancy payments.

The creation of the single European market allows free movement of capital across the EU, removing restrictions on direct investment using greenfield sites. Foreign direct investment through acquisition, however, may be subject to investigation under EC competition policy. American firms, in particular, sought to acquire European firms prior to 1992 in an attempt to secure a strong position in the face of the threat of 'Fortress Europe'.

The selection of international market entry mode is dependent on the trade-offs between the levels of control, resources and risk of losing proprietary information and technology. Figure 21.4 summarizes the levels associated with exporting using middlemen, exporting using company staff, licensing, joint ventures and direct investment.

Considerable research has gone into trying to understand the factors that have been shown to have an impact on selection of market entry method. Both external (country environment and buyer behaviour) and internal (company issues) factors have been shown to influence choice. A summary of these research findings is given in Table 21.1.

Developing International Marketing Strategy

Standardization or adaptation

A fundamental decision that managers have to make regarding their international marketing strategy is the degree to which they standardize or adapt their marketing mix around the world (these are referred to, respectively, as the **adapted marketing mix** and the **standardized marketing mix**). Many writers on the subject discuss standardization and adaptation as two distinct options but the literature on the subject is full of contradictions.[54] Pure standardization means that a company keeps the same marketing mix in all countries to which it markets. Such an approach is in line with Levitt's view that world markets are being driven 'towards a converging commonality'.[55] However, the world has moved on since Levitt made this comment. There are compelling arguments for and against standardization. The commercial reality is that few marketing mixes are totally standardized. Some brands that are most often quoted as being standardized are Coca-Cola, McDonald's and Levi Strauss. It is true that many elements of their marketing mixes are identical in a wide range of countries, but even here adaptation is found (Exhibit 21.1).

First, in Coca-Cola the sweetness and carbonization vary between countries. For example, sweetness is lowered in Greece and carbonization lowered in eastern Europe. Diet Coke's artificial sweetener and packaging differ between countries.[56] Second, Levi Strauss uses different domestic and international advertising strategies.[57] As Dan Chow Len, Levi's US advertising manager, commented:

> The markets are different. In the US, Levi's is both highly functional and fashionable. But in the UK, its strength is as a fashion garment. We've tested UK ads in American markets. Our primary target market at home is 16–20-year-olds, and they hate these ads, won't tolerate them, they're too sexy. Believe it or not, American 16–20-year-olds don't want to be sexy. . . . When you ask people about Levi's here, it's quality, comfort, style, affordability. In Japan, it's the romance of America.[58]

Third, in McDonald's, menus are changed to account for different customer preferences. For example, in France, McDonald's offers 'Croque McDo', its version of the French favourite the *croque monsieur*. It also works with French companies to offer local products such as yoghurts from Danone and coffee from Carte Noire, and buys 80 per cent of its products from French farmers. The proportion of meat in the hamburgers also varies between countries.

▲ EXHIBIT 21.1   McDonald's: a truly global brand.

Most global brands adapt to meet local requirements. Even high-tech electronic products have to conform to national technical standards and may be positioned differently in various countries.

How do marketers tackle the standardization–adaptation issue? A useful rule of thumb was cited at the start of this chapter: go global (standardize) when you can; stay local (adapt) when you must.

For example, HSBC recognizes the importance of acknowledging global and local requirements (see Exhibit 21.2).

Figure 21.5 provides a grid for thinking about the areas where standardization may be possible, and where adaptation may be necessary. There are many variations on which element is standardized and which is adapted. For example, IKEA's product offering and stores are largely standardized, but advertising is varied between countries. Seat's car models are standardized but its positioning alters. For example, it is positioned as a more upmarket brand in Spain than in the UK. Also, the Kronenbourg product is standardized, but it is positioned as more of a premium beer in the UK than in Germany. Occasionally the brand name changes for the same product. For example, Unilever's male toiletries brand is marketed as Lynx in the UK and Ireland, because of trademark problems, and as Axe across the rest of the world.[59]

Standardization is an attractive option because it can create massive economies of scale. For example, lower manufacturing, advertising and packaging costs can be realized. Also, the logistical benefit of being able to move stock from one country to another to meet low-stock situations should not be underestimated. This has led to the call to focus on similarities rather than differences between consumers across Europe, and the rest of the world. Procter & Gamble, for example, standardizes most of its products across Europe, so Pampers nappies and Pringles crisps are the same in all western European countries, although P&G's detergent Daz does differ.[60] However, there are a number of barriers to developing standardized global brands. These are discussed in Mini Case 21.1.

Developing global and regional brands requires commitment from management to a coherent marketing programme. The sensitivities of national managers need to be accounted

In the future, there will be no markets left waiting to emerge.

HSBC ◆▶

▲ EXHIBIT 21.2   HSBC recognizes the importance of acknowledging global and local requirements.

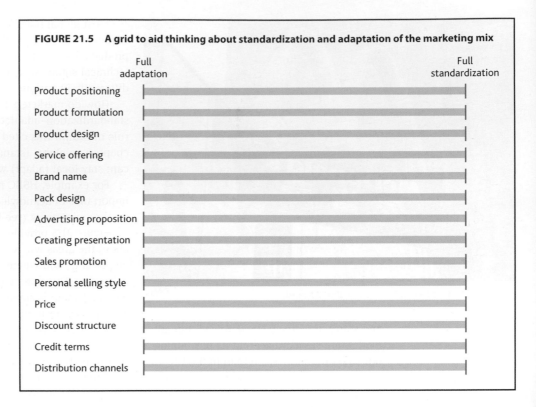

FIGURE 21.5 **A grid to aid thinking about standardization and adaptation of the marketing mix**

for as they may perceive a loss of status associated with greater centralized control. One approach is to have mechanisms that ensure the involvement of national managers in planning, and that encourage them to make recommendations. The key is to balance this local involvement with the need to look for similarities rather than differences across markets. It is the essential differences in consumer preferences and buyer behaviour that need to be recognized in marketing mix adaptation, rather than the minor nuances. Managers must also be prepared to invest heavily and over a long time period to achieve brand penetration. Success in international markets does not come cheaply or quickly. Market research should be used to identify the required positioning in each global market segment.[61]

This discussion has outlined the difficulties in achieving a totally standardized marketing mix package. Rather, the tried-and-tested approach of market segmentation based on understanding consumer behaviour and identifying international target markets, which allows the benefits of standardization to be combined with the advantages of customization, is recommended. The two contrasting approaches are summarized in Figure 21.6.

International marketing mix decisions

When developing an international marketing mix, marketers need to avoid falling into the trap of applying national stereotypes to country targets. As with domestic markets, overseas countries contain market segments that need to be understood in order to design a tailored marketing mix.

Before entering an overseas market a firm should develop an understanding of its target customers. This is to avoid the danger of using self-reference criteria where there is an assumption that the choice criteria, motivations and behaviour that are important to overseas customers are the same as those used by domestic customers.

For example, although Audi adopts a standardized approach to product design, it still researches overseas customers. For example, it sent members of its design team to California and China for eight weeks each, to live with families and better understand how they live

Mini Case 21.1 Barriers to Developing Standardized Global Brands

The cost of the logistical advantages of developing standardized global marketing approaches has meant that many companies have looked carefully at standardizing their approach to the European market. Mars, for example, changed the name of its chocolate bar Marathon in the UK to conform to its European brand name Snickers. Full standardization of the marketing mix is difficult, however, because of five problems.

1 *Culture and consumption patterns*: different cultures demand different types of product (e.g. beer and cheese). Some countries use Marmite to cook with rather than to spread on bread as a savoury spread—for example, in India; people in different countries wash clothes at different temperatures; UK consumers like their chocolate to be sweeter than people in mainland Europe; and in South America hot chocolate is a revitalizing drink to have at breakfast, whereas in the UK it is a comfort drink to have just before going to bed. In South America there are two female beer drinkers to every three males, while in the USA one in four women drinks beer. Yet, in the UK only 10 per cent of women drink beer. In China a fashionable drink is red wine with a dash of Coca-Cola, and in Singapore Guinness is drunk out of shared jugs as though it were Sangria. The failure of KFC in India is believed to be due to its standardized offering of plain fried chicken, while McDonald's has succeeded by adapting its offering—for example, the Maharajeh Mac made from chicken and local spices—to the Indian palate. Coca-Cola also had to change its Minute Maid orange juice for the UK market. After spending almost two years trying to understand what the British consumer wanted, Coca-Cola changed its US formulation of concentrate and water to fresh orange juice without concentrate. Consumer electrical products are less affected, though.

2 *Language*: brand names and advertising may have to change because of language differences. For example, one of the oldest soft drinks in French is called PSCHITT. If it were to be launched in the UK the name might have to be adapted because of English pronunciation.

3 *Regulations*: while national regulations are being harmonized in the single market, differences still exist—for example, with colourings and added vitamins in food.

4 *Media availability and promotional preferences*: varying media practices also affect standardization. For example, wine cannot be advertised on television in Denmark, but in the Netherlands this is allowed. Beer cannot be advertised on television in France, but this is allowed in most other European countries. In Italy levels of nudity in advertising that would be banned in some other countries are accepted. Sales promotions may have to change because of local preferences depending on the propensity of the target audience to seek bonus packs or use discount vouchers.

5 *Organizational structure and culture*: the changes necessary for a standardized approach may be difficult to implement where subsidiaries have, historically, enjoyed considerable power. Also where growth had been achieved through acquisition, strong cultural differences may lead to differing views about pan-European brand strategy.

As discussed, standardization is rarely possible. Even brands that are regarded as global, such as Sony, Nike, Visa, IBM, Disney, Heineken, McDonald's and Pringles, are not as globally identical as they may first appear. For example, Visa uses different logos in some countries, Heineken is positioned as a mainstream beer in some countries but as a premium beer in others, Pringles uses different flavours and advertising executions in different countries and, although McDonald's core food items are consistent across countries, some products are customized to local tastes. Setting the objective as being to develop a standardized global brand should not be the priority; instead, global brand leadership—strong brands in all markets backed by effective global brand management—should be the goal.

Questions:

1 Discuss the issues you might face if you are developing standardized communication messages for a global brand.
2 Suggest how you might overcome the issues identified in your answer to question 1.
3 Investigate the name changes within the insurance group Aviva, whose former names include Norwich Union and General Accident.

Based on: De Chernatony (1993);[62] Kirby (2000);[63] Aaker and Joachimsthaler (2002);[64] Luce (2002);[65] Benady (2003);[66] Charles (2008);[67] Lovell (2008)[68]

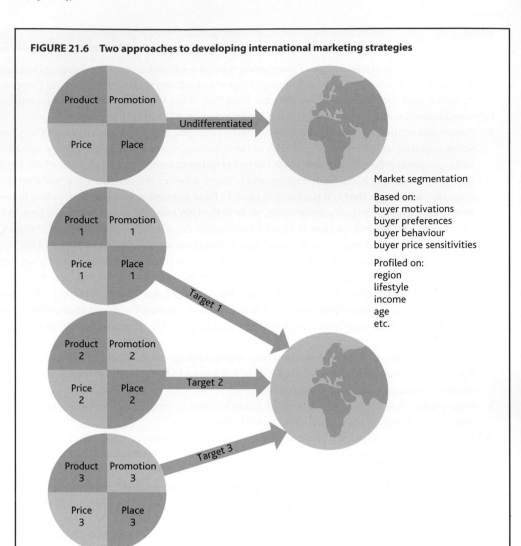

FIGURE 21.6 Two approaches to developing international marketing strategies

Undifferentiated

Market segmentation

Based on:
buyer motivations
buyer preferences
buyer behaviour
buyer price sensitivities

Profiled on:
region
lifestyle
income
age
etc.

Target 1

Target 2

Target 3

and drive. Its research in the USA persuaded Audi to put cup and bottle holders on its car doors. Also, Chinese drivers' liking of tea led to the installation of a cup holder in its A8 that can be heated or cooled. Rather than incur the expense of changing designs for specific countries, Audi has made these features standard globally. The cup holder used by Chinese drivers for green tea is promoted for use as a baby bottle holder elsewhere. About 98 per cent of its cars are the same globally, with the 2 per cent caused by legal differences (such as Canada's demanding requirements for bumpers), or colour and trim features where tastes differ.[69,70]

Expanding into overseas markets is notoriously difficult. Marks & Spencer failed in continental Europe, B&Q withdrew from South Korea and Tesco itself pulled out of France and its Fresh & Easy convenience supermarket launch in the USA struggled. Nevertheless, marketing research can provide dividends, with Tesco's in-depth study of overseas markets being the platform that has led it to build over half of its retailing space overseas, with 700 stores in Europe and over 1000 in Asia.

Once a thorough understanding of the target market has been achieved, marketing managers can then tailor a marketing mix to fit those requirements. We will now explore some of the special considerations associated with developing an effective *international marketing mix*.

Product

Some companies rely on global markets to provide the potential necessary to justify their huge research and development costs. For example, in the pharmaceutical industry GlaxoSmithKline's Zantac and Zovirax could not have been developed (R&D costs exceeded £30 million in both cases) without a worldwide market. Canon's huge research and development budget is also justified by the potential of global markets. For example, the bubble-jet and laser-beam computer printers it invented formed the basis upon which it has built world market shares of 30 and 65 per cent, respectively.[71] Once developed, the company can offer a standardized product to generate huge positive cash flow as the benefits that these products provide span national boundaries. Many car companies also standardize as much of their car models as possible, particularly those parts that are not visible to drivers, such as the air-conditioning system, suspension and steering column.

A second situation that supports a standardized product is where the brand concept is based on *authentic national heritage* across the globe: Scotch whisky, Belgian chocolate and French wine are relevant examples. Clearly, there are sound marketing reasons for a standard product. A third basis for standardization is where a global market segment of like-minded people can be exploited. This is the basis for the success of such products as Swatch and Rolex watches, Gucci fashion accessories and Chanel perfume. Where brands make statements about people, the *international properties* of the brand add significantly to its appeal.

In other cases, however, products need to be modified. Product adaptations come in two forms: permanent and temporary.[72] A company may make a fairly standard product worldwide, but make adaptations for particular markets. For example, the Barbie doll is a standardized product for most countries but in Japan, following market research, it had to be redesigned by making it smaller, darkening hair colour and giving it smaller breasts. This was a *permanent adaptation*. However, the change may be only a *temporary adaptation* if the local consumer needs time to adjust gradually to a new product. This often occurs with food products. For example, when McDonald's entered Japan it had to alter the red meat content of its hamburgers because Japanese consumers preferred fat to be mixed with beef. Over time, the red meat content has been increased, making it almost as high as it is in the USA. Also, when Mister Donut was introduced in Japan, the cinnamon content was reduced as market research had shown that the Japanese customers did not like the taste. Over time, the cinnamon content was increased to US levels.[73]

Many products that appear to be the same are modified to suit differing tastes. For example, the ubiquitous Mars bar has different formulations in northern and southern Europe, with northern Europeans favouring a sweeter taste. Also, the movement of large multinational companies to seek global brand winners can provide opportunities for smaller companies to exploit emerging market segments. For example, in the Netherlands, a small company took the initiative to sell environmentally friendly products, and captured one-quarter of the household cleaning market.[74]

Brand names may require modification because of linguistic idiosyncrasies. Many companies are alive to this type of problem now. Mars, for example, changed the name of its Magnum ice cream in Greece to Magic. However, in France McVitie's had problems trying to convince consumers that the word 'digestive' has nothing to do with stomach disorders. Brand name changes also occur in the UK with Brooke Bond PG Tips being called Scottish Blend in Scotland and coming in distinctive Scottish packaging.[75]

Promotion

Go to the website and compare how Schweppes and Fox's Biscuits use British stereotypes to promote their brand. www.mcgraw-hill.co.uk/ textbooks/jobber

A survey of agency practitioners found that the use of standardized advertising campaigns is set to increase in the future.[76] Standard campaigns can realize cost economies and a cohesive positioning statement in a world of increasing international travel. Standardization allows the multinational corporation to maintain a consistent image identity throughout the world, and minimizes confusion among consumers who travel frequently.[77] As with all standardization–

adaptation debates, the real issue is one of degree. Rarely can a campaign be transferred from one country to another without any modifications because of language difference. The clever use of pop music (an international language) in Levi's advertising was one exception, however. Coca-Cola is also close to the full standardization position with its one-sound, one-sight, one-appeal philosophy. Audi has successfully used the strap-line '*Vorsprung durch Technik*' globally. Other examples of the same copy being used globally are McDonald's ('I'm Lovin' It'), Johnnie Walker ('Keep Walking') and HSBC ('The World's Local Bank'). Yet research has found that full standardization of advertising is rare.[78]

Other companies find it necessary to adopt different positions in various countries, resulting in the need for advertising adaptation. In Mexico, Nestlé managed to position the drinking of instant coffee as an upmarket activity. It is actually smarter to offer guests a cup of instant coffee than ground coffee. This affects the content of its advertising. When brands are used differently in various countries, the advertising may need to be changed accordingly. For example, Schweppes tonic water is very much a mixer (e.g. drunk with gin) in the UK and Ireland, but is drunk on its own in Spain and France. Marketing in Action 21.1 gives examples of regulations on advertising in various countries.

Marketing in Action 21.1 Global Advertising Taboos

Standardized advertising campaigns are hampered by the rules and regulations in various countries around the world. These prevent certain types of advertising from appearing. Here are some examples.

Restrictions on advertising

Tobacco	Advertising and sponsorship on television banned within the EU
Alcohol	In the EU, ethical principles control alcohol advertising. Young people are protected and are deemed to have the right to grow up away from the negative consequences of alcohol consumption. This means advertising cannot: target minors, be linked with enhanced physical performance, suggest it can contribute to sexual success, have therapeutic properties, encourage excess consumption or emphasize high alcohol content. Similar codes of advertising conduct exist in the USA. In Sweden the restrictions are greater and only light beer adverts are allowed. In Asia, Malaysia has a total ban on alcohol advertising on TV and radio
Junk food	In the UK regulations banning the advertising of food with high fat, salt or sugar content have been introduced. In Sweden more stringent regulations ban all advertising to under-12s.

Based on: BBC News (2012);[79] House of Commons (2004)[80]

An analysis of the extent of advertising adaptation that is necessary can be assisted by separating the advertising proposition from the creative presentation of that proposition. The advertising platform is the aspect of the seller's product that is most persuasive and relevant to the potential customer: it is the fundamental proposition that is being communicated. The *creative presentation* is the way in which that proposition is translated into visual and verbal statements.[81] Advertising platforms, being broad statements of appeal, are more likely to be transferable than creative presentations. If this is the case, the solution is to keep the platform across markets but change the creative presentation to suit local demands. In other cases both platform and presentation can be used globally, as is the case with the McDonald's 'I'm Lovin' It' campaign.

Advertising can be used to position brands using one of three strategies, as outlined below.[82]

1 **Global consumer culture positioning**: this strategy defines the brand as a symbol of a given global culture. For example, a jeans brand could be positioned as one worn by

Price

Price setting is a key marketing decision because price is the revenue-generating element of the marketing mix. Poor pricing decisions can undermine previous cost saving strategies. As Leszinski states:

> As Europe moves towards a single market, lack of attention to pricing is a serious problem. The stakes are unusually high. . . . On average, a 1 per cent increase results in a 12 per cent improvement in a company's operating margin. This is four times as powerful as a 1 per cent increase in its volume. But the sword cuts both ways. A price decrease of 5 to 10 per cent will eliminate most companies' profits. As the single market develops, decreases of this magnitude can easily happen: the existing price differentials across Europe for some products are in the region of 20 to 40 per cent.[92]

In the face of more intense global competition, international marketers need to consider six issues when considering cross-national pricing decisions:

1. calculating extra costs and making price quotations
2. understanding the competition and customers
3. using pricing tactics to undermine competitor actions
4. parallel importing
5. transfer pricing
6. counter-trade.

Each of these special considerations will now be explored.

Calculating extra costs and making price quotations: the extra costs of doing business in a foreign market must be taken into account if a profit is to be made. *Middlemen and transportation costs* need to be estimated. Distributors may demand different mark-ups and agents may require varying commission levels in different countries. The length of the distribution channel also needs to be understood, as do the margins required at each level before a price to the consumer can be set. These can sometimes almost double the price in an overseas market compared to at home. Overseas transportation may incur the additional costs of insurance, packaging and shipping. *Taxes and tariffs* also vary from country to country. Although there are moves to standardize the level of value added tax in the single market there are still wide variations. Denmark, in particular, is a high-tax economy. A tariff is a fee charged when goods are brought into a country from another country. Although tariff barriers have fallen among the member states of Europe, they can still be formidable between other countries. Companies active in international business need to protect themselves against the costs of *exchange rate fluctuations*. Nestlé, for example, lost $1 million in six months due to adverse exchange rate moves.[93] Companies are increasingly asking that transactions be written in terms of the vendor company's national currency, and *forward hedging* (which effectively allows future payments to be settled at around the exchange rate in question when the deal was made) is commonly practised.

Care should be taken when *quoting a price* to an overseas customer. The contract may include such items as credit terms, currency of exchange, quality standards, quantities, responsibilities for the goods in transit, and who pays insurance and transportation charges and specify the currency. The price quoted can vary considerably depending on these factors.

Understanding the competition and customers: as with any pricing decision these factors play a major role. The difference is that information is often more difficult to acquire for exporters because of the distances involved. When making pricing moves, companies need to be aware of the present *competitors' strategic degrees of freedom*, how much room they have to react, and the possibility of the price being used as a weapon by companies entering the market from a different industry. Where prices are high and barriers to entry low, incumbent firms are especially vulnerable.

Companies also need to be wary of using **self-reference criteria** when evaluating overseas customers' perceptions. This occurs when an exporter assumes that the choice criteria, motivations and behaviour that are important to overseas customers are the same as those used by domestic customers. The viewpoints of domestic and foreign consumers to the same product can be very different. For example, a small Renault car is viewed as a luxury model in Spain but utilitarian in Germany. This can affect the price position vis-à-vis competitors in overseas markets.

International marketers need to understand how to use such pricing tactics in the face of increasingly fierce global competition.

Parallel importing: a major consideration in international markets is the threat of parallel imports. These occur when importers buy products from distributors in one country and sell them in another to distributors who are not part of the manufacturer's normal distribution system. The motivation for this practice occurs when there are large price differences between countries, and the free movement of goods between member states means that it is likely to grow. Companies protect themselves by:

- lowering price differentials
- offering non-transferable service/product packages
- changing the packaging—for example, a beer producer by offering differently shaped bottles in various countries ensured that the required recyclability of the product was guaranteed only in the intended country of sale.[94]

Another means of parallel importing (or 'grey market' trading as it is sometimes called) is by supermarkets buying products from abroad to sell in their stores at reduced prices. A landmark legal battle was won by Levi Strauss to prevent Tesco, the UK supermarket chain, from selling Levi's jeans imported cheaply from outside Europe.

Transfer pricing: this is the price charged between profit centres (e.g. manufacturing company to foreign subsidiary) of a single company. Transfer prices are sometimes set to take advantage of lower taxation in some countries than others. For example, a low price is charged to a subsidiary in a low-tax country and a high price in one where taxes are high. Similarly, low transfer prices may be set for high-tariff countries. Transfer prices should not be based solely on taxation and tariff considerations, however. For example, transfer pricing rules can cause subsidiaries to sell products at higher prices than the competition even though their true costs of manufacture are no different.

Counter-trade: not all transactions are concluded in cash; goods may be included as part of the asking price. Four major forms of counter-trade are as follows.

1 *Barter*: payment for goods with other goods, with no direct use of money; the vendor then has the problem of selling the goods that have been exchanged.
2 *Compensation deals*: payment using goods and cash. For example, General Motors sold $12 million worth of locomotives and diesel engines to former Yugoslavia and received $8 million in cash plus $4 million worth of cutting tools.[95]
3 *Counter-purchase*: the seller agrees to sell a product to a buyer and receives cash. The deal is dependent on the original seller buying goods from the original buyer for all or part of the original amount.
4 *Buy-backs*: these occur when the initial sale involves production plant, equipment or technology. Part or all of the initial sale is financed by selling back some of the final product. For example, Levi Strauss set up a jeans factory in Hungary that was financed by the supply of jeans back to the company.

A key issue in setting the counter-trade 'price' is valuing the products received in exchange for the original goods, and estimating the cost of selling on the bartered goods. However, according to Shipley and Neale, this forms 20–30 per cent of world trade with yearly value exceeding $100 billion.[96]

Place

A key international market decision is whether to use importers/distributors or the company's own personnel to distribute a product in a foreign market. Initial costs are often lower with the former method, so it is often used as an early method of market entry. For example, Sony and Panasonic originally entered the US market by using importers. As sales increased they entered into exclusive agreements with distributors, before handling their own distribution arrangements by selling directly to retailers.[97]

International marketers must not assume that overseas distribution systems resemble their own. As we have mentioned, Japan is renowned for its long, complex distribution channels; in Africa the physical landscape and the underdeveloped transport infrastructure create many challenges. Nonetheless, Kenyan growers have established distribution networks that enable beans, mangoes and other fresh produce to be picked, processed, packed and transported to markets in Northern Europe and the USA within a few short days. An important consideration when evaluating a distribution channel is the power of its members. Selling directly to large powerful distributors such as supermarkets may seem attractive logistically but their ability to negotiate low prices needs to be taken into account.

Customer expectations are another factor that has a bearing on the channel decision. For many years in Spain yoghurt was sold through pharmacies (as a health product). As customers expected to buy yoghurt in pharmacies, suppliers had to use them as an outlet. Regulations also affect the choice of distribution channel. For example, over-the-counter (OTC) pharmaceuticals are sold only in pharmacies in Belgium, France, Spain and Italy, whereas in Denmark, the UK and Germany, other channels (notably grocery outlets) also sell them.

Nevertheless, there can be opportunities to standardize at least part of the distribution system. For example, BMW standardizes its dealerships so that customers have the same experience when they enter their showrooms around the world.[98] Fiat adopted a similar approach when launching the Fiat 500 in the US. The Italian car manufacturer insisted that all dealerships invested heavily to convert showrooms to create an 'Italian' feel to the customer experience.

As with domestic marketing, the marketing mix in a foreign market needs to be blended into a consistent package that provides a clear position for the product in the marketplace. Furthermore, managers need to display high levels of commitment to their overseas activities as this has been shown to be a strong determinant of performance.[99]

. . . .

Organizing for International Operations

The starting point for organizing for international marketing operations is, for many companies, the establishment of an export department. As sales, the number of international markets and the complexity of activities increase, so the export department may be replaced by a more complex structure. Bartlett and Ghoshal describe four types of structure for managing a worldwide business enterprise: international, global, multinational and transnational organization.[100]

International organization

The philosophy of management is that overseas operations are appendages to a central domestic operation. Subsidiaries form a coordinated federation with many assets, resources, responsibilities and decisions decentralized, but overall control is in the hands of headquarters. Formal management planning and control systems permit fairly tight headquarters–subsidiary links.

Global organization

The management philosophy is that overseas operations should be viewed as 'delivery pipelines' to a unified global market. The key organizational unit is the centralized hub that controls most strategic assets, resources, responsibilities and decisions. The centre enforces tight operational control of decisions, resources and information.

Multinational organization

A multinational mentality is characterized by a regard for overseas operations as a portfolio of independent businesses. Many key assets, responsibilities and decisions are decentralized. Control is through informal headquarters–subsidiary relationships supported by simple financial controls.

Transnational organization

This organizational form may be described as a complex process of coordination and cooperation in an environment of shared decision-making. Organizational units are integrated with large flows of components, products, resources, people and information among interdependent units. The transnational organization attempts to respond to an environment that is characterized by strong simultaneous forces for both global integration and national responsiveness.[101]

Centralization vs Decentralization

A key determinant of the way international operations are organized is the degree to which the environment calls for global integration (centralization) versus regional responsiveness (decentralization). **Centralization** reaps economies of scale and provides an integrated marketing profile to channel intermediaries that, themselves, may be international, and customers that are increasingly geographically mobile. Confusion over product formulations, advertising approaches, packaging design and labelling, and pricing is eliminated by a coordinated approach. (However, too much centralization can lead to the *not invented here syndrome*, where managers in one country are slow to introduce products that have been successful in others, or fail to fully support advertising campaigns that have been conceived elsewhere.)

Decentralization maximizes customization of products to regional tastes and preferences. Since decentralized decision-making is closer to customers, speed of response to new opportunities is quicker than with a centralized organizational structure. Relationships with the trade and government are facilitated by local decision-making.

Many companies feel the pressure of both sets of forces, hence the development of the transnational corporation. European integration has led many companies to review their overseas operations with the objective of realizing global economies wherever possible. European centralized marketing teams carry the responsibility for looking at the longer-term strategic picture alongside national marketing staff who deal less with advertising theme development and brand positioning, and more with handling retailer relationships.[102] The result is loss of responsibility and power for national marketing managers. This is a sensitive issue, and many companies are experimenting with the right blend of centralization and national power.[103] The fact that national marketing managers often lose responsibility and power in moves to a more centralized marketing approach means that simply preaching the virtues of globalization will not gain their commitment. Neither is compelling business logic likely to remove their opposition.

One approach to developing support is through the creation of *taskforces*. A business area is selected where the urgency of need is most clear; and where positive early results can begin a 'ripple effect', creating champions for change within the company. Procter & Gamble, for example, created a taskforce of national product managers to decide upon common brand requirements. A freight company, under intense pressure from international buying groups, set up a pricing taskforce to thrash out a coordinated European pricing strategy. One by-product of the taskforce approach is that it provides top management with a forum for identifying potential Euro-managers.

Companies such as Coca-Cola, McDonald's, Shell and HSBC employ a global marketing director to coordinate worldwide operations. Such a role is not for the faint-hearted: much of their time is spent travelling and they have to combine an ability to digest reams of consumer research with the talent to persuade, through powerful argument, local marketing executives to adopt a strategy. HSBC's global marketing chief managed to achieve the right balance between the need to create a global positioning statement for its advertising and local demands for a bank by the use of the tag-line 'HSBC—the world's local bank'.

To minimize conflict, some companies are trying to build tiered systems where the marketing decisions that are centrally determined and those that are subject to local control are clearly defined. For example, the brand positioning and advertising theme issues may be determined centrally but the creative interpretation of them is decided locally.

Whichever approach is used, a system that shares insights, methods and best practice should be established. The system should provide a global mechanism to identify first-hand observations of best practice, communicate them to those who would benefit from them, and allow access to a store of best-practice information when required. To do this, companies need to nurture a culture where these ideas are communicated. This can be helped by rewarding the people who contribute. Tracking employees who post insights and examples of best practice, and rewarding them during annual performance reviews is one method. Regular meetings can also aid communication, especially when they include workshops that engage the participants in action-orientated learning. Sometimes the sharing of information at these meetings is less important than the establishment of personal relationships that foster subsequent communications and interactions.

Technological developments can also make communication easier and quicker, such as the formation of intranets that allow global communication of best practice news, competitor actions and technological change. Of more lasting use, however, is the sending of teams to see best practice at first hand to facilitate the depth of understanding not usually achieved by descriptive accounts.

Online
LearningCentre

When you have read this chapter

log on to the Online Learning Centre at **www.mcgraw-hill.co.uk/textbooks/jobber** to explore chapter-by-chapter test questions, links and further online study tools for marketing.

Review

1 **The reasons why companies seek foreign markets**
- The reasons are to find opportunities beyond saturated domestic markets; to seek expansion beyond small, low-growth domestic markets; to meet customer expectations; to respond to competitive forces (e.g. the desire to attack an overseas competitor); to act on cost factors (e.g. to gain economies of scale); and to achieve a portfolio balance where problems of economic recession in some countries can be balanced by growth in others.

2 **The factors that influence which foreign markets to enter**
- The factors are macroenvironmental issues (economic, socio-cultural and political-legal) and microenvironmental issues (market attractiveness, which can be assessed by analysing market size and growth rate, degree of competition, the costs of serving the market, profit potential and market accessibility) and company capability profile (skills, resources, product adaptability and the ability to create a competitive advantage).

3 **The range of foreign market entry strategies**
- Foreign market entry strategies are indirect exporting (using, for example, domestic-based export agents), direct exporting (using, for example, foreign-based distributors); licensing (using, for example, a local licensee with access to a set of technologies or know-how); joint venture (where, for example, two or more companies form a partnership to share the risks, costs and profits) and direct investment (where, for example, a foreign producer is bought or new facilities built).

4 **The factors influencing foreign market entry strategies**
- The factors are the risk of losing proprietary information (for example, direct investment may be used to avoid this risk), resources (for example, when resources are low, exporting using agents or distributors may be favoured) and the desired level of control (for example, when high control is desired direct investment or exporting using the company's staff may be preferred).

5. **The influences on the degree of standardization or adaptation**
   - A useful rule of thumb is to go global (standardize) when you can and stay local (adapt) when you must.
   - The key influences are cost; the need to meet local regulations, language and needs; the sensitivities of local managers, who may perceive a loss of status associated with greater centralized control; media availability and promotional preferences; and organizational structure and culture (for example, where subsidiaries hold considerable power).

6. **The special considerations involved in designing an international marketing mix**
   - The special considerations are huge research and development costs, where a brand concept is based on an authentic national heritage that transcends global boundaries, where a global segment of like-minded people can be exploited, and where a cohesive positioning statement makes sense because of increasing global travel. All of these considerations favour a standardized marketing mix. Where there are strong local differences an adapted marketing mix is required.

7. **How to organize for international marketing operations**
   - Many companies begin with an export department but this may be replaced later by more complex structures.
   - Four types of structure for managing a worldwide business enterprise are: international (where overseas operations are appendages to a central domestic operation); global (where overseas operations are delivery pipelines to a unified global market); multinational (where overseas operations are managed as a portfolio of independent businesses); and transnational organizations (which are characterized by a complex process of coordination and cooperation in an environment of shared decision-making).

Key Terms

adapted marketing mix an international marketing strategy for changing the marketing mix for each international target market

centralization in international marketing it is the global integration of international operations

contractual joint venture two or more companies form a partnership but no joint enterprise with a separate identity is formed

counter-trade a method of exchange where not all transactions are concluded in cash; goods may be included as part of the asking price

decentralization in international marketing it is the delegation of international operations to individual countries or regions

direct exporting the handling of exporting activities by the exporting organization rather than by a domestically based independent organization

direct investment market entry that involves investment in foreign-based assembly or manufacturing facilities

equity joint venture where two or more companies form a partnership that involves the creation of a new company

foreign consumer culture positioning positioning a brand as associated with a specific foreign culture (e.g. Italian fashion)

franchising a form of licensing where a package of services is offered by the franchisor to the franchisee in return for payment

global consumer culture positioning positioning a brand as a symbol of a given global culture (e.g. young cosmopolitan men)

indirect exporting the use of independent organizations within the exporter's domestic market to facilitate export

licensing a contractual arrangement in which a licensor provides a licensee with certain rights, e.g. to technology access or production rights

local consumer culture positioning positioning a brand as associated with a local culture (e.g. local production and consumption of a good)

self-reference criteria the use of one's own perceptions and choice criteria to judge what is important to consumers. In international markets the perceptions and choice criteria of domestic consumers may be used to judge what is important to foreign consumers

standardized marketing mix an international marketing strategy for using essentially the same product, promotion, distribution, and pricing in all the company's international markets

transfer pricing the price charged between the profit centres of the same company, sometimes used to take advantage of lower taxes in another country

Study Questions

1 What are the factors that drive companies to enter international markets?

2 Discuss possible entry methods for markets in Europe.

3 For a company of your choice, research its reasons for expanding into new foreign markets, and describe the moves that have been made.

4 Using information in this chapter and from Chapter 17, on distribution, describe how you would go about selecting and motivating overseas distributors.

5 Why are so many companies trying to standardize their global marketing mixes? With examples, show the limitations to this approach.

6 What are the factors that influence the choice of market entry strategy?

7 Select a familiar advertising campaign in your country and examine the extent to which it is likely to need adaptation for another country of your choice.

8 Describe the problems of pricing in overseas markets and the skills required to price effectively in the global marketplace.

References

1. http://ec.europa.eu/trade/statistics/#_economic-sectors, April 2012.
2. UKTI (2012) About UKTI, http://www.ukti.gov.uk/uktihome/aboutukti.html, April 2012.
3. Chapman, M. (2012) Tesco plans rapid global expansion for F&F brand, *Marketing*, http://www.marketingmagazine.co.uk/news/1112325/Tesco-plans-rapid-global-expansion-F-F-brand/, 17 January.
4. Milmo, D. (2011) China helps BMW quadruple its profits, *The Guardian*, 5 May, 30.
5. See Aharoni, S. (1966) *The Foreign Investment Decision Process*, Boston, Mass: Harvard University Press; Agarwal, S. and S. N. Ramaswami (1992) Choice of Foreign Market Entry Mode: Impact of Ownership, Location and Internalisation Factors, *Journal of International Business Studies*, Spring, 1–27; Knickerbocker, F. T. (1973) *Oligopolistic Reaction and Multinational Enterprise*, Boston, Mass: Harvard University Press.
6. Whitelock, J. and D. Jobber (2004) An Evaluation of External Factors in the Decision of UK Industrial Firms to Enter a New Non-domestic Market: an Exploratory Study, *European Journal of Marketing* 38(1/2), 1437–56.
7. Schwartz, A. (2012) Economic change in Russia, CSIS Center for Strategic and International Studies, Washington, DC.
8. Litvak, I. A. and P. M. Banting (1968) A Conceptual Framework for International Business Arrangements, in King, R. L. (ed.) *Marketing and the New Science of Planning*, Chicago: American Marketing Association, 460–7.
9. Conway, T. and J. S. Swift (2000) International Relationship Marketing, *European Journal of Marketing* 34(1/2), 1391–413.
10. Johanson, J. and J.-E. Vahlne (1977) The Internationalisation Process of the Firm: A Model of Knowledge Development and Increasing Foreign Market Commitments, *Journal of International Business Studies* 8(1), 23–32.
11. Erramilli, M. K. (1991) Entry Mode Choice in Service Industries, *International Marketing Review* 7(5), 50–62.
12. Prasad, A. (2011) The Impact of Non-Market forces on Competitive Positioning Understanding Global Industry Attractiveness through the Eyes of M. E. Porter, *Journal of Management Research*, 11(3), 131–7.
13. Wiggins, J. (2008) Brands Make a Dash into Russia, *Financial Times*, 4 September, 12.
14. Ngwenyama, O. and O. Morawczynski (2009) Factors affecting ICT expansion in emerging economies: an analysis of ICT infrastructure expansion in five Latin American countries, *Information Technology for Development*, 15(4), 237–58.
15. Knickerbocker (1973) op. cit.
16. Birchall, J. and C. Parkers (2006) Assault on West Coast Market, *Financial Times*, 10 February, 21.
17. Wiggins, J. (2008) Multinationals Eat into the Russian Market, *Financial Times*, 18 June, 22.
18. Watts, J. (2006) Wal-Mart Leads Charge in Race to Grab a Slice of China, *The Guardian*, 25 March, 20.
19. Whitelock, J. and D. Jobber (1994) The Impact of Competitor Environment on Initial Market Entry in a New, Non-Domestic Market, *Proceedings of the Marketing Education Group Conference*, Coleraine, July, 1008–17.
20. Felsted, A. and B. Jopson (2011) Tesco highlights retailers' US travails, *Financial Times*, 6 September, 8.
21. Young, S., J. Hamill, C. Wheeler and J. R. Davies (1989) *International Market Entry and Development*, Englewood Cliffs, NJ: Prentice-Hall.
22. West, A. (1987) *Marketing Overseas*, London: Pitman.
23. Young *et al.* (1989) op. cit.
24. Bloomgarden, K. (2000) Branching Out, *Marketing Business*, April, 12–13.

25. Hopkinson, G. C. and S. Hogarth-Scott (1999) Franchise Relationship Quality: Microeconomic Explanations, *European Journal of Marketing* 33(9/10), 827–43.

26. Welford, R. and K. Prescott (2000) *European Business*, London: Pitman.

27. Wright, R. W. (1981) Evolving International Business Arrangements, in Dhawan, K. C., H. Etemad and R. W. Wright (eds) *International Business: A Canadian Perspective*, Reading, MA: Addison Wesley.

28. Young *et al.* (1989) op. cit.

29. Terpstra, V. and R. Sarathy (1999) *International Marketing*, Fort Worth, Texas: Dryden.

30. Rigby, E. and J. Leaky (2008) Tesco Finds its Passage to India, *The Guardian*, 13 August, 17.

31. Hooley, G., T. Cox, D. Shipley, J. Fahy, J. Beracs and K. Kolos (1996) Foreign Direct Investment in Hungary: Resource Acquisition and Domestic Competitive Advantage, *Journal of International Business Studies* 4, 683–709.

32. Terpstra and Sarathy (1999) op. cit.

33. *The Economist* (2008) The Challengers, 12 January, 61–3.

34. Smit, B. (1996) Dutch Bank Moves Deeper into the Mid West, *European*, 28 November–4 December, 25.

35. Ghauri, P. N. and K. Holstius (1996) The Role of Matching in the Foreign Market Entry Process in the Baltic States, *European Journal of Marketing* 30(2), 75–88.

36. Vodafone (2012) Expanding partner markets in a drive for international growth, http://www.vodafone.com/content/index/media/news/expanding_partnermarkets.html, 9 January.

37. Parker, A. (2010) Vodaphone selling China Mobile stake for £4.3. billion, *Financial Times*, 7 September.

38. *The Economist* (2008) Ringing Off, 31 May, 86.

39. Gapper, J. (2008) Global Brands Special Report, *Financial Times*, 21 April, 1–6.

40. Buckley, P. J., H. Mirza and J. R. Sparkes (1987) Foreign Direct Investment in Japan as a Means of Market Entry: The Case of European Firms, *Journal of Marketing Management* 2(3), 241–58.

41. Goodnow, J. D. and J. E. Hansz (1972) Environmental Determinants of Overseas Market Entry Strategies, *Journal of International Business Studies* 3(1), 33–50.

42. Contractor, F. J. (1984) Choosing between Direct Investment and Licensing: Theoretical Considerations and Empirical Tests, *Journal of International Business Studies* 15(3), 167–88.

43. Anderson, E. and A. T. Coughlan (1987) International Market Entry and Expansion via Independent or Integrated Channels of Distribution, *Journal of Marketing* 51, January, 71–82.

44. Klein, S. and J. R. Roth (1990) Determinants of Export Channel Structure: The Effects of Experience and Psychic Distance Reconsidered, *International Marketing Review* 7(5), 27–38.

45. See Agarwal and Ramaswami (1992) op. cit.; Knickerbocker (1973) op. cit.

46. Sharma, D. D. (1988) Overseas Market Entry Strategy: The Technical Consultancy Firms, *Journal of Global Marketing* 2(2), 89–110.

47. Johanson and Vahlne (1977) op. cit.

48. Johanson, J. and J.-E. Vahlne (1990) The Mechanisms of Internationalisation, *International Marketing Review* 7(4), 11–24.

49. Buckley *et al.* (1987) op. cit.

50. Sharma (1988) op. cit.

51. Klein and Roth (1990) op. cit.

52. Erramilli (1991) op. cit.

53. Buckley *et al.* (1987) op. cit.

54. Hise, R. and Y.-T. Choi (2010) Are US companies employing standardization or adaptation strategies in their international markets? *Journal of Business and Cultural Studies* 4, 1–29.

55. Levitt, T. (1983) The Globalization of Markets, *Harvard Business Review*, May/June, 92–102.

56. Quelch, J. A. and E. J. Hoff (1986) Customizing Global Marketing, *Harvard Business Review*, May–June, 59–68.

57. Banerjee, A. (1994) Transnational Advertising Development and Management: An Account Planning Approach and a Process Framework, *International Journal of Advertising* 13, 95–124.

58. Mayer, M. (1991) *Whatever Happened to Madison Avenue? Advertising in the '90s*, Boston, MA: Little, Brown, 186–7.

59. Lewis, E. (2006) Going Global, *The Marketer*, June (Issue 25), 7–9.

60. Mazur, L. (2002) No Pain, No Gain, *Marketing Business*, September, 10–13.

61. De Chernatony, L. (1993) Ten Hints for EC-wide Brands, *Marketing*, 11 February, 16.

62. De Chernatony (1993) op. cit.

63. Kirby, K. (2000) Globally Led, Locally Driven, *Marketing Business*, May, 26–7.

64. Aaker, D. A. and E. Joachimsthaler (2002) *Brand Leadership*, New York: Free Press, 303–9.

65. Luce, E. (2002) Hard Sell to a Billion Consumers, *Financial Times*, 15 April, 14.

66. Benady, D. (2003) Uncontrolled Immigration, *Marketing Week*, 20 February, 24–7.

67. Charles, C. (2008) Coors Seeks Feminine Touch, *Marketing*, 27 August, 16.

68. Lovell, C. (2008) Universal Truths Cross Booze Borders, *Campaign*, 15 August, 8.

69. Jones, H. (2008) How To . . . Tackle Foreign Markets, *Marketer*, September, 35–8.

70. Reed, J. (2008) Designs that Keep on Moving, *Financial Times*, 29 July, 12.

71. Dawkins, W. (1996) Time to Pull Back the Screen, *Financial Times*, 19 November, 14.

72. Dudley, J. W. (1989) *1992: Strategies for the Single Market*, London: Kogan Page.

73. Ohmae, K. (1985) *Triad Power*, New York: Free Press.

74. Mitchell, A. (1993) Can branding take on global proportions? *Marketing*, 29 April, 20–1.

75. Harris, P. and F. McDonald (1994) *European Business and Marketing: Strategic Issues*, London: Chapman.

76. Duncan, T. and J. Ramaprasad (1993) Ad Agency Views of Standardised Campaigns for Multinational Clients, Conference of the American Academy of Advertising, Chicago, IL, 17 April.

77. Papavassiliou, N. and V. Stathakopoulos (1997) Standardisation versus Adaptation of International Advertising Strategies: Towards a Framework, *European Journal of Marketing* 31(7), 504–27.

78. Harris, G. and S. Attour (2003) The International Advertising Practices of Multinational Companies: A Content Analysis Study, *European Journal of Marketing* 37(1/2), 154–68.

79. BBC News (2012) Children 'watch same level' of junk food ads despite TV rules, http://www.bbc.co.uk/news/health-17041347, 16 February.

80. House of Commons (2004) Children's Food Bill http://www.publications.parliament.uk/pa/cm200304/cmbills/110/2004110.htm.

81. Killough, J. (1978) Improved Pay-offs from Transnational Advertising, *Harvard Business Review*, July–Aug., 58–70.

82. Alden, D. L., J.-B. E. M. Steenkamp and R. Batra (1998) Brand Positioning Through Advertising in Asia, North America, and Europe: The Role of Global Consumer Culture, *Journal of Marketing*, 63, January, 75–87.

83. Weeks, R. and M. Stoves (2008) Defensive vs Disillusioned, *Campaign*, 28 November, 11.

84. Wachman, R. (2004) Papa of the Branded Bags, *Observer*, 25 July, 16.

85. Jobber, D. and G. Lancaster (2009) *Selling and Sales Management*, London: Pitman.

86. Campbell, N. C. G., J. L. Graham, A. Jolibert and H. G. Meissner (1988) Marketing Negotiations in France, Germany, the United Kingdom and the United States, *Journal of Marketing*, 52, April, 49–62.

87. Niss, N. (1996) Country of Origin Marketing Over the Product Life Cycle: A Danish Case Study, *European Journal of Marketing* 30(3), 6–22.

88. Whitehead, J. (2008) More to Citroën Campaign than Stereotypes, *The Guardian*, 22 September, 7.

89. See Powell, C. (2000) Why We Really Must Fly the Flag, *Observer*, Business Section, 25 April, 4 and Yip, G. (2003) *Total Global Strategy*, Englewood Cliffs, NJ: Prentice-Hall, 88.

90. Benady, A. (2004) Global Clients Queue Up at the Agency, *FT Creative Business*, 30 November, 10–11.

91. Benady, D. (2005) The End of the World, *Marketing Week*, 3 November, 26–7.

92. Leszinski, R. (1992) Pricing for the Single Market, *McKinsey Quarterly* 3, 86–94.

93. Cateora, P. R., J. L. Graham and P. J. Ghauri (2006) *International Marketing*, London: McGraw-Hill, 376.

94. Leszinski (1992) op. cit.

95. Cateora *et al.* (2006) op. cit.

96. Shipley, D. and B. Neale (1988) Countertrade: Reactive or Proactive, *Journal of Business Research*, June, 327–35.

97. Darlin, D. (1989) Myth and Marketing in Japan, *Wall Street Journal*, 6 April, B1.

98. *Campaign* (2005) When the World is your Market, 27 May, 46–7.

99. Chadee, D. D. and J. Mattsson (1998) Do Service and Merchandise Exporters Behave and Perform Differently?, *European Journal of Marketing* 32(9/10), 830–42.

100. Bartlett, C. and S. Ghoshal (2002) *Managing Across Borders: The Transnational Solution*, Cambridge, MA: Harvard Business School Press.

101. Ghoshal, S. and N. Nohria (1993) Horses for Courses: Organizational Forms of Multinational Corporations, *Sloan Management Review*, Winter, 23–35.

102. Mazur, L. (1993) Brands sans Frontières, *Observer*, 28 November, 8.

103. Ohbora, T., A. Parsons and H. Riesenbeck (1992) Alternative Routes to Global Marketing, *McKinsey Quarterly* 3, 52–74.

IKEA is a state of mind that revolves around contemporary design, low prices, wacky promotions and an enthusiasm that few institutions in or out of business can muster. Perhaps more than any other company in the world, IKEA has become a curator of people's lifestyles, if not their lives. At a time when consumers face so many choices for everything they buy, IKEA provides a one-stop sanctuary for coolness. It is a trusted safe zone that people can enter and immediately be part of a like-minded cost/design/environmentally sensitive global tribe.

If the Swedish retailer has its way, you too will live in a BoKlok home and sleep in a Leksvik bed under a Brunskära quilt. Beds are named after Norwegian cities; bedding after flowers and plants. IKEA wants to supply the food in your fridge, it also sells the fridge, and the soap in your shower.

The IKEA concept has plenty of room to run: the retailer accounts for just 5 to 10 per cent of the furniture market in each country in which it operates. It is, however, a global phenomenon. That is because IKEA is far more than a furniture merchant. It sells a lifestyle that consumers around the world embrace as a signal that they've arrived, that they have good taste and recognize value. 'If it wasn't for IKEA,' writes British design magazine *Icon*, 'most people would have no access to affordable contemporary design.' The magazine even voted IKEA founder Ingvar Kamprad the most influential tastemaster in the world today.

As long as consumers from Moscow to Beijing and beyond keep striving to enter the middle class, there will be a need for IKEA. Think about it. What mass-market retailer has had more success globally? Not Wal-Mart Stores Inc., which despite vast strengths has stumbled in Brazil, Germany and Japan. Not France's Carrefour, which has never made it in the USA. IKEA has had its slip-ups, too. But right now its 284 stores mainly in Europe, Asia, Australia and the USA are thriving, hosting over 500 million shoppers a year.

Why the uproar?

IKEA is the quintessential global cult brand. Just take those stunts. Before an Atlanta opening, IKEA managers invited locals to apply for the post of Ambassador of Kul (Swedish for fun). The five winners wrote an essay on why they deserved $2000 in vouchers. There was one catch. They would have to live in the store for three days before the opening, take part in contests and sleep in the bedding

department. 'I got about eight hours of sleep total because of all the drilling and banging going on,' says winner Jordan Leopold, a manager at Costco Wholesale.

Leopold got his bedroom set. And IKEA got to craft another story about itself—a story picked up in the press that drew even more shoppers. More shoppers, more traffic. More traffic, more sales. More sales, more buzz. Such buzz has kept IKEA's sales growing at a healthy clip: for the fiscal year ended 31 August 2011, in the midst of a recession, revenues rose 7 per cent to $32 billion with profits up by 10 per cent to $4 billion. IKEA maintains these profits even while it cuts prices steadily. 'IKEA's operating margins of approximately 10 per cent are among the best in home furnishing,' says Mattias Karlkjell of Stockholm's ABG Sundal Collier. They also compare well with margins of 5 per cent at Pier 1 Imports and 7.7 per cent at Target, both competitors of IKEA in the USA.

TABLE C41.1   IKEA at a glance

Privately owned home products retailer that markets flat-pack furniture, accessories, and bathroom and kitchen items globally.

Ikea is the world's largest furniture manufacturer.

Sales of $32 billion (2011).

Estimated profits of $4 billion (2011).

Number of stores in 2011: 287 in 26 countries, mainly in Europe, USA, Canada, Asia and Australia. The largest number of stores are in Germany (46) and USA (38).

To keep growing at that pace, IKEA has continued its new store openings around the world with up to 20 per year (although that number was reduced during the recent recession) at a cost of $70 million per store, on average. IKEA has boosted its profile in three of its fastest-growing markets: the USA, Russia (where IKEA is already a huge hit—today's Russian yuppies are called 'the IKEA generation', and China (now worth over $200 million in sales). In the USA the number of stores has grown from 25 in 2005 to 38 in 2011. IKEA is also investing in emerging markets such as Croatia, Slovenia and the Ukraine. In the UK IKEA has built smaller, multi-level, city stores in Coventry and Southampton in response to restrictions on the building of out-of-town retail establishments.

The key to these roll-outs is to preserve the strong enthusiasm IKEA evokes—an enthusiasm that has inspired endless shopper comment on the Internet. Examples: 'IKEA makes me free to become what I want to be' (from Romania). Or this: 'Half my house is from IKEA—and the nearest store is six hours away' (the USA). Or this: 'Every time, it's trendy for less money' (Germany).

The shopping experience

What enthrals shoppers and scholars alike is the store visit—a similar experience the world over. The blue-and-yellow buildings average 28,000 square metres in size, about equal to five football fields. The sheer number of items—7000, from kitchen cabinets to candlesticks—is a decisive advantage. 'Others offer affordable furniture,' says Bryan Roberts, research manager at Planet Retail, a consultancy in London. 'But there's no one else who offers the whole concept in the big shed.'

The global middle class, which IKEA targets, shares buying habits. The $120 Billy bookcase, $13 Lack side table and $190 Ivar storage system are best-sellers worldwide. Even spending per customer is similar. According to IKEA, the figure in Russia is $85 per store visit—exactly the same as in affluent Sweden.

Wherever they are, customers tend to think of the store visit as more of an outing than a chore. That's intentional. IKEA practises a form of 'gentle coercion' to keep you as long as possible. Right at the entrance, for example, you can drop off your kids at the playroom, an amenity that encourages more leisurely shopping.

Then, clutching your dog-eared catalogue (the print run is over 160 million—more than the Bible, IKEA claims), you proceed along a marked path through the warren of showrooms. 'Because the store is designed as a circle, I can see everything as long as I keep walking in one direction,' says Krystyna Gavora, an architect who frequents IKEA in Schaumburg, Illinois. Wide aisles let you inspect merchandise without holding up traffic. The furniture itself is arranged in fully accessorized displays, down to the picture frames on the nightstand, to inspire customers and get them to spend more. The settings are so lifelike that one writer staged a play at IKEA in Renton, Washington.

Along the way, one touch after another seduces the shopper, from the paper measuring tapes and pencils to strategically placed bins with items like pink plastic watering cans, scented candles and picture frames. These are things you never knew you needed but at less than $2 each you load up on them anyway. You set out to buy a $40 coffee table but end up spending $500 on everything from storage units to glassware. 'They have this way of making you believe nothing is expensive,' says Bertille Faroult, a shopper at IKEA on the outskirts of Paris. The bins and shelves constantly surprise. IKEA replaces a third of its product line every year.

Then, there's the stop at the restaurant, usually placed at the centre of the store, to give shoppers a breather and encourage them to keep going. You proceed to the warehouse, where the full genius of founder Kamprad is on display. Nearly all the big items are flat-packed, which not only saves IKEA millions in shipping costs from suppliers but also enables shoppers to haul their own stuff home—another saving. Finally, you have the fun, or agony, of assembling at home, equipped with nothing but an Allen key and those cryptic instructions.

A vocal minority rails at IKEA for its long queues, crowded car parks, exasperating assembly experiences and furniture that's hardly built to last. The running joke is that IKEA is Swedish for particle board. But the converts outnumber the critics. And for every fan who shops at IKEA, there seems to be one working at the store itself. The fanaticism stems from founder Ingvar Kamprad, 86, a figure as important to global retailing as Wal-Mart's Sam Walton. Kamprad started the company in 1943 at the age of 17, selling pens, Christmas cards and seeds from a shed on his family's farm in southern Sweden. In 1951 the first catalogue appeared. Kamprad penned all the text himself until 1963. His credo of creating 'a better life for many' is enshrined in his almost evangelical 1976 tract, *A Furniture Dealer's Testament*. Peppered with folksy titbits—'divide your life into 10-minute units and sacrifice as few as possible in meaningless activity', 'wasting resources is a mortal sin' (that's for sure: employees are the catalogue models) or the more revealing 'it is our duty to expand'—the pamphlet is given to all employees the day they start. Employees at IKEA will never get rich but they do get to enjoy autonomy, very little hierarchy and a family-friendly culture. In return they buy into the culture of frugality and style that drives the whole company.

Kamprad, though officially retired, is still the cheerleader for the practices that define IKEA culture. One is

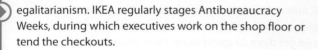

egalitarianism. IKEA regularly stages Antibureaucracy Weeks, during which executives work on the shop floor or tend the checkouts.

Prices and costs

A feature of IKEA is its steely competitiveness. You get a sense of that at one of IKEA's main offices, in Helsingborg, Sweden. At the doorway, a massive bulletin board tracks weekly sales growth, names the best-performing country markets and identifies the best-selling furniture. The other message that comes across loud and clear: cut prices. IKEA designers found a way to pack the Ektorp three-seater sofa more compactly, doubling the amount of sofa they could get into a given space. The cost saving meant that $135 could be shaved from its price.

The montage vividly illustrates IKEA's relentless cost cutting. The retailer aims to lower prices across its entire offering by an average of 2 per cent to 3 per cent each year. It goes deeper when it wants to hit rivals in certain segments. 'We look at the competition, take their price and then slash it in half,' says Mark McCaslin, manager of IKEA Long Island, in Hicksville, NY.

It helps that frugality is as deeply ingrained in the corporate DNA as the obsession with design. Managers fly economy, even top brass. Steen Kanter, who left IKEA in 1994 and now heads his own retail consultancy in Philadelphia, Kanter International, recalls that while flying with founder Ingvar Kamprad once, the boss handed him a coupon for a car rental he had ripped out from an in-flight magazine.

This cost obsession fuses with the design culture. 'Designing beautiful-but-expensive products is easy,' says Josephine Rydberg-Dumont, president of IKEA of Sweden. 'Designing beautiful products that are inexpensive and functional is a huge challenge.'

No design—no matter how inspired—finds its way into the showroom if it cannot be made affordable. To achieve that goal, the company's 12 full-time designers at Almhult, Sweden, along with 80 freelances, work hand in hand with in-house production teams to identify the appropriate materials and least costly suppliers, a trial-and-error process that can take as long as three years. Example: for the PS Ellan, a $39.99 dining chair that can rock back on its hind legs without tipping over, designer Chris Martin worked with production staff for a year and a half to adapt a wood-fibre composite, an inexpensive blend of wood chips and plastic resin used in highway noise barriers, for use in furnishings. Martin also had to design the chair to break down into six pieces, so it could be flat-packed and snapped together without screws.

With a network of 2000 suppliers in over 50 countries, IKEA works overtime to find the right manufacturer for the right product. It once contracted with ski makers—experts in bent wood—to manufacture its Poang armchairs, and it has tapped makers of supermarket carts to turn out durable sofas. Simplicity, a tenet of Swedish design, helps keep costs down. The 50' Trofé mug came only in blue and white, the least expensive pigments. IKEA's conservation drive extends naturally from this cost cutting. For its new PS line, it challenged 28 designers to find innovative uses for discarded and unusual materials. The results: a table fashioned from reddish-brown birch heartwood (furniture makers prefer the pale exterior wood) and a storage system made from recycled milk cartons.

Adaptation to local tastes

Adding to the challenge, the suppliers and designers have to customize some IKEA products to make them sell better in local markets. In China, the 250,000 plastic placemats IKEA produced to commemorate the year of the rooster sold out in just three weeks. Julie Desrosiers, the bedroom line manager at IKEA of Sweden, visited people's houses in the USA and Europe to peek into their closets, learning that 'Americans prefer to store most of their clothes folded, and Italians like to hang'. The result was a wardrobe that features deeper drawers for US customers.

The American market poses special challenges for IKEA because of the huge differences inside the USA. 'It's so easy to forget the reality of how people live,' says IKEA's US interior design director, Mats Nilsson. For example, IKEA realized it might not be reaching California's Hispanics, so its designers visited the homes of Hispanic staff. They soon realized they had set up the store's displays all wrong. Large Hispanic families need dining tables and sofas that fit more than two people, the Swedish norm. They prefer bold colours to the more subdued Scandinavian palette and display tons of pictures in elaborate frames. Nilsson warmed up the showrooms' colours, adding more seating and throwing in numerous picture frames.

IKEA is particularly concerned about the USA since it is key to expansion—and since IKEA came close to blowing it. 'We got our clocks cleaned in the early 1990s because we really didn't listen to the consumer,' says Kanter. Stores weren't big enough to offer the full IKEA experience, and many were in poor locations. Prices were too high. Beds were measured in centimetres, not king, queen and twin. Sofas weren't deep enough, curtains were too short and kitchens didn't fit US-size appliances. 'American customers were buying vases to drink from because the glasses were too small,' recalls Goran Carstedt, the former head of IKEA North America, who helped engineer a turnaround. Parts of the product line were adapted (no more metric measurements), new and bigger store locations chosen, prices slashed and service improved. Now US managers are paying close attention to the tiniest details. 'Americans want more comfortable sofas, higher-quality textiles, bigger glasses, more spacious entertainment units,' says Pernille Spiers-Lopez, head of IKEA North America.

The future

Can the cult keep thriving? IKEA has stumbled badly before. A foray into Japan 30 years ago was a disaster (the Japanese wanted high quality and great materials, not low price and particle board). The company returned to Japan in 2006. IKEA is also seeing more competition than ever. In the USA, Target Corp. recruited top designer Thomas O'Brien to develop a range of low-priced furnishings. An IKEA-like chain called Fly is popular in France. In Japan, Nitori Co. is the major player in low-cost furniture. ILVA is successfully selling upmarket furniture in Denmark and Sweden although its foray into the UK market was unsuccessful.

Perhaps the bigger issue is what happens inside IKEA. 'The great challenge of any organization as it becomes larger and more diverse is how to keep the core founding values alive,' says Harvard Business School Professor Christopher A. Bartlett. IKEA is still run by managers who were trained and groomed by Kamprad himself—and who are personally devoted to the founder. As the direct links with Kamprad disappear, the culture may start to fade.

For now, the fans keep clamouring for more. At least once a year, Jen Segrest, a 36-year-old freelance web designer, and her husband make a 10-hour round-trip from their home in Middletown, Ohio, to IKEA in Schaumburg, Illinois, near Chicago. 'Every piece of furniture in my living room is IKEA— except for an end table, which I hate. And next time I go to IKEA I'll replace it,' says Segrest. To lure the retailer to Ohio, Segrest has even started a blog called OH! IKEA. The banner on the home page reads 'IKEA in Ohio—Because man cannot live on Target alone.'

Questions

1. IKEA has chosen to enter new markets by direct investment. What advantages does this form of entry give it? Why doesn't IKEA use franchising like McDonald's and Benetton?

2. How would you categorize IKEA's approach to developing an international marketing strategy in terms of standardization and adaptation?

3. What are the factors that have helped IKEA to build a successful global brand?

This case was written by David Jobber, Professor of Marketing, University of Bradford.

The Smirnoff Nightlife Exchange Project
Global Marketing in Action

Introduction

Smirnoff is the world's best-selling vodka and the biggest brand in the cabinet of spirits and wine giant Diageo. Smirnoff traces its heritage back to nineteenth-century Russia and today is sold in 130 countries worldwide. In 2010 the Power 100 Report carried out by strategy consultancy Intangible Business was topped by Smirnoff, described as possessing a 'modern, cool image'.[1]

According to James Thomson, President of Global Marketing Spirits at Diageo, Smirnoff is an 'iconic' brand that appeals to consumers around the world. 'It's a truly global brand and there aren't many truly global brands around. The key to its success has been finding the right distribution and communicating an international message in particular markets.'[2]

Changing focus

Over the years, Diageo have built Smirnoff into the iconic international brand it is today. This has been achieved through several successful international marketing campaigns; however, the focus of these campaigns has changed over the years. In the early noughties Smirnoff found themselves faced with steep competition in the crowded vodka market and were eager to find a way to leapfrog the competition and get closer to their customers. They wanted a way to develop and maintain a loyal customer following. Their experience with traditional media wasn't working and they recognised that the energy in the brand's relationship had shifted from them to the consumer. Their previous focus was on the purity of the brand, but Smirnoff now wanted to shift to a lifestyle positioning. To accomplish their brand objectives, they changed their branding theme from 'Clearly Original' to 'Be There'. In July 2009 Diageo launched their new global marketing campaign for Smirnoff vodka, a direct call to action inviting consumers to 'Be There'—to create, seek out and participate in extraordinary shared experiences. To introduce this new approach, they cut back on traditional advertising significantly and sponsored a series of local social events where consumers could create buzz in advance and tell their friends 'Be There'.[3]

Smirnoff launched online ads promoting its website and asking visitors to the website to come up with ideas for their fantasy night out. Diageo would fund and help to put on the most creative suggestions—the only condition was that Smirnoff had to be served at these events. To foster engagement, they co-created several integrated social media campaigns using Facebook, Twitter, Flickr and YouTube. These parties evolved through online social media, with 'Be There' events being held all over the world. The events featured world-famous DJs and visual and performing artists, which all added excitement to the parties.[4]

Diageo also decided to add a couple of catchphrases to the events that were linked to their ads and became popular terms—'Life is Calling, Be There' and 'Can You Say I Was There'. These events were a huge success and raised the profile of the brand internationally. Smirnoff believes their success was due to their willingness to do things differently: that when you overturn convention or simply change one of the ingredients of a night out, you can create something special, something extraordinary—a night that you can look back on and are proud to say 'I was there'.[5]

The Nightlife Exchange Project

In 2010 Smirnoff launched one of the brand's most audacious missions yet—a new global integrated promotion campaign, called the Smirnoff Nightlife Exchange Project. The activity continued the 'Be There' campaign which was underpinned by the strategy of helping people enjoy one-of-a-kind experiences. While the digital age has made the world seem smaller than ever, global culture remains endlessly diverse. To celebrate that diversity and to explore different cities and others' local nightlife scene and cultures, Smirnoff created the Smirnoff Nightlife Exchange Project.[6]

This project set out to show the world how other cultures party. It was a call to action inviting consumer-generated ideas from 14 countries, which were then transformed into event experiences. Hailing from six continents, the 14 countries taking part were the United States, Great Britain, Argentina, Australia, Brazil, Canada, Germany, India, Ireland, Lebanon, Poland, South Africa, Thailand and Venezuela.[7] This initiative was aimed at discovering and celebrating the best nightlife from around the world. Consumers were invited to make suggestions for what represented the best of nightlife in their country on the Smirnoff Facebook page. Users could make suggestions about the fashion, food, music, dance moves, bands, DJs and more, that represented the best of their country's nightlife. These suggestions were reviewed by a local expert in each country, who made the decision as to what would represent the very best of each country's nightlife in the exchange.[8]

Each country's concepts were packed in a shipping crate as event experiences, with the campaign culminating on 27 November 2010, when each of the 14 countries involved exchanged the best of their nightlife with a partner country. Canada and India were paired, as were the UK and the US, Australia with Brazil, Argentina with Ireland, Germany with South Africa, Lebanon with Thailand and Poland with Venezuela.[6]

Having already rallied a global online community of over 2 million like-minded people, the Smirnoff Nightlife Exchange Project put these fans and the general public at its very centre. The campaign was anchored in the brand's Facebook page and included a global partnership with MTV, who drove the collaboration through webisodes and news segments hosted on the MTV site. The campaign also used a blogger outreach programme, a mobile channel (Smirnoff.mobi), PR drives and a TV and web advertising campaign.[9]

Smirnoff launched their Nightlife Exchange project through a TV advertisement, although the feel of the advert was more that of a teaser than a prime-time high budget advert. The purpose of the advertisement was to inform people of the Exchange Project and tease them to find out more through their social media pages. It worked! Customers flocked to the social media pages in the hope of finding a project near them and getting tickets. The TV campaign included video footage of consumers describing what in their view was the best of their country's nightlife in the exchange. This video footage was shot during a tour of the countries involved in the initiative. A crate with a mobile diary room inside toured each country and recorded the public's views on what was best about their local scene via a vox-pop booth. Those visiting the crate and recording their views were in with a chance to gain a special wristband which entitled them to selected discounts on drinks and complimentary access to a number of Smirnoff's on-trade partners' bars for the night.[10]

The results were revealed on 22 October 2010, when each country began the task of packing up its best nightlife for one of the other countries to experience. On 27 November 2010, 14 parties took place simultaneously in cities as far-reaching as Sydney, New Dehli, Buenos Aires and Miami.[11]

Evaluation

Drinks companies know that sponsoring nightlife events is good advertising, since most people attending will be drinking alcohol. By creating a branded exchange project, Smirnoff offered something new and exclusive, but also worldwide, to its potential customers.[12] Many alcohol brands sponsor and/or run a nightlife event, but none allow exclusive access to a new idea, a new type of nightlife. Smirnoff did and they offered it to the world! Their formula for a successful integrated campaign lies in giving the customer something they wanted, presenting the benefit in a totally different way to the competition and allowing customers to take part in the campaign.[13]

This campaign allowed customers to interact with the brand image. Consumers then felt that they had a personal relationship with the brand, reinforcing their brand loyalty and the image of the brand. Also, the campaign offered something that the competitors did not. Smirnoff has shown how a brand can engage consumers by using cultural exchange parties between cities around the world.[13]

Feedback from these parties was very positive, with consumers saying they were 'very excited' about the parties and thanking Smirnoff for an 'unforgettable evening'. This cross-pollination of nightlife around the world created an iconic and global moment.[14] Following on from the continent-straddling international extravaganza of the Nightlife Exchange Project, Smirnoff have decided to take this one step further and bring the Nightlife Exchange on tour. In 2011 Smirnoff will attempt to sustain this interest in and engagement with the brand as the Nightlife Exchange goes on the road in several of the participating countries. For example, in the UK, Smirnoff is offering the public the chance to bring a taste of Miami nightlife to a town near them in May 2011 on www.facebook.com/Smirnoff.[12]

▶ References

1 http://www.intangiblebusiness.com/Brand-Services/
   Marketing-services/Press-coverage/Smirnoff-named-
   most-valuable-drinks-brand-~3358.html

2 http://www.intangiblebusiness.com/Brand-Services/
   Marketing-services/Press-coverage/Smirnoff---a-no-
   nonsense-truly-global-vodka~230.html

3 http://www.brandingcommunications.com/case-
   stories/case-story-smirnoff.html

4 http://www.cityswitchlab.blogspot.com2010/02/
   project-name-and-url-smirnoff-be-there-html

5 http://www.newswire.ca/en/releases/archive/
   September2010/12/c8076.html

6 http://www.brandfreak.com/2010/11/smirnoff-and-jwt-
   learn-how-the-whole-wide-world-likes-to-party.html

7 http://www.psfk.com/2010/09/smirnoffs-nightlife-
   exchange-project.html

8 http://www.marketingweek.co.uk/sectors/food-and-
   drink/alcohol/smirnoff-plans-global-nightlife-
   campaign/3018122.article

9 http://www.marketingweek.co.uk/sectors/food-and-
   drink/alcohol/smirnoff-plans-global-nightlife-
   campaign/3018122.article

10 http://www.brandrepublic.com/go/news/article/1027983/
   smirnoff-kicks-off-international-nightlife-exchange-
   project/

11 http://www.promomarketing.info/the-smirnoff-co-
   announces-worlds-first-global-nigh/P003890/

12 http://www.mixmag.net/2011/02/17/smirnoff-launch-
   nightlife-exchange-uk-tour/

13 http://www.quatreus.com/Default.aspx?pagename=
   News-articles&newsarticletitle=Integrating-Advertising
   %2C-Social%2C-and-Live-Marketing&newsarticleid=1119

14 http://wave.wavemetrix.com/content/social-media-gets-
   consumers-raving-Smirnoff-Nightlife-Exchange-parties-
   00661

Questions

1 Comment on the factors that have led to Smirnoff's success as a global brand.

2 Why are so many brands such as Smirnoff standardizing their marketing strategies? What are the benefits and drawbacks associated with standardization?

3 Identify the challenges associated with a global marketing campaign like the 'Smirnoff Nightlife Exchange Project'. What macro-environmental trends have led to the success of this campaign?

This case was prepared by Marie O' Dwyer, Lecturer in Marketing, Waterford Institute of Technology, from various published sources, as a basis for class discussion rather than to illustrate either effective or ineffective management.

PART 5

Marketing Implementation and Application

SHOWCASE

A Marketing Showcase video featuring an interview with Intel's Marketing Director is available to lecturers for presentation and class discussion.

22 Managing marketing implementation, organization and control 812

CHAPTER 22

Managing marketing implementation, organization and control

However beautiful the strategy, you should occasionally look at the results.
SIR WINSTON CHURCHILL 1874–1965,
ENGLISH STATESMAN[1]

There is nothing more difficult than to take the lead in the introduction of a new order of things.
MACHIAVELLI

LEARNING OBJECTIVES

After reading this chapter, you should be able to:

1 describe the relationship between marketing strategy, implementation and performance

2 identify the stages that people pass through when they experience disruptive change

3 describe the objectives of marketing implementation and change

4 discuss the barriers to the implementation of the marketing concept

5 discuss the forms of resistance to marketing implementation and change

6 explain how to develop effective implementation strategies

7 describe the elements of an internal marketing programme

8 discuss the skills and tactics that can be used to overcome resistance to the implementation of the marketing concept and plan

9 discuss marketing organizational structures

10 explain the nature of a marketing control system

Designing marketing strategies and positioning plans that meet today's and tomorrow's market requirements is a necessary but not a sufficient condition for corporate success. They need to be translated into action through effective implementation. In this chapter we explore the following issues: the importance of implementation for business outcomes, the relationship between strategy, implementation and performance, how people react to change, and the objectives of implementation. We also explore resistance to change that might result from implementing the marketing strategy, and the skills and tactics marketing managers can use to bring about marketing implementation and change. Finally, we examine how companies organize their marketing activities and establish control procedures to check that objectives have been achieved.

Marketing Strategy, Implementation and Performance

Marketing strategy concerns the issues of *what* should happen and *why* it should happen. Implementation focuses on actions: *who* is responsible for various activities, *how* the strategy should be carried out, *where* things will happen and *when* action will take place. Lou Gerstner, the man admired for reviving IBM's fortunes, once said that the last thing the company needed was another strategy. What he actually meant was that the company's problem was not developing great strategies, but in its willingness and ability to implement them.[2]

Managers devise marketing strategies to meet new opportunities, counter environmental threats and match core competences. The framework for strategy development was discussed in Chapter 2, as part of the marketing planning process. Although implementation is a consequence of strategy, it also affects planning and is an integral part of the strategy development process. The proposition is straightforward: without a well-organized implementation, even the best strategy is likely to fail. Implementation capability is an integral part of strategy formulation and the link between the two is shown in Figure 22.1. Implementation affects marketing strategy choice. For example, a company that traditionally has been a low-cost, low-price operator may have a culture that finds it difficult to implement a value-added, high-price strategy. Strategy also determines implementation requirements: for example, a value-added, high-price strategy may require the salesforce to refrain from price discounting.

FIGURE 22.1   Marketing strategy and implementation

Marketing strategy

Determines

Marketing implementation

Affects

Combining strategies and implementation

Bonoma has argued that combinations of appropriate/inappropriate strategy and good/poor implementation will lead to various business outcomes.[3] Figure 22.2 shows the four-cell matrix, with predicted performances.

Appropriate strategy—good implementation

This is the combination most likely to lead to success. No guarantee of success can be

FIGURE 22.2   Marketing strategy, implementation and performance

		Strategy	
		Appropriate	Inappropriate
Implementation	Good	Success	Roulette
	Bad	Trouble	Failure

Source: adapted from Bonoma, T. V. (1985) *The Marketing Edge: Making Strategies Work*, New York: Free Press, 12. Reprinted with the permission of the Free Press. Copyright © 1985 by the Free Press.

made, however, because of the vagaries of the marketplace, including competitor actions and reactions, new technological breakthroughs and plain bad luck; but with strong implementation backing sound strategy, marketing management has done all it can to build success.

Appropriate strategy—bad implementation

This combination is likely to lead to trouble if sub-standard performance is attributed to poor strategy. Management's tendency to look for strategy change in response to poor results will result in a less appropriate strategy being grafted on to an already wayward implementation system.

Inappropriate strategy—good implementation

Two effects of this combination can be predicted. First, the effective implementation of a poor strategy can hasten failure. For example, very effectively communicating a price rise (which is part of an inappropriate repositioning strategy) to customers may accelerate a fall in sales. Second, if good implementation takes the form of correcting a fault in strategy, then the outcome will be favourable. For example, if strategy implies an increase in sales effort to push a low margin *dog* product to the detriment of a new *star* product in a growing market (perhaps for political reasons), modification at the implementation level may correct the bias. The reality of marketing life is that managers spend many hours supplementing, subverting, overcoming or otherwise correcting shortcomings in strategic plans.

Inappropriate strategy—bad implementation

This obviously leads to failure, which is difficult to correct because so much is wrong. An example might be a situation where a product holds a premium price position without a competitive advantage to support the price differential. The situation is made worse by an advertising campaign that is unbelievable, and a salesforce that makes misleading claims leading to customer annoyance and confusion.

Implications

So what should managers do when faced with poor performance? First, strategic issues should be separated from implementation activities and the problem diagnosed. Second, when in doubt about whether the problem is rooted in strategy or implementation, implementation problems should be addressed first so that strategic adequacy can be assessed more easily.

Implementation and the Management of Change

A key factor in implementing a change programme is top management support. Without its clear, visible and consistent backing a major change programme is likely to falter under the inertia created by vested interests.[4] It is important for companies to monitor change and ensure that systems are in place to gather and disseminate information throughout the organization. For example, Cisco invites groups of key clients three or four times a year for workshops and discussions over several days with all functional areas of the company. The objectives are to analyse how the company is doing and how it should go forward to better serve key customer needs. This allows Cisco not only to gain first-hand knowledge of customer preferences, but also to ensure the entire organization is immediately aware of customers' experiences, demands and how the company should operate in the future.[5]

The implementation of a new strategy may have profound effects on people in organizations. Brand managers who discover their product is to receive fewer resources (harvested) may feel bitter and demoralized; a salesperson who loses as a result of a change in the payment system may feel equally aggrieved. The implementation of a strategy move is usually associated with the need for people to adapt to *change*. The cultivation of change, therefore, is an essential ingredient in effective implementation. Some companies have charismatic leaders, like Virgin and Richard Branson, which can help the cultivation of change and Xerox's CMO Christine Carone. Read Marketing in Action 22.1 to find out more about how she has made a difference.

Marketing in Action 22.1 Xerox's CMO Christine Carone

Christina Carone is the Chief Marketing Officer for Xerox, a world-leading provider of business process and document management solutions. Christina faced the challenge of how to change global perceptions of the brand from photocopiers manufacturer to business service provider. In 2008 Xerox was positioned in the document copier market but its business strategy had been moving more into providing business process services including call centres, outsourcing and accounting, which were generating over 50 per cent of its revenue.

Christina's vision for change was to position the brand as more relevant to customers and in doing so 'cultivated a business to people (B2P) marketing approach'. She wanted the brand to be perceived as being more personable and in-touch with the world of business. In pursuit of relevance, Christina discovered that many large companies see accounting and managing call centres as 'a necessary evil'. So, it became relatively straightforward to help companies by taking over these processes, thereby enabling them to get on with their *real* business interests. Xerox developed a value proposition based on scale and providing business services to many large corporate clients.

The change of strategy and implementation has had a positive effect on employees throughout the business as they have acquired a real sense of purpose because everyone is clear about what the business stands for and what it is trying to achieve. Darren Miniards, Head of Marketing Communication Xerox Europe, says that Christina has had a profound effect on the business . . . she has given an absolute shape and clarity to what Xerox is about. In addition, she has worked with the CEO Ursula Burns to turn the company which employs over 136,000 people into a nimble and flexible business.

Base on: Snoad (2012)[6]

Go to the website to find out how Xerox helps manage information in the digital age.
www.mcgraw-hill.co.uk/ textbooks/jobber

⬆ EXHIBIT 22.1   Change can be assisted by the presence of a charismatic leader like Richard Branson.

It is helpful to understand the emotional stages that people pass through when confronted with an adverse change. These stages are known as the **transition curve** and are shown in Figure 22.3.[7]

FIGURE 22.3   The transition curve

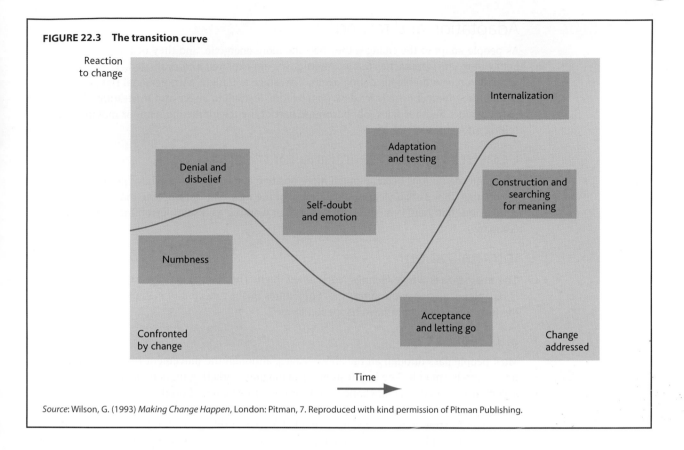

Source: Wilson, G. (1993) *Making Change Happen*, London: Pitman, 7. Reproduced with kind permission of Pitman Publishing.

Numbness

The first reaction is usually shock. The enormity of the consequences leads to feelings of being overwhelmed, despair and numbness. The outward symptoms include silence and lack of overt response. The news that a field salesforce is to be replaced by a telemarketing team is likely to provoke numbness in the field salespeople.

Denial and disbelief

Denial and disbelief may follow numbness, leading to trivializing the news, denying it or joking about it. The aim is to minimize the psychological impact of the change. News of the abandonment of the field salesforce may be met by utter disbelief, and sentiments such as 'They would never do that to us'.

Self-doubt and emotion

As the certainty of the change dawns, so personal feelings of uncertainty may arise. The feeling is one of powerlessness, of being out of control: the situation has taken over the individual. The likely reaction is one of anger: both as individuals and as a group, salesforce staff are likely to vent their anger and frustration on management.

Acceptance and letting go

Acceptance is characterized by tolerating the new reality and letting go of the past. This is likely to occur at an emotional low point but is the beginning of an upward surge as comfortable attitudes and behaviours are severed, and the need to cope with the change is accepted. In the salesforce example, salespeople would become accustomed to the fact that they would no longer be calling upon certain customers and receiving a particular salary.

Adaptation and testing

As people adapt to the changes they become more energetic, and they begin testing new behaviours and approaches to life. Alternatives are explored and evaluated. The classic case is the divorcee who begins dating again. This stage is fraught with personal risk, as in the case of the divorcee who is let down once more, leading to anger and frustration. Salespeople may consider another sales job, becoming part of the telemarketing team or moving out of selling altogether.

Construction and searching for meaning

As people's emotions become much more positive and they feel they have got to grips with the change, they seek a clear understanding of the new. The salespeople may come to the conclusion that there is much more to life than working as a salesperson for their previous company.

Internalization

The final stage is where feelings reach a new high. The change is fully accepted, adaptation is complete and behaviour alters too. Sometimes this is reflected in statements like 'That was the best thing that could have happened to me'.

Implications

Most people pass through all the above stages, although the movement from one stage to the next is rarely smooth. The implication for managing marketing implementation is that the acceptance of fundamental change such as the reprioritizing of products, jobs or strategic business units will take time for people to accept and come to terms with. The venting of anger and frustration is an accompanying behaviour to this transition from the old to the new, and should be accepted as such. Some people will leave as part of the fifth stage—the testing of new behaviours—but others will see meaning in and internalize the changes that have resulted from strategic redirection.

Objectives of Marketing Implementation and Change

The overriding objective of marketing implementation and change from a strategic standpoint is the successful execution of the marketing plan. This may include:

- gaining the support of key decision-makers in the company for the proposed plan (and overcoming the opposition of others)
- gaining the required resources (e.g. people and money) to be able to implement the plan
- gaining the commitment of individuals and departments in the company who are involved in frontline implementation (e.g. marketing, sales, service and distribution staff)
- gaining the cooperation of other departments needed to implement the plan (e.g. production and R&D).

For some people, the objectives and execution of the plan are consistent with their objectives, interests and viewpoints; gaining support from them is easy. But there are likely to be others who are involved with implementation who are less willing to support the planned change. They are the losers and neutrals. Loss may be in the form of lower status, a harder life or a reduction in salary. Neutrals may be left untouched overall with gains being balanced by losses. For some losers, support will never be forthcoming, for others they may be responsive to persuasion, whereas neutrals may be more willing to support change.

The ladder of support

What does support mean? Figure 22.4 illustrates the degree of support that may be achieved; this can range from outright opposition to full commitment.

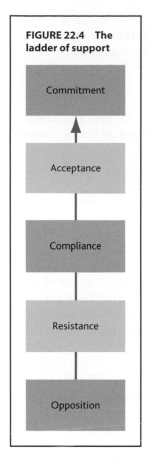

FIGURE 22.4 The ladder of support

- Commitment
- Acceptance
- Compliance
- Resistance
- Opposition

The Halifax Switching Team. Making it simple to move your current account.

It's now easier than ever to switch to a Halifax Reward Current Account, all thanks to our dedicated Switching Team who will move all your direct debits and standing orders for you. Better still, the service is completely free. Once you've switched, receiving your £5 is simple, all you need to do is pay in £1,000 each calendar month.

Switch your account in branch or by phone on 0845 122 1425.

WE MAKE **SWITCHING** EASY

HALIFAX
a little extra help

⬆ EXHIBIT 22.2   The Halifax bank uses members of staff when advertising its financial services products.

Opposition

The stance of direct opposition is taken by those with much to lose from the implementation of the marketing strategy, and who believe they have the political strength to stop the proposed change. Opposition is overt, direct and forceful.

Resistance

With resistance, opposition is less overt and may take a more passive form such as delaying tactics. Perhaps because of the lack of a strong power base, people are not willing to display open hostility but, nevertheless, their intention is to hamper the implementation process.

⬆ EXHIBIT 22.3   B&Q uses staff in advertisements as a sign of the importance of its employees.

Compliance

Compliance means that people act in accordance with the plan but without much enthusiasm or zest. They yield to the need to conform but lack conviction that the plan is the best way to proceed. These reservations limit the lengths to which they are prepared to go to achieve its successful implementation.

Staff feel valued when included in key organizational practices/activities. The Halifax bank uses members of staff when advertising its financial services products. Indeed, Howard Brown, bank employee, was so successful that he became the face of the Halifax for a number of years, appearing in a long run of advertising campaigns. However, in 2011, he left the bank after being dropped from the commercial for appearing 'too jolly'. Marketing strategists felt the tone of these campaigns was not appropriate for the period of austerity and recession.[8]

Acceptance

A higher level of support is achieved when people accept the worth of the plan and actively seek to realize its goals. Their minds may be won but their hearts are not set on fire, limiting the extent of their motivation.

Commitment

Commitment is the ultimate goal of an effective implementation programme. People not only accept the worth of the plan but also pledge themselves to secure its success. Both hearts and minds are won, leading to strong conviction, enthusiasm and zeal. This can be encouraged by making people feel valued. B&Q, a market-leading DIY chain in the UK, for example, uses members of staff in its television advertising to promote its garden products (Exhibit 22.3). Pizza Hut followed a similar approach using YouTube for an open casting call to find eight employees to feature in their ad campaigns. In this way they were able to involve many hundreds of employees. The Chief Marketing Officer said 'There is no better way to express the emotional side of the brand than through the employees that actually deliver the brand experience every day'.[9]

Go to the website to see how B&Q and Pizza Hut use employees in their adverts. www.mcgraw-hill.co.uk/textbooks/jobber

Barriers to the Implementation of the Marketing Concept

In this section we discuss forms of opposition and resistance towards implementation, and examine the skills and tactics which can be used to get over any such barriers. Increasingly, marketing managers need to be adept at managing the internal environment of the company as well as the external. First we shall examine barriers to the implementation of the marketing concept discussed in Chapter 1. Acceptance of marketing as a philosophy in a company is a necessary prerequisite for the successful development of marketing strategy and implementation.

The marketing concept states that business success will result from creating greater customer satisfaction than the competition. So why do so many companies score so badly at marketing effectiveness? The fact is that there are inherent *personal and organizational barriers* that make the achievement of marketing implementation difficult in practice. These are summarized in Figure 22.5.

High-cost solutions

Often giving what the customer wants involves extra costs. In highly competitive environments most companies will meet customers' low-cost solutions. Therefore many marketing recommendations to beat competition will involve higher costs. Travelworld, a travel agency, was founded on giving better service to its customers. The chief executive recognized that the competition often required customers to queue at peak periods when booking a holiday. This he felt was unacceptable when customers were involved in a major transaction: a holiday is one of the highest-expenditure items for families each year. The solution was to hire enough staff at his outlets to ensure that queuing was not a problem. He came from a marketing background and accepted the higher costs involved.

Meeting customer requirements can also conflict with production's desire to gain cost economies of scale, and the finance director's objective of inventory reduction. Customers invariably differ in their requirements—they have different personalities, experiences and lifestyles—and to meet individual requirements is clearly not feasible. A solution to this

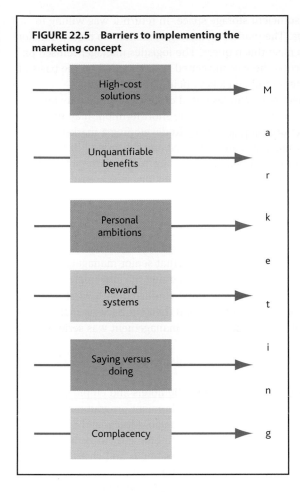

FIGURE 22.5   Barriers to implementing the marketing concept

M
a
r
k
e
t
i
n
g

High-cost solutions

Unquantifiable benefits

Personal ambitions

Reward systems

Saying versus doing

Complacency

problem is to group customers into segments that have similar needs and to target one product or service offering to each group. This allows the production manager to reap some economies of scale, and marketing to tailor offerings to the marketplace.

To a finance director stocks mean working capital tied up and on-going interest charges. To the marketing director stocks mean higher service levels and thus higher customer satisfaction. In the retailing of shoes, for example, an out-of-stock situation is likely to mean a lost customer. Once more the marketing approach of giving customers what they want is a high-cost solution. Clearly, a compromise needs to be reached and target market segmentation can provide its basis. Unipart, a supplier of spare parts for cars, recognized that inventory cost control procedures meant that the competition was holding low stocks. This resulted in customer dissatisfaction when an urgently needed part could not be provided when required. Unipart's strategy was to target motorists (do-it-yourselfers) who valued instant (or very quick) parts provision and were willing to pay a little more for the service. Its tag-line, 'The answer's yes. Now what's the question?', reflected the company's strategy. It identified a *high-price, high-service* segment and chose to serve those customers. In other situations, a *low-price, low-service* segment may be identified, and low stocks and a low price may be the appropriate response.

Unquantifiable benefits

A problem with marketing recommendations is that they are often unquantifiable and it is difficult to measure the exact increase in revenue (and profits) that will result from their implementation. For example, a business school faced with a customer problem: the student car park was regularly being raided by thieves who stole radios and cars. One marketing solution was to employ at least one security guard. The extra cost could easily be quantified, not so the economic benefits to the business school, however. On a purely commercial basis, it is impossible to say what the marginal revenue would be. On a similar theme, what is likely to be the reduced revenue from removing one platform attendant from a railway station? The cost saving is immediate and quantifiable; the reduced customer satisfaction through not having someone to answer queries is not.

Personal ambitions

Personal ambitions can also hinder the progress of marketing in an organization. The R&D director may enjoy working on challenging, complex technical problems at the cutting edge of scientific knowledge. Customers may simply want products that work. Staff may want an easy life, which means that the customer is neglected.

Reward systems

It is a basic tenet of motivation theory that behaviour is influenced by reward systems.[10] Sometimes, organizations reward individuals in ways that conflict with marketing-orientated action. An example is the situation that occurred between a supplier of motor oil and a supermarket chain. The supplier delivered 200 litres of motor oil in cans to each supermarket petrol station at a time. The supermarket asked if it would be possible to deliver smaller quantities more often as it did not have sufficient storage space. In return it was willing to pay extra to cover the additional journeys. The marketing manager, anxious to please a major customer, asked the logistics manager to meet this request. The logistics manager refused on the grounds that it would raise delivery costs: he was measured and rewarded on the basis of efficiency. A classic case of a reward system (and efficiency) being in conflict with effectiveness. Sales staff who are rewarded by incentives based on sales revenue may be tempted to give heavy discounts, which secure easy sales in the short term but may ruin positioning strategies and profits. Webster argues that the key to developing a market-driven, customer-orientated business lies in how managers are evaluated and rewarded.[11] If managers are evaluated on the basis of short-term profitability and sales, they are likely to pay heed to these criteria and neglect market factors, such as customer satisfaction, which ensure the long-term health of an organization.

Saying versus doing

Another force that blocks the implementation of the marketing concept is the gap between what senior managers say and what they do. Webster suggests that senior management must give clear signals and establish clear values and beliefs about serving the customer.[12] However, Argyris found that senior executives' behaviour often conflicted with what they said—for example, they might say 'Be customer orientated' and then cut back on marketing research funds.[13] This resulted in staff not really believing that management was serious about achieving a customer focus.

For those companies preaching an ethical stance, their words need to be backed up by deeds.

For example the Accor Hotel chain, which operates over 4000 hotels and employs 180,000 staff worldwide, has recently launched its new sustainable development programme—Planet 21. The group, which includes brands Novotel, Ibis, Mercure, Adagio, Motel6 and Sofitel, develops about 40,000 new rooms every year. Their plan is to combine growth with respect for the environment and local communities, by involving all of its hotels and customers. Through Planet 21 Accor is making 21 commitments and goals: for example, employees trained in disease prevention in 95 per cent of hotels; 80 per cent of properties promoting balanced meals; 85 per cent of hotels using eco-labelled products; a 15 per cent reduction in water consumption; and a 10 per cent decrease in energy use.

In order to avoid 'saying rather than doing' and being accused of green washing, Accor plan to guarantee the credibility of this programme by only allowing hotels to use the Planet 21 messages if they achieve a certain agreed level of performance.[14]

Complacency

A final barrier to the implementation of marketing change is complacency, which can be fuelled by past success. For example, at BMW, whose engineers had been used to success based on building powerful gas-guzzling cars, there was strong resistance to the introduction of a new fuel-efficiency programme called Efficient Dynamics. Their argument was that there was no need for efficient dynamics. Given their past success they believed that dynamics was enough. To drive through the change required to meet new market requirements, BMW's chief executive had to successfully change this mindset.[15]

Implications

The implications are that marketing managers have to face the fact that some people in the organization will have a vested interest in blocking the introduction and growth of marketing in the organization, and will have some ammunition (e.g. the extra costs, unquantifiable benefits) to achieve their aims. Marketing implementation, then, depends on being able to overcome the opposition and resistance that may well surface as a result of developing market-driven plans. The following sections discuss the nature of such resistance, and ways of dealing with it.

Forms of Resistance to Marketing Implementation and Change

Opposition to the acceptance of marketing and the implementation of marketing plans is direct, open and conflict driven. Often, arguments such as the lack of tangible benefits and the extra expense of marketing proposals will be used to cast doubt on their worth. Equally likely, however, is the more passive type of *resistance*. Kanter and Piercy suggest 10 forms of resistance:[16,17]

1 criticism of specific details of the plan
2 foot-dragging
3 slow response to requests
4 unavailability
5 suggestions that, despite the merits of the plan, resources should be channelled elsewhere
6 arguments that the proposals are too ambitious
7 hassle and aggravation created to wear the proposer down
8 attempts to delay the decision, hoping the proposer will lose interest
9 attacks on the credibility of the proposer with rumour and innuendo
10 deflation of any excitement surrounding the plan by pointing out the risks.

Market research reports supporting marketing action can also be attacked. Johnson describes the reaction of senior managers to the first marketing research report commissioned by a new marketing director.[18]

> As a diagnostic statement the research was full, powerful, prescriptive. The immediate result of this analysis was that the report was rubbished by senior management and directors. The analysis may have been perceived by its initiator as diagnostic but it was received by its audience as a politically threatening statement.

Ansoff argues that the level of resistance will depend on how much the proposed change is likely to disrupt the culture and power structure of the organization and the speed at which the change is introduced.[19] The latter point is in line with the previous discussion about how people adapt to adverse change, requiring time to come to terms with disruptions. The greatest level of opposition and resistance will come when the proposed change is implemented quickly and is a threat to the culture and politics of the organization; the least opposition and resistance will be found when the change is consonant with the existing culture and political structure, and is introduced over a period of time. Further, Pettigrew states that resistance is likely to be low when a company is faced with a crisis, arguing that a common perception among people that the organization is threatened with extinction also acts to overcome inertia against change.[20]

Developing Implementation Strategies

Faced with the likelihood of resistance from vested interests, a **change master** should develop an implementation strategy that can deliver the required change.[21] For example, when Anne Mulcahy was CEO at Xerox, the company was in trouble and she had to act as a change master. She began by talking to customers and employees, to gain an understanding of what was wrong. She ran meetings differently, forcing people to face the tough decisions that were necessary, and used the severity of the crisis at Xerox to gain acceptance for the required changes, which included cutting $1 billion of overheads and closing unprofitable businesses.[22] The workforce was cut by almost 40 per cent, while gaps in Xerox's product portfolio were filled with lower-priced products. This gave the company its largest product portfolio and has made it more competitive. Mulcahy was succeeded in 2009 by Ursula Burns who was instrumental in pulling Xerox back from the brink of bankruptcy.[23] As discussed earlier, Christina Carone continues in this vein acting as change agent when required. A change master is a person who is responsible for driving through change within an organization. This necessitates a structure for thinking about the problems to be tackled and the way to deal with them. Figure 22.6 illustrates such a framework. The process starts with a definition of objectives.

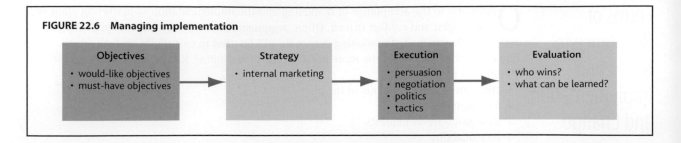

FIGURE 22.6 Managing implementation

Objectives	Strategy	Execution	Evaluation
• would-like objectives • must-have objectives	• internal marketing	• persuasion • negotiation • politics • tactics	• who wins? • what can be learned?

Implementation objectives

These are formulated at two levels: what we would like to achieve (*would-like objectives*) and what we must achieve (*must-have objectives*). Framing objectives in this way recognizes that we may not be able to achieve all that we desire. Would-like objectives are our preferred solution: they define the maximum that the implementer can reasonably expect.[24] Must-have objectives define our minimum requirements: if we cannot achieve these then we have lost and the plan or strategy will not succeed. Between the two points there is an area for negotiation, but beyond our must-have objective there is no room for compromise.

By clearly defining objectives at the start, we know what we would like, the scope for bargaining, and the point where we have to be firm and resist further concessions. For example, suppose our marketing plan calls for a move from a salary-only payment system for salespeople to salary plus commission. This is predicted to lead to strong resistance from salespeople and some sales managers, who favour the security element of fixed salary. Our would-like objective might be a 60:40 split between salary and commission. This would define our starting point in attempting to get this change implemented. But in order to allow room for concessions, our must-have objective would be somewhat lower, perhaps an 80:20 ratio between salary and commission. Beyond this point we refuse to bargain: we either win or lose on the issue. In some situations, however, would-like and must-have objectives coincide: here there is no room for negotiation, and persuasive and political skills are needed to drive through the issue.

Strategy

All worthwhile plans and strategies necessitate substantial human and organizational change inside companies.[25] Marketing managers, therefore, need a practical mechanism for thinking through strategies to drive change. One such framework is known as internal marketing, sometimes called the 'missing half' of the marketing programme.[26]

Originally the idea of internal marketing was developed within services marketing and it applied to the development, training, motivatation and retention of employees, in retailing, catering and financial services.[27] However, the concept can be expanded to include marketing to all employees with the aim of achieving successful marketing implementation. The framework is appealing as it draws an analogy with external marketing structures such as market segmentation, target marketing and the marketing mix. The people inside the organization to whom the plan must be marketed are considered *internal customers*. We need to gain the support, commitment and participation of sufficient of these to achieve acceptance and implementation of the plan. For those people where we fail to do this we need to minimize the effectiveness of their resistance. They become, in effect, our competitors in the internal marketplace.

Internal market segmentation

As with external marketing, analysis of customers begins with market segmentation. One obvious method of grouping internal customers is into three categories.

The internal marketing concept is approaching middle age. Its premise is concerned with internal products (jobs) that satisfy the needs of the internal audience (employees), while satisfying the objectives of the organisation.

This article looks at the leader's role in instilling the staff with a sense of togetherness within the organisation, often known as 'organizational identification' (OI). The authors go on to test the OI-transfer research model and offer evidence of the role leaders play in building staff identification.

Jan Wieseke, Michael Ahearne, Son K. Lam and Rolf van Dick (2009) The Role of Leaders in Internal Marketing,
Journal of Marketing, 73(March), 123–45.

Over 2000 years ago, Greek philosopher Heraclitus said, 'There is nothing permanent except change.' He may have been speaking today about organisations, as they are in a perpetual state of change to stay ahead of the competition, or just to stay alive. This article starts with a brief history of change theory, and goes on to discuss change agent strategies and techniques in managing change, as well as the implications for the people involved with the process.

Jonathan H. Westove (2010) Managing Organizational Change: Change Agent Strategies and Techniques to Successfully Managing the Dynamics of
Stability and Change in Organizations, International Journal of Management and Innovation, 2(1), 45–50.

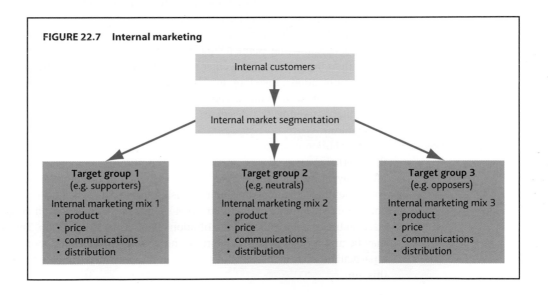

FIGURE 22.7   Internal marketing

1   *Supporters*: those who are likely to gain from the change or are committed to it.
2   *Neutrals*: those whose gains and losses are in approximate balance.
3   *Opposers*: those who are likely to lose from the change or are traditional opponents.
    These three market segments form distinct *target groups* for which specific *marketing mix* programmes can be developed (see Fig. 22.7).

Internal marketing mix programmes

Product is the marketing plan and strategies that are being proposed, together with the values, attitudes and actions that are needed to make the plan successful. Features of the product may include increased marketing budgets, extra staff, different ways of handling customers, different pricing, distribution and advertising, and new product development strategies. The product will reflect our would-like objectives; however, it may have to be modified slightly to gain acceptance from our opponents. Hence the need for must-have objectives.

The *price* element of the marketing mix is what we are asking our internal customers to pay as a result of accepting the marketing plan. The price they pay may be lost resources, lower status, fear of the unknown, harder work and rejection of their pet projects because of lack of funds. Clearly, price sensitivity is a key segmentation variable that differentiates supporters, neutrals and opposers.

Communications is a major element of the internal marketing mix and covers the communications media and messages used to influence the attitudes of key players. A combination of personal (presentations, discussion groups) and non-personal (the full report, executive summaries) can be used to inform and persuade. Communication should be two-way: we should listen as well as inform. We should also be prepared to adapt the product (the plan) if necessary in response to our internal customers' demands. It may also be necessary to fine-tune the language of marketing (e.g. eliminating jargon) to fit the corporate culture and background of the key players.[28]

Communication objectives will differ according to the target group, as follows.

- *Supporters*: to reinforce existing positive attitudes and behaviour, mobilize support from key players (e.g. chief executive).
- *Neutrals*: the use of influence strategies to build up perception of rewards and downgrade perceived losses; display key supporters and explain the benefits of joining 'the team'; negotiate to gain commitment.
- *Opposers*: disarm and discredit; anticipate objections and create convincing counterarguments; position them as 'stuck in their old ways'; bypass by gaining support of opinion and political leaders; negotiate to lower resistance.

Opposition to the proposals may stem from a misunderstanding on the part of staff of the meaning of marketing. Some people may equate marketing with advertising and selling rather than the placing of customer satisfaction as central to corporate success. An objective of communications, therefore, may be to clarify the real meaning of marketing, or to use terms that are more readily acceptable such as 'improving service quality'.[29]

Digital Marketing 22.1 discusses how company intranets can aid communication within companies.

Distribution describes the places where the product and communications are delivered to the internal customers such as meetings, committees, seminars, informal conversations and away-days. Consideration should be given to whether presentations should be direct (proponents to customers) or indirect (using third parties such as consultants). Given the conflicting viewpoints of the three target segments, thought should be given to the advisability of using different distribution channels for each group. For example, a meeting may be arranged with only supporters and neutrals present. If opponents tend to be found in a particular department, judicious selection of which departments to invite may accomplish this aim.

Execution

In order to execute an implementation strategy successfully, certain skills are required, and particular tactics need to be employed. Internal marketing has provided a framework to structure thinking about implementation strategies. Within that framework, the main skills are persuasion, negotiation and politics.

Persuasion

The starting point of persuasion is to try to understand the situation from the internal customer's standpoint. The new plan may have high profit potential, the chance of real sales growth and be popular among external customers but if it is perceived to cause grief to individuals and/or internal departments resistance is likely to occur. As with personal selling, the proponents of the plan must understand the needs, motivations and problems of their customers before they can hope to develop effective messages. For example, appealing to a production manager's sense of customer welfare will fail if that person is interested only in

Digital Marketing 22.1 Company Intranets: Open Access to Information

Internal communications are important to the success of implementation strategies. Internal customers should be understood in the same way as external customers. In other words, their needs and wants, attitudes and behaviours, all need to be taken into account. Increasingly, companies are using digital technologies as a means of communicating with employees and other internal stakeholders. Company intranets provide remote access through virtual private networks across the Internet to large resources of company information, and facilitate collaborative working. Intranets can be used in different ways to communicate with internal stakeholders (e.g. daily news updates, induction and training programmes, support systems, publishing repository, information resources, web applications). If implemented correctly, intranets can improve workforce productivity and communications and save time. At Aviva the CEO has been using the intranet to gauge staff opinions of the new business strategy, and Sainsbury's has been delving into how its 'live well for less' campaign is affecting its work force via the intranet.

The Open University, the world-leading provider of distance learning, has an intranet that provides access to information and support resources to its central academic staff and over 18,000 associate lecturers. However, having an intranet, and providing access to vast stores of information, is only part of the story. According to Daniel, 'the average knowledge worker spends around 10 per cent of their working time trying to find the information within their organization that they need to do their job'. She has five key recommendations, which can help to maximize the value of a company's information resources:

1   Ownership: all information should be assigned an owner to ensure effective stewardship.
2   Identification of all documents so they can be classified and retrieved easily.
3   Life cycle: documents become out of date and should be archived when no longer current.
4   Storage: systems should enable relevant staff to access the document they need at the time they need it. The maxim for many organizations is 'store once, use many'.
5   Audit: organizations should regularly review information stored, information requested, and the cost and value of the company's information resources.

Based on: Mortimer (2011);[30] *Mockler and Gartenfeld (2010);*[31] *Daniel (2006)*[32]

smooth production runs. In such a situation the proponent of the plan needs to show how smooth production will not be affected by the new proposals, or how disruption will be marginal or temporary.

The implementer also needs to understand how the features of the plan (e.g. new payment structure) confer customer benefits (e.g. the opportunity to earn more money). Whenever possible, evidence should be provided to support claims. Objectives should be anticipated and convincing counter-arguments produced. Care should be taken not to bruise egos unnecessarily.

Negotiation

Implementers have to recognize that they may not get all they want during this process. By setting would-like and must-have objectives (see earlier in this chapter) they are clear about what they want and have given themselves negotiating room wherever possible. Two key aspects of negotiation will be considered next: concession analysis and proposal analysis.

The key to **concession analysis** is to value the concessions the implementer might be prepared to make from the viewpoint of the opponent. By doing this it may be possible to identify concessions that cost the implementer very little and yet are highly valued by the opponent. For example, if the must-have objective is to move from a fixed salary to a salary plus commission, a salesperson's compensation plan conceding that the proportions should be 80:20 rather than 70:30 may be trivial to the implementer (an incentive to sell is still there) and yet highly valued by the salesperson as they will gain more income security and value the psychological bonus of winning a concession from management. By trading concessions that are highly valued by the opponent and yet cost the implementer little, painless agreement can be reached.

Proposal analysis: another sensible activity is to try to predict the proposals and demands that opponents are likely to make during the process of implementation. This provides time to prepare a response to them rather than relying on quick decisions during the heat of negotiation. By anticipating the kinds of proposals opponents are likely to make, implementers can plan the types of counter-proposal they are prepared to make.

Politics

Success in managing implementation and change also depends on the understanding and execution of political skills. Understanding the sources of power is the starting point from which an assessment of where power lies and who holds the balance can be made. The five sources are reward, expert, referent, legitimate and coercive power.[33]

Reward power derives from the implementer's ability to provide benefits to members in the organization. The recommendations of the plan may confer natural benefits in the form of increased status or salary for some people. In other cases, the implementer may create rewards for support—for example, promises of reciprocal support when required, or backing for promotion. The implementer needs to assess what each target individual values and whether the natural rewards match those values, or whether created rewards are necessary. A limit on the use of reward power is the danger that people may come to expect rewards in return for support. Created rewards, therefore, should be used sparingly.

Expert power is based on the belief that implementers have special knowledge and expertise that renders their proposals more credible. For example, a plan outlining major change is more likely to be accepted if produced by someone who has a history of success rather than a novice. Implementers should not be reluctant to display their credentials as part of the change process.

Referent power occurs when people identify with and respect the architect of change. That is why charismatic leadership is often thought to be an advantage to those who wish to see change implemented.

Legitimate power is wielded when the implementer insists on an action from a subordinate as a result of their hierarchical relationship and contract. For example, a sales manager may demand compliance with a request for a salesperson to go on a training course or a board of directors may exercise its legitimate right to cut costs.

The strength of **coercive power** lies with the implementer's ability to punish those who resist or oppose the implementation of the plan. Major organizational change is often accompanied by staff losses. This may be a required cost-cutting exercise but it also sends messages to those not directly affected that they may be next if further change is resisted. The problem with using coercive power is that, at best, it results in compliance rather than commitment.

Applications of power

The balance of power will depend on who holds the sources of power and how well they are applied. Implementers should pause to consider any sources of power they hold, and also the sources and degree of power held by supporters, neutrals and opposers. Power held by supporters should be mobilized, those neutrals who wield power should be cultivated, and tactics should be developed to minimize the influence of powerful opposers. The tactics that can be deployed will be discussed shortly, but two applications of power will be discussed first: overt and covert power plays.

Overt power plays are the visible, open kind of power plays that can be used by implementers to push through their proposals. Unconcealed use of the five sources of power is used to influence key players. The use of overt power by localized interests, who battle to secure their own interests in the process of change, has been well documented.[34]

Covert power plays are a more disguised form of influence. Their use is more subtle and devious than that of overt power plays. Their application can take many forms including agenda setting, limiting participation in decisions to a few select individuals/departments, and defining what is and what is not open to decision for others in the organization.[35]

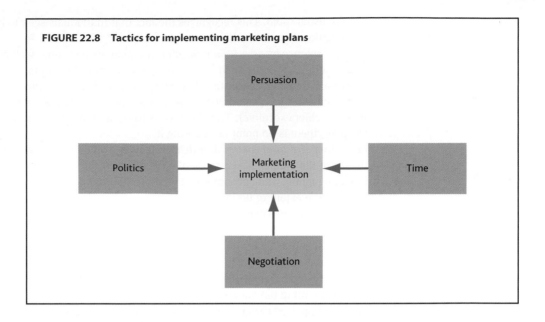

FIGURE 22.8   Tactics for implementing marketing plans

Tactics

The discussion of overt and covert power plays has introduced some of the means by which implementers and change agents can gain acceptance of their proposals and overcome opposition. Now we examine in more detail the tactics and skills needed to win implementation battles and how they can be applied in the face of some hostile reaction within the organization. These can be grouped into tactics of persuasion, politics, time and negotiation (see Fig. 22.8), and are based on the work of a number of authorities.[36] They provide a wide-ranging checklist of approaches to mobilizing support and overcoming resistance.

Persuasion

- *Articulate a shared vision*: the vision of where the organization is heading and the desired results of the change need to be clearly stated to key players in the organization. For example, if the marketing plan calls for a reduction in staffing levels, the vision that this is required to reposition the company for greater competitiveness needs to be articulated. Without an understanding of the wider picture, people may regard the exercise as 'just another cost drive'.[37] Since most change involves risk and discomfort, a clear vision of its purpose and consequences can make the risk acceptable and the discomfort endurable.
- *Communicate and train*: implementation of the marketing concept or a fundamentally different marketing plan means that many individuals have to reorientate and engage in new activities. To achieve this requires a major commitment to communicating the nature and purpose of the change, as well as to training staff in the new skills to be mastered. Major changes require face-to-face communication at discussion sessions and management education seminars. Formal training programmes are needed to upgrade skills and introduce new procedures.
- *Eliminate misconceptions*: a major part of the communication programme will be designed to eliminate misconceptions about the consequences of the change. Unfounded fears and anxieties should be allayed. Certain individuals will exaggerate the negative consequences of the proposed changes, and their concerns need to be addressed.
- *Sell the benefits*: the needs of key players have to be identified and the benefits of the change sold to them on that basis. The benefits may be economic (e.g. increased salary) or psychological (e.g. increased status, enhanced power). Whereas shared vision provides evidence of a wider general benefit (e.g. increased competitiveness) personal benefits

should also be sold. This recognizes the fact that individuals seek to achieve not only organizational goals but also personal ambitions.

● *Gain acceptance by association*: position the plan against some well-accepted organizational doctrine such as *customer service or quality management*. Because the doctrine is heavily backed, the chances of the plan being accepted and implemented are enhanced. Another positioning strategy is to associate the plan with a powerful individual (e.g. the chief executive). The objective is to create the viewpoint that if the boss wants the plan, there is no point in opposing it.

● *Leave room for local control over details*: leaving some local options or local control over details of the plan creates a sense of ownership on the part of those responsible for implementation, and encourages adaptation to different situations. Thought should be given to the extent of uniformity in execution, and the areas where local adoption is both practical and advisable.

● *Support words with action*: when implementation involves establishing a more marketing-orientated culture, it is vital to support words with corresponding action. As we saw when discussing resistance to the marketing concept, it is easy for managers to contradict their words with inappropriate actions (e.g. stressing the need to understand customers and then cutting the marketing research budget). An illustrative case of how management actions supported the culture they were trying to create is the story of a regional manager of US company United Parcel Service (UPS), who used his initiative to untangle a misdirected shipment of Christmas presents by hiring an entire train and diverting two UPS-owned 727s from their flight plans.[38] Despite the enormous cost (which far exceeded the value of the business), when senior management learned what he had done they praised and rewarded him: their actions supported and reinforced the culture they wanted to foster. As this story became folklore at UPS, its staff knew that senior management meant business when they said that the customer had to come first.

● *Establish two-way communication*: it is important that the people who are responsible for implementation feel that they can put their viewpoints to senior management, otherwise the feeling of top-down control will spread and resistance will build up through the belief that 'no one ever listens to us'. It is usually well worth listening to people lower down the management hierarchy and especially those who come face to face with customers. One way of implementing this approach is through staff suggestion schemes, but these need to be managed so that staff believe it is worth bothering to take part.

Asda, the UK supermarket chain acquired by Wal-Mart, is well known for its policy of tapping into the collective wisdom of its 85,000 staff. It encourages them to put forward suggestions for improved customer service and the best ideas are presented at an annual meeting called the National Circle. It also invites staff to write directly to its chief executive officer, with the most promising ideas being rewarded with 'star points' that staff can redeem against a catalogue of offers including clothes and holidays.

Politics

● *Build coalitions*: the process of creating allies for the proposed measures is a crucial step in the implementation process. Two groups have special significance: power sources that control the resources needed for implementation such as information (expertise or data), finance and support (legitimacy, opinion leadership and political backing); and stakeholders, who are those people likely to gain or lose from the change.[39] Discussion with potential losers may reveal ways of sharing some rewards with them ('Invite the opposition in'). At the very least, talking to them will reveal their grievances and so allow thought to be given to how these may be handled. Another product of these discussions with both potential allies and foes is that the original proposals may be improved by accepting some of their suggestions.

● *Display support*: having recruited powerful allies these should be asked for a visible demonstration of support. This will confirm any statements that implementers have made about the strength of their backing ('gain acceptance by association'). Allies should be invited to meetings, presentations and seminars so that stakeholders can see the forces behind the change.

- *Invite the opposition in*: thought should be given to creating ways of sharing the rewards of the change with the opposition. This may mean modifying the plan and how it is to be implemented to take account of the needs of key players. So long as the main objectives of the plan remain intact, this may be a necessary step towards removing some opposition.

- *Warn the opposition*: critics of the plan should be left in no doubt as to the adverse consequences of opposition. This has been called *selling the negatives*. However, the tactic should be used with care because statements that are perceived as threats may stiffen rather than dilute resistance, particularly when the source does not have a strong power base.

- *Use of language*: in the political arena the potency of language in endorsing a preferred action and discrediting the opposition has long been apparent. Language can be used effectively in the implementation battle. For example, critics of the new plan may be being labelled 'outdated', 'backward looking' and 'set in their ways'. In meetings, implementers need to avoid the temptation to *overpower* in their use of language. For people without a strong power base (such as young newcomers to a company) using phrases like 'We must take this action' or 'This is the way we have to move' to people in a more senior position (e.g. a board of directors) will provoke psychological resistance even to praiseworthy plans. Phrases like 'I suggest' or 'I have a proposal for you to consider' recognize the inevitable desire on the part of more senior management to feel involved in the decision-making rather than being treated like a rubber stamp.

- *Decision control*: this may be achieved by agenda setting (i.e. controlling what is and is not discussed in meetings), limiting participation in decision-making to a small number of allies, controlling which decisions are open for debate in the organization, and timing important meetings when it is known that a key critic is absent (e.g. on holiday, or abroad on business).

- *The either/or alternative*: finally, when an implementation proposal is floundering, a powerful proponent may decide to use the either/or tactic in which the key decision-maker is required to choose between two documents placed on the desk: one asks for approval of the implementation plan, the other tenders the implementer's resignation.

Time

- *Incremental steps*: people need time to adjust to change, therefore consideration should be given to how quickly change is introduced. Where resistance to the full implementation package is likely to be strong, one option is to submit the strategy in incremental steps. A small, less controversial strategy is implemented first. Its success provides the impetus for the next implementation proposals, and so on.

- *Persistence*: this tactic requires the resubmission of the strategy until it is accepted. Modifications to the strategy may be necessary on the way but the objective is to wear down the opposition by resolute and persistent force. Implementation can be a battle of wills, and requires the capability of the implementer to accept rejection without loss of motivation.

- *Leave insufficient time for alternatives*: a different way of using time is to present plans at the last possible minute so that there is insufficient time for anyone to present or implement an alternative. The proposition is basically 'We must move with this plan as there is no alternative'.

- *Wait for the opposition to leave*: for those prepared to play a waiting game, withdrawing proposals until a key opposition member leaves the company or loses power may be feasible. Implementers should be alert to changes in the power structure in these ways as they may present a window of opportunity to resubmit hitherto rejected proposals.

Negotiation

- *Make the opening stance high*: when the implementer suspects that a proposal in the plan is likely to require negotiation, the correct opening stance is to start high but be realistic. There are two strong reasons for this. First, the opponent may accept the proposal without modification; second, it provides room for negotiation. When deciding how high to go, the limiting factor is the need to avoid unnecessary conflict. For example, asking for a move from a fixed salary to a commission-only system with a view to compromising with salary plus commission is likely to be unrealistic and to provoke unnecessary antagonism among the salesforce.

- *Trade concessions*: sometimes it may be possible to grant a concession simply to secure agreement to the basics of the plan. Indeed, if the implementer has created negotiating room, this may be perfectly acceptable. In other circumstances, however, the implementer may be able to trade concession for concession with the opponent. For example, a demand from the salesforce to reduce list price may be met by a counter-proposal to reduce discount levels. A useful way of trading concessions is by means of the *if . . . then* technique: '*If* you are prepared to reduce your discount levels from 10 to 5 per cent, I am *then* prepared to reduce list price by 5 per cent.'[40] This is a valuable tool in negotiation because it promotes movement towards agreement and yet ensures that concessions given to the opponent are matched by concessions in return. Whenever possible, an attempt to create win-win situations should be made where concessions that cost the giver very little are highly valued by the receiver.

Evaluation

Finally, during and after the implementation process, evaluation should be made to consider what has been achieved and what has been learned. Evaluation may be in terms of the degree of support gained from key players, how well the plan and strategy have been implemented in the marketplace (e.g. by the use of customer surveys), the residual goodwill between opposing factions, and any changes in the balance of power between the implementers and other key parties in the company.

Some important lessons for implementing change programmes are identified when contrasting the fortunes of the move from Waterloo to St Pancras stations for the Eurostar cross-channel train service, and the opening of Heathrow airport's Terminal 5 (see Mini Case 22.1).

. . . .

Marketing Organization

Marketing organization provides the context in which marketing implementation takes place: companies may have no marketing departments; those that do may have functional, product-based market-centred or matrix organizational structures.

No marketing department

As we have seen this is a common situation. Small companies that cannot afford the luxury of managerial specialism, or production- or financially driven organizations that do not see the value of a marketing department. In small companies, the owner-manager may carry out some of the functions of marketing, such as developing customer relationships, and product development. In larger companies, which may use the traditional production, finance, personnel and sales functional division, the same task may be undertaken by those departments, especially sales (e.g. customer feedback, sales forecasting). The classic case of a company that has scorned the popular concept of marketing was the Body Shop. Despite being based on many of the essentials of marketing (e.g. a clearly differentiated product range, clear, consistent positioning and effective PR), the Body Shop refused to set up a marketing department. However, the growth of me-too brands led to the need to reappraise the role of marketing through the establishment of a marketing department in 1994.[41]

Mini Case 22.1 Change at St Pancras and Heathrow

Managers deal with change as a fundamental part of their job, but with varying degrees of success. Within months of each other London played host to two mammoth change programmes: the relocation of the cross-channel train service Eurostar from Waterloo to St Pancras stations, and the opening of Heathrow airport's Terminal 5. Their contrasting outcomes highlight the importance of preparation and communication in change management.

When Eurostar opened for business, it managed 97 per cent punctuality on the first day. The relocation not only meant a massive redesign of St Pancras station but also the move of 1600 employees, including 400 engineering and maintenance staff from south to north London. The keys to success were preparation and communication. Preparations began 18 months earlier and managers appreciated that the move was going to be an enormous event for their employees, both physically and emotionally. Business psychologists from the consultancy Kaisen were employed to advise managers. A huge two-way communication effort with staff was made to win their emotional engagement, as well as training them physically in how to work on the new site.

The Heathrow project was also a success—in terms of the construction of the site, which was completed on budget and on time. But, in spite of British Airways running a three-year change programme called 'Fit for 5', the opening day was a disaster, with over 30 flights cancelled as the baggage-handling operation ground to a halt. The baggage handlers had tried to warn their managers about the problems they could foresee. A key problem was that on the new, huge, site employees, who had not had enough training, simply did not know where they were supposed to go, and not enough time had been allowed to get staff from their locker rooms to the arrival and departure gates. The lockers themselves were too small to hold all the baggage handlers' clothing, and parking space was inadequate. All these problems had been communicated to managers beforehand.

So, what lessons can be learned? First, change requires preparation that includes practical training (a BA baggage handler complained that his training resembled guided tours of the terminal rather than hands-on practice). Second, managers need to recognize that employees (internal customers) may have useful things to say about the reality of the work they are doing, and that their insights should be built in to the change management programme.

Questions:

1 Identify issues that managers at St Pancras anticipated.
2 Suggest which models might help you plan for change.
3 In most organizations internal marketing is almost as important as external marketing. Compare and contrast these two concepts.

Based on: Jones (2008);[42] *Milmo (2008);*[43] *Stern (2008)*[44]

Marketing is likely to assume greater importance now that the Body Shop is owned by L'Oréal.[45]

It should be noted that not all companies that do not have a marketing department are poor at marketing; nor does the existence of a marketing department guarantee marketing orientation. Nevertheless, marketing should be seen as a company-wide phenomenon, not something that should be delegated exclusively to the marketing department.

Functional organization

As small companies grow, a formal marketing structure might emerge as a section within the sales department. As the importance of marketing is realized and the company grows, a marketing manager could be appointed with equivalent status to the sales manager who reports to a marketing director (see Fig. 22.9a). If the marketing director title is held by the previous sales director, little may change in terms of company philosophy: marketing may subsume a sales support role. This is the case in many companies where a more appropriate name for the person given the title 'marketing manager' would be 'communications manager'. An alternative route is to set up a *functional structure* under a sales director and a marketing director (see Fig. 22.9b). Both have equal status and the priorities of each job may

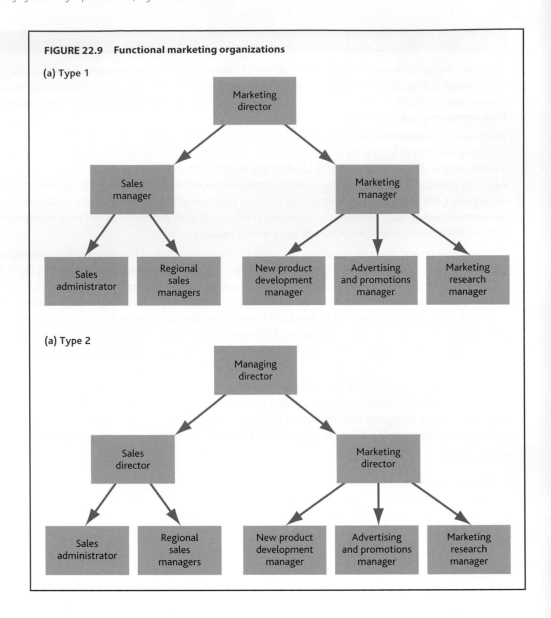

FIGURE 22.9   Functional marketing organizations

(a) Type 1

- Marketing director
  - Sales manager
    - Sales administrator
    - Regional sales managers
  - Marketing manager
    - New product development manager
    - Advertising and promotions manager
    - Marketing research manager

(a) Type 2

- Managing director
  - Sales director
    - Sales administrator
    - Regional sales managers
  - Marketing director
    - New product development manager
    - Advertising and promotions manager
    - Marketing research manager

lead to conflict[46] (see Table 22.1). A study of Fazer, a Finnish confectionery firm, showed that these conflicts can be heightened by the different backgrounds of marketing people who had business training and salespeople who relied more on personal experience and skills.[47] The preferred solution, then, is to appoint a marketing director who understands and has the power to implement marketing strategies that recognize sales as one (usually a key) element of the marketing mix.

Functionalisms bring the benefit of specialization of task and a clear definition of responsibilities, and is still the most common form of marketing organization.[48] However, as the product range widens and the number of markets served increases, the structure may become unwieldy with insufficient attention being paid to specific products and markets since no one has full responsibility for a particular product or market.

Product-based organization

The need to give sufficient care and attention to individual products has led many companies (particularly in the fast-moving consumer goods field) to move to a product-based structure. For example, Nestlé has moved from a functional to a product management system. A

TABLE 22.1 Potential areas of conflict between marketing and sales

Area	Sales	Marketing
Objectives	Short-term sales	Long-term brand/market building
Focus	Distributors/retail trade	Consumers
Marketing research	Personal experience with customers/trade	Market research reports
Pricing	Low prices to maximize sales volume. Discount structure in the hands of the salesforce	Price set consistent with positioning strategy. Discount structure built in to the marketing implementation plan
Marketing expenditure	Maximize resources channelled to the salesforce	Develop a balanced marketing mix using a variety of communication tools
Promotion	Sales literature, free customer give-aways, samples, business entertainment, sales promotions	Design a well-blended promotional mix including advertising, promotion and public relations

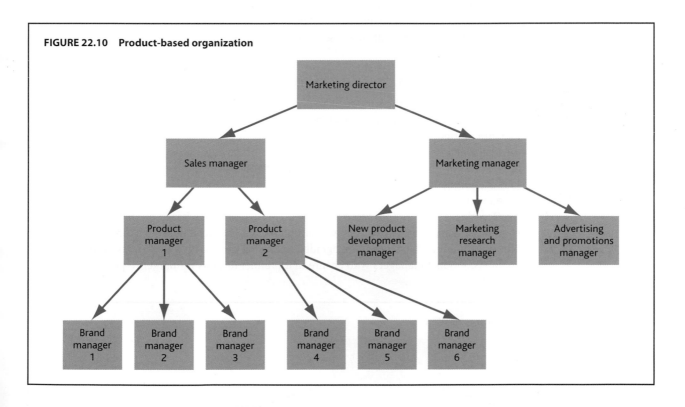

FIGURE 22.10   Product-based organization

common structure is for a product manager to oversee a group of brands within a product field (e.g. lagers, shampoos) supported by brand managers who manage specific brands (see Fig. 22.10). Their role is to coordinate the business management of their brands. This involves dealing with advertising, promotion and marketing research agencies, and function areas within the firm. Their dilemma stems from the fact that they have responsibility for the commercial success of their brands without the power to force through their decisions as they have no authority over other functional areas such as sales, production and R&D. They act as ambassadors for their brands, attempting to ensure adequate support from the salesforce, and sufficient marketing funds to communicate to customers and the trade through advertising and promotion.

The advantages of a *product-based organization* are that adequate attention is given to developing a coordinated marketing mix for each brand. Furthermore, assigning specific responsibility means that speed of response to market or technological developments is quicker than relying on a committee of functional specialists. A by-product of the system is it provides excellent training for young business people as they come into contact with a wide range of business activities.

The drawbacks with this approach are:

- Healthy rivalry between product managers can become counter-productive, negatively competitive and cause conflict.
- The system can lead to new layers of management, which can be costly—brand managers might be supplemented by assistants—as brands increase and additional brand managers are recruited. Companies like Procter & Gamble and Unilever are eliminating layers of management in the face of increasing demands from supermarkets to trim prices (and thus increase efficiency).
- Brand managers can be criticized for spending too much time coordinating in-company activities and too little time talking to customers. **Category management** can be an effective solution, which involves management of brands in a group, or *category* with specific emphasis on the retail trade's requirements. Suppliers such as Unilever, Heinz and L'Oréal have moved to category management to provide greater clarity in strategy across brands in an age where retailers themselves are managing brands as categories.[49]

Market-centred organization

Where companies sell their products to diverse markets, *market-centred organizations* should be considered. Instead of managers focusing on brands, *market managers* concentrate their energies on understanding and satisfying the needs of particular markets. The salesforce, too, may be similarly focused. For example, Figure 22.11 shows a market-centred organization for a hypothetical computer manufacturer. The specialist needs and computer applications in manufacturing, education and financial services justify a sales and marketing organization based on these market segments.

Occasionally, hybrid product/market-centred organizations based on distribution channels are appropriate. For example, at Philips, old organizational structures based on brands or products have been downgraded, replacing them with a new focus on distribution channels. Product managers who ensure that product designs fit market requirements still

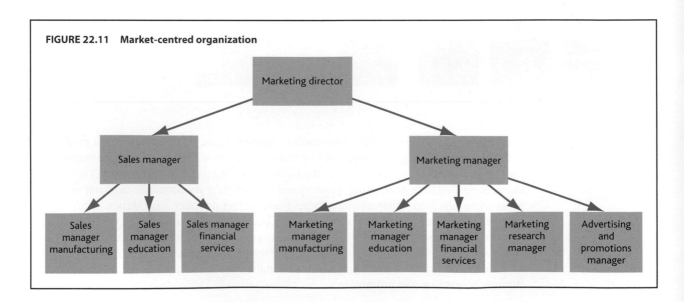

FIGURE 22.11 Market-centred organization

FIGURE 22.12 Matrix organization

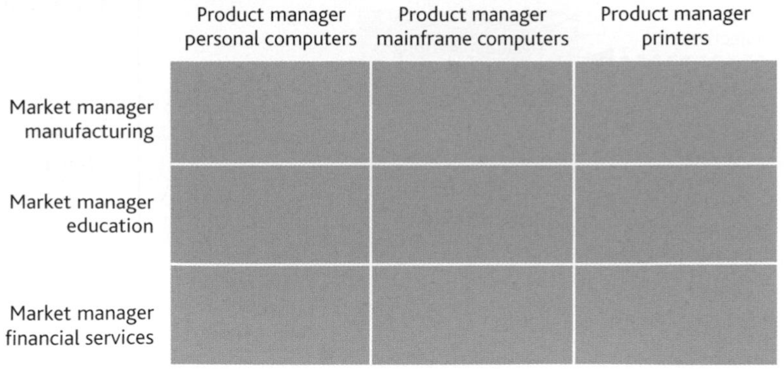

exist. However, under a new combined sales and marketing director the emphasis has moved to markets. Previously, different salespeople would visit retailers selling different products from the Philips range. This has been replaced by dedicated sales teams concentrating on channels such as the multiples, the independents and mail order.[50]

The enormous influence of the trade in many consumer markets has forced other firms, besides Philips, to rethink their marketing organization. This has led to the establishment of **trade marketing** teams, which serve the needs of large retailers.

The advantage of the market-centred approach is the focus it provides on the specific customer requirements of new opportunities, and developing new products that meet their customer needs. By organizing around customers, it embodies the essence of the marketing concept. However, for companies competing in many sectors it can be resource-hungry.

Matrix organization

For companies with a wide product range selling in diverse markets, a *matrix structure* may be necessary. Both product and market managers are employed to give due attention to both facets of marketing activity. The organizational structure resembles a grid, as shown in Figure 22.12, again using a hypothetical computer company. Product managers are responsible for their group of products' sales and profit performance, and monitor technological developments that impact on their products. Market managers focus on the needs of customers in each market segment.

For the system to work effectively, clear lines of decision-making authority need to be drawn up because of the possible areas of conflict. For example, who decides the price of the product? If a market manager requires an addition to the product line to meet the special needs of some customers, who has the authority to decide if the extra costs are justified? How should the salesforce be organized: along product or market lines? Also, it is a resource-hungry method of organization. Nevertheless, the dual specialism does promote the careful analysis of both product and markets so that customer needs are met.

Marketing organization and implementation are inevitably intertwined as the former affects the day-to-day activities of marketing managers. It is important that we understand the organizational world as marketing managers have come to understand it, in particular the activities that constitute their job.[51]

Marketing Control

Marketing control is an essential element of the marketing planning process because it provides a review of how well marketing objectives have been achieved. A framework for controlling marketing activities is given in Figure 22.13. The process begins

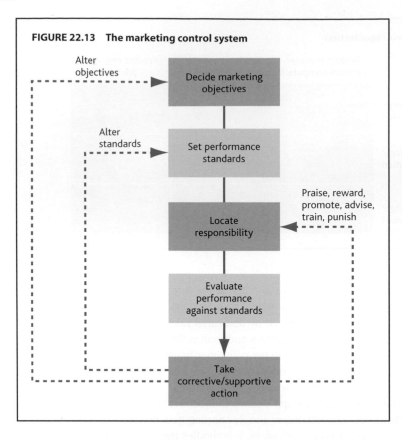

FIGURE 22.13 The marketing control system

Alter objectives

Alter standards

Decide marketing objectives

Set performance standards

Locate responsibility

Praise, reward, promote, advise, train, punish

Evaluate performance against standards

Take corrective/supportive action

by deciding marketing objectives, leading to the setting of performance standards. For example, a marketing objective of 'widening the customer base' might lead to the setting of the performance standard of 'generating 20 new accounts within 12 months'. Similarly the marketing objective of 'improving market share' might translate into a performance standard of 'improving market share from 20 per cent to 25 per cent'. Some companies set quantitative marketing objectives, in which case performance standards are automatically derived.

The next step is to locate responsibility. In some cases responsibility ultimately falls on one person (e.g. the brand manager), in others it is shared (e.g. the sales manager and salesforce). It is important to consider this issue since corrective or supportive action may need to focus on those responsible for the success of marketing activity.

Performance is then evaluated against standards, which relies on an efficient information system, and a judgement has to be made about the degree of success and/or failure achieved, and what corrective or supportive action is to be taken. This can take various forms.

- First, failure that is attributed to poor performance of individuals may result in the giving of advice regarding future attitudes and actions, training and/or punishment (e.g. criticism, lower pay, demotion, termination of employment). Success, on the other hand, should be rewarded through praise, promotion and/or higher pay.
- Second, failure that is attributed to unrealistic marketing objectives and performance standards may cause them to be lowered for the subsequent period. Success that is thought to reflect unambitious objectives and standards may cause them to be raised next period.
- Third, the attainment of marketing objectives and standards may also mean modification next period. For example, if the marketing objective and performance standard of opening 20 new accounts is achieved, this may mean the focus for the next period may change. The next objective may focus on customer retention, for instance.
- Finally, the failure of one achieved objective to bring about another may also require corrective action. For example, if a marketing objective of increasing calls to new accounts does not result in extra sales, the original objective may be dropped in favour of another (e.g. improving product awareness through advertising).

Strategic Control

Two types of control system may be used. The first concerns major strategic issues and answers the question 'Are we doing the right thing?' It focuses on company strengths, weaknesses, opportunities and threats, and the process of control is through a marketing audit. This was discussed in depth in Chapter 2 under the heading 'The process of marketing planning'.

Operational Control and the Use of Marketing Metrics

The second control system concerns tactical ongoing marketing activities, and is called operational control. An array of measures (often referred to as **marketing metrics**) are available to marketing managers who wish to measure the effectiveness of their activities.[52] However, it is often difficult to determine the exact contribution of marketing efforts because outcomes are usually dependent on several factors. For example, higher sales may be caused by increased (or better) advertising, a more motivated salesforce, weaker competition, more favourable economic conditions, and so on. This makes it difficult to justify, for example, increased advertising expenditure, because it is hard to quantify the past effects of advertising. This contrasts with production, where the effects of the introduction of a new machine can be calculated by measuring output; or finance, where a cost-cutting programme's effect on costs is easily calculated.

Despite these problems, there are now demands on marketing to become accountable for its activities. In order to be accountable, marketing managers are using *marketing metrics*, which are quantitative measures of the outcomes of marketing activities and expenditures. No longer can marketing executives attend budget meetings expecting to spend more money on advertising, promotion, direct marketing and other marketing activities without quantitative justification of these expenditures. The new mantra is **marketing accountability**: the requirement to justify marketing investment by using marketing metrics. Without such justification it is hardly surprising that marketing budgets are often the first to be cut in an economic downturn.

A research study has identified the kinds of marketing metrics being employed by companies, and the 10 most used metrics are shown in Table 22.2, together with an importance measure.[53] Although discussed under operational issues, the information can also usefully be fed into the marketing audit for strategic purposes.

Each of these metrics—as shown in Figure 22.14—will now be assessed, and specific measures identified, together with their calculation.

TABLE 22.2 The use of marketing metrics in UK firms			
Rank	**Metric**	**% using measure**	**% rating it as important**
1	Profit/profitability	92	80
2	Sales: value and/or volume	91	71
3	Gross margin	81	66
4	Awareness	78	28
5	Market share (value/volume)	78	37
6	Number of new products	73	18
7	Relative price	70	36
8	Customer dissatisfaction	69	45
9	Customer satisfaction	68	48
10	Distribution/availability	66	18

Source: Ambler, T., F. Kokkinaki and S. Puntoni (2004) Assessing Marketing Reasons for Metric Selection, *Journal of Marketing Management* 20, 475–98.

Profit/profitability

Typical metrics	**Calculation**
Profit	Profit = total revenue − total costs
Return on investment (ROI)	$ROI = \dfrac{\text{net profit}}{\text{investment}}$

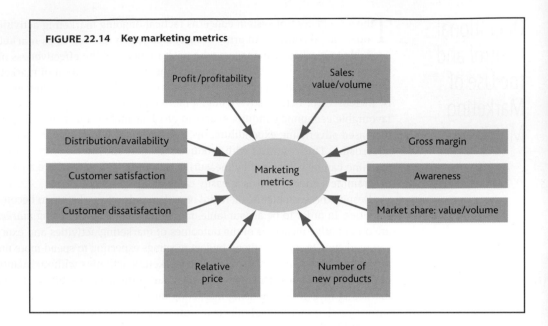

FIGURE 22.14   Key marketing metrics

Profit is the financial objective of most organizations so it is the most used metric. Similarly, profitability, which measures the profit return on investments such as products or advertising campaigns, is a popular metric since it relates to the financial objectives of companies. It is usually measured as return on investment (ROI) and, increasingly, marketers are attempting to measure return on marketing investment, although, as discussed earlier, accounting for marketing contribution to a sales (and hence profit) increase is sometimes difficult. What is required is a baseline figure (i.e. what would have happened without the marketing expenditure). Apart from direct marketing, where experiments can be conducted to test effects, such baseline figures can be difficult to establish. Also ROI is usually measured over a short time period (e.g. a year) and so such calculations can underestimate the full effects of marketing investments, which, through brand building, often have positive long-term effects.[54]

For operational control, **profitability analysis** can provide useful information on the profit performance of key aspects of marketing, such as products, customers or distribution channels. The example given focuses on products. The hypothetical company sells three types of product: paper products, printers and copiers. The first step is to measure marketing inputs to each of these products. These are shown in Table 22.3. Allocation of sales calls to products is facilitated by separate sales teams for each group.

TABLE 22.3   Allocating functional costs to products

Products	Salesforce (number of sales calls per year)	Advertising (number of one-page ads placed)	Order processing (number of orders placed)
Paper products	500	20	1000
Printers	400	20	800
Copiers	250	10	200
Total	1150	50	2000
Total cost	£190,000	£130,000	£80,000
Functional cost per unit	£165 per call	£2600 per ad	£40 per order

TABLE 22.4 Profitability statement for products (£)

	Paper products	Printers	Copiers
Sales	1,000,000	700,000	300,000
Cost of goods sold	500,000	250,000	250,000
Gross margin	500,000	450,000	50,000
Marketing costs			
Salesforce (at £165 per call)	82,500	66,000	41,250
Advertising (at £2600 per advertisement)	52,000	52,000	26,000
Order processing (at £40 per order)	40,000	32,000	8,000
Total cost	174,500	150,000	72,250
Net profit (or loss) before tax	325,500	300,000	(25,250)

If the sales teams were organized on purely geographic lines, an estimate of how much time was devoted to each product, on average, at each call would need to be made. Table 22.3 shows how the costs of an average sales call, advertising insertion and order are calculated. This provides vital information to calculate profitability for each product.

Table 22.4 shows how the net profit before tax is calculated. The results show how copiers are losing money. Before deciding to drop this line the company would have to take into account the extent to which customers expect copiers to be sold alongside paper products and printers, the effect on paper sales of dropping copiers, the possible annoyance caused to customers that already own one of its copiers, the extent to which copiers cover overheads that otherwise would need to be paid for from paper products and printer sales, the scope for pruning costs and increasing sales, and the degree to which the arbitrary nature of some of the cost allocations has unfairly treated copier products.

Sales

Typical metrics	Calculation
Sales revenue	Sales revenue = unit sales × price
Sales volume	Sales volume = unit sales
Sales revenue against target	Variance = sales revenue − target sales revenue

Processing sales revenue and sales volume is easy and the metrics are important determinants of marketing investments. Sales increases are normally sought to justify higher marketing expenditures, but without corresponding profit metrics can be misleading. This is because sales can be bought with excessive discounting, leading to higher sales but lower profit. For this reason, rewarding salesforces for higher sales without also measuring profits can be harmful.

Despite these dangers, **sales analysis** of actual against target sales revenue can be useful for operational control. Negative variance may be due to lower sales volume or lower prices. Product, customer and regional analysis will be carried out to discover where the shortfall arose. A change in the product mix could account for a sales fall, with more lower-priced products being sold. The loss of a major customer may also account for a sales decline. Regional analysis may identify a poorly performing area sales manager or salesperson. These findings would point the direction of further investigations to uncover the reasons for such outcomes.

Gross margin

Typical metrics	Calculation
Gross margin per unit (GMU)	GMU = price − cost of goods sold (material plus labour)
Gross margin percentage (GMP)	$GMP = \dfrac{GMU \times 100}{price}$

The third most popular metric is gross margin. Different industries can achieve widely varying gross margins. For example, high-volume, low-price supermarkets achieve low single-digit margins, while traditional jewellers typically require and achieve 50 per cent or more gross margins because their business is lower volume. Calculated as a percentage, gross margin is an indication of the percentage of the selling price that is a contribution to profit. It is not necessarily actual profit, as other expenses such as sales, marketing, distribution and administrative costs have not been deducted. A problem with using gross margin as a marketing metric is that it can be misleading if these other expenses are high. The answer is to calculate unit margin, where all costs are included.

Awareness

Typical metrics	Calculation
Recall	Survey respondents are asked to name all the brands in a product category that they can think of
Recognition	Survey respondents are shown a list of brands and asked to name those that they have heard of

Awareness is an important metric because it measures whether a marketing communications campaign is entering target consumers' minds. Awareness measures before and after a campaign are particularly useful. However, awareness does not necessarily raise purchase levels if the brand is not liked. It is therefore best used alongside other communications-orientated metrics such as measures of beliefs, liking, willingness to recommend, and purchase intention.

Market share

Typical metrics	Calculation
Market share (value)	$Market\ share\ (value) = \dfrac{sales\ revenue}{total\ market\ revenue}$
Market share (unit)	$Market\ share\ (unit) = \dfrac{unit\ sales}{total\ market\ unit\ sales}$
Relative market share	$Relative\ market\ share = \dfrac{brand's\ market\ share}{largest\ competitor's\ share}$

Market share analysis evaluates a company's performance in comparison to that of its competitors. Sales analysis may show a healthy increase in revenues but this may be due to market growth rather than an improved performance over competitors. An accompanying decline in market share would sound warning bells regarding relative performance. This would stimulate further investigation to root out the causes.

It should be recognized that a market share decline is not always a symptom of poor performance. This is why outcomes should always be compared to marketing objectives and performance standards. If the marketing objective was to harvest a product, leading to a performance standard of a 5 per cent increase in profits, its achievement may be accompanied by a market share decline (through the effect of a price rise). This would be a perfectly satisfactory outcome given the desired objective. Conversely, a market share gain may not signal improved performance if it was brought about by price reductions that reduced profits.

The relative market share metric (%) was used when calculating a brand's position on the Boston Consulting Group matrix (see Chapter 11, Managing products: product life-cycle, portfolio planning and product growth strategies). When a brand is a market leader, relative market share has a value greater than one.

Number of new products

Typical metrics	Calculation
Number of new products	Number of new products launched per year
Number of successful new products	Number of new products achieving objectives
Proportion of sales attributable to new products (PSANP)	$PSANP = \dfrac{\text{sales revenue of products on the market for less than n years}}{\text{total sales revenue}}$

Innovation is the lifeblood of success and as a consequence it is not surprising that an important marketing metric is the number of new products. However, simply counting the number of new products launched per year does not take into account their success rate. Two other metrics can be used to indicate success: the number (and proportion) of successful launches, where success is recognized when objectives are achieved, can be measured; also the proportion of sales revenue (and profits) attributable to new products within a given time period can be used. For example, 3M measures the proportion of sales attributable to new products launched within six years as a check on their innovative capability.

Care needs to be taken when defining what is a new product. As we saw in Chapter 12, Developing new products, there are many categories of new product, stretching from brand extensions to radical innovation (new-to-the-world products). Therefore it can be sensible to categorize each of the metrics according to type of new product.

Relative price

Typical metrics	Calculation
Ratio of brand A's price to the average price charged in the product category (RPAP)	$RPAP = \dfrac{\text{brand A's price}}{\text{average price in the product category}}$
Ratio of brand A's price to the price of its main competitor (RPPM)	$RPPM = \dfrac{\text{brand A's price}}{\text{price of its main competitor}}$

The relative price metric indicates the extent to which a brand is operating at a price premium or discount in a product category. A benchmark is required, which is usually the average price charged, the price of the brand's main competitor or the market leader. If brand A was priced at £4 and the average price charged was £3, the RPAP would be 1.33, demonstrating that the brand was charging a price premium (over the market average) of 33 per cent. If this metric was supported by market leadership (indicated by using a market share metric), this would suggest a strong differential advantage for the brand: not only does the brand outsell its rivals but it does so with a higher price. Therefore, when used with other metrics, relative price measures can be indicative of the strength of a brand (brand equity).

Customer dissatisfaction

Typical metrics	Calculation
Number of customer complaints	Number of complaints per period
Number of lost customers	Number of lost customers per period
Proportion of lost customers (PLC)	$PLC = \dfrac{\text{number of lost customers per period}}{\text{total number of customers at the start of the period}}$

Companies measure customer dissatisfaction because it is associated with losing customers. Companies monitor customer complaints to assess weaknesses in the product offering, including service levels. The outcomes of customer complaints should also be measured as research has shown that the successful resolution of a complaint can cause customers to feel more positive about the firm than before the service failure.[55] The number and proportion of lost customers are also useful metrics. These can be measured for consumer packaged goods by consumer panels and for business-to-business accounts directly from sales data.

Customer satisfaction

Typical metrics	Calculation
Satisfaction rating scales	Responses to 'Very dissatisfied' to 'Very satisfied' rating scales
Satisfaction compared to expectations	Responses to 'Worse than expected' to 'Better than expected' rating scales
Willingness to recommend	Responses to 'Would you recommend brand X to a friend or colleague?' question

An increasingly common barometer of marketing success is **customer satisfaction measurement**, which is encouraging as customer satisfaction is at the heart of the marketing concept. Although this measure does not appear directly on a company's profit and loss account, it is a fundamental condition for corporate success. The process involves the setting of customer satisfaction criteria, the design of a questionnaire to measure satisfaction on those criteria, the choice of which customers to interview, and the analysis and interpretation of results. The use of a market research agency is advised, to take advantage of its skills and unbiased viewpoint. A potential problem is that its measurement can lead to harmful behaviour on the part of the employees whose performance is being measured. For example, in one company salespeople gave price concessions to customers simply to build up goodwill that they hoped would improve their scores on a customer satisfaction questionnaire.[56]

One business-to-business marketing research agency advocates interviewing three customer groups to give a valid picture of customer satisfaction and marketing effectiveness:

1 10 current customers
2 10 lapsed customers (who bought from us in the past but do not now)
3 10 non-customers (who are in the market for the product but hitherto have not bought from us).

Invaluable information can be gained concerning customer satisfaction, how effective the salesforce is, why customers have switched to other suppliers, and why some potential customers have never done business with our company.

A powerful question to ask customers is 'Would you recommend brand X to a friend or colleague?' It provides insight into the strength of customer relationships and, therefore, likely future performance. Research by Reichheld into 14 companies in six industries in the USA showed that the answers to this question provided the first or second best predictor of future customer behaviour in 11 out of 14 tests.[57] Responses are given on a scale of 1 to 10, with 9s and 10s being defined as promoters, and 6s and below as detractors. The difference between the two gives the Net Promoter Score (NPS). A major benefit of this is its simplicity, but it has been criticized because a given NPS score can arise from very different sets of responses. For example, an NPS of 40 may arise from 70 per cent promoters and 30 per cent detractors, or one of 40 per cent promoters and zero detractors. Also the method does not allow measurement of satisfaction of particular aspects of the product offering such as product performance, service quality and salesperson satisfaction. In practice, the question is normally followed by the open-ended 'why' question, to tease out these elements. It also tends to be used alongside the normal customer satisfaction rating scales, rather than as a replacement for them.[58]

Distribution/availability

Typical metrics	Calculation
Availability ratio (AR)	$AR = \dfrac{\text{number of outlets stocking brand A}}{\text{total number of outlets}}$
Out of stock ratio (OSR)	$OSR = \dfrac{\text{number of outlets where brand A is listed but unavailable}}{\text{total number of outlets where brand A is listed}}$

The availability of a brand in distribution outlets is an important marketing metric because, if an outlet is out of stock, a consumer may be unwilling to visit another shop, preferring the convenience of buying a rival brand instead. Two important metrics are the availability ratio, which measures the proportion of outlets stocking the brand, and the out-of-stock ratio, which measures the proportion of outlets that normally stock the brand but are out of stock at a particular point in time. Poor scores on these ratios mean that the causes need to be identified and remedial action taken.

Other important metrics appear throughout this book, in the relevant chapters. For example, a brand equity metric is explained in Chapter 9, Managing products: brand and corporate identity management; in Chapter 11 Personal selling and sales management; and the lifetime value of a customer metric is discussed in Chapter 16. Website site metrics are discussed in Chapter 18.

In practice, marketing managers need to decide on the set of metrics that are relevant to their business, and seek ways of gathering them, which may mean employing a marketing research agency.

When you have read this chapter

log on to the Online Learning Centre at **www.mcgraw-hill.co.uk/textbooks/jobber** to explore chapter-by-chapter test questions, links and further online study tools for marketing.

Review

1 **The relationship between marketing strategy, implementation and performance**
- Appropriate strategy with good implementation will have the best chance of successful outcomes; appropriate strategy with bad implementation will lead to trouble, especially if the substandard implementation leads to strategy change; inappropriate strategy with good implementation may hasten failure or may lead to actions that correct strategy and therefore produce favourable outcomes; and inappropriate strategy with bad implementation will lead to failure.

2 **The stages that people pass through when they experience disruptive change**
- The stages are numbness, denial and disbelief, self-doubt and emotion, acceptance and letting go, adaptation and testing, construction and meaning, and internalization.

3 **The objectives of marketing implementation and change**
- The overall objective is the successful execution of the marketing plan.
- This may require gaining the support of key decision-makers, gaining the required resources and gaining the commitment of relevant individuals and departments.

4 **The barriers to the implementation of the marketing concept**
- The barriers are the fact that new marketing ideas often mean higher costs; the potential benefits are often unquantifiable; personal ambitions (e.g. the desire of R&D staff to work on leading-edge complex problems) may conflict with the customer's desire to have simple but reliable products; reward systems may reward short-term cost savings, sales and profitability rather than long-term customer satisfaction; and there may be a gap between what managers say (e.g. 'be customer-orientated') and what they do (e.g. cut back on marketing research funds).

5 **The forms of resistance to marketing implementation and change**
- The 10 forms of resistance are criticisms of specific details of the plan; foot-dragging; slow response to requests; unavailability; suggestions that, despite the merits of the plan, resources should be channelled elsewhere; arguments that the proposals are too ambitious; hassle and aggravation created to wear the proposers down; attempts to delay the decision; attacks on the credibility of the proposer; and pointing out the risks of the plan.

6 **How to develop effective implementation strategies**
- A change master is needed to drive through change.
- Managing the implementation process requires the setting of objectives ('would like' and 'must have'), strategy (internal marketing), execution (persuasion, negotiation, politics and tactics) and evaluation (who wins, and what can be learned).

7 **The elements of an internal marketing programme**
- An internal marketing programme mirrors the structures used to market externally such as market segmentation, targeting and the marketing mix.
- The individuals within the organization are known as internal customers. These can be segmented into three groups: supporters, neutrals and opposers. These form distinct target markets that require different internal marketing mixes to be designed to optimize the chances of successful adoption of the plan.

8 **The skills and tactics that can be used to overcome resistance to the implementation of the marketing concept and plan**
- The skills are persuasion (the needs, motivations and problems of internal customers need to be understood before appealing messages can be developed), negotiation (concession and proposal analysis) and political skills (the understanding of the sources of power, and the use of overt and covert power plays).

- The tactics are persuasion (articulating a shared vision, communicating and training, eliminating misconceptions, selling the benefits, gaining acceptance by association, leaving room for local control over details, supporting words with action, and establishing two-way communication); politics (building coalitions, displaying support, inviting the opposition in to share the rewards, warning the opposition of the consequences of opposition, the use of appropriate language, controlling the decision-making process and the use of the either/or alternative—either accept or I tender my resignation); timing (incremental steps, persistence, leaving insufficient time for alternatives, and waiting for the opposition to leave); and negotiation (starting high and trading concessions).

9 **Marketing organizational structures**
- The options are no marketing department, functional, product-based, market-centred or matrix organizational structures.

10 **The nature of a marketing control system**
- There are two types of marketing control: strategic and operational control systems.
- Strategic control systems answer the question 'Are we doing the right things?' and are based on a marketing audit.
- Operational control systems concern tactical ongoing marketing activities. Marketing metrics are used for this purpose and to justify marketing investments. The most commonly used metrics are profit/profitability, sales (value and/or volume), gross margin, awareness, market share, number of new products, relative price, customer dissatisfaction, customer satisfaction, and distribution/availability.

Key Terms

category management the management of brands in a group, portfolio or category, with specific emphasis on the retail trade's requirements

change master a person that develops an implementation strategy to drive through organizational change

coercive power power inherent in the ability to punish

concession analysis the evaluation of things that can be offered to someone in negotiation valued from the viewpoint of the receiver

covert power play the use of disguised forms of power tactics

customer satisfaction measurement a process through which customer satisfaction criteria are set, customers are surveyed and the results interpreted in order to establish the level of customer satisfaction with the organization's product

expert power power that derives from an individual's expertise

legitimate power power based on legitimate authority, such as line management

market share analysis a comparison of company sales with total sales of the product, including sales of competitors

marketing accountability the requirement to justify marketing investment by using marketing metrics

marketing control the stage in the marketing planning process or cycle when performance against plan is monitored so that corrective action, if necessary, can be taken

marketing metrics quantitative measures of the outcomes of marketing activities and expenditures

overt power play the use of visible, open kinds of power tactics

profitability analysis the calculation of sales revenues and costs for the purpose of calculating the profit performance of products, customers and/or distribution channels

proposal analysis the prediction and evaluation of proposals and demands likely to be made by someone with whom one is negotiating

referent power power derived by the reference source, e.g. when people identify with and respect the architect of change

reward power power derived from the ability to provide benefits

sales analysis a comparison of actual with target sales

trade marketing marketing to the retail trade

transition curve the emotional stages that people pass through when confronted with an adverse change

Study Questions

1 Think of a situation when your life suffered from a dramatic change. Using Figure 22.3 for guidance, recall your feelings over time. How closely did your experiences match the stages in the figure? How did your feelings at each stage (e.g. denial and disbelief) manifest themselves?

2 Can good implementation substitute for an inappropriate strategy? Give an example of how good implementation might make the situation worse and an example of how it might improve the situation.

3 Why do some companies fail to implement the marketing concept?

4 Describe the ways in which people may resist the change that is implied in the implementation of a new marketing plan. Why should they wish to do this?

5 What is internal marketing? Does the marketing concept apply when planning internal marketing initiatives?

6 What tactics of persuasion are at the implementer's disposal? What are the advantages and limitations of each one?

7 Discuss the options available for organizing a marketing department. How well is each form likely to serve customers?

8 Discuss the problems involved in setting up and implementing a marketing control system.

References

1. http://www.12manage.com/quotes_s.html.
2. Hirst, C. (2008) Time for Less Talk, More Action, *Marketing Week*, 7 June, 23.
3. Bonoma, T. V. (1985) *The Marketing Edge: Making Strategies Work*, New York: Free Press.
4. Johannessen, J.-A., J. Olaisen and A. Havan (1993) The Challenge of Innovation in a Norwegian Shipyard Facing the Russian Market, *European Journal of Marketing* 27(3), 23–38.
5. Calder, M. (2004) Customer Listening, Strategic Customer Management Conference, Warwick Business School, 10 November.
6. Snoad, L. (2012) Taking personal control of mission redefinition, *Marketing Week*, 26 January, 16–19.
7. Wilson, G. (1993) *Making Change Happen*, London: Pitman.
8. Mailonline (2011) Howard's end: bank employee who became face of the Halifax walks out after being dropped from ad campaign, http://www.dailymail.co.uk/news/article-1389417, 22 May.
9. Bruno Ken (2010) Marketers turn employees into Ad stars, http://www.forbes.com/sites/marketshare/2010/09/23/marketers-advertising-employees-yum-pizza-hut-bp-cathay-pacific/.
10. Stanton, W. J., R. H. Buskirk and R. Spiro (2002) *Management of a Sales Force*, Boston, Mass: Irwin.
11. Webster, F. E. Jr (1988) Rediscovering the Marketing Concept, *Business Horizons* 31 (May–June), 29–39.
12. Webster (1988) op. cit.
13. Argyris, C. (1966) Interpersonal Barriers to Decision Making, *Harvard Business Review* 44 (March–April), 84–97.
14. Hasek, G. (2012) Accor's Planet 21 program brings sustainability to all its hotels, greenbiz.com, http://www.greenbiz.com/news/2012/04/17/accors-planet-21-program-brings-sustainability-all-its-hotels, 17 April 2012.

15. Reed, J. and D. Schäfer (2008) BMW's Accelerator of Change, *Financial Times*, 6 October, 18.
16. Kanter, R. M. (1997) *The Change Masters*, London: Allen & Unwin.
17. Piercy, N. (2008) *Marketing-Led Strategic Change*, Oxford: Butterworth-Heinemann.
18. Johnson, G. (1987) *Strategic Change and the Management Process*, Oxford: Basil Blackwell.
19. Ansoff, I. and E. McDonnell (1990) *Implanting Strategic Management*, Englewood Cliffs, NJ: Prentice-Hall.
20. Pettigrew, A. M. (1985) *The Awakening Giant: Continuity and Change in ICI*, Oxford: Basil Blackwell.
21. Kanter (1997) op. cit.
22. London, S. and A. Hill (2002) A Recovery Strategy Worth Copying, *Financial Times*, 16 October, 12.
23. McGregor, J. (2009) An Historic Succession at Xerox, *Business Week*, 8 June, 18–22.
24. Kennedy, G., J. Benson and J. MacMillan (1987) *Managing Negotiations*, London: Business Books.
25. Piercy, N. (1990) Making Marketing Strategies Happen in the Real World, *Marketing Business*, February, 20–1.
26. Piercy, N. and N. Morgan (1991) Internal Marketing: The Missing Half of the Marketing Programme, *Long Range Planning* 24(2), 82–93.
27. See Grönroos, C. (1985) Internal Marketing: Theory and Practice, in Bloch, T. M., G. D. Upah and V. A. Zeithaml (eds) *Services Marketing in a Changing Environment*, Chicago: American Marketing Association; Gummesson, E. (1987) Using Internal Marketing to Develop a New Culture: The Case of Ericsson Quality, *Journal of Business and Industrial Marketing* 2(3), 23–8; Mudie, P. (1987) Internal Marketing: Cause of Concern, *Quarterly Review of Marketing*, Spring–Summer, 21–4.

28. Research conducted by Oxford Strategic Marketing and Hunter Miller Executive Search and reported in *Marketing Business* (2005) 100 Days, June, 15–17.

29. Laing, A. and L. McKee (2001) Willing Volunteers or Unwilling Conscripts? Professionals and Marketing in Service Organizations, *Journal of Marketing Management* 17(5/6), 559–76.

30. Mortimer, R. (2011) Celebrate the success of internal marketing, *Marketing Week*, 10 November, 3.

31. Mockler, R. and Gartenfeld, M. (2010) Intranets as Part of a Company's E-Business, Proceedings of the Northeast Business & Economics Association (NBEA), 610–13.

32. Daniel, E. (2006) The World According to Google, Open2.net, January, http://www.open2.net/money/briefs_20060120information. html.

33. French, J. R. P. and B. Raven (1959) The Bases of Social Power, in Cartwright, D. (ed.) *Studies in Social Power*, Ann Arbor: University of Michigan Press, 150–67.

34. See Hickson, D. J., C. R. Hinings, C. A. Lee, R. E. Schneck and J. M. Pennings (1971) A Strategic Contingencies Theory of Intraorganizational Power, *Administrative Science Quarterly* 16(2), 216–29; Hinings, C. R., D. J. Hickson, J. M. Pennings and R. E. Schneck (1974) Structural Conditions of Intraorganizational Power, *Administrative Science Quarterly* 19(1), 22–44.

35. Wilson, D. C. (1992) *A Strategy of Change: Concepts and Controversies in the Management of Change*, London: Routledge.

36. See Kanter, R. M., B. A. Stein and T. D. Jick (1992) *The Challenge of Organizational Change*, New York: Free Press; Kanter, R. M. (1983) *The Change Masters*, London: Allen and Unwin; Piercy, N. (2008) *Market-led Strategic Change*, Oxford: Butternorth-Heinemann; Ansoff and McDonnell (1990) op. cit.

37. Kanter, Stein and Jick (1992) op. cit.

38. Bonoma, T. V. (1984) Making your Marketing Strategy Work, *Harvard Business Review* 62 (March–April), 68–76.

39. Kanter, Stein and Jick (1992) op. cit.

40. Kennedy, G., J. Benson and J. McMillan (1980) *Managing Negotiations*, London: Business Books.

41. Hewitt, M. (1994) Body Shop Opens its Doors to Marketing, *Marketing*, 26 May, 20.

42. Jones, A. (2008) Shambolic But Totally Predictable, *The Guardian*, 28 March, 3.

43. Milmo, D. (2008) Passengers Fume in the Chaos of Terminal 5's First Day, *The Guardian*, 28 March, 2.

44. Stern, S. (2008) Managers Who Bring About Change We Can Believe In, *Financial Times*, 10 June, 14.

45. Benady, D. (2006) Body Shop, L'Oréal Plot Food Range, *Marketing Week*, 23 March, 3.

46. Dewsnap, B. and D. Jobber (2006) A Social Psychological Study of Marketing and Sales Relationships, University of Bradford School of Management Working Paper.

47. Eriksson, P. and K. Räsänen (1998) The Bitter and the Sweet: Evolving Constellations of Product Mix Management in a Confectionery Company, *European Journal of Marketing* 32(3/4), 279–304.

48. Workman J. P. Jr, C. Homburg and K. Gruner (1998) Marketing Organisation: an Integrative Framework of Dimensions and Determinants, *Journal of Marketing* 62 July, 21–41.

49. For further insights into category management see D. Aaker (2009) *Brand Leadership*, New York: Free Press; and T. Ambler (2001) Category Management is Best Deployed for Brand Positioning, *Marketing*, 29 November, 18.

50. Mitchell, A. (1994) Dark Night of Marketing or a New Dawn?, *Marketing*, 17 February, 22–3.

51. Brownlie, D. and M. Saren (1997) Beyond the One-Dimensional Marketing Manager: The Discourse of Theory, Practice and Relevance, *International Journal of Research in Marketing* 14, 147–61.

52. Faris, P. W., N. T. Bendle, P. E. Pfeifer and D. J. Reibstein (2006) *Key Marketing Metrics*, Harlow: Pearson.

53. Ambler, T., F. Kokkinaki and S. Puntoni (2004) Assessing Marketing Performance: Reasons for Metrics Selection, *Journal of Marketing Management* 20, 475–98.

54. Ambler, T. and J. H. Roberts (2008) Assessing Marketing Performance: Don't Settle For a Silver Metric, *Journal of Marketing Management* 24, 733–50.

55. Maxham III, J. G. and R. G. Netemeyer (2002) A Longitudinal Study of Complaining Customers' Evaluations of Multiple Service Failures and Recovery Efforts, *Journal of Marketing* 66, October, 57–71.

56. Piercy, N. and N. A. Morgan (1995) Customer Satisfaction Measurement and Management: A Processual Analysis, *Journal of Marketing Management* 11, 817–34.

57. Reichheld, F. (2006) *The Ultimate Question*, Boston: Harvard Business School Press.

58. Mitchell, A. (2008) The Only Number You Need to Know Does Not Add Up To Much, *Marketing Week*, 6 March, 15–16.

Bupa Great North Run
Changes in Marketing Implementation

Introduction and Race History

The 'Great North Run' is the world's biggest half marathon, which has taken place annually in Newcastle every September since it was first staged in 1981. The first race had over 10,000 competitors which has since grown to a staggering 54,000 participants each year. In addition to the runners themselves, thousands of supporters line the course's path with live music playing throughout the event, making it a truly special occasion. There are a number of major charity partners who take part such as The British Heart Foundation and Cancer Research UK, which has been a big part of the Bupa Great North Run experience for many runners. Every year race participants raise over £28 million for charity as well as bringing their own unique and personal stories to the event.

In recent years competitors from over 40 different countries have participated in the race, reflecting how the audience has diversified over time. A number of sporting legends have taken part in the event such as Sir Bobby Robson, Paula Radcliffe and marathon icon Haile Gebrselassie.

The evolution of 'The Great Run' and adapting to market changes

The 1970s' Olympian Brendan Foster founded the race with a team of colleagues after experiencing something similar in New Zealand. According to the race's current marketing manager, Catherine Foster, the evolution of 'The Great Run' brand has been quite organic. As the Great North Run grew it was obvious that a demand existed amongst the UK population for such a competition. A number of sporadic events were launched including the Great South Run in 1990 and the Edinburgh Run after that. In the late 1990s and early 2000s it was realized that, although there were a number of individual runs being implemented across the UK, a brand had emerged in the form of 'The Great Run', with a premium positioning that offers a safe, high-quality and well-managed sporting event with top-calibre sponsors.

Nova International was set up in 1988 as a vehicle to drive forward and grow the brand. The company's marketing approach has drastically changed over the years due to the different drivers in the industry. According to Foster, the organizers used to simply rely on the race itself to attract participants: however, the management took a step back and looked to form a more structured approach to targeting. The race provides a very specific demographic

type in runners, who are looking to improve their lifestyle, health and fitness. However, it is difficult to use traditional targeting methods throughout this market segment as the race appeals to all types of runners, ranging from highly competitive runners to those who are just keen to be a part of the whole occasion. Therefore, the messages themselves are based on a variety of elements of the great run that appeal to the diversity of customers. For example, an emphasis is placed on the pace of the run and competing with the elite when targeting the more ambitious runners out there.

Managerial challenges and changes to market implementation strategy

With regard to competing in the market, the Great North Run has a unique selling point in that it receives four to five hours of uninterrupted television exposure from the BBC. This is certainly an attraction to many sponsors who wish to be associated with such an event. Bupa's brand image fits in perfectly with the identity that has been build around the Great North Run as a premium brand that is all about being healthy, keeping fit and living an active lifestyle. The history and foundation of the race also provides a high degree of credibility, which has proved to be appealing to sponsors such as Asics and Powerade.

Foster alludes to how the sheer volume of running events in the UK has led to saturation in the market and has driven a natural change in the organization's marketing strategy in order to maintain market share. The manager stresses that the firm has stuck to its premium pricing position even though competitors have introduced a number of alternatives. The key change has come about in the way that the brand communicates to its customers as there is now much more focus on building relationships and brand loyalty. Foster believes that with each competitor comes not only a new audience, but a 16-week communication plan which is predominantly executed through the use of pre- and post-race emails. The company's most recent and innovative way of reaching customers is through their new website, aimed at providing customers with training tips, plans and trackers to help them with their progress. The post-race emails not only allow the customers to view their results but also provide access to race pictures and the opportunity to fill out a post-race questionnaire. After that communication is primarily directed at promoting re-registration for the following year, providing information on other 'Great Run' events and also collecting further customer feedback. A statistic that Foster is working to change is that the feedback has shown that 85–92 per cent of participants say they will race again yet the actual repeat entry rate is around 27–30 per cent.

Another key challenge that Nova faces is that the course itself is run through the city centre of Newcastle; obviously this can cause a lot of disruption due to the required road closures and the amount of public interest that surrounds the event. This potential challenge is turned on its head by Foster who sees it as an opportunity to raise awareness, referring to the firm's motto of 'maximum input from maximum disruption'.

Nova, like many others, has been impacted by the economic downturn and consequently has been forced to adapt in order to maintain its market position. It was the commercial side that suffered the most as regional development agencies used to fund the event as the exposure was seen as a positive for the local area. However, this revenue stream has since been cut leaving holes in certain budgets. This has meant that management has had to increase the amount of commercial partners sponsoring the event in order to narrow these gaps.

Having said this, Foster clearly highlights that the firm is still a relatively small business who take a very holistic approach to implementation. As part of an entrepreneurial company, all departments buy into the marketing objectives and are quite flexible in terms of adjusting to meet any new criteria.

Marketing objectives, current implementation structure and future developments

Nova's marketing objectives are both coordinated and complementary to the sponsor's objectives in order to provide a multi-dimensional approach. For example, Foster states that both Nova and the sponsors have shifted their communications strategy from brand building to engaging the customers through a number of marketing tools.

The implementation strategy of the firm consists of, first, establishing the marketing objectives, which are built around the participants, TV exposure and commercial income. A three-year plan is then constructed around the objectives followed by the various teams in the organization forming a general strategy. From a marketing perspective it is built very much from a customer communications point of view aimed at entry generation, as well as a PR impact point of view. The PR campaign will primarily include stories from those who have competed for a charity and those who have used running to turn their lives around. This will generate an emotional response from the audience and ultimately provoke conversation about the event.

The media mix is formed using projected percentages of uptake for each media vehicle—for example, local advertising and database communications. The cost of customer acquisition and retention has received a lot of interest from Foster and has been used to justify areas of budget spending in order to make the campaign as cost effective as possible.

As 'The Great North Run' is an established market leader, Nova International can be proud that it is now a specialist in 'the development, design, organization and rights management of mass participation, televised sporting events and is structured to deliver total event solutions from conception to implementation'.

Questions

1. What barriers do you think Catherine Foster may have encountered when implementing the marketing concept?

2. Explain the skills and tactics required to execute an implementation strategy, using this case study as reference.

3. Over 85 per cent of participants say they will race again. Yet the figures show only about 30 per cent do so. What marketing communication activities would you put in place to dramatically increase that figure?

This case was written by Brian Searle and Fred Silcock, Loughborough University. Special thanks to Catherine Foster, Great Run Marketing Manager, Nova International.

Subway Germany
Sink or Swim

The world loves fast food*. And Germany is no exception. Burgers? Pizza? Kebab? Currywurst? There has never been a wider choice of fast food offerings. The German fast food market is the third largest in Europe, accounting for 15.2 per cent of market share, and valued in excess of $6 billion in 2011.

So what is driving fast food consumption in Europe's largest economy? First, the increase in the number of fast food outlets means that a quick bite is within easy reach. Second, aggressive pricing strategies, for example, a cheeseburger or a cappuccino at McDonald's costs just 1 euro. Third, consumers are attracted to the convenience of fast food. Hectic lifestyles means that time has become a scarce commodity. Fast food saves all the time and hassle of cooking at home. Next, fast food outlets have become a social space to spend quality time with family and friends. The Starbucks experience has been extended to other settings such as McCafé where consumers are trading up to enjoy a Latte with a muffin or cupcake. Finally, the fast food industry has responded to consumer health concerns with the introduction of healthier options. For example, a choice of salads and wraps are now available at McDonald's.

Go to the website to see how Subway is trying to reinforce its value proposition to the German consumer.
www.mcgraw-hill.co.uk/textbooks/jobber

Subway: The Track to Global Success . . .

This would all seem to be good news for the restaurant chain, Subway, which has been positioned as a healthier fast food alternative. It is claimed that the sandwich was invented by John Montagu, the fourth Earl of Sandwich in 1762. Fast forward more than three hundred years to 1965 when Fred DeLuca and Peter Buck opened the first Subway store in the US state of Connecticut and consumers rediscovered a new way to eat sandwiches. The submarine sandwich (known as a Sub) was born. Growth in the US has reached over 25,108 outlets. The advertising slogan 'Eat

Fresh' explains how every sandwich is made to order—right in front of the customer using a variety of baked breads, fillings, toppings and sauces. With all the choices available, there is something for everyone![1]

The Subway Sub may not present a major product innovation breakthrough, but it has become an exponential global market success. Subway opened its first international restaurant in Bahrain in 1984. This was the start of a rapid global expansion plan. The franchise format ensured Subway's expansion, not only quickly, but with limited capital investment required by the franchisee. Subway has since overtaken McDonald's as the world's largest restaurant chain. Subway has currently 36,982 outlets (at the time of writing) in 100 countries with outlets from Afghanistan to Zambia. Subway claims on its website that 'We've become the leading choice for people seeking quick, nutritious meals that the whole family can enjoy'.

Subway Germany: Side-tracked?

Subway continues to open new stores across the globe with one exception—Germany. The first Subway restaurant opened in Berlin in 1999 and was able to expand as in other international markets with a franchise model that emphasises small, low-cost outlets. In 2009 the Subway chain grew to 798 outlets. While Subway was able to capture a growing share of the fast food dollar in other

---

*Marketline defines the fast food market as the sale of food and drinks for immediate consumption either on the premises or in designated eating areas shared with other foodservice operators, or for the consumption elsewhere.

TABLE C44.1   Fast food key players in Germany

	Turnover in millions of euros			Number of outlets		
Year:	2011	2010	2009	2011	2010	2009
McDonald's, McCafé	3,195	3,017	2,909	1,415	1,386	1,361
Burger King	780	750	765.5	678	687	681
Nordsee	300	296.9	297.5	345	344	351
Subway	175	203	226	612	703	798
KFC	122	103	93	76	72	65
Pizza Hut	58	54	55	62	63	63

Source: Bundesverband der Systemgastronie (BdS)

TABLE C44.2   German fast food market value

Year	$ million	€ million	% Growth
2008	5,785.7	4,158.8	
2009	5,985.1	4,302.1	3.4%
2010	5,993.9	4,308.4	0.1%
2011	6,009.8	4,319.9	0.3%

Source: MARKETLINE

TABLE C44.3   Fast food market geography segmentation: $ million, 2011

Geography	2011	%
United Kingdom	8,254.8	20.9
France	6,617.7	16.7
Germany	6,009.8	15.2
Spain	2,509.4	6.3
Italy	2,196.3	5.6
Rest of Europe	13,938.9	35.3
Total	39,526.9	100%

Source: MARKETLINE

European markets, German consumers were voting with their feet (or rather their mouths!). According to the Bundesverbandes der Systemgastronomie (a German industry association), Subway's sales turnover in 2011 was 175 million euros. This was down almost 23 per cent compared to 2009. Weak sales have hit the bottom line of the franchisee holder. 186 Subway outlets have closed for business since 2009 and there are now only 612 Subway restaurants in Germany. Indeed, Subway is facing competition from many of these former franchise holders who have opened rival chains such as Starsub, Fresh! and Mr Sub. Furthermore, it seems that the banks have also lost

confidence in the Subway franchise. In April 2010 it was reported that Deutsche Bank will no longer offer loans to prospective Subway franchise holders.[2]

While McDonald's was able to break the 3 billion euros revenue barrier in 2010 and continue its impressive growth in 2011, Subway is fighting to stay afloat at the same time as the German economy remains resilient to the eurozone crisis. However, the decline of Subway was not unexpected by everyone. In 2007 the President of the Franchisee Association Germany stated that 'A conservative estimate would be that 30% of the Subway franchisees in Germany are just scraping by at the subsistence level'.[3] So why are Germans turning their up noses at Subway?

Subway: Can't afford the ticket?

Icon Added Value & Brand Rating reported in a 2007 survey that Subway is perceived as being too expensive by German consumers. This might well be a critical factor as Germans are regarded as being particularly value-conscious consumers. In contrast, McDonald's was rated as delivering excellent quality at a fair price. A Subway 'meal deal' consisting typically of a sandwich, drink and cookie goes for 6.50 euros. This compares to a McDeal Menü of 3.79 euros. Subway has however attempted to boost sales and increase restaurant frequency with the launch of 'sub of the day' ('*Sub des Tages*'). Customers can enjoy a different sandwich each day for a set price of 2.49 euros. This is supported by a tongue-in-cheek TV commercial that shows an athlete throwing a javelin as far as 2.49 metres to reinforce its value-for-money proposition.

Crossed rails: culture shock?

German consumers should actually be leading sandwich connoisseurs. Germans eat the most bread in Europe— the average German eating almost 85 kilos of bread each year! However, it may be this passion for bread that is turning the Germans off the Subway sandwich. There are more than 300 different varieties of bread in Germany and it may be that Germans do not wish to compromise on quality and taste. How difficult would it be to sell Californian wine to the French or Australian beer to the Germans? It seemed that many fillings, such as Barbecue Ribs, were too strange and foreign to the German palate. This is in contrast to McDonald's who have adapted to the culinary needs of the German market. For example, more than 1 million sausages, 'Nurnberger', were sold in a 3-month promotion in 2010.

Brand image down the tube?

Executives take advantage of having informal meetings in a local Starbucks. Families choose to celebrate children's birthdays in McDonald's. Brands are appealing to the emotions of the fast food consumer to win over the hearts and minds (and pockets). Is Subway failing to connect emotionally with the fast food consumer? Subway's brand advertising support has been minimal compared to other fast food brands. According to Nielsen Media Research, McDonald's is one of Germany's top 10 advertisers and that doesn't take into account the sponsorship of major sporting events such as the Olympics and Euro Championship in 2012. McDonald's and other fast food brands have also invested in improving their overall corporate image. Critics may argue that the decision to change the McDonald's logo to green was a greenwashing publicity stunt. However, the publication of the McDonald's Corporate Responsibility Report[4] sets out to demonstrate its commitment as a responsible company. Moreover, it has undergone to improve its restaurant visual design. The French designer, Phillippe Avanzi, has revamped many of the McDonald's restaurant outlets in Germany to create a chic ambience and an appealing fast food restaurant experience.

Poorly conducted franchise management?

The success or failure of the franchise model is based on a strong working relationship between the franchisee and franchiser. Franchisees at Subway pay a fee of 12.5 per cent of their monthly sales turnover to the franchiser in which 4.5 per cent is put aside for advertising support.

The franchisee is able to benefit from Subway's franchise support system that includes training, product development, advertising, purchasing cooperative and field support. However, the Subway franchise model has received widespread criticism.

It is alleged that it has become too easy to become a Subway franchise holder. It has been argued that franchise holders lack the necessary basic management skills and competences to run a successful business. Subway franchisee holders participate in a two-week training course compared to an 18-month training programme at McDonald's. Many Subway franchisee holders have complained that they are not receiving adequate ongoing support from the franchiser. The relationship between franchiser and franchisee is no longer sweet but has turned rather sour.

Competition: A red light for Subway?

McDonald's is undoubtedly the giant of the German fast food market. However, the fast food market in Germany remains fairly fragmented and diverse giving the consumer greater choice. Has Subway underestimated the competitive intensity of the German market? It is estimated that there are between 10,000 and 15,000 independent doner kebab outlets generating an annual turnover of 2.5 billion euros. Moreover, Subway is not the only restaurant chain to offer so-called 'better-for-you' meals. There are approximately 15,000 master bakeries, with around 44,500 sales outlets in Germany that can be found on any high street. For instance, the bakery chains Kamps and Wiener Feinbäcker have about 840 outlets in Germany. These bakeries sell bread rolls (*Brötchen*) that are freshly prepared with conventional fillings such as ham and cheese with a slice of pickle using traditional German bread. Lunchtime queues are not uncommon as consumers seek the convenience of consistent home style quality closer to their workplace.

Back on track?

Many Subway franchise holders are fighting for survival and are looking towards the franchiser for an action plan to revive their business fortunes. William Walker was recently appointed the new Area Development Manager for Germany, Austria, Luxembourg and Switzerland. With almost 25 years' experience at McDonald's, it is hoped that Walker's industry expertise will help put the company back on track in a market that has reached near-maturity.

2012 has already seen a number of marketing initiatives. Subway was the first fast food player in Germany to launch an electronic loyalty card. The Subcard, which is also available as an App, encourages customers to collect points for purchases made at Subway which can be redeemed for Subway products. It also launched a quirky TV brand commercial that strikes a chord with the notorious scene in the movie *When Harry met Sally*, to dramatize the sensual pleasure of eating a freshly made Chicken Teriyaki sandwich.

Is the brand starting to connect with its customer base? Subway Germany has now over 400,000 followers on Facebook (McDonald's Germany has 1.6 million) that allows customers to give direct feedback on their store visit. There may be light at the end of the tunnel as an increasingly overweight German population becomes aware of the need to adopt healthier eating habits that does not necessarily have to be bland.

Food for thought

The German market has however been traditionally difficult for many foreign retailers. Wal-Mart, Virgin and GAP have all exited from the German market. Will Subway become another casualty of the German market or will it be able to prevent itself from sinking into oblivion?

References

1 Student & Educator Resource Guide is available at http://www.subway.com/subwayroot/AboutSubway/StudentGuide.pdf

2 Probleme bei Subway spitzen sich zu, http://www.wiwo.de/unternehmen-maerkte/probleme-bei-subway-spitzen-sich-zu-426518/

3 Subway Franchisees Unhappy in Germany, http://www.businessweek.com/globalbiz/content/mar2007/gb20070319_454968.htm

4 http://www.aboutmcdonalds.com/content/dam/AboutMcDonalds/Sustainability/Sustainability%20Library/2010-CSR-Report.pdf

Questions

1. Using additional data from Internet sources, such as from company websites and media reports, conduct a competitor analysis of the German fast food market.

2. Conduct a SWOT analysis of Subway Germany. Prioritize your key findings and discuss options for Subway Germany to deal with them.

3. What has been Subway Germany's competitive strategy and why has it been ineffective?

4. What specific actions can Subway take to become more competitive in the German market?

5. What future consumer trends should Subway consider in its long-term marketing strategies?

6. Taking into account the franchising strategy, advise Subway Germany on the development of an internal marketing approach.

This case was prepared by Glyn Atwal, ESC Dijon-Bourgogne, and Douglas Bryson, ESC Rennes School of Business, France, from various published sources as a basis for classroom discussion rather than to show effective or ineffective management.

Glossary

A

ad hoc research a research project that focuses on a specific problem, collecting data at one point in time with one sample of respondents

adapted marketing mix an international marketing strategy for changing the marketing mix for each international target market

administered vertical marketing system a channel situation where a manufacturer that dominates a market through its size and strong brands may exercise considerable power over intermediaries even though they are independent

advertising any paid form of non-personal communication of ideas or products in the prime media, i.e. television, the press, posters, cinema and radio, the Internet and direct marketing

advertising agency an organization that specializes in providing services such as media selection, creative work, production and campaign planning to clients

advertising message the use of words, symbols and illustrations to communicate to a target audience using prime media

agency an organization that specializes in providing services such as media selection, creative work, production and campaign planning to clients

attitude the degree to which a customer or prospect likes or dislikes a brand

augmented product the core product plus extra functional and/or emotional values combined in a unique way to form a brand

awareness set the set of brands that the consumer is aware may provide a solution to the problem

B

beliefs descriptive thoughts that a person holds about something

benefit segmentation the grouping of people based on the different benefits they seek from a product

blog short for weblog; a personal diary/journal on the web; information can easily be uploaded on to a website and is then available for general consumption by web users

bonus pack giving a customer extra quantity at no additional cost

brainstorming the technique where a group of people generate ideas without initial evaluation; only when the list of ideas is complete is each idea then evaluated

brand a distinctive product offering created by the use of a name, symbol, design, packaging, or some combination of these, intended to differentiate it from its competitors

brand assets the distinctive features of a brand

brand domain the brand's target market

brand equity a measure of the strength of a brand in the marketplace by adding tangible value to a company through the resulting sales and profits

brand extension the use of an established brand name on a new brand within the same broad market or product category

brand heritage the background to the brand and its culture

brand personality the character of a brand described in terms of other entities such as people, animals and objects

brand reflection the relationship of the brand to self-identity

brand stretching the use of an established brand name for brands in unrelated markets or product categories

brand valuation the process of estimating the financial value of an individual or corporate brand

brand values the core values and characteristics of a brand

broadcast sponsorship a form of sponsorship where a television or radio programme is the focus

business analysis a review of the projected sales, costs and profits for a new product to establish whether these factors satisfy company objectives

business ethics the moral principles and values that guide a firm's behaviour

business mission the organization's purpose, usually setting out its competitive domain, which distinguishes the business from others of its type

buyers generally refers to professionals in procurement. A buyer makes business decisions on purchasing

buying centre a group that is involved in the buying decision (also known as a *decision-making unit*)

buying signals statements by a buyer that indicate s/he is interested in buying

buzz marketing the passing of information about products and services by verbal or electronic means in an informal person-to-person manner. It is also about identifying triggers that will prompt new conversations from target audiences

bypass attack circumventing the defender's position, usually through technological leap-frogging or diversification

 C

campaign objectives goals set by an organization in terms of, for example, sales, profits, customers won or retained, or awareness creation

catalogue marketing the sale of products through catalogues distributed to agents and customers, usually by mail or at stores

category management the management of brands in a group, portfolio or category, with specific emphasis on the retail trade's requirements

cause-related marketing a commercial activity by which businesses and charities or causes form a partnership with each other to market an image or product for mutual benefit

centralization in international marketing it is the global integration of international operations

change master a person that develops an implementation strategy to drive through organizational change

channel integration the way in which the players in the channel are linked

channel intermediaries organizations that facilitate the distribution of products to customers

channel of distribution the means by which products are moved from the producer to the ultimate consumer

channel strategy the selection of the most effective distribution channel, the most appropriate

level of distribution intensity and the degree of channel integration

choice criteria the various attributes (and benefits) people use when evaluating products and services

classical conditioning the process of using an established relationship between a stimulus and a response to cause the learning of the same response to a different stimulus

coercive power power inherent in the ability to punish

cognitive dissonance post-purchase concerns of a consumer arising from uncertainty as to whether a decision to purchase was the correct one

cognitive learning the learning of knowledge and development of beliefs and attitudes without direct reinforcement

combination brand name a combination of family and individual brand names

communications-based co-branding the linking of two or more existing brands from different companies or business units for the purposes of joint communication

competitive advantage the achievement of superior performance through differentiation to provide superior customer value or by managing to achieve lowest delivered cost

competitive behaviour the activities of rival companies with respect to each other; this can take five forms—conflict, competition, co-existence, cooperation and collusion

competitive bidding drawing up detailed specifications for a product and putting the contract out to tender

competitive positioning consists of three key elements: target markets, competitor targets and establishing a competitive advantage

competitive scope the breadth of a company's competitive challenge, e.g. broad or narrow

competitor analysis an examination of the nature of actual and potential competitors, and their objectives and strategies

competitor audit a precise analysis of competitor strengths and weaknesses, objectives and strategies

competitor targets the organizations against which a company chooses to compete directly

concept testing testing new product ideas with potential customers

concession analysis the evaluation of things that can be offered to someone in negotiation valued from the viewpoint of the receiver

consumer a person who buys goods or services for personal use

consumer decision-making process the stages a consumer goes through when buying something—namely, problem awareness, information search, evaluation of alternatives, purchase and post-purchase evaluation

consumer movement an organized collection of groups and organizations whose objective it is to protect the rights of consumers

consumer panel household consumers who provide information on their purchases over time

consumer panel data a type of continuous research where information is provided by household consumers on their purchases over time

consumer pull the targeting of consumers with communications (e.g. promotions) designed to create demand that will pull the product into the distribution chain

consumerism organized action against business practices that are not in the interests of consumers

continuous research repeated interviewing of the same sample of people

contractual joint venture two or more companies form a partnership but no joint enterprise with a separate identity is formed

contractual vertical marketing system a franchise arrangement (e.g. a franchise) that ties together producers and resellers

control the stage in the marketing planning process or cycle when the performance against plan is monitored so that corrective action, if necessary, can be taken

core competences the principal distinctive capabilities possessed by a company—what it is really good at

core marketing strategy the means of achieving marketing objectives, including target markets, competitor targets and competitive advantage

core product anything that provides the central benefits required by customers

corporate identity the ethos, aims and values of an organization, presenting a sense of its individuality, which helps to differentiate it from its competitors

corporate social responsibility the ethical principle that an organization should be accountable for how its behaviour might affect society and the environment

corporate vertical marketing system a channel situation where an organization gains control of distribution through ownership

counter-offensive defence a counter-attack that takes the form of a head-on counter-attack, an attack on the attacker's cash cow or an encirclement of the attacker

counter-trade a method of exchange where not all transactions are concluded in cash; goods may be included as part of the asking price

covert power play the use of disguised forms of power tactics

culture the traditions, taboos, values and basic attitudes of the society in which an individual lives

customer analysis a survey of who the customers are, what choice criteria they use, how they rate competitive offerings and on what variables they can be segmented

customer-based brand equity the differential effect that brand knowledge has on consumer response to the marketing of that brand

customer benefits those things that a customer values in a product; customer benefits derive from product features

customer relationship management the methodologies, technologies and e-commerce capabilities used by firms to manage customer relationships

customer satisfaction measurement a process through which customer satisfaction criteria are set, customers are surveyed and the results interpreted in order to establish the level of customer satisfaction with the organization's product

customer satisfaction the fulfilment of customers' requirements or needs

customer value perceived benefits minus perceived sacrifice

customers a term used in both consumer and organizational purchasing situations. These are individuals and companies that have an established relationship with a seller (e.g. retailers, producers, manufacturers)

customized marketing the market coverage strategy where a company decides to target individual customers and develops separate marketing mixes for each

 D

data the most basic form of knowledge, the result of observations

database marketing an interactive approach to marketing that uses individually addressable marketing media and channels to provide information to a target audience, stimulate demand and stay close to customers

decentralization in international marketing it is the delegation of international operations to individual countries or regions

decision-making process the stages that organizations and people pass through when purchasing a physical product or service

decision-making unit (DMU) a group of people within an organization who are involved in the buying decision (also known as the buying centre)

demography changes in the population in terms of its size and characteristics

depth interviews the interviewing of consumers individually for perhaps one or two hours, with the aim of understanding their attitudes, values, behaviour and/or beliefs

descriptive research research undertaken to describe customers' beliefs, attitudes, preferences and behaviour

differential advantage a clear performance differential over the competition on factors that are important to target customers

differential marketing strategies market coverage strategies where a company decides to target several market segments and develops separate marketing mixes for each

differentiated marketing a market coverage strategy where a company decides to target several market segments and develops separate marketing mixes for each

differentiation strategy the selection of one or more customer choice criteria and positioning the offering accordingly to achieve superior customer value

diffusion of innovation process the process by which a new product spreads throughout a market over time

digital marketing the application of digital technologies that form channels to market (the Internet, mobile communications, interactive television and wireless) to achieve corporate goals through meeting and exceeding customer needs better than the competition

digital promotion the promotion of products to consumers and businesses through electronic media

direct cost pricing the calculation of only those costs that are likely to rise as output increases

direct exporting the handling of exporting activities by the exporting organization rather than by a domestically based independent organization

direct investment market entry that involves investment in foreign-based assembly or manufacturing facilities

direct mail material sent through the postal service to the recipient's house or business address promoting a product and/or maintaining an ongoing relationship

direct marketing (1) acquiring and retaining customers without the use of an intermediary; (2) the distribution of products, information and promotional benefits to target consumers through interactive communication in a way that allows response to be measured

direct response advertising the use of the prime advertising media such as television, newspapers and magazines to elicit an order, enquiry or request for a visit

disintermediation the removal of channel partners by bypassing intermediaries and going directly from manufacturer to consumer via the Internet

distribution analysis an examination of movements in power bases, channel attractiveness, physical distribution and distribution behaviour

distribution push the targeting of channel intermediaries with communications (e.g. promotions) to push the product into the distribution chain

divest to improve short-term cash yield by dropping or selling off a product

 E

ecology the study of living things within their environment

economic order quantity the quantity of stock to be ordered where total costs are at the lowest

economic value to the customer (EVC) the amount a customer would have to pay to make the total life-cycle costs of a new and a reference product the same

effectiveness doing the right thing, making the correct strategic choice

efficiency a way of managing business processes to a high standard, usually concerned with cost reduction; also called 'doing things right'

e-commerce involves all electronically mediated transactions between an organization and any third party it deals with, including exchange of information

e-marketing a term used to refer to the use of technology (telecommunications and Internet-based) to achieve marketing objectives and bring the customer and supplier closer together

encirclement attack attacking the defender from all sides, i.e. every

market segment is hit with every combination of product features

entry barriers barriers that act to prevent new firms from entering a market, e.g. the high level of investment required

entry into new markets (diversification) the entry into new markets by new products

environmental scanning the process of monitoring and analysing the marketing environment of a company

environmentalism the organized movement of groups and organizations to protect and improve the physical environment

equity joint venture where two or more companies form a partnership that involves the creation of a new company

ethical consumption the taking of purchase decisions not only on the basis of personal interests but also on the basis of the interests of society and the environment

ethics the moral principles and values that govern the actions and decisions of an individual or group

ethnography a form of qualitative research which involves detailed and prolonged observation of consumers in the situations which inform their buying behaviour

event sponsorship sponsorship of a sporting or other event

evoked set the set of brands that the consumer seriously evaluates before making a purchase

exaggerated promises barrier a barrier to the matching of expected and perceived service levels caused by the unwarranted building up of expectations by exaggerated promises

exchange the act or process of receiving something from someone by giving something in return

exclusive distribution an extreme form of selective distribution where only one wholesaler, retailer or industrial distributor is used in a geographical area to sell the products of a supplier

exhibition an event that brings buyers and sellers together in a commercial setting

experience curve the combined effect of economies of scale and learning as cumulative output increases

experimental research research undertaken in order to establish cause and effect

experimentation the application of stimuli (e.g. two price levels) to different matched groups under controlled conditions for the purpose of measuring their effect on a variable (e.g. sales)

expert power power that derives from an individual's expertise

exploratory research the preliminary exploration of a research area prior to the main data-collection stage

fair trade marketing the development, promotion and selling of fair trade brands and the positioning of organizations on the basis of a fair trade ethos

family brand name a brand name used for all products in a range

fighter brands low-cost manufacturers' brands introduced to combat own-label brands

flanking attack attacking geographical areas or market segments where the defender is poorly represented

flanking defence the defence of a hitherto unprotected market segment

focus group a group normally of six to twelve consumers brought together for a discussion focusing on an aspect of a company's marketing

focused marketing a market coverage strategy where a company decides to target one market segment with a single marketing mix

foreign consumer culture positioning positioning a brand as associated with a specific foreign culture (e.g. Italian fashion)

franchise a legal contract in which a producer and channel intermediaries agree each other's rights and obligations; usually the intermediary receives marketing, managerial, technical and financial services in return for a fee

franchising a form of licensing where a package of services is offered by the franchisor to the franchisee in return for payment

frontal attack a competitive strategy where the challenger takes on the defender head on

full cost pricing pricing so as to include all costs and based on certain sales volume assumptions

geodemographics the process of grouping households into geographic clusters based on information such as type of accommodation, occupation, number and age of children, and ethnic background

global branding achievement of brand penetration worldwide

global consumer culture positioning positioning a brand as a symbol of a given global culture (e.g. young cosmopolitan men)

going-rate pricing pricing at the rate generally applicable in the market, focusing on competitors' offerings rather than on company costs

group discussion a group, usually of six to eight consumers, brought together for a discussion focusing on an aspect of a company's marketing

guerrilla attack making life uncomfortable for stronger rivals through, for example, unpredictable price discounts, sales promotions or heavy advertising in a few selected regions

hall tests bringing a sample of target consumers to a room that has been hired so that alternative marketing ideas (e.g. promotions) can be tested

halo customers customers that are not directly targeted but may find the product attractive

harvest objective the improvement of profit margins to improve cash flow even if the longer-term result is falling sales

hold objective a strategy of defending a product in order to maintain market share

inadequate delivery barrier a barrier to the matching of expected and perceived service levels caused by the failure of the service provider to select, train and reward staff adequately, resulting in poor or inconsistent delivery of service

inadequate resources barrier a barrier to the matching of expected and perceived service levels caused by the unwillingness of service providers to provide the necessary resources

indirect exporting the use of independent organizations within the exporter's domestic market to facilitate export

individual brand name a brand name that does not identify a brand with a particular company

industry a group of companies that market products that are close substitutes for each other

information combinations of data that provide decision-relevant knowledge

information framing the way in which information is presented to people

information processing the process by which a stimulus is received, interpreted, stored in memory and later retrieved

information search the identification of alternative ways of problem-solving

ingredient co-branding the explicit positioning of a supplier's brand as an ingredient of a product

innovation the commercialization of an invention by bringing it to market

inseparability a characteristic of services, namely that their production cannot be separated from their consumption

intangibility a characteristic of services, namely that they cannot be touched, seen, tasted or smelled

integrated marketing communications the concept that companies coordinate their marketing communications tools to deliver a clear, consistent, credible and competitive message about the organization and its products

intensive distribution the aim of this is to provide saturation coverage of the market by using all available outlets

interaction approach an approach to buyer–seller relations that treats the relationships as taking place between two active parties

internal marketing training, motivating and communicating with staff to cause them to work effectively in providing customer satisfaction; more recently the term has been expanded to include marketing to all staff with the aim of achieving the acceptance of marketing ideas and plans

Internet surveys various methods of gathering qualitative (and in some cases quantitative) data using email or Web-based surveys

invention the discovery of new methods and ideas

just-in-time (JIT) this concept aims to minimize stocks by organizing a supply system that provides

materials and components as they are required

key account management an approach to selling that focuses resources on major customers and uses a team selling approach

learning any change in the content or organization of long-term memory as the result of information processing

legitimate power power based on legitimate authority, such as line management

licensing a contractual arrangement in which a licensor provides a licensee with certain rights, e.g. to technology access or production rights

life-cycle costs all the components of costs associated with buying, owning and using a physical product or service

lifestyle the pattern of living as expressed in a person's activities, interests and opinions

lifestyle segmentation the grouping of people according to their pattern of living as expressed in their activities, interests and opinions

local consumer culture positioning positioning a brand as associated with a local culture (e.g. local production and consumption of a good)

macroenvironment a number of broader forces that affect not only the company but the other actors in the environment, e.g. social, political, technological and economic

macrosegmentation the segmentation of organizational markets by size, industry and location

manufacturer brands brands that are created by producers and bear their chosen brand name

market analysis the statistical analysis of market size, growth rates and trends

market development to take current products and market them in new markets

market expansion the attempt to increase the size of a market by converting non-users to users of the product and by increasing usage rates

market penetration to continue to grow sales by marketing an existing product in an existing market

market segmentation the process of identifying individuals or organizations with similar characteristics that have significant implications for the determination of marketing strategy

market share analysis a comparison of company sales with total sales of the product, including sales of competitors

market testing the limited launch of a new product to test sales potential

marketing accountability the requirement to justify marketing investment by using marketing metrics

marketing audit a systematic examination of a business's marketing environment, objectives, strategies and activities with a view to identifying key strategic issues, problem areas and opportunities

marketing concept the achievement of corporate goals through meeting and exceeding customer needs better than the competition

marketing control the stage in the marketing planning process or cycle when performance against plan is monitored so that corrective action, if necessary, can be taken

marketing environment the actors and forces that affect a company's capability to operate effectively in providing products and services to its customers

marketing ethics the moral principles and values that guide behaviour within the field of marketing

marketing information system a system in which marketing information is formally gathered, stored, analysed and distributed to managers in accordance with their informational needs on a regular, planned basis

marketing metrics quantitative measures of the outcomes of marketing activities and expenditures

marketing mix a framework for the tactical management of the customer relationship, including product, place, price, promotion (the 4-Ps); in the case of services three other elements to be taken into account are process, people and physical evidence

marketing objectives there are two types of marketing objective: strategic thrust, which dictates which products should be sold in which markets, and strategic objectives, i.e. product-level objectives, such as build, hold, harvest and divest

marketing-orientated pricing an approach to pricing that takes a range of marketing factors into account when setting prices

marketing orientation companies with a marketing orientation focus on customer needs as the primary drivers of organizational performance

marketing planning the process by which businesses analyse the environment and their capabilities, decide upon courses of marketing action and implement those decisions

marketing research the gathering of data and information on the market

marketing structures the marketing frameworks (organization, training and internal communications) upon which marketing activities are based

marketing systems sets of connected parts (information, planning and control) that support the marketing function

media channel the means used to transmit a message, including spoken words, print, radio, television or the Internet. Also called the *medium*

media class decision the choice of prime media, i.e. the press, cinema, television, posters, radio, or some combination of these

media planning an advertising strategy most commonly employed to target consumers using a variety of informational outlets. Media planning is generally conducted by a professional media planning or advertising agency and typically finds the most appropriate media outlets to reach the target market

media relations the communication of a product or business by placing information about it in the media without paying for time or space directly

media type (also referred to as a *content type*) is a general category of data content, such as: application (executable program), audio content, an image, a text message, a video stream, and so forth

media vehicle decision the choice of the particular newspaper, magazine, television spot, poster site, etc.

message the use of words, symbols and illustrations to communicate to a target audience using prime media

microblogging the posting of short messages on social media sites like Twitter, Reddit

microenvironment the actors in the firm's immediate environment

that affect its capability to operate effectively in its chosen markets—namely, suppliers, distributors, customers and competitors

microsegmentation segmentation according to choice criteria, DMU structure, decision-making process, buy class, purchasing structure and organizational innovativeness

misconception barrier a failure by marketers to understand what customers really value about their service

mobile defence involves diversification or broadening the market by redefining the business

mobile marketing the sending of text messages to mobile phones to promote products and build relationships with consumers

modified rebuy where a regular requirement for the type of product exists and the buying alternatives are known but sufficient change (e.g. a delivery problem) has occurred to require some alteration to the normal supply procedure

money-off promotions sales promotions that discount the normal price

motivation the process involving needs that set drives in motion to accomplish goals

multichannel involves an organization that is using different channels—for example, physical retailer stores, the Web and mobile, to enable its customers to buy, communicate, gain access to information or pay for goods and services. The organization in return provides consistent levels of service and marketing mix across all of the channels

new task refers to the first-time purchase of a product or input by an organization

niche objective the strategy of targeting a small market segment

o

omnibus survey a regular survey, usually operated by a marketing research specialist company, which asks questions of respondents for several clients on the same questionnaire

operant conditioning the use of rewards to generate reinforcement of response

overt power play the use of visible, open kinds of power tactics

own-label brands brands created and owned by distributors or retailers

P

parallel co-branding the joining of two or more independent brands to produce a combined brand

parallel importing when importers buy products from distributors in one country and sell them in another to distributors who are not part of the manufacturer's normal distribution; caused by big price differences for the same product between different countries

PEEST analysis the analysis of the political/legal, economic, ecological/physical, social/cultural and technological environments

perception the process by which people select, organize and interpret sensory stimulation into a meaningful picture of the world

perishability a characteristic of services, namely that the capacity of a service business, such as a hotel room, cannot be stored—if it is not occupied, this is lost income that cannot be recovered

personal selling oral communication with prospective purchasers with the intention of making a sale

personality the inner psychological characteristics of individuals that lead to consistent responses to their environment

place the distribution channels to be used, outlet locations, methods of transportation

portfolio planning managing groups of brands and product lines

position defence building a fortification around existing products, usually through keen pricing and improved promotion

positioning the choice of target market (where the company wishes to compete) and differential advantage (how the company wishes to compete)

positioning strategy the choice of target market (*where* the company wishes to compete) and differential advantage (*how* the company wishes to compete)

pre-emptive defence usually involves continuous innovation and new product development, recognizing that attack is the best form of defence

premiums any merchandise offered free or at low cost as an incentive to purchase

price (1) the amount of money paid for a product; (2) the agreed value placed on the exchange by a buyer and seller

price unbundling pricing each element in the offering so that the price of the total product package is raised

price waterfall the difference between list price and realized or transaction price

product a good or service offered or performed by an organization or individual, which is capable of satisfying customer needs

product-based co-branding the linking of two or more existing brands from different companies or business units to form a product in which the brand names are visible to consumers

product churning a continuous and rapid spiral of new product introductions

product development increasing sales by improving present products or developing new products for current markets

product features the characteristics of a product that may or may not convey a customer benefit

product life-cycle a four-stage cycle in the life of a product illustrated as sales and profits curves, the four stages being introduction, growth, maturity and decline

product line a group of brands that are closely related in terms of the functions and benefits they provide

product mix the total set of products marketed by a company

product placement the deliberate placing of products and/or their logos in movies and television, usually in return for money

product portfolio the total range of products offered by the company

production orientation a business approach that is inwardly focused either on costs or on a definition of a company in terms of its production facilities

profile segmentation the grouping of people in terms of profile variables, such as age and socio-economic group, so that marketers can communicate to them

profitability analysis the calculation of sales revenues and costs for the purpose of calculating the profit performance of products, customers and/or distribution channels

project teams the bringing together of staff from such areas as R&D, engineering, manufacturing, finance and marketing to work on a project such as new product development

promotional mix advertising, personal selling, sales promotions, public relations, direct marketing, and Internet and online promotion

proposal analysis the prediction and evaluation of proposals and demands likely to be made by someone with whom one is negotiating

proprietary-based brand equity is derived from company attributes that deliver value to the brand

psychographic segmentation the grouping of people according to their lifestyle and personality characteristics

public relations the management of communications and relationships to establish goodwill and mutual understanding between an organization and its public

 Q

QR codes a form of barcode which, once scanned, can link the user directly to Web content, digital adverts and other available content. They are easy to use and smartphones can read the codes

qualitative research exploratory research that aims to understand consumers' attitudes, values, behaviour and beliefs

quantitative research a structured study of small or large samples using a predetermined list of questions or criteria

 R

reasoning a more complex form of cognitive learning where conclusions are reached by connected thought

rebranding the changing of a brand or corporate name

reference group a group of people that influences an individual's attitude or behaviour

referent power power derived by the reference source, e.g. when people identify with and respect the architect of change

reintermediation the introduction of new forms of channel intermediaries, which provide services that link members of the supply chain: e.g. Web service providers and retailers

relationship marketing the process of creating, maintaining and enhancing strong relationships with customers and other stakeholders

repositioning changing the target market or differential advantage, or both

research brief a written document stating the client's requirements

research proposal a document defining what the marketing research agency promises to do for its client and how much it will cost

retail audit a type of continuous research tracking the sales of products through retail outlets

retail audit data used to establish whether the promotion was associated with retail outlets increasing their stock levels or a rise in the number of outlets handling the brand, as well as for measuring sales effects

retail positioning the choice of target market and differential advantage for a retail outlet

reverse marketing the process whereby the buyer attempts to persuade the supplier to provide exactly what the organization wants

reward power power derived from the ability to provide benefits

rote learning the learning of two or more concepts without conditioning

 S

safety (buffer) stocks stocks or inventory held to cover against uncertainty about resupply lead times

sales analysis a comparison of actual with target sales

sales promotion incentives to customers or the trade that are designed to stimulate purchase

salesforce evaluation the measurement of salesperson performance so that strengths and weaknesses can be identified

salesforce motivation the motivation of salespeople by a process that involves needs, which set encouraging drives in motion to accomplish goals

sampling process a term used in research to denote the selection of a sub-set of the total population in order to interview them

secondary research data that have already been collected by another researcher for another purpose

selective attention the process by which people screen out those stimuli that are neither meaningful to them nor consistent with their experiences and beliefs

selective distortion the distortion of information received by people according to their existing beliefs and attitudes

selective distribution the use of a limited number of outlets in a geographical area to sell the products of a supplier

selective retention the process by which people only retain a selection of messages in memory

self-reference criteria the use of one's own perceptions and choice criteria to judge what is important to consumers. In international markets, the perceptions and choice criteria of domestic consumers may be used to judge what is important to foreign consumers

service any deed, performance or effort carried out for the customer

services marketing mix product, place, price, promotion, people, process and physical evidence (the '7-Ps')

simultaneous engineering the involvement of manufacturing and product development engineers in the same development team in an effort to reduce development time

social media a term used to refer to online community websites, with individuals who can become members, share ideas and interests, e.g. Facebook; publish and distribute articles and video and other multimedia content, such as YouTube; carry out social commerce activities like writing reviews, buying and selling, e.g. TripAdvisor; or play games across communities, for example, Zynga

societal marketing focuses on consumers' needs and long-term welfare as keys to satisfying organizational objectives and responsibilities by taking into account consumers' and societies' wider interests rather than just their short-term consumption

sponsorship a business relationship between a provider of funds, resources or services and an individual, event or organization that offers in return some rights and association that may be used for commercial advantage

stakeholder an individual or group that either (i) is harmed by or benefits from the company, or (ii) whose rights can be violated or have to be respected by the company

stakeholder theory this contends that companies are not managed purely in the interests of their shareholders alone but a broader group including communities associated with the company, employees, customers and suppliers

standardized marketing mix an international marketing strategy for using essentially the same product, promotion, distribution, and pricing in all the company's international markets

straight rebuy refers to a purchase by an organization from a previously approved supplier of a previously purchased item

strategic alliance collaboration between two or more organizations through, for example, joint ventures, licensing agreements, long-term purchasing and supply arrangement, or a joint R&D contract to build a competitive advantage

strategic business unit a business or company division serving a distinct group of customers and with a distinct set of competitors, usually strategically autonomous

strategic focus the strategies that can be employed to achieve an objective

strategic issues analysis an examination of the suitability of marketing objectives and segmentation bases in the light of changes in the marketplace

strategic objectives product-level objectives relating to the decision to build, hold, harvest or divest products

strategic thrust the decision concerning which products to sell in which markets

strategic withdrawal holding on to the company's strengths while getting rid of its weaknesses

strong theory of advertising the notion that advertising can change people's attitudes sufficiently to persuade people who have not previously bought a brand to buy it; desire and conviction precede purchase

supplier analysis an examination of who and where suppliers are located, their competences and shortcomings, the trends affecting them and the future outlook for them

sustainable marketing focuses on reducing environmental damage by creating, producing and delivering sustainable solutions while continuing to satisfy customers and other stakeholders

SWOT analysis a structured approach to evaluating the strategic position of a business by identifying its strengths, weaknesses, opportunities and threats

target accounts organizations or individuals whose custom the

company wishes to obtain

target audience the group of people at which an advertisement or message is aimed

target market a market segment that has been selected as a focus for the company's offering or communications

target marketing the choice of which market segment(s) to serve with a tailored marketing mix

team selling the use of the combined efforts of salespeople, product specialists, engineers, sales managers and even directors to sell products

team sponsorship sponsorship of a team—for example, a football, cricket or motor racing team

telemarketing a marketing communications system whereby trained specialists use telecommunications and information technologies to conduct marketing and sales activities

test marketing the launch of a new product in one or a few geographic areas chosen to be representative of the intended market

total quality management the set of programmes designed to constantly improve the quality of physical products, services and processes

trade marketing marketing to the retail trade

trade-off analysis a measure of the trade-off customers make between price and other product features so that their effects on product preference can be established

transfer pricing the price charged between the profit centres of the same company, sometimes used to take advantage of lower taxes in another country

transition curve the emotional stages that people pass through when confronted with an adverse change

undifferentiated marketing a market coverage strategy where a company decides to ignore market segment differences and develops a single marketing mix for the whole market

value analysis a method of cost reduction in which components are examined to see if they can be made more cheaply

value chain the set of a firm's activities that are conducted to design, manufacture, market, distribute and service its products

variability a characteristic of services, namely that, being delivered by people, the standard of their performance is open to variation

vicarious learning learning from others without direct experience or reward

weak theory of advertising the notion that advertising can first arouse awareness and interest, nudge some consumers towards a doubting first trial purchase and then provide some reassurance and reinforcement; desire and conviction do not precede purchase

Companies and Brands Index

Page locators in **bold** refer to main entries and those in *italics* refer to illustrations

Subjects and Authors Index

HUMAN HISTOLOGY

Second Edition

Alan Stevens
MBBS FRCPath

Senior Lecturer in Histopathology
University of Nottingham Medical School
Nottingham UK

James S. Lowe
BMedSci, BMBS, DM, FRCPath

Professor of Neuropathology
University of Nottingham Medical School
Nottingham UK

 Mosby

London   Baltimore   Barcelona   Bogotá   Boston   Buenos Aires   Carlsbad, CA   Chicago
Madrid   Mexico City   Milan   Naples, FL   New York   Philadelphia   St. Louis
SeoulSingapore   Sydney   Taipei   Tokyo   Toronto   Wiesbaden

Preface

We have written this book for students of medicine and human biology who require a detailed but readable textbook of medically relevant histology to complement the teaching they receive in cell biology, anatomy and pathology.

There has been a sad perception among students that histology is tedious and boring, with the result that they are unenthusiastic about reading and learning it. One reason for this is that histology is often taught in isolation at an early stage of most courses, where its relevance to human disease is not appreciated. A second reason is that it is sometimes taught in immense detail, often using the histology of lower animals, and the detail is excessive and inappropriate for an appreciation of the situation in humans. Times are changing; while it was once possible for students to get by with only a patchy and superficial knowledge of histology, advances in biology and in clinical medical practice now make this impossible.

Histology has never been such an important part of the medical and biology curriculum as it is today. The teaching of biochemistry and physiology increasingly revolves around the new discipline of cell biology and so a knowledge of cellular histology and ultrastructure is of paramount importance. Thanks to new technology, histology has also become a central part of the practice of clinical medicine. More and more, diagnosis of disease rests on the histological examination of small samples of tissue which are now obtainable from virtually every part of the body by safe painless techniques of biopsy. An understanding of the causes, mechanisms and effects of disease is increasingly dependent on a knowledge of histology, ultrastructure and cell biology.

Students are often dissatisfied with their histology textbooks. The main complaints are that textbooks are difficult to read, are either overburdened with detail of animal histology (not always relevant to humans), or are pictorial atlases lacking textual substance. Importantly, many students feel that histology textbooks give little to indicate the clinical importance of the subject and the relevance of histology to biology.

Today's students demand books which are easy to read yet sufficiently detailed to satisfy examination require-ments. In this book we have addressed the problems of presenting a modern view of human histology in a compact form. The text has a 'user-friendly' layout representing the best of contemporary design, and the material is presented in a variety of visually attractive ways.

In the first edition of this book, in the section at the front called 'About This Book', we invited comment and criticism from teachers and students about both the content and method of presentation of the book. We were gratified by the response from both groups and have tried to incorporate the constructive suggestions into this second edition. As a result we have presented the material second time around in a slightly different manner, with summary headings, Key Facts summaries, and some basic review questions based on the material dealt with in each chapter.

Some teachers courteously questioned the accuracy of some of our statements, pointing out what they perceived as errors of fact. We checked all of these and corrected those where we had truly erred. However, many of the factual discrepancies were due to the differences between animals from the lower orders, particularly rodents, and humans. Some of the details of structure taught and learnt in histology courses refer only to certain species, and are not true in human beings. We have stuck very firmly to our original intention that this book shall be about *human* histology, and have changed the title of the book to reflect this. We were occasionally criticised (quite rightly in some cases) about the fact that better electron micrographs could have been obtained with better, prompter, fixation of tissues, but this would have compromised our principal tenet that one cannot teach human histology and ultrastructure by using electron micrographs of the two-toed sloth, even if perfectly fixed by glutaraldehyde injection.

As working histopathologists with a responsibility for teaching medical students and students of human biology, we feel well-equipped to present a balanced view of histology which is relevant to human biology and clinical practice. Students have only a short time to assimilate an immense amount of knowledge, and we hope that our efforts in this book ease the way.